Proceedings

The 19th Annual International Symposium on COMPUTER ARCHITECTURE

acm ACM SIGARCH
COMPUTER ARCHITECTURE NEWS
Volume 20, Number 4
May 1992

The 19th Annual
International Symposium on

COMPUTER ARCHITECTURE

Proceedings

The 19th Annual International Symposium on COMPUTER ARCHITECTURE

May 19–21, 1992 Gold Coast, Australia

Association for Computing Machinery
New York, NY

Published by The Association for Computing Machinery
1515 Broadway
New York, New York 10036

Cover designed by Jack I. Ballestero

Printed in the United States of America

ACM Order Number 415920
Soft Cover ISBN 0-89791-509-7
Series Hard Cover ISBN 0-89791-510-0
IEEE Computer Society Order Number 2940
Library of Congress Number 85-642899
IEEE Catalog Number 92CH3156-7
Perfect Bound Number 0-8186-2940-1
ISBN 0-8186-2941-X (microfiche)
ISBN 0-8186-2942-8 (case)

Additional copies can be ordered from:

ACM
Order Department
P.O. Box 64145
Baltimore, MD 21264
1-800-342-6626
1-410-528-4261 (Outside USA, MD and AK)

IEEE Computer Society Press
Customer Service Center
10662 Los Vaqueros Circle
P.O. Box 3014
Los Alamitos, CA 90720-1264

IEEE Computer Society
13, Avenue de l' Aquilon
B-1200 Brussels
BELGIUM

IEEE Computer Society
Ooshima Building
2-19-1 Minami-Aoyama,
Minato-Ku
Tokyo 107, JAPAN

IEEE Service Center
445 Hoes Lane
P.O. Box 1331
Piscataway, NJ
08855-1331

Association for Computing Machinery

General Co-Chairs' Message

Welcome to Australia's Gold Coast for the 19th Annual Symposium on Computer Architecture. Three years ago the suggestion of taking the conference to the southern hemisphere was greeted enthusiastically; so this year is the first time ISCA will be held in winter. We hope the Gold Coast lives up to its reputation of mild winters and gives you an opportunity to see a little of Australia's characteristic coast line.

Australia's computer science and computer engineering community is small but very active. A recent workshop in computer architecture, held before the annual Australian Computer Science Conference, demonstrated the range of architecture projects being undertaken in Australian research sites. It therefore gives us great pleasure to be able to offer an international symposium of the standing of ISCA to Australian academics. Likewise, we hope our international visitors will enjoy interacting with local researchers.

This year we chose to include a number of industry sponsored keynote addresses in addition to the normal keynote talks. The speakers have been selected from a number of locally represented multi-national computer vendors, and will give us some interesting details on the architectures of commercial machines. We would like to thank these companies for their contribution, a list of whom will be made public at the time of the symposium.

No conference can be successful without the efforts of the conference and program committees. To them, we extend our deepest gratitude.

The co-chairs would particularly like to acknowledge the support of their employers, the Commonwealth Scientific and Industrial Research Organisation, the Royal Melbourne Institute of Technology and the University of Southern California. They have not only provided us with the time and facilities with which to organize the symposium, but have also made the Pacific Ocean a little smaller by sponsoring the countless electronic messages exchanged during the last 3 years.

As in past years, workshops are associated with the main Symposium. These workshops provide an ideal opportunity for fellow researchers to get together and discuss their work in detail. These workshops will be held on Hamilton Island; whilst stranded on this barren rocky outcrop of the Australian coast, we trust that the participants will be able to focus their minds on technical matters.

Welcome to Australia and welcome to ISCA92.

David Abramson & Jean-Luc Gaudiot.

Program Chair's Message

Welcome to Australia! It has been an honor and (mostly) a great pleasure to be the program chair for the 1992 International Symposium on Computer Architecture. My thanks to David and Jean-Luc, the conference chairs, for selecting me and to the members of the program committee (PC) who conducted the PC meeting at NYU in a workshop-like manner. Their names are listed in these Proceedings. Special thanks to the members of my Ultracomputer project, especially Nancy Cruz, who pitched in with the not-so-much fun parts—like sealing envelops and printing address labels.

The committee received 173 papers for consideration of which 39 (23%) were accepted for oral presentation and appear in these proceedings. An additional 36 (21%) were accepted for poster presentation. The authors of twenty-four of these 36 papers have agreed to a poster presentation and have written short abstracts, which appear in the proceedings.

Each submitted paper was sent to one PC member to act as primary PC reviewer and another to act as secondary. The primary PC reviewer was to read the paper personally; the secondary reviewer could have colleagues at his/her institution read the paper but was to be familiar with it. All reviewing was blind. Although blind refereeing was mentioned in the call for papers, it was omitted from various summaries of the call and many papers contained the author's names and affiliations. Before these papers were sent out, we obliterated the information from title pages but did not pre-read the papers and remove other identification. In addition, each paper was sent to two referees outside the program committee for further blind refereeing. For all papers, reviewers were not from the same institution as any of the authors.

The program committee met for one and a half days, with nearly all the work finished on the first day. Although there were a few strong disagreements (e.g. a paper received the max and min possible grades from the two PC reviewers, both of whom were present), there were no fights and the only criteria used to select papers were scientific quality and value to attendees. I have characterized the atmosphere as workshop-like and was pleased to attend. This was primarily do to my good fortune in having such a high quality committee but another contributing factor might have been our policy of not permitting PC members to submit papers.

We received many excellent papers and I believe we have assembled a strong program. I hope you agree. So enjoy the talks, study the papers, and, for those of you like me from the other hemisphere, look up at night.

Allan Gottlieb
New York University

1992 ISCA Organizing Committee

Program Chair

Allan Gottlieb, New York University, USA

General Co-Chairs

David Abramson, CSIRO, Australia
Jean-Luc Gaudiot, University of Southern California, USA

Symposium Committee

Greg Egan, Swinburne Institute of Technology, Australia (local arrangements)
Rhys Francis, CSIRO, Australia (registration)
Mark Franklin, Washington University, USA (travel grants)
Walid Najjar, Colorado State University, USA (posters)
John Rosenberg, University of Sydney, Australia (finance)
Andrew Wendelborn, University of Adelaide, Australia (publicity & publications)

Program Committee

Anant Agarwal, MIT, USA
George Almasi, IBM Corporation, USA
Makoto Amamiya, Kyushu University, Japan
Prith Banerjee, University of Illinois, USA
Alan Berenbaum, AT&T Bell Labs, USA
Mike Flynn, Stanford University, USA
Allan Gottlieb, New York University, USA (Chair)
Lee Hoevel, NCR Corporation, USA
Harry Jordan, University of Colorado, USA
Kai Li, Princeton University, USA
Neil Lincoln, SSESCO, USA
Gerald Maguire, Columbia University, USA
Dan Reed, University of Illinois, USA
Marc Snir, IBM Corporation, USA
Patricia J. Teller, New Mexico State University, USA
Kam-Fai Wong, ECRC, Germany

Workshop Organizers

Lubomir Bic, University of California, Irvine (Chair)
John Feo, Lawrence Livermore National Laboratory, USA
James R. Goodman, The University of Wisconsin, Madison, USA
Trevor Mudge, University of Michigan, Ann Arbor, USA

Tutorial Organizers

Guang R. Gao, McGill University, USA
Dave O'Hallaron, Carnegie Mellon University, USA
Edward Lee, University of California, Berkeley, USA (Chair)
Akhilesh Tyagi, University of North Carolina, USA

Panel Organizers

Gary Koob, Office of Naval Research, USA
H.J. Siegel, Purdue University, USA (Chair)

1992 ISCA List of Referees

A. Abnous
N. Aboulenein
S. Abraham
N. Abu-Ghazaleh
S. Addanki
S. Adve
B. Aichinger
S. Akhtar
A. Al-Khalili
N. Alexandridis
M. Algudady
M. Algududy
B. Alleyne
H. Ando
J. Archibald
J. Arora
T. Austin
A. Ayers
J. Baer
N. Bagherzadeh
J. Balasz
S. Bandyopadhyay
L. Barroso
P. Bates
B. Bederson
K. Bhat
R. Bianchini
L. Bic
A. Bohm
B. Boothe
B. Bray
E. Brewer
S. Brobst
R. Brown
R. Bryant
D. Brzezinski
T. Casavant
D. Chaiken
A. Cheese
G. Chen
C. Chen
J. Chen
A. Chien
W. Ching
T. Chiueh
P. Chow
R. Clark
L. Coraor
A. Cox
B. Cuclik
D. Culler
W. Dally
B. Dally
W. Dally
C. Das
D. DeWitt
W. Delaney
S. Dickey
T. Diep
M. Dorochevsky
C. Dubnicki
H. Dwyer
K. Ebcioglu
J. Edler
K. Ekanadham
E. Elnozahy
P. Emma
R. Engelbrecht
P. Evripidou
B. Fagin
R. Fanfelle
K. Farkas
S. Fineberg
J. Fisher
E. Freudenthal
K. Gharachorloo
C. Glass
S. Goldstein
G. Goodes
J. Goodman
R. Groves
A. Gupta
R. Hammaker
T. Heil
J. Hennessy
D. Hensgen
V. Heuring
M. Hill
R. Hiromoto
M. Holliday
M. Horowitz
W. Hsu
A. Huang
P. Hulina
D. James
T. Joe
E. Johnson
J. Johnson
K. Johnson
N. Jouppi
K. Kaeli
R. Kain
R. Karne
R. Katz
S. Keckler
P. Keleher
R. Kenner
J. Kim
E. Koldinger
S. Konstantinidou
J. Kubiatowicz
M. Kumar
L. Kurian
P. Lacroute
K. Lai
M. Lam
J. Laudon
T. Leblanc
F. Lee
D. Lenoski
R. Lethin
L. Li
X. Li
L. Liang-Liang
D. Liljo
B. Lim
J. Lin
R. Lin
Y. Liu
A. Louri
C. Love
W. Lynch
G. Maa
K. Mackenzie
A. Malony
J. Maneatis
R. Matick
N. Matloff
K. McAuliffe
R. McLellan
S. Mcfarling
P. Melliar-Smith
J. Menon
C. Metcalf
W. Miller
B. Mishra
M. Misra
P. Mohapatra
R. Moore
L. Moser

T. Mudge
M. Mutka
J. Na
W. Najjar
A. Naylor
B. Nelson
G. Newman
P. Ng
J. Nguyen
L. Ni
R. Nikhil
S. Novello
D. Nussbaum
P. Nuth
S. Olariu
K. Olukotun
C. Ortancil
J. Ottos
P. Ouyang
K. Padmanabhan
S. Pan
G. Panneerselvam
G. Papadopoulos
A. Park
D. Patterson
J. Pezaris
J. Pfeiffer
G. Pfister
A. Pleszkun
A. Pletszkun
S. Prakash
G. Pratt
T. Puzak
N. Quach
J. Quinlan
M. Raghunath
J. Rahmeh
U. Ramachandran
A. Ramanan
J. Ramanathan
S. Ramaswamy
T. Ramesh
B. Ramkumar
D. Ramsey
B. Rau
N. Reddy
S. Richardson
J. Salmon
J. Sanz
K. Schauser
C. Scheurich
E. Schonberg
J. Schwartz
E. Schwarz
S. Scott
C. Selvidge
G. Shah
D. Shea
B. Shirazi
R. Simoni
J. Singh
G. Singh
J. Smith
B. Smith
A. Smith
J. Smith
B. Smith
R. Smith
M. Smith
B. Smith
G. Sohi
H. Soliman
A. Sood
P. Stenstrom
L. Stevens
S. Stolfo
H. Stone
M. Stumm
H. Sung
S. Takkar
M. Talluri
J. Tang
S. Tanimoto
V. Taylor
R. Tessier
M. Thazhuthaveetil
C. Thekkath
H. Torng
J. Traff
K. Traub
G. Tyson
N. Tzeng
A. Uht
S. Vajapeyam
A. Varma
Z. Vranesic
J. Vucetic
C. Walrath
W. Wang
S. Ward
P. Wilsey
D. Wingard
M. Wisam
C. Wittenbrink
C. Wittinbrink
P. Woest
K. Wong
I. Wu
L. Wu
W. Wulf
P. Yale
M. Yang
Q. Yang
T. Yeh
J. Yen
D. Yeung
R. Yomtov
A. Youssef
A. Youssof
C. Yu
L. Zhiyong
R. Zucker

Table of Contents

Session 5: Multithreaded Architecture

Session 6: Caches

Session 7: Multithreading

Session 8: Memory Systems

Session 8A: Panel Session II

Session 9: Message Routing Networks

Session 10: I/O Systems

Session 11: Program Performance

Session 12: Vectors and Streams

Session 13: System Performance

Poster Abstracts

Session 1: Consistency for Shared Memory Multi-Processors

A Performance Study of Memory Consistency Models

Richard N. Zucker* and Jean-Loup Baer
Department of Computer Science and Engineering, FR-35
University of Washington
Seattle, WA 98195

Abstract

Recent advances in technology are such that the speed of processors is increasing faster than memory latency is decreasing. Therefore the relative cost of a cache miss is becoming more important. However, the full cost of a cache miss need not be paid every time in a multiprocessor. The frequency with which the processor must stall on a cache miss can be reduced by using a relaxed model of memory consistency.

In this paper, we present the results of instruction-level simulation studies on the relative performance benefits of using different models of memory consistency. Our vehicle of study is a shared-memory multiprocessor with processors and associated write-back caches connected to global memory modules via an Omega network. The benefits of the relaxed models, and their increasing hardware complexity, are assessed with varying cache size, line size, and number of processors. We find that substantial benefits can be accrued by using relaxed models but the magnitudes of the benefits depend on the architecture being modeled, the benchmarks, and how the code is scheduled. We did not find any major difference in levels of improvement among the various relaxed models.

1 Introduction

Recent advances in technology are such that the speed of processors is increasing faster than memory latency is decreasing. Therefore the relative cost of a cache miss is becoming more important, since processors are left idle for a greater number of cycles. This performance loss is even more noticeable in multiprocessors because of the higher miss rates [9] and because memory access times are increased by the latency of and contention for the interconnect that links processors and memory modules.

We can alleviate the high cost of cache misses by reducing the frequency with which the processor must stall on a cache miss. In the case of multiprocessors, one approach is to use relaxed models of consistency. Under such models, the hardware is not required to stall every time there is an outstanding memory reference. However, for correct executions parallel programs must not exhibit data races and primitive synchronization operations must be visible to the hardware. In return the system appears sequentially consistent [17] and is generally faster than a truly sequentially consistent machine.

In this paper we present the results of simulation studies of shared-memory multiprocessors that indicate the relative performance benefits of various implementations of systems that are sequentially consistent, weakly ordered, and release consistent. Our studies show that relaxed models of consistency provide performance improvements from 1% to 36% over sequentially consistent systems. The magnitude of improvement depends mostly upon the benchmark and cache parameters (line and cache sizes). The single best predictor of the level of benefit provided by the relaxed models is the cache hit rate, but it is not always an accurate predictor. We also observed that programs may need to be written or compiled differently to obtain the highest performance on machines with different memory models.

Section 2 defines the various memory models, gives the rules that these models impose on programmers, and indicates how more freedom is allowed in the sequencing of memory accesses as the models become more relaxed (for a more in depth explanation, see [1]). The simulated architecture, the choices made in the implementations of the various models, and the selected benchmarks are described in section 3. In section 4 we present the results of our study. We analyze both the characteristics of the benchmarks for which there is clearly a performance gain in using a relaxed memory model and the hardware features that yield the most benefits. Section 5 compares our results to a previous study of relaxed consistency models based on a simulation of DASH [12]. As will be seen, our results are qualitatively in agreement with those of that previous study. The

*Supported by a DARPA/NASA Research Assistantship in Parallel Processing administered by the Institute for Advanced Computer Studies, University of Maryland

This work was supported in part by NSF Grants CCR-9101541, CCR-8904190 and CCR-8702915.

quantitative differences can be explained by the architectural features being simulated. Section 6 concludes with an assessment of the performance gains that can be exploited by building shared-memory multiprocessors with relaxed models of memory consistency.

2 Consistency Models

2.1 Sequential Consistency

Memory models impose rules on programs to ensure correct executions. On a uniprocessor, the implicit model is that of sequential consistency (SC), which is so intuitive that programmers who implicitly follow it do not even realize that they are adhering to a model's rules. SC is defined as [17]:

> [A system is sequentially consistent if] the result of any execution is the same as if the operations of all the processors were executed in some sequential order, and the operations of each individual processor appear in this sequence in the order specified by its program.

In a sequentially consistent multiprocessor the result of the program must be the same as if each shared access had completed before the next shared access is started; these accesses are executed in program order. If this order is not maintained, then communication between processes, that is, synchronization, using loads and stores (e.g. Dekker's Algorithm [7]) may not work correctly.

Until recently SC had been the usual model of memory access for multiprocessors. However, SC's strict ordering rules can lead to performance inefficiencies. For example, there is (very) limited use of write buffers and the execution of memory accesses must be in program order. Because of SC's restrictions, other memory access models have been proposed. In the following sections, we review those models that we will consider in our performance evaluations.

2.2 Weak Ordering

In systems using relaxed memory models, not all memory accesses need to be sequentially consistent; only the synchronization operations do, which allows for greater freedom in the ordering of memory accesses. The first proposed relaxed memory model was weak ordering, which is defined in [8, 1] as:

1. accesses to global synchronizing variables are sequentially consistent and
2. no access to a synchronizing variable is issued in a processor before all previous global data accesses have been performed and
3. no access to global data is issued by a processor before a previous access to a synchronizing variable has been performed.

The formal definition of "performed" is given in [8]. Basically a store is performed when the value stored by the processor executing the instruction can be seen by all other processors. A load is performed when the value to be returned by the load has been set and cannot be changed.

Under this weak ordering model, writing parallel programs, already a difficult task, becomes even more difficult. However, it has been shown that weakly ordered hardware can appear sequentially consistent to programs with minimal constraints [1], only two of which are significant: programs must not contain data races and all synchronization operations must be visible to the hardware. The first condition is not much of a restriction since a data race is usually an error in a sequentially consistent program (chaotic relaxation is an exception). The second condition is not a significant restriction either since most multiprocessors already provide hardware support for synchronization (e.g., Test-and-Set), and these primitives are those generally used for synchronization.

In a weakly ordered system there are minimal restrictions on the access order of non-synchronizing memory references. The access order must obey the program's own data and control dependencies. Also, the second and third rules of weak ordering say that whenever a synchronization operation is performed, all references to shared data must be performed and no new references to shared data may be issued until the synchronization has completed. Except for this, the accesses may be performed in any order. Thus an order that maximizes system performance may be used.

2.3 Release Consistency

In [14], Gharachorloo et al. proposed the release consistency model. As in weak ordering, the release consistency model has minimal restrictions on the ordering of the performing of normal accesses. There are some restrictions on the ordering of synchronization accesses.

In release consistency synchronizing accesses are categorized as either acquire or release operations. An acquire indicates that a processor needs to "see" the latest values for the next part of its program. A release indicates to the system that some values have been updated and can now be "seen" by other processors. For example, a lock/unlock pair corresponds to an acquire/release operation; a barrier is a release followed by an acquire. The processor treats acquire and release operations differently. An acquire causes the processor to stall until the acquire has completed, since the processor must be certain that it is "seeing" the new values before it continues. However, unlike a weakly ordered system, it is not necessary that all of its previous accesses have been performed before the acquire is issued. A release cannot be performed until all outstanding accesses have been globally performed. However, the processor does not need to stall until the release is completed. Only the release operation itself needs to be delayed. The final difference between weak ordering and release consistency follows from this. There can be an outstanding release operation when an acquire is completed (assuming no data dependency). Gharachorloo et al. also showed that under program restrictions similar to those mentioned above for weak ordering, a release consistent system behaves in a sequentially consistent manner [11].

3 Methodology

3.1 Base Architecture

The architecture that we simulated is a typical "dance-hall" architecture (see Figure 1). It consists of a number of processors, each with a local memory for private data and its own cache, and a number of memory modules for global memory that contain shared data. Processors and global memory are connected via two identical Omega networks, one for the processor requests to memory and one for memory's responses. Cache coherence is enforced by a full directory scheme [5].

We used the Cerberus instruction-level simulator [4] for our simulation studies. The processor it simulates is a RISC processor similar to the Ridge 32 [20]. The caches are two-way set associative and use a write-back write-allocate policy; we experimented with a range of cache and line sizes. The caches are only for shared data. We assume that there are no instruction cache misses and that the private data can be accessed from local memory. We configured the simulator to use 4×4 switches in the interconnection networks. There is a four element buffer between the processor and the request network as well as between the memory and the response network. The memory latency (no contention) for the fetching of the first word of the line is 18 cycles for 16 processors and 20 cycles for 32 processors. The memory latency is independent of the line size due to the pipelined nature of the network and of the memory accesses. However, the length of time that the response network and the memory are busy is proportional to the line size.

3.2 Model Implementations

We simulated four system types. Two are sequentially consistent, one is weakly ordered, and one is release consistent. A summary is given in Table 1.

Sequentially Consistent 1 - SC1 SC1, a sequentially consistent model, is our baseline system. The programmer has complete freedom for the scheduling of inter-processor communication and synchronization. The hardware does not allow a subsequent memory access if one access is already outstanding. However, we allowed one optimization, namely non-blocking loads. Therefore, the processor only stalls if it tries to read from a register that is the destination of an uncompleted load or it attempts another memory access. Since there can be only one outstanding reference at a time, lockup-free caches [16] are not necessary; however, some form of register interlock or scoreboarding is needed for the correctness of register-register operations. In the case of a cache hit, the loads are delayed loads, and the value is not available for four cycles[1]. The processor also does not stall in the case of a write miss. The value to be written is sent to the cache where the write is performed when the line is received from memory. At the same time the source register may be overwritten by a register-register operation.

Sequentially Consistent 2 - SC2 A more aggressive version of SC that does not change the programmer's view of the system was also simulated. Non-binding prefetches on stalls, as suggested in [13], were added to SC1. The processor still stalls when there is an outstanding memory reference and another memory reference is about to be made. But a request for this second access is nonetheless sent to the cache. If the access to the corresponding cache line results in a miss, the line is prefetched into the cache. Note that this prefetch is non-binding; the contents of the prefetched line are still visible to the cache coherence mechanism since no value has been loaded into a register in the case of a load, nor has a new value been written into the line in the case of a store. The performance advantage brought upon by this prefetch is that the miss rate, or at the very least the perceived memory latency, is reduced since the memory accesses are pipelined.

For SC2 the cache is more complicated. The cache controller must be able to handle a prefetch request while there is an outstanding reference. SC1 only needed to distinguish between coherence requests and a line returning from memory, of which there could be only one. SC2 must be able to determine which of its (two) outstanding requests is returning from memory, and whether or not the processor can now be unstalled.

Weakly Ordered 1 - WO1[2]. The first relaxed memory model we simulated obeys the definition for weak ordering given in section 2. With a WO1 implementation the programmer is limited to synchronization that is visible to the hardware. WO1 provides special synchronization instructions in the *lock* and *barrier* routines. The programmer also has the option of using a SYNC instruction to indicate a synchronization point, such as when writing into a shared flag. With respect to the hardware, the processor must now stall at each synchronization point until all outstanding memory references complete. Except for that restriction, memory accesses are allowed to complete in any order as long as the data and control dependencies are observed.

With WO1 several memory references can be outstanding at a time and hence the cache must be lockup-

[1] Our simulator forced us to use a (arguably long) delay of four cycles. We have since repeated the experiments with a smaller delay and found the absolute benefits of the models to be the same. See [21].

[2] A variation of WO1, called WO2, allowing bypassing of stores by loads was also simulated. See [21].

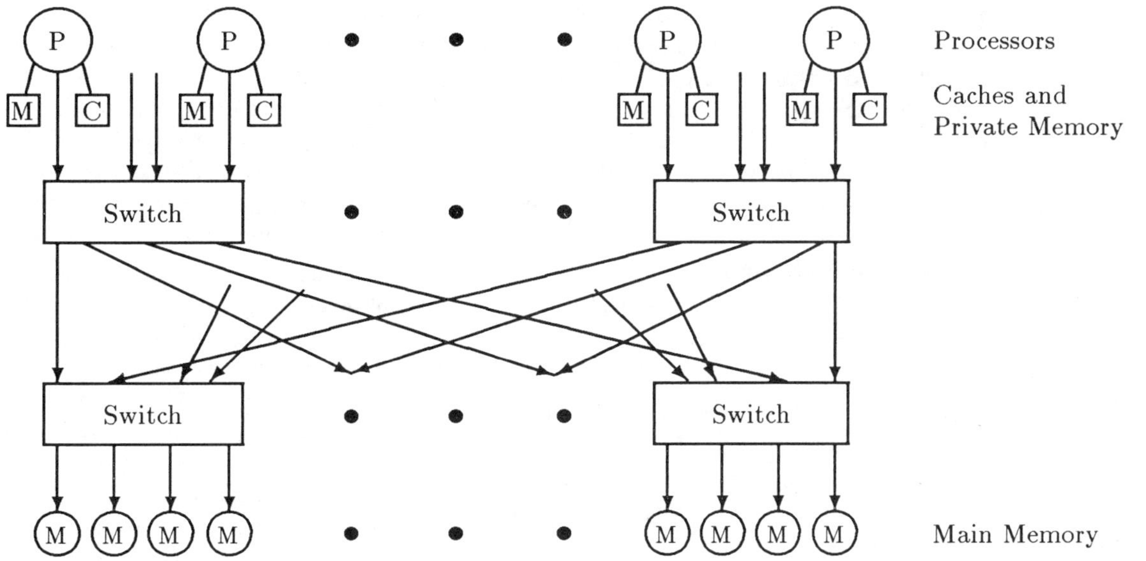

Figure 1: Model Architecture

System	Major Features		
SC1	sequentially consistent, non-blocking loads		
SC2	SC1	+	hardware directed non-binding prefetch at stalls
WO1	SC1	+	hw visible synchronization operations, no stalls on memory access while outstanding references
RC	WO1	+	no stalling while a release completes

Table 1: Summary of Implementation Features

free. Information on each outstanding reference must be maintained in a miss information/status holding register (MSHR) [16] (we simulate five MSHR's). The MSHR's will cause the processor to stall when it makes a reference which must be delayed due to data dependency requirements. In a WO1-like system, the non-blocking loads can be especially useful since several loads can be initiated successively, even in the absence of intervening register-register operations. The overlap of the memory accesses can hide some of their latency[3].

The hardware costs of WO1 can be significant. The cache must be lockup-free; its MSHR's must be (associatively) consulted when requests return from memory, for cache coherence messages, and each time the processor issues a reference (in order to check for an outstanding reference to that line and for data dependencies). Hardware recognizable synchronization instructions are required. The processor must stall when it encounters such an instruction if there are any outstanding references and be able to restart when all references have completed. This requires the use of a counter and an associated stall/restart mechanism.

[3]Both read and write latency is hidden here. In [21] we use blocking loads, and determine how much of the hidden latency is due to reads and how much is due to writes.

Release Consistent - RC In the release consistent system the acquire and release synchronization operations are treated differently, thus requiring the programmer to be aware of the type of synchronization needed. However, the need to make this distinction will not usually be a problem if system-provided synchronization routines are used. Under our simulated RC, when an acquire operation is attempted, the processor stalls until the acquire completes. It does not matter if there are any outstanding memory accesses.

There are several possible situations which can occur when a release operation is encountered in the instruction stream. In all cases though, the processor continues executing past that point in the program. The release operation can be issued if there are no outstanding accesses. However, the release cannot proceed immediately if the locations it operates on are not in the cache. In that case the request to do the release is sent to the cache which will delay issuing the operation until the necessary lines arrive from memory. If there are outstanding references when a processor encounters a release operation, then a special bit is set in all the valid MSHR entries and a counter is set equal to the number of such entries. Whenever an outstanding reference is resolved, this bit in the corresponding MSHR entry is checked. If it is set, the counter is decremented. When the counter is decremented to zero, the pending release operation is issued. This scheme requires an extra bit in the MSHRs, a counter for the number of references still outstanding from the time of the release operation (as opposed to a general counter of outstanding references as in WO1), and the ability to keep track of the pending release operation since the processor has continued executing past the location in the instruction stream where the release was encountered.

3.3 Benchmarks

The benchmark programs used to compare the various memory models are all written using PCP [3], a simple parallel extension to C. They were compiled to the simulator's machine code and linked using Cerberus's compiler. Due to compiler limitations there is no static allocation of private data. Any variable allocated globally is a shared variable and resides in a shared memory module. The only private data are variables declared in functions. Since the architecture supports non-blocking loads, the compiler attempts to schedule the code so that loads to registers are issued far enough ahead of their use so that the processor will hopefully not have to stall if there is a cache miss.

Our four benchmark programs are described below. Table 2 shows statistics on the benchmarks for 16 processors for various cache and line sizes under SC1 and their run-times are given in Figure 2. The exact number of memory references can change based upon the consistency model, and this can impact the hit rates.

Gauss *Gauss* [6] performs the gaussian elimination of a 250 × 250 matrix. This program exhibits a large amount of spatial locality, as can be seen from the 16K cache data in Table 2 and Figure 2. The larger line sizes result in large performance gains: the 64 byte line configuration shows a speed-up over 8 byte lines of almost 50% and over 16 byte lines of almost 25%. This gain is to be expected since the hit ratios increase from 64% for 8 byte lines to 81% for 16 bytes and to 94% for 64 bytes. However, when 64K caches are used the hit ratios are uniformly high and the run-times vary very little with the line sizes. Clearly the data set of each processor fits in a 64K cache, but not in a 16K one.

Qsort *Qsort* [15] executes a parallel quicksort of 500,000 integers. It is dynamically scheduled, unlike the other benchmarks which are statically scheduled. Units of work are pushed onto and popped off of a shared stack and allocated to processors on a FCFS basis. Since any change in the architecture influences the relative rate of execution of each processor, the order of the tasks on the stack can change and thereby affect the way the work is partitioned as well as the size of the partitions [15], thus demonstrating the effect of dynamic scheduling. This natural variability prevents us from reaching general conclusions from a single run of the benchmark. Because of the severe load on CPU time brought upon by instruction-level simulations, we have not yet had the time to repeat this experiment with different seeds and to compute appropriate confidence intervals. We will not discuss the generally small variations in performance we observed, since we cannot isolate the likely causes due to the dynamic nature of the program.

As shown in Table 2, the hit ratios of *Qsort* are fairly low (69-81%). This is to be expected due to its sequential access pattern. Also, when partitioned among the 16 processors, each processor's data set is still too large to fit into even the 64K cache. As long as the cache capacity is too small, for a given line size we see very little variation in *Qsort*'s hit ratio between 16K and 64K caches. The line size does affect the run-time. The systems with 64 byte lines are somewhat slower in spite of their higher hit rates (for more detailed explanations see [15] and [21]).

Relax *Relax* is an iterative relaxation procedure using a nine point stencil over a 514 x 514 matrix. Its main computation consists of averaging the values of nine grid points laid out in a square. If the compiler produces code that loads a value and adds it into the sum before loading the next value, the processor will stall whenever it tries to add in a value whose loading is still pending because of a cache read miss, and this is independent of the consistency model (our compiler's instruction scheduling is discussed in section 4.1). With an 8 byte line size and a matrix of doubles, there is a read miss and a write miss per relaxation (for 16 byte lines misses occur every two relaxations and for 64 byte lines, every eight relaxations). However, after the write, there are a number of register-register operations which hide the latency of the memory access even in SC1.

This grid computation dominates *Relax* so much that the memory access pattern is extremely regular. The cache hit rates and the number of references are almost the same for all processors. As long as the cache is large enough to hold three rows or columns of the submatrix the processor is processing (whether it is a row or column depends upon the loop structure), then the hit rates can be calculated ahead of time very easily. The observed cache hit rates match up almost exactly with those we predicted. Unlike *Gauss*, the data set size would need to be significantly larger for there to be a large change in the cache hit rate.

Psim *Psim* is the simulator of the multi-stage network that the simulator itself uses. It simulates a 64 processor network using 4 x 4 switches with each processor issuing 513 references. *Psim* differs from the other benchmarks in various ways. We observe that 70% of its cache misses are invalidation misses, which is indicative of a high level of sharing. This increases the traffic on the Omega network. Also, Psim's accesses to memory

Program	References		Hit Rate (%) by line and cache size					
			16K cache			64K cache		
	Reads	Writes	8 bytes	16 bytes	64 bytes	8 bytes	16 bytes	64 bytes
Gauss	1074	314	64.3	80.9	94.4	95.9	97.4	98.8
Qsort	1171	310	69.0	74.9	80.7	72.9	74.8	81.4
Relax	2132	329	78.8	89.3	97.0	79.6	89.7	97.2
Psim	1827	319	88.4	88.6	90.7	89.5	89.6	91.3

Table 2: Benchmark Statistics for SC1 for 16K and 64K caches
References are averages per processor and are in 1000's.

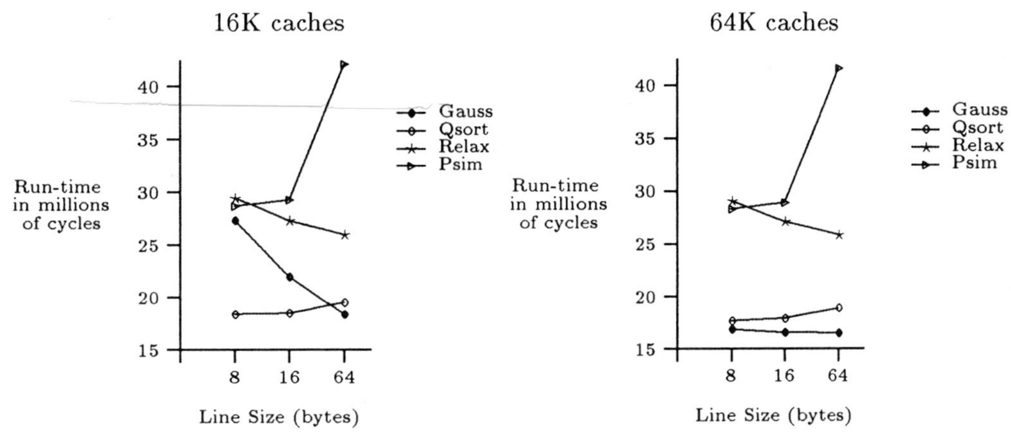

Figure 2: Performance by Line Size for SC1

are not spread out evenly across the memory modules. The utilization of the modules varies by as much as a factor of six, which produces some minor hot spots. Both of these factors result in a much higher actual memory latency in *Psim*. The latency is proportional to the line size, and as seen in Figure 2, can have a major performance impact. The data set of *Psim* is fairly small and fits into a 16K cache. So, its performance is fairly insensitive to the cache size. The hit rate is also insensitive to the line size. Finally, *Psim* has the highest synchronization rate of any of the benchmarks (over 80,000 synchronizations per processor. See [21]).

4 Simulation Results

Our experiments were instruction-level simulations of 16 processor systems for all benchmarks and of 32 processor systems for *Gauss* only because of time limitations. We ran the simulations with cache line sizes of 8, 16 and 64 bytes and two cache sizes: 16K and 64K bytes. The results for 16 processors and 16K caches are shown in Figure 3, the results for 16 processors and 64K caches are shown in Figure 4, and the results for *Gauss* with 32 processors are shown in Figure 5. In these figures, each graph has plots for each of the three line sizes. The y-axes show the relative (percent) performance improvements of the various memory models over the SC1 system for that line size. Note that the scales of the y-axes are different for each benchmark.

In the following sections we discuss the results for each benchmark and compare the results for the various models. This will allow us to draw some conclusions on the relative merits of each hardware addition.

4.1 Analysis of Benchmarks

Gauss The greatest performance improvement from using relaxed models is attained in the *Gauss* benchmark. In the case of 16K caches with 8 byte lines the systems implementing relaxed models show a performance gain of over 35%. With 16 byte lines the gain is about 20% and with 64 byte lines 8%. The greater gain for 8 byte lines is due to the lower hit ratios since cache misses provide the opportunity to draw benefits from the relaxed models. With the relaxed models there is also less of a gap between the performance of the different line sizes. Under WO1 there is only a 16% and 10% improvement for 64 byte and 16 byte lines over the 8 byte line versus the 50% and 25% mentioned earlier for SC1.

The case of the 64K cache is quite different. As mentioned above, the cache hit rates for 64K caches are quite high. Therefore we cannot expect much gain from the relaxed models; the benefits never reach 2%.

The 32 processor results show the same trends that

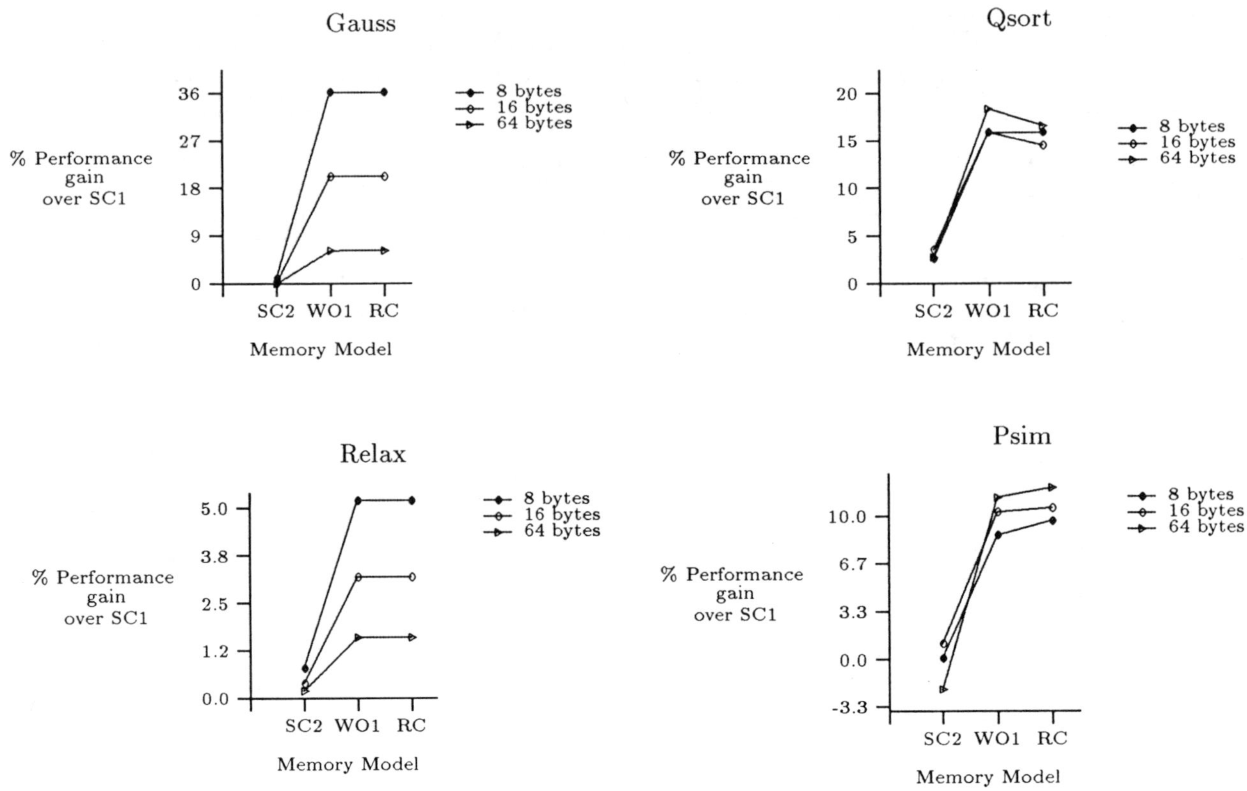

Figure 3: 16 processors, 16K caches

The performance improvement is relative to SC1 for that line size.
Note that the scale of the y axis in each graph is different.

are seen with 16 processors. The data set still does not fit in the cache when 16K caches are used. The performance benefit for each line size is slightly higher than was observed with 16 processors. This is to be expected since the memory latency is higher due to the extra level needed in the network. Despite the slight increase in memory latency, the speed-up with 32 processors was good. The system was faster by 80-86% with one instance of 76%. The relaxed models showed a 1-4% better speed-up than SC1 did when using the same cache structure.

One should not reach undue conclusions from the 64K cache experiment. Recall that the data set was of a size that made it amenable to be run on a simulator. A 250x250 matrix of doubles occupies only half a megabyte of memory. Gaussian elimination on such a matrix takes about 10 CPU seconds on a modern workstation. The problems we expect to run on a real parallel processor will be much larger. The data sets will probably be too large for the cache and the hit ratios will be more like those recorded for the 16K cache.

Qsort The performance of *Qsort* is significantly improved by the implementation of relaxed models. The benefits range from 13% to 18% and are realized for both cache sizes. These improvements stem from a moderately low hit rate (69-81% for both cache sizes since neither cache has the capacity to store the program's working set) accompanied by memory access patterns that allow overlapping. As mentioned in section 3.3, the variability of results for the various line sizes and models is caused by dynamic scheduling effects.

Relax As can be seen in Figures 3 and 4, *Relax* obtains very little benefit from the relaxed models. The largest gain is 5%. Part of the reason for the lack of improvement is *Relax*'s high cache hit rate, from 79% to 98% depending mostly on the line size. Note that the 79% hit rate is comparable to *Qsort*'s and for that latter benchmark the relaxed models yield better improvements. The compounding reason for *Relax*'s low improvement is its access pattern. The relaxed models cannot hide much of the memory latency. As described in section 3.3, most of it is already hidden in the case of a write miss (in all implementations) by the register-register operations following the write, or it cannot be hidden in the case of a read miss that causes a stall almost immediately when the destination register is used (see a more detailed analysis in [21]).

This analysis of *Relax* made us realize that how the program is written or compiled for peak performance depends upon the memory model to be used. If the

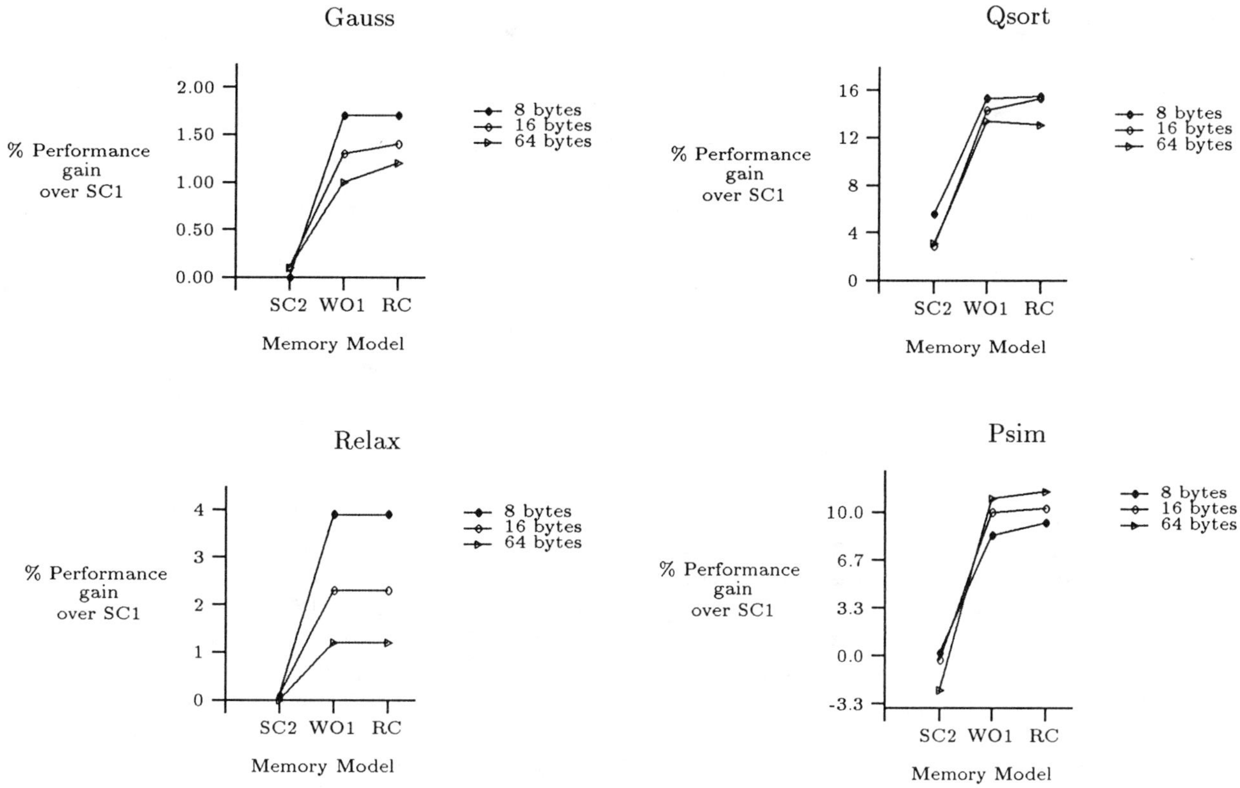

Figure 4: 16 processors, 64K caches

The performance improvement is relative to SC1 for that line size.
Note that the scale of the y axis in each graph is different.

compiler can rearrange the code to schedule all the loads at the top of loop, then there may be some benefit from the relaxed models for *Relax* for 8 byte lines. The access that will cause the miss should be done first among the nine loads, thereby allowing the main memory access to be done while loading the other eight registers from cache. For larger lines with high hit rates (over 90%), we expect the effect of this optimization, for this size data set, to be minimal. Note that even in SC1 the code can be rearranged to minimize the memory access penalty. All the loads should again be done at the top of the loop, but the one that causes the miss should be done last. Otherwise the processor will stall when attempting a load after the miss. While the line is being fetched from memory, the other eight values can be summed so that by the time the register whose value was coming from main memory is added into the sum, the line has arrived from memory (this can also be done for the relaxed models). The optimizer in our compiler does reorganize the code so that all the loads are at the top of the loop. However, it is not smart enough to realize which load will miss in the cache and schedule the code accordingly[4].

[4] See [21] for the effect of hand-scheduled code.

Psim *Psim* has a moderate (8-10%) performance improvement from the relaxed models which is to be expected given its hit rate of approximately 90%. Since *Psim* has a much higher average memory latency due to its high level of sharing and skewed memory access distribution, it gets greater benefit than *Relax*.

4.2 Performance of the Consistency Models

Relaxed Model Benefits As a general rule, the relaxed models show a non-negligible performance improvement as long as the cache hit rates are not too high. If hit rates are in the high nineties, then the memory access times are less important and, as could be expected, the use of sequential consistency won't degrade performance. In the case of lower hit rates, the benefits of relaxed models can be mitigated if either a single non-blocking load (as in SC1) allows a substantial overlap of memory access and computation, or, conversely, if a fetch for some value is almost immediately followed by its use. In the latter situation, it is likely that the code could be reorganized to take better advantage of the relaxed models, especially if the architecture supplies a sufficient number of registers. We further discuss the general benefits of the relaxed models in section 5.2.

RC versus WO1 In all of the runs RC and WO1

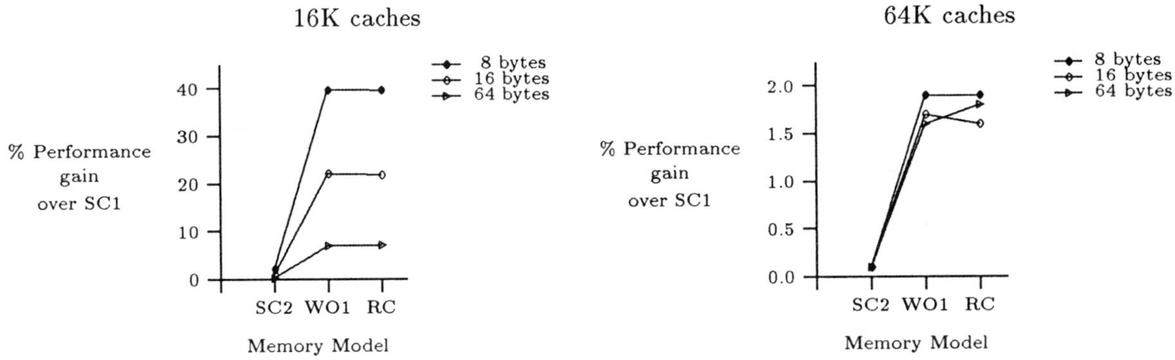

Figure 5: 32 processors, Gauss

The performance improvement is relative to SC1 for that line size.
Note that the scale of the y axis in each graph is different.

performed in a similar manner. If there was any difference, RC's improvement over SC1 was slightly better. The largest instance, less than 1% better relative to SC1, occurred for *Psim*, the program with the most synchronizations, and hence, the most releases. Recall that RC and WO1 differ only in the way acquires and releases are implemented. Under RC when a release is encountered the processor does not stall either for outstanding references or for the release to complete, whereas under WO1, the processor does stall. Also, for an acquire it does not stall while outstanding memory accesses complete. Clearly neither of these events were frequent enough for the processor to spend a significant portion of its time stalling at releases in the WO1 system. From these benchmarks there is nothing to indicate that it is worthwhile implementing RC instead of WO1 if implementing RC would in any way be more costly or detrimental to the processor's cycle time.

SC2 versus SC1 In general there is very little benefit in prefetching one line when a processor is stalled due to a cache miss. In fact, for *Psim* with 64 byte lines prefetching was detrimental because it increased the congestion in the network. As noted earlier, that benchmark has a high level of network traffic due to coherence effects and the network traffic was exacerbated by the large line size. SC2 causes a clustering of memory requests that further saturate the network, resulting in a net rise in the memory latency, the opposite of what we sought. The probable cause for the general lack of performance gain in SC2 is that the opportunity for it to be of any help, i.e., to have consecutive cache misses to different lines without an intervening register interlock causing a processor stall, is rare. This paucity of limited prefetches increases for programs with good locality.

5 Related Work and Comparisons

5.1 Methodology

Simulation performance studies of relaxed consistency models have been done on two different architectures: a shared-bus multiprocessor [2] and a mesh connected multiprocessor based on DASH, an experimental system being built at Stanford [12, 19]. Our previous study [2] should not be compared to this one due to the modest number of processors (nine to twelve), the low memory latency, and the limitations of its trace-driven nature. However, the Stanford study, which used instruction-level simulation, is similar in scope to our current study but their architectural framework and memory model implementations are significantly different.

The Stanford study is based on a variant of the DASH [18] architecture with 16 processors connected in a mesh-like fashion. Memory is globally distributed with a portion of global memory being associated with each processor and forming its local, or home, memory; the remainder of the global memory is the remote (for that processor) memory. Each processor has a two-level cache hierarchy with a write-through first level and a write-back second level cache. There is a write buffer between the two caches and if a relaxed consistency model is being implemented, loads can bypass the stores that are in the write buffer. The first level cache has a one word line size and a fetch size on read misses of four words [10]. Cache coherence is enforced by a hardware full directory scheme with the directories being associated with the home memories. The memory latency depends upon the type of memory reference (read, write, synchronization), the memory location of the missing line (home or remote), and the state of the line (clean or dirty). The memory latencies range from 20 to 80 cycles in the case of no contention on the interconnect.

Gharachorloo et al. [12] studied a number of consistency models including: two forms of sequentially consistent systems, a weakly ordered system, and a release consistent system. The major difference between the systems involved the selection of events that led to processor stalls. Specifically:

- In all four cases, after the issue of a read or an acquire the processor stalls until the operation completes, i.e., *blocking loads* are used.

- In all systems except the release consistent one, all writes have to be performed before an acquire or a release is issued.
- In the release consistent system, releases are delayed until all writes are performed but the processor is not stalled. Pending writes do not cause the processor to stall at an acquire.
- Upon issue of a write, either:
  - the processor stalls until the writes are performed (base sequentially consistent)
  - writes are sent to the write buffer but reads won't be allowed until writes are performed (aggressive sequentially consistent)
  - writes are sent to the write buffer and the processor continues on (weak ordering, release consistency)

Note that since blocking loads are used, no read latency is being overlapped with computation. Only write latency is.

5.2 Results and Comparisons

Our experiments show that a relaxed memory model (WO1) using non-blocking loads, lock-up free caches, synchronization primitives visible to the hardware, and stalls on all synchronization points when outstanding memory references are present is worthwhile. Performance improvements over an aggressive sequential consistency model can reach 35%. However, with high cache hit rates the benefit is limited.

The trends observed in the Stanford study were the same as ours, but their maximum reported performance gain, 40% over their base system in the case of the most aggressive models, was higher. There are several reasons for the quantitative differences. First, the memory latencies for the Stanford study are much larger, thus giving a greater advantage to relaxed memory models. Second, the implementation of our base system, SC1, is more aggressive since we use non-blocking loads. Third, the cache structures that were used are different. In the Stanford study the first level cache is direct-mapped and write-through (although write hits in the second level cache take only two cycles). Therefore, writes are not performed as quickly as in our write-back cache and consequently the relaxed models have more opportunity to gain since all writes take several cycles to complete. Also, while simulating several cache organizations, we showed that the benefit could vary greatly depending upon the cache and line size; it would be interesting to see whether this is true too of a DASH-like architecture.

There was one case where we reached different conclusions about the benefit of one of the models. In the Stanford study one benchmark, *Pthor*, was found to have significant performance improvement when run on RC compared to when run on WO1. In our comparable benchmark, *Psim*, which had a similar hit rate and a high level of synchronization, although still only a third of *Pthor*'s, the benefits of RC and WO1 were essentially the same. We believe that there are three main reasons for the difference in the level of improvement: (i) *Pthor*'s higher synchronization rate and, as observed earlier, the more frequent synchronization, the greater the opportunity to benefit from RC, (ii) the higher memory latency in the DASH-like system results in a greater likelihood of a write being outstanding at a release (it is not expected that a read would be outstanding at a release since its value would need to have been used before the release), and (iii) even though the write hit rates are roughly the same, the number of write misses per unit time of *Pthor* is over double that of *Psim*, thereby increasing the chances of a write being outstanding at a release. All three factors provide RC with a greater opportunity for a benefit over WO1.

6 Conclusions

We have studied the performance benefits of several implementations of models of relaxed memory consistency in shared-memory multiprocessors where each processor has a private cache and the interconnect is a multistage network. Using instruction-level simulations, we have shown that under different and more aggressive architectural choices the performance benefits that might arise from using relaxed models of consistency depend significantly on the cache structure and on the program characteristics and much less so on the sophistication of the model implemented.

Our results are qualitatively similar to those presented in a simulation of the DASH architecture. Programs with high cache hit rates, little sharing, and good locality will not benefit much, as expected, from relaxed consistency. The line and cache sizes, which are very important factors in determining the hit rates, will also greatly influence the utility of relaxed consistency. When the hit rates are lower, relaxed models will usually be advantageous. However, our study shows that the gains are proportional to the memory latency and the rate of misses per unit time as well as being dependent upon the ability of the compiler to schedule the code to take advantage of the relaxed models.

The main hardware features that allow relaxed models to be beneficial are non-blocking loads and lockup-free caches. Prefetching of one line when there is already an outstanding miss, and extra flexibility to prevent the processor from stalling at some synchronization points had only minimal secondary effects. As memory latency increases, it will clearly be worthwhile to develop multiprocessors with lock-up free caches and hardware visible synchronization points so that some form of relaxed consistency can be implemented. Relaxed consistency should be implemented in conjunction with other memory latency reducing techniques such as more sophisticated prefetching, speculative execution, fast context-switching or multithreaded architectures.

The effect of relaxed consistency on the programmer and the compiler needs to be investigated. We have shown, through an example, how the optimal code reordering depends upon the model of consistency implemented. Although we know what the constraints of relaxed consistency models are to the writer of correct parallel programs, the impact of these relaxed models on programming for efficiency is an open area of study.

We could not close this paper without a word of caution. Both our study and the Stanford study used time-consuming instruction-level simulations which limited the size of the benchmarks. It is unclear what the performance of a full size data set would be. It is also unclear what other methodology should be used, if any, to avoid the overbearing consumption of CPU resources. For example, limiting the cache size proportionally to the data set size might be an approach but we have shown that not all benchmarks (e.g., *Qsort*) would have been sensitive to that effect. This methodological question is one that certainly deserves further study.

Acknowledgements We would like to thank the MPCI Project of Lawrence Livermore National Labs for hosting the first author and providing the Cerberus Simulator and some of the benchmarks. Simon Kahan wrote *Qsort* and was of great help in explaining its intricacies. We thank Craig Anderson and Tien-Fu Chen for various forms of assistance, the UW architecture lunch, and Cathy McCann in particular, as well as Sarita Adve and Kourosh Gharachorloo, for numerous and excellent comments on earlier versions of this paper. Diane Gorenberg provided assistance with the writing style and overall readability.

References

[1] Sarita Adve and Mark Hill. Weak Ordering - A New Definition. In *17th ISCA*, pages 2–14, 1990.

[2] Jean-Loup Baer and Richard N. Zucker. On Synchronization Patterns of Parallel Programs. In *1991 ICPP*, pages II–60–67, 1991.

[3] E. D. Brooks III. PCP: A Parallel Extension of C that is 99% Fat Free. Tech. Rep. UCRL-99673, Lawrence Livermore National Laboratory, 1988.

[4] E. D. Brooks III, T. S. Axelrod, and G. A. Darmohray. The Cerberus Multiprocessor Simulator. In G. Rodrigue, editor, *Parallel Processing for Scientific Computing*, pages 384–390. SIAM, 1989.

[5] Lucien M. Censier and Paul Feautrier. A New Solution to Coherence Problems in Multicache Systems. *IEEE Transactions on Computers*, C-27(12):1112–1118, December 1978.

[6] Gregory A. Darmohray. Gaussian Techniques on Shared-Memory Multiprocessors. Master's thesis, University of California, Davis, April 1988.

[7] Edgar W. Dijkstra. Cooperating Sequential Processes. In F. Genuys, editor, *Programming Languages*. Academic Press, 1968.

[8] Michel Dubois, Christoph Scheurich, and Faye Briggs. Memory access buffering in multiprocessors. In *13th ISCA*, pages 434–442, 1986.

[9] Susan J. Eggers and Randy H. Katz. The Effect of Sharing on the Cache and Bus Performance of Parallel Programs. In *Third ASPLOS*, pages 257–270, 1989.

[10] Kourosh Gharachorloo. personal communication.

[11] Kourosh Gharachorloo, Sarita Adve, Anoop Gupta, John Hennessy, and Mark Hill. Programming for Different Memory Consistency Models. *Journal of Parallel and Distributed Computing*, to appear.

[12] Kourosh Gharachorloo, Anoop Gupta, and John Hennessy. Performance Evaluation of Memory Consistency Models for Shared-Memory Multiprocessors. In *Fourth ASPLOS*, pages 245–257, 1991.

[13] Kourosh Gharachorloo, Anoop Gupta, and John Hennessy. Two Techniques to Enhance the Performance of Memory Consistency Models. In *1991 ICPP*, pages I–355–364, 1991.

[14] Kourosh Gharachorloo, Daniel Lenoski, James Laudon, Phillip Gibbons, Anoop Gupta, and John Hennessy. Memory Consistency and Event Ordering in Scalable Shared-Memory Multiprocessors. In *17th ISCA*, pages 15–26, 1990.

[15] Simon Kahan and Larry Ruzzo. Parallel Quicksand: Sorting on the Sequent. Technical Report 91-01-01, Department of Computer Science, University of Washington, January 1991.

[16] David Kroft. Lockup-free Instruction Fetch/-Prefetch Cache Organization. In *8th ISCA*, pages 81–87, June 1981.

[17] Leslie Lamport. How to Make a Multiprocessor Computer That Correctly Executes Multiprocess Programs. *IEEE Transactions on Computers*, C-28(9):690–691, September 1979.

[18] Dan Lenoski, James Laudon, Kourosh Gharachorloo, Anoop Gupta, and John Hennessy. The Directory-Based Cache Coherence Protocol for the DASH Multiprocessor. In *17th ISCA*, pages 148–159, 1990.

[19] Todd Mowry and Anoop Gupta. Tolerating Latency Through Software-Controlled Prefetch in Shared-Memory Multiprocessors. *Journal of Parallel and Distributed Computing*, 12(2):87–106, June 1991.

[20] Ridge Computers. *Ridge 32 User's Guide*.

[21] Richard N. Zucker and Jean-Loup Baer. A Performance Study of Memory Consistency Models. Technical Report 92-01-02, Department of Computer Science, University of Washington, March 1992.

Lazy Release Consistency for Software Distributed Shared Memory

Pete Keleher, Alan L. Cox, and Willy Zwaenepoel
Department of Computer Science
Rice University

Abstract

Relaxed memory consistency models, such as *release consistency*, were introduced in order to reduce the impact of remote memory access latency in both software and hardware distributed shared memory (DSM). However, in a software DSM, it is also important to reduce the number of messages and the amount of data exchanged for remote memory access. *Lazy release consistency* is a new algorithm for implementing release consistency that *lazily* pulls modifications across the interconnect only when necessary. Trace-driven simulation using the SPLASH benchmarks indicates that lazy release consistency reduces both the number of messages and the amount of data transferred between processors. These reductions are especially significant for programs that exhibit false sharing and make extensive use of locks.

1 Introduction

Over the past few years, researchers in hardware distributed shared memory (DSM) have proposed relaxed memory consistency models to reduce the *latency* associated with remote memory accesses [1, 8, 9, 10, 14]. For instance, in release consistency (RC) [9], writes to shared memory by processor p_1 need to be performed (become visible) at another processor p_2 only when a subsequent *release* of p_1 performs at p_2. This relaxation of the memory consistency model allows the DASH implementation of RC [12] to combat memory latency by pipelining writes to shared memory (see Figure 1). The processor is stalled only when executing a release, at which time it must wait for all its previous writes to perform.

In software DSMs, it is also important to reduce the *number* of messages exchanged. Sending a message in a software DSM is more expensive than in a hardware DSM, because it may involve traps into the operating system kernel, interrupts, context switches, and the execution of several layers of networking software. Ideally, the number of messages exchanged in a software DSM should equal the number of messages exchanged in a message passing implementation of the same application. Therefore, Munin's write-shared protocol [6], a software implementation of RC, buffers writes until a release, instead of pipelining them as in the DASH implementation. At the release, all writes going to the same destination are merged into a single message (see Figure 2).

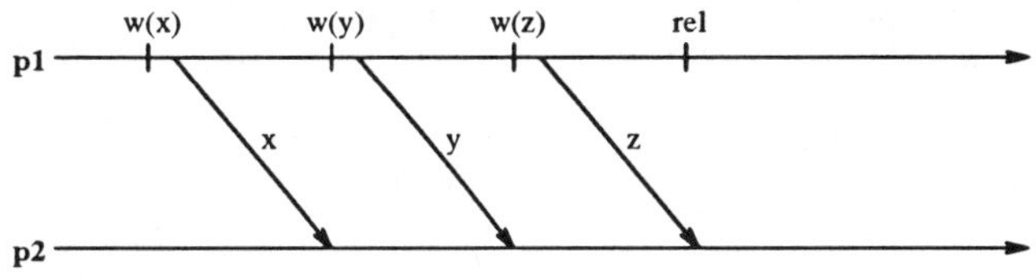

Figure 1: Pipelining Remote Memory Accesses in DASH.

Even Munin's write-shared protocol may send more messages than a message passing implementation of the same application. Consider the example of Figure 3, where processors p_1 through p_4 repeatedly acquire the lock l, write the shared variable x, and then release l. If an update policy is used in conjunction with Munin's write-shared protocol, and x is present in all caches, then all of these cached copies are updated at every release. Logically, however, it suffices to update each processor's copy only when it acquires l. This results in a single message exchange per acquire, as in a message passing implementation. This problem is not peculiar to the use of an update policy. Similar examples can be constructed for an invalidate policy.

Lazy release consistency (LRC) is a new algorithm for implementing RC, aimed at reducing both the number of messages and the amount of data exchanged. Unlike *eager* algorithms such as Munin's write-shared protocol, *lazy* algorithms such as LRC do not make modifications globally visible at the time of a release. Instead, LRC guaran-

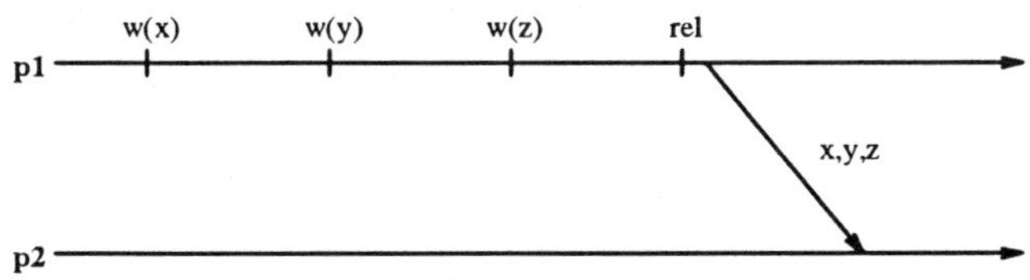

Figure 2: Merging of Remote Memory Updates in Munin.

This work is supported in part by NSF Grant No. CDA-8619893 and Texas ATP Grant No. 0036404013. Pete Keleher was supported by a NASA Fellowship.

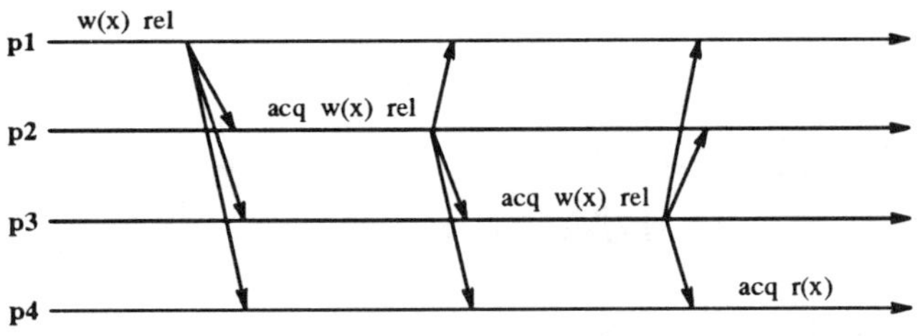

Figure 3: Repeated Updates of Cached Copies in Eager RC.

tees only that a processor that acquires a lock will see all modifications that "precede" the lock acquire. The term "preceding" in this context is to be interpreted in the transitive sense: informally, a modification precedes an acquire, if it occurs before any release such that there is a chain of release-acquire operations on the same lock, ending with the current acquire (see Section 4 for a precise definition). For instance, in Figure 3, all modifications that occur in program order before any of the releases in p_1 through p_3 precede the lock acquisition in p_4. With LRC, modifications are propagated at the time of an acquire. Only the modifications that "precede" the acquire are sent to the acquiring processor. The modifications can be piggybacked on the message that grants the lock, further reducing message traffic. Figure 4 shows the message traffic in LRC for the same shared data accesses as in Figure 3. l and x are sent in a single message at each acquire.

By not propagating modifications globally at the time of the release, and by piggybacking data movement on lock transfer messages, LRC reduces both the number of messages and the amount of data exchanged. We present the results of a simulation study, using the SPLASH benchmarks, that confirms this intuition. LRC is, however, more complex to implement than eager RC because it must keep track of the "precedes" relation. We intend to implement LRC to evaluate its runtime cost. The message and data reductions seen in our simulations seem to indicate that LRC will outperform eager RC in a software DSM environment.

The outline of the rest of this paper is as follows. In Section 2, we state the definition of RC. In Section 3, we present an eager implementation of RC based on Munin's write-shared protocol. In Section 4, we define LRC and outline its implementation. In Section 5, we describe a comparison through simulation of eager RC and LRC. We briefly discuss related work in Section 6, and we draw conclusions and explore avenues for further work in Section 7.

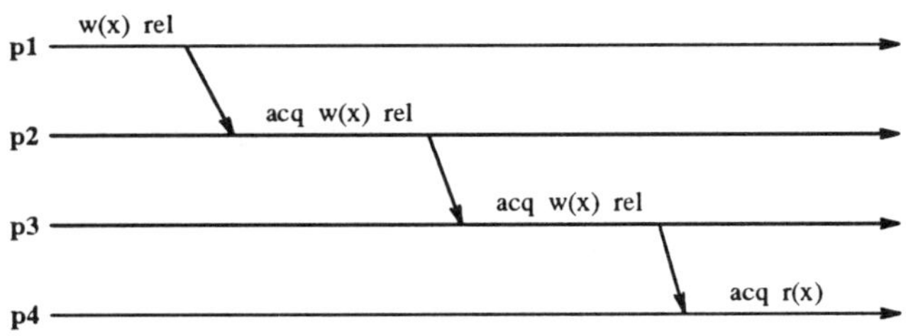

Figure 4: Message Traffic in LRC.

2 Release Consistency

Release consistency (RC) [9] is a form of relaxed memory consistency that allows the effects of shared memory accesses to be delayed until certain *specially labeled* accesses occur. RC requires shared memory accesses to be labeled as either *ordinary* or *special*. Within the *special* category, accesses are divided into those labeled *sync* and *nsync*, and *sync* accesses are further subdivided into *acquires* and *releases*.

Definition 2.1 *A system is* release consistent *if:*

1. *Before an ordinary access is allowed to perform with respect to any other processor, all previous* acquires *must be performed.*
2. *Before a* release *is allowed to perform with respect to any other processor, all previous ordinary reads and writes must be performed.*
3. Special *accesses are sequentially consistent with respect to one another.*

A write is performed with respect to another processor when reads by that processor return the new write's (or a subsequent write's) value. Reads are performed with respect to another processor when a write issued by that processor can no longer affect the value returned by the read. Accesses are *performed* when they are performed with respect to all processors in the system.

Properly labeled programs [9] produce the same results on RC memory as they would on sequentially consistent memory [11]. Informally, a program is properly labeled if there are "enough" accesses labeled as acquires or releases, such that, for all legal interleavings of accesses, each pair of conflicting ordinary accesses is separated by a release-acquire chain. Two accesses *conflict* if they reference the same memory location, and at least one of them is a write.

RC implementations can delay the effects of shared memory accesses as long as they meet the constraints of Definition 2.1.

3 Eager Release Consistency

We base our eager RC algorithm on Munin's write-shared protocol [6]. A processor delays propagating its modifications to shared data until it comes to a *release*. At that time, it propagates the modifications to all other processors that cache the modified pages. For an invalidate protocol, this simply entails sending invalidations for all modified pages to the other processors that cache these pages. In order to limit the amount of data exchanged, an update protocol sends a *diff* of each modified page to other cachers. A *diff* describes the modifications made to the page, which are then merged in the other cached copies. In either case, the release blocks until acknowledgments have been received from all other cachers.

No consistency-related operations occur on an acquire. The protocol locates the processor that last executed a release on the same variable, and the resulting value is sent from the last releaser to the current acquirer.

On an access miss, a message is sent to the directory manager for the page. The directory manager forwards the request to the current owner, and the current owner sends the page to the processor that incurred the access miss.

4 Lazy Release Consistency

In LRC, the propagation of modifications is further postponed *until the time of the acquire*. At this time, the acquiring processor determines which modifications it needs to see according to the definition of RC. To do so, LRC uses a representation of the *happened-before-1* partial order introduced by Adve and Hill [2]. The *happened-before-1* partial order is a formalization of the "preceding" relation mentioned in Section 1.

4.1 The *happened-before-1* Partial Order

We summarize here the relevant aspects of the definitions of *happened-before-1* [2].

Definition 4.1 *Shared memory accesses are partially ordered by* happened-before-1, *denoted* $\stackrel{hb1}{\rightarrow}$, *defined as follows:*

- *If* a_1 *and* a_2 *are accesses on the same processor, and* a_1 *occurs before* a_2 *in program order, then* $a_1 \stackrel{hb1}{\rightarrow} a_2$.
- *If* a_1 *is a release on processor* p_1, *and* a_2 *is an acquire on the same memory location on processor* p_2, *and* a_2 *returns the value written by* a_1, *then* $a_1 \stackrel{hb1}{\rightarrow} a_2$.
- *If* $a_1 \stackrel{hb1}{\rightarrow} a_2$ *and* $a_2 \stackrel{hb1}{\rightarrow} a_3$, *then* $a_1 \stackrel{hb1}{\rightarrow} a_3$.

RC requires that before a processor may continue past an acquire, all shared accesses that precede the acquire according to $\stackrel{hb1}{\rightarrow}$ must be performed at the acquiring processor. LRC guarantees that this property holds by propagating *write-notices* on the message that effects a release-acquire pair. A write-notice is an indication that a page has been modified in a particular interval, but it does not contain the actual modifications. Write-notices and actual values of modifications may be sent t different times in different messages.

4.2 Write-Notice Propagation

We divide the execution of each processor into distinct *intervals*, a new interval beginning with each special access executed by the processor. We define a *happens-before-1* partial order between intervals in the obvious way: an interval i_1 precedes an interval i_2 according to $\stackrel{hb1}{\rightarrow}$, if all accesses in i_1 precede all accesses in i_2 according to $\stackrel{hb1}{\rightarrow}$. An interval is said to be performed at a processor if all modifications made during that interval have been performed at that processor.

Let $V^p(i)$ be the *vector timestamp* [15] for interval i of processor p. The number of elements in the vector $V^p(i)$ is equal to the number of processors. The entry for processor p in $V^p(i)$ is equal to i. The entry for processor $q \neq p$ in $V^p(i)$ denotes the most recent interval of processor q that has performed at p.

On an acquire, the acquiring processor, p, sends its current vector timestamp V^p to the previous releaser, q. Processor q uses this information to send p the write-notices for all intervals of all processors that have performed at q but have not yet performed at p. Releases are purely local operations in LRC, no messages are exchanged.

4.3 Data Movement Protocols

4.3.1 Multiple Writer Protocols

Both Munin and LRC allow *multiple-writer* protocols. Multiple processors can write to different parts of the same page concurrently, without intervening synchronization. This is in contrast to the exclusive-writer protocol used, for instance, in DASH [9], where a processor must obtain exclusive access to a cache line before it can be modified. Experience with Munin [6] indicates that multiple-writer protocols perform well in software DSMs, because they can handle false sharing without generating large amounts of message traffic. Given the large page sizes in software DSMs, false sharing is an important problem. Exclusive-writer protocols may cause falsely shared pages to "ping-pong" back and forth between different processors. Multiple-writer protocols allow each processor to write into a falsely shared page without any message traffic. The modifications of the different processors are later merged using the *diffs* described in Section 3.

4.3.2 Invalidate vs. Update

In the case of an invalidate protocol, the acquiring processor invalidates all pages in its cache for which it received write-notices. In the case of an update protocol, the acquiring processor updates those pages. Let i be the current interval. For each page in the cache, *diffs* must be obtained from all *concurrent last modifiers*. These are all intervals j, such that $j \stackrel{hb1}{\rightarrow} i$, the page was modified in interval j, and there is no interval k, such that $j \stackrel{hb1}{\rightarrow} k \stackrel{hb1}{\rightarrow} i$, in which the modification from interval j was overwritten.

4.3.3 Access Misses

On an access miss, a copy of the page may have to be retrieved, as well as a number of *diffs*. The modifications summarized by the *diffs* are then merged into the page before it is accessed.

On an access miss during interval i, *diffs* must be obtained for all intervals j, such that $j \stackrel{hb1}{\rightarrow} i$, the missing page was modified in interval j, and there is no interval k, such that $j \stackrel{hb1}{\rightarrow} k \stackrel{hb1}{\rightarrow} i$, in which the modification from interval j was overwritten.

If the processor still holds an (invalidated) copy of the page, LRC does not send the entire page over the interconnect. The write-notices contain all the information necessary to determine which *diffs* need to be applied to this copy of the page in order to bring it up-to-date. The *happened-before-1* partial order specifies the order in which the *diffs* need to be applied. This optimization reduces the amount of data sent.

5 Simulation

We present the results of a simulation study based on multiprocessor traces of five shared-memory application programs from the SPLASH suite [17]. We measured the number of messages and the amount of data exchanged by each program for an execution using each of four protocols: lazy update (LU), lazy invalidate (LI), eager update (EU), and eager invalidate (EI). We then relate the communication

	Access Miss	Locks	Unlocks	Barriers
LI	2m	3	0	2(n-1)
LU	2m	3+2h	0	2(n-1)+2u
EI	2 or 3	3	2c	2(n-1) + v
EU	2	3	2c	2(n-1) + 2u

m = # concurrent last modifiers for the missing page
h = # other concurrent last modifiers for any local page
c = # other cachers of the page
n = # processors in system
p = # pages in system
$u = \sum_{i=1}^{n}$ (# other cachers of pages modified by i)
$v = \sum_{i=1}^{p}$ (# excess invalidators of page i)

Table 1: Shared Memory Operation Message Costs

behavior to the shared memory access patterns of the application programs.

5.1 Methodology

A trace was generated from a 32-processor execution of each program using the Tango multiprocessor simulator [7]. These traces were then fed into our protocol simulator. We simulated page sizes from 512 to 8192 bytes.

We assume infinite caches and reliable FIFO communication channels. We do not assume any broadcast or multicast capability of the network.

5.2 Message Counts

The SPLASH programs use barriers and exclusive locks for synchronization. Communication occurs on barrier arrival and departure, on lock and unlock, and on an access miss. Table 1 shows the message count for each of these events under each of the protocols.

A miss costs either two or three messages for the eager protocols, depending on whether or not the directory manager has a valid copy of the page (see Section 3). For the lazy protocols, a miss requires collecting *diffs* from the *concurrent last modifiers* of the page (see Section 4.3.2).

For a lock operation, three messages are used by all four protocols for finding and transferring the lock. In addition, in LU, the new lock holder collects all the *diffs* necessary to bring its cached pages up-to-date, causing $2h$ additional messages. No extra messages are required at this time for LI, because the invalidations are piggybacked on the lock transfer message. Also, no additional messages are required for EU and EI.

On unlocks, the eager protocols send write-notices to all cachers of locally modified pages, using $2c$ messages. The lazy protocols do not communicate on unlocks.

Barriers are implemented by sending an arrival message to the *barrier master* and waiting for the return of an exit message. Consequently, $2(n-1)$ messages are used to implement a barrier. In addition, both update protocols require $2u$ messages to send updates to all processors caching modified pages. The LI protocol requires no additional messages, because invalidations are piggybacked on the messages used for implementing the barrier. The EI protocol may require

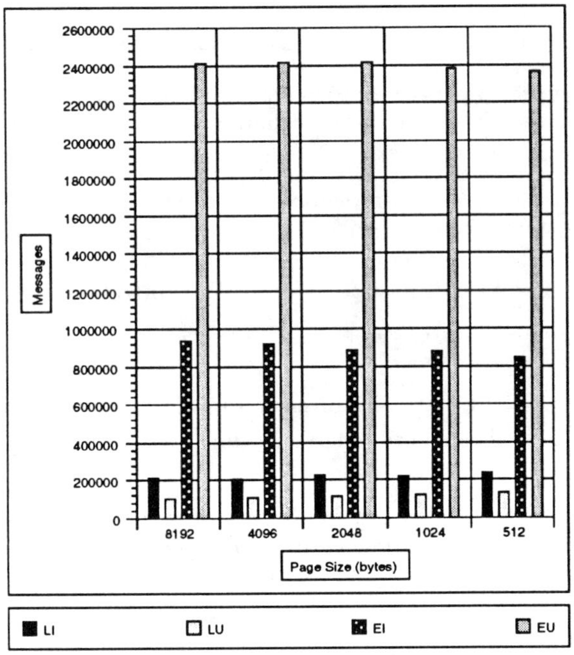

Figure 5: LocusRoute Messages.

a small number of additional messages v to resolve multiple invalidations of a single page.

5.3 SPLASH Program Suite

5.3.1 LocusRoute

`LocusRoute` is a VLSI cell router. The major data structure is a cost grid for the cell, a cell's cost being the number of wires already running through it. Work is allocated to processors a wire at a time. Synchronization is accomplished almost entirely through locks that protect access to a central task queue.

Data movement in `LocusRoute` is largely migratory [18]: locks dominate the synchronization, and data moves according to lock accesses. As page size increases, false sharing also becomes important. Both of these factors favor lazy protocols.

Figures 5 and 6 show `LocusRoute`'s performance. The lazy protocols reduce the number of messages and the amount of data exchanged, for all page sizes.

5.3.2 Cholesky Factorization

`Cholesky` performs the symbolic and numeric portions of a `Cholesky` factorization of a sparse positive definite matrix. Locks are used to control access to a global task queue and to arbitrate access when simultaneous supernodal modifications attempt to modify the same column. No barriers are used.

Data motion in `Cholesky` is largely migratory, as in `LocusRoute`. The resulting performance of `Cholesky` is therefore also similar to that of `LocusRoute`: Figures 7 and 8 show that the lazy protocols reduce the number of messages and the amount of data exchanged, for all page sizes.

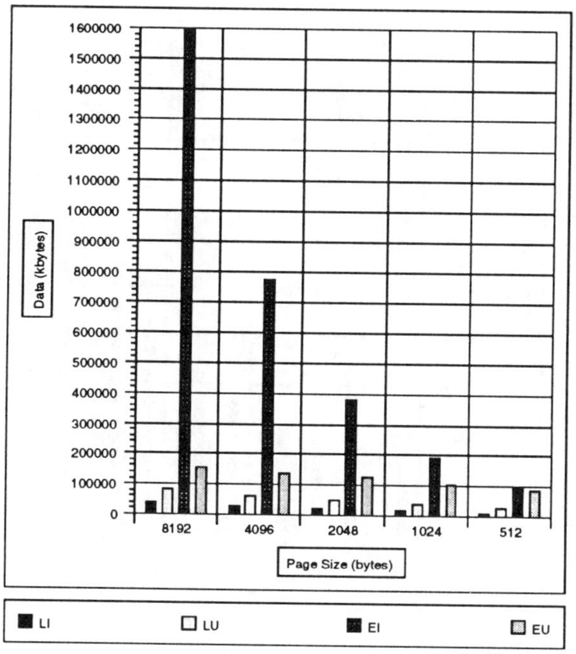

Figure 6: LocusRoute Data.

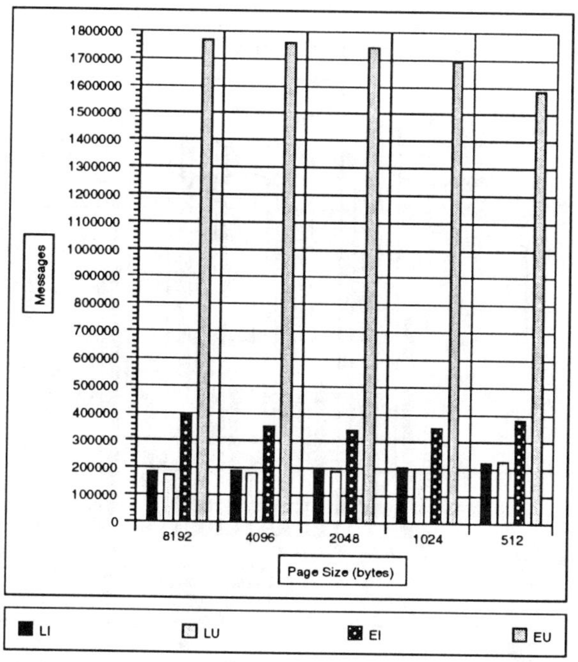

Figure 7: Cholesky Messages.

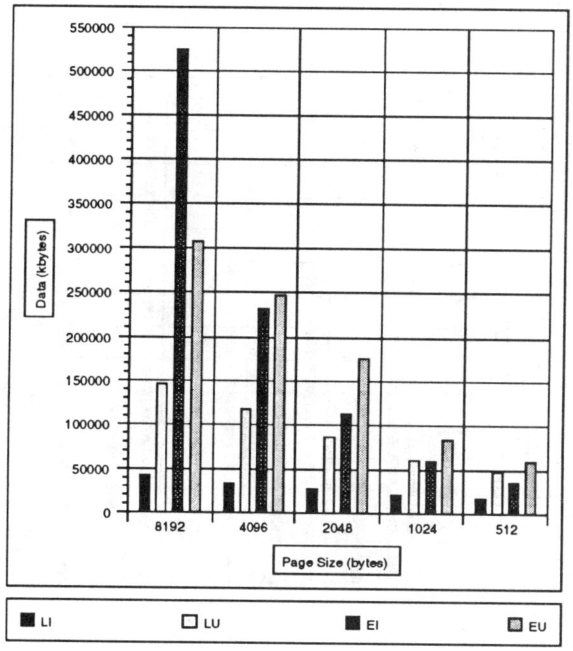

Figure 8: Cholesky Data.

5.3.3 MP3D

`MP3D` simulates rarefied hypersonic airflow over an object using a Monte Carlo algorithm. Each timestep involves several barriers, with locks used to control access to global event counters.

The message traffic for `MP3D` is dominated by access misses. Figures 9 and 10 show `MP3D`'s performance. The lazy protocols exchange less data than the eager ones, because they only need to send *diffs* on an access miss and not full pages, as do the eager protocols. The update protocols exchange fewer messages, because they incur fewer access misses.

5.3.4 Water

`Water` performs an N-body molecular dynamics simulation, evaluating forces and potentials in a system of water molecules in the liquid state. At each timestep, every molecule's velocity and potential is computed from the influences of other molecules within a spherical cutoff range. Several barriers are used to synchronize each timestep, while locks are used to control access to a global running sum and to each molecule's force sum.

Of the five benchmark programs, `Water` has the least communication. Figures 11 and 12 show the message and data traffic for `Water`. While the lazy protocols use only slightly fewer messages than eager protocols for large page sizes, their data totals are significantly lower because they can often avoid bringing an entire page across the network on an access miss.

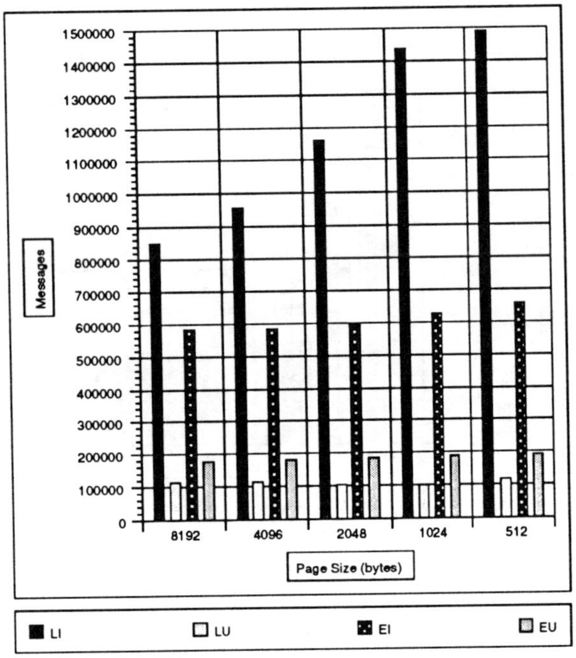

Figure 9: MP3D Messages.

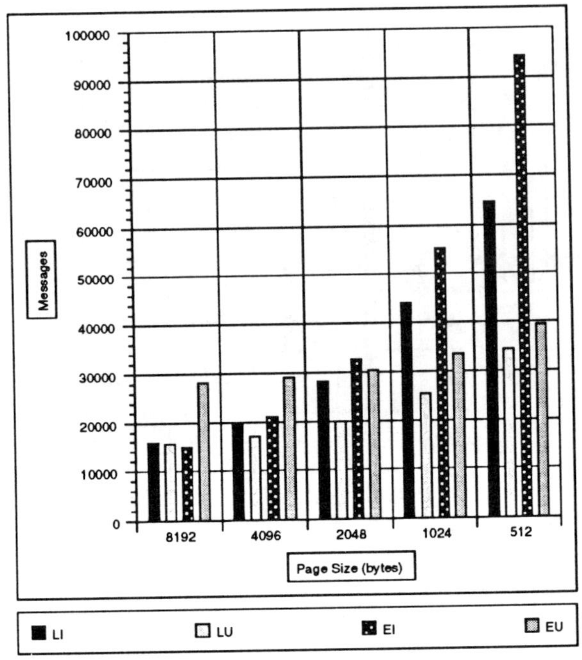

Figure 11: Water Messages.

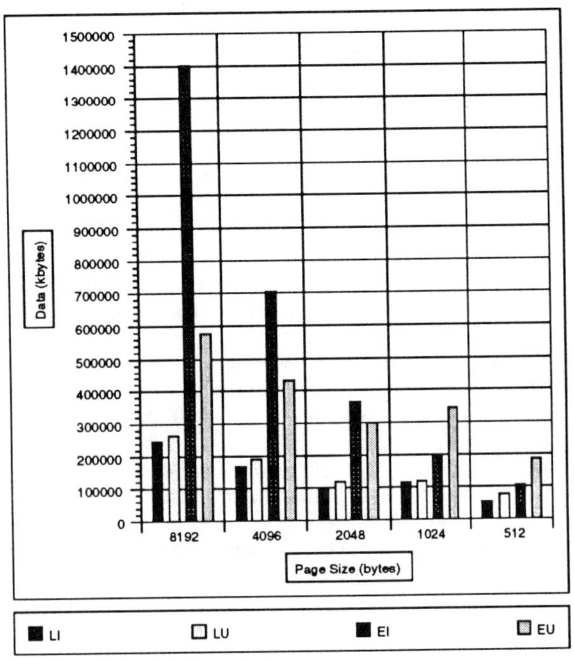

Figure 10: MP3D Data.

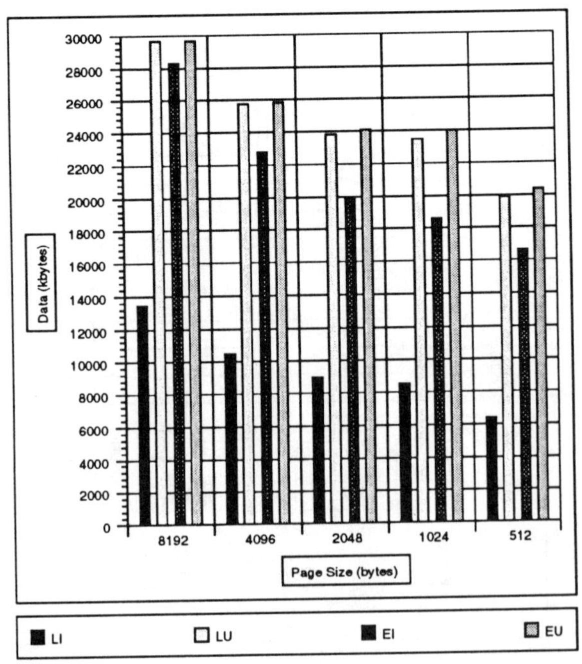

Figure 12: Water Data.

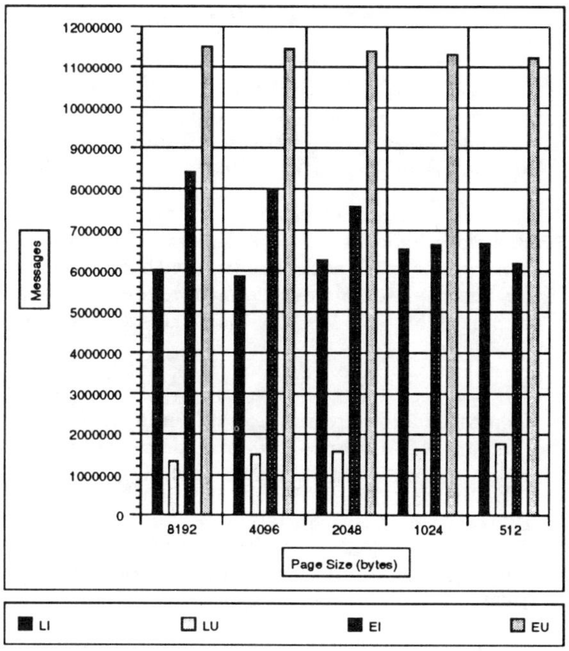

Figure 13: Pthor Messages.

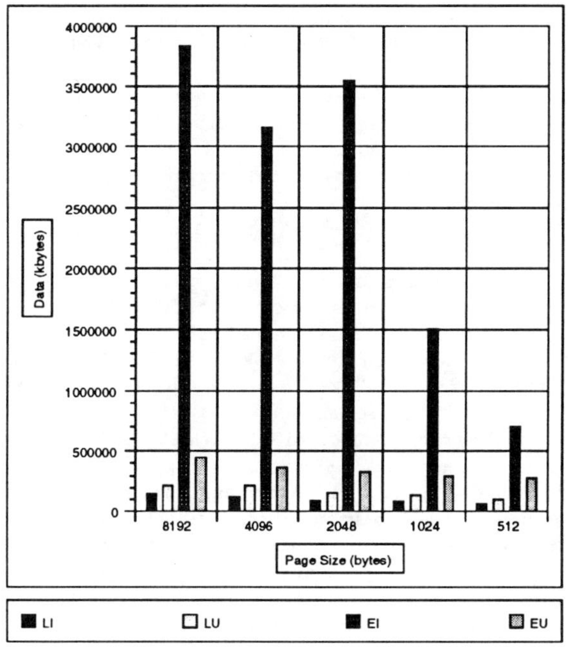

Figure 14: Pthor Data.

5.3.5 Pthor

`Pthor` is a parallel logic simulator. The major data structures represent logic elements, wires between elements, and per-processor work queues. Locks are used to protect access to all three types of data structures. Barriers are used only when deadlock occurs and all task queues are empty.

In `Pthor`, each processor has a set of pages that it modifies. However, these pages are also frequently read by the other processors. Under an invalidation protocol, this causes a large number of invalidations and later reloads.

Figures 13 and 14 show `Pthor`'s performance. Data totals for EI are particularly high, because frequent reloads cause the entire page to be sent. The message count for LI is higher than for LU, because LI has more access misses.

5.4 Summary

The SPLASH programs can be divided into two categories based on their synchronization and sharing behavior. The first category is characterized by heavy use of barrier synchronization. This category includes the `MP3D` and `Water` programs. These programs performed poorly with invalidate protocols and large page sizes. Although barriers result in nearly the same number of messages under both eager and lazy protocols, even these programs have enough lock synchronization for the lazy protocols to reduce the number of messages and the amount of data exchanged.

The second category is characterized by migratory access to data that is controlled by locks. This category includes `LocusRoute`, `Cholesky` and `Pthor`. In `Cholesky` and `Pthor`, the locks protect centralized work queues, while the locks in `LocusRoute` protect access to individual cost array elements. The use of locks tends to cause the sharing patterns to closely follow synchronization. Since the lazy protocols move data according to synchronization, they handle this type of synchronization much better than eager protocols.

LU performed well for both categories of programs. In contrast, EU often performed worse than the invalidate protocols, because it does not handle migratory data very well. LU sends fewer messages than EU for migratory data because updates are only sent to the next processor to acquire the lock that controls access to the data.

In all of the programs, the number of processors sharing a page is increased by false sharing. Multiple-writer RC protocols reduce the impact of false sharing by permitting ordinary accesses to a page by different processors to be performed concurrently. However, the eager protocols still perform communication at synchronization points between processors sharing a page, but not the data within the page. Lazy protocols eliminate this communication, because processors that falsely share data are unlikely to be causally related. This observation is consistent with the results of our simulations.

6 Related Work

Ivy [13] was the first page-based distributed shared memory system. The shared memory implemented by Ivy is sequentially consistent, and does not allow multiple writers.

Clouds [16] uses program-based *segments* rather than pages as the granularity of consistency. In addition, Clouds permits segments to be locked down at a single processor to prevent "ping-ponging".

Release consistency was introduced by Gharachorloo *et al.* [9]. It is a refinement of weak consistency, defined by Dubois and Scheurich [8]. The DASH multiprocessor takes advantage of release consistency by pipelining remote memory accesses [12]. Pipelining reduces the impact of remote memory access latency on the processor.

Munin [6] was the first software distributed shared memory system to use release consistency. Munin's implementation of release consistency merges updates at release time, rather than pipelining them, in order to reduce the number of messages transferred between processors. Munin uses multiple consistency protocols to further reduce the number of messages.

Ahamad *et al.* defined a relaxed memory model called *causal memory* [3]. Causal memory differs from RC because conflicting pairs of *ordinary* memory accesses establish causal relationships. In contrast, under RC, only *special* memory accesses establish causal relationships.

Entry consistency, defined by Bershad and Zekauskas [5], is another related relaxed memory model. EC differs from RC because it requires all shared data to be explicitly associated with some synchronization variable. As a result, when a processor acquires a synchronization variable, an EC implementation only needs to propagate the shared data associated with the synchronization variable. EC, however, requires the programmer to insert additional synchronization in shared memory programs, such as the SPLASH benchmarks, to execute correctly on an EC memory. Typically, RC does not require additional synchronization.

7 Conclusions

The performance of software DSMs is very sensitive to the number of messages and the amount of data exchanged to create the shared memory abstraction. We have described a new algorithm for implementing release consistency, *lazy release consistency*, aimed at reducing both the number of messages and the amount of data exchanged. Lazy release consistency tracks the causal dependencies between writes, acquires, and releases, allowing it to propagate writes lazily, only when they are needed.

We have used trace-driven simulation to compare lazy release consistency to an eager algorithm for implementing release consistency, based on Munin's write-shared protocol. Traces were collected from the programs in the SPLASH benchmark suite, and both update and invalidate protocols were simulated for lazy and eager RC. The simulations confirm that the number of messages and the amount of data exchanged are generally smaller for the lazy algorithm, especially for programs that exhibit false sharing and make extensive use of locks. Further work will include an implementation of lazy release consistency to assess the runtime cost of the algorithm.

References

[1] S. Adve and M. Hill. Weak ordering: A new definition. In *Proceedings of the 17th Annual International Symposium on Computer Architecture*, pages 2–14, May 1990.

[2] S. V. Adve and M. D. Hill. A unified formalization of four shared-memory models. Technical Report CS-1051, University of Wisconsin, Madison, September 1991.

[3] M. Ahamad, P. W. Hutto, and R. John. Implementing and programming causal distributed shared memory. In *Proceedings of the 11th International Conference on Distributed Computing Systems*, pages 274–281, May 1991.

[4] J.K. Bennett, J.B. Carter, and W. Zwaenepoel. Toward large-scale shared memory multiprocessing. In M. Dubois and S. Thakkar, editors, *Scalable Shared Memory Multiprocessors.* Kluwer Academic Publishers, 1991.

[5] B.N. Bershad and M.J. Zekauskas. Midway: Shared memory parallel programming with entry consistency for distributed memory multiprocessors. Technical Report CMU-CS-91-170, Carnegie-Mellon University, September 1991.

[6] J.B. Carter, J.K. Bennett, and W. Zwaenepoel. Implementation and performance of Munin. In *Proceedings of the 13th ACM Symposium on Operating Systems Principles*, pages 152–164, October 1991.

[7] H. Davis, S. Goldschmidt, and J. L. Hennessy. Tango: A multiprocessor simulation and tracing system. Technical Report CSL-TR-90-439, Stanford University, 1990.

[8] M. Dubois and C. Scheurich. Memory access dependencies in shared-memory multiprocessors. *IEEE Transactions on Computers*, 16(6):660–673, June 1990.

[9] K. Gharachorloo, D. Lenoski, J. Laudon, P. Gibbons, A. Gupta, and J. Hennessy. Memory consistency and event ordering in scalable shared-memory multiprocessors. In *Proceedings of the 17th Annual International Symposium on Computer Architecture*, pages 15–26, Seattle, Washington, May 1990.

[10] J.R. Goodman. Cache consistency and sequential consistency. Technical Report Technical report no. 61, SCI Committee, March 1989.

[11] L. Lamport. How to make a multiprocessor computer that correctly executes multiprocess programs. *IEEE Transactions on Computers*, C-28(9):690–691, September 1979.

[12] D. Lenoski, J. Laudon, K. Gharachorloo, A. Gupta, and J. Hennessy. The directory-based cache coherence protocol for the DASH multiprocessor. In *Proceedings of the 17th Annual International Symposium on Computer Architecture*, pages 148–159, May 1990.

[13] K. Li and P. Hudak. Memory coherence in shared virtual memory systems. *ACM Transactions on Computer Systems*, 7(4):321–359, November 1989.

[14] R.J. Lipton and J.S. Sandberg. Pram: A scalable shared memory. Technical Report CS-TR-180-88, Princeton University, September 1988.

[15] F. Mattern. Virtual time and global states of distributed systems. In Michel Cosnard, Yves Robert, Patrice Quinton, and Michel Raynal, editors, *Parallel & Distributed Algorithms*, pages 215–226. Elsevier Science Publishers, Amsterdam, 1989.

[16] U. Ramachandran, M. Ahamad, and Y.A. Khalidi. Unifying synchronization and data transfer in maintaining coherence of distributed shared memory. Technical Report GIT-CS-88/23, Georgia Institute of Technology, June 1988.

[17] J.P. Singh, W.-D. Weber, and A. Gupta. Splash: Stanford parallel applications for shared-memory. Technical Report CSL-TR-91-469, Stanford University, April 1991.

[18] W.-D. Weber and A. Gupta. Analysis of cache invalidation patterns in multiprocessors. In *Proceedings of the 3th Symposium on Architectural Support for Programming Languages and Operating Systems*, pages 243–256, April 1989.

Hiding Memory Latency using Dynamic Scheduling in Shared-Memory Multiprocessors

Kourosh Gharachorloo, Anoop Gupta, and John Hennessy

Computer Systems Laboratory
Stanford University, CA 94305

Abstract

The large latency of memory accesses is a major impediment to achieving high performance in large scale shared-memory multiprocessors. Relaxing the memory consistency model is an attractive technique for hiding this latency by allowing the overlap of memory accesses with other computation and memory accesses. Previous studies on relaxed models have shown that the latency of write accesses can be hidden by buffering writes and allowing reads to bypass pending writes. Hiding the latency of reads by exploiting the overlap allowed by relaxed models is inherently more difficult, however, simply because the processor depends on the return value for its future computation.

This paper explores the use of dynamically scheduled processors to exploit the overlap allowed by relaxed models for hiding the latency of reads. Our results are based on detailed simulation studies of several parallel applications. The results show that a substantial fraction of the read latency can be hidden using this technique. However, the major improvements in performance are achieved only at large instruction window sizes.

1 Introduction

The performance of large scale shared-memory multiprocessors can be severely limited by the long latency of remote memory accesses. Overlapping of memory accesses with other computation and accesses is an attractive method for hiding the memory latency. The degree to which such overlap is allowed within the same thread is determined by the memory consistency model chosen for the architecture.

The *sequential consistency* (SC) model [22] proposed by Lamport is the most commonly assumed memory consistency model; it requires the execution of a parallel program to appear as some interleaving of the execution of the parallel threads on a sequential machine. Unfortunately, this requirement places severe restrictions on the allowable ordering of shared memory accesses within the same thread. To allow for more overlap among memory accesses, several relaxed consistency models have been proposed [1, 6, 10, 12]. One of the more relaxed models is *release consistency* (RC) [10]. RC allows for significant overlap among memory accesses as long as synchronization operations are appropriately identified.

Relaxed models such as release consistency allow read and write accesses between synchronizations to be overlapped with one another, thus presenting the opportunity to hide the latency arising from both read and write accesses. Whether this opportunity is exploited depends on the aggressiveness of the processor architecture and the memory subsystem. For example, a processor that blocks for the return value of a read access (typical for current commercial processors) cannot hide the latency of the read. Similarly, a cache that stalls while servicing a cache miss cannot exploit the allowable overlap among multiple misses.

The performance gain from relaxing the consistency model has been previously studied for processors that block on read accesses [7]. These studies have shown that the latency of writes can be effectively hidden as long as the write buffer and the cache allow reads to be serviced while there are pending writes. However, exploiting relaxed models for hiding the latency of reads remains unexplored.

Hiding the latency of reads through overlap with other computation and accesses is inherently more difficult than hiding write latency, simply because the computation following the read usually depends on the return value. To hide this latency, the processor needs to find other independent computation and memory accesses to process while awaiting the return value for the read. To achieve this in hardware implies an aggressive processor architecture with a decoupled decode and execution unit and capability for dynamic scheduling, branch prediction, and speculative execution. Given expected memory latencies ranging from tens to hundreds of processor cycles, there are serious concerns as to whether such a processor architecture allows for effective overlap of read latencies and whether the added complexity is justifiable.

This paper explores the use of dynamically scheduled processors to exploit the overlap allowed by relaxed models for hiding the latency of reads. The study is based on detailed simulation results of five parallel applications. The applications are a particle-based simulator used in aeronautics (MP3D) [26], an LU-decomposition program (LU), a digital logic simulation program (PTHOR) [35], a standard cell placement and routing program (LOCUS) [30], and a program for simulating large scale ocean currents (OCEAN) [31]. The simulated processor environment is based on an architecture proposed by Johnson [18].

Our results show that dynamic scheduling in combination with relaxed consistency models is successful in hiding a substantial fraction of the read latency. However, to fully realize these gains requires large instruction lookahead windows. The window size is varied from 16 to 256 in our experiments. With memory latency of 50 cycles, we observe that there is a noticeable gain from increasing the window size from 16 to 32 and from 32 to 64 instructions. However, the performance levels off past a window size of 64. Our results for a latency of 100 cycles show similar trends [9]. The lower performance at the smaller window sizes is primarily attributed to data dependences at short distances and the inability of the processor to overlap independent operations that are farther apart than the size of the lookahead window. Except for PTHOR, the branch behavior of the applications does not hinder lookahead until we reach very large window sizes.

The next section provides background information on memory consistency models and describes architectural features that are necessary to exploit the full potential of a relaxed consistency model. Section 3 presents details of the processor architecture used in our study. The simulation environment and the five parallel applications are also described in this section. Simulation results are presented in Section 4. Sections 5 and 6 discuss the results and the related work. Section 7 concludes the paper.

2 Background

This section begins with a brief description of several memory consistency models that have been proposed in the literature. The latter part of the section discusses processor and memory system features that are necessary to fully exploit the overlap of accesses and computation allowed by the relaxed consistency models.

2.1 Memory Consistency Models

Overlapping memory accesses is an attractive technique for hiding the large memory latency in multiprocessors. However, as a result of the distribution of memory and interconnection resources, multiple requests issued by a processor may complete out of order. This can lead to incorrect behavior if a program depends on completion of accesses in a certain order. Consequently, we need to impose certain restrictions on the completion order of memory accesses to provide a reasonable programming model for an architecture. This function is fulfilled by the memory consistency model.

A memory consistency model specifies the constraints on ordering of shared memory accesses. *Sequential consistency* (SC) [22] is the most commonly assumed memory model. Sequential consistency requires the execution of a parallel program to appear as some interleaving of the execution of the parallel processes on a sequential machine. *Processor consistency* (PC) [12] relaxes some of the restrictions of SC. While PC requires writes issued from a process to be seen in program order by all other processes, it allows reads to be reordered with respect to previous writes from a process. The constraints for satisfying PC are specified formally in [10].

Dubois et al. [6] have proposed a further relaxation of consistency constraints by relating ordering to synchronization points in the program. The *weak ordering* (WO) model (also known as weak consistency) is based on this idea and ensures consistency only at synchronization points. WO provides considerable flexibility for overlapping accesses between synchronization points. The *release consistency* model (RC) [10] extends this framework by further classifying synchronization into *acquires* and *releases*. An acquire is a read operation that gains permission to access a set of data (e.g., a lock operation or waiting for a flag to be set), while a release is a write operation that gives away such permission (e.g., an unlock or setting of a flag). This information is used to further relax the ordering between data and synchronization accesses. The *data-race-free-0* (DRF0) [1] model proposed by Adve and Hill is similar to RC, although it does not explicitly distinguish between acquire and release accesses.

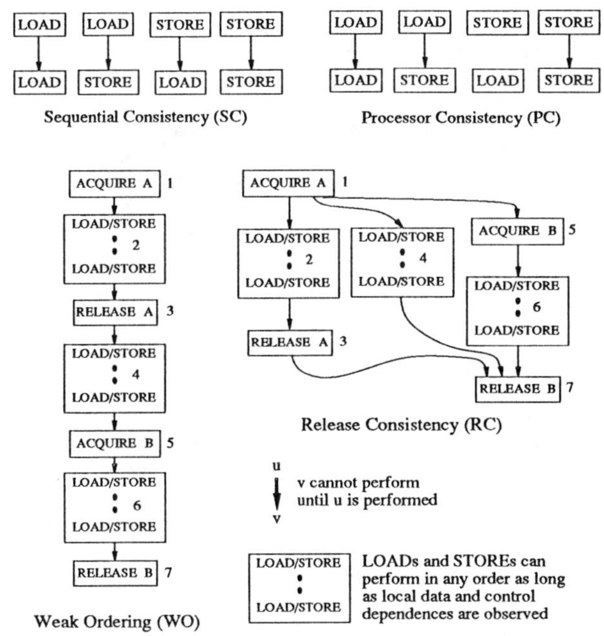

Figure 1: Ordering restrictions on memory accesses. The numbers beside the blocks indicate the program order.

The constraints imposed by a consistency model can be satisfied by restricting when an access is allowed to perform. A read is considered *performed* (or completed) when the return value is bound and cannot be modified by other write operations while a write is considered *performed* (or completed) once the value written is visible to all processors. Figure 1 shows the restriction on completion order of accesses from the same process for straightforward implementations of the four consistency models discussed above.

As shown in Figure 1, SC can be guaranteed by performing accesses within each process in a serial manner. PC provides more flexibility by allowing reads to bypass writes in the same process. WO and RC provide further flexibility by exploiting information about synchronization accesses. Both models allow accesses between synchronization to be overlapped. The figure also shows how RC exploits the acquire and release information to further relax ordering constraints.

While relaxed models such as WO and RC permit considerable overlap among shared accesses, whether such overlap takes place depends on the aggressiveness of the processor architecture and the memory system. The next section describes the corresponding design issues.

2.2 Processor Architecture and Memory System Issues

To effectively hide the latency of memory accesses, the processor requires the ability to continue past pending accesses to find other computation and memory accesses to execute. The extent of this ability is primarily determined by the technique used for scheduling instructions.

Processors that use *static scheduling* [16] check for data and structural hazards at decode time. The issue of the instruction is delayed in case there is a hazard, leading to an in-order issue and execution of instructions. Static scheduling depends on software and compiler techniques to schedule instructions for minimizing such stalls. On the other hand, *dynamic scheduling* [16] decouples the decoding of an instruction from its issue and execution, with the execution unit assuming the responsibility for detecting structural and data hazards. The out-of-order issue and execution of instructions allows the processor to continue decoding and executing instructions even though some previous instructions may be delayed due to data dependences or busy functional units.

Most current commercial microprocessors are statically scheduled. Load and store instructions are often handled in a special manner, however. Stores are normally placed in a store buffer and the store buffer issues the store whenever the memory subsystem can accept another access. The processor can continue executing instructions even though there may be stores outstanding, thus overlapping the write latency with other computation and accesses. This has been shown to be an effective way to hide the latency of writes in multiprocessors [7]. Load instructions, on the other hand, are scheduled in one of two ways. The most common technique is to stall the processor for the return value. This removes the need for checking data dependence later. The second method simply issues the load, delaying the stall up to the next instruction that actually uses the return value. The former technique disallows any type of overlap with future instructions for the purposes of masking the latency of the read. Although the latter technique allows the processor to continue past the load, it is likely that the processor will stall within a few instructions due to data dependence, unless the compiler can successfully schedule instructions to avoid such a stall.

Dynamic scheduling provides the opportunity for the processor to continue past an outstanding load and the instructions that are dependent on the return value. The use of dynamic scheduling to hide memory latency dates back to the IBM Stretch [5] and IBM 360/91 [36]. In order to be effective in hiding latencies in the range of tens to hundreds of cycles, dynamic scheduling needs to be complemented with *register renaming* [19], *dynamic branch prediction* [23], and *speculative execution*. Register renaming alleviates write-after-read (WAR) and write-after-write (WAW) dependences that in turn may delay the execution of future instructions. Dynamic branch prediction increases the lookahead capability of the processor while speculative execution allows the processor to execute instructions past unresolved branches. Several of these techniques have been proposed for use in dynamically scheduled superscalar designs for multiple issue of instructions (e.g. [18, 27]). However, in this paper, we are mainly concerned with the use of these techniques for hiding memory latency. The degree to which these techniques succeed in hiding the latency of reads is determined by the size of the lookahead buffer from which the processor chooses instructions to execute, the predictability of branches, and finally the data dependence characteristics of the program, which determines the degree of independence among instructions. Our experimental results will shed more light on the effect of each of these factors on performance.

Overlapping memory accesses to hide latency also imposes several requirements on the memory system. In general, these requirements involve providing high bandwidth and avoiding serialization points. Let us first consider the memory subsystem within the processor environment. To effectively hide the latency of writes, the store buffer needs to allow reads to bypass pending writes. In addition, it is important for the caches to be lockup-free [21] in order to allow the servicing of reads while previous writes are being serviced. Overlap of multiple reads clearly extends the requirement on the cache to allow simultaneous service of reads also. Regarding the interconnection network and memory modules, it is important to allow accesses that are issued in an overlapped manner to be serviced concurrently. This requires sufficient bandwidth and the need to avoid serialization points within the interconnection network and at the memory modules.

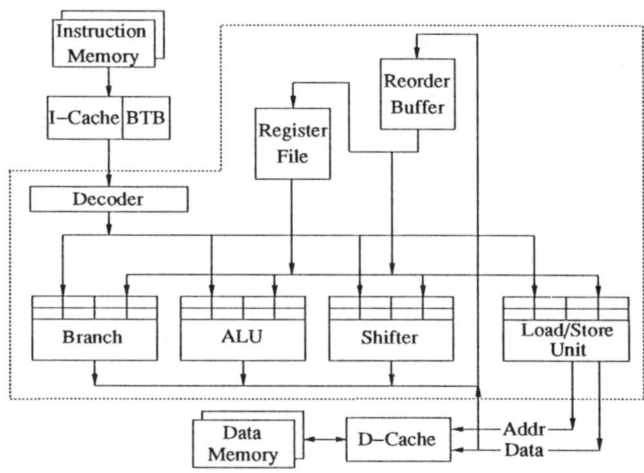

Figure 2: Overall structure of Johnson's dynamically scheduled processor.

3 Simulation Methodology

This section presents the different components used in our simulation environment. The first subsection discusses architectural details of the processor. The second subsection explains the coupling of the multiprocessor simulation with the processor simulator. Finally, the last subsection presents the benchmark applications used in our study.

3.1 Simulated Processor Architecture

The base processor used in our study is derived from an architecture proposed by Johnson [18]. Only a brief description is provided here; the interested reader is referred to [18] for more detail.

Figure 2 shows the overall structure of the processor. The processor consists of a number of functional units with associated *reservation stations* [36]. Although not shown in the figure, there are another four floating point units for performing floating point add, multiply, divide, and conversion.[1] The reservation stations are instruction buffers that decouple instruction decoding from instruction execution and allow for dynamic scheduling of instructions. Decoded instructions and operands are placed into the appropriate reservation station by the decoder. The reservation station can issue an instruction as soon as the instruction has its data dependences satisfied and the functional unit is free.

The reorder buffer [34] shown in Figure 2 is responsible for several functions in this architecture. The first function is to eliminate storage conflicts through register renaming [19]. Each instruction that is decoded is dynamically allocated a location in the reorder buffer and a tag is associated with its result register. The tag is updated to the actual result value once the instruction completes. Correct execution is achieved by providing the value or tag in the reorder buffer (instead of the value in the register file) to later instructions that attempt to read this register. Unresolved operand tags in the reservation stations are updated when the corresponding instruction completes.

[1] While Johnson assumes the floating point units reside on a coprocessor, we assume they are on the same chip as the integer units.

The second function for the reorder buffer is to provide the rollback mechanism necessary for supporting speculative execution past unresolved branches. The architecture uses a branch target buffer (BTB) [23] to provide dynamic branch prediction. The rollback mechanism for mispredicted branches works as follows. Decoded instructions enter the reorder buffer in program order. When an instruction at the head of the buffer completes, the entry belonging to it is deallocated and the result value is written to the register file. Since instructions enter the reorder buffer in program order and are retired in the same order, updates to the register file take place in program order. Therefore, instructions that depend on an unresolved branch are not committed to the register file until the branch completes. Similarly, memory stores are also held back (the reorder buffer controls the retiring of stores from the store buffer).[2] If a branch is mispredicted, all instructions past the branch are invalidated from the reorder buffer, the reservation stations, and the appropriate buffers, and decoding and execution is started from the correct branch target. The mechanism provided for handling mispredicted branches is also used to provide precise interrupts. This allows the processor to restart quickly without the need to save and restore complex state information.

For our study, we have assumed a single cycle latency for all functional units except the load/store unit. The latency for loads and stores is assumed to be one cycle in case of a cache hit. The scheduling of instructions within each functional unit is allowed to be out-of-order. This pertains to the load and store unit also as long as the memory consistency constraints allow it. Furthermore, for consistency models that allow it, load operations can bypass the store buffer and dependence checking is done on the store buffer to assure a correct return value for the load.

Regarding the caches, we simulate a lockup-free data cache [21] that allows for multiple outstanding requests. We ran our simulations assuming a single cache port, thus limiting the number of loads and stores executed to at most one per cycle. The branch target buffer size was set to 2048 entries with a 4-way set-associative organization. For simplicity, all instructions are assumed to hit in the instruction cache.

The next section describes how our processor simulator is coupled to the multiprocessor simulation.

3.2 Multiprocessor Simulation

Our multiprocessor simulation is done using Tango Lite, the lightweight thread version of the Tango simulation environment [11]. The simulation assumes a simple multiprocessor architecture. The architecture consists of 16 processors, each with a 64K data cache that is kept coherent using an invalidation-based scheme. The caches are direct mapped, write-back caches with a line size of 16 bytes. The simulated processors are simple in-order issue processors with blocking reads. Writes are placed in a write buffer. The consistency model assumed for the multiprocessor simulation is release consistency, thus the latency arising from writes is effectively hidden. The latency of memory is assumed to be 1 cycle for cache hits and a fixed number of cycles for cache misses. In our experiments, we use a 50 cycle penalty for cache misses (results for a 100 cycle penalty are provided in [9]). Queuing and contention effects in the interconnection network are not modeled.

The above simulation generates a dynamic instruction trace for each of the simulated processes. The generated trace is augmented with other dynamic information including the effective address for load and store instructions and the effective latency for each memory and synchronization operation.

[2] A store at the head of the reorder buffer is retired as soon as its address translation completes and the consistency constraints allow its issue. The store buffer is free to issue the store after this point.

To simulate the effects of dynamic scheduling, we choose the dynamic instruction trace for one of the processes from the multiprocessor simulation and feed it through our processor simulator (described in the previous section). Since the pertinent information about the multiprocessor cache simulation and the synchronization behavior is already contained in the trace, the processor simulator simply uses this information to determine the latency of memory accesses and synchronization.

The use of trace-driven simulation in our study may introduce some inaccuracies in our results [20]. This is because the trace is generated assuming a different processor architecture than the processor we eventually simulate. Thus, although the exact global interleaving of shared accesses may be different given the two processor architectures, we use the same ordering for both. The extent to which this affects results depends both on the application behavior and on the characteristics being studied. For our study, the program characteristics that determine how well dynamically scheduled processors hide memory latency are the cache miss behavior, the data dependence characteristics between memory accesses and computation, and the predictability of branches. We do not expect these characteristics to vary greatly due to slightly different global interleaving of the accesses.

One characteristic that can vary greatly due to different interleavings is the synchronization latency and load balance in an execution. Thus, synchronization times need to be treated cautiously in trace-driven simulations. In this study, we mainly focus on the fraction of read latency that can be hidden and the overhead of synchronization does not fundamentally affect the ability of dynamic scheduling techniques in hiding this latency. Synchronization times are only reported to provide an estimate for the fraction of execution time that corresponds to memory latency. Overall, we believe that our results are only minimally affected by the use of traces in our simulations.

3.3 Benchmark Applications

The applications chosen for this study are representative of algorithms used in an engineering and scientific computing environment. The five applications that we study are MP3D, LU, PTHOR, LOCUS, and OCEAN. The first four applications are written in C. OCEAN is written in Fortran. The applications use synchronization primitives provided by the Argonne National Laboratory macro package [4]. The first three applications have already been used in a previous study on consistency models [7]. Except for LU, the other four applications are part of the SPLASH suite from Stanford [32].

MP3D [26] is a 3-dimensional particle simulator used to study the pressure and temperature profiles created by an object flying at high speed through the upper atmosphere. The overall computation of MP3D consists of evaluating the positions and velocities of molecules over a sequence of time steps. During each time step, the molecules are picked up one at a time and moved according to their velocity vectors. Collisions of molecules among themselves and with the object and the boundaries are all modeled. The simulator is well suited to parallelization because each molecule can be treated independently at each time step. The main synchronization consists of barriers between each time step. For our experiments we ran MP3D with 10,000 particles in a 64x8x8 space array, and simulated 5 time steps.

LU performs LU-decomposition for dense matrices. The primary data structure in LU is the matrix being decomposed. Columns are statically assigned to the processors in an interleaved fashion. Each processor waits for the current pivot column, and then uses that column to modify all the columns that it owns. The processor that produces the current pivot column releases any processors waiting for that column. For our experiments we performed LU-decomposition on a 200x200 matrix.

PTHOR [35] is a parallel distributed-time logic simulator based on the Chandy-Misra simulation algorithm. The primary data structures associated with the simulator are the logic elements (e.g., AND-gates, flip-flops), the nets (wires linking the elements), and the task queues which contain activated elements. Each processor executes the following loop. It removes an activated element from one of its task queues and determines the changes on that element's outputs. It then schedules the newly activated elements onto the task queues. For our experiments we simulated five clock cycles of a small RISC processor consisting of the equivalent of 11,000 two-input gates.

LOCUS [30] is a commercial quality VLSI standard cell router. The program evaluates standard cell circuit placement with the objective of finding an efficient routing that minimizes area. The main data structure is a cost array that keeps track of the number of wires running through each routing cell of the circuit. The parallelism exists at many levels. The many wires in a circuit can be routed in parallel. The routing of each wire can also be done in parallel since it involves determining paths for all independent two-pin segments of the wire. Finally, the several routes for finding the best path for each two-pin segment can be evaluated in parallel. For our experiments we used a circuit with 1266 wires and a 481-by-18 cost array.

OCEAN [31] models the role of eddy and boundary currents in influencing large-scale ocean movements. The simulation is performed for many time-steps until the eddies and mean ocean flow attain a mutual balance. The work in each time-step involves solving a set of spatial partial differential equations. The principle data structure consists of a set of two-dimensional arrays holding discretized values of the various functions associated with the model's equations. The two-dimensional structures are statically allocated as 200-by-200 double precision floating point arrays, and there are approximately 25 such arrays in the program. For our experiments we simulated a 98-by-98 point square grid.

Table 1 provides some statistics on data references for the five applications. This data is from the Tango Lite multiprocessor simulation assuming memory latency of 50 cycles. The numbers are for a single processor in the 16 processor simulation. The column marked busy cycles in Table 1 specifies the number of useful cycles (or instructions) in the application for a single processor. We should point out that the 64K data caches (per processor) are large relative to the problem sizes we are simulating. Thus, the cache misses reported mainly reflect inherent communication misses. Table 2 provides similar information about the synchronization references (wait event and set event implement general event synchronization for producer/consumer interactions). Since branch behavior is an important factor in determining the performance of dynamically scheduled processors, we also provide some statistics on branches in Table 3.

4 Simulation Results

This section studies the effect of relaxing the consistency model in conjunction with dynamically scheduled processors. Section 4.1 presents simulation results comparing statically and dynamically scheduled processors given different consistency models. The above results assume single instruction issue processors. Section 4.2 briefly discusses the effect of higher latency and using multiple instruction issue (simulation results for Section 4.2 appear in the full version of the paper [9]).

Table 1: Statistics on data references. Numbers are for a single processor in the 16 processor simulation. Numbers in parentheses are rates given as references per thousand instructions.

Program	*Busy Cycles*	*reads* ($\times$*1,000*)	*writes* ($\times$*1,000*)	*read misses* ($\times$*1,000*)	*write misses* ($\times$*1,000*)
MP3D	550,000	127 (230)	63 (114)	13.4 (24.3)	12.4 (22.5)
LU	2,277,000	697 (306)	345 (151)	16.4 (7.2)	5.5 (2.4)
PTHOR	1,758,000	701 (399)	147 (83)	41.2 (23.5)	15.2 (8.7)
LOCUS	3,325,000	697 (210)	180 (54)	30.9 (9.3)	18.4 (5.5)
OCEAN	5,141,000	1,550 (302)	585 (114)	112 (21.7)	202 (39.3)

Table 2: Statistics on synchronization. Numbers are for a single processor in the 16 processor simulation. Numbers in parentheses are rates given as references per thousand instructions.

Program	*locks*	*unlocks*	*wait event*	*set event*	*barriers*
MP3D	40 (0.07)	40 (0.07)	0	0	30 (0.05)
LU	0	0	199 (0.09)	13 (0.00)	2 (0.00)
PTHOR	6,038 (3.43)	6,039 (3.44)	134 (0.08)	0	249 (0.14)
LOCUS	356 (0.11)	356 (0.11)	2 (0.00)	0	1 (0.00)
OCEAN	21 (0.00)	21 (0.00)	0	0	150 (0.03)

4.1 Static versus Dynamic Scheduling

Figure 3 shows the simulation results comparing statically and dynamically scheduled processors with variation of the memory consistency model. The left-most column in each graph shows the breakdown of the execution time on an in-order execution processor (BASE) which completes each operation before initiating the next one (i.e., no overlap in execution of instructions and memory operations). The bottom section of this column represents busy time or useful cycles executed by the processor. The black section above it represents the time that the processor is stalled waiting for acquire synchronization (i.e., locks, wait events, barriers). The two sections on top of this show the contribution of read miss and write miss latencies to the execution time. Release operations are included in the total write miss time. The penalty for cache misses is assumed to be 50 cycles in these simulations.

The next three groups of columns in each graph correspond to varying the consistency model. The models evaluated are sequential consistency (SC), processor consistency (PC), and release consistency (RC). For each model, we evaluate three different processor architectures. The first is a simple statically scheduled processor with blocking reads (SSBR). The second is a statically scheduled processor with non-blocking reads (SS). This processor is allowed to execute past read misses and the stall is delayed up to the first use of the return value. We assume a 16 word deep write buffer for the above processors. The SS processor also has a 16 word deep read buffer. Finally, we evaluate the dynamically scheduled processor (DS) described in Section 3.1. To allow us to better isolate the effects on hiding memory latency, we have limited the decode and issue rate for the DS processor to a maxi-

Table 3: Statistics on branch behavior.

Program	Percentage of Instructions	Avg. Distance bet. Branches (in instructions)	Percentage Correctly Predicted	Avg. Distance bet. Mispredictions (in instructions)
MP3D	6.1%	16.4	90.8%	176.9
LU	8.0%	12.5	98.0%	618.1
PTHOR	15.3%	6.5	81.2%	34.7
LOCUS	15.6%	6.4	92.1%	81.6
OCEAN	6.0%	16.6	97.9%	778.9

mum of 1 instruction per cycle. The size of the reorder buffer (or lookahead window) used is denoted at the bottom of each column. This size corresponds to the maximum number of instructions that can reside in the window at any given time. The window size is varied from 16 to 256 for the RC model. For SC and PC, we only show the results for the most aggressive buffer size since the gains from dynamic scheduling are relatively small for these models. All simulations assume an aggressive memory system with lockup-free caches, write buffers that allow reads to bypass writes, and the ability to issue one access per cycle from each node. Of course, the extent to which these features are exploited depends on the consistency model and the processor architecture.

Some general observations that can be made from the simulation results are: (i) SC does not allow the read and write latency to be hidden regardless of the processor architecture; (ii) PC is in general successful in hiding the latency of writes with statically scheduled processors and does not gain much from the use of dynamic scheduling; (iii) RC fully hides the latency of writes under static scheduling and can substantially reduce the read latency given dynamically scheduled processors with large window sizes. Section 4.1.1 briefly discusses the results for static scheduling. Sections 4.1.2 and 4.1.3 analyze the results for dynamic scheduling in greater detail.

4.1.1 Static Scheduling Results

In this section, we briefly discuss the results for the two statically scheduled processors (SSBR and SS). We first concentrate on the results for the SSBR processor. The effect of consistency models on statically scheduled processors with blocking reads (SSBR) has been previously studied [7], and our results simply reconfirm the findings in the previous study. Thus, we simply state some of the interesting results from our simulation and refer the interested reader to the previous study for a more in-depth analysis. As can be seen in Figure 3, the SC model is not successful in hiding the latency of either reads or writes. The PC model, on the other hand, is in general successful in hiding the latency of writes by allowing reads to bypass previous writes. This latency is fully hidden for three of the applications (MP3D, LU, and PTHOR). The small amount of write latency in LOCUS is mainly due to the bursty nature of writes in the application which results in the write buffer filling up and stalling the processor once in a while (4% of the cycles). OCEAN is different since PC is only successful in hiding part of the write latency and a substantial amount remains. The reason arises from the fact that the number of write misses is substantially larger than the number of read misses in this application. Normally, the fact that the processor stalls on read misses gives the write buffer sufficient time to retire previous writes without filling up. However, this condition does not hold if the total latency due to write misses exceeds the latency from read misses [7]. In OCEAN, the write buffer stalls the processor due to being full for about 29% of the cycles under PC. The results for RC are as expected. RC successfully hides the latency of writes in all the applications and the problems that arise with PC are not present since RC allows writes to be overlapped, thus reducing the likelihood of the write buffer filling up.

We now consider the results for the SS processor. The difference between SS and SSBR is that SS does not block on read accesses and delays this stall until the first use of the return value. Therefore, there is the potential for hiding the latency of reads in the region between the read access and its first use. However, as the results indicate, the improvement over SSBR is minimal. This is mainly because the object code has not been rescheduled to exploit non-blocking reads (by moving the load access further away from the use of the return value). Thus, the processor is effectively stalled a short distance away from a read miss since the use of the return value is normally within a few instructions away. In the future, we plan to study the effect of compiler rescheduling to exploit non-blocking reads as an alternative to using dynamic scheduling techniques in hardware.

4.1.2 Dynamic Scheduling Results

We begin by building some intuition for the different factors that affect the performance of dynamically scheduled processors, specifically in their ability to hide read latencies. We then analyze the results based on this intuition. Section 4.1.3 presents more simulation results to further isolate the factors that influence performance.

Three factors determine the effectiveness of dynamic scheduling in hiding memory latency. Two of these factors relate to the characteristics of the application: (i) data dependence behavior and (ii) control (or branch) behavior. The third factor is the size of the lookahead window (or reorder buffer) provided by the architecture.

The data dependence characteristics of an application is the most fundamental factor influencing performance. Dynamic scheduling depends on the presence of independent accesses and computation for hiding memory latency. For the applications we are considering, independent operations are present at different granularities. Typically, the applications exploit parallelism at the task or loop iteration level and each processor is assigned a set of tasks or loop iterations. One source of independent operations is within the task or loop iteration boundary. Another source of independence is operations from two different tasks or loop iterations that have been assigned to the same processor. The availability of such independent operations and the distance between them determines the feasibility of a hardware technique in finding and overlapping them.

The behavior of branches in an application is also a key factor that affects performance. The frequency of branches and their predictability determines whether it is feasible for hardware to find distant independent operations.

Finally, the size of the lookahead window determines the maximum distance between independent operations that can be overlapped by the hardware. Therefore, to overlap two independent accesses, the size of the lookahead window needs to be at least as large as the distance between the two accesses. Furthermore, to fully overlap the latency of memory accesses with computation requires enough independent instructions to keep the processor busy for the duration of the latency. This requires the window size to be at least as large as the latency of memory. For example, with the latency of 50 cycles, we require a window size of at least 50 instructions. Smaller window sizes overlap only a fraction of this latency (proportional to the size).

We now consider the results with dynamically scheduled processors for the SC and PC models (Figure 3). Under SC, the implementation delays each access until the previous access is completed. Therefore, it is likely that the processor will stall

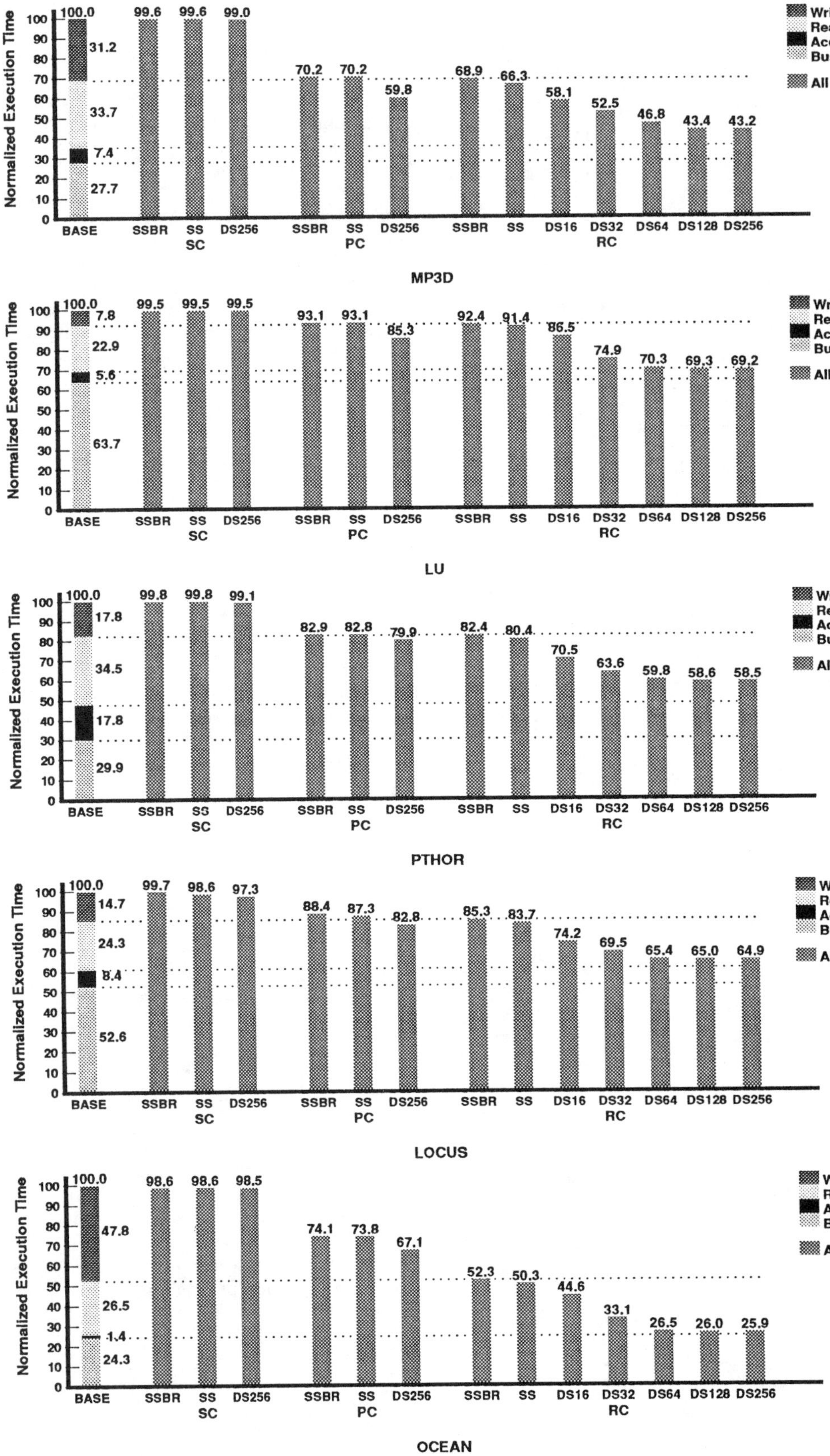

Figure 3: Simulation results for memory latency of 50 cycles.

shortly after a read or write miss due to its inability to complete future reads. As expected, the results for SC with the aggressive window size of 256 show virtually no improvement over static scheduling.

The PC model is slightly more relaxed than SC in that reads can bypass or overlap previous writes. This allows write latencies to be hidden. However, read accesses are still serialized. Due to this serialization, PC is in general not successful in hiding much of the read latency either, even with the aggressive window size of 256. The more noticeable gains in MP3D and LU most likely arise from the presence of independent computation on data that already resides in registers, which in turn allows the processor to continue past read misses for a short time without requiring another read value. As for OCEAN, the increase in performance compared to static scheduling mainly arises from the larger write buffer used for the DS processor which reduces the frequency of stalls due to a full write buffer.

Before analyzing the results for RC, let us first consider the bound on the gain achievable by dynamic scheduling given that read and write accesses can be overlapped between synchronization points. Since we limit issue to a maximum of one instruction per cycle, the time due to the computation (busy/useful time) cannot be diminished. In addition, acquire synchronization overhead arising from load imbalance or contention for synchronization variables is also impossible to hide with the techniques we are considering. On the other hand, the fraction of the synchronization overhead arising from the memory latency to access synchronization variables can be hidden in the same way that normal memory latency is hidden. For example, the latency to access a free lock can be hidden by overlapping this time with the computation prior to it. Relating this to the applications, our detailed simulation results show that virtually all of the acquire overhead in MP3D, LU, LOCUS, and OCEAN arises from load imbalance and contention. Therefore, the best dynamic scheduling can do for these applications is to fully hide the read and write (including release) latency. In PTHOR, however, approximately 30% of the acquire overhead is due to latency for accessing free locks. Therefore, in PTHOR, it is theoretically possible to hide a fraction of the acquire overhead as well.

Referring to the results for RC in Figure 3, we notice that there is a gradual increase in performance as we move from window size of 16 to window size of 256, with the performance increasing more rapidly for the small window sizes and leveling off at the larger windows. For LU and OCEAN, dynamic scheduling hides virtually all memory latency at window size of 64. For LOCUS, almost all latency, except for 16% of the read latency, is hidden at the larger window sizes. For MP3D, 24% of the read latency remains even at the larger window sizes. Similarly, PTHOR has 31% of its read latency remaining.

Data dependence and small window size effects are most likely the two factors that influence performance at the small window sizes (16 and 32). Based on the average distance between mispredicted branches shown in Table 3, branch behavior is not expected to be a determining factor for the small windows, except possibly in PTHOR. The factors shift at the larger window sizes. In LU and OCEAN, performance levels off at larger windows simply because the memory latency is virtually all hidden at the smaller window sizes. On the other hand, the leveling off of performance in MP3D, PTHOR, and LOCUS is most likely due to the fact that the branch prediction falls short of effectively using such large window sizes.

4.1.3 Detailed Analysis of Dynamic Scheduling

This section provides simulation results to further isolate the effects of different factors influencing the performance of dynamically scheduled processors. Figure 4 presents these results for all five applications. The left-most column in each graph repeats the data presented in Figure 3 for the BASE processor. The next five columns in each graph provide performance results for the different window sizes assuming perfect branch prediction. The last five columns in each graph present the results given for the case where branch prediction is perfect and data dependences are being ignored.[3] Since the gains from dynamic scheduling were substantial only under the RC model, the results in this section all assume this model.

To isolate the effect of branches on performance, we can compare the performance for each window size with and without perfect branch prediction (left side of Figure 4 and right side of Figure 3). For LU and OCEAN, the branch prediction is already so good that we see virtually no gain from perfect branch prediction even at the largest window size of 256. For LOCUS, perfect branch prediction performs slightly better at the large window sizes of 128 and 256. For MP3D, noticeable gain from perfect branch prediction starts at window size of 64. PTHOR, which has the worst branch behavior of all the applications, seems to noticeably gain from perfect branch prediction even at the small window sizes of 16 and 32. Thus, except for PTHOR, the branch behavior of the applications does not seem to affect the performance until we reach the 128 and 256 window sizes.

To isolate the effect of data dependences, we can look at the improvement in performance at each window size when we move from perfect branch prediction to additionally ignoring data dependences (left and right side in Figure 4). For LU and OCEAN, there is little or no gain from ignoring data dependences, pointing to the fact that data dependences do not hinder performance in these two applications (this is as expected since it was possible to hide all memory latency for these two applications). For MP3D, PTHOR, and LOCUS, we observe that ignoring data dependences increases the performance more at the small window sizes. In fact, at window size of 256, the performance with and without ignoring data dependences is virtually the same in these three applications. This points to the fact that there are some data dependences at short distances (within a task or loop iteration), however, by looking ahead at substantially larger distances, it is possible to find more independent operations (across tasks or loop iterations). Although this is an interesting observation, from a practical point of view, it is not possible to exploit such independence at large distances with hardware techniques simply because the branch prediction falls short of providing such lookahead distances.

Our detailed simulation results also confirm the presence of data dependences at short distances. One such result measures the delay of each read miss from the time the instruction is decoded and placed in the reorder buffer to the time the read is issued to memory. Below, we consider this measure for the window size of 64 given perfect branch prediction. In LU and OCEAN, we find that read misses are rarely delayed more than 10 cycles. This clearly points to the fact that read misses are independent from one another in these two applications. Results for MP3D show that about 15% of the read misses are delayed over 40 cycles. Similarly, in LOCUS, more than 20% of read misses are delayed over 40 cycles. This indicates the presence of read misses that are data dependent on one another, with one read miss affecting the address of the next read miss. Data dependences have the most serious effect in PTHOR. For PTHOR, around 50% of the read misses are delayed over 50 cycles. This is indicative of dependence chains formed by multiple misses. One effect of such dependence chains is that there are fewer independent accesses to overlap. Furthermore, it is more difficult to fully hide the latency of read misses in such a chain by overlap with independent

[3]Dependences arising from consistency constraints, for example from an acquire to the following access, are still respected.

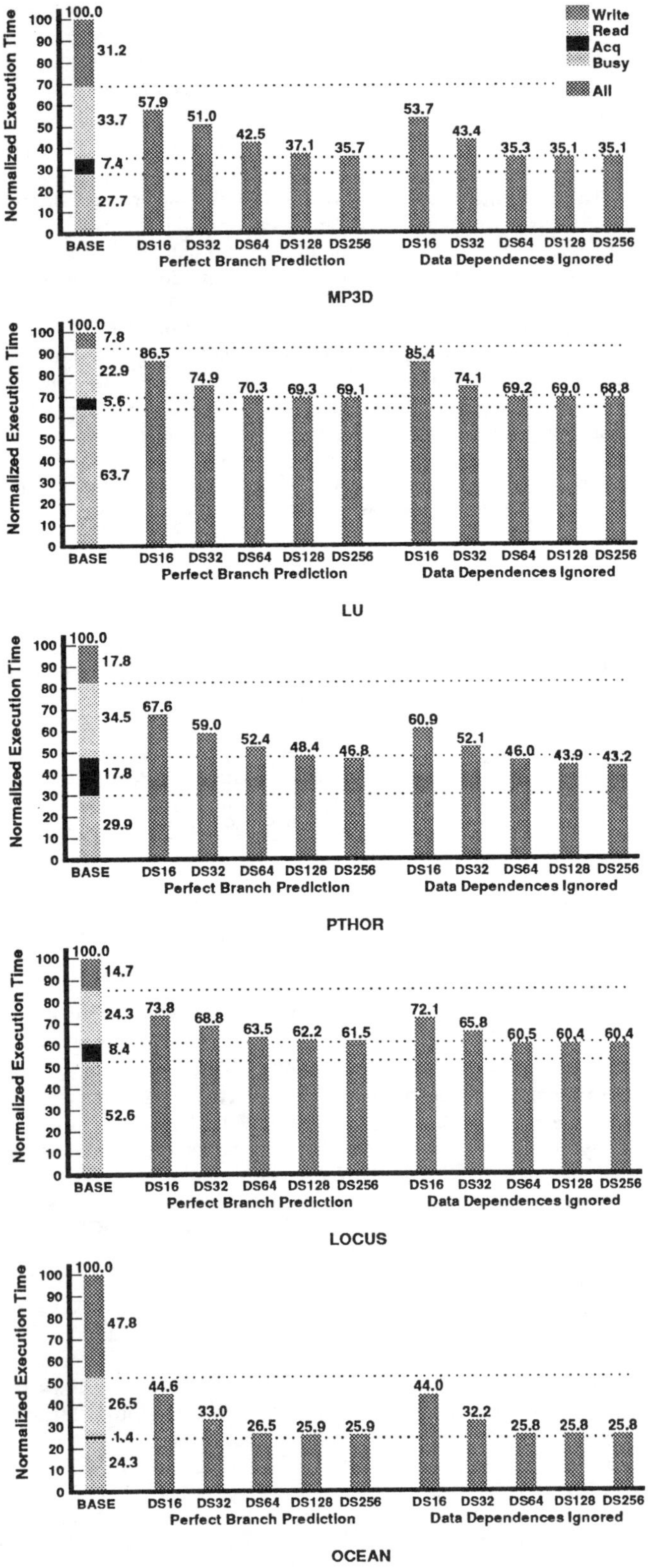

Figure 4: Effect of perfect branch prediction and ignoring data dependences for dynamic scheduling under RC.

computation, simply because the misses in the chain behave like a single read miss with double or triple the effective memory latency. This is the main reason why it takes window sizes of up to 256 to fully hide the latency of read misses in MP3D and PTHOR even with perfect branch prediction.

Finally, we can isolate the effect of window size by further analyzing the results for when both branch prediction is perfect and data dependences are ignored (right hand side in Figure 4). In this case, the only remaining factor that can affect performance is the window size. Looking at the results, we notice that window sizes of 16 and 32 do not fully hide the latency of reads. As explained in the previous section, the reasons for this are (i) small window sizes do not find independent operations that are farther apart than the window size, and (ii) to fully overlap latency with computation, the window size (in instructions) needs to be at least as large as the latency of access (in cycles). Relating to (i), our detailed simulation data for LU show that 90% of the read misses are a distance of 20-30 instructions apart. Thus, the window size of 16 performs relatively poorly compared to other applications. Similarly, in OCEAN, about 55% of the read misses are 16 to 20 instructions apart. Again, the reason for the poor performance at window size of 16 is that the distance between independent accesses exceeds the window size. Regarding reason (ii), we observe from the results that once we reach window size of 64 (which exceeds the memory latency), the latency can be fully overlapped with computation given the assumed lack of data dependences.[4]

In summary, data dependence and branch predictability do not hinder performance in LU and OCEAN. The performance of LOCUS and MP3D are primarily affected by data dependence at small window sizes and by branch predictability at large window sizes. Finally, PTHOR is affected by both data dependence and branch behavior at all window sizes.

4.2 Effect of Higher Latency and Multiple Instruction Issue

We briefly discuss the effect of higher memory latency and multiple instruction issue in this section. The simulation results for these experiments are presented in the full version of the paper [9].

We repeated the simulations assuming a higher memory latency of 100 cycles. The trends were similar to what we observed for the 50 cycle memory latency. The most obvious difference was that the performance leveled off at the window size of 128 instead of 64. This arises from the fact that the window size needs to exceed the latency in order to fully overlap memory latency with computation. Another observation was that the relative gain in performance from hiding memory latency was consistently larger for the higher latency of 100 cycles.

We also did a preliminary study of the effect of multiple instruction issue. In [9], we present some simulation results for issuing a maximum of four instructions per cycle. As with the higher latency results, the performance was still increasing when we moved from window size of 64 to 128 under RC, while without multiple issue, the performance virtually leveled off at window size of 64 (see Figure 3). This arises from the fact that multiple issue speeds up the computation, while memory latency remains at 50 cycles. Thus, a larger window size is needed to fully overlap the memory latency with computation time. Our preliminary results also indicated that the relative performance gains from multiple issue over

[4]Given perfect branch prediction and the assumed lack of dependence, the execution times for MP3D, LU, LOCUS, and OCEAN asymptotically approach the time for the computation plus the acquire overhead. For PTHOR, however, some of the acquire overhead is also being hidden. As explained in the previous section, the reason for this is that about 30% of the acquire overhead in PTHOR arises from latency for accessing free locks.

single issue were larger with RC than with SC. We are planning to do further simulations to better understand the interaction between multiple issue and hiding large memory latencies.

5 Discussion

Previous work has shown that relaxed models are effective in hiding latency arising from write accesses [7]. The goal of this study has been to evaluate relaxed models with respect to hiding read latency. We used a dynamically scheduled processor to exploit the overlap allowed by relaxed models for hiding this latency.

The choice of the application domain clearly influences our results. The scientific and engineering parallel programs used in this study typically exhibit sufficient instruction-level parallelism that can be exploited to hide memory latency. Furthermore, the branch predictability in these applications is usually better than for most uniprocessor programs.

Our architectural assumptions also influence the results. Our results are somewhat optimistic since we assume a high bandwidth memory system. In addition, we do not model the effect of contention in the network or at memory modules. However, the results are pessimistic in that we did not consider the effect of compiler help to schedule code to allow the processor to use the lookahead window more effectively. In addition, the FIFO retirement of instructions from the lookahead window (to provide precise interrupts) is a conservative way of using the window since instructions that have already been executed may remain in the window, disallowing new instruction from being considered for overlapped execution. Other techniques for providing precise interrupts may allow for better use of the window space. More aggressive branch prediction strategies may also allow higher performance for the applications with poor branch prediction. Finally, our simulation results are based on relatively large memory latencies. Smaller memory latencies will require proportionally smaller window sizes to achieve good performance.

The factors that determine the viability of dynamically scheduled processors are numerous. The most important concern about such processors is the extra hardware complexity and its effect on cycle time. These factors have to be considered in determining the actual gain from dynamic scheduling. In addition, other techniques for hiding latency need to be considered. For example, the overlap of memory accesses allowed by relaxed models can also be exploited by the compiler for scheduling read misses to mask their latency on a statically scheduled processor with non-blocking reads. Other competitive techniques for hiding latency include the use of multiple contexts [2, 15, 17, 33, 37] and prefetching [13, 24, 28, 29]. Choosing among these different techniques requires a careful study of the tradeoffs of each technique [14]. In fact, some combination of these techniques may be the most viable choice.

6 Related Work

This section discusses the related work on hiding memory latency. We begin by describing related work in the context of uniprocessors and then discuss the work directly related to shared-memory multiprocessors.

Baer and Chen [3] have suggested a dynamic hardware technique for uniprocessors that prefetches accesses into the cache before they are used. The technique depends on dynamically detecting regular access patterns and issuing prefetches before the processor issues the access. Although this scheme may achieve reasonable gains for applications with regular access behavior (e.g., LU and OCEAN), the technique would probably fail to hide latency for applications that do not have such regular characteristics (e.g., MP3D, PTHOR, LOCUS).

Melvin and Patt [27] have observed that dynamically scheduled processors are less sensitive to higher memory latency than statically scheduled processors. Their study was done in the context of multiple issue of instructions in uniprocessors and the largest cache miss penalty used was 10 cycles. In addition, the behavior (e.g., cache miss, data dependence, and branch behavior) of the uniprocessor applications they studied is substantially different from the parallel applications used in our study.

Lee et al. [25] have studied the effect of a hardware-controlled prefetching scheme in a multiprocessor architecture with software-based cache coherence. They use sixteen subroutines to evaluate the gains from prefetching assuming a memory latency of 20 cycles and instruction lookahead buffers of up to 16 entries. Since caches are kept coherent by software, any shared access that cannot be analyzed by the compiler is marked as non-cacheable. Lee et al. conservatively treat these non-cacheable accesses as synchronization, effectively imposing consistency constraints at these points. Thus, the performance of their scheme depends heavily on whether the compiler can identify enough shared accesses as cacheable in order to avoid the serialization that occurs at non-cacheable accesses. Since the compiler is usually conservative, we expect the serialization due to non-cacheable accesses to have hindered the ability to achieve full overlap among accesses (as is allowed in a relaxed model such as RC). Their results show that the performance gain is indeed mainly limited due to the presence of such serialization points and in some cases due to poor branch prediction.

Regarding the role of memory consistency models in hiding memory latency in multiprocessors, two new techniques have been recently proposed for boosting the performance of sequential consistency relative to other relaxed models [8]. These techniques aggressively overlap memory accesses without violating SC. The first technique involves a non-binding prefetch of values for the accesses that are delayed due to consistency constraints. The second technique employs speculative execution on read values to allow the processor to proceed with reads even though the consistency constraints disallow this in general (there is rollback ability if a violation of SC is detected). The degree to which these techniques boost the performance of strict consistency models remains to be fully studied. While the success of these techniques may deemphasize the correctness aspect of overlapping memory accesses in multiprocessors at the hardware level, the underlying mechanisms that enable and exploit such overlap still remain important.

7 Concluding Remarks

Relaxing the consistency model has been proposed as an attractive way to hide the large memory latency in shared-memory multiprocessors. A previous study evaluated the performance of relaxed models in the context of invalidation-based cache coherent multiprocessors [7]. The results of the study showed that relaxed models such as processor consistency and release consistency are effective in fully hiding the latency of writes. However, the opportunity to overlap read accesses, as allowed by models such as release consistency, was not exploited due to the use of statically scheduled processors with blocking reads. Therefore, the effect of relaxed models on hiding the latency of reads remained unexplored.

In this paper, we have explored the performance of relaxed models for hiding read latency using dynamically scheduled processors. The study was based on simulation results using five scientific and engineering parallel applications. Assuming a memory latency of 50 cycles, the average percentage of read latency that was hidden across the five applications was 33% for window size of 16, 63% for window size of 32, and 81% for window size of 64. For two of the applications, LU and OCEAN, read latency was fully hidden at the 64 window size. In general, larger window sizes did not increase the performance substantially. The trends for a memory latency of 100 cycles were similar, except that larger windows were needed to fully hide the read latency. In isolating the different factors that affect performance, we identified data dependences at short distances and small lookahead as the limiting factors for small windows and branch prediction as the limiting factor for large windows.

These results show that a substantial fraction of the memory latency can be hidden by overlapping accesses as allowed by relaxed models. However, whether the use of dynamically scheduled processors is viable for exploiting this overlap in hardware depends more on the feasibility of building such processors, especially with large window sizes. As future research, it would be interesting to evaluate compiler techniques that exploit relaxed models to schedule reads early. Such compiler rescheduling may allow dynamic processors with small windows or statically scheduled processors with non-blocking reads to effectively hide read latency with simpler hardware.

8 Acknowledgements

We thank the anonymous reviewers for their comments. We also thank the following people for providing useful comments on an earlier version of the paper: Sarita Adve, Phillip Gibbons, Michael Smith, Per Stenstrom, and Rick Zucker. We greatly appreciate the help of several people who made it possible to do the simulations. Stephen Goldschmidt provided us with the Tango Lite environment. The dynamically scheduled processor simulator was based on a simulator previously developed at Stanford by Mike Johnson. We thank him and Michael Smith for helping us extend the simulator for our experiments. We thank the application writers for their applications: Jeff McDonald for MP3D, Ed Rothberg for LU, Larry Soule for PTHOR, Jonathan Rose for LOCUS, and Jaswinder Pal Singh for OCEAN. Charles Orgish was instrumental in providing us with enough workstations to complete the simulations in a timely fashion. Finally, we thank Rohit Chandra for the many useful discussions.

This research was supported by DARPA contract N00039-91-C-0138. Kourosh Gharachorloo is partly supported by Texas Instruments. Anoop Gupta is partly supported by a NSF Presidential Young Investigator Award.

References

[1] Sarita Adve and Mark Hill. Weak ordering - A new definition. In *Proceedings of the 17th Annual International Symposium on Computer Architecture*, pages 2–14, May 1990.

[2] Anant Agarwal, Beng-Hong Lim, David Kranz, and John Kubiatowicz. April: A processor architecture for multiprocessing. In *Proceedings of the 17th Annual International Symposium on Computer Architecture*, pages 104–114, May 1990.

[3] Jean-Loup Baer and Tien-Fu Chen. An effective on-chip preloading scheme to reduce data access penalty. In *Proceedings of Supercomputing '91*, pages 176–186, November 1991.

[4] James Boyle et al. *Portable Programs for Parallel Processors.* Holt, Rinehart and Winston, Inc., 1987.

[5] W. Buchholz, editor. *Planning a Computer System: Project Stretch.* McGraw-Hill, 1962.

[6] Michel Dubois, Christoph Scheurich, and Fayé Briggs. Memory access buffering in multiprocessors. In *Proceedings of the 13th Annual International Symposium on Computer Architecture*, pages 434–442, June 1986.

[7] Kourosh Gharachorloo, Anoop Gupta, and John Hennessy. Performance evaluation of memory consistency models for shared-memory multiprocessors. In *Fourth International Conference on Architectural Support for Programming Languages and Operating Systems*, pages 245–257, April 1991.

[8] Kourosh Gharachorloo, Anoop Gupta, and John Hennessy. Two techniques to enhance the performance of memory consistency models. In *Proceedings of the 1991 International Conference on Parallel Processing*, pages I:355–364, August 1991.

[9] Kourosh Gharachorloo, Anoop Gupta, and John Hennessy. Hiding memory latency using dynamic scheduling in shared-memory multiprocessors. Technical report, Stanford University, April 1992.

[10] Kourosh Gharachorloo, Dan Lenoski, James Laudon, Phillip Gibbons, Anoop Gupta, and John Hennessy. Memory consistency and event ordering in scalable shared-memory multiprocessors. In *Proceedings of the 17th Annual International Symposium on Computer Architecture*, pages 15–26, May 1990.

[11] Stephen R. Goldschmidt and Helen Davis. Tango introduction and tutorial. Technical Report CSL-TR-90-410, Stanford University, 1990.

[12] James R. Goodman. Cache consistency and sequential consistency. Technical Report Computer Sciences #1006, University of Wisconsin, Madison, February 1991.

[13] E. Gornish, E. Granston, and A. Veidenbaum. Compiler-directed data prefetching in multiprocessors with memory hierarchies. In *International Conference on Supercomputing*, pages 354–368, 1990.

[14] Anoop Gupta, John Hennessy, Kourosh Gharachorloo, Todd Mowry, and Wolf-Dietrich Weber. Comparative evaluation of latency reducing and tolerating techniques. In *Proceeding of the 18th Annual International Symposium on Computer Architecture*, pages 254–263, May 1991.

[15] Robert H. Halstead, Jr. and Tetsuya Fujita. MASA: A multithreaded processor architecture for parallel symbolic computing. In *Proceedings of the 15th Annual International Symposium on Computer Architecture*, pages 443–451, June 1988.

[16] John L. Hennessy and David A. Patterson. *Computer Architecture: A Quantitative Approach.* Morgan Kaufmann Publishers, Inc., 1990.

[17] R. A. Iannucci. Toward a dataflow/von Neumann hybrid architecture. In *Proceedings of the 15th Annual International Symposium on Computer Architecture*, pages 131–140, June 1988.

[18] Mike Johnson. *Superscalar Microprocessor Design.* Prentice Hall, 1991.

[19] R. M. Keller. Look-ahead processors. *Computing Surveys*, 7(4):177–195, 1975.

[20] Eric J. Koldinger, Susan J. Eggers, and Henry M. Levy. On the validity of trace-driven simulation for multiprocessors. In *Proceedings of the 18th Annual International Symposium on Computer Architecture*, pages 244–253, May 1991.

[21] D. Kroft. Lockup-free instruction fetch/prefetch cache organization. In *Proceedings of the 8th Annual International Symposium on Computer Architecture*, pages 81–85, 1981.

[22] Leslie Lamport. How to make a multiprocessor computer that correctly executes multiprocess programs. *IEEE Transactions on Computers*, C-28(9):241–248, September 1979.

[23] J. K. F. Lee and A. J. Smith. Branch prediction strategies and branch target buffer design. *IEEE Computer*, 17:6–22, 1984.

[24] Roland L. Lee. *The Effectiveness of Caches and Data Prefetch Buffers in Large-Scale Shared Memory Multiprocessors*. PhD thesis, Department of Computer Science, University of Illinois at Urbana-Champaign, May 1987.

[25] Roland L. Lee, Pen-Chung Yew, and Duncan H. Lawrie. Data prefetching in shared memory multiprocessors. In *Proceedings of the 1987 International Conference on Parallel Processing*, pages 28–31, August 1987.

[26] Jeffrey D. McDonald and Donald Baganoff. Vectorization of a particle simulation method for hypersonic rarified flow. In *AIAA Thermodynamics, Plasmadynamics and Lasers Conference*, June 1988.

[27] Stephen Melvin and Yale Patt. Exploiting fine-grained parallelism through a combination of hardware and software techniques. In *Proceedings of the 18th Annual International Symposium on Computer Architecture*, pages 287–296, May 1991.

[28] Todd Mowry and Anoop Gupta. Tolerating latency through software-controlled prefetching in shared-memory multiprocessors. *Journal of Parallel and Distributed Computing*, 12(2):87–106, June 1991.

[29] Allan K. Porterfield. *Software Methods for Improvement of Cache Performance on Supercomputer Applications*. PhD thesis, Department of Computer Science, Rice University, May 1989.

[30] Jonathan Rose. Locusroute: A parallel global router for standard cells. In *Design Automation Conference*, pages 189–195, June 1988.

[31] Jaswinder Pal Singh and John L. Hennessy. Parallelizing the simulation of ocean eddy currents. Technical Report CSL-TR-89-388, Stanford University, August 1989.

[32] Jaswinder Pal Singh, Wolf-Dietrich Weber, and Anoop Gupta. SPLASH: Stanford Parallel Applications for Shared Memory. Technical Report CSL-TR-91-469, Stanford University, May 1991.

[33] Burton J. Smith. Architecture and applications of the HEP multiprocessor computer system. *SPIE*, 298:241–248, 1981.

[34] J. E. Smith and A. R. Pleszkun. Implementation of precise interrupts in pipelined processors. In *Proceedings of the 12th Annual International Symposium on Computer Architecture*, pages 36–44, June 1985.

[35] Larry Soule and Anoop Gupta. Parallel distributed-time logic simulation. *IEEE Design and Test of Computers*, 6(6):32–48, December 1989.

[36] R. M. Tomasulo. An efficient hardware algorithm for exploiting multiple arithmetic units. *IBM Journal*, 11:25–33, 1967.

[37] Wolf-Dietrich Weber and Anoop Gupta. Exploring the benefits of multiple hardware contexts in a multiprocessor architecture: Preliminary results. In *Proceedings of the 16th Annual International Symposium on Computer Architecture*, pages 273–280, June 1989.

Session 2: Instruction Level Parallelism

Effects of Building Blocks on the Performance of Super–Scalar Architectures

Edil S. T. Fernandes and Fernando M. B. Barbosa

COPPE-Sistemas and Instituto de Matemática
Universidade Federal do Rio de Janeiro
Caixa Postal 68511
21945 – Rio de Janeiro – RJ, Brazil

Abstract

The inherent low level parallelism of Super-Scalar architectures plays an important role in the processing power provided by these machines: independent functional units promote opportunities for executing several machine operations simultaneously. From the viewpoint of the hardware designer it is very important to assess the influence of each functional unit, and the way they communicate, on the overall performance of the machine. Particularly, it is highly desirable to determine an upper bound in the number of additional functional units which give significant performance improvement ratios.

This work describes experiments that have been carried out to assess the effect of alternative instruction issue mechanisms, multiple functional units, instruction queues, common data bus and other hardware solutions on the performance of Super-Scalar machines. The assessment was obtained by interpreting non optimized object code of an actual processor on some basic machine models. The paper outlines the main aspects of the research, and shows that speed-up ratios of up to 3.35 times were observed during the interpretation of benchmark programs.

1. Introduction

The development of computer architectures comprising several independent functional units which can be programmed to perform concurrent operations is a current trend in the design of parallel machines. These processors —known as **Super-Scalar** machines— incorporate advanced concepts inherited from early efforts in the Computer Architecture field, especially those studies exploiting the potential power of μ-programmed architectures with horizontal μ-instructions.

Classical contributions leading to the development of Super-Scalar processors were the design of the CDC-6600 (Control Data) [THOR64], the IBM-360/91 [ANDE67], the decoupled architectures [SMIT82], the specification of the HPS machine[PATT85], and so on. Another major step towards the design of Super-Scalar machines was the development of global compaction techniques [TOKO78], [FISH81] and [NICO85].

As a consequence of the global compaction techniques, Very Long Instruction Word architectures (VLIW) have been specified and implemented [FISH84]. In these machines, each instruction has sufficient fields to exercise direct control over the resources of the hardware, and it is left to the compiler the task of specifying which functional units should be active during each machine cycle. For this reason, before the execution of a program on a

This work is supported by the Brazilian agencies CAPES, CNPq, and FAPERJ.

VLIW machine, a sequence of single (long) instructions should be produced [KRIC91]. The instruction issue mechanism used by VLIW architectures is very simple, and it is similar to the way machine instructions are issued in conventional processors: the activities are obeyed in the original order as scheduled by the compaction algorithm.

Alternatively, the architecture can have a hardware mechanism to identify, at execution time, which instructions can be executed simultaneously. The mechanism is embedded in the underlying hardware, and it significantly contributes to increasing the occupation level of the functional units. Such an issue scheme was implemented in some Super-Scalar machines, as for example, in the Intel 80960CA [INTE89] and IBM RS/6000 [GROH90]. Publications dealing with instruction issue algorithms are:

• The issue mechanisms proposed in [TJAD70] and [TJAD73];

• A comparison of some issue methods for pipelined supercomputer is in [WEIS84];

• The instruction dispatch approach proposed by Keller in [KELL85];

• The CONDEL model, which extracts concurrency from static instruction streams, presented by Uht in [AUTH85];

• The issue mechanism employing a dispatch stack containing instructions to be executed described in [ACOS86];

• Experiments carried out on a CRAY-like processor model, measuring the performance impact of some hardware features, reported in [PLES88];

• A survey on instruction sequencing presented in [KRIC91].

Instead of proposing a new machine design, in this work we describe experiments that have been carried out to identify the effectiveness of classical hardware solutions on the overall performance of Super-Scalar architectures. To achieve this objective, four basic machine models oriented for scalar operations (non-vector) have been specified. In this study, we have decided to incorporate multiple **non-pipelined** functional units because, as pointed out in [PLES88], there is no substantial performance improvement in pipelining the units on a non-vector machine.

Our basic models can be distinguished by their instruction issue mechanism. Within one model, machine configurations comprising a different mix of functional units were specified. For each machine configuration, we have evaluated both the occupation percentage of its hardware resources and the processing time required in the execution of benchmark programs. These metrics are valuable instruments in determining an upper bound on the number of additional machine blocks which give significant performance improvement ratios.

Algorithms reproducing the behaviour of the instruction issue mechanisms of the basic machine models have been specified and implemented. The algorithms are updated versions of traditional instruction issue methods, and take into account the current trends in contemporary μ-architectures. Variations of the hardware solutions introduced in the CDC-6600 [THOR64] and IBM-360/91 [TOMA67] such as *Scoreboard, Common Data Bus*, and *reservation station* were incorporated in the machine models of our experiments.

Reservation Stations (RS) can be viewed as virtual devices: they are attached to the functional units and act as buffers holding the necessary information (data and control) for the execution of an instruction.

The Common Data Bus (CDB) interconnects all the machine units. Results produced by the functional units can be directly transferred through the CDB —in a associative fashion— to the reservation stations. In this way, machine instructions waiting for an input operand which is still being evaluated by another functional unit, are allowed to proceed after receiving the corresponding unit output when it is propagated by the CDB. The CDB and RS concepts were used in the IBM-360/91 to detect data dependencies among instructions. In the CDC-6600, data dependencies among instructions are detected through the scoreboard which keeps track of the status of each machine resource.

This paper is organized in five sections. Next, we present the architecture model of our experiments. Section 3 describes a framework for evaluating the effectiveness of each model configuration. Section 4 explains the experiments and shows the main results. Section 5 provides the conclusions.

2. Architecture Model

The architecture model of our experiments represents a family of machines. The basic architecture includes several independent functional units and two multi-port register files. Each family member is fully described through parameters indicating the number of functional units, the presence of reservation stations attached to these units, if there exists a common data bus interconnecting all the machine components, etc. By changing the values of the parameters, different machine configurations are defined, allowing assessment of the effect of specific component mixes on the execution time required by benchmark programs.

2.1 Functional Blocks

The functional blocks of our target architecture are similar to the units of contemporary RISC processors. In our models, target components are based on the Intel i860 processor [MARG90], and includes at least one of the following blocks:

- Core Unit: executes branches and ALU operations (32-bit integer);
- Floating-point Units: consists of an adder and a multiplier capable of performing addition and multiplication in parallel;
- Graphic Unit: implements graphical primitives, and executes register transfers between the register files;
- Main Memory Controller: performs multiple main memory transfers in an interleaving scheme.

In addition to these functional blocks, the following are available:

- Reservation Stations: as in Tomasulo's model [TOMA67], some basic machine versions incorporate this intermediary device type.
- Common Data Bus (CDB): basic machine configurations can include this type of device which interconnects all the functional blocks.

Irrespective of the basic model, every machine configuration includes two Register Files (integer and floating-point registers), each one with 32 32-bit registers, and a queue from which instructions are fetched.

2.2 Target Instructions and Latencies

The basic machine instructions are analogous to the i860 repertoire except for the dual instruction mode subset (each dual instruction is decomposed and interpreted as two single instructions). As in the i860 processor, in our basic machine main memory operations are carried out via load and store instructions, core operations specify from one to three operand registers, and there are register transfer operations. We have decided to model the on-chip cache memory for instructions (of the i860) as the instruction queue of our basic machines. In this study, we are supposing that the the on-chip cache memory for data of that processor is disabled. Instead of modelling the branch predictor mechanism that always knows the next instruction address [BUTL91] (which would be immediate in our framework), we preferred to take into account the latencies required by the conditional branches instructions.

All the execution latencies are measured in terms of machine sub-cycles (cycles for short), and they are passed as parameters to the basic models. The following latencies were used during our experiments:

- instruction fetch, decode, and input operands fetch: one clock cycle each;
- addition and subtraction: three clock cycles;
- multiplication and division: six or nine clock

cycles for single or double precision operations respectively;
o main memory operations: 18 cycles for up to 64-bits being transferred or 36 clock cycles for 128-bit data transfers;
o graphical operations: three clock cycles;
o branches: three or four clock cycles (depending on whether the branch will be taken or not).

2.3 Machine Models

In addition to these components, target machines can be distinguished by the hardware mechanism responsible for the dispatch of the instructions. We have the following machine models:
(a) – only the scoreboard is used by the instruction issue mechanism. In this model, instructions are directly dispatched to the functional blocks, and the results are transferred to the destination registers before being read by waiting instructions;
(b) – there is a CDB connecting all the functional blocks of the machine. Through the CDB, results produced by the functional blocks are transferred to the destination registers and to the units waiting for the results;
(c) – attached to each machine component there is at least one reservation station (RS). The operation code and the operands are transferred to the RS before the actual execution by the corresponding functional unit. Since **there is no CDB**, reservation stations requiring an operand which is still being evaluated, have to read it from the source register;
(d) – the data path includes a CDB, and attached to each functional block there is at least one reservation station. Results produced by a functional block can be transferred to the reservation stations and to the destination register simultaneously.

2.4 Instruction Issue Mechanisms

We assume the existence of a program counter which points to the instruction queue. Within each machine cycle, the issue mechanism examines the instruction pointed to by the program counter. The instruction is fetched from the queue and decoded by the mechanism, and if there exists a functional block (or an RS) available, the instruction operands are read from the register banks and transferred, together with the operation code, to the appropriate functional block (or RS). If there are no data dependencies, the instruction execution starts. Otherwise, the execution is deferred until the instruction operands become available. Irrespective of the instruction execution being initiated, the issue mechanism starts treating the next instruction. Issuing will only stop if either there is no functional block (or reservation station) available or if the last instruction is a conditional branch.

The stop conditions above are common to all models. There is an additional stop condition for models (a) and (c): whenever the destination register specified by the current instruction has already been designated to hold the result of a previous instruction, the mechanism also stops.

3. A Framework for Evaluation

We have developed a framework to evaluate the role of different mixes of functional blocks, common data bus, reservation stations, and instruction issue mechanisms in the execution time of test programs. Particularly, we want to determine the utilization level of each functional block, and the bounds on the number of functional units resulting in performance improvement.

Two steps are required to perform the evaluation: trace generation, and simulation of the instruction issue mechanisms. By using an interpreter of the Intel i860, trace files related to the benchmark programs are generated. This step is executed only once: the same trace file is utilized by the simulation of alternative instruction issue mechanisms, it being unnecessary to repeat the interpretation.

For each architecture model, a specific algorithm reproducing the behaviour of the corresponding instruction issue mechanism was specified and implemented. The algorithm accepts as input the dynamic sequence of instructions related to the interpretation of test programs, and dispatches the instructions to the appropriate functional units as specified by the issue mechanism. The occupation ratio of each machine resource, the elapsed time, the number of functional units being used concurrently, upper and lower bounds on the number of functional units, and a global profile of the target machine are examples of the data produced during the simulation of each machine configuration.

3.1 Trace Driven Simulation

Test programs written in C language are translated into the object code for the i860 processor by a commercial compiler. For validation purposes, the code is executed in the Intel processor. Next, the code is fed into the i860 interpreter and the corresponding trace file is generated. This trace contains the sequence of the instructions which were interpreted and other information required by the different instruction issue mechanisms of the experiments. Typical information gathered at interpretation time include the current program counter contents; the i860 machine instruction being interpreted; machine status; elapsed time; addresses of the main memory words accessed by load/store instructions, and other data related to the test program interpretation.

For each basic machine model, an algorithm reproducing the behaviour of the instruction issue mechanism described in Section 2.4, has been developed. Since we have the dynamic sequence of the instructions, the algorithm *does not execute the code again.* It reads the next trace file instruction, and (if possible) depending on the basic machine model, the instruction is dispatched either to the appropriate functional unit or to the reservation station. Next, the status of each machine component is examined, the simulated time is updated, and other book keeping tasks are performed.

Whenever an operation is concluded, the scoreboard entries related to the resources used by the instruction are updated. If the basic machine model incorporates a common data bus, the algorithm performs (*virtual*) transfers of the operation result both to the destination register and to the functional blocks or reservation stations which are waiting for that operand. Otherwise, only the destination register is updated. In both cases, operations waiting for a resource which became available are allowed to proceed.

In order to dispatch the main memory operations, the algorithms use the memory word addresses contained in the trace file to decide which memory bank will carry out the operation. Main memory banks are regarded as resources, and for this reason each bank has a scoreboard entry associated to it. Both the number of memory banks and the amount of reservation stations attached to each memory controller are simulation parameters. Conflicts in the use of mutually exclusive resources (e.g., memory banks, CDB, and register files ports) are modelled and handled by the algorithms.

4. Experiments

The performance of alternative machine configurations was evaluated through four sets of experiments, one for each basic machine model. By varying the number of functional blocks and reservation stations, several machine configurations were defined. Test programs were submitted to each configuration, and the machine performance was generated by the instruction issue algorithm.

The benchmark used in our experiments consists of eight test programs. They are: The **Livermore Loop** number 24 (Liv) which finds the index of the minimum component in a one-dimensional array of floating-point numbers [MCMA83]; **LU Decomposition** (LU) [FORS67]; **Hu-Tucker** (Hu) [YOHE72]; The

Branch (Brc) program described in [DITZ87]; **BCD-BIN** (Bcd) [AUHT85]; **Integral** (Int) evaluation of a function through the trapezoidal rule [CONT65]; **Quick-Sort** (Qck) and **Bubble-Sort** (Bub) [KNUT73].

4.1 Performance Figures

A hypothetical machine was used as a **reference** to evaluate the performance of the various basic machine configurations. The reference machine has only one unit of each type, and there is neither a common data bus nor are there reservation stations. The instruction execution times are the same as in our machine models, and object code is executed in a sequential fashion: an instruction is only dispatched when the previous one has finished. The speed-up and reduction ratios presented along the text were obtained with respect to the execution time required by each benchmark program on the reference machine. Table I shows the execution time and the number of i860 instructions executed by each functional block within the reference machine.

Prog	Core	FMu	FAd	Mem	Gra	Cycles
Int	2683	396	991	995	100	53,546
LU	1749	90	84	714	10	27,566
Hu	1159	0	0	575	0	18,990
Brc	7686	0	0	0	0	44,070
Bcd	330	0	0	40	0	2,771
Liv	1589	0	0	635	0	22,711
Qck	3705	0	0	933	0	53,068
Bub	3208	0	0	1676	0	54,176

Table I: Operations per Functional Block and Execution Times

As can be seen in Table I, the floating-point units are only used by the two first test programs. This is the actual code generated by the i860 C compiler, and such distribution reflects our interest in choosing typical application programs encountered in non-vector machines. As mentioned before, the execution times (expressed in terms of cycles) will be used as the reference unit to evaluate the performance gains of the basic models.

A very important aspect regarding the specification of a Super-Scalar architecture is how to determine the number of each functional unit type (i.e., the components mix) forming its data path. Determining the components mix is a complex task because a very large number of simulations can be required. During our experiments we have been forced to tackle this problem: since there were machine configurations with up to ten parameters (five functional unit types and five RS types) which must be jointly dimensioned, our tuning task towards a balanced configuration was very complex. Thus, it is essential to devise a suitable methodology to carry out the tuning process. In order to discard irrelevant machine configurations, our first step towards the tuning consisted in determining an upper bound on the number of components.

Attributing a very high number to each machine parameter in all basic models, and monitoring the percentage of the time in which machine components remained occupied, gave us such a bound. In our experiments, we have fixed in 64 the number of each machine component. The number of functional blocks actually used together with the execution times can be found in [FERN92].

Determining the maximum number of functional blocks which were activated simultaneously is not sufficient to give an idea of the concurrency level. For this reason, we have assessed the percentage of execution time in which groups of functional blocks remain working together. Figure I shows this percentage for groups of FP Adders during the execution of the *LU Decomposition* program on the Basic Model (b). As we can see, all the units remained idle during 71.09% of the execution time, and only in 3.59% two FP Adders were occupied simultaneously. This means that a single unit would satisfy the processing requirements in 96.41% of the execution time.

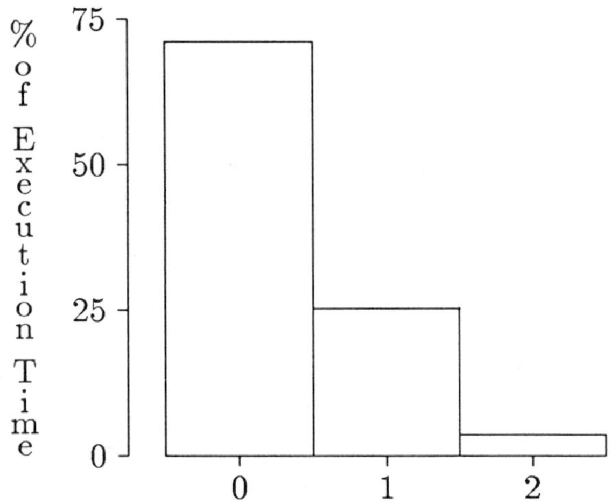

Figure 1: Concurrently Active FP Adders

On the other hand, examining the occupation percentages of the Core Units during the execution of the *Livermore Loop* program on Model (b), a more even distribution is observed. Figure 2 shows this percentage distribution.

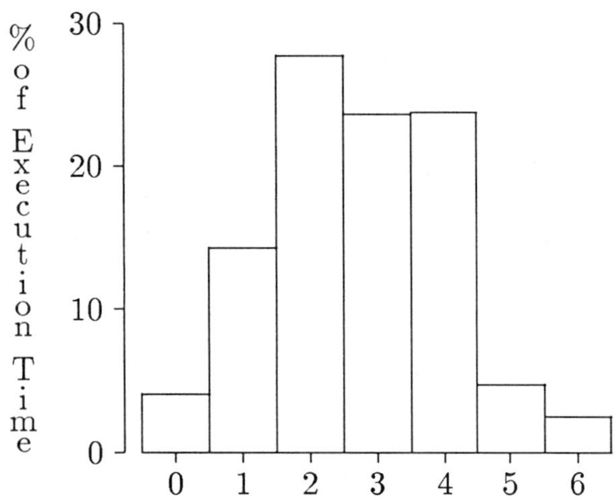

Figure 2: Concurrently Active Core Units

As illustrated in Figure 2, no more than four Core Units were required during 91.78% of the execution time. Since there are 1,589 instructions to be executed by the Core Units, one might expect that, by removing two of the six units, the execution time would be increased by the execution of 8.22% of these instructions (about 131 instructions). Unfortunately that is not quite simple. For example, the percentage of execution time in which all the Core Units remained idle could be decreased while the occupation ratios of the other Core Units (and perhaps the overall execution time as well) could be augmented. It is obvious that doing such a removal will disturb the occupation ratio of other machine components, and this is the reason for the need of a jointly dimensioning, mentioned early.

The next step in our experiments consisted in determining how long each functional block remained waiting for an input operand. Through these waiting time values it was possible to assess the actual contribution of each machine component on the global performance of each target architecture.

Following the waiting time evaluation, we started the tuning process. Based on the occupation ratios, functional units (and RS) were removed/included, and the effect on the performance was evaluated. For each basic model, this tuning process was carried out for each benchmark component (i.e., the tuning process was performed in 32 machine configurations). Since there are several machine parameters, this task required a very large number of simulations.

Due to the nature of the experiment, we preferred to conduct the tuning interactively because by examining the performance evaluation graphic it was easier to select the number of units from which the performance gain curve flattens off. For example, as illustrated in Figure 3, varying the number of Memory Controllers from four to 16 units, results in the execution time being reduced from 12,567 to 12,244 cycles, reaching the 12,363 cycles mark with eight Controllers.

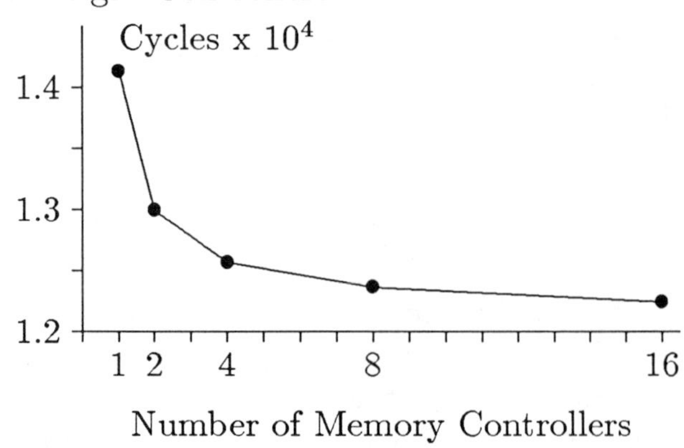

Figure 3: Effect of Memory Controllers on the Performance

The graphic shown in Figure 3 was obtained by issuing the instructions of the *Livermore Loop* program in Model (d). From the performance viewpoint it was better to select the configuration including 16 units because the corresponding execution time is more reduced than the others. However, if we consider the configuration costs, by reducing the amount of Controllers by a quarter, results in a degradation of 2.64% in the execution time. It remains to be seen whether the same percentage degradation will hold for other test programs, and depending on the results produced by the configuration with eight Controllers, perhaps the costs should be penalized in favour of a faster execution time.

As a consequence of the above, several simulations have been carried out. For each test program being executed in the same basic model, we found a configuration incorporating a lower number of components without degrading the machine performance too much.

Based on the values attributed to each machine component, a final tuning was performed. The main objective of this step was to find a balanced configuration to be used in all the models. Through this configuration it will be possible to assess the role of each issue mechanism on the performance of a Super-Scalar machine. A first choice of the component mix comprising the common configuration was based on the distribution of the numbers of each machine component used in the various resulting configurations. The numbers with highest relative frequencies were selected, and the corresponding component mix was used to evaluate the models. The resulting performance figures were compared with the previous ones, and further adjustments have been done –each one followed by the corresponding simulation of the benchmark. Based on the *cost x performance* criteria, we obtained the following values for the reservation stations (RS) and functional units (FU) comprising the final configuration:

Type	RS	FU
Core Unit	3	2
FP Multiplier	2	2
FP Adder	2	2
Mem. Controller	4	4
Graphic Unit	1	1

Tables II and III indicate the number of machine cycles taken by the basic models, and the corresponding speed-up ratios.

	Model (a)		Model (b)	
Prog	Cycles	Speed-up	Cycles	Speed-up
Int	21,550	2.49	17,299	3.10
LU	18,010	1.53	14,548	1.90
Hu	10,593	1.79	8,906	2.13
Brc	29,724	1.48	28,698	1.54
Bcd	2,095	1.32	1,821	1.52
Liv	15,314	1.48	12,937	1.76
Qck	31,156	1.70	27,092	1.96
Bub	32,127	1.69	25,926	2.09

Table II: Final Configuration Performance in Models (a) and (b)

	Model (c)		Model (d)	
Prog	Cycles	Speed-up	Cycles	Speed-up
Int	21,549	2.49	16,905	3.17
LU	17,276	1.60	13,886	1.99
Hu	10,558	1.80	8,825	2.15
Brc	29,724	1.48	28,696	1.54
Bcd	1,952	1.42	1,741	1.59
Liv	15,314	1.48	12,567	1.81
Qck	30.840	1.72	26,270	2.02
Bub	32,127	1.69	25,926	2.09

Table III: Final Configuration Performance in Models (c) and (d)

4.2 Interpretation of Results

Examining the results listed in Tables II and III, we can see that Model (a) presented speed-up ratios varying from 1.32 up to 2.49. Nearly the same amount of improvement is achieved by Model (c). Consequently, we can conclude that replacing some functional blocks by reservation stations does not improve the target machine performance.

Models (b) and (d) achieved better performance improvements. Their speed-up ratios range from 1.52 up to 3.10 and from 1.54 up to 3.17 respectively. The presence of a common data bus, providing full connectivity among target machine components, is responsible for such improvements: a high degree of low level concurrency is achieved with the output operands being propagated to the register banks and other machine devices simultaneously. The presence of reservation stations is responsible for the slightly superior improvement level presented by Model (d) with respect to the speed-up ratios of Model (c).

The occupation ratios of each functional block type reflect the characteristics of the benchmark programs. For example, *LU – Decomposition* and *Integral* programs make use of the floating-point units while the other programs do not. The main memory bottleneck is evidenced by the high occupation ratios observed in all the test programs. The only exception is the *Branch* program which consists of a loop evaluating the sum of odd and even numbers ranging from 1 up to 1024.

5. Conclusions

A framework to evaluate Super-Scalar architectures was specified and implemented. It assess the effect of functional blocks, common data bus and reservation stations on the overall performance of alternative target machine designs. The framework is able to handle machine models with different instruction issue mechanisms.

In order to evaluate the performance of machines with specific functional blocks mix, we carried out several experiments with the actual machine code of an existing processor. This code was generated from a set of test programs, and the behaviour profiles of Super-Scalar machines were obtained. From these results it is possible to assess the contribution of each component on the machine performance. The occupation ratio of each functional block during the processing time and the period in which they remained waiting for input operands are examples of valuable design parameters provided by the framework. Through these data is possible to determine lower/upper bounds in the number of effective functional units which should be incorporated in the design of Super-Scalar machines.

As demonstrated by the performance results, the role played by a common data bus interconnecting all the processor components is a very important feature: it increases the low-level concurrency within the μ-architecture. The importance of the instruction issue mechanisms were evidenced by the speed-up ratios achieved by our models with the instructions being executed out of the original order.

It should be emphasized that the object code used by the experiments was not optimised. For this reason, we believe that more significant speed-up ratios should be obtained after optimising the target code. Another research topic which is being pursued regards the main memory bottleneck. The issue algorithms will be modified to take into account the presence of presence of a cache memory for data. The work continues.

References

[ACOS86] R.D. Acosta, J. Kjelstrup, and H.C. Torng, "An Instruction Issuing Approach to Enhancing Performance in Multiple Functional Unit Processors," IEEE Transactions on Computers, Vol. C-35, No. 9, September 1986, pp. 815–828.

[ANDE67] D.W. Anderson, F.J. Sparacio, and R.M. Tomasulo, "The IBM System/360 Model 91: Machine Philosophy and Instruction Handling," IBM Journal, No. 11, 1967, pp. 2–7.

[AUHT85] Augustus K. Uht, "Hardware Extraction of Low Level Concurrency from Sequential Instruction Streams," Ph.D. Thesis, Carnegie-Mellon University, December 1985.

[BUTL91] M. Butler, T. Yeh, Y. Patt, M. Alsup, H. Scales, and M. Shebanow, "Single Instruction Stream Parallelism Is Greater than Two," Proceedings of the 18th Annual International Symposium on Computer Architecture, May, 1991, pp. 276–286.

[CONT65] S. D. Conte, "Elementary Numerical Analysis," McGraw-Hill Book Co., New York, NY, USA, 1965.

[DITZ87] David R. Ditzel, and Hubert R. Mclellan, "Branch Folding in the CRISP Microprocessor: Reducing Branch Delay to Zero," Proceedings of the 14th Annual International Symposium on Computer Architecture, 1987, pp. 2–9.

[FERN92] Edil S. T. Fernandes, and Fernando M. B. Barbosa, "Effects of Building Blocks on the Performance of Super–Scalar Architectures," Technical Report, COPPE/Sistemas, UFRJ, January 1992, 18 pages.

[FISH81] Joseph A. Fisher, "Trace Scheduling: A Technique for Global Microcode Compaction," IEEE Transactions on Computers, Vol. C-30, No. 7, July 1981, pp. 478–490.

[FISH84] Joseph A. Fisher, "VLIW Machine: A Multiprocessor for Compiling Scientific Code," Computer, July 1984, pp. 45–53.

[FORS67] G. Forsythe, and C. B. Moler, "Computer Solution of Linear Algebraic Systems," Prentice Hall, Englewood Cliffs, New Jersey, 1967.

[GROH90] G. F. Grohoski, "Machine Organization of the IBM RISC System/6000 Processor," IBM Journal of Research and Development, Vol. 34. No. 1, January 1990, pp. 37–58.

[INTE89] Intel, "Intel 80960CA User's Manual," Intel, 1989.

[KELL75] R. M. Keller, "Look-Ahead Processors," Computing Surveys, Vol. 7, No. 4, December 1975, pp. 177–195.

[KNUT73] D. Knuth, "Art of Computer Programming," Addison-Wesley Publishing Co., USA, 1973.

[KRIC91] R. F Krick and A. Dollas, "The Evolution of Instruction Sequencing," IEEE Computer, April 1991, pp. 5–15.

[MARG90] N. Margulis, "i860 Microprocessor Internal Architecture," Microprocessors and Microsystems, Vol. 14, No. 2, March 1990, pp. 89–96.

[MCMA83] F. H. McMahon, " Fortran Kernels: MFLOPS," Lawrence Livermore National Laboratory, 1983.

[NICO85] A. Nicolau, "Percolation Scheduling: A Parallel Compilation Technique," Technical Report TR 85-678, Department of Computer Science, Cornell University, May 1985.

[PATT85] Y. N. Patt, W. Hwu, and M. C. Shebanow, "HPS, a New Microarchitecture: Rationale and Introduction," Proceedings of the 18th International Microprogramming Workshop, December 1985, pp. 103–108.

[PLES88] A. R. Pleszkun and G. S. Sohi, "The Performance Potential of Multiple Functional Unit Processors," Proceedings of the 15th Annual International Symposium on Computer Architecture, 1988. pp. 37–44.

[SMIT82] J. Smith "Decoupled Access / Execute Computer Architectures," Proceedings of the 9th International Symposium on Computer Architecture, April 1982, pp. 113–119.

[THOR64] J. E. Thornton, "Parallel Operation in the Control Data 6600." AFIPS Proceedings FJCC, pt 2, Vol. 26, 1964, pp. 33–40.

[TJAD70] G.S. Tjaden and M. Flynn, "Detection and Parallel Execution of Independent Instructions," IEEE Transactions on Computers, Vol. C-19, No. 10, October 1970, pp. 889–895.

[TJAD73] G.S. Tjaden and M. Flynn, "Representation of Concurrency with Ordering Matrices," IEEE Transactions on Computers, Vol. C-22, No. 8, August 1973, pp. 752–761.

[TOMA67] R. M. Tomasulo, "An Efficient Algorithm for Exploiting Multiple Arithmetic Units," IBM Journal, No. 11, 1967, pp. 25–33.

[TOKO78] M. Tokoro, T. Takizuka, E. Tamura, and I. Yamaura, "A Technique of Global Optimization of Microprograms," Proceedings of the 11th Annual Microprogramming Workshop, 1978, pp. 41–50.

[WEIS84] Shlomo Weiss and James E. Smith, "Instruction Issue Logic for Pipelined Supercomputers," Proceeding of the 11th Annual International Symposium on Computer Architecture, June 1984, pp. 110–118.

[YOHE72] J. M. Yohe, "Hu-Tucker Minimum Redundancy Alphabetic Coding Method [Z]," CACM, Vol. 15, No. 5, May 1972, pp. 360–362.

Limits of Control Flow on Parallelism

Monica S. Lam and Robert P. Wilson
Computer Systems Laboratory
Stanford University, CA 94305

Abstract

This paper discusses three techniques useful in relaxing the constraints imposed by control flow on parallelism: control dependence analysis, executing multiple flows of control simultaneously, and speculative execution. We evaluate these techniques by using trace simulations to find the limits of parallelism for machines that employ different combinations of these techniques. We have three major results. First, local regions of code have limited parallelism, and control dependence analysis is useful in extracting global parallelism from different parts of a program. Second, a superscalar processor is fundamentally limited because it cannot execute independent regions of code concurrently. Higher performance can be obtained with machines, such as multiprocessors and dataflow machines, that can simultaneously follow multiple flows of control. Finally, without speculative execution to allow instructions to execute before their control dependences are resolved, only modest amounts of parallelism can be obtained for programs with complex control flow.

1 Introduction

The potential for parallelism can be evaluated from two different perspectives. The first is to propose an actual system design; the performance of such a system is a lower bound on the amount of available parallelism. The second is to perform studies on the limits of parallelism for a particular approach by enforcing only the constraints associated with the approach and relaxing all other constraints. If the upper bound of performance is found to be unacceptably low, then the approach is inadequate. On the other hand, if the upper bound is within expectations, the only conclusion is that the approach may be sufficient. It is only from low limits that we can draw interesting conclusions.

This research was supported in part by DARPA contract N00039-91-C-0138 and by an NSF graduate fellowship.

A recent study by Wall [17] contains a surprising result that suggests a severe limitation in current approaches. One of the experiments in that study examines the performance of a processor that uses an aggressive hardware algorithm to predict the outcomes of branches. Instructions along the predicted path of a branch are *speculatively* executed before the branch is resolved. The processor has perfect memory disambiguation, perfect register renaming, unlimited instruction fetching, and a very large number of functional units. The reported speedups for this processor on a set of non-numeric programs range from 4.1 to 7.4. Given the assumptions of perfect memory disambiguation and a large number of functional units, these speedups are quite small.

Wall's result constrasts sharply with experiments that assume perfect branch prediction [10, 12]. Since a machine with perfect branch prediction requires foreknowledge, we refer to such a machine as an *oracle*. The effects of control flow on parallelism are essentially eliminated on an oracle machine because all of the branch outcomes are known in advance. Much more parallelism is available on an oracle machine, suggesting that the bottleneck in Wall's experiment is due to control flow.

The ultimate goal of our study is to discover ways to increase parallelism by an order of magnitude beyond current approaches. In this paper, we focus on control flow. Through a study of the limits of parallelism, we hope to establish the inadequacy of current approaches in handling control flow and identify promising new directions.

This paper offers evidence that the limit of parallelism discussed in Wall's paper is likely to apply to many more non-numeric programs than those measured. A processor that uses speculation to only exploit local parallelism found between mispredicted branches is fundamentally limited. A compiler can locate more global parallelism in the code by extracting the true *control dependence* of the program. However, this increased opportunity for parallelization cannot be fully exploited unless the machine can simultaneously pursue multiple flows of control. The degree of parallelism is fundamentally limited by the von Neumann architecture. Higher performance can be obtained with machines that can simultaneously follow multiple flows of control.

In this paper, we analyze the techniques of speculative execution, control dependence analysis, and following multiple flows of control. We evaluate these techniques empirically by computing the limits of parallelism for a set of programs on machines that employ different combinations of these techniques. So far, research on superscalar and multiprocessor architectures has mostly been conducted independently. This work studies how instruction and processor levels of parallelism interact. Our study also suggests that a useful characteristic for predicting the parallelism in a program is whether the control flow is data dependent.

We first introduce the major concepts of the paper in Section 2. We explain speculative execution, control dependence analysis, and pursuing multiple flows of control. Section 3 presents a set of abstract machine models that use these three techniques in various combinations. In Section 4, we describe the experimental framework used to evaluate the limits of parallelism. Section 5 presents the results of these experiments and analyzes the parallelism for each machine model. Finally, Section 6 presents the conclusions of our study and describes its implications for some specific architectures that have been proposed and implemented.

2 Relaxing Control Flow Constraints

The perfect branch prediction of an oracle machine is an upper bound of all other techniques to relax control flow constraints. Unfortunately, it is also an unrealistic upper bound. Because branch outcomes are known in advance on an oracle machine, no instructions have to wait for branches to be resolved. To achieve the same performance, a machine must speculatively execute all possible paths through a program. This requires hardware resources exponential in the number of outstanding conditional branches. Since perfect branch prediction is not realistic, more practical techniques are required to handle control flow. This section examines three techniques: speculation with branch prediction, control dependence analysis, and following multiple flows of control.

2.1 Speculation with Branch Prediction

While speculation on all possible paths is infeasible in practice, limited speculation is commonly used throughout computer systems to improve performance. For example, almost all modern processors prefetch the instructions following a conditional branch. Some machines such as the IBM 360/91 pursue both execution paths by also prefetching the instructions at the branch target.

A common technique to improve the efficiency of speculation is to only speculate on instructions from the most likely execution path. The success of this approach depends on the accuracy of branch prediction. Even for non-numeric code, both hardware and software prediction algorithms have been shown to be accurate over 85% of the time [6, 8].

Extending speculative instruction fetching to speculative execution creates additional parallelism. However, unlike instruction fetching, speculatively executing an instruction may generate unwanted side effects. These side effects must be discarded if the branch prediction is incorrect. Both hardware and software techniques can be used to implement speculative execution.

Various hardware structures have been proposed to support speculative execution [7, 11, 13, 16]. These structures store the results of the speculative instructions until the branch direction is determined. If the branch prediction was correct the results are committed, otherwise they are discarded. Hardware scheduling, however, is limited by the fact that an instruction simply cannot execute before it is fetched. It is difficult to fetch instructions from far ahead along the predicted execution path, especially for programs with complex control flow.

Software techniques overcome instruction fetch limitations by reordering instructions. Trace scheduling identifies the most commonly executed trace and schedules the instructions within the trace as if they belong to one large basic block [2, 4]. However, implemented trace scheduling algorithms only employ very limited forms of speculation. Smith et al. extend software scheduling with hardware support for speculative execution [15]. Instructions to be speculatively executed are *boosted* before a conditional branch. These instructions are labeled so that their results are discarded or committed when the branch condition is determined. This combines the ability of software to eliminate fetch limitations and the ability of hardware to speculatively execute instructions with side effects.

2.2 Control Dependence Analysis

For most hardware instruction schedulers, all speculatively executed instructions must be discarded when a conditional branch is mispredicted. This constraint is, however, unnecessarily strict. Consider the following simple example:

```
if (a < 0)
     b = 1;
c = 2;
```

While the assignment `b = 1` is executed only if `a < 0`, the assignment `c = 2` is always executed regardless of the value of `a`. We say that `b = 1` is *control dependent* on the condition `a < 0` and that `c = 2` is *control independent*. We refer to the branch on which an instruction is control dependent as its *control dependence branch*.

A hardware scheduler generally cannot determine which instructions are control independent. In this example, suppose the scheduler speculatively executes `c = 2` before the condition is resolved. If the branch is mispredicted, the hardware must discard the assignment to `c` only so that it can repeat the identical assignment later. A compiler can compute the control dependence and eliminate this inefficiency. More generally, control dependence analysis allows instructions to be moved across many branches. By expanding the range of code from which parallelism can be extracted, control dependence analysis increases the available parallelism.

Control dependence is an intuitively simple concept. For block-structured programs, the immediate control dependence for an instruction is simply the condition in the closest enclosing control construct. For example, in the following code,

```
for (i = 0; i < 100; i++)
    if (A[i] > 0) foo();
bar();
```

the call of the `foo` function is control dependent on the condition `A[i] > 0`, which in turn is control dependent on the loop exit condition `i < 100`. The `bar` function is not control dependent on any part of the loop and can execute in parallel with the loop, assuming there is no data dependence between `foo` and `bar`.

Control dependences in programs with arbitrary control flow can easily be computed in a compiler using the *reverse dominance frontier* algorithm [3]. Hardware techniques for analyzing control dependences have also been considered [9], but they can only detect a small subset of the control independent instructions and require complex hardware.

2.3 Executing Multiple Flows of Control

Control dependence analysis discovers parallelism from across different regions of code, each of which may have its own flow of control. In the example above, control dependence analysis shows that the `bar` function can run concurrently with the preceding loop. However, a uniprocessor can typically only follow one flow of control at any time. A uniprocessor cannot fetch and execute the instructions from within the loop while following the arbitrary control flow that may be present in the `bar` function.

Support for following multiple flows of control is necessary to fully exploit the parallelism uncovered by control dependence analysis. Multiprocessor architectures are a general means of providing this support. Each processor of a MIMD multiprocessor can follow an independent flow of control. At the other extreme, it is sometimes possible to generate uniprocessor code that corresponds to pursuing multiple flows of control in the original computation. A small number of code segments can be packed together by generating different versions of the code for every possible combination of control flow. However, in general, combining independent control flows can lead to significant code expansion.

3 Abstract Machine Models

To establish the fundamental limits of these three techniques for relaxing control flow constraints, we define a set of abstract machine models and analyze the parallelism for each machine under ideal conditions. Each machine model uses a different combination of the three techniques. Our approach is to examine a set of instruction traces from real programs and compute the available parallelism by simply enforcing true data dependence constraints and the control flow constraints associated with each abstract machine model. Other constraints due to imperfect memory disambiguation, reuse of variables, and limited resources are ignored.

We define seven abstract machines. The BASE machine uses none of the three techniques and provides a baseline for comparison. The ORACLE machine has perfect branch prediction, and its performance represents an upper bound of parallelism given the assumptions in our experiments. The other five machines use combinations of control dependence analysis (CD), following multiple flows of control (MF), and speculative execution with branch prediction (SP). There are only five interesting combinations because we cannot recognize independent flows of control without control dependence analysis.

Each machine is distinguished by its ability to handle control flow. We model these abilities by imposing the sequencing constraints shown in Figure 1 on the execution of instructions in dynamic traces. More aggressive machines have less restrictive constraints. Since the BASE machine uses none of the three techniques, its control flow constraint is the most severe; it prevents instructions from executing before any preceding branches. The CD machine has perfect control dependence information, and thus, instructions that are not dependent upon a branch need not wait for it to be resolved. To reflect the limitation of following one flow of control, we also impose an ordering on the branch instructions. To model the behavior of current compilers [1], this ordering requires all branches in the program to execute in the original sequential execution order. The CD-MF machine may follow an unlimited number of flows of control and does not require a branch ordering constraint.

All of the machines with speculative execution in this study only speculatively execute instructions on the most likely execution path, Simultaneously executing instructions on alternate paths would require that some instructions be cancelled regardless of the branch outcomes. However, in the various SP machines, all of the speculative instructions are potentially useful, making these machines more realistic than the ORACLE machine.

The SP machine can speculate on an infinite number of consecutive branch outcomes. This essentially creates an infinitely long path of predicted instructions through a program. Instructions from anywhere along this path may execute in parallel. However, when a branch is mispredicted, all of the instructions on the predicted path following the

BASE An instruction cannot execute until the immediately preceding branch in the trace is resolved. This implies that branch instructions must execute in order, one per cycle.

CD An instruction cannot execute until its control dependence branches are resolved. In addition, branch instructions must execute in order, one per cycle, to reflect the inability to pursue multiple flows of control simultaneously.

CD-MF An instruction cannot execute until its control dependence branches are resolved. Multiple branch instructions can execute in parallel and need not be ordered.

SP An instruction cannot execute until the immediately preceding mispredicted branch in the trace is resolved. This implies that a branch instruction must wait for all preceding mispredicted branches.

SP-CD An instruction cannot execute until its mispredicted control dependence branches are resolved. In addition, a branch instruction must wait for all preceding mispredicted branches, not just the ones it is control dependent on.

SP-CD-MF An instruction cannot execute until its mispredicted control dependence branches are resolved. There are no additional constraints on branches.

ORACLE There are no constraints due to control flow.

Figure 1: Control Flow Constraints of Abstract Machines

branch must be cancelled. Only those instructions that are not cancelled appear in the traces that we analyze. Therefore, the control flow constraint on an instruction in a trace is that it cannot execute until all of the preceding mispredicted branches are resolved. As long as the branch predictions are correct, the flow of control does not change and the branch instructions can execute in any order. A mispredicted branch requires that the flow of control transfer to the unpredicted branch path, and thus, only one mispredicted branch can execute in each cycle.

The SP-CD machine differs from the SP machine in its treatment of mispredicted branches. Instead of cancelling all of the instructions along the predicted path, only those instructions that are actually control dependent on the mispredicted branch are cancelled. Due to following a single flow of control, the mispredicted branches must still be executed in order. The SP-CD-MF machine can follow multiple flows of control simultaneously, and thus mispredicted branches can execute in parallel.

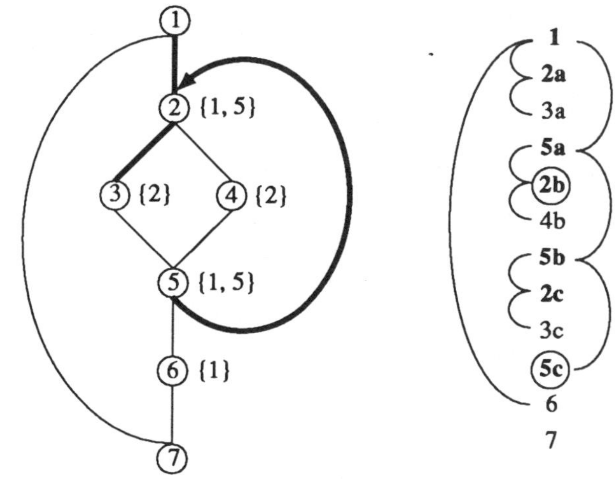

Figure 2: Example Flow Graph and Trace

To illustrate the power of the different abstract machine models, consider the flow graph in Figure 2. Assume that there are no data dependences in this program. Each node in the graph consists of a single instruction. Next to each node is the set of branch instructions on which it is immediately control dependent. The edges represent the possible flow of control, with the more likely branch outcomes highlighted by bold arcs. One possible trace through this graph is also shown in Figure 2. Each instruction in the trace is identified by the instruction node number and a letter to distinguish the specific instance. Branch instructions are written in boldface and circled if they are mispredicted. The edges in the trace represent the control dependence relationships.

Since there are no data dependences in the program, the ORACLE machine simply executes all of the instructions in one cycle. The executions of the other machine models are shown in Figure 3, where the edges represent the dependences due to control flow and instructions at the same level execute at the same time.

The BASE machine executes all of the branches sequentially and each non-branch instruction one cycle after the preceding branch. The CD machine executes instructions 6 and 7 earlier because they are not control dependent on the immediately preceding branches. The CD-MF machine need not execute the branches in order; the edges are simply the control dependence edges from the trace in Figure 2. The SP machine executes all of the instructions between mispredicted branches in parallel. The SP-CD machine behaves similarly but executes instructions 3c, 6, and 7 earlier because they are not control dependent on the mispredicted branches. Finally, the SP-CD-MF machine executes all but one of the instructions in one cycle. Since instruction 4b is not on the predicted path, the machine does not speculatively execute the instruction. The instruction is therefore not executed until the processor discovers that it

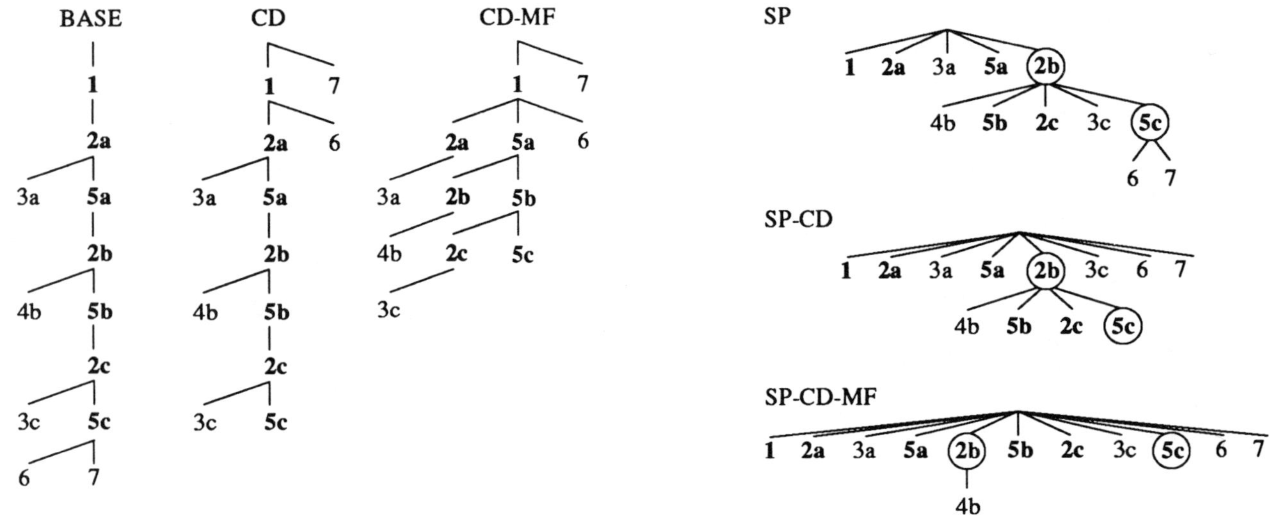

Figure 3: Execution of the Abstract Machines

has mispredicted the branch 2b. In contrast, to achieve the performance of the ORACLE machine, both instructions 3 and 4 must be executed in parallel on every iteration. This illustrates the fundamental difference between SP-CD-MF and ORACLE: the SP-CD-MF machine does not pursue alternate paths simultaneously.

4 Experimental Framework

This section describes the methodology used to analyze the parallelism for each machine model. Since we are only interested in evaluating techniques for handling control flow, we limit the scope of the experiment to include only the fundamental constraints related to control flow.

4.1 Data Dependence

We assume an idealistic approach to handling data dependences. The only data dependence constraint enforced is that a read operation in the trace must only wait for the immediately preceding write operation to the same location. This relaxes many constraints in reality.

First, since we are enforcing only true data dependences (reads after writes), we have eliminated all the anti-dependences (writes after reads) and output dependences (writes after writes) for all register as well as memory accesses. In practice, various renaming techniques can be used to remove some of these spurious data dependences.

Second, we also assume that memory references are perfectly disambiguated; that is, the machines can determine if two addresses are identical even before they have been computed. This perfect disambiguation is an upper bound for what can be achieved by compiler analysis and by speculative hardware disambiguation.

Third, an instruction must wait until it can be determined that no preceding instructions will alter the instruction's operands. Different data dependences may occur along different control flow paths, as shown in the following example:

```
b = 0;
if (a < 0)
    b = 1;
c = b;
```

Depending on the outcome of the a < 0 condition, the b = 1 assignment may or may not be executed. Therefore, the value assigned to c depends on the outcome of the condition. The potential data dependence between c = b and b = 1 delays the assignment to c at least until the condition a < 0 is resolved.

Since potential data dependence constraints force instructions to wait for branches, speculation with branch prediction can relax these constraints. For example, if we predict that b = 1 will not execute, c = b can execute speculatively with the assumption that b is 0. If the prediction was incorrect, the assignment must be re-executed with the correct value of b.

We are unable to include the potential data dependence constraints in our experiment because only one execution path is captured in a trace. These constraints must be analyzed statically. Static analysis, however, cannot be completely accurate in the presence of indirect memory references because perfect disambiguation is only possible when analyzing a trace. To ensure that our results are upper bounds, we must avoid introducing constraints based on imperfect disambiguation, and so we ignore the potential data dependence constraints.

4.2 Program Transformations

Procedure calls and loops are two control constructs that are commonly implemented in ways that introduce unnecessarily serializing constraints. These constraints can be eliminated by alternate implementation techniques and simple transformations such as procedure inlining and loop unrolling. Our study tries to model an upper bound of these techniques.

Procedure calls and returns introduce unnecessary control flow and cause problems for branch prediction. Furthermore, a new stack frame is typically allocated and deallocated in every procedure by incrementing and decrementing the stack pointer. Since there is a true data dependence between every increment and decrement, these stack pointer manipulations must be executed sequentially. For programs with many small procedures, this may limit the parallelism. To simulate the optimal case of inlining all procedures, including recursive procedures, we ignore all call and return instructions in a trace, as well as all instructions that manipulate the position of the stack pointer.

Parallelism in many loops is inhibited by dependences on the loop index variables. Loop index variables and induction variables are incremented in every loop iteration[1], creating true data dependences between iterations. However, these dependences are only a result of the way code is generated for scalar processors and are not an inherent part of the loop semantics. Loop unrolling is a simple technique that compilers use to reduce such effects.

In our experiment, we simulate perfect and complete unrolling. First, we analyze the object code to discover the loops in the program. We then use iterative data flow analysis to identify registers that are incremented by a constant exactly once per loop iteration. We only check the registers and not memory locations because we assume that the compiler has allocated the index variables in registers. If the index variables could not be register allocated, the loop index update is unlikely to be in the critical path of the loop execution. Finally, the analysis marks all instructions that increment loop index and induction variables, comparisons of loop indices with loop invariant values, and branches based on the results of such comparisons. These instructions are ignored when they occur in the trace.

Admittedly, many more transformations could be applied. A sophisticated compiler may be able to translate a program into an equivalent one that is more amenable to parallelization. This experiment does not, by any means, establish the limit of parallelism for the problem solved by a program. Finding such a limit is an undecidable problem. This experiment only establishes the limits of parallelism for the particular code generated by the compiler and subject to all of the assumptions in our experiment. If the resulting limits are considered inadequate, other techniques not considered in this study must be used.

[1]This assumes that the compiler has identified the induction variables and performed strength-reduction.

Program	Language	Description
awk	C	pattern scanning/processing
ccom	C	front-end of a C compiler
eqntott	C	truth table generation
espresso	C	logic minimization
gcc (cc1)	C	Gnu C compiler
irsim	C	simulator for VLSI layouts
latex	C	document preparation system
matrix300	FORTRAN	matrix multiplication
spice2g6	FORTRAN	circuit simulation
tomcatv	FORTRAN	mesh generation

Table 1: Benchmark Programs

4.3 Benchmark Programs

Our benchmark suite consists of the six SPEC programs and the four other benchmarks shown in Table 1. We have included three of the FORTRAN SPEC programs for comparison with the non-numeric programs. The standard inputs were used for the SPEC benchmarks. The programs were compiled for a MIPS R3000 processor by the MIPS C and FORTRAN compilers with full optimization. The traces were obtained using the MIPS pixie tool, and each program was simulated for up to 100 million instructions. Our instruction traces include library routines but not system calls, so we ignore dependences that occur within the operating system.

4.4 Simulation Algorithm

The basic simulation algorithm is to determine the execution time of each instruction in a trace. The completion time of the last instruction to execute is the total execution time for the trace. The resulting parallelism is the ratio of the sequential execution time to the parallel execution time. Since we want to measure the actual parallelism and not the speedup for a realistic machine, we use one clock cycle latencies for all instructions. With non-unit latencies, some of the parallelism would be used to fill pipeline bubbles. The instructions removed because of our perfect inlining and perfect unrolling do not contribute to the sequential time, so the parallelism does not include any speedup due to removing those instructions.

Our experiment allows instructions arbitrarily far apart in the program trace to execute in parallel. This is necessary to detect parallelism that could be exposed by aggressive compiler transformations, such as loop interchange. Since the simulator cannot record the data dependences in a limited scheduling window, it records the time of the most recent write to each register and memory location. A large hash table is used to record writes to memory. Each bucket in this table may contain entries for several different locations, and additional space is allocated if a bucket overflows.

For each instruction, the simulator first determines when the operands are available. This is straightforward for register operands. For memory operands, we read the actual address from the trace and check the hash table for the time of the last write to that address. Next the simulator determines when the control flow constraints are satisfied. For the BASE machine, the execution time of the most recent branch in the trace is recorded, and all subsequent instructions must wait until that time. The implementations of the control flow constraints for the other machine models are described below. Given the constraints of control flow and operand availability, the instruction execution time is the minimum time satisfying all of these constraints. Finally, the simulator records when the instruction result is written. For store instructions, the actual address of the destination is read from the trace, and the time is entered into the hash table.

4.4.1 Control Dependence Analysis

For the CD and CD-MF machines, the control flow constraint is that an instruction cannot execute until after its immediate control dependence branch has executed. Control dependence analysis is performed in two stages. We first compute the control dependences within each procedure by analyzing the object code. Interprocedural control dependences are handled dynamically as the traces are analyzed.

To analyze the control dependences within a procedure, we must first build a control flow graph. We use the MIPS pixie tool to identify the basic block boundaries. We then decode and analyze the instructions from the object file to determine the successors of each basic block. Using the flow graph, the analysis computes all of the immediate control dependences by finding the reverse dominance frontier of each basic block [3]. All of the instructions within a basic block are immediately control dependent on the branches in the reverse dominance frontier of the block.

An instruction may be immediately control dependent on multiple branches. However, each dynamic instance of an instruction only depends immediately on one of these branches. For example, instruction 2 in Figure 2 is control dependent upon both instructions 1 and 5. If control flows from instruction 1 to instruction 2, we need to consider only the dependence on instruction 1. This is accomplished by sequentially numbering each basic block in the trace, and as we analyze the trace, the simulator records for each basic block in the code the sequence number of its most recent instance. The immediate control dependence of an instance of an instruction is simply the branch within its reverse dominance frontier with the latest sequence number.

Interprocedural control dependences are handled by maintaining a stack that contains the control dependence information for each active procedure. This stack records the control dependence for each calling instruction and the sequence number at the start of each procedure. Each procedure simply inherits the control dependence of the instruction that calls that procedure. Without recursion, the control dependence for an instance of an instruction is either the control dependence on the top of the stack or an instance of a branch in its reverse dominance frontier, whichever is most recent.

With recursion, the control dependence for an instruction is either the dependence on the top of the stack or an instance of a branch in its reverse dominance frontier *from the same procedure invocation*. For expediency, our simulations do not keep track of all the necessary information to accurately compute the control dependence in a recursive procedure. For each basic block in the code, along with the sequence number of its most recent instance, the simulator also remembers the sequence number at the start of its procedure. Recursion is detected when any branch in an instruction's reverse dominance frontier has a procedure sequence number greater than the current procedure. At that point, to provide an upper bound on the control dependence, we simply ignore the control dependence for that instance of the instruction.

4.4.2 Speculative Execution

Our simulations of speculative execution use static branch predictions based on profile information. These statistics were collected from running the benchmarks with the same inputs used in the simulations. Our prediction rates are therefore an upper bound for static branch prediction techniques. Dynamic techniques provide similar performance [8]. Table 2 shows the branch prediction rates for conditional branches in each benchmark. We do not attempt to predict computed jumps.

A mispredicted branch in a trace is easily identified by comparing the actual branch outcome with the predicted outcome. The simulator for the SP machine simply remembers the execution time of the most recent mispredicted branch, and no subsequent instructions in the trace can execute before that time. For the SP-CD and SP-CD-MF machines, an instruction must wait for its last mispredicted control dependence branch. By recording for each branch in the code whether its most recent instance was mispredicted, the simulator can compute this control flow constraint.

5 Evaluation and Analysis

The parallelism for each machine model is shown in Table 3. The following sections examine these results for the non-numeric benchmarks and discuss the implications. The results for the numeric benchmarks are presented in Sec-

Program	Prediction Rate	Dynamic Instructions Between Branches
awk	93.48	6.8
ccom	92.02	7.5
eqntott	91.92	3.4
espresso	85.64	6.0
gcc (cc1)	89.29	7.9
irsim	87.71	6.7
latex	87.11	9.4
matrix300	99.02	20.0
spice2g6	97.66	13.1
tomcatv	99.09	58.8

Table 2: Branch Statistics

tion 5.3, and Section 5.4 discusses the effects of perfect loop unrolling.

The BASE machine provides a standard for comparison by determining the amount of parallelism when no special effort is made to reduce the control flow constraints. For the non-numeric benchmarks, the BASE machine has a harmonic mean parallelism of 2.14, which is larger than in other studies of similar machines because our assumptions are very different. First, the BASE machine allows some instruction scheduling across basic blocks. An instruction can execute as soon as the previous conditional branch is resolved, even if other instructions before the branch have not completed. In addition to this overlap, basic blocks that are not separated by conditional branches may also be executed in parallel. Second, whereas all operations in our machines execute in only one clock cycle, some previous studies used realistic operation latencies. Since non-unit latency operations consume some parallelism to fill pipeline bubbles, the reported speedups do not measure all of the parallelism. Finally, we do not include any limitations on fetching instructions [14].

At the other extreme is the upper bound of the ORACLE machine. As expected, the amount of parallelism is quite large and varies significantly between benchmarks. This reflects the different types of algorithms in the programs. For example, `eqntott` primarily executes a quicksort function which contains few data dependences. On the other hand, `ccom` and `latex` are composed of algorithms with much less inherent parallelism. Several factors cause our numbers to be considerably larger than in previous experiments with perfect branch prediction. Our unlimited scheduling window exposes parallelism across the entire program trace. Anti-dependences and output data dependences are not considered. Our simulation of procedure inlining also removes the instructions that adjust the stack pointer at the entry and exit of most procedures. This is significant in the case of the ORACLE machine because the stack pointer increments and decrements often lengthen the critical path of a program.

5.1 Control Dependence Analysis

The CD machine has more parallelism than the BASE machine because basic blocks with the same control dependences can be executed in parallel. However, the harmonic mean parallelism of 2.39 for the CD machine is only slightly better than for the BASE machine. Figure 4 shows the parallelism for each benchmark compared to the BASE machine. The parallelism for the CD machine is primarily limited by the constraint that branches must be executed in order. Since conditional branches occur frequently in our benchmarks, executing one branch at a time is a serious bottleneck. Table 2 shows the average number of dynamic instructions between conditional branch instructions in the program traces. For the non-numeric programs, a branch instruction occurs about every six instructions in a trace. When all of these branches are ordered, it is difficult to find much parallelism.

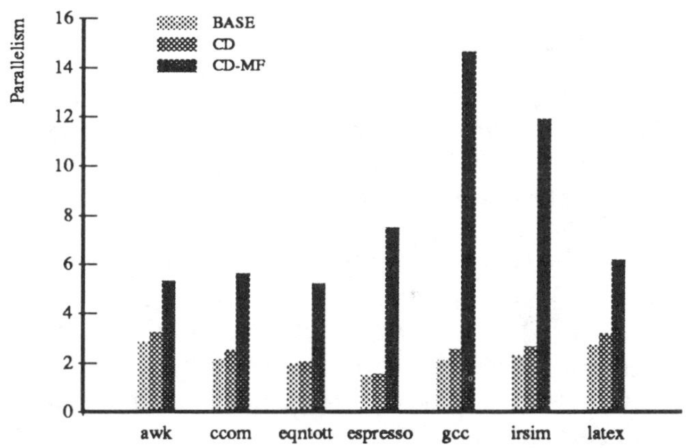

Figure 4: Parallelism with Control Dependence Analysis

When the constraint on branches is removed in the CD-MF machine, only the true control and data dependences must be observed. The parallelism for each benchmark is shown in comparison to the parallelism for the CD machine in Figure 4. The parallelism increases for all of the programs, and especially for `gcc`, `irsim`, and `espresso`. However, there is still not a massive amount of parallelism. This is really not too surprising when one considers the types of benchmarks that we are analyzing. There may be some parallelism within individual components of these programs, but the overall algorithms are simply not very parallel.

Since the constraints for the CD-MF machine only require that true data and control dependences be observed, the parallelism for this machine is a limit for all systems without speculative execution. Dataflow architectures, for example, are able to execute programs with only these essential dependences. Since there are not massive amounts

	BASE	CD	CD-MF	SP	SP-CD	SP-CD-MF	ORACLE
awk	2.85	3.24	5.32	9.22	12.89	41.88	242.77
ccom	2.13	2.51	5.61	6.92	9.83	18.05	46.80
eqntott	1.98	2.05	5.21	6.40	18.09	225.90	3282.91
espresso	1.51	1.54	7.49	4.16	19.55	402.85	742.30
gcc (cc1)	2.10	2.55	14.63	7.76	13.18	66.29	174.50
irsim	2.31	2.66	11.89	8.40	15.82	45.86	265.42
latex	2.71	3.17	6.18	7.60	9.72	18.65	131.69
Harmonic Mean	2.14	2.39	6.96	6.80	13.27	39.62	158.26
matrix300	293	432	68324	36192	108575	180632	188470
spice2g6	2.14	2.29	16.80	8.11	25.28	196.76	843.60
tomcatv	22.23	42.77	3237	124	1881	3918	3918

Table 3: Parallelism for each Machine Model

of parallelism, any machine attempting to exploit parallelism in non-numeric programs without speculative execution must have low overhead to be effective.

5.2 Speculative Execution

The parallelism for the SP machine ranges from 4.16 to 9.22, with a harmonic mean of 6.80. Figure 5 shows the parallelism for each benchmark compared to the BASE machine. These results are comparable to Wall's results for a similar machine [17]. The differences can be attributed to procedure inlining, perfect loop unrolling, and the unlimited scheduling window in our simulator. The parallelism for the SP machine is fairly consistent across the different benchmarks. The following measurements offer an explanation for the consistency and suggest that this limit of parallelism will probably apply to many more non-numeric applications.

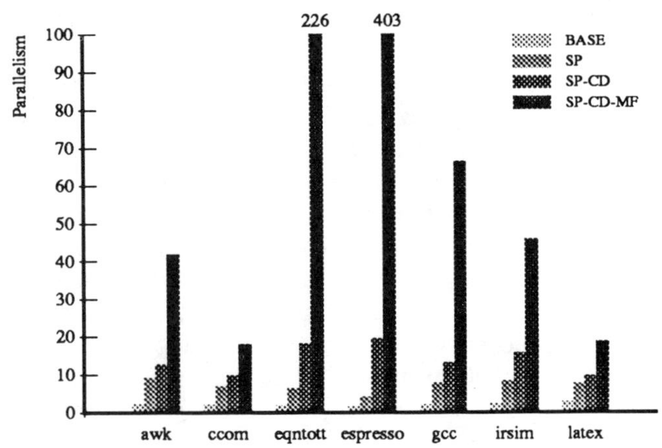

Figure 5: Parallelism with Speculative Execution

In the SP machine, a misprediction cancels the execution of all instructions following the branch, so mispredictions are barriers to instruction scheduling. Parallelism can only be found among the instructions between mispredicted branches. Therefore, the overall limit of parallelism for the SP machine is actually an average over many discrete segments of code separated by mispredicted branches. Each of these segments has two vital characteristics: the degree of parallelism and the *misprediction distance*, that is, the number of instructions in the segment. In our experiments, we recorded the number of occurrences of each misprediction distance. The cumulative distributions of these misprediction distances for each program are shown in Figure 6. These distributions are quite consistent across the different benchmarks, with over 80% of the mispredictions occurring within a distance of 100 instructions. We expect other non-numeric programs to have similar distributions.

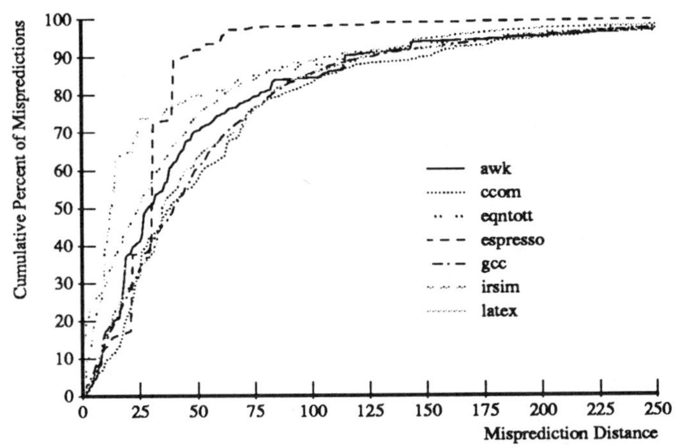

Figure 6: Cumulative Distribution of Misprediction Distances

We also recorded the degree of parallelism for each segment of code between two mispredicted branches and found that the relationship between the degree of parallelism and the misprediction distance is similar for all of the benchmarks. Figure 7 is a combination of the statistics for all of the programs. For each misprediction distance, we plot the harmonic mean of the parallelism for all segments of that size. To reflect differences in the significance of these numbers, the bars for frequently occurring misprediction distances are shaded darker. For short misprediction distances, there is little parallelism. Instructions within these short segments tend to be closely related and have many data dependences between them, and thus the parallelism is limited. For longer misprediction distances, there is a greater chance of having unrelated instructions within the segments and more parallelism can be found. However, as shown by the distributions, long misprediction distances do not occur very frequently. Therefore, non-numeric programs with predominantly short misprediction distances have limited parallelism on the SP machine due to the data dependence in short segments of instructions.

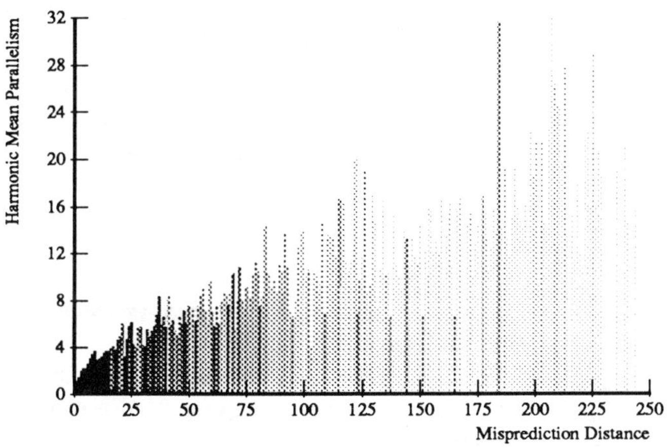

Figure 7: Parallelism vs. Misprediction Distance

The SP-CD machine does not need to discard all instructions following a mispredicted branch, and thus it can exploit parallelism across mispredicted branches. As a result, the harmonic mean parallelism for this machine increases to 13.27. Figure 5 compares the parallelism for each benchmark to the parallelism for the SP machine. The branch constraint for this machine requires that a branch cannot execute before a preceding misprediction. This is much less restrictive than the branch constraint for the CD machine. The flow of control only changes when a branch is mispredicted, and since mispredictions are relatively infrequent, the branch constraint is not a bottleneck.

Finally, the parallelism for the SP-CD-MF machine is much larger. Figure 5 illustrates the parallelism for each benchmark. The `eqntott` and `espresso` programs have especially large amounts of parallelism, and there is a large increase for all of the benchmarks.

The SP-CD-MF model provides us with an interesting data point. It is more aggressive than the SP machine but also more realistic than the ORACLE machine. To achieve the performance of the ORACLE machine, instructions from alternate paths must be executed simultaneously, and only the instructions from one of the paths will be useful. On the other hand, as long as branches are correctly predicted, the SP-CD-MF machine does not have to cancel any instructions.

5.3 Numeric Applications

Numeric programs, programs which operate on floating-point data and which are commonly written in FORTRAN, are generally considered to contain more parallelism than non-numeric programs. This section examines the parallelism for our three FORTRAN benchmarks and shows that the type of control flow in a program is a more useful indication of the available parallelism. The parallelism measured by our experiments for the FORTRAN benchmarks is shown in Table 3.

The `matrix300` and `tomcatv` programs have much higher parallelism for all of the machine models. From the ORACLE machine, we observe that there is less data dependence in these programs. The CD-MF machine achieves a large fraction of the ORACLE machine parallelism. Because the control flow in these programs is not dependent on the results of the computation, the control dependence analysis exposes parallelism across different levels of nested loops and across outer loops. As a result, speculation is not as important. In comparison to the CD-MF machine, the SP-CD and SP-CD-MF machines only compress the critical path of each inner loop by a small constant factor. Thus it is the data independent control flow that sets these programs apart from the non-numeric programs.

Among the FORTRAN benchmarks, the behavior of `spice2g6` is clearly different. The control flow in `spice2g6` is highly data dependent, thus causing it to behave like the non-numeric programs in this study. As numeric programs evolve to model more complex phenomena, they are likely to have increasingly complex control flow and data structures. Distinctions based on the source language and type of arithmetic will become less meaningful. Our study suggests that a more relevant characteristic for predicting the parallelism in a program is whether the control flow is data dependent.

5.4 Effects of Perfect Loop Unrolling

Previous studies on limits of parallelism did not remove all of the dependences on induction variables [17]. A question often raised is whether the induction variable dependences significantly affect the results of these studies. We performed two experiments, one with and one without removing the induction variable dependences. Table 4 shows the percent change in parallelism compared to the case when perfect loop unrolling is not performed. That is, a positive percent change means that removing the induction variable

	BASE	CD	CD-MF	SP	SP-CD	SP-CD-MF	ORACLE
awk	30	36	10	48	52	41	-22
ccom	0	1	2	3	2	-2	-2
eqntott	-1	-1	-54	11	11	-4	3
espresso	-6	-6	134	-2	-16	15	-21
gcc (cc1)	0	2	-2	14	18	-3	-4
irsim	2	3	9	17	4	-9	-9
latex	0	0	-1	0	0	0	29
matrix300	2911	4317	16	182136	5488	2	0
spice2g6	12	12	35	21	23	0	-1
tomcatv	47	126	-9	149	13	-12	-12

Table 4: Percent Change in Parallelism due to Perfect Loop Unrolling

dependences improves parallelism. We discovered that removing these data dependences and the associated control dependences has mixed effects.

Although our simulation of perfect loop unrolling always decreases the program execution times, this does not necessarily imply that the parallelism increases. In fact, perfect unrolling has two competing effects on parallelism. By removing index variable dependences and loop branches, more parallelism is exposed. However, at the same time, removing the loop overhead instructions decreases the opportunities for overlapping those instructions with the rest of the computation in the loop, thereby decreasing the parallelism. Either one of these effects may dominate depending on the benchmark and the machine model.

For most of the non-numeric programs, unrolling has little effect. For example, `ccom` and `latex` have almost no change at all. These programs primarily contain loops with a lot of control and data dependences, so the dependences removed by unrolling are not very significant. The loops in these programs also tend to iterate a small number of times.

The CD-MF machine is most sensitive to perfect unrolling. Removing induction variable dependences allows multiple iterations with arbitrary control flow to execute in parallel. This can improve parallelism, as in the case of `espresso`. However, the loop overhead constitutes much of the parallelism found in some loops. Thus, parallelism decreases when we remove such instructions, as in the case of `eqntott`.

Perfect unrolling has the biggest impact on `matrix300` and, to a lesser extent, `tomcatv`. These programs primarily execute simple loops where index variable dependences limit the parallelism. For these programs, the SP machine benefits the most from perfect unrolling. For nested loops, each iteration of an outer loop is separated by a mispredicted branch from the end of the inner loop. This prevents the outer loop iterations from executing in parallel. Perfect unrolling removes the loop branches, essentially coalescing the loops, so that these serializing mispredictions do not occur.

In general, the effects of loop index and induction variable dependences on parallelism vary depending on the application program and the machine model. As expected, the matrix-oriented numeric programs benefit significantly from perfect loop unrolling. For programs with complex control flow, unrolling often makes no significant difference.

6 Conclusion

This paper shows that control flow in a program can severely limit the available parallelism. The control flow of many non-numeric programs and also some numeric programs is complex and highly data dependent. To increase the available parallelism beyond the current level, the constraints imposed by control flow must be relaxed.

This paper discusses three basic techniques for handling control flow: speculative execution, control dependence analysis, and following multiple flows of control. Through a study of abstract machines that utilize different combinations of these techniques, we have established the importance of each technique. These basic techniques also form a useful set of criteria with which to evaluate real architectures.

This study suggests that some of the current highly parallel architectures lack adequate support for control flow. For example, a VLIW (Very Long Instruction Word) machine can only follow one flow of control. It cannot find sufficient parallelism in programs whose control flow is highly data dependent. In contrast, a dataflow machine can execute from many different parts of a program simultaneously. However, our study shows that even if instructions are executed as soon as all their data and control dependences are satisfied, the parallelism is still quite limited. Speculation is necessary to find sufficient parallelism in these programs.

This study of abstract machines also helps to identify useful architectural features. The concept of boosting [15], which relies on software for scheduling and a small degree of hardware to support speculative execution, appears particularly promising. Another interesting concept is *guarded instructions* [5]. A guarded instruction is conditionally executed based on a value stored in a general register. This allows a compiler to specify some amount of control dependence information, that only the action is control dependent on the guard. Furthermore, using guarded instructions, a basic block can contain code from different conditional statements by simply capturing their conditions in the guards. Guarded instructions are particularly interesting when combined with support for speculative execution, since they help increase the distance between mispredicted branches. Though guarded instructions give the processor some ability to execute from different regions of the source code, they are inefficient for following multiple complex flows of control simultaneously. If higher performance is desired, a small-scale multiprocessor system with guarded instructions and speculative execution support would be an interesting possibility.

References

[1] D. Bernstein and M. Rodeh. Global Instruction Scheduling for Superscalar Machines. In *Proceedings of the ACM SIGPLAN'91 Conference on Programming Language Design and Implementation*, pages 241–255, June 1991.

[2] R. P. Colwell, R. P. Nix, J. J. O'Donnell, D. B. Papworth, and P. K. Rodman. A VLIW Architecture for a Trace Scheduling Compiler. *IEEE Transactions on Computers*, C-37(8):967–979, August 1988. Also in ASPLOS-3 pp. 180-192.

[3] R. Cytron, J. Ferrante, B. K. Rosen, M. N. Wegman, and F. K. Zadeck. An Efficient Method of Computing Static Single Assignment Form. In *Proceedings of the 16th Annual ACM Symposium on Principles of Programming Languages*, pages 25–35, January 1989.

[4] J. A. Fisher. Trace Scheduling: A Technique for Global Microcode Compaction. *IEEE Transactions on Computers*, C-30(7):478–490, July 1981.

[5] P. Y. Hsu. *Highly Concurrent Scalar Processing*. PhD thesis, University of Illinois at Urbana-Champaign, 1986.

[6] W. W. Hwu, T. M. Conte, and P. P. Chang. Comparing Software and Hardware Schemes For Reducing the Cost of Branches. In *Proceedings of the 16th Annual International Symposium on Computer Architecture*, pages 224–233, May 1989.

[7] M. Johnson. *Superscalar Microprocessor Design*. Prentice Hall, Englewood Cliffs, NJ, 1990.

[8] S. McFarling and J. Hennessy. Reducing the Cost of Branches. In *Proceedings of the 13th Annual International Symposium on Computer Architecture*, pages 396–404, June 1986.

[9] K. Murakami, N. Irie, M. Kuga, and S. Tomita. SIMP (Single Instruction Stream/Multiple Instruction Pipelining): A Novel High-Speed Single-Processor Architecture. In *Proceedings of the 16th Annual International Symposium on Computer Architecture*, pages 78–85, May 1989.

[10] A. Nicolau and J. A. Fisher. Measuring the Parallelism Available for Very Long Instruction Word Architectures. *IEEE Transactions on Computers*, C-33(11):968–976, November 1984.

[11] Y. N. Patt, S. W. Melvin, W. W. Hwu, and M. Shebanow. Critical Issues Regarding HPS, A High Performance Microarchitecture. In *Proceedings of the 18th Annual Workshop on Microprogramming*, pages 109–116, December 1985.

[12] E. M. Riseman and C. C. Foster. The Inhibition of Potential Parallelism by Conditional Jumps. *IEEE Transactions on Computers*, C-21(12):1405–1411, December 1972.

[13] J. E. Smith and A. R. Pleszkun. Implementation of Precise Interrupts in Pipelined Processors. In *Proceedings of the 12th Annual International Symposium on Computer Architecture*, pages 36–44, June 1985.

[14] M. D. Smith, M. Johnson, and M. A. Horowitz. Limits on Multiple Instruction Issue. In *Proceedings of the Third International Conference on Architectural Support for Programming Languages and Operating Systems*, pages 290–302, April 1989.

[15] M. D. Smith, M. S. Lam, and M. A. Horowitz. Boosting Beyond Static Scheduling in a Superscalar Processor. In *Proceedings of the 17th Annual International Symposium on Computer Architecture*, pages 344–354, May 1990.

[16] G. S. Sohi and S. Vajapeyam. Instruction Issue Logic for High-Performance, Interruptible Pipelined Processors. In *Proceedings of the 14th Annual International Symposium on Computer Architecture*, pages 27–34, June 1987.

[17] D. W. Wall. Limits of Instruction-Level Parallelism. In *Proceedings of the Fourth International Conference on Architectural Support for Programming Languages and Operating Systems*, pages 176–188, April 1991.

The Expandable Split Window Paradigm for Exploiting Fine-Grain Parallelism

Manoj Franklin and Gurindar S. Sohi
Computer Sciences Department
University of Wisconsin-Madison
1210 W. Dayton Street
Madison, WI 53706

Abstract

We propose a new processing paradigm, called the Expandable Split Window (ESW) paradigm, for exploiting fine-grain parallelism. This paradigm considers a window of instructions (possibly having dependencies) as a single unit, and exploits fine-grain parallelism by overlapping the execution of multiple windows. The basic idea is to connect multiple sequential processors, in a decoupled and decentralized manner, to achieve overall multiple issue. This processing paradigm shares a number of properties of the restricted dataflow machines, but was derived from the sequential von Neumann architecture. We also present an implementation of the Expandable Split Window execution model, and preliminary performance results.

1. INTRODUCTION

The execution of a program, in an abstract form, can be considered to be a dynamic dataflow graph that encapsulates the data dependencies in the program. The nodes of the graph represent *computation* operations, and the arcs of the graph represent *communication* of values between the nodes. The execution time of a program is the time taken to perform the computations and communication in its dynamic dataflow graph. If there are altogether n communication arcs in the graph, and at a time a maximum of m communication arcs can be carried out, then the execution time involves a minimum of n/m communication steps, no matter how many parallel resources are used for computations. With the continued advance in technology, switching components become smaller and more efficient. The effect is that computation becomes faster and faster. Communication speed, on the other hand, seems to be restricted by the speed of light, and eventually becomes the major bottleneck.

The abstract dataflow graph hides information about the distances involved in the inter-node or inter-operation communication. When a dataflow graph is mapped onto a processing structure, interesting dynamics are introduced into the picture. First, depending on the matching between the dataflow graph and the processing structure, adjacent nodes in the graph (those directly connected by a communication arc) may get mapped to either the same processing element, physically adjacent (communication-wise adjacent) processing elements, or distant processing elements. Based on the mapping used, the communication arcs of the graph get "stretched" or "shrunk", causing changes in the communication cost because it takes more time to send values over a distance. Second, since there can only be a finite amount of fast storage for temporarily storing the intermediate computation values, the values have to be either consumed immediately or stored away into some form of backup storage (for example, main memory), creating more nodes and communication arcs.

An inspection of the dynamic dataflow graph of many sequential programs reveals that there exists a large amount of theoretically exploitable instruction-level parallelism [2, 3, 5, 13, 24], *i.e.*, a large number of computation nodes that can be executed in parallel, provided a suitable processor model with a suitable communication mechanism backed up by a suitable temporary storage mechanism exists. Where is this parallelism most likely to be found in a dynamic execution of the sequential program? Because most programs are written in an imperative language for a sequential machine with a limited number of architectural registers for storing temporary values, it is quite likely that instructions of close proximity are data dependent. This means that most of the parallelism can be found only further down in the dynamic instruction stream. The obvious way to get to that parallelism is to use a large window of dynamic instructions. This motivates the following bipartite question: "What is the best way to identify a large number of independent operations every cycle, especially if they are to be extracted from a large block of operations intertwined with intricate dependencies, and at the same time reduce the communication costs and the costs of storing temporary results?" The design of a fine-grain parallel processor, to a large extent, revolves around how one attempts to answer this question and the train of questions that arise while attempting to answer it. A good scheme should optimize not only the number of operations executed in parallel, but also the communication costs by reducing the communication distances and the temporary storing away of values, thereby allowing expandability. We consider a processor model to be expandable if its abilities can be expanded easily, as hardware and software technology advances. This requires the processor model to have no centralized resources that can become potential bottlenecks.

Several processing paradigms have been proposed over the years for exploiting fine-grain parallelism. The most general one, the dataflow model, considers the entire dataflow graph to be a single window and uses an unconventional programming paradigm to expose the maximum amount of parallelism present in the application. Such a general model allows the maximum number of computation nodes to be active simultaneously, but incurs a large performance penalty due to the "stretching" of the communication arcs. It also suffers from the inability to express critical sections and imperative operations that are essential for the efficient execution of operating system functions, such as resource management [5, 17]. (Of late, more restricted forms of dataflow architecture have been proposed [9, 14, 16, 17].) This is where the power of sequentiality comes in. By ordering the computation nodes in a suitable manner, sequentiality can be used to introduce (and exploit) different kinds of temporal locality to minimize the costs of communication and intermediate result storage. This has the effect of combining several adjacent nodes into one, because the communication arcs between them become very short when temporal locality is exploited by hardware means. A good example of this phenomenon are the vector machines, which exploit the "regular" type of parallelism found in many numeric applications effectively by hardware means such as *chaining* (*i.e.*, forwarding a result directly from a producer to a consumer without intermediate storage).

Sequential execution can be augmented to exploit the "irregular" type of parallelism found in most non-numeric applications. Superscalar processors [10, 12, 15, 18] and VLIW processors [4] do exactly this; they stay within the realm of sequential execution, but attempt to execute multiple operations every cycle. For achieving this, superscalars scan through a window of (sequential) operations every cycle and dynamically detect independent operations to be issued in a cycle. These von Neuman based machines use the conventional programming paradigm, but require a sufficiently large centralized window (obtained by going beyond several basic blocks), if even moderate sustained issue rates are to be desired. The hardware required to extract independent instructions from a large centralized window and to enforce data dependencies typically involves wide associative searches, and is non-trivial. Furthermore, superscalars require multi-ported register files and wide paths from the instruction cache to the issue unit. Although dynamic scheduling with a large centralized window has the potential for high issue rates, a realistic implementation is not likely to be possible because of its complexity, unless novel schemes are developed to reduce the complexity.

VLIW processors partially circumvent this problem by detecting parallelism at compile time, and by using a large instruction word to express the multiple operations to be issued in a cycle. A major limitation of static scheduling is that it has to play safe, by always making worst-case assumptions about information that is not available at compile time. VLIW processors also require some of the centralized resources required by superscalars, such as the multi-ported register files, crossbars for connecting the computation units, and wide paths to the issue unit. These centralized resources can easily become bottlenecks and be a severe limitation on the performance of these machines.

Looking at these existing models, we see that the concept of sequential execution with a large window is good, but definitely not sufficient by itself. The following additional criteria are very important.

- The creation of the large window should be accurate. That is, the window should consist mostly of instructions that are guaranteed to execute, and not instructions that "might" be executed.
- Factors such as the ability to feed instructions into this window, should not be a limitation. That is, it should be possible to get farther down in the instruction stream, without fetching and decoding the instructions in between.
- There should be provision to issue loads before proper address disambiguation, *i.e.*, in a speculative manner.

We also need a powerful way of decentralizing the critical resources in the system. Our objective is to use the conventional sequential programming paradigm with dynamic scheduling and large windows, but augmented with novel techniques to decentralize the critical resources. This is achieved by splitting a large operation window into small windows, and executing many such small windows in parallel. The principle of dataflow is used in a restricted manner to pass values efficiently across the multiple windows in execution; the execution model within each window can be a simple, sequential processor. As we will see later in this paper, such an approach has the synergistic effect of combining the advantages of the sequential and the dataflow execution models, and the advantages of static and dynamic scheduling.

1.1. Organization of the Paper

We have outlined the important issues pertaining to designing a high-performance fine-grain parallel processor. The rest of this paper is organized as follows. Section 2 describes the basic philosophy behind the Expandable Split Window (ESW) processing paradigm. Section 3 describes a possible implementation of this paradigm. The description includes details of the instruction issue mechanism (distributed instruction caches), the distributed register file, the distributed memory disambiguation unit, and the distributed data cache. Section 4 presents preliminary performance results for the new paradigm, obtained from a simulation study using the SPEC benchmarks. Section 5 provides a summary of the research done so far, and the future course of work.

2. THE EXPANDABLE SPLIT WINDOW PROCESSING PARADIGM

To have an expandable system that can handle large windows in an efficient manner, and whose ability can be expanded easily as technology advances, we need to decentralize all the critical resources in the system. These include the hardware for dependency enforcement and identification of independent operations within the window, the instruction supply mechanism, and the memory address disambiguation mechanism. A convenient way of simplifying the hardware for identification of independent operations is to split the large window into smaller windows (c.f. Figure 1) so that the task of searching a large window can be split into 2 smaller subtasks: (i) independent searches (if need be) in small windows, all of which can be done in parallel, and (ii) enforcement of control and data dependencies between the smaller windows. The dynamic scheduling hardware can then be divided into two hierarchical units — a distributed top-level unit that enforces dependencies between the small windows, and

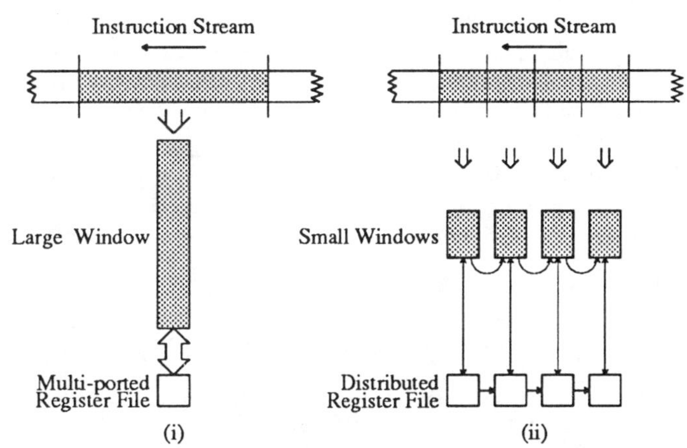

Figure 1: Splitting a large window of instructions into smaller windows
(i) A single large window (ii) A number of small windows

several independent lower-level units at the bottom level, each of which enforces dependencies within a small window and identifies the independent instructions in that window. Each of these lower-level units can be a separate execution unit akin to a simple (possibly sequential) execution datapath.

Having decided to split the large operation window, the next question is where to split. There are several issues to be considered here. First, the overall large window would invariably consist of many basic blocks, obtained through dynamic branch prediction. When a prediction is found to be incorrect, we would like not to discard the part of the window before the mispredicted branch. Second, it would be ideal if (at least some of) the information available at compile time is conveyed to the dynamic scheduling hardware. With these views in mind, we propose to consider a single-entry loop-free call-free block of (dependent) instructions (or a **basic window**) as a single unit, *i.e.*, each such block forms a small window[1]. Splitting the *dynamic* instruction stream at such *statically* determined boundaries has the following advantages:

(1) If a basic window is a basic block or a subset of a basic block, then it is a straight-line piece of code that is entirely executed once it is entered, and the registers read and written are the same for any execution of that basic window. Ironically, the dynamic scheduling hardware expends quite a bit of effort to reconstruct this information. This information can be statically determined and conveyed to the hardware in a concise manner (explained in Section 3.3.3), which simplifies the hardware for the enforcement of register value dependencies between the basic windows. If a basic window is a superset of several basic blocks, then also it is possible to express this information, but the information will be conservative, as it has to consider all possible paths through the basic window.

(2) The control flow graph of most programs are embedded with diamond-shaped structures (reconvergent fanouts, typically due to **if-then** and **if-then-else** statements), which tend to have low branch prediction accuracies. In such situations, there is merit in encompassing the diamond-shaped part within a basic window so as to allow subsequent windows to start execution earlier with no fear of being discarded later due to an incorrect branch prediction at an earlier stage.

(3) By merging small basic blocks into one basic window, we can tide over the problem of poor utilization of an execution unit when small, data-dependent basic blocks appear next to each other in the dynamic instruction stream. This situation arises frequently in non-numeric benchmarks, where the mean basic block size is typically 5-6 instructions.

Example: The basic idea behind the new paradigm is best illustrated by an example. Consider the following loop, which adds the number 10 to 100 elements of an array and sets an element to 1000 if it is greater than 1000. This is a typical **for** loop with an **if** statement enclosed within.

```
A:  R1  =  R1 + 1
    R2  =  [R1, base]
    R3  =  R2 + 10
    BLT  R3, 1000, B
    R3  =  1000
B:  [R1, base]  =  R3
    BLT  R1, 100, A
```

In this example, all the instructions in one iteration except the last instruction can be executed only in strict sequential order. We can consider each iteration of this loop to be a basic window; at run time, the loop gets expanded into multiple basic windows as shown below.

	Basic Window 1		Basic Window 2
A_1:	$R1_1$ = $R1_0$ + 1	A_2:	$R1_2$ = $R1_1$ + 1
	$R2_1$ = [$R1_1$, base]		$R2_2$ = [$R1_2$, base]
	$R3_1$ = $R2_1$ + 10		$R3_2$ = $R2_2$ + 10
	BLT $R3_1$, 1000, B_1		BLT $R3_2$, 1000, B_2
	$R3_1$ = 1000		$R3_2$ = 1000
B_1:	[$R1_1$, base] = $R3_1$	B_2:	[$R1_2$, base] = $R3_2$
	BLT $R1_1$, 100, A_2		BLT $R1_2$, 100, A_3

Multiple instances of a register are shown with different subscripts, for example, $R1_1$ and $R1_2$. Although the instructions of a basic window in this example are sequentially dependent, a new basic window can start execution once the first instruction of the previous basic window has been executed. Our idea is to execute these multiple basic windows in parallel, with distinct execution units. Notice that among the two branches in an iteration, branch prediction is performed only for the second one, which can be predicted much more accurately than the other. The low confidence branch (the first one) has been incorporated within the basic window so that a poor branch prediction does not result in an inaccurate dynamic window. For a general program, the compiler divides the instruction stream into basic windows based on the following factors: (i) the pattern of data dependencies between instructions, (ii) maximum size allowed for a basic window, and (iii) predictability of branch outcomes.

3. IMPLEMENTATION OF THE ESW PARADIGM

As mentioned earlier, to be expandable, there should be no centralized resources that could become potential bottlenecks. Designing a dynamically scheduled fine-grain parallel processor with decentralized resources poses several challenges, some of which are: (i) an adequate decentralized instruction issue mechanism, (ii) adequate CPU resources, and (iii) an adequate decentralized memory system. Other issues, of no less magnitude, that pose challenges especially when doing speculative execution are: (i) efficient means of forwarding results from one instruction to another when a number of instructions are simultaneously active, (or efficient means of detecting and enforcing register dependencies), (ii) disambiguating memory addresses and enforcing memory dependencies, (iii) good branch handling/prediction schemes that allow the dynamic window to be expanded fairly accurately, and (iv) efficient mechanisms to recover a precise state when special events such as incorrect branch predictions and exceptions occur.

In this section, we discuss a possible implementation of the new processing paradigm. In the ensuing subsections, it will

[1] If a single-entry loop-free call-free block is too large, or if it is a collection of blocks with few data dependencies between them, then it can be split into appropriate smaller blocks. In this paper, quite frequently we use a basic block as a basic window for illustration purposes, although a basic window could be a subset or a superset of basic blocks. We are still investigating the issues involved in creating a basic window that is larger than a basic block. We are also investigating the implications of removing the "loop-free" requirement. The basic window discussed in this paper should therefore be considered only as one example of a basic window of instructions.

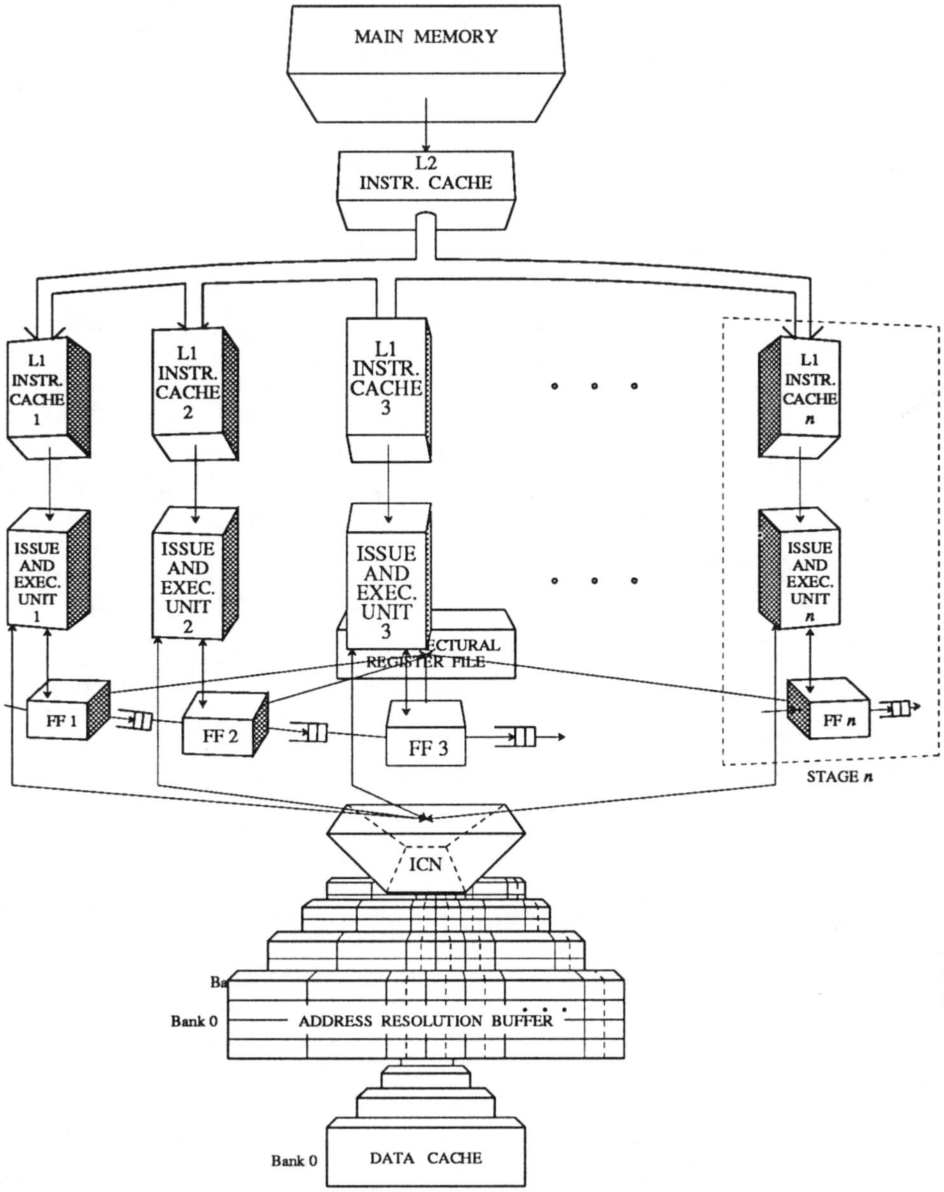

Figure 2: Block Diagram of the Expandable Split Window Paradigm Implementation

become evident that throughout the design we have emphasized two points — *decentralization* (which facilitates expandability) and *realizability*. Several novel techniques have been used to decentralize the resources, without which the potential of the new paradigm could not have been exploited. The techniques used for decentralizing the different parts of the system are different, because their workings and the way they fit into the system are different. As the purpose of this paper is to introduce the paradigm and present an overall view, and because of space restrictions, some of the intricate design details are not presented here.

Figure 2 presents the block diagram of our machine. The processor consists of several independent, identical *stages*, each of which is equivalent to a typical datapath found in modern processors. The stages conceptually form a circular queue, with hardware pointers to the head and tail of the queue. These pointers are managed by a control unit (not shown in Figure 2 for clarity), which also performs the task of assigning basic windows to the stages. Dynamic branch prediction is used (if required) to decide new basic windows, and every cycle, the control unit assigns a new window to a stage unless the circular stage queue is full. It is important to note that all that the control unit does when it assigns a window to a stage unit is to tell the stage to execute a basic window starting at a particular PC (program counter) value; it is up to the stage to fetch the required instructions, decode them and execute them (most likely in serial order) until the end of the basic window is reached. The control unit does not perform instruction decoding. (A major purpose of "decoding" instructions in a superscalar processor is to establish register dependencies between instructions. We shall see in section 3.3 how we enforce the register dependencies without dynamically decoding the instructions.) Because the task of the control unit is relatively straightforward, it does not become a potential bottleneck. (Control units with instruction decoders that feed centralized windows are a major impediment to performance in superscalar processors, as shown in [21].)

The active stages, the ones from the head to the tail, together constitute the large dynamic window of operations, and the stages contain basic windows, in the sequential order in which the windows appear in the dynamic instruction stream. When all the instructions in the stage at the head have completed execution, the window is committed, and the control unit moves the head pointer forward to the next stage. Consequently, the big window is a *sliding* or *continuous* window, and not a fixed big window, a feature that allows more parallelism to be exploited [24]. The major parts of the ESW implementation are described below.

3.1. Distributed Issue and Execution Units

Each stage has as its heart an Issue and Execution (IE) unit, which takes operations from a local instruction cache and pumps them to its functional units after resolving their data dependencies. An IE unit is comparable to the Instruction Issue and Execution Unit of a conventional processor in that it has its own set of functional units. Notice that if the cost of functional units (especially the floating point units) is a concern, infrequently used functional units may be shared by multiple stages. It is also possible to have a small interconnect from the IE units to a common Functional Unit Complex. In any given cycle, up to a fixed number of ready-to-execute instructions begins execution in each of the active IE units. It is possible to have out-of-order execution in an IE unit, if desired.

3.2. Distributed Instruction Supply Mechanism

The proposed scheme for exploiting instruction-level parallelism by the execution of multiple basic windows in parallel will bear fruit only if instructions are supplied to the IE units at an adequate rate. Supplying multiple IE units in parallel with instructions from different basic windows can be a difficult task for an ordinary centralized instruction cache. We need novel instruction cache designs, ones that are suited to the issue strategy and the execution model used.

We propose to use a two-level instruction cache, with the level 1 (L1) (the level closest to the IE units) split into as many parts as the number of stages, one for each stage, as shown in Figure 2. An IE unit accesses instructions from its L1 cache. If a request misses in the L1 cache, it is forwarded to the L2 instruction cache. If the window is available in the L2 cache, it is supplied to the requesting L1 cache (a fixed number of instructions are transferred per cycle until the entire window is transferred — a form of intelligent instruction prefetch). If the transferred window is a loop, the L1 caches of the subsequent stages can also grab the window in parallel, much like the *snarfing* (*read broadcast*) scheme proposed for multiprocessor caches [8]. If the request misses in the L2 cache, it is forwarded to main memory. Notice that several IE units can simultaneously be fetching instructions from their corresponding L1 caches, and several L1 caches can simultaneously be receiving a basic window (if the window is a loop) from the L2 cache, in any given cycle.

3.3. Distributed Inter-Instruction Communication Mechanism

A high-speed inter-instruction communication mechanism is central to the design of any processor. Earlier we saw that a centralized register file can become a bottleneck for the VLIW and superscalar processors. In our processor, at any one time there could be more than 100 active operations, many of which may be executed simultaneously. Clearly, a centralized architectural register file cannot handle the amount of register traffic needed to support that many active operations; we need a decentralized inter-instruction communication mechanism. The main criteria to be considered in coming up with a good decentralized scheme is that it should tie well with the distributed, speculative execution feature of our model. (For instance, the split register file proposed for the VLIW and superscalars cannot be of much help to our model.)

In order to do a careful design of the decentralized register file, we first conducted a quantitative study of the traffic handled by the architectural registers in a load/store architecture (MIPS R2000). In particular, we studied how soon newly created register instances are used up by subsequent instructions and are eventually overwritten. These studies showed that: (i) a significant number of register instances are used up in the same basic block in which they are created, and (ii) most of the rest are used up in the subsequent basic block. The first result implies that if we have a local register file for each stage, much of the register traffic occurring in a stage can be handled by the local register file itself. Only the last updates to the registers in a stage need be passed on to the subsequent stages. The second result implies that most of these last updates need not be propagated beyond one stage. Thus we can exploit the *temporal locality of usage of register values* to design a good decentralized register file structure that ties well with our execution model, and that is exactly what we do.

3.3.1. Distributed Future File

In our proposed design, each stage has a separate register file called a *future file*. These distributed future files are the working files used by the functional units in the IE units. In that sense, they work similar in spirit to the *future file* discussed in [20] for implementing precise interrupts in pipelined processors. As we will see in section 3.5, the distributed future file simplifies the task of recovery when incorrect branch predictions are encountered. If out-of-order execution within IE units is desired, then each IE unit should also have some means of forwarding results within the unit (possibly reservation stations [23]). Another advantage of the distributed future file structure in that case is that it allows independent register renaming for each stage. An architectural register file is maintained to facilitate restart in the event an exception occurs in the IE unit at the head of the queue, and to bring the processor to a quiescent state before system calls.

3.3.2. Register Data Dependencies Within a Stage

Register dependencies within a basic window are enforced by either doing serial execution within an IE unit, or using reservation stations (or renamed registers) with data forwarding.

3.3.3. Register Data Dependencies Across Stages

The burden of enforcing register data dependencies across multiple basic windows becomes light when windows are ordered in a sequence, and the data flowing into and out of basic window boundaries are monitored. To keep the discussion simple, we shall explain the working of the scheme for the case when basic windows are either basic blocks or subsets of basic blocks. For a given basic block, the registers through which externally-created values flow into the basic block and the registers through which internally-created values flow out of the basic block are invariants for any execution of that basic block. We express these invariants concisely by bit maps called **`use`** and **`create masks`**.

The **create** and **use masks** capture a good deal of the information (related to register traffic) in a basic block in a simple and powerful way. If there were no **create masks**, each instruction in the large dynamic window has to be decoded before identifying the destination register and setting the corresponding "busy bit" in the register file. Subsequent instructions in the overall large window, even if independent, have to wait until all previous instructions are decoded, and the "busy bits" of the appropriate registers are set. The advantage of having a **create mask** is that all the registers that are written in a basic block are known immediately after the mask is fetched, *i.e.*, even before the entire basic block is fetched from the instruction cache and decoded. (As mentioned earlier, this "decoding" problem is a major problem in the superscalar processors proposed to date.) Independent instructions from subsequent basic windows can thus start execution, possibly from the next cycle onwards, and the hardware that allows that is much simpler than the hardware required to decode a large number of instructions in parallel and compare their source and destination registers for possible conflicts.

Generation of Register Masks

If adequate compile-time support is available, the masks can be generated by the compiler itself[2]. If the use of compile-time support is not an option (for example if object code compatibility is required), or if the additional code space overhead due to the masks is considered intolerable, the masks can be generated at run time by hardware the first time the block is encountered, and stored in a dynamic table for later reuse.

Forwarding of Register Values

When an instruction completes execution, its results are forwarded to subsequent instructions of that stage. If the result is a register's *last update* in that basic block, the result is written to the future file of that stage, and forwarded to the future files of the subsequent stages as well, one stage at a time. When a result from a previous stage reaches a future file, the appropriate register is updated. If the register entry appears in the **use mask** of that stage, then the reservation stations in that unit are checked for possible matchings. The result is also forwarded to the subsequent future file in the next cycle. The **create** and **use masks** helps to reduce the forwarding traffic and the associative search involved in forwarding the results. When the result of an instruction (*i.e.*, a new register instance) is forwarded to a future file, the reservation stations in the corresponding IE unit need be searched for possible matchings only if the register entry appears in its **use mask**. Similarly, if the register entry appears in a **create mask**, then the result need not be forwarded to the subsequent stages, because they need a different instance of that register[3]. Notice that data from several stages can simultaneously be traveling to subsequent stages in a pipelined fashion. Queues are used to facilitate this forwarding.

[2] All optimizing compilers invariably do dataflow analysis [1,7]; the `create` and `use` masks are similar to the `def` and `use` variables computed by these compilers for each basic block, except that the former pair represent architectural registers and the latter pair represent variables of the source program.

[3] Since most of the register instances are used up either in the same basic block in which they are created or in the subsequent basic block, we can expect a significant reduction in the forwarding traffic because of the `create mask`.

When the IE unit at the head commits, the last updates in that window are written to the architectural register file for purposes of precise state recovery (see section 3.5).

3.4. Distributed Data Memory System

When a processor attempts to issue and execute many instructions in parallel, it is imperative that the memory system should be capable of supporting multiple memory references per cycle, preferably with small latencies [22]. The latency can be reduced by using a data cache. In line with our objective of expandability, the memory system also has to be decentralized.

Decentralizing the memory system is harder than most of the other parts. When a system performs speculative execution, a store operation can be allowed to proceed to the memory system only when it is guaranteed to commit; otherwise the old memory value is lost and recovery will not be possible. Nevertheless, succeeding loads (from speculatively executed code) to the same location do require the new value, and not the old value. Thus, there must be some means of forwarding "uncommitted" memory values to subsequent loads, just like the forwarding of "uncommitted" register values. In the case of register values, the distributed register files served as good temporary platforms to hold these "uncommitted" register values, and the **create** and **use masks** served to enforce the dependencies between them. But such a straightforward replication scheme will not work for the memory system, because of the following reasons.

(1) Even if replication of data caches was feasible, we still have the problem of maintaining consistency among the multiple copies, and that too, with the restriction that values have to be written onto a memory location in the order given by the sequential semantics of the program.

(2) With register values, maintaining this consistency was easily done by using the static **create** and **use masks**. In the case of memory values, the number of memory locations is much too large to permit the use of such bitmaps. Furthermore, memory addresses, unlike register addresses, are computed at run time, and therefore have the *aliasing* problem. Although some addresses could be disambiguated statically, many others, especially those arising from pointer variables in the source program, can be determined only at run time. This is reflected in the fact that even if the data cache is decentralized, we still need to do a global memory disambiguation within the large active window.

3.4.1. Enforcing Memory Data Dependencies

To guarantee correctness of execution, before a load operation is issued, the load address has to be checked (for possible conflicts) with the addresses of all pending stores in the same basic window as well as the preceding active basic windows. Whereas performing this (centralized) associative search is one problem, the more serious problem is that the memory addresses of some of the previous stores may not be determined yet. If worst-case assumptions are made about possible memory hazards and a load operation is made to wait until the addresses of all pending stores are determined, parallelism is inhibited and performance might be affected badly. What we need to do is to allow for the execution of load instructions without proper disambiguation, with facilities provided for recovery actions when it is determined that an incorrect value has been loaded. For this recovery, we can use the same facility that has been provided for fast recovery in times of incorrect branch prediction. Our analysis of the memory traffic in programs indicates that most of the stored values are not reloaded in the immediate future, say within the next 100 instructions (a good compiler would keep soon-to-be-used values in registers). Therefore, we expect that most of the time, the unresolved loads will fetch the correct values from the data cache/main memory.

To detect if an unresolved load fetched an incorrect value, we need to perform global memory disambiguation within the large active window. On first glance, this appears to be a sequential process, or one requiring a large associative search; but we have developed a decentralized scheme for carrying this out. The scheme, called an *Address Resolution Buffer (ARB)*, is the solution that we settled on after considering several other options.

3.4.2. Interleaved Address Resolution Buffer

As with all other major resources, the ARB is also decentralized. The ARB is a special cache for storing information relevant to the loads and stores that have been issued from the active large window. It is interleaved (based on the memory address) to permit multiple accesses per cycle. Figure 3 shows the block diagram of a 2-way interleaved ARB. Each ARB bank would typically have provision for storing 4 - 8 addresses and related information. Associated with each address entry is a bitmap with twice as many bits as the number of stages. Of the 2 bits per stage, one is used for indicating if a (partially resolved) load has been performed from the corresponding stage, and the other is for indicating if a store has been performed from that stage. There is also a *value* field associated with each address entry to store one memory value for that location.

Within each stage, memory disambiguation is done in a strict serial order with the help of a local queue-like structure, which also has provision for forwarding values from stores to loads within that stage. When a load is properly resolved locally within its stage (automatic if each unit executes sequentially), it is ready to be issued. When the load is issued, the addresses of the entries in the appropriate ARB bank are associatively checked (notice that this associative search is only 4-way or 8-way, searching for a single key) to see if the same address is present in the ARB. If the address is not present, an ARB entry is allotted to the new address. If the address is present in the ARB, then a check is made in its bitmap to see if an earlier store has been made to the same address from a previous stage. If so, then it takes the value stored in the *value* field of the entry. Finally, the load bit corresponding to the stage is set to 1.

When a store is performed, a similar associative check is performed to see if the address is already present in the ARB. If not, an entry is allotted to the new address. The bitmap corresponding to the store address is updated to reflect the fact that a store has been performed from a particular stage. The value to be stored is deposited in the *value* field of the bitmap. If the store address was already present in the ARB, then a check is also performed to see if an earlier load has been made to the same address from a succeeding stage. If so, recovery action is initiated so that all stages beyond the one that made the incorrect load are nullified, and restarted. Since there is provision for storing only one "store value" at a time for any address, special recovery actions are taken when a second store request occurs to an address.

When the stage at the head is retired, all load and store marks corresponding to that stage are erased immediately. This requires a facility to clear all the bits in 2 columns of the ARB in 1 cycle. Similarly, when the tail pointer is moved backwards during recovery, the columns corresponding to the stages stepped over by the tail pointer are also cleared immediately. An ARB entry is reclaimed for reuse when all the load and store bits associated with the entry are cleared.

The ARB scheme has the full power of a hypothetical scheme that performs associative compares of the memory addresses in the entire large window. Here also, we use the concept of splitting a large task (memory disambiguation within a large window) into smaller subtasks. Furthermore, it ties well with our execution model. It allows speculative loads and speculative stores! It also allows forwarding of memory values when loads are performed, and all stores are effectively "cache hits" because the value is stored only in the ARB until its stage is committed.

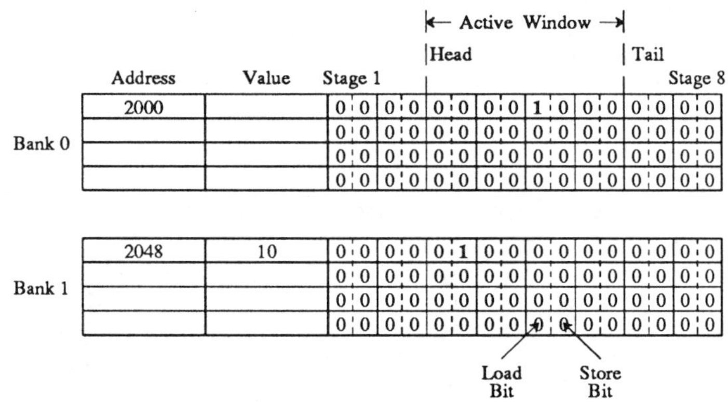

Figure 3: A Two-Way Interleaved Address Resolution Buffer

We feel that the ARB is a very powerful, decentralized (and thus expandable) way of dynamically disambiguating memory references. We are considering the performance impact of set-associative mappings in the ARB, as well as other performance implications of this "cache besides the cache".

3.4.3. Interleaved Data Cache

As seen from the discussion so far, conventional data caches are not appropriate for the ESW paradigm; the exact nature of the data caches is a subject of our future research. Currently we propose to use an interleaved non-blocking cache similar to the one proposed in [22].

3.5. Enforcing Control Dependencies

Dynamic branch prediction is used (if required) to fetch new basic windows. When a conditional branch instruction or a return instruction is executed in an IE unit, its outcome is compared with the earlier prediction. If there is a mismatch, then all subsequent windows are discarded. This is easily done by advancing the tail pointer (of the circular stage queue) to the stage that succeeds the one containing the mispredicted branch. In the next cycle, the IE unit at the tail starts fetching the correct set of instructions. Notice that the distributed future file system helps to maintain precise states at each basic window boundary, which eases the implementation of the recovery mechanism significantly.

4. PERFORMANCE ISSUES

4.1. Preliminary Experimental Results

We are in the process of conducting several simulation studies, both to verify the potential of the new processor design and to study the effects of compiler optimizations. A sound evaluation of the execution model can be done only after the development of a compiler that considers the idiosyncrasies of the model and exploits its potential. In this section, we present some of the preliminary results obtained in our simulation studies. These results should be viewed as a realistic starting point.

The simulator that we developed uses the MIPS R2000 - R2010 instruction set and functional unit latencies. All important features of the ESW paradigm, such as the split instruction caches, distributed address resolution buffer, and data caches, have been included in the simulator. The simulator accepts executable images of programs, and executes them; it is not trace driven. Its features are listed below:

- Number of stages can be varied.
- Up to 2 instructions are fetched/decoded/issued from each of the active IE units, every cycle; out-of-order execution is used in each stage.
- A basic window can have up to 32 instructions.
- The data cache is 64Kbytes, direct-mapped, and has an access latency of **2 cycles** (one cycle to pass through the interconnect between the IE units and the cache, and another to access the ARB and the cache in parallel). The interleaving factor of the data cache and the ARB is the smallest power of 2 that is equal to or greater than twice the number of stages. (For instance, if the number of stages is 6, the interleaving factor used is 16.) The cache miss latency is 4 cycles.
- Each stage has a 4Kword L1 instruction cache.
- The L2 instruction cache has not been included in the simulator; instead, we assume 100% hit ratio for the L2 instruction cache.
- The branch prediction mechanism for conditional branches uses the 3-bit counter scheme proposed in [19]. For effectively predicting the return addresses of procedure calls, there is a stack-like mechanism similar to the one discussed in [11], with a stack depth of 20.

The simulator is not equipped to detect basic windows that are supersets of basic blocks (which needs a control flow analysis within each procedure to make sure that each basic window has only a single entry); currently it uses basic blocks (or smaller blocks if a basic block is larger than 32) as basic windows.

For benchmarks, we used the SPEC benchmark suite. The benchmark programs were compiled for a DECstation 3100; notice that the `a.out` executables so obtained have been compiled for a single-IPC machine. The C benchmarks were simulated to completion; the FORTRAN benchmarks were simulated up to approximately `1 billion` instructions.

Table 1 presents the results obtained with code generated for an ordinary single IPC machine, and with basic blocks used as basic windows. The latter feature affects the performance of the integer benchmarks because they contain several small basic blocks with poor predictability, as is evident from the "Mean Basic Block Size" column and the "Branch Prediction Accuracy" column. The C benchmarks are executed with 4 stages and the FORTRAN benchmarks with 10 stages.

From Table 1 we see that, even using basic blocks as basic windows, we get fairly impressive completion rates, ranging from 1.81 to 2.04 for the C programs, and 1.92 to 5.88 for the FORTRAN benchmarks, even using code that is not compiled/scheduled for our machine model. (Notice that the actual speedup numbers would be higher because the instruction completion rate of a conventional processor is ≤ 1.)

Table 1: Instruction Completion Rates with Unmodified Code

Benchmarks	Mean Basic Block Size	No. of Stages	Branch Prediction Accuracy	Completion Rate
eqntott	4.19	4	90.14%	2.04
espresso	6.47	4	83.13%	2.06
gcc	5.64	4	85.11%	1.81
xlisp	5.04	4	80.21%	1.91
dnasa7	26.60	10	99.13%	2.73
doduc	12.22	10	86.90%	1.92
fpppp	113.42	10	88.86%	3.87
matrix300	21.49	10	99.35%	5.88
spice2g6	6.14	10	86.95%	3.23
tomcatv	45.98	10	99.28%	3.64

In comparing our results to other results in the literature, we see that we are achieving issue rates similar to Butler, *et. al.* [3], with similar resources but larger window sizes (our results are slightly better in several cases), and much better than the issue rates achieved by Smith, *et. al* [21]. This is despite the fact that we include all stalls, specifically stalls due to: instruction and data cache misses (instruction cache miss stalls cause a noticeable degradation in performance in many schemes), data cache bank contention (including contention due to speculative loads), recovery due to incorrect speculative loads (we do not assume disambiguated memory operations), and recovery due to branch prediction with a real predictor (our predictor does not do too well, as can be seen in Table 1), whereas the other studies make optimistic assumptions in these cases.

We tried using more stages for the C benchmarks, and our results improved somewhat, but not significantly (about 20-30% increase in performance) because of our using a basic block as a basic window, and the small average size of a basic block in the code compiled for a single-IPC machine.

4.2. Role of the Compiler

The compiler has the opportunity to play an important role in bringing to reality the full potential of this processing paradigm. The compiler can introduce helpful transformations that are tailored to the idiosyncrasies of the execution model. For instance, if the compiler partitions the instruction stream into basic windows that are larger than basic blocks, or if the compiler knows how the instruction stream would be dynamically partitioned into windows, it can attempt to move up within a window the operations whose results are needed early on in the following window. Similarly, it can perform a static memory disambiguation, and push down (within a window) those loads which are guaranteed to conflict with stores in the previous windows. Many other "optimizations" are also possible. The important ones include:

- Partition the program into basic windows that are supersets of basic blocks and convey this to the hardware. This would allow a more accurate expansion of the dynamic window to get at more parallelism. (This information is present in the control flow graph constructed by the compiler.) In case the basic block is large, decide where to split.

- Perform static code re-scheduling based on the idiosyncrasies of the ESW model, as described earlier. For example, pack all *dependent* instructions into a basic window.

Table 2 gives a feel of the improvements we can expect to see when some of the above points are incorporated. The results in Table 2 were obtained by manually performing the optimizations in one or two important routines in some of the benchmarks. Hand code scheduling was performed only for those benchmarks which spend at least 50% of the time in a limited portion of the code, so that manual analysis is possible. The only transformations that were performed are: (i) moving up within a basic window those instructions whose results are needed in the critical path in the following basic windows. (Such instructions typically include induction variables, which are usually incremented at the end of a loop when code is generated by an ordinary compiler.) (ii) in the *cmppt* routine of **eqntott**, we expand a basic window to a superset of 3 basic blocks. (iii) in the *compl_lift* and *elim_lowering* routines of **espresso**, we consider basic windows that are supersets of basic blocks.

Table 2: Instruction Completion Rates with Modified Code

Benchmarks	No. of Stages	Prediction Accuracy	Completion Rate
eqntott	4	95.58%	4.23
	8	96.14%	4.97
espresso	4	92.17%	2.30
dnasa7	10	98.95%	7.17
matrix300	10	99.34%	7.02
tomcatv	10	99.31%	4.49

Even the simple optimizations implemented for Table 2 boost performance considerably in the cases considered — **eqntott** is achieving close to 5 instructions per cycle, and **matrix300** and **dnasa7** are able to sustain over 7 instructions per cycle (the completion rate for **dnasa7** has improved from 2.73 to 7.17 with this simple code scheduling). We expect that with such simple compiler enhancements (for example facilitating the hardware's task of recovering part of the control structure of the program), we will be able to double the performance of the C benchmarks. We base our expectation on an analysis of the C programs which suggests that expanding the basic window into a sequence of basic blocks will not only increase the average size of the basic window (in terms of useful instructions executed) by a factor of about 2, but also allow us to get past of many of the "badly predicted" branches since they become part of the basic window and do not prevent us from accurately expanding the dynamic window. (Notice that the branch prediction accuracies for **eqntott** in Table 2 are much better than those in Table 1 for precisely this reason; the prediction accuracies are different for 4 and 8 stages because the exact dynamic instruction stream that enters the IE units differs with different number of stages.) For the FORTRAN programs, the primary impediment to greater performance in most cases is the hardware limitation, though in some cases, such as **tomcatv**, static memory disambiguation would assist in reducing the cycles lost due to incorrect speculative loads.

5. SUMMARY AND FUTURE WORK

5.1. Summary

We have proposed a new processing paradigm for exploiting fine-grain parallelism. The model, which we call the Expandable Split Window (ESW) paradigm, shares a number of properties with the restricted dataflow machines, but was derived from the von Neumann architecture. The essence of dynamic dataflow execution is captured by simple data forwarding schemes for both register and memory values. The fundamental properties of the von Neumann architecture that we retained includes a sequential instruction stream, which relies on inter-instruction communication through a set of registers and memory locations. The result is a simple architecture that accepts ordinary sequential code, but behaves as a fairly restricted dataflow machine.

We proposed an implementation of the proposed model. In our view, the beauty of the ESW model and its implementation lies in its realizability, not to mention its novelty. It draws heavily on the recent developments in microprocessor technology, yet goes far beyond the centralized window-based superscalar processors in exploiting "irregular" fine-grain parallelism. It has no centralized resource bottlenecks that we are aware of. This is very important, because many existing execution models are plagued by the need for centralized resources. Almost all the parts of our implementation are found in conventional serial processors, the only exception is the Address Resolution Buffer (ARB); yet these parts have been arranged in such a way as to extract much more parallelism than was thought to be realistically possible before. The ARB scheme presented in this paper is, to the best of our knowledge, the first decentralized design for memory disambiguation with a large window of instructions[4].

Another feature of the ESW paradigm is its expandability. When advances in technology allow more transistors to be put on a chip, our implementation can be easily expanded by adding more stages; there is no need to redesign the implementation/architecture.

The performance results are also very promising. We are able to achieve about 2 instructions per cycle, with 4 stages, for the C programs, and more for the FORTRAN programs, with no special code transformations, and taking all stalls that degrade performance into account. When we applied some optimizations suited to the ESW model to some of the benchmarks, the performance was enhanced substantially; the completion rate increased by a factor of 2.5 for **eqntott** and a factor of 2.6 for **dnasa7**. We strongly feel that the ESW model has significant potential for becoming the model of choice for future fine-grain parallel processors. It encompasses many of the strengths of the VLIW, superscalar, decoupled, systolic, and restricted dataflow models of computation, and overcomes most of their drawbacks.

5.2. Future Work

We would like to conduct a series of studies to determine what a basic window of instructions should be. Currently, we use a single-entry call-free loop-free block of instructions as a basic window. We are investigating the implications of removing the "loop-free" requirement. Studies are also needed to determine the optimum number of stages and the maximum number of

[4] There is an ongoing independent work on hardware support for dynamic disambiguation of memory references in the context of a VLIW processor in industry [6].

instructions to be issued from each IE unit in a cycle. Another issue worth investigating is the benefit of out-of-order execution within an IE unit when it contains a straight-line piece of code. If a window consists mostly of dependent operations, serial execution within each IE unit might suffice, thereby saving the associative hardware and reservation stations required within each IE unit to perform out-of-order execution.

The design of our fine-grain parallel processor is at a stage where many of the hardware issues have been investigated, and the arena slowly shifts to software issues. We expect to conduct further analysis of programs for the purpose of software development, especially a suitable compiler for the machine. We feel that the compiler effort would not be as detailed as that required for some other fine-grain parallel models since most of the tasks that we ask of the compiler, such as the construction of the basic window and simple code scheduling are routinely done by compliers, and some of the harder tasks, such as static memory disambiguation are helpful, but not essential to our execution model.

ACKNOWLEDGEMENTS

The foundation for this work was laid in discussions with Jim Smith in the 1988-1989 time frame, and continued discussions with him have helped to refine the work. We would like to thank Mitch Alsup and Kemal Ebcioglu for their insightful comments on the paper, and Joel Emer and Bob Rau for discussions that helped to refine some of the ideas presented in this paper. Financial support for this work was provided by NSF grant CCR-8919635 and by an IBM Graduate Fellowship.

REFERENCES

[1] A. V. Aho, R. Sethi, and J. D. Ullman, *Compilers: Principles, Techniques, and Tools.* Addison-Wesley Publishing Company, 1986.

[2] T. M. Austin and G. S. Sohi, "Dynamic Dependency Analysis of Ordinary Programs," *Proc. 19th Annual International Symposium on Computer Architecture*, 1992.

[3] M. Butler, T. Yeh, Y. Patt, M. Alsup, H. Scales, and M. Shebanow, "Single Instruction Stream Parallelism Is Greater than Two," *Proc. 18th Annual International Symposium on Computer Architecture*, pp. 276-286, 1991.

[4] R. P. Colwell, R. P. Nix, J. J. O'Donnell, D. B. Papworth, and P. K. Rodman, "A VLIW Architecture for a Trace Scheduling Compiler," *IEEE Transactions on Computers*, vol. 37, pp. 967-979, August 1988.

[5] D. E. Culler and Arvind, "Resource Requirements of Dataflow Programs," *Proc. 15th Annual International Symposium on Computer Architecture*, pp. 141-150, 1988.

[6] J. S. Emer and R. P. Nix, "Personal Communication," June 1991.

[7] C. N. Fischer and R. J. LeBlanc, Jr., *Crafting A Compiler.* Menlo Park, CA: The Benjamin/Cummings Publishing Company, Inc., 1988.

[8] J. R. Goodman and P. J. Woest, "The Wisconsin Multicube: A New Large-Scale Cache-Coherent Multiprocessor," *Proc. 15th Annual Symposium on Computer Architecture*, pp. 422-431, June 1988.

[9] R. A. Iannucci, "Toward a Dataflow / von Neumann Hybrid Architecture," *Proc. 15th Annual International Symposium on Computer Architecture*, pp. 131-140, 1988.

[10] N. P. Jouppi and D. W. Wall, "Available Instruction-Level Parallelism for Superscalar and Superpipelined Machines," *Proc. ASPLOS III*, pp. 272-282, 1989.

[11] D. R. Kaeli and P. G. Emma, "Branch History Table Prediction of Moving Target Branches Due to Subroutine Returns," *Proc. 18th Annual International Symposium on Computer Architecture*, pp. 34-42, 1991.

[12] K. Murakami, N. Irie, M. Kuga, and S. Tomita, "SIMP (Single Instruction Stream / Multiple Instruction Pipelining): A Novel High-Speed Single-Processor Architecture," *Proc. 16th Annual Symposium on Computer Architecture*, pp. 78-85, May 1989.

[13] A. Nicolau and J. A. Fisher, "Measuring the Parallelism Available for Very Long Instruction Word Architectures," *IEEE Transactions on Computers*, vol. C-33, pp. 968-976, November 1984.

[14] R. S. Nikhil and Arvind, "Can Dataflow Subsume von Neumann Computing?," *Proc. 16th International Symposium on Computer Architecture*, pp. 262-272, June 1989.

[15] R. R. Oehler and R. D. Groves, "IBM RISC System/6000 Processor Architecture," *IBM Journal of Research and Development*, vol. 34, pp. 23-36, January 1990.

[16] G. M. Papadopoulos and D. E. Culler, "Monsoon: An Explicit Token-Store Architecture," *Proc. 17th Annual International Symposium on Computer Architecture*, pp. 82-91, May, 1990.

[17] G. M. Papadopoulos and K. R. Traub, "Multithreading: A Revisionist View of Dataflow Architectures," *Proc. 18th Annual International Symposium on Computer Architecture*, pp. 342-351, 1991.

[18] Y. N. Patt, W. W. Hwu, and M. Shebanow, "HPS, A New Microarchitecture: Rationale and Introduction," *Proc. 18th Annual Workshop on Microprogramming*, pp. 103-108, December 1985.

[19] J. E. Smith, "A Study of Branch Prediction Strategies," *Proc. 8th International Symposium on Computer Architecture*, pp. 135-148, May 1981.

[20] J. E. Smith and A. R. Pleszkun, "Implementing Precise Interrupts in Pipelined Processors," *IEEE Transactions on Computers*, vol. 37, pp. 562-573, May 1988.

[21] M. D. Smith, M. Johnson, and M. A. Horowitz, "Limits on Multiple Instruction Issue," *Proc. ASPLOS III*, pp. 290-302, 1989.

[22] G. S. Sohi and M. Franklin, "High-Bandwidth Data Memory Systems for Superscalar Processors," *Proc. ASPLOS IV*, pp. 53-62, 1991.

[23] R. M. Tomasulo, "An Efficient Algorithm for Exploiting Multiple Arithmetic Units," *IBM Journal of Research and Development*, pp. 25-33, January 1967.

[24] D. W. Wall, "Limits of Instruction-Level Parallelism," *Proc. ASPLOS IV*, pp. 176-188, 1991.

Session 3: Multi-Processor Architecture

TOWARDS A SHARED-MEMORY MASSIVELY PARALLEL MULTIPROCESSOR

Daniel Litaize, Abdelaziz Mzoughi, Christine Rochange, Pascal Sainrat
Institut de Recherche en Informatique de Toulouse
118 route de Narbonne 31062 Toulouse Cedex, France
Tél: (33) 61 55 64 16 E-mail: litaize@irit.fr

ABSTRACT

A set of ultra high throughput (more than one Gigabits per second) serial links used as processor-memory network can lead to the starting up of a shared-memory massively parallel multiprocessor. The bandwidth of the network is far beyond values found in present shared-memory multiprocessor networks. To feed this network the memory must be serially multiported. Such a multiprocessor can actually be build with current technologies.

This paper analyzes the characteristics of such a novel architecture, presents the solutions that must be considered and the practical problems associated with close of experiments. These results show then the way to effectively build this multiprocessor, taking into account main topics such as data coherency, latency time and scalability.

KEY WORDS: multiprocessors, shared memory, caches, networks, serial links.

I. INTRODUCTION

Rapid IC technology improvements have led to a high growth rate of CPU and to an increase in memory performance. Both have benefited from the increase in the number of transistors available on a chip, but architectural advances like RISC ideas, pipelining and caches have shown profit only for CPUs. The gap between DRAM (used as main memory) cycle times and processor cycle times (measuring in fact the instruction and data needs) is therefore growing ineluctably. The effect of this gap is fortunately smoothed by the use of integrated SRAM caches, but this gap remains the main problem to be solved, especially in multiprocessors, in which specific problems are added. For these reasons, sophisticated memory hierarchies are needed, that keep the average access time low and provide high bandwidth [HeJo91].

Current shared-memory multiprocessors are mainly based on a common bus. If we increase the number of CPUs connected to this bus we need to increase the bus bandwidth. The intensive use of caches leads us to consider the block as the logical data transfer unit, and a natural way to increase the bandwidth is to widen the bus. The physical data transfer unit can therefore be doubled and doubled again until the logical data transfer unit is reached.

Widening the bus is not the best solution. Hopper and al., in their study [HOLJ89], have shown that considering two to four n bits busses gives in many cases a better global performance than considering one 2n to 4n bits bus.

Another approach is on the contrary to shrink the bus, providing a higher bit rate, the lower limit being a one bit bus. In this limit case, a 32 bits bus equivalent bandwidth is obtained with a 32 time faster data rate transfer. For example, a 50 MHz 32 bits bus needs the use of a 1.6 GHz serial link data rate to get an equivalent bandwidth. This data rate can nowadays be considered, but only if it is a point to point link, so as to control precisely the electrical (optical) characteristics of the transmission medium.

The latter remark prevents us from considering a common data bus using the same data rate. A 32 bits common bus connecting 32 CPU modules to a main memory cannot be expected to work faster than a few tens of Mhz, giving a bandwidth of, saying, 200 MBytes per second, whereas 32 serial links connecting each CPU module to the main memory give a global bandwidth of 6400 MBytes per second using 1.6 GHz links.

However the resulting architectures are not the same. We move from a common bus structure to a fully interconnected one. This means that the main memory must be designed in a serial multiported fashion (this term will be defined later, but suggests the idea of having one private entry for each serial link). To ensure a sufficient bandwidth, the main memory must classically be composed of independent banks. The point to point feature leads then to the architecture given by Figure 1, which can be qualified as Serially Multiported Multiprocessor SMM.

Each processor module is tied to every memory module by a private serial connection used for address and data transfers. The interconnection bandwidth available for each processor module implies we should consider a cluster of processors at that place. A memory module, in addition to the RAM, owns logic for address and data block recording and data coherency processing.

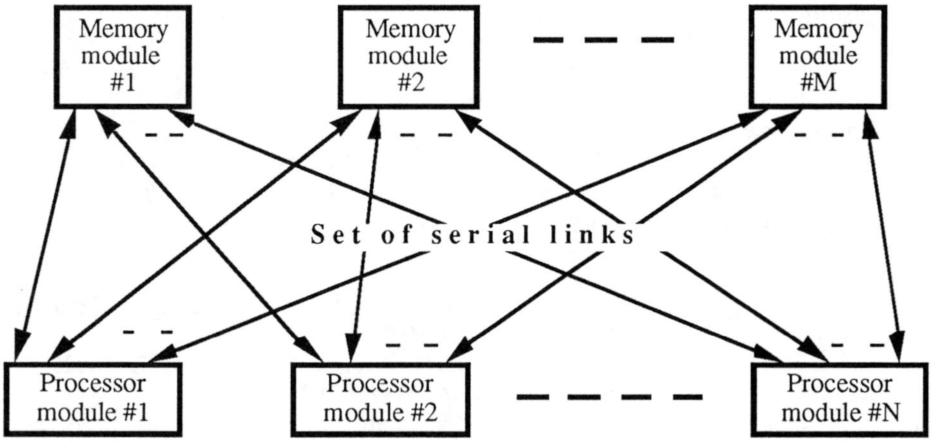

Figure 1 : Serially multiported multiprocessor

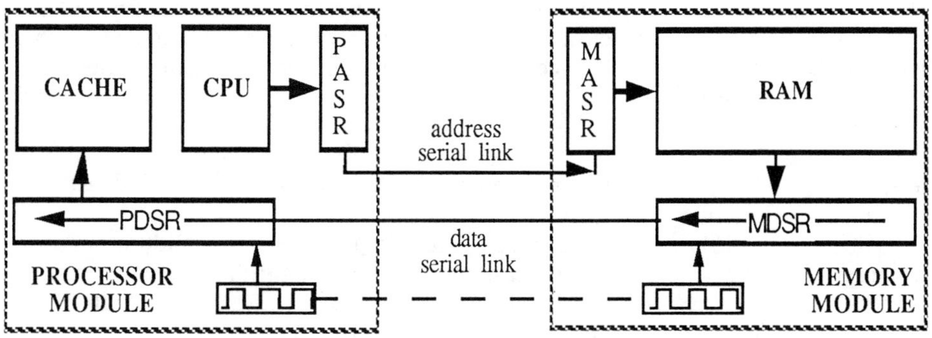

Figure 2 : conceptual view of a serial connection

All these points will now be studied further on, the accent being put on the possibility of building nowadays such an architecture with a significant number of CPUs. References will be made to the experiments done for the prototype under construction at our laboratory, presented in [LHLM89] [Sain91], and called "M3S" project (French acronym for "Multiprocesseur à Mémoire Multiport Série"), and whose aim is to make the main aspects of such an architecture possible.

Section 2 will present the level of performance reachable with serial connections used in this context. Interfaces at each end of the serial interconnection will then be studied, at processor side in section 3 and at memory side in section 4. Sections 5,6,7,8 each develop some important features: data coherency, bandwidth, latency time and scalability. Section 9 is the conclusion.

2. ULTRA HIGH SPEED SERIAL CONNECTIONS

2.1. CONCEPTUAL ASPECT

Figure 2 presents a conceptual view of a serial connection used in such a SMM architecture. The term connection specifies here the bonding between modules. A connection is considered to be composed of two unidirectional links.

A data block transfer due to, for example, a cache miss needs then the execution of the following steps :

- the loading of the Processor Address Shift Register PASR with the address of the requested data block,
- the transfer of the content of the register PASR to the Memory Address Shift Register MASR through the serial link connecting the two registers,
- the memory reading of the data block, then loaded into the Memory Data Shift Register MDSR,
- the transfer of the content of the register MDSR to the Processor Data Shift Register PDSR through the serial link connecting the two registers,
- the writing of the PDSR content into the cache.

The size of the memory data shift register is that of a data block, the size of the processor data shift register is that of a cache word (a word being a data cache transfer unit). The transfer is done as usual, i.e. the requested word being placed in front of the data block and block transfer being overlapped with cache words writing.

The transmission speed is of course the key factor of performance. The numerous experiments made for the M3S prototype have allowed a throughput of 1.5 Gigabits per second, using standard off the shelves GaAs integrated circuits and ordinary coaxial cables as transmission support. Considering the length of the connections used here (less than one meter), the physical transmission support used is not a limiting factor to the speed increase. It must be noticed that this kind of transmission is well adapted to a fiber optic support, but the speed considered here is beyond the current possibilities of the transducers.

As an example, we will consider, in this presentation, a throughput of 2 Gigabits per second (noted 2 Gbs) on the serial links, on the understanding that a shift register GaAs IC full custom made today could handle close to twice this rate. At this rate, the time needed to transfer a 32 bit address is below 20 nanoseconds and for a 16 byte data block (144 bits, including parity bits) is below 80 ns, corresponding to a time under 20 nanoseconds for a 32 bit first word access.

The memory data shift register MDSR being of a data block size, a memory read or write is done in one memory cycle, this operation corresponding to an optimal solution: no more can be done with actual RAM IC.

Moreover, a wraparound mechanism is easy to

implement, the data being picked from the shift register at a word boundary, while the tail of the register is looped back to its head.

At the processor level, the overlapping of the data transfer with the cache writing needs the use of two shift registers working in flip-flop. However the data rates considered here lead to avoid such a solution. We have then to consider as many registers as words in a block, each of them being sequentially stopped at each word boundary. This interface structure is probably the one giving the greatest speed possibility.

2.2. PRACTICAL ASPECT

The serial connection presented in Figure 2 is composed of two unidirectional links, one used for the address transfer and the other used for the data transfer. It seems that a bidirectionnal link working in a half-duplex manner is adequate due to the alternation of information transfer. This scheme is not sufficient for the system to work properly. Due to the need of block flushes, the serial links must have an equal access to the address and data shift registers. Considering a bidirectional link leads then to consider bidirectional data shift registers.

For the following reasons we will consider two unidirectional serial links connected each to a couple of shift registers, one for the address and one for the data :

- the full duplex use of the connection gives the highest level of performance when the cache is full, because block flushes can be done in parallel with block loading,
- the multiprocessor environment necessitates the transfer of messages between memory modules and processor modules in order to maintain the data coherency in the various caches. The exact alternation mentioned early is then no longer respected and a contention problem appears in the half duplex mode,
- perhaps with less obvious consequences, shift clocks must be synchronized. Experiments made for the M3S prototype [LHSP90] [Sain91] have shown that a common clock distributed all over the multiprocessor is satisfactory for a data rate up to 1 Gbs and a number of links lower than 128. In the general case, the clock must be recovered from the data. In a half duplex connection, a special bit stream must then be sent before each data transfer, and the time taken to send this synchronization sequence is added to the information transfer time: this extra time is not acceptable for performance reasons.

Clock recovery is a classical problem in low data transfer and needs a data encoding. We will consider here a 4B/5B data encoding used in FDDI, as in TAXI chips at 150 Mbits per second [TAXI90], Hotrod chip from Gazelle working at 1 Gbs [GAZE90], or HPPI from Gigabit Logic. Given rates represent useful data transfer rate, the throughput on the link being in fact raised to a 5/4 ratio.

A 2 Gbs useful rate needs then a 2.5 Gbs rate on the serial link.

So, the use of two unidirectional links solves the problem of clock synchronization, dead times being filled with synchronizing sequences, and the problem of contention, messages being sent in a full duplex manner.

We have to notice that the same physical medium can be used for a full duplex data transfer: addition of current or voltage, distinct light wavelength.

Last but not least feature, experiments made for the M3S prototype have shown that all the very high speed logical parts must be integrated into one IC to work properly at these desired frequencies.

3. LINK INTERFACE AT THE PROCESSOR MODULE LEVEL

3.1. CASE OF ONE PROCESSOR PER PROCESSOR MODULE

Taking into account the preceding characteristics, the interface between the serial link and the memory side of the cache could be designed like a Hotrod type chip integrating some message decoding facilities. To define them more closely, we must consider the kind of messages exchanged between a processor module and the memory modules.

From processor to memory a message can be :

- a block request following a cache miss. The message is composed of a header coding the kind of request followed by the block number.
- a request for data coherency. Without giving any precision about the exact algorithm used, we can expect that such a message has the same format as in the preceding case.
- a block flush. The message is formed by the nature of the request, an address block and the corresponding data block.

We can notice that a message is always composed of the same format first word.

From memory to processor a message can be :

- a data block, in response to a block request.
- a request for data coherency. Still without precision about the exact algorithm used, such a message is composed of a header and a block number, the header coding a flush or an invalidation request.
- a block flush acknowledge. This kind of message is necessary due to the fact that the memory resources associated to the serial link must be free before the sending out of a new request.

To indicate the kind of message, a data block must then be preceded by a code.

The fact that very few types of messages are to be transmitted, three in each direction, suggests encoding them using the free codes of the 4B/5B encoding. Latency for a request is then reduced to a minimum value (corresponding to 4 useful bits in the worst case) but the interface is now slightly involved in the transaction.

3.2. GENERAL CASE

However this interface would not have sufficient capabilities for actual use. A processor module is build at least around an Harvard processor architecture, or is itself a cluster of processors. A processor module is connected to

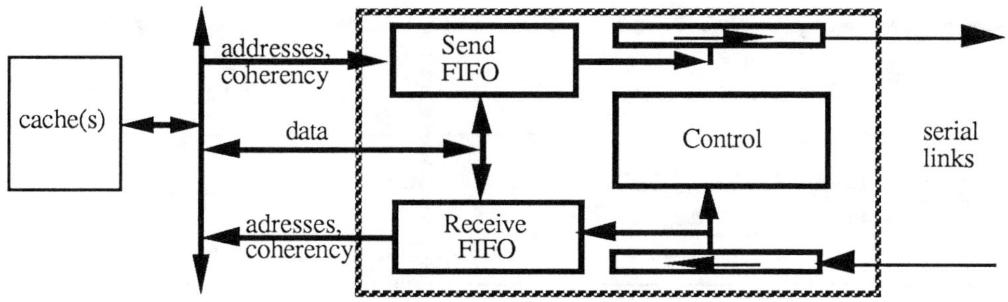

Figure 3 : one serial interconnection interface

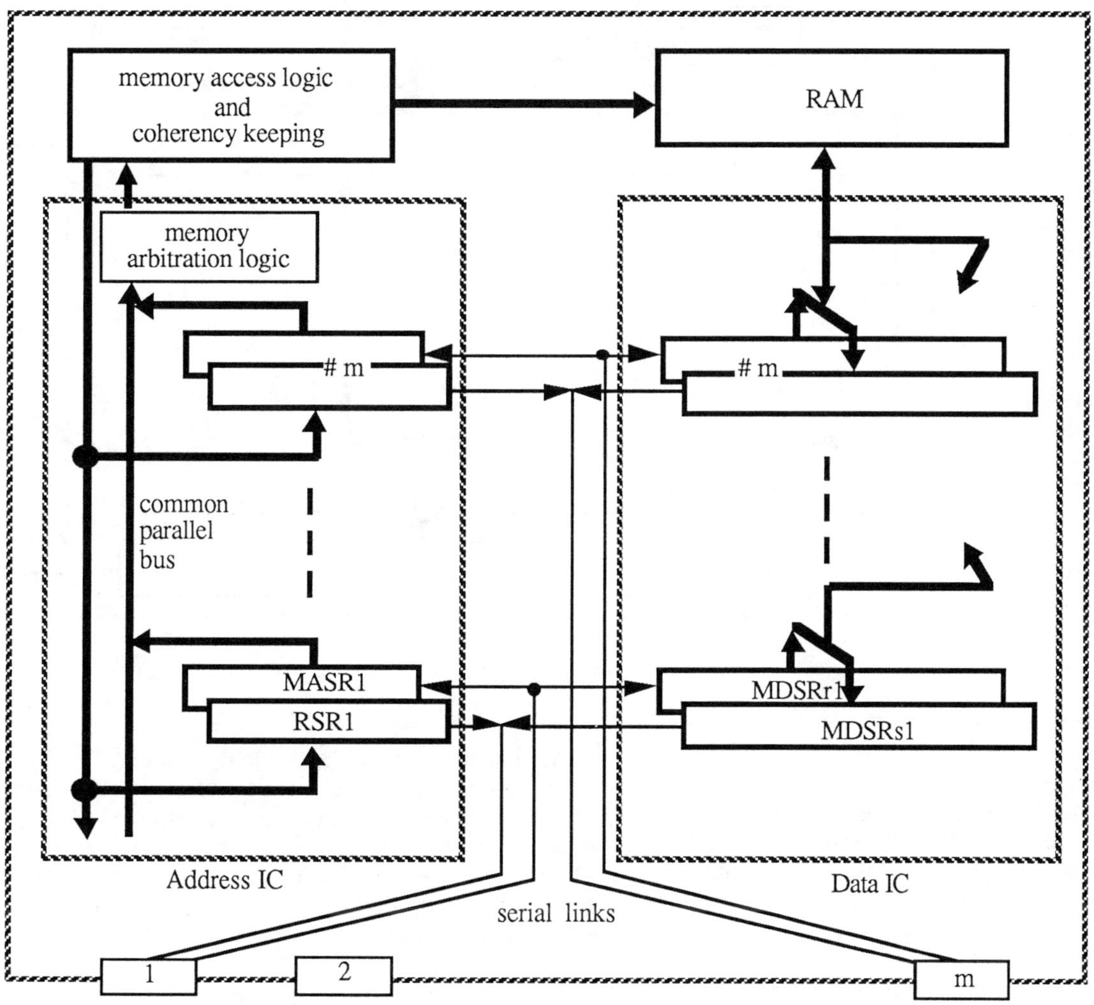

Figure 4 : general structure of a memory module

many memory modules and for scalability reasons, the IC interface chip does not handle the whole set of serial connections. At most there are as many interfaces as memory modules. All these resources, caches and interfaces, must then be connected together and the simplest manner to connect them is to consider a common local bus, as shown on Figure 3.

A new level of parallelism appears, as many requests can be in progress simultaneously in different memory modules. In this case, the control part of an interface must record the cache number and the requested block number since the return block order can be different from the request order, due to coherency wait at the memory level. Blocks in response must then be identified.

Requests can be queued in the interface, with separate queues for blocks requests and data coherency requests. This also suggests having separate busses.

The coherency bus width is at the most that of a block address size.

The data bus is larger for two reasons: first, performance, but above all, to match the serial data rate on the links: 2 Gbs means 62.5 Megawords per second (assuming 32 bit words).

The interface complexity leads to a hierarchical structure based on technology. The serial links of the interface are replaced by parallel busses which are connected to Hotrod type ICs since the HotRod uses a parallel/serial interface.

The various points studied in this section show that the processor module interface is not a difficult problem to solve. A multiprocessor with a large number of processors leads to a large number of processor modules, and fortunately to a smaller number of memory modules. As each processor module is connected to all memory modules, a processor module can therefore be equipped with 8, 16 or 32 serial interfaces. As we will see in section 6.2, these values give a very high level of performance.

On the other hand, each memory module must be connected to all processor modules and the number of connecting points makes its design more difficult.

4. LINK INTERFACE AT THE MEMORY LEVEL

Figure 1 shows that each processor module must be connected to every memory module. In fact this can be done in two distinct ways :

- the connection goes from memory module to memory module in a daisy chain manner. This solution has no drawback in the processor to memory direction (each memory module must recognize itself) if we suppose that no block requests are interleaved, which is not the case. In the memory to processor direction, the problem is more complex as each memory module is able to send a coherency request at any moment.

Moreover, in the two cases, clock recovery problems and electrical adaptation problems of the links have to be reconsidered. Rebuffering doubles the number of connecting points, which is a major drawback.

- Each memory module has an interface with every processor module. This leads to a private connection. This solution is ideal from any point of view, the main advantage probably being the electrical or optical adaptation of the links.

The connection being the only communication link between a processor module and a memory module, the latter must do the following work :

- process the address block and execute the corresponding request (read, write, coherency),
- ensure the data block transfer in each direction,
- manage state information about data blocks in order to maintain the data coherency in the various caches of the multiprocessor. This can lead to send one or more coherency messages.

These three points lead to a general structure of a memory module given by Figure 4.

As already noted, the high speed logic must be integrated into only one circuit. At the memory level, adresses and data blocks can be handled separately. Addresses are processed in an address IC and data in a data IC.

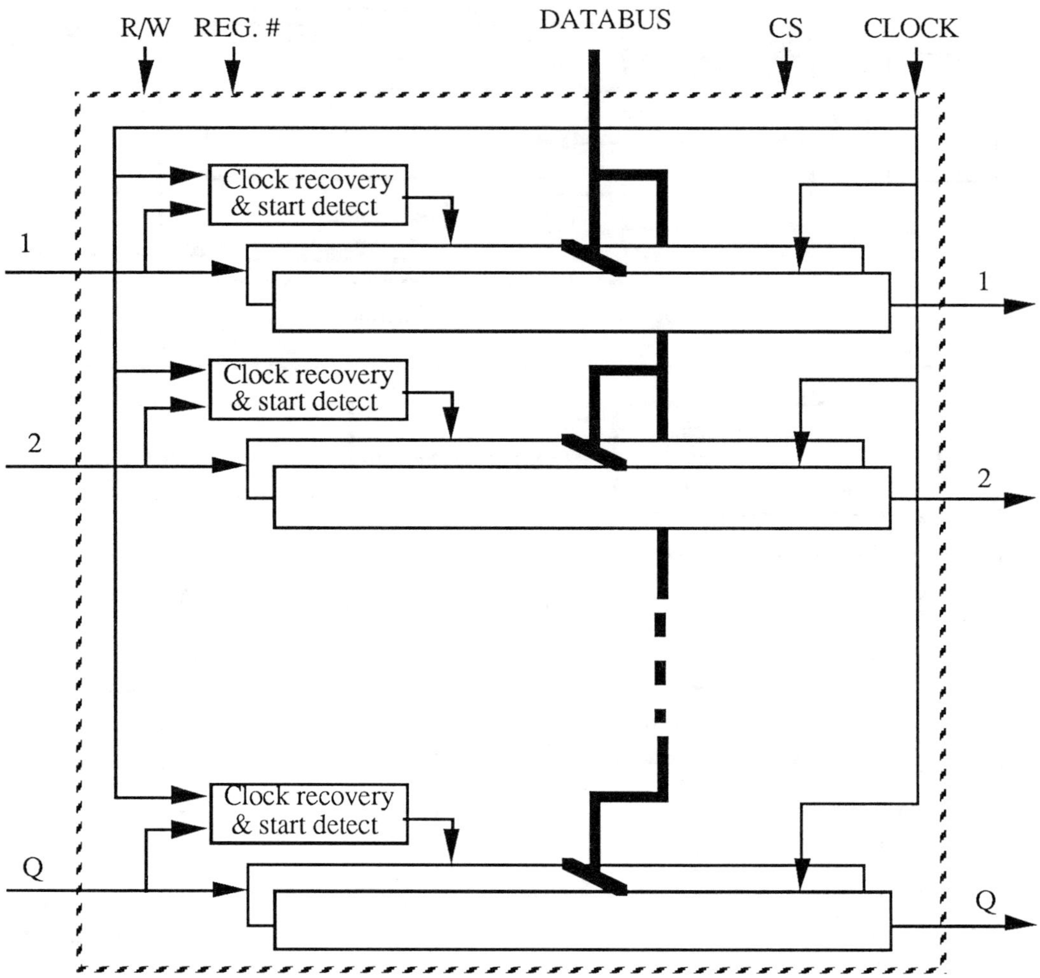

Figure 5 : general structure of a data IC

The header and the address part of a message coming from a processor module are recorded into the MASR shift register. If the message is a flush, the data part is recorded in the receive Memory Data Shift register, MDSRr. The request is then submitted through a local common address bus to arbitration logic.

The general process is the following :

- in case of a flush, the data block is written at the right place in memory from the MDSRr, the coherency state information is updated, and a free-link message is sent over the right link through the response shift register RSR.
- in case of a read or a write request, one of the two following cases can occur :

* the request can be satisfied immediately: the block is read from memory, loaded in the send Memory Data Shift Register MDSRs and immedially sent. During the read, the coherency state information is updated.

* the request must be put in a waiting state, as the updated block is not in memory. This will lead to the emission of one or more coherency messages.

We will see in paragraph 4.2 how the wait state is implemented.

- A coherency message is send over the right link through the response shift register RSR.

These points will now be studied more deeply.

4.1. DATA BLOCK PROCESSING

A block is loaded into a shift register (SR) of a block size. Two such SR are needed by each connection, one in each direction. The shift rate of 2Gbs can nowadays be implemented only in GaAs and soon in BiCMOS technologies and must, as mentioned earlier, be integrated into only one IC. The limiting factor being primarily the number of pins, a minimum number is reached if each register uses only one pin, as presented in Figure 4. This supposes that each receive register is able to recover the clock and analyse the kind of message in order to stop the shift automatically in case of a block flush. The mechanism is enabled again after the memory block write. This supposes also, in the other direction, that the data block is automatically sent after a block memory read and that the output of the send register is automatically put in a quiet state just after the last bit shift. The latter condition is due to the presence of the response register tied to the link. The send clock is common to all the send registers.

Figure 5 gives the general architecture of such a data IC.

All these mechanisms are simple to implement, and can be done by the way of control shift registers. Futhermore the structure of this SR IC is regular as each connection is identical. The loading/unloading of a data block is done sequentially through the parallel data bus, at memory speed.

The number of pins will quickly become a bottleneck with the increasing number of connections and block size. For example, a block size of 16 bytes with parity needs roughly 150 pins at the RAM side (10-20 MHz), and 64 serial connections lead to 128 pins (2GHz). Fortunately, this organization is well adapted to bit slicing, and combined with a "nibble dispatcher" (ND) a hierarchy of technology can again be considered, as shown in Figure 6.

The ND receives a flow of 4B/5B encoded nibbles. Each nibble is recorded at the given rate at the link side and sent to its corresponding slice at a rate one to nine times slower. Synchronization nibbles are sent in the same manner but the start nibble is duplicated 9 times and sent to the 9 "lower rated" links.

Each slice chip has the same characterictics as the first one, but with a rate divided by 9.

In the other direction, a simpler mechanism is needed as the nibbles can be collected synchronously at a 1/9 of the transmission rate.

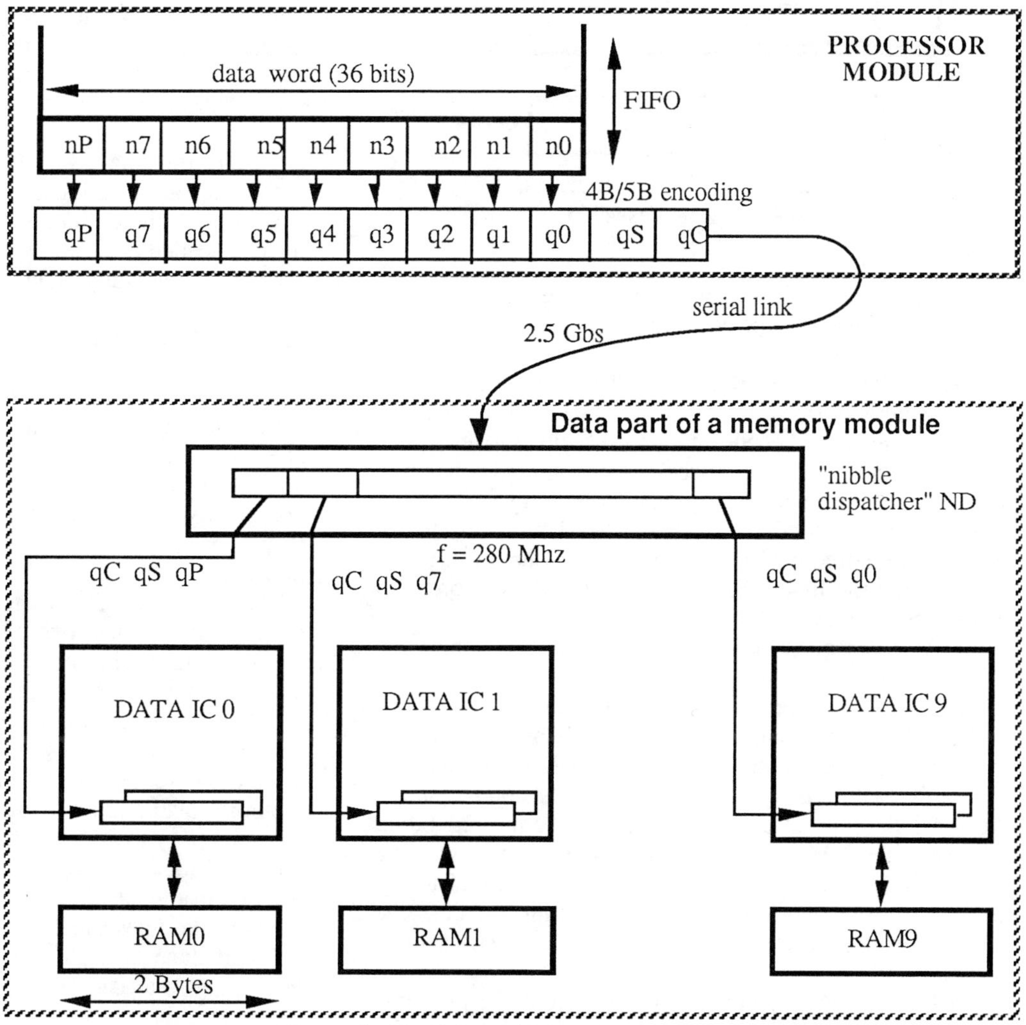

Figure 6 : bit slicing with speed slowdown

With the previously given value, a SR IC can now be made using MOS technology, and the number of pins at the memory side is about 30.

The data part of a memory module is now composed of 9

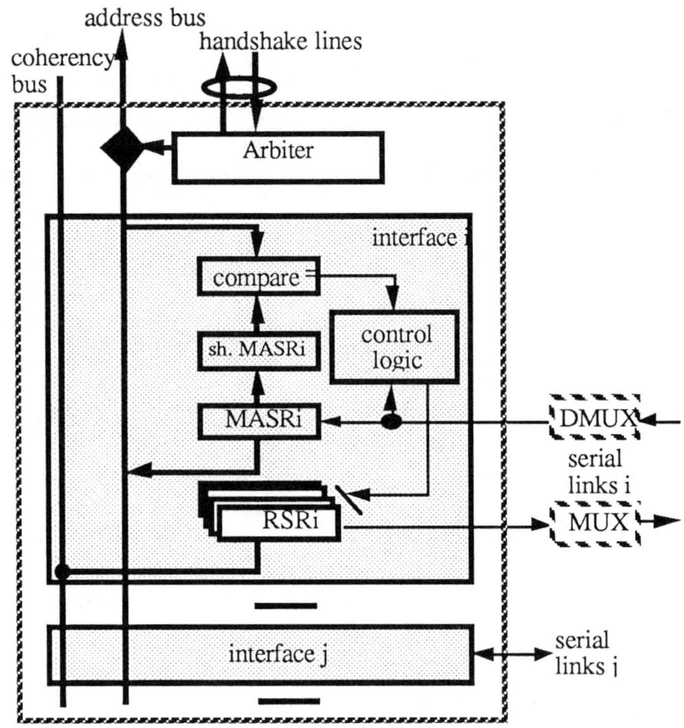

Figure 7 : the address chip

SR IC (cascadable), each connection having its own couple of IC ND and NC (nibble collector).

4.2. ADDRESS BLOCK PROCESSING

As already noticed on Figure 4, the address part is recorded in register MASR and then submitted to an arbiter which controls the memory accesses through the coherency logic. This request must be put in a waiting state if the block is not immediately available. This is done by copying the content of the MASR into a shadow MASR so as to free the link for further flush requests in order to avoid crossed waits.

Putting the request in a wait state leads to a coherency action whose aim is to force the processor owning the block to flush it, which is done through the right response register. Some time later, this flush will be observed on the local common bus. In fact the goal of the shadow MASR is double: first to free the link and second to snoop the local bus, so as to know when the requested block becomes available. As soon as possible, the waiting request is put back in the MASR and resubmitted to the arbiter. If more than one request is waiting for the same block the preceding mechanism is reactivated until completion.

Since many requests can be sent sequentially to the same processor module, the response register RSR must be replaced by a queue. If the processor module is a multiprocessor then more than one request can be put in waiting state and the shadow register must be replaced by a set of such registers.

Figure 7 presents an "address manager" IC corresponding to the preceding characteristics. This organization is well suited to a large-scale integration due to its regular structure. If the component is in a very high speed technology then each connection needs only two pins. Address and coherency busses can be multiplexed as they are the same size. Such a 200 pin IC can therefore manage 64 serial connections.

A hierarchy of technologies can also be used, as presented in Figure 6 for the data part. Such "address manager" ICs can also be associated in parallel on their busses with a two level arbitration logic. Combining these two characteristics and using the preceding described nibble dispatcher and collector leads to an association of 4 such MOS IC for 64 connections, each IC managing 16 connections with roughly 340 pins. Figure 8 gives a general structure of a memory module. Each ND IC has two output busses, one for the data part and one for the address part. This is consistent with our experiments which show that at a 300 Mhz rate, a well electricaly adapted connection is needed, the best case being a point to point link. For the same reason, each NC IC has two input busses, one for data part and one for address part.

Assuming that the IC being described have been achieved, a 64 connection point memory module could easily be designed on a single printed board. The number of ICs needed is currently practical, given the performance and packaging values considered above.

5. DATA COHERENCY

A SMM architecture implies the use of a directory based algorithm for data coherency. This directory can be distributed over the memory modules or chained on the caches themselves. The various possible options are nowadays well known although the performance level is not exactly known for an architecture with a great number of processors [CFKA90] [ASHH88]. Scalability induces one to use some kind of "Scalable Coherence Interface" [JLGS90] [AKGJ90]. In this algorithm, used block pointers are chained over the caches, the last pointer being at the memory level. In this case coherency messages travel from cache to cache:

- the owner of a dirty block is recorded at the memory level and a flush request is sent along the right link,
- the last requester of a clean block is also known at the memory level and an invalidation request is sent primarily from memory to a cache and then from cache to cache until the last block keeper has been reached. These messages travel through a memory module and as many paths as memory modules can be used.

In the case of a block flush due to a loss of place and belonging to a list, then :

- a simple chaining involves an invalidation of all successors,
- a double chaining needs to establish a link between the predecessor and the successor, which leads again to send a message through the serial links.

We can notice that if this algorithm is well adapted to a SMM architecture, other algorithms like Dir_iB can also be planned, addressed or broadcast message being sent from a

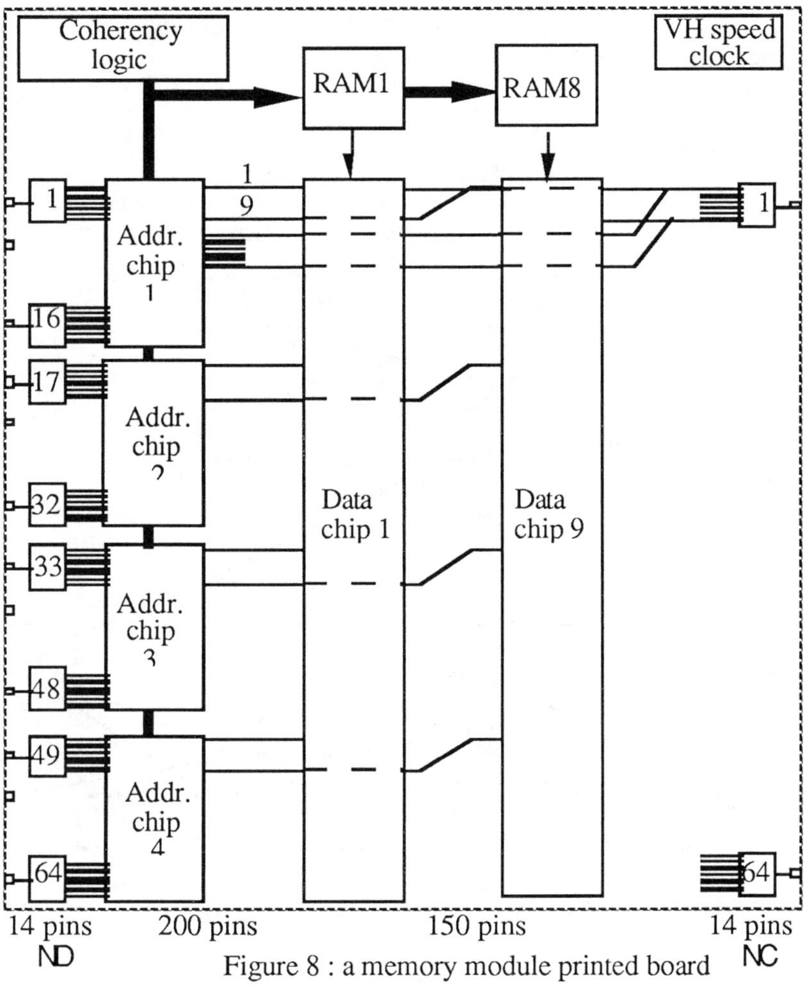

Figure 8 : a memory module printed board

memory module over the existing links or through a specialized (serial) link. The latter solution can be considered as such messages are always sent from a memory module to all caches.

6. THE BANDWIDTH

6.1. NETWORK BANDWIDTH

A connection between a processor module and a memory module that is composed of two serial links with a useful data rate of 2Gbs each leads to a theoretical bandwidth of 500 MBytes per second. Assuming an 8 memory module multiprocessor and usual address interleaving, each processor module has a network bandwidth of 4 Gigabytes. For 32 processor modules, the theoretical bandwidth of the network is about 128 gigabytes per second. This value is far beyond current shared-memory multiprocessors bandwidth.

However this bandwidth can only be reached if the memory has the same bandwidth.

6.2. MEMORY BANDWIDTH

The time spent to transfer a 16+2 bytes block size over a 2 Gbs serial link is approximately 80 nanoseconds, corresponding to the access time of standard cheap IC memories. Considering the previously described memory module, the maximum bandwidth is reached only if the memory can feed all the 64 connections i.e. 128 links at a time, which means 128 memory cycles every 80 ns !

The usual techniques to increase the memory bandwidth are:

1. use faster memories. The expected improvement can be factor of 4 to 8 using the fastest BiCMOS memory chips.
2. interleave memory banks at the memory module level. The expected improvement cannot exceed 4 to 8 also. This is due to the higher and higher memory capacity: since using a 16 Mbit chip and 8-way interleaving, a memory module has a 128 Mblock capacity which leads to a 16 Gigabyte memory capacity ! (assuming 8 memory modules and 16 byte blocks).
3. enlarge the memory front and at the same time the block size. This point must be considered with a 2-level cache hierarchy, which is out of the scope of this presentation.

A factor of 32 seems to be a fair combining the two first characteristics. In this case the memory module bandwidth is the 1/4 of the interconnection bandwidth. The spare bandwidth of the interconnection network can then be used for the message coherency traffic.

The performance level of the memory can therefore be further improved only by considering some kind of multiported serial memory IC, as suggested in [LHMR91].

It remains however that a multiprocessor with 8 previous described memory modules would have the following characteristics :

- maximum number of processor modules: 64.
- theoretical bandwidth of one processor module with its memory: 8*0.5 = 4 Gigabytes per second (1/4 usable for data transfer)
- theoretical bandwidth of the interconnection network : 64*4 = 256 Gigabytes per second.
- maximum number of serial interconnections : 64*8 = 512.

7. LATENCY TIME

The latency time can be calculated by adding all the elementary times corresponding to each following step :

t1: bus arbitration time at processor module level and request transfer time to the interface level: 50 ns.

t2: request transfer time on the serial link: 20 ns (2Gbs) + 10 ns of second order delays.

t3: waiting time at memory level (bus arbitration, coherency check): 100 ns.

t4: RAM access time: 80 ns.

t5: block transfer time, taking into account only the first word: 20 ns +10 ns of second order delays.

t6: bus arbitration time at processor module, first word cache writing time with processor by-pass: 70 ns.

The total time from t1 to t6 is about 360 ns for the first word and 420 for the whole block (20 ns access time cache), 80 ns of this time corresponding to the block transfer time. The ratio processor cycle (40 ns) to block transfer time is better than 1 :: 11, value to be compared with RPP, crossbar based multiprocessor, which is 1 :: 24 (processor cycle: 60 ns) [MMFU89] and DASH, mesh based multiprocessor, which is 1::80 to 1:: 120 (processor cycle: 40 ns) [LLGG90] [DASH91]. Moreover, for a read, t2 can be overlapped with t3 if serial address processing logic is used.

We can notice that the transfer time itself represents 1/4 to 1/5 of the total block transfer time: the latency time is probably the parameter which is the less sensitive to the increasing number of resources.

8. SCALABILITY

A processor module can be designed so that serial interfaces can be added on. The modularity could be 1, 2 or more, as the IC interface chip could manage more than one interface at a time.

Cascadability of address and data IC leads to some modularity in the design of a memory module, involving memory module with a range of 16, 32 ... serial ports.

Connections between memory modules and processor modules do not need to be done on a one to one basis: more than one serial link could bind two modules, and symmetry does not need to be respected, as there could be more links in one way, in the memory to processor direction for example, as it is more heavily loaded.

The number of memory modules must grow according to some ratio with the number of processor modules, until the upper limit given by the maximum number of serial ports of a memory module is reached. Indeed, in this case the number of processors can still be increased by multicomputer replication techniques. Replication techniques can double and double again many times the number of memory modules and the number of processor modules, each of them able to address only 1/2 and 1/4 and so on of memory space.

A replication example is given in Figure 9.

Using the characteristics of the multiprocessor decribed in section 6, the maximum multicomputer is obtained by $\log_2 8$ times replications which leads to the following characteristics :

256 memory modules, 1024 processor modules, 16K serial interconnections, 32K CPU, 8K Gbytes/second theoretical bandwidth. Each processor can then address 1/8 of the memory space and the maximum distance between processors is 4.

The resulting values are very large. This architecture combines multiprocessor and multicomputer techniques. Considering a cluster of 4 processors -or more- at each processor module level leads us to some form of massively parallel multiprocessor.

9. CONCLUSION

As a conclusion we can highlight the following points, all of them evolving the right direction with technology :

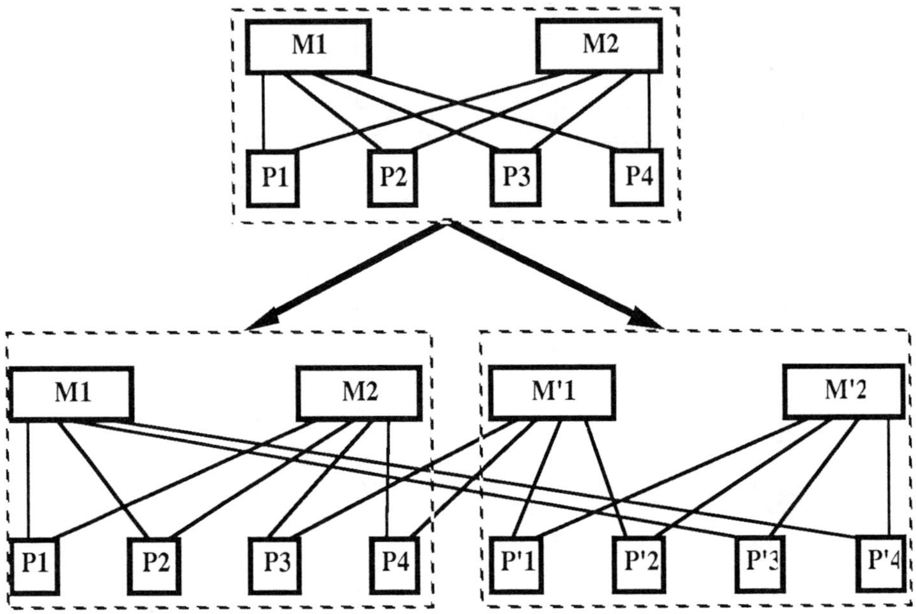

Figure 9 : one time replication of a SMM multiprocessor

-> high speed technology is needed,

-> high integration level is needed,

-> point to point serial links are needed [StCo91], well suited to optical fiber,

-> any directory data coherency algorithm actually known can be used and recent works in this important area [GuWM90] [SiHo91] can be applied to SMM,

-> latency time grows proportionally slower with the number of processors than in other networks and this point is also a major one [GHGM91],

-> spare bandwidth makes prefetching more attractive,

-> SMM architectures throw a bridge between multiprocessors and multicomputers,

-> serial link tranfer time represents 1/4 to 1/5 of the total block transfer time with a 2 Gbs data rate. The latter point must be commented on. It seems that the higher the rate is, the better the performance. This is of course true but we have just noticed that the transfer time occupies only 1/4 to 1/5 of the whole block transfer time. We have also noticed that if the transfer time is too quick, the memory has no time to feed other registers during shifting. It appears that there is an optimum data rate for a given memory technology. In our opinion, for present technologies, this optimum is between 1 and 2 Gbs. All the values considered through this presentation can be relevant today.

The M3S project being built in our laboratory is an

outline of such a SMM architecture and has been presented in [LHMS91]. Performance evaluations for a M3S architecture have been done by modeling technics and results are presented in [Elkh89][LELM89]. This kind of data transmission in a SMM environment and the needed associated serial multiported memory chips have been the object of a patent [LSME88].

REFERENCES

[AKGJ90] K. Alnaes, E.H. Kristiansen, D.B. Gustavson, D.V. James: *"Scalable Coherent Interface"*. CompEuro 90, Tel Aviv, Israel, May 7-9, 1990.

[ASHH88] A. Agarwal, R. Simoni, J. Hennessy, M. Horowitz : *"An Evaluation of Directory schemes for cache coherence"*. Proc. of the 15th ISCA, June 1988, pp. 280-289.

[CFKA90] D. Chaiken, C. Fields, K. Kurihara, A. Agarwal: *"Directory-based cache coherence in large-scale multiprocessors"*. Computer, June 90, pp. 49-58.

[DASH91] D. Lenoski, J. Laudon, K. Gharachorloo, W.D. Weber, A. Gupta, J. Hennessy, M. Horowitz, M. Lam: *"The stanford DASH Multiprocessor"*. Second workshop on scalable shared-memory multiprocessors, Toronto, May 24-25 1991.

[EgKa89] S.J. Eggers, R.H. Katz: *" The effect of sharing on the cache and bus performance of parallel programs"*. Proc. of ASPLOS-III (Architectural support for programming langage and operating systems), April 89, pp.257-270.

[Elkh89] F. Elkhlifi: *"Modélisation et évaluation de performance d'architectures multiprocesseur à mémoire multiport série"*. PhD Thesis, Université Paul Sabatier, Toulouse, July 89.

[GAZE90] Gazelle *"Hotrod chip"*, Technical note, 90.

[GHGM91] A. Gupta, J. Hennessy, K. Gharacharloo, T. Mowry and W-D. Weber: *"Comparative Evaluation of Latency Reducing and Tolerating Techniques"*. Proc. of the 18 th ISCA, Toronto, May 27-30, 1991, pp.254-263.

[GuWM90] A. Gupta, W-D Weber ,T. Mowry: *"Reducing Memory and Traffic Requirements for Scalable Directory-Based Cache Coherence Schemes"*. Proc. of the 1990 ICPP, August 1990, vol. I, pp. 312-321.

[HeJo91] J.L. Hennessy, N.P. Juoppi: *"Computer Technology and Architecture: An Evolving Interaction"*. Computer Vol. 24 num. 9, September 91, pp. 18-29.

[HoJL89] A. Hopper, A. Jones, D. Lioupis: *"Multiple vs wide shared-bus multiprocessors"*. Proc. of the 16th ISCA, June 89, pp. 300-306.

[JLGS90] D.V. James, A.T. Laundrie, S. Gjessing, G.S.Sohi : *"Scalable Coherent Interface"*. Computer, June 90, pp. 74-78.

[LELM89] D. Litaize, F. Elkhlifi, M. Lalam, A. Mzoughi, P. Sainrat, J-C Salinier: *"Multiprocessors with serial multiport memories"*. Conference on parallel architectures and languages Europe - PARLE89, Eindhoven, The Netherlands, June 12-16, 1989 pp 34-51.

[LHLM89] D.Litaize,O. Hammami, M.Lalam, A. Mzoughi, P. Sainrat: *"Multiprocessors with a serial multiport memory and a pseudo crossbar of serial links used as processor - Memory switch"*. Computer Architecture News, SIGARCH newsletter, December 1989, pp. 8-21.

[LHSP90] D.Litaize, O.Hammami, P. Sainrat, R. Pulou: *"Les liaisons série du multiprocesseur M3S : justification, problèmes techniques, solutions"*. 2ème symposium Architectures Nouvelles de Machines, Toulouse France 12-14 September 90, pp. 243-265.

[LHMR91] D.Litaize, O.Hammami, A. Mzoughi, C. Rochange, R. Pulou, P. Sainrat: *"Multiprocesseur Massivement Parallèle à Mémoire Multiport Série"*. 3ème symposium sur les Architectures Nouvelles de Machines, Palaiseau, France, june 91, pp. 155-175

[LHMS91] D.Litaize, O.Hammami, A. Mzoughi, P. Sainrat: *"The M3S project"*. Second workshop on scalable shared-memory multiprocessors, Toronto, May 24-25 1991.

[LLGG90] D. Lenoski, J. Laudon, K. Gharachotloo, A. Gupta, J. Hennessy: *"The directory based cache coherence protocol for the DASH multiprocessor"*. Proc. of the 17th ISCA, June 1990, pp. 148-159.

[LSME88] D. Litaize, JC Salinier, A. Mzoughi, F. Elkhlifi, M. Lalam, P. Sainrat: *" Système multiprocesseur, procédé d'échange d'informations mis en oeuvre et composant mémoire multiport série suceptible d'équiper ledir système"*. Patent France n° 87.18103 (14/12/87). PCT/FR 88/00608 (9/12/88).

[MMFU89] K.Murak*ami, S. Mori, A. Fukuda, T. Sueyoshi, S. Tomita: "The Kyushu University Reconfigurable Parallel Processor - Design Philosophy and architecture"*. Proc. of the 11th World Comp. congress, San Francisco, August 89, pp. 995-1000.

[Sain91] P. Sainrat: *"Réseau d'interconnexion du multiprocesseur M3S: étude et mise en oeuvre"*. PhD Thesis, Université Paul Sabatier, Toulouse, Jan. 91.

[SiHo 91] R. Simoni , M. Horowitz: *"Modeling the Performance ol Limited Pointers Directories for Cache Coherence"*. Proc. of the 18 th ISCA, Toronto, May 27-30 1991, pp. 309-318.

[StCo91] H. S. Stone, J. Cocke: *"Computer architecture in the 1990s"*. Computer Vol. 24 num. 9, September 91, pp. 30-38.

[TAXI90] AMD: *"Am7968A/Am7969A"*, technical note, 90.

[WiAn87] Wilson, Andrew W. Jr.: *"Hierarchical cache/bus architecture for shared-memory multiprocessors"*. Proc. of the 14th ISCA, June 87, pp. 244-252.

Comparative Performance Evaluation of Cache-Coherent NUMA and COMA Architectures

Per Stenström†, Truman Joe, and Anoop Gupta

Computer Systems Laboratory
Stanford University, CA 94305

Abstract

Two interesting variations of large-scale shared-memory machines that have recently emerged are *cache-coherent non-uniform-memory-access* machines (CC-NUMA) and *cache-only memory architectures* (COMA). They both have distributed main memory and use directory-based cache coherence. Unlike CC-NUMA, however, COMA machines automatically migrate and replicate data at the main-memory level in cache-line sized chunks. This paper compares the performance of these two classes of machines. We first present a qualitative model that shows that the relative performance is primarily determined by two factors: the relative magnitude of capacity misses versus coherence misses, and the granularity of data partitions in the application. We then present quantitative results using simulation studies for eight parallel applications (including all six applications from the SPLASH benchmark suite). We show that COMA's potential for performance improvement is limited to applications where data accesses by different processors are finely interleaved in memory space and, in addition, where capacity misses dominate over coherence misses. In other situations, for example where coherence misses dominate, COMA can actually perform worse than CC-NUMA due to increased miss latencies caused by its hierarchical directories. Finally, we propose a new architectural alternative, called COMA-F, that combines the advantages of both CC-NUMA and COMA.

1 Introduction

Large-scale multiprocessors with a single address-space and coherent caches offer a flexible and powerful computing environment. The single address space and coherent caches together ease the problem of data partitioning and dynamic load balancing. They also provide better support for parallelizing compilers, standard operating systems, and multiprogramming, thus enabling more flexible and effective use of the machine. Currently, many research groups are pursuing the design and construction of such multiprocessors [12, 1, 10]. As research has progressed in this area, two interesting variants have emerged, namely CC-NUMA (cache-coherent non-uniform memory access machines) and COMA (cache-only memory architectures). Examples of the CC-NUMA machines are the Stanford DASH multiprocessor [12] and the MIT Alewife machine [1], while examples of COMA machines are the Swedish Institute of Computer Science's Data Diffusion Machine (DDM) [10] and Kendall Square Research's KSR1 machine [4].

Common to both CC-NUMA and COMA machines are the features of distributed main memory, scalable interconnection network, and directory-based cache coherence. Distributed main memory and scalable interconnection networks are essential in providing the required scalable memory bandwidth, while directory-based schemes provide cache coherence without requiring broadcast and consuming only a small fraction of the system bandwidth. In contrast to CC-NUMA machines, however, in COMA the per-node main memory is converted into an enormous secondary/tertiary cache (called *attraction memory* (AM) by the DDM group) by adding tags to cache-line sized chunks in main memory. A consequence is that the location of a data item in the machine is totally decoupled from its physical address, and the data item is automatically migrated or replicated in main memory depending on the memory reference pattern.

The main advantage of the COMA machines is that they can reduce the average cache miss latency, since data are dynamically migrated and replicated at the main-memory level. However, there are also several disadvantages. First, allowing migration of data at the memory level requires a mechanism to locate the data on a miss. To avoid broadcasting such requests, current machines use a hierarchical directory structure, which increases the miss latency for global requests. Second, the coherence protocol is more complex because it needs to ensure that the last copy of a data item is not replaced in the attraction memory (main memory). Also, as compared to CC-NUMA, there is additional complexity in the design of the main-memory subsystem and in the interface to the disk subsystem.

Even though CC-NUMA and COMA machines are being built, so far no studies have been published that evaluate the performance benefits of one machine model over the other. Such a study is the focus of this paper. We note that the paper focuses on the relative performance of the two machines, and

† Per Stenström's address is Department of Computer Engineering, Lund University, P.O. Box 118, S-221 00 LUND, Sweden.

not on the hardware complexity. We do so because without a good understanding of the performance benefits, it is difficult to argue about what hardware complexity is justified.

The organization of the rest of the paper is as follows. In the next section, we begin with detailed descriptions of CC-NUMA and COMA machines. Then in Section 3, we present a qualitative model that helps predict the relative performance of applications on CC-NUMA and COMA machines. Section 4 presents the architectural assumptions and our simulation environment. It also presents the eight benchmark applications used in our study, which include all six applications from the SPLASH benchmark suite [14]. The performance results are presented in Section 5. We show that COMA's potential for performance improvement is limited to applications where data accesses by different processors are interleaved at a fine spatial granularity and, in addition, where capacity misses dominate over coherence misses. We also show that for applications which access data at a coarse granularity, CC-NUMA can perform nearly as well as a COMA by exploiting page-level placement or migration. Furthermore, when coherence misses dominate, CC-NUMA often performs better than COMA. This is due to the extra latency introduced by the hierarchical directory structure in COMA. In Section 6, we present a new architectural alternative, called COMA-F (for COMA-FLAT), that is shown to perform better than both regular CC-NUMA and COMA. We finally conclude in Section 7.

2 CC-NUMA and COMA Machines

In this section we briefly present the organization of CC-NUMA and COMA machines based on the Stanford DASH multiprocessor [12] and the Swedish Institute of Computer Science's Data Diffusion Machine (DDM) [10]. We discuss the basic architecture and the coherence protocols, directory structure and interconnection network requirements, and finally the software model presented by the architectures.

2.1 CC-NUMA Architecture

A CC-NUMA machine consists of a number of processing nodes connected through a high-bandwidth low-latency interconnection network. Each processing node consists of a high-performance processor, the associated cache, and a portion of the global shared memory. Cache coherence is maintained by a directory-based, write-invalidate cache coherence protocol. To keep all caches consistent, each processing node has a directory memory corresponding to its portion of the shared physical memory. For each memory line (aligned memory block that has the same size as a cache line), the directory memory stores identities of remote nodes caching that line. Thus, using the directory, it is possible for a node writing a location to send point-to-point messages to invalidate remote copies of the corresponding cache line. Another important attribute of the directory-based protocol is that it does not depend on any specific interconnection network topology. Therefore, any scalable network, such as a mesh, a hypercube, or a multi-stage network, can be used to connect the processing nodes.

Handling a cache miss in a CC-NUMA machine requires knowledge about the *home node* for the corresponding physical address. The home node is the processing node from whose main memory the data is allocated. (It is usually determined by the high-order bits of the physical address.) If the local node and the home node are the same, a cache miss can be serviced by main memory in the local node. Otherwise, the miss is forwarded to the *remote* home node. If the home node has a clean copy, it returns the block to the requesting cache. (We call this a 2-hop miss since it requires two network traversals — one from the requesting node to the home node, and the other back.) Otherwise, the read request is forwarded to the node that has the dirty copy. This node returns the block to the requesting node and also writes back the block to the home node. (We call this a 3-hop miss, as it takes three network traversals before the data is returned to the requesting node.)

If the block is not exclusively owned by a processor that issues a write request, a read-exclusive request is sent to the home node. The home node returns ownership and multicasts invalidation requests to any other nodes that have a copy of the block. Acknowledgments are returned directly to the issuing node so as to indicate when the write operation has completed. A write request to a dirty block is forwarded (the same way as a read request) to the node containing the dirty copy, which then returns the data.

The Stanford DASH multiprocessor [12] is an example of a CC-NUMA machine. The prototype is to consist of 16 processing nodes, each with 4 processors, for a total of 64 processors. Each processor has a 64 Kbytes first-level and a 256 Kbytes second-level cache. The interconnection network is a wormhole routed 2-D mesh network. The memory access latencies for a cache hit, local memory access, 2-hop, and 3-hop read misses are approximately 1, 30, 100, and 135 processor clocks respectively.

The CC-NUMA software model allows processes to be attached to specific processors and for data to be allocated from any specific node's main memory. However, the granularity at which data can be moved between different node's main memories (transparently to the application) is page sized chunks. We note that the allocation and movement of data between nodes may be done explicitly via code written by the application programmer, or automatically by the operating system [3]. This is in contrast to the COMA machines where such migration and replication happens automatically at the granularity of cache blocks.

2.2 COMA Architecture

Like CC-NUMA, a COMA machine consists of a number of processing nodes connected by an interconnection network. Each processing node has a high-performance processor, a cache, and a portion of the global shared memory. The difference, however, is that the memory associated with each node is augmented to act as a large cache, denoted *attraction memory* (AM) using DDM terminology [10]. Consistency among cache blocks in the AMs is maintained using a write-invalidate protocol. The AMs allow transparent migration and replication of data items to nodes where they are referenced.

In a COMA machine, the AMs constitute the only memory in the system (other than the disk subsystem). A consequence is that the location of a memory block is totally decoupled from its physical address. This creates several problems. First, when a reference misses in the local AM, a mechanism is needed to trace a copy of that block in some other node's AM. Unlike CC-NUMA, there is no notion of a home node for a block. Second, some mechanism is needed to ensure that the last copy of a block (possibly the only valid copy) is not purged.

To address the above problems and to maintain cache and memory consistency, COMA machines use a *hierarchical directory scheme* and a corresponding hierarchical interconnection network (at least logically so[1]). Each directory maintains state information about all blocks stored in the subsystem below. The state of a block is either exclusive in exactly one node or shared in several nodes. Note that directories only contain state information to reduce memory overhead; data are not stored.

Upon a read miss, a read request locates the closest node that has a copy of that block by propagating up the hierarchy until a copy in state shared or exclusive is found. At that point, it propagates down the hierarchy to a node that has the copy. The node returns the block along the same path as the request. (A directory read-modify-write needs to be done at each intermediate directory along the path, both in the forward and return directions.) Because of the hierarchical directory structure, COMA machines can exploit *combining* [7]; if a directory receives a read request to a block that is already being fetched, it does not have to send the new request up the hierarchy. When the reply comes back, both requesters are supplied the data.

A write request to an unowned block propagates up the hierarchy until a directory indicates that the copy is exclusive. This directory, the root directory, multicasts invalidation requests to all subsystems having a copy of the block and returns an acknowledgement to the issuing processor.

As stated earlier, decoupling the home location of a block from its address raises the issue of replacement in the AMs. A shared block (i.e., one with multiple copies) that is being replaced is not so difficult to handle. The system simply has to realize that there exist other copies by going up the hierarchy. Handling an exclusive block (the only copy of a block, whether in clean or dirty state) is, however, more complex since it must be transferred to another attraction memory. This is done by letting it propagate up in the hierarchy until a directory finds an empty or a shared block in its subsystem that can host the block.

Examples of COMA machines include the Swedish Institute of Computer Science's DDM machine [10] and Kendall Square Research's KSR1 machine [4]. The processing nodes in DDM are also clusters with multiple processors, as in DASH. However, the interconnect is a hierarchy of buses, in contrast to the wormhole-routed grid in DASH. In KSR1, each processing node consists of only a single processor. The interconnect consists of a hierarchy of slotted ring networks.

In summary, by allowing individual memory blocks to be migrated and replicated in attraction memories, COMA machines have the potential of reducing the number of cache misses that need to be serviced remotely. However, because of the hierarchy in COMA, latency for remote misses is usually higher (except when combining is successful); this may offset the advantages of the higher hit rates. We study these tradeoffs qualitatively in the next section.

[1]Wallach and Dally are investigating a COMA implementation based on a hierarchy embedded in a 3-dimensional mesh network [16].

3 Qualitative Comparison

In this section, we qualitatively evaluate the advantages and disadvantages of the CC-NUMA and COMA models. In particular, we focus on application data access patterns that are expected to cause one model to perform better than the other. We show that the critical parameters are the relative magnitudes of different miss types in the cache, and the spatial granularity of access to shared data. We begin with a discussion of the types of misses observed in shared-memory parallel programs, and discuss the expected miss latencies for CC-NUMA and COMA machines.

3.1 Miss Types and Expected Latencies

Since both CC-NUMA and COMA have private coherent caches, presumably of the same size, the differences in performance stem primarily because of differences in the miss latencies. In shared-memory multiprocessors that use a write-invalidate cache coherence protocol, cache misses may be classified into four types: cold misses, capacity misses, conflict misses, and coherence misses.

A *cold miss* is the result of a block being accessed by the processor for the first time. A *capacity miss* is a miss due to the finite size of the processor cache and a *conflict miss* is due to the limited associativity of the cache. For our discussion below, we do not distinguish between conflict and capacity misses since CC-NUMA and COMA respond to them in the same way. We collectively refer to them as capacity misses. A *coherence miss* (or an invalidation miss) is a miss to a block that has been referenced before, but has been written by another processor since the last time it was referenced by this processor. Coherence misses include both *false sharing misses* as well as *true sharing misses* [15]. False sharing misses result from write references to data that are not shared but happen to reside in the same cache line. True sharing misses are coherence misses that would still exist even if the block size were one access unit. They represent true communication between the multiple processes in the application.

We now investigate how the two models respond to cache misses of different types. Beginning with cold misses, we expect the average miss penalty to be higher for COMA, assuming that data is distributed among the main memory modules in the same way. The reason is simply that cold misses that are not serviced locally have to traverse the directory and network hierarchy in COMA. The only reason for a shorter latency for COMA would be if combining worked particularly well for an application.

For coherence misses, we again expect COMA to have higher miss latencies as compared to CC-NUMA. The reason is that the data is guaranteed not to be in the local attraction memory for COMA, and therefore it will need to traverse the directory hierarchy.[2] In contrast to CC-NUMA, the latency for COMA can, of course, be shortened if combining is successful, or if the communication is localized in the hierarchy.

Finally, for capacity misses, we expect to see shorter miss latencies for COMA. Most such misses are expected to hit in the local attraction memory since it is extremely large and

[2]We assume one processor per node. If several processors share the same AM (or local memory), a coherence miss can sometimes be serviced locally.

organized as a cache. In contrast, in CC-NUMA, unless data referenced by a processor are carefully allocated to local main memory, there is a high likelihood that a capacity miss will have to be serviced by a remote node.

In summary, since there are some kinds of misses that are serviced with lower latency by COMA and others that are serviced with lower latency by CC-NUMA, the relative performance of an application on COMA or CC-NUMA will depend on what kinds of misses dominate.

3.2 Application Performance

In this subsection, we classify applications based on their data access patterns, and the resulting cache miss behavior, to evaluate the relative advantages and disadvantages of COMA and CC-NUMA. A summary of this classification is presented in Figure 1. As illustrations, we use many applications that we evaluate experimentally in Section 5.

On the left of the tree in Figure 1, we group all applications that exhibit low cache miss-rates. Linear algebra applications that can be blocked, for example, fall into this category [11]. Other applications where computation grows at a much faster rate than the data set size, e.g., the $O(N^2)$ algorithm used to compute interaction between molecules in the Water application [14], often also fall into this category. In such cases, since the data sets are quite small, capacity misses are few and the miss penalty has only a small impact on performance. Overall, for these applications that exhibit a low miss rate, CC-NUMA and COMA should perform about the same.

Looking at the right portion of the tree, for applications that exhibit moderate to high miss rates, we differentiate between applications where coherence misses dominate and those where capacity misses dominate. Focusing first on the former, we note that this class of applications is not that unusual. High coherence misses can arise because an application programmer (or compiler) may not have done a very good job of scheduling tasks or partitioning data, or because the cache line size is too large causing false sharing, or because solving the problem actually requires such communication to happen. Usually, all three factors are involved to varying degrees. In all of these cases, CC-NUMA is expected to do better than COMA because the remote misses take a shorter time to service. As we will show in Section 5, even when very small processor caches are used (thus increasing the magnitude of capacity misses), at least half of the applications in our study fall into this category.

The situation where COMA has a potential performance advantage is when the majority of cache misses are capacity misses. Almost all such misses get serviced by the local attraction memory in COMA, in contrast to CC-NUMA where they may have to go to a remote node. CC-NUMA can deliver good performance only if a majority of the capacity misses are serviced by local main memory.

We believe that it is possible for CC-NUMA machines to get high hit rates in local memory for many applications that access data in a "coarse-grained" manner. By coarse grained, we mean applications where large chunks of data (greater than page size) are primarily accessed by one process in the program for significant periods of time. For example, many scientific applications where large data arrays are statically partitioned among the processes fall into this class. A specific example is the Cholesky sparse factorization algorithm that we evaluate later in the paper. In the Cholesky application, contiguous columns with similar non-zero structure (called supernodes) are assigned to various processors. If the placement is done right for such applications, the local memory hit rates can be very high.

Even if the locus of accesses to these large data chunks changes from one process to another over time, automatic replication and migration algorithms implemented in the operating system (possibly with hardware support) can ensure high hit rates in local memory for CC-NUMA. In fact, we believe that an interesting way to think of a CC-NUMA machine is as a COMA machine where the line size for the main-memory cache is the page size, which is not unreasonable since main memory is very large, and where this main-memory cache is managed in software. The latter is also not an unreasonable policy decision because the very-large line size helps hide the overheads.

In applications where many small objects that are collocated on a page are accessed in an interleaved manner by processes, page-level placement/migration obviously can not ensure high local hit-rates. An example is the Barnes-Hut application for simulating the interaction of N-body problems (discussed in Section 5). In this application multiple bodies that are accessed by several processors reside on a single page and, as a result, page placement does not help CC-NUMA.

In summary, we expect the relative performance of CC-NUMA and COMA to be similar if the misses are few. When the miss rate is high, we expect CC-NUMA to perform better than COMA if coherence misses dominate; CC-NUMA to perform similar to COMA if the capacity misses dominate but the data usage is coarse grained; and finally, COMA to perform better than CC-NUMA if capacity misses dominate and data usage is fine grained.

4 Experimental Methodology

This section presents the simulation environment, the architectural models, and the benchmark applications we use to make a quantitative comparison between CC-NUMA and COMA.

4.1 Simulation Environment

We use a simulated multiprocessor environment to study the behavior of applications under CC-NUMA and COMA. The simulation environment consists of two parts: (i) a functional simulator that executes the parallel applications and (ii) the two architectural simulators.

The functional simulator is based on Tango [5]. The Tango system takes a parallel application program and interleaves the execution of its processes on a uniprocessor to simulate a multiprocessor. This is achieved by associating a virtual timer with each process of the application and by always running the process with the lowest virtual time first. By letting the architectural simulator update the virtual timers according to the access time of each memory reference, a correct interleaving of all memory references is maintained. The architectural simulator takes care of references to shared data; instruction fetches and private data references are assumed to always hit in the processor cache.

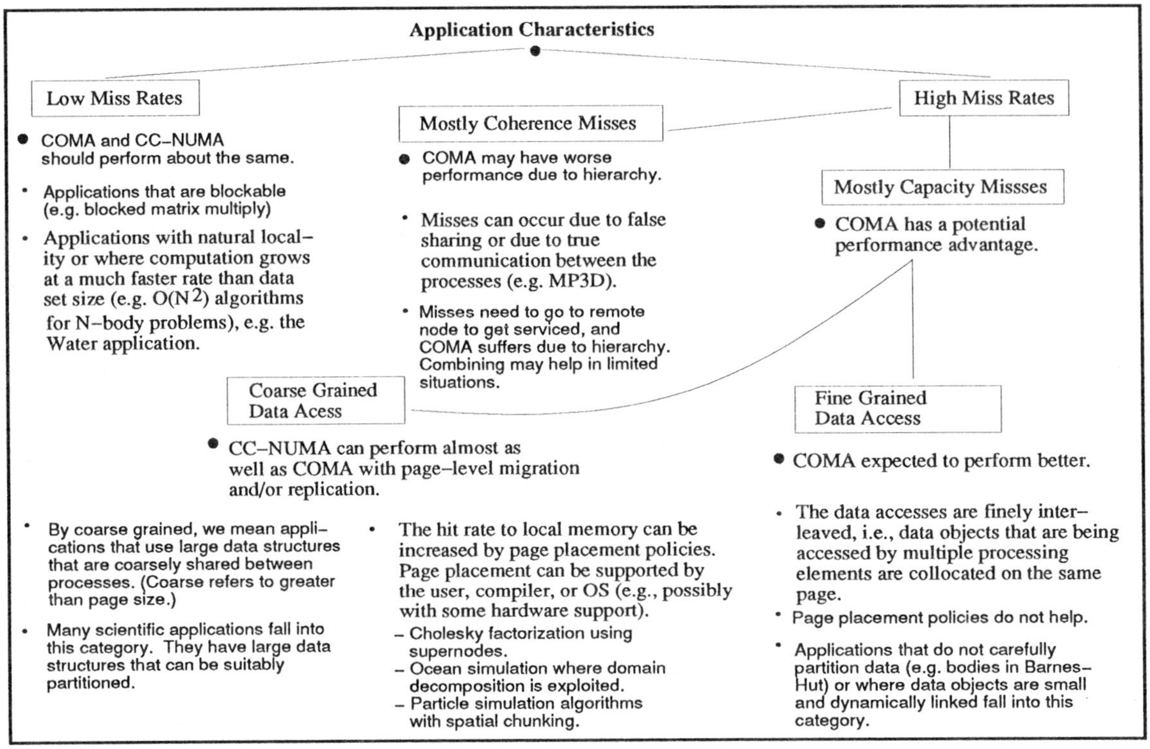

Figure 1: Prediction of relative performance between CC-NUMA and COMA based on relative frequency of cache miss types and application data access pattern.

4.2 Architecture Simulators

Both architectures consist of a number of processing nodes connected via low-latency networks. In our simulations we assume a 16 processor configuration, with one processor per processing node. (Figure 2(a) shows the organization of the processing node.) We assume a cache line size of 16 bytes. In the default configurations, we use a processor cache size of 4 Kbytes, and in the case of COMA, infinite attraction memories. For COMA we assume a branching factor of 4, implying a two-level hierarchy.

The reasons for choosing this rather small default processor cache size are several. First, since the simulations are quite slow, the data sets used by our applications are smaller than what we may use on a real machine. As a result, if we were to use full-size caches (say 256 Kbytes), then for some of the applications all of the data would fit into the caches and we would not get any capacity misses. This would take away all of the advantages of the COMA model, and the results would obviously not be interesting. Second, by using very small cache sizes, we favor the COMA model, and our goal is to see whether there are situations where CC-NUMA can still do better. Third, 4 Kbytes is only the default, and we also present results for larger cache sizes. As for use of infinite attraction memories, our choice was motivated by the observation that the capacity miss-rates are expected to be extremely small for the attraction memories. As a result, the complexity of modeling finite sized attraction memories did not seem justified.

We now focus on the latency of cache misses in CC-NUMA and COMA. To do this in a consistent manner, we have defined a common set of primitive operations that are used to

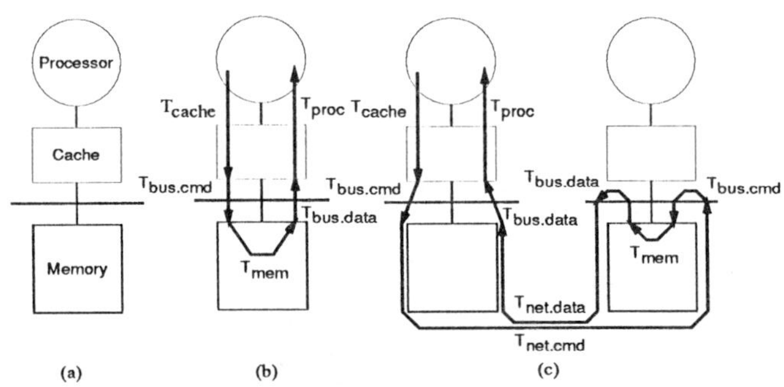

Figure 2: Node organization (a) and latency calculations for local and remote misses for CC-NUMA (b) and (c).

construct protocol transactions for both architectures. We can then choose latency values for these operations and use them to evaluate the latency of memory operations. In the following subsections, we describe reference latencies for the two architectures in terms of these primitive operations. Table 1, located at the end of this section, summarizes these primitive operations and lists the default latency numbers, assuming a processor clock rate of 100 MHz.

4.2.1 CC-NUMA Latencies

For CC-NUMA, a load request that hits in the cache incurs a latency of a cache access, T_{cache}. For misses, the processor is stalled for the full service latency of the load request.

In Figure 2(b) we depict the memory latency for a load

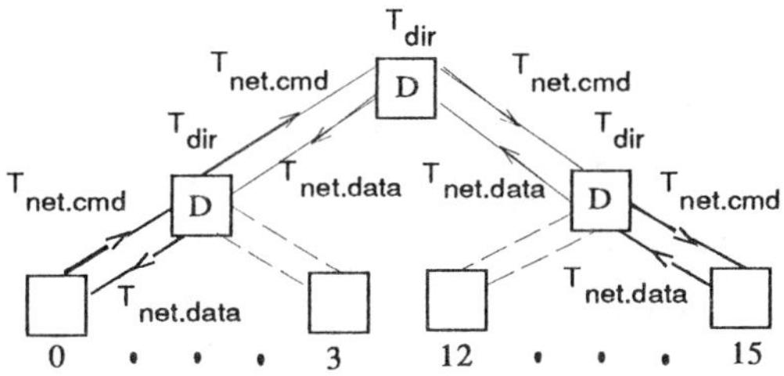

Figure 3: Latency model for global read requests in COMA.

request that hits in the local memory. The load first checks the cache (T_{cache}), it then arbitrates for the local bus and places the request onto the bus ($T_{bus.cmd}$), it then accesses memory (T_{mem}), the data is placed on the local bus ($T_{bus.data}$), and finally the cache loads data from the bus and restarts the processor (T_{proc}).[3] Similarly, in Figure 2(c) we show the latency for a load request to a shared block whose home is not the local node. $T_{net.cmd}$ is the network latency to send the load request to the home node, and $T_{net.data}$ is the network latency for the return data packet. If the block is dirty in a node other than the home node, an additional latency that consists of another network traversal and node memory access is needed.

Stores are handled according to the weakly ordered consistency model [6] by a write buffer which sits between the processor and the cache. Hence, the processor is not stalled on a store request. However, on a synchronization request, the processor is stalled until all pending invalidation acknowledgements have been received.

The default network latency numbers assume a 4×4 wormhole-routed synchronous mesh clocked at 100 MHz with 16-bit wide links.

4.2.2 COMA Latencies

For COMA, the processor cache hit latency is the same as CC-NUMA. The latency for a hit in the attraction memory is the same as a request serviced by local memory in CC-NUMA. For requests that need to go to a remote processing node, we illustrate the latency using a simple example. Figure 3 shows a request made by processor 0 and serviced by processor 15. The latency consists of a check in processor cache (T_{cache}); request issue on local bus ($T_{bus.cmd}$); check in local attraction memory (T_{mem}); traversal up through the hierarchy ($T_{net.cmd} + T_{dir}$ at each level); traversal down the hierarchy ($T_{net.cmd} + T_{dir}$ at each level); lookup in the memory of processor 15 ($T_{bus.cmd} + T_{mem} + T_{bus.data}$); traversal back up the hierarchy ($T_{net.data} + T_{dir}$ at each level); traversal down to the requesting node ($T_{net.data} + T_{dir}$ at each level); and finally back to the processor ($T_{bus.data} + T_{proc}$). Latency for other requests can be similarly derived. The protocol follows that used by DDM [10], assuming infinite write buffers and a weakly ordered consistency model. The effects of request combining in the hierarchy are also modeled in our simulator. However, we do not model contention at any of the buses or directories.

A hierarchical network with point-to-point links with a width of 32-bits and synchronous data transfers is assumed. Since a hierarchical layout makes it difficult to achieve high clock rates (unlike a mesh), we assume that the links are clocked at 50 MHz yielding the latency numbers $T_{net.cmd} = 4$ and $T_{net.data} = 12$ pclocks, respectively.

[3] Note: The latency for $T_{bus.data}$ is only one bus cycle (2 pclocks) in Figure 2(b) because the return of data overlaps with the latency for processor restart T_{proc}.

Table 1: Default latencies for primitive operations in processor clock cycles (1 pclock $\approx$ 10 ns).

Primitive Operation	Parameter	Latency (pclocks)
Cache Access Time	T_{cache}	1
Cache Fill and Restart	T_{proc}	6
Local Bus Request Time	$T_{bus.cmd}$	4
Local Bus Reply Time	$T_{bus.data}$	2
Com. Net. Latency (CC-NUMA)	$T_{net.cmd}$	12
Data Net. Latency (CC-NUMA)	$T_{net.data}$	20
Com. Net. Latency (COMA)	$T_{net.cmd}$	4
Data Net. Latency (COMA)	$T_{net.data}$	12
Memory and AM	T_{mem}	20
Directory Update (rd-mod-wr)	T_{dir}	20

Table 2: Default latencies for various read operations.

Read Operation	Latency (pclocks)
Cache Hit	1
Fill from Local Node	33
2-hop Remote Fill (CC-NUMA)	71
3-hop Remote Fill (CC-NUMA)	109
1-level Remote Fill (COMA)	131
2-level Remote Fill (COMA)	243

In Table 2, we show the default latencies for read requests satisfied at various levels in the memory hierarchy, based on the default latencies for the primitive operations from Table 1. Note that these are just default latencies. We will present results for other architectural assumptions as well in Section 5.6.

4.3 Benchmark Programs

To understand the relative performance benefits of CC-NUMA and COMA we use a variety of scientific and engineering applications, including all six SPLASH benchmarks [14]. A summary of the eight applications that we use is given in Table 3.

The data sets used for our eight applications are as follows. MP3D was run with 10K particles for 10 time steps. PTHOR was run with the RISC circuit for 5000 time steps with incremental deadlock detection turned on. LocusRoute used the circuit Primary1.grin which has 1266 wires and a 481x18 cost array. Water was run with 288 molecules for 4 time steps. Cholesky was run using the matrix bcsstk14 from the Boeing-Harwell benchmark matrices, and it has 1806 equations and 61648 non-zeroes. LU was run on a 200×200 random matrix. Barnes-Hut [13] was run using 2048 bodies in a plummer distribution simulated for 10 time steps with a tolerance of 1.0. Finally, Ocean was run with a 98×98 grid with a convergence tolerance of 10^{-7} and w set to 1.15. Statistics acquisition is

Table 3: Benchmark programs.

Benchmark	Description
MP3D	Particle-based wind tunnel simulation
PTHOR	Distributed-time logic simulation
LocusRoute	VLSI standard cell router
Water	Molecular dynamics code: Water
Cholesky	Cholesky factorization of sparse matrix
LU	LU decomposition of dense matrix
Barnes-Hut	N-body problem solver O(NlogN)
Ocean	Ocean basin simulation

started when the parallel section of the application is entered (see SPLASH report [14]), because the initialization part is expected to be negligible for full-scale runs.

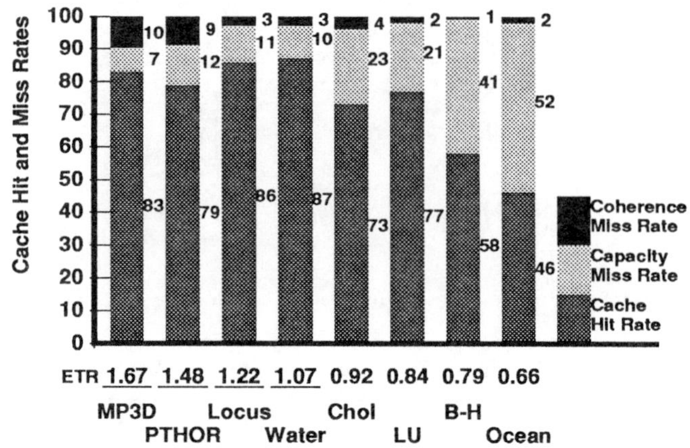

Figure 4: Cache hit-rate, capacity miss-rate, and coherence miss-rate assuming 4 Kbyte caches. ETR is the execution time for COMA divided by the execution time for CC-NUMA.

5 Quantitative Evaluation

In this section, we provide experimental results that show the advantages and disadvantages of CC-NUMA and COMA. We begin by investigating how the relative frequency of capacity and coherence misses impacts the relative performance of CC-NUMA and COMA. Then in Sections 5.2, 5.3, and 5.4, we explore how page migration and initial page placement can help CC-NUMA reduce the penalty of capacity misses, thus improving its performance. Finally, in Sections 5.5 and 5.6, we study how our results are affected by variations in architectural parameters.

5.1 Performance of CC-NUMA and COMA

Since performance of CC-NUMA and COMA machines is closely tied to the cache hit-rate achieved and the types of cache misses incurred, in Figure 4 we present relevant statistics. For each application, the bottom dark-gray section gives the cache hit-rate, the middle light-gray section gives the capacity miss-rate, and the top black section gives the coherence miss-rate. We do not show cold miss-rates separately because they are very small (0.9% for Cholesky, 0.26% for LocusRoute, and less than 0.1% for the remaining applications), and in Figure 4 they are lumped with capacity misses.

As can be seen from Figure 4, there is a large variation in the relative magnitude of capacity and coherence misses across the applications; for example, while coherence misses dominate in MP3D, capacity misses dominate in Ocean. To see how this impacts the relative performance of CC-NUMA and COMA, we also measured the *node hit-rate* for the applications, that is, the fraction of references that get serviced by the cache or the local memory. Although we do not present these data here directly, for COMA machines, the node hit-rate is essentially the cache hit-rate plus the capacity miss-rate, since all capacity misses are serviced by the local attraction memory. In contrast, for CC-NUMA, the node hit-rate is highly dependent on the way in which the data are distributed among the processing nodes. If we assume that the data pages are distributed randomly or in a round-robin manner (as default in this paper, we use the round-robin strategy), then node hit-rate for CC-NUMA is expected to be the cache hit-rate plus the capacity miss-rate divided by the number of processors. Given that the number of processors is quite large, 16 in our case, the node hit-rate for CC-NUMA is approximately the same as the cache hit-rate. Thus the difference in the node hit-rate between COMA and CC-NUMA is roughly the middle light-gray section in Figure 4.

The question now becomes how the differences in node hit-rate and node miss penalty for CC-NUMA and COMA impact their relative performance. We use *execution time ratio* (ETR) of COMA to CC-NUMA as a measure of the relative performance. Thus ETR > 1 implies that CC-NUMA is performing better than COMA. In Figure 4, we show the ETR beneath the hit/miss rate bar for each application. As expected, for applications where the coherence miss-rate is a significant part of the overall miss-rate (MP3D, PTHOR, LocusRoute, and Water), COMA exhibits worse performance than CC-NUMA due to the higher node miss penalty incurred by COMA. For the other four applications (Cholesky, LU, Barnes-Hut, and Ocean), the capacity miss-rate dominates the overall miss-rate, and as expected, COMA shows better performance. We also observe that the overall swing in the relative performance is quite large; while CC-NUMA does 67% better than COMA for MP3D, COMA does 52% better than CC-NUMA for Ocean.

To study whether combining is playing an important role in the higher performance of COMA, we measured the percentage of node misses that get combined in the hierarchical directory structure. Combining turned out to be significant in one case only — in LU, 47% of all remote requests get combined. This is because the pivot column is read by all processors as soon as all modifications to it have been completed. Except for the LU application, combining was of little help in reducing the node miss penalty as incurred by the hierarchical directory structure in COMA — in Barnes-Hut, 6% of remote requests get combined, and for all remaining applications, less than 1% of remote requests get combined.

To summarize, we have shown that the relative frequency of capacity and coherence misses has a first order effect on the relative performance of CC-NUMA and COMA. We observed that four of the eight applications perform worse on COMA because of the coherence miss penalty associated with the hierarchical network. We also observed that request combining

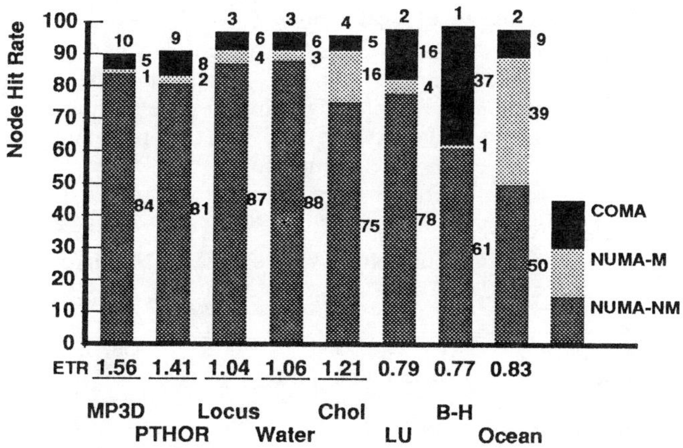

Figure 5: Node hit-rate for CC-NUMA with no migration (NUMA-NM), CC-NUMA with migration (NUMA-M), and COMA assuming 4 Kbytes pages. ETR is the execution time for COMA divided by the execution for NUMA-M.

has only a small impact in hiding the higher network latency incurred by the hierarchy in COMA.

5.2 CC-NUMA: Page Migration

As stated in Section 3, if large chunks of data (greater than page size) are primarily accessed by one process in the program for significant periods of time, intelligent page migration and replication algorithms can help CC-NUMA reduce the penalty for capacity misses. In this subsection, we focus on the performance gains for CC-NUMA if the operating systems performed page migration. We consider a fairly aggressive competitive page migration algorithm proposed by Black et al. [2]. Note, our purpose here is to explore the performance potential of page migration rather than advocating the use of this particular page migration algorithm.

Our migration algorithm associates N counters with each page, given N processing nodes. A remote access to a page increments the corresponding counter and decrements some other randomly chosen counter. When a counter exceeds twice the migration cost (measured in units of remote access cost), the page is migrated to the corresponding node. We have estimated the software overhead of migration by examining the operating system code associated with page transfers. It includes invocation of the page management software (800 pclocks); invalidation of all TLB entries for the page ($300+40n$ pclocks, assuming n processors have TLB entries); and finally, migration of the page ($T_{mem}P/B$, where P is the page size and $B = 16$ is the block size). We also assume that the page is blocked from being accessed while it is being moved.

To see how well page migration manages to improve the node hit-rate for CC-NUMA, in Figure 5 we show the node hit-rate for CC-NUMA with no page migration (NUMA-NM), CC-NUMA with page migration (NUMA-M), and COMA assuming 4 Kbyte pages. The number on top of each bar represents the coherence miss-rate. We see that the node hit-rate improves significantly for Cholesky and Ocean for NUMA-M, since data usage in both applications is coarse grained. The Cholesky application works with groups of contiguous columns, called supernodes, that are often larger than a page. The Ocean application works with arrays of data objects that are coarsely partitioned and assigned to each processor in chunks which are typically larger than 4 Kbytes.

Table 4: Node hit-rate and execution time for NUMA-M (with different page sizes) relative to NUMA-NM (with 4Kbyte pages).

Page Size	LU Node HR	LU Rel. Exec.	LU Mig. Count	Ocean Node HR	Ocean Rel. Exec.	Ocean Mig. Count
NUMA-NM	78	1.00	–	50	1.00	–
NUMA-M 4K	82	1.06	2.7K	89	0.79	6.6K
NUMA-M 2K	86	1.02	4.6K	93	0.68	6.6K
NUMA-M 1K	89	0.97	3.8K	96	0.64	4.7K
NUMA-M .5K	90	0.93	4.0K	96	0.66	7.8K
COMA	98	0.84	–	98	0.66	–

Finally, to show the overall benefits of page migration, we present the execution time ratio (ETR) of COMA to NUMA-M beneath each bar in Figure 5. The four applications where previously NUMA-NM did better than COMA (MP3D, PTHOR, LocusRoute, and Water), NUMA-M continues to do better than COMA. The performance advantage is, however, slightly smaller now — in these applications the software overhead of migration is slightly larger than the benefits. However, for Cholesky, where previously NUMA-NM did worse than COMA (see Figure 4), NUMA-M does significantly better than COMA (ETR = 1.21). For Ocean, NUMA-M substantially decreases the performance advantage of COMA than before. For LU and Barnes-Hut the performance is essentially unchanged between NUMA-NM and NUMA-M. We speculate that one reason why the gains are small is that we have been using small data sets for our applications. To study the effects of larger data sets, we consider page size variations next.

5.3 Page Migration: Impact of Page Size

As stated in Section 4, the data set size we use for the applications is smaller than what we may use on real machines. Consequently, for applications that use coarse data partitioning, we expect data chunks to be larger for full-sized problems. For example, as matrix size is increased for LU, the columns will get larger. In this section, we indirectly study the performance gains from migration for larger data sets by instead considering smaller page sizes (512b, 1K, and 2K pages). Due to space limitations, we only present results for LU and Ocean. These two are among the three applications that are currently doing worse under COMA; the results for Barnes-Hut, the third application, are not expected to change with page size.

Table 4 shows the node hit-rate and the execution time relative to NUMA-NM (4 Kbyte pages) for various page sizes for LU and Ocean. We see that the node hit-rate increases as the page size is decreased. The explanation is that as the page size is decreased, the data partitions in these applications start becoming larger than the pages. As a result, pages are primarily referenced by only a single processor, and quickly migrate to that processor. In contrast, with larger pages there is false sharing with multiple processors referencing a page, and the migration algorithm can not satisfy all referencing processors. Responding to increasing node hit-rates, execution times go down as the page size is reduced. For 512 byte pages, the difference between the performance of NUMA-M and COMA is less than 10% for LU and none for Ocean.

For Ocean, it is interesting to note that the minimum execution time occurs for 1 Kbyte pages and not for 512 byte pages. The reason is simply the overhead due to page migrations. To understand this, we also show the number of migrations that occur for a given page size in Table 4. For Ocean, the number of migrations follows a U-shaped curve. For page sizes much larger than data objects, we have many migrations because of false sharing. For page sizes much smaller than data objects, we have many migrations because bringing each object closer takes multiple page migrations. For LU, it is interesting to note that the node hit-rates for NUMA-M never reach close to that achieved by COMA. The reason is that columns in the matrix do not occupy an integer number of pages. Since successive columns are assigned to different processors, the migration algorithm never succeeds in totally satisfying all processors. In contrast, COMA with its 32-byte memory blocks does very well in bringing data close to the processors.

To summarize, we see that for the scaled down problems used in this paper, migration with smaller page sizes is quite effective. In turn, the results also indicate that for full-sized problems, we are likely to be able to get good performance while using migration with regular sized pages. Of course, page migration is not expected to work for all applications. For applications such as Barnes-Hut, where data chunks are much smaller than the page size, the migration overheads are likely to exceed the benefits.

5.4 CC-NUMA: Benefits from Initial Placement

A disadvantage of using page migration algorithms is that they can require substantial hardware and software support. An alternative is to let the compiler/programmer spend some effort in partitioning the data set and in placing the pages so as to improve the local memory hit-rate. To study the benefits of initial placement, without doing the placement ourselves, we adopted the following scheme. We evaluated the performance of the applications using the same page migration algorithm as in the last subsection, but with only a single migration allowed for each page. In Table 5, we show the node hit-rate, the execution time ratio, and the number of migrations for LU and Ocean under this scheme (NUMA-I) with various page sizes. (The reasons for considering only LU and Ocean are the same as in the previous subsection.)

First, we note that the node hit-rate increases as the page size is reduced. This is what we expect since false sharing of pages is reduced. Second, execution time also drops as the page size goes down. Third, looking at the number of migrations, the general trend is that the migration count goes up as page size is decreased. The reason is that twice as many pages must be migrated when the page size is reduced by a factor of two.

Comparing the relative performance of NUMA-I and NUMA-M, we see that LU does significantly better with single migrations than with multiple migrations (see Table 4), in fact, even better than COMA with 512 byte pages. The reason is that we have significantly reduced the number of page migrations (e.g., down from 2.7K to 135 migrations for 4 Kbyte pages), thus reducing the software overhead of migration. When multiple migrations are allowed, a page in LU may thrash back-and-forth between the various processors that have columns allocated on that page, without really improving the overall hit-rate in local memory.

For Ocean, the performance for single versus multiple page migrations is essentially the same. Although the node hit-rate is lower when only a single migration per page is allowed, this is compensated by the fact that there are fewer page migrations and hence lower software overhead.

Table 5: Node hit-rate and execution time for CC-NUMA with single page migration (NUMA-I) relative to NUMA-NM for various page sizes.

Model	LU			Ocean		
	Node HR	Rel. Exec	Mig. Count	Node HR	Rel. Exec	Mig. Count
NUMA-NM	78	1.00	–	50	1.00	–
NUMA-I 4K	83	0.96	135	87	0.74	581
NUMA-I 2K	87	0.88	270	89	0.66	1091
NUMA-I 1K	90	0.87	511	95	0.62	2218
NUMA-I .5K	91	0.79	948	94	0.64	4250
COMA	98	0.84	–	98	0.66	–

In summary, we show that initial placement manages to eliminate most performance differences between CC-NUMA and COMA for LU and Ocean. (All other applications, with the exception of Barnes-Hut, already do quite well with CC-NUMA.) Of course, proper intial placement requires extra effort from the compiler/programmer, and this must be traded off against the higher implementation complexity of COMA. COMA, however, is expected to be more responsive to dynamically changing workloads (e.g., multiprogrammed workloads).

5.5 Impact of Cache Size Variations

All experiments so far have been based on 4 Kbyte caches. In this subsection we study how the relative frequency of capacity and coherence misses changes as the cache size is increased, while keeping the problem size fixed.

An important effect of increasing the cache size is that while the capacity misses go down, the coherence misses remain the same. As a result, with larger caches, we expect coherence misses to start dominating, thus making the relative performance of CC-NUMA better than COMA. In Table 6 we show this data for the four applications (Cholesky, LU, Barnes-Hut, and Ocean) that did worse on CC-NUMA than COMA in Section 5.1.

As the cache size is increased, we clearly see that the ca-

Table 6: Capacity miss-rate (on left) and execution time ratio of COMA versus NUMA-NM (on right) for various cache sizes. The bottom line of the Table shows the coherence miss-rate for the applications.

Cache Size	Cholesky	LU	B-H	Ocean
4 K	23/0.92	21/0.84	41/0.79	52/0.66
16 K	6/1.52	8/1.08	20/0.89	28/0.79
64 K	3/1.58	3/1.35	5/1.01	15/0.91
Coher. MR	4	2	1	2

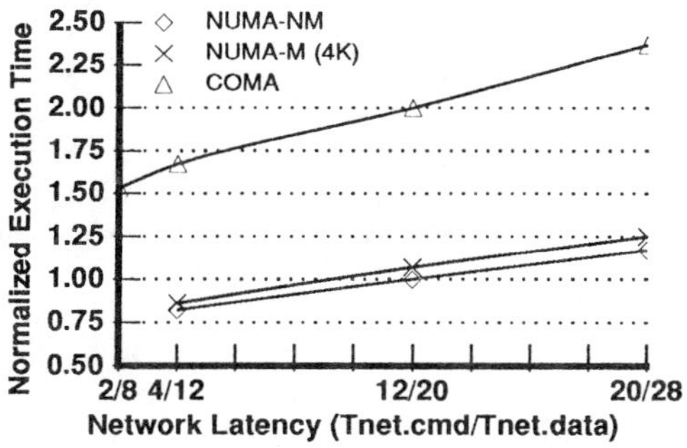

Figure 6: Network latency variation for MP3D.

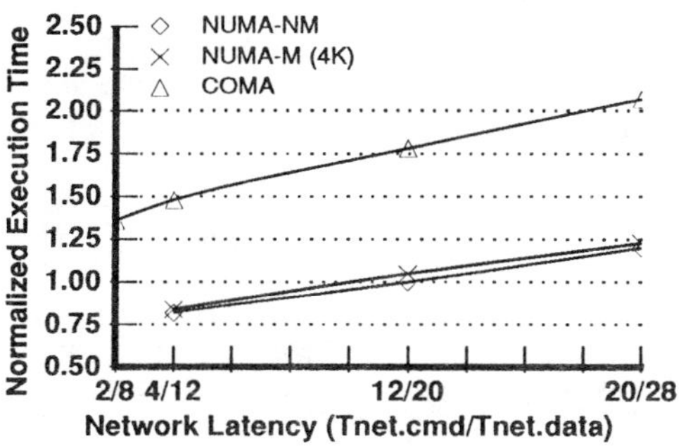

Figure 7: Network latency variation for PTHOR.

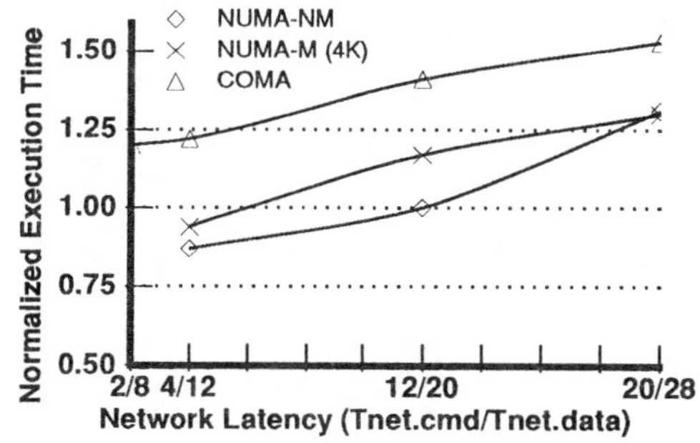

Figure 8: Network latency variation for LocusRoute.

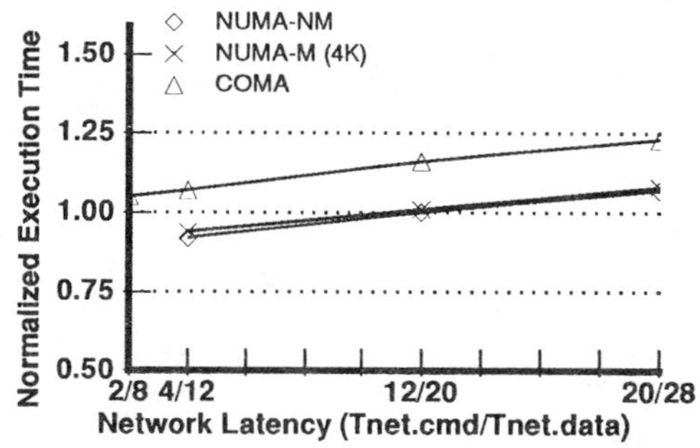

Figure 9: Network latency variation for Water.

pacity miss-rate is reduced and the coherence miss-rate starts to dominate. As expected, with larger caches the execution time ratio increases indicating that CC-NUMA is starting to perform better. As the data show, with 64 Kbyte caches, the performance of CC-NUMA (with no migration) is better for all applications except Ocean.

5.6 Impact of Network Latency Variations

We have seen that COMA's performance is limited primarily by the larger latency incurred by its hierarchical directory structure. In this subsection we explore how variations in the network latency and directory access times influence the relative performance. Due to space limitations, we only present results for MP3D, PTHOR, LocusRoute, and Water. By picking this set of applications that perform better on CC-NUMA, we wish to see if it is possible for COMA to perform better if a more aggressive network implementation is assumed. We will first study variations in network latency and then consider more aggressive directory implementations.

As default values for network latency, we have so far assumed a synchronous point-to-point hierarchy for COMA with latency numbers $T_{net.cmd} = 4$ and $T_{net.data} = 12$ pclocks. For CC-NUMA, we have assumed a synchronous mesh with default latency numbers $T_{net.cmd} = 12$ and $T_{net.data} = 20$ pclocks. In Figures 6–9 we show the relative performance of COMA, NUMA-M (with 4 Kbyte pages), and NUMA-NM under different network latency assumptions. All execution times are shown relative to NUMA-NM with default parameters. An important observation is that even if we consider a very aggressive point-to-point hierarchy for COMA ($T_{net.cmd} = 2$ and $T_{net.data} = 8$), default NUMA-NM outperforms COMA for MP3D, PTHOR, LocusRoute, and Water. We study variations in directory access time for COMA next.

The directory access time is another important contributor to the node miss penalty associated with COMA. A directory access consists of a read-modify-write cycle in order to modify the state information. More specifically, the following basic actions and latencies are associated with a directory access, assuming 80ns DRAM-based directories and a 100 MHz processor clock rate: (i) arbitration among the multiple inputs into a directory (2 pclocks); (ii) directory DRAM access plus data buffering (10 pclocks); (iii) tag comparison and decision about next action (4 pclocks); (iv) directory DRAM update (6 pclocks); and (v) precharge before next directory access (8 pclocks). The busy time thus adds up to 30 pclocks. If the network load is low, the directory update and precharge operations can be overlapped by network transfers. We have partly taken this into account in our default directory access time by assuming $T_{dir} = 20$ pclocks. However, for applications with high coherence miss-rates, less overlap is expected. In Table 7 we show the execution time of COMA relative to CC-NUMA with default parameters, assuming less directory overlap ($T_{dir} = 28$ pclocks). We see that for applications with a significant coherence miss-rate, such as MP3D and PTHOR, less overlap can substantially degrade the performance of COMA.

One could reduce the node miss penalty for COMA by using faster (and more expensive) SRAM-based directories. In order to study the effect of faster directories, in Table 7 we show the performance of COMA (relative to CC-NUMA with default parameters), assuming directories built from 30ns SRAMs and where the update and precharge operations are completely overlapped by the network transfer ($T_{dir} = 12$ pclocks). We see that even for such an aggressive directory implementation, COMA performs worse than CC-NUMA for all four applications.

In summary, we note that even for more aggressive im-

Table 7: Execution time ratio of COMA to NUMA-NM as directory access time is varied.

T_{dir}	MP3D	PTHOR	Locus	Water
28	1.92	1.68	1.42	1.12
20	1.67	1.48	1.22	1.07
12	1.41	1.26	1.19	1.03

plementations of the hierarchical directory structure, COMA suffers from the higher network latency for applications with a significant coherence miss-rate.

6 COMA-F: A Flat COMA

We have seen that COMA's primary advantage is small capacity-miss penalties due to the large attraction memories, and its primary disadvantage is large coherence-miss penalties due to the hierarchical directory structure. The hierarchy is fundamental to COMA's coherence protocol because it helps locate copies of a memory block in the system. It also helps to support combining of requests. In contrast, CC-NUMA has an explicit home node for each memory block, and the directory at the home node keeps track of all copies of that memory block. Consequently, a copy of a memory block can be located without traversing any hierarchy, resulting in lower remote-miss latencies. In this section, we propose a new architecture called COMA-F (for COMA-FLAT) that provides the benefits of both COMA and CC-NUMA (low capacity-miss penalties and low coherence-miss penalties). To avoid confusion, we denote previously proposed COMA machines as COMA-H, for hierarchical COMA.

COMA-F has no hierarchy. However, like COMA-H, COMA-F supports migration and replication of cache blocks at the main-memory level by organizing its main memory as an attraction memory (i.e., there are tags associated with each memory block). In addition, like CC-NUMA, each memory block has a clear notion of a home node, and the directory memory there keeps track of all copies of that block. However, unlike CC-NUMA, the home node does not reserve its main memory for blocks for which it keeps directory entries (thus, blocks whose home is some other processing node can come and reside there). Below, we present an overview of the memory coherence protocol for COMA-F — the detailed protocol is described in [8].

We begin with the structure of the directory entries. Each entry contains a pointer to one of the copies denoted MASTER, and a list of other nodes having a copy of the block, called the sharing list. The state of a directory entry can either be SHARED or EXCLUSIVE. The state of an attraction-memory block can be one of INVALID, SHARED, MASTER-SHARED, or EXCLUSIVE. If a block is in MASTER-SHARED or EXCLUSIVE state, it implies that the directory entry considers the local node to be the MASTER. As for directory-memory overhead for COMA-F, we note that it should be possible to use limited-pointer directory schemes as proposed for CC-NUMA, but sparse directories are not expected to work well [9].

If a read request misses in the attraction memory, it is sent to the HOME node. The HOME forwards the read request to the MASTER node which responds with a copy of the data to the requesting node. The HOME also updates the sharing list. If the MASTER copy was in state EXCLUSIVE, the state of the directory entry is changed to SHARED and the block state in the MASTER node is changed to MASTER-SHARED. Note, in contrast to CC-NUMA, accessing a clean block in COMA-F may take three instead of two network traversals. Also in contrast to COMA-H, there is no hardware combining in COMA-F.

A read-exclusive request is also first sent to the HOME node. As before, the HOME node forwards the request to the MASTER node which responds with a copy of the block to the requesting node. In addition, the requesting node now becomes the new MASTER node and all other copies are invalidated. Acknowledgements are sent directly to the new MASTER node.

Since there is no physical memory backing up the attraction-memory cache blocks, replacements need special care in order to avoid replacing the last remaining copy. A node that initiates replacement of a SHARED block can simply discard it and then inform the HOME node to remove itself from the sharing list. However, if the state of the block is either EXCLUSIVE or MASTER-SHARED, then the initiating node is currently the MASTER node and it must send the replaced block to the HOME node. The HOME node must now nominate a new MASTER node. If there are other nodes with copies, an arbitrary node among them is nominated as the MASTER. If there are no other copies, then we need to get fresh space for the replaced block. While there are many different strategies possible, one reasonable strategy is to make a place for the replaced block in the HOME node itself. While this may cause another replacement, the chain of replacements is expected to be short.

We have investigated the performance of COMA-F using the protocol mentioned above, assuming infinite attraction memories. In Table 8, we present execution times for COMA-H and NUMA-NM relative to COMA-F, assuming 4 Kbyte pages and default latency numbers. As expected, COMA-F outperforms both COMA and NUMA-NM. Compared to COMA-H, COMA-F manages to reduce the coherence-miss penalty (as seen from performance of MP3D and PTHOR) and as compared to CC-NUMA, COMA-F manages to reduce the capacity-miss penalty (as seen from performance of LU, Barnes-Hut, and Ocean).

7 Conclusion

We have studied the relative performance of two different approaches to designing large-scale shared-memory multiprocessors, CC-NUMA and COMA. We have found that for applications with low miss rates, the two styles of machines achieve nearly identical performance. The performance differences arise as a result of the efficiency with which they handle cache misses. The COMA style handles capacity misses more efficiently than CC-NUMA. The replication and migration of small blocks of data at the main-memory level allows COMA to service a majority of such misses locally. The CC-NUMA style handles coherence misses more efficiently than COMA. The hierarchical directory structure that is needed by COMA results in a much larger latency than the flat structure in CC-NUMA. We have observed through simulation that the relative performance of these two machine models is easily predicted by the relative frequency of these two types of misses.

In contrast to COMA machines, CC-NUMA can replicate

Table 8: Execution time ratio of COMA-H and NUMA-NM relative to COMA-F.

	MP3D	PTHOR	Locus	Water	Chol	LU	B-H	Ocean
COMA-H	1.90	1.73	1.30	1.16	1.35	1.27	1.04	1.11
NUMA-NM	1.14	1.18	1.09	1.09	1.46	1.51	1.32	1.68

and migrate data at the main-memory level only in large page-sized chunks. However, we show that proper initial placement and smart migration of pages can still be quite effective for scientific applications that use coarse-grained data partitions. Overall, with page migration turned on, we show that CC-NUMA performs better than COMA or is competitive with COMA for seven of the eight benchmark applications that we evaluate.

Finally, by combining the notion of a home location for directory information with the feature of replication of cache-block sized chunks at the main-memory level, we have outlined a COMA-F architecture that does not rely on a hierarchical directory structure. Our preliminary results show that such an architecture can offer significant performance improvements. However, we believe it is still an open question whether the additional complexity and hardware overhead of COMA machines is justified by the expected performance gains; this question is especially critical for hierarchical COMA machines.

Acknowledgments

We would like to thank Ed Rothberg, Kourosh Gharachorloo, Rohit Chandra, John Hennessy, and Kunle Olukotun for discussions and helpful comments on earlier drafts of this paper. This work has been supported by DARPA contract N00039-91-C-0138. Per Stenström is supported by STU contract 9001797. Anoop Gupta is also supported by an NSF Presidential Young Investigator Award.

References

[1] Anant Agarwal, Beng-Hong Lim, David Kranz, and John Kubiatowicz. APRIL: A processor architecture for multiprocessing. In *Proceedings of the 17th Annual International Symposium on Computer Architecture*, pages 104–114, May 1990.

[2] David L. Black, Anoop Gupta, and Wolf-Dietrich Weber. Competitive management of distributed shared memory. In *Proceedings of Compcon 1989*, March 1989.

[3] William J. Bolosky, Michael L. Scott, Robert P. Fitzgerald, Robert J. Fowler, and Alan L. Cox. NUMA policies and their relation to memory architecture. In *Proceedings of the 4th International Conerfernce on Architectural Support for Programming Languages and Operating Systems*, pages 212–221, 1991.

[4] Henry Burkhardt III, Steven Frank, Bruce Knobe, and James Rothnie. Overview of the KSR1 Computer System. Technical Report KSR-TR-9202001, Kendall Square Research, Boston, February 1992.

[5] Helen Davis, Stephen R. Goldschmidt, and John L. Hennessy. Multiprocessor simulation and tracing using Tango. In *Proceedings of International Conference on Parallel Processing*, pages 99–107, 1991. Vol. II.

[6] Michel Dubois, Christoph Scheurich, and Faye Briggs. Memory access buffering in multiprocessors. In *Proceedings of the 13th Annual International Symposium on Computer Architecture*, pages 434–442, 1986.

[7] Alan Gottlieb, Ralph Grishman, C. Kruskal, Kevin McAuliffe, Larry Rudolph, and Mark Snir. The NYU Ultracomputer - Designing a MIMD, shared memory parallel machine. *IEEE Transactions on Computers*, 32(2):175–189, February 1983.

[8] Anoop Gupta, Truman Joe, and Per Stenström. Comparative performance evaluation of cache-coherent NUMA and COMA architectures. Technical report, Stanford University, March 1992.

[9] Anoop Gupta, Wolf-Dietrich Weber, and Todd Mowry. Reducing memory and traffic requirements for scalable directory-based cache coherence schemes. In *Proceedings of International Conference on Parallel Processing*, August 1990.

[10] Erik Hagersten, Seif Haridi, and David H.D. Warren. The cache-coherence protocol of the data diffusion machine. In Michel Dubois and Shreekant Thakkar, editors, *Cache and Interconnect Architectures in Multiprocessors*. Kluwer Academic Publishers, 1990.

[11] Monica S. Lam, Edward E. Rothberg, and Michael E. Wolf. The cache performance and optimizations of blocked algorithms. In *Proceedings of the 4th International Conerfernce on Architectural Support for Programming Languages and Operating Systems*, pages 63–74, 1991.

[12] Daniel E. Lenoski, James P. Laudon, Kourosh Gharachorloo, Anoop Gupta, and John L. Hennessy. The directory-based cache coherence protocol for the DASH multiprocessor. In *Proceedings of the 17th Annual International Symposium on Computer Architecture*, pages 148–159, 1990.

[13] Jaswinder P. Singh, Chris Holt, Takashi Totsuka, Anoop Gupta, and John L. Hennessy. Load balancing and data locality in parallel hierarchial N-body simulation. Technical Report CSL-TR-92-505, Stanford University, February 1992.

[14] Jaswinder P. Singh, Wolf-Dietrich Weber, and Anoop Gupta. SPLASH: Stanford parallel applications for shared-memory. Technical Report CSL-TR-91-469, Stanford University, April 1991.

[15] Joseph Torrellas, Monica S. Lam, and John L. Hennessy. Shared data placement optimizations to reduce multiprocessor cache miss rates. In *Proceedings of the International Conference on Parallel Processing*, pages 266–270, 1990. Vol. II.

[16] Deborah A. Wallach. A scalable hierarchial cache coherence protocol. Bachelor of Science Thesis, Massachuesetts Institute of Technology, May 1990.

The DASH Prototype: Implementation and Performance

Daniel Lenoski, James Laudon, Truman Joe, David Nakahira, Luis Stevens, Anoop Gupta and John Hennessy

Computer Systems Laboratory
Stanford University, CA 94305

Abstract

The fundamental premise behind the DASH project is that it is feasible to build large-scale shared-memory multiprocessors with hardware cache coherence. While paper studies and software simulators are useful for understanding many high-level design trade-offs, prototypes are essential to ensure that no critical details are overlooked. A prototype provides convincing evidence of the feasibility of the design, allows one to accurately estimate both the hardware and the complexity cost of various features, and provides a platform for studying real workloads. A 16-processor prototype of the DASH multiprocessor has been operational for the last six months. In this paper, the hardware overhead of directory-based cache coherence in the prototype is examined. We also discuss the performance of the system, and the speedups obtained by parallel applications running on the prototype. Using a sophisticated hardware performance monitor, we characterize the effectiveness of coherent caches and the relationship between an application's reference behavior and its speedup.

1.0 Introduction

For parallel architectures to achieve widespread usage it is important that they efficiently run a wide variety of applications without excessive programming difficulty. To maximize both high performance and wide applicability, we believe a parallel architecture should provide (i) the ability to support hundreds to thousands of processors, (ii) high-performance individual processors, and (iii) a single shared address space.

One important question that arises in the design of such large-scale single-address-space machines is whether or not to allow caching of shared writeable data. The advantage, of course, is that caching allows higher performance to be achieved by reducing memory latency; the disadvantage is the problem of cache coherence. While solutions to the cache coherence problem are well understood for small-scale multiprocessors, they are unfortunately not so clear for large-scale machines. In fact, large-scale machines currently do not support cache coherence, and it has not been clear what the benefits and costs will be.

For the past several years, the DASH (Directory Architecture for SHared memory) project has been exploring the feasibility of building large-scale single-address-space machines with coherent caches. The key ideas are to distribute the main memory among the processing nodes to provide scalable memory bandwidth, and to use a distributed directory-based protocol to support cache coherence. To evaluate these ideas, we have constructed a prototype DASH machine. The full prototype will consist of sixty-four 33MHz MIPS R3000/R3010 processors, delivering up to 1600 MIPS and 600 scalar MFLOPS. An initial 16-processor prototype has been working for the past several months, and we are currently expanding this to the full 64-processor configuration.

This paper examines the hardware cost and performance characteristics of the prototype DASH system. Cost is measured in terms of the logic gates and the bytes of dynamic and static memory in the base system and the added directory logic. Performance is measured in terms of memory system bandwidth and latency, and in terms of parallel application speedups. For a representative set of the measured applications, we also present detailed reference statistics and relate these statistics to the observed application speedups. Finally, we describe the structure of the performance monitor logic which was used to take the detailed reference measurements.

The paper is organized as follows. Section 2 gives an overview of the DASH architecture. Section 3 introduces the DASH prototype and describes the logic used for the directory-based coherence protocol. Section 4 details the hardware costs of the system. Section 5 outlines the structure and function of the performance monitor logic, and Section 6 presents the performance of the memory system, and the speedups obtained by parallel applications running on the prototype. We conclude in Section 7 with a summary of our experience with the DASH prototype.

2.0 The DASH Architecture

The DASH architecture has a two-level structure shown in Figure 1. At the top level, the architecture consists of a set of processing nodes (clusters) connected through a mesh interconnection network. In turn, each processing node is a bus-based multiprocessor. Intra-cluster cache coherence is implemented using a snoopy bus-based protocol, while inter-cluster coherence is maintained through a distributed directory-based protocol.

The cluster functions as a high-performance processing node. In addition, the grouping of multiple processors on a bus within each cluster amortizes the cost of the directory logic and the network interface. This grouping also reduces the directory memory requirements by keeping track of cached lines at a cluster as opposed to processor level. (We will more concretely discuss the role of clustering in reducing overhead in Section 4).

© 1992 ACM 0-89791-509-7/92/0005/0092 $1.50

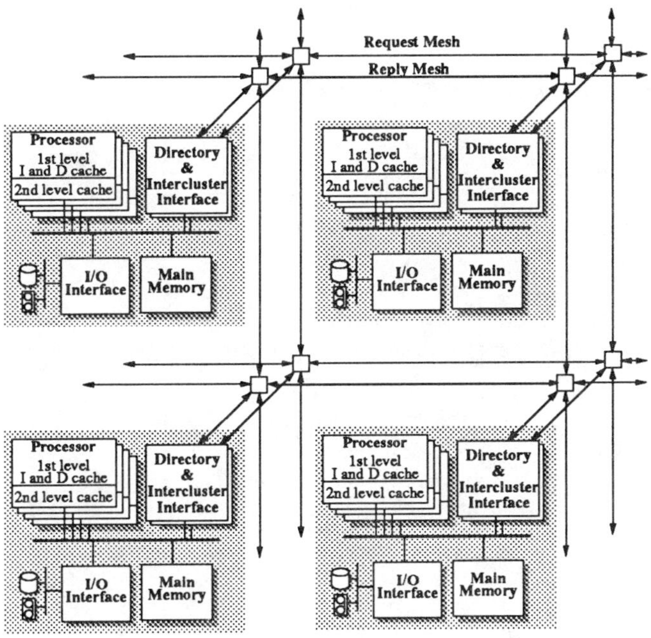

Figure 1. Block diagram of a 2x2 DASH prototype.

The directory-based protocol implements an invalidation-based coherence scheme. A memory location may be in one of three states: *uncached*, that is not cached by any processing node at all; *shared*, that is in an unmodified state in the caches of one or more nodes; or *dirty*, that is modified in the cache of some individual node. The directory keeps the summary information for each memory line, specifying the clusters that are caching it.

The DASH memory system can be logically broken into the four level hierarchy shown in Figure 2. The level closest to the processor is the processor cache and is designed to match the speed of the processor. A request that cannot be serviced by the processor cache is sent to the second level in the hierarchy, the *local cluster* level. This level consists of other processors' caches within the requesting processor's cluster. If the data is locally cached, the request can be serviced within the cluster, otherwise the request is sent to the *directory home* level. The home level consists of the cluster that contains the directory and physical memory for a given memory address. For some addresses, the local and home cluster are the same and the second and third level access occur simultaneously. In general, however, the request will travel through the interconnect to the home cluster. The home cluster can usually satisfy a request, but if the directory entry is in the dirty state, or in the shared state when the requesting processor requires exclusive access, the fourth, *remote cluster* level, must be accessed. The remote cluster level responds directly to the local cluster level while also updating the directory level.

In addition to providing coherent caches to reduce memory latency, DASH supports several other techniques for hiding and tolerating memory latency. DASH supports the *release consistency* model, that helps hide latency by allowing buffering and pipelining among memory requests. DASH also supports *software-controlled non-binding prefetching* to help hide latency of read operations. Finally, DASH supports efficient spin locks in hardware and fetch-and-incr/decr primitives to help reduce the overhead of synchronization. Since we will primarily be focussing on the basic cache coherence protocol in this paper, we will not

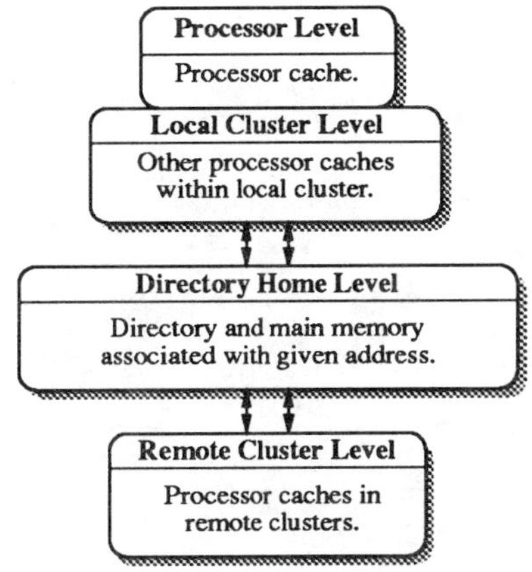

Figure 2. Logical memory hierarchy of DASH.

describe the details of these optimizations. For a more detailed discussion of the protocol and the optimizations, see [7, 8].

3.0 The DASH Prototype

To focus our effort on the novel aspects of the design and speed completion of a usable system, the base cluster hardware of the prototype is a commercially available bus-based multiprocessor. While there are some constraints and compromises imposed by the given hardware, the prototype still makes an interesting research vehicle.

The prototype system is based on a Silicon Graphics POWER Station 4D/340 as the base cluster [3]. The 4D/340 system consists of four MIPS R3000 processors and R3010 floating-point coprocessors running at 33 MHz. Each R3000/R3010 combination can achieve execution rates up to 25 VAX MIPS and 10 MFLOPS. Each CPU contains a 64 Kbyte instruction cache and a 64 Kbyte write-through data cache. The 64 Kbyte data cache interfaces to a 256 Kbyte second-level write-back cache. The interface consists of a read buffer and a 4 word deep write-buffer. Both the first and second-level caches are direct-mapped and support 16 byte lines. The first-level caches run synchronously to their associated 33 MHz processors while the second-level caches run synchronous to an independent 16 MHz memory bus clock.

The second-level processor caches are responsible for bus snooping and maintaining coherence among the caches in the cluster. Since the first-level caches satisfy most memory requests, the second-level caches do not need duplicate snooping tags. Coherence is maintained with a MESI (Illinois) protocol[12], and inclusion of the first-level cache by the second-level. The main advantage of using the Illinois protocol in DASH is the cache-to-cache transfers specified in this protocol. While they do little to reduce the latency for misses serviced by local memory, local cache-to-cache transfers can greatly reduce the penalty for remote memory misses. The set of processor caches effectively act as a cluster cache for remote memory.

The memory bus (MPBUS) of the 4D/340 is a synchronous bus and consists of separate 32-bit address and 64-bit data buses. The MPBUS is pipelined and supports memory-to-cache and cache-to-cache transfers of 16 bytes every 4 bus clocks with a latency of 6 bus clocks. This results in a maximum bandwidth of 64 Mbytes/sec.

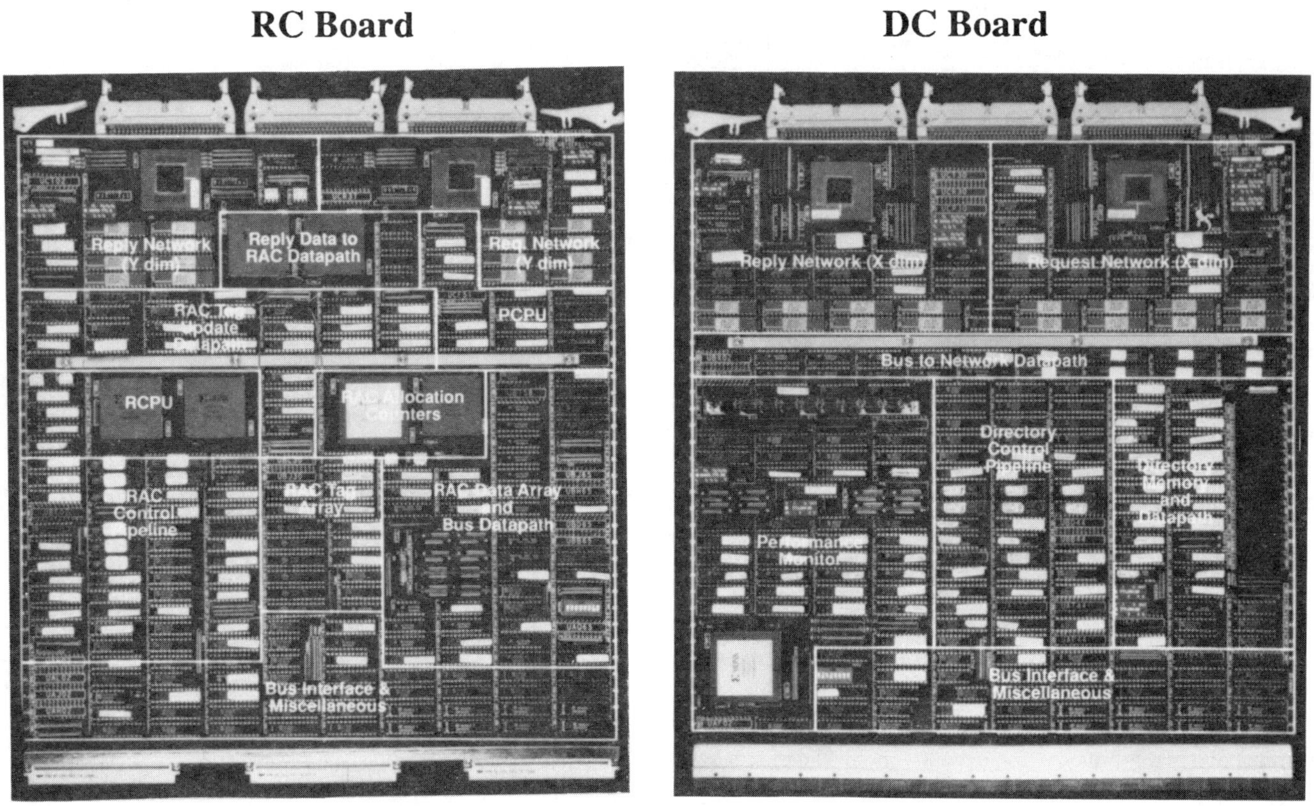

Figure 3. Directory and Reply Controller boards.

To use the 4D/340 in DASH, we have had to make minor modifications to the existing system boards and design a pair of new boards to support the directory memory and inter-cluster interface. The main modification to the existing boards is to add a bus retry signal that is used when a request requires service from a remote cluster. The central bus arbiter has also been modified to accept a mask from the directory which holds off a processor's retry until the remote request has been serviced. This effectively creates a split transaction bus protocol for requests requiring remote service. The new directory controller boards contain the directory memory, the intercluster coherence state machines and buffers, and a local section of the global interconnection network.

While the prototype, with minor modifications, could scale to support hundreds of processors, the current version is limited to a maximum configuration of 16 clusters and 64 processors. This limit was dictated primarily by the physical memory addressability of the 4D/340 system (256 Mbytes) which would severely limit the memory per processor in a larger system.

The directory logic in DASH is responsible for implementing the directory-based coherence protocol and interconnecting the clusters within the system. Pictures of the directory boards are shown in Figure 3. The directory logic is split between the two boards along the lines of the logic used for outbound and inbound portions of inter-cluster transactions.

The DC board contains three major subsections. The first section is the *directory controller* (DC) itself, which includes the directory memory associated with the cachable main memory contained within the cluster. The DC logic initiates all out-bound network requests and replies. The second section is the performance monitor which can count and trace a variety of intra- and inter-cluster events. The third major section is the request and reply outbound network logic together with the X-dimension of the network itself.

The second board is the RC board which also contains three major sections. The first section is the *reply controller* (RC) which tracks outstanding requests made by the local processors and receives and buffers replies from remote clusters using the *remote access cache* (RAC). The second section is the *pseudo-CPU* (PCPU), which is responsible for buffering incoming requests and issuing these requests onto the cluster bus. The PCPU mimics a CPU on this bus on behalf of remote processors except that responses from the bus are sent out by the directory controller. The final section is the inbound network logic and the Y-dimension of the mesh routing networks.

Directory memory is accessed on each bus transaction. The directory information is combined with the type of bus operation, the address, and the result of snooping on the caches to determine what network messages and bus controls the DC will generate. The directory memory organization is similar to the original directory scheme proposed by Censier and Feautrier [4]. Directory pointers are stored as a bit vector with 1 bit for each of the 16 clusters. While a full bit vector has limited scalability, it was chosen because it requires roughly the same amount of memory as a limited-pointer directory [2, 6, 11, 1] given the size of the prototype, and it allows for more direct measurements of the caching behavior of the machine. Each directory entry contains a single state bit that indicates whether the clusters have a shared or dirty copy of the data. The directory is implemented using DRAM technology, but performs all necessary actions within a single bus transaction.

The reply controller stores the state of on-going requests in the remote access cache (RAC). The RAC's primary role is the coordination of replies to inter-cluster transactions. This ranges from the simple buffering of reply data between the network and bus to the accumulation of invalidation acknowledgments and the enforcement of release consistency. The RAC is organized as a 128Kbyte direct-mapped snoopy cache with 16byte cache lines. One port of the RAC services the in-bound reply network while the other snoops on bus transactions. The RAC is lockup-free in that it can handle several outstanding remote requests from each of the local processors. RAC entries are allocated when a remote request is initiated by a local processor and persist until all inter-cluster transactions relative to that request have completed. The snoopy nature of the RAC naturally lends itself to merging requests made to the same cache block by different processors within the cluster, and it takes advantage of the cache-to-cache transfer protocol supported between the local processors. The snoopy structure also allows the RAC to supplement the function of the processor caches. This includes support for a dirty-sharing state for a cluster (normally the Illinois protocol would force a write-back) and operations such as prefetch.

As stated in the architecture section, the DASH coherence protocol does not rely on a particular interconnection network topology. The prototype system uses a pair of *wormhole* routed meshes to implement the interconnection network. One mesh handles request messages while the other is dedicated to replies. The networks are based on variants of the mesh routing chips developed at Caltech where the datapaths have been extended from 8 to 16 bits[5]. Wormhole routing allows a cluster to forward a message after receiving only the first flit (flow unit) of the packet, greatly reducing the latency through each node (≈ 50ns per hop in our network). The bandwidth of each self-timed link is limited by the round trip delay of the request-acknowledge signals. In the prototype flits are transferred at approximately 30 MHz, resulting in a peak bandwidth of 120 Mbytes/sec in and out of each cluster.

4.0 Gate Count Summary

One important result of building the DASH prototype is that it provides a realistic model of the cost of directory-based cache coherence. While some of these costs are tied to the specific prototype implementation (e.g., the full DRAM directory vector), they provide a complete picture of one system.

At a high level, the cost of the directory logic can be estimated by the fact that a DASH cluster includes six logic cards, four of which represent the base processing node and two of which are used for directory and inter-cluster coherence. This is a very conservative estimate, however, because Silicon Graphics' logic, in particular the MIPS processor chips and Silicon Graphics' gate arrays, are more highly integrated than the MSI PALs and LSI FPGAs used in the directory logic.

Table 1 summarizes the logic for a DASH cluster at a more detailed level. The table gives the percent of logic for each section and the totals in terms of thousands of 2-input gates, kilobytes of static RAM, megabytes of dynamic RAM, and 16-pin IC equivalents. RAM bytes include all error detecting or correcting codes and cache tags. 16-pin IC equivalent is a measure of board area (0.36 sq. inch), assuming through-hole technology (i.e. DIPs and PGAs) was used throughout the design. (Actually about 1/4 of the CPU logic is implemented in surface mount technology, but the IC Equivalent figures used here assume through-hole since all of the logic could have been designed in surface mount.) The number of 2-input gates is an estimate based on the number of gate-array 2-input gates needed to implement each function. For each type of logic used in the prototype the equivalent gate complexity was calculated as:

Custom VLSI	Estimate based on part documentation.
CMOS Gate Array	Actual gate count or estimate based on master-slice size and complexity.
PAL	Translation of 2-level minimized logic into equivalent gates.
PROM	Espresso minimized PROM files translated into 2-input gates. This includes the primary state machines in the DC and RC, but not the boot EPROMs for the CPUs.
TTL	Gates in equivalent gate array macros.

Table 1. Percent of all logic in a DASH cluster.

Section	Gates (000's)	SRAM (KB)	DRAM (MB)	IC Equiv
Processors/Caches	69.3%	86.0%	0.0%	32.4%
Main Memory	3.3%	0.0%	75.8%	12.7%
IO Board	8.3%	0.0%	1.4%	13.5%
Directory Controller	4.4%	0.0%	12.0%	8.2%
Reply Controller	8.4%	7.3%	0.0%	12.0%
PCPU	0.5%	0.0%	0.0%	1.2%
Network Outbound	2.8%	0.7%	0.0%	4.3%
Network Inbound	1.1%	0.7%	0.0%	2.4%
Performance Mon.	1.8%	5.3%	10.8%	3.5%
Total	535	2420	83	2603

The numbers in Table 1 are somewhat distorted by the extra logic in the base Silicon Graphics' hardware and the directory boards that is not needed for normal operations. This includes (i) the performance monitor logic on the directory board; (ii) the diagnostic UARTs and timers attached to each processor; (iii) the Ethernet and VME bus interfaces on the Silicon Graphics' I/O board.[1] Table 2 shows the percentage of this *core* logic assuming the items mentioned above are removed.

As expected, only when measured in terms of IC equivalents (i.e. board area), is the cost of the directory logic approximately33%. When measured in terms of logic gates the portion of the cluster dedicated to the directory is 20%, and the SRAM and DRAM overhead is 13.9% and 13.7% respectively.

Note that in the above analysis, we do not account for the hardware cost of snooping on the local bus separately because these costs are very small. In particular, the processor's two-level cache structure doesn't require duplicate snooping tags, and the processor's bus interface accounts for only 3.2% of the gates in a cluster. Even if the second-level cache tags were duplicated, it would represent only 4.0% of a cluster's SRAM. In practice, we expect most future systems will use microprocessors with integrated first-level caches (e.g., MIPS R4000, DEC Alpha, etc.) and to incorporate an external second-level cache (without duplicate tags) to improve uniprocessor performance. Thus, the extra SRAM cost for snooping (e.g., extra state bits) is expected to be negligible.

1. Each I/O board would still include a SCSI interface for disk interfacing.

Table 2. Percent of *core* logic in a DASH cluster.

Section	Gates (000's)	SRAM (KB)	DRAM (MB)	IC Equiv
Processors/Caches	70.8%	90.8%	0.0%	45.2%
Main Memory	3.9%	0.0%	86.3%	13.9%
IO Board	5.1%	0.0%	0.0%	10.3%
Directory Controller	5.2%	0.0%	13.7%	9.0%
Reply Controller	9.9%	7.7%	0.0%	13.1%
PCPU	0.6%	0.0%	0.0%	1.3%
Network Outbound	3.3%	0.8%	0.0%	4.7%
Network Inbound	1.3%	0.8%	0.0%	2.6%
Performance Mon.	0.0%	0.0%	0.0%	0.0%
Total	456	1268	73	2286

Looking at the numbers in Table 2 in more detail also shows additional areas where the directory overhead might be improved. In particular, the prototype's simple bit vector directory grows in proportion to the number of clusters in the system, and in inverse proportion to cache line size. Thus, increasing cache line size from 16 to 32 or 64 bytes would reduce the directory DRAM overhead to 6.9% and 3.4% respectively, or it could allow the system to grow to 128 or 256 processors with the same 13.7% overhead. For larger systems, a more scalable directory structure [2, 6, 11, 1] could be used to keep the directory overhead at or below the level in the prototype. The directory's overhead in SRAM could also be improved. The 128KB remote access cache (RAC) is the primary use of SRAM in the directory. The size of the RAC could be significantly reduced if the processor caches were lockup-free. With enhanced processor caches, the primary use of the RAC would be to collect invalidation acknowledgments and to receive granted locks. This would allow a reduction in size by at least a factor of four, and result in an SRAM overhead of less than 2%. Likewise, a closer coupling of the base cluster logic and bus protocol to the inter-cluster protocol might reduce the directory logic overhead by as much as 25%. Thus, the prototype represents a conservative estimate of directory overhead. A more ideal DASH system would have a logic overhead of 18-25%, an SRAM overhead of 2-8% and a DRAM overhead 3-14%. This is still significant,[2] but when amortized over the cluster the overhead is reasonable.

The prototype logic distributions can also be extrapolated to consider other system organizations. For example, if the DASH cluster-based node was replaced by a uniprocessor node, the overhead for directory-based cache-coherence would be very high. Ignoring the potential growth in directory storage (that would need to track individual processor caches instead of clusters), the percent of directory logic in a uniprocessor node would grow to ≈44% (a 78% overhead). Thus, a system based on uniprocessor nodes would lose almost a factor of two in cost/performance relative to a uniprocessor or small-scale multiprocessor.

Another possible system organization is one based on a general memory or messaging interconnect, but without support for global hardware cache coherence (e.g., the BBN TC2000 or Intel Touchstone). An optimistic assumption for such a system is that it would remove all of the directory DRAM and support, the RAC and its datapath, and 90% of the RC and DC control pipelines. Under these assumptions, the fraction of logic dedicated to the inter-cluster interface falls to 10% of a cluster, and the memory overhead becomes negligible. Thus, the cost of adding inter-cluster coherence to a large-scale, non-cache coherent system is approximately 10%. If more than a 10% performance gain is realized by this addition, then the overall cost/performance of the system will improve. Our measurements on DASH indicate that caching improves performance by far more than 10%, and support for global cache coherence is well worth the extra cost.

Finally, by examining the required gate, memory, and connectivity requirements, one can estimate how the prototype logic might be integrated into a small number of VLSI components. As examined in detail in [9], such a system could consist of clusters based on the following:

- Four single-chip microprocessors with direct control of their second-level caches and a their interface to the cluster's snoopy bus.
- A single memory control chip interfaced to local DRAM and the cluster bus.
- An I/O interface chip connecting the cluster to a high-speed fiber optic I/O links (e.g., fibre channel).
- A single directory controller chip interfacing to an external mixed SRAM-DRAM sparse directory, the cluster bus, and a network chip.[3]
- A single mesh routing chip supporting two logical 3-D meshes.

This integrated system could maintain a similar directory logic and memory overhead as the prototype, while supporting cache coherence for 2K processors and 128 GBytes of memory.

5.0 Performance Monitor

One of the prime motivations for building the DASH prototype was to study real applications with large data sets running on a large ensemble of processors. To enable more insight into the behavior of these applications when running on the prototype, we have dedicated over 20% of the DC board to a hardware performance monitor. Integration of the performance monitor with the base directory logic allows non-invasive measurements of the complete system without any external hardware. The performance hardware is controlled by software, and it provides low-level information on software reference characteristics and hardware resource utilizations. The monitor hardware can trace and count a variety of bus, directory and network events. The monitor is controlled by a software programmable Xilinx gate array (FPGA) [15] allowing flexible event selection and sophisticated event preprocessing.

A block diagram of performance logic is shown in Figure 4. It consists of three major blocks. First, the FPGA which selects and preprocesses events to be measured and controls the rest of the performance logic. Second, two banks of 16Kx32 SRAMs and increment logic that count event occurrences. Third, a 2M x 36 trace DRAM which captures 36 or 72 bits of information on each bus transaction.

The counting SRAMs together with the FPGA support a wide variety of event counting. The two banks of SRAM are addressed by events selected by the FPGA. They can be used together to trace events that occur on cycle by cycle basis, or the banks can be used independently to monitor twice as many events. By summing over all addresses with a particular address bit high or low the number of occurrences of that event can be determined. Likewise, the con-

2. Approximately equal to the complexity of a entire processor with its caches.

3. A small associative RAC would be kept on-chip.

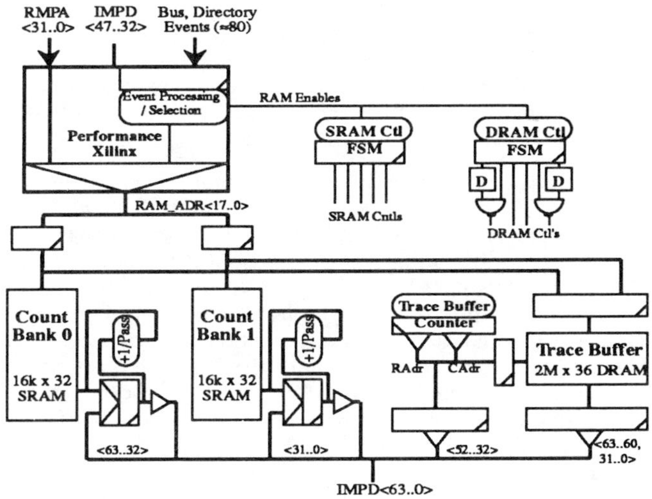

Figure 4. Block diagram of the performance monitor logic

junction or disjunction of any set of events can be determined by summing over the appropriate address ranges. Another use of the count SRAM is as a histogram array. In this mode, certain events are used to start, stop and increment a counter inside the FPGA. The stop event also triggers the counter to be used as a SRAM address to increment.

The current use of the counting SRAM in the prototype increments the two banks of SRAM independently on each bus transaction. The data in the first bank allows access type frequencies, bus utilization, access locality, RAC performance, remote caching statistics and network message frequency to be calculated. The second bank of SRAM is addressed with the local cache snoop results and histogram counters of remote latency. The snoop data allows one to determine the effectiveness of cache-to-cache sharing within the cluster. The remote latency histogram dedicates an internal FPGA counter to each CPU which is enabled whenever a processor is waiting for a remote access. This allows a complete distribution of remote access latencies to be determined. Furthermore, when combined with the count of local bus cycles an estimate of processor utilization can be made.

The other resource of the performance monitor is a 2 M x 36 trace array. Again, what information is traced can vary based on programming of the FPGA, but the current use of the trace logic has two modes. In the first configuration, up to 2M memory addresses together with the issuing processor number and read/write status are captured. The second mode can capture only 1 M addresses, but adds additional bus and directory state, and a bus idle count to each trace entry. This trace information can be used to do detailed analysis of reference behavior or as input to a memory simulator. With software assistance the tracer can be used to capture much longer traces and trace all memory references.

6.0 Prototype Performance

This section examines the performance of the initial hardware prototype of DASH which includes 16 processors in four clusters. The first part summarizes the memory latencies measured on the prototype hardware. The second part describes the speedups obtained by parallel applications run on the actual machine.

6.1 Processor Issue Bandwidth and Latency

Although the coherent caches in DASH significantly reduce the number of remote accesses made by a processor, it is still essential to minimize the latency when misses do occur. Table 3 lists the processor bandwidth and latency for cache memory operations in DASH assuming no contention. *(PClocks* refer to processor clocks which are 30ns in the prototype.) The delays are based on measurements of the hardware, but extrapolated to a full 4x4 cluster configuration. In the table, the best-case numbers assume stride-one access, with one cache miss every four references (cache lines are 16 bytes). The worst-case numbers assume stride-four accesses with no reuse of cache lines.

The table presents data separately for reads and writes. For reads, the access latency is given by the last column of the table. The latency can vary by more than two orders of magnitude depending on where a read access is serviced in the memory hierarchy. The read bandwidth also varies considerably, from a high of 133 Mbytes/sec from the primary cache to a meager 4 Mbytes/sec if all of the data is dirty in a remote non-home cluster. While, beyond a point, not much can be done about reducing the latency in large-scale machines, the bandwidth can be increased via pipelining, and it is for this reason we have provided non-blocking prefetch operations in DASH. The times given for store operations are the rate at which writes are retired from the write buffer into the second-level cache after acquiring ownership. Release consistency is assumed so that the processor need not wait for the write to retire, and invalidations do not affect write latency.

Table 3. Cache operation bandwidth and latencies.

Cache Operation	Best Case		Worst Case	
	MB/ sec	Clock/ word	MB/ sec	Clock/ word
Read from 1st-level cache	133.3	1.0	133.3	1.0
Fill from 2nd-lev. cache	29.6	4.5	8.9	15.0
Fill from local bus	16.7	8.0	4.6	29.0
Fill from remote	5.1	26.0	1.3	101.0
Fill from dirty-remote	4.0	33.8	1.0	132.0
Write retired in cache	32.0	4.2	32.0	4.2
Write retired on local bus	18.3	7.3	8.0	16.7
Write retired on remote	5.3	25.3	1.5	88.7
Write retired on dirty-rem.	4.0	33.0	1.1	119.7

A more detailed break-down of the latency for local and remote cache misses is given in Figure 5. The latency for a local miss that is serviced within the cluster is based entirely on the base SGI hardware (i.e., the hardware we have added to the SGI clusters does not slow the system down). In the prototype, a simple remote miss (i.e., a miss that is serviced by a remote home cluster) takes ≈3.5 times longer than a local miss. The final case illustrated in Figure 5 represents the latency for fetching a location that is dirty in a cluster other than its home. In this case, an extra 30 clocks (or 1 μsec) of delay is incurred in forwarding the request to the dirty cluster. The DASH protocol supports the direct transfer of the dirty data between the dirty and requesting cluster, reducing latency by 20% over a simpler protocol that first causes a writeback to the home cluster and then replies to the requesting processor.

While latencies in the DASH prototype (when measured in microseconds) are far from optimal, we believe that the delays when measured in processor clocks are quite indicative of what we expect to see in future large-scale machines. The reason is that

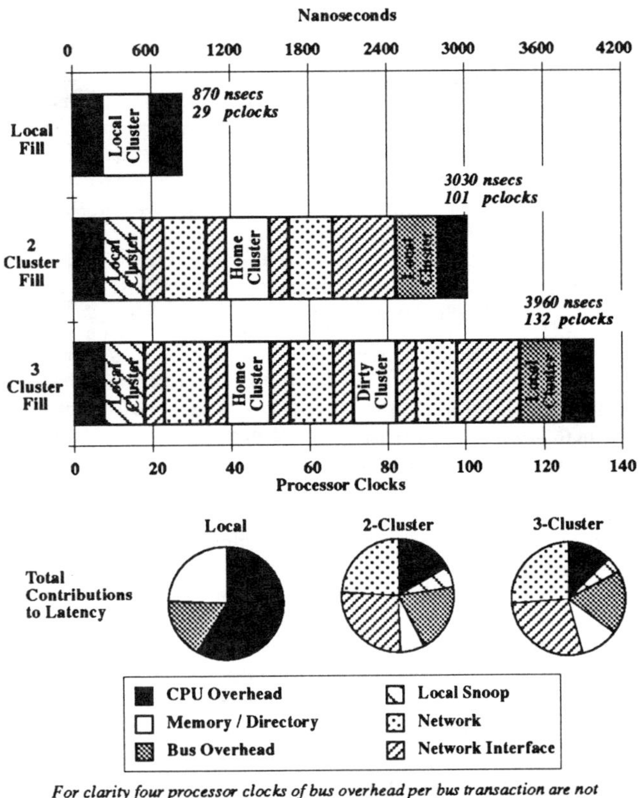

Figure 5. Cache fill latency in the DASH prototype.

while state-of-the-art technology (with integration and optimization) would allow us to reduce the prototype's latencies by a factor of about three [9], state-of-the-art processor clock rates are also about three times the 33 MHz used in the prototype. As a result, we expect that exploiting cache and memory locality will continue to be important in future large-scale machines, as will mechanisms that help hide or tolerate latency.

6.2 Parallel Application Performance

This subsection outlines the performance actually achieved on the prototype for a number of parallel applications. We begin by describing the software environment available on the prototype and how the measurements were made. We then present the speedup for nine parallel programs representing a variety of application domains. Three of these applications are studied more in greater detail using data captured by the performance monitor.

6.2.1 Application Runtime Environment

The operating system running on the prototype DASH is a modified version of IRIX; a variant of UNIX System V.3 developed by Silicon Graphics. The applications for which we present results are coded in C that has been augmented with the Argonne National Labs (ANL) parallel macros[10] to control a MIMD, shared-memory programming model.

Before giving the speedup results in the next subsection, we first state the assumptions used in measuring the speedups. The speedup were measured as the time for the uniprocessor to execute the parallel version of the application code (i.e. not all synchronization code is removed) divided by the time for the parallel application to run on a given number of processors. The runs were averaged over a number of executions to eliminate any scheduling anomalies in UNIX. In some applications, the serial start-up time is ignored from the measurement because the runs used shortened executions of the application (less time steps, etc.) to reduce measurement time. In production runs the start-up time would be negligible.

For our measurements, each application process is attached to a processor for its lifetime, and we fully use one cluster before assigning processors to new clusters. Physical memory pages used by the application are allocated only from the clusters that are actively being used, as long as the physical memory in those clusters is enough. Thus, for an application running with 4 processes, all memory is allocated from the local cluster, and all misses cost about 30 clocks. However, with 8 processes, some misses may be to a remote cluster and cost over 100 clock cycles. Most of the programs allocate shared data randomly or in a round-robin fashion from the clusters being actively used, but some include explicit system calls to control memory allocation.[4] Finally, all applications were run under processor consistency mode, i.e., writes were not retired from the write-buffer until all invalidation acknowledgments had been received, and no prefetching has been added.

6.2.2 Application Speedups

Figure 6 gives the speedup for nine parallel applications running on the hardware prototype using from 1 to 16 processors. The applications cover a variety of domains. There are some scientific applications (Barnes-Hut and Water), several engineering applications (Radiosity, MP3D, PSIM4, Locusroute) and two kernels (Cholesky, Matrix Multiply and Mincut). Four of the programs (Water, LocusRoute, MP3D and Cholesky) are taken from the SPLASH parallel application suite[14]. We begin with a quick overview of all nine applications and then present the detailed reference behavior and performance of three of the applications (Barnes-Hut, Water, and LocusRoute).

Starting with the applications with the best speedup, the Radiosity application is from the domain of computer graphics. It computes the global illumination in a room given a set of surface patches and light sources using a variation of hierarchical n-body techniques. The particular problem instance solved starts with 364 surface patches, and ends with over 10,000 patches. While the data structures used are a complex oct-tree and a binary-space partition tree, we see that caches work quite well and we get a speedup of over 14 with 16 processors. The second application, Barnes-Hut, is an N-body galactic simulation solved using the Barnes-Hut algorithm (an O(*N*log*N*) algorithm). Again we see that although the structure of the program is complex, good speedups are obtained.

The next application is Mincut. It performs graph partitioning using parallel simulated annealing. We ran Mincut to find the minimum bisection of a graph containing 500 nodes. Mincut achieves good speedups because there is extensive cache reuse as processors traverse the graph and repeatedly consider moving nodes as the graph partition and annealing temperature change.

The next application is a scaled matrix multiply. It uses 88x88 square matrices on a single processor (obtaining 8.8 DP MFLOPS on a single processor) and 1408x1408 matrices on 16 processors (obtaining 125 DP MFLOPS). The application below that is the Water code (the parallelized version of the MDG code from the

4. Currently all operating system code and data are allocated from cluster-0's memory. This causes cluster 0 to become a hot spot for OS misses, and causes some degradation in speedups. We are in the process of fixing this problem.

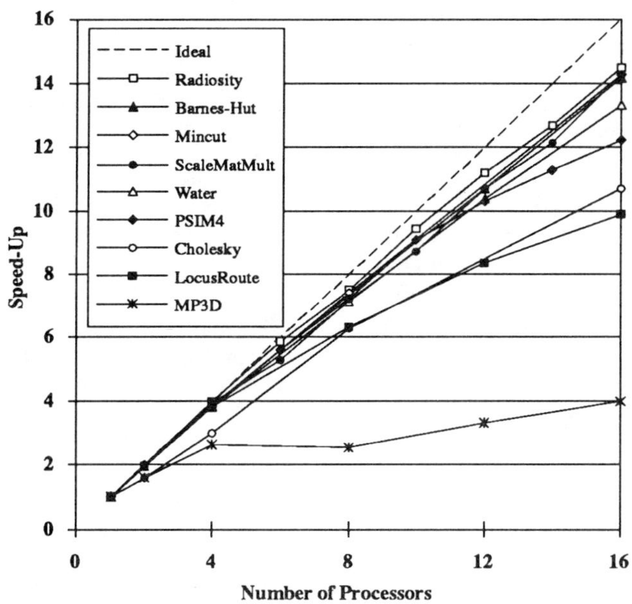

Figure 6. Speedup of applications on the DASH prototype.

Perfect Club benchmarks), a molecular dynamics code. We measured runs using 512 water molecules.

PSIM4 is an application from NASA-Ames, that is a particle-based simulator of a wind tunnel. PSIM4 is an enhanced version of the MP3D code (the application with the poorest speedup), both in terms of functionality (it models multiple types of gases and it models chemistry) and in terms of locality of memory accesses (it uses spatial decomposition of simulated space to distribute work among processors). The 16 processor run is done with over 100,000 particles and it achieves a scaled speedup of over 12 in contrast to a speedup of about 4 achieved by the older MP3D code. While the changes in functionality make a direct comparison of absolute execution time for PSIM4 and MP3D impossible, the speedup improvements of PSIM4 over MP3D are very encouraging.

The next application is Cholesky. It performs factorization of sparse positive-definite matrices using supernodal techniques (data blocking techniques that enhance the performance of caches both for uniprocessors and multiprocessors). Here it is used to solve a 256x256 grid problem. We note that much of the fall off in speedup that we see is due to the trade-off between large data block sizes (which increase processor efficiency, but decrease available concurrency and cause load balancing problems) and small data block sizes. As we go to a large number of processors, we are forced to use smaller block sizes unless the problem size is scaled to unreasonably large sizes. The next application is LocusRoute which performs global routing of standard cells. It will be discussed later in this section.

Finally, as stated before, MP3D is a particle-based wind-tunnel simulator. The measured runs simulated 40,000 particles. The speedups for MP3D are poor because the particles are statically allocated to processors, but the space cells (representing physical space in the wind tunnel) are referenced in a relatively random manner depending on the location of the particle being moved. Since each move operation also updates the corresponding space cell, as the number of processors increases, it becomes more and more likely that the space cell being referenced will be dirty in another processor's cache. Thus, even with four processors, the speedup is poor. When a second cluster is added, speedup is flat because roughly half of the misses are now remote. MP3D's speedups improve for 12 and 16 processors, but this does not compensate for the initial inefficiencies encountered with 4 and 8 processors.

Overall, we see that many applications achieve good speedups, even though they have not been specially optimized on the DASH prototype. Almost all get over ten times improvement on sixteen processors, and some get above fourteen times speedup.

6.2.3 Detailed Case Studies

To get a better understanding of the detailed reference behavior of these applications, we now examine Barnes-Hut, Water, and LocusRoute in more detail. We also extend the results for these applications with preliminary results from the 32-processor DASH system (which has just been up for the last two weeks). As expected from Figure 6, Barnes-Hut and Water achieve good speedups on 32 processors (27.5 and 24.5 respectively), but the speedups for LocusRoute fall-off significantly (9.9 at 16, but only 13.2 at 32). These applications were chosen because they achieved a range of speedups, and we were able to get results for them on the larger 32-processor system. We expect that once the 32-processor kernel is better tuned the speedups will improve.

6.2.3.1 Barnes-Hut

The Barnes-Hut program [13] models the dynamic evolution of a system of galaxies under gravitational forces. Using the Barnes-Hut algorithm, the possible N^2 interactions are reduced to $N \log N$ by a hierarchical decomposition of the galaxies and by approximating groups of distant bodies by a single point at their center of mass. The input to the measured runs consisted of two interacting Plummer-model galaxies with 16384 bodies each.

Table 4 gives a detailed memory reference profile of Barnes-Hut running on DASH as measured by the hardware performance monitor.[5] Table 5 is broken into four sections: (i) overall performance and processor utilization; (ii) memory request distribution; (iii) request locality and latency and (iv) bus and network utilization.

The first section of the table gives the overall speedup, efficiency relative to the uniprocessor, and processor utilization. Unfortunately, processor utilization cannot be measured directly from the bus, so the number in the table is an estimate that assumes the processor is doing active work whenever it is not waiting for a bus transaction to complete. This ignores internal stalls due to first-level cache misses satisfied by the second-level, TLB miss handling, and floating-point interlocks.[6] The number of busy clocks between stalls (third row) give an indication of cache hit rate and the application's sensitivity to memory latency.

As indicated by Table 4, Barnes-Hut has a high and nearly constant cache-hit ratio, and a large fraction of its misses are local. Thus, processor efficiency and speedup are very good as the number of

5. The results given in the table are averaged over all active clusters. This implies some inaccuracies for the one and two processor runs due to the overhead of the idle processors running the UNIX scheduler and daemons (e.g., slightly lower processor utilization for 1 and 2 processors than for 4 processors).

6. Since writes are buffered, they are not assumed to stall the processor directly. Instead, it is assumed that the processor can execute for 20 clocks before stalling. This delay is an estimate of the time for the processor to fill the other 3 words to the write-buffer (i.e. assuming 15% instructions are writes). In reality, the processor may not issue writes at this rate, or may stall earlier due to a first-level cache miss.

processors increases. There is a small drop in efficiency as the first remote cluster is added, but the degradation beyond this is slight.

The second section of Table 4 gives a breakdown of the memory reference types. This breakdown indicates the type of accesses that cause bus transactions and whether synchronization references are significant. In Barnes-Hut, cache read misses dominate and there are few synchronizations.

The third section of Table 5 lists the fraction of local cache fills, the fraction of remote fills satisfied by a dirty-remote cluster (ratio of 3 cluster to 2 cluster fills), and the latency for local and remote cache fills. The locality figure counts any references satisfied in a single bus transaction as local, while any that must be repeated are considered remote. Thus, a remote reference that was satisfied by a local cache-to-cache transfer between processors would be considered local, and a local reference that was dirty-remote would be considered remote.[7]

For Barnes-Hut, cluster locality is high and decreases only slightly as clusters are added. The actual locality of references (not given in the table) does decrease as clusters are added, but most communication is with nearby processors. Thus, even though the home for the data is remote, many remote accesses are satisfied by a local cache-to-cache transfer from another processor in the cluster. In addition, of the references that are remote, most misses are serviced by the home cluster. This results from the fact that most of these misses are to global data, and only the first processor needs to fetch this data from the producing (i.e. dirty) cluster. The others read the shared data from the home.

The final section of Table 4 indicates the load on the cluster bus and on the bisection of the mesh networks. Bus utilization is measured directly by the performance monitor, while the network bisection utilizations are estimates assuming uniform network traffic. The bisection utilizations are calculated by knowing the total number of network messages sent, assuming half of the messages cross the bisection of the mesh, and dividing by the bandwidth provided across the bisection.[8] For Barnes-Hut, both the buses and networks are lightly loaded.

In Barnes-Hut, as in the other applications studied, the bus loading is higher than the network bisection loading. This is due to the relatively slow cluster bus used in the prototype, and the retry mechanism used for the remote references which implies that each remote reference includes at least three bus accesses, but only one network request and one network reply. For the size of the prototype, the individual cluster buses limit total memory bandwidth. In larger systems with more nodes and faster split-transaction cluster buses, we expect that the network bisection will limit aggregate memory bandwidth if accesses are uniformly distributed.

6.2.3.2 Water

Water is a molecular dynamics code from the field of computational chemistry. The application computes the interaction between a set of water molecules over a series of time steps. The algorithm is $O(N^2)$ in that each molecule interacts with all other molecules in the system. As shown in Figure 6, the Water application achieves good speedup on the DASH hardware.

Table 5 shows that cache-locality is high in Water, and the time between processor stalls indicates that it is not highly sensitive to memory latency. The table does show some reduction in the busy clocks between stalls, especially when going from 2 to 4 processors, but the decrease is slight after this initial drop. In comparison with Barnes-Hut, Water achieves a slightly lower speedup due to lower cluster locality which increases the average miss penalty. As indicated by the fraction of dirty-remote cache reads, many more of the misses in Water are satisfied directly by the producing processor than in Barnes-Hut.

Looking at the breakdown of memory reference types in Water, the percentage of synchronization references is fairly high. This is due in part to the high cache hit rates, and to the fact that every successful lock acquire or release references the bus in the prototype. Given the percentage of locks and unlocks are almost identical, this data also indicates that lock contention is not a problem in Water.

Finally, we see that like Barnes-Hut, Water does not put a heavy load on the memory system. While the table does indicate an increase in remote memory latency, this is due to the increasing fraction of remote misses that are dirty-remote as opposed to larger queuing delays.

6.2.3.3 LocusRoute

LocusRoute is a standard-cell placement tool that uses actual routed area to evaluate the quality of a given placement. Thus, the task that LocusRoute performs is the routing of a given cell placement. LocusRoute exploits parallelism at two levels. First, multiple wires are routed simultaneously. Second, different routes for the same wire are evaluated in parallel. The runs shown in Figure 6 were for the route of a circuit consisting of 3817 wires and 20 routing channels.

LocusRoute achieves a respectable 9.9 times speedup on 16 processors, but speedup does not increase linearly when more than 16 processors are used (only 13.2 times speedup on 32 processors). Comparing the reference behavior of LocusRoute shown in Table 6 with that of Water, it is clear why LocusRoute does not achieve the same speedup. First, its cache hit rate (busy pclocks between stalls) is lower than Water. This makes it more sensitive to the increase in memory latency when going to multiple clusters. Second, as in Water, locality falls off with more processors and the fraction of dirty-remote references also increases.

Considering the application data structures and algorithms, these effects are not surprising. In LocusRoute, most misses are due to the *cost array* which tracks the number of signals routed in a given section of a channel. The cost array is actively updated by each processor, and there is only limited reuse of the data structure as wires are routed. The result is a lower hit rate than Water and more sensitivity to locality.

Looking at system loading, it is clear that LocusRoute puts more stress on the memory system than Barnes-Hut or Water. Bus utilization is moderate (35-40%). The large latencies for remote memory references when using 24 or 32 processors are due in part to hot spotting for the cost array. In the current implementation, this array is allocated only out of cluster 0's memory. For the 32-processor run, this cluster has over 65% bus utilization (as compared to the average of 37%), and we suspect there is substantial queuing at the PCPU. While removing this hot spot should improve performance, we expect that LocusRoute will achieve significantly better speedup on more than 16 processors only with larger problems.

7. The 20-25% dirty-remote fills when using 1-4 processors are background OS activity. This is only 20-25% of the 0.5-3.0% of the misses that are remote. Local misses caused by the application dominate. When using 8 processors, the dirty-remote percentages are low because there are never any three cluster fills because there is only two active clusters.

8. The factor of two increase when going from 12 to 16 processors arises because the 32-processor DASH is arranged in a 4x2 grid. Currently, processors are numbered and allocated first in the X-dimension so that the 16 processors run in a 4x1 ensemble. Thus, a single X-dimension path sees the load of all four clusters.

Table 4. Barnes-Hut memory access characteristics

Execution Attribute	1 Proc.	2 Proc.	4 Proc.	8 Proc.	12 Proc.	16 Proc.	24 Proc.	32 Proc.
Speedup	1.0	2.0	3.9	7.4	10.7	14.2	20.6	27.5
Efficiency (relative to uniprocessor)	1.00	0.99	0.96	0.92	0.89	0.89	0.86	0.86
Busy Pclks between Proc. Stalls	526.3	633.8	602.7	606.8	534.6	602.7	564.5	560.9
Est. Processor Utilization (%)	94.6	95.6	95.5	94.2	92.9	93.4	92.5	92.3
Cache Read (%)	85.6	90.3	88.5	91.5	92.0	90.7	90.5	90.4
Cache Read Exclusive (%)	9.7	6.8	10.1	6.5	6.1	6.9	6.7	6.7
Cache Lock (%)	2.3	1.4	0.7	1.1	1.2	1.6	2.0	2.0
Cache Unlock (%)	2.1	1.3	0.7	0.8	0.7	0.8	0.6	0.6
Fraction of Reads Local (%)	97.8	99.0	99.5	89.8	86.8	84.9	82.6	82.5
Fraction of Rem. Rds. Dirty-Rem (%)	21.8	21.0	21.2	9.1	6.4	5.7	5.5	5.3
Avg Local Cache Fill (Pclks)	29.2	29.2	29.3	29.4	29.4	29.4	29.4	29.4
Avg Rem Cache Fill (Pclks)	106.6	107.4	105.7	104.2	106.2	109.1	110.9	113.1
Bus Utilization (%)	5.2	6.3	9.1	9.8	11.0	10.2	10.9	11.0
Req. Net Bisection Util. (%)	0.6	0.7	0.7	0.8	0.9	1.7	1.9	2.0
Reply Net Bisection Util. (%)	0.5	0.5	0.5	0.9	1.1	2.2	2.5	2.6

Table 5. Water memory access characteristics

Execution Attribute	1 Proc.	2 Proc.	4 Proc.	8 Proc.	12 Proc.	16 Proc.	24 Proc.	32 Proc.
Speedup	1.0	2.0	3.8	7.1	10.4	13.3	19.3	24.6
Efficiency (relative to uniprocessor)	1.00	0.99	0.95	0.89	0.87	0.83	0.80	0.77
Busy Pclks between Proc. Stalls	935.9	955.0	614.6	528.3	515.0	523.7	553.8	506.3
Est. Processor Utilization (%)	97.5	97.7	97.2	93.2	91.1	90.6	89.2	88.0
Cache Read (%)	46.0	45.2	46.7	46.9	45.2	45.2	44.6	47.0
Cache Read Exclusive (%)	11.9	7.3	25.1	29.6	30.9	30.9	31.7	30.8
Cache Lock (%)	20.9	23.8	14.1	12.1	12.4	12.5	12.3	11.8
Cache Unlock (%)	20.8	23.7	14.1	11.4	11.6	11.4	11.5	10.5
Fraction of Reads Local (%)	96.9	97.2	99.4	68.9	55.1	51.6	40.9	42.8
Fraction of Rem. Rds. Dirty-Rem (%)	21.4	21.6	22.6	9.2	18.3	27.0	48.0	50.0
Avg Local Cache Fill (Pclks)	29.2	29.2	29.4	29.6	29.7	29.7	29.7	29.8
Avg Rem Cache Fill (Pclks)	102.8	107.5	106.9	104.5	108.1	111.6	118.3	120.6
Bus Utilization (%)	4.6	5.7	10.2	14.5	16.3	16.6	17.7	18.8
Req. Net Bisection Util. (%)	0.7	0.8	0.7	1.5	2.0	4.6	6.1	6.7
Reply Net Bisection Util. (%)	0.5	0.6	0.5	1.8	2.5	5.3	6.3	6.7

Table 6. LocusRoute memory access characteristics

Execution Attribute	1 Proc.	2 Proc.	4 Proc.	8 Proc.	12 Proc.	16 Proc.	24 Proc.	32 Proc.
Speedup	1.0	2.0	3.8	6.3	8.4	9.9	11.9	13.2
Efficiency (relative to uniprocessor)	1.00	0.99	0.95	0.79	0.70	0.62	0.50	0.41
Busy Pclks between Proc. Stalls	342.8	312.4	258.0	196.1	179.4	175.4	179.9	181.2
Est. Processor Utilization (%)	92.7	92.9	92.0	79.1	73.1	69.5	64.8	59.4
Cache Read (%)	74.0	70.3	68.8	64.5	69.0	69.3	69.8	70.1
Cache Read Exclusive (%)	15.8	21.9	25.8	31.3	27.5	27.2	26.5	26.0
Cache Lock (%)	5.0	3.9	2.7	2.3	2.0	2.1	2.4	2.7
Cache Unlock (%)	5.0	3.8	2.6	2.0	1.5	1.4	1.3	1.0
Fraction of Reads Local (%)	97.1	98.4	99.6	63.7	60.7	54.4	46.5	41.3
Fraction of Rem. Rds. Dirty-Rem (%)	24.9	24.7	22.8	2.9	20.8	28.0	33.6	35.0
Avg Local Cache Fill (Pclks)	29.1	29.3	29.7	30.4	30.8	31.0	31.0	30.9
Avg Rem Cache Fill (Pclks)	108.2	106.9	107.3	109.1	119.6	128.7	149.6	183.0
Bus Utilization (%)	5.9	8.9	17.1	30.8	36.1	38.2	38.5	36.8
Req. Net Bisection Util. (%)	0.6	0.6	0.7	3.8	5.9	14.2	16.1	16.1
Reply Net Bisection Util. (%)	0.5	0.5	0.5	4.9	6.7	15.4	16.8	16.6

6.2.4 Application Speedup Summary

Overall, a number of conclusions can be drawn from the speedup and reference statistics presented in previous sections. First, it is possible to get near linear speedup on DASH for a number of real applications. Applications with the best speedup have good cache and cluster locality. Since most of the degradation in memory latency occurs when adding the first remote cluster, we expect most of the applications will perform well on 32 and 64 processors. Speedup for many of the applications should be more than 24 on 32 processors, and more than 45 on 64 processors, especially if problem size is increased.

In absolute terms, the number of busy clocks between bus accesses indicates that caching of shared data improves performance significantly. For example, earlier simulation work with the SPLASH benchmarks [14] indicates that the reference rates for Water and LocusRoute to shared data (with 32 processors) is roughly one reference every 20 and 11 instructions respectively. Given the number of busy clocks between misses for Water and LocusRoute given in Table 5 and Table 6 (or even assuming that the number of processor instructions between stalls is optimistic by a factor of two due to internal stalls), caches are satisfying 92% of the shared references in Water (i.e. there are at least $506/2/20 \approx 12$ shared references for every miss), and 88% of the shared references in LocusRoute. Thus, processor utilization without caching would be only 26% in Water and only 13% in LocusRoute.[9] Overall, this implies that caching of shared data improves performance by a factor of 3.4-4.5 in these applications, but as shown earlier, only adds 10% to system cost.[10]

Even with caches, however, locality is still important. If locality is very low and communication misses are frequent (as in MP3D), then speedup will be poor. However, for many applications, the natural locality of the applications is enough (e.g., Barnes-Hut, Radiosity, Water) that good speedups can be achieved without algorithmic or programming contortions. Even in applications where natural locality is limited, DASH's shared-address space model allows the programmer to focus on the few critical data structures that are causing loss in performance, rather than having to explicitly manage (replicate and place) all data objects in the program.

7.0 Conclusions

This paper has outlined our experience in building and starting to use the DASH prototype system. The first result from building the prototype is that such systems are feasible. While the coherence protocol and hardware are not trivial, such systems can be built. Looking in more detail at the logic and memory costs exhibited by the prototype, we have shown that the logic overhead for supporting distributed shared memory (without coherence) is about 10%. Supporting cache coherence adds another 10%-14% in logic and memory overhead if clustering is used.

The second result of building the prototype has been an analysis of the memory system performance. At the lowest level, it is clear that remote memory latencies are significant. We believe this will remain true as processor speeds increase relative to the inherent delays of a large system. Thus, both cache and cluster locality are important in this class of machines, and latency hiding techniques (e.g., prefetch) may be very useful.

The prototype system has also allowed us to measure applications with large data sets using the performance monitor hardware. A number of parallel applications have been run and most achieve good speedup. Many of these applications achieve better than 12 times speedup on 16 processors, and the preliminary results with the 32-processor machine indicate that many will also work well with 32 and 64 processors.

9. This assumes the locality of shared references is the same as the locality given in the table. This is optimistic since there would be no cache-to-cache sharing.

10. The extra overhead costs for caching is conservative because we ignore any added costs in the uncached system that would be necessary to increase the bandwidth to main memory.

Acknowledgments

This research has been supported by DARPA contract N00039-91-C-0138. Dan Lenoski is supported by Tandem Computers Inc. James Laudon is supported by IBM. Anoop Gupta is partly supported by a NSF Presidential Young Investigator Award.

References

[1] Agarwal, A., B.-H. Lim, D. Kranz, and J. Kubiatowicz. LimitLESS Directories: A Scalable Cache Coherence Scheme. In *Proc. Fourth Int. Conf. on Architectural Support Programming Languages and Operating Systems*. pp. 224-234, 1991.

[2] Agarwal, A., R. Simoni, J. Hennessy, and M. Horowitz. An Evaluation of Directory Schemes for Cache Coherence. In *Proc. 15th Int. Symp. on Computer Architecture*. pp. 280-289, 1988.

[3] Baskett, F., T. Jermoluk, and D. Solomon. The 4D-MP Graphics Superworkstation: Computing + Graphics = 40 MIPS + 40 MFLOPS and 100,000 Lighted Polygons per Second. In *Proc. Compcon Spring 88*. pp. 468-471, 1988.

[4] Censier, L. and P. Feautrier, A New Solution to Coherence Problems in Multicache Systems. *IEEE Trans. on Computers,* C(27):1112-1118, 1978.

[5] Flaig, C.M., *VLSI Mesh Routing Systems*. Technical Report 5241:TR:87, California Institute of Technology, May 1987.

[6] Gupta, A., W.-D. Weber, and T. Mowry. Reducing Memory and Traffic Requirements for Scalable Directory-Based Cache Coherence Schemes. In *Proc. 1990 Int. Conf. on Parallel Processing*. pp. I:312-321, 1990.

[7] Lenoski, D., J. Laudon, K. Gharachorloo, A. Gupta, and J. Hennessy. The Directory-Based Cache Coherence Protocol for the DASH Multiprocessor. In *Proc. 17th Int. Symp. on Computer Architecture*. pp. 148-159, 1990.

[8] Lenoski, D., J. Laudon, K. Gharachorloo, W.-D. Weber, A. Gupta, J. Hennessy, M. Horowitz, and M. Lam, The Stanford DASH Multiprocessor. *Computer,* **25**(3), 1992.

[9] Lenoski, D.E., *The Design and Analysis of DASH: A Scalable Directory-Based Multiprocessor*. Ph.D. Thesis. Stanford University. 1991. Also available as Stanford University Technical Report CSL-TR-92-507

[10] Lusk, E., R. Overbeek, J. Boyle, R. Butler, T. Disz, B. Glickfeld, J. Patterson, and R. Stevens, *Portable Programs for Parallel Processors*. Holt, Rinehard and Winston, Inc.1987.

[11] O'Krafka, B.W. and A.R. Newton. An Empirical Evaluation of Two Memory-Efficient Directory Methods. In *Proc. 17th Int. Symp. on Computer Architecture*. pp. 138-147, 1990.

[12] Papamarcos, M.S. and J.H. Patel. A Low Overhead Coherence Solution for Multiprocessors with Private Cache Memories. In *Proc. 11th Int. Symp. on Computer Architecture*. pp. 348-354, 1984.

[13] Singh, J.P., C. Holt, T. Totsuka, A. Gupta, and J.L. Hennessy, *Load Balancing and Data Locality in Parallel N-body Techniques.* Technical Report CSL-TR-92-505, Stanford University, 1991.

[14] Singh, J.P., W.-D. Weber, and A. Gupta, *SPLASH: Stanford Parallel Applications for Shared Memory*. Technical Report CSL-TR-91-469, Stanford University, 1991.

[15] Xilinx, *The Programmable Gate Array Data Book.* 1991.

Session 4: Processor Elements

Performance Evaluation of a Decoded Instruction Cache for Variable Instruction-Length Computers

Gideon Intrater
National Semiconductor (I.C.) Ltd.
P.O.Box 3007, Herzlia B. 46104, ISRAEL
E-mail gideon@nsc.nsc.com

Ilan Spillinger
Department of Electrical Engineering
TECHNION - Israel Institute of Technology
Haifa 32000, ISRAEL

ABSTRACT

A Decoded INstruction Cache (DINC) serves as a buffer between the instruction decoder and the other instruction-pipeline stages. In this paper we explain how techniques that reduce the branch penalty based on such a cache, can improve CPU performance. We analyze the impact of some of the design parameters of DINCs on variable instruction-length computers, e.g., CISC machines.

Our study indicates that tuning the mapping function of the instructions into the cache, can improve the performance substantially. This tuning must be based on the instruction length distribution for a specific architecture. in addition, the associativity degree has a greater effect on the DINC's performance, than on the performance of regular caches. We also discuss the difference between the performance of DINCs and other caches, when longer cache lines are used. The results presented were obtained by both analytical study and trace-driven simulations of several integer UNIX™ applications.

1. INTRODUCTION

Pipelined single-processor computers reach high performance by overlapping the execution of different instructions. A fundamental disadvantage of pipelining is the performance loss incurred, due to branches that require stalling or flushing of the pipeline. A combination of hardware, software and architectural techniques are used to reduce the branch penalty [1], [2]. Each technique contributes to the processor performance.

Branch folding [3] is a promising method to reduce the branch penalty. Branches are folded into other instructions, making it unnecessary to execute them as separate instructions. As in microprograms, an instruction issued for execution specifies both the operation code, and a conditional branch. At the end of the operation, the processor performs the (folded) branch if the condition is true. If the condition is false, the next sequential instruction is executed. Since branches are executed in parallel with other instructions, the branch penalty can be eliminated. In all the other branching techniques, branch execution requires at least one cycle, to issue the branch instruction in the pipeline.

To implement branch folding, two instructions must be examined in parallel. Folding can be implemented during compilation (as in the CCI Regulus [4]), but this increases the code size, and does effect existing code. A possible hardware solution is to merge the two instructions in the decoding stage of the pipeline. This is a demanding task for a single pipeline stage, especially on variable instruction-length computers, where the second instruction cannot be decoded before the length of the first one is known. The hardware required to implement such parallel decoding is complex and bulky.

A simpler method is to use a Decoded INstruction Cache (DINC) [3]. A DINC is a buffer between the instruction decoder, and the rest of the pipeline stages (**Figure 1**). Each entry in the DINC contains a decoded instruction, a branch condition, and a branch target address. Providing a branch target address for every instruction in the cache, has the same effect as turning every instruction into a potential branch instruction. This way, no specific branch instructions are required within the processor (except for indirect branches). Branches exist only in the machine language program.

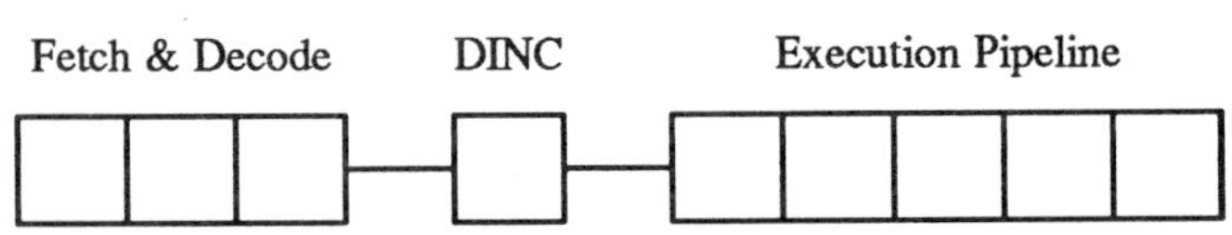

Figure 1. Instruction execution path for a processor with a DINC

The folding algorithm can be performed before storing the instructions into the DINC. This eliminates the requirement to examine two instructions in the same cycle. Usually, folded instructions are fetched from the DINC. On a DINC miss, instructions must be folded while being fetched. As misses are infrequent, a single instruction decoder can be used with very little penalty.

Since most of the world's software runs on variable instruction-length machines (e.g., Intel-86, VAX and IBM-370), and users want to upgrade their system's performance without changing the existing code. A DINC seems to be a promising way to achieve this goal. In this work we study several design parameters and their effect on DINC performance in a CISC environment.

© 1992 ACM 0-89791-509-7/92/0005/0106 $1.50

The outline of this paper is as follows. Section 2 describes the potential CPU performance. Problems in achieving a high cache hit rate in a DINC used in a CISC environment, are shown in Section 3. Our analytical model for DINC behavior with different mapping functions, is introduced in Section 4. Section 5 presents simulation results for various associativity schemes. In Section 6 we suggest a new method to improve DINC performance using large line sizes. Conclusions are summarized in Section 7.

2. BRANCH PENALTY

The execution time of a program can be expressed by: $Path\_Length \times CPI \times Cycle\_Time$. $Path\_Length$ is the dynamic size of the program (i.e., number of executed instructions), CPI is the average number of Cycles Per Instruction, and $Cycle\_Time$ is the basic clock time unit of the processor. Techniques to minimize branch penalty increase the CPU performance by reducing the CPI and sometimes the $Cycle\_Time$. In this section we estimate the performance potential of different branching techniques. For our analyses we use a typical CISC instruction pipeline with 6 stages, like the one found in Zilog Z80000 [5] and Motorola 68040 [6] microprocessors.

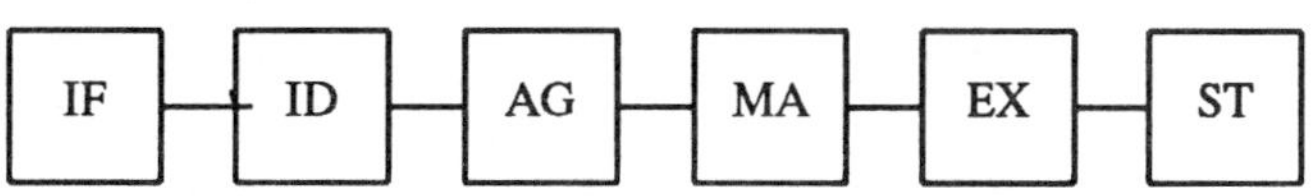

Figure 2. A basic *CISC* instruction pipeline

The pipeline stages are:

IF: Instruction Fetch - Fetches the next instruction from memory or the instruction cache.

ID: Instruction Decode - Decodes the instruction, reads registers for address calculation (for instructions with an operand in memory) and calculates the branch target (for a branch instruction).

AG: Address Generation - For a memory operand, calculates its address and sends it to the Data Cache.

MA: Memory Access - Reads the operand from the Register File or from the Data Cache.

EX: EXecute - Executes the instruction. A No-Operation for LOAD and STORE instructions.

ST: STore result - Writes result to the Register File, Data Cache, or to memory.

Execution of up to 6 different instructions can be overlapped, to reach a peak of one instruction completion per cycle (1 *CPI*). For sequential execution, the pipeline speed is limited by dependencies between instructions in the pipeline, and by storage delays (for a comprehensive discussion see [7]). For non-sequential execution (i.e., when branch instructions are introduced), the execution of the branch depends on the calculation of the branch target, and on the condition code. In our pipeline model, the condition codes are calculated in the **EX** stage, and the branch target is calculated in the **ID** stage.

To minimize the branch penalty, a branch-prediction mechanism is usually incorporated [8]. The processor predicts which direction the conditional branch will take, and starts to fetch instructions from that address. If the prediction was wrong, the processor needs to flush all the instructions that were prefetched from the wrong stream, and start to fetch from the correct address. The simplest branch prediction techniques are *Always-Taken* and *Never-Taken*. Under the *Never-Taken* strategy the **IF** continues fetching from the sequential stream. When the *Always-Taken* strategy is used, the **IF** fetches instructions beginning at the branch target. In **Table 1** we summarize the four possible cases for the above branch predictions and their branch penalties. Note that the penalty is the sum of the time to execute the branch instruction (1 cycle), and the number of empty stages in the pipeline.

	Prediction	
Outcome	*Never-Taken*	*Always-Taken*
Branch Not-Taken	1 + 0	1 + 3
Branch Taken	1 + 3	1 + 1

TABLE 1. Branch penalty using simple prediction techniques (in cycles)

Better branch prediction strategies can be employed [2] [8] to achieve about 85% correct predictions. The wrong prediction penalty can be reduced by using *branch spreading*. The compiler tries to re-order the compare and conditional branch instructions. If the compare instruction can be executed two or more instructions before the branch instruction, the penalty for wrong prediction is reduced to a single cycle (execution of the branch instruction itself). There are cases where the compare and branch instructions can not be spreaded. In [9], where a machine with the pipeline described in **Figure 2** runs code generated for the Series 32000™ architecture [10], the authors show that *branch spreading* reduces the penalty for wrong branch prediction to 2.8 cycles. In [9], the authors also show that an average of 62.4% of the conditional branches are taken and 37.6% are not taken. Using the above, the average branch penalty is: $1 + 1 \times 0.85 \times 0.624 + 2.8 \times 0.15 = 1.95$ cycles. The three terms in the formula are: the cost of the branch instruction (1 cycle), the penalty associated with branches that were predicted *taken* and were actually taken, and the penalty associated with branches where the prediction was wrong.

	Prediction	
Outcome	*Never-Taken*	*Always-Taken*
Branch Not-Taken	1 + 0	1 + 2.8
Branch Taken	1 + 2.8	1 + 0

TABLE 2. Branch penalty while using a DINC

A DINC reduces the average number of cycles per branch as shown in **Table 2.** The **IF** stage fetches the next instruction according to the branch prediction mechanism, either from the next sequential address, or from the branch target address stored in the DINC. On a predicted-taken branch in a DINC, the **IF** stage does not need to wait a full cycle to let the **ID** stage calculate the branch target. Therefore, the branch penalty of taken branches that were predicted as such, becomes zero. Hence, the average branch penalty is: $1 + 2.8 \times 0.15 = 1.42$ cycles.

Another reduction in the branch penalty can be achieved by implementing *branch folding* [3]. Since each instruction in the

DINC has a next address field, each instruction can easily incorporate a branch instruction by adding few more bits to specify the conditions for which the branch is actually taken. If all the branch instructions are folded into the previous instruction, the penalty for branches is reduced (see **Table 3**). The branch instruction is usually folded into the previous compare instruction. In case of a wrong prediction the four instructions in the next pipeline stages have to be flushed (one more instruction than in the non-folded case). *Branch spreading* reduces this penalty to 3.8 cycles [9]. The branch penalty here reduces to: $3.8 \times 0.15 = 0.57$ cycles.

	Prediction	
Outcome	*Never-Taken*	*Always-Taken*
Branch Not-Taken	0	3.8
Branch Taken	3.8	0

TABLE 3. Branch penalty while using folded branches in a DINC

Now that we know the branch penalty for each technique we can evaluate the performance of the processor. We have to add the number of *CPI* without the branch instructions, to the branch penalty in each pipeline type. The average *CPI* in the 6 stage pipeline is 1.22 *CPI* (assuming 1 cycle per branch) and the conditional branch frequency is 16.56% [9]. Thus the *CPI* is given by: $1.22 + 0.1656 \times (\text{branch penalty} - 1)$. The results are presented in the following table (note that these results are without the penalty for instruction cache misses). The term RINC in **Table 4** stands for Regular INstruction Cache.

Method	CPI	Relative Performance
RINC, Branch Prediction and Branch Spreading	1.38	100%
DINC, Branch Prediction and Branch Spreading	1.29	107%
DINC, Branch Prediction, Branch Spreading and Branch Folding	1.15	120%

TABLE 4. CPU Performance

We see that a DINC with branch folding offers a 20% potential improvement in the CPU performance. This improvement assumes the same cache hit ratio for DINC and RINC with the same capacity. In the next section we show that to achieve this hit ratio, the DINC designer must follow some subtle architectural guidelines.

3. MAPPING INSTRUCTIONS INTO A DINC

Let us organize the DINC in a similar structure to a RINC, as a set-associative cache with a tag for each entry [11]. Instructions are mapped into the cache according to their address. The *m* address bits are separated into two fields, the *n* less significant bits form an index, and the rest form a tag.

tag	index
m ... n	n-1 ... 0

Figure 3. Tag and index address fields

For direct mapping, the index specifies the cache set, and the tag is compared with the most significant bits of the address stored in the entry. In the following example, we show how direct mapping of variable length instructions causes *empty sets* in a DINC.

Example 1: On a machine with a 1-way set associative (i.e., direct mapped) DINC with 8 sets, we map one decoded instruction into each set. Given an instruction stream with three instructions I_1, I_2 and I_3, lengths 3, 2 and 2 bytes and addresses 00000, 00011 and 00101, respectively. **Table 5** shows that each instruction is followed by *empty sets* (sets 001, 010, 100, 110 and 111). No matter how long the instructions are, the decoded instructions are of the same size, the size of the cache entry.

Instruction address	Set number	Instruction
00000	000	I_1
	001	—
	010	—
00011	011	I_2
	100	—
00101	101	I_3
	110	—
	111	—

TABLE 5. Direct mapping into a 1-way set associative DINC

Empty sets might increase the miss rate as illustrated in the following example.

Procedure A		Procedure B		DINC	
Address	Inst.	Address	Inst.	Set	Instruction
00000	I_{A1}			000	I_{A1}
		10001	I_{B1}	001	I_{B1}
00010	I_{A2}	10010	I_{B2}	010	I_{A2}, I_{B2}
				011	—
00100	I_{A3}			100	I_{A3}
		10101	I_{B3}	101	I_{B3}
00110	I_{A4}	10110	I_{B4}	110	I_{A4}, I_{B4}
				111	—

TABLE 6. Mapping two procedures into a 1-way DINC

Example 2: Assuming the same DINC of **Example 1**, we map two procedures, A and B, into the DINC. Procedure A consists of four 2-byte instructions I_{A1}, I_{A2}, I_{A3} and I_{A4} in addresses 00000, 00010, 00100 and 00110, respectively. Procedure B consists of instructions I_{B1}, I_{B2}, I_{B3} and I_{B4}, lengths 1, 3, 1 and 3 bytes, and addresses 10001, 10010, 10101 and 10110 respectively.

Clearly, after both procedures have been executed once (A and then B), all the instructions except for I_{A2} and I_{A4} are in the cache (**Table 6**). The instructions of the two procedures are intermixed in the DINC. In the case where procedures A and B execute alternately, a miss occurs on each execution of instructions I_{A2}, I_{B2}, I_{A4} and I_{B4}.

To reduce the number of *empty sets* that might cause misses, the index can be extracted from higher bits of the instruction address. For the above example, the index can be extracted from bits 1 to n+1 i.e., shifted by one bit (1-shift), as shown in **Figure 4.** **Table 7** shows that this mapping results in a better cache utilization.

tag	index	tag
m … n+1	n … 1	0

Figure 4. Tag and index address fields with 1-shift

Procedure A		Procedure B		DINC	
Address	Inst.	Address	Inst.	Set	Instruction
00000	I_{A1}	10001	I_{B1}	000	I_{A1}, I_{B1}
00010	I_{A2}	10010	I_{B2}	001	I_{A2}, I_{B2}
00100	I_{A3}	10101	I_{B3}	010	I_{A3}, I_{B3}
00110	I_{A4}	10110	I_{B4}	011	I_{A4}, I_{B4}

TABLE 7. Mapping two procedures into a 1-way DINC (with 1-shift)

Usually, a good prefetching policy can eliminate most of the misses. An example of such a policy is to fetch ahead the next instructions as long as they are missing from the cache. The bus is tuned for block transfers, so only the first instruction causes a miss, while the following (consecutive) instructions are fetched at a rate equal to the throughput of the pipeline, and are actually not counted as misses. When such a prefetching policy is used for the above example, a miss occurs only once, at the beginning of each procedure. Mapping the same procedures into a RINC results in the same number of misses.

Using the 1-shift mapping function, an *empty set* is created only when two consecutive instructions are 3 bytes long each. If, on the other hand, the processor has also a single byte instruction length, the 1-shift mapping may cause a *collision* whenever such an instruction is located in an even address. In the general case, a CISC architecture supports several instructions lengths, and the average length is few bytes. In this case it is obvious that mapping instructions with 0-shift (the index is given by the least significant bits of the address) causes *empty sets*, while mapping with non 0-shift (index is extracted from higher order address bits) may introduce *collisions* between consecutive instructions. These *collisions* have a direct effect on the miss-ratio. The two colliding instructions are always executed sequentially, so each one of them causes a miss!

Misses are also caused by another DINC characteristic that does not exist in a RINC. In a DINC with 2-way associativity or more, mapping with a shift will cause consecutive instructions to reside in several entries within one set. Therefore, two procedures that can be mapped side by side, in a RINC, will collide in a DINC as shown in the next example.

Example 3: Let us use a machine with a 2-way set associative DINC (4 sets), a 1-shift mapping function, and an LRU replacement algorithm. **Table 8** shows the mapping of two procedures A and B into the DINC. Each of the procedures can be mapped into the DINC without *collisions*. Note that I_{B1} and I_{B2} are not colliding, since there are two entries in each set. When each of these procedures is executed once (procedure A and then B), all the instructions except for I_{A2} reside in the cache. If these procedures execute alternately, a miss will occur for each of the instructions I_{A2}, I_{B1} and I_{B2}. We will refer to it as a *full set* effect.

Procedure A		Procedure B		DINC	
Address	Inst.	Address	Inst.	Set	Instruction
00000	I_{A1}			00	I_{A1}
		10010	I_{B1}	01	I_{A2}, I_{B1}, I_{B2}
00011	I_{A2}	10011	I_{B2}		
		10101	I_{B3}	10	I_{B3}
00110	I_{A3}			11	I_{A3}

TABLE 8. Mapping two procedures into a 2-way DINC with a 1-shift

We see that *empty sets* cause scattered misses because of intermixed procedures. To solve it, we use a non-zero shift that might cause *collisions* and *full sets*. Both effects increase the miss ratio. In the next section we introduce a novel model to estimate the optimal mapping function to minimize the miss ratio, without using extensive trace driven simulations.

4. EVALUATION OF DINC BEHAVIOR

Intuitively, a DINC performs optimally if the number of *collisions*, *full sets* and *empty sets* are minimal. To estimate these numbers we developed the following probabilistic model.

First, let us define a *memory line* as a group of L consecutive addresses (bytes) mapped to the same DINC set. Also, $P(Len_1{=}i)$ is the probability that the length of a given instruction is i. A *collision* in a 1-way set associative DINC occurs whenever two or more instructions start in the same *memory line*. This happens whenever an instruction I with length i starts in a *memory line* ML, with less than $L-i$ occupied bytes. The instructions preceding I occupy less than $L-i$ bytes of ML. Instruction I uses i bytes of ML, thus the instruction that follows I will also start in ML and be mapped into the same set. Assuming that on variable instruction-length machines there is an equal probability that an instruction ends at any of the L bytes in a *memory line*, the *collision* probability in a 1-way set associative DINC, $P_c(1)$, is given by:

$$P_c(1) = \frac{1}{L}\sum_{i=1}^{L}(L-i)\,P(Len_1{=}i) \qquad (1)$$

In a similar way, the *collision* probability of an N-way set associative DINC, $P_c(N)$, is given by:

$$P_c(N) = \frac{1}{L} \sum_{i=1}^{L} (L-i)\, P(Len_N = i) \qquad (2)$$

Where $P(Len_N=i)$ is the probability that the length of N consecutive instructions is i. Here, N instructions in the same *memory line* can fit into the N ways of the set associative cache. A *collision* occurs when the length of N instructions is smaller than $L-i$ (i.e., the following instruction is also mapped into the same set).

Our workload is a set of four Series 32000 UNIX applications (*ls*, *grep*, *opt* and *dc*). **Table 9** summarizes some characteristics of this workload.

Name	Instructions in Trace	Static Code Size	Average Instruction Length
ls	22551	19320 Bytes	3.26 Bytes
dc	531789	33780 Bytes	3.32 Bytes
grep	697463	16944 Bytes	3.20 Bytes
opt	430323	31276 Bytes	3.70 Bytes

TABLE 9. The UNIX workload

The following table shows the *collision* probability evaluated by equations (1) and (2) using the measured instruction length distribution of our workload, for several cache associativity schemes and different mapping functions. Note that we used only simple mapping functions employing shifts of the index. Other mapping functions can also be used but may require the use of complex hardware. The results in **Table 10** show that with higher associativity, more shifts (and therefore less *empty sets*) can be used without getting any *collisions*.

Mapping	0-shift	1-shift	2-shift	3-shift	4-shift
1-way	0	0	0.273	0.580	0.790
2-way	0	0	0	0.214	0.579
4-way	0	0	0	0	0.191
8-way	0	0	0	0	0
16-way	0	0	0	0	0

TABLE 10. Collision probability as a function of the mapping and associativity

The probability of *full sets* in a DINC can be calculated using the equation for *collision* probability. A *memory line* causes a fully occupied set in an associativity of N, if in an N-1 associativity it causes a *collision*, and it does not cause a *collision* in an N-way associativity. E.g., two instructions that reside in the same set in a 2-way DINC cause a *collision* in a 1-way DINC, since only one instruction can fit in the single instruction slot of the set. Thus, the probability of *full sets* in an N-way DINC, $P_f(N)$, is:

$$P_f(N) = P_c(N-1) - P_c(N) \qquad (3)$$

In the following table we show the probability of *full sets* evaluated using equation (3). Note that in this table we start with associativity of 2-way. In 1-way associativity, the behavior of DINCs and RINCs is similar, each time an instruction is mapped into a specific set, this set is fully occupied, and cannot be used for other instructions without removing the previous one.

Mapping	0-shift	1-shift	2-shift	3-shift	4-shift
2-way	0	0	0.273	0.366	0.211
4-way	0	0	0	0.047	0.181
8-way	0	0	0	0	0
16-way	0	0	0	0	0

TABLE 11. Probability of *full sets* as a function of the mapping and associativity

An instruction causes *Empty sets* whenever its length i is greater than the *memory line* size L, and crosses a *memory line* boundary. In this case the following instruction is not mapped to the consecutive cache set. Our model for number of *empty sets*, E, is:

$$E = \sum_{i=L}^{MAX} \left(\frac{i}{L} - 1\right) P(Len_1 = i) \qquad (4)$$

Where MAX is the maximal instruction length. It is easy to see that the average number of *empty sets* does not depend on the associativity of the DINC. In **Table 12** we use equation (4) to evaluate the average number of *empty sets*.

Mapping	0-shift	1-shift	2-shift	3-shift	4-shift
Empty Sets	2.369	0.685	0.116	0	0

TABLE 12. An estimate to the average number of *empty sets*

We see that low number of shifts cause higher number of *empty sets*. When either 3-shift or 4-shift is used, the number of *empty sets* becomes zero. The reason is that in our workload there are only few instructions with length greater than 7.

Summarizing the above discussion, we see that whenever a *collision* occurs there is a miss in the DINC. A *full set* will cause a miss only if another procedure cannot be mapped into a parallel associative way of the DINC. *Empty sets* will cause a miss only if they cause the instructions of two procedures to be mapped in an intermixed order into the DINC, and to collide.

To choose the mapping function which reduces the miss ratio we have to minimize the number of *collisions*, *full sets* and *empty sets*. According to the above study, *collisions* have the largest effect on the miss ratio. We also feel that eliminating the probability of *full sets* is a second priority, and that minimizing the number of *empty sets* is of the lowest importance.

For the 32000 architecture, and our workload analyses (see **Tables 9, 10** and **11**), we choose a mapping function that will eliminate both *collisions* and *full sets* in all the associativity levels. From the set of mapping functions that meet the above criteria, we choose one that minimizes (but not always eliminates) the number of empty sets. According to these rules, for a 1-way associativity, shifts by 0 and 1 eliminate *collisions* and *full sets*. We will choose a shift by 1 where the number of *empty sets* is minimal. In a similar way, we will choose a shift by 1 and 2 for 2- and 4-way associativity, respectively. In 8- and 16-way associativity, shifts by 3 and 4 eliminate the *collisions*, *full sets* and *empty sets*. We can choose any of these mapping functions to achieve similar results.

To validate these decisions, we ran trace-driven simulations of our workload. We measured the miss rate for different DINC organizations and mapping functions. The DINC capacity was modeled with 128, 256 and 512 instructions, and simulated with 1-, 2-, 4-, 8- and 16-way set associative organization. Note that to simulate a multitasking environment, our simulator flushed the whole instruction cache every 100,000 instructions. **Figure 5** shows the geometric average [12] of the miss rate over all four applications and DINC capacities.

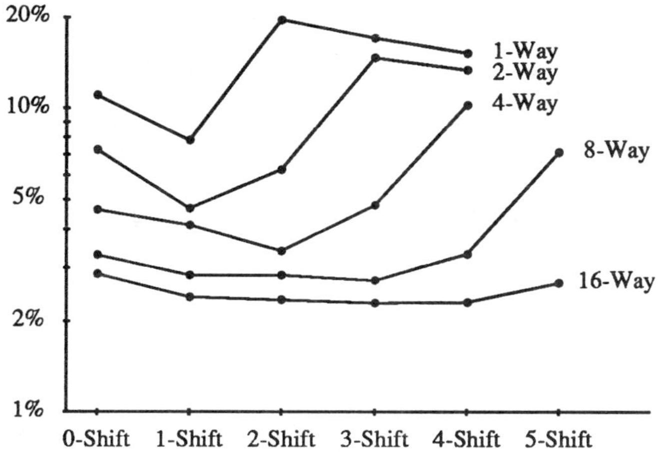

Figure 5. Average number of misses as a function of associativity and mapping

These results match the conclusions that followed our analysis presented above. In the next section we focus on the influence of different associativity degrees on the DINC performance.

5. ASSOCIATIVITY IN DINC

In the previous section we determined the best mapping function for each associativity degree of a DINC. Usually, to choose the best associativity scheme, the designer has to consider the chip-area and the complexity of different associativity degrees [13]. We simulated DINCs and RINCs of comparable capacities to evaluate the improvement in miss rate when the associativity degree increases. The DINC was modeled with 128, 256 and 512 instructions. The RINC was modeled with 512, 1024 and 2048 bytes (average instruction length is close to 4 bytes, in our workload, so we compared a DINC of m entries with a RINC of $4 \times m$ bytes). Both the DINC and the RINC were simulated with 1-, 2-, 4-, 8- and 16-way set associative organizations. **Figure 6** presents the geometric mean of the miss rate over all the applications and cache capacities.

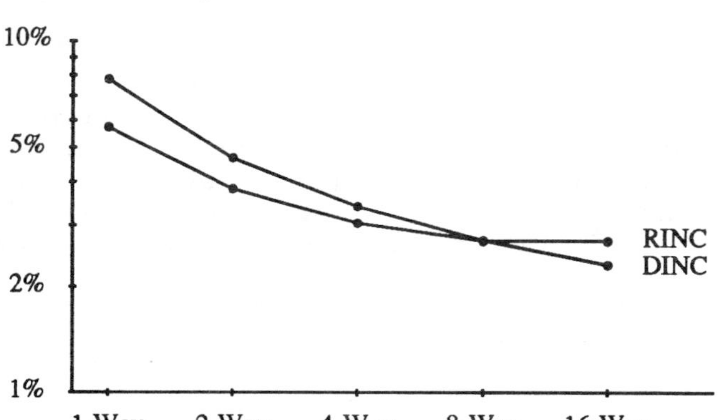

Figure 6. Average miss rates for DINCs and RINCs

As expected, the miss rate in RINC decreases as the associativity degree increases [6]. The main factor is the higher flexibility in choosing the place for a new instruction. As follows from Section 4 above, associativity has greater effect on DINCs (see the slope of the DINC's curve).

From **Figure 6**, it follows that for high associativity degrees, the performance of the DINC and the RINC is comparable. This is due to the negligible number of *collisions*, *full sets* and *empty sets* in DINCs with high associativity degrees. The fact that a 8-way is the lowest associativity degree for DINC performance comparable to a RINC, matches the results presented in Section 4, where it is the lowest associativity degree to overcome the *collisions*, *full sets* and the *empty sets* problems.

It should be pointed out that although the instruction capacities of the DINC and the RINC we compared, are similar, the actual area to implement a DINC is larger. In the DINC we have modeled, we decode each instruction into a vertical microcode format with a fixed length of four bytes each (similar to the instruction encoding in RISC machines [7]). This format can be used only for a subset of the machine instructions (which will be executed at the full throughput of the pipeline). In our workload, the length of more than 60% of the instructions is less than or equal to 4 bytes, most of them are 2 or 3 bytes long. By changing the encoding of all the short instructions and some of the long instructions to 4 bytes, we can achieve a high percentage of instructions decoded in 4 bytes. We assume that the number of instructions that cannot be mapped to 4 bytes is negligible, and therefore choose not to map them into the DINC. It can be shown that two more bytes can contain all the rest of the information needed in a DINC representation (the branch condition, and the branch target address). Thus the number of bytes needed for storing an instruction in a DINC is six, four bytes for the instruction, and another two for the folded branch. In the next section, we evaluate the performance of DINCs with various line sizes.

6. LINE SIZE EFFECT ON DINCS

In the DINC structures we discussed above, we assumed that the DINC incorporates single instruction lines. A common method to increase the performance of regular caches is to use a larger line size [14]. In the following we show that it is not trivial to obtain the same advantage in a DINC.

Each cache line stores several instructions and a single tag, see **Figure 7** below (this is more efficient for a given cache area, when both the data and the tag area are considered [13]). Such a structure implies that only a stream of instructions that are executed sequentially can be mapped into a single line, where branches cause access to a new cache line. This limits the number of instructions in each cache line to the basic block size (i.e., the number of instructions between two consecutive branches).

tag	instruction 1	instruction 2	instruction 3	instruction 4

Figure 7. Structure for LDINC with 4 instructions per line

To implement such a cache structure, the Instruction Fetch (**IF**) stage of the pipeline has to search for the next instruction in two possible places: the current cache line (i.e., in the instruction slot following the instruction currently in the Instruction Decode stage), or in the first slot of a cache line pointed by the instruction address. This technique may require a buffer to hold the current cache line (or part of it). We call such a decoded instruction cache, LDINC (*Line Decoded INstruction Cache*).

To exploit the performance of caches with large line size, prefetching techniques need to be used. In the following we will concentrate on one possible prefetching policy: prefetch a full line. Each cache miss causes the **IF** to prefetch instructions to fill the whole cache line.

We have simulated LDINCs and RINCs with several comparable capacities, and line sizes. **Figures 8** and **9** present the appropriate results.

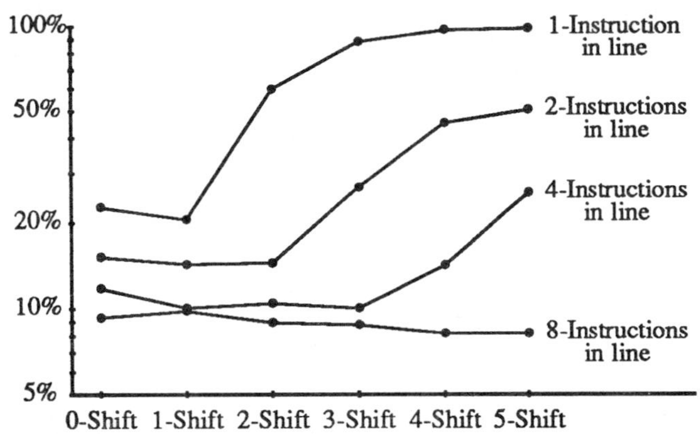

Figure 8. Average percentage of misses in an LDINC

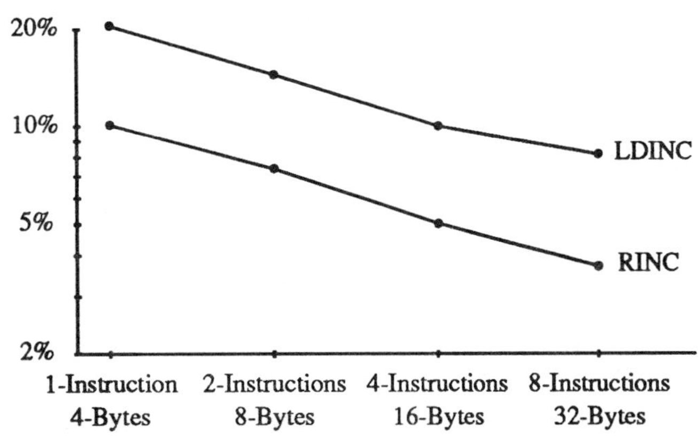

Figure 9. Average percentage of misses in RINC and LDINC

Figure 8 shows that the minimal number of misses is achieved with a higher number of shifts in longer cache lines. **Figure 9** shows that a RINC achieves a much better hit rate than an LDINC with comparable capacity. In other words, we see that the LDINC does not exploit to full advantage the longer lines as does a RINC (refer to [14]). There are three LDINC characteristics that cause this performance degradation. The first one is that branch targets are not mapped to the beginning of *memory lines*. A second problem is the irregularity of the length of *n* instructions in a *memory line*, due to the variable instruction length. This causes *full sets*, *empty sets* and more *collisions* (depending on the mapping function). The third problem is that the basic block size is small (4-5 instruction on average), thus long cache lines cannot be fully utilized. A possible way to tackle the first two problems is to use the compiler to tune the code, so that instructions fit the *memory lines*, using the following alignment algorithm.

The goal of the algorithm is to group together at most *n* instructions (*n* will be the number of instruction slots in a cache line) with a length of exactly *m* bytes (i.e., *memory line* with $L=m$). If the length of the set of instructions grouped together is less then *m*, we "pad" this group with a branch instruction to the aligned address of the next *memory line* (this address is of course a multiple of *m*). Also, we do not allow grouping together a set of instructions whose length exceeds the limit of *m* bytes, although the number of instructions in the group is less then *n*. Regardless of the process described above, if we encounter an instruction that is a possible target for a branch instruction, we assign this instruction to an aligned address (i.e., as a first instruction in a new group). Notice that the branch instructions that we use for the padding adjust each group size to *m*. These instructions will not map into the LDINC due to the use of the *branch folding* technique [3].

This algorithm applies only for software that can be re-compiled, and benefit from the better cache performance. Existing code can still run on the LDINC correctly. To quickly evaluate the potential for the above compiler technique, we modified our workload traces (by changing instruction addresses) to produce a trace with aligned instructions. Note that a compiler tuned for the DINC structure can produce a more efficient code.

In **Figure 10** we summarize the results for RINC and the two kinds of LDINC: LDINC without code alignment, and LDINC using code alignment (ALDINC). The line size *m* is $4 \times n$ bytes, and the mapping function uses $Log_2(m)$ shifts.

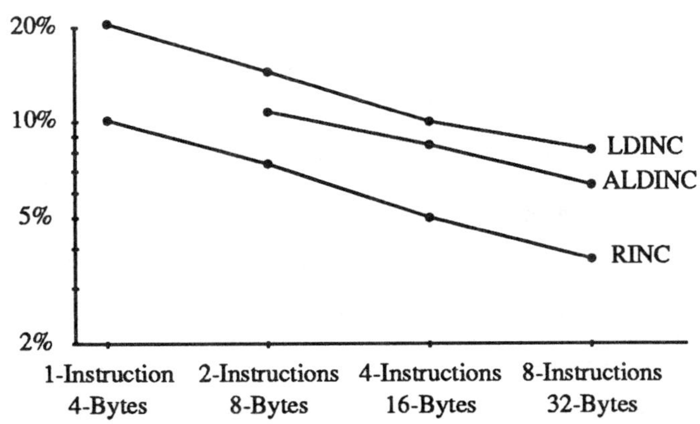

Figure 10. Average percentage of misses in an Aligned LDINC

It is clear from the above results that the alignment algorithm improves the LDINC performance. We should point out that for 2 and 4 instructions per line, the alignment algorithm increases the code size from 50% to 100% (i.e., the code size is duplicated in lines with 4 instructions). Aligning for larger line size is not cost effective, due to the increase in the code size (e.g., for the case of eight instructions per line, the code increase by 217%). Larger lines cannot be fully utilized, due to the size of basic blocks.

7. SUMMARY

We have described how branch folding and spreading can be used together to greatly improve performance. These techniques can enhance the performance of existing programs without compiling them again for a new architecture. The demand for such improvement is very great because of the high cost of recompiling the billions of bytes of code running on the popular architectures, e.g., Intel-86, VAX and IBM-370.

An efficient way to implement branch folding is to use a DINC. We wanted to simplify the implementation of a DINC for variable instruction length computers, and to design a DINC that would take advantage of the performance improvement potential of the branch folding technique.

We have explained the correlation between instruction length distribution, and mapping into a DINC. This correlation enables the DINC designer to choose the best function for mapping into a DINC, using a minimum number of simulation runs. We have also shown that, even though designers should usually choose direct mapped caches [15], high associativity degrees are necessary to enable hit rates that compare favorably with those of RINCs.

Longer cache lines can also enhance the performance of a DINC, because less memory is required for tags. However, they do not enhance performance as much as might be expected. We described three factors that prevent high hit rates in an LDINC. We proposed a way to eliminate two of these three factors, by having the compiler tune the code to the cache. Code that was recompiled achieved better hit rates. However, the basic block size continued to restrict the performance of the LDINC.

Finally, we succeeded in designing a DINC whose hit rate is comparable to that of an RINC. We were able to actualize the 20% improvement in processor performance that is possible using DINCs. We suggest that further work be done with DINCs on superscalar CISC machines, to determine how DINCs can simplify the logic used to issue instructions.

8. ACKNOWLEDGMENTS

We would like to thank Raya Leviatan, Sara Bitan, and Eran Gluska from National Semiconductor for their help with the instruction tracer that provided the Series 32000 traces. Special thanks to Don Alpert from Intel and Gabriel M. Silberman from IBM for their help during the various stages of this work.

9. REFERENCES

[1] S. McFarling and J. Hennessy, "Reducing the Cost Of Branches," *Proc. of the 13th Annual Symposium on Computer Architecture*, 1986, pp. 396-403.

[2] D. J. Lilja, "Reducing the Branch Penalty in Pipelined Processors," *IEEE Computer*, Vol. 21, No. 7, July 1988, pp. 47-54.

[3] D. Ditzel and H. McLellan, "Branch Folding in the CRISP Microprocessor: Reducing Branch Delay to Zero," *Proc. of the 14th Annual Symposium on Computer Architecture*, 1987, pp. 2-9.

[4] J. Letz, and J. Slingwine, "Living with RISC: Software Issues in the Regulus Architecture," *Proc. of 1987 IEEE International Conference on Computer Design: VLSI in Computers and Processors (ICCD-87)*, 1987, pp 549-557.

[5] D. Philips, "Z80000 Microprocessor," *IEEE Micro*, Vol. 5, No. 6, December 1985, pp. 23-36.

[6] R. W. Edenfield *et al.*, "The 68040 Processor, Part 1, Design and Implementation," *IEEE Micro*, Vol. 10, No. 1, February 1990, pp. 66-78.

[7] J. L. Hennessy and D. A. Patterson, *Computer Architecture: A Quantitative Approach*, Morgan Kaufman 1989.

[8] J. Lee and A. Smith, "Branch Prediction Strategies and Branch Target Buffer Design," *IEEE Computer*, Vol. 17, No. 1, January 1984, pp. 6-22.

[9] D. Alpert, A. Averbuch, and O. Danieli, Performance Comparison of Load/Store and Symmetric Instruction Set Architectures," *Proc. of the 17th Annual Symposium on Computer Architecture*, 1990, pp. 172-181.

[10] Colin Hunter, "Series 32000 Programmer's Reference Manual," Prentice-Hall Inc., 1987.

[11] A. J. Smith, "Cache Memories," *ACM Computing Surveys*, Vol. 14, No. 3, 1982, pp. 473-530.

[12] P. J. Fleming, and J. J. Wallace, "How Not to Lie with Statistics: The correct Way to Summarize Benchmark Results," *CACM*, Vol. 29, No. 3, March 1986, pp. 218-221.

[13] D. Alpert, *Performance Tradeoffs for Microprocessor Cache Memories*, Computer System Laboratory Technical Note 83-239, Stanford University, Stanford, CA, December 1983.

[14] A. J. Smith, "Line (Block) Size Choice for CPU Cache Memories," *IEEE Transactions on Computers*, Vol. C-36, No. 9, September 1987, pp. 1063-1075.

[15] M. D. Hill, "A Case for Direct-Mapped Caches," *IEEE Computer*, Vol. 21, No. 12, December 1988, pp. 25-40.

1 Series 32000 is a trademarks of National Semiconductor Corporation.

2 UNIX is a trademark of AT&T.

A Simulation Based Study of TLB Performance

J. Bradley Chen
School of Computer Science
Carnegie Mellon University
5000 Forbes Avenue
Pittsburgh, PA 15213

Anita Borg
Norman P. Jouppi
Western Research Laboratory
Digital Equipment Corporation
250 University Avenue
Palo Alto, CA 94301

Abstract

This paper presents the results of a simulation-based study of various translation lookaside buffer (TLB) architectures, in the context of a modern VLSI RISC processor. The simulators used address traces, generated by instrumented versions of the SPECmarks and several other programs running on a DECstation 5000. The performance of two-level TLBs and fully-associative TLBs were investigated. The amount of memory mapped was found to be the dominant factor in TLB performance. Small first-level FIFO instruction TLBs can be effective in two level TLB configurations. For some applications, the cycles-per-instruction (CPI) loss due to TLB misses can be reduced from as much as 5 CPI to negligible levels with typical TLB parameters through the use of variable-sized pages.

1. Introduction

In computer systems with virtual memory, a TLB is typically used to provide fast translation of virtual addresses generated by instruction execution to physical addresses needed for cache tag comparisons. Both physically and virtually addressed caches require address translation. With physically addressed caches, the TLB lookup is in the critical path of cache access, so low latency and miss rates are crucial for memory system performance. The TLB is a cache, speeding up access to entries in the page table, where complete information on virtual to physical memory mappings is maintained. Most modern machines use split instruction and data caches, and this configuration is assumed (unless stated otherwise) in the remainder of this paper. Given this context, we consider several possibilities for the TLB implementation:

- **A single TLB shared between instruction and data caches.** To reduce contention, the TLB can be dual-ported. This introduces complex circuitry, doubling the size of the TLB without increasing its capacity.
- **Independent TLBs for instruction and data caches.** The instruction TLB should be made smaller than the data TLB, as instruction reference streams exhibit greater locality than those for data. The appropriate size tradeoff is difficult to determine and once made is fixed. If the instruction TLB is too small, performance will suffer. If it is too large, the space available for the data TLB is compromised and again performance suffers.
- **Two-level TLB architectures.** A small instruction TLB (i.e., *micro-TLB*), can be refilled from a larger single-ported shared TLB, primarily used for data references. This option is described in more detail below.

A micro-TLB is a fully associative TLB with a very small number of entries (probably less than eight) which is reloaded in hardware from a larger shared TLB. A number of recent machines use micro-TLBs, including the MIPS R4000 [7], though they are invisible at the architecture level. A micro-TLB is accessed in parallel with the instruction cache. On a miss, the micro-TLB is reloaded from the shared TLB. As the larger TLB is single ported, the CPU may stall for a few cycles, with data references suspended while the TLB is busy, but this penalty is much less expensive than that of a full TLB miss. We assume 3 cycles as the micro-TLB miss penalty in this paper. Because of the high locality in instruction reference streams, and the relatively small miss penalty, acceptable miss rates can be achieved with a small micro-TLB. The balance of instruction and data entries in the shared TLB is determined dynamically, unlike in the second option above. In addition the shared TLB need not be dual-ported, so the extra space can be used to increase its capacity. No previous research known to the authors characterizes the design space for the micro-TLB.

Because the TLB can be in the critical path of memory access, good TLB performance is essential to good overall performance of a machine. TLB design has been complicated in several recent architectures with split instruction and data TLBs. To date, such designs have received negligible attention in the research literature. Experimental results are presented herein to characterize the behavior of split as well as shared TLBs.

Another feature found in several recent architectures is TLB entries that can map variable size pages. When such a TLB entry is loaded with a new mapping, it is also loaded with the size of the page to be mapped. Typically, the size is restricted to a power of two and may range from 4K bytes to a gigabyte [5, 7]. Although there are several obvious applications of variable size pages, such as mapping operat-

© 1992 ACM 0-89791-509-7/92/0005/0114 $1.50

ing system text and graphics frame buffers, it is not yet understood to what degree they can be used to improve the execution rate of application code. Performance of applications which concentrate references on a contiguous segment could improve if that segment were accessed as a single page with a single TLB entry. Applications which scatter references across a sparse address space have little hope of benefiting from large pages without significantly increased memory usage. Address traces and reference counting tools can be used to record dynamic patterns of memory access, to aid in understanding the applicability of these structures.

The many recent studies on memory system behavior and performance have concentrated almost exclusively on cache design [10, 9]. Little attention has been given to TLB performance. Early studies have shown that TLB miss penalties consume 6% of all machine cycles [4] and 4% of execution time [3], and hence can have a significant impact on machine performance. However, these results were for VAX computers with 512 byte page sizes, an order of magnitude smaller than is typical today, and main memory sizes two orders of magnitude smaller than those considered in this study.

Wood [12, 11] proposed in-cache address translation as an alternative to a TLB. His work has shown that such methods are effective for programs such as Lisp applications and operating systems, where the working set is spread over a large address space. They are less useful for behavior such as is seen with typical C programs, where memory activity is concentrated in the bottom of several segments. His methods also become less applicable when memory access times become large with respect to processor speed.

Finally, previous TLB studies [3, 11] have considered set-associative or direct-mapped organizations. These were common when TLBs were made from discrete MSI and LSI RAMs. Recently, however, VLSI RISC microprocessors (e.g., [5, 7]) typically make use of fully-associative TLBs, since these require about the same area as set-associative TLBs when implemented within a VLSI chip. Thus the TLB implementations studied in this paper are all fully-associative designs.

This paper is concerned with TLB performance. Understanding the relation between TLB performance and overall machine performance is a different question, involving the balance of compulsory to capacity misses and the relative ability of caches and TLBs to map multiple localities. The first access to a page results in a *Compulsory* TLB miss. In this situation, cache misses also occur, the cost of which might overshadow the TLB penalties. Other TLB misses are *capacity* misses, when a program returns to a locality that has been replaced out of the TLB, though it might still be present in the cache. This phenomena becomes more common as cache sizes increase. In this paper, CPI effects of TLB performance are discussed assuming perfect memory system performance. This can be deceptive, as it trivializes the question of cache performance. More exact results require simulation of a more complete memory system.

The remainder of the paper is structured as follows. First we give some brief details on our methodology. This is followed by a discussion of instruction TLB behavior, both for micro-TLBs and for independent instruction TLBs. Data and shared TLB results are presented next, followed by a discussion of variable size pages, and finally some concluding notes.

2. Methodology

The tracing and simulations were done on a DECstation 5000, using an updated version of the WRL address tracing tools [2]. Application programs are instrumented by inserting code at the start of each basic block and before each load or store instruction to make entries in a per-process trace buffer. The contents of the per-process buffer are appended to a system trace buffer each time the kernel is invoked, and whenever the per-process buffer becomes full. The kernel makes additional entries in the system buffer to record context switches, system calls, and other such events. When the system buffer becomes full, traced processes are suspended and an analysis program, in this case a TLB simulator, is started. The analysis program runs until the contents of the kernel buffer have been consumed, at which time tracing may continue. The system permits multi-process traces and on-the-fly analysis of trace data with minimum distortion to the traces. System references are not included in the traces.

In simulating the various TLB configurations, a variety of workloads were used, including each of the SPECmarks, plus a number of other workloads meant to anticipate more realistic future workloads. *Tree* is a recursive, data intensive benchmark written in C-Scheme [1]. *Magic* [8] is a VLSI layout tool. In this run it was extracting the MultiTitan CPU chip [6]. A multi-tasking mix was also used, running the following programs:

- *gcc*
- *magic* extracting the MultiTitan CPU chip
- *ld* loading *magic*
- *tree* with a 10 megabyte heap
- a loop running the shell programs *cp*, *cat*, *sed*, *ls*, *ps*, and *rm*.

Short running programs were put in loops, so that their execution would continue throughout the entire run. This mix is is meant to be comparable to the mix used in previous trace-based studies by Borg et.al. [2].

3. Instruction TLB results

Instruction reference streams place lesser demands on TLB resources than data reference streams. Instruction references generally exhibit higher locality, both spatial and temporal. Also there is generally less memory involved. The largest text segment of the SPECmarks, when compiled for the DECstation, is the Gnu C compiler *gcc* with 688K bytes. The average text segment size is around 200K bytes. Data segments are frequently much larger. Data references for *nasa7*, a benchmark for numeric computation, range over a space of over three megabytes.

Because of the different performance characteristics of TLBs and micro-TLBs, they are discussed separately.

3.1. Micro-TLBs

Micro-TLBs were simulated with sizes varying from one to eight entries and *Least Recently Used* (LRU) or *Least Recently Replaced* (FIFO) replacement algorithms. Page sizes of 4K and 16K bytes were used for the simulations.

Figure 3-1 is a plot of the simulation results for the *eqntott* benchmark, illustrative of micro-TLB behavior. The

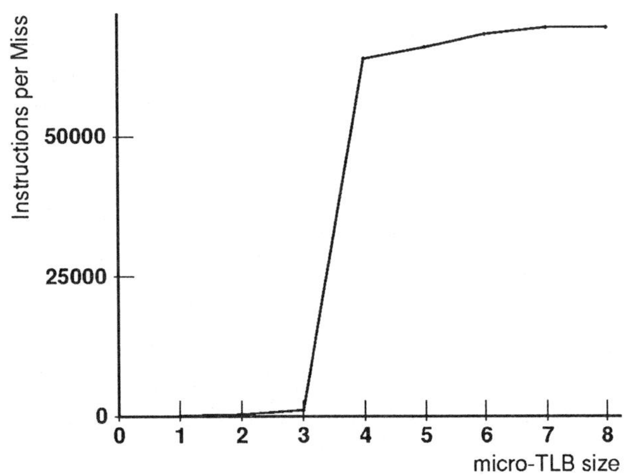

Figure 3-1: ***Eqntott*** **micro-TLB behavior**
FIFO replacement, 4K byte pages

number of entries in the micro-TLB varies along the x axis. The y axis is scaled in instructions per miss, the reciprocal of the miss rate. Plots of instructions per miss are used because they illustrate interesting behavior more clearly than plots of miss rate, with data points corresponding to good performance towards the top of the graph, poor performance toward the bottom, and points spaced in a meaningful way, rather than disappearing along the X axis.

There are three general regimes of behavior to be observed. Notice the flatness of the curve to the left side of the graph. In this region, thrashing is occurring. The number of micro-TLB entries is well under the number of instruction pages in the working set of the program, and consequently micro-TLB performance is relatively poor: 442 instructions per miss with two micro-TLB lines, 1490 instructions per miss with three.

After the flat part of the curve comes a region where performance improves rapidly. For *eqntott* this occurs between three and four micro-TLB entries. Lastly comes another relatively flat region, where the micro-TLB has enough entries to map the entire working set of the program. In this region, additional micro-TLB entries do little to improve performance.

One issue which turned out to be uninteresting is the effect of context switches on the micro-TLB. One alternative in simulations is to be pessimistic about preserving the contents of the micro-TLB, and flush it after every context switch. An optimistic alternative is to preserve the contents of the micro-TLB between context switches. It was found in the optimistic simulations that behavior improved in regions of already good behavior, but that there was little change where behavior was poor. In regions of good behavior, all micro-TLB misses are compulsory. In the optimistic simulations, only one compulsory miss is taken for each referenced page. In the pessimistic simulations, the micro-TLB is flushed, and so a compulsory miss occurs for every context switch. Preserving the micro-TLB reduces the number of compulsory misses, hence improving good behavior. During poor micro-TLB behavior, the vast majority of misses are not compulsory but capacity misses, and so changing the number of compulsory misses has a negligible effect on the overall results. The simulations used to generate data for this paper use the pessimistic model.

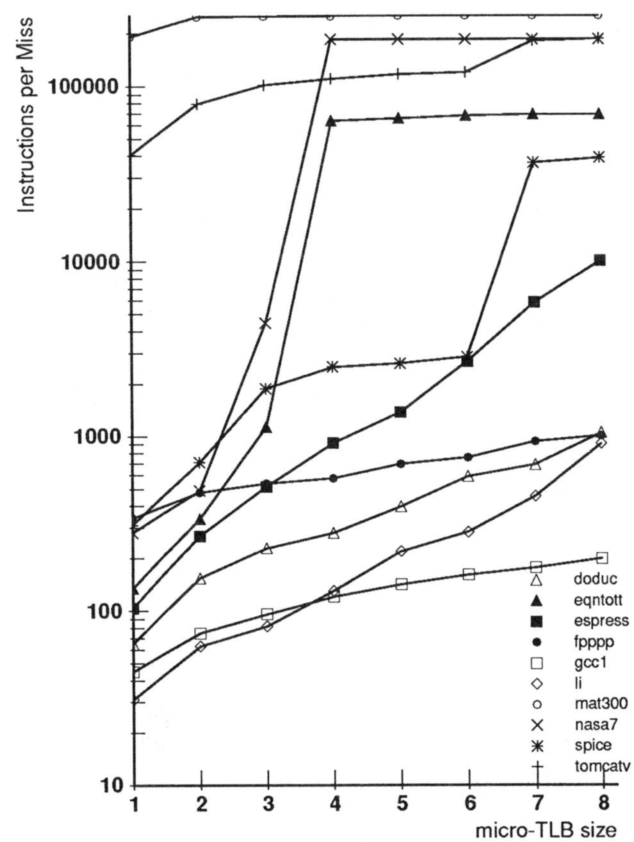

Figure 3-2: SPECmark micro-TLB Behavior
FIFO replacement, 4K byte pages

Figure 3-2 illustrates micro-TLB performance for the SPECmarks. Notice a log scale is used for the y axis of this graph, while the y axis in Figure 3-1 used a linear scale. Although the log scale tends to obscure the different domains of behavior, it makes it possible to compare all the SPECmarks on the same graph. If a micro-TLB miss penalty of 3 cycles is assumed and the average number of instructions per miss is 333 or less, then about one machine cycle per one hundred instructions (i.e. 0.01 cycles per instruction - CPI) is lost to micro-TLB misses. With one micro-TLB entry, more than half the SPECmarks have this much of a penalty. With a two entry micro-TLB, 40% are at this penalty level.

Four of the SPECmarks have particularly mediocre micro-TLB performance. *Fpppp* and *doduc* are both floating-point benchmarks. Both of them are noted for their poor instruction cache performance, predictive of the observed micro-TLB behavior. The miss rate for *fpppp* for a simulated 4K byte instruction cache with 16 byte lines is 23%, due to its particularly long basic blocks (an average of 130 instructions per branch for the entire run). Computation in *doduc* is spread over a large number of procedures, and has a simulated 4K byte I-cache miss rate of 11%.

Two language processing programs, *gcc*, the Gnu C compiler, and *li*, a lisp interpreter, have the worst micro-TLB performance. The I-cache miss rates for *gcc* and *li* are 10% and 2%, respectively. Their micro-TLB behavior is explained in considering the structure of the programs. *Gcc* for example, has a large amount of code and it tends to make many nested procedure calls. We believe that the observed behavior results from there being eight or more procedures involved in most of *gcc*'s localities, and that these procedures tend to be spread over more than eight pages.

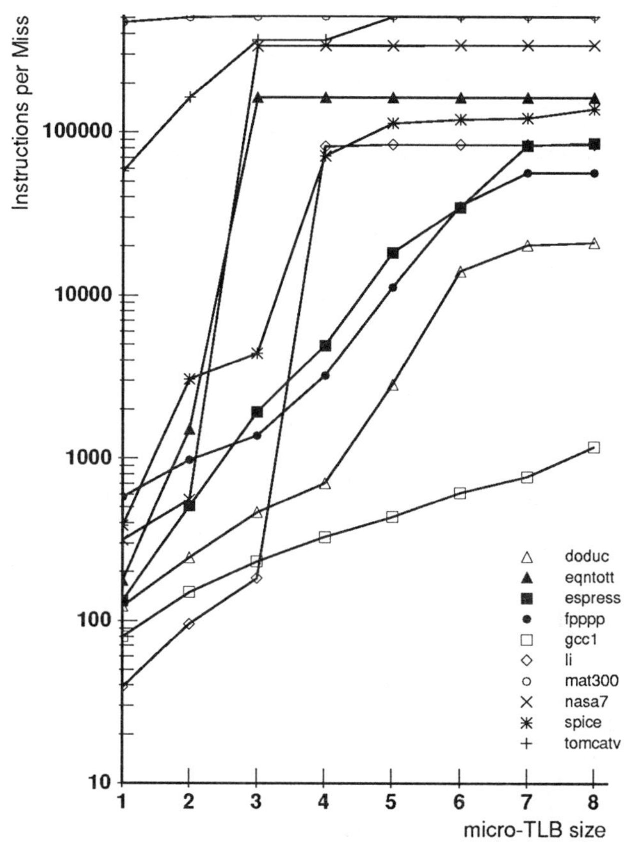

Figure 3-3: SPECmark micro-TLB Behavior
FIFO replacement, 16K byte pages

The SPECmarks were also simulated for micro-TLBs using an instruction page of size 16K bytes. The results are shown in Figure 3-3. At this page size, with 7 micro-TLB entries, the working set of virtually all the programs appears to have been reached, with the exception of *gcc*. The amount of memory fragmentation induced by the change to 16K byte pages can be inferred from the change in TLB resource demands of the programs. For example, *eqntott* uses 4 × 4K = 16K bytes of instruction memory with 4K pages, and 48K bytes with 16k pages. Spice grows from 28K to 64K bytes. Fragmentation for 16K byte pages could be reduced with compilers and loaders that used heuristics or feedback information to locate the most active code adjacent in memory.

Another micro-TLB design parameter that was considered is replacement policy. For two entries, LRU is easily implemented in hardware. For more than two entries, hardware LRU becomes more difficult. An interesting alternative for micro-TLBs is *least recently replaced.* This has the advantage of a relatively straightforward hardware implementation as a first-in first-out queue. *FIFO* is used in this exposition to refer to this replacement policy.

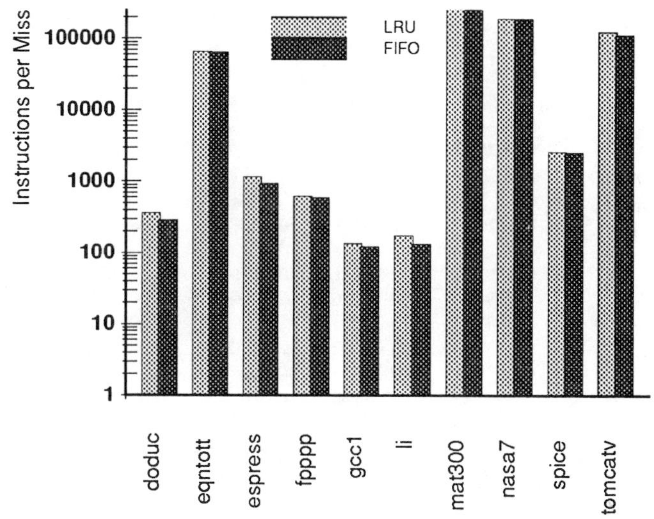

Figure 3-4: LRU vs. FIFO Replacement
4 entry micro-TLB, 4K byte pages

Figure 3-4 shows relative performance of LRU and FIFO replacement policies for the ten SPECmarks. LRU is uniformly better, but not by a large amount. Again, the log scale makes it possible to compare all the benchmarks in the same graph, although it tends to obscure the real difference in performance, sometimes as much as a factor of two. Nonetheless, FIFO performance is always comparable with LRU performance when the overall affect on CPI is considered, establishing it as an interesting replacement policy for micro-TLBs of size greater than two.

Simulations were also run to compare LRU, FIFO and Random replacement policies in full size data TLBs. It was found that FIFO performs uniformly better than Random, failing only in pathological worst case situations. For most machines with hardware to support Random replacement, FIFO can be easily implemented, although it is expected that Random replacement will be used to avoid pathologic worst case behavior.

Table 3-1 shows miss rates for the ten SPECmarks, plus *tree* and *magic*. Under the assumption of a 3 cycle miss penalty, figures in bold-face indicate where the micro-TLB penalty is greater than 0.01 CPI. Again, with 4K byte pages, it is observed that most of the SPECmarks achieve reasonable performance with a two entry micro-TLB, although improvement is observed with larger sizes. Figure 3-5 shows how data from Table 3-1 can be used to estimate CPI contribution for a given SPECmark, micro-TLB configuration, and miss penalty.

Note that the micro-TLB performance for *tree* is particularly poor. With 4K byte pages, a two entry micro-TLB absorbs about 0.10 CPI. Micro-TLB performance for *tree* begins to improve rapidly beyond four micro-TLB entries. There are two effects that could conceivably be contributing to the degraded performance: the working set size of the computation, and conflicts between the garbage collector and the rest of the computation. The garbage collector and the program behave as independent co-routines or threads in the single address space. In the case of *tree*, most of the observed miss rate is due to locality properties of the com-

	1×4KB pg 1×16KB pg	2×4KB pg 2×16KB pg	4×4KB pg 4×16KB pg	8×4KB pg 8×16KB pg
doduc	**0.015415**	**0.006433**	**0.003552**	0.000953
	0.008111	**0.004078**	0.001416	0.000047
eqntott	**0.007415**	0.002951	0.000016	0.000014
	0.005647	0.000661	0.000006	0.000006
espress	**0.009610**	**0.003687**	0.001089	0.000099
	0.007500	0.001966	0.000202	0.000012
fpppp	0.002936	0.002085	0.001727	0.000988
	0.001723	0.001022	0.000309	0.000018
gcc1	**0.021989**	**0.013269**	**0.008288**	**0.005010**
	0.012539	**0.006648**	0.003042	0.000844
li	**0.031792**	**0.015781**	**0.007661**	0.001097
	0.025473	**0.010456**	0.000012	0.000012
mat300	0.000005	0.000004	0.000004	0.000004
	0.000002	0.000002	0.000002	0.000002
nasa7	**0.003544**	0.002037	0.000005	0.000005
	0.003180	0.001788	0.000003	0.000003
spice	0.003199	0.001407	0.000399	0.000026
	0.002598	0.000326	0.000014	0.000007
tomcatv	0.000025	0.000013	0.000009	0.000005
	0.000017	0.000006	0.000002	0.000002
ccom	**0.030306**	**0.016114**	**0.007844**	**0.004098**
	0.017705	**0.008653**	0.001761	0.000174
sed	**0.033778**	**0.008355**	0.000070	0.000064
	0.009710	0.000031	0.000031	0.000031
tree	**0.074999**	**0.034553**	**0.017515**	0.001264
	0.062228	**0.021160**	0.002427	0.000215
magic	**0.014811**	**0.007654**	0.002853	0.000606
	0.013080	**0.006197**	0.001599	0.000287

Table 3-1: SPECmark FIFO micro-TLB Miss Rates

2 entry FIFO micro-TLB with 4K byte page
3 cycle miss penalty

CPI Contribution = 3 * 0.0133 = 0.0399 CPI

Figure 3-5: Estimating micro-TLB CPI Contribution for *gcc*

piled Scheme code, as co-routine exchanges between the garbage collector and the program execution are much too infrequent[1] to account for the observed miss rates.

Although multi-thread effects were not important with *tree*, it is worth noting that, in as much as threads tend to execute in independent code localities, tightly coupled threads executing in a single address space will lead to degraded micro-TLB performance. This effect will be exaggerated with very small micro-TLBs.

3.2. Instruction TLBs

We simulated instruction TLBs with sizes in powers of two from 8 to 64 entries, and page sizes in powers two from 4K to 64K bytes. In examples used to illustrate TLB performance, an approximation of 100 cycles is used for the TLB miss penalty. It is assumed that a TLB miss will cause two memory references, corresponding to a page table lookup, and that the latency of these memory references will dominate the miss penalty. The penalty of 100 cycles corresponds to a futuristic microprocessor with a cycle time of under five nanoseconds, and is meant to be somewhat less than the time for two references to main memory and somewhat more than the time for two references to an off chip cache. Under these assumptions, with TLB performance of 10000 instructions per miss, 0.01 CPI is lost to the TLB. This is used as a somewhat arbitrary lower bound on reasonable TLB performance.

The behavior of single-benchmark workloads in instruction-only TLBs is mostly uninteresting, as *gcc* is the only SPECmark that presents a significant demand on resources. Figure 3-6 illustrates the behavior for *gcc*. Again log scales are used. Solid lines connect TLB configurations with the same page size. Dashed lines connect TLBs that map the same amount of memory. The amount of memory mapped by a TLB will be referred to as its *mapping size*, to discriminate between that measure of size and others, such as the number of lines in a TLB.

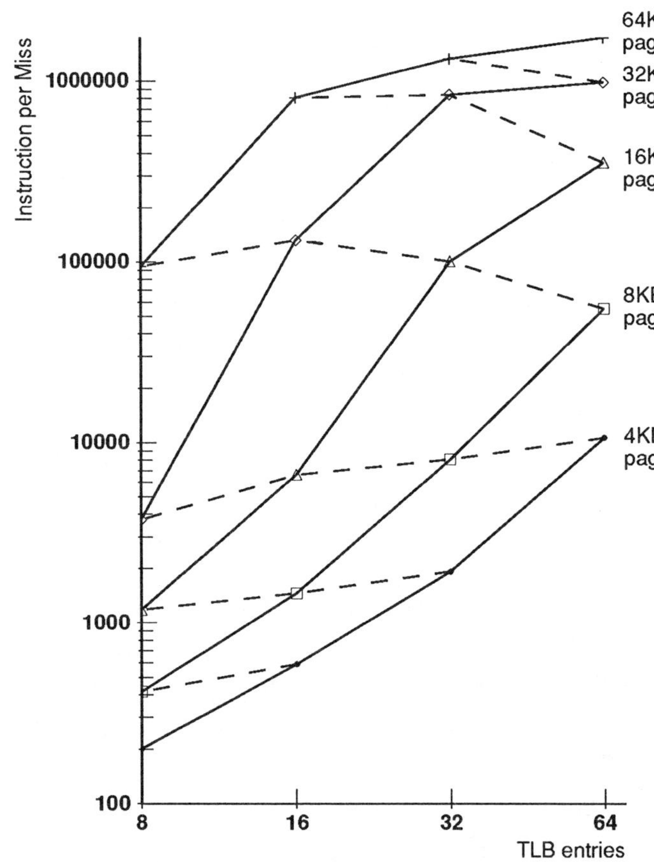

Figure 3-6: *Gcc* Instruction TLB Behavior.
Random Replacement, Full-Associative.

As with the micro-TLB, there are three regimes of behavior to be observed. The placement of data points is more compact in the lower portion of the graph, with relatively little improvement for larger TLB configurations. This represents thrashing, trying to operate with TLB resources well below the working set size of the program. In the next region, performance improves quickly as working set size is approached. This figure shows that *gcc* approaches the TLB resources to map its working set with an instruction TLB mapping size of 512K bytes. Once the working set

[1]The *tree* execution takes about 147 seconds, of which 2 seconds are spent collecting garbage. Garbage collections were observed to occur every 8-15 seconds.

size of the program has been reached, increasing the mapping size has a reduced effect on performance, and the points again become more closely spaced. Such behavior is observed at the top of the graph. These three regimes of behavior become more pronounced for shared and data TLBs, as in Figure 4-1.

Note that in the lower part of the graph, the dashed lines that connect TLBs with the same mapping size tend to slope upward slightly, while at the top of the graph they slope down. An application that uses sparse, non-contiguous data tends to have better TLB performance with more smaller pages of memory than with a few larger pages. Such behavior is observed in the lower part of the graph. In the upper part of the graph, the dashed lines tend to slope down, hence better performance with fewer larger pages. As a TLB becomes large enough to map all of a program's working set, smaller pages mean that TLB misses occur for each of several small pages, rather than once for a single large page. Similar behavior is observed when a program accesses contiguous data, as in Figure 4-1.

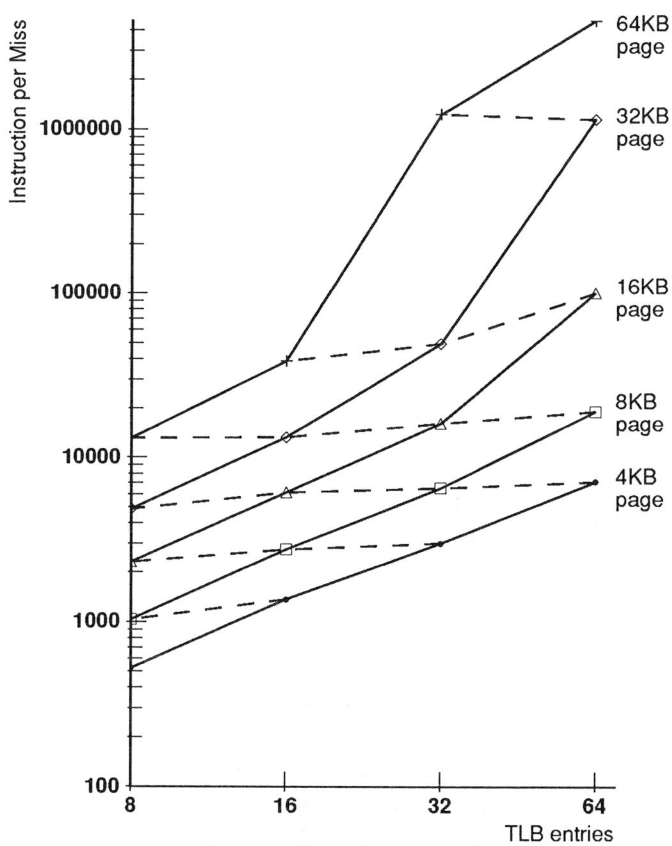

Figure 3-7: Multi-task instruction TLB behavior.
Random Replacement, Full-Associative.

Figure 3-7 illustrates instruction TLB performance for the multi-task mix. For this workload, the flat dashed lines suggest that TLB performance is determined entirely from mapping size, and that the configuration of page size and number of entries has little effect. TLB performance crosses the 10000 instruction per miss performance boundary at a mapping size of 512K bytes, and appears to have reached the working set size for mapping sizes over 2 megabytes.

Table 3-2 gives miss rates for selected benchmarks for a number of instruction-only TLB configurations. The benchmarks not included have very low miss rates.

	16x4KB	32x4KB	64x4KB	16x16KB	32x16KB
gcc1	**0.001688**	**0.000516**	0.000094	0.000151	0.000010
magic	**0.000275**	0.000059	0.000000	0.000041	0.000000
tree	**0.000309**	0.000000	0.000000	0.000000	0.000000
ccom	**0.001969**	0.000032	0.000003	0.000001	0.000001
mixA	**0.000728**	**0.000331**	**0.000140**	**0.000163**	0.000062

Table 3-2: Instruction TLB Miss Rates.
Random Replacement, Full-Associative.

Our experiments suggest that an instruction TLB with 16 entries and 16K byte pages is adequate for most application workloads. One shortcoming of these experiments is that they do not consider the effects of operating system instruction references. It is known that system code generally exhibits worse instruction locality than applications. Certain operating systems are known to be particularly ill behaved. When designing an architecture to support a specific operating system, this should be a consideration.

4. Data and Shared TLB Results

Data-only TLBs and shared TLBs behave similarly. Most programs have well behaved instruction reference patterns, so in the shared case behavior is dominated by data references. Although the following discussion is in terms of shared TLBs, the analysis can be applied to the data-only case as well.

Shared TLBs were simulated with sizes in powers of two from 32 to 256 entries, page sizes in powers of two from 4K to 64K bytes, and with LRU and Random replacement policies. All TLBs simulated were fully associative.

Figure 4-1 shows the shared TLB behavior for *mat300*, which was found to be the SPECmark with the worst TLB performance. Note that the TLBs in this figure are a factor of four larger than those considered with instruction TLBs, ranging from 32 to 256 entries as opposed to 8 to 64 entries. With a miss penalty of 100 cycles and a 64 entry TLB with 4K byte pages, *mat300* spends 5 CPI on the TLB. *Mat300* does matrix operations on three matrices with a total size of approximately 2.5 megabytes. The contents of these three matrices are accessed in regular patterns, sometimes sequentially and sometimes stepping by columns. This explains the poor behavior when the TLB maps less than 2.5 megabytes, and rapid improvement as that barrier is reached and surpassed. Observe that lines connecting TLBs with the same mapping size always slope down, consistent with the observation that *mat300* accesses its data contiguously.

Figure 4-2 shows the TLB behavior for *tree* running with a 10 megabyte heap. Memory is allocated from 5 megabytes of the heap, while the other 5 megabytes is reserved for garbage collection. As expected, performance improves steadily through a mapping size of 5 megabytes (16k pages × 256 entries), after which the rate of improvement begins to diminish, shown by the downward sloping lines connecting configurations with equal mapping sizes. Note that below the 5 megabyte boundary, the lines connecting TLBs with the same mapping size are nearly horizontal. This indicates that TLB performance for this benchmark depends exclusively on the mapping size. Other TLB parameters are unimportant.

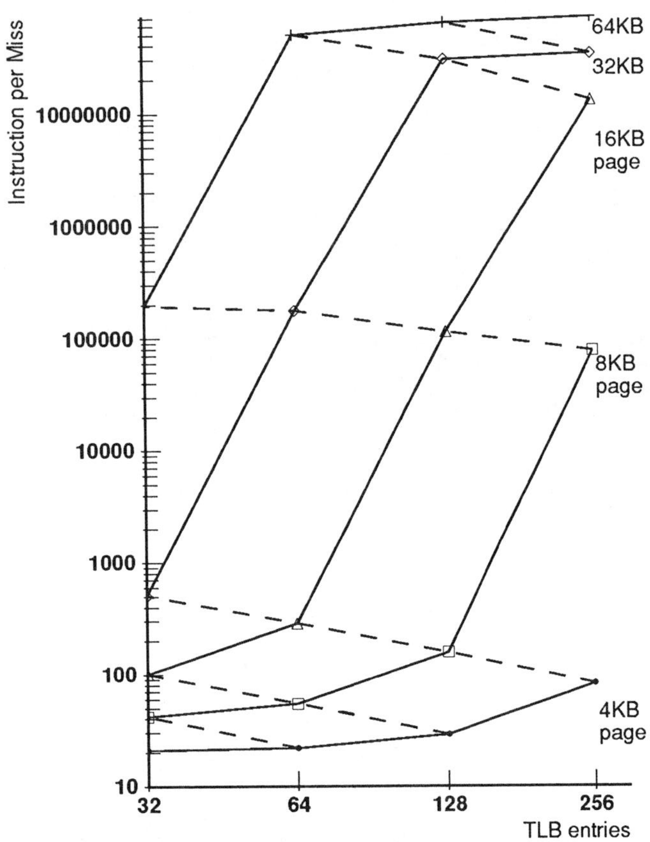

Figure 4-1: ***Mat300*** **Shared TLB Behavior**

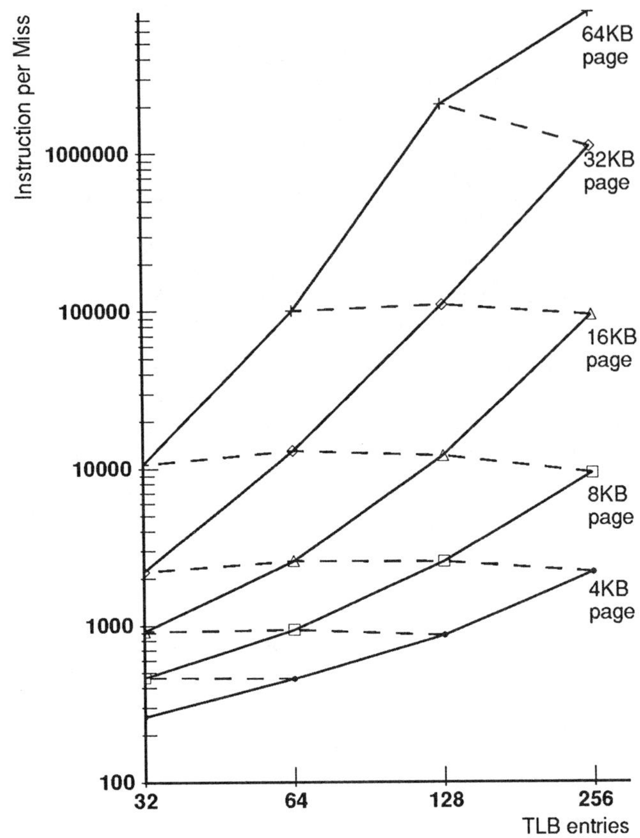

Figure 4-2: ***Tree*** **Shared TLB Behavior.**
Random Replacement Full-Associative

As a last illustration of shared TLB behavior, Figure 4-3 shows a plot for the multi-task mix. Several conclusions are immediate. First, as for *tree*, the mapping size of the TLBs is the dominant factor in performance. Only after a mapping size of eight megabytes do the dashed lines stop looking horizontal. Also, most of the plot is fairly compact. Data points become less compact beyond a mapping size of eight megabytes, as the working set size is approached. Lastly, for all TLBs with a mapping size of one megabyte or less, assuming a 100 cycle miss penalty, at least 0.05 CPI is lost to the TLB, a significant performance penalty. This suggests that, if a machine with a TLB is to execute such a workload efficiently, the TLB must have a significantly larger mapping size.

Table 4-1 shows TLB miss rates for the ten SPECmarks, plus several other workloads of interest. This table is highlighted to indicate where the TLB penalty is more than 0.01 CPI. With the exceptions of *nasa7* and *mat300*, both of which are oriented towards scientific/vector machines, the SPECmarks perform better than this with a 64x16k TLB, suggesting that such a configuration provides adequate TLB performance. The smaller configurations don't perform as well. This suggests that sometime in the near future, TLBs with larger mapping sizes will be needed, especially for machines running numeric programs.

Table 4-2 gives miss rates for a number of data-only TLB configurations.

Figure 4-4 compares miss rates for shared and split TLBs. All TLBs use 64 entries and 4K byte pages. For all but *gcc* and the multi-task mix, the instruction miss rates are inconsequential. Note that the sum of the split instruction and data miss rates is generally less than the miss rate for the shared TLB. This difference represents competition for TLB entries between instruction and data references. This comparison is not meant to suggest two specific implementation alternatives, as the split TLBs illustrated use twice the resources of the shared TLB.

5. Variable Size TLB Entries

An interesting question for future work is how to make use of the variable size TLB entries that have appeared in recent architectures [5, 7]. Maps of the dynamic patterns of memory access are useful to understand this problem. Figure 5-1 shows the pattern of data memory accesses for *mat300*. Page address varies in the x dimension, from 0x10000000 on the left to 0x1021e000 on the right, a range of about 2.2 megabytes. Instruction count (i.e. time) varies along the y dimension, ranging from 0 at the top to 2.63 billion at the bottom. Each dark square represents one or more accesses to a 16K byte page during a 1000000 instruction interval.

The three matrices used by *mat300* are clearly visible from the usage patterns in the address space. The compactness and predictability of the *mat300* accesses show that the use of larger pages could virtually eliminate TLB misses, provided that adequate memory resources were available.

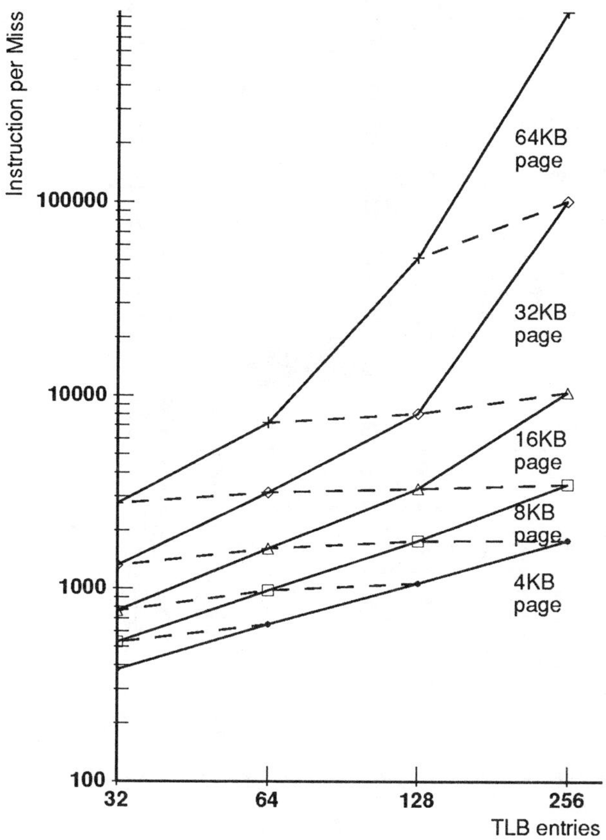

Figure 4-3: Multiprocess Mix TLB Behavior.
Random Replacement, Full-Associative.

	64x4KB	128x4KB	256x4KB	64x16KB	64x32KB
doduc	0.000014	0.000000	0.000000	0.000000	0.000000
eqntott	**0.000410**	**0.000162**	0.000002	0.000020	0.000000
espress	0.000004	0.000001	0.000001	0.000000	0.000000
fpppp	0.000001	0.000000	0.000000	0.000000	0.000000
gcc1	**0.001143**	**0.000244**	**0.000132**	0.000053	0.000013
li	0.000000	0.000000	0.000000	0.000000	0.000000
mat300	**0.049097**	**0.036378**	**0.012669**	**0.003461**	0.000006
nasa7	**0.016526**	**0.011955**	**0.005183**	**0.002024**	0.000000
spice	0.000052	0.000005	0.000000	0.000000	0.000000
tomcatv	**0.000151**	**0.000138**	0.000121	0.000033	0.000012
ccom	**0.000283**	0.000009	0.000006	0.000005	0.000002
sed	0.000017	0.000017	0.000015	0.000006	0.000005
tree	**0.004683**	**0.002749**	**0.001015**	**0.000224**	0.000069
magic	**0.000644**	**0.000139**	0.000003	**0.000106**	0.000086
mixA	**0.001527**	**0.000937**	**0.000563**	**0.000620**	**0.000316**

Table 4-1: Shared TLB Miss Rates.
Random Replacement, Full-Associative.

Tree, the lisp benchmark, also shows interesting data reference patterns, illustrated in figure 5-2. Note that a page size of 64K bytes was used. The address space represented in this figure is about 11 megabytes. The descending staircase pattern shows the behavior of the memory allocator as it walks across the heap. Solid vertical bands show where garbage collection has compacted the heap into frequently accessed regions. The pattern of memory references for

	64x4KB	128x4KB	256x4KB	64x16KB	128x16KB
doduc	0.000000	0.000000	0.000000	0.000000	0.000000
eqntott	**0.000355**	**0.000140**	0.000002	0.000016	0.000000
espress	0.000001	0.000001	0.000000	0.000000	0.000000
fpppp	0.000000	0.000000	0.000000	0.000000	0.000000
gcc1	**0.000152**	**0.000104**	0.000067	0.000022	0.000014
li	0.000000	0.000000	0.000000	0.000000	0.000000
mat300	**0.045666**	**0.034275**	**0.012050**	**0.003460**	0.000008
nasa7	**0.016521**	**0.011947**	**0.005178**	**0.002022**	0.000001
spice	0.000034	0.000000	0.000000	0.000000	0.000000
tomcatv	**0.000149**	**0.000137**	0.000120	0.000033	0.000021
ccom	0.000005	0.000004	0.000003	0.000001	0.000001
sed	0.000011	0.000010	0.000009	0.000005	0.000004
tree	**0.001804**	**0.001002**	**0.000420**	**0.000288**	0.000076
magic	**0.000270**	0.000038	0.000003	0.000059	0.000002
mixA	**0.001358**	**0.000866**	**0.000511**	**0.000546**	**0.000258**

Table 4-2: Data TLB Miss Rates
Random Replacement, Full-Associative.

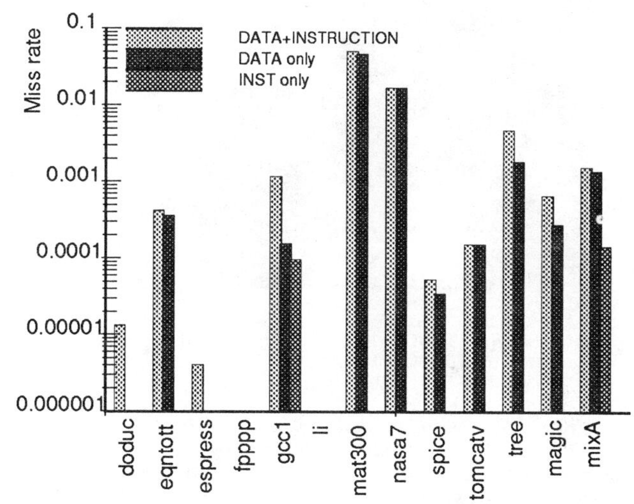

Figure 4-4: Shared vs. Split TLBs. 64 entries, 4KB pages
Random Replacement, Full-Associative

tree is sparse relative to *mat300*.[2] This, along with the size of the address space, suggests that lisp workloads such as *tree* are relatively poor candidates for variable size pages.

Interesting patterns of reference are the exception rather than the rule in memory access patterns. Most of the benchmarks concentrate on a small number of unclustered pages, resulting in a few dark vertical bars from the top to the bottom of the map, with occasional horizontal excursions.

Figure 5-3 shows a map of instruction references for *gcc.* Each point represents one or more references to a 4k byte page during an interval of 100000 instructions. The address space spanned in this figure is 684K bytes, the largest text segment of any of the SPECmarks. The number of different

[2]This is more readily seen in grayscale maps, with darkness indicating frequency of reference. Figures in these proceedings are black and white, as the grayscale maps reproduce poorly.

Figure 5-1: *mat300* **Data Memory Access Patterns**

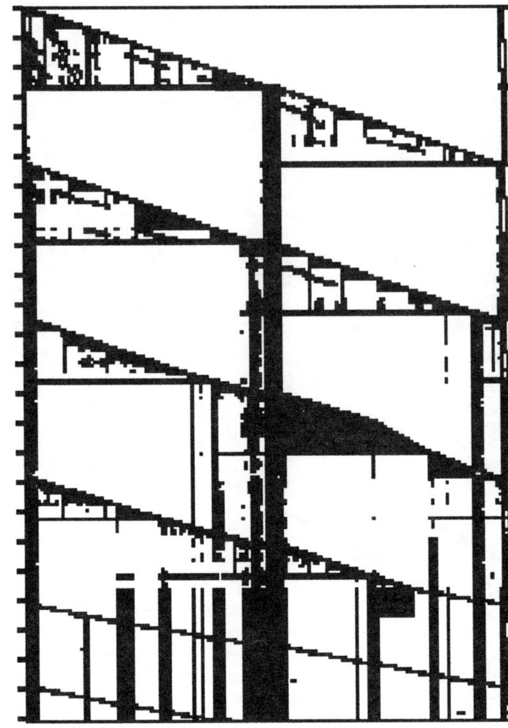

Figure 5-2: *tree* **Data Memory Access Patterns**

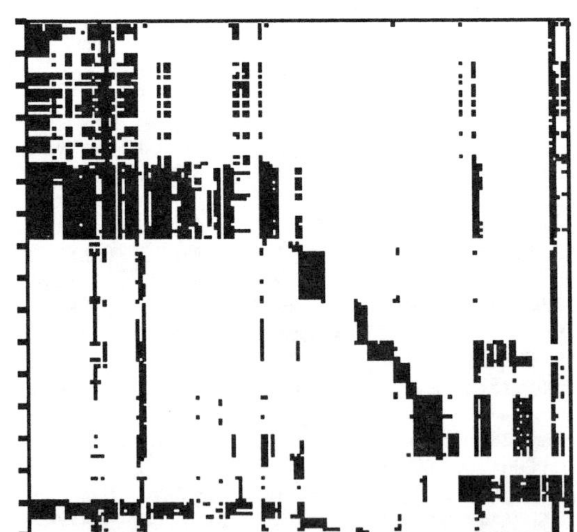

Figure 5-3: *gcc* **Data Memory Access Patterns**

pages touched during a single 100000 instruction interval illustrates clearly why *gcc* places high demands on the TLB. If variable size memory pages were to be used to improve *gcc* performance, the only solution would be load the entire program text into a contiguous segment.

For instruction references, compilers might use feedback information on performance critical applications to locate active text contiguously, making the use of a single larger TLB entry a more attractive option. Such techniques are more difficult to apply to data references, as heap allocated structures are allocated dynamically, and so their location is not under the control of the compiler. With the relocatable nature of lisp data, it might be possible to tune garbage collectors to improve the locality of reference. For uncollected memory allocation schemes, a tool using feedback information could make suggestions of how to order heap data allocation to improve contiguity of data.

6. Conclusions

This study has investigated the performance of one and two-level instruction TLBs, data TLBs, and shared TLBs, as well as analyzing the potential performance implications of variable-sized pages. In contrast to previous studies, this work concentrated on fully-associative TLB organizations and split instruction and data reference streams.

For instruction TLBs, programs such as *gcc* and *li* that make many nested calls to small procedures are the hardest to satisfy. For most of the SPECmarks, 4K byte pages and a two entry micro-TLB (whose misses are serviced in several cycles by a shared TLB) perform reasonably well. For example, with a 3 cycle micro-TLB miss penalty (i.e., assuming that the reference hits in the 2nd-level TLB) all SPECmarks except *gcc* and *li* incur a CPI of less than 0.03 due to microTLB misses. *gcc* and *li* can achieve this level of performance with 4-entry micro-TLBs, but incur a CPI penalty of about 0.06 with a 2-entry micro-TLB. A FIFO replacement policy performs almost as well as LRU for micro-TLBs.

In single-level instruction, data, and shared TLBs, TLB performance is usually dominated by how much memory is mapped. Single-level fully-associative instruction TLBs (or the second level of a two-level organization) with more that 32 entries, 4K byte pages, and a 100 cycle miss penalties incur CPIs of under 0.1 even for *gcc*. Performance on other benchmarks and with larger TLBs is better. With the larger capacities and miss penalties of full size instruction TLBs, multi-tasking and system effects also become important.

A data or shared TLB mapping 256K byte in 4K byte pages (i.e., 64 entries) with 100 cycle miss penalty incurs 0.1 CPI or less for all of the SPECmarks except *nasa7* and *mat300*. Both of these are scientific/vector oriented programs with large data sets. Furthermore, column access (i.e., non-unit stride) can result in successive data references to successive pages, disastrous for TLB performance unless the entire data set is mapped at the same time. *nasa7* and *mat300* incur a CPI of 1.7 and 4.9, respectively, for the TLB parameters given above. This is not reduced to under 0.1 CPI for *mat300* until the TLB can map 2 megabytes (e.g., 256 entry TLB with 8K byte pages). Work with more demanding workloads suggests that future TLBs must map significantly more memory.

One way to increase the amount of memory mapped without requiring an unreasonably large number of TLB entries is the use of variable-sized pages. Memory access plots suggest that the use of very large pages (e.g., 256K byte or greater) for the data space of *mat300* and *tree*, and the instruction space of *gcc* could vastly reduce the size of the TLB required for good performance while decreasing its miss rate.

One significant shortcoming of this TLB analysis is the inability to consider operating system effects. We are currently involved in completing a new tracing system which includes system traces, with the intention of performing a thorough exploration of operating system memory behavior on modern RISC processors.

7. Acknowledgements

We would like to thank David Wall for keeping the compiler aspects of the tracing project in tiptop shape. We would also like to thank Joel Bartlett for consultations on Scheme. Thanks to Brian Bershad and John Ousterhout for their useful comments on this paper.

References

1. J. F. Bartlett. SCHEME->C: A Portable Scheme-to-C Compiler. WRL Research Report 89/1, Digital Equipment Western Research Laboratory, 1989.

2. Anita Borg, R.E. Kessler, Georgia Lazana, and David Wall. Long Address Traces from RISC Machines: Generation and Analysis. WRL Research Report 89/14, Digital Equipment Western Research Laboratory, 1989.

3. Douglas W. Clark and Joel S. Emer. "Performance of the VAX 11/780 Translation Buffer: Simulation and Measurement.". *ACM Transactions on Computer Systems 3*, 1 (February 1985).

4. Douglas W. Clark, Peter J. Bannon, and James B. Keller. Measuring VAX 8800 Performance with a Histogram Hardware Monitor. Proceedings of the 15th Annual International Symposium on Computer Architecture, June, 1988, pp. 176-185.

5. Daniel Dobberpuhl, et. al. A 200Mhz 64b Dual-Issue CMOS Microprocessor. The 39th International Solid-State Circuits Conference, IEEE Computer Society Press, February, 1992, pp. 106-107. See also slide supplement.

6. Norman P. Jouppi. Architectural and Organizational Tradeoffs in the Design of the MultiTitan CPU. Proceedings of the 16th Annual International Symposium on Computer Architecture, May, 1989, pp. 281-289.

7. Sunil Mirapuri, Michael Woodacre, and Nader Vasseghi. "The MIPS R4000 Processor". *IEEE Micro 12*, 4 (April 1992), .

8. J. Ousterhout, G. Hamachi, R. Mayo, W. Scott, and G.S. Taylor. "The Magic VLSI Layout System". *IEEE Design and Test of Computers 2*, 1 (February 1985), 19-30.

9. Steven A. Przybylski. *Cache Design: A Performance-Directed Approach.* Morgan-Kaufmann, San Mateo, CA, 1990.

10. Alan Jay Smith. "Cache Memories". *ACM Computer Surveys 14*, 3 (September 1982), 473-530.

11. David A. Wood, et. al. An In-Cache Address Translation Mechanism. The 13th Annual Symposium on Computer Architecture, IEEE Computer Society Press, June, 1986, pp. 358-365.

12. David A. Wood. *The Design and Evaluation of In-Cache Address Translation.* Ph.D. Th., Department of Computer Science, UC Berkeley, March 1991. Report Number UCB/CSD 90/565.

Alternative Implementations of Two-Level Adaptive Branch Prediction

Tse–Yu Yeh and Yale N. Patt
Department of Electrical Engineering and Computer Science
The University of Michigan
Ann Arbor, Michigan 48109-2122

Abstract

As the issue rate and depth of pipelining of high performance Superscalar processors increase, the importance of an excellent branch predictor becomes more vital to delivering the potential performance of a wide-issue, deep pipelined microarchitecture. We propose a new dynamic branch predictor (Two-Level Adaptive Branch Prediction) that achieves substantially higher accuracy than any other scheme reported in the literature. The mechanism uses two levels of branch history information to make predictions, the history of the last k branches encountered, and the branch behavior for the last s occurrences of the specific pattern of these k branches. We have identified three variations of the Two-Level Adaptive Branch Prediction, depending on how finely we resolve the history information gathered. We compute the hardware costs of implementing each of the three variations, and use these costs in evaluating their relative effectiveness. We measure the branch prediction accuracy of the three variations of Two-Level Adaptive Branch Prediction, along with several other popular proposed dynamic and static prediction schemes, on the SPEC benchmarks. We show that the average prediction accuracy for Two-Level Adaptive Branch Prediction is 97 percent, while the other known schemes achieve at most 94.4 percent average prediction accuracy. We measure the effectiveness of different prediction algorithms and different amounts of history and pattern information. We measure the costs of each variation to obtain the same prediction accuracy.

1 Introduction

As the issue rate and depth of pipelining of high performance Superscalar processors increase, the amount of speculative work due to branch prediction becomes much larger. Since all such work must be thrown away if the prediction is incorrect, an excellent branch predictor is vital to delivering the potential performance of a wide-issue, deep pipelined microarchitecture. Even a prediction miss rate of 5 percent results in a substantial loss in performance due to the number of instructions fetched each cycle and the number of cycles these instructions are in the pipeline before an incorrect branch prediction becomes known.

The literature is full of suggested branch prediction schemes [6, 13, 14, 17]. Some are static in that they use opcode information and profiling statistics to make predictions. Others are dynamic in that they use run-time execution history to make predictions. Static schemes can be as simple as always predicting that the branch will be taken, or can be based on the opcode, or on the direction of the branch, as in "if the branch is backward, predict taken, if forward, predict not taken" [17]. This latter scheme is effective for loop intensive code, but does not work well for programs where the branch behavior is irregular. Also, profiling [6, 13] can be used to predict branches by measuring the tendency of a branch on sample data sets and presetting a static prediction bit in the opcode according to that tendency. Unfortunately, branch behavior for the sample data may be very different from the data that appears at run-time.

Dynamic branch prediction also can be as simple as in keeping track only of the last execution of that branch instruction and predicting the branch will behave the same way, or it can be elaborate as in maintaining very large amounts of history information. In all cases, the fact that the dynamic prediction is being made on the basis of run-time history information implies that substantial additional hardware is required. J. Smith [17] proposed utilizing a branch target buffer to store, for each branch, a two-bit saturating up-down counter which collects and subsequently bases its prediction on branch history information about that branch. Lee and A. Smith proposed [14] a Static Training method which uses statistics gathered prior to execution time coupled with the history pattern of the last k run-time executions of the branch to make the next prediction as to which way that branch will go. The major disadvantage of Static Training methods has been mentioned above with respect to profiling; the pattern history statistics gathered for the sample data set may not be applicable to the data that appears at run-time.

In this paper we propose a new dynamic branch predictor that achieves substantially higher accuracy than any other scheme reported in the literature. The mechanism uses two levels of branch history information to make predictions. The first level is the history of the

© 1992 ACM 0-89791-509-7/92/0005/0124 $1.50

last k branches encountered. (Variations of our scheme reflect whether this means the actual last k branches encountered, or the last k occurrences of the same branch instruction.) The second level is the branch behavior for the last s occurrences of the specific pattern of these k branches. Prediction is based on the branch behavior for the last s occurrences of the pattern in question.

For example, suppose, for $k = 8$, the last k branches had the behavior 11100101 (where 1 represents that the branch was taken, 0 that the branch was not taken). Suppose further that $s = 6$, and that in each of the last six times the previous eight branches had the pattern 11100101, the branch alternated between taken and not taken. Then the second level would contain the history 101010. Our branch predictor would predict "taken."

The history information for level 1 and the pattern information for level 2 are collected at run time, eliminating the above mentioned disadvantages of the Static Training method. We call our method Two-Level Adaptive Branch Prediction. We have identified three variations of Two-Level Adaptive Branch Prediction, depending on how finely we resolve the history information gathered. We compute the hardware costs of implementing each of the three variations, and use these costs in evaluating their relative effectiveness.

Using trace-driven simulation of nine of the ten SPEC benchmarks [1], we measure the branch prediction accuracy of the three variations of Two-Level Adaptive Branch Prediction, along with several other popular proposed dynamic and static prediction schemes. We measure the effectiveness of different prediction algorithms and different amounts of history and pattern information. We measure the costs of each variation to obtain the same prediction accuracy. Finally we compare the Two-Level Adaptive branch predictors to the several popular schemes available in the literature. We show that the average prediction accuracy for Two-Level Adaptive Branch Prediction is about 97 percent, while the other schemes achieve at most 94.4 percent average prediction accuracy.

This paper is organized in six sections. Section two introduces our Two-Level Adaptive Branch Prediction and its three variations. Section three describes the corresponding implementations and computes the associated hardware costs. Section four discusses the Simulation model and traces used in this study. Section five reports the simulation results and our analysis. Section six contains some concluding remarks.

2 Definition of Two-Level Adaptive Branch Prediction

2.1 Overview

Two-Level Adaptive Branch Prediction uses two levels of branch history information to make predictions. The first level is the history of the last k branches encountered. (Variations of our scheme reflect whether this means the actual last k branches encountered, or the last k occurrences of the same branch instruction.) The second level is the branch behavior for the last s occurrences of the specific pattern of these k branches. Prediction is based on the branch behavior for the last s occurrences of the pattern in question.

To maintain the two levels of information, Two-Level Adaptive Branch Prediction uses two major data structures, the branch history register (HR) and the pattern history table (PHT), see Figure 1. Instead of accumulating statistics by profiling programs, the information on which branch predictions are based is collected at run-time by updating the contents of the history registers and the pattern history bits in the entries of the pattern history table depending on the outcomes of the branches. The history register is a k-bit shift register which shifts in bits representing the branch results of the most recent k branches.

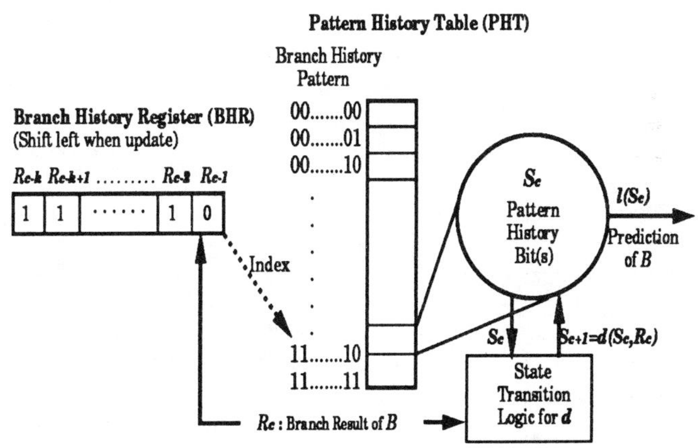

Figure 1: Structure of Two-Level Adaptive Branch Prediction.

If the branch was taken, then a "1" is recorded; if not, a "0" is recorded. Since there are k bits in the history register, at most 2^k different patterns appear in the history register. For each of these 2^k patterns, there is a corresponding entry in the pattern history table which contains branch results for the last s times the preceding k branches were represented by that specific content of the history register.

When a conditional branch B is being predicted, the content of its history register, HR, denoted as $R_{c-k}R_{c-k+1}......R_{c-1}$, is used to address the pattern history table. The pattern history bits S_c in the addressed entry $PHT_{R_{c-k}R_{c-k+1}......R_{c-1}}$ in the pattern history table are then used for predicting the branch. The prediction of the branch is

$$z_c = \lambda(S_c), \tag{1}$$

where λ is the prediction decision function.

After the conditional branch is resolved, the outcome R_c is shifted left into the history register HR in the least significant bit position and is also used to update the pattern history bits in the pattern history table entry $PHT_{R_{c-k}R_{c-k+1}......R_{c-1}}$. After being

[1]The Nasa7 benchmark was not simulated because this benchmark consists of seven independent loops. It takes too long to simulate the branch behavior of these seven kernels, so we omitted these loops.

updated, the content of the history register becomes $R_{c-k+1}R_{c-k+2}......R_c$ and the state represented by the pattern history bits becomes S_{c+1}. The transition of the pattern history bits in the pattern history table entry is done by the state transition function δ which takes in the old pattern history bits and the outcome of the branch as inputs to generate the new pattern history bits. Therefore, the new pattern history bits S_{c+1} become

$$S_{c+1} = \delta(S_c, R_c). \quad (2)$$

A straightforward combinational logic circuit is used to implement the function δ to update the pattern history bits in the entries of the pattern history table. The transition function δ, predicting function λ, pattern history bits S and the outcome R of the branch comprise a finite-state Moore machine, characterized by equations 1 and 2.

State diagrams of the finite-state Moore machines used in this study for updating the pattern history in the pattern history table entry and for predicting which path the branch will take are shown in Figure 2. The automaton *Last-Time* stores in the pattern history only the outcome of the last execution of the branch when the history pattern appeared. The next time the same history pattern appears the prediction will be what happened last time. Only one bit is needed to store that pattern history information. The automaton $A1$ records the results of the last two times the same history pattern appeared. Only when there is no taken branch recorded, the next execution of the branch when the history register has the same history pattern will be predicted as not taken; otherwise, the branch will be predicted as taken. The automaton $A2$ is a saturating up-down counter, similar to the automaton used in J. Smith's branch target buffer design for keeping branch history [17].

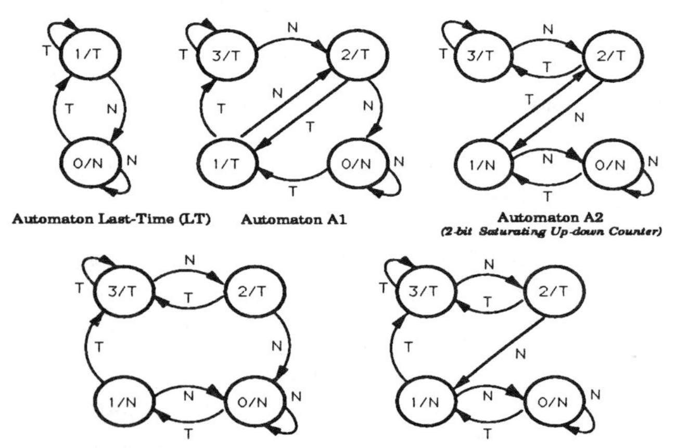

Figure 2: State diagrams of the finite-state Moore machines used for making prediction and updating the pattern history table entry.

In J. Smith's design the 2-bit saturating up-down counter keeps track of the branch history of a certain branch. The counter is incremented when the branch is taken and is decremented when the branch is not taken. The branch path of the next execution of the branch will be predicted as taken when the counter value is greater than or equal to two; otherwise, the branch will be predicted as not taken. In Two-Level Adaptive Branch Prediction, the 2-bit saturating up-down counter keeps track of the history of a certain history pattern. The counter is incremented when the result of a branch, whose history register content is the same as the pattern history table entry index, is taken; otherwise, the counter is decremented. The next time the branch has the same history register content which accesses the same pattern history table entry, the branch is predicted taken if the counter value is greater or equal to two; otherwise, the branch is predicted not taken. Automata $A3$ and $A4$ are variations of $A2$.

Both Static Training [14] and Two-Level Adaptive Branch Prediction are dynamic branch predictors, because their predictions are based on run-time information, i.e. the dynamic branch history. The major difference between these two schemes is that the pattern history information in the pattern history table changes dynamically in Two-Level Adaptive Branch Prediction but is preset in Static Training from profiling. In Static Training, the input to the prediction decision function, λ, for a given branch history pattern is known before execution. Therefore, the output of λ is determined before execution for a given branch history pattern. That is, the same branch predictions are made if the same history pattern appears at different times during execution. Two-Level Adaptive Branch Prediction, on the other hand, updates the pattern history information kept in the pattern history table with the actual results of branches. As a result, given the same branch history pattern, different pattern history information can be found in the pattern history table; therefore, there can be different inputs to the prediction decision function for Two-Level Adaptive Branch Prediction. Predictions of Two-Level Adaptive Branch Prediction change adaptively as the program executes.

Since the pattern history bits change in Two-Level Adaptive Branch Prediction, the predictor can adjust to the current branch execution behavior of the program to make proper predictions. With these run-time updates, Two-Level Adaptive Branch Prediction can be highly accurate over many different programs and data sets. Static Training, on the contrary, may not predict well if changing data sets brings about different execution behavior.

2.2 Alternative Implementations of Two-Level Adaptive Branch Prediction

There are three alternative implementations of the Two-Level Adaptive Branch Prediction, as shown in Figure 3. They are differentiated as follows:

Two-Level Adaptive Branch Prediction Using a Global History Register and a Global Pattern History Table (GAg)

In GAg, there is only a single global history register (GHR) and a single global pattern history table (GPHT) used by the Two-Level Adaptive Branch Pre-

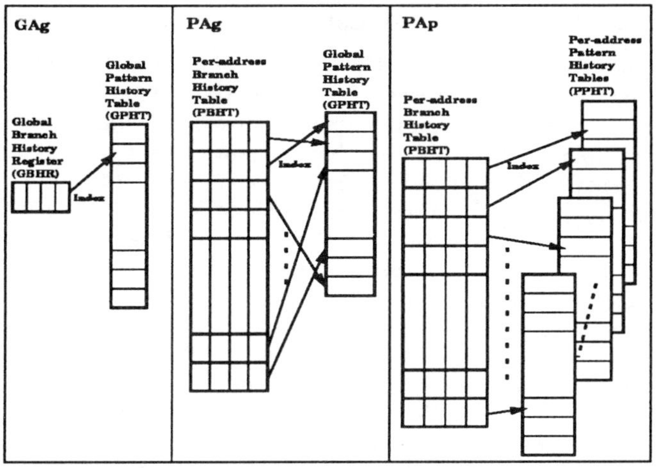

Figure 3: Global view of three variations of Two-Level Adaptive Branch Prediction.

diction. All branch predictions are based on the same global history register and global pattern history table which are updated after each branch is resolved. This variation therefore is called Global Two-Level Adaptive Branch Prediction using a global pattern history table (GAg).

Since the outcomes of different branches update the same history register and the same pattern history table, the information of both branch history and pattern history is influenced by results of different branches. The prediction for a conditional branch in this scheme is actually dependent on the outcomes of other branches.

Two-Level Adaptive Branch Prediction Using a Per-address Branch History Table and a Global Pattern History Table (PAg)

In order the reduce the interference in the first level branch history information, one history register is associated with each distinct static conditional branch to collect branch history information individually. The history registers are contained in a per-address branch history table (PBHT) in which each entry is accessible by one specific static branch instruction and is accessed by branch instruction addresses. Since the branch history is kept for each distinct static conditional branch individually and all history registers access the same global pattern history table, this variation is called Per-address Two-Level Adaptive Branch Prediction using a global pattern history table (PAg).

The execution results of a static conditional branch update the branch's own history register and the global pattern history table. The prediction for a conditional branch is based on the branch's own history and the pattern history bits in the global pattern history table entry indexed by the content of the branch's history register. Since all branches update the same pattern history table, the pattern history interference still exists.

Two-Level Adaptive Branch Prediction Using Per-address Branch History Table and Per-address Pattern History Tables (PAp)

In order to completely remove the interference in both levels, each static branch has its own pattern history table a set of which is called a per-address pattern history table (PPHT). Therefore, a per-address history register and a per-address pattern history table are associated with each static conditional branch. All history registers are grouped in a per-address branch history table. Since this variation of Two-Level Adaptive Branch Prediction keeps separate history and pattern information for each distinct static conditional branch, it is called Per-address Two-Level Adaptive Branch Prediction using Per-address pattern history tables (PAp).

3 Implementation Considerations

3.1 Pipeline Timing of Branch Prediction and Information Update

Two-Level Adaptive Branch Prediction requires two sequential table accesses to make a prediction. It is difficult to squeeze the two accesses into one cycle. High performance requires that prediction be made within one cycle from the time the branch address is known. To satisfy this requirement, the two sequential accesses are performed in two different cycles as follows: When a branch result becomes known, the branch's history register is updated. In the same cycle, the pattern history table can be accessed for the next prediction with the updated history register contents derived by appending the result to the old history. The prediction fetched from the pattern history table is then stored along with the branch's history in the branch history table. The pattern history can also be updated at that time. The next time that branch is encountered, the prediction is available as soon as the branch history table is accessed. Therefore, only one cycle latency is incurred from the time the branch address is known to the time the prediction is available.

Sometimes the previous branch results may not be ready before the prediction of a subsequent branch takes place. If the obsolete branch history is used for making the prediction, the accuracy is degraded. In such a case, the predictions of the previous branches can be used to update the branch history. Since the prediction accuracy of Two-Level Adaptive Branch Prediction is very high, prediction is enhanced by updating the branch history speculatively. The update timing for the pattern history table, on the other hand, is not as critical as that of the branch history; therefore, its update can be delayed until the branch result is known. With speculative updating, when a misprediction occurs, the branch history can either be reinitialized or repaired depending on the hardware budget available to the branch predictor. Also, if two instances of the same static branch occur in consecutive cycles, the latency of prediction can be reduced for the second branch by using the prediction fetched from the pattern history table directly.

3.2 Target Address Caching

After the direction of a branch is predicted, there is still the possibility of a pipeline bubble due to the time it takes to generate the target address. To eliminate this bubble, we cache the target addresses of branches. One extra field is required in each entry of the branch history table for doing this. When a branch is predicted taken, the target address is used to fetch the following instructions; otherwise, the fall-through address is used.

Caching the target addresses makes prediction in consecutive cycles possible without any delay. This also requires the branch history table to be accessed by the fetching address of the instruction block rather than by the address of the branch in the instruction block being fetched because the branch address is not known until the instruction block is decoded. If the address hits in the branch history table, the prediction of the branch in the instruction block can be made before the instructions are decoded. If the address misses in the branch history table, either there is no branch in the instruction block fetched in that cycle or the branch history information is not present in the branch history table. In this case, the next sequential address is used to fetch new instructions. After the instructions are decoded, if there is a branch in the instruction block and if the instruction block address missed in the branch history table, static branch prediction is used to determine whether or not the new instructions fetched from the next sequential address should be squashed.

3.3 Per-address Branch History Table Implementation

PAg and PAp branch predictors all use per-address branch history tables in their structure. It is not feasible to have a branch history table large enough to hold all branches' execution history in real implementations. Therefore, a practical approach for the per-address branch history table is proposed here.

The per-address branch history table can be implemented as a set-associative or direct-mapped cache. A fixed number of entries in the table are grouped together as a set. Within a set, a Least-Recently-Used (LRU) algorithm is used for replacement. The lower part of a branch address is used to index into the table and the higher part is stored as a tag in the entry associated with that branch. When a conditional branch is to be predicted, the branch's entry in the branch history table is located first. If the tag in the entry matches the accessing address, the branch information in the entry is used to predict the branch. If the tag does not match the address, a new entry is allocated for the branch.

In this study, both the above practical approach and an Ideal Branch History Table (IBHT), in which there is a history register for each static conditional branch, were simulated for Two-Level Adaptive Branch Prediction. The branch history table was simulated with four configurations: 4-way set-associative 512-entry, 4-way set-associative 256-entry, direct-mapped 512-entry and direct-mapped 256-entry caches. The IBHT simulation data is provided to show the accuracy loss due to the history interference in a practical branch history table implementations.

3.4 Hardware Cost Estimates

The chip area required for a run-time branch prediction mechanism is not inconsequential. The following hardware cost estimates are proposed to characterize the relative costs of the three variations. The branch history table and the pattern history table are the two major parts. Detailed items include storage space for keeping history information, prediction bits, tags, and LRU bits and the accessing and updating logic of the tables. The accessing and updating logic consists of comparators, MUXes, LRU bits incrementors, and address decoders for the branch history table, and address decoders and pattern history bit update circuits for the pattern history table. The storage space for caching target addresses is not included in the following equations because it is not required for the branch predictor.

Assumptions of these estimates are:

- There are a address bits, a subset of which is used to index the branch history table and the rest are stored as a tag in the indexed branch history table entry.
- In an entry of the branch history table, there are fields for branch history, an address tag, a prediction bit, and LRU bits.
- The branch history table size is h.
- The branch history table is 2^j-way set-associative.
- Each history register contains k bits.
- Each pattern history table entry contains s bits.
- Pattern history table set size is p. (In PAp, p is equal to the size of the branch history table, h, while in GAg and PAg, p is always equal to one.)
- C_s, C_d, C_c, C_m, C_{sh}, C_i, and C_a are the constant base costs for the storage, the decoder, the comparator, the multiplexer, the shifter, the incrementor, and the finite-state machine.

Furthermore, i is equal to $log_2 h$ and is a non-negative integer. When there are k bits in a history register, a pattern history table always has 2^k entries.

The hardware cost of Two-Level Adaptive Branch Prediction is as follows:

$$
\begin{aligned}
& Cost_{Scheme}(BHT(h,j,k), p \times PHT(2^k, s)) \\
&= Cost_{BHT}(h,j,k) + p \times Cost_{PHT}(2^k, s) \\
&= \{BHT_{Storage\_Space} + BHT_{Accessing\_Logic} + \\
&\quad BHT_{Updating\_Logic}\} + p \times \{PHT_{Storage\_Space} + \\
&\quad PHT_{Accessing\_Logic} + PHT_{Updating\_Logic}\} \\
&= \{[h \times (Tag_{(a-i+j)\_bit} + HR_{k\_bit} + Prediction\_Bit_{1\_bit} \\
&\quad + LRU\_Bits_{j\_bit})] + \\
&\quad [1 \times Address\_Decoder_{i\_bit} + 2^j \times \\
&\quad Comparators_{(a-i+j)\_bit} + 1 \times 2^j X1\_MUX_{k\_bit}] + \\
&\quad [h \times Shifter_{k\_bit} + 2^j \times LRU\_Incrementors_{j\_bit}]\} + \\
&\quad p \times \{[2^k \times History\_Bits_{s\_bit}] + \\
&\quad [1 \times Address\_Decoder_{k\_bit}] + [State\_Updater_{s\_bit}]\}
\end{aligned}
$$

$$= \{h \times [(a-i+j)+k+1+j] \times C_s + [h \times C_d + 2^j \times (a-i+j) \times C_c + 2^j \times k \times C_m] + [h \times k \times C_{sh} + 2^j \times j \times C_i]\} + p \times \{[2^k \times s \times C_s] + [2^k \times C_d] + [s \times 2^{s+1} \times C_a]\}, \quad a+j \geq i. \quad (3)$$

In GAg, only one history register and one global pattern history table are used, so h and p are both equal to one. No tag and no branch history table accessing logic are necessary for the single history register. Besides, pattern history state updating logic is small compared to the other two terms in the pattern history table cost. Therefore, cost estimation function for GAg can be simplified from Function 3 to the following Function:

$$Cost_{GAg}(BHT(1, \ , k), 1 \times PHT(2^k, s))$$
$$= Cost_{BHT}(1, \ , k) + 1 \times Cost_{PHT}(2^k, s)$$
$$\simeq \{[k+1] \times C_s + k \times C_{sh}\} + \{2^k \times (s \times C_s + C_d)\} \quad (4)$$

It is clear to see that the cost of GAg grows exponentially with respect to the history register length.

In PAg, only one pattern history table is used, so p is equal to one. Since j and s are usually small compared to the other variables, by using Function 3, the estimated cost for PAg using a branch history table is as follows:

$$Cost_{PAg}(BHT(h, j, k), 1 \times PHT(2^k, s))$$
$$= Cost_{BHT}(h, j, k) + 1 \times Cost_{PHT}(2^k, s)$$
$$\simeq \{h \times [(a + 2 \times j + k + 1 - i) \times C_s + C_d + k \times C_{sh}]\} + \{2^k \times (s \times C_s + C_d)\}, \quad a+j \geq i. \quad (5)$$

The cost of a PAg scheme grows exponentially with respect to the history register length and linearly with respect to the branch history table size.

In a PAp scheme using a branch history table as defined above, h pattern history tables are used, so p is equal to h. By using Function 3, the estimated cost for PAp is as follows:

$$Cost_{PAp}(BHT(h, j, k), h \times PHT(2^k, s))$$
$$= Cost_{BHT}(h, j, k) + h \times Cost_{PHT}(2^k, s)$$
$$\simeq \{h \times [(a + 2 \times j + k + 1 - i) \times C_s + C_d + k \times C_{sh}]\} + h \times \{2^k \times (s \times C_s + C_d)\}, \quad a+j \geq i. \quad (6)$$

When the history register is sufficiently large, the cost of a PAp scheme grows exponentially with respect to the history register length and linearly with respect to the branch history table size. However, the branch history table size becomes a more dominant factor than it is in a PAg scheme.

4 Simulation Model

Trace-driven simulations were used in this study. A Motorola 88100 instruction level simulator is used for generating instruction traces. The instruction and address traces are fed into the branch prediction simulator which decodes instructions, predicts branches, and verifies the predictions with the branch results to collect statistics for branch prediction accuracy.

4.1 Description of Traces

Nine benchmarks from the SPEC benchmark suite are used in this branch prediction study. Five are floating point benchmarks and four are integer benchmarks. The floating point benchmarks include *doduc*, *fpppp*, *matrix300*, *spice2g6* and *tomcatv* and the integer ones include *eqntott*, *espresso*, *gcc*, and *li*. *Nasa7* is not included because it takes too long to capture the branch behavior of all seven kernels.

Among the five floating point benchmarks, *fpppp*, *matrix300* and *tomcatv* have repetitive loop execution; thus, a very high prediction accuracy is attainable, independent of the predictors used. *Doduc*, *spice2g6* and the integer benchmarks are more interesting. They have many conditional branches and irregular branch behavior. Therefore, it is on the integer benchmarks where a branch predictor's mettle is tested.

Since this study of branch prediction focuses on the prediction for conditional branches, all benchmarks were simulated for twenty million conditional branch instructions except *gcc* which finished before twenty million conditional branch instructions are executed. *Fpppp*, *matrix300*, and *tomcatv* were simulated for 100 million instruction because of their regular branch behavior through out the programs. The number of static conditional branches in the instruction traces of the benchmarks are listed in Table 1. History register hit rate usually depends on the number of static branches in the benchmarks. The testing and training data sets for each benchmark used in this study are listed in Table 2.

Benchmark Name	Number of Static Cnd. Br.	Benchmark Name	Number of Static Cnd. Br.
eqntott	277	espresso	556
gcc	6922	li	489
doduc	1149	fpppp	653
matrix300	213	spice2g6	606
tomcatv	370		

Table 1: Number of static conditional branches in each benchmark.

Benchmark Name	Training Data Set	Testing Data Set
eqntott	NA	int_pri_3.eqn
espresso	cps	bca
gcc	cexp.i	dbxout.i
xlisp	tower of hanoi	eight queens
doduc	tiny doducin	doducin
fpppp	NA	natoms
matrix300	NA	Built-in
spice2g6	short greycode.in	greycode.in
tomcatv	NA	Built-in

Table 2: Training and testing data sets of benchmarks.

In the traces generated with the testing data sets, about 24 percent of the dynamic instructions for the integer benchmarks and about 5 percent of the dynamic instructions for the floating point benchmarks are branch instructions. Figure 4 shows about 80 percent of the dynamic branch instructions are conditional branches; therefore, the prediction mechanism for conditional branches is the most important among the prediction mechanisms for different classes of branches.

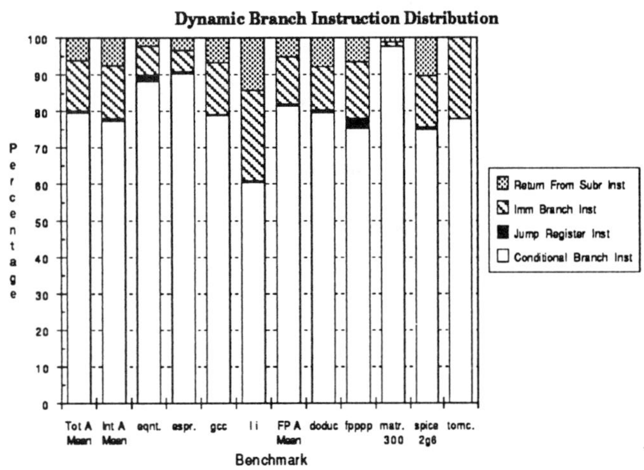

Figure 4: Distribution of dynamic branch instructions.

4.2 Characterization of Branch Predictors

The three variations of Two-Level Adaptive Branch Prediction were simulated with several configurations. Other known dynamic and static branch predictors were also simulated. The configurations of the dynamic branch predictors are shown in Table 3. In order to distinguish the different schemes we analyzed, the following naming convention is used: *Scheme*(*History*(*Size*, *Associativity*, *Entry_Content*), *Pattern_Table_Set_Size* × *Pattern*(*Size*, *Entry_Content*), *Context_Switch*). If a predictor does not have a certain feature in the naming convention, the corresponding field is left blank.

Scheme specifies the scheme, for example, GAg, PAg, PAp or Branch Target Buffer design (BTB) [17]. In *History*(*Size*, *Associativity*, *Entry_Content*), *History* is the entity used to keep history information of branches, for example, HR (A single history register), IBHT, or BHT. *Size* specifies the number of entries in that entity, *Associativity* is the associativity of the table, and *Entry_Content* specifies the content in each branch history table entry. When *Associativity* is set to 1, the branch history table is direct-mapped. The content of an entry in the branch history table can be any automaton shown in Figure 2 or simply a history register.

In *Pattern_Table_Set_Size* × *Pattern*(*Size*, *Entry_Content*), *Pattern_Table_Set_Size* is the number of pattern history tables used in the scheme, *Pattern* is the implementation for keeping pattern history information, *Size* specifies the number of entries in the implementation, and *Entry_Content* specifies the content in each entry. The content of an entry in the pattern history table can be any automaton shown in Figure 2. For Branch Target Buffer designs, the *Pattern* part is not included, because there is no pattern history information kept in their designs. *Context_Switch* is a flag for context switches. When *Context_Switch* is specified as *c*, context switches are simulated. If it is not specified, no context switches are simulated.

Since there are more taken branches than not taken branches according to our simulation results, a history register in the branch history table is initialized to all 1's when a miss on the branch history table occurs. After the result of the branch which causes the branch history table miss is known, the result bit is extended throughout the history register. A context switch results in flushing and reinitialization of the branch history table.

Model	BHT Config.			PHT	PHT Config.	
Name	# of Entr.	Asc	Entry Cont.	Set Size	# of Entr.	Entry Cont.
GAg(HR(1, ,*r*-sr), 1×PHT(2^r,A2),[c])	1		*r*-bit sr	1	2^r	Atm A2
PAg(BHT(256,1,*r*-sr), 1×PHT(2^r,A2),[c])	256	1	*r*-bit sr	1	2^r	Atm A2
PAg(BHT(256,4,*r*-sr), 1×PHT(2^r,A2),[c])	256	4	*r*-bit sr	1	2^r	Atm A2
PAg(BHT(512,1,*r*-sr), 1×PHT(2^r,A2),[c])	512	1	*r*-bit sr	1	2^r	Atm A2
PAg(BHT(512,4,*r*-sr), 1×PHT(2^r,A1),[c])	512	4	*r*-bit sr	1	2^r	Atm A1
PAg(BHT(512,4,*r*-sr), 1×PHT(2^r,A2),[c])	512	4	*r*-bit sr	1	2^r	Atm A2
PAg(BHT(512,4,*r*-sr), 1×PHT(2^r,A3),[c])	512	4	*r*-bit sr	1	2^r	Atm A3
PAg(BHT(512,4,*r*-sr), 1×PHT(2^r,A4),[c])	512	4	*r*-bit sr	1	2^r	Atm A4
PAg(BHT(512,4,*r*-sr), 1×PHT(2^r,LT),[c])	512	4	*r*-bit sr	1	2^r	Atm LT
PAg(IBHT(inf, ,*r*-sr), 1×PHT(2^r,A2),[c])	∞		*r*-bit sr	1	2^r	Atm A2
PAp(BHT(512,4,*r*-sr), 512×PHT(2^r,A2),[c])	512	4	*r*-bit sr	512	2^r	Atm A2
GSg(HR(1, ,*r*-sr), 1×PHT(2^r,PB),[c])	1		*r*-bit sr	1	2^r	PB
PSg(BHT(512,4,*r*-sr), 1×PHT(2^r,PB),[c])	512	4	*r*-bit sr	1	2^r	PB
BTB(BHT(512,4,A2), ,[c])	512	4	Atm A2			
BTB(BHT(512,4,LT), ,[c])	512	4	Atm LT			

Asc – *Table Set-Associativity*, **Atm** – *Automaton*, **BHT** – *Branch History Table*, **BTB** – *Branch Target Buffer Design*, **Config.** – *Configuration*, **Entr.** – *Entries*, **GAg** – *Global Two-Level Adaptive Branch Prediction Using a Global Pattern History Table*, **GSg** – *Global Static Training Using a Preset Global Pattern History Table*, **IBHT** – *Ideal Branch History Table*, **inf** – *Infinite*, **LT** – *Last-Time*, **PAg** – *Per-address Two-Level Adaptive Branch Prediction Using a Global Pattern History Table*, **PAp** – *Per-address Two-Level Adaptive Branch Prediction Using Per-address Pattern History Tables*, **PB** – *Preset Prediction Bit*, **PSg** – *Per-address Static Training Using a Preset Global Pattern History Table*, **PHT** – *Pattern History Table*, **sr** – *Shift Register*.

Table 3: Configurations of simulated branch predictors.

The pattern history bits in the pattern history table entries are also initialized at the beginning of execution. Since taken branches are more likely for those pattern history tables using automata *A*1, *A*2, *A*3, and *A*4, all entries are initialized to state 3. For *Last-Time*, all entries are initialized to state 1 such that the branches at the beginning of execution will be more likely to be predicted taken. It is not necessary to reinitialize pattern history tables during execution.

In addition to the Two-Level Adaptive schemes, Lee and A. Smith's Static Training schemes, Branch Target Buffer designs, and some dynamic and static branch prediction schemes were simulated for comparison purposes. Lee and A. Smith's Static Training scheme is similar in structure to the Per-address Two-Level Adaptive scheme with an IBHT but with the important difference that the prediction for a given pattern is pre-determined by profiling. In this study, Lee and A. Smith's Static Training is identified as PSg, meaning per-address Static Training using a global preset pattern history table. Similarly, the scheme which has a similar structure to GAg but with the difference that the second-level pattern history information is collected from profiling is abbreviated PSg, meaning Global Static Training using a preset global pattern history table. Per-address Static Training using per-address pattern history tables (PSp) is another application of Static Training to a different structure; however, this scheme requires a lot of storage to keep track of pattern behavior of all branches statically. Therefore, no PSp schemes were simulated in this study. Lee and A. Smith's Static Training schemes were simulated with the same branch history table configurations as used by the Two-Level Adaptive schemes for a fair comparison. The cost to implement Static Training is not less expensive than the cost to implement the Two-Level Adaptive Scheme because the branch history table and the pattern history table required by both schemes are similar. In Static Training, before program execution starts, extra time is needed to load the preset pattern prediction bits into the pattern history table.

Branch Target Buffer designs were simulated with automata *A2* and *Last-Time*. The static branch prediction schemes simulated include the Always Taken, Backward Taken and Forward Not Taken, and a profiling scheme. Always Taken scheme predicts taken for all branches. Backward Taken and Forward Not Taken (BTFN) scheme predicts taken if a branch branches backward and not taken if the branch branches forward. The BTFN scheme is effective for loop-bound programs, because it mispredicts only once in the execution of a loop. The profiling scheme counts the frequency of taken and not-taken for each static branch in the profiling execution. The predicted direction of a branch is the one the branch takes most frequently. The profiling information of a program executed with a training data set is used for branch predictions for the program executed with testing data sets, thus calculating the prediction accuracy.

5 Branch Prediction Simulation Results

Figures 5 through 11 show the prediction accuracy of the branch predictors described in the previous session on the nine SPEC benchmarks. "Tot GMean" is the geometric mean across all the benchmarks, "Int GMean" is the geometric mean across all the integer benchmarks, and "FP GMean" is the geometric mean across all the floating point benchmarks. The vertical axis shows the prediction accuracy scaled from 76 percent to 100 percent.

5.1 Evaluation of the Parameters of the Two-Level Adaptive Branch Prediction Branch Prediction

The three variations of Two-Level Adaptive Branch Prediction were simulated with different history register lengths to assess the effectiveness of increasing the recorded history length. The PAg and PAp schemes were each simulated with an ideal branch history table (IBHT) and with practical branch history tables to show the effect of the branch history table hit ratio.

5.1.1 Effect of Pattern History Table Automaton

Figure 5 shows the efficiency of using different finite-state automata. Five automata *A1*, *A2*, *A3*, *A4*, and *Last-Time* were simulated with a PAg branch predictor, having 12-bit history registers in a four-way set-associative 512-entry BHT. *A1*, *A2*, *A3*, and *A4* all perform better than *Last-Time*. The four-state automata *A1*, *A2*, *A3*, and *A4* maintain more history information than *Last-Time* which only records what happened the last time; they are therefore more tolerant to the deviations in the execution history. Among the four-state automata, *A1* performs worse than the others. The performance of *A2*, *A3*, and *A4* are very close to each other; however, *A2* usually performs best. In order to show the following figures clearly, each Two-Level Adaptive Scheme is shown with automaton *A2*.

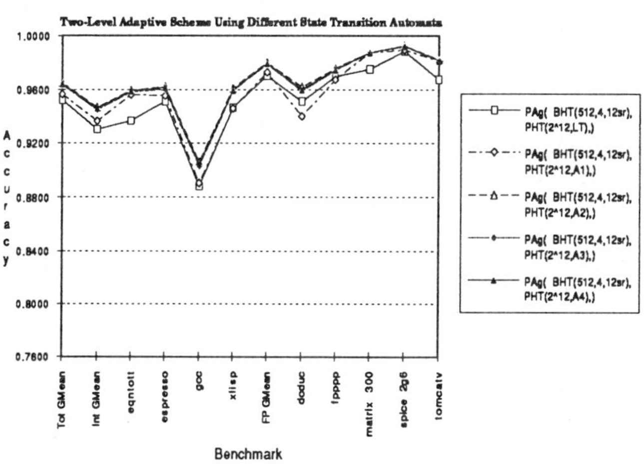

Figure 5: Comparison of Two-Level Adaptive Branch Predictors using different finite-state automata.

5.1.2 Effect of History Register Length

Three variations using history registers of the same length

Figure 6 shows the effects of history register length on the prediction accuracy of Two-Level Adaptive schemes. Every scheme in the graph was simulated with the same history register length. Among the variations, PAp performs the best, PAg the second, and GAg the worst.

GAg is not effective with 6-bit history registers, because every branch updates the same history register, causing excessive interference. PAg performs better than GAg, because it has a branch history table which reduces the interference in branch history. PAp predicts the best, because the interference in the pattern history is removed.

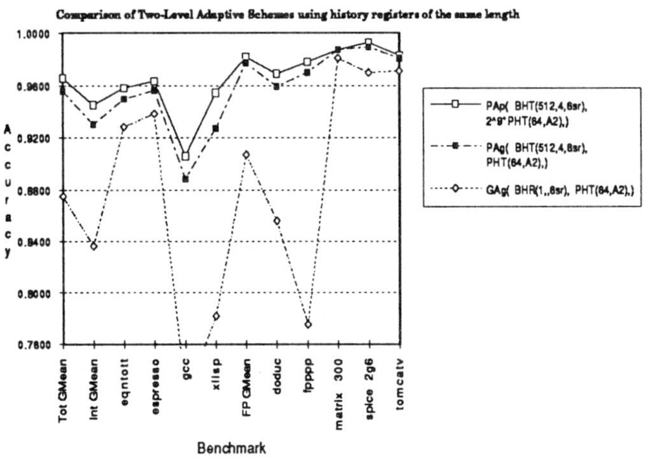

Figure 6: Comparison of the Two-Level Adaptive schemes using history registers of the same length.

Effects of various history register lengths

To further investigate the effect of history register length, Figure 7 shows the accuracy of GAg with various history register lengths. There is an increase of 9 percent in accuracy by lengthening the history register from 6 bits to 18 bits. The effect of history register length is obvious on GAg schemes. The history register length has smaller effect on PAg schemes and even smaller effect on PAp schemes because of the less interference in the branch history and pattern history and their effectiveness with short history registers.

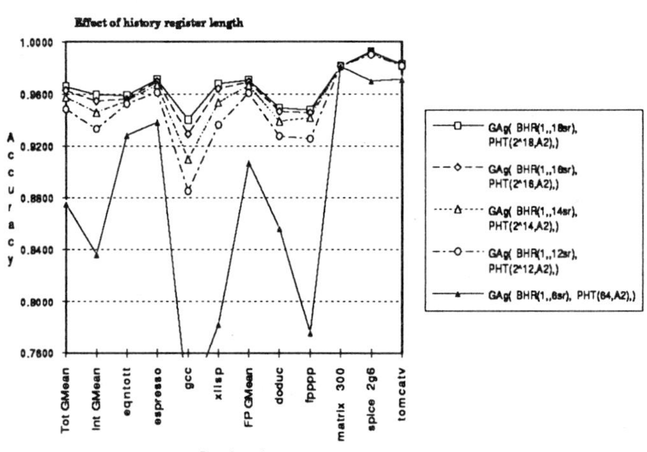

Figure 7: Effect of various history register lengths on GAg schemes.

5.1.3 Hardware Cost Efficiency of Three Variations

In Figure 6, prediction accuracy for the schemes with the same history register length were compared. However, the various Two-Level Adaptive schemes have different costs. PAp is the most expensive, PAg the second, and GAg the least, as you would expect. When evaluating the three variations of Two-Level Adaptive Branch Prediction, it is useful to know which variation is the least expensive when they predict with approximately the same accuracy.

Figure 8 illustrates three schemes which achieve about 97 percent prediction accuracy. One scheme is chosen for each variation to show the variation's configuration requirements to obtain that prediction accuracy. To achieve 97 percent prediction accuracy, GAg requires an 18-bit history register, PAg requires 12-bit history registers, and PAp requires 6-bit history registers. According to our cost estimates, PAg is the cheapest among these three. GAg's pattern history table is expensive when a long history register is used. PAp is expensive due to the required multiple pattern history tables.

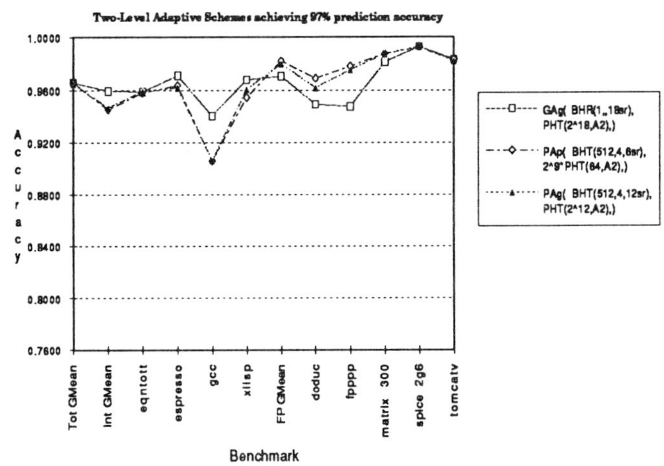

Figure 8: The Two-Level Adaptive schemes achieve about 97 percent prediction accuracy.

5.1.4 Effect of Context Switch

Since Two-Level Adaptive Branch Prediction uses the branch history table to keep track of branch history, the table needs to be flushed during a context switch. Figure 9 shows the difference in the prediction accuracy for three schemes simulated with and without context switches. During the simulation, whenever a trap occurs in the instruction trace or every 500,000 instructions if no trap occurs, a context switch is simulated. After a context switch, the pattern history table is not re-initialized, because the pattern history table of the saved process is more likely to be similar to the current process's pattern history table than to a re-initialized pattern history table. The value 500,000 is derived by assuming that a 50 MHz clock is used and context switches occur every 10 ms in a 1 IPC machine. The average accuracy degradations for the three schemes are all less than 1 percent. The accuracy degradations for *gcc* when PAg and PAp are used are much greater than those of the other programs because of the large number of traps in *gcc*. However, the excessive number of traps do not degrade the prediction accuracy of the GAg scheme, because an initialized global history register can be refilled quickly. The prediction accuracy of *fpppp* using GAg actually increases when context switches are simulated. There are very few conditional branches in *fpppp* and all the conditional branches have regular behavior; therefore, initializing the global history register helps clear out the noise.

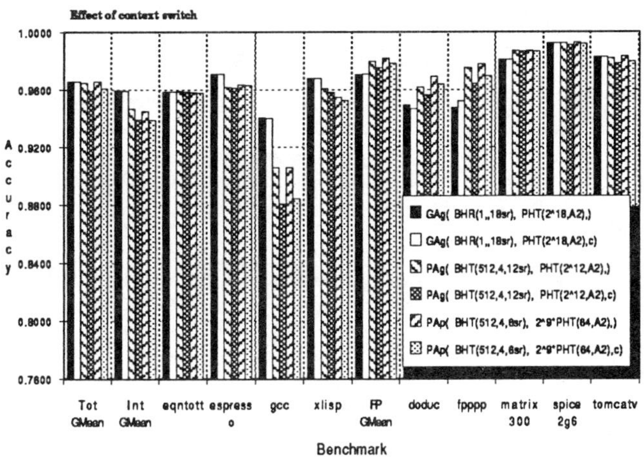

Figure 9: Effect of context switch on prediction accuracy.

5.1.5 Effect of Branch History Table Implementation

Figure 10 illustrates the effects of the size and associativity of the branch history table in the presence of context switches. Four practical branch history table implementations and an ideal branch history table were simulated. The four-way set-associative 512-entry branch history table's performance is very close to that of the ideal branch history table, because most branches in the programs can fit in the table. Prediction accuracy decreases as table miss rate increases, which is also seen in the PAp schemes.

5.2 Comparison of Two-Level Adaptive Branch Prediction and Other Prediction schemes

Figure 11 compares the branch prediction schemes. The PAg scheme which achieves 97 percent prediction accuracy is chosen for comparison with other well-known schemes, because it costs the least among the three variations of Two-Level Adaptive Branch Prediction.

The 4-way set-associative 512-entry BHT is selected to be used by all schemes which keep the first-level branch history information, because it is simple enough to be implemented. The Two-Level Adaptive scheme and the Static Training scheme were chosen on the basis of similar costs.

The top curve is achieved by the Two-Level Adaptive scheme whose prediction accuracy is about 97 percent.

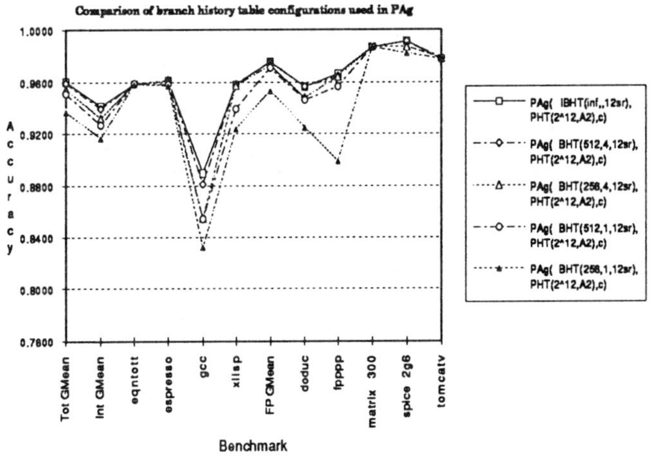

Figure 10: Effect of branch history table implementation on PAg schemes.

Since the data for the Static Training schemes are not complete due to the unavailability of appropriate data sets, the data points for *eqntott*, *fpppp*, *matrix*300 , and *tomcatv* are not graphed. PSg is about 1 to 4 percent lower than the top curve for the benchmarks that are available and GSg is about 4 to 19 percent lower with average prediction accuracy of 94.4 percent and 89 percent individually. Note that their accuracy depends greatly on the similarities between the data sets used for training and testing. The prediction accuracy for the branch target buffer using 2-bit saturating up-down counters [17] is around 93 percent. The Profiling scheme achieves about 91 percent prediction accuracy. The branch target buffer using *Last-Time* achieves about 89 percent prediction accuracy. Most of the prediction accuracy curves of BTFN and Always Taken are below the base line (76 percent). BTFN's average prediction accuracy is about 68.5 percent and Always Taken's is about 62.5 percent. In this figure, the Two-Level Adaptive scheme is superior to the other schemes by at least 2.6 percent.

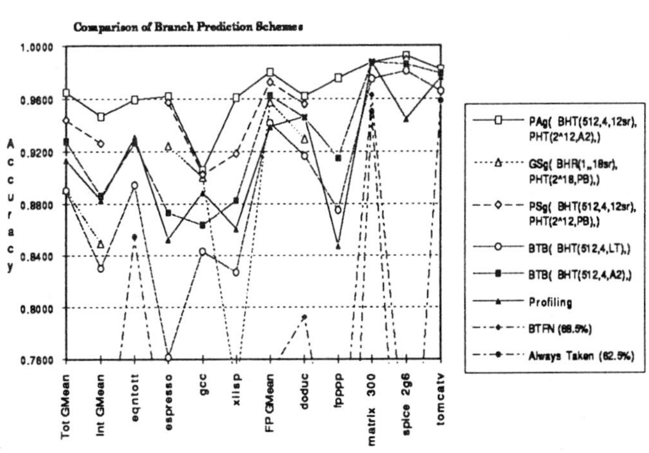

Figure 11: Comparison of branch prediction schemes.

6 Concluding Remarks

In this paper we have proposed a new dynamic branch predictor (Two-Level Adaptive Branch Prediction) that achieves substantially higher accuracy than any other scheme that we are aware of. We computed the hardware costs of implementing three variations of this scheme and determined that the most effective implementation of Two-Level Adaptive Branch Prediction utilizes a per-address branch history table and a global pattern history table.

We have measured the prediction accuracy of the three variations of Two-Level Adaptive Branch Prediction and several other popular proposed dynamic and static prediction schemes using trace-driven simulation of nine of the ten SPEC benchmarks. We have shown that the average prediction accuracy for Two-Level Adaptive Branch Prediction is about 97 percent, while the other known schemes achieve at most 94.4 percent average prediction accuracy.

We have measured the effects of varying the parameters of the Two-Level Adaptive predictors. We noted the sensitivity to k, the length of the history register, and s, the size of each entry in the pattern history table. We reported on the effectiveness of the various prediction algorithms that use the pattern history table information. We showed the effects of context switching.

Finally, we should point out that we feel our 97 percent prediction accuracy figures are not good enough and that future research in branch prediction is still needed. High performance computing engines in the future will increase the issue rate and the depth of the pipeline, which will combine to increase further the amount of speculative work that will have to be thrown out due to a branch prediction miss. Thus, the 3 percent prediction miss rate needs improvement. We are examining that 3 percent to try to characterize it and hopefully reduce it.

Acknowledgments The authors wish to acknowledge with gratitude the other members of the HPS research group at Michigan for the stimulating environment they provide, and in particular, for their comments and suggestions on this work. We are also grateful to Motorola Corporation for technical and financial support, and to NCR Corporation for the gift of an NCR Tower, Model No. 32, which was very useful in our work.

References

[1] T-Y Yeh and Y.N. Patt, "Two-Level Adaptive Branch Prediction", *Technical Report CSE-TR-117-91, Computer Science and Engineering Division, Department of EECS, The University of Michigan*, (Nov. 1991).

[2] T-Y Yeh and Y.N. Patt, "Two-Level Adaptive Branch Prediction", *The 24th ACM/IEEE International Symposium and Workshop on Microarchitecture* , (Nov. 1991), pp. 51-61.

[3] M. Butler, T-Y Yeh, Y.N. Patt, M. Alsup, H. Scales, and M. Shebanow, "Instruction Level Parallelism is Greater Than Two", *Proceedings of the 18th International Symposium on Computer Architecture*, (May. 1991), pp. 276-286.

[4] D. R. Kaeli and P. G. Emma, "Branch History Table Prediction of Moving Target Branches Due to Subroutine Returns" , *Proceedings of the 18th International Symposium on Computer Architecture*, (May 1991), pp. 34-42.

[5] Motorola Inc., "M88100 User's Manual", *Phoenix, Arizona*, (March 13, 1989).

[6] W.W. Hwu, T.M.Conte, and P.P.Chang, "Comparing Software and Hardware Schemes for Reducing the Cost of Branches", *Proceedings of the 16th International Symposium on Computer Architecture*, (May 1989).

[7] N.P. Jouppi and D. Wall, "Available Instruction-Level Parallelism for Superscalar and Superpipelined Machines.", *Proceedings of the Third International Conference on Architectural Support for Programming Languages and Operating Systems*, (April 1989), pp. 272-282.

[8] D. J. Lilja, "Reducing the Branch Penalty in Pipelined Processors ", *IEEE Computer*, (July 1988), pp.47-55.

[9] W.W. Hwu and Y.N. Patt, "Checkpoint Repair for Out-of-order Execution Machines", *IEEE Transactions on Computers*, (December 1987), pp.1496-1514.

[10] P. G. Emma and E. S. Davidson, "Characterization of Branch and Data Dependencies in Programs for Evaluating Pipeline Performance" , *IEEE Transactions on Computers*, (July 1987), pp.859-876.

[11] J. A. DeRosa and H. M. Levy, "An Evaluation of Branch Architectures ", *Proceedings of the 14th International Symposium on Computer Architecture*, (June 1987), pp.10-16.

[12] D.R. Ditzel and H.R. McLellan, "Branch Folding in the CRISP Microprocessor: Reducing Branch Delay to Zero", *Proceedings of the 14th International Symposium on Computer Architecture*, (June 1987), pp.2-9.

[13] S. McFarling and J. Hennessy, "Reducing the Cost of Branches", *Proceedings of the 13th International Symposium on Computer Architecture*, (1986), pp.396-403.

[14] J. Lee and A. J. Smith, "Branch Prediction Strategies and Branch Target Buffer Design", *IEEE Computer*, (January 1984), pp.6-22.

[15] T.R. Gross and J. Hennessy, "Optimizing Delayed Branches", *Proceedings of the 15th Annual Workshop on Microprogramming*, (Oct. 1982), pp.114-120.

[16] D.A. Patterson and C.H. Sequin, "RISC-I: A Reduced Instruction Set VLSI Computer", *Proceedings of the 8th International Symposium on Computer Architecture*, (May. 1981), pp.443-458.

[17] J.E. Smith, "A Study of Branch Prediction Strategies", *Proceedings of the 8th International Symposium on Computer Architecture*, (May. 1981), pp.135-148.

[18] T. C. Chen, "Parallelism, Pipelining and Computer Efficiency", *Computer Design*, Vol. 10, No. 1, (Jan. 1971), pp.69-74.

Session 5: Multithreaded Architecture

An Elementary Processor Architecture with Simultaneous Instruction Issuing from Multiple Threads

Hiroaki Hirata, Kozo Kimura, Satoshi Nagamine, Yoshiyuki Mochizuki, Akio Nishimura, Yoshimori Nakase and Teiji Nishizawa

Media Research Laboratory,
Matsushita Electric Industrial Co., Ltd.
1006 Kadoma Osaka. 571 Japan
(hirata@isl.mei.co.jp)

Abstract

In this paper, we propose a multithreaded processor architecture which improves machine throughput. In our processor architecture, instructions from different threads (not a single thread) are issued simultaneously to multiple functional units, and these instructions can begin execution unless there are functional unit conflicts. This parallel execution scheme greatly improves the utilization of the functional unit. Simulation results show that by executing two and four threads in parallel on a nine-functional-unit processor, a 2.02 and a 3.72 times speed-up, respectively, can be achieved over a conventional RISC processor.

Our architecture is also applicable to the efficient execution of a single loop. In order to control functional unit conflicts between loop iterations, we have developed a new static code scheduling technique. Another loop execution scheme, by using the multiple control flow mechanism of our architecture, makes it possible to parallelize loops which are difficult to parallelize in vector or VLIW machines.

1 Introduction

We are currently developing an integrated visualization system which creates virtual worlds and represents them through computer graphics. However, the generation of high quality images requires great processing power. Furthermore, in order to model the real world as faithfully as possible, intensive numerical computations are also needed. In this paper, we present a processor architecture[1] used as the base processor in a parallel machine which could run such a graphics system.

In the field of computer graphics, ray-tracing and radiosity are very famous algorithms for generating realistic images. In these algorithms, intersection tests account for a large part of the processing time for the whole program. This test has inherent coarse-grained parallelism and can easily create many threads(parallel processes) to be executed on multiprocessing systems. Each thread, however, executes a number of data accesses and conditional branches. In the case of a distributed shared memory system, low processor utilization can result from long latencies due to remote memory access. On the other hand, low utilization of functional units within a processor can result from interinstruction dependencies and functional operation delays. Another obstacle to the optimization of the single thread execution arises if the past performance of a repeatedly executed conditional branch does not help in predicting the target of future executions.

In order to overcome these problems, we introduced two kinds of multithreading techniques into our processor architecture: *concurrent multithreading* and *parallel multithreading*. The concurrent multithreading technique attempts to remain active during long latencies due to remote memory access. When a thread encounters an absence of data, the processor rapidly switches between threads. On the other hand, parallel multithreading within a processor is a latency-hiding technique at the instruction level. When an instruction from a thread is not able to be issued because of either a control or data dependency within the thread, an independent instruction from another thread is executed. This technique is especially effective in a deeply pipelined processor.

Our goal is to achieve an efficient and cost-effective processor design which is oriented specifically for use as an elementary processor in a large scale multiprocessor system rather than for use in an uniprocessor system. The idea of parallel multithreading arose from hardware resource optimization where several processors are

© 1992 ACM 0-89791-509-7/92/0005/0136 $1.50

united and reorganized so that functional units could be fully used. Figure 1(a) shows a general multiprocessor system organization. Multiple threads are executed on each physical processor. For example, assume that the utilization of the busiest functional unit of a processor in Figure 1(a) is about 30% because of the instruction level dependency. The utilization of the functional unit is defined as $U = \frac{N \cdot L}{T} \times 100[\%]$, where N is the number of invocations of the unit, L is an issue latency of the unit, and T represents the total execution cycles of the program. In this case, three processors could be united into one as shown in Figure 1(b), so that the utilization of the busiest functional unit could be expected to be improved nearly to 30×3=90%. Consequently, on the united processor, multiple instructions from different threads are issued simultaneously and executed unless they conflict with one another to compete for the same functional unit.

The programmer's view of the *logical processor* in Figure 1(b) is almost as same as the view of physical processor in Figure 1(a), although the physical organization is different. In the field of numerical computation, parallel loop execution techniques developed for multiprocessor, such as *doall* or *doacross* techniques which assign iterations to processors, are also applicable to our processor.

In this paper, we will concentrate most of our architectural interest upon parallel multithreading and restrict ourselves to simply outlining concurrent multithreading. The rest of this paper is organized as follows. In section 2, our multithreaded processor architecture is addressed. Section 3 demonstrates the effectiveness of our architecture via simulation results. In section 4, preceding works on multithreaded architectures are presented to be compared with our architecture. Concluding remarks are made in section 5.

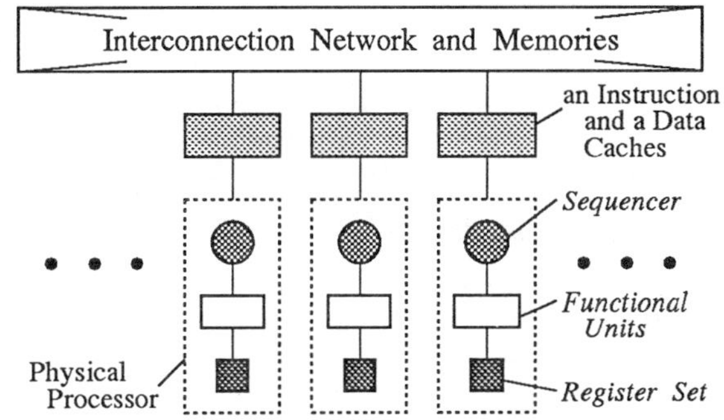

(a) Conventional organization

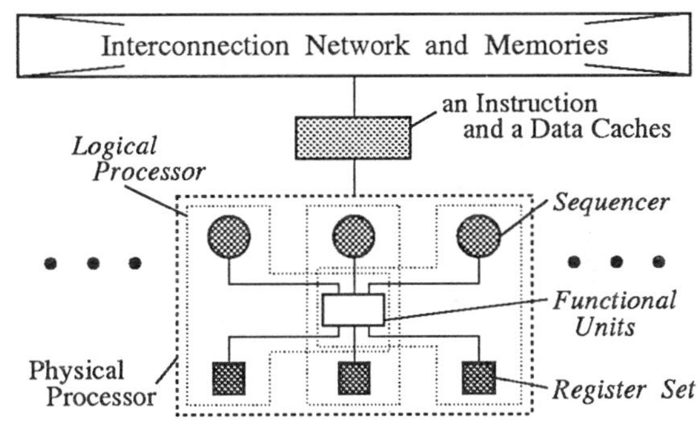

(b) Organization using united elementary processors

Figure 1: Multiprocessor system organization

2 Processor Architecture

2.1 Machine Model

2.1.1 Hardware Organization

As shown in Figure 2, the processor is provided with several instruction queue unit and decode unit pairs, called *thread slots*. Each thread slot, associated with a program counter, makes up a *logical processor*, while an instruction fetch unit and all functional units are physically shared among logical processors.

An instruction queue unit has a buffer which saves some instructions succeeding the instruction indicated by the program counter. The buffer size needs to be at least $B = S \times C$ words, where S is the number of thread slots, and C is the number of cycles required to access the instruction cache.

An instruction fetch unit fetches at most B instructions for one thread every C cycles from the instruction cache, and attempts to fill the buffer in the instruction queue unit. This fetching operation is done in an interleaved fashion for multiple threads. So, on the average, the buffer in one instruction queue unit is filled once in B cycles. When one of the threads encounters a branch instruction, however, that thread can preempt the fetching operation. The instruction cache and fetch unit might become bottleneck for a processor with many thread slots. In such a case, another cache and fetch unit would be needed.

A decode unit gets an instruction from an instruction queue unit and decodes it. The instruction set is based on a RISC type, and a load/store architecture is assumed. Branch instructions are executed within the decode unit. The data dependencies of an instruction are checked using the scoreboarding technique, and issued if it is free of dependencies. Otherwise, issuing is interlocked.

Issued instructions are dynamically scheduled by *instruction schedule units* and delivered to functional units. Unless an instruction conflicts with other instructions issued from other decode units over the same

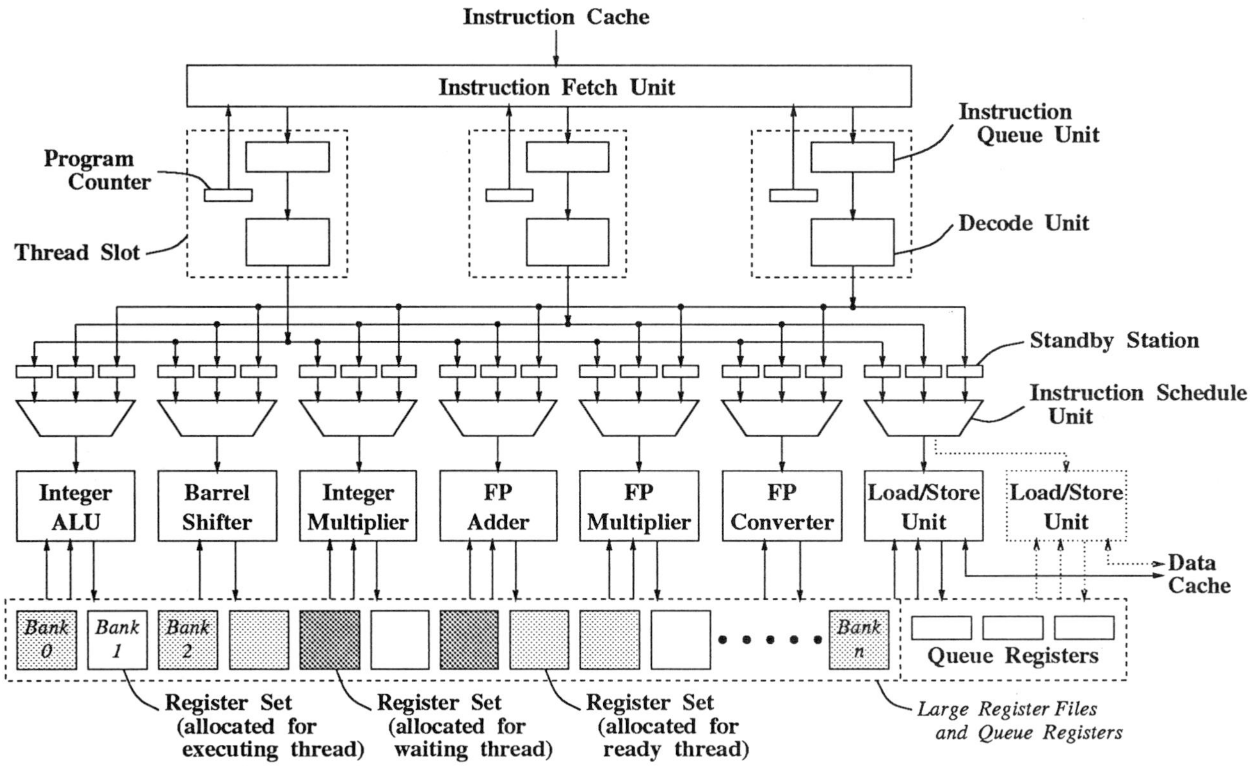

Figure 2: Hardware organization with three thread slots

functional unit, the instruction is sent immediately to the functional unit and executed. Otherwise, the instruction is arbitrated by the instruction schedule unit.

When an instruction is not selected by an instruction schedule unit, it is stored in a *standby station* and remains there until it is selected. Standby stations can allow decode units to proceed with their operations even if previously issued instructions cause resource conflicts. For example, while a shift instruction stays in a standby station, a succeeding add instruction from the same thread could be sent to the ALU. Consequently, instructions from a thread are executed out of order, though they are issued from a decode unit in order. A standby station is a simple latch whose depth is one, and differs from a reservation station in Tomasulo's algorithm[2] because issued instructions are guaranteed to be free of dependencies in our architecture.

A large general-purpose register file, as well as floating-point one, is divided into banks, each of which is used as a full register set private to a thread. Each bank has two read ports and one write port. More read ports are unnecessary because operand data can be stored in standby stations. In order to support concurrent multithreading, the physical processor is provided with more register banks than thread slots. When a thread is executed, the bank allocated for the thread is logically bound to the logical processor. The exclusive one-to-one binding between a logical processor and a register bank guarantees that the logical processor does not access any register banks other than the bank bound to it. In contrast, *queue registers* are special registers which enable communications between logical processors at the register-transfer level.

Some disadvantages with our machine model include the hardware cost of register files, multiple thread slots, and dynamic instruction scheduling facilities. The increased complexity in the network between functional units and register banks is also a disadvantage.

2.1.2 Instruction Pipeline

Figure 3(a) shows the instruction pipeline of the logical processor, which is a modification of a superpipelined RISC processor as shown in Figure 3(b). In the logical processor pipeline, two instruction fetch(IF) stages are followed by two decode(D) stages, followed by a schedule(S) stage, followed by multiple execution(EX) stages, followed by a write(W) stage.

The IF stages are shown for convenience, and, in fact, an instruction is read from a buffer of an instruction queue unit in one cycle. In stage D_1, the format or type of the instruction is tested. In stage D_2, the instruction is checked if it is issuable or not. Stage S is inserted for the dynamic scheduling in instruction schedule units.

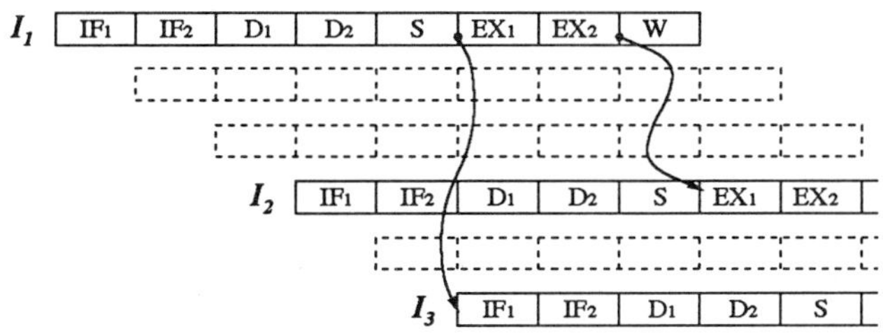

(a) Instruction pipeline of multithreaded processor

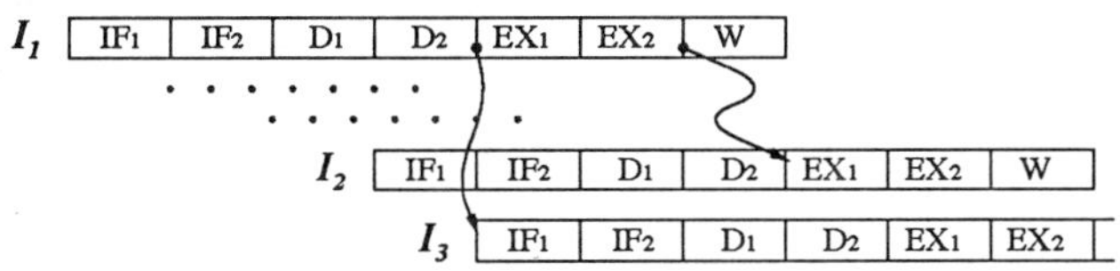

(b) Instruction pipeline of base RISC processor

Figure 3: Instruction pipeline

Table 1: Functional unit and issue/result latencies of instructions

functional unit	category of instructions	latency (cycle) issue	latency (cycle) result
Integer ALU	add/subtract	1	2
	logical	1	2
	compare	1	2
Barrel Shifter	shift	1	2
Integer Multiplier	multiply	1	6
	divide	1	6
FP Adder	add/subtract	1	4
	compare	1	4
	absolute/negate	1	2
	move	1	2
FP Multiplier	multiply	1	8
	divide	1	24
FP Converter	convert	1	4
Load/Store	load	2	4
	store	2	(4)

The number of EX stages is dependent on the kind of instruction. For example, in our simulation (section 3), we assumed each operation had latencies as listed in Table 1. The result latency means the number of cycles before the instruction finishes execution (i.e. the number of EX stages), and the issue latency is the number of stages before another instruction of the same type may be issued. Since two cycles are assumed to be required to access the data cache as well as the instruction cache, the issue latency of load/store instructions is two cycles. Other instructions can be accepted in every cycle. So, the issue latency of these instructions is one cycle. In stage W, the result value is written back to a register.

Required operands are read from registers in stage S. A scoreboarding bit corresponding to a destination register is flaged on in stage S and off in the last of the EX stages. This can avoid additional delay on the initiation of data-dependent instructions. That is, assuming instruction I_2 uses the result of instruction I_1 as a source, at least three cycles are required between I_1 and I_2 in Figure 3(a). The same cycles are also required in the base RISC pipeline in Figure 3(b).

In the case of branch instructions, an instruction fetch request is sent to the instruction fetch unit at the end of stage D_1, even if a conditional branch outcome is still unknown at that point. Assume I_1 is a branch instruction and I_3 is an instruction executed immediately after I_1. In Figure 3(b), the delay between I_1 and I_3 is four cycles. But the delay in Figure 3(a) is five. What is worse, it could become more than five if some threads encounter branches at the same time. It is obvious that the single thread performance is damaged. In our architecture, however, while some threads are blocked because of branches, other types of instructions from other threads are executed. Consequently, the parallel multithreading scheme has a potential to hide the delay of branches as well as other arithmetical operation delays, and enhance machine throughput.

2.1.3 Support of Concurrent Multithreading

Each pair of general purpose and floating-point register sets, together with an *instruction address save register* and a *thread status register*, is conceptually grouped into a single entity called a *context frame*, and allocated to a thread. An instruction address save register and a thread status register are used as save areas for the program counter and program status words (which hold various pieces of thread-specific state), respectively.

Since the processor has more context frames than thread slots, context switching is achieved rapidly by changing the logical binding between a logical processor and a context frame. As long as the number of threads to be scheduled does not exceed the number of physical context frames, threads can be resident on the physical processor, reducing the overhead to save or restore contexts to/from memory.

Another important element of the context frame is the *access requirement buffer*, which contains outstanding memory access requirements. When a thread in running state issues load/store instructions, these instructions are copied and recorded in the access requirement buffer, and deleted when they are performed.

The processor is pipelined and standby stations enable out-of-order execution of instructions. This makes

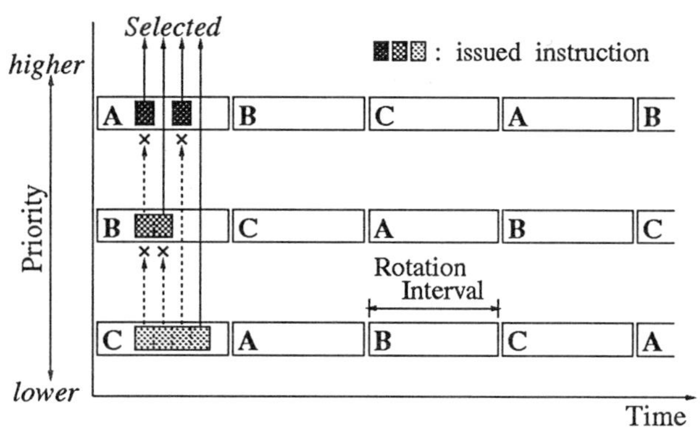

Figure 4: Dynamic instruction selection policy in instruction schedule unit (A, B, and C denote thread slots.)

the restart mechanism of programs somewhat complex. Before the thread is switched out, the logical processor should wait until all issued instructions but load/store instructions are performed. A load/store instruction is not always performed in short latency, and this is the main source of context switching in our architecture. Therefore, the load/store instructions in the execution pipeline could be flushed. But the restarting of threads is possible because such outstanding memory access requests are also saved as a piece of the context. When the thread is resumed, instructions in the access requirement buffer are decoded again and re-executed, being followed by the instruction indicated by the instruction address save register. This mechanism also ensures imprecise but restartable interrupts on page fault. Mechanisms similar to this can be applied to floating-point exception handling.

Context switching is triggered by a data absence trap. Detailed conditions concerning such traps must be considered with care, because incorrect choices can create starvation and thrashing problems. We will report our solution including cache/memory architecture in another paper in the future.

2.2 Instruction Scheduling Strategy

In this section, we present the dynamic instruction selection policy in the instruction schedule unit. Simple selection policy is preferable, so as not to enlarge the instruction pipeline pitch.

Figure 4 illustrates an example of the policy with multi-level priorities. A unique priority is assigned to each thread slot. Unless an issued instruction conflicts with other instructions from other thread slots to which higher priorities are assigned, it is selected by the instruction schedule unit. In order to avoid starvation, the priorities are rotated. The lowest priority is assigned to the thread slot which had the highest priority before the rotation.

The instruction schedule unit works in one of two modes: *implicit-rotation mode* and *explicit-rotation mode*. The mode is switched to the alternative mode through a privileged instruction. In the implicit-rotation mode, priority rotation occurs at a given number of cycles(*rotation interval*), as shown in Figure 4. On the other hand, in the explicit-rotation mode, the rotation of priority is controlled by software. The rotation is done when a *change-priority instruction* is executed on the logical processor with the highest priority.

There are two reasons why our architecture supports the explicit-rotation mode. One is to aid the compiler to schedule the code of threads executed in parallel when it is possible. The other is to parallelize loops which are difficult to parallelize using other architectures. These features are discussed in section 2.3.2 and 2.3.3, respectively.

2.3 Parallel Execution of a Single Loop

2.3.1 Overview

Parallel execution of a single loop is available on our multithreaded machine, by assigning iterations to logical processors. For example, in the case of a physical processor with n thread slots, the kth logical processor executes the $ni+k$th$(i = 0, 1, \cdots)$ iteration respectively.

The explicit-rotation mode presented in section 2.2 is one of the facilities supporting parallel execution of a loop. In this mode, a context switch due to data absence is suppressed and a physical processor is occupied entirely by the threads from a loop. In the usual case, a change-priority instruction is inserted at the end of each iteration by the compiler.

A *fast-fork instruction* generates the same number of threads as logical processors by setting its own next instruction address to program counters of other thread slots and activating them. It also sets unique logical processor identifiers to special registers corresponding to each logical processor. Each thread, therefore, can be informed which iterations it executes.

In the case of *doall* type of loops, it is unnecessary for logical processors to communicate with one another. But the execution of *doacross* type of loops requires communication between logical processors. One solution would be communication through memory. But in order to reduce the communication overhead, we provide the processor with queue registers. They are queue-structured registers connected to functional units.

The connection topology among logical processors through queue registers is important when considering the trade-offs between hardware cost and its effect. One simple and effective connection topology is a ring net-

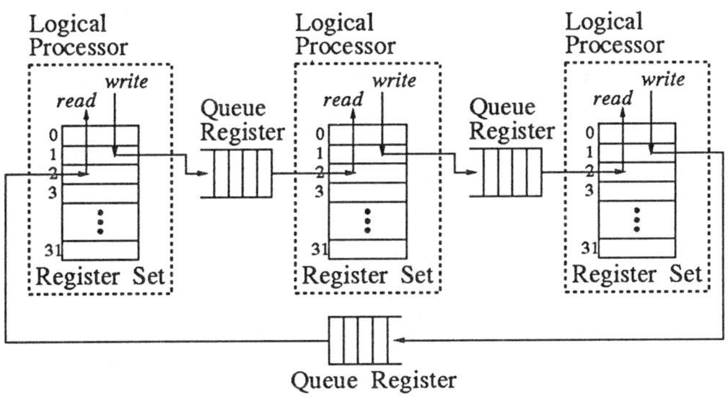

Figure 5: Logical view of queue registers

work, as shown in Figure 5. Many *doacross* type of loops encountered in practice have one iteration difference. When a loop has more than one iteration difference, data should be relayed through several logical processors. This could create overhead. Some techniques, however, are available to convert loops so that the iteration difference is reduced to one. Loop unrolling is one such technique[3].

Queue registers are enabled and disabled by special instructions. When enabled, two queue registers, for reading from the previous and writing to the next logical processor respectively are mapped into two general-purpose or floating-point registers. The reference to such registers is interpreted as the reference to queue registers, reducing data move overheads between queue registers and general/floating-point registers. *Full/empty bits* attached to queue registers are available as scoreboarding bits.

2.3.2 Static Code Scheduling

As mentioned in section 1, in the case of computer graphics programs, it is often difficult to predict the control sequence of a thread before execution, because the sequence is determined dynamically by data-dependent branches. In such cases, in order to obtain high throughput, the compiler could employ no other techniques than a simple list scheduling algorithm[4]. The compiler reorders the code without consideration of other threads, and concentrates on shortening the processing time for each thread. Short processing time of a single thread means a high issuing rate of instructions because the number of instructions is constant whether scheduled or not. Though this scheduling approach does not have control over resource conflicts, it aims at flooding functional units with sufficient instructions by parallel execution of such scheduled code.

On the other hand, in the case of numerical computation programs, it is often possible to predict the execution-time behavior of a loop. Therefore, the compiler employs more judicious code scheduling techniques.

For example, software pipelining[5, 6], which is an effective code scheduling technique for VLIW architectures, employs a resource reservation table to avoid resource conflicts. Such a technique is also applicable to our architecture. But it might postpone the issue of instructions which would cause a resource conflict. So, straight use of the algorithm could miss opportunities to issue instructions. Consequently, we have developed a new algorithm which makes the most of the function of standby stations and instruction schedule units.

Our algorithm employs not only a resource reservation table but also a standby table whose entry corresponds to a standby station. Our algorithm differs from software pipelining in the point described below. When all of the instructions without dependencies at an issuing cycle have resource conflicts, a software pipeliner would generate a NOP code. Our code scheduler, however, checks entries of the standby table for those instructions. If an entry is not marked, the instruction is determined to be issued and the entry is marked. This means the instruction is stored in a standby station. The explicit-rotation mode enables the compiler to know which instruction is selected. The resource reservation table is not used only to determine if there is a resource conflict, but also to tell the compiler when the instruction in the standby station is executed.

2.3.3 Eager Execution of Sequential Loop Iterations

Using an example, this section shows that our architecture can parallelize loops which are difficult to parallelize using vector or VLIW architectures.

The source code fragment of a sample program is shown in Figure 6. This program traverses a linear linked list. Although it is a simple example, it demonstrates the application of our execution scheme using a loop structure that is fundamental to many application programs.

```
ptr = header;
while ( ptr != NULL ) {
        tmp = a * ((ptr->point)->x)
              + b * ((ptr->point)->y) + c;
        if ( tmp < 0 )
            break;
        ptr = ptr -> next;
}
```

Figure 6: A sample program (written in C)

Each iteration is executed on a logical processor, and the value of ptr is passed through queue registers. The

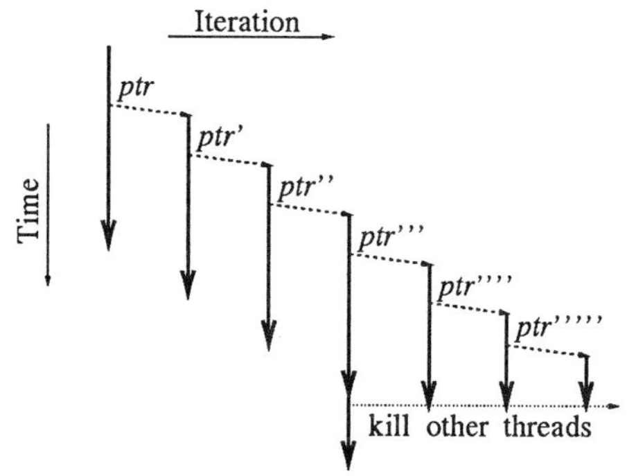

Figure 7: Parallel execution of while loop

compiler generates multiple versions for a variable `ptr` so that iterations can be initiated without having to wait for preceding iterations to complete. Such optimization with respect to a variable is a variation of the use of variables in dataflow machines. Figure 7 illustrates the parallel execution scheme. Each thread receives the value of `ptr` from the thread executed in the immediately preceding iteration, and passes the next value to the thread executed in the immediately succeeding iteration. After that, the thread continues to execute the rest of the loop body.

A thread can initiate an iteration which might not have been executed in the sequential execution. So, we call this scheme *eager execution*.

The instruction selection policy in instruction schedule units plays an important part in preserving the semantics of the sequential program. The execution of an iteration is not acknowledged until the thread gets the highest priority. It is the thread with the highest priority who executes the earliest iteration remaining at that point. By using multilevel priority, the instruction selection policy guarantees the execution of succeeding iterations does not hinder the execution of preceding iterations.

When a thread has exited from the loop, it tries to stop the operation of other thread slots and to kill other running threads. Such a special instruction is valid only for the thread with the highest priority. When a thread without the highest priority tries to execute this instruction, it is put into an interlocked state until it is given the highest priority.

If the variable `tmp` is global and alive after the loop, the compiler should use the special store instruction which is performed only by the thread with the highest priority. This guarantees that writes to the memory location of `tmp` are performed in order with respect to the source code. Some instructions are also provided to ensure consistency between contexts of threads before and after the execution of the loop.

3 Estimation

3.1 Simulation Model and Assumptions

In the following four sections, we present simulation results of our parallel multithreading architecture. Since cache simulation has not yet been implemented in our simulator, we assumed that attempts to access caches were all hit.

We used two kinds of functional unit configurations (see Figure 2). One consists of seven heterogeneous units. The other consists of those units with another load/store unit. In practice, a data cache might consist of several banks in order to be accessed simultaneously by two load/store units. But our simulation assumed there was no bank conflict. Latencies of each instruction are listed in Table 1. All machines simulated in this paper are not equipped with delayed branch mechanisms, branch prediction facilities, or overlapped register windows.

In order to estimate our architecture, we use the speed-up ratio as a criterion. It is defined as the proportion of total cycles required by multithreaded execution to those by sequential execution. Sequential execution means the execution of the sequential version of program on a RISC based processor whose instruction pipeline is shown in Figure 3(b).

3.2 Speed-up by Parallel Multithreading

This section presents simulation results of our multithreaded machine. As an application program, we have chosen a ray-tracing program, which can be easily parallelized at every pixel. The program written in C was compiled by a commercial RISC compiler with an optimization option. The object code was executed on a workstation, and traced instruction sequences were translated to be used for our simulator.

Table 2 lists speed-up ratios when the rotation interval in the instruction schedule unit is eight cycles. In the case of a processor with one load/store unit, an 1.83 times speed-up is gained by parallel execution of two instruction streams, although all of the hardware of a single-threaded processor is not duplicated in the processor. A performance improvement of a factor of 2.89 is still possible with four thread slots, though it is less effective (2.89/1.83=1.58) than the improvement attained by increasing from one to two thread slots (1.83). When eight thread slots are provided, the utilization of the busiest functional unit, the load/store unit, becomes 99%. This is the reason why the speed-up ratio is saturated at only 3.22 times. Addition of another load/store unit improves speed-up ratios by 10.4~79.8%.

Table 2: Speed-up ratio by parallel multitthreading

no. of thread slots	with one load/store unit		with two load/store units	
	without standby station	with standby station	without standby station	with standby station
2	1.79	1.83	2.01	2.02
4	2.84	2.89	3.68	3.72
8	3.22	3.22	5.68	5.79

Standby stations improve the speed-up ratio by 0~2.2%. This low improvement is due to poor parallelism within an instruction stream. In the case of application programs whose thread is rich in fine-grained parallelism, greater improvement can be achieved.

We also simulated a machine whose thread slots are provided with private instruction caches and instruction fetch units. Such organization does provide a slight speed-up. Achieved speed-up ratios are the same as those in Table 2, except that 1.79 and 5.79 is respectively replaced by 1.80 and 5.80. This shows that the delay due to instruction fetch conflicts is hidden and sharing an instruction cache between thread slots is possible.

We also examined the execution cycles with various rotation intervals (2^n cycles, where n is 0~8). But, in this application program, rotation interval did not have much influence on the performance, though using eight or sixteen cycles seems slightly superior.

3.3 Multithreading with Superscalar Design

In our simulator, each thread slot can support multiple instruction issuing from a single instruction stream similar to superscalar architectures. In this section, using the same program as in section 3.2, we discuss hybrid architectures which employ both coarse- and fine-grained parallelism.

A hybrid processor is represented here by (D,S)-processor, where D is the maximum number of instructions which a thread slot issues each cycle, and S is the number of thread slots. For a fair comparison, the hardware cost of (d,s)-processor is almost as same as that of $(1,d\times s)$-processor. For example, the instruction fetch bandwidth is $d\times s$ words per cycle in both processors. Although $(d\times 2,s/2)$-processor is provided with a half register set of (d,s)-processor, it requires double the number of register ports. Each thread slot checks the dependencies of instructions in the instruction window of size D, and issues instructions without dependencies every cycle. The instruction window is filled every cycle. Some techniques[7, 8] are proposed to boost the superscalar performance, but they are not provided for the thread slot because they requires additional hardware.

Table 3: Tradeoff between speed-up and employed parallelism (speed-up ratio)

total no. of issued instructions $(D\times S)$	no. of issued instructions from each thread slot (D)			
	1	2	4	8
2	2.02	1.31	—	—
4	3.72	2.43	1.52	—
8	5.79	4.37	2.79	1.66

Table 3 lists the simulation results. Values in the table are speed-up ratios. Simulated processors are composed of eight functional units. We used the instruction pipeline shown in Figure 3(b) for a $(d,1)$-processor, and the pipeline shown in Figure 3(a) for others. This table demonstrates that the increase of S produces a more significant speed-up than the increase of D.

The main objective of multithreading is to enhance the machine throughput. On the other hand, the main objective of superscalar architecture is to improve the single thread performance. This difference of objectives makes a simple comparison of the two architectures impossible. But, from the viewpoint of cost-effectiveness, it is clear that D=1 is the best choice if parallel multithreading is introduced into a processor architecture.

3.4 Effect of Static Code Scheduling

We will compare static code scheduling strategies discussed in section 2.3.2. The sample program is the Livermore Kernel 1. The source code is shown in Figure 8.

```
     DO 1 K = 1,N
 1   X(K) = Q+Y(K)*(R*Z(K+10)+T*Z(K+11))
```

Figure 8: Livermore Kernel 1 (written in FORTRAN)

Table 4 lists average execution cycles for one iteration. The source code was compiled by a commercial compiler, and the generated object code was scheduled by our code schedulers. The simulated machine has one load/store unit. Strategy A represents a simple list scheduling approach, and strategy B represents the list scheduling approach with a resource reservation table and a standby table.

Strategy B is overall superior to other strategies. It achieves the performance improvement by 0~19.3%

Table 4: Comparison of static code scheduling

no. of thread slots	optimization strategy		
	non-optimized	strategy A	strategy B
1	50	42	—
2	25	21.5	21
3	16.7	15	14
4	12.75	11.25	11
5	10.4	9	9
6	8.83	8	8
7	8.125	8	8
8 ~	8	8	8

(unit: cycle)

over non-optimized code. The differences between effectiveness of strategy A and strategy B, however, are small in this program. Although strategy A achieves nearly the same effectiveness at a lower cost, strategy B should be employed in order to optimize the program.

The object code contains three load instructions and one store instruction, so at least (3+1)×2=8 cycles are required for one iteration. This is the reason of performance saturation.

3.5 Effect of Eager Execution

In section 2.3.3, the eager execution scheme of sequential loop iterations is addressed. This section reports simulation results of the execution of the sample program shown in Figure 6. The simulated machine has one load/store unit.

The execution of the sequential version of the object code requires 56 cycles for one iteration. Table 5 lists the average execution cycles of the parallel version for one iteration. With a small number of thread slots, when a new value of `ptr` is passed to the next thread through a queue register, the thread is still executing a preceding iteration. An increase in the number of thread slots enables a thread to initiate an iteration as soon as the data is available, but the speed-up ratio is limited by the inter-loop dependency of `ptr`.

Since parallel code includes more overhead in loop headers and footers than sequential code, sequential execution performs better than parallel execution when the number of iterations is small. As the number of iterations increases, the maximum speed-up ratio becomes closer to 56/17=3.29 times.

4 Related Works

The concept of concurrent multithreading is discussed in HEP[9], MASA[10], Horizon[11], and P-RISC[12].

Table 5: Evaluation of eager execution of sequential loop iterations

no. of thread slots	execution cycle for one iteration
2	32.5
3	21.67
4 ~	17

These processors support cycle-by-cycle interleaving of instructions from multiple instruction streams. In order to improve poor performance of single thread execution in these machines, APRIL[13], and [14] support block interleaving in which a thread keeps control until it encounters a remote memory access. The hybrid data-flow/von Neumann machine[15] also employs the latter type of interleaving. Our concurrent multithreading scheme builds on such a block interleaving architecture. In our architecture, however, combination with parallel multithreading enables other threads to continue working during context switches.

Farrens and Pleszkun[16] take a multithreading approach to increase instruction issuing rate. This idea is closely allied to the basic one of our parallel multithreading. In their architecture, two instructions from two threads compete with each other to be issued, but the total number of issued instructions each cycle is still at most one. On the other hand, in our architecture, multiple instructions can be issued unless there are resource conflicts.

Daddis and Torng[17] propose a superscalar architecture which uses multiple threads to increase functional unit utilization. Prasadh and Wu[18] present a VLIW architecture which does the same. In our opinion, such hybrid architectures are not as cost-effective as a multithreaded non-superscalar architecture as mentioned in section 3.3. Functional unit utilization is an important factor, but the instruction fetch bandwidth sufficient to sustain multiple functional units must also be considered. For example, although Prasadh's four-threaded, eight-functional-unit processor achieves about eight times speed-up, it requires an instruction fetch bandwidth of thirty-two words per cycle.

5 Concluding Comments

In this paper, we proposed a multithreaded architecture oriented for use as a base processor of multiprocessor systems. Through the simulation using a ray-tracing program, we ascertained that a two-threaded, two-load/store-unit processor achieves a factor of 2.02 speed-up over a sequential machine, and a four-threaded processor achieves a factor of 3.72 speed-up. We also examined the performance of multi-threaded architecture combined with superscalar technique. This evaluation, however, shows the best cost-effectiveness is achieved when a processor employs only coarse-grained parallelism and ignores fine-grained parallelism.

We developed a static code scheduling algorithm applicable for our architecture, which is derived from idea of software pipelining. We also investigate possibilities for broadened use of parallel multithreading scheme. One instance of such intention is presented as an eager loop execution scheme. It parallelizes loops which are difficult to be parallelized with other architectures.

One weak point of this paper is the poor variety of tested programs. We should confirm the effectiveness of our architecture by using many other application programs. We are currently working on evaluating finite cache effects and the detailed design of the processor.

References

[1] H. Hirata, Y. Mochizuki, A. Nishimura, Y. Nakase and T. Nishizawa, "A Multithreaded Processor Architecture with Simultaneous Instruction Issuing," In *Proc. of Intl. Symp. on Supercomputing, Fukuoka, Japan*, pp. 87-96, November 1991.

[2] R.M.Tomasulo, "An Efficient Algorithm for Exploiting Multiple Arithmetic Units," In *IBM Journal of Research and Development*, vol. 11, no. 1, pp. 25-33, January 1967.

[3] A. Munshi and B. Simons, "Scheduling Sequential Loops on Parallel Processors," In *IBM Technical Report 5546*, 1987.

[4] E.G. Coffman, In *Computer and Job-Shop Scheduling Theory*, 1976.

[5] R.F. Touzeau, "A Fortran Compiler for the FPS-164 Scientific Computer," In *Proc. of the ACM SIGPLAN'84 Symp. on Compiler Construction*, pp. 48-57, June 1984.

[6] M. Lam, "Software Pipelining: An Effective Scheduling Technique for VLIW Machines," In *Proc. of the SIGPLAN'88 Conf. on Programming Language Design and Implementation*, pp. 318-328, June 1988.

[7] K. Murakami, N. Irie, M. Kuga and S. Tomita, "SIMP (Single Instruction Stream / Multiple Instruction Pipelining): A Novel High-Speed Single Processor Architecture," In *Proc. of the 16th Annual Intl. Symp. on Computer Architecture*, pp. 78-85, May 1989.

[8] M.D. Smith, M.S. Lam and M.A. Horowitz, "Boosting Beyond Static Scheduling in a Superscalar Processor," In *Proc. of the 17th Annual Intl. Symp. on Computer Architecture*, pp. 344-354, May 1990.

[9] B.J. Smith, "A Pipelined, Shared Resource MIMD Computer," In *Proc. of the 1978 Intl. Conf. on Parallel Processing*, pp. 6-8, August 1978.

[10] R.H. Halstead and T. Fujita, "MASA: A Multithreaded Processor Architecture for Parallel Symbolic Computing," In *Proc. of the 15th Annual Intl. Symp. on Computer Architecture*, pp. 443-451, June 1988.

[11] M.R. Thistle and B.J. Smith, "A Processor Architecture for Horizon," In *Proc. of 1988 Supercomputing Conf.*, pp. 35-41, November 1988.

[12] R.S. Nikhil and Arvind, "Can Dataflow Subsume von Nuemann Computing?" In *Proc. of the 16th Annual Intl. Symp. on Computer Architecture*, pp. 262-272, June 1989.

[13] A. Agarwal, B.H. Lim, D. Kranz and J. Kubiatowicz, "APRIL: A Processor Architecture for Multiprocessing," In *Proc. of the 17th Annual Intl. Symp. on Computer Architecture*, pp. 104-114, June 1990.

[14] W.D. Weber and A. Gupta, "Exploring the Benefits of Multiple Hardware Contexts in a Multiprocessor Architecture: Preliminary Results," In *Proc. of the 16th Annual Intl. Symp. on Computer Architecture*, pp. 273-280, June 1989.

[15] R.A. Iannucci, "Toward a Dataflow/von Neumann Hybrid Architecture," In *Proc. of the 15th Annual Intl. Symp. on Computer Architecture*, pp. 131-140, June 1988.

[16] M.K. Farrens and A.R. Pleszkun, "Strategies for Achieving Improved Processor Throughput," In *Proc. of the 18th Annual Intl. Symp. on Computer Architecture*, pp. 362-369, May 1991.

[17] G.E. Daddis Jr. and H.C. Torng, "The Concurrent Execution of Multiple Instruction Streams on Superscalar Processors," In *Proc. of the 20th Intl. Conf. on Parallel Processing*, pp. I:76-83, August 1991.

[18] R.G. Prasadh and C. Wu, "A Benchmark Evaluation of a Multi-Threaded RISC Processor Architecture," In *Proc. of the 20th Intl. Conf. on Parallel Processing*, pp. I:84-91, August 1991.

Thread-based Programming for the EM-4 Hybrid Dataflow Machine

Mitsuhisa SATO*, Yuetsu KODAMA, Shuichi SAKAI,
Yoshinori YAMAGUCHI, Yasuhito KOUMURA†

Electrotechnical Laboratory
1-1-4 Umezono, Tsukuba-shi, Ibaraki 305, JAPAN

Abstract

In this paper, we present a thread-based programming model for the EM-4 hybrid dataflow machine, where parallelism and synchronization among threads of sequential execution are described explicitly by the programmer. Although EM-4 was originally designed as a dataflow machine, we demonstrate that it provides effective architectural support for a variety of programming styles, including message passing and distributed data sharing in imperative languages. Our approach allows the programmer to control the parallelism and maintain data locality explicitly to achieve high performance. EM-4 can be thought of as a multi-threaded architecture that can exploit both von Neumann and dataflow compiling technology. Thread-based programming provides the first step to explore better programming/compiling technology for a hybrid dataflow machine as well as EM-4.

1 Introduction

EM-4 is a highly parallel hybrid dataflow architecture, which is designed to have more than 1000 processing elements (PEs). We have built a prototype of EM-4 consisting of 80 PEs which has been operational since April 1990. The architecture of EM-4 is a hybrid of the dataflow and von Neumann architectures — it can execute sequential, register-based code efficiently, and it can also use dataflow-like mechanisms to allow cheap synchronization and communication between threads of sequential execution.

*E-mail: msato@etl.go.jp
†SANYO Electric Co., Ltd.

In this paper, we present a thread-based programming model for the EM-4, where parallelism and synchronization among threads of sequential execution are described explicitly by the programmer. Our approach differs from traditional approaches to programming dataflow computers, because we allow synchronization and parallelism to be expressed explicitly, rather than implicitly, such as in functional languages. We seek to provide the appropriate tools to enable the programmer to write parallel applications based on multiple threads of sequential execution.

From the viewpoint of an executing sequential thread, EM-4 can be thought of as either a distributed-memory or shared-memory multi-processor. Each PE has its own local memory, and threads within a PE operate only on the local memory – in this sense, EM-4 is a distributed-memory machine. There is no "global" shared memory, but hardware support for word-sized packet communication allows EM-4 to be used effectively as a shared-memory machine, since word-sized remote memory references can be done via hardware packet communication.

Dataflow mechanisms within the architecture support allow multiple sequential threads within a processor to interact efficiently. To express parallelism explicitly, a set of functions is provided for forking threads, passing messages between threads, and sharing data via remote memory access.

The dataflow computational model has been attractive because it allows the exploitation of parallelism at the instruction, loop, procedure, and task levels. In the pure dataflow model, instructions are dynamically scheduled based on the availability of data. "Pure" dataflow machines have overhead because each dyadic instruction requires dynamic operand matching, and because extra instructions are needed to make copies of data when a particular value is required by several instructions. When a static schedule can be computed at compile-time, the von Neumann character of the hybrid architecture enables the compiler to schedule instructions to eliminate the overhead of run-time synchronization between instructions by allowing communication via registers.

Using such a machine as a bridge between existing systems and new dataflow machines would make the transition much less traumatic. Thread-based programming provides a deeper understanding of the strengths and weakness of both the dataflow and von Neumann architectures, and their current programming models.

Although EM-4 was originally designed as a dataflow machine, we demonstrate that it provides effective architectural support for a variety of programming styles, including message passing and distributed data sharing in imperative languages [5].

In Section 2, we first give the EM-4 architecture and its basic dataflow execution model briefly. The sequential thread execution of an imperative language on EM-4 is described in Section 3. Section 4 describes the library functions to implement the programming model. We present preliminary observations on different programming styles and discuss their performance on EM-4 in Section 5. Concluding remarks are made in Section 6.

2 The EM-4 Architecture

The main design principle of the EM-4 was to construct a high performance parallel system in a compact implementation. EM-4 consists of single chip processors, EMC-R's, connected in a Circular Omega Network. As the first step toward a 1000 PE system, we have built an EM-4 prototype system with 80 PEs. The performance of the EMC-R processor chip is 12.5 MIPS. The interconnection network has a 60.9 Mbytes/s/port transfer rate. A more detailed description of the EM-4 architecture is given in [11, 7].

2.1 Dataflow Model of EM-4

As a dataflow machine, the architecture of EM-4 is based on a modified dataflow model called the *strongly connected arc model.* In this model, dataflow graph arcs are classified into two categories: *normal arcs* and *strongly connected arcs.* A set of nodes connected by strongly connected arcs is called a *strongly connected block* (SCB). The strongly connected arc model provides additional firing rules for nodes within an SCB to execute exclusively. An SCB is invoked by tokens through normal arcs, and the SCB is executed as if it were a single basic node in the dataflow graph.

In EM-4, an SCB is implemented as an uninterrupted sequence of instructions. The SCB is executed in a single PE just as in a register-based RISC architecture. From the viewpoint of the dataflow computational model, SCB tokens are stored in registers, instead of

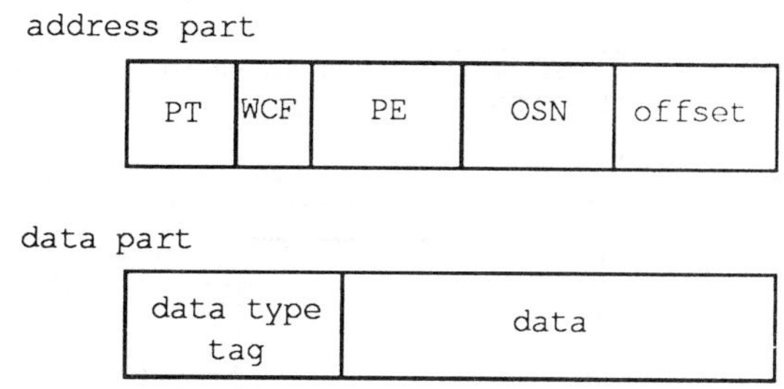

Figure 1: Packet Format

being transferred as tokens, reducing the cost of communication and operand matching.

SCB execution is controlled with a program counter, rather than by recirculating tokens in a circular pipeline. The pipeline of EMC-R is designed to integrate register-based von Neumann execution and packet-based dataflow execution.

2.2 Executing Function with SCBs

A function can consist of several SCBs. Function frames which are required for function invocations are allocated the caller at invocation-time. In EM-4, these are called *operand segments.* The code for each function is stored in another area called the *template segment.* Since each segment is aligned on a 128 words boundary, a segment number specifies a 128 words block. The template segment number is stored into the first word of the operand segment to link code of a function.

The unit of all communication in the system is the packet. A token of dataflow computation is delivered with a packet. Packets arrive from the network and are buffered in the packet queue. The address portion of each packet specifies the SCB to be invoked for that packet. The format of a packet is shown in Figure 1. `PE` is the processing element number and `OSN` is the operand segment number. The offset is used to calculate the address of the invoked SCB. `WCF` is a two bit waiting condition flag which specifies one of four *firing rules* for the token: operand for monadic operator (`1op`), right operand (`2opR`) and left operand (`2opL`) for dyadic operator, and operand for dyadic operator with a constant operand (`imm`). `PT` is a packet type which is used to implement special packet facility. A `1op` token invokes the execution of an SCB immediately.

In order to reduce the overhead of operand matching, a *direct matching scheme* is introduced in the EM-4. If a packet has WCFs for dyadic operators, `2opL` or `2opR`, the location of the specified offset in the operand segment is checked to see whether the other operand has arrived: the WCF bits in the word indicate the matching state. If the partner is absent, the data part

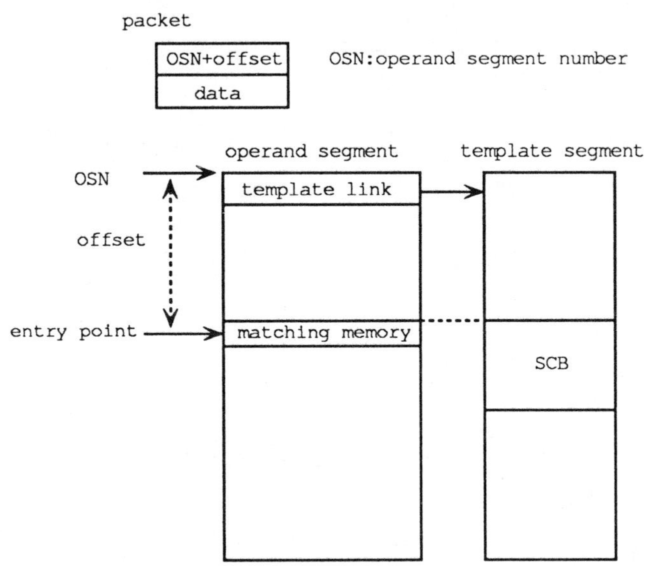

Figure 2: Entry point of SCB and direct matching

of the token is stored in the matching word. When the partner is present or a token has an immediate partner, the SCB is invoked. The operation of the direct match is shown in Figure 2. Each packet thus only contains the matching address as its address portion. To use direct matching for dyadic operators, the address of the entry of the SCB in the template segment must have a one-to-one correspondence with its matching word in the operand segment. We call the address specified in the packet an *entry point* for the instance of the SCB.

Each instruction has a bit to indicate whether to continue the execution of the SCB. These bits correspond with the strongly connected arcs. Once an SCB is invoked, the execution continues until an instruction whose bit is not set is encountered.

2.3 Basic Instruction Set

EM-4 executes instructions in an SCB with a RISC instruction set. Most instructions execute in one cycle except LOAD/STORE instructions. Instructions take register operands except the first instruction of an SCB, which operates on input tokens for the SCB. The data of the input tokens are loaded into *left operand register* `r0` and *right operand register* `r1`. EM-4 has 10 general purpose registers and 6 special purpose registers including a program counter and operand segment register. Each register is 38 bits long, containing a data type tag and data. During the execution of an SCB, the address of the current operand segment is set in the *operand segment register*. LOAD/STORE instructions access the local memory of the PE.

Within an SCB, *branch* instructions control the execution. Because of EM-4's RISC architecture, branch instructions are implemented with delayed semantics. The dataflow *switch operator* can be implemented as an SCB using branch instructions and MKPKT instructions.

2.4 Packet Generation

The MKPKT instruction sends a packet whose address portion and data portion are specified by its operands. The instruction `mkpkt r0,r1` sends a packet containing the value of `r0` to the address specified by `r1`, where the value of `r1` must have the same format as the address port of the packet. The MKPKT instruction can generate several forms of packet addresses. For example, consider the following code fragment:

```
     mkpkt r0,L.1
     op ...   :break
     ...
L:   op @l,@r
```

The MKPKT instruction sends a packet to the entry point specified by `L` in the same operand segment. The optional specifier ``:break'' terminates the SCB. To send to an entry point of segment in a different PE, the destination can be specified using the form `(reg L.1)` where `reg` contains the operand segment number with the appropriate PE number.

The GET instruction sends the address of an entry point in the current operand segment as data, and it is used to send a return entry point continuation for function calls.

2.5 Special Packet Facility

Packets with packet types other than the NORM packet type are called *special packets*. Special packets are generated by MKPKT or GET instructions. To handle special packets, the SCB for the *special packet routine* associated with its packet type is executed. When a special packet routine is executed, the SCB of the routine can take the address part in the segment register as an argument as well as the data in left operand register.

This type of a packet is used for remote memory access and resource management. For example, remote memory read is specified as follows:

```
     get C.v,r0 :ptype=MEM_READ :break
C:   op @v
```

where `r0` is the *global address* to be fetched, which contains the PE number and the local address, and `:ptype=MEM_READ` specifies the packet type for the remote memory special packet routine. The GET instruction sends the continuation `C.v` as its packet data. After sending the special packet, the execution continues.

The code for the `MEM_READ` special packet routines is as follows:

```
MEM_READ:
    l [seg],r1           ; fetch local memory at seg
    mkpkt r1,r0 :break   ; send it back
```

The continuation in the received packet is loaded into r0. Using the special packet facility, global I-structure memory [1] can be implemented by emulating the operations.

Special packet routines are loaded into system area of each PE at boot time and work as an operating system or a part of hardware. The special packet facility makes the EM-4 system flexible and extensible.

3 Multiple Threads in EM-4

A thread is an independent instruction stream. In EM-4, threads can be implemented simply by passing tokens between several SCBs to execute those SCBs sequentially. As a multi-threaded processor, each PE has many sequential threads of controls. Dataflow mechanisms allow new threads to be created cheaply. This leads to an entirely different view of computation from dataflow model, and allows execution of programs written in familiar imperative languages such as C or FORTRAN.

EM-4 is a memory-distributed multi-processor; each PE has its own local memory. Threads in each PE can interact with each other by communicating with messages, or by accessing remote memory rather than consuming tokens and firing of instructions as in the dataflow model. *Thread library* functions are provided to express parallelism and communication between threads in application program written in imperative languages. We have developed a "sequential" C compiler for EMC-R to write programs for threads. The thread library functions can be called from this C compiler.

3.1 Thread with SCBs

An SCB is a short sequential uninterrupted thread of control. During the execution of an SCB, each instruction operates on the register file as well as local memory. At the end of SCB, values in the registers can be spilled out into the function invocation frame.

From the view point of the execution of a thread, a packet between SCBs can be thought of as the minimum state of a thread:

- The program counter.
- The function frame, or the operand segment.
- One word of internal state.

Though the address portion of a packet contains only an operand segment number and an offset, the current instruction address can be obtained from its operand segment.

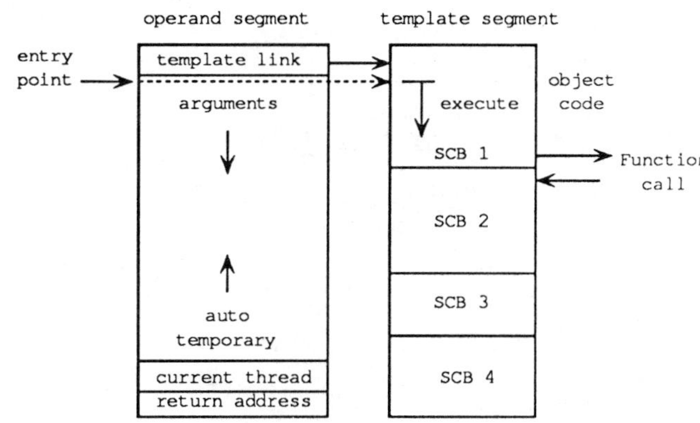

Figure 3: Function Frame

Before the SCB is terminated, the packet with lop WCF is sent back to the packet queue to continue the next SCB. A packet is automatically dequeued from the packet queue to resume the execution of the associated thread whenever a processor requires work. When packets for other threads are waiting in the packet queue, SCBs of different threads can start to execute. The packet queue works like the process ready queue of a conventional operating system, but it is scheduled efficiently in hardware. While the execution time of an SCB is arbitrary, its size determines the granularity of the uninterruptable block [1].

3.2 Function Call within Thread

To call a function within the same thread, the caller allocates an operand segment for the function invocation frame. Within the function, local variables and temporaries can be allocated in the operand segment. A function frame is illustrated in Figure 3. As threads do not span processors, the function frame is allocated locally. The caller writes arguments into the callee's frame, and sends its return address with a packet to the entry point of the function. The caller's code looks like this:

```
    s [ftop+ARG1],arg1   ; write arg 1
    ....                 ; write arg 2 ...  arg n
    add ftop,ENTRY,r0    ; calculate entry point
    get C.v,r0           ; send a continuation
    ls [ftop],$foo,ftop :break
    ; link the free segment to the function "foo"
C:  op @v
    ; continue ....
```

where ftop is a special register maintaining free operand segments list. After the function call, the SCB of the caller is terminated. The callee sends its return value as a packet to the caller's continuation point. Receiving a result packet from the callee resumes the execution of the caller [2].

3.3 Thread Function Library

Using threads as described above, a programmer can view the EM-4 as a distributed-memory multiprocessor. The *thread library* allows the programmer to express parallelism explicitly. Most library functions can be expanded inline by a compiler.

Creating threads — There are two kinds of threads: *named threads* and *simple threads.*

```
fork(PE,func,n,arg1,...,argn)
port=create_thread(PE,func,n,arg1,...,argn)
```

The function `create_thread` creates a named thread on the specified PE, and returns its port which represents the created thread. A named thread can be regarded as a black box with internal state which can communicate with other threads. Simple threads are used to compute on distributed data. The function `fork` spawns a simple thread on the specified PE.

Message passing — The function `msg_send` is used to send a message containing data from one thread to the port of another named thread. The function `msg_recv` reads messages sent to the current named thread: only a named thread can use this function.

```
msg_send(port,msg_type,msg,nbytes)
msg = msg_recv(msg_type)
```

The parameter `msg_type` selects a particular type of received messages among several messages sent to the current thread.

Message passing is asynchronous and buffered: the send operation blocks the current thread until the entire message is sent, but does not waits for the message to be received. The port of a named thread maintains message queues to hold sent messages which have not been received yet. The receive operation blocks the current thread until the message is received. In addition, the functions `word_send` and `word_recv` can send and receive one word message efficiently.

Packet communication — Packet communication is more efficient than message passing communication between threads, because it makes use of the direct matching mechanism of EM-4. The function `pkt_output` sends a packet containing one word data to the port. The function `pkt_input` receives the word sent to the current thread.

[1] Usually, function call terminates the SCB in thread. Programmers can terminate explicitly by calling the *dummy function* which is compiled into breaking the SCB.

[2] Actually, a large function may require several template segments. For such a large code, the current template segment is re-linked to the operand segment before calling other functions.

```
pkt_output(port,slot,word)
word = pkt_input(slot)
```

Unlike message passing, the packet is not queued. When the sent packet is not received, subsequent send operations cause an error.

Remote memory access — The remote memory access facility enables a different programming style in thread-based programming. It provides the illusion of global memory shared among PEs, where threads can share data and synchronize with each other.

To access memory in a different PE, the functions `mem_write` and `mem_read` are used explicitly.

```
mem_write(global_addr,word)
word = mem_read(global_addr)
```

The global address `global_addr` contains the PE number as well as a local address in that PE.

Distributed data structure — In EM-4, I-structure memory is also implemented using the special packet mechanism. For I-structure memory access, `I_write` and `I_read` are used instead. If a word is not written by `I_write` at the specified location yet, `I_read` operation blocks the execution of the current thread. The subsequent `I_write` operation resumes the execution of the thread blocked by `I_read`. Our I-structure is extended to allow multiple-reader/multiple-writer. It can be used to implement shared variables.

The created thread starts from a given main function. When the main function returns, the executing thread disappears. A thread can notify its termination by sending messages or accessing distributed data.

4 Implementation

4.1 Special packet routines

The special packet routines play an important role in implementing thread library functions. The following special packet routines are provided:

`MEM_READ`: Fetch the word form the location specified by the address portion, and send the data back to the continuation in the data portion.

`MEM_WRITE`: Store the data portion of the packet at the location specified by the address potion.

`I_READ`: Similar to `MEM_READ`, fetch the word and return it to the continuation if the tag of the word is not undefined. Otherwise, store the continuation at the word instead. If the word contains another continuation, it is kept in the queue associated to the location.

`I_WRITE`: Similar to `MEM_WRITE`, write the data portion into the location specified by the address portion if the previous word is undefined. If a continuation is already stored at the location, send the data to the continuation and store the undefined word. Otherwise, it is kept in the queue associated to the location.

GET_OSN: Allocate a new operand segment on the PE and link it to the template segment specified by the address portion. Return its operand segment number to the continuation specified in the data portion of the packet.

MEM_ALLOC: Allocate a memory area whose size is specified in the address portion, and return its global address to the continuation in the data portion.

NULL: Receive a packet, and do nothing. This entry point is used to terminate a thread.

The mutual exclusion operation for resource mangement is guaranteed as these routines are executed within one SCB.

The remote read functions **mem_read** and **I_read** send packets to the special packet routines **MEM_READ** and **I_READ** respectively. Within the sending threads, the SCB is terminated after sending the packet. Receiving the fetched data resumes the execution of the current thread. The requests for write operation never block the current thread.

4.2 Fork/Terminate a thread

In order to fork a new thread, a token is generated from the current SCB to the entry address of the new thread, and the current thread continues execution. If an SCB generates no tokens, the thread of the SCB is terminated.

Creating a simple thread is similar to a function call, but is different in that it may create a thread in a different PE. The function **fork** is performed in the following steps:

1. Allocate an operand segment for the main function of a thread in a different PE using the special packet routine **GET_OSN**.
2. Write the arguments into the operand segment using **MEM_WRITE**.
3. Send the address of the **NULL** routine as a return address to the entry point of the main function. On returning from the main function, the created thread is terminated.
4. Unlike a function call, continue execution of the current thread.

4.3 Thread kernel for message passing

A port of a named thread is an object which receives messages and maintains the message queue. A port is implemented as an operand segment linked to a special template segment called the *thread kernel*. We call this operand segment the *thread segment*. The structure of a named thread is illustrated in Figure 4. The thread segment has the following entry points:

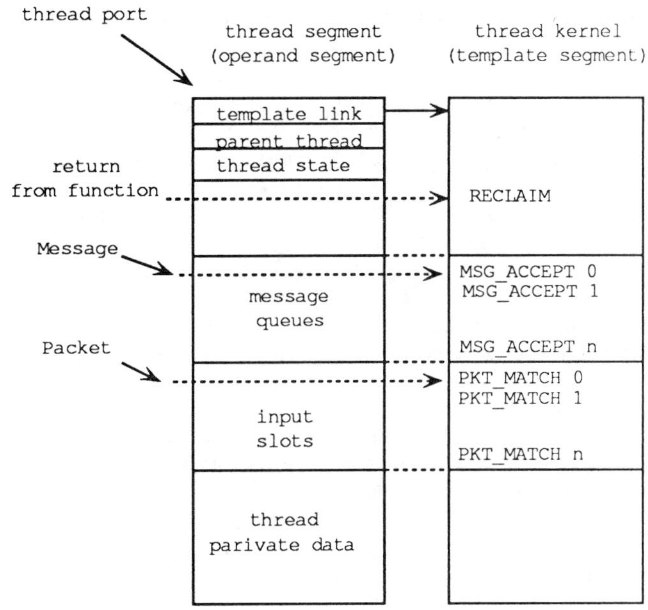

Figure 4: Thread segment

MSG_ACCEPT 0 ... n: Accept an incoming message to put into the message queue associated with its message type. The thread segment has this kind of entry points for each message type. If a corresponding word in the thread segment contains a continuation, the incoming message resumes the execution of the thread.

PKT_MATCH 0 ... n: Match an incoming packet generated by **pkt_output** and a continuation from **pkt_input**. This operation is done by operand matching. The thread segment also has this kind of entry points for each slot of packet.

RECLAIM: Reclaim the thread segment itself. This entry is used as the return address of a named thread's main function. On returning from the main function, this entry point reclaims the thread segment.

The message queue is manipulated exclusively by executing within one SCB. A few words in the thread segment are available to store private data for the thread.

The function **create_thread** allocates a thread segment and an operand segment for the thread main function respectively in a different PE using **GET_OSN**, and sends the thread segment's **RECLAIM** entry point to its function's entry point as the return address. The function **create_thread** returns its thread segment number to the caller as its port.

The messages are bound to the thread segment associated to the port. For example, the function **word_send** is performed in the following code:

```
; r0 is a port, r1 is the message type,
; r2 is a word to be sent
  add r0,MSG_ACCEPT0,r0   ; r0 is its thread segment
  mul r1,MSG_ENT_SIZE,r1  ; calculate the entry point
  add r0,r1,r0            ; for the message type
  mkpkt r2,r0 :wcf=1op    ; send the word
                          ; with WCF bits 1op
```

When messages are sent to the entry point MSG_ACCEPT n, the following code is invoked:

```
MSG_ACCEPT:
   nop @v              ; data portion in r0
   l [seg],r1          ; load queue head
   bntype r1,CONT_TYPE,enqueue
   nop                 ; if continuation is stored,
   br r1               ; jump to the continuation
   clr [seg]           ; clr queue
enqueue:
   ; enqueue messages into queue
```

When executing a named thread, the current thread segment is stored in the operand segment of the function. The receive operation fetches the data from the message queue:

```
; r0 is a message type to be received.
   l [seg+CUR_THREAD],r1     ; load thread segment
   add r1,MSG_ACCEPT0,r1     ;
   mul r0,MSG_ENT_SIZE,r0    ; calculate entry point
   add r0,r1,r0
   l [r0],r1
   bntype r1,UNDEF_TYPE,dequeue
   nop
   l [seg+RET_ADDR],r1       ; load continuation
   s [r0],r1 :break          ; store continuation
                             ; and suspend
dequeue:
   ; dequeue messages ...
```

If no message has arrived, the continuation is stored instead, and execution resume on the arrival of the message. To send a large message, MEM_ALLOC is used to allocate the memory area for massages remotely on the PE to which the messages are sent. The function **msg_send** writes message data by remote memory access to the buffer, and sends its global address.

At the PKT_MATCH entry point, the following instruction is executed:

```
PKT_MATCH:
     ; match the continuation and input packet
     mkpkt @l,@r :break
```

While **pkt_input** sends the continuation to the entry point as right operand, **pkt_output** sends the data as left operand. The invoked MKPKT instruction sends the data to the continuation.

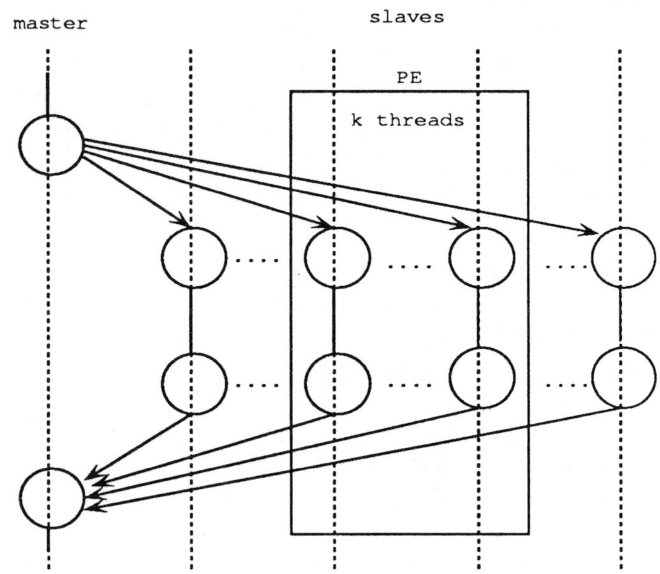

Figure 5: Master and slaves

5 Discussion

5.1 Preliminary Experience

For thread-based programming, EM-4 allows the programmer to use a variety of programming styles: message passing style with named threads and shared memory styles with remote memory access. SPMD (single program, multiple data) programs are being developed where synchronized threads in each PE works on local memory data [12]. We now show how different parallel programming styles affect the performance with a very simple program that computes the inner product of a large array, in both integer and single-precision floating point. For the parallel program, as shown in Figure 5, a master thread distributes the work to slave threads to compute partial results, and goes into a loop to get the results from the slaves. Each slave sends its result to the master. We consider the following variations on data distribution and memory access for the program:

Message passing/Centralized (M/C) — The master holds a large array, and distribute parts of the array to slaves at run-time by sending them as messages.

Remote access/Centralized (R/C) — The master sends the global address of the partial array to slaves. Each slaves accesses the array in the master by remote access at run-time.

Local access/Distributed (L/D) — The array is already distributed to each local memory. Each slave computes the partial result locally.

Remote access/Interleaved (R/I) — The array is allocated across the slaves' local memory in an interleaved manner: the next element in the array is placed in the next PE. Each slave accesses the interleaved array by remote access as a global common memory. In this case, each slave computes the partial result for the partial array spread out across PEs.

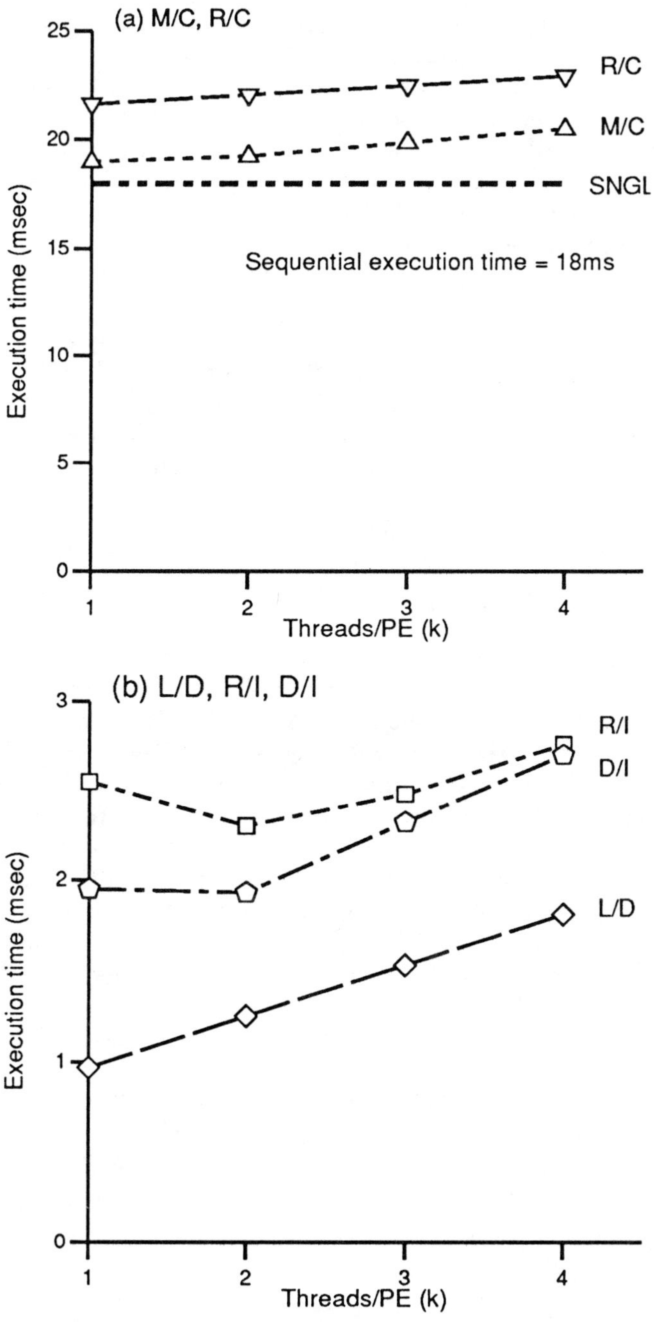

Figure 6: Execution time of integer inner product

Dataflow access/Interleaved (D/I) — Similar to **R/I**, however, each iteration computes in manner of dataflow computation using *split-phase transactions*. A memory request is issued and computation continues while the request is processed concurrently.

The programs are executed in parallel with 79 processors; one for the master thread and 78 for slaves[3]. The size of the array is 18720 words. When the array is distributed over slaves, 240 words are allocated in the local memory for each slave. To increase parallelism, we ran k slave threads in each PE for each program. Figure 6 and 7 shows the execution time.

An iteration in the inner product computation executes in 10 cycles for the integer version and 200 cycles for the floating point version. Because EM-4 has no hardware floating point unit, the floating point operations are emulated in software.

It is obvious that the **local/distributed** case has the best performance, since most of the computation is performed locally. In the case of centralized data, the time for distributing data to the slave PEs dominates the total execution time. For the integer version, centralized data causes the parallel execution to be much slower than the sequential execution in a single PE. The reason is that the communication time is much larger than the time for effective computation.

Remote memory access is slower than message passing. The remote memory access may increase the network traffic, because each slave must send request packets and receive data packets, whereas writing a word of messages requires only one packet. In addition, sometimes the packet conflict is caused because remote access requests are generated at run-time. Since EMC-R has no output buffer to the network, the network conflict forces the execution in PE to stop. The split-phase transaction improves the performance than in thread-based execution in small k. But, as can be seen in Figure 6(b), network conflict degrades the performance because more packets are generated. For message passing, the master sends all data sequentially so that no network conflict occurs.

In the case of message passing, slaves have to wait to receive the entire message. As the network switch unit of EM-4 can work independently from the instruction execution, partitioning a messages into smaller messages make the execution unit active during receiving the other messages.

More parallelism does not necessarily improve the performance. A few threads in the same PE are sufficient to tolerate the communication latency, result in the performance improvement. As the number of threads k in each PE increases, however, more time is

[3]Unfortunately, the optimization of our C compiler has not yet been completed. The programs were compiled by hand.

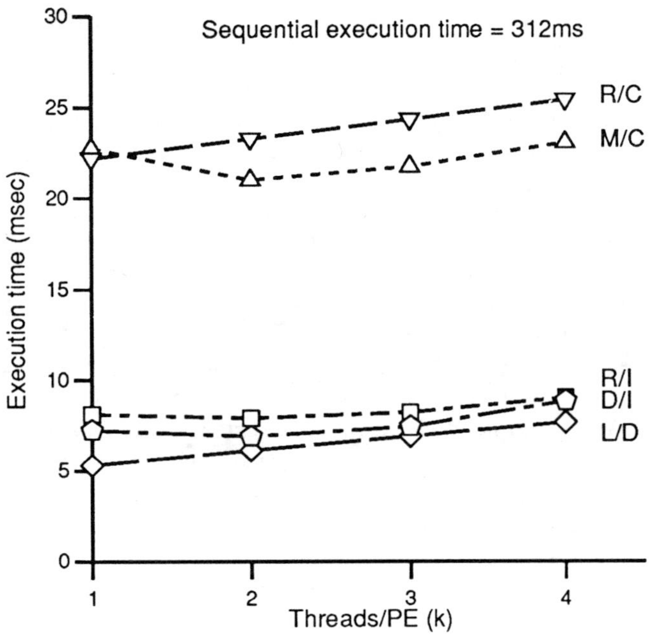

Figure 7: Execution time of floating point inner product

needed to add up the partial result on the master, and network traffic increases, resulting in longer total execution time.

5.2 Comparison with dataflow execution

Recently, several von Neumann/dataflow hybrid architectures have generated considerable interest in the area of dataflow architectures [4] [10] [3] [8]. The recent paper of MIT's Monsoon [9] presents a different view of hybrid dataflow machines where dataflow execution is re-defined in the terms of threads of control. In contrast with their definition of "thread", a thread described here is explicitly declared and controlled by programmers with the thread library functions.

The technique of *split-phase transactions* is often used to tolerate long latency for remote memory access. Such fine-grain parallelism might be exploited by the compiler optimization even in the thread-based programming model. The compiler splits the programmer's thread into more fine-grain threads to synchronize them using the dataflow operand matching mechanism.

In thread-based programming, several threads in the same PE can be used to tolerate the latency of the other activities. For example, when iterations of a loop are distributed onto more than two threads in the same PE, one thread can continue the computation during the processing of the remote memory request issued by the other.

The dataflow computational model relies upon global memory, where sufficient parallelism masks the long latency to the global memory. When parallelism cannot be exploited, the long latency incurred causes performance degradation. On the other hand, too much parallelism may increase the network traffic, resulting in even worse performance.

With message passing, threads operate on local memory by moving the data between PEs explicitly. Latency to the local memory is small and predictable enough that it can be tolerated. In this case, the code can be scheduled statically at compile-time, rather than dynamically at run-time in dataflow graph. If a task can be performed in a single SCB, active variables can be referenced in registers to execute the sequential codes efficiently. When the work is distributed into several threads, the balance between the cost of communication and the distributed task must be taken into account. If it takes a long time to distribute data, a subsequent task may use these data locally once data is distributed. When a program uses remote memory access, values in registers must be spilled into memory since waiting for fetched data terminates an SCB.

The explicit usage of operand matching hardware is restricted in thread-based programming. Within a thread, matching is done only with a continuation and input data. It is not clear that this restriction affects the performance in thread-based programming. This situation can also be found in P-RISC [8], which eliminates the wait-matching unit.

5.3 Scheduling

In EM-4, the SCB is an unit of scheduling: the execution of an SCB is not interrupted until it is explicitly terminated. Since the state of a thread is maintained in a packet, context switching is performed very efficiently on the packet queue by hardware. However, the hardware implementation sometimes reduces the flexibility of scheduling. Consider two tasks which can be executed in parallel. If one of these tasks is in the critical path of total execution, it should be executed with higher priority. But if the SCB of the task is terminated and an SCB of other task executes a long time, the delay of the task makes total execution time longer.

One solution is to restrict an SCB to a basic block. Usually the length of a basic block is relatively small so that threads are executed in a certain granularity. In this case, the values in registers must be spilled out at the end of every basic block. Otherwise, the programmer must be careful to control the parallelism as to prevent such a situation.

5.4 Message passing in EM-4

We define the message passing facility in the von Neumann/dataflow hybrid framework. Message passing systems assume that some memory is local to each processor but none is globally accessible. In EM-4, we can access other processors' memory by remote memory access alternatively. As mentioned above, a program involving remote memory access tends to increase network traffic, sometimes resulting in poor performance.

Compared with other message passing architectures such as iPSC or NCube, EM-4's message passing is more efficient due to its high transfer rate and self-routing packet communication. In these machines, it takes a long time to create a header and set up the communication channel. Although such overhead is amortized when a greater number of bytes are sent, it often causes a *performance bug* in the parallel programming. While large message are often supported by DMA in these message passing computers, EM-4 needs a number of instructions to send packets and copy packets to send large messages. In order to send large messages more efficiently, additional hardware is need to handle remote memory access packet. Dividing a large message into certain small pieces is an effective technique to tolerate message communication time since the packet switching unit of EM-4 works independently from the execution unit [6].

Message Driven Processor in the J-machine [2] supports small message passing efficiently for object-oriented concurrent programming. As in EM-4, it supports hardware queue for messages and a message invokes exection of the associated method. A named thread of our programming system can also work as an concurrent object. Method selection is performed in the thread in software.

6 Conclusion

In this paper, we have demonstrated the effectiveness of thread-based programming on a hybrid dataflow machine, EM-4, in which threads interact with each other by sending messages and accessing remote memory. EM-4 can be thought of as a multi-threaded architecture that can exploit both a von Neumann and dataflow compiling technology. It allows a variety of programming styles in von Neumann/dataflow framework to make use of parallel processing element effectively. We have shown that even a message passing system can be implemented and executed efficiently.

Essentially, EM-4 is a distributed-memory multiprocessor. One of the most important issues in getting high performance in parallel processing is maintaining data locality and controlling parallelism. In the thread-based programming model, the programmer handles such issues explicitly. We believe that our approach is the first step to explore better programming/compiling technology including dataflow computational model for a hybrid dataflow machine.

Acknowledgement

We wish to thank Dr. Toshitsugu Yuba, Director of the Computer Science Division, and Mr. Toshio Simada, Chief of the Computer Architecture Section for supporting this research, and also the staff of the Computer Architecture Section for their fruitful discussion. We specially thank Mr. Andrew Shaw for his careful reading of this paper and Prof. Amamiya and the referees for their valuable suggestions.

References

[1] Arvind, R. S. Nikhil, and K. K. Pingali. "I-Structure: Data Structure for Parallel Computing", Technical Report Computation Structure Group Memo 269, MIT Laboratory for Computer Science, February 1987.

[2] W. Dally, L. Chao, A. Chien, S. Hassoun, W. Horwat, J. Kaplan, P. Song, B. Totty and S. Wills, "Architecture of a Message-Driven Processor", *Proc. of the 14th Annual International Symposium on Computer Architecture*, pp. 189-196, June 1987.

[3] V. G. Grafe and J. E. Hoch, "The Epsilon-2 Hybrid Dataflow Architecture", *Proc. of Compcon 90*, pp 88-93, March 1990.

[4] R. A. Iannucci, "Toward a Dataflow/von Neumann Hybrid Architecture", *Proc. of the 15th Annual International Symposium on Computer Architecture*, pp. 131-140, 1988.

[5] Alan H. Karp. "Programming for Parallelism", *IEEE Computer*, pp.43-57, May 1987.

[6] S. Kim, S. S. Pande, D. P. Agrawal and J. Mauney, "A Message Segmentation Technique to Minimize Task Completion Time", *Proc. of 5th International Parallel Processing Symposium*, pp. 519-524, April 1991.

[7] Y. Kodama, S. Sakai, Y. Yamaguti. "A Prototype of a Highly Parallel Dataflow Machine EM-4 and its Preliminary Evaluation", *Proc. of Info Japan '90*, pp. 291-298, 1990.

[8] R. S. Nikhil and Arvind, "Can Dataflow Subsume von Neumann Computing?", *Proc. of the 16th Annual International Symposium on Computer Architecture*, pp. 262-272, June 1989.

[9] G. M. Papadopoulos and K. R. Traub, "Multithreading: A Revisionist View of Dataflow Architectures", *Proc. of the 18th Annual International Symposium on Computer Architecture*, pp. 342-351, June 1991.

[10] G. M. Papadopoulos and D. E. Culler, "Monsoon: an Explicit Token-Store Architecture", *Proc. of the 17th Annual International Symposium on Computer Architecture*, 1990.

[11] S. Sakai, Y. Yamaguti, K. Hiraki, Y. Kodama and T. Yuba, "An Architecture of a Dataflow Single Chip Processor", *Proc. of the 16th Annual International Symposium on Computer Architecture*, pp. 46-53, June 1989.

[12] A. Shaw, Y. Kodama, M. Sato and Y. Yamaguchi, "Data-Parallel Programming on the EM-4 Dataflow Parallel Supercomputer", to appear in *Proc. of JSPP in Japan*, 1992.

*T: A Multithreaded Massively Parallel Architecture

R. S. Nikhil [00]
Digital Equipment Corp.

G. M. Papadopoulos [01]
MIT

Arvind [11]
MIT

Abstract

What should the architecture of each node in a general purpose, massively parallel architecture (MPA) be? We frame the question in concrete terms by describing two fundamental problems that must be solved well in any general purpose MPA. From this, we systematically develop the required logical organization of an MPA node, and present some details of *T (pronounced *Start*), a concrete architecture designed to these requirements. *T is a direct descendant of dynamic dataflow architectures, and unifies them with von Neumann architectures. We discuss a hand-compiled example and some compilation issues.

1 Introduction

There appears to be widespread consensus that general purpose supercomputers of the future will be Massively Parallel Architectures (MPA's) consisting of a number of nodes in a high speed, regular interconnection network. This view has been eloquently summarized in the slogan "attack of the killer micros" by Eugene Brooks of Lawrence Livermore Laboratories [8]. In this paper, we focus on the organization of each node in such an MPA.

In an MPA, inter-node communication latency is expected to be high and caching global locations is difficult. In Section 2 we present this issue in concrete terms by describing two specific latency-related problems that must be performed well by MPA nodes. In Section 3 we systematically develop the logical node organization of *T, that addresses these problems. Pronounced *Start*, it is named after the principal communication instruction in the machine. It can also be read as an acronym for "multi- (*) Threaded", a principal feature of the machine. In Section 4 we present some instruction set details of the logical organization of *T, and in Section 5 we discuss the coding of DAXPY. In Section 6 we discuss possibilities for physical implementation of *T, and we conclude in Section 7 with some discussion of compilation issues.

*T is the latest step in the evolution of dynamic dataflow architectures, starting with the MIT Tagged-Token Dataflow Architecture (TTDA, [5, 7]), the Manchester dataflow machine [16] and the ETL SIGMA-1 [19]. In 1987-88, the associative waiting-matching store of these machines was replaced by an explicitly managed, directly addressed token store, by Papadopoulos and Culler in the Monsoon architecture [25, 10]. Nikhil and Arvind's P-RISC architecture [24] then split the "complex" dataflow instructions into separate synchronization, arithmetic and fork/control instructions, eliminating the necessity of presence bits on the token store (also known as "frame memory"). P-RISC also permitted the compiler to assemble instructions into longer threads, replacing some of the dataflow synchronization with conventional program counter-based synchronization (in retrospect, Monsoon could also be viewed in this light [26]). *T is the latest step in this direction, eliminating the prior distinction between processor and I-structure nodes, and attempting also to be compatible with conventional MPA's based on von Neumann processors.

Throughout this evolution, our *system view* of an MPA (*i.e.,* viewing each node of an MPA as a black box) has remained constant, and is in fact quite unique to dataflow architectures. Inter-node traffic consists of tokens (*i.e.,* messages) which contain a *tag* (or *continuation*, a pair comprising a context and instruction pointer) and one or more values. All inter-node communications are performed with *split-phase* transactions (request and response messages); processors never block when issuing a remote request, and the network interface for message handling is well integrated into the processor pipeline. Thus, TTDA, Monsoon, P-RISC and *T are properly viewed as steps in the evolution of the *node architecture* of dataflow MPA's.

Important architectural influences in our thinking have been the seminal Denelcor HEP [30] and Iannucci's Dataflow/von Neumann Hybrid architecture [20], which incorporated some dataflow ideas into von Neumann processors for MPA's (similar ideas were also expressed by Buehrer and Ekanadham [9]). ETL's EM-4 [28], Sandia's Epsilon [15], Dennis and Gao's Argument-Fetching Dataflow machine [14], and Dennis' multithreaded architecture [13] are also dataflow machines supporting threads. Finally, the Network Interface Chip by Henry and Joerg [18] has had a direct influence on our implementation of *T.

---

[00] This work was done while the author was at MIT. *Address*: Digital Cambridge Research Laboratory, One Kendall Square, Bldg 700, Cambridge, MA 02139, USA;
email: nikhil@crl.dec.com; *phone*: 1 (617) 621 6639

[01,11] *Address*: MIT Laboratory for Computer Science, 545 Technology Square, Cambridge, MA 02139, USA;
email: {greg,arvind}@mit.edu; *phone*: 1 (617) 253 {2623,6090}

Funding for the work at MIT is provided in part by the Advanced Research Projects Agency of the Department of Defense under Office of Naval Research contract N00014-89-J-1988.

Software considerations, *i.e.*, compiling, have played an equally important role in the design of *T. Compilation of the high-level parallel programming language Id has been central to our research since the beginning [7]. Nikhil, in [23], and Culler *et al* in [11] proposed P-RISC-like compilation models extended to allow additional instruction sequencing constraints, making explicit the notion of a thread. Culler's model, the Threaded Abstract Machine (TAM) has been implemented by his group and has been in use for almost two years, providing a wealth of data on the nature of threads, locality and synchronization [29]. This experience has directly influenced the *T design.

Many researchers have arrived at similar mechanisms starting from other vantage points (*e.g.*, Halstead and Fujita's MASA [17] and Maurer's SAM [22]). There are very interesting comparisons to be made between *T and recent multithreaded architectures, notably the Tera Computer System [3] (a descendant of the HEP), Alewife [1] and the J-Machine with Message Driven Processors (MDPs) [12]. Undoubtedly, aspects of these machines will influence concrete *T designs.

2 Fundamental Problems in an MPA

A general purpose Massively Parallel Architecture (MPA) consists of a collection of nodes that communicate using a pipelined, message based interconnection network (see Figure 1). Each node contains a processor and some local memory.

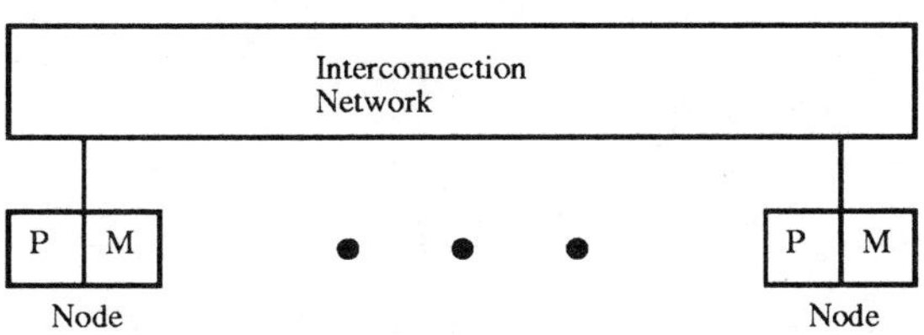

Figure 1: Structure of a massively parallel architecture.

Given a node N, we refer to its own memory as *local memory* and to other memories as *remote memories*.

A consequence of message based communication is that remote accesses must be structured as *split transactions*. If node N1 wants to read the contents of location A in node N2, it involves two messages: a request message from N1 to N2 carrying the address A and a return address identifying N1, followed by a response message from N2 to N1 carrying the contents of location A.

Memory addressing: although we believe it is important, we do not consider here the issue of whether the memories in the different nodes belong to a single, global address space or whether the memory in each node has its own local address space. We also do not consider here the issue of virtual memory.

Locality and memory latencies: In an MPA, the latencies of local *vs.* remote memory accesses typically vary by orders of magnitude. Further, remote memory latencies grow with machine size— the best-case scenario is that remote access time will vary with $\log N$, where N is the number of nodes.

We now present two problems which, we hope the reader will agree, a general purpose MPA must solve efficiently in order to have good performance over a wide variety of applications [6].

2.1 The Latency of Remote Loads

The remote load situation is illustrated in Figure 2. Variables A and B are located on nodes N2 and N3, respectively, and need to be brought to node N1 in order to compute the difference A-B in variable C. The basic intent of the computation is expressed by the following statement sequence executing on N1:

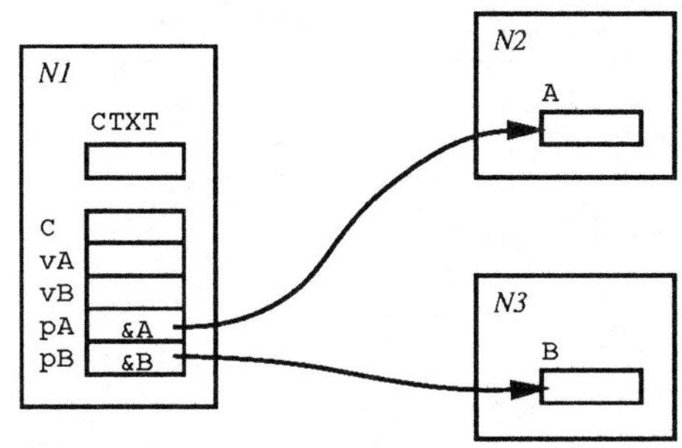

Figure 2: The remote load problem: Node N1 to compute difference of variables in nodes N2 and N3

```
vA = rload pA
vB = rload pB
C = vA - vB
```

where pA and pB are pointers to A and B, respectively. The first two statements perform remote loads, copying values from A and B into vA and vB, respectively. The last statement computes the difference and stores it in C.

The figure also shows a variable CTXT, which is the *context* of the computation on N1. It could be, for example, a stack pointer, a frame pointer, a "current-object" pointer in an object-oriented system, a process identifier, *etc*. In general, variable names like vA, vB and C are interpreted relative to CTXT.

The key issue in remote loads is how to deal with the long latencies in the communication system, *i.e.*, how to avoid idling N1's processor during the remote load operations. Note that in most architectures, these latencies are predictable because they depend mainly on the distance between the nodes.

2.2 Idling due to Synchronizing Loads

We extend the remote load problem by now assuming that A and B are computed by concurrent processes, and we are not sure exactly when they will be ready for node N1 to read. We need some form of synchronization to ensure that the remote loads from N1 read the values only after they have been produced. This is an example of producer-consumer parallelism.

Unlike the remote load problem, the latency here is not just an architectural property— it also depends on scheduling, and the time it takes to compute A and B, which may be much longer than the transit latency. In particular, the unpredictable latencies of synchronizing loads are a problem *even when they are local.*

3 Solutions

3.1 Caches

Classically, caches are used to mask memory latency, and we could add a cache to each node to hold copies of remote locations. However, *cache coherence* is a then significant problem: multiple copies of a location residing in different nodes' caches must be kept consistent. Further, a processor may still idle when there is a cache miss. A possible solution for the distributed cache coherence problem is to use *directories*; and for the cache miss problem, to multiplex between a small number of contexts to cover cache loading. Implementing this appears non-trivial (see MIT's MASA [17] and Alewife [1], and Stanford's DASH [21], for example). In any case, *the proposals in this paper may be seen as orthogonal to cacheing solutions.* Further, while distributed cacheing helps in the remote load situation, it does not offer anything for the synchronizing load problem.

3.2 Multithreading

Another solution is to multiplex amongst many threads: when one thread issues a remote load request, the processor begins work on another thread, and so on. Clearly, the cost of thread-switching should be much smaller than the latency of the remote load, or else the processor might as well wait for the remote load's response.

Continuations on messages: A consequence of multithreading is that *messages should carry continuations*. Suppose, after issuing a remote load from thread T1, we switch to thread T2 which also issues a remote load. The responses may not arrive in the same order— for example, the requests may travel different distances, through varying degrees of congestion, to destination nodes whose loads differ greatly, *etc.* Thus, each remote load and response should carry an identifier for the appropriate thread so that it can be re-enabled on the arrival of a response. We refer to these thread identifiers as *continuations.*

Adequate continuation namespace: The longer the latency of remote loads, the more threads we need to avoid idling the processor. Thus, it is important that we have a *continuation namespace* that is large enough to name an adequate number of threads waiting for remote responses.

The size of this namespace can greatly affect the programming model. If the latency of a single remote load is l, we would expect that at any given time, we need no more than about l active threads in the processor to cover remote loads. However, if the programmer (or compiler) cannot predict the scheduling of these threads precisely, he may need *many more than* l threads in the hope that, dynamically, l of them are ready to run at any given time. Thus, if the continuation namespace is too small, it requires more precise scheduling of threads, which in turn limits the programming model.

If we generalize our remote transaction model to include not just remote loads, but (a) synchronizing remote loads and (b) remote parallel procedure calls, then it becomes extremely difficult for the programmer/compiler to schedule threads precisely. Therefore, it is essential to have a large continuation namespace.

The size of the hardware-supported continuation namespace varies greatly in existing designs: from 1 in DASH [21], 4 in Alewife [1], 64 in the HEP [30], and 1024 in the Tera [3], to the local memory address space in Monsoon [25], Hybrid Dataflow/von Neumann [20], MDP [12] and *T. Of course, if the hardware-supported namespace is small, one can always virtualize it by multiplexing in software, but this has an associated overhead.

3.3 Fine Grain Multithreading: forks and joins

So far, we have only talked about efficient multiplexing amongst existing threads. However, if thread creation and synchronization are also sufficiently cheap, the multithreading idea can be advantageously taken further. Instead of the `rload-rload-subtract` sequence earlier, we could fork separate threads for the two `rloads` and synchronize them when both have completed. Then, instead of taking four message-transit times, we could perhaps do it in two (since they occur in parallel):

```
    fork M1
L1: vA = rload pA   ; (A)
    jump N

M1: vB = rload pB   ; (B)
    jump N

N:  join 2 J        ; synchronization of responses
    C = vA - vB
```

This kind of parallelism is available in all dataflow architectures [4]. `Fork` initiates a new thread at label `M1`. The parent thread continues at `L1`, issuing the remote load (A), which suspends to await the response. This allows the just-forked thread at `M1` to run, which issues the remote load (B), which also suspends to await the response. When the first response arrives (say, (A)), the first thread resumes, completing the instruction at `L1` by storing the arriving value into `vA`, and jumps to `N`. Similarly, when the second response arrives (B), the second thread resumes, completing the instruction at `M1` by storing the arriving value in `vB` and also jumping to `N`.

The `join` instruction at `N` is executed twice, once by each thread. Each time, it increments `J` (initialized to 0, we assume) and compares it to the terminal count (2). If `J < 2`, the thread dies, otherwise it continues. In general, if the terminal count is c, then $c - 1$ threads arriving at `N` will die and the only the last one continues to perform the sequel.

Again, the cost of `fork` and `join` should be small compared to the latencies of the remote loads that we are trying to cover. Note that modern RISC techniques such as delayed loads, cache prefetching, *etc.* are also modest, "peephole" examples of the use of fork-join parallelism to overlap long-latency loads with useful computation, but they do not generalize well to remote loads in MPA's.

The behavior at N is called a *join synchronization*, and is very important. A significant number of messages entering a node may be destined for join synchronizations. In an inner-product, at each index we remote load $A[j]$ and $B[j]$, join the responses, and multiply. Note that for all but the last thread entering a join, the amount of work done is very small— the thread increments a counter, tests it and dies. For a two-way join, this may be as small as testing and setting one bit. It is important that the processor not take a large hiccup to do this.

Exactly the same kind of join synchronization is also needed for *software* reasons. For example, a function that sums the nodes of a binary tree may have exactly the same structure as the above program with the two `rload`s simply replaced by remote function calls to sum the left and right subtrees, respectively, and the subtraction in the final line replaced by addition. Now, the latencies include both communication and the time to perform the subcomputations.

This leads to another observation: for messages that arrive at highly unpredictable times (as in the tree sum) or at widely separate times (even if predictable) the rendezvous point `J` for join synchronization must typically be *in memory, not registers*. The reason: processor utilization will be low if registers remain allocated to a process for unpredictable and possibly very long durations.

3.4 Messages and Message-Handling

Our first approximation to a message format is:

```
NA: < msg_type, arg1, arg2, ...>
```

Node address NA is used for routing, and may be consumed in transit. `Msg_type` specifies how the message should be handled. The remaining arguments depend on the message type. Figure 3 shows the messages for an `rload` where `&A` and `*A` mean the address and contents of `A`, respectively.[1] The values `N1`, `L1` and `CTXT` together constitute a *continuation*, *i.e.*, a complete specification of the thread awaiting the response.

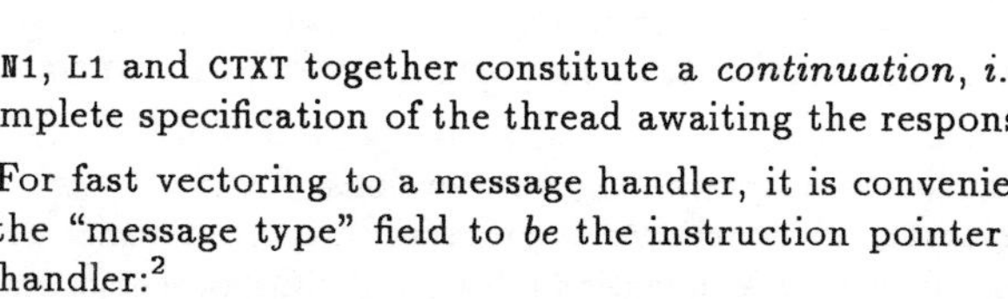

Figure 3: Messages to perform a remote load.

For fast vectoring to a message handler, it is convenient for the "message type" field to *be* the instruction pointer of the handler:[2]

```
NA: < IP, arg1, arg2, ...>
```

To keep up with high incoming message rates, a hardware *network interface* can accept and queue them, to be consumed by the processor at its convenience (Figure 4). Of course, this may add to the latency of a remote load. The *message formatter* constructs outgoing messages.

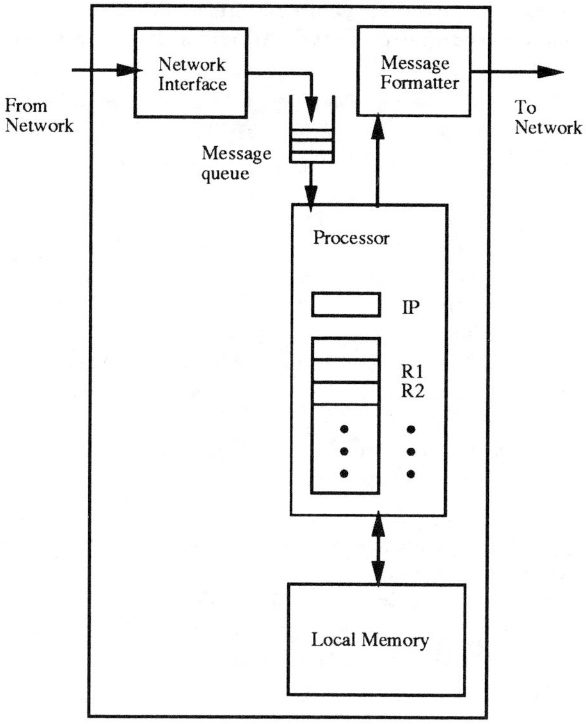

Figure 4: A node with network interface.

The actual handling of an `rload` request at N2 is simple and short: read location `A` and send the response message to N1. Handling the response at N1 may be broken into two parts: (a) completing the unfinished `rload` instruction, and (b) continuing the execution of the thread. Part (a) is always brief. Part (b) is also brief if it just executes a failing `join`.

Both N1 and N2 will typically be executing some other thread when these messages arrive. How can we handle these messages quickly (so that latency is low) and with minimum disruption, *i.e.*, how well is message-handling integrated with normal processing in the node? *The answer to this question is crucial to the efficient operation of an MPA.* The overhead can vary from hundreds of instruction-times in Thinking Machines' CM-5 and Intel's Touchstone, where message-handling is not well integrated, down to under ten instruction-times in the MDP [12], and further down to a single instruction-time in machines like Monsoon [25] and the EM-4 [28] where message-handling is totally integrated into the processor pipeline.

There is good reason to insist that message-handling *should not compromise excellent single-thread performance* in an MPA node. First, existing SIMD/SPMD applications have long sequential threads. Second, even in more dynamic applications, certain sequential critical sections (such as storage allocators) must be executed as quickly as possible. Third, users may wish to develop code on a 1-node MPA. Fourth, uniprocessor libraries should be portable to MPA nodes without degrading their performance. We note that

[1] Figure 3 depicts the logical information in messages; clever encoding can compress it significantly.

[2] Dally's Message Driven Processor [12] also uses an IP in the first field of a message.

competitive single-thread performance is an important goal in the Alewife [1] and Hybrid Dataflow/von Neumann [20] machines.

Interrupts are inadequate: An arriving message could interrupt the processor, which responds, and then resumes normal computation. Modern processors achieve high speeds through deep pipelining and more processor state (registers, caches), and any change in context incurs a large penalty draining, saving, flushing, reloading, *etc.* Thus, frequent short threads, such as `rload` handlers and messages that go into failing joins are likely to be severely disruptive. This may be alleviated by replicating processor state so that the main thread's state does not have to be saved and restored during interrupts. Still, the main thread's performance is affected adversely, because each incoming message takes away cycles and may require processor pipelines to drain and refill. Frequent interrupts for message handling are thus not desirable.

Separate Coprocessors: We can offload the burden of short, simple handlers into separate, asynchronous coprocessors, as shown in Figure 5. This is only a functional decomposition, or logical organization of the node; we will discuss physical organizations in Section 6.

We will refer to the original, conventional main processor as the *data processor* (DP). It executes threads supplied through the *continuation queue* and is optimized for long, sequential runs.

The *remote memory request coprocessor* RMEM handles incoming `rload` requests. It accesses local memory, and sends the response directly, without disturbing DP. Similarly, RMEM also handles `rstore` requests.

The *synchronization coprocessor* SP handles `rload` responses returning to this node. The contents of the message are loaded directly into its registers, with the first message field (IP) loaded into its PC, so that it is vectored directly to the appropriate handler. The basic action of SP is thus to repeatedly load a message from its message queue and run it to completion; the run is always non-suspensive and is expected to be very short. SP completes the unfinished `rload` by storing the value from the message (now in `sV1`) into the destination location. After this, it places the `<L1+1,CTXT>` continuation into the *continuation queue*, to be picked up later by the main processor DP. Even better, if the next instruction is a `join`, SP executes it and enqueues the continuation only if it succeeds. Thus, the main processor dP does not have to execute disruptive `join` instructions at all.

3.5 Handling Synchronized Loads

We observed the need for synchronization if the remote loads for `A` and `B` must wait for corresponding producer computations. We follow the well-known idea of appending *presence bits* to each memory location indicating whether it is FULL or EMPTY.[3] The variables `A` and `B` are initially marked EMPTY. When values are written there, they are marked FULL, *e.g.*, by the RMEMs when they perform the stores. Thus, the remote loads should succeed only after the locations become FULL.

[3] Our development does not depend on it— presence bits could be interpreted in ordinary memory.

Busy waiting: When N1's `rload` request for `A` arrives, N2 could simply return the entire location, presence bits and all. N1 would then test the response, and may choose to try again, perhaps after some delay. Unfortunately, this can waste network bandwidth, and may also waste cycles on N1 in order to test and perform the retries. This is essentially the solution in the Tera [3] and Alewife [1], using traps instead of explicit tests.

A data driven solution: We extend the presence bits to have an additional state, PENDING. For a remote synchronizing load, node N1 executes an `iload` instruction instead of `rload`:

```
L1: vA = iload pA
```

The only difference in the request message is a different IP:

```
N2: <iload_request, &A, N1,L1,CTXT>
```

At N2, the `iload_request` handler tests the presence bits of `A`. If FULL, it responds just like the `rload_request` handler. If EMPTY, it attaches the arguments (`N1,L1,CTXT`) to location `A`, marks it PENDING, and *produces no response*. When the producer later stores the value at `A`, N2 again checks the presence bits. If EMPTY, it simply stores the value there and marks it FULL. If PENDING, it not only stores the value there, but also constructs and sends the response to the waiting load. In all cases, N2's response message for an `iload` looks identical to an `rload` response.

In general, many loads may be pending at `A`, so N2 needs to remember a set of pending requests at location `A`. Thus, one of the costs is that N2 must perform some storage management to construct this set. However, a simple free-list strategy may be used, since set components are of fixed size and are not shared. Thus, it does not matter if the remote load request arrives before the value is ready— it simply waits there until it is ready. There is no additional message traffic for the synchronizing remote load, and N1 does no busy waiting at all. As far as N1 is concerned, an `iload` is just an `rload` that may take a little longer— the interface is identical.

This is essentially the dataflow notion of *I-structures* [7], but we note that it is more general— a variety of other synchronization primitives (such as Fetch-and-ϕ [2]) could be implemented using the same methodology. Finally, note that these message handlers are still simple enough to be handled entirely by the RMEM coprocessor, without disturbing DP.

4 *T Instruction Set Architecture

Figure 5 depicts the logical view of a *T node with three separate, asynchronous coprocessors, each of which can be regarded as a conventional (*e.g.*, RISC) processor with a few extensions. In this section, we flesh out this view by describing these extensions. Since RMEM and SP are very similar, our description here will not distinguish them (we postpone to Section 6 a more detailed discussion of physical implementations that may separate or multiplex them).

Both SP and DP execute instruction streams. For clarity, we distinguish labels for the two coprocessors by the subscripts S and D, respectively (*e.g.*, L_S, L_D, M_S, M_D, ...).

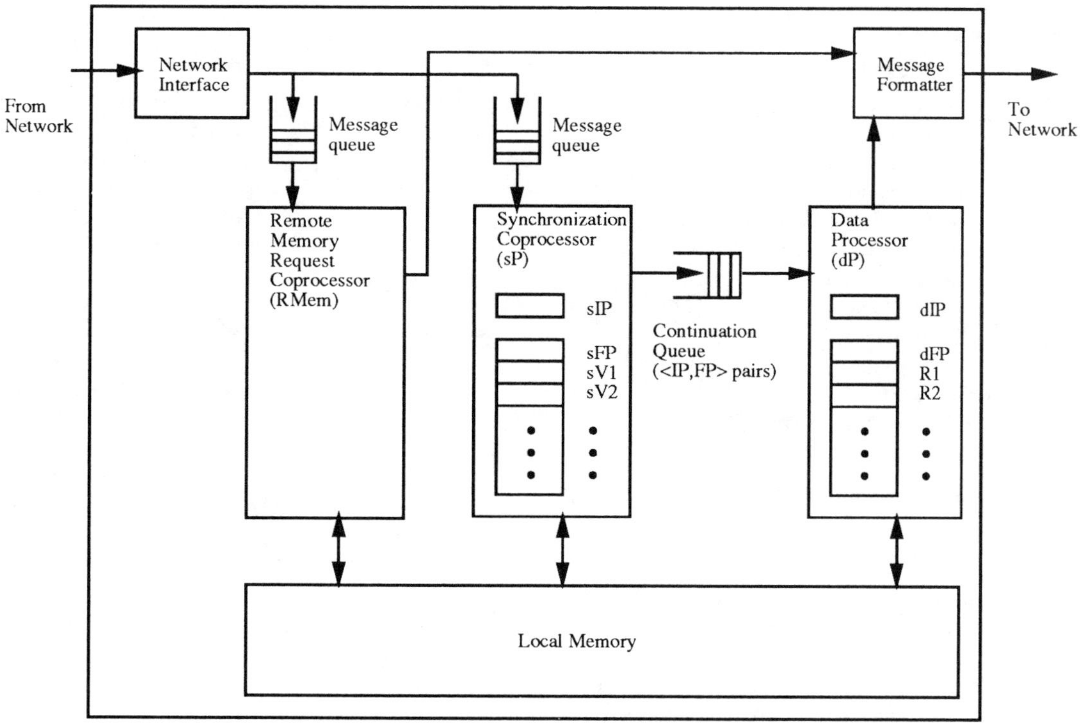

Figure 5: A *T node: separate coprocessors for short threads.

We will look at messages in more detail shortly, but for now it is enough to know that each message has the form:

<*IP*, *Address*, *Value1*, *Value2*, ...>

`Address` is a global address that identifies a unique destination node in the MPA, and is typically a frame pointer `FP` or an address of a location in the heap. The message is automatically routed there. Of course, messages from a node to itself are short-circuited back directly.

We assume that a *context* for a computation is represented simply by an address in memory. In the spaghetti stack model, this may be a stack pointer or a pointer to a frame in the stack. In an object oriented model, this may be a pointer to an object. For uniformity, we will use the term *Frame Pointer* `FP` to refer to a context.

We assume that frames or contexts do not span nodes in the MPA, *i.e., each context resides entirely within one node* of the MPA. Thus, `FP` may be regarded as a pointer to the collection of local variables of that context. A frame pointer encodes a node number. Thus, a continuation is given by `<IP, FP>` where `IP` is a pointer to an instruction on the same node encoded by `FP`. This model of locality is not restrictive in any way— parallel procedure calls and loop iterations may be distributed to different nodes by giving them separate contexts (see [23] and [11, 29] for more on programming and compilation).

It may be desirable to allow contexts to migrate across MPA nodes for load balancing and locality reasons. However, that capability is orthogonal to our discussion here and, for simplicity, we assume that frames, once allocated, do not migrate (a virtual-to-physical FP mapping, plus forwarding, may be added in the manner of the MDP [12] or Empire.[4]

4.1 The Data Processor

The Data Processor DP is a superset of a conventional RISC processor, with a conventional repertoire of register-to-register instructions and ability to manipulate local memory using conventional load and store instructions. Its program counter is called `dIP` ("Data processor Instruction Pointer"). One of its registers, called `dFP`, is assumed, by convention, to contain the current Frame Pointer for the thread being executed by the DP. Being a conventional RISC processor, the Data Processor is optimized to run sequential threads efficiently. It obtains the starting points of these threads from the continuation queue using a `next` instruction. Each such thread is run to completion, *i.e.*, there is no concept of a thread "suspending" in the Data Processor. On completion of a thread, if there is no new thread available from the continuation queue, the Data Processor simply waits until one is available.

In addition to conventional RISC instructions, the Data Processor can execute a few additional instructions which are summarized in Figure 6. (The notation `Register[j]` refers to the j'th DP register.) Most of them send messages into the network. These are non-blocking, *i.e.*, the Data Processor continues executing after sending a message (so, they are implicit forks). The message can cause threads to be scheduled on the other nodes or on the same node, and a later response may deposit values in the sender's frame.

The `start` instruction starts a new thread in a different

[4] Empire was the machine being built at IBM Research based on Iannucci's Dataflow/von Neumann Hybrid Architecture [20].

DP instruction	Semantics
start rIP, rFP, rV	Send message: <L_S, FP, V>
next	Load (L_D,FP') from continuation in continuation queue into registers (dIP,dFP) (so, execution continues at L_D)
rload rIP, rA	Send message: <rload_handler$_S$, A, L_S, FP>
rstore rA, rV, rIP	Send message: <rstore_handler$_S$, A, V, L_S, FP>

L_S = Register[rIP], FP = Register[rFP],
V = Register[rV], A = Register[rA]

Figure 6: DP extensions to conventional instruction set.

sP instruction	Semantics
start rIP', rFP, rV	Send message: <L_S, FP', V>
next	Load (L_S,A,V1,V2, ...) from message in message queue into registers sIP,sFP,sV1,sV2,... (so, execution continues at L_S)
post rIP, rFP	Post <FP', L_D> into continuation queue
join *ctr*, *tc*, rIP	Memory[FP + *ctr*] := Memory[FP + *ctr*] + 1 If Memory[FP + *ctr*] $\geq$ *tc* then Post <FP, L_D> into continuation queue Memory[FP + *ctr*] := 0

L_S = Register[rIP'], L_D = Register[rIP],
FP' = Register[rFP], FP = Register[sFP]
V = Register[rV], A = Register[rA]

Figure 7: sP extensions to conventional instruction set.

context. For example, suppose function F calls another function G. The frames for these functions may be on different nodes (hence, different contexts). Thus, start instructions are used by F to send arguments and initiate threads in G, and start instructions are used by G to to send results and resume threads in F. Since start instructions are non-blocking, it is possible to perform parallel function calls and coroutines. Note that instruction pointer L_S on the start message is a label for the target node's sP, not DP.[5]

The next instruction terminates the present DP thread by loading a new continuation, after which the DP is executing a new thread. Note that there is no implicit saving or restoring of registers. In general, at the beginning of a new thread, no assumptions can be made about the contents of any DP registers except dFP. We also say that registers are "volatile" or "ephemeral" across threads. This instruction is similar in effect to Monsoon's STOP instruction [25] and the MDP's SUSPEND [12].

We will discuss the rload and rstore instructions shortly, after describing the Synchronization Coprocessor.

4.2 The Synchronization Coprocessor

sP, the Synchronization Coprocessor, also looks very much like a conventional RISC microprocessor— it has a program counter sIP, general purpose registers, and it can load and store to local memory. Unlike a conventional RISC, it is tuned for very rapid disposition of incoming messages instead of the computation of arithmetic expressions. In particular, some of its registers (sIP, sFP, sV1, sV2, ...) are loaded directly from messages, there is datapath support for join operations, and it can post <FP,L_D> pairs into the continuation queue. In the following, we do not disinguish it from RMEM, which is very similar.

Like a dataflow processor, sP is triggered by the arrival of a network message (it simply waits, if there is none available). When it picks up a message, its registers sIP, sFP, sV1, sV2, *etc.* are loaded with the corresponding values from the message, after which it begins executing instructions from the address in sIP. The unconventional instructions of sP are summarized in Figure 7. (The notation Register[j] refers to the j'th sP register.)

The start instruction is identical to the Data Processor's start instruction— it starts a new thread in a different context. This allows it to respond to incoming messages directly. For example, in an rload request message, the *IP* field points to rload_handler$_S$, the *address* field contains the address to be read, and the *V1* and *V2* fields contain the return continuation (return IP, return FP). The handler code looks like this:

```
rload_handlerS:
  load   rX, sFP[0]     -- sFP has addr to read (A)
  start  sV1, sV2, rX  -- create response message
  next                 -- done; handle next message
```

Similarly, here is the handler for remote stores (the message's *V1*, *V2* and *V3* fields contain the value to be stored and the return continuation, respectively):

```
rstore_handlerS:
  store  sFP[0], sV1   -- sFP has addr to write (A)
  start  sV2, sV3, 0   -- create acknowledgment message
  next                 -- done; handle next message
```

The acknowledgement may be used to ensure serial consistency— the destination thread executes under a guarantee that the store has completed— or to return miscellaneous status information. Omitting the return continuation from the message and the start instruction from the handler implements unacknowledged stores. Similar handlers may also be coded on the MDP [12].

The next instruction ends the present sP thread by reloading its registers from the next message, after which it is executing that message's handler.

The post instruction allows sP to post a thread to DP by inserting a continuation into the continuation queue. Recall, this thread will be executed by the DP when it is popped off

[5] A start message corresponds exactly to a dynamic dataflow token [7]— FP is the context or color, L_S is the instruction pointer or statement number and, of course, V is the value on the token.

the continuation queue by the DP issuing a next instruction. Here is a typical sP code sequence that executes for an incoming message that loads label L_S into sIP (for example, this message may be the response to a remote load):

```
LS:
  store  sFP[T], sV1 --  store incoming val at frame offset T
  post   LD, sFP     --  enable thread LD with
                     --      this frame in DP
  next               --  done; handle next message
```

The DP thread at L_D is assured that the remote load has completed.

The join instruction allows fast join synchronization using synchronization counters in the frames. Because this is a very frequent operation for the sP, we provide special hardware support to accelerate join operations. The join instruction implements an atomic test-and-increment semaphore on a location in the current activation frame called a *join counter*. The join instruction *conditionally posts* a thread to the continuation queue only if incrementing the join counter causes it to reach the terminal count (given by *tc*). It is assumed that a newly allocated activation frame will have all of its join counter locations initialized to zero. Observe, the join instruction implements a self-cleaning protocol by returning the counter to zero after the terminal count has been reached (this is similar to the wait-match operation in dataflow architectures [4]).

sP message handlers correspond almost exactly to *inlets* in the TAM model [11]. This style of message handling is also easy to code for the MDP [12], although there is no dedicated logic for fast n-ary join synchronization. The salient difference is that in *T the message handlers (inlets) and the computation threads are processed by two logically distinct and asynchronous processors.

Turning back to DP, it can initiate remote loads and stores using rload and rstore instructions, each of which sends a message. The destination node is implicit in the global address A, which is used to route the message there. We have already shown the remote rload handler code. Observe, the response contains FP in its *address* field, so it is routed back to the node that issued the rload. Since rload and rstore are also forks, we can initiate many remote accesses before receiving any response. The responses may return in any order.

Note that the typical rload sequence copies a remote value into a local *frame* location, and not a register. Although this means that another (local) load instruction is necessary to move it from the frame to a register, the choice is deliberate: it allows the thread that issued the rload to easily relinquish DP before the result comes back. Our choice recognizes the fact that storing the value in the frame would be necessary anyway if rload returned to a failing join or if it was a synchronizing load.

Address Hashing: It is useful to have different kinds of address maps for different kinds of objects. For example, we may wish to interleave large data structures such as vectors and matrices across the MPA nodes. On the other hand, we may wish code segments, stack frames and small objects to be addressed linearly within a node's local memory. Of course, these variations in address hashing could be performed in software, but with large overhead. In *T we intend to provide hardware support for address randomization in a manner similar to the IBM RP3 [27] or the Tera [3]. A logical place for this mapping is in the Message Formatter.

5 An example: DAXPY

DAXPY is the inner loop of the Linpack benchmark:

```
for i = 1 to N do
    Y[i] = a * X[i] + Y[i]
```

We assume that the current frame (context) contains the following data, with symbolic names for the frame slots shown at left (in the codes below, the dFP and sFP registers point at this frame):

	...
N	Loop trip
XP	*pointer to* X[1]
YP	*pointer to* Y[1]
A	*loop constant* A
YLim	*pointer to* Y[N]
	...

5.1 Uniprocessor Code

Uniprocessor *T code for the DAXPY loop is shown below (in a uniprocessor, there is only local memory, which contains arrays X and Y). We use names beginning with "r" as symbolic names for general purpose registers. For clarity, the loop has not been unrolled (a compiler would typically do this).

```
  load  rXP, dFP[XP]      --  load ptr to  X
  load  rYP, dFP[YP]      --  load ptr to  Y
  load  rA,  dFP[A]       --  load loop const: a
  load  rYlim, dFP[YLim]  --  load loop const: Y  ptr limit
  cmp   rB,rYP,rYLim      --  compare ptr to  Y  with limit
  jgt   rB, OUT           --  zero-trip loop if greater

LOOP:
  load  rXI, rXP          -- X[i]  into rXI    (L1)
  load  rYI, rYP          -- Y[i]  into rYI    (L2)
  add   rXP,rXP,8         --  incr ptr to  X
  fmul  rTmp,rA,rXI       --  a*X[i]
  fadd  rTmp,rTmp,rYI     --  a*X[i] + Y[i]
  store rYP, rTmp         --  store into  Y[i]    (S1)
  add   rYP,rYP,8         --  incr ptr to  Y
  cmp   rB,rYP,rYLim      --  compare ptr to  Y  with limit
  jle   rB, LOOP          --  fall out of loop if greater

OUT:
  ... loop sequel ...
```

The code runs entirely within the Data Processor (in a uniprocessor, sP plays no role).

5.2 Multiprocessor Code: Using rloads to Mask Latency

Suppose X[I] and Y[I] are on remote nodes of a multiprocessor. The two loads **(L1)** and **(L2)** need to be changed to remote loads. We will issue rloads to initiate the movement of X[i] and Y[i] into the local frame, and we will free up the processor to do other work. Each response arrives at sP, deposits the value into the frame, and tries to join with the other response at frame location c1. When the join succeeds, sP enables the thread in the Data Processor that computes with these data, executes an `rstore` and continues to the next iteration.

When the loop completes, it gives up the Data Processor by executing a `next` instruction. Meanwhile, the `rstore` acknowledgments all arrive at sP and join at frame location c2. The continuation of this join is the loop sequel; the sequel executes only after all `rstore`s have completed. Here is the augmented frame layout and the new code (it is easier to start reading the code at the Data Processor section):

	...
N	Loop trip
XP	*pointer to* X[1]
YP	*pointer to* Y[1]
A	*loop constant* A
YLim	*pointer to* Y[N]
XI	*copy of* X[I]
YI	*copy of* Y[I]
c1	*join counter for* rloads
c2	*join counter for* rstores
	...

```
;;
;;  Synchronization Processor Message Handlers
;;
L1_S:
   store sFP[XI],   rV1      -- store away incoming  X[I]
   join  c1, 2, CONTINUE_D   -- attempt continuation of loop
   next                      -- next message

L2_S:
   store sFP[YI],   rV1      -- store away incoming  Y[I]
   join  c1, 2, CONTINUE_D   -- attempt continuation of loop
   next                      -- next message

S1_S:
   load  rN, sFP[N]          -- total number of stores
   join  c2, rN, OUT_D       -- sequel when all stores complete
;;
;;  Data Processor Threads
;;
   load  rXP, dFP[XP]        -- load ptr to  X
   load  rYP, dFP[YP]        -- load ptr to  Y
   load  rYlim, dFP[YLim]    -- load loop const: Y  ptr limit
   cmp   rB,rYP,rYLim        -- compare ptr to  Y  with limit
   jgt   rB, OUT_D           -- zero-trip loop if greater

LOOP_D:
   rload rXP, L1_S           -- initiate load X[i]   (L1)
   rload rYP, L2_S           -- initiate load Y[i]   (L2)
   next

CONTINUE_D:
   load  rXI, dFP[XI]        -- load copy of  X[I]
   load  rYI, dFP[YI]        -- load copy of  Y[I]
   load  rA,  dFP[A]         -- load loop const:  a
   load  rXP, dFP[XP]        -- load ptr to  X
   load  rYP, dFP[YP]        -- load ptr to  Y
   load  rYLim, dFP[YLim]    -- load loop const:  Y  ptr limit

   fmul  rTmp,rA,rXI         -- a*X[i]
   fadd  rTmp,rTmp,rYI       -- a*X[i] + Y[i]
   rstore rYP, rTmp,S1_S     -- store into Y[i]  (S1)
   add   rXP,rXP,8           -- increment ptr to  X
   add   rYP,rYP,8           -- increment ptr to  Y
   store dFP[XP],   rXP      -- store ptr to  X
   store dFP[YP],   rYP      -- store ptr to  Y
   cmp   rB,rYP,rYLim        -- compare ptr to  Y  with limit
   jle   rB, LOOP_D          -- fall out of loop if greater
   next

OUT_D:
   ... loop sequel ...
```

5.3 Analysis of Multiprocessor Code

Here we see the clear and unpleasant consequence of our choice that `rload`s deposit into the frame and not into registers. Now, the Data Processor performs more loads and stores on the current frame than in the uniprocessor case. The reason is that since we relinquish the Data Processor at the `next` instruction after the `rload`s, the registers may have changed by the time we get the Data Processor back at label CONTINUE$_D$. Thus, we have to repeatedly reload the the `X` and `Y` pointers and the loop constants `A` and `YLim`, and repeatedly store the incremented `X` and `Y` pointers back.

Now, in a multiprocessor, all these extra instructions may actually pay off when compared with nodes built with conventional processors, because *none of them are long latency operations,* they are all local. Suppose we have an MPA built with conventional processors and the same load/store instructions are used for remote locations (*i.e.*, the code looks like the uniprocessor code presented earlier). Here is a comparison of the dynamic instruction counts of the Data Processor for the body of the inner loop for the two codes, generalized for k-way unrolling:

	Arith	Br	Local Ld	Local St	Remote Ld	Remote St
Conventional processor	$1+4k$	1	0	0	$2k$	k
*T	$1+4k$	2	$4+2k$	2	$2k$	k

Ld = `load`, St = `store`, k = degree of unrolling

Of the five arithmetic operations in the loop body, only the `cmp` is not replicated on loop unrolling. For *T, even in an unrolled loop, the two loop constants and the two pointers to `X` and `Y` need to be loaded only once and the two incremented pointers need to be stored only once; also, we count the `next` instruction as a branch.

Assume that arithmetic, branch and local loads and stores cost one time unit. For the conventional processor, assume that the remote loads cost an average of l units (the processor stalls waiting for the reference to complete), and assume that each remote store costs only 1 unit because it is likely to find the just-loaded `Y[i]` in the cache. For *T, we charge one unit for `rload`s and `rstore`s, since they are non-blocking message sends. We charge no additional cost for the thread switch at `next`, assuming sufficient parallelism in the continuation queue to keep the processor busy with other work. Therefore, *T will take less overall execution time when,

$$9k + 9 \leq 2kl + 5k + 2$$

If the loop is unrolled 8 times ($k = 8$) then the *T code is preferred whenever the average global penalty is $l \geq 2.4$. That is, if the expected value of the remote load/store penalty is about 3 units or more, then the extra local instructions executed by the multiprocessor code are worth it.

As a calibration point, consider a cache coherent multiprocessor with miss penalty of 100 units (see for example the

Stanford DASH[21]). If the cache miss rate exceeds about 2–3% then the multithreaded code would be prefered to relying on the cache.

5.4 Other Optimizations

Speculative Avoidance of the extra `load`*'s and* `store`*'s*: The multithreaded code and coherent caching are not mutually exclusive. If fact, as Culler has observed [11], the multithreaded code overhead can be mitigated by speculating that the `rloads` and `rstores` will hit the cache. We only pay the cost of a thread switch in case the cache misses. In many ways, this is the same tradeoff offered by the April processor used in Alewife [1]. Here is the modified code.

```
;;
;;  Synchronization Processor Message Handlers
;;
L1_S:
  store sFP[XI],     rV1   --  store away incoming  X[I]
  join  c1, 3, CONTINUE_D --  attempt continuation of loop
  next                     --  next message

L2_S:
  store sFP[YI],     rV1   --  store away incoming  Y[I]
  join  c1, 3, CONTINUE_D --  attempt continuation of loop
  next                     --  next message

L3_S:
  join  c1, 3, CONTINUE_D --  attempt continuation of loop
  next                     --  next message

S1_S:
  load  rN, sFP[N]         --  total number of stores
  join  c2, rN, OUT_D      --  sequel when all stores complete
  next                     --  next message
;;
;;  Data Processor Threads
;;
  load  rXP, dFP[XP]       --  load ptr to  X
  load  rYP, dFP[YP]       --  load ptr to  Y
  load  rA,  dFP[A]        --  load loop const: a
  load  rYlim, dFP[YLim]   --  load loop const: Y  ptr limit
  cmp   rB,rYP,rYLim       --  compare ptr to  Y  with limit
  jgt   rB, OUT_D          --  zero-trip loop if greater

LOOP_D:
  rload rXP, L1_S          --  initiate load X[i]   (L1)
  rload rYP, L2_S          --  initiate load Y[i]   (L2)

  load  rC1, dFP[c1]       --  load join counter          (L3)
  cmp   rB, 2, rC1         --  Two responses arrived?  (C1)
  jeq   rB, FAST_CONTINUE_D --  yes, skip save/restore  (J1)
                           --  gamble failed; save modified regs
  store dFP[XP],    rXP    --  store ptr to  X            (S2)
  store dFP[YP],    rYP    --  store ptr to  Y            (S3)
  start L3_S, dFP, 0       --  start 3rd synch thread   (S4)
  next                     --  do something else

CONTINUE_D:                --  gamble failed; restore regs
  load  rA,  dFP[A]        --  load loop const: a
  load  rXP, dFP[XP]       --  load ptr to  X
  load  rYP, dFP[YP]       --  load ptr to  Y
  load  rYlim, dFP[YLim]   --  load loop const: Y  ptr limit

FAST_CONTINUE_D:           --  directly here if gamble succeeds
  store dFP[c1], 0         --  re-initialize join counter
  load  rXI, dFP[XI]       --  load copy of  X[I]
  load  rYI, dFP[YI]       --  load copy of  Y[I]

  fmul  rTmp,rA,rXI        --  a*X[i]
  fadd  rTmp,rTmp,rYI      --  a*X[i] + Y[i]
  rstore rYP, rTmp,S1_S    --  store into Y[i]               (S1)
  add   rXP,rXP,8          --  increment ptr to X
  add   rYP,rYP,8          --  increment ptr to Y
  cmp   rB,rYP,rYLim       --  compare ptr to  Y  with limit
  jle   rB, LOOP_D         --  fall out of loop if greater
  next

OUT_D:
  ... loop sequel ...
```

Unlike the previous version, the data processor now loads all relevant values into registers before the loop, including the loop constants `a` and `ylim`, gambling that it can keep them there. After issuing the two `rloads` in statements **L1** and **L2**, it peeks at the join counter `c1` (**L3**, **C1**). If the two `rload` responses have already arrived (say, because of a cache hit), `c1` will have been incremented from 0 to 2; the gamble succeeds and we jump directly to $\texttt{FAST\_CONTINUE}_D$. In this case, we only load the values that arrived on the message; the loop constants and `X` and `Y` pointers are already in registers. Note also that after the two pointer increments (`add` instructions), we no longer store the pointers back into the frame.

If the gamble fails (`c1` < 2 in statement **C1**), we save modified registers (**S2**, **S3**), start a third (trivial) message handler in `sP` which will synchronize with the returning `rload` responses (**S4**), and switch to another thread. In `sP`, when the three message handlers at $\texttt{L1}_S$ $\texttt{L2}_S$, and $\texttt{L3}_S$ have executed (two `rload` responses, one started locally at **S4**), the data processor thread at $\texttt{CONTINUE}_D$ is initiated, which reloads the two loop constants and the two pointers into registers before proceeding.

A number of tricks could be used to improve the probability that the gamble succeeds. Other useful instructions could be executed after the `rloads` and before peeking at the join counter. For example, if the loop is unrolled n times, all $2n$ `rloads` could be issued before looking for the responses for the first pair. We could even busy-wait a little, polling the join counter a few times before giving up.

Loop splitting: The loop can be split into several loops working on independent chunks of the arrays, so that the remote loads of one loop are overlapped with computation in other loops, and vice versa.

Clearly, there are a number of challenging compilation issues. We will discuss some software issues in Section 7.

6 Implementation Considerations

So far, *T should be viewed as a *logical* model for a node in a multithreaded MPA; specialized, separate coprocessors are otherwise familiar RISC processors extended with instructions for the rapid creation and consumption of network messages, and for the efficient synchronization and scheduling of lightweight threads (in fact, many of the "extended" instructions can be realized as memory-mapped operations). In this section we explore possible physical realizations of the *T node architecture.

6.1 Coprocessor Data Sharing and Loading Issues

All three coprocessors share the same local memory, and their view must be consistent. Generally speaking, there is a significant sharing of data between the sP and dP, but relatively little sharing between either of these and the RMEM. The data values on *every* message handled by the sP are written into frames and are subsequently read by the dP. It is also likely that the dP will initialize join counters (or query them) which are subsequently modified by the sP. In contrast, data sharing between the dP and RMEM is limited to those structures which are both globally accessed by other nodes using split phase transactions, and locally accessed using traditional load/store operations. Thus, if the three coprocessors are implemented as distinct units (presumably with each having a cache for local memory) then we can expect a large volume of coherence traffic between the sP and dP coprocessors.

The relative load among the coprocessors will also influence an implementation. The sP typically executes several more threads than the dP but the threads are apt to be proportionately shorter. Assuming an average `join` arity of about four messages corresponding to an average data thread length of approximately 15 instructions, then the two coprocessors should execute roughly the same number of instructions (assuming three or four instructions per sP message handler).

In terms of network messages, the accounting is straightforward. Every `rload` or `rstore` request generated by a dP is processed by some RMEM which subsequently generates a `start` message for the requester's sP. Added to the remote memory traffic are dP-generated `start` messages corresponding to function arguments and results. For many applications the remote memory traffic dominates this extra traffic. Thus, assuming a uniform distribution of remote memory requests, an RMEM will process about as many messages as an sP.

6.2 Multiplexing the Coprocessors

While the workload appears nicely balanced among the coprocessors, engineering considerations may suggest multiplexing them on common resources. For example, we are actively pursuing a design where the sP and dP are combined onto a single chip. The pipeline and caches are time multiplexed on a thread-by-thread basis. By sharing the same data cache the sP–dP coherence traffic is eliminated. Obviously, the throughput of the node will suffer because we will not be able to exploit concurrency between the sP and dP. A more subtle consequence is pressure on the incoming message queue. Data processor threads are typically several times longer than message handlers. If data threads execute to completion before executing message handlers, then the variance on message service times will cause increased queuing of network messages.

In the ETL EM-4 [28], the Fetch and Matching Unit (FMU) corresponds to our sP and the Execution Unit (EU) corresponds to our dP. There is no separate RMEM— its function is performed by the EU. Further, the FMU is not programmable like our sP; rather, it is specialized for various *wait-match* operations similar to Monsoon [25] (two-way joins on frame presence bits, accompanied by a single frame read/write). Also, the FMU and the EU share a single port to local memory.

An implementation might go further and multiplex all three coprocessors onto the same shared resource (as in the MDP). This might be considered when remote memory operations are network bandwidth limited anyway. However, we would still consider this an improvement over, say, a CM-5 node (represented by Figure 4), because it still provides exceptionally efficient support for `join`, `start`, `rload`, `rstore`, and `next`. That is, we distinguish *T architectures by their direct implementation of synchronization and scheduling primitives for a potentially large set of very lightweight threads *in addition to* a tightly integrated network interface wherein internode communication is exposed to the compiler.

An orthogonal dimension of multiplexing is that multiple threads can be interleaved in the processor pipeline, as in the HEP [30], the Tera [3] and Monsoon [25]. This can simplify the pipeline, since the pressure due to inter-instruction dependencies is less, but it also degrades single thread performance by the degree of multiplexing.

7 Software for *T

We believe that *T will efficiently support code developed for HEP/Tera, the J-machine, EM-4, *etc.*, because in each case it provides a superset of their capabilities. Thus, any compiler techniques developed for these machines are directly applicable to *T. Further, we believe that *all* these architectures will efficiently support SIMD/SPMD programming models, again because they are more general.

The real challenge is to provide general purpose programming models in which applications can have much more dynamic structure. Here, the problem is the extraction of *excess parallism*, *i.e.*, parallelism that is reasonably greater than the number of nodes in the MPA. This will allow each node to have sufficient threads so that even though some may be waiting for incoming messages, there is a high probability that other threads are ready to run.[6].

A very promising approach is to start with *declarative languages* where the compiler can effortlessly extract large amounts of fine grain parallelism. Nikhil [23] and Culler *et al* [11] have proposed compiler flowgraph formalisms which, inspired by dataflow graphs and the P-RISC model, make explicit the notion of threads as a unit of scheduling. Culler's Threaded Abstract Machine (TAM) has been implemented and is in use for over two years on a variety of platforms (RISC uniprocessors, shared memory multiprocessors, NCUBE/2, *etc.*). His experiments have provided much data on achievable thread lengths, frequency of synchronization, instruction counts, comparisons with dataflow instructions, *etc.*, all of which have had a strong influence on *T, which almost directly mirrors the TAM compilation model. The TAM work is an existence proof that compilation of large, non-trivial programs with massive amounts of parallelism

[6] A MIMD is a terrible thing to waste!

for *T is possible. Nevertheless, there remain serious research issues concerning dynamic storage management, load balancing, *etc.*

Acknowledgements: MIT and Motorola, Inc. are collaborating on the design and construction of a real *T machine. Bob Greiner and Ken Traub of Motorola have contributed significantly towards the architecture and software systems, respectively.

References

[1] A. Agarwal, B.-H. Lim, D. Kranz, and J. Kubiatowicz. APRIL: A Processor Architecture for Multiprocessing. In *Proc. 17th Ann. Intl. Symp. on Computer Architecture, Seattle, WA*, pages 104–114, May 1990.

[2] G. S. Almasi and A. Gottlieb. *Highly Parallel Computing.* Benjamin/Cummings, Redwood City, CA, 1989.

[3] R. Alverson, D. Callahan, D. Cummings, B. Koblenz, A. Porterfield, and B. Smith. The Tera Computer System. In *Proc. Intl. Conf. on Supercomputing, Amsterdam*, June 1990.

[4] Arvind and D. E. Culler. Dataflow Architectures. In *Annual Reviews in Computer Science*, volume 1, pages 225–253. Annual Reviews Inc., Palo Alto, CA, USA, 1986.

[5] Arvind, D. E. Culler, R. A. Iannucci, V. Kathail, K. Pingali, and R. E. Thomas. The Tagged Token Dataflow Architecture. Technical report, MIT Lab. for Computer Science, Aug. 1983. Revised October, 1984.

[6] Arvind and R. A. Iannucci. Two Fundamental Issues in Multiprocessing. In *Proc. DFVLR - 1987 Conf. on Parallel Processing in Science and Engineering, Bonn-Bad Godesberg, W. Germany (Springer-Verlag LNCS 295)*, June 1987.

[7] Arvind and R. S. Nikhil. Executing a Program on the MIT Tagged-Token Dataflow Architecture. *IEEE Trans. on Computers*, 39(3):300–318, Mar. 1990.

[8] E. Brooks. The Attack of the Killer Micros, 1989. Teraflop Computing Panel, Supercomputing '89, Reno, Nevada.

[9] R. Buehrer and K. Ekanadham. Incorporating Dataflow Ideas into von Neumann Processors for Parallel Execution. *IEEE Trans. on Computers*, C-36(12):1515–1522, Dec. 1987.

[10] D. E. Culler and G. M. Papadopoulos. The Explicit Token Store. *J. Parallel and Distributed Computing*, Dec. 1990.

[11] D. E. Culler, A. Sah, K. E. Schauser, T. von Eicken, and J. Wawrzynek. Fine-grain Parallelism with Minimal Hardware Support: A Compiler-Controlled Threaded Abstract Machine. In *Proc. 4th Intl. Conf. on Arch. Support for Programming Languages and Systems (ASPLOS), Santa Clara, CA*, pages 164–175, Apr. 1991.

[12] W. Dally, L. Chao, A. Chien, S. Hassoun, W. Horwat, J. Kaplan, P. Song, B. Totty, and S. Wills. Architecture of a Message-Driven Processor. In *Proc. 14th. Ann. Intl. Symp. on Computer Architecture, Pittsburgh, PA*, pages 189–196, June 1987.

[13] J. B. Dennis. The Evolution of "Static" Data-Flow Architecture. In *Advanced Topics in Data-flow Computing, J-L. Gaudiot and L. Bic (eds.)*, pages 35–91. Prentice-Hall, 1991.

[14] J. B. Dennis and G. R. Gao. An Efficient Pipelined Dataflow Processor Architecture. In *Proc. Supercomputing, Orlando, FL*, pages 368–373, Nov. 1988.

[15] V. Grafe, G. Davidson, J. Hoch, and V. Holmes. The Epsilon Dataflow Processor. In *Proc. 16th. Ann. Intl. Symp. on Computer Architecture, Jerusalem, Israel*, pages 36–45, May 1989.

[16] J. R. Gurd, C. Kirkham, and I. Watson. The Manchester Prototype Dataflow Computer. *Comm. of the ACM*, 28(1):34–52, Jan. 1985.

[17] R. H. Halstead Jr. and T. Fujita. MASA: A Multithreaded Processor Architecture for Parallel Symbolic Computing. In *Proc. 15th Ann. Intl. Symp. on Computer Architecture, Honolulu, Hawaii*, June 1988.

[18] D. S. Henry and C. F. Joerg. The Network Interface Chip. Technical Report CSG Memo 331, MIT Laboratory for Computer Science, 545 Technology Square, Cambridge MA 02139, June 1991.

[19] K. Hiraki, K. Nishida, S. Sekiguchi, T. Shimada, and T. Yuba. The SIGMA-1 Dataflow Supercomputer: A Challenge for New Generation Supercomputing Systems. *J. of Information Processing*, 10(4):219–226, 1987.

[20] R. A. Iannucci. Toward a Dataflow/von Neumann Hybrid Architecture. In *Proc. 15th Ann. Intl. Symp. on Computer Architecture, Honolulu, Hawaii*, pages 131–140, June 1988.

[21] D. Lenoski, J. Laudon, K. Gharachorloo, A. Gupta, and J. Hennessy. The Directory-Based Cache Coherence Protocol for the DASH Multiprocessor. In *Proc. 17th. Ann. Intl. Symp. on Computer Architetecture, Seattle, WA*, pages 148–159, May 1990.

[22] P. M. Maurer. Mapping the Data Flow Model of Computation onto an Enhanced von Neumann Processor. In *Proc. Intl. Conf. on Parallel Processing*, pages 235–239, Aug. 1988.

[23] R. S. Nikhil. The Parallel Programming Language Id and its Compilation for Parallel Machines. In *Proc. Wkshp. on Massive Parallelism, Amalfi, Italy*, October 1989.

[24] R. S. Nikhil and Arvind. Can dataflow subsume von Neumann computing? In *Proc. 16th. Ann. Intl. Symp. on Computer Architecture, Jerusalem, Israel*, pages 262–272, May 1989.

[25] G. M. Papadopoulos. *Implementation of a General Purpose Dataflow Multiprocessor.* MIT Press, 1991.

[26] G. M. Papadopoulos and K. R. Traub. Multithreading: A Revisionist View of Dataflow Architectures. In *Proc. 18th. Intl. Symp. on Computer Architecture, Toronto*, Mar. 1991.

[27] G. Pfister, W. Brantley, D. George, S. Harvey, W. Kleinfelder, K. McAuliffe, E. Melton, V. Norton, and J. Weiss. The IBM Research Parallel Processor Prototype (RP3): Introduction and Architecture. In *Proc. Intl. Conf. on Parallel Processing*, pages 764–771, Aug. 1985.

[28] S. Sakai, Y. Yamaguchi, K. Hiraki, and T. Yuba. An Architecture of a Dataflow Single Chip Processor. In *Proc. 16th Ann. Intl. Symp. on Computer Architecture, Jerusalem, Israel*, pages 46–53, May 1989.

[29] K. E. Schauser, D. E. Culler, and T. von Eicken. Compiler-Controlled Multithreading for Lenient Parallel Languages. In *Proc. 5th ACM Conf. on Functional Programming Languages and Computer Architecture, Cambridge, MA (Springer-Verlag LNCS 523)*, pages 50–72, Aug. 1991.

[30] B. J. Smith. A Pipelined, Shared Resource MIMD Computer. In *Proc. Intl. Conf. on Parallel Processing*, pages 6–8, 1978.

Session 6: Caches

Adjustable Block Size Coherent Caches

Czarek Dubnicki Thomas J. LeBlanc

Department of Computer Science
University of Rochester
Rochester, New York 14627-0226

Abstract

Several studies have shown that the performance of coherent caches depends on the relationship between the granularity of sharing and locality exhibited by the program and the cache block size. Large cache blocks exploit processor and spatial locality, but may cause unnecessary cache invalidations due to false sharing. Small cache blocks can reduce the number of cache invalidations, but increase the number of bus or network transactions required to load data into the cache. In this paper we describe a cache organization that dynamically adjusts the cache block size according to recently observed reference behavior. Cache blocks are split across cache lines when false sharing occurs, and merged back into a single cache line to exploit spatial locality. To evaluate this cache organization, we simulate a scalable multiprocessor with coherent caches, using a suite of memory reference traces to model program behavior. We show that for every fixed block size, some program suffers a 33% increase in the average waiting time per reference, and a factor of 2 increase in the average number of words transferred per reference, when compared against the performance of an adjustable block size cache. In the few cases where adjusting the block size does not provide superior performance, it comes within 7% of the best fixed block size alternative. We conclude that an adjustable block size cache offers significantly better performance than every fixed block size cache, especially when there is variability in the granularity of sharing exhibited by applications.

1 Introduction

Several studies have shown that the performance of coherent caches depends on the relationship between the granularity of sharing and locality exhibited by a program and the cache block size (the amount of data stored in a single cache line) [7; 8; 11]. Large cache blocks improve application performance when there is substantial processor and spatial locality (i.e. all words allocated to one cache line are accessed by one processor in some window of time). If cache blocks are smaller than the data objects used on a per-processor basis, then accessing a single object can generate references to multiple cache lines, increasing the number of invalidations and decreasing the beneficial effects of prefetching [11]. However, if cache blocks are too large, then *false sharing* [15] is introduced (wherein two data items not being shared happen to reside in the same cache line), which also increases the number of invalidations [8]. Since the granularity of sharing can vary widely among programs, the likelihood of a mismatch between the block size and the object sizes used by some programs is high.

The mismatch between block size and program sharing patterns has been studied both in the context of bus-based machines and scalable multiprocessors. Eggers and Katz [7; 8] examined the effect of sharing on cache and bus performance using traces from four application programs. They showed that miss ratios for some parallel programs increase when the cache line size increases, while for other programs the miss ratio decreases with an increase in line size. This behavior is caused by the different degree of sharing in the various applications. For those programs exhibiting fine-grain sharing, the number of invalidation misses rises with block size; when there is spatial locality on a per-processor basis, invalidation misses decrease with block size. Both false sharing and per-processor locality were shown to be important factors affecting cache performance when a larger block size was used (32 bytes versus 4 bytes). Coherency overhead (expressed in terms of bus cycles needed to maintain coherency) for a write-invalidate protocol increased by over 75% for two applications, and decreased by 48% and 66% for the other two programs.

Simulation results of three parallel applications on the VMP multiprocessor also show that no single block size is best for all programs [6]. The best block size for the three programs considered varied between 32 and 132 bytes.

Gupta and Weber [11] examined the effect of cache block size on the number and size of invalidations in a multiprocessor system with a directory-based cache coherency protocol. [1] With four-byte blocks, most shared writes generated one invalidation. In some cases, larger block sizes (16 and 64 bytes) increased the number of invalidations substantially (over 50% in one case) and the size of invalidations (increasing the percentage of shared writes affecting more than one processor from 13% to 22%). In other cases, an increase in block size reduced the average number of invalidations from 1.77 to 0.34. Once again, these discrepancies were traced to different sharing patterns in the various applications.

Each of these studies concluded that a close match be-

[0] This research was supported by the National Science Foundation under grant CDA-8822724.

[1] The size of an invalidation is the number of caches containing the data to be invalidated.

tween the degree of sharing in an application and the block size is desirable. One general technique to achieve such a match is to structure the application based on knowledge of the cache organization, allocating separate objects to separate cache lines [15], grouping objects according to sharing patterns [5; 9], and avoiding fine-grain sharing [8]. Using a variety of program restructuring techniques, Cheriton *et al* [5] were able to achieve an order of magnitude improvement in the cache miss ratio for shared data in large (128 bytes) cache lines.

In this paper we describe a cache organization with an adjustable block size that offers a compromise between the advantages of small cache blocks for fine-grain sharing and large cache blocks for spatial locality. In this cache organization, the hardware dynamically adjusts the amount of data stored in a cache line according to recently observed data reference patterns. Cache blocks are split across cache lines when false sharing occurs; cache blocks are merged back into a single cache line to exploit spatial locality. By relaxing the standard assumption that the size of a cache block is fixed, and instead varying the block size according to observed reference behavior, we hope to improve on the performance of coherent caches when application programs exhibit a range of sharing patterns.

The remainder of this paper is organized as follows. We first provide a brief overview of our proposed cache organization in section 2. In section 3 we describe the details of this cache organization and the interaction with the coherence protocol in the context of a scalable multiprocessor architecture. In section 4 we use simulation to compare the performance of caches with a fixed block size to a cache with an adjustable block size. In section 5 we examine the performance impact of the parameters used to control changes in block size in the adjustable block size cache organization. We present our conclusions in section 6.

2 Overview of Adjustable Block Size Caches

We propose a coherent cache organization that adjusts the cache block size to match the granularity of sharing observed during program execution. We use a power-of-two buddy scheme to split and merge cache blocks across cache lines based on recent access patterns. Under this scheme, the cache block stored in a single cache line is split in two when processors reference only one half of the cache block. Two adjacent cache blocks of the same size are merged within a single cache line when both halves of both blocks are referenced by a single processor.

We assume that processor caches are fully associative; each cache line may hold any data block. (A direct-mapped organization is discussed at the end of this section). In addition to the address tag field (which must be large enough to identify the smallest possible cache blocks), each cache line includes the following fields:

- *size* - Indicates the size of the data block currently in the cache line. The size may be any integer power of two from *MinBlockSize* to *MaxBlockSize* (the size of a cache line).
- *LU* - Reference bits for the lower and upper half of the data block stored in the cache line. Each time data is referenced in one half of the data block, the corresponding reference bit is set. Each half of a block is called *a sub-block*.
- *split-merge counter* - Records the number of processors that accessed only the lower or upper half of the cache block while it was resident in their cache. The counter is incremented if only one half the cache block was accessed, and is decremented if both halves of the cache block were accessed.

A cache block may be split or merged when it has been modified by one processor and is then requested by another processor. [2] The decision to split a cache block is based on the value of the split-merge counter associated with the cache line containing the data block. The counter is updated according to the value of the reference bits when the cache line is requested by another processor; the value of the split-merge counter is transferred to the requesting processor with the contents of the cache line. A positive counter suggests that processors do not on average access both halves of the data block, and therefore the cache block should be split in two. A negative split-merge counter suggests that processors do access both halves, and therefore the cache block should not be split.

The decision to merge two adjacent cache blocks is based on the value of their respective split-merge counters. Merging is encouraged when adjacent cache blocks of the same size both have negative counters.

Within this basic organization, there are several parameters that can affect how quickly and accurately the cache block size converges to the desired value. The maximum block size, which is also the cache line size, must be small enough so that cache space is effectively utilized, and yet large enough to exploit spatial locality. The minimum block size must be small enough to avoid false sharing, and large enough to avoid an excessive waste of cache space. The initial block size must be close to the average block size, if cache blocks are to converge to an appropriate size quickly.

The accuracy of the reference information and the way it is used also affects how quickly we reach the desired block size. Rather than allow the short-term reference pattern of a single processor to determine when to split or merge cache blocks, we define separate split and merge threshold values that must be exceeded before a split or merge occurs. High thresholds can discourage excessive splitting or merging, but the thresholds must not be so high as to prevent splitting or merging. When the split (merge) threshold is N, a cache block must have been modified and then requested by another processor N times before the block can be split (merged).

Regardless of the specific values chosen for these parameters, the main advantage of this cache organization is that the size of data blocks maintained in a cache line varies depending on references to the data. When appropriate, the largest possible block size is used, minimizing the number of bus or network transactions needed to retrieve the data. False sharing causes a data block to be split across cache lines, reducing the number of subsequent invalidations. We would expect this adaptive scheme to produce fewer invalidations than a cache with a large, fixed block size, and require fewer bus or network transactions than a cache with a small, fixed block size.

One consequence of this caching scheme is that some portions of the processor cache go unused. Under this scheme, the effective line size of the cache is equal to the average

[2] We restrict block size adjustment to modified blocks because there is only one copy to consider. It is possible to adjust the block size of read-shared blocks, but we would incur the cost of reaching a global consensus on the new block size.

data block size, which could be much smaller than the actual line size. If cache space were to become a serious concern, we could decrease the amount of unused cache space by increasing the minimum block size. Alternatively, we could use multiple sub-caches, each with a different line size. Large cache blocks would be stored in a sub-cache with a large line size, while small cache blocks would be stored in a separate sub-cache with a small line size. To find a particular cache block, we would search each sub-cache in parallel.

One advantage to using multiple sub-caches is that size bits would not have to be stored in the cache. Moreover, each sub-cache can be direct-mapped, which makes a large adjustable block size cache feasible, and results in a shorter cycle time.

In general, we would expect an adjustable block size cache to be used as a second-level cache. Doing so would shield the processor from the effects on cycle time caused by complications in the logic of an adjustable block size cache. The first-level cache could use very short lines (say, one word) and be direct-mapped. None of the fields introduced above would have to be stored in the first-level cache. The reference bits for a line in the second-level cache would be updated on the first reference to a sub-block, when the sub-block is brought into the first-level cache. Subsequent references to the sub-block would not require accesses to the second-level cache, as long as the data remains in a first-level cache.

In the remainder of this paper, we will ignore the details of interaction between the first and second-level caches, focusing instead on the role of the adjustable block size cache.

3 Implementation in a Scalable Multiprocessor

We will now illustrate the use of an adjustable block size cache in a scalable, shared-memory multiprocessor. We describe a representative multiprocessor organization and coherence protocol, and detail the role of the coherence protocol in adjusting the size of cache blocks.

3.1 Architectural Assumptions

We will consider a multiprocessor architecture consisting of processor nodes connected by an interconnection network. Each processing node contains a processor, a processor cache, and a memory module. Data coherence is maintained in hardware using a directory protocol [4].

There are four levels in the memory hierarchy. The first level consists of the local processor caches. Local memory is the second level. The third level includes the caches of all other nodes. The fourth level consists of all nonlocal memory modules.

Each memory module contains random access memory and a tag cache [13], which is used to implement a distributed directory. Each tag cache is indexed by block address. A tag cache line maintains a bit vector of nodes that currently have a copy of the data block indexed by the tag cache line. In addition, each tag cache entry contains a field for the size of the data block. Both processor caches and tag caches are fully associative.

3.2 Coherency Protocol

Data coherence is maintained using a variant of the write-invalidate, ownership protocol for the DASH multiprocessor [12]. Under this protocol, each data block is assigned to a memory module. The node containing the memory module to which a given data block is assigned is called the *home node* for the data block.

A data block can be in one of three states: *uncached* data is not cached by any processor; *read-shared* (*shared-remote*) data is cached in an unmodified state by one or more processors; *modified* (*dirty-remote*) data is cached in a modified state on a single processor. The processor containing a data block in the *modified* state is called the *owner* of the data block. There are also in-transit states indicating that an operation is in progress on a particular data block.

The simplest operation occurs when a node wants to read data and the corresponding data block is in the *read-shared* state. On a cache miss, the requesting node sends a read request message to the home node of the data block. The home node fetches the data from memory, updates its directory information, and returns the requested data in a read reply message.

When the requested data block is in the *modified* state, a read request is forwarded to the owner of the block. The owner provides the requesting processor with the data, and writes the data back to the home node. The new state of the data block is *read-shared.*

On a write request, the home node must invalidate all copies (if any) of the requested data. In the *read-shared* state, the home node immediately sends the data to the requesting node. This message also contains the number of invalidation acknowledgements the requesting node should receive before the write can be regarded as having been performed globally. Next, the home node sends invalidations to all nodes containing copies of the data block. Those nodes invalidate their copies and send invalidation acknowledgements to the original requesting node. The new state of the data block is *modified.*

When a write to modified data is requested, the home node forwards the write request to the owner node. This node sends the data to the requesting node indicating that one acknowledgement should arrive. The owner then notifies the home node about the change in ownership. The home node in turn acknowledges completion of the write transaction.

3.3 Adjusting the Block Size

In addition to maintaining data coherency, the coherency protocol must distribute reference information, and choose when to split or merge cache blocks.

The reference bits associated with a cache line record reference information on a per-processor basis. These bits are used to update the split-merge counter, which records reference information across processors. The split-merge counter is updated as follows:

- When a requesting node receives data directly from the home node, it clears its split-merge counter.
- When a data block changes owner, the previous owner updates its split-merge counter based on the current values of its reference bits, and includes the new value of its counter with the data. The new owner initializes its counter to this value. If the change in ownership results in a split or merge, the new owner initializes its split-merge counter to zero.
- When a node receives invalidation acknowledgements from other nodes containing copies of a data block, the acknowledgements include the split-merge counters for

each copy. The requesting node adds these values to its split-merge counter.

The decision to split a data block is made by the owner on a transition in ownership. When an owner receives a request forwarded from the home node, it updates its split-merge counter and compares the new value to the split threshold. If the split-merge counter exceeds the split threshold, a split occurs. The owner provides the requesting node with the half of the original block containing the requested offset within a block. The original owner maintains ownership of half the block (clearing the split-merge counter for the block), and transfers ownership of the other half (containing the requested offset). The home node updates its tag cache and memory (if necessary) when notified of the split by the original owner, as part of the sharing-writeback message or ownership-change message. Thus, no additional messages are required to implement a split, and the amount of data transferred is actually less than in the case where a split does not occur. The directory entry remains locked until the information about a potential split is received, so the home node always has an up-to-date value for the block size.

Two adjacent cache blocks of equal size can be merged to form a single block within a line at two different points:

1. If we load the tag for the longest possible line on a tag cache miss, we implicitly merge blocks after the block tags are evicted from the tag cache.

2. A merge can be ordered by the owner when a block in the *modified* state is requested by another node. The following conditions should be met when a merge is ordered by the owner: (a) both blocks are owned by the same node, (b) the split-merge counters of both blocks are less than the merge threshold.

The owner invalidates the processor cache lines containing the two subblocks being merged on a write request, and changes the state of the blocks to *read-shared* on a read request. The owner also sends a *reply* message containing the merged blocks to the requesting node. Merging does not require extra messages, since the home node is notified as part of the sharing-writeback message or ownership-change message, but the amount of data transferred is increased because both the requested block and its neighbor are sent to the requesting node.

4 Performance Evaluation

To quantify the performance benefits of varying the block size in coherent caches, we simulated the scalable multiprocessor organization described in the previous section using both fixed block size caches and adjustable block size caches. The simulator is written in C++ and runs on SUN SPARCstations under SunOS and the Silicon Graphics 480/GTX under IRIX. The simulations use a suite of memory reference traces of parallel programs collected on the IBM ACE multiprocessor. For each simulation, we measured the average waiting time per memory reference, and the number of 4-byte words transferred per reference. In this section, we describe the memory reference traces, the simulation model, and the results of the simulations.

4.1 Memory Reference Traces

We use memory reference traces collected on an 8-node IBM ACE multiprocessor workstation to drive our simulations. In addition to our work, these traces have been used by others to study memory management policies and the performance benefits of disabling coherence to minimize short-term false sharing [2].

The programs in our trace suite fall into three different classes:

- *C-threads applications* - The majority of the programs were implemented using the C-threads package on a non-uniform memory access (NUMA) multiprocessor. *Sorbyr* and *sorbyc* implement red-black successive over-relaxation. The two programs differ in the order of their inner loops: *sorbyr* operates on rows, while *sorbyc* operates on columns. *Plytrace* is a scene rendering program. *Matmult* implements matrix multiplication. Both *bsort* and *kmerge* perform a merge sort; in *bsort* half the processors drop out in each phase, whereas in *kmerge* all processors are busy until the end. *Gauss* is a Gaussian elimination program. All of these programs exhibit coarse-grain parallelism and good processor locality.

- *SPLASH applications* - Two programs were taken from the SPLASH suite [14]. These programs were written in C using the Argonne macros for parallel constructs [3]. *S-cholesky* performs parallel factorization of a sparse matrix; *S-mp3d* solves a problem in fluid flow simulation. Both programs, which were written for a bus-based multiprocessor, exhibit fine-grain sharing and poor processor locality.

- *Presto applications* - Four programs were implemented in Presto [1]. *P-life* is a parallel implementation of Conway's game of life, *p-qsort* implements parallel quicksort, *p-matmult* is a matrix multiplication program, and *p-gauss* is a Gaussian elimination program. Like the SPLASH programs, these applications were written for a bus-based multiprocessor, and exhibit fine-grain sharing and poor processor locality.

Each of these programs was executed on the IBM ACE and detailed memory reference traces were collected. The number of memory references made by each program and the fraction of writes is presented in Table 1. Both the total number of references and the faction of writes varies widely among the programs.

Application	Millions of References	Fraction of Writes
sorbyr	104	0.21
sorbyc	105	0.21
plytrace	15.4	0.34
matmult	4.64	0.03
kmerge	10.9	0.36
bsort	23.6	0.36
gauss	270	0.17
s-cholesky	38.7	0.23
s-mp3d	20	0.43
p-life	72	0.20
p-quicksort	24.5	0.25
p-matmult	6.74	0.04
p-gauss	28	0.29

Table 1: Summary of Reference Traces.

4.2 Simulation Model

In order to preserve the original interleaving of references in the traces, we use a synchronous trace-driven simulation. That is, we simulate one memory reference at a time. As a consequence of this simulation approach, we do not model contention. In addition, we cannot use program execution time as our evaluation metric. Instead, we use two other metrics:

- Average waiting time per reference - the number of cache cycles, on average, a processor has to wait for data.
- Average number of words transferred - the average number of words in a message transferred between nodes, including message headers.

The first metric is sensitive to the particular constants used in the simulation, especially the time required to send a message. Other than the assumption that messages have 2-word headers, the second metric is not sensitive to the specific values used in the simulation.

We simulated seven different cache organizations: caches with a fixed line (block) size of 1, 2, 4, 8, 16, and 32 4-byte words, and an adjustable block size cache. We simulated an adjustable block size cache with a minimum block size of 1 word, a maximum block size of 32 words, an initial block size of 16 words, a split threshold of 2, and a merge threshold of 1. We chose these particular default values to admit the greatest possible range of block sizes, and to minimize the number of splits or merges required to converge to an appropriate block size. The split and merge thresholds were set so as to encourage changes in the size of cache blocks, slightly favoring merges over splits. Although our choice of initial block size and merge threshold were influenced somewhat by the bias towards coarse-grain sharing in our application programs, small fluctuations in these values do not affect the relative performance of the various cache organizations.

We assume that the cache cycle time is the same for each cache organization. In the case of the adjustable block size cache, we incur additional cache cycles for split and merge operations. Every time we allocate a new cache line or change the contents of an existing cache line, we pay at least one cache cycle. When a split occurs, or when notification of a split arrives at the home node, we pay one cache cycle. When we attempt a merge operation, we pay one cycle to lookup the buddy block. If the merge is successful, we pay an additional cache cycle to invalidate one cache line and update the contents of another. [3]

The processor cache cycle time and the tag cache cycle time are normalized to 1. To eliminate the effect of cache size and to simplify our simulations, we assume that both the processor caches and tag caches are infinite. Each main memory access requires 5 cache cycles and up to 32 consecutive words can be written or read from memory in one access.

Messages are sent between caches. All messages are assumed to be no longer than 32 words of data plus header. A transfer of a message of length X between different nodes costs A*X + B. Since communication channels are one word wide, the length of a message is given in words. B is the cost of preparing and sending a message of length zero. This parameter is equal to 40 in our simulations, reflecting our assumption that sending a message to an arbitrary node in a large-scale multiprocessor will be expensive. The incremental cost of sending an additional word in a message is A. This parameter is equal to 10 in our simulations.

These parameter values are representative of the costs we would expect to incur in a scalable multiprocessor. As in the DASH multiprocessor [10], a cache fill from a remote node can be expensive. For example, it costs about 100 cache cycles to satisfy a cache miss from remote memory, including 40 cycles to send a request for data to another node, 50 cycles or more to send the reply, and 5 cycles to retrieve the data from memory.

4.3 Comparison of Cache Organizations

We simulated the execution of each of the applications in our trace suite for each cache organization described above. During each simulation we recorded the average waiting time per reference, and the average number of words transferred per reference. Table 4.3 summarizes our results by presenting the best value achieved for each metric, and the block size responsible for producing that value. We see that in most cases, varying the block size produced the best result for both metrics. In a small number of cases, a single fixed block size produced a better average waiting time or a smaller number of words transferred. In only two cases (*kmerge* and *bsort*) did a single fixed block size produce a better result for both metrics.

In every case, the adjustable block size cache was within 7% of the best result for each metric. In two cases (*matmult* and *p-life*), the adjustable block size cache lowered the average waiting time per reference by 20% or more when compared with the best fixed block size cache. Furthermore, in the case of *matmult*, the average number of words transferred by the best fixed block size cache organization was 64% greater than the number of words transferred by the adjustable block size cache organization; for *gauss*, the adjustable block size cache shows a factor of 3 improvement over the next best alternative. These results suggest that an adjustable block size cache is never much worse than the best fixed block size cache, and in some cases is much better than any fixed block size cache.

There is good agreement between the figures in Table 4.3 and what we would expect given the description of each application presented earlier. The C-threads programs, having been written for a NUMA machine, exhibit good processor locality, which is reflected in the metrics. The C-threads programs have a very low average waiting time per reference, and are the only programs for which the average number of words transferred per reference is below 0.1. The SPLASH and Presto programs on the other hand, were not written to maximize locality, which is also reflected in the metrics. For the most part, the SPLASH and Presto applications have a high average waiting time per reference, and the number of words transferred per reference is 0.5 or higher.

The last column of Table 4.3 lists the best fixed block size organization for each of the two metrics. Where a single block size is given, it is the best fixed block size for both metrics. Where two sizes are given, the first produces the best average waiting time per reference, the second produces the lowest average number of words transferred per reference. Examining this column, we see that no single block size is best across all of our applications. The best fixed block size varied between 4 and 32 words for the first metric, and between 2 and 32 words for the second metric. This observation

[3] Our results are not sensitive to the exact overhead of a split or merge operation because both of these operations occur relatively infrequently.

Application	Shortest Average Waiting Time Per Reference			Lowest Average Number of Words Per Reference			BestFixed
	value	block size	BestFxd/Variable	value	block size	BestFxd/Variable	
sorbyr	1.16	Variable	1.01	0.015	Variable	1.04	32
sorbyc	1.50	Variable	1.01	0.033	4	0.94	8,4
plytrace	2.61	Variable	1.03	0.140	Variable	1.04	8,4
matmult	1.42	Variable	1.20	0.033	Variable	1.64	8,4
kmerge	1.72	32	0.94	0.081	32	0.93	32
bsort	1.50	32	0.96	0.052	32	0.93	32
gauss	1.07	Variable	1.15	0.007	Variable	3.28	16
s-cholesky	6.77	8	0.99	0.497	Variable	1.04	8
s-mp3d	17.19	Variable	1.05	1.214	Variable	1.11	4
p-life	7.87	Variable	1.24	0.554	Variable	1.33	4
p-quicksort	9.16	Variable	1.13	0.574	Variable	1.07	4,2
p-matmult	2.37	Variable	1.10	0.105	Variable	1.10	8,4
p-gauss	10.11	Variable	1.11	0.717	Variable	1.07	4,2

Table 2: The Best Cache Organization for Each Application and Metric.

holds even within a single class of program. For example, the best block size for the C-threads programs ranges between 4 and 32 words for the two metrics.

Even within a single application, no one block size is best, as evidenced by the performance of the adjustable block size organization. For almost every program, varying the block size produced better results than every fixed block size alternative.

More detailed results are presented in Figure 1. The performance of each fixed block size cache is contrasted directly with the performance of the adjustable block size cache. Values lower than 1 in Figure 1 indicate cases where a fixed block size cache was able to perform better than the adjustable block size cache.

Figure 1 illustrates the range of reference behavior exhibited by our application suite. Some programs prefer large cache blocks (*sorbyr*, *kmerge*, and *bsort*), while most others prefer medium-size cache blocks. There was not enough fine-grain sharing to justify a fixed block size of 1 or 2 words in any of our experiments, although the number of words transferred in the case of *p-qsort* is smallest when the block size is 2 words. Only *gauss* was not particularly sensitive to block size.

From Figure 1 we see that both large and small cache blocks introduce significant overhead for some programs. For example, when the cache block size is one word, the average waiting time per reference for *matmult*, *kmerge*, *bsort*, and *cholesky* is more than twice that of the adjustable block size cache. A block size of 2 doesn't help much for *kmerge* and *bsort*, and introduces more than 50% overhead for *sorbyr*, *matmult*, and *cholesky*. At the other extreme, a block size of 32 words doubles the average waiting time per reference for *p-life*, *q-sort*, and *p-gauss*, and introduces more than 50% overhead for *matmult*, *cholesky*, and *s-mp3d*. With a block size of 16 words, five programs suffer 30% or more overhead in average waiting time when compared against the adjustable block size cache.

Even caches with medium-size blocks do not always perform well. With a block size of 4 words, two programs (*kmerge* and *bsort*) suffer 65% overhead in the average waiting time per reference, and three other programs (*sorbyr*, *matmult*, and *p-life*) suffer 25-30% overhead. With a block size of 8 words, six programs suffer 20% overhead or more, and up to 34% in one case (*p-life*).

The results are not very different when we consider the average number of words transferred per reference. Caches with either large or small cache blocks transfer significantly more data than an adjustable block size cache. Every single fixed block size cache transfers twice as many words as the adjustable block size cache for some program. The best fixed block size is 8 words, but even in that case, three programs require an increase in the number of words transferred of between 45% (*p-gauss*) and 67% (*matmult*), and one program requires an increase of a factor of 3 (*gauss*).

4.4 Splits and Merges

Our simulations of an adjustable block size cache all assume an initial block size of 16 words. For programs that prefer a larger or smaller block size, splits or merges have to occur in order to reach the best block size. As seen in Figure 1, three programs (*sorbyr*, *kmerge*, and *bsort*) perform best with a block size of 32 words, five programs (*sorbyc*, *plytrace*, *matmult*, *cholesky*, and *p-matmult*) prefer a block size of 8 words, four programs (*smp3d*, *p-life*, *p-qsort*, and *p-gauss*) prefer a block size of 4 words, and only one program (*gauss*) performs best with a block size of 16 words. The threshold values for splits and merges determines how quickly the cache is able to adjust the block size to these values during execution.

Ideally, we would like to converge to the right block size without an excessive number of splits or merges. Table 3 presents the statistics for the number of splits, merges, and merge attempts. [4] As expected, only a very small fraction of references actually cause a split or merge to occur. Only the SPLASH programs had more than 0.1% of all references produce a split or merge; in every other case, fewer than 0.05% of all references were followed by a split or merge. Merge attempts occur much more frequently (6% of all references in *s-mp3d*, but less than 3% of all references in the other cases), but only cost one cache cycle.

It is somewhat surprising that so few split or merge operations can have such a significant impact. In particular,

[4] A merge attempt occurs when the split-merge counter for a referenced cache block is decremented below the merge threshold. If the counter for the buddy block is also below the threshold value (we pay one cache cycle to check), a merge occurs. If it is not below the threshold value, we record a failed merge attempt.

Figure 1: Performance of fixed block size caches relative to adjustable block size cache for each metric. For each application, the 6 bars represent the fixed block size caches in increasing size from 1 word (uppermost bar) to 32 words (lowermost bar).

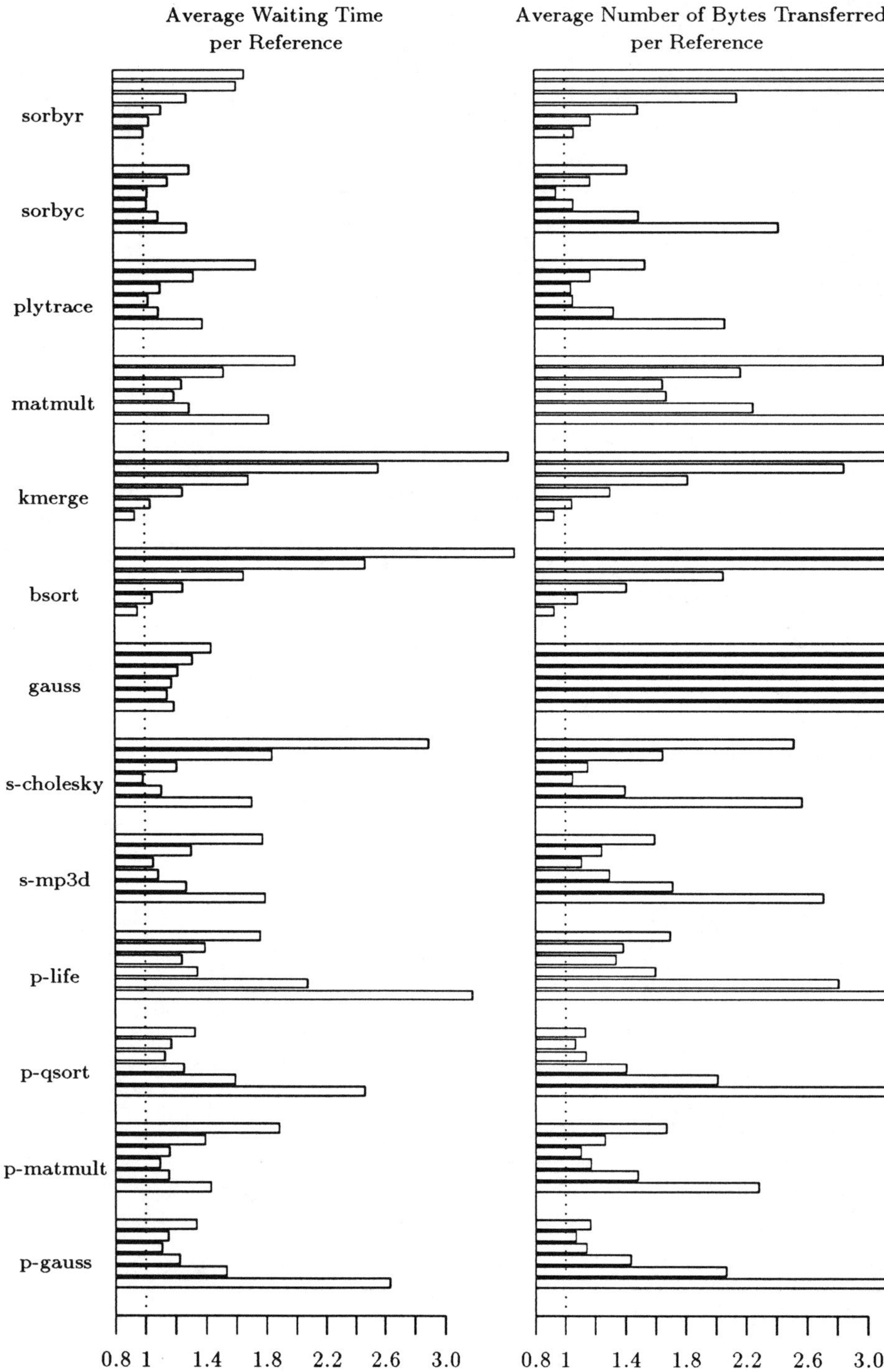

Application	Splits	Merges	Failed Merges	Fraction of References
sorbyr	148	425	1700	0.000022
sorbyc	19409	1870	72073	0.000891
plytrace	5780	689	46078	0.003413
matmult	267	148	3668	0.000879
kmerge	33	3991	9752	0.001260
bsort	25	5121	12889	0.000763
gauss	929	7010	16038	0.000089
s-cholesky	51061	54539	393371	0.012903
s-mp3d	14524	9857	1282708	0.064393
p-life	125	153	1521841	0.020911
p-qsort	2250	1398	471455	0.019405
p-matmult	73	19	16998	0.002449
p-gauss	858	689	814019	0.028481

Table 3: Number of splits, merges, and failed merges, and the fraction of all references that cause one of the three operations.

only 929 splits and 7010 merges take place during the execution of *gauss*, which contains over 270 million references. Nevertheless, these few operations lower the average waiting time per reference by 15% and the average number of words transferred by a factor of 3.

Figure 2 illustrates how successful the adjustable block size cache organization is at adapting the block size to different programs. It shows the fraction of cache blocks of a given size transferred between processors when using an adjustable block size cache. The C-threads programs, which have good processor locality, mostly transfer large cache blocks, while the Presto programs, which exhibit fine-grain sharing, mostly transfer one word blocks. Nearly every program used all the block sizes eventually, however in many cases, block sizes of 8, 4, and 2 words are used only while collecting sufficient reference information to continue splitting into smaller blocks.

The large percentage of one-word blocks among the Presto applications suggests that a cache block size of one word might be best for those programs. But Figure 1 shows that a block size of 4 or 8 words is best for the Presto programs, which suggests that the amount of fine-grain sharing at the level of a single word in those programs is not sufficient to offset the benefits of a longer block size for exploiting processor locality. As can be inferred from Figure 2 significant number of words are transferred in larger blocks, even though there is fine-grain sharing in the Presto programs. This illustrates the advantage of an adjustable block size cache; a large percentage of all words are transferred in large blocks, but small blocks are used as necessary to eliminate false sharing.

Figure 2 also explains why a cache with a fixed block size of 32 words performs better than an adjustable block size cache on *kmerge* and *bsort*. In both cases, the ideal block size is 32 words, so an adjustable block size cache with an initial block size of 16 words must merge all the buddy blocks over time. We can see from Figure 2 that in fact 25-30% of all transfers did use blocks of size 32 words, but there simply were not enough merge opportunities over the lifetime of the execution to allow all the buddy blocks to merge. There were more merge opportunities during the execution of *sorbyr*, which was able to merge often enough so that 70% of all transfers were of size 32 words.

Figure 2: Fraction of block transfers of a given size using an adjustable block size cache. For each application, the 6 bars represent the fixed block size caches in increasing size from 1 word (uppermost bar) to 32 words (lowermost bar).

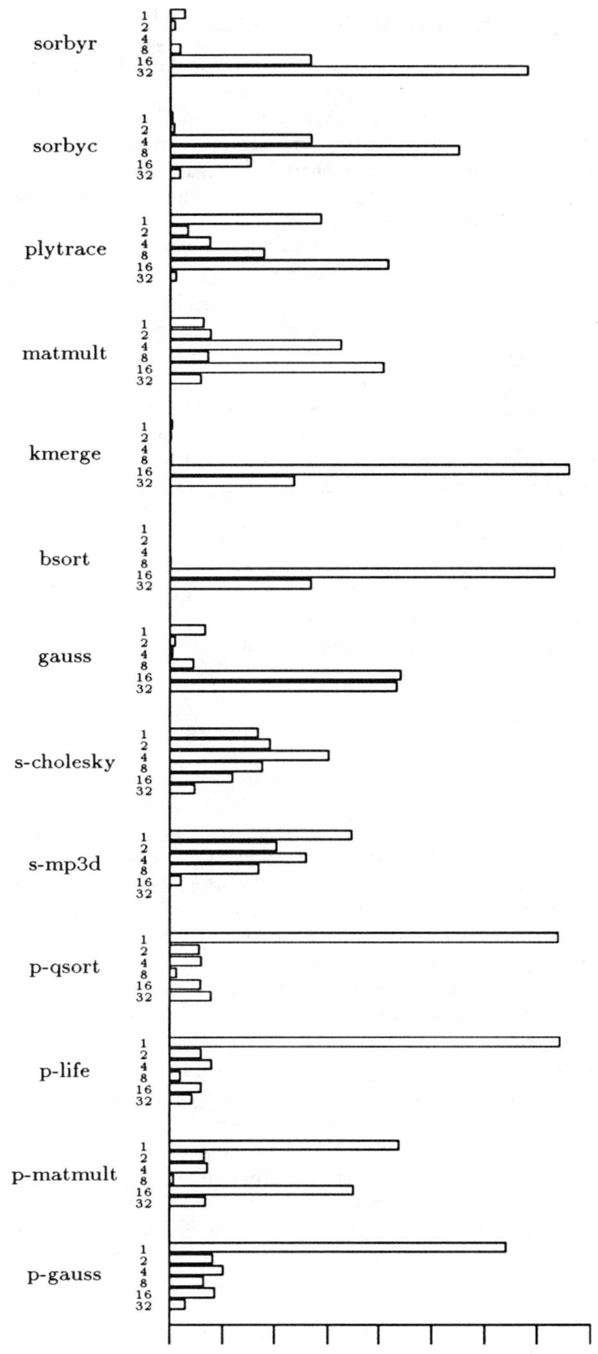

5 Effects of Adjustable Block Size Cache Parameters

In this section we discuss the tradeoffs to be considered when selecting the split and merge threshold values, the initial block size, the maximum and minimum block size, and the amount of reference history maintained in the split-merge counter. We also quantify the effect of each of these parameters in our simulations.

5.1 Split and Merge Thresholds

The split and merge thresholds determine how quickly the block size adjusts to reference behavior. By choosing small values for these thresholds, we can encourage both splits and merges to occur. In our simulations, we set the split threshold to 2 and the merge threshold to 1. We chose small values for both to encourage changes in the block size; we chose a slightly smaller value for the merge threshold because the conditions for merge arise less frequently.

Additional simulations showed that small changes in the split threshold do not alter the results significantly. For example, setting the split threshold to 1 instead of 2 for *s-cholesky* increased the average waiting time per reference by 6%, and the number of words transferred by 2%. No other program was affected this much by the change in split threshold. Raising the split threshold to 3 increased both metrics by 1% for *qsort*, but improved the metrics for *s-cholesky* by 3%. The *C-threads* programs were insensitive to these changes in the split threshold.

Small changes in the merge threshold did not affect performance much either. Even for programs that prefer large cache blocks (such as *bsort* and *kmerge*), raising the merge threshold to 2 increased the average waiting time per reference by only 3%, and the number of words transferred by 5%.

5.2 Initial Block Size

The initial block size is an important parameter for the adjustable block size cache because it sets the starting point from which we attempt to converge to the optimal block size. The smaller the number of steps (in splits or merges) between the initial block size and the optimal block size for a given piece of data within an application, the better the performance of the adjustable block size cache.

In our application suite, the optimal block size varies between 4 words and 32 words, therefore it would be reasonable to set the initial block size to either 8 or 16 words. We chose 16 words as the initial block size because the conditions for a split are easier to satisfy than the conditions for a merge. However, changing the initial block size to 8 words did have a significant effect in some cases. For example, lowering the initial block size to 8 words increased both the average waiting time per reference and the number of words transferred by about 20% for *kmerge*, which prefers longer lines. For this same program, increasing the initial block size from 16 words to 32 words improved the average waiting time per reference by 7% and decreased the average number of words transferred by 24%.

Similar changes in the initial block size had the opposite effect on the Presto programs, which require lots of splits. Raising the initial block size to 32 words increased the average waiting time per reference of *p-qsort* by 11%, and the number of words transferred per reference by 40%. On the other hand, lowering the initial block size to 8 words improved the average waiting time per reference of *p-qsort* by 9%. The smaller initial block size did not help *p-matmult* however, where it increased the average waiting time per reference by 5%.

It is somewhat surprising that the best fixed block size for a given program is not always the best initial block size for that program. For example, an initial block size of 16 words proved to be the best for *p-matmult*, even though a cache with a fixed line size of 8 words performs better than a cache with a fixed line size of 16 words on that program. We can see from Figure 2 that when the initial block size is 16 words, the vast majority of all transfers are of size 1 word or 16 words. Although only 8% of all transfers are of size 32 words, these transfers account for 25% of all the data transferred. If we change the initial block size to 8 words, too few merge operations occur. As a result, only a few transfers use a cache block with 16 words, and none use a cache block with 32 words. It is this lack of merge operations that causes a cache with an initial block size of 8 words to perform worse on *p-matmult* than a cache with an initial block size of 16 words, even though a fixed line size of 8 words provides better performance than a fixed line size of 16 words on this same program.

5.3 Maximum Block Size

The maximum block size is determined by the size of a cache line. A single cache line should be big enough to exploit spatial locality, but not so big that most of the cache line goes unused. Thus, there is a tradeoff between the performance benefits of a larger cache line and the cost of unused cache space.

As seen in Figure 1, three applications (*sorbyr*, *kmerge*, and *bsort*) perform best when the line size is 32 words. The average waiting time per reference increases by about 10% when the line size is fixed at 16 words, and by 30% or more when the line size is fixed at 8 words. This data suggests that shrinking the maximum block size in an adjustable block size cache would adversely affect the performance of these programs. On the other hand, shrinking the maximum block size could actually help the performance of other programs, since doing so might preclude unnecessary merge operations.

To see the effect of a smaller cache line size (maximum block size) on cache performance, we ran several simulations of the adjustable block size cache using 16 words as the maximum block size. We would expect *sorbyr* to suffer the most, since (as seen in Figure 2) this is the only program that uses 32 word blocks for the majority of all transfers. Restricting the maximum block size to 16 words produced a 14% increase in the number of words transferred by *sorbyr*, but only a 3% increase in average waiting time. For *kmerge*, which also performs best when the block size is 32 words, the average waiting time per reference degraded by only 3% as well; even when the maximum block size is 32 words, the vast majority of block transfers are 16 words in size.

The performance of two other programs improved with the smaller cache line size. The average waiting time per reference for *p-matmult* and *p-qsort* decreased by 3-4% with the smaller line size; the average number of words transferred per reference decreased by about 10%.

These results point out the relationship between the merge threshold and the maximum block size. When the merge threshold is low (as it was in our simulations), some unnecessary merges take place, as in the case of *p-matmult* and *p-qsort*. For these programs and others, a large maximum block size simply increases the opportunity for unnecessary merge operations. Shrinking the maximum block size or raising the merge threshold would prevent unnecessary merges, but either alternative would adversely affect the performance of other programs that require merge operations to produce an appropriate block size. Raising the merge threshold makes it difficult for programs such as *kmerge*, *qsort*, and *sorbyr* to quickly adjust the block size upwards, while shrinking the maximum block size prevents these programs from ever achieving the desired block size of 32 words. Given the relationship between the maximum block size and the merge threshold, and the relatively small performance improvements offered by large cache lines, we can attain most of the performance advantages of an adjustable block size cache with 32-word cache lines by using 16-word cache lines and a small merge threshold.

5.4 Minimum Block Size

Several programs perform best with a fixed block size equal to 32 words. There is no program that performs best with a fixed block size equal to 1 word, however. In fact, every program performs better with at least three other block sizes than with the minimum block size of 1 word. This fact suggests that limiting the possible block sizes to 2 words or larger would not seriously affect the performance of the adjustable block size cache. Figure 2 suggests the opposite conclusion however, since in several cases a majority of all cache block transfers are 1 word in size. In particular, 75% of all transfers in *p-qsort* and *p-life* contain 1 word cache blocks. We would expect these programs to suffer disproportionately when the minimum block size is greater than 1.

Raising the minimum block size to 2 words increases the average waiting time per reference by 5% and the average number of words transferred by 7% for *p-qsort*; a minimum block size of 4 words increases the two metrics by 11% and 18%, respectively. By contrast, raising the minimum block size to 4 words improves the performance of *s-cholesky* by 9% and 5% respectively for the two metrics. The reason for this improvement can be seen in Figure 1; *s-cholesky* performs poorly when the block size is small, and our small split threshold allows too many small blocks to be created when the minimum block size is less than 4 words.

The relationship between the minimum block size and split threshold is analogous to the relationship between the maximum block size and the merge threshold. When the split threshold is low and the minimum block size is small, too many splits can occur. This situation arises whenever a program initializes adjacent data from different processors (which causes splits), but then exhibits good processor locality for subsequent accesses. On the other hand, some programs perform best with a small block size, and a low split threshold that allows blocks to shrink quickly. An increase in the split threshold or the minimum block size penalizes these programs.

To see the effect of the block size range on performance, we reran several of the simulations from the previous section using a minimum block size of 2 words, a maximum block size of 16 words, an initial block size of 16 words, a split threshold of 2, and a merge threshold of 1. The greatest impact we observed occurred during execution of *matmult*, which saw an increase in the average waiting time per reference of 7%, and a 22% increase in the number of words transferred. The two metrics increased by 5% and 8% respectively for *bsort*, and 2% and 9% respectively for *sorbyr*. There was essentially no change in the metrics for *p-qsort*, *kmerge* and *s-cholesky*. The two metrics for *p-matmult* actually improved by 4% and 7%, respectively. Once again, we conclude that most of the performance advantages of an adjustable block size cache can be had by avoiding extremes in the range of blocks sizes, and using small split and merge thresholds.

5.5 Reference History

The split-merge counter records the reference history for a cache block as it moves from one cache to another. We would like the information in the counter to be as current as possible without resorting to timestamps or aging. We would also like to ensure that slight changes in reference behavior do not cause an excessive number of splits or merges to occur.

One way to control the ease with which the cache adjusts to changes in reference behavior is to limit the size of the split-merge counter. With a small counter, reference information is quickly replaced, ensuring that information accumulated during an earlier phase of execution cannot prevent splits or merges during a subsequent phase. With a large counter, the cache is less sensitive to short-term reference patterns. Of course the counter must be big enough to hold the integers between the (negative) merge threshold and the split threshold, but a larger counter can also record reference information that temporarily exceeds the thresholds, such as occurs when reference information from several copies of a cache block is brought together.

All of our previous experiments used a 4-bit split-merge counter. To test the sensitivity of our results to this parameter we reran our experiments with a 3-bit counter and an 8-bit counter. All other parameters remained the same. Several applications, including *sorbyr*, *matmult*, and *kmerge*, showed no sensitivity to the size of the split-merge counter, which suggests there are no changes in reference behavior during execution of these applications. For *s-cholesky*, the two metrics improved by 5% and 2% respectively when the 8-bit counter was used; this was the only case where a larger counter improved performance. The performance of *bsort* was unaffected by the use of a 3-bit counter, but the 8-bit counter caused an increase of 5% and 8% respectively in our two metrics. The performance of *p-qsort* and *p-matmult* improved a little with the 3-bit counter, and deteriorated somewhat under the 8-bit counter (a 7% increase in average waiting time and a 15% increase in the number of words transferred). We conclude from these experiments that small split-merge counters (say, 3 or 4 bits) not only save space, but may also provide the best performance across a range of applications.

6 Conclusions

The performance of scalable coherent caches is extremely sensitive to the degree of sharing and spatial locality exhibited by application programs. Unfortunately, these attributes vary widely across applications. For programs with a significant amount of write-sharing, a small cache blocks minimize the number of expensive invalidations. For programs with a high degree of spatial locality, large cache blocks minimize the number of expensive transfers from one node to another. A mismatch between the block size and the granularity of sharing can cause serious performance degradation, over 300% in some cases.

To achieve the best match between the cache block size and the degree of sharing and spatial locality exhibited by different programs, we introduced a cache organization that dynamically adjusts the block size based on the reference behavior of a program. Using simulation we showed that an adjustable block size cache provides the best performance over a range of applications. For every fixed block size, at least one program suffered a 33% increase in the average waiting time per reference, and a factor of 2 increase in the average number of words transferred per reference, when compared against the adjustable block size cache. For most programs only two fixed block sizes (4 words and 8 words) were competitive with the adjustable block size cache, and in both cases the average waiting time per reference was never better than that produced by the adjustable block size cache, and was 25% higher for at least 4 programs. In one case, a block size of 4 words lowered the average number of words transferred per reference by 6%, but in three cases it increased the number of words referenced by a factor of 2 or more. When we consider all the applications in our simulations, there are only a few cases where adjusting the block size did not provide the best performance, and even then it was within 7% of the best fixed block size alternative. We conclude that adjusting the block size can significantly improve cache performance, especially when there is variability in the granularity of sharing exhibited by applications.

Acknowledgments

William Bolosky, Rob Fowler, Evangalos Markatos and Michael Scott provided many helpful comments on earlier versions of this paper.

References

[1] B.N. Bershad, E.D. Lazowska, and H.M. Levy. Presto: A system for object-oriented parallel programming. *Software - Practice and Experience*, 18(8), August 1988.

[2] W.J. Bolosky, M.L. Scott, R.P. Fitzgerald, R.J. Fowler, and A.L. Cox. NUMA policies and their relation to memory architecture. *Proc. 4th ASPLOS*, pages 212–221, 1991.

[3] L. Bomans, D. Roose, and R. Hempel. The Argonne/GMD macros in FORTRAN for portable parallel programming and their implementation on the intel iPSC/2. *Journal of Parallel Computing*, 15:119–132, September 1990.

[4] L.M. Censier and P. Feautier. A new solution to coherence problems in multicache systems. *IEEE Transactions on Computers*, 27:1112–1118, December 1978.

[5] D.R. Cheriton, H.A. Goosen, and P. Machanick. Restructuring a parallel simulation to improve cache behavior in a shared-memory mutiprocessor: A first experience. In *Intl. Symp. on Shared Memory Multiprocessing*, April 1991.

[6] D.R. Cheriton, A. Gupta, P.D. Boyle, and H.A. Goosen. The VMP multiprocessor: Initial experience, refinements, and performance evaluation. In *15 International Symposium on Computer Architecture*, pages 410–421, June 1988.

[7] S.J. Eggers and R.H. Katz. A characterization of sharing in parallel programs and its application to coherency protocol evaluation. In *15 International Symposium on Computer Architecture*, pages 373–383, May 1988.

[8] S.J. Eggers and R.H. Katz. The effect of sharing on the cache and bus performance of parallel programs. In *Proc. 3rd ASPLOS*, pages 257–270, April 1989.

[9] S.J. Eggers and Jeremiassen T.E. Eliminating false sharing. Technical report, Department of Computer Science and Engineering, University of Washington, December 1990.

[10] A. Gupta, J. Hennessy, K. Gharachorloo, Todd Mowry, and W.D. Weber. Comparative evaluation of latency reducing and tolerating techniques. In *18 International Symposium on Computer Architecture*, pages 254–263, May 1991.

[11] A. Gupta and W.D. Weber. Analysis of cache invalidation patterns in shared-memory multiprocessors. In *Cache and Interconnect Architectures in Multiprocessors*, pages 83–108. Kulwer Academic Publishers, 1990.

[12] D. Lenoski, J. Laudon, K. Gharachorloo, A. Gupta, and J. Hennessy. The directory-based cache coherence protocol for the DASH multiprocessor. In *17 International Symposium on Computer Architecture*, pages 148–159, May 1990.

[13] B.W. O'Krafka and R.A. Newton. An empirical evaluation of two memory-efficient directory methods. In *17 International Symposium on Computer Architecture*, pages 138–147, June 1990.

[14] J.P. Singh, W-D. Weber, and A. Gupta. Splash: Stanford parallel applications for shared-memory. Technical report, Department of Computer Science, Stanford University, April 1991.

[15] J. Torrellas, M.S. Lam, and J.L. Hennessy. Shared data placement optimizations to reduce multiprocessor cache miss rates. In *Proc. 1990 ICPP Volume II*, pages 266–270, August 1990.

Performance Optimization of Pipelined Primary Caches *

Kunle Olukotun
Computer Systems Laboratory
Stanford University, CA 94305

Trevor Mudge and Richard Brown
Dept. Electrical Engineering and Computer Science
University of Michigan, Ann Arbor, MI 48109

Abstract

The CPU cycle time of a high-performance processor is usually determined by the the access time of the primary cache. As processors speeds increase, designers will have to increase the number of pipeline stages used to fetch data from the cache in order to reduce the dependence of CPU cycle time on cache access time. This paper studies the performance advantages of a pipelined cache for a GaAs implementation of the MIPS based architecture using a design methodology that includes long traces of multiprogrammed applications and detailed timing analysis. The study evaluates instruction and data caches with various pipeline depths, cache sizes, block sizes, and refill penalties. The impact on CPU cycle time of these alternatives is also factored into the evaluation. Hardware-based and software-based strategies are considered for hiding the branch and load delays which may be required to avoid pipeline hazards. The results show that software-based methods for mitigating the penalty of branch delays can be as successful as the hardware-based *branch-target buffer* approach, despite the code-expansion inherent in the software methods. The situation is similar for load delays; while hardware-based dynamic methods hide more delay cycles than do static approaches, they may give up the advantage by extending the cycle time. Because these methods are quite successful at hiding small numbers of branch and load delays, and because processors with pipelined caches also have shorter CPU cycle times and larger caches, a significant performance advantage is gained by using two to three pipeline stages to fetch data from the cache.

1 Introduction

The organization of the cache has a significant impact on CPU performance for two reasons. First, the access time of the cache usually sets the CPU cycle time. Second, the miss rate of the cache determines how much of the time the CPU is stalled waiting for data to be fetched from main memory. The access time and miss rate of a cache are determined by its size and its set-associativity. Making the cache smaller or less set-associative will reduce the cache access time and increase the cache miss rate.

As the speeds of CPUs increase relative to the speed of DRAM-based main memory, the cost of missing the cache increases. This presents computer designers with the problem of building a cache that has both a low miss rate and a short access time. A low miss rate ensures that the high cost of cache misses do not dominate execution time and a short access time ensures that the cache does not slow down the rest of the CPU. A partial solution to this cache design problem is to provide more than one level of cache memory. In a two-level cache hierarchy, the level one (primary) cache is made small and fast to match the CPU speed and the level two (secondary) cache is made slower and much larger to keep the overall cache miss rate low. Although this is better than having a single large cache, the primary cache will still limit the CPU cycle time. The only way to reduce the effect of cache access time on processor cycle time is to increase the number of cache pipeline stages. This spreads the fixed delay of the cache access time over more CPU cycles making it possible for the CPU cycle time to be reduced. Implementing a pipelined cache involves splitting the access of the cache into two or more stages and placing latches between each stage. Some of the pipelining may be implemented inside the SRAM itself [CCS+91]. An example of a processor that uses this technique is the MIPS R4000 which takes two pipeline stages to access an on-chip cache [KH92]. It is likely that as microprocessor speeds increase we will see wider use of pipelined caches.

While cache performance evaluation has received considerable attention [Smi78, Hil87, Prz90], the effect of pipelining cache access has received far less attention. This paper presents a methodology for accurately evaluating and optimizing the performance of pipelined primary caches and a study that shows the performance improvement that pipelined caches can provide.

This study was done during the design of microprocessor based on the MIPS instruction set architecture (ISA) [KH92] that is to implemented in GaAs direct-coupled FET logic with multichip module packaging [MBB+91]. A general block diagram of the processor, annotated with the ranges of parameters considered in this study, is shown in Figure 1. The two-level cache organization is necessary to hide the large disparity in speeds between the processor and main memory. The level one (L1) cache is split in to instruction (L1-I) and data (L1-D) halves to provide an instruction or data access every cycle. The justification of these design choices is discussed in detail in [Olu91].

Increasing the number of cache pipeline stages can reduce the CPU cycle time, but it will increase the number of load and branch delay cycles due to pipeline hazards. If no useful instructions are executed during these delay cycles they will increase the number of

*This work was supported by Defense Advanced Research Projects Agency under DARPA/ARO Contract No. DAAL03-90-C-0028

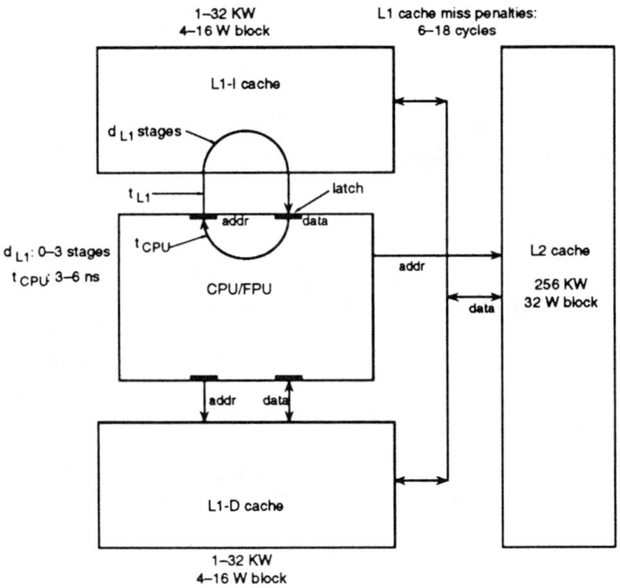

Figure 1: The basic system architecture and the range of parameters that are considered in this study. The access paths of the pipelined primary instruction cache are shown.

cycles a program takes to execute, and potentially overwhelm the performance benefits of pipelining. Our experiments show that as many as three load or branch delay cycles can be hidden by static compile-time instruction scheduling or by dynamic hardware-based methods. Static schemes are more effective at hiding branch delay cycles, but dynamic methods are more effective at filling load delay slots. When these results are combined with results from cache simulation and timing analysis the conclusions are that the caches with two to three pipeline stages have higher performance than caches with less pipeline stages.

The organization of the rest of this paper is as follows. The next section of the paper defines the pipelined cache optimization problem and describes the design optimization methods used in this study. Sections 3 shows how the number of clocks per instruction (CPI) are affected by the primary instruction and data cache organizations. In particular, the impact of pipelining is examined. Section 4 shows how the cycle time, t_{CPU}, are affected by the size of the primary cache. The results of Sections 3 and 4 are combined to yield the final performance evaluation of pipelined primary caches in Section 5. Concluding remarks are given in Section 6.

2 The Primary Cache Optimization Problem

A widely recognized metric for architectural performance comparison is the time it takes to execute a realistic set of benchmarks [HP90]. Given a specific ISA and compiler, a performance metric that is directly proportional to execution time is *time per instruction* (TPI). The equation for TPI can be written as,

$$\mathrm{TPI} = \mathrm{CPI} \times t_{CPU} \tag{1}$$

In this paper we use TPI as the performance metric.

The objective of primary (L1) cache optimization is to select a cache organization that minimizes TPI subject to implementation technology constraints. To solve this optimization problem, we must determine the effect cache organization, including the number of cache pipeline stages, has on t_{CPU} and CPI.

If the L1 cache access is on the critical timing path, t_{CPU} depends on the access time of L1, t_{L1}, and its pipeline depth, d_{L1}. The value of t_{L1} is defined as the elapsed time, measured in nanoseconds, between sending an address to the cache and receiving the data from that address. The value of t_{CPU} is related to t_{L1} and d_{L1}, as follows,

$$t_{CPU} = \frac{t_{L1}}{d_{L1}} \tag{2}$$

Although the details of the timing are more complicated, for the purposes of this discussion, the access path to the L1 cache can be viewed as part of a circular pipeline with $(d_{L1} + 1)$ stages clocked at intervals of t_{CPU}, see Figure 1. The address generation takes one cycle and the cache access takes d_{L1}. From (2), it follows that fixing d_{L1} causes t_{CPU} to get longer as t_{L1} increases. In particular, larger or more set-associative caches which have longer access times result in longer CPU cycle times. Increasing the value of d_{L1} by placing more latches along the L1 access path to increase pipelining makes it possible to reduce t_{CPU}. The amount of reduction depends upon the placement of the latches, the latch delay overhead, and the clocking scheme [Olu91].

Given a constant time L1 miss penalty, then CPI depends on t_{CPU}, d_{L1}, and the miss rate of the cache, m_{L1}. As the cache is made larger or more set-associative m_{L1} gets smaller and so does CPI. With a constant time L1 miss penalty, CPI decreases with increasing t_{CPU} because fewer CPU cycles are required to handle a miss. The dependence of CPI on d_{L1} is more subtle. In general, CPI is an increasing function of d_{L1} because increasing d_{L1} will increase the number of load and branch delay cycles that cannot be hidden. Furthermore, software techniques used to hide branch delays often replicate code, resulting in larger static code sizes which in turn may lead to higher L1 instruction (L1-I) cache miss ratios.

As we have seen, CPI and t_{CPU} depend on both the organization which specifies the pipeline depth, size and associativity of the cache and the hardware implementation technology which determines the access time of the cache and the delays of the rest of the CPU. It is evident that organization and technology are interdependent because CPI is dependent on t_{CPU} and both are dependent on d_{L1}. The further dependence of CPI on the workload of the CPU necessitates that t_{CPU} and CPI be determined by using a simulation-based multilevel design methodology that considers the organization and technology aspects of cache design together.

The multilevel optimization design methodology that we use in this study combines the optimization of the traditionally separate organization and implementation phases of system design [OBL+91]. This results in a system design that is optimized for performance in a specific technology. The process of multilevel optimization uses optimizing compilers, trace-driven simulation, delay macro-modeling, and timing analysis to accurately predict the TPI of an architecture [Olu91]. Delay macro-modeling and timing analysis are used to predict t_{CPU} while trace-driven simulation of optimized code is used to predict CPI. The timing analyzer used in this study, $minT_C$, is capable of finding the minimum clock cycle time of a synchronous digital circuit [SMO90]. The compiler used in this study is one that was developed by MIPS for the R2000 instruction set architecture [MIP88]. The trace-driven simulator used in this study, `cacheUM`, is capable of evaluating a variety of two-level cache organizations and techniques for reducing the effect of load and branch delays [Olu91].

The process of multilevel optimization systematically improves the performance of a base architecture. A base architecture is defined by a register transfer level (RTL) organization and implementation technology. The main requirement of a suitable base architecture is that it be as simple as possible in order to accurately assess the performance impact of adding to it. Taking the base architecture as a starting point in the design space, and using the performance analysis tools, multilevel optimization proceeds as

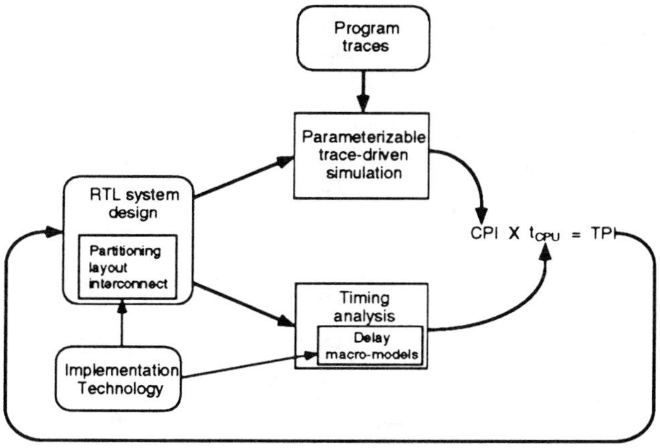

Figure 2: Multilevel design optimization.

follows. The base architecture is simulated to establish a base level of performance. To explore the effect of changes in the base architecture a set of candidate designs is encoded into the trace-driven simulator and changes to the RTL model are made to reflect the new organization. The compiler is also changed to produce code that is optimized for the new RTL organizations. The performance of the set of designs is simulated using trace-driven simulation to reveal the general nature of the CPI-t_{CPU} tradeoffs. Once these tradeoffs has been established, delay modeling, timing analysis and floor planning provide the technology constraints. These technology constraints make the CPI-t_{CPU} tradeoffs specific and allow the selection of the highest performing design alternative. The RTL specification represented by this design choice becomes the new base architecture. This process of generation and evaluation of different organizations continues until the design meets the performance specifications or the costs of further changes in organization are not justified by the performance improvements they provide. The multilevel design methodology is diagrammed in Figure 2.

In the remainder of this paper the multilevel optimization design approach is used to study the performance of pipelined primary caches. The trace-driven simulations used in this study use multiprogramming traces created from the benchmark programs listed in Table 1. The CPI values presented in this paper represent the weighted harmonic mean of all of the benchmarks in this table. The weights for each benchmark correspond its fraction of total execution time. The instruction count used to calculate CPI is that of optimized MIPS R2000 code for for an architecture with no load or branch delay cycles.

3 CPI Measurements

3.1 The effect of branch delays

As long as the CPU is executing instructions sequentially, the pipeline depth of the L1-I cache access has no effect on CPI. However, when a control transfer instruction (CTI) is executed, the next instruction to be fetched must be delayed until its address is known. Assuming that the branch condition of a conditional branch CTI can be evaluated in one cycle the pipeline depth of the L1-I cache, d_{L1-I}, is the number of cycles by which the next instruction is delayed. These cycles are called *branch delay cycles*. Since most applications dynamically execute control transfer instructions 10–20 % of the time (Table 1), a unit increase in d_{L1-I} will result in a 10–20 % increase in CPI. A number of hardware and software schemes have been proposed to limit this effect on CPI [Smi81, LS84, MH86, Lil88, HCC89, KT91]. Two representative schemes are evaluated here: a hardware-based branch-target buffer, and a software-based delayed branches with optional squashing.

A branch-target buffer (BTB) is a cache whose entries contain address tags and target addresses of branch instructions. Every instruction address is checked against the tags in the BTB. Those addresses that hit are predicted to be branches (CTI). The BTB simulated here uses the 2 b (bit) prediction scheme described in [LS84]. If the BTB predicts a branch taken, the target address is used as the next instruction address. If the BTB can be accessed in a single cycle and its prediction is correct, it can completely hide the branch delay. However, when the BTB miss predicts a branch, we assume a one cycle stall is required to fill the BTB with the correct information in addition to the stall cycles necessary for branch delay. This penalty is the minimum that can be expected. The size of the BTB that will be evaluated in this study is 256 entries. With two 32 b addresses plus 2 b of prediction per entry, the BTB requires approximately 2 KB of SRAM storage. This size represents the upper limit of an SRAM having single cycle access if we assume that the ALU adder sets the lower bound on cycle time [Olu91].

In the other approach evaluated, delayed branches with optional squashing, each branch instruction is followed by a number of instructions called *branch delay slots* equal to the number of branch delay cycles in the architecture. The compiler must rearrange the code so that these delay slots contain useful instructions. For each branch there are three potential sources of useful instructions: (1) before the branch instruction, (2) after the branch instruction, or (3) from the branch target. Rearrangements that move instructions from before the branch are always correct no matter what direction the branch takes. In contrast, instructions from after the branch must be squashed if the branch is taken and instructions from the branch target must be squashed if the branch is not taken in order to preserve program correctness. Squashing dynamically converts delay slots instructions to `noop` instructions. In addition, there is a code expansion penalty associated with using instructions from the branch target because these instructions must be replicated. We will consider a delay slot to be "hidden" if it is filled with useful instructions that do not require squashing.

To evaluate the performance of these schemes for reducing the impact of branch delay cycles we need to know the number of delay cycles, the number of these that are hidden, the effect on CPI, and the effect of the expanded static code size associated with delayed branches. Because we did not have access to a retargetable compiler, a post-processor for MIPS object code was developed to collect this information. This post-processor can schedule code for architectures having differing numbers of branch delay slots. It creates a translation file that contains a mapping of instruction addresses from the MIPS code, which assumes one branch delay slot without squashing, to those of an architecture that may have a different number of delay slots with optional squashing.

A translation file for an architecture with zero delay cycles is used in the BTB experiments. Such a file is produced by removing all `noop` instructions that appear after CTIs in the original MIPS object code and then recording the mapping between the basic block entry points of the original object code and the transformed code.

The object code for a one cycle branch delay architecture is the same as that produced by the MIPS compiler. However, the MIPS ISA does not include optional squashing and so it has less freedom to move instructions from after the branch and from the branch target into the branch delay slot. Cases where the compiler was unable to move any instructions into the branch delay slot have a `noop` instruction following CTI. The procedure that is followed in such cases is covered in the general (two or more) delay slot insertion scheme described below.

In the description of the general delay slot insertion procedure that follows, b is the number of branch delay cycles (slots) in the

Benchmark	Description	Inst. (M)	Loads (% inst.)	Stores (% inst.)	Branches (% inst.)	Syscalls
5diff	File comparison (I)	218.3	15.3	3.4	20.7	305
awk	String matching and processing (I)	209.5	19.0	12.6	14.3	101
doducd	Monte Carlo simulation (D)	96.3	31.0	10.0	8.7	427
espresso	Logic minimization (I)	238.0	19.9	5.6	16.2	17
gcc	C compiler (I)	235.7	23.3	13.8	20.1	487
integral	Numerical integration (D)	110.5	37.0	10.4	7.6	12
linpackd	Linear equation solver (D)	4.0	37.4	19.7	5.4	10
loops	First 12 Livermore kernels (D)	275.5	29.3	10.9	5.3	3
matrix500	500 x 500 matrix operations (S)	202.2	24.3	3.5	3.5	10
nroff	Text formatting (I)	15.7	22.4	10.8	24.6	1701
small	Stanford small benchmarks (I/S)	16.7	19.9	8.8	19.6	0
spice2g6	Circuit simulator (S)	297.3	29.8	8.6	8.0	395
tex	Typesetting (I)	133.8	30.2	14.2	11.7	697
wolf33	Simulated annealing placement (I)	115.4	30.0	7.5	14.8	407
xlswins	X-windows application (I)	52.2	22.5	17.7	17.1	65294
yacc	Parser generator (I)	193.9	19.6	2.4	25.2	49
Total		2414.9	24.7	8.7	13	69915

Table 1: Benchmarks that were used to create the multiprogramming traces. Integer benchmarks are denoted by (I), single precision floating point benchmarks by (S), and double precision floating point by (D). The heading "Branches" represents all control transfer instructions.

Delay slots	% code increase
1	6
2	14
3	23

Table 2: Static code size increase versus the number of branch delay slots.

architecture that is being simulated. The term r is the number of branch delay slots that can be filled from before the branch and s is the number of delay slots that must be filled from the sequential path, from the branch-target path, or, in the case of register-indirect jumps, with noop instructions ($b = r + s$). The steps in the procedure are:

1. Check to see if the MIPS compiler inserted a noop instruction after the CTI. If it did, the CTI cannot be moved any higher in the basic block, Therefore, set $r = 0, s = b$ and go to step 3.

2. Move the CTI up in the basic block as far as the data dependencies of the preceding instructions allow. No attempt is made to rearrange the ordering of any other instructions in the basic block besides the CTI. The number of instructions that the CTI can be moved is r and, then, $s = b - r$.

3. Determine the prediction of the CTI. Backward branches and unconditional jumps are predicted to be *taken*. Forward branches are predicted to be *not taken*.

4. Insert s noop instructions after CTI that are predicted to be taken in order to simulate the instructions that are replicated from the target path.

When this procedure is completed, each CTI will have associated with it a value for s, the number of instructions in the delay slots that may need to be squashed, and a flag that indicates whether the CTI is predicted to be taken or not-taken. In the case of register-indirect jumps, set $s = 0$ because the target of these jumps is not computable at compile time and noop instructions will have to be fetched. The translation file contains values for s, the branch prediction flags, and the basic-block entry-point mappings.

Table 2 shows, for 1 to 3 branch delay slots, the average static code size increase for the benchmarks of this study compared to that of an architecture that has no delay slots. The code size increase comes from filling the delay slots of the 60 % of CTIs that are statically predicted to be taken. Measurements taken from our benchmarks indicate that the MIPS compiler is able to fill 54 % of all first branch delay slots with instructions from before the CTI. For CTIs predicted to be taken, this number decreases to 52 %. The rest of the delay slots for these CTIs must be filled with instructions from the target. The delay slots of register-indirect jumps cannot be filled with target instructions and so are filled with noop instructions. Register-indirect jumps make up roughly 10 % of all CTIs in our benchmarks.

Translation files enable us to use a trace from a computer with an ISA that has one branch delay slot and no squashing to simulate the instruction referencing behavior of a computer with b branch delay slots and optional squashing. Thus the translation files can be used to simulate the instruction cache behavior as follows. Each basic block entry-point instruction address that comes from an instrumented benchmark is translated to a new address using the data in the translation file. This address is used to simulate l sequential instruction references, where l is the length of the new basic-block.

For accurate cache simulation, we need not be concerned with the specific mechanism used to squash instructions in the delay slots, we need only ensure that the correct instruction reference stream is produced. To get the correct reference stream, it is necessary to check the prediction at each CTI. If the prediction at the CTI is that it will be taken and the prediction is correct, then the value of s associated with the CTI is added to the instruction address of the target basic block thus leaving $l - s$ instructions to be executed in the target basic block. This assumes that s instructions of the target basic block have been executed in the delay slots of the CTI. If there are fewer than s instructions in the target basic block, then the delay slots are assumed to be padded with noop instructions. If the prediction is that the CTI will be taken and the prediction is incorrect, then the instruction address of the sequential basic block is left unchanged. This simulates the effect of the extra delay slot instruction references. If the prediction is that the CTI will not be taken and the prediction is correct, then no action is taken because the sequential instructions are in the delay slots of the CTI. However, if the CTI is predicted not to be taken and the prediction is incorrect, then s extra instruction references are made in the sequential basic block before control is transferred to the target basic block.

Our experiments show that CPI increases as the number of branch delay slots is increased. This increase comes from two sources: (1) increases in the number of L1-I cache misses due to the larger code size and (2) the extra useless instruction references that are executed when the static branch prediction is incorrect. To measure the effect of the extra L1-I cache misses, various L1 cache configurations were simulated as the number of branch delay slots was varied from 0 to 3. Apart from delay slots, the other major parameters of

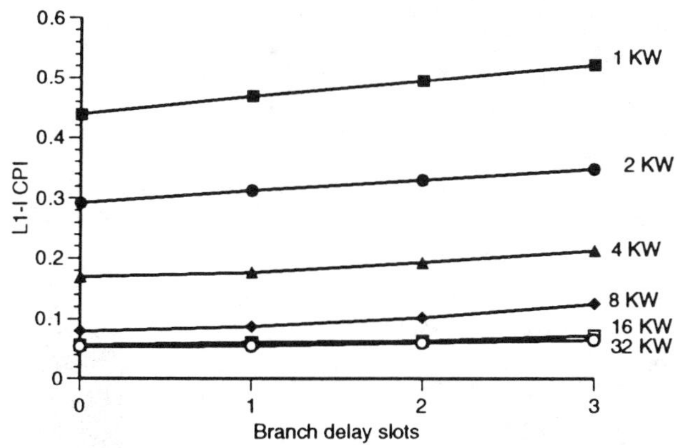

Figure 3: Effect of cache misses due to branch delay slots on L1-I performance: $B_{L1} = 4\,W$, $P_{L1} = 10\,cycles$.

the cache organization that were varied in these simulations were the L1-I cache size, S_{L1}, the line or block size, B_{L1}, and the L1 miss penalty, P_{L1}.

Cache experiments were performed for L1-I cache sizes that varied from 1 KW to 32 KW; for block sizes of 4 W, 8 W, and 16 W; and for L1 miss penalties of 6, 10, and 18 cycles. The miss penalties correspond to refill rates of 4, 2 and 1 word per cycle plus a 2 cycle startup. For each value of miss penalty the block size was selected to achieve the lowest CPI. The results of the experiment for the case $B_{L1} = 4$, $P_{L1} = 10$ are shown in Figure 3. For smaller miss penalties the slope and intercept of the lines is reduced and for larger miss penalties the slope and the intercept of the lines is increased. This reveals that the number of delay slots has a measurable impact on the performance of the L1-I cache. This impact diminishes as the cache size is increased and the miss penalty is decreased. For the smallest L1-I cache size of 1 KW (4 KB) the rate of increase in CPI is roughly 0.06 per delay slot for a miss penalty of 18 cycles. When the miss penalty is reduced to 6 cycles the rate of CPI increase drops to 0.015 per delay slot. For the largest L1-I cache size of 32 KW, the rate of increase in CPI is quite small. The rate of increase varies from 0.014 to 0.004 CPI per delay slot as the miss penalty is varied form 18 to 6 cycles.

Table 3 lists, for 1, 2 and 3 delay slots, the static branch prediction statistics, cycles per branch, and additional CPI due to extra instruction reference cycles. The data in this table support two conclusions. First, static branch prediction with optional squashing is an effective scheme for mitigating the branch-delay penalty. For example, since 13 % of instructions executed are CTIs, three branch delay slots could increase CPI by 39 %; in fact, the increase is only 8.7 %, due to good branch prediction. Secondly, the effect of instruction cache misses should not be ignored when considering the performance of aggressive static branch prediction schemes. Though this is less important for large caches and small miss penalties, it is noteworthy that the increase in CPI due to increased cache misses with three delay slots is 9 % for a 1 K-W L1-I cache with a 10-cycle miss penalty (see Figure 3).

Experiments with the hardware approach for hiding branch delay cycles show that the BTB achieves a hit rate of over 91 %; however, incorrect predictions reduce this hit rate to a branch prediction accuracy of 86%. This is still better than the static prediction accuracy of 70%. However, the overall effectiveness of the BTB method is reduced because an extra cycle is required to update the BTB with the correct information every time there is a BTB miss or an incorrect prediction. When these cycles are included in the branch penalty, the performance of the BTB is reduced to that shown in Table 4.

Delay cycles	Cycles per CTI	Extra CPI
1	1.44	0.057
2	1.65	0.082
3	1.85	0.110

Table 4: BTB prediction performance.

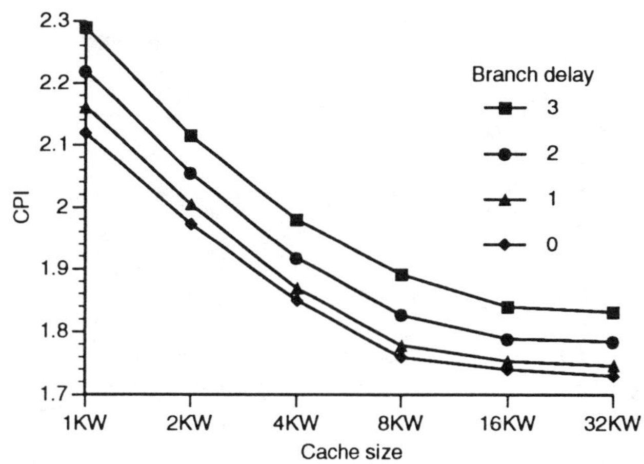

Figure 4: Branch delay slots versus L1-I cache size: $B_{L1} = 4\,W$, $P_{L1} = 10\,cycles$.

A comparison of Tables 3 and 4 shows that the static scheme performs better. This is because static rearrangement allows 0.5 to 0.8 of the delay slots to be filled with instructions from before the CTI, so that fewer cycles are wasted even if the CTI prediction is incorrect. The BTB scheme loses one cycle per delay slot every time a CTI misses the BTB or the CTI prediction is incorrect. One could argue that the relatively small size of the BTB compromises its performance; recall, though, that the BTB was restricted to 256 entries to ensure single cycle access, which is necessary to make this scheme worthwhile. Though they did not investigate the effects of code expansion, other researchers have also shown that static branch prediction techniques using sophisticated program profiling and fetch strategies are competitive with much larger BTBs [HCC89, KT91]. Of course, for static prediction, the additional CPI due to increased L1-I misses (see Figure 3) must be considered; for small cache sizes and large miss penalties, this would give the performance edge to the BTB approach. Nevertheless, because its performance is roughly comparable and its hardware cost is lower, the static prediction scheme is used in the remainder of the L1 cache experiments.

Figure 4 plots the total CPI for the same values of L1-I cache size, numbers of delay slots, and penalty that was used in Figure 3 This figure shows that for L1-I cache sizes of 1–16 KW, it is always possible to decrease the CPI of the system by doubling the cache size and increasing the number of delay slots by one. The reason for this is that in this region of L1-I cache size the relative increase in CPI from increasing the number of delay slots (0.03–0.15) is less than the decrease in CPI from doubling the cache size (0.05–0.2).

Finally, an example of the dependence of CPI on t_{CPU} is illustrated in Figure 5 which plots CPI versus t_{CPU} for various cache sizes in a system having two branch delay slots and a miss penalty of 10 cycles. Smaller caches are affected more by the code size increase that comes with additional delay slots. Likewise, the higher miss ratios of smaller caches means that they experience more performance loss as the miss penalty is increased. Figure 5 shows

Delay slots	CTIs Predicted Taken		CTIs Predicted Not-Taken		Cycles per CTI	Additional CPI
	% of total	% correct	% of total	% correct		
1	47	93	53	49	1.092	0.012
2	47	93	53	49	1.339	0.044
3	47	93	53	49	1.670	0.087

Table 3: Performance of branch prediction versus number of branch delay slots. The numbers of predict-taken and predict-not-taken CTIs are expressed as percentages of the total number of executed CTIs. CTIs make up 13 % of all executed instructions.

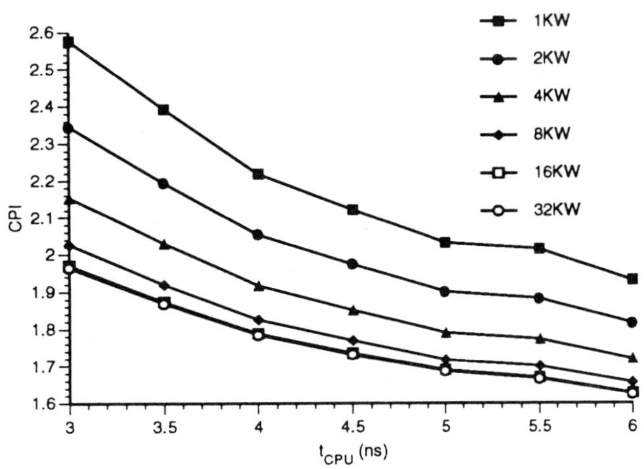

Figure 5: t_{CPU} versus L1-I cache size: $b = 2$, $B_{L1} = 4$ W, $P_{L1} = 10$ cycles. The curves are not smooth because of the need to make the L1 miss penalty an integer number of cycles.

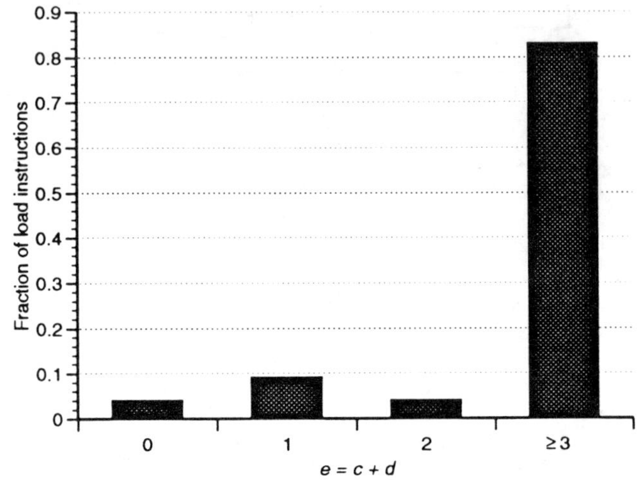

Figure 6: Histogram of ϵ values for benchmark suite used in this study.

that CPI decreases as t_{CPU} increases because the miss penalty (in cycles) decreases with increasing t_{CPU}.

3.2 The effect of load delays

The L1-D cache supplies data to the CPU when *load* instructions are executed. The number of CPU cycles between the execution of a load instruction and the time at which the data arrives at the CPU is determined by the pipeline depth of the L1-D cache, d_{L1-D}. These cycles are called load delay slots.

The MIPS ISA has only one memory addressing mode for all load instructions. This mode, called *register plus displacement*, uses a 16 b signed displacement from a 32 b general purpose register. To aid our discussion of load delay cycles, the following fragment of code, including an `lw` (load word) instruction is given as an example:

```
subu r5, r5, r4  ---
  •               | c
  •               |
  •              ---
lw r3, 100(r5)   ---
  •               | d
  •               |
  •              ---
addu r4, r3, r2
```

The `lw` instruction loads a word from memory location 100 plus the contents of address register `r5` into `r3`. It is preceded by an instruction that subtracts the contents of `r4` from `r5` and places the contents in `r5`. It is followed by instruction that adds the contents of `r3` to `r2` and places their sum into `r4`.

We define the following terms: 1) c is the number of instructions between the last instruction to modify the address register and the load instruction; 2) d is the number of instructions between the load instruction and the first instruction that uses the result of the load; 3) ϵ is the sum of c and d; and 4) l is the number of load delay cycles in the architecture. In this example, it is possible to execute the `lw` directly after the `subu` instruction, implying $c \geq 0$, but the `add` instruction can not be executed until l cycles after the `lw` instruction.

If nothing is done to hide the lost cycles due to load delays, the CPI will increase by the fraction of instructions that are loads, times the number of delay cycles per load. In the benchmark suite used in our experiments this fraction is 0.25. To reduce the effect of load delay cycles, load instructions can be rescheduled so that load delays do not result in stall cycles. The rescheduling may be done statically at compile time or dynamically at execution time. The restriction that a load instruction must execute after the instruction that modifies its address register limits the the number of delay cycles that can be hidden in this manner to ϵ.

The number of delay cycles that can be hidden is determined from the dynamic distribution of values for ϵ, given in Figure 6. The large fraction (over 80 %) of loads that have ϵ values of three or more indicates a great opportunity for moving load instructions away from where their results are used. The reason for this high percentage of loads having $\epsilon \geq 3$ is that many variable references are to global static variables or to local automatic variables whose address registers do not change often. Program measurements reveal that over 90% of array and structure references are to global variables and over 80% of scalar references are to local variables [PS82]. The MIPS compiler allocates most global static variables from a 64 KB area of memory called the *gp area*. Variables in this area are addressed using a single dedicated register that is set once at the beginning of the program. Local automatic variables

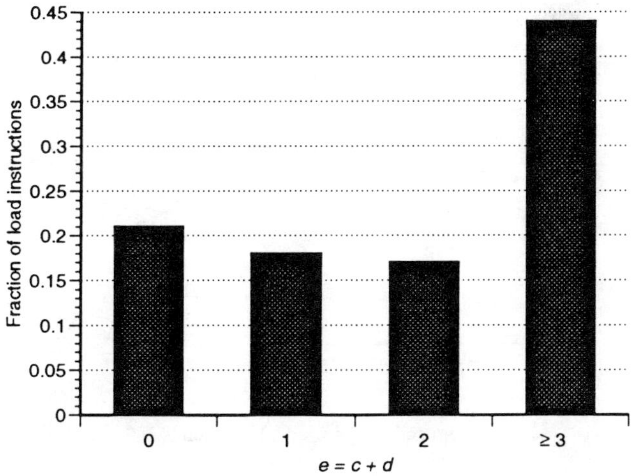

Figure 7: Histogram of ϵ values with with restrictions due to basic-block boundaries.

Delay slots	Static Delay cycles per load	Static CPI	Dynamic Delay cycles per load	Dynamic CPI
1	0.21	0.05	0.04	0.01
2	0.62	0.18	0.19	0.05
3	1.21	0.29	0.39	0.08

Table 5: The increase in CPI due to load delay cycles.

are addressed using the stack pointer register, which only changes at procedure call entry points. Furthermore, the MIPS compiler attempts to address as many memory locations as possible from the same address register [CCH+87].

Though Figure 6 would indicate that most load delay cycles can be hidden dynamically for an architecture with $l \leq 3$, the presence of control transfer instructions reduces the number of opportunities for hiding load delay cycles at compile time. Delayed loads assume l delay slot instructions before an instruction that uses the result of the load. A compiler attempts to fill these delay slots with useful instructions from within the basic block that appear before the load instruction. These instructions must be independent of the load. If enough independent instructions cannot be found to fill all the delay slots of a load the excess delay slots are filled with noop instructions. Not being able to look beyond a basic block greatly restricts the ability of the compiler to statically hide delay cycles compared to a completely dynamic technique. Figure 7 illustrates this by presenting the data of Figure 6 with the restrictions introduced by basic block boundaries. These boundaries prevent a load instruction from being moved away from the instructions that uses its result, causing the value of c to be reduced. A comparison of Figures 6 and 7 shows clearly that these boundaries change the distribution of ϵ, so that far fewer delay slots can be hidden in an architecture having $0 < l \leq 3$. However, even Figure 6 is optimistic in that it represents the best static scheduling for load instructions within a basic block. This scheduling assumes that only true dependencies are preserved and includes perfect memory address disambiguation which allows a load to be moved before a store if their addresses do not reference the same word.

Table 5 shows the CPI increase that results from 1, 2 and 3 load delay cycles. The data in this table is calculated using a dynamic frequency for load instructions of 0.25 from Table 1, and the data in Figures 6 and 7. Even though the data in Table 5 shows that dynamic

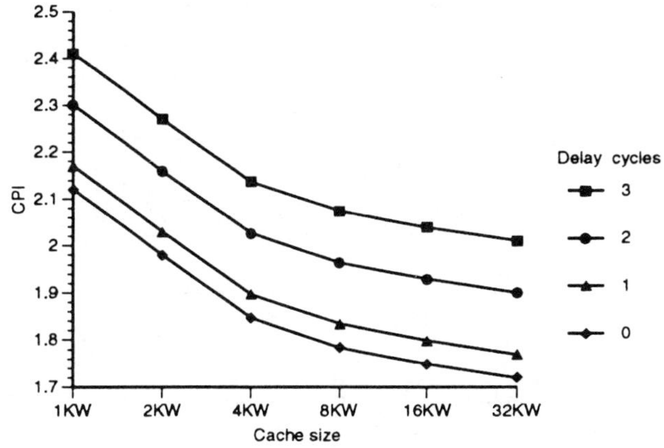

Figure 8: CPI versus L1-D cache size for different load delay cycles: $B_{L1} = 4\,W$ and $P_{L1} = 10$ cycles.

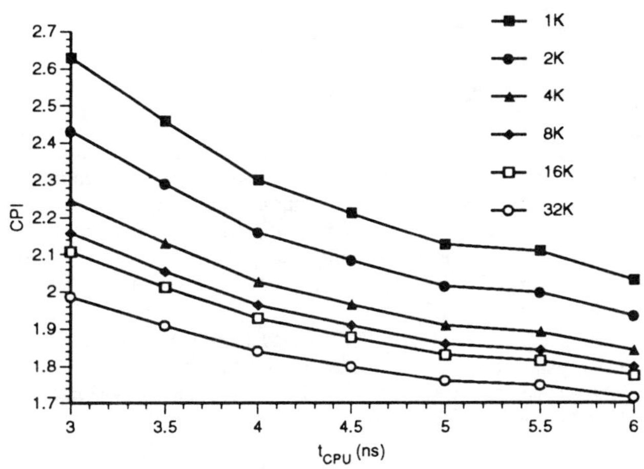

Figure 9: t_{CPU} versus L1-D cache size: $l = 2$, $B_{L1} = 4\,W$, $P_{L1} = 10$ cycles.

load delay slot hiding could potentially be much better at hiding load delay slots than static instruction scheduling, dynamic schemes would require out-of-order instruction execution, extra register-file ports, and a separate load address adder. This extra hardware will increase the cycle time. Rather than trying to estimate the change in t_{CPU}, we assume static instruction scheduling in the remainder of our analysis, and refer to Table 5 to estimate the performance of dynamic scheduling or to estimate how much the t_{CPU} could be increased in a dynamic scheme before it has less performance than static instruction scheduling.

Figure 8 shows CPI versus L1-D cache size for 0 through 3 delay cycles. As in the L1-I experiments, the block sizes of the caches have been optimized for the refill latency and miss penalty. This figure also shows the effect that load delay cycles have on CPI. We have assumed that load instructions are interlocked. This avoids the code expansion associated with the need to insert noop instructions into load delay slots which cannot be filled with useful instructions. The figure shows that the code expansion effect becomes more significant for delay values greater than one cycle. In fact, in order to decrease CPI after increasing the number of load delay cycles from one to two requires at least a four-fold increase in cache size.

Figure 9 combines the effects of varying t_{CPU} with the variation of L1-D size. The parameters used in this figure are two load delay cycles and a miss penalty of 10 cycles. This plot shows CPI for L1-

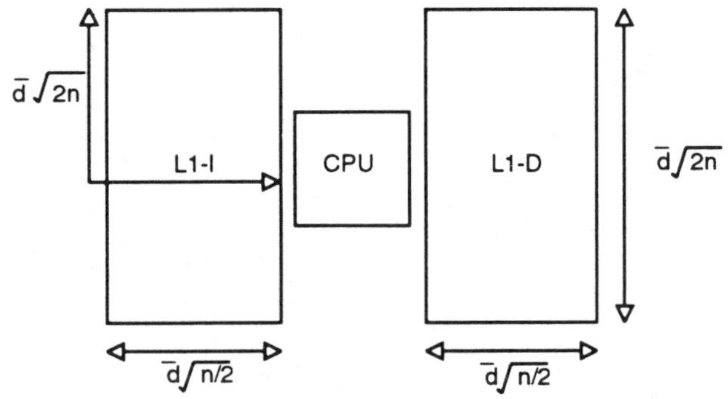

Figure 10: The minimum delay arrangement of $2n$ L1 cache SRAM chips.

D caches with 2 delay cycles and perfect compile time instruction scheduling to hide load delays. The curves in this figure will be shifted up or down by the same distances as the curves in Figure 8 for different numbers of delay cycles.

4 Cache Access Time

In this section we develop a macro-model, or simple expression, to estimate the access time of a direct-mapped cache that is implemented from GaAs SRAM chips mounted as bare die directly on an multichip module (MCM). It will be seen from the macro-model that t_{L1} increases linearly with number of chips. In the next section the results of Sections 3 and this section are combined to find an optimum primary cache organization.

The access time of an MCM-based L1 cache t_{L1} can be divided in two parts: the on-chip access time of the SRAM array, t_{SRAM}, and the round trip delay from the CPU to the cache and back, t_{MCM}. The equation for t_{L1} is given by,

$$t_{L1} = t_{SRAM} + 2t_{MCM} \qquad (3)$$

In general, t_{MCM} is dependent upon the electrical characteristics of the MCM interconnect (R, L and C) and the longest distance from the CPU to any cache SRAM. Given n, the number of SRAM chips in the L1-I or L1-D (L1 data) cache, t_{MCM} can be approximated by the following linear equation

$$t_{MCM} = k_0 + k_1 n \qquad (4)$$

where k_0 is a constant term associated with the delay of the off-chip drivers and receivers and k_1 is a linear coefficient that represents the additional delay per chip.

If n is the number of SRAM chips in the L1-I or L1-D cache, then to minimize interconnection delay these chips should be arranged as closely as possible to a $\sqrt{n/2} \times \sqrt{2n}$ rectangle as shown in Figure 10. If the CPU is placed in the middle of the long side of this rectangle, the maximum length l of a wire from the CPU to any chip is $\bar{d}\sqrt{2n}$ where $\bar{d}$ is the average chip pitch. More specifically, the term $\bar{d}$ is defined as the average of the horizontal and vertical pitches of the chip, including the width of adjacent wiring channels.

The value of the linear coefficient can be expressed as

$$k_1 = Z_0 C_{bond} + 2\bar{d}^2 R_{MCM} C_{MCM} \qquad (5)$$

where Z_0 is the characteristic impedance of the MCM interconnect and R_{MCM} and C_{MCM} are the resistance and capacitance per unit length of interconnect. This equation is a modified form of an equation for the packaging delay of interconnect presented in [Bak90]. The first term of (5) is the delay due to parasitic capacitance (C_{bond}) of the bonding method and the pad that connects the chip to the MCM. The second term is the distributed RC delay of the MCM interconnection lines and is proportional to the square of the length of the MCM interconnect that is being driven. However, this length is proportional to the square root of the number of chips in the cache n, making the second term proportional to n. Equation (5) assumes the interconnect is quite lossy and so neglects any delay from transmission line behavior. The value of k_1 calculated using (5) is within 1 % of the value calculated using SPICE circuit analysis of real layouts [Olu91].

Equations (3)-(5) can be combined to produce the following expression for t_{L1}

$$t_{L1} = t_{SRAM} + 2k_0 + 2n\left[Z_0 C_{bond} + 2\bar{d}^2 R_{MCM} C_{MCM}\right] \qquad (6)$$

Equation (6) defines t_{L1} for an MCM based direct-mapped L1 cache as a function of its size in SRAM chips. This equation can be combined with the pipeline depth of the L1 cache, d_{L1}, to determine the value of t_{CPU}.

The macro-model for t_{L1} defined by (6) is, of course, specific to particular SRAM chips and MCM technology. In general, the L1 cache may be on a PCB or, more likely, in the future, on the same chip as the CPU. Whatever the case, the important point from the multilevel optimization viewpoint is to develop a macro-model for t_{L1} as a function of cache organization.

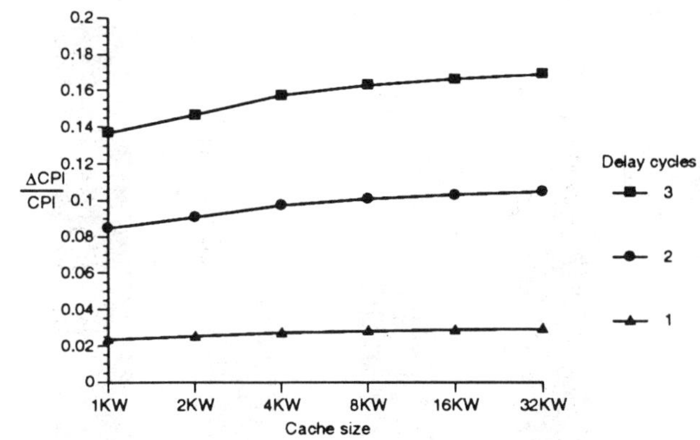

Figure 11: $\frac{\Delta CPI}{CPI}$ for L1-D caches.

5 Calculating TPI

In Figures 5 and 9, it was shown, among other things, that CPI decreases with increase in t_{CPU}. Equation (2) shows that t_{CPU} in turn is simply the cache access time scaled by the pipeline depth, $\frac{t_{L1}}{d_{L1}}$. Thus CPI will decrease with increase in t_{L1}. Increasing d_{L1}, or pipelining cache access, has the potential to decrease t_{CPU} without decreasing t_{L1}, however, as discovered in Section 3, increasing the pipeline depth also increases CPI (Figures 4 and 8).

If we consider incremental changes to the quantities in (1), the following equation can be obtained,

$$\frac{\Delta TPI}{TPI} = \frac{\Delta CPI}{CPI} + \frac{\Delta t_{CPU}}{t_{CPU}} \qquad (7)$$

Thus, although pipelining cache access has the potential to decrease t_{CPU}, in order to increase system performance, the relative decrease in t_{CPU}, $\frac{\Delta t_{CPU}}{t_{CPU}}$, must be greater than the relative increase in CPI, $\frac{\Delta CPI}{CPI}$. In Figure 11 $\frac{\Delta CPI}{CPI}$ is plotted for L1-D caches in order to measure the t_{CPU} change required to improve performance. The

L1 size	L1-I(0)	L1-I(1)	L1-I(2)	L1-I(3)	L1-D(0)	L1-D(1)	L1-D(2)	L1-D(3)
1KW	10.0	5.0	3.5	3.5	9.2	4.6	3.5	3.5
2KW	10.1	5.1	3.5	3.5	9.4	4.7	3.5	3.5
4KW	10.3	5.2	3.5	3.5	9.6	4.8	3.5	3.5
8KW	10.9	5.4	3.6	3.5	10.1	5.1	3.5	3.5
16KW	12.0	6.0	4.0	3.5	11.2	5.6	3.7	3.5
32KW	14.2	7.1	4.7	3.5	13.4	6.7	4.5	3.5

Table 6: Optimal cycle times for L1 caches for $B_{L1} = 4$. All times are in nanoseconds. The numbers in parentheses specify the pipeline depth of the caches.

relative CPI is plotted against cache size for an architecture with no load delay cycles. This figure shows that as the number of delay cycles is increased, the relative decrease in t_{CPU} required to improve performance grows larger. For 2 delay cycles, the decrease is less than 10%. This indicates that performance will be improved if t_{CPU} can be reduced by more than 10%. The figure also shows that as the cache size grows, the required improvement in t_{CPU} grows larger, suggesting that pipelining the cache access path is less effective for large caches. In general, Figure 11 shows that if the CPI of a system is low, deep pipelining will require a greater reduction in t_{CPU} before the performance of the system increases.

To determine exactly how t_{CPU} varies with cache size and pipeline depth we used the timing analyzer developed in [SMO90] to estimate t_{CPU} for L1 cache sizes of 1 to 32 KW and L1 access pipeline depth values of 0 to 3. The value of t_{L1} is estimated using the delay model for MCM-based caches that was developed in the Section 4. We have assumed that the SRAM chips have both address and data registers. The overhead delay of these latches was included in all timing analyses. In each case, the timing analyzer was used to optimize the timing of the circuit using a multiphase clocking scheme. Optimized clocking produces a t_{CPU} which increases by a factor of $\frac{1}{d_{L1}+1}$ for each unit increase in the access time, t_{L1}, of the L1 cache. The factor $d_{L1} + 1$ is the number of pipeline stages, including the ALU, in the the address calculation path and the cache access path (see Figure 1). This means that there is a smaller dependence of t_{CPU} on cache access time in deeper cache pipelines.

The results of the timing analysis are tabulated in Table 6. The minimum cycle time (3.5 ns) shown in the table is set by the time required to add two integer operands in the ALU (2.1 ns) and feed the result back to the ALU (1.4 ns). The pipeline depth of this path is one.

The data in Table 6 shows that for a pipeline depth of 0 the L1-I and L1-D caches limit t_{CPU} to more than 10 ns. This demonstrates that requiring the L1 cache to be accessed in the same cycle as the execution unit will lead to excessively long cycle times compared to the ALU add time which is 2.1 ns. When the pipeline depth of the L1-I and L1-D caches are increased to 3, the feedback loop around the ALU is critical for all cache sizes, and the cycle time is limited to 3.5 ns.

The L1 cache experiments have been presented above in terms of L1-I or L1-D. In order to combine a particular L1-I organization and an L1-D organization we take the maximum t_{CPU} of each, as the new system cycle time t_{CPU}. These are combined with the results of Figures 4 and 8 to give Figure 12.

A number of conclusions can be drawn from Figure 12. It shows that when the L1 cache is divided equally between L1-I and L1-D, performance is maximized when the number of branch delay slots is equal to the number of load delay slots, *i.e.*, $b = l$. The reason for this is that pipelining the different sides of the L1 cache to different depths causes the t_{CPU} set by one side to be shorter than that of the other. Since, the side with the longest cycle time will set the system cycle time, the extra pipelining on the other side will be wasted, *i.e.*, there will be extra CPI without the benefit of reducing t_{CPU}. Figure 12 also shows that for every combination of load

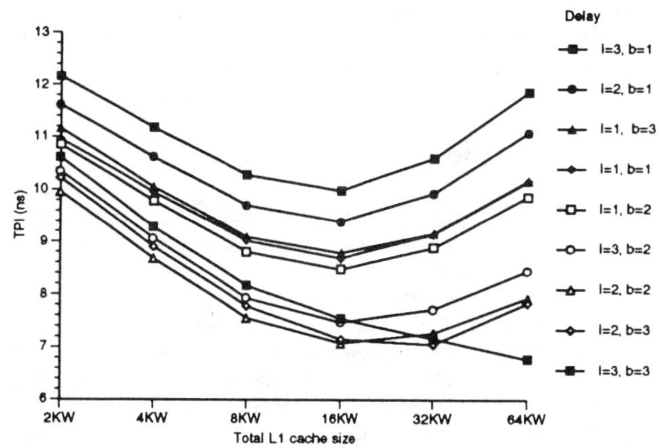

Figure 12: TPI versus cache size for various instruction and data cache delay-slot combinations; $B_{L1} = 4\,W$ and $P_{L1} = 10$ cycles.

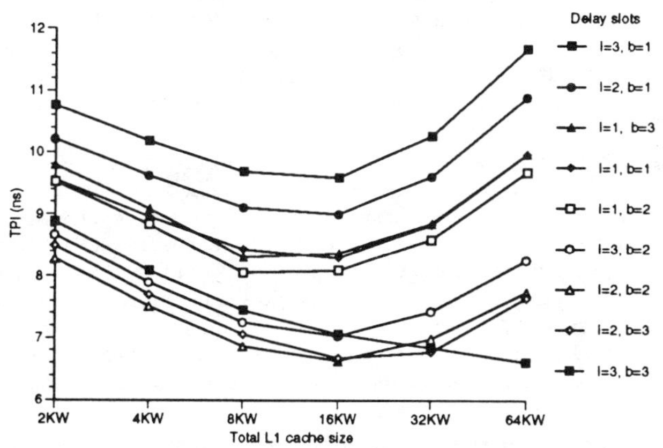

Figure 13: TPI versus cache size for a number of delay-slot combinations, with $B_{L1} = 4\,W$ and $P_{L1} = 6$ cycles.

and branch delay slots, there is an L1 cache size that maximizes performance. Maximum performance is reached for medium size caches at TPI = 6.8ns, when $b = 3$, $l = 3$, $S = 64$ KW, and $t_{CPU} = 3.5$ ns. The final conclusion is that increasing the number of branch and load delay slots is able to increase performance because doing so reduces the dependence of t_{CPU} on the size of the cache. This allows larger caches to be accessed without increasing cycle time.

If dynamic out-of-order load execution were used instead of static load instruction scheduling, a new maximum performance of TPI = 6.2ns could be reached when the number of branch and load delay slots are both equal to three ($l = 3, b = 3$) and the combined L1 cache size is 64 KW. The value of TPI is strongly dependent on the cycle time. We calculate that if the implementation of out-of-order load execution required more than a 10% increase in t_{CPU}, the performance of the dynamic scheme would be worse than the performance of the best static load delay scheduling organization.

Different L1 penalties change the performance and location of the optimal design points: higher penalties increase both the L1 cache size and pipeline depth. Lower penalties have the opposite effect, as shown in Figure 13, where maximum performance is reached at TPI = 6.61ns ($b = 2$, $l = 2$, $S_{L1} = 16$ KW, and $t_{CPU} = 3.5$ ns). Smaller refill penalties also make it possible to take advantage of the fact that increasing the number of branch delay slots increases CPI less than a comparable increase in load delay slots. This can be done by using a larger size L1-I cache than L1-D cache and pipelining the access of the L1-I cache more deeply. When this is done, the maximum performance is reached at TPI = 6.5ns ($S_{\rm L1-I} = 32$ KW and $S_{\rm L1-D} = 8$ KW).

6 Conclusions

The performance of pipelined primary caches of various configurations has been evaluated using a multilevel design optimization procedure. The objective is to reduce the cycle time by pipelining cache, while minimizing the penalty from the branch and load delay cycles. For the instruction cache, we found that delayed branching with optional squashing results in a lower CPI than does a branch-target buffer that is small enough to allow single cycle access. However, for small cache sizes and high miss penalties, the extra cache misses caused by the larger code size of the delayed branching scheme make the performance of these two schemes comparable.

Tradeoffs among cache-access pipeline depth, primary cache size, and $t_{\rm CPU}$, were investigated using timing analysis. We found that in systems having no delay slots for cache access, the value of $t_{\rm CPU}$ can be up to five times the integer-addition delay. However, even for the largest caches that were considered, pipelining the cache with 2 or 3 stages ensured that the ALU, rather than cache, was the critical path.

This study has shown significant performance benefits from pipelining the primary cache of a CPU which has a peak execution rate of one instruction per cycle. The extra cycles added through pipelining can be hidden often enough that overall performance improves. Furthermore, pipeline depth is better tolerated on the instruction side than on the data side, where basic-block boundaries make static instruction scheduling less effective at hiding load-delay slots. This suggests that for maximum performance, the instruction cache should be larger and more deeply pipelined than the data cache.

Finally, we have shown that the benefits of pipelining are twofold. First, it reduces the $t_{\rm CPU}$ and the dependence of $t_{\rm CPU}$ on cache access time. Second, it allows larger caches to be accessed without increasing $t_{\rm CPU}$, thus lowering CPI. These results suggest that the cache size versus set-associativity tradeoff may need to be re-examined. If $t_{\rm CPU}$ is less dependent on the access time of pipelined L1 caches, then increasing the associativity of the cache to lower the miss ratio will have a larger performance benefit for pipelined caches.

References

[Bak90] H. B. Bakoglu, *Circuits, Interconnections, and Packaging for VLSI*. Reading, Massachusetts: Addison-Wesley Publishing Company, 1990.

[CCH+87] F. Chow, S. Correll, M. Himestei, E. Killian, and L. Weber, "How many addressing modes are enough?," in *Proc. 2nd Int. Conf. Architectural Support for Programming Languages and Operating Systems (ASPLOS-II)*, pp. 117–121, Oct. 1987.

[CCS+91] T. I. Chappell, B. A. Chappell, S. E. Schuster, J. W. Allan, S. P. Klepner, R. V. Joshi, and R. L. Franch, "A 2-ns cycle, 3.8-ns access 512-kb CMOS ECL SRAM with a fully pipelined architecture," *IEEE Jour. of Solid-State Circuits*, vol. 26, pp. 1577–1585, Nov. 1991.

[HCC89] W. W. Hwu, T. M. Conte, and P. P. Chang, "Comparing software and hardware schemes for reducing the cost of branches," in *Proc.16th Annual Int. Symp. Computer Architecture*, pp. 224–233, June 1989.

[Hil87] M. D. Hill, *Aspects of Cache Memory and Instruction Buffer Performance*. PhD thesis, University of California, Berkeley, 1987.

[HP90] J. L. Hennessy and D. A. Patterson, *Computer Architecture A Quantitative Approach*. San Mateo, California: Morgan Kaufman Publishers, Inc., 1990.

[KH92] G. Kane and J. Heinrich, *MIPS RISC Architecture*. Englewood Cliffs, New Jersey: Prentice Hall, 1992.

[KT91] M. Katevenis and N. Tzartzanis, "Reducing the branch penalty by rearranging instructions in a double-width memory," in *Proc. 4th Int. Conf. Architectural Support for Programming Languages and Operating Systems (ASPLOS-IV)*, pp. 15–27, Apr. 1991.

[Lil88] D. J. Lilja, "Reducing the branch penalty in pipelined processors," *IEEE Computer Magazine*, vol. 21, pp. 47–55, July 1988.

[LS84] J. K. F. Lee and A. J. Smith, "Branch prediction strategies and branch target buffer design," *IEEE Computer Magazine*, vol. 17, pp. 6–22, Jan. 1984.

[MBB+91] T. N. Mudge, R. B. Brown, W. P. Birmingham, J. A. Dykstra, A. I. Kayssi, R. J. Lomax, O. A. Olukotun, K. A. Sakallah, and R. Millano, "The design of a micro-supercomputer," *IEEE Computer Magazine*, vol. 24, Jan. 1991.

[MH86] S. McFarling and J. Hennessy, "Reducing the cost of branches," in *Proc.13th Annual Int. Symp. Computer Architecture*, pp. 396–403, june 1986.

[MIP88] MIPS Computer Systems, Inc, *MIPS RISCompiler Languages Programmer's Guide*, Dec. 1988.

[OBL+91] O. A. Olukotun, R. B. Brown, R. J. Lomax, T. N. Mudge, and K. A. Sakallah, "Multilevel optimization in the design of a high-performance GaAs microcomputer," *IEEE J. Solid-State Circuits*, vol. 26, May 1991.

[Olu91] O. A. Olukotun, *Technology-Organization Tradeoffs in the Architecture of a High Performance Processor*. PhD thesis, The University of Michigan, Ann Arbor, 1991.

[Prz90] S. A. Przybylski, *Cache and Memory Hierarchy Design*. San Mateo, California: Morgan Kaufman Publishers, Inc., 1990.

[PS82] D. Patterson and C. Séquin, "A VLSI RISC," *IEEE Computer Magazine*, vol. 15, pp. 8–21, Sept. 1982.

[Smi78] A. J. Smith, "A comparative study of set associative memory mapping algorithms and their use for cache and main memory," *IEEE Trans. Software Engineering*, vol. SE-4, pp. 121–130, Mar. 1978.

[Smi81] J. E. Smith, "A study of branch prediction strategies," in *Proc. 8th Annual Int. Symp. Computer Architecture*, pp. 135–147, July 1981.

[SMO90] K. A. Sakallah, T. N. Mudge, and O. A. Olukotun, "*checkT$_c$* and *mint$_c$* : Timing verification and optimal clocking of synchronous digital circuits," in *Proc. IEEE Conf. Computer-Aided Design*, (Santa Clara, California), Nov. 1990.

Cache Replacement with Dynamic Exclusion

Scott McFarling
DEC Western Research Laboratory
250 University
Palo Alto, CA 94301

Abstract

Most recent cache designs use direct-mapped caches to provide the fast access time required by modern high speed CPU's. Unfortunately, direct-mapped caches have higher miss rates than set-associative caches, largely because direct-mapped caches are more sensitive to conflicts between items needed frequently in the same phase of program execution.

This paper presents a new technique for reducing direct-mapped cache misses caused by conflicts for a particular cache line. A small finite state machine recognizes the common instruction reference patterns where storing an instruction in the cache actually harms performance. Such instructions are dynamically excluded, that is they are passed directly through the cache without being stored. This reduces misses to the instructions that would have been replaced.

The effectiveness of dynamic exclusion is dependent on the severity of cache conflicts and thus on the particular program and cache size of interest. However, across the SPEC benchmarks, simulation results show an average reduction in miss rate of 33% for a 32KB instruction cache with 16B lines. In addition, applying dynamic exclusion to one level of a cache hierarchy can improve the performance of the next level since instructions do not need to be stored on both levels. Finally, dynamic exclusion also improves combined instruction and data cache miss rates.

1 Introduction

In recent years, the dramatic rise of CPU speed has increasingly stressed memory system performance. Even though DRAM chips are now much denser, their speed has not kept pace with CPU cycle times. This trend increases the importance of cache design to provide the instruction and data bandwidth required by modern CPU's. Furthermore, short CPU cycle times often require both instruction and data caches to be on the same chip as the CPU since crossing chip boundaries lead to unacceptable cache access times. On-chip caches must necessarily be small. These factors leads to caches with relatively high miss rates and large miss penalties.

For a given cache size, set-associative caches have a significantly lower miss rate than direct-mapped caches. In a set-associative cache, every memory item can be stored in one of multiple cache lines. Thus, any two items can be simultaneously stored in a set-associative cache. In a direct-mapped cache, each item can be stored in only one cache line. Thus, a direct-mapped cache can have many more misses if two items are needed repeatedly in the same phase of program execution and they both must be stored in the same cache line. In spite of this issue, direct-mapped caches often have better overall performance because they have lower access times.

This paper presents a new hardware technique that improves the miss rate of direct-mapped caches, particularly instruction caches. When two instructions compete for the same cache line, the technique attempts to keep one instruction in the cache and the other instruction out of the cache. We call this selection of instructions to keep out of the cache the *dynamic exclusion* replacement policy. Here, replacement policy refers to deciding whether an instruction should be replaced when a competing instruction is needed or if the competing instruction should just be passed on to the processor.

The key to dynamic exclusion is the recognition of the common instruction execution patterns. These patterns are typically determined by the loops in the program. Section 3 describes the common loop structures, the resulting execution patterns, and the optimal replacement policy for these patterns. Section 4 describes a simple finite state machine that can recognize these patterns and guide a direct-mapped cache toward the optimal replacement policy. Section 5 describes how the dynamic exclusion state can be stored in cache. Also, methods of handling and reducing misses in the next level cache are discussed. Section 6 describes the interaction between dynamic exclusion and caches with block

© 1992 ACM 0-89791-509-7/92/0005/0191 $1.50

sizes larger than one instruction. Section 7 discusses using dynamic exclusion on data and combined caches. Finally, Section 8 gives some concluding remarks. First however, we begin with a short discussion of related work in the area of cache design.

2 Related Work

The design of caches to improve memory system performance has been studied extensively. For an overview, see Smith [Smi82]. One area of strong interest has been cache organization. In this paper, we assume caches are direct mapped. Several studies have shown that direct-mapped caches have better overall performance than set-associative caches because of their lower access times [Prz88, PHH89, PHH88, Hil87].

Many cache replacement policies have also been studied. Belady [Bel66] gave an optimal replacement policy in the context of page replacement for virtual memories. Belady's algorithm uses future information to establish a theoretical upper bound on the performance of any other replacement policy. This paper attempts to predict the future and match optimal replacement by recognizing the execution patterns caused by loops. Smith and Goodman [SG85] also used a loop model to compared the effectiveness of different instruction cache replacement policies. Loops models have also been used to improve cache performance with compiler techniques [HC89, PH90, WL91, McF89, McF91b].

In [McF89, McF91b], cache performance was improved by reordering instructions so that more frequent instructions are kept in in the cache and less frequent instructions are kept out. The less frequent instructions were either excluded by address or reordered to only interfere with other less frequent instructions. Reordering significantly reduced instruction cache miss rates, but required instruction frequency information to be provided to the compiler. The technique described in this paper also excludes less frequent instructions. However, by using hardware techniques, no changes to the compiler are required.

Jouppi [Jou90] also studied a hardware method of reducing the sensitivity of direct-mapped caches to conflicts. A small second level associative cache, called a victim cache, was used to avoid pathological conflicts between two frequently accessed items that use the same cache line. Victim caches work well for data references where the number of conflicting items may be small. For instruction references, there are usually many more conflicting items than a victim cache can hold. This is where dynamic exclusion is most effective. Jouppi also shows how to reduce the effective instruction cache miss penalty by prefetching instructions into a stream buffer. Since stream buffers do not change the number of conflict misses, stream buffers and dynamic exclusion are complementary.

3 Common Reference Patterns

To understand how direct-mapped cache performance can be improved, we need to look at the misses that occur for common instruction reference patterns. For now, we assume that each cache miss brings one instruction into the cache. Typically, misses are caused by the interference between the pairs of instructions known as *conflicting instructions* that cannot both be stored in cache at the the same time. Conflicts between three or more instructions also occur, but less frequently. Normally, when execution of two conflicting instructions alternate, there are two misses as each instruction must be brought into the cache. Our goal is to change the replacement policy so that whenever possible there will only be one miss. To explain how this can be done, we will examine the three most common sources of instruction conflicts:

1. conflict between instructions in two different loops
2. conflict between an instruction inside a loop with an instruction outside the loop.
3. conflict between two instructions within the same loop.

To guide our choice of a new replacement policy, we will compare a conventional direct-mapped cache with an optimal direct-mapped cache. By optimal direct-mapped cache, we mean that the cache stores instructions in the same place that a direct-mapped cache would, but the cache has an optimal replacement policy. With this optimal policy, the cache retains the instructions that will be used soonest in the future among those instructions that map to each location in the cache. Furthermore, we assume an instruction can be passed directly to the CPU without ever being stored in the cache. This allows the instruction in the cache to be retained if it will be used sooner in the future than the current instruction will be needed again.

3.1 Conflict Between Loops

An example of conflict between instructions in different loops can be seen in the following example, where instructions a and b map to the same cache location.

```
for (i = 1, i <= 10, i++) {
    for (j = 1, j <= 10, j++)
        instruction a
    for (j = 1, j <= 10, j++)
        instruction b
}
```

Ignoring the instructions associated with the for loops, this example has the execution sequence:

$$(a^{10}b^{10})^{10}$$

In this paper, exponents give the number of times a subsequence is repeated. The subscripts h and m refer to instructions that hit or miss respectively. For the above sequence, both conventional and optimal direct-mapped caches have the behavior:

$$(a_m a_h^9 b_m b_h^9)^{10}$$

with miss rates:

$$m_{DM} = m_{OPTDM} = 10\%$$

Every time an instruction is executed, it is either already in the cache or should be placed in the cache because it is also the next instruction to be executed. Thus, a conventional direct-mapped cache already has optimal performance. Any new replacement strategy for direct-mapped caches should not change this performance.

3.2 Conflict Between Loops Levels

The following example shows a conflict between an instruction inside a loop with another instruction outside the loop:

```
for (i = 1, i <= 10, i++) {
    for (j = 1, j <= 10, j++)
        instruction a
    instruction b
}
```

Here, the behavior of an conventional direct-mapped cache is:

$$(a_m a_h^9 b_m)^{10}$$

$$m_{DM} = 18\%$$

The behavior of an optimal direct-mapped cache is:

$$a_m a_h^9 b_m (a_h^{10} b_m)^9$$

$$m_{OPTDM} = 10\%$$

In the conventional direct-mapped cache, each access to b causes two misses. Not only does instruction b miss, b knocks a out of the cache and causes a to miss the next time it is executed. In the optimal cache, instruction a is kept in the cache even when b is executed. Instruction a will only miss once. To achieve the optimal cache behavior, a new replacement method should recognize instructions that will only be executed once before some other instruction is repeated, and not add such instructions to the cache.

3.3 Conflict within Loops

The final example below illustrates the behavior when two instructions within a single loop compete for space in the cache.

```
for (i = 1, i <= 10, i++) {
    instruction a
    instruction b
}
```

Here, the behavior of a conventional direct-mapped cache is:

$$(a_m b_m)^{10}$$

$$m_{DM} = 100\%$$

The behavior of an optimal direct-mapped cache is:

$$a_m b_m (a_h b_m)^9$$

$$m_{OPTDM} = 55\%$$

In a conventional cache, both instructions continuously knock each other out of the cache. Neither hits. Conversely, the optimal cache selects one instruction to keep in the cache. This selected instruction will hit on later executions. To improve on the conventional direct-mapped cache, the replacement policy should recognize when two instructions are alternating and select one to be kept in the cache.

4 Dynamic Exclusion Policy

We now present a new method for improving direct-mapped cache performance. The basic idea is to recognize the patterns presented in the previous section and mimic the behavior of an optimal direct-mapped cache. The recognition process treats each cache line independently. In this section, we assume each cache line can hold a single instruction at a time. Section 6 will generalize the result to larger cache line sizes.

In a conventional direct-mapped cache, the most recent reference is always placed in the cache. As we saw in Section 3, optimal direct-mapped caches can get fewer misses by excluding some instructions from the cache. We now consider a new cache replacement policy that reduces the number of misses by dynamically determining which instructions should be excluded from the cache. The determination uses a simple finite-state machine (FSM) in conjunction with two new state bits associated with each cache line. These new bits are called *sticky* and *hit-last* and are denoted s and $h[\,]$ respectively.

The sticky bit gives the cache some inertia to reduce thrashing. No longer will cached instructions always be replaced

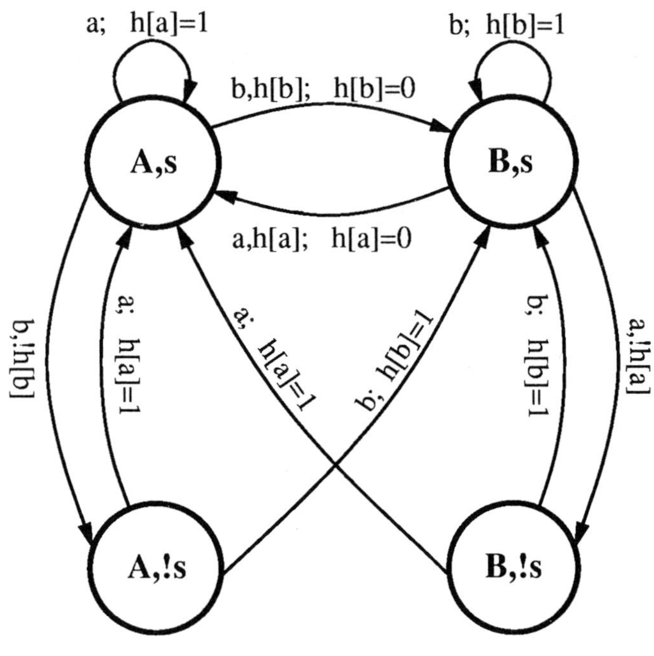

Figure 1: Dynamic Exclusion State Diagram

when a conflicting instruction is executed. However, if an instruction is kept in the cache despite a conflict it will be replaced the next time a conflicting instruction is executed unless the original instruction is executed first. One sticky bit is associated with each cache line.

The hit-last bit tells whether an instruction hit the last time it was in the cache. More precisely, the hit-last bit tells whether an instruction should be immediately loaded into the cache despite the value of the sticky bit. In principle, there is one hit-last bit in memory associated with each instruction. In practice, this is impossible, since the hit-last bits need to be used on each cache access. Section 5 discusses methods of storing the hit-last bits in cache.

Figure 1 gives the state transition diagram for the dynamic exclusion FSM. Only the states and transitions for two instructions, a and b, are shown. The behavior for other instructions is symmetrical. The notation A and B indicate instruction a or b is in the cache respectively. s and $!s$ indicate whether the sticky bit associated with the current cache line is set or reset respectively. Thus, the transition $A, !s \rightarrow B, s$ indicates that instruction b is fetched and replaces instruction a in the cache. In addition, the sticky bit is set. The notation $h[x]$ refers to the hit-last bit associated with instruction x. The semicolons in arc labels separate the input conditions on the left from the hit-last state changes on the right. As in the language C, assignment is represented by an equal sign.

The state diagram can be understood by examining its behavior for the three common instruction reference patterns described in Section 3. Consider first the conflict between loops in the pattern $(a^{10}b^{10})^{10}$. The initial states of the sticky bit, the hit-last bits, and the current instruction in the cache are unknown. However, for all possible initial states, instruction a will be loaded into the cache after at most two misses. During sequential executions of a, the cache will remain in State A, s and the hit-last bit $h[a]$ will be set since a will hit several times. When b is executed the initial action depends on the initial state of $h[b]$. However, after at most two misses, b will be loaded into the cache and subsequently $h[b]$ will be set.

At this point, both $h[a]$ and $h[b]$ are set, indicating that both a and b are repeated whenever they are executed. Subsequently, the cache behavior is the same as an optimal direct-mapped cache. Whenever either a or b is executed, the instruction will either already be in the cache or be immediately loaded just as an optimal cache would. Thus, for this pattern, a direct-mapped cache with dynamic exclusion has at most two more misses than an optimal direct-mapped cache depending on the initial state.

In the conflict between loop levels pattern $(a^{10}b)^{10}$, a direct-mapped cache with dynamic exclusion again matches the behavior of an optimal direct-mapped cache, perhaps after some initial training time. The initial executions of instruction a are identical to the earlier pattern. After at most three executions, a will be in the cache and $h[a]$ will be set. Instruction b will be loaded only if $h[b]$ is initially set. However, even in this case, $h[b]$ is reset and the sticky bit will keep b from ever being loaded again. Again, a direct-mapped cache with dynamic exclusion has at most two more misses than an optimal direct-mapped cache. This is significantly better than a normal direct-mapped cache where each execution of b causes two misses.

Finally, in the pattern of conflict within a loop $(ab)^{10}$, a direct-mapped cache with dynamic exclusion again acts like an optimal direct-mapped cache after some initial activity to correctly set the $h[\ ]$ and s bits. Depending on the initial conditions, either instruction a or b may be kept in the cache. However, eventually one instruction will be kept in. For example, if a is initially in the cache, the finite state machine will cycle between states A, s and $A, !s$. Again, after some initial misses, the direct-mapped cache with dynamic exclusion has only half the misses of a normal direct-mapped cache.

Before going further, we should note that the state diagram in Figure 1 occasionally sets the the $h[x]$ bit even when instruction x does not hit. For example, this occurs in the transition $A, !s \rightarrow B, s$. This would occur if the initial state was $A, s, !h[b]$ and instruction b was executed twice. Here, the $h[b]$ bit means that instruction b *should* have hit the last time it was executed. This transition improves the cache performance by allowing more random references to get in the cache sooner. This is especially useful for data and mixed caches.

To evaluate the effectiveness of dynamic exclusion, we will use the SPEC benchmarks[SPE90] shown in Figure 2. These benchmarks include a mix of symbolic and numeric applications. However, to limit cache simulation time, only

benchmark	description
doduc	Monte Carlo simulation
eqntott	conversion from equation to truth table
espress	minimization of boolean functions
fpppp	quantum chemistry calculations
gcc	GNU C compiler
li	lisp interpreter
mat300	matrix multiplication
nasa7	NASA Ames FORTRAN Kernels
spice	circuit simulation
tomcatv	vectorized mesh generation

Figure 2: SPEC Benchmarks Used for Evaluation

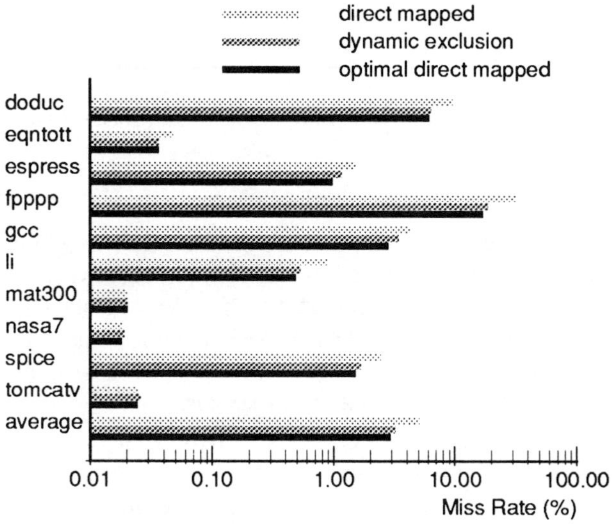

Figure 3: Instruction Cache Performance for Various Benchmarks (S=32KB, b=4B)

the first 10 million references from each benchmark were used. Results using the full reference streams are similar. Execution traces were obtained on a DECstation 3100 using the pixie tracing facility[Kil86, Smi91].

Figure 3 shows the instruction cache performance for each of the SPEC benchmarks for a normal direct-mapped cache, a direct-mapped cache with dynamic exclusion, and an optimal direct-mapped cache, all at a cache size of 32KB and line size of 4B. The improvement varies between benchmarks largely depending on the relative frequency of the patterns discussed in Section 3. All the benchmarks with a high instruction cache miss rate show a significant improvement. Benchmarks nasa7 and tomcatv show a slight increase in misses with dynamic exclusion. This is caused by a small increase in cold-start misses while the dynamic exclusion state bits are initialized. For the full instruction reference streams, this increase is negligible.

Dynamic exclusion improves miss rates because of the prevalence of the three common reference patterns described

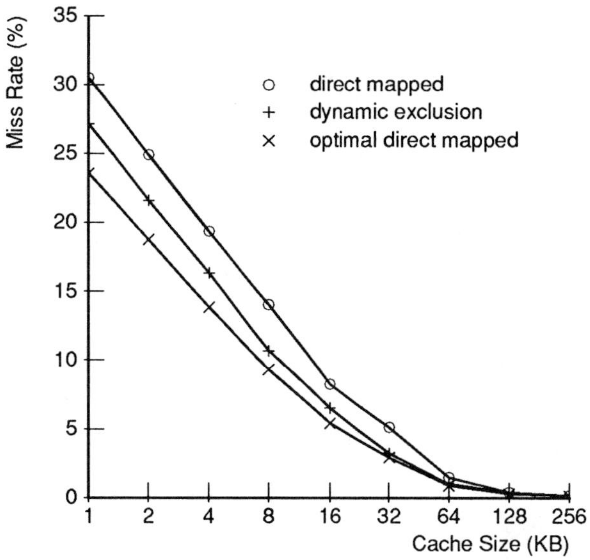

Figure 4: Instruction Cache Dynamic Exclusion Performance for Various Cache Sizes (b=4B)

in Section 3. However, for several of the benchmarks, dynamic exclusion has a significantly higher miss rate than a direct-mapped cache with optimal replacement. Typically, this is caused by the startup time needed to recognize the current pattern and by the occasional occurrence of more complex patterns. One such pattern, is the sequence $(abc)^{10}$ that occurs when a loop has three instructions that map to a single cache line. Both a direct-mapped cache and a dynamic-exclusion cache using the FSM in Figure 1 miss on all references. The miss rate can be improved by locking instruction a in the cache. This could be done with dynamic exclusion by adding additional sticky bits. However, this produces mixed results because additional startup time is required and because the miss rate for other patterns increases. For example, if instruction a is locked in the cache for the pattern $(abb)^{10}$, the miss rate would be higher than with a single sticky bit. For more information on the use of additional sticky bits, see reference [McF91a].

Figure 4 shows the average instruction cache miss rate across the SPEC benchmarks for a range of cache sizes with the same three types of caches as in Figure 3. Figure 5 shows the percentage reduction from the normal direct-mapped cache miss rate. For very large caches, the potential improvement decreases since there are no conflicts when the programs fit in the cache. For very small cache sizes, the conflicts are more likely to involve more than two instructions and thus not be recognizable by the FSM in Figure 1. The potential improvement is also smaller. This is reflected by the decline in the percentage improvement for an optimal direct-mapped cache for these small cache sizes. The average improvement for dynamic exclusion peaks at 37% at a cache size of 32KB.

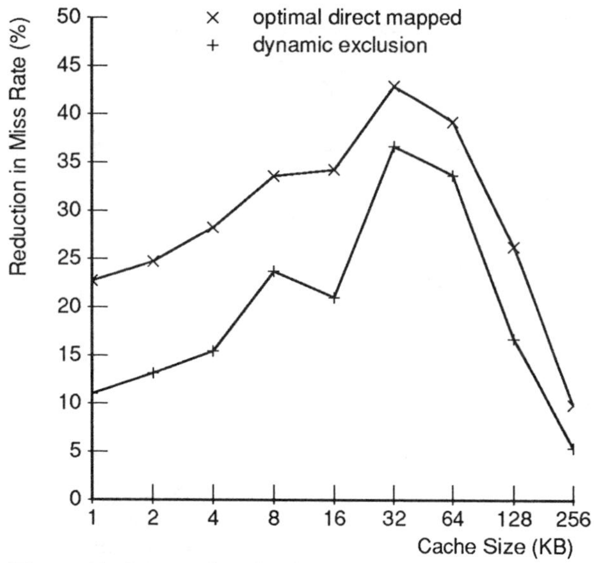

Figure 5: Instruction Cache Performance Improvement for Various Cache Sizes (b=4B)

5 State Storage Choices

In this section, we consider alternate methods of storing the dynamic exclusion state information in cache. Each sticky bit is logically associated with a line in the first level of cache. Thus, it is natural to store the sticky bit along with this cache line. In contrast, the hit-last bit must be remembered while an instruction is not in the cache. In addition, the value associated with an instruction is only used when that instruction misses. Thus, one natural place to store the hit-last bits is in the next lower level in the memory hierarchy. However, even if the value is not used, the hit-last bit could be set on any first level cache access. Normally, the second level cache is too slow to be written this frequently. One solution to this problem is to keep a copy of the hit-last bit in the first level cache. Whenever the hit-last bit needs to be set, the L1 copy is set. This copy is then transferred to the L2 cache when the instruction in the L1 cache is replaced. Figure 6 shows the cache organization using this approach. The Level 1 (L1) cache contains both the sticky and hit-last bits. The Level 2 cache contains only the hit-last bit.

If the second level cache is large, the hit-last bits flushed out of the L1 cache are likely to be found in the L2 cache. However, we also need to consider what to do when the hit-last bits are not found in the L2 cache. In particular, we will consider three ways a cache with dynamic exclusion could respond to an L2 miss:

1. use the existing hit-last bit (hashed)
2. assume the hit-last bit is set (assume-hit)
3. assume the hit-last bit is not set (assume-miss)

The first option has a significant structural advantage. The hit-last bits previously kept in the L2 cache can be kept in the L1 cache since there is no need to insure that the current instruction matches the instruction stored in L2. This avoids the need to communicate the hit-last information between the caches and even the need for the L2 cache to know that the L1 cache is using dynamic exclusion. Also, there is no need for the original hit-last bit in L1 since the bits previously stored in L2 can be accessed directly at L1 speeds.

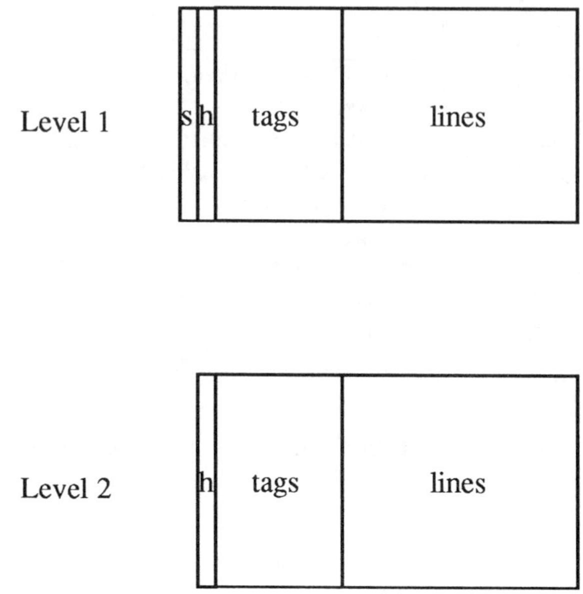

Figure 6: Direct-Mapped Cache with Dynamic Exclusion State Bits

Figure 7 shows the L1 miss rates with dynamic exclusion using each of the three options as the L2 cache size is increased. For most L2 cache sizes, the assume-hit option has slightly fewer L1 misses. Assuming instructions will hit is usually correct. However, if the L2 cache is the same size as the L1 cache, the assume-hit option gives no improvement since the cache degenerates to conventional direct-mapped behavior. With all three schemes, most of the performance is achieved as long as the L2 cache is at least 4 times as large as the L1 cache. This is large enough to insure that most L1 misses are found in the L2 cache. This also implies that the hashing strategy needs only four hit-last bits for each cache line to get good performance.

Figures 8 and 9 show the results of the three options on the L2 miss rates. With the hashed and assume-miss strategies, all instructions stored in the L1 cache do not need to be stored in the L2 cache. This allows the L2 cache to store other instructions and get a lower miss rate. This could be particularly useful if the L2 cache is on the same chip as the CPU and needs to to be kept small. As the figures show, the assume-miss strategy is best at improving the L2 miss rate. This is because it maximizes the difference between the two caches. The hashed strategy also has a significant improvement. The assume-hit strategy does not help the L2 cache because everything in the L1 cache will also be in the L2 cache.

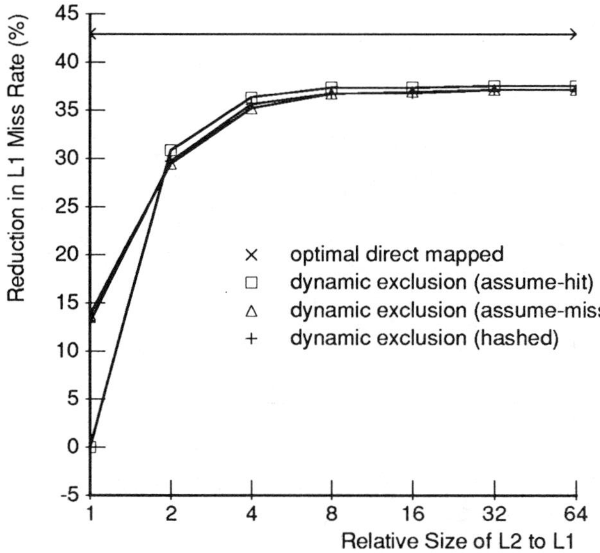

Figure 7: Dynamic Exclusion L1 Performance for Various L2 Cache Sizes (L1=32KB, b=4B)

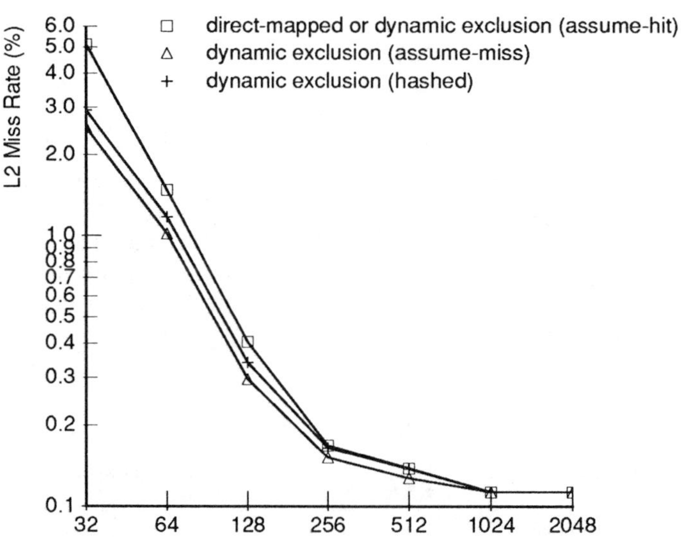

Figure 8: Dynamic Exclusion L2 Performance for Various L2 Cache Sizes (L1=32KB, b=4B)

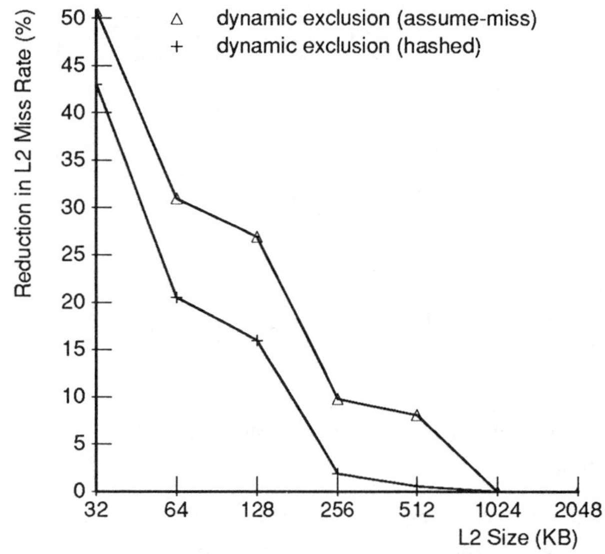

Figure 9: Dynamic Exclusion L1 Performance Improvement for Various L2 Cache Sizes (L1=32KB, b=4B)

6 Caches with Longer Line Sizes

In the discussion so far, we have assumed each cache line contains one instruction. Larger cache lines present two problems. First, the sequence of instructions that use each tag is much different. If the dynamic exclusion state bits are updated whenever a given tag is accessed, the patterns described in Section 3 will no longer be seen. Using the same finite state machine, cache lines would rarely be excluded because there are almost always several instructions executed sequentially that use the same tag. The second problem is that even if the FSM excluded whole cache lines, this would result in poor performance as each sequential instruction generated a new miss.

We can solve both these problems once we recognize that the pattern of references to each position within a cache line is highly correlated since the instructions are often in the same basic block. If we treat the sequential references to each cache line as one reference, the sequence of these references is very similar to the sequence of references to each instruction within the line. Moreover, the patterns of these line references is the same as the patterns discussed in Section 3. If each cache line holds one instruction, we were able to reduce the number of misses by excluding instructions that are only used once before a competing instruction is executed. A similar improvement is possible with larger line sizes if we recognize lines that will only be used for sequential instruction executions. These lines should be excluded from the cache, but they do need to be held somewhere so that only one miss is required for the sequential references in the line. This allows dynamic exclusion to be used without losing the benefits of spatial locality.

There are three particularly simple methods of implementing exclusion of longer cache lines:

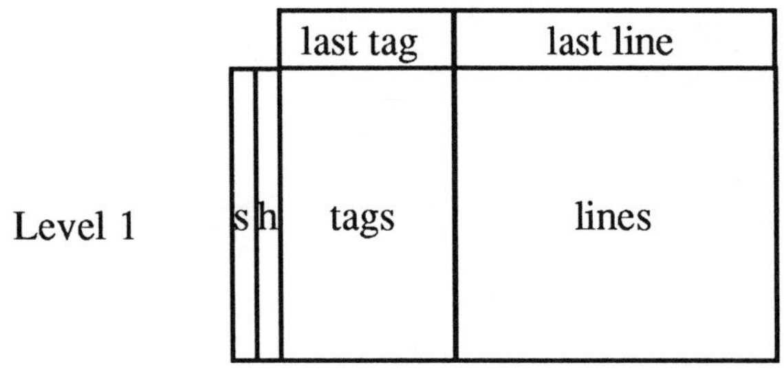

Figure 10: Dynamic Exclusion Structure with Longer Cache Lines

1. use an instruction register the same size as the L1 cache line.

2. logically add a special line to the cache with its own tag to hold the most recently referenced line.

3. leave excluded instructions in the stream buffer.

In the first alternative, missing lines are always stored in the instruction register. However, the line is only stored in the L1 cache if the dynamic exclusion FSM suggests it should be. Sequential requests for the next instructions are taken from the instruction register without changing the dynamic exclusion state. It is only necessary to access the cache again when there is a taken branch or the program counter rolls over to the next line.

The structure for the second alternative is shown in Figure 10. All missing lines are stored in the special *last-line* area. Subsequent sequential references are taken from the last-line when there is a match to the *last-tag* field. Lines are only stored to the L1 cache as directed by the dynamic exclusion FSM. Finally, the dynamic exclusion state is only changed when the current instruction address does not match last-tag.

The third scheme is probably the simplest if the machine already uses a stream buffer. For best results, the CPU needs to be able to access sequential instructions in the stream buffer as quickly as instructions in the L1 cache.

Figure 11 shows the performance of the second scheme as the cache line size increases with a 32KB instruction cache. The percentage improvement in the miss rate declines progressively from 37% with 4 byte lines to 25% at 64 byte lines. This loss in efficiency tracks the internal fragmentation problem of long cache lines. In particular, two instructions that do not conflict with a small line size may conflict with a longer line size. These added conflicts can prevent the FSM from finding a line that can be excluded to improve performance. Figure 12 shows the performance improvement from dynamic exclusion for a range of cache sizes at a cache line size of 16 bytes.

The extra space required for dynamic exclusion including a last-line buffer is small relative to the increase in performance. As an example, Figure 13 compares the efficiency of adding dynamic exclusion with simply increasing cache

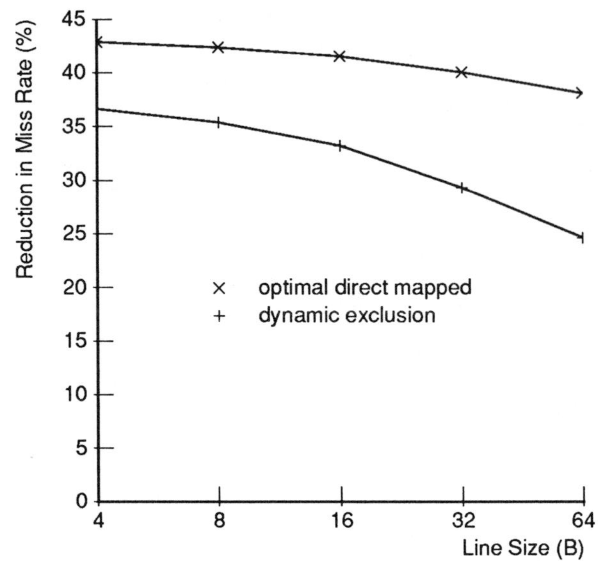

Figure 11: Instruction Cache Dynamic Exclusion Performance for Various Line Sizes (S=32KB)

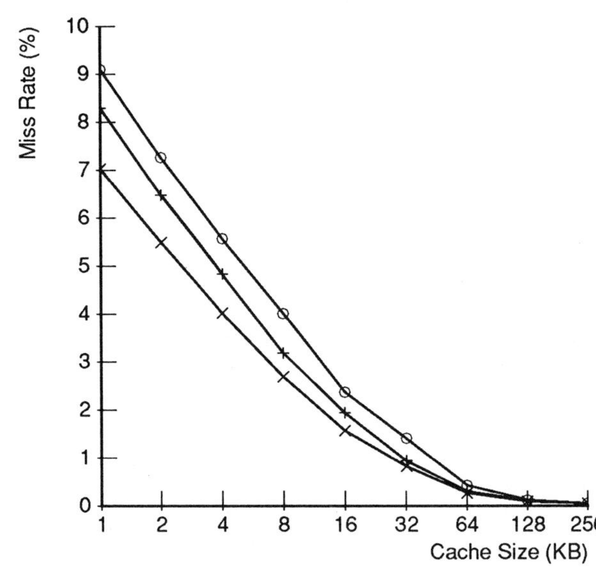

Figure 12: Instruction Cache Dynamic Exclusion Performance for Various Cache Sizes (b=16B)

	8KB DM	8KB DE	16KB DM
Δ size		3.4%	100%
miss rate	4.02	3.18	2.38
Δ miss rate		21%	41%
$\frac{\Delta \text{miss rate}}{\Delta \text{size}}$		6.1	0.41

Figure 13: Dynamic Exclusion Efficiency (b=16B)

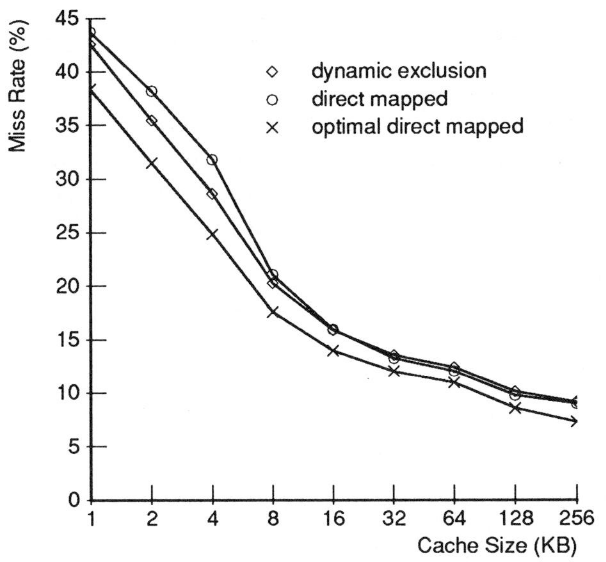

Figure 14: Data Cache Dynamic Exclusion Performance for Various Cache Sizes (b=4B)

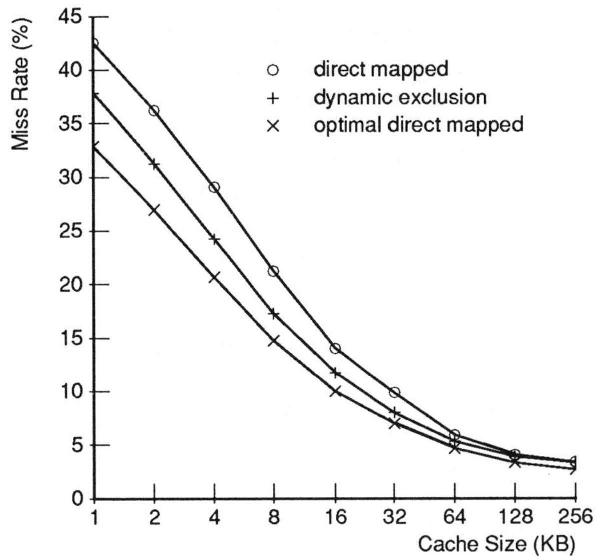

Figure 15: Dynamic Exclusion Performance for Various Combined I and D Cache Sizes (b=4B)

size. The baseline cache is a 8KB direct mapped cache (DM) with 16B lines. The alternate designs are a cache with dynamic exclusion (DE) with the same capacity and a direct-mapped cache with twice the capacity. We assume the cache with dynamic exclusion has a 16B last-line buffer and uses the hashing strategy with four hit-last bits per L1 cache line. Adding dynamic exclusion is roughly 15 times more efficient than adding capacity.

7 Data and Mixed Caches

The previous sections have only discussed instruction caches. A natural question is whether the same techniques can be applied to data caches as well. Figure 14 shows the result of using the single bit dynamic exclusion FSM to the data references from the SPEC benchmarks. Again, only the first 10 million references were used to keep simulation time reasonable. For small cache sizes there is a small improvement. However, for larger cache sizes, the dynamic exclusion FSM has slightly worse performance than a direct-mapped cache. The common data reference patterns are different than those for instructions. In addition, a normal direct-mapped cache is closer to optimal for data references than for instruction references. Thus, there is less potential for dynamic exclusion to help.

Figure 15 shows the performance of dynamic exclusion for various sizes of combined data and instruction caches with a line size of 4 bytes. For smaller cache sizes, the improvement is nearly as large as the improvement for instruction caches. For large caches, the improvement is smaller. With these benchmarks, instruction references dominate the miss rate for small caches and data references dominate for large caches. Dynamic exclusion is most useful where instruction reference patterns predominate.

8 Conclusions

This paper has presented a new technique named dynamic exclusion that reduces the miss rate of direct-mapped caches. The technique uses a small finite state machine to recognize the common instruction reference patterns. By keeping instructions that will not hit anyway out of the cache, the remaining instructions have fewer misses. The reduction in miss rate depends on the benchmark and the cache size. However, for a 32KB instruction cache with 4B lines, the average miss rate for the SPEC benchmarks is reduced by 37%. This improvement decreases with increasing cache line size, but even with 64B lines, there is still a 25% reduction. In addition, dynamic exclusion can improve the performance of the second level cache since some instructions only need to be stored in the first level cache. Finally, by reducing the number of instruction misses, dynamic exclusion may also be useful for combined instruction and data caches.

9 Acknowledgments

Michael Smith helped me get started using pixie. The reviewers detailed comments were very useful.

References

[Bel66] L.A. Belady. A study of replacement algorithms for a virtual-storage computer. *IBM Systems J.*, 5(2):78–101, 1966.

[HC89] W. W. Hwu and P. H. Chang. Achieving high instruction cache performance with an optimizing compiler. In *Proc. 16th Sym. on Computer Architecture*, Israel, May 1989.

[Hil87] M.D. Hill. *Aspects of Cache Memory and Instruction Buffer Performance*. PhD thesis, University of California, Berkeley, November 1987.

[Jou90] N. P. Jouppi. Improving direct-mapped cache performance by the addition of a small fully-associative cache and prefetch buffers. In *Proc. 17th Sym. on Computer Architecture*, Seattle, May 1990.

[Kil86] E. A. Killian. In *RISCompiler and C Programmer's Guide*. MIPS Computer Systems, 930 Arques Ave., Sunnyvale, CA 94086, 1986.

[McF89] S. McFarling. Program optimization for instruction caches. In *Proceedings of ASPLOS III*, Boston, MA, April 1989.

[McF91a] S. McFarling. Cache replacement with dynamic exclusion. WRL Technical Note TN-22, Digital Western Research Laboratory, November 1991.

[McF91b] S. McFarling. *Program Analysis and Optimization for Machines with Instruction Cache*. PhD thesis, Stanford University, September 1991. Available as CSL-TR-91-493.

[PH90] K. Pettis and R. C. Hansen. Profile guided code positioning. In *Proceedings of the ACM SIGPLAN '90 Conference on Programming Language Design and Implementation*, pages 16–27, 1990.

[PHH88] S. Przybylski, M. Horowitz, and J.L. Hennessy. Performance tradeoffs in cache design. In *Proc. 15th Sym. on Computer Architecture*, Honolulu, Hawaii, June 1988.

[PHH89] S. Przybylski, M. Horowitz, and J. Hennessy. Characteristics of performance-optimal multi-level cache heirarchy. In *Proc. 16th Sym. on Computer Architecture*, Israel, May 1989.

[Prz88] S. A. Przybylski. *Performance-Directed Memory Heirarchy Design*. PhD thesis, Stanford University, September 1988.

[SG85] J. E. Smith and J. R. Goodman. Instruction cache replacement policies and organizations. *IEEE Transactions on Computers*, C-34(3):234–241, March 1985.

[Smi82] A. J. Smith. Cache memories. *Computing Surveys*, 14(3):473–530, September 1982.

[Smi91] M. D. Smith. Tracing with pixie. Technical Report CSL-TR-91-497, Computer Systems Laboratory, Stanford University, November 1991.

[SPE90] SPEC. *The SPEC Benchmark Report*. Waterside Associates, Fremont, CA, January 1990.

[WL91] M. E. Wolf and M. S. Lam. A data locality optimizing algorithm. In *Proceedings of the ACM SIGPLAN '91 Conference on Programming Language Design and Implementation*, pages 30–44, 1991.

Session 7: Multithreading

Processor Coupling: Integrating Compile Time and Runtime Scheduling for Parallelism*

Stephen W. Keckler and William J. Dally
Artificial Intelligence Laboratory and Laboratory for Computer Science
Massachusetts Institute of Technology
Cambridge, Massachusetts 02139

Abstract

The technology to implement a single-chip node composed of 4 high-performance floating-point ALUs will be available by 1995. This paper presents processor coupling, a mechanism for controlling multiple ALUs to exploit both instruction-level and inter-thread parallelism, by using compile time and runtime scheduling. The compiler statically schedules individual threads to discover available intra-thread instruction-level parallelism. The runtime scheduling mechanism interleaves threads, exploiting inter-thread parallelism to maintain high ALU utilization. ALUs are assigned to threads on a cycle by cycle basis, and several threads can be active concurrently. We provide simulation results demonstrating that, on four simple numerical benchmarks, processor coupling achieves better performance than purely statically scheduled or multi-processor machine organizations. We examine how performance is affected by restricted communication between ALUs and by long memory latencies. We also present an implementation and feasibility study of a processor coupled node.

1 Introduction

By 1995, improvements in semiconductor technology will allow multiple high performance floating point units and several megabits of memory to reside on a single chip. One possible use of these multiple arithmetic units is to organize them in a single processor to exploit instruction-level parallelism. Controlling concurrent function units presents a challenge. Applications exhibit an uneven amount of instruction-level parallelism during their execution [11]. In some parts of a program, all of the function units will be used, while in others, serial computations with little instruction-level parallelism dominate. The amount of available parallelism depends upon both the computation at hand and the accessibility of data. Long memory latencies can stifle the opportunities to exploit instruction-level parallelism. The ideal multiple function unit processing node should provide a task the use of as many function units as it needs, but also allow unused units to be assigned to other tasks. In addition to being effective as a uniprocessor, such a node serves well in a parallel computing environment since many tasks are available. Furthermore, exploiting instruction-level parallelism in conjunction with coarser grained algorithmic concurrency improves machine performance.

*The research described in this paper was supported in part by a National Defense Science and Engineering Graduate Fellowship, by the Defense Advanced Research Projects Agency under contracts N00014-88K-0738 and N00014-87K-0825, and by a National Science Foundation Presidential Young Investigator Award, grant MIP-8657531, with matching funds from General Electric Corporation, IBM Corporation, and AT&T.

Processor Coupling

Processor coupling is a runtime scheduling mechanism in which multiple function units execute operations from a multiple instructions stream and place results directly in each other's register files. Several threads may be active simultaneously, sharing use of the function unit pipelines. Instruction level parallelism within a single thread is exploited using static scheduling techniques similar to those demonstrated in the Multiflow Trace system [4]. At runtime, the hardware scheduling mechanism interleaves several threads, exploiting inter-thread parallelism to maintain high utilization of function units.

Figure 1 demonstrates how processor coupling dynamically interleaves instruction streams from multiple threads across multiple function units. The operations from threads **A**, **B**, and **C** are scheduled independently at compile time as shown in the top of the figure. Each column in a thread's instruction stream represents an operation field for a single function unit. Each row holds operations that may be executed simultaneously. The empty boxes indicate that there is insufficient instruction-level parallelism to keep all of the function units busy. During execution, arbitration for function unit usage is performed on a cycle by cycle basis. When several threads are competing for a given function unit, one is granted use and the others must wait. For example, operations **A3** and **A4** are locked out during the second cycle because thread **C** is granted those units instead. Figure 2 illustrates the mapping of function units to threads, as a result of runtime arbitration, for the first two cycles shown in Figure 1.

Note that operations scheduled in a single long instruction word need not be executed simultaneously. Allowing the static schedule to slip provides for finer grain sharing of function units between threads. In Figure 1, operations **A3-A6** are scheduled on the same instruction word in thread **A**. Operations **A3**, **A5**, and **A6** are all issued during cycle 3, while **A4** is not issued until cycle 4. However, **A4** must be issued before **A7** and **A8**.

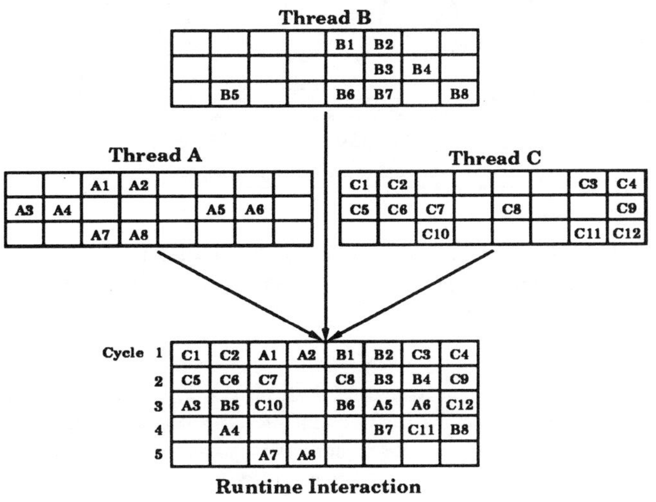

Figure 1: Interleaving of instruction streams: threads A, B, and C are scheduled separately and their instruction streams are shown at the top of the diagram. Each column of the instruction stream is a field for a particular function unit and each row holds those operations which are allowed to execute simultaneously. The bottom box shows a runtime interleaving of these threads in which some operations are delayed due to function unit conflicts.

A compiler can be used to extract the maximum amount of statically available instruction-level parallelism from a program fragment. However, compile time scheduling is limited by unpredictable memory latencies and by some dependencies, such as data dependent array references, which cannot be statically determined. Furthermore, although trace scheduling [5] and software pipelining techniques [14] can be used, branch boundaries tend to limit the number of operations that can be scheduled simultaneously. By interleaving multiple threads, the hardware runtime scheduling mechanisms of processor coupling address the limits of static scheduling due to dynamic program behavior. Additional information and further analysis of processor coupling can be found in [12].

Related Work

Processor coupling incorporates ideas from research in compile time scheduling, multiple instruction issue architectures, multithreaded machines, and runtime scheduling. Very long instruction word (VLIW) processors such as the Multiflow Trace series [3] use only compile time scheduling to manage instruction-level parallelism and resource use. Superscalar processors execute multiple instructions simultaneously by relying upon runtime scheduling mechanisms to determine data dependencies [18, 10]. The proposed XIMD [19] architecture employs compile time techniques to statically schedule instructions as well as threads, but does not dynamically interleave multiple thread execution. Using multiple threads to hide memory latencies and pipeline delays has been explored in [7, 8, 13, 17]. Dataflow and hybrid dataflow approaches such as [2, 9] have decomposed programs into large numbers of threads, consisting of one or a few instructions which are dynamically scheduled. Fisher and Rau summarize many instruction-level parallelism techniques in [6].

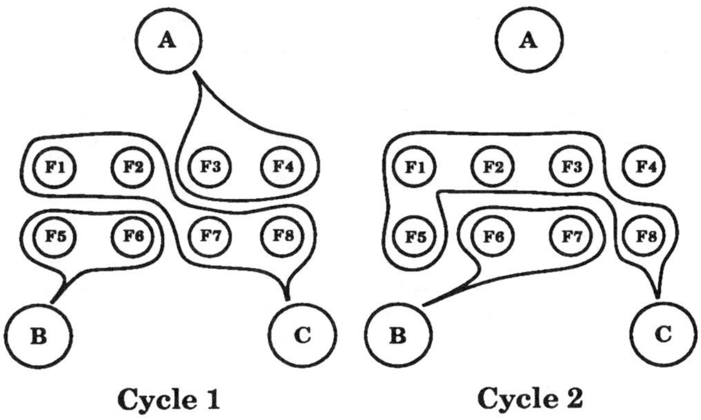

Figure 2: Two mappings of function units to threads. These mappings correspond to the first two cycles shown in Figure 1.

Context of Processor Coupling

Processor coupling is useful in machines ranging from workstations based upon a single multi-ALU node to massively parallel machines such as the MIT M-Machine, which is currently being designed. The M-Machine will consist of thousands of multi-ALU processor coupled nodes and will have many threads to be interleaved at each node. The machine will thus take advantage of a hierarchy of parallelism, ranging from coarse-grained algorithmic parallelism to extremely fine-grained instruction-level parallelism. However, as will be demonstrated in Section 4, processor coupling can be effective on only a single node. This paper will consider only a single node instance of processor coupling.

Outline

The next section examines in more detail the architecture of a processor coupled node. Section 3 presents a prototype compiler for processor coupling, as well as a simulator to evaluate processor coupled performance. Experimental assumptions, benchmarks, and results are described in Section 4. Section 5 sketches an implementation of processor coupling, while Section 6 shows that building a processor coupled node will be feasible. Finally, Section 7 proposes further directions for research in this area.

2 Discussion of Architecture

A processor coupled node, as shown in Figure 3 consists of a collection of function units, register files, memory banks, and interconnection networks. A function unit may perform integer operations, floating point operations, branch operations, or memory accesses. Function units are grouped into *clusters*, sharing a register file among them. A cluster can write to its own register file or to that of another cluster through the Unit Interconnection Network. Clusters access memory banks through the Memory Interconnection Network.

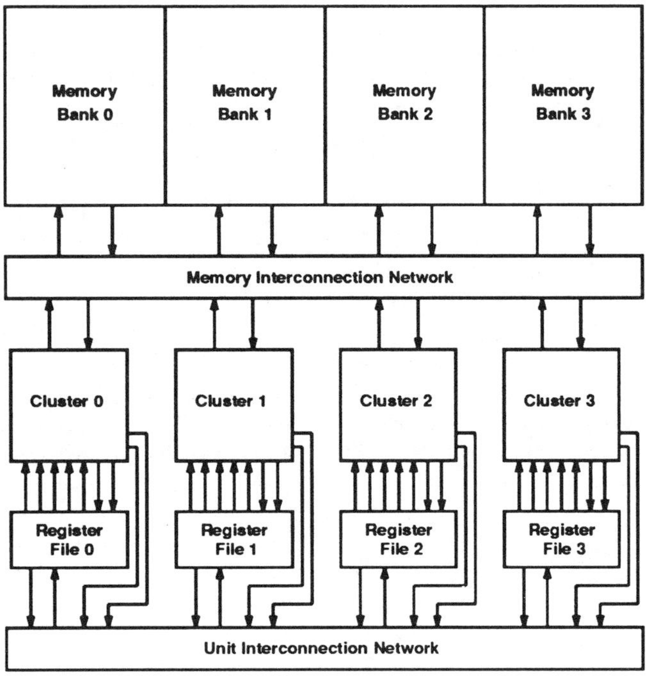

Figure 3: This sample machine consists of four clusters, each of which contains an arithmetic unit and a memory unit. The units communicate with each other through the unit interconnection network and through memory.

A function unit may be generic, such as an integer ALU, or more specialized, such as a branch calculation unit or a floating point multiplier; a unit may be be pipelined to arbitrary depth. A thread's instruction stream can be considered to be a sparse matrix of *operations*, as seen in Figure 1. To keep signal propagation delays as short as possible, control is distributed throughout the clusters. Each function unit contains an *operation cache* and an *operation buffer*. When summed over all function units the operation caches form the instruction cache. The operation buffer holds a pending operation from each active thread. A cluster's register file is multi-ported to allow multiple read and write operations per cycle. Although execution of a thread's instruction does not take place in lock step, global management of an instruction pointer prevents operations from issuing out of order. Section 5 discusses the architecture of a function unit in more detail.

Intra-thread Synchronization

Processor coupling uses data presence bits in registers for low level synchronization within a thread. An operation will not be issued until all of its source registers are valid. When an operation is issued, the valid bit for its destination register is cleared. The valid bit is set when the operation completes and writes data back to the register file. To move data between function units, an operation may specify destination registers in other clusters. Thus registers are used to indicate data dependencies between individual operations and to prevent operations from executing before their data requirements are satisfied.

Reference	Precondition	Postcondition
load	unconditional	leave as is
	wait until full	leave full
	wait until full	set empty
store	unconditional	set full
	wait until full	leave full
	wait until empty	set full

Table 1: Loads and stores can complete if the addressed location's valid bit satisfies the reference's precondition. When an memory reference completes, it sets the valid bit to the specified postcondition.

An operation can issue only if all of its data dependencies are satisfied and all of the previous instruction's operations have issued. Because different function units may have different pipeline latencies, this discipline ensures in-order operation issue, but not necessarily in-order completion.

Multiple Threads

Hardware is provided to sequence and synchronize a small number of active threads. Each thread has its own instruction pointer and logical set of registers, but shares the function units and interconnect bandwidth. A thread's register set is distributed over all of the clusters that it uses. The combined register set in each cluster can be implemented as separate register files or as a collection of virtually mapped registers [15]. Communication between threads takes place through the shared memory on the node; synchronization between threads is on the presence or absence of data in a memory location.

Each function unit determines independently, through examination of dynamic data dependencies, the next operation to issue. That operation may be from any thread in the active set. The function unit examines simultaneously the data requirements for each pending operation by inspecting the valid bits in the corresponding register files. The unit selects a ready operation, marks its destination register invalid, and issues it to the execution pipeline stages.

A processor coupled system must provide a set of thread management functions. If a thread in the active set idles, it may be swapped out in favor of another thread waiting to execute. The process of spawning new threads and of terminating threads must occur with low latency as well. Thread management is beyond the scope of this paper and will not be further discussed.

Memory System

The memory system is used for storage, synchronization, and communication between threads. Like the registers, each memory location has a valid bit. Different flavors of loads and stores are used to access memory locations. The capabilities of memory reference operations are similar to those in the Tera machine description [1] and are summarized in Table 1. These mechanisms can be used to build producer-consumer relationships, atomic updates, semaphores, and other types of synchronization schemes.

On-chip memory is used as a cache and is interleaved into banks to allow concurrent access to multiple memory locations.

Memory operations that must wait for synchronization are held in the memory system. When a subsequent reference changes a location's valid bit, waiting operations reactivate and complete. This split transaction protocol reduces memory traffic and allows memory units to issue other operations.

3 Experimental Environment

In order to evaluate the performance of processor coupling, we built an experimental environment consisting of a compiler and a simulator. The compiler is implemented in Common Lisp and the simulator in C++.

Compiler

The compiler source language has simplified C semantics with Lisp syntax. A configuration file for the machine to be simulated specifies the number and type of function units, each function unit's pipeline latency, and the grouping of function units into clusters. The compiler uses configuration information to statically schedule thread operations.

Partitioning of a benchmark program into multiple threads is made explicit in the source code using `fork` and `forall` constructs. A `fork` causes the enclosed expression to be compiled separately, and at runtime the forked thread runs concurrently with the host thread.

Code can be compiled in two ways, depending on value of the `mode` flag. If set to `single`, each thread's code is scheduled on the function units of a single cluster. The compiler chooses upon which cluster a given thread will be scheduled. If set to `unrestricted`, each thread may use as many of the function units as it needs. The compiler assigns a ordered list of clusters to each thread, which determines the function unit access pattern. Using different orderings for different threads serves as a simple form of load balancing.

The compiler performs several optimizations including constant propagation, common subexpression elimination, and static evaluation of expressions with constant operands. Live variables are kept in registers across basic block boundaries. The compiler does not perform register allocation, assuming that an infinite number of registers are available. Simulation results show that the realistic machine configurations all have a peak of fewer than 60 live registers per cluster, for each of the selected benchmarks. Averaging over these benchmarks, each cluster uses a peak of 27 registers. Only ideal mode simulations, in which loops are unrolled extensively by hand, require as many as 490 registers.

Scheduling is done according to critical path analysis of each basic block, in which the most critical operations are scheduled first. Operations are placed to minimize the amount of communication between function units.

The compiler does not perform trace scheduling or software pipelining, and does not schedule or move code across basic block boundaries. Loops must be unrolled by hand and procedures are implemented as macro-expansions. Although a few modern compilers do perform trace scheduling and software pipelining, this compiler provides a good lower bound on the quality of generated code. Using more sophisticated scheduling techniques should benefit processor coupling at least as much other machine organizations.

The compiler produces assembly code, a diagnostic file, and a modified configuration file with information concerning register and memory requirements.

Simulator

Like the compiler, the simulator is parameterized for processor configurations. The simulator takes the configuration file and the assembly code produced by the compiler, runs the program, and generates statistics including dynamic cycle count, operation count, and function unit utilization.

Simulation is at a functional level, rather than at a register transfer level, but the simulator is accurate in counting the number of cycles and operations executed. Certain assumptions were made in order to simplify simulation. Each thread is allocated its own set of registers while the function units, the communication channels, and the memory system are shared. No thread management is considered as all executing threads are assumed to be a part of the active set. New threads are spawned by the `fork` instruction which initiates a new thread context. The number of available registers is specified by the compiler, and integers and floating point numbers reside in the same register files.

The memory system is modeled statistically. The configuration file specifies the hit latency, the miss rate, and a minimum and maximum miss penalty. If a miss occurs, the number of penalty cycles is randomly chosen from the penalty range. Also, no bank conflicts are modeled, as a memory operation can always access the necessary bank. No instruction cache misses or operation prefetch delays are included.

Additionally, the configuration file describes the behavior of the interconnection between function units. The simulator manages arbitration for buses between function units if conflicts arise.

Simulation Modes

Since an input program specifies the amount of threading, and the compiler can adjust how operations are assigned to clusters, four different modes of operation are possible. Each mode corresponds to a different type of machine and is described below:

1. Sequential (SEQ): The program is written using only a single thread, with the compiler scheduling the operations on only one cluster. This is similar to a statically scheduled machine with an integer unit, a floating point unit, a memory unit, and a branch unit.

2. Statically Scheduled (STS): Like Sequential mode, only a single thread is used, but there is no restriction on the clusters used. This approximates a VLIW machine without extensive trace scheduling.

3. Ideal: The program is single threaded, has its loops unrolled as much as possible, and is completely statically scheduled. This mode is not available for those benchmarks with data dependent control structures, as they cannot be statically scheduled.

4. Thread per element (TPE): Multiple threads are specified, but each thread is restricted to run on only one cluster. Static load balancing is performed to schedule different threads on different clusters. A thread may not migrate to other clusters, but the benchmark programs are written to divide work evenly among the clusters.

5. Coupled: Multiple threads are allowed and function unit use is not restricted.

4 Experiments

Benchmarks

We selected four simple benchmarks to test the effectiveness of processor coupling. The benchmarks suite includes applications that exhibit both data parallelism and data dependent control parallelism. Each benchmark is written so that it can be partitioned easily into separate threads. This is intended to provide a set of benchmarks that each machine model can perform well upon.

Matrix is a 9×9 matrix multiply of floating point numbers, with the inner loop unrolled completely. The threaded versions execute all of the iterations of the outer loop in parallel. The ideal version of this benchmarks has all of the loops unrolled and entire computation is statically scheduled by the compiler.

FFT is a 32 point decimation-in-time fast-Fourier-transform of complex numbers. A sequential data movement routine places the input vector in bit-flipped order. The threaded version executes concurrently all of the butterfly computations within a single stage. The ideal version unrolls the inner loop completely, statically scheduling all of the operations within a single stage.

LUD solves a sparse system of linear equations using the lower-upper decomposition technique. The input data is a 64×64 adjacency matrix of an 8×8 mesh. After selecting a source row, the threaded version updates all of the target rows concurrently. No loops are unrolled and there is no ideal version since the control flow depends upon the input data.

Model is a model evaluator from an VLSI circuit simulator in which the change in current for each node in the network is computed based upon previous node voltages. The input circuit is a 20 device CMOS operational amplifier. The threaded version creates a new thread to evaluate each device on each iteration of a master loop. Like **LUD**, no loops are unrolled.

Although they are small and well contained problems, these benchmark programs can be used as building blocks for larger numerical applications. For example, the compute intensive portions of a circuit simulator such as SPICE include a model evaluator and sparse matrix solver [16].

Using these benchmarks, we first compare the performance of the different types of simulated machines. Further experiments explore issues concerning restricted connectivity between function units, variable memory latencies, and different mixes of function units.

Baseline Comparisons

The baseline machine consists of four arithmetic clusters and two branch clusters. Each arithmetic cluster contains an integer unit, a floating point unit, a memory unit, and a shared register file, while a branch cluster contains only a branch unit and a register file. The branch cluster may be used by any thread for all modes of simulation. Although processor coupling does not preclude multiple branch units, since the current version of the compiler allows each thread to issue at most one branch operation per cycle, one branch cluster is sufficient. Each function unit has a pipeline latency of one cycle.

Benchmark	Mode	#Cycles	Compared to Coupled	Utilization FPU	Utilization IU
Matrix	SEQ	1992	3.12	0.69	0.90
Matrix	STS	1182	1.85	1.16	1.52
Matrix	TPE	629	0.99	2.19	2.83
Matrix	Coupled	638	1.00	2.16	2.79
Matrix	Ideal	350	0.55	3.93	0.28
FFT	SEQ	3377	3.06	0.24	0.61
FFT	STS	1792	1.63	0.45	1.24
FFT	TPE	1977	1.79	0.40	1.05
FFT	Coupled	1102	1.00	0.73	2.03
FFT	Ideal	402	0.36	1.99	2.54
Model	SEQ	993	2.69	0.21	0.10
Model	STS	771	2.09	0.27	0.13
Model	TPE	395	1.07	0.54	0.64
Model	Coupled	369	1.00	0.57	0.70
LUD	SEQ	57975	2.69	0.14	0.45
LUD	STS	33126	1.54	0.24	0.78
LUD	TPE	22627	1.05	0.35	1.35
LUD	Coupled	21543	1.00	0.37	1.42

Table 2: Cycle count comparison of different types of machines. Floating point unit (FPU) utilization is given as the average number of floating point operations executed each cycle. Integer Unit (IU) utilization is calculated similarly.

In the baseline machine, an operation can specify at most two simultaneous register destinations. A function unit can write a result back to any cluster's register file, each of which has enough buses and ports to prevent resource conflicts. Memory units perform the operations required for address calculation. Memory references take a single cycle and have no bank conflicts.

Assuming that the compiler produces the best possible schedule, the number of cycles executed by the fully unrolled instance of a benchmark is a lower bound for this particular machine configuration. Sequential mode operation provides an upper bound since only the parallelism within a single cluster can be exploited. Table 2 shows the cycle counts for each machine mode. Floating point utilization is given as the average number of floating point operations executed each cycle. Integer unit utilization is calculated similarly. Figure 4 displays the cycle counts graphically.

Considering the statically scheduled benchmarks, STS mode requires on average 1.7 times fewer cycles than SEQ, since STS allows use of all the function units. Since the Ideal mode's program is fully unrolled and statically scheduled, loop overhead operations and redundant address calculations are eliminated. This reduced operation count permits the ideal machine to execute in an average of 7 times fewer cycles than SEQ.

In threaded mode, the cycle count for Coupled and TPE are nearly equivalent for the **Matrix**, **LUD**, and **Model** benchmarks, which have been stripped of nearly all sequential execution sections, and are easily partitionable. TPE is as fast as Coupled since

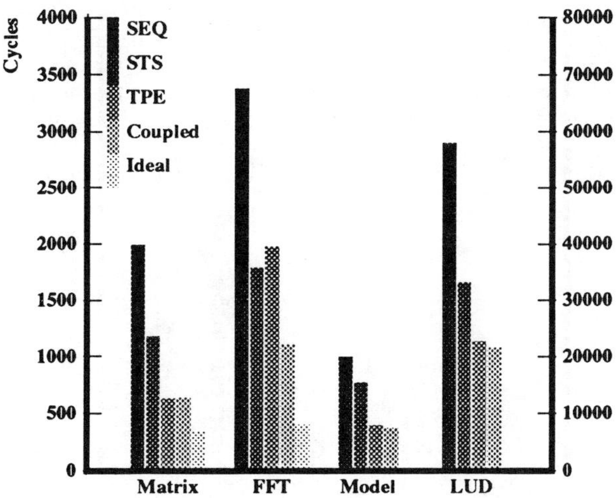

Figure 4: Baseline cycle counts for the five simulation modes. **Matrix**, **FFT**, and **Model**, are referenced to the left axis, while the scale for **LUD** is on the right. Ideal is only implemented for **Matrix** and **FFT**.

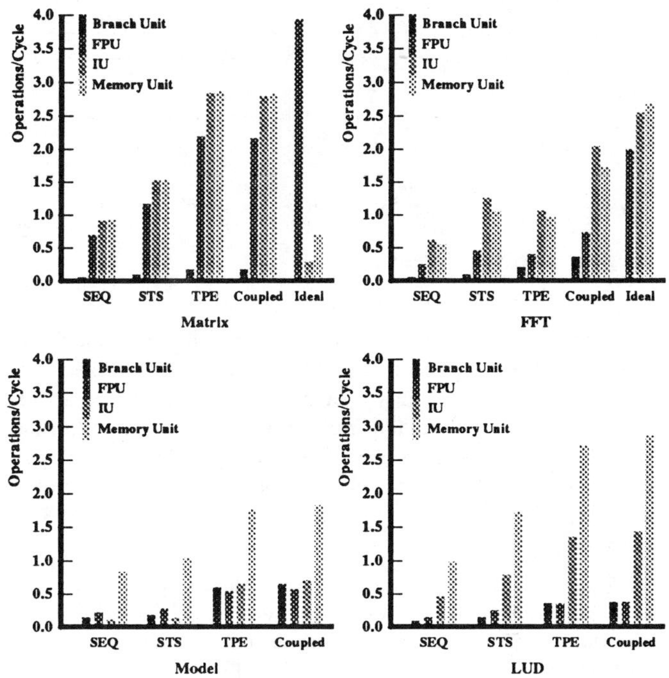

Figure 5: Function unit utilization for all four benchmarks. FPU utilization is the average number of FPU operations per cycle. Other unit utilizations are calculated similarly.

the load is balanced across the its clusters. Processor coupling will have an advantage in less intrinsically load balanced computations, as long as threads are not allowed to migrate between clusters.

FFT, however, has a large sequential section that cannot be partitioned. Since each TPE thread can execute on only one cluster, the performance of TPE in the sequential section is no better than SEQ. In fact, because of the dominance of the sequential section, TPE does not even perform as well as STS for the entire benchmark. Coupled, on the other hand, performs as well as STS on sequential code. The available instruction level parallelism can be exploited by Coupled, but not by TPE. Thus, one advantage of Coupled over TPE is found in sequential code execution. Since parallel speedup of a program is limited by the amount of sequential code, single thread performance is vital.

The dynamic scheduling capability of Coupled mode allows it to execute in an average of 55% fewer cycles than the statically scheduled STS mode. TPE, with its multiple threads, also executes faster than STS for all benchmarks but **FFT**. This reduced cycle count in TPE and Coupled is due to the fine grained interleaving of threads. The multiple threads of Coupled mode result in much higher function unit utilization, and therefore a lower cycle count, than STS. One of processor coupling's advantages over a statically scheduled scheme is the increased unit utilization allowed by dynamic scheduling.

Utilization

Figure 5 shows for each benchmark, the utilization of the floating point units, integer units, memory units, and branch units. In all benchmarks, unit utilization increases as the simulation mode approaches Ideal. For **Matrix**, utilization is balanced for FPUs, IUs, and memory units, up to the Coupled mode. In Ideal mode, the FPU utilization is 3.9, indicating that the compiler has filled nearly every floating point operation slot. Note that since the compiler has eliminated loop overhead operations and common subexpressions in array index calculation, very few integer and branch operations are required. Furthermore, a significant fraction of the memory operations have been replaced by register operations.

Aside from the ideal mode, **FFT** utilization is similar. The multiple active threads available in TPE and Coupled modes drive memory unit utilization up. This rise results from the many read and write operations performed by the butterfly calculations of the inner loop. Memory utilization in the Ideal mode is still high because the compiler was unable to replace memory references with register references. The **Model** and **LUD** benchmarks are dominated by memory operations. Thus, even in Coupled and TPE mode, the integer and floating point utilizations are still quite small.

Interference

For multithreaded versions of the benchmarks programs, the statically scheduled threads interfere with one another, causing the runtime cycle count to be longer than the compile time schedule would suggest. To demonstrate this dilation, we use a slightly different version of the **Model** benchmark in Coupled mode. Four threads are created when the program starts. Each thread accesses a common priority queue of devices to be evaluated, chooses a device, updates the queue, and then evaluates the device. This loop is repeated by all threads until the queue is empty. A new input circuit with identical devices, each at the same operating point, al-

Mode	Thread	Compile Time Schedule	Runtime Cycle Count	Devices Evaluated
STS	1	25	25.0	20
Coupled	1	23	28.0	8
Coupled	2	23	38.7	6
Coupled	3	23	77.3	3
Coupled	4	23	80.7	3

Table 3: Average cycle counts for each iteration of the inner loop of the **Model** benchmark for STS and Coupled, with threads assigned different priorities.

lows extraneous code in the source program to be removed. Thus, every operation specified in the new source program is executed. This provides us with ability to compare runtime cycle count with the number of instructions generated by the compiler. With the modified benchmark, the effect of the priority assigned to a thread on its runtime schedule can be seen more clearly. We compare the Coupled benchmark to a similarly altered version of an STS mode program.

Table 3 shows the compile time schedule length and the average runtime cycle count to evaluate one model for each of the four threads in Coupled mode. The higher priority threads in Coupled mode execute in fewer cycles. In STS mode, there is only one thread, and it runs in the same number of cycles as the static schedule predicts.

In addition, contention between threads for the shared queue arises in Coupled mode as even the highest priority thread requires more cycles than the schedule predicts. Taking a weighted average across the four threads, Coupled mode requires 46.5 cycles per device evaluation. Although STS requires only 25 cycles per evaluation, the multiple threads of Coupled allows evaluations to overlap such that the aggregate running time is shorter (274 cycles versus 505 for STS). On single threaded code, Coupled and STS perform equally well; on threaded code, Coupled mode will execute in fewer cycles.

Restricting Communication

Data may need to be transferred from one cluster to another for several reasons. When two independent operations executing simultaneously on different clusters produce results needed by a subsequent operation, at least one of the results must be transferred. Thus data movement comes as a result of the compiler trying to exploit the maximum instruction level parallelism. Another source of data movement comes from operation results that must be used by multiple subsequent operations. One example is an eliminated common subexpression, such as redundant array index calculations. These values might be distributed to multiple clusters.

Since the number of buses and register input ports required to support fully connected function units is prohibitively expensive, some compromises must be made. Restricting communication between function units reduces cost without significantly affecting cycle count. The five different communication configurations that were simulated are described below:

1. Full: The function units are fully connected with no restrictions on the number of buses or register file write ports.

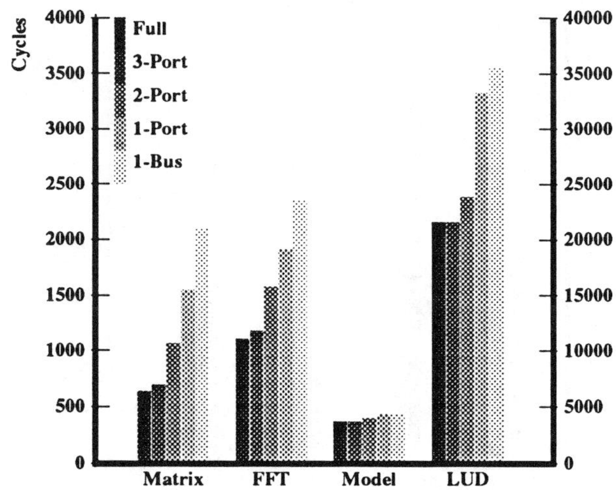

Figure 6: Cycle counts for restricted communication schemes of processor coupling on all benchmarks. **Matrix, FFT,** and **Model,** are referenced to the left axis, while the scale for **LUD** is on the right. Cycle count increases dramatically when single buses and ports are used, but the Tri-Port scheme is nearly as effective as the fully connected configuration.

2. Tri-port: Each register file has three write ports. One port is used locally within a cluster by those units sharing the register file. The other two ports have their own buses and can be used by any function unit in another cluster.

3. Dual-port: Each register file has two write ports. This is similar to Tri-Port, with only one global register port.

4. Single-port: Each register file has a single write port with its own bus. Any function unit can use the port without interfering with writes to other register files.

5. Shared-bus: Each register file has two ports. One port is for use within a cluster, while the other port is is connected to a globally shared bus. Arbitration is performed to decide which function unit may use the bus on a given cycle.

Figure 6 demonstrates how processor coupled performance is affected by restricting the amount of communication between function units. As expected, the number of cycles increases when function units must contend for buses and register ports.

Matrix, FFT, and **LUD,** have high integer unit utilization because they calculate many common array indices, and are sharply affected when using a Single-Port or Single-Bus network. **Model** exhibits less instruction level parallelism, has low unit utilization, and is hardly affected by changing communication strategies.

Any restricted communication scheme trades chip area for increased cycle count. Tri-Port performs the best of the restricted configurations examined, requiring an average of only 4% more cycles than the fully connected configuration. Tri-port can be implemented using only 2 global buses per cluster. The number of buses to implement a fully connected scheme, on the other hand, is proportional to the number of function units times the number of clusters. Furthermore, the completely connected configuration

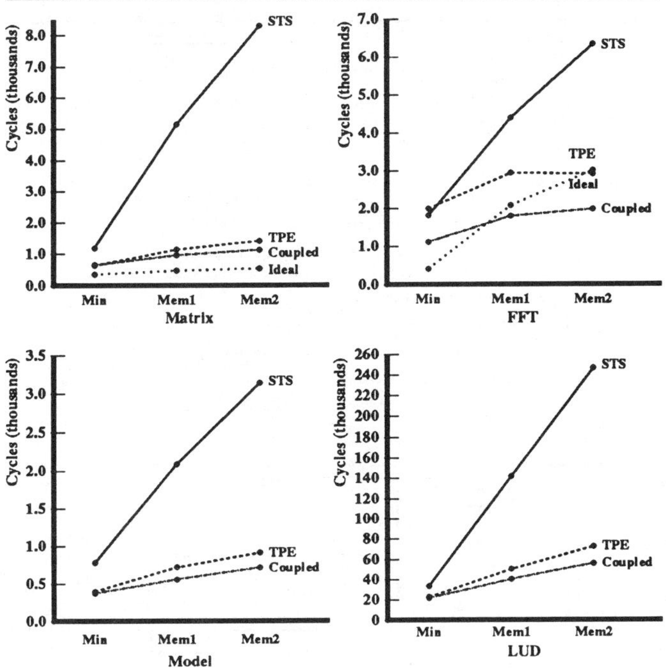

Figure 7: Cycle counts when memory latency is varied for all of the benchmarks. Increased memory latency affects the single threaded modes (STS and Ideal) more than the threaded modes (Coupled and TPE).

will require additional register ports. In a four cluster system the interconnection and register file area for Tri-Port is 28% that of complete connection.

Variable Memory Latency

Long memory latencies due to synchronization or remote references degrade performance of any machine. Statically indeterminant memory latencies are particularly damaging for STS mode machines since long delays stall the entire computation. Multithreaded machines hide long memory latencies by executing other threads.

A five to ten percent miss rate is assumed for an on-chip cache, depending on its size and organization. If a cache miss occurs, the memory reference must go off chip. When the requested data is in local memory, the reference might complete in 20 cycles. References to physically remote nodes can take 100 or more cycles. The three models of memory system performance used in simulations are:

- **Min**: single cycle latency for all memory references.
- **Mem1**: single cycle hit latency, 5% miss rate, and a miss penalty evenly distributed between 20 and 100 cycles.
- **Mem2**: similar to **Mem1** with a 10% miss rate.

Figure 7 shows how the cycle counts for different machine models are affected by long memory latencies. Since the compiler is able to use 490 registers in Ideal mode for **Matrix**, very few memory references need to be made. Thus long latencies hardly affect the ideal machine's cycle count. In **FFT**, however, the cycle count for Ideal mode increases dramatically, because many loads and stores are required, and each delayed memory reference halts computation. Cycle count for STS mode rises in all benchmarks with increasing memory latency for similar reasons. Nearly 5.5 times as many cycles are needed on average for execution with **Mem2** parameters as with **Min** for STS.

The cycle count for Coupled does not increase as greatly in any of the benchmarks since other threads are executed when one thread is waiting for a long latency reference. On average, execution with **Mem2** parameters requires twice as many operations as **Min**. If the compiler knew which references would cause long delays, it could create a schedule to try to mask long latencies. However, since memory latencies cannot be statically determined, runtime scheduling techniques, like those of processor coupling, must be used to mask the delay. Memory latencies can be quite long in a distributed memory parallel machine; masking of latency is a major advantage of Coupled over STS.

TPE is affected only a little more severely than Coupled by long memory latencies. Execution in **Mem2** mode requires 2.3 times as many operations as **Min**. Like Coupled mode, TPE has other threads to run while waiting for long latency memory references. However, threads are allocated statically to specific clusters. If only one thread is resident on a cluster and it stalls waiting for a reference, the processor resources on that cluster go unused.

Number and Mix of Function Units

To determine the proper ratio between different types of units, we simulated all processor coupled machine configurations with up to four IUs and four FPUs, while keeping the number of memory units constant at four. For our applications, simulation showed that a single branch unit is sufficient. Figure 8 displays the cycle counts for all the benchmarks as a function of the number of IUs and FPUs. The number of FPUs and IUs are on the X and Y axes. Cycle count is displayed on the Z axis.

The function unit requirements depend greatly upon the application. For **Matrix**, cycle count is highest when only one IU and one FPU are used, and decreases when more units are added. If the number of IUs is held constant and the number of FPUs is increased, the cycle count drops. The same holds true if the number of FPUs is constant and the number of IUs is varied. One FPU will saturate a single IU, but two IUs are needed to saturate a single FPU. Even though each benchmark consists primarily of floating point operations, this shows that integer units, which are used for synchronization and loop control, can also be a bottleneck. With a fixed number of function units, cycle count is minimized when the number of FPUs and IUs are equal.

The results for **FFT** are similar to those of **Matrix**. However, with four FPUs and one IU, the cycle count increases. This is due to additional IU operations required to move floating point array indicies to remote memory units. Like **Matrix**, one FPU will saturate a single IU, but each additional IU improves performance. **LUD** shows much the same behavior as **FFT** with cycle count increasing as FPUs are added.

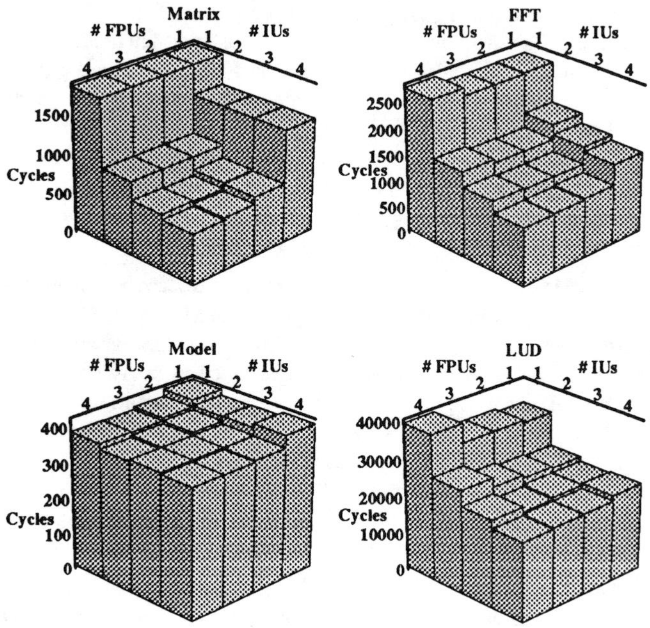

Figure 8: Cycle count as a function of number of Floating Point Units (FPUs) and Integer Units (IUs) for all four benchmarks. Cycle count is minimized when the number of IUs and FPUs is equal.

Model exhibits much less instruction level parallelism and does not benefit as greatly as the other benchmarks from additional function units. Cycle count is still minimized when four IUs and four FPUs are used.

For these benchmarks, the incremental benefit in cycles decreases as more function units are added. The results indicate that performance of a processor coupled node does not increase significantly for the sample benchmarks when more than four IUs and FPUs are used.

5 Implementation

Function Unit Pipeline

A block diagram of a function unit is shown in Figure 9. The function unit has as a five-stage pipeline consisting of operation fetch (OF), scoreboard check (SC), register read (RR), execution (EX), and write back (WB) stages.

Operation Fetch: During the operation fetch (OF) stage, an active thread addresses the operation cache, reading an operation into the operation prefetch buffer. The prefetch buffer holds one prefetched operation for each active thread. The thread instruction stream to fetch from is determined by the operation issued to the RR stage. If thread j's operation i is issued into the RR stage, then j's next operation $i+1$ is read into the operation buffer, and operation $i+2$ is fetched into the prefetch buffer. This allows a single thread the capability to issue an operation each cycle.

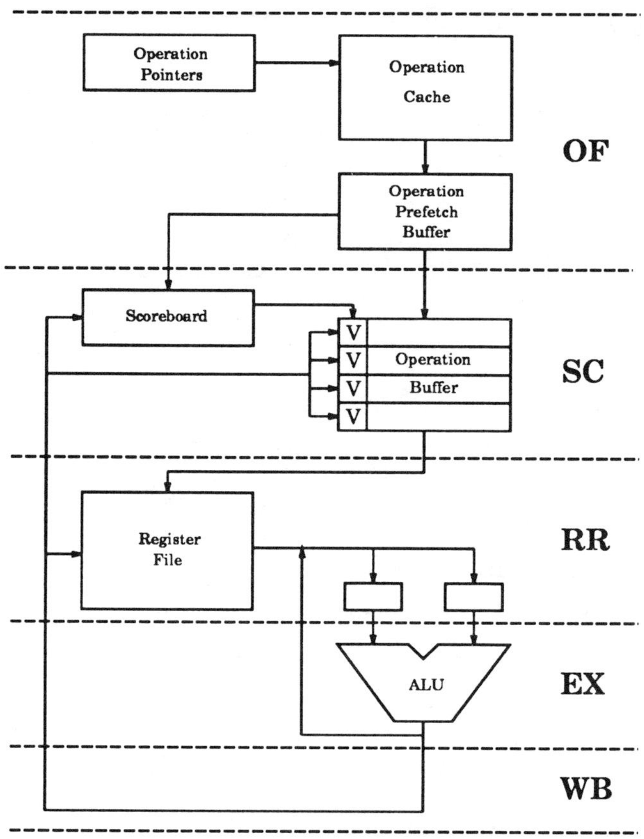

Figure 9: A Sample function unit with a single EX stage. OF fetches an operation from the Operation Cache, SC checks the scoreboard to determine which of the source registers are ready, RR reads the register file, EX executes the operation, and WB writes back the result.

Scoreboard Check: An operation accesses the scoreboard during the scoreboard check (SC) stage. The scoreboard determines which of the source registers required by the operation are ready. The operation, along with the register status obtained from the scoreboard is deposited in the operation buffer. The operation buffer can hold one pending operation from each active thread.

The operation buffer maintains the status for each pending operation to determine when that operation is ready to issue. Its function is similar to that of a reservation station [18]. An operation is enabled to issue when all of its source registers are ready and when all operations from previous instructions in that thread have issued. A pending operation's status is updated as source registers become available and as operations from previous instructions complete. This update is performed directly in-place and does not require access to the scoreboard. An operation that finds all of its registers ready when it accesses the scoreboard may move directly from the SC stage to the RR stage, without entering the operation buffer.

Register Read: Each cycle, the operation buffer selects an enabled operation and forwards it to the register read (RR) stage,

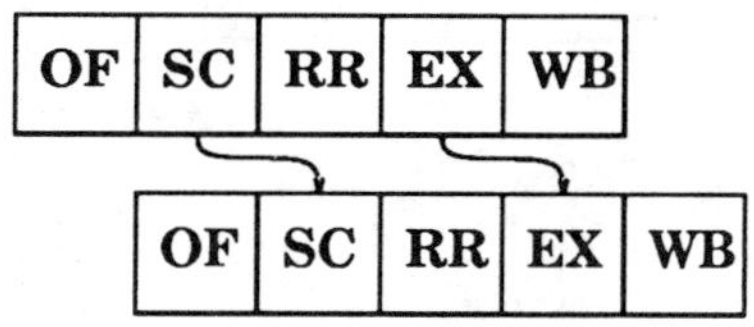

Figure 10: A five stage pipeline corresponding to the function unit in Figure 9. The first operation updates the scoreboard as it issues to the RR stage. The next operation can use the bypassed result. Data can be bypassed from one EX stage to the next.

where the selected operation reads its source registers. These registers are guaranteed to be available since only operations with all dependencies satisfied are issued to the RR stage. The RR stage is the only pipeline stage that uses the register read ports. The presence bits used for synchronization are kept instead in the scoreboard and are accessed during the SC stage.

Execution: The operation along with its arguments proceeds to the execution (EX) stage(s). All operations, including arithmetic operations, loads, stores, and branches, are executed during EX stages. Depending on the type of operation performed, more than one cycle may be required for execution. Some operations, such as memory references take a variable number of cycles to complete. Out of order completion of operations is permitted since the scoreboard manages data dependencies.

Write Back: The results of the operation are written to the destination register file in the register write (RW) stage. A destination register may reside in a local register file or in a remote register file. Writes to the local register file can use the local bypass paths, and the results can be used without delay. However, remote writes must proceed through the WB stage.

Scoreboard Update

Two cycles before an operation is to complete, the destination register file's scoreboard is updated to indicate that the register is available. This allows an operation to issue in time to use a result that is bypassed directly from the execution unit. Figure 10 shows an operation pipeline with a one stage execution unit. The first operation updates the scoreboard as soon it issues to the RR stage. This permits the subsequent operation to issue in the next cycle and use the bypassed result. The path for data to be bypassed from one EX stage to the next is also shown.

The scoreboard requires the same number of read ports and write ports as the register file. The read ports are used during the SC stage to check the status of operation source registers, while the write ports are used two cycles before RW so that the scoreboard will reflect all register writes. Any arbitration required for access to the register file write ports is performed at the same time as the scoreboard update.

Comparison to Conventional Pipeline

The processor coupled function unit adds a scoreboard check stage to the conventional four-stage execution pipeline. In a conventional pipeline, instructions check the availability of their operands in parallel with the register read. These speculative register reads before dependencies are satisfied cause the pipeline to stall whenever a source register is not available. Because the register read ports have been consumed by the stalled instruction, no other instruction is available to proceed to the execution unit on the next cycle. A bubble is inserted into the pipeline and resources are wasted.

In a processor coupled pipeline, dependencies are examined in the SC stage without using the register read ports. Only operations that are enabled by having all dependencies satisfied are issued to the RR stage. This early check permits an operation from another thread to be issued from the operation buffer if the operation just accessing the scoreboard is not ready for issue. The scoreboard check adds a stage to the pipeline and thus increases the branch penalty by one cycle. It does not increase arithmetic latency, however, since the scoreboard can be updated early to permit immediate use of bypassed arithmetic results.

Inter-Cluster Communication

An operation must read its source registers from the local register file but may write its result to a register in a different cluster. An inter-cluster interconnection network is provided to support this communication. Several alternative structures for this network were evaluated in Section 4. For these networks, a single cycle is required to transport a result to a remote cluster. A result produced in cycle i, can be used by the execution unit in the local cluster during cycle i, but will not be available to a remote cluster until cycle $i + 1$.

Arbitration for shared communication resources is performed at the time of scoreboard update, two cycles before the result is available. An operation that wins the arbitration updates the scoreboard in the remote cluster immediately and uses the data paths granted by the arbitration two cycles later to provide the result. An operation that loses the arbitration stalls its pipeline and retries on subsequent cycles until the data paths are granted. The networks discussed in Section 4 are designed so that all resources (paths and register ports) are granted in a single arbitration cycle; multiple arbitrations that could potentially lead to deadlock are not required.

Inter-Cluster Synchronization

To provide in-order execution of operations from a given thread, a wire-or NOTDONE line is provided for each active thread. If a function unit holds an unenabled operation from a thread's previous instruction, the unit will assert the corresponding NOTDONE line. When all non-null operations in a particular thread's previous instruction have issued, this line is deasserted. As long as the line remains deasserted, each function unit is capable of issuing an operation from that thread every cycle. The OF and SC stages fill the operation buffer with operations from each active thread, independent of the state of the thread's NOTDONE lines. Thus a

Component	Area
64-bit FPU	$8\times10^7\lambda^2$
Integer Unit	$10^7\lambda^2$
128 64-bit Registers	$4\times10^7\lambda^2$
Operation Cache (16Kbits)	$2\times10^7\lambda^2$
Operation Buffer	$10^6\lambda^2$
Scoreboard	$5\times10^6\lambda^2$
Control	$2\times10^7\lambda^2$
Total	$1.8\times10^8\lambda^2$

Table 4: Cluster components with area estimates. Area estimates are made using λ design rules from current technologies.

function unit is able to issue an operation for a thread as soon as the NOTDONE line is deasserted.

Memory System

Each memory unit sees the memory system as a request port and a response port. A memory unit sends read and write requests to the request port. Each request consists of an address, data (for writes), and a destination specifier (for reads). Results of read operations are directed to the response port for the cluster specified. Each response updates the scoreboard and stores its data into the specified register.

The details of the memory system implementation are beyond the scope of this paper. We expect that an interleaved cache will be required on-chip to satisfy the bandwidth demands of the arithmetic units. This on-chip cache will be backed by a larger off-chip memory and by the global machine memory accessed over an inter-node interconnection network.

6 Chip Area Estimates

In 1995, CMOS process technology will have $0.5\mu m$ gate lengths and three layers of metal interconnect. Chips $17.5mm$ on a side, providing $4.9\times10^9\lambda^2$ of area, will be economical.[1]

A four cluster coupled multi-ALU processor (MAP) with resources for four active threads is feasible with 1995 technology. Table 4 lists each component, with a corresponding area estimate, of a cluster. Area estimates are made using λ design rules for current technologies. Each cluster requires a total area of $1.8\times10^8\lambda^2$. With 6λ wire pitch, 512 cluster interconnect wires running the length of four function units ($5\times10^4\lambda$) consumes $1.5\times10^8\lambda^2$. Area for interconnect to the on-chip cache is $8\times10^7\lambda^2$. The remaining $4\times10^9\lambda^2$ is used for 8Mbits of SRAM. Figure 6 shows a floorplan for the processor coupled chip.

The additional components required by each cluster to implement processor coupling are the operation cache ($2\times10^7\lambda^2$), the scoreboard ($5\times10^6\lambda^2$), the operation buffer ($10^6\lambda^2$), and approximately half of the control ($10^7\lambda^2$). This overhead is $3.6\times10^7\lambda^2$ per cluster for a total of $1.4\times10^8\lambda^2$, which is 20 percent of the entire cluster area, but only 3 percent of the chip area.

In terms of speed and area, building register files with more than six ports is inefficient. Replacing the partitioned register sets

[1] The parameter λ is, to first order, process independent and is equivalent to one half of the minimum feature size. For a $0.5\mu m$ process, λ is 0.25.

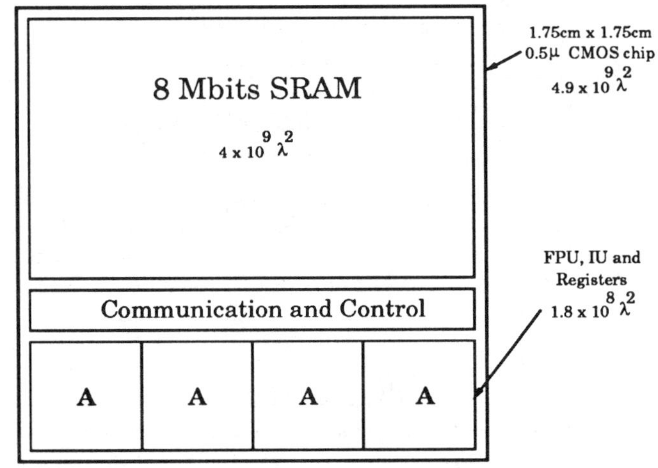

Figure 11: Floorplan of a four cluster multi-ALU node.

with a unified register file would require each register cell to have roughly 32 ports. Each cell needs at least 32 word lines and 32 bit lines. If a 6λ wiring pitch is used, a cell will be nearly 200λ on a side with an area of $4\times10^4\lambda^2$. The area of a 512 register 64-bit register file, which is specified above for a processor coupled node, would be $1.3\times10^9\lambda^2$. This is more than one-quarter of the total chip area. Furthermore, the long wires required by a single register file are likely to induce clock speed limiting delays. The processor coupling approach distributes the registers into individual register files local to a cluster. Partitioning a cluster's registers further reduces the number of ports required. The area of a six-ported register cell is $5\times10^3\lambda^2$. Building eight register files of 64 64-bit registers requires $1.6\times10^8\lambda^2$. With the function unit interconnect area of $1.5\times10^8\lambda^2$ needed to move data from cluster to cluster, the total area required is $3.1\times10^8\lambda^2$. This is less than seven percent of the total chip area. Although distributing the register files will require more operations to be executed, cycle time is reduced and area for other important components becomes available.

7 Conclusion

Processor coupling combines compile-time and run-time scheduling to exploit instruction level parallelism while maintaining high function unit utilization. A compiler schedules each thread across multiple ALUs to exploit instruction level parallelism. The schedules of several active threads are interleaved at runtime by coupling threads to ALUs on a cycle-by-cycle basis. This interleaving makes use of resources that would otherwise be left idle due to both holes in a single thread's schedule and stalls caused by synchronization and statically undetermined latencies. Processor coupling combines the ability to exploit parallelism at the level of a single operation as in a VLIW machine with the latency tolerance and high utilization of a multithreaded architecture.

Four simple benchmarks (**Matrix**, **FFT**, **Model**, and **LUD**) were run on several types of simulated machines. On these particular benchmarks, a processor coupled node executes in 60% fewer cycles, and achieves almost twice the utilization of a statically scheduled processor without coupling. Processor coupling is tolerant of variable memory and execution unit latencies. In our experiments with variable memory latency, a processor coupled node executes in 75% fewer cycles than a statically scheduled processor.

The inter-function unit interconnection greatly affects performance. Our simulations suggest the use of an interconnection scheme with three write ports on each register file. One port is devoted to intra-cluster communication, and the remaining ports are connected to buses that can be driven by function units in other clusters. This configuration gives nearly the same performance as complete connection (only 4% more cycles) for less cost (28% of the interconnect area for a four cluster machine). Performance also depends on the right balance of function unit types. Our simulations suggest a configuration with four floating point units, four integer units, and one branch unit.

Processor coupling is implemented by adding a scoreboard check (SC) stage containing an operation buffer to a standard four-stage pipeline. The SC stage ensures that an operation is enabled to be issued only if all of its dependencies are satisfied. This check avoids wasting register bandwidth reading operands for instructions that are not ready. Adding this stage to the pipeline adds one cycle to the penalty for an incorrectly predicted branch but does not affect arithmetic latency. Preliminary circuit estimates indicate that since the machine's cycle time will be dominated by arithmetic and memory latencies, processor coupling will not affect clock speed.

A single-chip, four-cluster, multi-alu processor is feasible with 1995 technology (0.5μ CMOS). Each cluster of such a chip consists of a floating point unit, integer unit, registers, and control, occupying $1.8\times10^8\lambda^2$. The remaining area is allocated to on-chip communication ($2.3\times10^8\lambda^2$) and 8Mbits of memory ($4\times10^9\lambda^2$). The additional control logic required to implement processor coupling adds only 3% to the area cost of the chip.

The simulation results presented here suggest that processor coupling is an attractive method for controlling multi-ALU processors. To complement this examination of multi-ALU processor control, studies of high-bandwidth memory systems and mechanisms for thread management are needed. Parameters of the memory system, including the number of banks at each level of hierarchy, the split transaction protocol, and the cache organization must be studied in detail. Thread management functions such as synchronization between threads, the number of threads in the active set, and the mechanism for swapping threads in and out of the active set, require exploration as well.

Acknowledgements

Many thanks to the anonymous reviewers of this paper for their insightful suggestions. We thank Deborah Wallach for her careful review of early drafts of this paper, and Ricardo Telichevesky for his help in formulating the **LUD** benchmark. Finally we thank all the members of the MIT Concurrent VLSI Architecture group for their feedback and contributions to this to this work.

References

[1] Alverson, R., Callahan, D., Cummings, D., Koblenz, B., Porterfield, A., and Smith, B. The Tera computer system. In *Proceedings of the International Conference on Supercomputing* (June 1990), pp. 1–6.

[2] Arvind, and Culler, D. E. Dataflow architectures. *Annual Reviews in Computer Science 1* (February 1986), 225–53.

[3] Colwell, R. P., Hall, W. E., Joshi, C. S., Papworth, D. B., Rodman, P. K., and Tornes, J. E. Architecture and implementation of a VLIW supercomputer. In *Proceedings of Supercomputing '90* (November 1990), IEEE Computer Society Press, pp. 910–919.

[4] Colwell, R. P., Nix, R. P., O'Donnell, J. J., Papworth, D. B., and Rodman, P. K. A VLIW architecture for a trace scheduling compiler. *IEEE Transactions on Computers 37*, 8 (August 1988), 967–979.

[5] Ellis, J. R. *Bulldog: A Compiler for VLIW Architectures.* MIT Press, Cambridge, MA, 1986.

[6] Fisher, J. A., and Rau, B. R. Instruction-level parallel processing. *Science 253* (September 1991), 1233–1241.

[7] Gupta, A., and Weber, W.-D. Exploring the benefits of multiple hardware contexts in a multiprocessor architecture: preliminary results. In *Proceedings of the 16th Annual Symposium on Computer Architecture* (May 1989), IEEE, pp. 273–280.

[8] Halstead, R. H., and Fujita, T. MASA: A multithreaded processor architecture for parallel symbolic computing. In *Proceedings of the 15th Annual Symposium on Computer Architecture* (1988), IEEE, pp. 443–451.

[9] Ianucci, R. A. Toward a dataflow/Von Neumann hybrid architecture. In *Proceedings of the 15th Annual Symposium on Computer Architecture* (1988), IEEE, pp. 131–140.

[10] Johnson, W. M. *Superscalar Microprocessor Design.* Prentice Hall, Englewood Cliffs, NJ, 1991.

[11] Jouppi, N. P., and Wall, D. W. Available instruction level parallelism for superscalar and superpipelined machines. In *Proceedings of the Third International Conference on Architectural Support for Programming Languages and Operating Systems* (April 1989), ACM Press, pp. 272–282.

[12] Keckler, S. W. A coupled multi-ALU processing node for a highly parallel computer. Tech. Rep. 1355, Massachusetts Institute of Technology Artificial Intelligence Laboratory, Cambridge, MA 02139, 1992.

[13] Kuehn, J. T., and Smith, B. J. The Horizon supercomputing system: Architecture and software. In *Proceedings of Supercomputing '88* (Orlando, Florida, November 1988), pp. 28–34.

[14] Lam, M. Software pipelining: An effective scheduling technique for VLIW machines. In *ACM Sigplan '88 Conference on Programming Language Design and Implementation* (1988), pp. 318–328.

[15] Nuth, P. R., and Dally, W. J. A mechanism for efficient context switching. In *Proceedings of the International Conference on Computer Design* (October 1991), IEEE, pp. 301–304.

[16] Sadayappan, P., and Visvanathan, V. Circuit simulation on shared memory multiprocessors. *IEEE Transactions on Computers 37*, 12 (December 1988), 1634–1642.

[17] Smith, B. J. Architecture and applications of the HEP multiprocessor computer system. *SPIE 298* (1981), 241–248.

[18] Tomasulo, R. An efficient algorithm for exploiting multiple arithmetic units. *IBM Journal 11* (January 1967), 25–33.

[19] Wolfe, A., and Shen, J. P. A variable instruction stream extension to the VLIW architecture. In *Proceedings of the Fourth International Conference on Architectural Support for Programming Languages and Operating Systems* (April 1991), ACM Press, pp. 2–14.

Improved Multithreading Techniques for Hiding Communication Latency in Multiprocessors

Bob Boothe* Abhiram Ranade*

Computer Science Division
University of California, Berkeley, CA 94720

Abstract

Shared memory multiprocessors are considered among the easiest parallel computers to program. However building shared memory machines with thousands of processors has proved difficult because of the inevitably long memory latencies. Much previous research has focused on cache coherency techniques, but it remains unclear if caches can obtain sufficiently high hit rates. In this paper we present improved multithreading techniques that can easily tolerate latencies of hundreds of cycles, and yet only require a small number of threads per processor. High performance is achieved by introducing an explicit context switch instruction that can be used by a simple optimizing compiler to group together several shared accesses. This grouping of shared accesses dramatically reduces the frequency of context switches compared to simpler multithreading models. The combination of our techniques achieves efficiencies of 80% or higher on a broad set of applications.

1 Introduction

Large shared memory multiprocessors will have very long latencies for remote memory accesses. For a 1024 processor machine, we expect latencies of hundreds of cycles[7, 9]. These long latencies are inevitable because of the size and complexity of any interconnection network that can connect thousands of processors and memories and support high bandwidth. Without some means of tolerating memory latency, a 1024 processor shared memory multiprocessor would spend a large fraction of its time waiting for shared accesses to complete.

Memory latency has traditionally been hidden by caches, and many researchers have tried to extend cache coherency schemes to allow cacheing to be used on scalable shared memory machines. [5, 9, 18]. Caches, however, do not actually hide memory latency, but instead, they hope to eliminate enough of the memory accesses that the latencies of the few remaining accesses will have only a small impact on the execution time. Consider a simple example where a program accesses shared memory every tenth cycle and where the memory latency is 200 cycles. Without any means of hiding latency, the program will execute for ten cycles and then wait 200 cycles for the result to return. The processor utilization will be only 5%. If we add a cache that can achieve a 90% hit rate, only every tenth access will have to wait, but that access will still wait 200 cycles. The efficiency has risen only to 33%. Recent simulation results from the DASH project[9] confirm this simple argument. They measured hit rates on shared-read references ranging from 66% to 80%, and processor utilizations ranging from 20% to 28% under a release consistency model. Other simulation studies have also reported low processor utilizations[5]. O'Krafka[18] reported more promising hit rates, but overall, cacheing alone does not appear to be an adequate solution to the latency problem.

Prefetching of data is another potential solution. If data can be prefetched far enough in advance, it will have returned from the memory network by the time the processor needs to use it. For many scientific codes prefetching works well[8, 9, 13]. But on less regular codes, such as those that traverse complex linked data structures, the sequence of references can not be predicted and prefetching will not be possible. Prefetching alone is not a general solution to the latency problem.

Multithreading is an alternative technique for hiding memory latency. If several threads are assigned to each processor, memory latency can be hidden by rapidly context switching to a different thread rather than waiting for a memory access to complete. While previous studies have shown mixed results when using multithreading as an adjunct to cacheing[1, 9, 25], in this paper we study multithreading on its own merits and find it to be very effective.

1.1 Overview

First we look at a simple multithreading model that context switches on every load from shared memory (Section 4). For a few applications the shared loads are spaced far enough apart that a small number of threads are able to hide the memory latency and utilize the available processing power. However for most applications, shared loads occur too frequently (as often as once every 5 cycles) and too close together (often in bunches) to allow a small number of threads

*This work is supported by the Air Force Office of Scientific Research (AFOSR/JSEP) under contract F49620-90-C-0029 and NSF Grant Number 1-442427-21936. Computing resources were provided by NSF Infrastructure Grant number CDA-8722788.

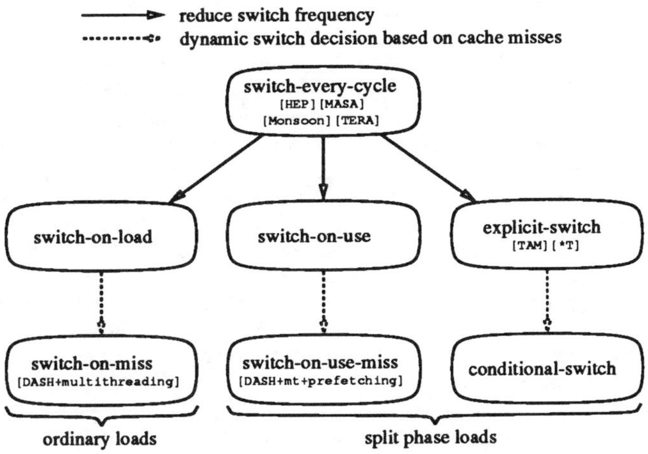

Figure 1: Evolution of Multithreading Models

to hide the latency. For these applications we need a better multithreading model.

For this next model (Section 5), we introduce the idea of grouping accesses together to eliminate unnecessary context switches. This grouping lets the processors wait for several accesses together rather than waiting for each access individually. The frequency of context switches decreases by as much as a factor of 5, and most of the closely spaced accesses can be grouped together. This one change allows all of the applications to execute with 70% or better efficiency on a multithreading machine with less than ten threads per processor.

The main problem with the previous model is that it requires a large bandwidth to shared memory. To address this problem we introduce a third multithreading model that adds a cache but still maintains the benefits of grouping (Section 6). For many of the applications this proves effective in both reducing the memory bandwidth and in further decreasing the multithreading level needed to achieve good performance.

Before we present our simulation results, we first present a structured overview of previous multithreading research (Section 2), and a description of the multiprocessor model and applications used in this study (Section 3).

2 Previous Work

Previous multithreading research has been motivated by four concerns: tolerating memory latency, building a fast pipeline, supporting a threaded execution model, and as an adjunct to cacheing. Figure 1 shows the evolution of multithreading models and some of the motivations for moving from one model to another. Some of these models have not been studied previously but can be predicted based on the motivations.

The costs of multithreading are the larger number of threads needed, the larger register file, the increased scheduling complexity, and the cycles lost to context switching overhead. These costs are influenced by when and how often context switching is performed.

The oldest model **switch-every-cycle** was used in the Denelcor HEP [14] and in MASA [11]. After each instruction, the processor switches to a different thread. This allows a fast CPU pipeline to be built because it eliminates data dependencies between instructions in the pipeline by interleaving different threads. It also allows memory latencies to be tolerated by not scheduling a thread until its references have completed. Unfortunately this model requires a complex scheduling mechanism and a large number of threads. By interleaving the instructions from many threads, a single thread is limited to a small fraction of the processing power. The Monsoon[20], P-RISC[17], and TERA[2] projects also switch every cycle, but have changed the scheduling policy so that scheduling decisions are made at a coarser granularity than every instruction.

With a normal RISC CPU pipeline, there is no need to context switch every cycle. The compiler can schedule instructions so as to hide the small pipeline delays. Context switches are needed only to hide the long memory latency of remote accesses.

The **switch-on-load** model switches on load instructions which access shared memory. Loads from local memory and other instructions all complete quickly, and can be scheduled by the compiler. Shared stores don't wait for their completion and therefore don't cause context switches either. The advantage of this model over **switch-every-cycle** is that a single thread can execute at full speed until it context switches. Fewer threads are needed to cover the latency since threads aren't being used to schedule individual instructions in the pipeline. Simpler hardware is needed since context switches are less frequent.

The **switch-on-load** model sometimes context switches sooner than it needs to. If a compiler can order instructions so that a load is issued several cycles before the value is used, the context switch does not have to occur until the actual use of the value. This allows a thread to hide some of its own memory latency by prefetching data. This mechanism is facilitated by using split phase instructions. The first instruction, `load`, issues the reference into the network, and a second instruction, `use`, waits for the result. The **switch-on-use** multithreading model context switches on the `use` instructions rather than the `load` instructions.

A benefit of the **switch-on-use** model is that several load instructions can be grouped together so that all of the loads in the group can be issued into the memory network before any of the results are used. This allows a single context switch (on the first of the uses) to wait for all of the loads in the group. For example, a simple computation may load two values from shared memory and then compute their average. Both loads should be issued into the memory network and then a single context switch performed upon the use of the first value. This allows waiting for both loads together rather than individually. The cost of this model is the addition of a `use` instruction for each shared memory load and hardware to count the results as they are returned.

An alternative method for grouping shared loads together is to add an explicit context switch instruction between the group of loads and their subsequent uses. This **explicit-switch** model is studied in this paper and is shown to eliminate from 50% to 80% of the context switches needed by the **switch-on-load** model. With fewer context switches, a smaller number of threads can be used to cover the latency. The most recent data flow research[6, 16] has adopted the **explicit-switch** model. Short threads execute until their completion at which point they cause a context switch to a new thread.

By adding caches to the previous models, the cache can satisfy many of the shared loads without going to shared memory. Only the shared loads that miss in the cache will have long latencies and cause context switches.

The **switch-on-miss** model switches at points where load instructions miss in the cache. An early study of this by Weber & Gupta[25] suggested substantial performance benefits were available, but a later study as part of the DASH project [9] had less optimistic results. Both of these studies restricted multithreading to at most 4 threads per processor. **Switch-on-miss** multithreading was also studied as part of the ALEWIFE project [1] and achieved good results with a few simple applications. One draw back of context-switching on cache misses is that the context switch is detected after a number of subsequent instructions have started down the CPU pipeline. These instructions must be canceled, and thus there will be a context switch cost of several cycles because of the wasted pipeline slots.

The **switch-on-use-miss** model context switches when a **use** instruction tries to use the value from a shared load that missed in the cache. The split phase instructions essentially provide a mechanism for prefetching data. The switch-on-use-miss model was studied (approximately) by the DASH project[9] when they looked at the combination of prefetching and multithreading. They found little benefit from prefetching when combined with multithreading, however they state that their prefetching method was meant for a single threaded processor and should be done differently for a multithreaded processor.

The **conditional-switch** model adds cacheing to the **explicit-switch** model. The code appears the same as that for the explicit-switch model: there is a group of load instructions, followed by a context switch instruction, followed by the instructions that use the loaded data. The difference is that the context switch instruction is treated as a *conditional* switch instruction. If any of the loads preceding the switch instruction missed in the cache, a context switch is performed as expected. But if all of the preceding loads hit, the context switch instruction is ignored and the thread continues executing. This model provides the same benefits of grouping and cacheing that were possible in the **switch-on-use-miss** model, but it may be simpler to implement.

In this paper we concentrate on the **switch-on-load**, **explicit-switch**, and **conditional-switch** models. This allows us to demonstrate the effectiveness of grouping in improving the performance of multithreading and in reducing the number of threads needed by each processor.

3 Multiprocessor Model

We have targeted this research at shared memory applications that use a fixed set of processes. This is typical for applications written in C or FORTRAN. The applications fork a set of processes and use that set for the entire computation by either statically or dynamically scheduling the work to be done.

For benchmarks, we use parallel programs written for the Sequent[19]. The Sequent allows shared storage to be allocated both statically (using a `shared` declaration) and dynamically (using `shmalloc()`). A potential problem arises because a pointer can point to either local or shared data. This would require dynamic address testing to determine whether or not an address is in shared memory. We avoid this difficulty by assuming that all memory references can be statically classified by the compiler as either local or shared. After looking at many programs, it is clear that this assumption is valid. Programmers write programs where they know which data is in shared memory. There are several techniques which could be used to determine this information. The simplest is to augment variable declarations to allow specifying which variables point to shared data. In our simulator we use trace analysis to determine this information.

For the CPU we assume a typical pipelined RISC processor, except that each thread has its own set of 32 integer and 32 floating-point registers. We use the instruction set and timings of the MIPS R3000[12], but we have supplemented it with a few additional instructions which are needed on a multiprocessor. We added `Load-Double` and `Store-Double` instructions to reduce the number of network messages, and we provided both local and shared versions of all load and store instructions. We added a `Fetch-and-Add` instruction as the synchronization primative and built higher level synchronization primatives such as locks and barriers out of `Fetch-and-Add`'s and spinning.

We assume that there is no overhead (in lost cycles) for context switching. This is consistent with switch-every-cycle machines[2, 11, 14, 17, 20] but in conflict with switch-on-miss machines[1, 9, 23, 25] which assume a cost of several cycles for clearing the processor pipeline. The key difference is the ability to recognize that an instruction will cause a context switch as that instruction enters the pipeline. This is possible for the switch-on-load and explicit-switch models studied in this paper since the context switch is implied by the opcode alone, and thus the context switch is identified while the instruction is in the decode stage of the cpu pipeline. At this point, the first instruction from the next thread to be executed should have already been prefetched. It can then be decoded on the next cycle and thus no cycles will be wasted.

We assume that remote accesses are returned in the same order in which they are sent, and, as a result, we use round-robin scheduling of the threads on a processor. Round-robin scheduling is optimal under ordered delivery since whenever the next thread in round-robin order must wait for an access to return, all other threads will be waiting for the return of accesses that were issued later. While some networks support ordered delivery of messages[22], most other large scale networks do not. Even on these networks round-robin scheduling may still be a good choice since it provides fairness in scheduling. Fairness is important for programs that use static load balancing since if one thread is scheduled less often than the others, that thread will finish later and delay the entire computation.

We expect that large shared memory multiprocessors will be built with multi-stage packed-switched networks such as the butterfly network used in the NYU Ultracomputer[8] and the IBM RP3[21], and that the network will support combining of messages. If hardware combining is not available, software combining techniques could be used for barriers[26]. We do not simulate the network, but instead assume that it has a constant 200 cycle round trip latency. We expect the average latency of a 1024 processor machine will fall in this range. Other researchers also expect latencies in the hundreds of cycles. The DASH project[9] has latencies of 90 cycles for a 16 processor machine when ignoring network congestion. With congestion, latencies will increase. Dally[7] found average round trip latencies of 144 cycles on a 64 processor butterfly when running at 50% utilization.

In a real network, access latencies depend on network loading, which is a function of both the network bandwidth and the bandwidth requirements of the application. There can also be a large variance in latency[7] because of congestion within the network. We have purposely chosen not to model a specific network because it would obscure the main focus of this research which is to evaluate the ability

Application	Lines	Cycles	Description & Problem size
sieve	242	106 M	counts primes < 4,000,000
blkmat	409	87 M	blocked matrix multiply — 200 × 200 matrices
sor	332	258 M	S.O.R. solver for Laplace's equation — 192 × 192 grid
ugray	10784	1353 M	ray tracing graphics renderer — gears (7169 faces), 20 × 512 slice of image
water	1368	1082 M	simulate a system of water molecules — 343 molecules, 2 iterations
locus	6347	665 M	route wires in a standard cell circuit — Primary2 (1290 cells × 20 channels)
mp3d	1510	192 M	simulate rarefied hypersonic flow — 100,000 particles, 10 iterations

Table 1: Parallel Applications

of multithreading to hide long memory latencies.

Caches are assumed for both instructions and local memory, but the effects of misses in these caches has been ignored. The instruction cache and local data cache are expected to have high hit rates just as on uniprocessors. Local data misses are serviced locally and would not cause a context switch. However instruction cache misses are serviced over the network and in a real machine, should cause a context switch. We believe these assumptions will not qualitatively affect the results.

3.1 Simulator

Simulating a 1024 processor machine requires enormous amounts of both time and memory. Far too much, in fact, to ever allow simulating large enough computations to keep such a machine busy. Since we are interested in the ability of multithreading to hide long memory latencies, we have reduced the number of processors simulated, but not the latency. We feel that this makes our latency tolerance results more directly applicable to a 1024 processor machine.

We have built a very fast simulator based on augmenting the object code of applications in a similar fashion to the `pixie`[15] profiling system for MIPS machines. With this code augmentation technique we are able to use optimized code as would be used on the actual machine. All applications were compiled at optimization level "-O2". Most instructions are directly executed by the host machine in a single cycle. A few additional cycles are used for loading and storing relevant registers, and counting execution cycles. On average, two instructions are added for each original instruction. Shared accesses are handled by the simulator, and require scheduling and context switching among many threads. These shared accesses take from 300 to 1000 cycles to simulate, but overall, the simulator is very fast since only a small fraction of instructions are shared accesses. Applications are typically simulated at speeds that range from 20 to 70 times slower than direct execution.

3.2 Applications

Table 1 lists the applications used in this study. `Sieve`, `blkmat`, and `sor` are toy applications developed by the authors. `Ugray` is from Berkeley[3]. And `water`, `locus`, and `mp3d` are from the Stanford SPLASH[24] benchmark set. We show the problem sizes and the number of cycles (in millions) that the applications would require on a single (0 latency) processor. It should be noted that these are much smaller than problems that would be solved on a real parallel machine. For example, a 100 mips workstation could solve the largest of these problems in under 14 seconds. Even at these small sizes, many of the applications already have sufficient parallelism for 1024 threads. Problems large enough for a 1024 processor parallel machine will likely have enough parallelism for hundreds of thousands of threads. More than enough for multithreading.

Figure 2 shows the performance of the seven applications on an ideal shared memory machine. This ideal machine has no contention and zero latency to shared memory. Such a machine would be impossible to build, but it corresponds to an upper bound on achievable performance. Rather than show the standard speedup curves, we have plotted the efficiency vs. the number of processors (efficiency = speedup / number of processors). For example, the `mp3d` program achieves a speedup of 778 when using 1024 processors, and thus has an efficiency of .76 = (778 / 1024). These curves are all computed with a fixed size problem. As the number of processors increases, the work is divided more finely and the efficiency drops. This lower efficiency at finer granularities results from uneven load balancing, synchronization overhead, and parallelization overhead. If, on the other hand, the problem sizes were increased, there would be more parallelism and thus more processors could be utilized.

Four of the applications (`sieve`, `blkmat`, `sor` and `mp3d`) have speedups of 700 or better with 1024 processors. Simulation time was too large for the other programs to allow simulating large enough problems to achieve these speedups. The `water` application stands out in the graph because of its erratic behavior. With 256 processors the efficiency is only .56, but with 343 processors the efficiency rises to .79 . This rise in performance results from the static load balancing used in the application. The load balancing works best when the number of processors divides evenly into the number of molecules (which is 343).

All programs studied in this paper have a single forked phase during which the parallel computation is performed. Any work done outside this forked phase has been excluded from the results presented in this paper. This excluded work typically consists of reading input files, performing initialization, and writing result files. There are a number of reasons for excluding this serial computation. First, as problem sizes are increased, the startup code becomes a smaller and smaller fraction of the total computation[10]. Second, many of these applications were written for today's small shared memory machines. Often much of the initialization could have been parallelized, but this wasn't deemed necessary for a small machine. Third, we expect that large parallel machines will do their input and output in parallel.

4 Switch-On-Load

In this section we evaluate the switch-on-load multithreading model. This is a simple model that works well for some applications but poorly for others. It serves as a baseline for comparison and helps motivate more sophisticated multithreading models.

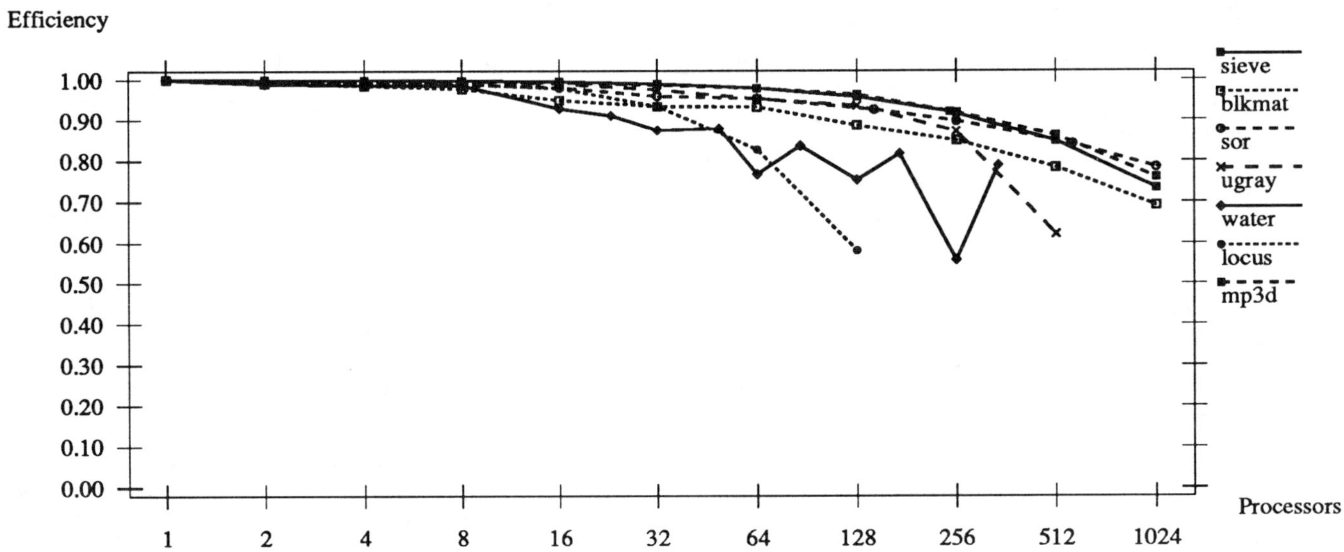

Figure 2: Efficiency on ideal (0 latency) machine.

	Distribution						
App.	1–9	10–19	20–29	30–39	40–49	50+	mean
sieve	—	95%	5%	—	—	—	19
blkmat	—	31%	1%	2%	3%	63%	137
sor	79%	19%	—	1%	2%	—	6
ugray	65%	10%	3%	11%	7%	4%	18
water	83%	8%	6%	—	—	4%	44
locus	93%	4%	2%	1%	—	1%	7
mp3d	81%	6%	5%	5%	—	3%	9

Table 2: Switch-On-Load: Run-Lengths Between Shared Loads

4.1 Run-Lengths Between Shared Loads

Table 2 shows the average run-lengths for the applications studied. Run-length is defined as the number of cycles between context switches. For example, if a shared load instruction occurs every 10 cycles, the run-length would be 10 since a context switch is done on every shared load. The mean run-length can be used to estimate the number of threads that will be need to hide the memory latency. For example, with a mean run-length of 10 cycles, 20 threads could hide the 200 cycle latency. Counting the thread whose latency is being hidden, a multithreading level of 21 would be sufficient. We would prefer to have a small multithreading level because it requires less total threads and allows small problems to be solved more efficiently.

Using the mean run-length to estimate the multithreading performance fails when there is variation in the run-length distribution. Sometimes all of the threads will execute run-lengths longer than the mean, and the latency will be covered easily. But at other times, threads will execute run-lengths shorter than the mean, and the full latency will not be covered. In this situation, either a higher multithreading level should be used or else some cycles will be wasted waiting for memory.

For the seven applications studied, only `sieve` has a fairly constant run-length distribution. (It runs through a large array marking numbers as non-prime at a constant rate.) The other applications, have more complex behavior. There are usually many different calculations being performed. Some require only a few cycles, while others require hundreds. This leads to large variations in run-lengths. The `blkmat` application stands out because of the exceptionally high mean run-length. This occurs because it makes private copies of data to reduce the number of shared accesses. The applications `sor`, `locus` and `mp3d` have very short run-lengths and will need large multithreading levels to hide their latency.

4.2 Performance

Figure 3 shows the performance of the `sieve` application under different levels of multithreading. The top curve shows the performance on an ideal (0 latency) shared memory multiprocessor. The other curves shown are with 200 cycle latency. Without multithreading, the processors are busy only 9% of the time. As extra threads are added, more of the latency is covered, and the efficiency rises, until at a multithreading level of 12, nearly 100% efficiency is achieved.

On the ideal machine, the efficiency of this application starts to drop when more than 100 processors are used. This drop in performance arises because of imperfect load balancing and the overheads of parallelization and synchronization. Under multithreading, the drop in performance occurs at the same point (100 threads), but because there are several threads assigned to each processor, the drop off in performance occurs at a proportionately lower number of processors. With larger problem sizes we expect that the region of linear speedup will extend further to the right. And thus with large enough problems for a 1024 processor machine, we expect to see the same multithreading behavior at 1024 processors that is observed here using a lesser number of processors.

The performance of the other applications is summarized

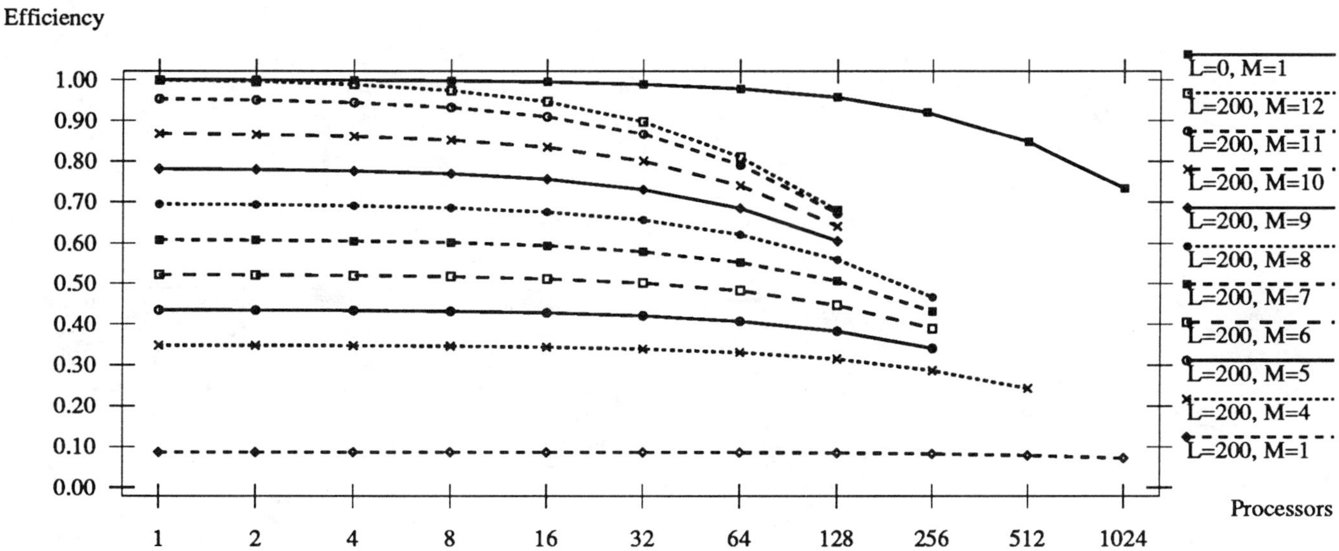

Figure 3: Multithreading Efficiency for sieve (L = Latency, M = Multithreading level)

Application (processors)	Desired Efficiency 50%	60%	70%	80%	90%
sieve (16)	6	7	9	10	11
blkmat (32)	1	2	2	4	—
sor (8)	28	40	—	—	—
ugray (8)	9	12	—	—	—
water (10)	5	7	10	12	—
locus (2)	17	21	25	32	—
mp3d (8)	13	15	19	22	28

Table 3: Switch-On-Load: Multithreading needed to achieve % efficiency.

in table 3. The multithreading levels needed to achieve 50, 60, 70, 80 and 90% efficiency are shown. Most of the applications could not achieve all of these efficiency levels. As the multithreading is increased, more total threads are used and the applications enter the domain where the problem sizes are too small for the number of threads. For the sieve application table 3 shows the results when using 16 processors. With a multithreading level of 11, the program uses 176 threads and runs at 90% efficiency. Note that in figure 3 we could have chosen any point from 1 to 16 processors and the multithreading level needed to achieve 90% efficiency would have remained the same. Similarly for each of the applications, we have reported the performance at a point just before the performance drops off.

While some of the applications achieve high efficiencies, other applications such as sor and ugray reach an upper bound around 60% efficiency. The reason for this bound involves the run-length distributions presented in table 2. With the sor application, for example, 39% of the run-lengths are 1 cycle and another 39% are 2 cycles. These short run-lengths contribute little towards hiding latency and it is inevitable that cycles are lost waiting for memory.

5 Explicit-Switch

We can do better than the switch-on-load model by looking at the data dependency structure of the applications. Most programs do not load a single value and then perform a calculation with it. Instead, they usually load several values and compare or combine them in a calculation. The processor should issue the group of loads together and then context switch only once, rather than context switching after every load.

5.1 Compiler Optimization

The grouping together of loads improves the performance of multithreading in two ways. First, by eliminating context switches, it increases the run-length (number of cycles) between context switches. With a longer run-length, less threads are needed to cover the memory latency. Second, it improves the distribution of run-lengths by eliminating many of the small run-lengths that result from back to back loads.

The inner loop of the sor application is shown in figure 4(a) as an example. Without grouping, the 5 loads are issued one at a time, with a context switch after each one. In figure 4(b) the code has been reorganized so that all 5 loads are grouped together and are then followed by a single context switch instruction. Rather than having four short run-lengths followed by one long run-length, there is now just a single long run-length.

A compiler designed for a multithreaded architecture will group shared loads whenever possible. Since the compilers we have today don't do this grouping, we wrote a post-processor which finds the basic blocks in an object file, does dependency analysis within the basic blocks, and then reorganizes the instructions so as to group shared loads together. It then inserts a single context switch instruction after each group of independent shared loads. Because we do this analysis at the assembly language level, we must

Application	Distribution						mean	loads / switch
	1–9	10–19	20–29	30–39	40–49	50+		
sieve	—	63%	37%	—	—	—	19	1.0
blkmat	—	23%	9%	2%	3%	63%	138	1.0
sor	—	—	80%	2%	17%	—	30	4.7
ugray	50%	17%	5%	15%	2%	11%	23	1.3
water	—	36%	9%	22%	13%	19%	210	4.8
locus	93%	3%	2%	1%	—	1%	8	1.05
mp3d	23%	23%	28%	19%	—	7%	23	2.3

Table 4: Explicit-Switch: Run-Lengths Between Context Switches

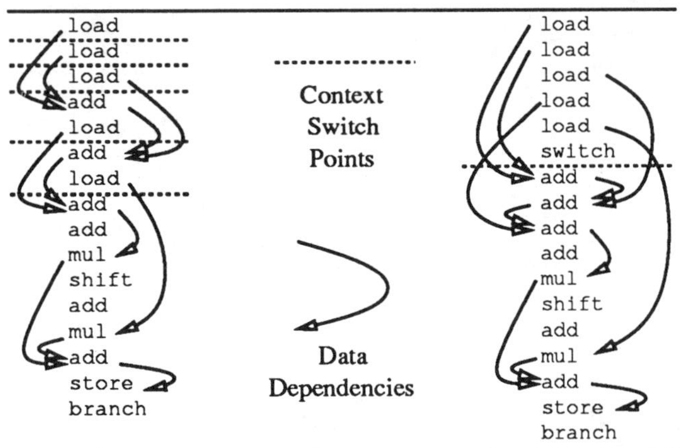

(a) switch-on_load (b) explicit-switch

Figure 4: Inner loop of **sor**.

make pessimistic assumptions[1] which restrict our ability to reorganize the code. Nevertheless our code reorganization works very well for basic blocks. Compiler based optimization could do even better by looking beyond the scope of a single basic block.

Table 4 shows the new run-length distributions for the applications. The last column shows the level of grouping achieved. The **sor** and **water** applications benefited the most. In the inner loop of **sor**, for example, 5 loads were grouped together between context switches. Where previously their run-length distributions were dominated by short run-lengths (of 1 or 2 cycles), now those short run-lengths have been completely eliminated. In contrast, the **locus** and **ugray** applications did not have much improvement. These applications have very short basic blocks, and grouping is needed beyond the scope of a single block. Two of the applications, **sieve** and **blkmat**, did not benefit at all from grouping, but this is unimportant since they access shared memory one item at a time and already have good run-length behavior.

Table 5 shows the improved performance results with the explicit-switch multithreading model. The applications now achieve higher performance and use fewer threads. For **locus** the mean run-length of 8 cycles is still too short to allow a small number of threads to cover the latency, but for the other applications, 14 or fewer threads are now sufficient to maximize performance.

One penalty of having explicit switch instructions is that

[1] We assume that every shared store might have a conflict with every shared load because of address aliasing.

Application (procs)	Desired Efficiency					grouping overhead
	50%	60%	70%	80%	90%	
sieve (16)	6	7	9	10	11	2%
blkmat (32)	1	2	2	4	—	0%
sor (16)	5	6	8	9	—	10%
ugray (8)	6	8	11	—	—	2%
water (20)	1	2	3	4	6	0%
locus (2)	16	20	26	—	—	11%
mp3d (16)	6	7	8	10	14	4%

Table 5: Explicit-Switch: Multithreading needed to achieve % efficiency. (Efficiency measurements account for grouping overhead.)

they take a cycle that might have otherwise been used for computation. A further penalty arises from the code reorganization. The original code is optimized so that the execution of floating point instructions is overlapped with that of the load instructions. When we reoptimize the code to group loads together, we often add a few cycles to the execution time because operations are no longer overlapped as tightly. The last column of table 5 shows the performance penalty due to the code reorganization and added context switch instructions. This penalty is often just a few percent, and in all cases it is overshadowed by the benefits of grouping.

5.2 Grouping Beyond Basic Blocks

For the **locus** and **ugray** applications we were disappointed that grouping did not perform better. After examing these programs, we found that both programs could benefit from inter-block grouping. We observed that the inter-block grouping opportunities often involved accesses to several fields in a small structure. These accesses were split among several basic blocks because of condition tests, but in fact could have all been issued before the condition tests were done.

Since we don't have a compiler which does inter-block grouping, we designed a simple experiment to estimate the potential grouping available. We simulate a very small cache associated with each thread. The cache has a line size of 32 words, but only one line. We assume that any loads which hit in this cache are in the same structure or array as the preceding reference and thus could have been grouped.

For **ugray** 42% of the loads hit in this cache, and the grouping factor increased from 1.3 to 1.9 . For **locus** the hit rate is 84%, and the grouping factor increased from 1.05 to 6.6 . This dramatically shows the potential for compiler based grouping. Table 6 shows the revised multithreading figures based on the additional grouping predicted by this experiment.

Application	explicit-switch cycles / access	explicit-switch bandwidth bits/cycle	conditional-switch hit rate	conditional-switch cycles / access	conditional-switch bandwidth bits/cycle
sieve	13.7	9.3	99%	3333	0.1
blkmat	114	1.4	65%	326	1.2
sor	5.3	30.2	98%	246	2.3
ugray	24.1	5.8	92%	228	1.3
water	44.1	3.4	93%	518	0.7
locus	8.3	15.4	91%	146	2.6
mp3d	6.4	20.2	72%	23	18.7

Table 7: Comparison of bandwidth requirement under explicit-switch and conditional-switch multithreading models.

Application (procs)	Desired Efficiency 50%	60%	70%	80%	90%	loads / switch
sieve (64)	2	2	3	5	—	11.3
blkmat (64)	1	1	2	3	—	1.4
sor (16)	5	6	8	9	—	5.0
ugray (12)	5	6	8	—	—	1.9
water (20)	1	2	2	3	5	8.1
locus (8)	4	5	6	7	—	6.6
mp3d (32)	4	5	6	8	11	3.3

Table 6: Explicit-Switch: estimated performance with interblock grouping.

This experiment is only a means to estimate the available grouping opportunities. To verify the results, we examined the code of `ugray` and `locus` to see where the cache hits were comming from. In `ugray` we found that 47% of the identified grouping opportunities were valid. These were cases where one field in a structure was examined, and if it met some condition, a second field was loaded and used in a computation. A smart compiler could group these two loads together by speculatively loading the second value in the expectation that the test would succeed and thus the second load would be needed. The other 53% of the grouping opportunities identified by the cache experiment turned out to be cases of coincidental memory allocation such as when two structures were allocated in the same cache line. While examing the code, however, we also found many interblock grouping opportunities that were missed by the cache. Overall, it remains unclear whether this experiment overestimated or underestimated the interblock grouping potential for `ugray`.

For the `locus` application, a single instruction was found to be responsible for 95% of the cache hits. This turned out to be in a loop that was stepping horizontally though a large two dimensional array. A compiler could easily group these loads by unrolling the loop. In addition, we found similar loops that stepped vertically through the array. The same compiler unrolling technique could group these loads as well, but they were missed by the cache. Thus for `locus` our experiment underestimated the potential for interblock grouping.

Research in compiler optimization is needed to fully explore the idea of grouping accesses. We have shown that grouping within basic blocks is simple and effective for many application, and that further grouping is available by looking beyond basic blocks. Much of this interblock grouping will come from compiler techniques such as unrolling loops and speculative loads. The speculative loads will need careful consideration since they will increase grouping at the cost of increased network bandwidth.

6 Conditional-Switch

The biggest problem with the explicit-switch model is that it requires a large bandwidth to shared memory. In this section we present preliminary results on the effects of adding a cache to a multithreaded processor. The cache is able to reduce the memory bandwidth requirement by filtering out a large fraction of the accesses. To be cost effective, however, the increased cost and complexity of adding caches must be more than compensated for by the reduced cost of the network.

6.1 Bandwidth

For this preliminary study we have chosen to look at small caches that could be included as part of a single chip processor. We experimented with several cache sizes and line sizes and found that a 64 K-Byte, write back cache, with a 16 byte line size and 4 way set associativity is a reasonable choice. Selection of an optimal cache configuration is beyond the scope of this paper.

Coherency is maintained with the Censier and Feautrier[4] invalidation based cache coherency protocol. This protocol maintains a full directory of owners for each data line. It serves as a convenient starting point for comparison with other research, however we expect that this may not be the most cost effective choice because of its large hardware cost[18].

Table 7 shows the applications' bandwidth requirements under the explicit-switch model compared to those under the conditional-switch model. We have shown both the access rate, which is shown in terms of the average number of cycles between accesses, and the bandwidth requirement which is shown in bits per cycle. The bandwidth figure includes the overhead of message headers and result, acknowledgement, and invalidation messages.[2] The bandwidth does not decrease proportionally to the access rate because of the extra coherency overhead and the larger message sizes needed to load a full line of data.

The cache works well for all of the applications except `mp3d`. The hit rates are above 90% and the bandwidth requirements are reduced to well under 4.0 bits per cycle. This bandwidth figure is the sum of both the forward and return traffic, and thus it suggests that a network with channels as narrow as 2 bits in each direction would have sufficient bandwidth to support these application. In reality the channels might need to be wider than this because traffic will be bursty and have periods of higher bandwidth requirements.

[2]We have excluded messages used in spinning on locks and barriers, since we expect a real machine to provide mechanisms to perform these operations without spinning.

Application (processors)	Desired Efficiency 50%	60%	70%	80%	90%
sieve (256)	1	1	1	1	—
blkmat (64)	1	1	2	3	—
sor (16)	1	1	3	4	—
ugray (32)	1	1	2	2	4
water (29)	1	1	1	2	3
locus (10)	1	2	2	4	—
mp3d (32)	3	4	5	6	9

Table 8: Conditional-Switch: Multithreading needed to achieve % efficiency.

Simulations using realistic networks are needed to fully explore this issue.

The mp3d application has very poor reference locality and thus benefits little from cacheing. To support this application as is, the network will have to supply much higher bandwidth. We would be interested in seeing if this application could be rewritten to improve is locality.

6.2 Multithreading Level

An additional benefit of cacheing is that it can further reduce the level of multithreading needed to achieve high performance. Since many context switches are not taken, the run-lengths between taken context switches increases, and this allows hiding the memory latency using fewer threads.

Skipping too many context switches, however, can causes problems. In the ugray application, for example, we found that long sequences of cache hits allowed threads to have some run-lengths that lasted for thousands of cycles. These long run-lengths caused problems when another thread on the same processor was in a critical region. The thread in the critical region would like to complete and exit the critical region as quickly as possible, but when the thread context switched, the other threads on the processor would sometimes execute for a very long time before the first thread was resumed and allowed to finish. The result was that locks ended up being held for much longer than they needed to be, and the increased lock contention hurt performance.

The simplest solution to this problem is to limit the interval between context switches. For this simulation we set a flag after a thread has executed for 200 cycles. When this flag is set, the next context switch instruction will cause a context switch regardless of whether there were any preceding cache misses. This mechanism is adequate for this study, but there is room for improvement by using more sophisticated scheduling policies such as priority scheduling of threads inside critical regions.

Table 8 shows the performance of the application under the conditional-switch multithreading model. Under this model execution efficiencies of 80% or better can be achieved with 6 threads or less. This small number of threads is important because it reduces the size of the register files need to support multithreading.

The conditional-switch multithreading model cannot always context switch in a single cycle as the switch-on-load and explicit-switch models could. The context switch decision is based on whether or not any of the preceding load instructions miss in the cache. If a miss occurs several cycles before the context switch instruction enters the CPU pipeline, the context switch will be correctly predicted, but if the outcome of a load is not known when the context switch instruction enters the pipeline, a few cycles may be wasted. For the applications studied here, this effect was minor.

The results from table 8 show that many of the applications were able to achieve efficiencies of 50 or 60% with just a single thread per processor. This is substantially better than previous results such as those from the Dash project[9] which reported processor utilizations ranging from 20% to 28% when using just a single thread per processor. The difference between their processor model and ours is that we are able to group references together because of the context switch instruction. This grouping lets us issue multiple accesses into the memory network before we wait for them to return. Our improved performance suggests that the grouping of shared accesses is an important capability that extends beyond multithreaded processors.

7 Conclusions

While previous studies of multithreading have shown mixed results, we study a broad set of applications and show that all of them can perform well under multithreading. The key idea introduced is to take advantage of the data dependency structure of the code and group shared loads together so that processors can avoid unnecessary context switches. This grouping is facilitated by the introduction of an explicit context switch instruction and compiler optimization techniques. Grouping increases the average run-length between context switches and also eliminates most of the troublesome short run-lengths from the run-length distributions.

It is difficult to compare results with other studies since different applications are studied, different problems sizes are used, and different latencies are assumed. One common point for comparison is possible with the DASH project. Gupta and Hennessy[9] studied the mp3d application under the switch-on-miss multithreading model. They reported an efficiency of 50% with a multithreading level of 4. The explicit-switch model studied here achieves similar efficiency at this multithreading level while tolerating a latency more than twice that used in the DASH study. The improved latency tolerance of the explicit-switch model shows the importance of grouping.

We have introduced a classification scheme for multithreading models and have started the exploration of this design space. With the explicit-switch model, 70% or better efficiency can be achieved without any cacheing of shared memory, and requiring only a moderate level of multithreading. The only difficulty is that the network bandwidth requirements are high for some applications. Cacheing together with the conditional-switch model addresses this problem and for most applications is able to reduce the bandwidth to acceptable levels.

References

[1] Anant Agarwal, Beng-Hong Lim, David Kranz, and John Kubiatowicz. APRIL: A Processor Architecture for Multiprocessing. In *The 17th Annual Int. Symp. on Computer Architecture*, pages 104–114, 1990.

[2] Robert Alverson, David Callahan, Daniel Cummings, et al. The TERA Computer System. In *1990 Int. Conf. on Supercomputing*, pages 1–6, 1990.

[3] Bob Boothe. Multiprocessor Strategies for Ray-Tracing. Master's thesis, U.C. Berkeley, September 1989. Report No. UCB/CSD 89/534.

[4] L. M. Censier and P. Feautrier. A New Solution to Coherence Problems in Multicache Systems. *IEEE Transactions on Computers*, C-27(12):1112–1118, December 1978.

[5] David Chaiken, Craig Fields, Kiyoshi Kurihara, and Anant Agarwal. Directory-Based Cache Coherency in Large-Scale Multiprocessors. *IEEE Computer*, 23(6):49–59, June 1990.

[6] David E. Culler, Anurag Sah, Klaus Erik Schauser, Thorsten von Eicken, and John Wawrzynek. Fine-grain Parallelism with Minimal Hardware Support: A Compiler-Controled Threaded Abstract Machine. In *ASPLOS-IV Proceedings*, pages 164–175, 1991.

[7] William J. Dally. Virtual-Channel Flow Control. In *The 17th Annual Int. Symp. on Computer Architecture*, pages 60–68, 1990.

[8] Allan Gottlieb, Ralph Grishman, Clyde P. Kruskal, Kevin P. McAuliffe, Larry Rudolph, and Marc Snir. The NYU Ultracomputer — Designing a MIMD, Shared-Memory Parallel Machine. In *Conf. Proc. of the 9th Annual Symposium on Computer Architecture*, pages 27–42, 1982.

[9] Anoop Gupta, John Hennessy, Kourosh Gharachorloo, Todd Mowry, and Wolf-Dietrich Weber. Comparative Evaluation of Latency Reducing and Tolerating Techniques. In *The 18th Annual Int. Symp. on Computer Architecture*, pages 254–263, 1991.

[10] J. L. Gustafson. Reevaluating Amdahl's Law. *Communications of the ACM*, pages 532–533, May 1988. Technical Note.

[11] Robert H. Halstead, Jr. and Tetsuya Fujita. MASA: A Multithreaded Processor Architecture for Parallel Symbolic Computing. In *The 15th Annual Int. Symp. on Computer Architecture*, pages 443–451, 1988.

[12] Gerry Kane. *MIPS RISC Architecture*. Prentice Hall, 1989.

[13] Alexander C. Klaiber and Henry M. Levy. An Architecture for Software-Controlled Data Prefetching. In *The 18th Annual Int. Symp. on Computer Architecture*, pages 43–53, 1991.

[14] Janusz S. Kowalik, editor. *Parallel MIMD computation : the HEP supercomputer and its applications*. MIT Press, 1985.

[15] MIPS Computer Systems. *MIPS language programmer's guide*, 1986.

[16] R. S. Nikhil, G. M. Papadopoulos, and Arvind. *T: A Killer Micro for A Brave New World. Technical report, MIT Lab. for Comp. Sci., 1991. Computation Structures Group Memo 325.

[17] Rishiyur S. Nikhil and Arvind. Can dataflow subsume von Neumann computing? In *The 16th Annual Int. Symp. on Computer Architecture*, pages 262–272, 1989.

[18] Brian W. O'Krafka and A. Richard Newton. An Empirical Evaluation of Two Memory-Efficient Directory Methods. In *The 17th Annual Int. Symp. on Computer Architecture*, pages 138–147, 1990.

[19] Anita Osterhaug, editor. *Guide to Parallel Programming on Sequent Computer Systems*. Prentice Hall, 1989.

[20] Gregory M. Papadopoulos and David E. Culler. Monsoon: an Explicit Token-Store Architecture. In *The 17th Annual Int. Symp. on Computer Architecture*, pages 82–91, 1990.

[21] G. F. Pfister, W. C. Brantley, D. A. George, S. L. Harvey, W. J. Kleinfelder, K. P. McAuliffe, E. A. Melton, V. A. Norton, and J. Weiss. The IBM Research Parallel Processor Prototype (RP3): Introduction and Architecture. In *Proc. 1985 Int. Parallel Processing Conf*, pages 764–771, 1985.

[22] Abhiram Gorakhanath Ranade. *Fluent Parallel Computation*. PhD thesis, Yale University, May 1989.

[23] Rafael H. Saavedra-Barrera, David E. Culler, and Thorsten von Eicken. Analysis of Multithreaded Architectures for Parallel Computing. In *ACM Symp. Paral. Alg. Arch.*, July 1990.

[24] Jaswinder Pal Singh, Wolf-Dietrich Weber, and Anoop Gupta. SPLASH: Stanford Parallel Applications for Shared-Memory. Technical report, Computer Systems Laboratory, Stanford, 1991. Tech. Rpt. #CSL-TR-91-469.

[25] Wolf-Dietrich Weber and Anoop Gupta. Exploring the Benefits of Multiple Hardware Contexts in a Multiprocessor Architecture: Preliminary Results. In *The 16th Annual Int. Symp. on Computer Architecture*, 1989.

[26] Pen-Chung Yew, Nian-Feng Tzeng, and Duncan H. Lawrie. Distributing Hot-spot Addressing in Large-Scale Multiprocessors. In *Int. Conf. on Parallel Processing*, pages 51–58, 1986.

Instruction-level Parallelism in Prolog: Analysis and Architectural Support

Alessandro De Gloria and Paolo Faraboschi

University of Genoa
Department of Biophysical and Electronic Engineering (DIBE)
Via Opera Pia 11a
I-16145 Genova, Italy
e-mail: adg@cpsi7.dibe.unige.it

ABSTRACT

The demand of increasing computation power for symbolic processing has given a strong impulse to the development of ASICs dedicated to the execution of Prolog. Unlike past microcoded implementation based on the Warren Machine model, novel trends in high performance Prolog processors suggest the implementation of RISC-based processors committed to Prolog only through the adoption of a few basic dedicated features, like the Berkeley Abstract Machine (BAM) processor.

Following the idea of using a smart compiler for a simple instruction set, the SYMBOL project represents an experiment in applying global compaction techniques and VLIW design philosophy to the static exploitation of instruction-level parallelism in Prolog.

This paper presents code analysis results and shows how we can approach the theoretical speed-up limit (about 3) imposed by Amdahl's law on shared memory models, by means of global code optimizations and a suitable architectural support. In addition, we show implemetation details and some preliminary data of a VLSI prototype architecture .

Keywords: *Prolog shared-memory model, Static Instruction-Level Parallelism, Global Compaction Techniques, VLIW architectures.*

1. INTRODUCTION

Logic programming, and Prolog in particular, has become a subject of much attention, as it can map complex problems into machine code more easily than traditional high-level languages [Clocksin81]. This is accomplished by relieving the programmer from the implementation of the control structures underlying the algorithms which are provided by the language engine itself [Kowalski79].

Unfortunately the necessity of handling tagged data in Prolog imposes heavy limits on general-purpose machine performance, since uncommitted datapaths lack in dedicated structures and need to execute complex mask constructs for simple operations, like tag insertion or branching.

Unlike early Prolog machines, which implemented microcoded interpreters of Warren Instructions [Warren83], such as the PLM [Dobry87] or the KCM [Benker89], novel approaches are based on RISC-based processors and sophisticated front-end compilation techniques, like the Berkeley Abstract Machine (BAM) [Holmer90]. By the adoption of data-flow and mode analysis and specialized unification, the BAM succeeds in exploiting the determinism in Prolog programs and eliminates all the redundancies of Warren Code, thus obtaining an impressive speedup with respect to previous WAM implementations.

This research aims at evaluating quantitatively the maximum benefit which can be obtained by adopting a compiler-driven VLIW architecture [Fisher83] for the BAM model of Prolog. The underlying idea is to utilize a simple load-store architecture with the minimum amount of language specific hardware features and to determine which is the degree of statically exploitable instruction-level concurrency in Prolog.

By applying sophisticated compilation techniques to simple hardware with only a limited application specific support, our approach benefits from the fine-grain parallelism of code, and at the same time does not compromise general-purpose computation capabilities and fexibility.

This paper presents the results of code analysis performed on Prolog benchmarks extracted from the Aquarius Benchmark Suite [Haygood89], and how they justify the adoption of global compilation techniques, which were originally developed for numeric code [Fisher81]. In section 3 we also sketch a description of the evaluation system and the code-compaction mechanisms we implemented in the back-end compiler. Finally, section 5 presents some preliminary data of a prototype VLSI processor which has been designed and is currently being tested in its operating environment.

2. THE BERKELEY ABSTRACT MACHINE

The Berkeley Abstract Machine (BAM) has been developed as part of the Aquarius Project at University of California, Berkeley [VanRoy90]. The BAM execution flow and data structure is similar to the Warren Abstract Machine (WAM) [Warren83], but it uses an instruction set which is much closer to a general-purpose architecture. This allows a higher possibility of low-level optimizations than the WAM. BAM code has been designed to be re-targetable to a wide range of architectures, by the adoption of an instruction set which is machine and implementation independent.

Some basic guidelines have been followed in the design of the BAM model:

- Development of techniques to exploit determinism in programs
- Development of techniques to specialize unification
- Development of a portable instruction set suitable for optimizations.

The basic idea of the BAM is to retain the good features of the WAM, but implementing an instruction set closer to RISC-based architectures. In addition, particular attention has been focused on unification, which has been specialized by means of a

© 1992 ACM 0-89791-509-7/92/0005/0224 $1.50

global dataflow analysis which derives information about the program structure at compilation time.

A first implementation of a BAM processor [Holmer90] reaches performance which are approximately a factor of ten faster than Warren-based implementation like the PLM [Dobry87]. The factor of ten comes from:

- a model improvement of the BAM versus the WAM abstract machine and more sophisticated compiler optimizations. This gives roughly a factor of three.
- a technological improvement in VLSI processor design. This allows a clock rate (30 MHz) about three times faster than the microcoded PLM (10 MHz).

3. THE EVALUATION SYSTEM

In order to quantitatively evaluate the data-path resources which can actually bring cost-effective performance gain to the BAM model, we have applied some general criteria which are valid for any domain specific architecture [DeGloria90].

The development of a domain specific architecture requires analysis and evaluation tools to guide the designer towards correct design choices, and must show some basic features:

- the starting point of the design must be the behavior of the architecture, specified by means of benchmarks which has to be free as much as possible from hardware hypotheses;
- the minimum set of hardware functionalities being able to speed up the execution of the application must be found out;
- a resource has to be introduced only if it is justified by its frequency of use and if it can be efficiently exploited by the available compiler technology.

Our analysis considers the class of parallel synchronous non-homogeneous architectures which we define through the following properties:

- There is one central control (one program counter).
- The Data Path is composed of several functional units.
- The functional units are connected by means of local or global buses.
- The functional units may work in pipeline or multi-cyclic mode.
- The machine instruction may be composed of several operations, each of them driving a different functional unit.
- Each functional unit requires a static predictable amount of execution time.
- A new instruction is issued at each machine cycle.
- Memory can be organized in a hierarchical fashion.

This architecture model represents a large set of architectures which encompass VLIW machines. No constraint is imposed on the complexity of the functional units, and the only restriction to the model is to be synchronous in order to manage parallelism in a static way.

During evaluation, hardware and software are considered tightly coupled components of the design process, and both architecture and compiler features can be analyzed. The evaluation system (Figure 1) starts from the program benchmarks and allows to obtain a set of measurements of various architecture configurations through a sequence of intermediate steps.

3.1. Front-end and Intermediate Code features

The front-end implies the translation of the Benchmarks into an Intermediate Code (IntCode), composed of simple instructions directly expressing primitive hardware functionalities. This is accomplished by means of two steps: Prolog compilation and Intermediate Code translation.

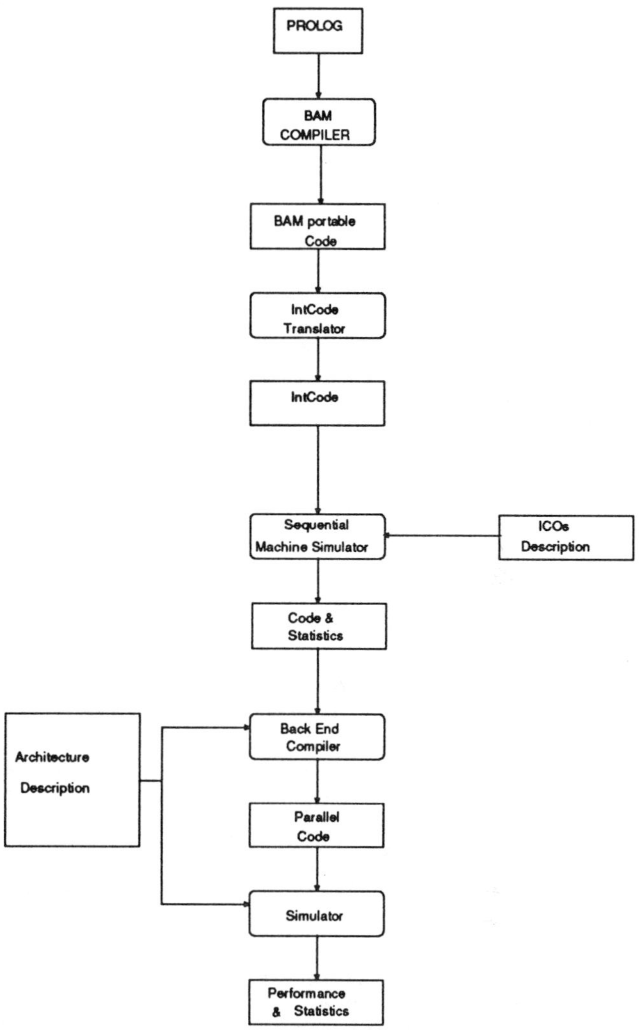

Fig. 1 - Flow diagram of the Evaluation System applied to Prolog

- We compile Prolog into the BAM abstract machine model by using the BAM compiler [VanRoy90] with the Automatic Mode analysis option in order to get high-performance code.
- BAM code is translated into machine-independent Intermediate Code Instructions (ICI). In this step we avoid all optimizations which are delayed to the back-end compiler. We only apply a variable renaming procedure in order to eliminate redundant data-dependencies.

The IntCode is composed of simple instructions directly expressing functionalities which, for the specific application, represent a good hardware/software tradeoff. Each ICI is directly executed by a machine hardware resource. ICIs specify functionality but contain no information about register allocation or hardware units. The general format of an ICI is:

$$Opcode\ Operand_1, \ldots, Operand_N,$$

where the operands may be variables or constants. Only direct and immediate addressing modes are supported while indirect addressing must be detailed with more instructions.

An IntCode Sequential Emulator extracts basic statistical information about the code generated by the front-end from Prolog Benchmarks, and validates the code itself. The emulator computes for each ICI the *Expect* (number of times it has been executed), and for each branch also the *Probability* (to take the branch). These information are used by the Parallelizing Compiler to guide global compaction.

3.2. Back-end Compilation

The back-end compiler extracts the parallelism from the Int-Code and maps it onto the resources of a target architecture.

It is based on a global parallelizing technique derived from the Trace Scheduling approach [Fisher81], which operates compaction on traces of instructions extending beyond each basic block of code. Trace choice is based on the statistical information about execution frequency extracted by preliminary simulation. Any instruction of any complexity can be modeled, with the only constraint that each operation must require a fixed and known amount of time to be executed.

The Code generator is implemented by means of a variation on the Bottom-Up-Greedy algorithm described in [Ellis85].

Functional units for operations and register are chosen with heuristic techniques which take into account:

- estimated completion cycle of an operation for each possible unit in the architecture;
- nearest allocated operands and destinations;
- possible bottleneck paths, using a priority assigned to each communication path;
- register movement insertion in order to have operands and destinations directly connected with the functional units;
- functional unit usage and register allocation balance;

An event-driven simulator has also been developed in order to obtain performance and statistics about resource utilization.

4. CODE ANALYSIS

Some important remarks have to be done about the evaluation methods.

- The analysis focuses only on the micro-architecture features without considering system related parameters. On this purpose, we assume to have a fixed access time for both data and code cache memory. The independency of the micro-architecture from other system components enables to scan a space of homogeneous micro-architectures.
- We intentionally avoid any reference to absolute cycle timing, highlighting technology-independent parameters. What we want to estimate is the performance/cost gain that can be obtained with the introduction of different architectural options in comparison with a pure sequential implementation. Absolute values (cycle time, chip area) are related only to available technology and have no influence on the presented analysis.

4.1. Data dependency and memory references

Dependency analysis is fundamental for parallelism discovery: it allows the compiler to exploit fine-grain instruction concurrency by transforming the program in a semantically equivalent form with a higher degree of parallelism. Dependency analysis is necessary in particular for memory disambiguation for parallel access on separate memory banks [Wolfe89]. The problem of data-dependency reduction is then outstanding from a parallel perspective, and in the numeric world a wide set of optimizations algorithms has already been developed [Aho86].

In this context, it is important to remark that the Abstract Execution Model of the BAM (as well as the WAM [VanRoy84]), separates data space in distinct stack areas (environment stack, choice point stack, heap, trail, push-down). Then it would seem natural to physically organize data cache memory in different banks in order to have an easy parallel memory access. Unfortunately, previous studies on the WAM [Tick87], which retain their validity for the BAM as well, have demonstrated that the majority of memory accesses are in the stack (environment and choice point: more than 70%) and cannot be disambiguated since most of the times deriving from an indirect (pointer) memory address. Since no valid technique has yet been developed for pointer disambiguation, memory references analysis cannot help to eliminate data-dependencies.

Moreover, optimizations which are commonly employed in numeric code, such as loop unrolling and interchanging, are nearly useless in Prolog due to the peculiar nature of symbolic computation. In fact, Prolog code is characterized by an absence of "traditional" loops, the only ones being built-in predicates (e.g. multiplication, division, hashing), dereferencing and detrailing, while iterative constructs are normally implemented through recursion. Since unrolling is mainly used to eliminate memory dependencies in array-based structures, it is completely ineffective in Prolog loops which basically perform pointer- chasing operations.

It is important to remind that distributed memory models for Prolog have already been developed in the past, although they have not had wide popularity, since in many cases the semantic of the language was altered, or the programmer was forced to specify program parallelism.

For these reasons we limit our research scope to shared-memory architectures, although the same compilation methods and algorithms can be easily extended to multiple memory access configurations, when suitable models will be developed.

4.2. Instruction Frequency and Amdahl's Law

Prolog programs spend a large part of time in data memory accesses. Measurements on instruction frequency on a subset of programs extracted form the Aquarius Benchmark Suite (Figure 2) show that memory operations take about 32% of the whole execution time. Data are computed as an average of the values obtained via sequential simulation of the benchmarks and with the hypothesis that all operations have the same duration.

We can apply well-known Amdahl's law [Amdahl67] to evaluate which is the maximum speed-up we can expect with a shared memory approach:

$$Speedup = \frac{1}{(1 - Fraction_{enhanced}) + \dfrac{Fraction_{enhanced}}{Speedup_{enhanced}}}$$

If we suppose to speed up ideally the execution of all operations but memory accesses, we can say that:

$$Fraction_{enhanced} \approx 0.68$$

$$Speedup_{enhanced} \rightarrow \infty$$

$$Speedup = \frac{1}{0.32} \approx 3.0$$

As a consequence, with a shared memory model, we will never be able to obtain a speed-up of more than 3.0 over a sequential implementation. Our opinion is that a value of 3.0 as an asymptotic speed-up is not to be considered marginal and can justify the research by itself. Obviously, we cannot speed-up ALU operations, data movements and control operations without limits, but we have to take into account implementation cost issues. Figure 3 gives an approximation of the maximum ideal speed-up which can be obtained by varying the enhancements of ALU and control operations. The dotted line shows the maximum hypothetical speed-up when supposing that memory operations are executed separate from computation. The continuous line, on the contrary, is based on the assumption that memory operations can be com-

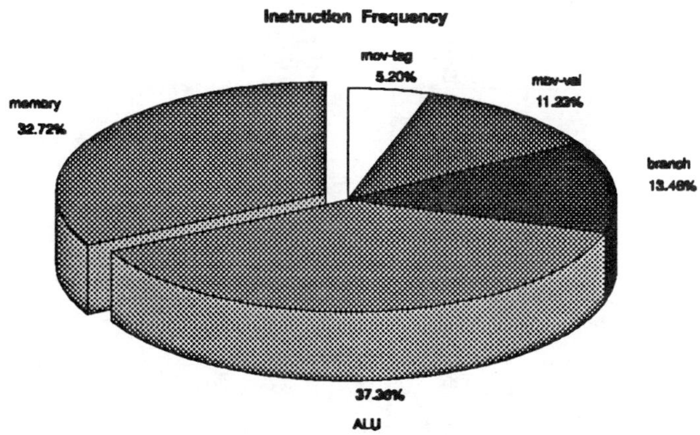

Fig. 2 - Execution frequency of IntCode instructions, organized in groups (data transport, memory access, data transformation-ALU, control operations). Data are obtained from sequential simulation supposing that all operations have the same duration.

pletely overlapped with computation. In the latter hypothesis, we can see how factors of concurrency greater than three are useless, since memory accesses constiutute the limiting factor.

In this context, it is important to remark that the graph shows an optimistic prevision of speed-up based on the hypothesis that:

- the code contains enough parallelism by itself
- the compiler is able to find the necessary concurrency in the code.

In the following sections, we show how this goal can be reached only by using global compaction techniques which extend their analysis beyond basic blocks of code.

4.3. Basic Blocks and Global Compaction

As we have seen, Prolog code promises a worthwhile degree of concurrency even for a shared memory architecture model, at the condition that an efficient compiler is able to exploit it.

The greatest problem in finding parallelism in Prolog code comes from the high percentage of branch operations (more than 15%) which make difficult to find reasonable degrees of instruction concurrency inside each basic block (composed of not more than 6-7 instructions).

To overcome the barrier of basic blocks, it is then necessary to apply Global Compaction techniques which extend their optimizations beyond basic blocks and consequently allow a higher possibility of code motion. An in-house arrangement of the "Trace Scheduling" technique has been chosen for the analysis, thus allowing to exploit parallelism beyond branches.

Quantitatively, Table 1 shows the available concurrency for each of the considered benchmarks, by limiting code compaction within basic blocks, and by considering global compaction applied to traces of instructions. It is possible to see how a global optimization technique increases the block size to 11-12 instructions, and performs about 30% faster than simple basic-blocks optimizations.

Hypotheses of measurements:

- All operations have duration 1, except memory (2 cycles in pipeline) and control (2 cycles in pipeline). This assumption is made for a realistic modeling of RISC-based machines.
- While computing maximum speed-ups, different kinds of data dependency have been considered: Memory dependency, Source-Destinations, Write-after-read, Write-after-write, Off-live. Also a constraint on the sequence of branches has been imposed in order to limit the possibility of code motion to avoid an exponential growth of instruction copies [Ellis85].

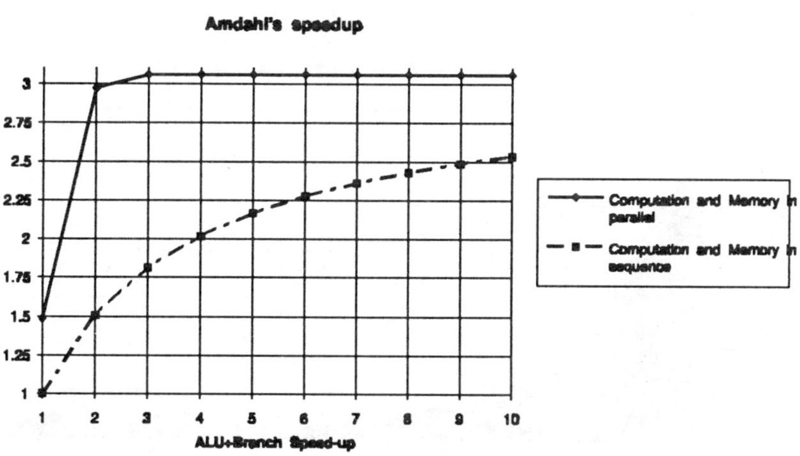

Fig. 3 - Maximum achievable speed-up according to Amdahl's law for shared-memory architectures. Speed-up is computed as a function of the enhancements of ALU and control operations. For instance, saying that *ALU+BRANCH Speed-up = 3* means that in the same cycle we are able to execute one memory access and 3 operations of the BRANCH and ALU classes. Data movement operations overhead is considered negligible assuming that they can be completely overlapped with computation.

Benchmark	Traces		Basic Blocks	
	Speedup vs. seq.	Average Length	Speedup vs. seq.	Average Length
conc30	1.65	11.88	1.55	6.35
divide10	1.98	13.35	1.63	7.49
log10	1.81	12.95	1.44	7.31
mu	2.28	6.94	1.52	3.58
nreverse	1.79	12.55	1.60	6.36
ops8	2.07	12.71	1.67	6.99
prover	2.20	14.64	1.66	7.11
qsort	1.93	14.87	1.72	7.56
queens_8	1.90	10.43	1.81	5.42
sendmore	3.18	8.83	1.53	4.53
serialise	2.68	11.11	1.71	5.82
tak	2.30	9.05	2.01	4.72
times10	2.08	13.35	1.64	7.15
zebra	2.27	10.08	1.60	6.48
Average	2.15	11.62	1.65	6.21

Table 1 - Speed-ups which can be obtained by applying Basic Block compaction or Trace Scheduling for shared memory architectures.

Having a higher degree of concurrency available means that higher possibilities of code motion are given to the code generator in order to keep the data path fully operative.

We notice also that this possibility is not achievable with microprogrammed machines models because branches operations are not exposed to the compiler and therefore only general optimization on single basic blocks of the microprogram can be applied. Only through the combination of an efficient execution model like the BAM and advanced compilation techniques, it is possible to reach this improvement.

4.4. Branch Prediction and validity of Trace Scheduling

Global Compaction approaches are based on statistic data on the execution flow of the program. The Trace Scheduling algorithm, in particular, operates compaction by choosing the "traces" of most frequently executed instructions. The trace-picking procedure follows the flow of the program, by choosing the most probable path at each branch instruction.

For these reasons, Trace Scheduling has been applied in the past only to highly regular scientific code. In loop-structured code it is easy to predict which direction is the most frequently followed at each branch instruction. In fact, most backward going branches are loop branches, whose typical probability to be taken is about 90%. Starting from these considerations, a well-known rule-of-thumb is derived, stating that about 90% of backward-going branches are taken while only about 50% of forward-going branches are taken (The *90/50 Branch-Taken Rule*) [Hennessy90]. This rule has been proved to be rather accurate for typical numeric/scientific code. If it were valid for Prolog code as well, the applicability of Trace Scheduling would be compromised, since the behavior of program execution flow would result unpredictable (branch probability around 50%), due to the absence of loops.

In order to evaluate the Predictability of Prolog code, we have measured the actual distribution of branch probability in the benchmarks.

We can define:

- **Probability of a Branch** ($P_{bt}(b)$): the probability of a branch to be taken,
- Probability of a Faulty Prediction of a Branch $P_{fp}(b)$: the probability that a branch usually taken is not taken, or that a branch usually not taken is taken. In formulas:

$$P_{fp}(b) = \begin{cases} P_{bt}(b), \text{ if } P_{bt}(b) \leq 0.5 \\ 1 - P_{bt}(b), \text{ if } P_{bt}(b) > 0.5 \end{cases}$$

During Trace Scheduling compilation, we pick the most probable traces of instructions by following the most probable executed branches. When the execution follows the most probable traces, performance gain is maximal. Otherwise, a penalty is paid in terms of additional cycles. Then the average value of $P_{fp}(b)$ represents a measure for the effectiveness of a Trace Scheduling approach: the smallest $P_{fp}(b)$, the smallest the probability and the penalty of making a wrong choice during trace picking.

Table 2 shows the average values of $P_{fp}(b)$ obtained through a dynamic analysis during simulation which computes an average of the probability weighted with the execution frequency of the branches. Figure 4 shows the distribution of P_{fp} for all the considered benchmarks.

We can notice how the average probability of a faulty prediction is about 0.14, value which guarantees a low performance decay due to run-time unpredictable execution flow. The statistic profile of distribution of Figure 4 shows also that the "90/50 Branch- Taken Rule" is not true for symbolic code, since most program branches (not belonging to the loop-backward class) are rather deterministic in their execution. Only a small percentage

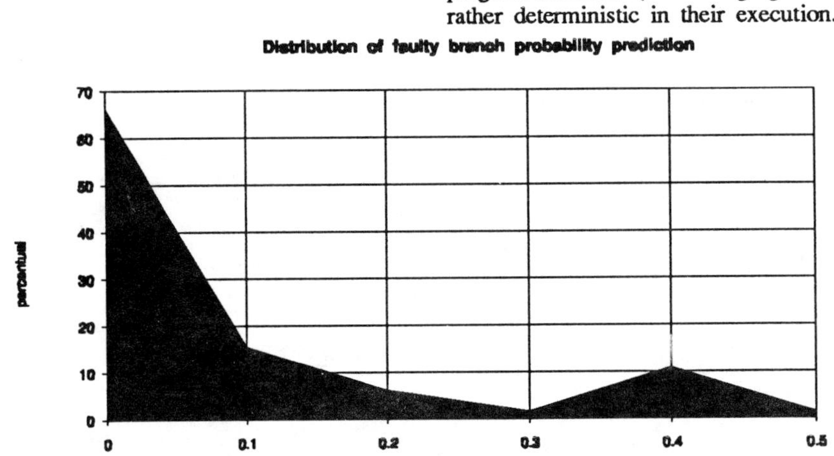

Fig. 4 - Distribution (percent) of the probability of making an erroneous prediction of the direction of a branch. As we can see, Prolog code is rather deterministic in its execution flow since branch instructions are often taken in the same direction.

Benchmark	Average Probability of Faulty Prediction of branch direction (P_{fp})
conc30	0.0292
crypt	0.0408
divide10	0.0935
log10	0.0354
mu	0.1215
nreverse	0.0523
ops8	0.1297
prover	0.0976
qsort	0.2376
queens_8	0.0973
query	0.1164
sendmore	0.0888
serialise	0.0896
tak	0.1994
times10	0.0935
zebra	0.1898
Average	**0.1475**

Table 2 - Probability of faulty prediction of branch targets for the considered benchmarks.

(represented as the peak around 0.4) is really data-dependent and represents the fraction of branches which actually decides the semantic of the programs.

These considerations, which are not intuitive, show how a Trace Scheduling approach could be effective also when applied to symbolic computation. Disadvantages of a larger code size due to the introduction of compensation copies, are overcome by the advantage of a faster execution of the most frequently executed parts. Moreover, if we consider a hierarchical memory organization, only a small frequently executed part of code will be kept in cache, while other large parts of program will be stored (and compacted) in slower memory.

4.5. Estimated performance of VLIW architectures

Starting from the results of the previous sections which demonstrate the opportunity of applying global compaction techniques to a shared-memory Prolog abstract machine, we can design an architecture to support the considered computational model.

By using the described evaluation system, we can estimate the performance of different machine configurations, expressed in terms of machine cycles, in order to get technology-independent comparisons.

As described in section 3, we consider the class of parallel synchronous non-homogeneous architectures with dedicated hardware for supporting Prolog intrinsic features. In order to maintain capabilities of general-purpose computation, we limit specialized hardware structures to the minimum set which is necessary for an efficient management of tagged data.

The target architectures have the block structure shown in Figure 5, and can be composed of a variable number of basic units. Each unit supports simple arithmetic, logic and control operations, with no interpretation level between instruction and hardware, is completely exposed to the compiler, and can execute in the same cycle a memory access, a control operation, an ALU operation and a local data movement. The Instruction Set is register-oriented, with only direct and immediate addressing modes, and the only instructions which can access memory are explicit *load* and *store* operations.

Prolog dedicated features are added to optimize datapath structure and branch management.

- The data path supports tagged data and registers are organized into independent data fields.
- In order to reduce the overhead of redundant compare operations, the sequencer can branch directly on the tag fields. Also delayed branches, overlapping and multi-way jumps are allowed.

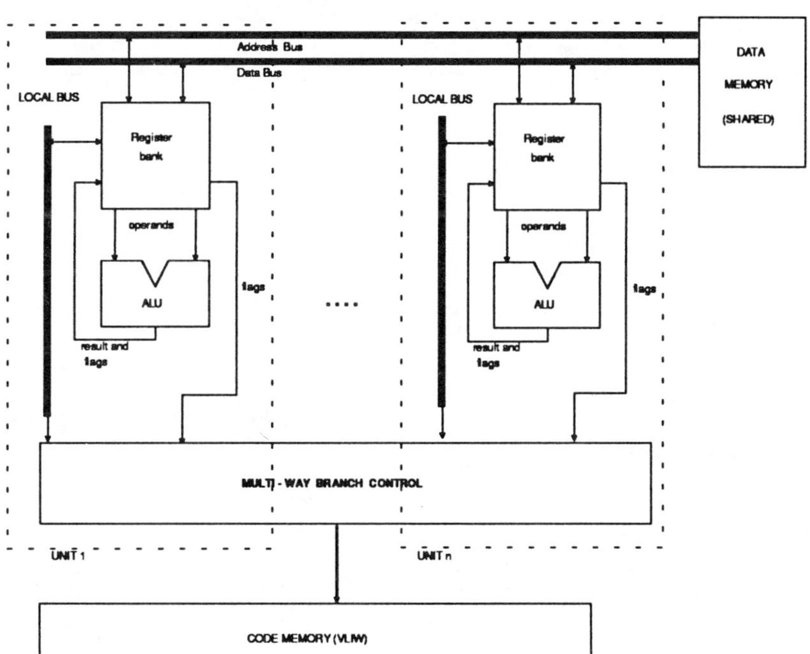

Fig. 5 - The structure of the architecture support used to evaluate the effectiveness of global compaction techniques.

Bench-mark	seq	BAM		1 unit		2 units		3 units		4 units		5 units	
		cycles	s.u.	cycles	s.u.	cycles	s.u.	cycles	s.u.	cycles	s.u.	cycles	s.u.
conc30	798	577	1.38	513	1.56	512	1.56	512	1.56	512	1.56	512	1.56
divide10	1902	1173	1.62	1101	1.73	1016	1.87	998	1.91	980	1.94	980	1.94
log10	626	610	1.03	368	1.70	341	1.84	339	1.85	338	1.86	338	1.86
mu	49099	25929	1.89	38281	1.28	27172	1.81	27035	1.82	26236	1.87	25352	1.94
nreverse	8925	6234	1.43	5542	1.61	5515	1.62	5515	1.62	5515	1.62	5515	1.62
ops8	1241	762	1.63	705	1.76	636	1.95	627	1.98	618	2.01	618	2.01
prover	53791	29460	1.83	33425	1.61	28575	1.88	27946	1.92	27260	1.97	27244	1.97
qsort	9564	6828	1.4	5244	1.82	5111	1.87	5111	1.87	5111	1.87	5111	1.87
queens_8	56924	36416	1.56	34338	1.66	31967	1.78	31919	1.78	31919	1.78	31919	1.78
sendmore	1859889	1282921	1.45	1075486	1.73	845423	2.2	826407	2.25	809759	2.3	809759	2.3
serialise	30080	15554	1.93	17847	1.69	14342	2.1	13735	2.19	13235	2.27	13161	2.29
tak	1364190	940817	1.45	732671	1.86	653498	2.09	653498	2.09	653498	2.09	653498	2.09
times10	1704	1047	1.63	958	1.78	872	1.95	854	1.99	836	2.04	836	2.04
zebra	5031109	2633032	1.91	2877146	1.75	2526207	1.99	2457727	2.05	2394038	2.1	2394038	2.1
Average			**1.58**		**1.68**		**1.89**		**1.92**		**1.95**		**1.95**

Table 3 - Cycles and speed-up versus a sequential machine of different parallel architectural configurations. The architectures are assumed to be composed of the units shown in Fig.5.

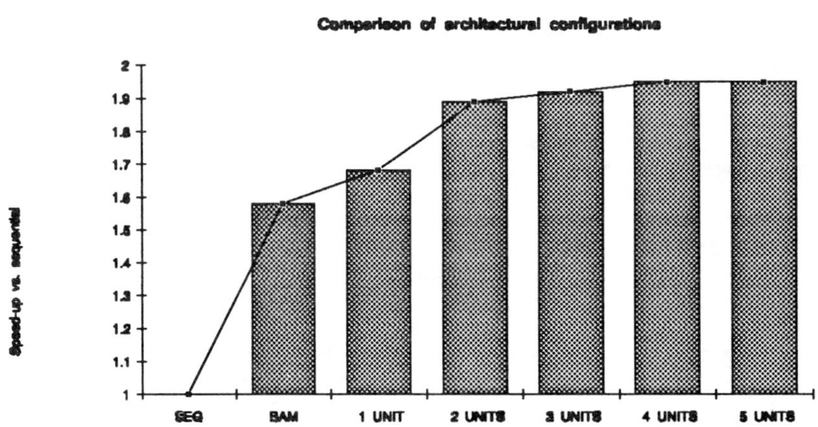

Fig. 6 - Performance comparison of different architectures (whose structure is described in FIgure 5), a pure sequential implementation and the BAM processor itself.

The system architecture can be composed of an arbitrary number of units, depending on the required cost/performance ratio. A single Very Long Instruction Word is issued at every cycle with a unique control flow.

The instruction set of the architecture is similar to the BAM, but with a lower level of complexity. Since the micro-architecture is completely compiler-driven, BAM instructions that require sequences (e.g.: dereference, unification) are implemented via primitive operations.

In order to verify the validity of global compaction techniques, we need to measure the variation of the speed-up with an increase in the number of units of the architecture. As terms of comparison, we use both a pure sequential machine, and the BAM processor itself. On this purpose, we suppose that the duration of the operations of the architecture is equal to the BAM ones.

Some consideration can be drawn from the analyis of Table 3 and Figure 6, which show the results of our analysis:

- For most benchmarks, there is a speed-up saturation for a number of units larger than 3-4, as it was forecast by Amdahl's law.
- We can notice how the BAM shows a speed-up of about 1.6 with respect to a pure sequential implementation. This is very close to the limit of basic blocks (1.65, see Table 2) and is obtained by an instruction set which has some parallelism features, and by the adoption of RISC optimizations techniques (like delayed branches).
- In any case, the cost/performance gain with respect to the BAM is not impressive for architectures with more than one unit.
- However, in high-end applications where performance is the key parameter, a global compilation technique represent the only viable chance with a shared memory model.

5. A VLIW PROTOTYPE

5.1. Architecture features

A first result of the SYMBOL project is a VLIW incremental architecture and compiler, intended to work as a Hardware Accelerator attached to a host workstation. The architecture is based on a VLSI processor, whose features conform to the description of a unit in section 4.5.

The architecture represents an experiment in building a real machine to test on the field the applicability of the described compilation techniques. The prototype will be used for research purposes and applied to control tasks in autonomous vehicle navigation problems.

In order to use completely automated layout tools for rapid prototyping, we have adopted a standard cell approach and we have been forced to reach a compromise between performance and cost issues. As a consequence, the implemented processors shows some limits in comparison with the unit described in section 4.5:

- For scalability and testability reasons, a single processor is self-sufficient, and contains registers, an ALU and a sequencer. When more sequencers are used for multi-way branches, synchronization among them is achieved by means of an external logic network. In fact, since multiple branch instructions can be issued in the same cycle, a strategy has to be used to solve conflicts when more than one condition is true. So the compiler includes bits in the instructions to specify the priority of the branch operations. At each branch, a controller decides which processor Program Counter will be enabled in the next cycle.
- For pinout limitations, we had to organize the instruction in two formats, one for ALU operations and one for control operations. Then the compiler has to choose, and parallelism is somewhat reduced. However, memory accesses can be issued in both formats.
- For on-board memory cost considerations, accesses to code and data space have been organized in a three-cycle pipeline. This does not compromise the peak rate of one access per cycle, but causes two-cycles delayed branches and a longer completion time of data memory operations.

5.2. The VLSI Processor

Machine instructions are horizontal, 64 bits wide and organized into two formats, one for direct and one for immediate addressing.

- Direct address format allows a memory access, an ALU operation and a register movement.
- Immediate address format allows a control operation (or immediate operand movement) and a memory access.

The datapath (Figure 7) is composed of:

- a multi-port Register Bank (16 registers),
- an Arithmetic-Logic Unit,
- a Sequencing unit,
- a Data Memory interface.

The Register bank is composed of 16 32-bits registers organized in separate and independently addressable fields:

- value (28 bits), used to store addresses or constants
- tag (3 bits), used to store data specifications (list, structure, atom, variables) as well as arithmetic flags deriving from compare operations
- cdr (1 bit), used for list concatenation and for some status flags, originally introduced for compatibility with the WAM.

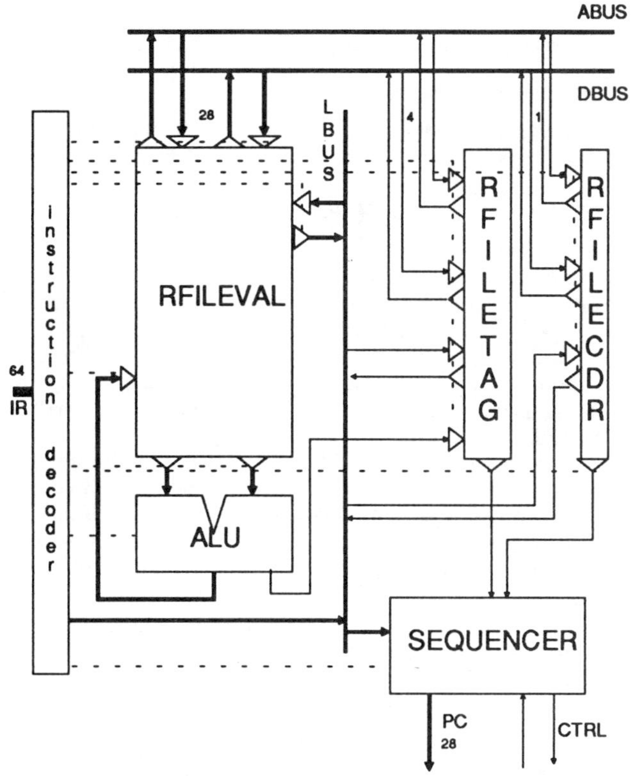

Fig. 7 - The micro-architecture of the prototype processor

Unlike common Prolog processors, there are no reserved registers (apart from the Program Counter) for environment variables. In this way the code generator is free to decide where to store a variable, to reduce the traffic on the buses connecting the processors. The processor has no dedicated status word, and flags resulting from ALU operations can be stored (only when necessary) in the tag field of any register.

As in other RISC machines, the sequencer has a reduced complexity, because of the simple control instructions supported that actually are only branch-on-condition and jump (direct and indirect). A little hardware support has been added for pipelined jumps management: when a jump is executed in any processor, sequencers of all processors must be disabled in the following two cycles, in order to preserve program flow correctness.

Data Memory is interfaced through non-multiplexed data and address buses, which are also used for processor-to-processor register movements. Addresses and the different fields of data can come from different processors with no constraints. Memory operations are organized in a three-stages pipeline, with the assumption of an external memory (or cache) with a single cycle access time. MAR and MDR registers are external to the processor, and transparent to the compiler.

The control part is just composed of decoders for the instructions fields, which are fixed for each format and directly control functional units and bank ports of the architecture. Code Memory access is organized in a three-cycle pipeline, also considering the decoding phase (which is very simple indeed). An external Program Counter and Instruction Register are included for the pipeline.

The RISC processor has been designed by using a hierarchical standard cell environment. The chip obtained has an area of 12.5 mm by 13.5 mm and is composed of about 100,000 transistors (Figure 8) [DeGloria91].

The measured operating frequency is 30 MHz.

5.3. Performance Measurements

Following [Hennessy90], performance of an architecture can be measured only by taking into account all of the following factors:

- Cycles Per Instructions (CPI). In our case CPI = 1.
- Clock Rate. In our case Clock Rate = 30 MHz
- Instruction Count.

For this reasons, instead of giving performance in terms of MLIPS (Millions of logical inferences per second), we prefer to show absolute execution times. However, for the NREVERSE benchmark, which is commonly used as a reference term for measuring logical inferences, we obtain a peak performance of 2.1 MLIPS.

Table 4 shows the (simulated) execution times of a three-processor architecture for the benchmarks (expressed in milliseconds) in comparison with other Prolog machine. We can see that absoulte performance of a three-processor architectures reaches only 83% of BAM performance. However, this fact does not affect the validity of the approach, since we must consider that:

- we have implemented an architecture which, although composed of three processors, is characterized by a remarkable design simplicity and has been realized with completely automated layout tools;
- we have used a slow technology (2 microns), and operation durations are consequently longer than the BAM processor.

In order to demonstrate the effectiveness of the Global Compaction technique, we can consider the speed-up of the architecture relative to a sequential implementation which obeys the same operation duration hypotheses (Table 5). We notice how a Trace Scheduling compilation succeeds in reaching a level of speedup (1.9) which is slightly higher than the BAM (1.5).

	Quintus	VLSI-PLM	KCM	BAM	Symbol-3
divide10	0.41	0.38	0.091	0.0387	0.0423
log10	0.15	0.109	0.039	0.0201	0.0146
mu	7.04	12.407	4.644	0.8557	1.2913
nreverse	1.62	2.10	0.65	0.2057	0.2401
ops8	0.24	0.214	0.059	0.0251	0.0274
prover	8.67	6.83	-	0.9722	1.2995
qsort	4.82	4.24	1.32	0.2253	0.2192
queens_8	21.20	28.80	1.205	1.2017	1.549
sendmore	490.00	-	-	42.3364	44.0939
serialise	3.10	2.47	1.22	0.5133	0.6556
tak	1120.00	940.00	-	31.047	32.067
times10	0.345	0.2470	0.082	0.0346	0.0363
zebra	423.00	-	-	86.890	119.184
average speed-up	(10.51)	(10.47)	(2.42)	(0.83)	(1.00)

Table 4 - Performance comparison of some Prolog implementations. Values are expressed in milliseconds. The last rows shows the speed-up relative to the SYMBOL-3 (three-processors) VLIW architecture. The values are computed without taking into account the cycle time difference, since it may be influenced by the adopted architectural model.

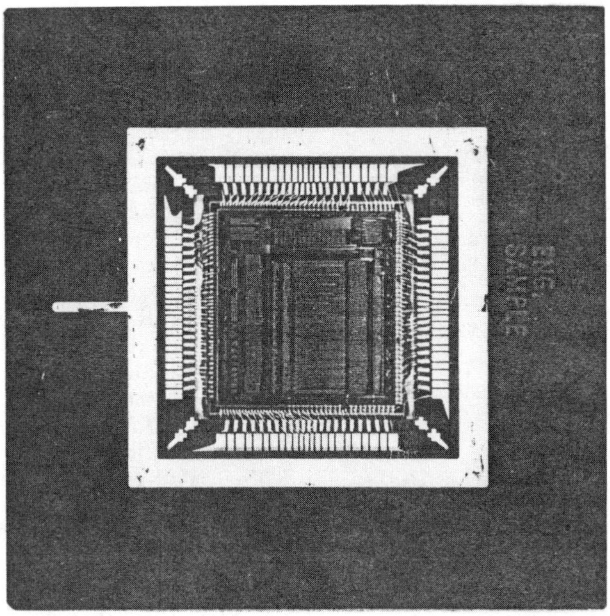

Fig. 8 - A photograph of the layout of the prototype processor

	BAM/ sequential (BAM)	SYMBOL-3/ sequential(SYMBOL)
divide10	1.62	1.88
log10	1.03	1.82
mu	1.89	1.80
nreverse	1.43	1.60
ops8	1.63	1.91
prover	1.83	1.88
qsort	1.40	1.89
queens_8	1.56	1.88
sendmore	1.45	2.10
serialise	1.93	2.05
tak	1.45	2.02
times10	1.63	1.94
zebra	1.91	2.01
average speed-up	(1.58)	(1.90)

Table 5 - Speed-ups of the BAM and the SYMBOL-3 architectures with respect to sequential machines with congruent hypotheses on operation duration.

6. CONCLUSIONS

In this paper we have presented results of a code analysis which show the effectiveness of a Global Compilation approach to the BAM model of Prolog.

The basic consideration which emerges from the analysis is that Prolog shared-memory models have almost reached their limits with the BAM architecture.

In this context, further improvements can come only from technology (designing faster processors), or architecture (adopting dynamic scheduling), and only marginally from a static exploitation of instruction-level parallelism. In any case, we can't overcome Amdahl's limit of speedup (about 3) with a shared memory model.

In our opinion, the only solution to break the barrier with a compiler-driven parallel approach is in the development of distributed memory models for Prolog. There, a global compaction algorithm can be really effective and reach order of magnitudes of improvement, but it is still an open field for future research.

ACKNOWLEDGEMENT

We would like to thank the Aquarius research group at University of California, Berkeley for key contributions to this research. In particular, thanks to Peter Van Roy for the BAM compiler and to Bruce Holmer for the BAM simulator.

REFERENCES

[Amdahl67] G. M. Amdahl, "Validity of the single processor approach to achieving large scale computing capabilities", Proc. *AFIPS 1967 Spring Joint Computer Conference* , N.J., 1967.

[Aho86] A. Aho, R. Sethi, D. Ullman, *Compilers: Principles, Techniques and Tools,* Addison Wesley, 1986.

[Benker89] H. Benker, J. Beacco, S. Bescos et al., " KCM: A Knowledge Crunching Machine", *16th International Symposium on Computer Architecture (ISCA16)* , pp. 186-194, 1989.

[Borriello86] G. Borriello, A. Cherenson, P. Danzig, M. Nelson, "Special or General-Purpose Hardware for Prolog: A Comparison", *Technical report*, University of California at Berkeley, 1986.

[Dobry87] T. Dobry, *A High Performance Architecture for Prolog*, PhD Thesis, University of California at Berkeley, 1987.

[Clocksin81] W.F.Clocksin, C.S. Mellish, *Programming in Prolog*, Springer-Verlag, New York, 1981.

[Ellis85] J. Ellis, *Bulldog: A Compiler for VLIW architectures*, The MIT Press, Boston, Mass., 1985.

[DeGloria90] A.De Gloria, P.Faraboschi, "An Evaluation System for Application Specific Architectures", *23rd International Workshop on Microprogramming and Microarchitecture (MICRO23),* 1990.

[DeGloria91] A.De Gloria, P.Faraboschi, E. Guidetti, "A VLIW Architecture for Prolog", *IEEE MicroArch*, Vol. 6, N. 1, Nov 1991, pp 27-32.

[Fisher81] J. Fisher, "Trace Scheduling: a technique for global microcode compaction", *IEEE Trans. on Computer*, vol. C-30, pp. 478-490, 1981.

[Fisher83] J. Fisher, "Very Long Instruction Word Architectures and the ELI-512" , *Proc. of 10th International Symposium on Computer Architecture (ISCA10)*, 1983.

[Haygood89] R. Haygood, *A Prolog Benchmark Suite for Aquarius*, Report. No. UCB/UCSD 89/509, University of California at Berkeley, Apr. 1989.

[Hennessy83] J. Hennessy, "VLSI Processor Architecture", *IEEE Trans. on Computer*, pp. 1221-1246, 1983.

[Hennessy90] J. Hennessy, D. Patterson. *Computer Architecture: a Quantitative Approach* , Morgan Kaufmann Publ., San Mateo, CA, 1990.

[Holmer90] B. Holmer, B. Sano, M. Carlton, P. Van Roy, R. Haygood, W. Bush, A. Despain, J. Pendleton, T. Dobry,"Fast Prolog with an Extended General Purpose Architecture", *17the International Symposium on Computer Architecture (ISCA17)* , pp. 282-291, 1990.

[Katevenis83] M. Katevenis, *Reduced Instruction Set computer for VLSI*, Computer Science Division (EECS) UCB/CSB 83/141, University of California At Berkeley, Oct. 1983.

[Kowalski79], R. Kowalski, *Logic for Problem Solving*, Elsevier Publ., North-Holland, 1979.

[Tick87] E. Tick, *Studies in Prolog Architectures*, Technical Report, Stanford University, 1987.

[VanRoy84] P. Van Roy, *A Prolog Compiler for the PLM*, Master Thesis, University of California at Berkeley, 1984

[VanRoy90] P. Van Roy, *Can Logic Programming Execute as Fast as Imperative Programming?* , PhD Thesis, Report No. UCB/CSD 90/600 (EECS) University of California at Berkeley, CA, Dec. 1990.

[Warren83] D. Warren, *An Abstract Prolog Instruction Set*, Artificial Intelligence Center, SRI International, 1983.

[Wolfe89] M. Wolfe, *Optimizing supercompilers for supercomputers*, The MIT Press, Boston, Mass. 1989.

Session 8: Memory Systems

Memory Latency Effects in Decoupled Architectures with a Single Data Memory Module*

Lizyamma Kurian, Paul T. Hulina and Lee D. Coraor
Department of Electrical and Computer Engineering
The Pennsylvania State University
University Park, PA 16802

Abstract

Decoupled computer architectures partition the memory access and execute functions in a computer program and achieve high performance by exploiting the fine-grain parallelism between the two. These architectures make use of an access processor to perform the data fetch ahead of demand by the execute process and hence are often less sensitive to memory access delays than conventional architectures. Past performance studies of decoupled computers used memory systems that are interleaved or pipelined. We undertake a simulation study of the latency effects in decoupled computers when connected to a single, conventional, non-interleaved data memory module so that the effect of decoupling is isolated from the improvement caused by interleaving. We compare decoupled computer performance to single processors with caches, study the memory latency sensitivity of the decoupled systems, and also perform simulations to determine the significance of data caches in a decoupled computer architecture. The Lawrence Livermore Loops and two signal processing algorithms are used as the simulation benchmark.

Keywords: Decoupled Architecture, Access Processor, Performance Evaluation, Memory Latency, Caches.

1 Introduction

Decoupled computer architectures exploit fine-grain parallelism existing between access and execute functions in a computer program. The memory access task and execution task required for accomplishing a job are actually two interrelated but independent processes. Decoupled computer implementations attempt to separate these two processes to provide concurrency between them and give high performance and increased flexibility.

Some separation of access and execute functions has been a feature of several early high performance computers such as the IBM 360/370, CDC 6600, CDC 7600 and CRAY-1. Several computer architectures have been proposed or built later, which partition access operations and computation functions in the program more distinctly. MAP-200 [4], DAE [18], PIPE [8] [22], SMA [14], SDP [16], FOM [2], ZS-1 [19] [24] [25] all belong to this category.

Performance of decoupled architectures has been studied in [23], [8], [25] etc. Smith et al [23] compared the performance of a pipelined decoupled architecture to that of scalar CRAY-1. This particular research effort also included studies on the effect of memory latency by varying the access time of main memory. Since a comparison is made with the CRAY-1, an interleaved memory configuration, (as in CRAY-1), is assumed. Memory bank conflicts are ignored too. Here memory access time was varied from 5 cycles to 32 cycles, but since the memory system is 16 way interleaved, the memory can be considered to be very fast. It is observed in this work that the performance improvement over the scalar CRAY-1 becomes more significant as the memory path length increases.

Goodman et al evaluated the performance of PIPE, a VLSI decoupled architecture [8]. The performance in decoupled mode is compared against the single processor mode. This work includes the effects of memory speed on performance by conducting studies on both a fast and a slow memory module. The fast memory had an access time of one clock cycle; the slow one had an access time of four clock cycles and was four way interleaved. They included a memory controller. With the overheads incurred in the controller, the effective delay seen in case of the fast memory is 3 cycles and it is 6 cycles for the slow memory [9]. They also ignore memory module conflicts in their study.

Smith, Abraham and Davidson [25] reported results on the effects of memory latency and fine grain parallelism on the Astronautics ZS-1, when connected to a pipelined memory system. They observed that once the slip limits were high, the computer system is almost insensitive to memory latency.

1.1 Objective

The performance study presented in this paper has three goals: first to compare the performance of decoupled computers to uniprocessor systems with caches, second to study memory latency sensitivity of decoupled computers with a single non-interleaved non-pipelined memory module, and third to determine the significance of a data cache in a decoupled architecture.

*This research was supported in part by the National Science Foundation under grant MIP-8912455.

© 1992 ACM 0-89791-509-7/92/0005/0236 $1.50

The performance of decoupled computers is compared against single processors without caches in the previous studies. Conceptually, in decoupled systems, we are using a processor to do the access task and eliminate the delay for data operands. In cache based systems, we utilize a cache to capture locality and eliminate the long delays required to access main memory. It would be interesting to find out how the two schemes compare to one another. In this paper, we investigate whether an access processor hides the memory latency of a computer system better than a data cache. Hence we perform comparison of the performance in decoupled mode against uniprocessors with caches.

Another objective of this paper is to study the sensitivity of a decoupled architecture to memory latency, when the memory is noninterleaved and nonpipelined. Previous studies report that decoupled computers have less sensitivity to memory path length than conventional systems. It is also reported that the speed up over single processor configuration becomes greater as the memory becomes slower. But as mentioned before, these studies used interleaved or pipelined memory systems. We want to study whether system behavior will exhibit a similar pattern even when the memory is noninterleaved.

A third objective of this paper is to study the significance of data caches in decoupled architectures when the memory system is not interleaved. Decoupled architectures generally do not have data caches. In the architectures mentioned above, only the ZS–1 has a data cache. The reduced sensitivity to memory access time observed in the previous studies tend to suggest that the improvement possible with a data cache would be minor [23]. Interleaving and memory pipelining obscure some of the memory latency and we suspect that, this is one reason for the insensitivity to longer memory cycle times in the studies in the past. We investigate whether a data cache would result in any serious performance advantage in decoupled architectures with noninterleaved memory units.

1.2 Overview

In section 2, we detail the decoupled architecture that is used to conduct our performance studies. This architecture is similar to many of the other architectures and especially to PIPE. It should be noted that this specific architecture is not critical to this research. We would expect to obtain similar results with any decoupled system. But we describe this specific architecture since our results were observed in the course of some other studies on this architecture. The description in section 2 illustrates that this architecture is considerably similar to other decoupled architectures and hence results obtained from this system should apply at least qualitatively to other decoupled architectures as well. In section 3, we analyze the mechanism by which decoupled computers alleviate the memory latency problem. In section 4, we explain our simulation tools and describe the benchmarks used. In section 5, we detail the simulation results obtained. We compare cache based uniprocessors to decoupled systems, study the sensitivity of decoupled systems to memory latency, examine the limitations of caches and decoupled architectures in eliminating memory latency, and study the significance of a data cache in a decoupled architecture. We conclude the paper in section 6.

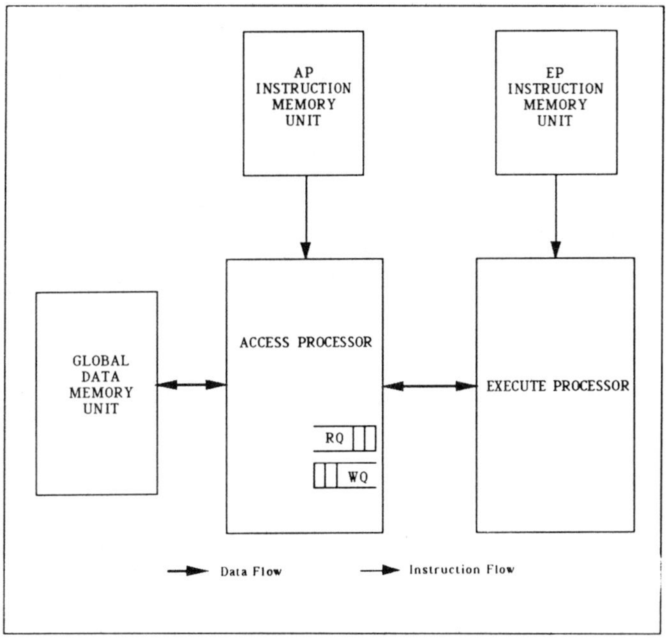

Figure 1: A Decoupled Architecture

2 A Decoupled Architecture

In this section, we describe the decoupled architecture, which was used to conduct our simulation studies. An overall view of the architecture is presented in section 2.1 and section 2.2 gives a description of the specific access processor used in the system.

2.1 The Architecture Overview

The architecture uses two processors, an Execute Processor (EP) and an Access Processor (AP) as shown in Fig. 1. As in standard DAE (decoupled access execute) architectures [18], the EP executes program instructions and performs all the required data computations. All accesses of the data memory are done by the AP. The two processors communicate through architectural queues. Access related instructions are fetched by the AP and computation instructions are fetched by the EP into their respective instruction caches. Data operands needed by the EP are fetched from the data memory unit by the AP and passed to the EP via architectural queues. Results of EP computations are deposited into the queues and transferred to the data memory by the AP. AP instructions are stored in an instruction memory private to the AP to avoid bus contentions with the data fetch. Since pin limitations of the AP in a VLSI implementation might pose a problem, the AP instructions could also be stored in the global data memory unit. This will not degrade the performance in problems with loops since the AP has an instruction cache. Our performance results in this paper are based on the architecture with AP instructions stored in the same memory unit as the data.

The two instruction streams run at their own speed, with the queues absorbing excess data. The AP fetches data elements into the Read Queue. The EP reads data from the Read Queue and stores its results into the Write Queue. Wherever coordination is required, the AP and EP use tokens to ensure correct operation. While accessing multiple-element data structures, the AP uses *End-of-Data* (EOD) tokens to separate batches of data such as an array, a column of a matrix, or the entire matrix. The AP can use the Read Queue to pass this EOD token to the EP. The EP uses these tokens to control its iterations. There is no potential problem due to sending such control information intermingled with data in the queues. Explicit instructions are used to deposit tokens and also to access them. Correctness of the program can be ensured as long as the EOD token is deposited only after the completion of any issued load instruction.

In problems with static data bounds, the AP has prior knowledge about when to insert the EOD tokens. In problems with dynamic bounds such as the C library string copy (*strcpy*) and string compare (*strcmp*) where the end of the string is not known until it is actually encountered, the scenario is different. To exploit any advantage of a decoupled architecture in such an application, the AP can fetch the string elements one by one without checking for the delimiter. The EP can perform the comparison to find the end of the string. Due to slip, the AP would have fetched beyond the end of the string by the time the EP finds the end of string. In such a case, the EP sends an EOD token to the AP whereupon the AP stops its fetch operation and also flushes any unnecessary data it has fetched. The EP can meanwhile continue operations on its own, but it should not read any data until the AP has flushed its queue. This can be accomplished if the AP sends a token to the EP to mark that it has flushed the queue, and the EP waits for the token before reading data operands from the queue again. This creates a certain amount of busy waiting but it seems to be inevitable, if any parallelism is to be exploited in such a problem.

We have not designed a specific EP, but intend to use our AP with any standard uniprocessor CPU with added queue accessing capability. We discuss the design of a 32-bit access processor in section 2.2.

2.2 The Access Processor

Efficient address generation for data structures is a primary goal in obtaining high performance in a computer system. The architecture of the AP and its instruction set is tailored to perform the address generation task efficiently.

The AP is comprised of a Read Queue, a Write Queue, an arithmetic unit, a register set and an instruction cache as in Fig. 2. The instruction set of the AP is classified into arithmetic, data transfer, control and queue manipulation groups. The arithmetic group consists of register add, immediate add, immediate multiply, register multiply, and register subtract instructions intended to aid in address calculations. The data transfer group consists of load and store instructions. There are byte, half-word and word loads and stores. In all the above instructions, the Read Queue can be specified as a destination and the Write Queue as a source. Any invalid operation on a queue (reading from an empty queue, writing to a full queue) causes that instruction to be temporarily blocked.

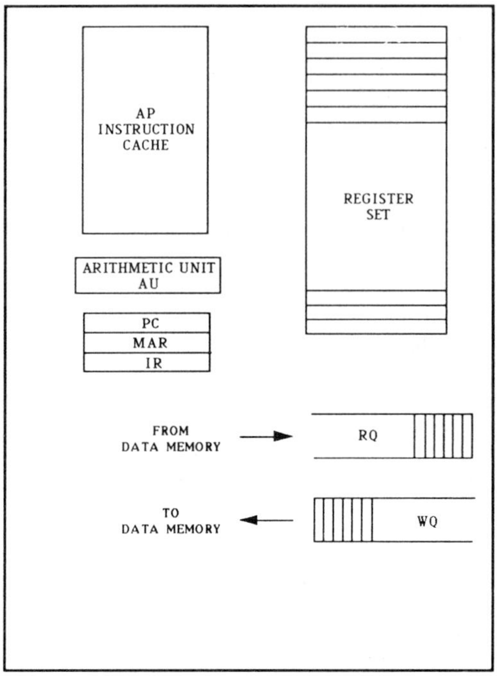

Figure 2: Block Diagram of the Access Processor

The control group consists of jump instructions and branches. The queue manipulation group consists of PUT EOD and Branch-on-no-end-of-data (BNEOD) instructions. The PUT EOD instruction is used to deposit EOD tokens into the queues. The BNEOD instruction is the counterpart of this instruction in the sense that whenever one processor inserts an EOD token, the other processor can check for the token using this instruction. Though only these two instructions are explicitly designated as queue manipulation instructions, it should be mentioned that other instructions can also operate on the queues by specifying the queue address in the register fields.

The *End-of-Data* token bit of the head of the queue is treated as an EOD flag. A data read from the queues will not occur if the EOD flag is set. The queue will be left unaffected in such cases. The BNEOD (Branch if no End-of-Data) instruction checks the EOD flag (or the token bit of the head of the queue) and if it is set, it clears the flag as well as the head of the queue. If the EOD flag is not set, the BNEOD instruction leaves the queue unaffected.

This 32-bit access processor could be used along with a standard RISC processor as the execute processor to form a usable decoupled architecture. The EP should also have queue manipulation instructions as in the AP instruction set. Even for the EP, one register bit pattern should indicate the queues and it should be possible to use the queue as the source or destination operand in any operation. It is possible to design instructions in such a way that both source operands come from the queue, but for sake of simplicity, we do not consider such instructions. It is quite possible to have the AP instruction set as a subset of the EP instruction set.

3 Memory Latency and the Access Processor

The Access Processor (AP) eliminates latency of main memory by performing the access process ahead of demand by the execute processor. When a program is looping, the access instruction stream often precedes the execution stream by at least one iteration. The Read Queue buffers the prefetched data. The execute processor does not have to wait to obtain data for its computations. The access processor would have already loaded the data into the Read Queue. Hence if sufficient slip is present, the EP obtains its operands with no delay. Similarly, in the case of memory writes, the EP can put the data into the Write Queue and proceed. The AP would store it back into the main memory later. It is assumed that the queue, like registers, can be accessed in a single cycle. Hence, if the AP can run ahead and load the queue with the data before the EP reaches the section of the code with a reference to the data, and if the Write Queue is long enough for the EP to dump its result and proceed, the EP never experiences a delay in accessing main memory. The AP thus hides memory latency from the EP.

The length of the queues is a critical factor in a decoupled architecture since often the distance the access process can run ahead is limited only by the queues. A slow memory access path can be compensated for by using longer queues [23]. With sufficiently long queues, a high average transfer rate can be achieved even with a memory of relatively low peak transfer rate capacity. The queues enable the system to utilize given memory bandwidth more efficiently. The memory latency insensitivity that can be achieved by a decoupled architecture depends on the slip that can be attained.

In the case of very fast memories, the address calculation instructions consume a significant amount of time and there is a limit on the slip that can be attained. With slower memories, the environment permits more slip. But memory poses a bottleneck and slip is limited again as the memory speed decreases beyond a certain point, which can be considered as an optimum memory speed. This optimum is not a constant, but will depend on the characteristics of the program under execution, such as the fraction of memory access instructions, etc.

4 Simulation Methodology

To realize the architecture, we use a RISC processor, actually the MIPS R2000 as the execute processor in combination with the AP described in section 2.2. Performance simulators were developed for the MIPS R2000 system and the decoupled system with the MIPS R2000 as the execute processor. Modifications necessary in the R2000 for queue operations and the EP-AP interface are assumed. The simulators are written in C and run on a DEC 3100 station under UNIX operating system. The results from the MIPS R2000 system form the baseline for comparison. Our simulators are mostly table driven so that the effect of changes in system parameters can be easily studied.

Both the EP and the AP are assumed to have a pipeline control similar to the MIPS R2000. The instruction pipeline is five stages deep, IF (instruction fetch), RD (read and decode), ALU, MEM (memory access) and WB (write back). Each of these steps requires approximately one CPU cycle [11]. The R2000 tries to achieve single cycle execution for its instructions by delayed load and delayed branch techniques. The uniprocessor that forms the baseline system for comparison as well as the EP in the decoupled implementation incorporate these techniques in identical manners so that the effect of decoupling could be easily identified. For the decoupled mode, the length of the queues was kept at 20 in our simulations. It has been reported that short queues are sufficient to achieve performance close to the maximum available with unbounded queues [23].

4.1 Benchmark Details

The simulation workload consists of some of the Lawrence Livermore Loops (LLLs) and some signal processing algorithms. The LLLs were chosen since they were used in research in the past [23] [8] and since they are important to a wide range of scientific algorithms and applications. In addition to the LLLs, we have synthesized a convolution and correlation algorithm as well. These signal processing algorithms are selected since they contain some addressing patterns other than purely sequential. They have been used in the past to benchmark special address generation units [10]. These algorithms exhibit good locality properties. Since our studies involve cache based systems, these algorithms are very relevant for our studies. We intended to include results from some large benchmarks like SPEC, but were unable to do so in the limited timeframe, due to lack of compiler support.

The LLLs can be classified as pure vector loops, linear recurrent loops and vector reduction loops [25]. We have picked up a few loops from each class so that the performance of the system for various types of code is obtained. We consider 'integerized' versions of the LLLs, since our execute processor is not a floating point processor. It would be possible to consider the EP as a system that has a fixed point unit and a floating point unit, say an R2000 and R2010. Our main purpose here is to study the performance enhancement contributed by the access processor, and hence considering data elements to be integer instead of floating point does not invalidate the results. At this point, it may be noted that integerized LLLs were used in the studies in [8] also.

Among the benchmarks we studied, LLL5 and LLL11 involve memory RAW (Read After Write) hazards. The loops can be optimized and RAW hazards avoided by storing intermediate results to a register and using the register content in the succeeding iteration, rather than again reading the data from memory. For loop 5, we consider only the optimized version. For loop 11, both versions are considered; the unoptimized version is labelled as loop 11a and the optimized version is denoted as loop 11b.

5 Discussion of Simulation Results

In this section we present our simulation results. We

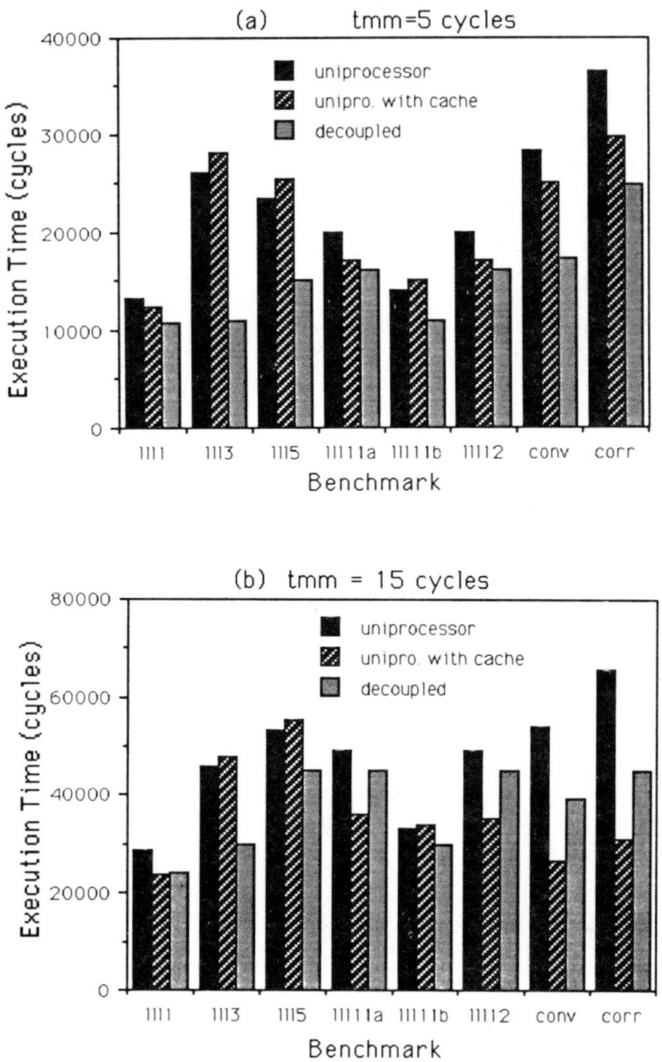

Figure 3: Performance of uniprocessor and decoupled systems

first compare the performance of decoupled systems with single processors with caches. In order to relate our work to previous research, we also simulate uniprocessors without caches. During simulation runs, we vary the main memory access time to find out the sensitivity of system performance to memory path length. The simulation results are analyzed to identify limitations of decoupled architectures and cache based systems. Finally, the relevance of a data cache in a decoupled architecture is studied by simulating a system with a cache in the AP. At this stage a comprehensive comparison of uniprocessors with and without caches and decoupled systems with and without caches is presented.

5.1 Comparison to Uniprocessors with Caches

The performance of the decoupled system in comparison with uniprocessors with and without caches is shown in Fig. 3. Since block sizes and cache sizes can have a critical effect on the performance of cache based systems, we performed simulations with a few different cache parameters. But in order not to clutter the figures with too much data, we plot only one typical organization of the cache with a size of 1024 bytes. (This cache size might look unrealistically small, but it should be remembered that the benchmarks are small too.) The cache is assumed to have a single cycle access time. It can be seen that in the 5 cycle case, the decoupled architecture executes the code faster than the uniprocessor with and without cache, while at 15 cycles the uniprocessor with cache performs better than the decoupled system for several of the traces.

5.2 Sensitivity of Performance to Memory Access Time

The effect of memory speed on performance is illustrated in Fig. 4 for both decoupled systems and cache based single processors. The total execution time is plotted as a function of the memory speed, for three representative traces, loop 3, loop 12 and the convolution algorithm. Loops 5 and 11b behave similar to loop 3; loops 1 and 11a are similar to loop 12 and correlation algorithm is similar to convolution. In Fig. 4a, the range of variation in execution time is the same for both types of systems. In Fig. 4b, uniprocessors with caches have a slightly lesser sensitivity to change in memory speed. The convolution and correlation benchmarks show the behavior in Fig. 4c. These algorithms have strong locality of reference and uniprocessors with caches are far more insensitive to memory speed than the decoupled architecture.

Fig. 5 illustrates the change in speed up of the decoupled system as the memory access time is varied. Results reported in [23] and [8] indicate that the speedup with a decoupled organization improves as the memory speed decreases. For most of the loops, we do observe the effect they reported, but we also notice that beyond a certain memory speed, the speedup declines. In [8], though it is mentioned that the performance advantage is more significant with a slower memory, 5 out of the 12 Lawrence Livermore loops they analyzed, show a smaller speedup for the slower memory module. Since they considered interleaved memories, this effect was not evident in the other loops in the ranges of memory speed they used.

5.3 Limitations Associated with Caches

Caches hide the latency of the main memory by capturing the temporal and spatial locality of the data references. Success of a cache organization depends on minimizing the miss ratio, the delay due to a miss, and the penalty for updating main memory. The number of fetches required to load a block of a given size, depends on the bus width. Larger block sizes capture spatial locality and may decrease the miss ratio, but increases both the delay due to a miss and also the updating penalty. Larger block sizes might increase the traffic ratio and actually increase the execution time. In several problems, precise tuning of the cache parameters is required to obtain performance advantage. For example, while running the convolution benchmark, it was noted that a system with a cache of size 1024 bytes is reasonably insensitive to memory speed when the block size is 4 bytes, but when the block size is 64 bytes, the 1024 byte size cache seems inadequate in eliminating latency.

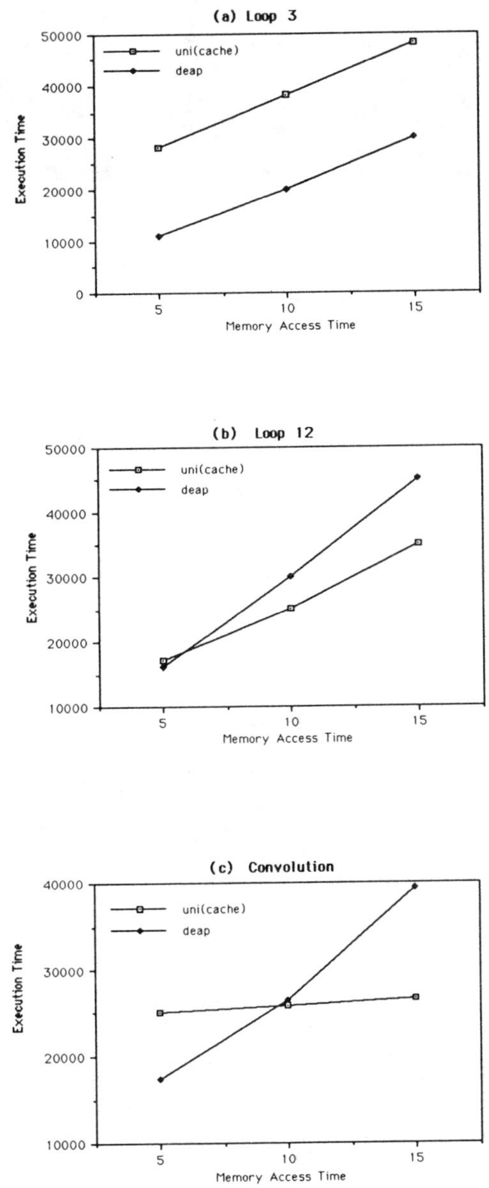

Figure 4: Execution Time vs Memory Speed

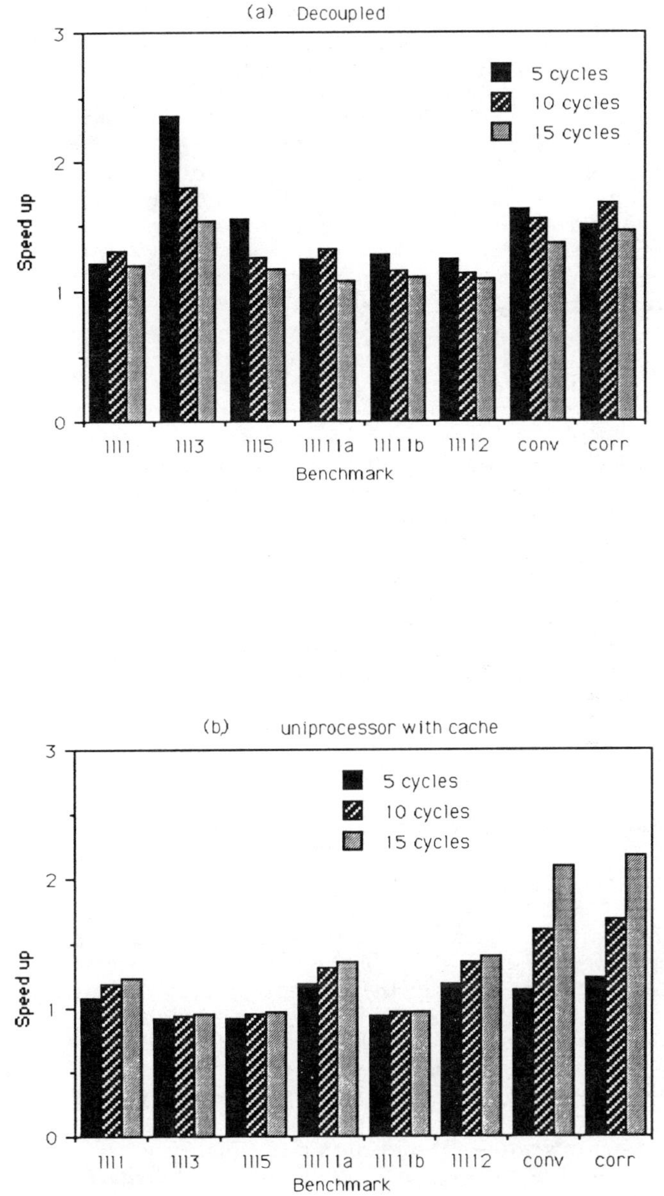

Figure 5: Speed up of decoupled system and cache based uniprocessor

Lack of temporal locality limits the capability of some problems to exploit the cache. In Fig. 3, one can notice that caches result in an increase of execution time in some of the benchmarks. Consider Lawrence Livermore Loop 3.

```
      q = 0.0
      do 3 k = 1,1000
3     q = q + z(k)*x(k)
```

Here the program steps through the arrays and hence there is spatial locality. In our study, the elements of the array have a 32-bit representation and the data bus width is 32 bits as well. The main memory is organized with a word size of 32 bits and each access furnishes one word or 32 bits. Considering memory traffic issues, the best choice for block size would be 4 bytes. (Let us ignore the directory costs just to give caches the maximum potential advantage.) If a block size of 4 bytes is used, only the array element in demand is loaded each time there is a miss. Since no array element is used again (or in other words there is no temporal locality), a cache of 4 byte blocks does not improve the performance. Having a larger block size would exploit the spatial locality, but since fetching a larger block requires a proportionately larger number of cycles, the cache does not decrease the total execution time. The cache can yield an advantage if some of these fetch cycles could run in parallel with computation cycles when the CPU is busy, but does not use the bus. Otherwise, the cache just slows down the system by adding the cache access time to each reference. This phenomenon can be observed in loop 3, loop 5 and loop 11b in Fig. 3. The execution time for the cache based system is higher than that for the system without the cache. If the data size is smaller than a word, or in other words, if more than one data element could be fetched at the expense of one fetch, performance improvement could be obtained. For this reason, problems with only spatial locality sometimes do not benefit from caches. As previously observed in [1] [12] [20] unless carefully designed and implemented, caches result in increasing the total execution time of a program.

5.4 Limitations of Decoupled Architectures

With the presence of slip, the access processor in a decoupled architecture performs address computations and accomplishes data fetch ahead of EP demand. The access processor can thus hide the long memory access times from being seen by the execute processor. But our simulations point to a limit to the performance enhancement that can be introduced by the AP. In conventional memories, if there are m memory accesses in the entire program and if t_{mm} is the main memory cycle time, a time of $(m * t_{mm})$ is required for the data access (assuming no cache and data size equal or greater than bus width). Irrespective of whether locality properties are exhibited by the data references or not, since the AP has to perform fetches for each individual reference, no reduction in the time $(m * t_{mm})$, is possible. Hence decoupled architectures can eliminate memory latency only as long as the total fetch time required can be accomodated within the time the execute processor would consume to complete its section of the code without having to wait for any operands. Beyond that point, the effect of memory latency will be clearly evident in the total execution time. This is clear from Fig. 6. The solid section indicates fetch time as a component of the total execution time in the decoupled mode. Optimizations can result in better performance in the $t_{mm} = 5$ cycles case (and certainly in $t_{mm} < 5$ cycles) but in $t_{mm} = 10$ cycles and $t_{mm} = 15$ cycles, there is no room for further improvement. In cases with slower memory, data accesses constitute almost the entire execution time. This explains the sensitivity that decoupled systems exhibited to memory access speed in our simulations. It might be noted that increasing the queue length cannot hide the latency, once memory has become a bottleneck like this.

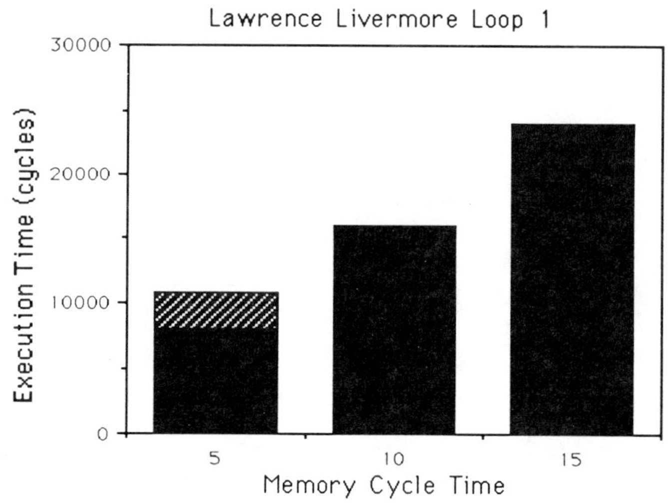

Figure 6: Fetch cycles as a fraction of total execution time

Another limitation of decoupled computers relate to the overhead incurred in the process of exploiting the access execute parallelism in the computing process. Slight code expansion results while AP-EP code is generated. Branch instructions must appear in both processors. If the execute processor does not support operations with both operands from the same queue, one of the operands has to be moved from the queue to a register which also contributes to code expansion.

In certain problems, like the transposition of a matrix, array copy, etc. the whole problem is of an access nature and there is no role that the execute processor can play. Effort to parallelize these problems can result in serious overheads that may increase the execution time more than the uniprocessor mode. If the compiler recognizes such problems, the DAE system should not be slower than a uniprocessor.

5.5 Significance of a Data Cache in a Decoupled Architecture

We observed that uniprocessors with data caches performed considerably better than decoupled architectures, for slow memories. (See t=15 cycle case in Fig. 3). This observation naturally leads to the question of whether a decoupled architecture could also benefit from caches. We performed simulations to investigate this and the results appear in Fig. 7. The total

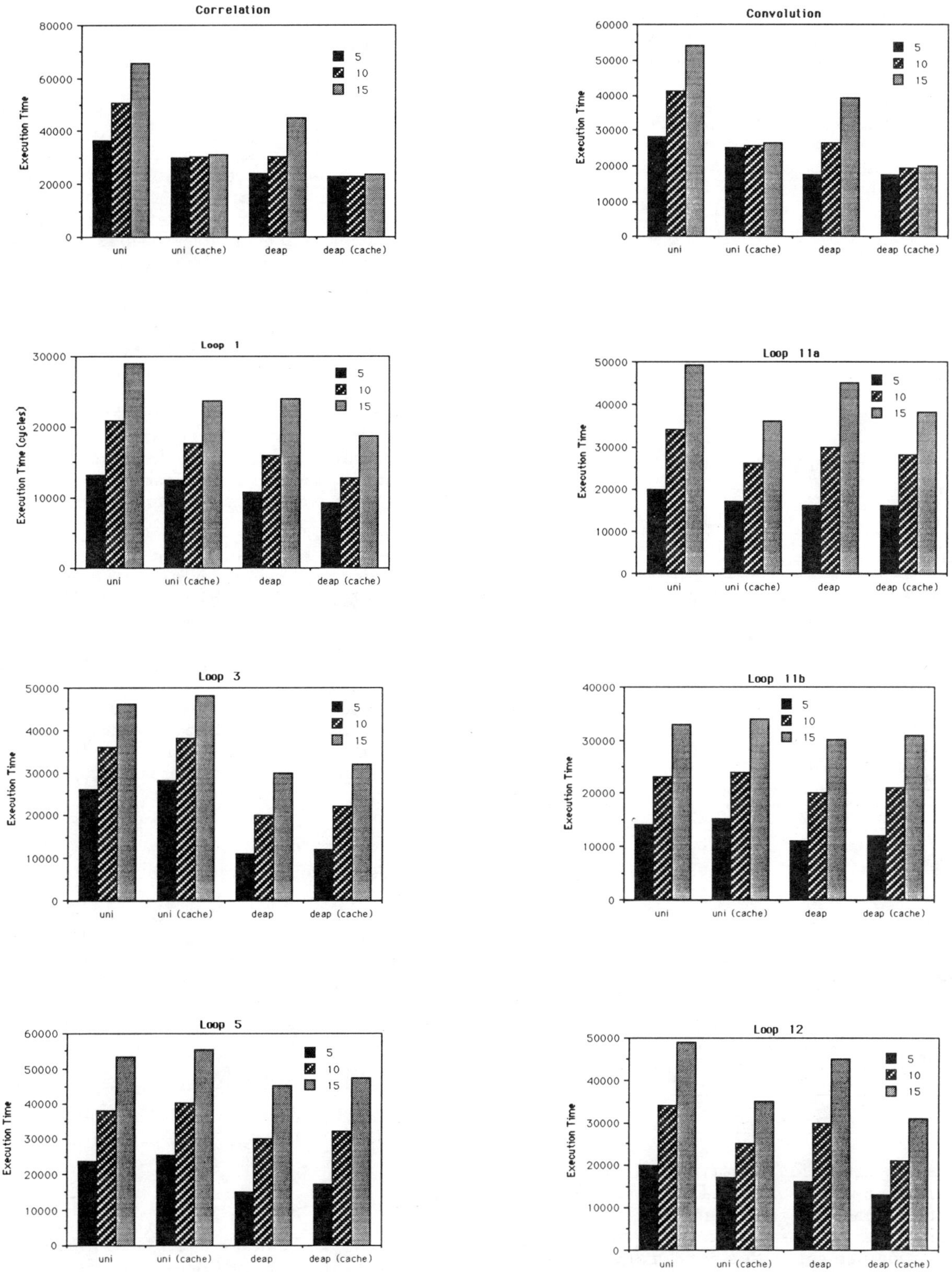

Fig.7. Performance comparison of decoupled systems with and without caches and uniprocessors with and without caches

execution time of each benchmark is plotted for decoupled systems with caches, uniprocessors with and without caches and ordinary decoupled architectures. The results are characteristic of the memory referencing behavior of each benchmark. For the convolution and correlation algorithms, the decoupled system with caches perform better than the other systems. This can be attributed to the strong temporal locality present in the data references in these benchmarks. The effect of caches is not so pronounced in benchmarks like Lawrence Livermore Loops 1, 11a and 12. Loop 3, loop 5 and loop 11b (loop 11 after optimization) do not benefit from caches. For these benchmarks, the cache has a similar effect in uniprocessors too.

t=15cycles

Benchmark	Uniproc with cache	Decoupled without cache	Decoupled with cache
LLL1	1.22	1.20	1.53
LLL3	0.95	1.53	1.44
LLL5	0.96	1.18	1.13
LLL11a	1.36	1.08	1.29
LLL11b	0.97	1.10	1.06
LLL12	1.39	1.08	1.58
Mean	1.14	1.20	1.34
Correlation	2.12	1.46	2.77
Convolution	2.04	1.37	2.71
Mean	2.08	1.42	2.74

t=5cycles

Benchmark	Uniproc with cache	Decoupled without cache	Decoupled with cache
LLL1	1.06	1.22	1.43
LLL3	0.92	2.35	2.16
LLL5	0.92	1.55	1.37
LLL11a	1.18	1.25	1.25
LLL11b	0.93	1.27	1.17
LLL12	1.18	1.25	1.53
Mean	1.03	1.48	1.49
Correlation	1.23	1.51	1.61
Convolution	1.13	1.60	1.61
Mean	1.18	1.55	1.61

Table I. Speedup comparison

The speedup figures for memory access time equal to 5 cycles and 15 cycles is presented in Table I. Speedup is calculated with reference to uniprocessors without caches. The mean values for Lawrence Livermore Loops and convolution and correlation benchmarks are shown separately. The contribution of caches is significant in the t=15 cycles case, but is minor in the t=5 cycles case. Optimized code often cannot exploit caches to the same degree as their unoptimized versions, and that is illustrated by the difference in performance for loops 11a and 11b. All the limitations associated with caches in uniprocessors seem to also apply to decoupled systems with caches. Nevertheless, the improvement resulting from caches in programs with temporal locality cannot be neglected.

6 Conclusion

We have presented simulation results for a decoupled architecture when connected to a noninterleaved memory. Since caches are a time-tested mechanism to solve the memory access problem, we also compared the decoupled architecture performance to uniprocessors with caches. We see that caches and decoupled systems achieve their best performance in different domains, since their mechanisms to alleviate memory bottleneck depend on different characteristics of a computer program. There are cases in which both might result in a performance advantage and there are problems where one scheme might not contribute significantly to the performance. Caches have the potential of efficiently hiding the main memory latency in programs that exhibit strong locality properties but it may also slow down the system if not carefully designed. If one fixed organization of the cache is going to be used for all applications, there is heavy risk of the cache affecting the system adversely under some conditions.

In the case of decoupled systems, we note that there is more scope for improvement from 'decoupling' and 'slip', once the main memory is fast enough so that the total data access time required can be accomodated within the runtime of the execute processor if it does not have to wait for any operands. With very slow memory, the effect of memory latency will be clearly evident in the total execution time. Memory poses a bottleneck here and decoupled computers cannot lower the execution time below the total memory access time. But even in that region, programs might benefit from caches if strong temporal locality is present. In spite of the memory posing a bottleneck in some cases, the speedup of the decoupled system relative to a non-cached uniprocessor is significant.

We also performed simulations to determine whether decoupled architectures can obtain performance advantage from data caches. The contribution of caches is minor when the main memory is fast. But in cases with strong temporal locality, decoupled architectures with caches achieve a level of memory path insensitivity superior to all other configurations. It can be concluded that caches are as relevant to decoupled computers as they are to uniprocessors.

7 Acknowledgements

We would like to thank Ali S. Berrached for his help during the development of the simulator.

References

[1] Alpert, D.B., Flynn M.J., "Performance Trade-offs for Microprocessor Cache Memories", IEEE Micro, August 1988, pp. 44-53.

[2] Brantley W.C., Weiss J.,"Organization and architecture tradeoffs in FOM", presented at IEEE Int. Workshop Comp. Syst. Organization, New Orleans, LA, March 1983.

[3] Coraor L.D., Hulina P.T. and Mannai D.N.,"A Queue- based Instruction Cache Memory", Proc. of the International Symposium on Computer Architecture and Digital Signal Processing, October 1989, Hong Kong, pp.281-286.

[4] Cohler E.U., Storer J.E., "Functionally parallel architectures for array processors", IEEE Computer, vol.14, pp.28–36, Sept.1981.

[5] Eickemeyer R.J., Patel J.H., "Performance Evaluation of On-chip Register and Cache Organizations", Proc. 15th Int. Symp. on Computer Architecture, 1988, pp. 64-72.

[6] Farrens M.K.,Pleszkun A.R., "Improving Performance of Small on-chip Instruction Caches", Proc. 16th Int. Symp. on Computer Architecture, 1989, pp. 234-241.

[7] Farrens M.K.,Pleszkun A.R., "Implementation of the PIPE processor", IEEE Computer, Jan. 1991, pp. 65–70.

[8] Goodman J.R., Hsieh J.T., Liou K., Pleszkun A.R., Schechter P.B., Young H.C., "PIPE: A VLSI Decoupled Architecture", 12th Annual International Symposium on Computer Architecture, June 17-19, 1985, Boston, Massachusetts, pp.20-27.

[9] Hsieh J.T., Pleszkun A.R. and Goodman J.R., "Performance Evaluation of the PIPE Computer Architecture", Technical Report #566, Computer Sciences Department, University of Wisconsin-Madison, Nov. 1984.

[10] Hulina P.T., Coraor L.D., Sun S.W., " Performance Analysis of an Address Generation Coprocessor", IEEE International Conference on Parallel Processing, 1991.

[11] Kane G., "MIPS RISC Architecture", Prentice-Hall, Englewood Cliffs, N.J., 1988.

[12] Kurian L., Hulina P.T., Coraor L.D., Mannai D.N., "Classification and Performance Evaluation of Instruction Buffering Techniques", 18th Intl. Symposium on Computer Architecture, May 1991, Toronto, Canada, pp. 150–159.

[13] Pleszkun A.R., "A Structured Memory Access Architecture", Computer Systems Group report CSG-10, Coordinated Science Lab, University of Illinois, Urbana, Oct 1982.

[14] Pleszkun A.R., Davidson E.S., "Structured Memory Access Architecture", Proc. IEEE International Conference on Parallel Processing 1983, pp 461–471.

[15] Pleszkun A.R., Kahalleh B.Z., Davidson E.S., "Features of the Structured Memory Access (SMA) Architecture", Third IEEE Computer Society International Conference, San Francisco, CA, March 1986.

[16] Shivley R.R., "Architecture of a Programmable Digital Signal Processor", IEEE Trans. on Computers, vol.C–31, Jan. 1982.

[17] Smith A.J., "Cache Memories", ACM Computing Surveys, Vol.14, No. 3, September 1982, pp. 473-530.

[18] Smith J.E., "Decoupled Access/Execute Computer Architecture", ACM Transactions on Computer Systems, Vol.2, No.4, November 1984, pp 289-308.

[19] Smith J.E., et .al., "The ZS–1 Central Processor", Proceedings of the Second International Conference on Architectural Support for Programming Languages and Operating Systems, Palo Alto, CA, pp 199–204, October 1987.

[20] Smith A.J., "Line (Block) Size Choice for CPU Cache Memories", IEEE Transactions on Computers, Vol. C-36, No. 9, September 1987, pp. 1063-1075.

[21] Smith J.E., " Dynamic Instruction Scheduling and the Astronautics ZS–1", IEEE Computer, July 1989.

[22] Smith J.E., Pleszkun A.R., Katz R.H., Goodman J.R., "PIPE: A High Performance VLSI Architecture", IEEE Workshop on Computer System Organization, New Orleans, LA, pp.131–138, March 1983.

[23] Smith J.E., Weiss S. and Pang N.Y, "A Simulation Study of Decoupled Architecture Computers", IEEE Transactions on Computers, Vol.C-35, No.8, August 1986.

[24] Smith W.M, Abraham S.G. and Davidson E.S, "A performance comparison of the IBM RS/6000 and the Astronautics ZS-1", IEEE Computer, January 1991.

[25] Smith W.M., Abraham S.G., Davidson E.S., "The Effects of Memory Latency and Fine–Grain Parallelism on Astronautics ZS–1 Performance", Proceedings of the 23rd Annual Hawaii Intl. Conf. on System Sciences, CS Press, Los Alamitos, Calif, Order No.2008, 1990, pp.288-296.

[26] Sohi G.S, Davidson E.S., "Performance of the Structured Memory Access Architecture", Proc. of the International Conference on Parallel Processing, pp.506–513, August 1984.

Interleaved Parallel Schemes: improving memory throughput on supercomputers

André Seznec, Jacques Lenfant
IRISA, Campus de Beaulieu
35042 Rennes Cedex, FRANCE
e-mail : seznec@irisa.fr

Abstract

On many commercial supercomputers, several vector register processors share a global highly interleaved memory in a MIMD mode. When all the processors are working on a single vector loop, a significant part of the potential memory throughput may be wasted due to the asynchronism of the processors.

In order to limit this loss of memory throughput, a SIMD synchronization mode for vector accesses to memory may be used. But an important part of the memory bandwidth may be wasted when accessing vectors with an even stride.

In this paper, we present IPS, a interleaved parallel scheme, which ensures an equitable distribution of elements on a highly interleaved memory for a wide range a vector strides. We show how to organize access to memory, such that unscrambling of vectors from memory to the vector register processors requires a minimum number of passes through the interconnection network.

Keywords

Vector register processor, SIMD synchronization, Interleaved Parallel Scheme, Interconnection Network

1 Introduction

As vector parallelism is easiest to detect and to exploit, a large number of vector processors have been built and commercialized.

Vector processors usually resort to the pipeline architecture (e.g., vector register machines as the Cray Series) or to the SIMD architecture where a single sequencing unit controls several identical processing elements (e.g. the Connection Machine).

On many commercial supercomputers (e.g., Cray series, Alliant series, ..), several vector register processors share a global highly interleaved memory in a MIMD mode. Even when all the processors are working on a single vector loop, a significant part of the potential memory througput may be wasted due to asynchrony of the processors. In order to limit this loss of memory throughput, one should synchronize the processors in a SIMD fashion.

In this paper, we consider a SIMD synchronization mode that could be implemented on a shared memory multiprocessor built with multiple vector register processors accessing vectors in memory.

When working in this mode, both SIMD and vector register machine performance on a specific vector instruction sequence will depend highly on the effective throughput of memory, i.e., on an adequate distribution of the vector elements over the memory banks and also on avoiding conflicts in the interconnection network during the unscrambling of the vector.

In section 2, we recall classical difficulties for accessing vectors in parallel on SIMD computers and vector register machines. In section 3, we point out that it may be easier to obtain maximum memory throughput for vector accesses on a shared memory multiprocessor built with vector register processors than on SIMD computers built with scalar registers or vector register uniprocessors.

In section 4, the Interleaved Parallel Scheme, IPS(d,q,n), is proposed. Using this new mapping induces more equitable distribution over memory banks for a wider set of vectors than when using the usual mappings.

However, equitable distribution on memory banks is not sufficient to guarantee parallel accessibility.

In section 5, we show that the parallel accessibility of vectors in memory is ensured by this storage scheme and SIMD synchronization of the processors. We show how to organize the unscrambling of data from memory to the processors avoiding conflicts in the interconnection network and obtaining effective high memory throughput on vector accesses for a very large range of access strides.

2 Accessing memory on SIMD machines and vector register processors

Many manufacturers of vector processors have adopted the following definition for a vector.

Definition: A vector is an ordered set of words whose addresses form an arithmetic series.

For example, rows, columns and diagonals of a matrix stored columnwise are vectors.

2.1 Mapping vectors onto a parallel memory

In both SIMD machines and vector register processors, several memory banks are used to build a large memory system with high potential thoughput. To obtain maximum memory throughput for a vector instruction, memory access conflicts must be avoided.

The usual mapping of data onto memory consists of mapping address A in memory bank $A \ mod \ N$ at local address $A \ / \ N$: this mapping is sometimes referred to as low order interleaving. When using this mapping, the distribution of the elements of a vector V stored with a stride R has the following property:

> $V(i)$ and $V(j)$ are stored in the same memory bank iff
> $i = j \bmod N/GCD(N, R)$

Then $N/GCD(N, R)$ consecutive elements of the vector are stored in distinct memory banks and then may be accessed in parallel.

To ensure conflict free parallel accesses to a maximum set of vectors, one may use a prime number of memory banks. This was used in the Burroughs Scientific Processor [KUC82]. Then address computation requires arithmetic modulo a prime number, however for simplicity in construction one generally prefers to use a power of two memory banks. Then by simply reordering the address lines, bank interleaved addressing is accomplished.

From now on, we shall assume that the number of memory banks is a power of two: $N = 2^n$.

As the ability to access a slice of a vector in parallel depends on the distribution of data in memory banks, we define here the equitable distribution of a set of data among the memory banks:

Definition: The distribution of a set S of $X * N$ elements on the N memory banks is equitable iff X elements of S are stored in each memory bank.

2.2 Vector register machines: time-multiplexed memory

In vector register machines, an interleaved memory is used because of the difference between processor cycle time and memory cycle time.

Let us consider a memory consisting in N memory banks. A memory bank is busy due to a request for t cycles. For simplicity, we consider a vector register machine with only one memory access port (as e.g. Cray 1 or Cray 2). In order to guarantee that no conflicts may arise between successive vector accesses, a delay of t cycles must occur between two successive requests to the same bank.

2.3 SIMD machines : space-multiplexed memory

Let us consider a SIMD processor with N memory banks and P processing elements (processors).

The structure is illustrated in Figure 1. Memory

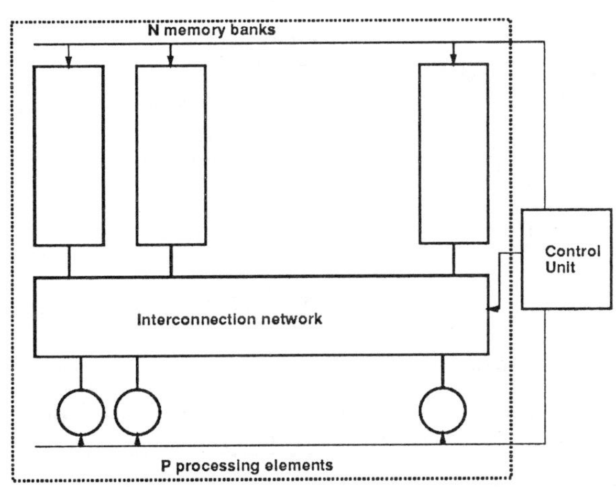

Figure 1: Simplified structure of a SIMD computer

banks are numbered from 0 to $N - 1$ and processors are numbered from 0 to $P - 1$.

Memory is accessed by the processors through the interconnection network.

For simplicity's sake, we also assume that $P = N = 2^n$ processors. If the vector stride is $R = 2^k r$ with r

odd and $k \leq n$, then 2^k cycles are needed for accessing a slice of N consecutive elements of a vector.

In [TAM85], it is pointed out that the distribution of the strides of accessed vectors in real applications is not random, but that about 80 % of the vectors are accessed with stride one, while the remaining 20% are accessed with approximatively random stride.

Let us consider the following distribution of vector accesses:

- 80 % of the vectors are accessed with stride one
- 10 % of the vectors are accessed with an odd stride distinct from one
- for $k \geq 1$, $10/2^k$ % of the accessed vectors have strides of the form $2^k r$

Then accessing 100 vectors of N elements will require at the average $90+(n+1)*10$ cycles: e.g., for $N = 512$, i.e., $n = 9$, (resp. $N = 64$, i.e., $n = 6$) the effective memory throughput is only of 53% (resp. 62.5 %) of the potential throughput.

As a key point, note that one of the major obstacles to the systematic use of the type COMPLEX in FORTRAN applications is the two-strided access it induces for accessing the vector of real (resp. imaginary) parts, resulting in half of the memory bandwidth being wasted.

In order to remove this penalty for accesses to vectors with an even stride, memory bandwidth is sometimes overdimensioned i.e., $N = 2P$ or $N = 4P$.

2.4 Using skewing schemes

In order to increase effective throughput, one can try to use skewing schemes [BUD71]. The following skewing scheme was proposed by Harper and Jump [HAR87] :

> let $m(A)$ be the number of the memory bank where a word at address A is stored. m(A) is given by:
>
> $$m(A) = (A + (A/N)) \ mod \ N$$

Figure 2 illustrates this skewing scheme.

0	1	2	3	4	5	6	7
0	1	2	3	4	5	6	7
15	8	9	10	11	12	13	14
22	23	16	17	18	19	20	21
29	30	31	24	25	26	27	28
36	37	38	39	32	33	34	35
43	44	45	46	47	40	41	42
50	51	52	53	54	55	48	49
57	58	59	60	61	62	63	56

Figure 2: Skewing scheme of Harper and Jump ($N = 8$)

This skewing scheme was proposed for improving the throughput of the interleaved memory of a vector register machine.

Using this skewing scheme on a vector register machine associated with buffers at input and output of each memory bank may dramatically improve the effective throughput of an interleaved memory on a vector register machine (see [HAR87]).

For SIMD computers, this skewing scheme allows parallel access to some vectors stored with even stride, but it does not allow parallel access to slices of N consecutive elements for most of the one-strided vectors, e.g. the vector starting at address 1 (see Figure 2).

3 Accessing vectors on shared memory supercomputers: a new challenge

3.1 Synchronizing processors in a SIMD fashion

On many commercial supercomputers (e.g., Cray Research Systems, ...), several vector register processors share a global memory in a MIMD mode.

The memory organization in these machines may be illustrated by figure 3: this memory is both space and time multiplexed. Several physical memory banks are connected to the same port of the interconnection network; we will refer to this set of memory banks as a logical memory bank.

In such a memory organization, the clasical mapping of data is:

> Word at address A is mapped to local address $A/2^{n+d}$ in physical bank $(A/2^n)$ mod 2^d in logical bank A mod 2^n.

Achieving high performance on vector applications on these machines depends highly on the effective throughput of the memory for vector accesses.

Even when all the processors are working on a single vector loop, a significant part of the potential memory throughput may be wasted due to asynchronism of the processors: access to vector V0 by processor P0 may interfere with access to vector V1 by processor P1 when strides and/or base addresses of the vectors are different.

In order to limit this loss of memory throughput, one may imagine synchronizing the sequencing of the distinct processors in a SIMD fashion, or at least to implement a specific synchronization mode for which the accesses to memory of the distincts processors are synchronized in a SIMD fashion. There is no systematic increase of the memory throughput for all the vector

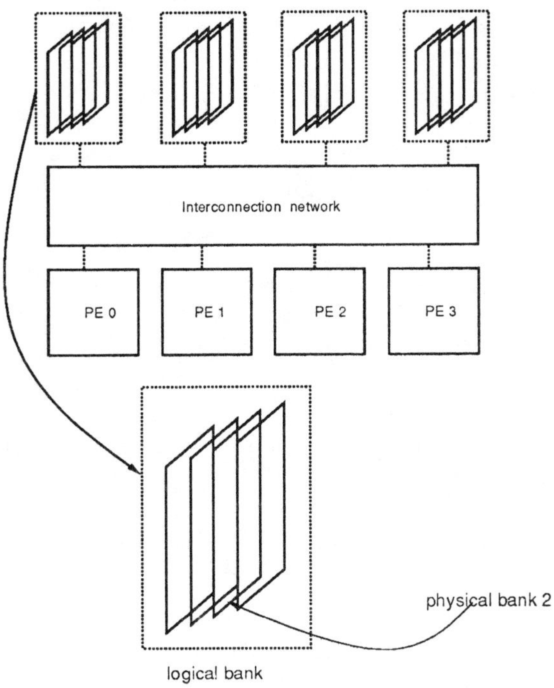

Figure 3: Memory organization on a vector register processor based multiprocessor

sections [1], but simulations show that on average there would be an increase of memory throughput.

Considering the same distribution of the vector strides as in section 2.3, for 64 (resp. 8) processors, 64 (resp. 8) logical memory banks and 8 physical banks per logical banks busy for 8 cycles by a memory request, only 38 % (resp. 41 %) of the theoretical memory throughput would be realized by a a quasi-infinite sequence of vector accesses without any synchronization of the processors versus 2/3 (resp. 74 %) of the theoretical memory throughput when using SIMD synchronization on the vector requests to memory.

It must be noted that these simulations are rather optimistic for 64 processors: in our simulation, a 64*64 crossbar network was assumed and we supposed that conflicts were resolved on the fly (i.e., a rejected request is submitted again at the next cycle). Implementation of such a large fast crossbar network and its associated control logic cannot be envisaged at the moment.

Distribution of the elements

When synchronizing the processors in a SIMD fashion, the distribution of the operations among the processors is naturally done as follows: element x of a vector is processed by processor $x \ mod \ 2^n$.

[1] e.g. consider the usual mapping of data in memory and a vector sequence accessing two two-strided vectors one with an even base address, the second with an odd base address

In the next sections, we show that the effective memory throughput on vector accesses may be improved by using a skewed storage scheme which will allow a maximum memory throughput on a wider family of vectors than allowed by the usual mapping.

3.2 Some notations

From now, we consider a multiprocessor where such a SIMD synchronization mode is implemented with the following parameters:

1. Each processor is a vector register machine: it may receive one word of data from memory per cycle.
2. The size of the vector register is $M = 2^m$ words.
3. The number of processors is $N = 2^n$.
4. The number of logical memory banks is also $N = 2^n$
5. The processors are connected to the memory banks through a N entry, N exit interconnection network.
6. A logical bank is built with $D = 2^d$ physical memory banks. We shall consider that a physical bank can deliver a word of data per D cycles.

Definition: A vector V is q-permissible if its storage stride is of the form $2^k r$ with $k \leq q$ and r odd.

3.3 The new challenge

In this architecture, the granularity of a vector instruction on the machine becomes $2^n * 2^m$ elements. To obtain the maximum throughput on vector accesses to the memory, the challenge has been changed:

> *slices of M*N consecutive elements of a vector have to be accessed from the memory and unscrambled in a minimum time to the vector registers of the distinct processors.*

Let us point out that the elements of the vectors which are accessed in parallel do not have to belong to the same slice of 2^n consecutive elements.

In the next section, we present the Interleaved Parallel Scheme IPS(d,q,n), $q \leq n$. When using this scheme, any slice of 2^{q+d+n} consecutive elements of any q-permissible vector is equitably distributed among the 2^{d+n} physical memory banks. Moreover in section 5, we show how to organize the access to a slice of $2^n * 2^m$ consecutive elements of a q-permissible vector in order to busy the distinct resources (memory banks, interconnection network, ..) during only 2^m cycles.

4 The Interleaved Parallel Scheme IPS(d,q,n)

4.1 The Logical Parallel Scheme

Let $0 < q \leq n$, let us consider the decomposition of the binary representation of an address A in four bit strings A_3, A_2, A_1 and A_0 respectively of $s-(n+q)$ bits, q bits, $n-q$ bits and q bits (see Figure4): $A = A_3 2^{s-(n+q)} + A_2 2^n + A_1 2^{n-q} + A_0$. We shall note also $A = (A_3, A_2, A_1, A_0)$.

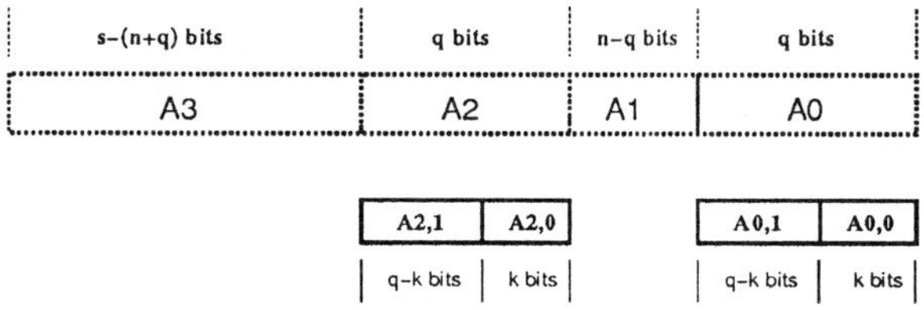

Figure 4: Decomposition of an address A into different bit strings

We define the Logical Parallel Scheme LPS(q,n) as follows:

Address A is mapped at local address (A_3, A_2) in logical bank $(A_1, A_2 \oplus A_0)$.

Other skewing schemes using exclusive-OR were considered in other contexts in [RAU89, NOR87, FRA85]. From now on, we assume that the LPS(q,n) skewing scheme is used for mapping data on to the memory. In order to achieve maximum throughput on a vector access, an equitable distribution over the logical memory banks is needed.

Theorem 1: Let V be a q-permissible vector, then for any arbitrary slice of 2^{n+q} consecutive elements of vector V, the distribution of the elements on the 2^n logical memory banks is equitable, i.e., 2^q per logical memory bank.

Proof:
Let V be a vector stored with stride $2^k r$ and base address F.
Let T be the slice of the first 2^{n+q-k} consecutive elements of the vector V,
let f be the application defined by :

$$\begin{array}{llll} f: & \{0,1,..,2^{n+q}-1\} & \rightarrow & \{0,1,..,2^s-1\} \\ & i & \rightarrow & L = \{0,1,..,2^s-1\} \end{array}$$

$f(i)$ is the address of element $V(i)$

Let us consider the previous binary decomposition of an address A: A_2 (resp. A_0) may be subdivided in two substrings $A_{2,1}$ and $A_{2,0}$ (resp. $A_{0,1}$ and $A_{0,0}$) of $q-k$ bits and k bits respectively.

Let us consider the applications P_1, P_2 and P_3 defined by :

$$\begin{array}{llll} P_1: & L & \rightarrow & \{0,1,..,2^{n+q}-1\} \\ & A & \rightarrow & (A_{2,1}, A_{2,0}, A_1, A_{0,1}) \\ P_2: & L & \rightarrow & \{0,..,2^k-1\} \\ & A & \rightarrow & A_{0,0} \\ P_3: & L & \rightarrow & \{0,1,..,2^{n+q}-1\} \\ & A & \rightarrow & (A_{2,1}, A_1, A_{0,1} \oplus A_{2,1}, A_{0,0} \oplus A_{2,0}) \end{array}$$

A second form of $P_1 of$ is : $P_1 of(i) = r * i + (F \ / \ 2^k)$;
A second form of $P_2 of$ is : $P_2 of(i) = F \ mod \ 2^k$;

Then $P_1 of$ is a bijection and $P_2 of$ is a constant application, this induces that $P_3 of$ is a bijection.

As $(A_1, A_{0,1} \oplus A_{2,1}, A_{0,0} \oplus A_{2,0})$ is the index of the logical memory bank where the word at address A is stored, 2^{q-k} elements of the slice T are stored in each memory bank. Q.E.D.

4.2 Physically Parallel Scheme

A logical memory bank is built with $D = 2^d$ physical memory banks; an equitable distribution of the elements in a vector slice among the logical memory banks is not sufficient to guarantee a maximum throughput for the memory on vector accesses. We must also guarantee an equitable distribution of the data among the physical memory banks. The usual low order interleaving at the logical memory bank level does not work as shown by Figure5: the physical memory banks may be partitionned into "odd" banks and "even" banks.

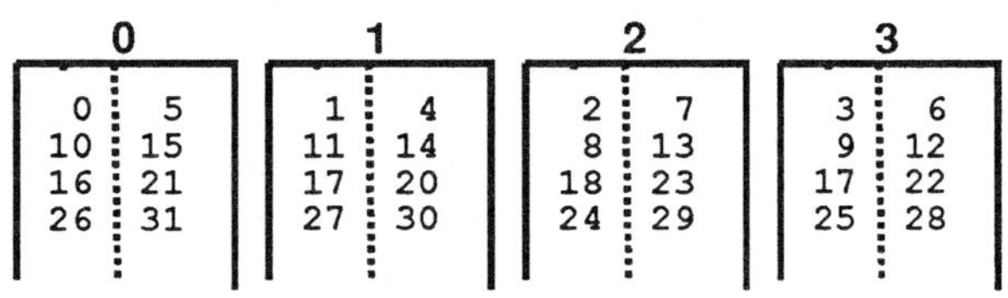

Figure 5: Low order interleaving of physical memory banks using $LPS(1,2)$

That is why, we also need to skew the storage inside each logical memory bank using the Physically Parallel Scheme PPS(d,q,n) described below:

The word at address A is mapped to physical bank number

$p_{d,q,n} = (A_3 \ mod \ 2^{min(d,q)} \oplus A_2 \ mod \ 2^d)$

We called the combination of the two schemes on physical and logical banks the Interleaved Parallel Scheme IPS(d,q,n)

IPS(1,2,2) is illustrated in Figure6.

Theorem 2: Let V be a q-permissible vector, then for any arbitrary slice T of 2^{n+q+d} consecutive elements of

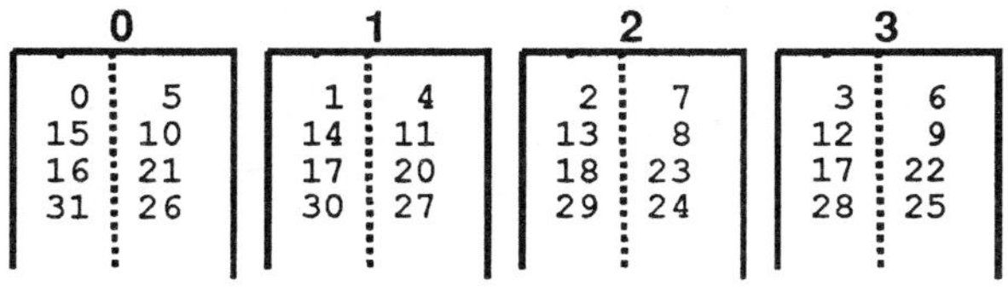

Figure 6: The IPS(1,2,2) skewing scheme

vector V, the distribution of the elements on the 2^{n+d} physical memory banks is equitable, i.e., 2^{q+d} per physical memory bank.

Proof: We give the proof for the case $d \leq q$. The proof for case $q < d$ is quite similar.

Let V be a vector stored with stride $2^k r$ and base address F.
Let T be the slice of the first 2^{n+q-k} consecutive elements of the vector V,
let f be a mapping from $S_k = \{0, 1, .., 2^{n+q} - 1\}$ in the space of addresses $L = \{0, 1, .., 2^s - 1\}$, where $f(i)$ is the address of element i in slice T,
and f is defined by $f(i) = 2^k r * i + F$.

Let us consider mappings P_3 and P_4 defined by

$$\begin{array}{llll} P_3: & L & \rightarrow & \{0, .., 2^d - 1\} \\ & A & \rightarrow & A_3 \ mod \ 2^d \\ P_4: & L & \rightarrow & \{0, .., 2^{q+n} - 1 \\ & A & \rightarrow & (A_2, A_1, A_0) \end{array}$$

For $0 \leq i < 2^{n+q}$, the restriction of P_4of to the set $\{i + 2^{n+q-k}x\}_{0 \leq x < 2^d}$ is a constant mapping :

$P_4of(i + 2^{n+q-k}x) = ((2^{n+q}x * r + f(i)) \ mod \ 2^{n+q} = f(i) \ mod \ 2^{n+q}$.

Then, for $0 \leq i < 2^{n+q}$, the elements $T(i + 2^{n+q-k}x)_{0 \leq x < 2^d}$ are stored in the same logical memory bank

For $0 \leq i < 2^{n+q}$, the restriction of P_3of to the set $\{i + 2^{n+q-k}x\}_{0 \leq x < 2^d}$ is a bijection: $P_3of(i + 2^{n+q-k}x) = [(f(i) + rx2^{n+q})/2^{n+q}] \ mod \ 2^d = (rx + Y_i) \ mod \ 2^d$

As element x of the slice T is stored in physical memory bank number $(P_4of(x)) \oplus ((P_3of(x)/2^n)$, then for $0 \leq i < 2^{n+q} - 1$, the elements $T(i + 2^{n+q-k}x)_{0 \leq x < 2^d}$ are stored in the different physical memory banks of a single logical memory bank.

Thus the elements of the slice T of vector V which are stored in logical memory bank I are equitably distributed among the physical memory banks. As we already know (theorem 1) that the slice T is equitably distributed among the logical memory banks, the slice T is equitably distributed among the 2^{n+d} physical memory banks. Q.E.D.

5 Parallel accessibility of data

In the previous section, we have shown that the Interleaved Parallel Scheme ensures an equitable distribution of data among the physical and logical memory banks for all the q-permissible vectors.

Paradoxally, when there is no SIMD synchronization of the processors, simulations show that, when using IPS(d,q,n) the effective memory throughput on a sequence on vector accesses is approximatively the same as the throughput obtained when using the usual mapping: all the benefits of a better data distribution are lost due to conflicts in the interconnection network, physical banks, ... *This explains why skewed storage schemes are not used on current vector register processor based multiprocessor.*

In order to feed the processors at a rate of one data element per cycle and per processor, we need to unscramble the elements from the memory to the processors through the interconnection network at a maximum rate, i.e., 2^n elements per cycle.

When looking at Figure 6, it is quite clear that slices of 2^n consecutive elements cannot be unscrambled by a permutation network in a single pass: there are conflicts in destinations. But as previously pointed out, the challenge is not to unscramble 2^n consecutive vector elements in a single pass through a 2^n entry, 2^n exit interconnection network, but to unscramble 2^{n+m} consecutive elements in 2^m passes through the interconnection network.

In this section, we shall show that SIMD synchronization of processors and the use the Interleaved Parallel Scheme IPS(d,q,n) in conjunction with our earlier results on controlling interconnection networks controlling interconnection networks for vector accesses [LEN85, ŚEZ87] allow us to unscramble any slice of 2^{n*m} consecutive elements of a q-permissible vector in a minimum number of passes through a 2^n entry, 2^n exit interconnection network.

5.1 Previous results on vector unscrambling through interconnection networks

Controlling an interconnection network for performing a permutation may require a quite complex hardware mechanisms. The use of a crossbar network (as in the BSP [KUC82]) seems efficient as a first approach. These networks can perform all the permutations between their P entries and their N exits. But a crossbar network requires $N * P$ switches; fast crossbar networks for large N and P are not be built because they cannot be easily partitioned: a crossbar network cannot be envisaged in vector register processor based multiprocessor with more than 15 or 20 processors.

In order to overcome this difficulty, multistage interconnection networks (like the Omega network [LAW75] or the Benes network [BEN68]) have been proposed: these interconnection networks can be partitionned and pipelined. The Benes network $B^{(n)}$ can perform any arbitrary permutation on its 2^n entries. It requires $(2n-1)$ stages consisting in 2^{n-1} $2*2$ switches and can be pipelined. But the algorithms to control this network for arbitrary permutations are time and space consuming [LEE85]: these algorithms cannot be used at execution time in vector applications because the permutation to be executed may change at each cycle. Pre-computing control of the interconnection network at code generation time may seem attractive; but the needed permutations must be known at compile time, this is generally incompatible with the use of separate compilation and library routines.

To overcome this difficulty, Lenfant [LEN85] defined FUM's (frequently used permutations). FUM's are a set of permutations on $E^{(n)} = \{0, 1, .., 2^n-1\}$ depending on a few parameters that are sufficient to execute most of the useful data manipulations on vectors when the usual mapping of data is used. Lenfant also presented efficient algorithms to compute the routing of Benes network for this family.

5.1.1 Frequently used permutations

In this section, we consider that the usual mapping of data on memory banks is used.

The family $\{\lambda_{J,K}^{(n)}\}$:

For executing the assignment $B := A$, when A and B are two vectors both stored with an odd increment, the interconnection network has to perform a permutation of the family $\{\lambda_{J,K}^{(n)}\}$ on slices of 2^n elements of A. For j odd, $\lambda_{J,K}^{(n)}$ is defined by $\lambda_{J,K}^{(n)}(x) = Jx + K \ mod\ 2^n$.

The Bit Permute Complement permutations (BPC): Permutations of the family $\{\lambda_{J,K}^{(n)}\}$ are not sufficient for accessing vectors stored with an even increment.

Let us consider a vector A stored with a stride $2^k r$ where r odd and $k \leq n$ and a vector B stored with an odd increment.

Assigning a slice of 2^{n-k} consecutive elements of a vector A in vector B may be decomposed in three steps:

1. Access to the 2^n first elements of the vector A' derived from vector A as follows: $A'(0)$ and $A(0)$ have the same address, A' is stored with increment r.
2. Alignment of the elements of vector A on the 2^{n-k} first positions
3. Realignment of the result vector in order to store the 2^{n-k} first elements in vector B.

The three steps induce permutations through the interconnection network: steps 1 and 3 induce permutations of the family $\{\lambda_{J,K}^{(n)}\}$ and step 2 may be realized by $\sigma_{(n)}^k$ where $\sigma_{(n)}$ is the perfect shuffle on the segment $E^{(n)} = \{0, 1, .., 2^n-1\}$.

The perfect shuffle, its powers, the bit-reversal and some other useful permutations belong to the class of Bit Permute Complement permutations (BPCs) [NAS81]:

Definition: A permutation M on $E^{(n)}$ is a BP (bit permute permutation) if there exists a permutation T on $\{1, 2, .., n\}$ such that, given $S = T^{-1}$ and $x_n x_{n-1} .. x_1$ the binary representation of x, $x_{S(n)} x_{S(n-1)} .. x_{S(1)}$. A permutation Ψ is BPC on $E^{(n)}$ if there exists a BP M, an integer x in $E^{(n)}$ such that $\Psi = \tau_x^{(n)} o M$, $\tau_x^{(n)}$ is the exclusive or by x.

The permutations of the family $\{\lambda_{J,K}^{(n)} o \tau_x^{(n)} o\ M\ o \lambda_{i,h}^{(n)}\}$ allow us to execute the assignment B:=A for all vectors in a minimum number of passes through the interconnection network.

Permutations of this family are referred to as EBPC's (Extended Bit Permute Complement permutations) [SEZ86, SEZ87].

In [LEN85], Lenfant gave algorithms with time complexity in $O(n)$ for controlling the 2^n entry, 2^n exit Benes network for the family $\{\lambda_{J,K}^{(n)}\}$ and the BPC's.

Seznec [SEZ86, SEZ87] proposed the Sigma network $\Sigma^{(n)}$ (Figure7) which is essentially the Benes preceeded and followed by a link realizing the bit-reverse permutation i.e, the BP induced by a symmetry of bits. Algorithms with time complexity $O(n)$ for controlling the 2^n entries, 2^n exits Sigma network $\Sigma^{(n)}$ for the EBPC's were also presented.

When implementing these algorithms in hardware, control of the Sigma network may be computed at execution time for the EBPC's (see [SEZ86]). [2]

5.2 Unscrambling q-permissible vectors

In this section, we consider that IPS(d,q,n) is used for memory.

The following result shows that synchronizing the processors in a SIMD fashion will allow us to unscramble all q-permissible vectors in a minimum number of passes through an interconnection network.

Theorem 3 : Let V be a q-permissible vector, then any arbitrary slice of 2^{n+q} consecutive elements of the vector V may be routed through 2^n entry, and 2^n exit

[2] In order to be able to route all the vectors from memory to the processors, permutations of family $\{\tau_x^{(n)} o\ \sigma_{(n)}^k\ o \lambda_{i,h}^{(n)}\}$ are sufficient i.e.,. $2^n * n * 2^{n-1} * 2^n$ permutations e.g., for N=64, 786432 permutations, for N =512, more than $600 * 10^6$ permutations!

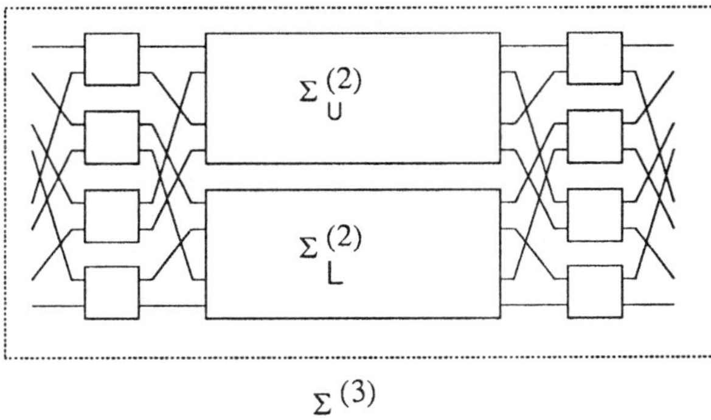

Figure 7: Recursive definition of the Sigma network$\Sigma^{(}3)$

interconnection network in 2^q passes (i.e.,., the minimum possible number) using only EBPC's.

Proof: Let V be a vector stored with stride $2^k r$ and base address F.
Let T be the slice of the first 2^{n+q-k} consecutive elements of the vector V,
let f be the mapping from $S_k = \{0, 1, .., 2^{n+q} - 1\}$ in the space of addresses $L = \{0, 1, .., 2^s - 1\}$ defined by $f(i) = 2^k r * i + F$. $f(i)$ is the address of element i in slice T.

Let us consider applications P_6 and P_7 defined by :

$$P_6 : L \rightarrow \{0, .., 2^n - 1\}$$
$$A \rightarrow (A_{2,0}, A_1, A_{0,1}) = (A/2^k) \ mod \ 2^n$$
$$P_7 : L \rightarrow \{0, .., 2^{q-k} - 1)$$
$$A \rightarrow A_{2,1} = (A/2^{n+k}) \ mod \ 2^{q-k}$$

For $0 \leq i < 2^n$, for $0 \leq x < 2^{q-k}$, $P_6 of(i + x2^n) = \lambda^{(n)}_{r,(F/2^k)}(i)$

For $0 \leq i < 2^n$, for $0 \leq x < 2^{q-k}$, $P_7 of(i + x2^n) = [[(2^k ri + F) + 2^{k+n} rx]/2^{k+n}] \ mod \ 2^{q-k}$
i.e., $P_7 of(i + x2^n) = (rx + C_i) \ mod \ 2^{q-k}$

Then for $0 \leq i < 2^n$, the restriction of $P_7 of$ to the elements accessed by Processing Element i (i.e., elements $i + x2^n$, $0 \leq x < 2^{q-k}$) is a bijection)

Then, for $0 \leq i < 2^n$, for $0 \leq t < 2^{q-k}$, there exists $0 \leq X(i, t) < 2^{q-k}$ such that $P_7 of(i + 2^n X(i, t)) = t$

Then, for $0 \leq t < 2^{q-k}$, the element $V(X(i, t))$ is stored in the logical memory bank $(2^k t + (F \ mod \ 2^k)) \oplus (\sigma^k_{(n)} o \lambda^{(n)}_{r,(F/2^k)}(i))$

Then the set of elements $(V(X(i, t)))_{0 \leq i < 2^n}$ may be routed in a single pass through the interconnection network using a EBPC i.e., : $(\tau^{(n)}_{2^k t \oplus (F \ mod \ 2^k)} o \sigma^k_{(n)} o \lambda^{(n)}_{r,(F/2^k)})^{-1}$.
Q.E.D.

This result shows how to organize subslices of 2^n non-consecutive elements of the vectors in order to access these subslices in parallel and to route the elements to their destination processors.

The set of permutations induced on the interconnection network by IPS(d,q,n) is the set induced by the usual low order interleaving scheme.

5.3 Using the IPS(d,q,n) skewing scheme

In this section, we suggest how to access a slice of $2^m * 2^n$ elements of a vector V stored with stride $2^k r$, r odd, $k \leq q$ and starting at base address F when using the proposed skewing scheme.

We assume that $m > d$, i.e., that a vector load hits several times each physical bank (when the data distribution is equitable for the vector).

We assume that the IPS(d,q,n) skewing scheme is used with parameter $q = min(n, m - d)$.

For the sake of simplicity, we assume here that $q = m - d$.

Accessing a slice T of 2^{m+n} consecutive elements of vector V may be executed in three steps as follows:

1. Address computation:
   For each processor, addresses for all the accessed elements in the slice are computed:
   in order to allow parallel access to the memory by all the processing elements, sub-slices of 2^n elements (one for each processor) are organized.

   In each processor i, the addresses of the vector elements are stored in a special address vector register Va as follows:

   the address B of element $T(i + 2^n x)$ is stored in Va at local address :

   $a_{T,i}(x) = (A_2 \oplus x \ mod \ 2^k, p_{d,q,n}(A))$

   The results from previous sections ensure that $a_{T,i}$ is a one-to-one mapping from $\{0, 1, .., 2^m - 1\}$ onto itself.
2. Access to memory:
   The addresses are sent to memory in usual order (i.e., increasing indices in the vector registers):
   Addresses of same rank $y = y1 * 2^{k+d} + x * 2^d + y0$ in the vector registers Va of the distinct processors are sent at the same cycle to memory; there is no conflict with the logical memory banks (theorem 1) and the permutation used for sending this set of addresses is: $\tau^{(n)}_{2^k y1 \oplus (F \ mod \ 2^k)} o \sigma^k_{(n)} o \lambda^{(n)}_{r,(F/2^k)}$ (theorem 3).

   Moreover there is no conflict with the physical banks: physical bank x in logical bank i receives one request in the subslice at rank y iff $y = x \ mod \ 2^d$.
3. Data are read from memory and routed back to the processors. In each processor, the data are reordered in the destination vector register by by $a^{-1}_{T,i}$.

These three steps may be pipelined, but step 2 cannot overlap the end of the execution of step 1.

Nevertheless, accessing two vectors may be chained; no inter-access delay is needed between two consecutive vector accesses: a throughput of one element per cycle per processor may be obtained in a sequence of accesses to q-permissible vectors.

If the number of processors is quite small (less or equal to 16), then using a crossbar may be envisaged. Otherwise another interconnection network must be used, for example the Sigma network.

Note that if a Sigma network Σ^n is used as the interconnection network, the performance demanded of the control unit of the interconnection is to compute the command for the permutation $\sigma^k_{(n)} o \lambda^{(n)}_{r,(F/2^k)}$ during step 1; the command for $\tau^{(n)}_{2^k y1 \oplus (F \ mod \ 2^k)} o \sigma^k_{(n)} o \lambda^{(n)}_{r,(F/2^k)}$ may then be deduced on the fly by very simple hardware mechanism (see [SEZ87]).

An example

Let us consider, a vector register processor based multiprocessor with $N = 64$ processors, 64 logical memory banks (i.e., $n = 6$) consisting of 8 physical banks (i.e., $d = 3$), a vector register size of 64 elements (i.e., $m = 6$).

The IPS(3,3,6) skewing scheme may be used; then access to slices of $64 * 64 = 4096$ consecutive elements of any vectors stored with strides of the form r, $2r$, $4r$ or $8r$ with r odd will be executed at full speed.

The number of cycles needed to access a slice of 4096 consecutive elements of a vector stored with a stride $2^k r$,r odd is:

- $k \leq 3$: 64 cycles
- $3 < k \leq 12$: $2^{k-3} * 64$ cycles
- $k \geq 12$: $512 * 64$ cycles

If we consider the same distribution of vector accesses as in section 2.1, then the average number of cycles needed for accessing 100 vector slices of 4096 elements is : $64 * (98.75 + 9 * \Sigma_{3<k\leq 12} 10 * 2^{k-3}/2^k + 10 * 512/2^{12})=$ $64 * 111.25$ cycles, i.e., about 90 % of the maximum achievable throughput compared with the 53% achieved when using low order interleaving.

For 8 processors, 8 logical banks and 8 physical banks per logical bank, the average memory throughput on vector accesses would be of 93 % of the maximum throughput.

6 Conclusion

High performance vector processors generally are generally organized as vector register processors or SIMD machines. For these architectures, a highly interleaved structure of memory is used; the performance may be limited by conflicts in memory accesses and by routing in the interconnection network.

In this paper, we have considered a shared memory multiprocessor based on vector registers processors. In order to feed the processing elements with data, the memory must be interleaved in a two-way fashion: space multiplexing (2^n data must be accessed in parallel) and time multiplexing (memory cycle time is longer than processor cycle time). When the distinct processors are working on the same vector sequence, synchronizing processors' accesses to vectors in memory limits the contention on the interconnection network and may be an alternative to the use of overdimensioned memory bandwidth in current commercial supercomputers.

But using the usual low order interleaving scheme on memory and a power of two as number of memory banks would lead to unsatisfactory memory throughput on vectors stored with an even stride.

Using SIMD synchronization of vector register processors changes the challenge of accessing 2^n consecutive vector elements in parallel in a SIMD computer to the challenge of accessing a slice of $2^n * 2^m$ consecutive vector elements in 2^m cycles.

The IPS(d,q,n) skewing scheme allows access in a minimum time to a wide range of vectors (all vectors stored with stride of form $2^k r$ with $0 \leq k \leq q$):

- Slices of 2^{n+m} consecutive vector elements are equitably distributed over the memory banks.
- Data may be routed in a minimum number of passes through an interconnection network: the permutations induced on the interconnection network are EBPC's. Realistic control algorithms for executing the EBPC's on the Sigma network were given in [SEZ87].

We have also noted is that simulations have shown that using the Interleaved Parallel Scheme does not degrade the memory throughput when the distinct processors execute independent vector accesses streams in MIMD mode on the memory.

When using SIMD synchronization of vector register processors and the IPS(d,q,n) skewing scheme on memory, the granularity of a vector access to memory is a slice of 2^{d+q+n} elements, i.e., access time to a slice of x consecutive elements of a vector, $x \leq 2^{d+q+n}$ is approximatively the same as for the complete slice of 2^{d+q+n} elements; but when usual low order interleaving is used, the granularity of a vector access to memory is a slice of 2^{d+n} elements and delays between consecutive vector accesses must be inserted. Moreover there exist vector applications with a very high granularity: the commercial success of the Connection Machine (64 K processors) proves it.

Acknowledgement

The authors are endebted to the program committee member G.Q. Macquire for carefully polishing the english in the final version of the paper.

References

[BEN68] V.E. Benes, "Mathematical Theory of connecting networks and telephone traffic", New York: Academic, 1968

[BUD71] P.Budnick, D.Kuck "The organization and use of parallel memories" IEEE Transaction On Computers, Dec. 1971

[FRA85] J.M. Frailong, W.Jalby, J.Lenfant "XOR-schemes: a flexible organization in parallel memories" Proceedings of 1985 International Conference on Parallel Processing, Aug. 1985

[KUC82] D.J.Kuck, R.A.Stokes, "The Burroughs Scientific Processor (BSP)" IEEE Transactions on Computers, May 1982.

[HAR86] D.T. Harper, J.R. Jump "Performance evaluation of vector accesses in parallel memories using a skewed storage scheme ", Proceedings of the 13th International Symposium on Computer Architecture, June 1986

[HAR87] D.T. Harper, J.R. Jump "Vector accesses in parallel memories using a skewed storage scheme " IEEE Transactions on Computers, Dec. 1987

[LAW75] D.H. Lawrie "Access and alignment of data in array computer" IEEE Transactions on Computers, Dec. 1975

[LEE85] K.Y. Lee, "On the rearrangeability of a (2 log N - 1) stage permutation network" IEEE Transactions on Computers, May 1985.

[LEN78] J.Lenfant, "Parallel permutations of data : A Benes network control algorithm for frequently used permutations" IEEE Transactions on Computers, July 1978.

[LEN85] J.Lenfant, " A versatile mechanism to move data in an array processor" IEEE Transactions on Computers, June 1985

[NAS81] D.Nassimi, S.Sahni "A self-routing Benes network and permutation algorithms" IEEE Transactions on Computers, May 1981.

[NOR87] A.Norton, E.Melton "A class of boolean linear transformations for conflict-free power-of-two stride access", Proceedings of the International Conference on Parallel Processing, 1987

[RAU89] B.Rau, M.Schlander, D. Yen " The Cydra 5 stride insensitive memory system", Proceedings of the International Conference on Parallel Processing, 1989

[SEZ86] A.Seznec, "An efficent routing control unit for the Sigma network $\Sigma^{(4)}$", Proceedings of the 13th International Symposium on Computer Architecture, June 1986

[SEZ87] A.Seznec, "A new interconnection network for SIMD computers: the Sigma network $\Sigma^{(n)}$" IEEE Transactions on Computers, July 1987

[TAM85] H.Tamura, Y.Shinkai, F.Isobe "The Supercomputer FACOM VP system" Fujitsu Sc. Tech. J., March 1985

Active Messages: a Mechanism for Integrated Communication and Computation

Thorsten von Eicken
David E. Culler
Seth Copen Goldstein
Klaus Erik Schauser

{tve,culler,sethg,schauser}@cs.berkeley.edu
Computer Science Division — EECS
University of California, Berkeley, CA 94720

Abstract

The design challenge for large-scale multiprocessors is (1) to minimize communication overhead, (2) allow communication to overlap computation, and (3) coordinate the two without sacrificing processor cost/performance. We show that existing message passing multiprocessors have unnecessarily high communication costs. Research prototypes of message driven machines demonstrate low communication overhead, but poor processor cost/performance. We introduce a simple communication mechanism, *Active Messages*, show that it is intrinsic to both architectures, allows cost effective use of the hardware, and offers tremendous flexibility. Implementations on nCUBE/2 and CM-5 are described and evaluated using a split-phase shared-memory extension to C, *Split-C*. We further show that active messages are sufficient to implement the dynamically scheduled languages for which message driven machines were designed. With this mechanism, latency tolerance becomes a programming/compiling concern. Hardware support for active messages is desirable and we outline a range of enhancements to mainstream processors.

1 Introduction

With the lack of consensus on programming styles and usage patterns of large parallel machines, hardware designers have tended to optimize along specific dimensions rather than towards general balance. Commercial multiprocessors invariably focus on raw processor performance, with network performance in a secondary role, and the interplay of processor and network largely neglected. Research projects address specific issues, such as tolerating latency in dataflow architectures and reducing latency in cache-coherent architectures, accepting significant hardware complexity and modest processor performance in the prototype solutions. This paper draws on recent work in both arenas to demonstrate that the utility of exotic message-driven processors can be boiled down to a simple mechanism and that this mechanism can be implemented efficiently on conventional message passing machines. The basic idea is that the control information at the head of a message is the address of a user-level instruction sequence that will extract the message from the network and integrate it into the on-going computation. We call this *Active Messages.* Surprisingly, on commercial machines this mechanism is an order of magnitude more efficient than the message passing primitives that drove the original hardware designs. There is considerable room for improvement with direct hardware support, which can be addressed in an evolutionary manner. By smoothly integrating communication with computation, the overhead of communication is greatly reduced and an overlap of the two is easily achieved. In this paradigm, the hardware designer can meaningfully address what balance is required between processor and network performance.

1.1 Algorithmic communication model

The most common cost model used in algorithm design for large-scale multiprocessors assumes the program alternates between computation and communication phases and that communication requires time linear in the size of the message, plus a start-up cost[9]. Thus, the time to run a program is $T = T_{compute} + T_{communicate}$ and $T_{communicate} = N_c(T_s + L_c T_b)$, where T_s is the start-up cost, T_b is the time per byte, L_c is the message length, and N_c is the number of communications. To achieve 90% of the peak processor performance, the programmer must tailor the algorithm to achieve a sufficiently high ratio of computation to communication that $T_{compute} \geq 9T_{communicate}$. A high-performance network is required to minimize the communication time, and it sits 90% idle!

If communication and computation are overlapped the situation is very different. The time to run a program becomes $T = \max(T_{compute} + N_c T_s,\ N_c L_c T_b)$. Thus, to achieve high processor efficiency, the communication and compute times need only balance, and the compute time need only swamp the communication overhead, *i.e.*, $T_{compute} \gg N_c T_s$. By examining the average time between communication phases ($T_{compute}/N_c$) and the time for message transmission, one can easily compute the per-processor bandwidth through the network required to sustain a given level of processor utilization. The hardware can be designed to reflect this balance. The essential properties of the communication mechanism are that the start-up cost must be low and that it must facilitate the overlap and co-ordination of communication with on-going computation.

1.2 Active Messages

Active Messages is an asynchronous communication mechanism intended to expose the full hardware flexibility and performance of modern interconnection networks. The underlying idea is simple: each message contains at its head the address of a user-level handler which is executed on message arrival with the message body as argument. The role of the handler is to get the message out of the network and into the computation ongoing on the processing node. The handler must execute quickly and to completion. As discussed below, this corresponds closely to the hardware capabilities in most message passing multiprocessors where a privileged interrupt handler is executed on message arrival, and represents a useful restriction on message driven processors.

Under Active Messages the network is viewed as a pipeline operating at a rate determined by the communication overhead and with a latency related to the message length and the network depth. The sender launches the message into the network and continues computing; the receiver is notified or interrupted on message arrival and runs the handler. To keep the pipeline full, multiple communication operations can be initiated from a node, and computation proceeds while the messages travel through the network. To keep the communication overhead to a minimum, Active Messages are not buffered except as required for network transport. Much like a traditional pipeline, the sender blocks until the message can be injected into the network and the handler executes immediately on arrival.

Tolerating communication latency has been raised as a fundamental architectural issue[1]; this is not quite correct. The real architectural issue is to provide the ability to overlap communication and computation, which, in-turn, requires low-overhead asynchronous communication. Tolerating latency then becomes a programming problem: a communication must be initiated sufficiently in advance of the use of its result. In Sections 2 and 3 we show two programming models where the programmer and compiler, respectively, have control over communication pipelining.

Active Messages is not a new parallel programming paradigm on par with send/receive or shared-memory: it is a more primitive communication *mechanism* which can be used to implement these paradigms (among others) simply and efficiently. Concentrating hardware design efforts on implementing fast Active Messages is more versatile than supporting a single paradigm with special hardware.

1.3 Contents

In this paper, we concentrate on message-based multiprocessors and consider machines of similar base technology representing the architectural extremes of processor/network integration. Message passing machines, including the nCUBE/2, iPSC/2, iPSC/860 and others, treat the network essentially as a fast I/O device. Message driven architectures, including Monsoon[17, 16] and the J-Machine[5], integrate the network deeply into the processor. Message reception is part of the basic instruction scheduling mechanism and message send is supported directly in the execution unit.

Section 2 examines current message passing machines in detail. We show that send/receive programming models make inefficient use of the underlying hardware capabilities. The raw hardware supports a simple form of Active Messages. The utility of this form of communication is demonstrated in terms of a fast, yet powerful asynchronous communication paradigm. Section 3 examines current message driven architectures. We show that the power of message driven processing, beyond that of Active Messages, is costly to implement and not required to support the implicitly parallel programming languages for which these architectures were designed. Section 4 surveys the range of hardware support that could be devoted to accelerating Active Messages.

2 Message passing Architectures

In this section we examine message passing machines, the one architecture that has been constructed and used on a scale of a thousand high-performance processors. We use the nCUBE/2 and the CM-5 as primary examples.

The nCUBE/2 has up to a few thousand nodes interconnected in a binary hypercube network. Each node consists of a CPU-chip and DRAM chips on a small double-sided printed-circuit board. The CPU chip contains a 64-bit integer unit, an IEEE floating-point unit, a DRAM memory interface, a network interface with 28 DMA channels, and routers to support cut-through routing across a 13-dimensional hypercube. The processor runs at 20 Mhz and delivers roughly 5 MIPS or 1.5 MFLOPS.

The CM-5 has has up to a few thousand nodes interconnected in a "hypertree" (an incomplete fat tree). Each node consists of a 33 Mhz Sparc RISC processor chip-set (including FPU, MMU and cache), local DRAM memory and a network interface to the hypertree and broadcast/scan/prefix control networks. In the future, each node will be augmented with four vector units.

We first evaluate the machines using the traditional programming models. Then we show that Active Messages are well-suited to the machines and support more powerful programming models with less overhead.

2.1 Traditional programming models

In the traditional programming model for message passing architectures, processes communicate by matching a *send* request on one processor with a *receive* request on another. In the synchronous, or crystalline[9] form, send and receive are blocking — the send blocks until the corresponding receive is executed and only then is data transferred. The main advantage of the blocking send/receive model is its simplicity. Since data is only transferred after both its source and destination addresses are known, no buffering is required at the source or destination processors.

Blocking send/receive communication exacerbates the effects of network latency on communication latency[1]: in order to match a send with a receive a 3-phase protocol, shown in Figure 1, is required: the sender first transmits a request to the receiver which returns an acknowledgement upon executing a matching receive operation and only then is data transferred. With blocking send/receive, it is impossible to overlap communication with computation and thus the network bandwidth cannot be fully utilized.

To avoid the three-phase protocol and to allow overlap of communication and computation, most message passing implementations offer non-blocking operation: *send* appears instantaneous to the user program. The message layer buffers the message until the network port is available, then the message is transmitted to the recipient, where it is again buffered until a matching *receive* is executed. As shown in the ring communication example in Figure 2, data can be exchanged while computing by executing all sends before the computation phase and all receives afterwards.

[1]We call communication latency the time from initiating a send in the user program on one processor to receiving the message in the user program on another processor, *i.e.*, the sum of software overhead, network interface overhead and network latency.

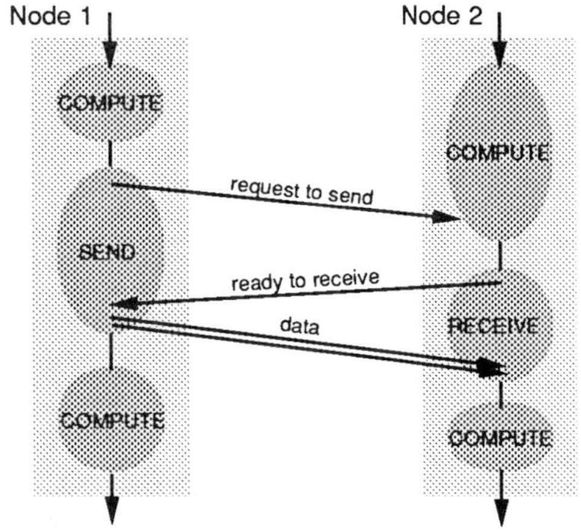

Figure 1: *Three-phase protocol for synchronous send and receive. Note that the communication latency is at best three network trips and that both send and receive block for at least one network round-trip each.*

Table 1 shows the performance of send/receive on several current machines. The start-up costs are on the order of a thousand instruction times. This is due primarily to buffer management. The CM-5 is blocking and uses a three-phase protocol. The iPSC long messages use a three-phase protocol to ensure that enough buffer space is available at the receiving processor. However, the start-up costs alone prevent overlap of communication and computation, except for very large messages. For example, on the nCUBE/2 by the time a second send is executed up to 130 bytes of the first message will have reached the destination. Although the network bandwidth on all these machines is limited, it is difficult to utilize it fully, since this requires multiple simultaneous messages per processor.

Machine	T_s [μs/mesg]	T_b [μs/byte]	T_{fp} [μs/flop]
iPSC[8]	4100	2.8	25
nCUBE/10[8]	400	2.6	8.3
iPSC/2[8]	700	0.36	3.4
	390†	0.2	
nCUBE/2	160	0.45	0.50
iPSC/860[12]	160	0.36	0.033[7]
	60†	0.5	
CM-5‡	86	0.12	0.33[7]

†: messages up to 100 bytes
‡: blocking send/receive

Table 1: *Asynchronous send and receive overheads in existing message passing machines. T_s is the message start-up cost (as described in Section 1.1), T_b is the per-byte cost and T_{fp} is the average cost of a floating-point operation as reference point.*

2.2 Active Messages

Although the hardware costs of message passing machines are reasonable, the effectiveness of the machine is low under traditional send/receive models due to poor overlap of communication and computation, and due to high communication overhead. Neither of these shortcomings can be attributed to the base hardware: for example, initiating a transmission on the nCUBE/2 takes only two instructions, namely to set-up the DMA[2]. The discrepancy between the raw hardware message initiation cost and the observed cost can be explained by a mismatch between the programming model and the hardware functionality. Send and receive is not native to the hardware: the hardware allows one processor to send a message to another one and cause an interrupt to occur at arrival. In other words the hardware model is really one of launching messages into the network and causing a handler to be executed asynchronously upon arrival. The only similarity between the hardware operation and the programming model is in respect to memory address spaces: the source address is determined by the sender while the destination address is determined by the receiver[3].

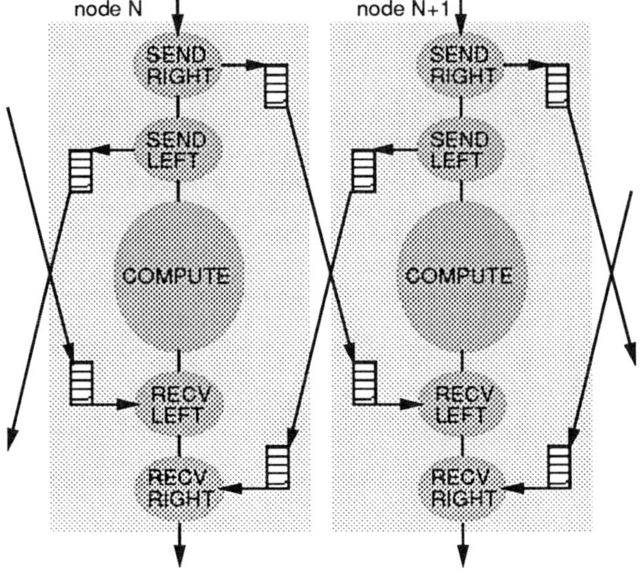

Figure 2: *Communication steps required for neighboring processors in a ring to exchange data using asynchronous send and receive. Data can be exchanged while computing by executing all sends before the computation phase and all receives afterwards. Note that buffer space for the entire volume of communication must be allocated for the duration of the computation phase!*

Active Messages simply generalize the hardware functionality by allowing the sender to specify the address of the handler to be invoked on message arrival. Note that this relies on a uniform code image on all nodes, as is commonly used (the SPMD programming model). The handler is specified by a user-level address and thus traditional protection models apply. Active Messages differ from general remote procedure call (RPC) mechanisms in that the role of the Active Message handler is not to perform computation on the data, but to extract the data from the network and integrate it into the ongoing computation with a small amount of work. Thus, concurrent communication and computation is fundamental

[2] On the nCUBE/2, each of the 13 hypercube channels has independent input and output DMAs with a base-address and a count register each. Sending or receiving a message requires loading the address and the count.

[3] Shared-memory multiprocessor advocates argue that this is the major cause of programming difficulty of these machines.

to the message layer. Active Messages are not buffered, except as required for network transport. Only primitive scheduling is provided: the handlers interrupt the computation immediately upon message arrival and execute to completion.

The key optimization in Active Messages compared to send/receive is the elimination of buffering. Eliminating buffering on the receiving end is possible because either storage for arriving data is pre-allocated in the user program or the message holds a simple request to which the handler can immediately reply. Buffering on the sending side is required for the large messages typical in high-overhead communication models. The low overhead of Active Message makes small messages more attractive, which eases program development and reduces network congestion. For small messages, the buffering in the network itself is typically sufficient.

Deadlock avoidance is a rather tricky issue in the design of Active Messages. Modern network designs are typically deadlock-free provided that nodes continuously accept incoming messages. This translates into the requirement that message handlers are not allowed to block, in particular a reply (from within a handler) must not busy-wait if the outgoing channel is backed-up.

2.2.1 Active Messages on the nCUBE/2

The simplicity of Active Messages and its closeness to hardware functionality translate into fast execution. On the nCUBE/2 it is possible to send a message containing one word of data in 21 instructions taking $11\mu s$. Receiving such a message requires 34 instructions taking $15\mu s$, which includes taking an interrupt on message arrival and dispatching it to user-level. This near order of magnitude reduction ($T_c = 30\mu s$, $T_b = 0.45\mu s$) in send overhead is greater than that achieved by a hardware generation. Table 2 breaks the instruction counts down into the various tasks performed.

Task	Instruction count send	receive
Compose/consume message	6	9
Trap to kernel	2	–
Protection	3	–
Buffer management	3	3
Address translation	1	1
Hardware set-up	6	2
Scheduling	–	7
Crawl-out to user-level	–	12
Total	21	34

Table 2: *Breakdown into tasks of the instructions required to send and receive a message with one word of data on the nCUBE/2. "Message composition" and "consumption" include overhead for a function call and register saves in the handler. "Protection" checks the destination node and limits message length. "Hardware set-up" includes output channel dispatch and channel ready check. " Scheduling" accounts for ensuring handler atomicity and dispatch. "Crawling out to user-level" requires setting up a stack frame and saving state to simulate a return-from-interrupt at user-level.*

The Active Message implementation reduces buffer management to the minimum required for actual data transport. On the nCUBE/2 where DMA is associated with each network channel, one memory buffer per channel is required. Additionally, it is convenient to associate two buffers with the user process: one to compose the next outgoing message and one for handlers to consume the arrived message and compose eventual replies. This set-up reduces buffer management to swapping pointers for a channel buffer with a user buffer. Additional buffers must be used in exceptional cases to prevent deadlock: if a reply from within a handler blocks for "too long", it must be buffered and retried later so that further incoming messages can be dispatched. This reply buffering is not performed by the message layer itself, rather REPLY returns an error code and the user code must perform the buffering and retry. Typically the reply (or the original request) is saved onto the stack and the handlers for the incoming messages are nested within the current handler.

The breakdown of the 55 instructions in Table 2 shows the sources of communication costs on the nCUBE/2. A large fraction of instructions (22%) are used to simulate user-level interrupt handling. Hardware set-up (15%) is substantial due to output channel selection and channel-ready checks. Even the minimal scheduling and buffer management of Active Messages is still significant (13%). Note however, that the instruction counts on the nCUBE/2 are slightly misleading, in that the system call/return instructions and the DMA instructions are far more expensive than average.

The instruction breakdown shows clearly that Active Messages are very close to the absolute minimal message layer: only the crawl-out is Active Message specific and could potentially be replaced. Another observation is that most of the tasks performed here in software could be done easily in hardware. Hardware support for active messages could significantly reduce the overhead with a small investment in chip complexity.

2.2.2 Active Messages on the CM-5

The Active Messages implementation on the CM-5 differs from the nCUBE/2 implementation for five reasons[4]:

1. The CM-5 provides user-level access to the network interface and the node kernel time-shares the network correctly among multiple user processes.

2. The network interface only supports transfer of packets of up to 24 bytes (including 4 bytes for the destination node) and the network routing does not guarantee any packet ordering.

3. The CM-5 has two identical, disjoint networks. The deadlock issues described above are simply solved by using one network for requests and the other for replies. One-way communication can use either.

4. The network interface does not have DMA. Instead, it contains two memory-mapped FIFOs per network, one for outgoing messages and one for incoming ones. Status bits indicate whether incoming FIFOs hold messages and whether the previous outgoing message has been successfully sent by the network interface. The network interface discards outgoing messages if the network is backed-up or if the process is time-sliced during message composition. In these cases the send has to be retried.

5. The network interface generally does not use interrupts in the current version due to their prohibitive cost. (The hardware and the kernel do support interrupts, but their usefulness is limited due to the cost.) For comparison, on the nCUBE/2 the interrupt costs the same as the system call which would have to be used instead since there is no user-level access to the network interface.

[4] The actual network interface is somewhat more complicated than described below, we only present the aspects relevant to this discussion.

Sending a packet-sized Active Message amounts to stuffing the outgoing FIFO with a message having a function pointer at its head. Receiving such an Active Message requires polling, followed by loading the packet data into argument registers, and calling the handler function. Since the network interface status has to be checked whenever a message is sent (to check the send-ok status bit), servicing incoming messages at send time costs only two extra cycles. Experience indicates that the program does not need to poll explicitly unless it enters a long computation-only loop.

Sending multi-packet messages is complicated by the potential reordering of packets in the network. For large messages, set-up is required on the receiving end. This involves a two-phase protocol for GET, and a three-phase protocol for PUT (discussed below). Intermediate-sized messages use a protocol where each packet holds enough header information (at the expense of the payload) that the arrival order is irrelevant.

The performance of Active Message on the CM-5 is very encouraging: sending a single-packet Active Message (function address and 16 bytes of arguments) takes $1.6\mu s$ (≈ 50 cycles) and the receiver dispatch costs $1.7\mu s$. The largest fraction of time is spent accessing the network interface across the memory bus. A prototype implementation of blocking send/receive on top of Active Messages compares favorably with the (not yet fully optimized) vendor's library: the start-up cost is $T_c = 23\mu s$ (vs. $86\mu s$) and the per byte cost is $T_b = 0.12\mu s$ (identical). Note that due to the three-phase protocol required by send/receive, T_c is an order of magnitude larger than the single packet send cost. Using different programming models such as Split-C, the cost off communication can be brought down to the Active Message packet cost.

2.3 Split-C: an experimental programming model using Active Messages

To demonstrate the utility of Active Messages, we have developed a simple programming model that provides split-phase remote memory operations in the C programming language. The two split-phase operations provided are PUT and GET: as shown in Figure 3a, PUT copies a local memory block into a remote memory at an address specified by the sender. GET retrieves a block of remote memory (address specified by sender) and makes a local copy. Both operations are non-blocking and do not require explicit coordination with the remote processor (the handler is executed asynchronously). The most common versions of PUT and GET increment a separately specified flag on the processor that receives the data. This allows simple synchronization through checking the flag or busy-waiting. Operating on blocks of memory can yield large messages which are critical to performance on current hardware as seen below.

The implementations of PUT and GET consist of two parts each: a message formatter and a message handler. Figure 3b shows the message formats. PUT messages contain the instruction address of the PUT handler, the destination address, the data length, the completion-flag address, and the data itself. The PUT handler simply reads the address and length, copies the data and increments the flag. GET requests contain the information necessary for the GET handler to reply with the appropriate PUT message. Note that it is possible to provide versions of PUT and GET that copy data blocks with a stride or any other form of gather/scatter[5].

To demonstrate the simplicity and performance of Split-C, Figure 4 shows a matrix multiply example that achieves 95% of peak

[5]Split-C exposes the underlying RPC mechanism the programmer as well, so that specialized communication structures can be constructed, e.g., enqueue record.

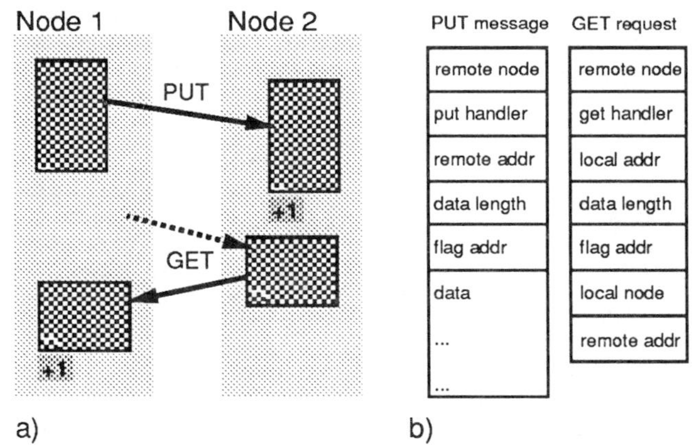

Figure 3: *Split-C* PUT *and* GET *perform split-phase copies of memory blocks to/from remote nodes. Also shown are the message formats.*

performance on large nCUBE/2 configurations. In the example, the matrices are partitioned in blocks of columns across the processors. For the multiplication of $C = A \times B$ each processor GETs one column of A after another and performs a rank-1 update (DAXPY) with the corresponding elements of its own columns of B into its columns of C. To balance the communication pattern, each processor first computes with its own column(s) of A and then proceeds by getting the columns of the next processor. Note that this algorithm is independent of the network topology and has a familiar shared-memory style. The remote memory access and its completion are made explicit, however.

The key to obtaining high performance is to overlap communication and computation. This is achieved by GETting the column for the next iteration while computing with the current column. It is now necessary to balance the latency of the GET with the time taken by the computation in the inner loops. Quantifying the computational cost is relatively easy: for each GET the number of multiply-adds executed is Nm (where m is the number of local columns of B and C) and each multiply-add takes $1.13\mu s$. To help understand the latency of the GET, Figure 6 shows a diagram of all operations and delays involved in the unloaded case.

The two top curves in Figure 5 show the performance predicted by the model and measured on a 128 node nCUBE/2, respectively, as the number of columns per processor of A is varied from 1 to 32. N is kept constant ($N = 128$) and R is adjusted to keep the total number of arithmetic operations constant ($R = 262144/M$). The matrix multiply in the example is computation bound if each processor holds more than two columns of A (*i.e.*, $m > 2$). The two bottom curves show the predicted and measured network utilization. The discrepancy between the model and the measurement is due to the fact that network contention is not modeled. Note that while computational performance is low for small values of m, the joint processor and network utilization is relatively constant across the entire range. As the program changes from a communication to a computation problem the "overall performance" is stable.

2.4 Observations

Existing message passing machines have been criticized for their high communication overhead and the inability to support global

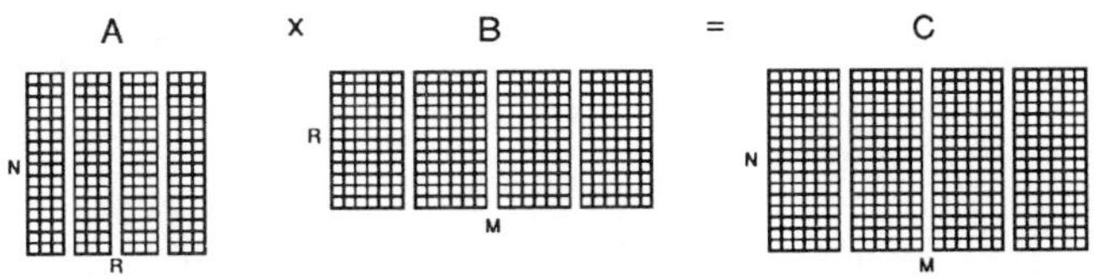

The matrices are partitioned in blocks of columns across the processors. For the multiplication of $C_{N\times M} = A_{N\times R} \times B_{R\times M}$ each processor GETs *one column of A after another and performs a rank-1 update (DAXPY) with its own columns of B into its columns of C. To balance the communication pattern, each processor first computes with its own column(s) of A and then proceeds by getting the columns of the next processor. This network topology independent algorithm achieves 95% of peak performance on large nCUBE/2 configurations.*

```
int N, R, M;   /* matrix dimensions */
double A[R/P][N], B[M/P][R], C[M/P][N];
int i, j, k;   /* indices */
int j0, nj;    /* initial j, next j */
int dj;        /* delta j (j=j0+dj) */
int P, p;      /* num of procs, my proc */
int Rp = R/P;
double V0[N], V1[N]; /* remote col bufs */
double *V=V0;   /* current column */
double *nV=V1;  /* next column */
double *tV;     /* temp column */
static int flag = 0; /* sync. flag */
extern void get(int proc, void *src, int size,
                void *dst, int &flag);

j0 = p * Rp;           /* starting column */
get(p, &A[0][0], N*sizeof(double),
    nV, &flag);        /* get first col of A */
/* loop over all columns of A */
for(dj=0; dj<R; dj++) {
  j = (j0+dj)%R;       /* this column index */
  nj = (j0+dj+1)%R; /* next column index */
  /* wait for previous get to complete */
  while(!check(1, &flag)) ;
  tV=V; V=nV; nV=tV;/* swap curr&next col */
  /* if not done, get next column */
  if(nj != j0) get(nj/Rp, &A[nj%Rp][0],
         N*sizeof(double), nV, &flag);
  /* accum. V into every column with scale */
  for(k=0; k<M/P; k++)
      for(i=0; i<N; ++) /* unroll! */
          C[i][k] = C[i][k] + V[i]*B[j][k];
}
```

Figure 4: Matrix multiply example in Split-C.

memory access. With Active Messages we have shown that the hardware is capable of delivering close to an order of magnitude improvement today if the right communication mechanism is used, and that a global address space may well be implemented in software. Split-C is an example of how Active Messages can be incorporated into a coarse-grain SPMD (single-program multiple-data) programming language. It generalizes shared memory read/write by providing access to blocks of memory including simple synchronization. It does not, however, address naming issues.

Using Active Messages to guide the design, it is possible to improve current message passing machines in an evolutionary, rather than revolutionary, fashion. In the next section, we examine research efforts to build hardware which uses a different approach to provide another magnitude of performance improvement.

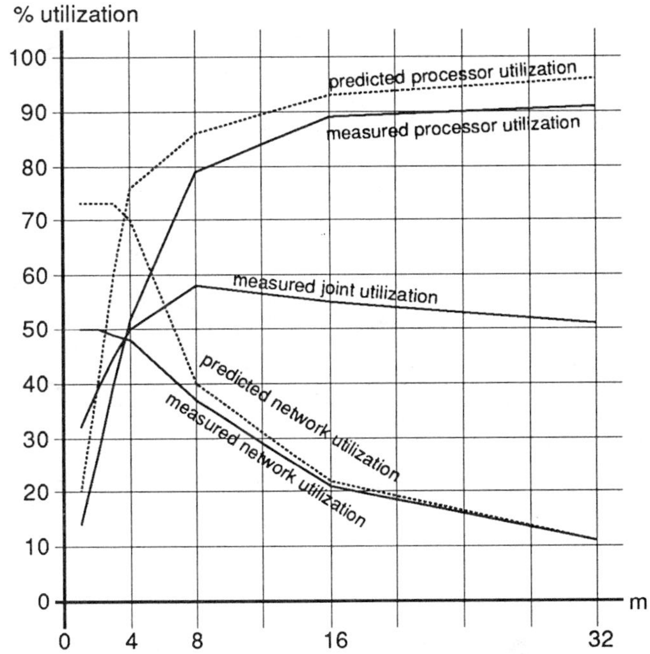

Figure 5: *Performance of Split-C matrix multiply on 128 processors compared to predicted performance using the model shown in Figure 6.*

3 Message driven architectures

Message driven architectures such as the J-Machine and Monsoon expend a significant amount of hardware to integrate communication into the processor. Although the communication performance achieved by both machines is impressive, the processing performance is not. At first glance this seems to come from the fact that the processor design is intimately affected by the network design and that the prototypes in existence could not utilize traditional processor design know-how. In truth, however, the problem is deeper: in message driven processors a context lasts only for the duration of a message handler. This lack of locality prevents the processor from using large register sets. In this section, we argue that the hardware support for communication is partly counter-productive. Simpler, more traditional, processors can be built without unduly compromising either the communication or the processing performance.

3.1 Intended programming model

The main driving force behind message driven architectures is to support languages with dynamic parallelism, such as Id90[14],

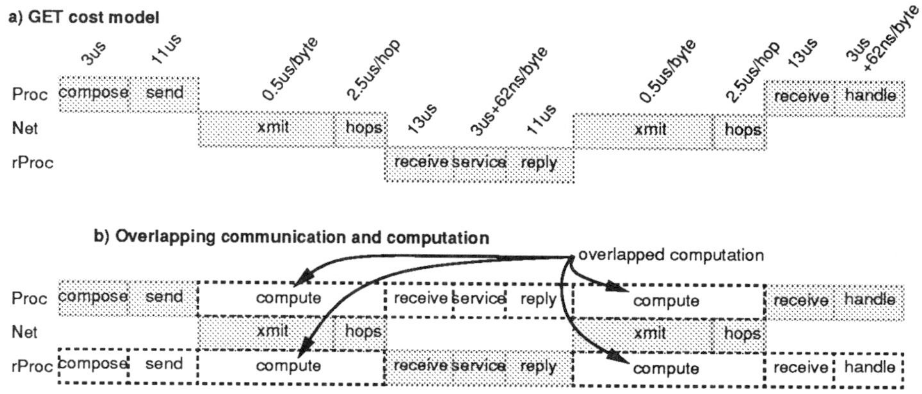

Figure 6: *Performance model for* GET. Compose *accounts for the time to set-up the request.* Xmit *is the time to inject the message into the network and* hops *is the time taken for the network hops.* Service *includes for copying the data into the reply buffer and* handle *for the time to copy the data into the destination memory block.*

Multilisp[10], and CST[11]. Computation is driven by messages, which contain the name of a handler and some data. On message arrival, storage for the message is allocated in a scheduling queue. When the message reaches the head of the queue, the handler is executed with the data as arguments. The handler may perform arbitrary computation, in particular it may synchronize and suspend. This ability to suspend requires general allocation and scheduling on message arrival and is the key difference with respect to Active Messages.

In the case of the J-Machine, the programming model is put forward in object-oriented language terms[6]: the handler is a method, the data holds the arguments for the method and usually one of them names the object the method is to operate on. In a functional language view, the message is a closure with a code pointer and all arguments of the closure. Monsoon is usually described from the dataflow perspective[17] and messages carry tokens formed of an instruction pointer, a frame pointer and one piece of data. The data value is one of the operands of the specified instruction, the other is referenced relative to the frame pointer.

The fundamental difference between the message driven model and Active Messages is where computation-proper is performed: in the former, computation occurs in the message handlers whereas in the latter it is in the "background" and handlers only remove messages from the network transport buffers and integrate them into the computation. This difference significantly affects the nature of allocation and scheduling performed at message arrival.

Because a handler in the message driven model may suspend waiting for an event, the lifetime of the storage allocated in the scheduling queue for messages varies considerably. In general, it cannot be released in simple FIFO or LIFO order. Moreover, the size of the scheduling queue does not depend on the rate at which messages arrive or handlers are executed, but on the amount of excess parallelism in the program[4]. Given that the excess parallelism can grow arbitrarily (as can the conventional call stack) it is impractical to set aside a fraction of memory for the message queue, rather it must be able to grow to the size of available memory.

Active Message handlers, on the other hand, execute immediately upon message arrival, cannot suspend, and have the responsibility to terminate quickly enough not to back-up the network. The role of a handler is to get the message out of the network transport buffers. This happens either by integrating the message into the data structures of the ongoing computation or, in the case of remote service requests, by immediately replying to the requester. Memory allocation upon message arrival occurs only as far as is required for network transport (*e.g.* if DMA is involved) and scheduling is restricted to interruption of the ongoing computation by handlers. Equivalently, the handlers could run in parallel with the computation on separate dedicated hardware.

3.2 Hardware Description

The Monsoon and J-Machine hardware is designed to support the message driven model directly. The J-Machine has a 3-D mesh of processing nodes with a single-chip CPU and DRAM each. The CPU has a 32-bit integer unit with a closely integrated network unit, a small static memory and a DRAM interface (but no floating-point unit). The hardware manages the scheduling queue as a fixed-size ring buffer in on-chip memory. Arriving messages are transferred into the queue and serviced in FIFO order. The first word of each message is interpreted as an instruction pointer and the message is made available to the handler as one of the addressable data segments. The J-Machine supports two levels of message priorities in hardware and two independent queues are maintained. Each message handler terminates by executing a SUSPEND instruction that causes the next message to be scheduled.

In Monsoon, messages arrive into the token queue. The token queue is kept in a separate memory proportional in size to the frame store. It provides storage for roughly 16 tokens per frame on average[6]. The queuing policy allows both FIFO and LIFO scheduling. The ALU pipeline is 8-way interleaved, so eight handlers can be active simultaneously. As soon as a handler terminates or suspends by blocking on a synchronization event, a token is popped from the queue and a new handler starts executing in the vacated pipeline interleave.

A common characteristic of both machines is that the amount of state available to an executing handler is very small: four data and three address registers in the J-Machine, an accumulator and three temporary registers in Monsoon. This reflects the fact that the computation initiated by a single message is small, typically less than ten arithmetic operations. This small amount of work cannot

[6] A token queue store of 64K tokens for 256K words of frame store and an expected average frame size of 64 words.

utilize many registers and since no locality is preserved from one handler to the next, no useful values could be carried along.

It is interesting to note that the J-Machine hardware does not actually support the message driven programming model fully in that the hardware message queue is managed in FIFO order and of fixed size. If a handler does not run to completion, its message must be copied to an allocated region of non-buffer memory by software. This happens for roughly 1/3 of all messages. The J-Machine hardware does support Active Messages, however, in which case the message queue serves only as buffering. Close to 1/3 of the messages hold a request to which the handler immediately replies and general allocation and scheduling is not required.

In Monsoon, the fact that tokens are popped from the queue means that the storage allocated for an arriving message is deallocated upon message handler execution. If a handler suspends, all relevant data is saved in pre-allocated storage in the activation frame thus, unlike the J-Machine, Monsoon does implement the message driven model, but at the cost of a large amount of high-speed memory.

3.3 TAM: compiling to Active Messages

So far, we have argued that the message driven execution model is tricky to implement correctly in hardware due to the fact that general memory allocation and scheduling are required upon message arrival. Using hardware that implements Active Messages, it is easy to simulate the message driven model by performing the allocation and scheduling in the message handler. Contrary to expectation this does not necessarily result in lower performance than a direct hardware implementation because software handlers can exploit and optimize special cases.

TAM[3] (Threaded Abstract Machine), a fine-grain parallel execution model based on Active Messages, goes one step further and requires the compiler to help manage memory allocation and scheduling. It is currently used as a compilation target for implicitly parallel languages such as Id90. When compiling for TAM, the compiler produces sequences of instructions, called *threads*, performing the computation proper. It also generates handlers, called *inlets*, for all messages to be received by the computation. Inlets are used to receive the arguments to a function, the results of called (child) functions, and the responses of global memory accesses. All accesses to global data structures are split-phase, allowing computation to proceed while requests travel through the network.

For each function call, an *activation frame* is allocated. When an inlet receives a message it typically stores the data in the frame and schedules a thread within the activation. Scheduling is handled efficiently by maintaining the scheduling queue within the activation frame: each frame, in addition to holding all local variables, contains counters used for synchronizing threads and inlets, and provides space for the *continuation vector* — the addresses of all currently enabled threads of the activation. Enabling a thread simply consists of pushing its instruction address into the continuation vector and possibly linking the frame into the ready queue. Figure 7 shows the activation tree data structure.

Service requests, such as remote reads, can typically be replied-to immediately and need no memory allocation or scheduling beyond what Active Messages provides. However, in exceptional cases requests must be delayed either for a lack of resources or because servicing inside the handler is inadequate. To amortize memory allocation, these requests are of fixed size and queue space is allocated in chunks.

Maintaining thread addresses in frames provides a natural two-level scheduling hierarchy. When a frame is scheduled (*activated*),

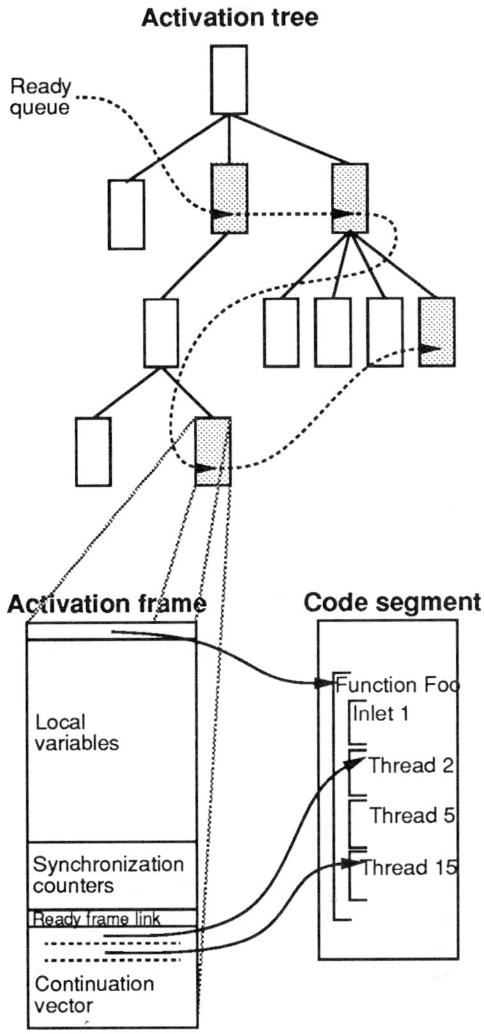

Figure 7: *TAM activation tree and embedded scheduling queue. For each function call, an activation frame is allocated. Each frame, in addition to holding all local variables, contains counters used to synchronize threads and inlets, and provides space for the* continuation vector *— the addresses of all currently enabled threads of the activation. On each processor, all frames holding enabled threads are linked into a ready queue. Maintaining the scheduling queue within the activation keeps costs low: enabling a thread simply consists of pushing its instruction address into the continuation vector and sometimes linking the frame into the ready queue. Scheduling the next thread within the same activation is simply a pop-jump.*

enabled threads are executed until the continuation vector is empty. When a message is received, two types of behavior can be observed: either the message is for the currently active frame and the inlet simply feeds the data into the computation, or the message is for a dormant frame in which case the frame may get added to the ready queue, but the ongoing computation is otherwise undisturbed.

Using the TAM scheduling hierarchy, the compiler can improve the locality of computation by synchronizing in message handlers and enabling computation only when a group of messages has arrived (one example is when all prerequisite remote fetches for an inner loop body have completed). This follows the realization that while the arrival of one message enables only a small amount of computation, the arrival of several closely related messages can enable a significant amount of computation. In cases beyond the power of compile-time analysis, the run-time scheduling policy dynamically enhances locality by servicing a frame until its continuation vector is empty.

As a result of the TAM compilation model, typically no memory allocation is required upon message arrival. Dynamic memory allocation is only performed in large chunks for activation frames and for global arrays and records. Locality of computation is enhanced by the TAM scheduling hierarchy. It is possible to implement TAM scheduling well even without any hardware support: on a uniprocessor[7] the overall cost for dynamic scheduling amounts to doubling the number of control-flow instructions relative to languages such as C. However, the overall performance depends critically on the cost of Active Messages. Table 3 summarizes the frequency of various kinds of messages in the current implementation. On average, a message is sent and received every eight TAM instructions (equivalent to roughly 20 RISC instructions). Note that these statistics are sensitive to optimizations. For example, significant changes can be expected from a software cache for remote arrays.

Message types	data words	frequency
Frame-frame	0	1%
	1	10%
	2	1%
Store request	1	8%
Fetch request	0	40%
Fetch reply	1	40%

Table 3: *Frequency of various message types and sizes (represented by the number of data values transmitted) in the current implementation of TAM. On average, a message is sent and received every 8 TAM instructions. These statistics are sensitive to compiler optimizations and, in some sense, represent a worst case scenario.*

4 Hardware support for Active Messages

Active messages provide a precise and simple communication mechanism which is independent of any programming model. Evaluating new hardware features can be restricted to evaluating their impact on Active Messages. The parameters feeding into the design are the size and frequency of messages, which depend on the expected workload and programming models.

Hardware support for active messages falls into two categories: improvements to network interfaces and modifications to the processor to facilitate execution of message handlers. The following subsections examine parts of the design space for each of these points of view.

4.1 Network interface design issues

Improvements in the network interface can significantly reduce the overhead of composing a message. Message reception benefits from these improvements as well, but also requires initiation of the handler.

Large messages: The support needed for large messages is a superset of that for small messages. To overlap computation with large message communication, some form of DMA transfer must be used. To set-up the DMA on the receiving side, large messages must have a header which is received first. Thus, if small messages are well supported, a large message should be viewed as a small one with a DMA transfer tacked-on.

Message registers: Composing small messages in memory buffers is inefficient: much of the information present in a small message is related to the current processor state. It comes from the instruction stream, processor registers and sometimes from memory. At the receiving end, the message header is typically moved into processor registers to be used for dispatch and to address data. Direct communication between the processor and the network interface can save instructions and bus transfers. In addition, managing the memory buffers is expensive.

The J-Machine demonstrates an extreme alternative for message composition: in a single `SEND` instruction the contents of two processor registers can be appended to a message. Message reception, however, is tied to memory buffers (albeit on-chip). A less radical approach is to compose messages in registers of a network coprocessor.

Reception can be handled similarly: when received, a message appears in a set of registers. A (coprocessor) receive instruction enables reception of the next message. In case a coprocessor design is too complex, the network interface can also be accessed as a memory mapped device (as is the case in the CM-5).

Reuse of message data: Providing a large register set in the network interface, as opposed to network FIFO registers, allows a message to be composed using portions of other messages. For example, the destination for a reply is extracted from the request message. Also, multiple requests are often sent with mostly identical return addresses. Keeping additional context information such as the current frame pointer and a code base pointer in the network interface can further accelerate the formatting of requests.

Single network port: Multiple network channels connected to a node should not be visible to the message layer. On the nCUBE/2, for example, a message must be sent out on the correct hypercube link by the message layer, even though further routing in the network is automatic. The network interface should allow at least two messages to be composed simultaneously or message composition must be atomic. Otherwise, replies within message handlers may interfere with normal message composition.

Protection: User-level access to the network interface requires that protection mechanisms be enforced by the hardware. This typically includes checking the destination node, the destination process and, if applicable, the message length. For most of these checks a simple range check is sufficient. On reception, the message head (*i.e.*, the handler address and possibly a process id) can be checked using the normal memory management system.

[7] Id90 requires dynamic scheduling even on uniprocessors.

Frequent message accelerators: A well-designed network interface allows the most frequent message types to be issued quickly. For example in the *T[15] proposal, issuing a global memory fetch takes a single store double instruction (the network interface is memory mapped). The 64-bit data value is interpreted as a global address and translated in the network interface into a node/local-address pair. For the return address the current frame pointer is cached in the network interface and the handler address is calculated from the low-order bits of the store address.

4.2 Processor support for message handlers

Asynchronous message handler initiation is the one design issue that cannot be addressed purely in the network interface: processor modifications are needed as well. The only way to signal an asynchronous event on current microprocessors is to take an interrupt. This not only flushes the pipeline, but enters the kernel. The overhead in executing a user-level handler includes a crawl-out to the handler, a trap back into the kernel, and finally the return to the interrupted computation[8]. Super-scalar designs tend to increase the cost of interrupts.

Fast polling: Frequent asynchronous events can be avoided by relying on software to poll for messages. In execution models such as TAM where the message frequency is very high, polling instructions can be inserted automatically by the compiler as part of thread generation. This can be supported with little or no change to the processor. For example, on Sparc or Mips a message-ready signal can be attached to the coprocessor condition code input and polled using a branch on coprocessor condition instruction.

User-level interrupts: User-level traps have been proposed to handle exceptions in dynamically typed programming languages[13] and floating-point computations. For Active Messages, user-level interrupts need only occur between instructions. However, an incoming message may not be for the currently running user process and the network interface should interrupt to the kernel in this case.

PC injection: A minimal form of multithreading can be used to switch between the main computational thread and a handler thread. The two threads share all processor resources except for the program counter (PC). Normally instructions are fetched using the computation PC. On message arrival, instruction fetch switches to use the handler PC. The handler suspends with a `swap` instruction, which switches instruction fetch back to the computation PC. In the implementation the two PCs are in fact symmetrical. Switching between the two PCs can be performed without pipeline bubbles, although fetching the `swap` instruction costs one cycle. Note, that in this approach the format of the message is partially known to the network interface, since it must extract the handler PC from the message.

Dual processors: Instead of multiplexing the processor between computation threads and handlers, the two can execute concurrently on two processors, one tailored for the computation and a very simple one for message handlers (*e.g.*, it may have no floating-point). The crucial design aspect is how communication is handled between the two processors. The communication consists of the data received from the network and written to memory, *e.g.*, into activation frames, and the scheduling queue.

A dual-processor design is proposed for the MIT *T project. It uses an MC88110 for computation and a custom message processor. In the *T design, the two processors are on separate die and communicate over a snooping bus. If the two processors were integrated on a single die, they could share the data cache and communication would be simpler. The appealing aspect of this design is that normal uniprocessors can be used quite successfully.

For coarse-grain models, such as Split-C, it is most important to overlap computation with the transmission of messages into the network. An efficient network interface allows high processor utilization on smaller data sets. On the other extreme, implicitly parallel language models that provide word-at-a-time access to globally shared objects are extremely demanding of the network interface. With modest hardware support, the cost of handling a simple message can be reduce to a handful of instructions, but not to one. Unless remote references are infrequent, the amount of resources consumed by message handling is significant. Whether dual processors or a larger number of multiplexed processors is superior depends on a variety of engineering issues, but neither involves exotic architecture. The resources invested in message handling serve to maintain the efficiency of the background computation.

5 Related work

The work presented in this paper is similar in character to the recent development of optimized RPC mechanisms in the operating system research community[18, 2]. Both attempt to reduce the communication layer functionality to the minimum required and carefully analyze and optimize the frequent case. However, the time scales and the operating system involvement are radically different in the two arenas.

The RPC mechanisms in distributed systems operate on time-scales of 100s of microseconds to milliseconds, and operating system involvement in every communication operation is taken for granted. The optimizations presented reduce the OS overhead for moving data between user and system spaces, marshaling complex RPC parameters, context switches and enforcing security. Furthermore, connecting applications with system services is a major use of operating system RPCs, so the communication partners must be protected from one another.

In contrast, the time scale of communication in parallel machines is measured in tens of processor clock cycles (a few μs) and the elimination of all OS intervention is a central issue. Security is less of a concern given that the communication partners form a single program.

Another difference is that in the distributed systems arena the communication paradigm (RPC) is stable, whereas we propose a new mechanism for parallel processing and show how it is more primitive than and subsumes existing mechanisms.

6 Conclusions

Integrated communication and computation at low cost is the key challenge in designing the basic building block for large-scale multiprocessors. Existing message passing machines devote most of

[8]It may be possible for the user-level handler to return directly to the computation.

their hardware resources to processing, little to communication and none to bringing the two together. As a result, a significant fraction of the processor is lost to the layers of operating system software required to support message transmission. Message driven machines devote most of their hardware resources to message transmission, reception and scheduling. The dynamic allocation required on message arrival precludes simpler network interfaces. The message-by-message scheduling inherent in the model results in short computation run-lengths, limiting the processing power that can be utilized.

The fundamental issues in designing a balanced machine are providing the ability to overlap communication and computation and to reduce communication overhead. The active message model presented in this paper minimizes the software overhead in message passing machines and utilizes the full capability of the hardware. This model captures the essential functionality of message driven machines with simpler hardware mechanisms.

Under the active message model each node has an ongoing computational task that is punctuated by asynchronous message arrival. A message handler is specified in each message and serves to extract the message data and integrate it into the computation. The efficiency of this model is due to elimination of buffering beyond network transport requirements, the simple scheduling of non-suspensive message handlers, and arbitrary overlap of computation and communication. By drawing the distinction between message handlers and the primary computation, large grains of computation can be enabled by the arrival of multiple messages.

Active messages are sufficient to support a wide range of programming models and permit a variety of implementation tradeoffs. The best implementation strategy for a particular programming model depends on the usage patterns typical in the model such as message frequency, message size and computation grain. Further research is required to characterize these patterns in emerging parallel languages and compilation paradigms. The optimal hardware support for active messages is an open question, but it is clear that it is a matter of engeneering tradeoffs rather than architectural revolution.

Acknowledgements

We thank our good friends at MIT for the work on Id90, Monsoon and the J-Machine, which stimulated this investigation. nCUBE/2 time was gratefully provided by Sandia National Laboratories and nCUBE Corp. nCUBE also provided access to Vertex kernel sources and a mini nCUBE/2 configuration to reboot at leisure. Guidance and encouragement from hard working folks at Thinking Machines Corp. was instrumental throughout the development of Active Messages on the CM-5.

This work was supported by National Science Foundation PYI Award (CCR-9058342) with matching funds from Motorola Inc. and the TRW Foundation. Thorsten von Eicken is supported by the Semiconductor Research Corporation Grant 91-DC-008. Seth Copen Goldstein is supported by Sandia National Laboratories Contract 87-0212. Klaus Erik Schauser is supported by an IBM Graduate Fellowship. CM-5 computational resources were provided by the NSF Infrastructure Grant CDA-8722788.

References

[1] Arvind and R. A. Iannucci. Two Fundamental Issues in Multiprocessing. In *Proc. of DFVLR - Conf. 1987 on Par. Proc. in Science and Eng.*, Bonn-Bad Godesberg, W. Germany, June 1987.

[2] B. N. Bershad, T. E. Anderson, E. D. Lazowska, and H. M. Levy. Lightweight Remote Procedure Call. *ACM Trans. on Computer Systems*, 8(1), February 1990.

[3] D. Culler, A. Sah, K. Schauser, T. von Eicken, and J. Wawrzynek. Fine-grain Parallelism with Minimal Hardware Support: A Compiler-Controlled Threaded Abstract Machine. In *Proc. of 4th Int. Conf. on Architectural Support for Programming Languages and Operating Systems*, Santa-Clara, CA, April 1991. (Also available as Technical Report UCB/CSD 91/591, CS Div., University of California at Berkeley).

[4] D. E. Culler and Arvind. Resource Requirements of Dataflow Programs. In *Proc. of the 15th Ann. Int. Symp. on Comp. Arch.*, pages 141–150, Hawaii, May 1988.

[5] W. Dally and et al. Architecture of a Message-Driven Processor. In *Proc. of the 14th Annual Int. Symp. on Comp. Arch.*, pages 189–196, June 1987.

[6] W. Dally and et al. The J-Machine: A Fine-Grain Concurrent Computer. In *IFIP Congress*, 1989.

[7] J. J. Dongarra. Performance of Various Computers Using Standard Linear Equations Software. Technical Report CS-89-85, Computer Science Dept., Univ. of Tennessee, Knoxville, TN 37996, December 1991.

[8] T. H. Dunigan. Performance of a Second Generation Hypercube. Technical Report ORNL/TM-10881, Oak Ridge Nat'l Lab, November 1988.

[9] G. Fox. *Programming Concurrent Processors*. Addison Wesley, 1989.

[10] R. H. Halstead, Jr. Multilisp: A Language for Concurrent Symbolic Computation. *ACM Transactions on Programming Languages and Systems*, 7(4):501–538, October 1985.

[11] W. Horwat, A. A. Chien, and W. J. Dally. Experience with CST: Programming and Implementation. In *Proc. of the ACM SIGPLAN '89 Conference on Programming Language Design and Implementation*, 1989.

[12] Intel. Personal communication, 1991.

[13] D. Johnson. Trap Architectures for Lisp Systems. In *Proc. of the 1990 ACM conf. on Lisp and Functional Programming*, June 1990.

[14] R. S. Nikhil. The Parallel Programming Language Id and its Compilation for Parallel Machines. In *Proc. Workshop on Massive Parallelism, Amalfi, Italy, October 1989*. Academic Press, 1991. Also: CSG Memo 313, MIT Laboratory for Computer Science, 545 Technology Square, Cambridge, MA 02139, USA.

[15] R. S. Nikhil, G. M. Papadopoulos, and Arvind. *T: A Killer Micro for A Brave New World. Technical Report CSG Memo 325, MIT Lab for Comp. Sci., 545 Tech. Square, Cambridge, MA, January 1991.

[16] G. M. Papadopoulos. Implementation of a General Purpose Dataflow Multiprocessor. Technical Report TR432, MIT Lab for Comp. Sci., 545 Tech. Square, Cambridge, MA, September 1988. (PhD Thesis, Dept. of EECS, MIT).

[17] G. M. Papadopoulos and D. E. Culler. Monsoon: an Explicit Token-Store Architecture. In *Proc. of the 17th Annual Int. Symp. on Comp. Arch.*, Seattle, Washington, May 1990.

[18] A. Thekkath and H. M. Levy. Limits to Low-Latency RPC. Technical Report TR 91-06-01, Dept. of Computer Science and Engineering, University of Washington, Seattle WA 98195, 1991.

Session 9: Message Routing Networks

Planar-Adaptive Routing: Low-cost Adaptive Networks for Multiprocessors

Andrew A. Chien and Jae H. Kim
achien@cs.uiuc.edu *kim@cs.uiuc.edu*
Department of Computer Science
University of Illinois at Urbana-Champaign
1304 W. Springfield Avenue
Urbana, IL 61801

Abstract

Network throughput can be increased by allowing multipath, adaptive routing. Adaptive routing allows more freedom in the paths taken by messages, spreading load over physical channels more evenly. The flexibility of adaptive routing introduces new possibilities of deadlock. Previous deadlock avoidance schemes in k-ary n-cubes require an exponential number of virtual channels [17]. We describe a family of deadlock-free routing algorithms, called *planar-adaptive routing* algorithms which require only a constant number of virtual channels, independent of network size and dimension. Planar adaptive routing algorithms reduce the complexity of deadlock prevention by reducing the number of choices at each routing step. In the fault-free case, planar-adaptive networks are guaranteed to be deadlock-free. In the presence of network faults, the planar-adaptive router can be extended with misrouting to produce a working network which remains provably deadlock free and is provably livelock free. In addition, planar adaptive networks can simultaneously support both in-order and adaptive, out-of-order packet delivery.

Planar-adaptive routing is of practical significance. It provides the simplest known support for deadlock-free adaptive routing in k-ary n-cubes of more than two dimensions (with $k > 2$). Restricting adaptivity reduces the hardware complexity, improving router speed or allowing additional performance-enhancing network features. The structure of planar-adaptive routers is amenable to efficient implementation.

Keywords: Multicomputers, Routing Networks, Adaptive Routing, Deadlock Avoidance, Transmission-Order Preservation, Fault Tolerance

1 Introduction

In concurrent computers, interconnection networks are used by the processing nodes to exchange data and synchronize with each other. Network performance is often critical, as the performance of large-scale parallel machines is sensitive to network latency and throughput. While multicomputers have been touted as scalable parallel architectures, their scalability is limited by the performance of their interconnection networks.

An interconnection network is defined by its topology, routing, and flow control. The topology is the pattern of network node interconnection via physical communication channels. The routing algorithm specifies how packets choose paths through the network. Flow control deals with the allocation of channel and buffer resources to packets as they proceed through the network. This paper focuses on the issue of routing. In particular, we describe a class of adaptive routing algorithms which require only local information and modest hardware support. While our discussion is in the context of k-ary n-cube networks, the same ideas can be applied to other networks with regular topologies. Likewise, though we present the ideas in the context of cut-through routing (virtual cut-through or wormhole routing) the ideas apply to store-and-forward networks as well.

2 The Problem

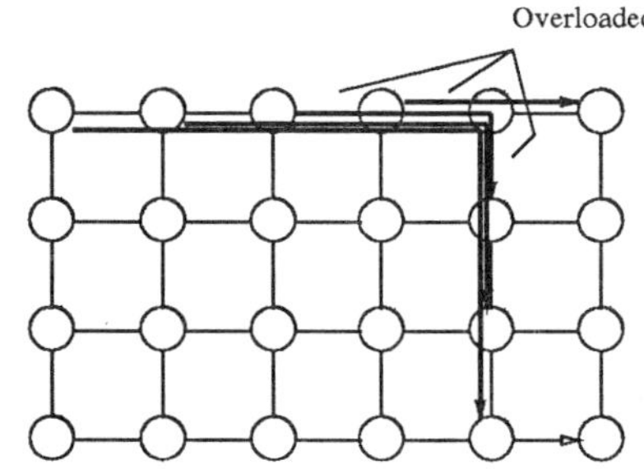

Figure 1: Four packets and their routing paths under deterministic, dimension-order routing.

Most existing multicomputer routing networks use deterministic routing [22, 20, 8, 21]. Although there are numerous paths between any source and destination, in order to avoid deadlock, *deterministic routing* defines a single path from source to destination. This means that the interconnection networks cannot make effective use of the density of their physical interconnection because the physical channels are used inflexibly. Unfortunately, for any choice of fixed paths, some traffic patterns will produce performance which is much poorer than should be possible, given the physical interconnect. *Deterministic routing prevents the use of productive network resources to complete the communication.* An example of this situation is portrayed in Figure 1. In the figure, the circles represent nodes which are connected in a two-dimensional mesh. Four nodes are sending packets to the destinations indicated. In this case, the deterministic routing algorithm used to avoid deadlock requires routing horizontally, then vertically. Despite the presence of many other possible paths all four packets are forced to traverse the overloaded channel. The result is poor performance.

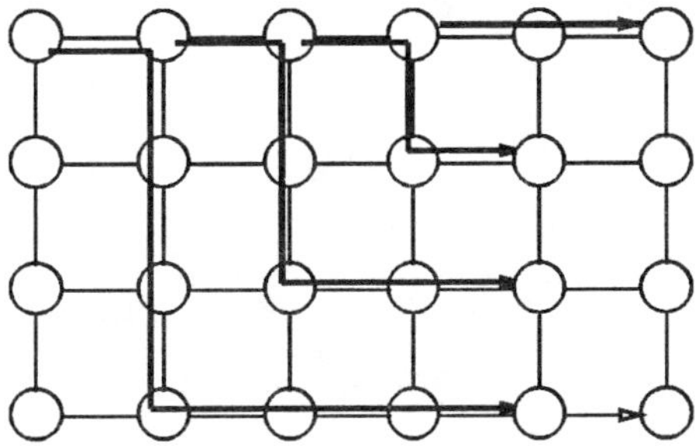

Figure 2: The same four packets and potential routing paths under a more flexible routing scheme.

Adaptive routing allows packet routing to take advantage of the density of network interconnection. Typically, in adaptive schemes, packets can take one of a number of paths. This situation is depicted in Figure 2. In the figure, the same four packets are routed using an adaptive algorithm. Packet routes are adapted based on whether channels are busy when a packet header arrives. If the desired physical channel is busy, another channel leading towards the destination may be chosen. In this case, the result is that none of the packets need to share physical channels. The key observation is that the best choice of paths depends on current network loading. To achieve good performance on all traffic loads, routing algorithms must be *adaptive*, e.g. choose paths based on network conditions. The additional flexibility in adaptive routers can improve performance under both uniform and non-uniform loading. In general, in adaptively-routed systems, path choices can be made on the basis of any local information. The distinction we make between deterministic and adaptive routing is sometimes termed oblivious versus non-oblivous routing.

3 Overview

In the paper, we begin by briefly discussing some of the most relevant work in adaptive routers for k-ary n-cubes. In particular, we highlight the cost of deadlock-avoidance in these systems. In Section 5, we introduce the *planar-adaptive* routing algorithm which allows adaptive routing at much lower hardware cost than previous techniques. Planar-adaptive routing is proven to be deadlock-free in k-ary n-cubes with no wraparounds with only three virtual channels. Following that, we show how to extend the router to support fault-tolerance by adding disciplined misrouting. The resulting routing algorithm is termed a fault-tolerant, planar-adaptive router. Misrouting may result in non-minimal packet routes, but the routing algorithm remains deadlock-free. In addition, we prove that the fault-tolerant, planar-adaptive routing algorithm is livelock-free. In Section 6, we consider the issue of message delivery order. The planar-adaptive routing algorithm can also simultaneously support both in-order and adaptive, out-of-order packet transmission. We demonstrate how this can be done. Section 7 discusses implementation issues for planar-adaptive routers with a focus on hardware complexity and speed. Finally, Section 8 concludes the paper with a discussion of the ramifications and future directions.

4 Background

All adaptive routers choose from several paths based on channel loading, channel failure, or other dynamic information. The paths from which the router may select define a basic distinction amongst adaptive routers. This distinction separates adaptive routers which choose from a set of minimal paths (wasting no work) and non-minimal paths (potentially wasting routing work in exchange for increased routing freedom). These two types of adaptive routing algorithms are described below:

Minimal or productive adaptive routing. Packets are routed along paths of minimal distance to their destination. Packets never move away from their destination.

Non-minimal or misrouting-based adaptive routing. Packets may temporarily move away from their destination (misrouting), but eventually arrive at their destination. Due to misrouting, the distance a packet travels may not be minimal. The network may do some unnecessary work.

Significant work has explored non-minimal approaches [19, 15]. While such efforts have produced interesting routers which can outperform minimal adaptive routers in some cases, the use of misrouting makes prevention of livelock a difficult problem. Complex schemes for packet priority and aging have been proposed, but they complicate the router logic required for routing and arbitration decisions. One interesting non-deterministic approach to livelock prevention is the Chaos router [15], but its efficiency and cost are still under evaluation. The use of misrouting in non-minimal adaptive routing also makes it difficult to preserve packet transmission order. Order-preserving packet delivery can significantly reduce the number of packets required to implement serialization protocols [16].

Minimal routers are attractive because they do not waste any effort. Since packets are never transmitted away from their destination, it's possible to utilize the full wire capacity[1] of the network productively. Minimal routers can also support order-preserving routing efficiently. For these reasons, we focus on minimal routers.

Planar-adaptive routing is a minimal, adaptive routing algorithm which is provably deadlock-free. Under appropriate reconfiguration algorithms, planar-adaptive networks are also fault-tolerant. In addition, planar-adaptive routing can be extended to support in-order packet delivery and adaptive, unordered packet delivery simultaneously. The designated in-order traffic is delivered in sequence, the other packet arrive in unspecified order. In all cases, the planar-adaptive networks are both deadlock and livelock free.

[1]We define network capacity as the bandwidth of all network wires being used simultaneously.

4.1 The Cost of Deadlock Avoidance

Adaptive routing algorithms increase routing flexibility, multiplying the possibilities for deadlock. In multiprocessor networks, routing decisions must be made in a single cycle, and thus cannot incorporate complex distributed deadlock prevention and detection algorithms.

Consequently, we focus on deadlock prevention schemes based on restricting the routing algorithm [3]. Because the physical network has cycles naive routing schemes can produce deadlock, so we virtualize the network by introducing virtual channels (really only extra buffers) and define routing functions on the virtual networks. The new routing functions are from virtual channel to virtual channel and define a network with no cycles. This technique is useful in both deterministic and adaptive routing systems and is based on ideas from data networks found in [12, 11].

We focus particularly on two families of networks, k-ary n-cubes and multi-dimensional meshes (k-ary n-cubes without wraparounds) and assume cut-through [13] or wormhole routing [6]. Dally and Seitz use virtual channels and restrict routing to implement deadlock-free routing in k-ary n-cubes [3]. However, their scheme assumes a deterministic routing algorithm, dimension-order routing.

A minimal adaptive routing scheme described by Linder and Harden [17] extends the techniques of Dally and Seitz to allow adaptive routing while preventing deadlock. However, the hardware cost of their approach is significant, requiring a large number of virtual channels per physical channel. Such hardware complexity typically reduces attainable network speed.

Dally and Aoki have described an adaptive routing algorithm based on the notion of "dimension-reversals" [5]. Each dimension-reversal is a departure from dimension-order routing. In their static scheme, one additional virtual channel is required for each allowed dimension-reversal in order to prevent deadlock. Consequently, that scheme supports only a fixed number of dimension reversals. Their dynamic scheme can support an arbitrary number of dimension-reversals by tagging each message a dimension-reversal count and terminating adaptive routing if blocked by a packet with a lower number of reversals. Updating reversal counts and making routing decisions on that basis may increase router complexity significantly. We do not consider adaptive schemes which are only applicable to binary hypercubes, not other types of k-ary n-cubes [14].

A table comparing the virtual channel hardware requirements of existing techniques and planar-adaptive routing is given in Figure 3[2]. We include only those techniques which are deadlock-free over a variety of k-ary n-cubes, particularly those with larger radixes ($k > 2$).

As can be seen in the figure, deterministic routing requires only one or two virtual channels to prevent deadlock for networks of all dimensions. All of the adaptive routing algorithms require greater numbers of virtual channels. The Linder-Harden (LH) algorithm which permits fully adaptive routing[3], requires a number of virtual channels exponential in n. Practically speaking, the number is quite large even for a three or four-dimensional network. In contrast, the planar-adaptive routing algorithm requires only three or six virtual channels to prevent deadlock for networks of any dimension.

[2]The numbers shown for planar-adaptive routing are for the fault-free case. For the fault-tolerant case, preventing deadlock and livelock requires three virtual channels for the 2D mesh and six virtual channels for the 2D cube.

[3]Any productive channel toward the destination may be used.

Topology	Determ.	L-H	P-Adaptive
2D Mesh	1	2	2
2D Cube (Torus)	2	6	4
3D Mesh	1	4	3
3D Cube	2	16	6
4D Mesh	1	8	3
4D Cube	2	40	6
n-D Mesh	1	2^{n-1}	3
n-D Cube	2	$2^{n-1}(n+1)$	6

Figure 3: Virtual channel requirements for deadlock-free routing algorithms for k-ary n-cubes. The virtual channel requirements for Dally and Aoki's scheme is omitted as they depend on the number of dimension reversals permitted.

The cost advantage of planar-adaptive routing can be dramatic for higher-dimensional networks. Such networks are of increasing interest. Large-scale machines increase the effect of node latency, favoring networks with greater connectivity. Looser constraints on wiring bisection and pin-bounds also make higher-dimensional networks more attractive. Furthermore, recent results indicate that higher-dimensional networks may exhibit more robust performance over a range of communication locality [1].

Cost Metrics In routing networks, the most expensive part is the wires for the physical channels. Following that, the second most expensive elements are the buffers and switching hardware (crossbar or other). Only if routing algorithms become very complex is routing logic a significant contributor. Since we will compare different routing schemes with respect to a fixed topology, the physical channel cost is constant. The issue is how to get the best performance out of the wires. Since the networks we consider are wormhole-routed, the main contribution to the buffering is the number of "virtual channels" which is the same as the minimum number of buffers. The number of switch ports in a crossbar affects both its cost and setup latency. Switch cost is superlinear in the number of ports, so partitionable switches will be cheaper and faster. We return to this issue when we discuss implementation issues in Section 7. Meanwhile, we focus on virtual channel requirements as a cost metric. Hardware cost savings are significant as they not only save chip area, they may also allow the router to run at higher speeds.

5 Planar-Adaptive Routing

Fully adaptive, minimal routing allows the use of any channels that move a packet towards its destination. As shown in Figure 4, packets are routed in the n-dimensional subcube of the network defined by the source and destination. It is possible to reduce the cost of deadlock avoidance by restricting routing flexibility (adap-

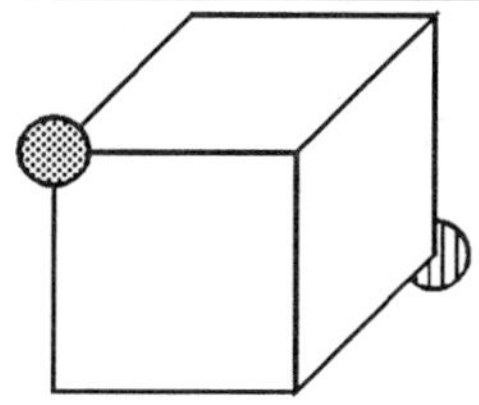

Figure 4: A fully adaptive, minimal router allows a packet to be routed in the n-dimensional subcube defined by the source and destination. This subcube is shown for the case of a three-dimensional network.

tivity). The motivation for this approach is the following observation about Linder and Harden's deadlock prevention scheme.

Observation: The requirement of a large number of virtual channels to prevent deadlock arises from the freedom to route in the n dimensions in arbitrary order.

By constraining the routing freedom to a few dimensions at a time, the hardware requirements for deadlock avoidance can be greatly reduced. Compared to fully adaptive routing, the planar-adaptive approach sacrifices some routing freedom to drastically reduce the possibilities of deadlock. Planar-adaptive routing limits its routing freedom to two dimensions at a time. The reduced freedom make it possible to prevent deadlock with only a fixed number of virtual channels, independent of the number of network dimensions.

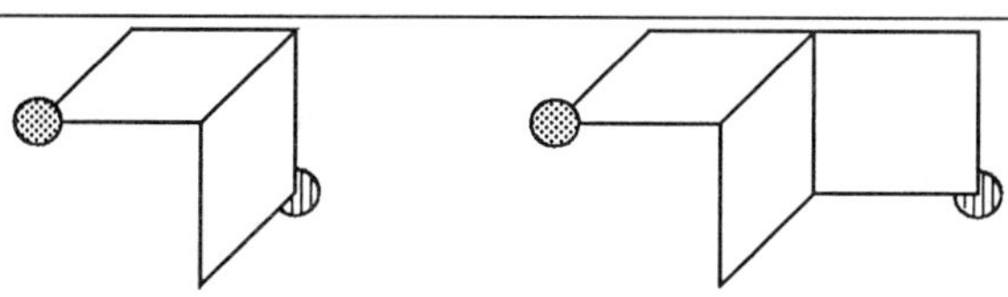

Figure 5: Planar, adaptive routing allows the packet to be routed on a series of two-dimensional surfaces, adaptive planes. Planar-adaptive routing for three and four dimensions is illustrated.

Though there is less routing freedom than with fully adaptive routing, planar-adaptive routing still allows choice from a large number of paths from source to destination. Routing proceeds on a series of adaptive planes (2-dimensional surfaces). The routing freedom available in planar-adaptive routing is pictured in Figure 5. Within each adaptive plane, packets may use any channels leading toward their destination. Restricting the adaptivity in this fashion reduces the coupling between network dimensions, reducing the possibilities for inter-dimensional resource cycles. Consequently fewer resources are needed to avoid deadlock.

5.1 Notation and Terminology

We adopt notation similar to that in [4, 17]. We presume for the purposes of discussion, a physical topology of a k-ary n-cube with no wraparound paths. The generalization to cubes with wraparound paths is straightforward.

k	=	# of nodes along a dimension
n	=	# of dimensions, 2*n = # of physical channels per node
$d_{i,j}$	=	dimension i, virtual channel j.
$p_{i,j,k}$	=	Node with addresses i, j, k in dimensions $0, 1, 2$ respectively.

As a k-ary n-cube, the network has k^n nodes. $d_{i,j}$ specifies a set of virtual channels, j, in dimension i of the network. It specifies two for each node, one in the positive direction, one in the negative direction in the i dimension. We denote the positive direction channels as $d_{i,j}+$ and the negative direction channels as $d_{i,j}-$. Each node has a unique label $p_{i,j,k}$. For example, $p_{1,3,2}$ denotes a node with address 1 in dimension 0, address 3 in dimension 1, and address 2 in dimension 2 of a k-ary 3-cube. Throughout this paper, we use the terms message and packet synonymously to indicate a unit of routing in the network.

5.2 Planar-Adaptive Routing

The idea in planar-adaptive routing is to provide adaptivity in two dimensions at all times. Thus, a packet is routed adaptively in a series of two-dimensional planes. As the packet progresses towards its destination the routing dimensions change. Eventually, the packet is routed in all dimensions and delivered to its destination. By limiting the adaptivity to two dimensions and structuring the passage from one adaptive plane to the next, we reduce network cost while maintaining deadlock-freedom.

In a k-ary n-cube with no wraparound paths, planar-adaptive routing requires three virtual channels for each physical channel. We claim and will show that these three channels are sufficient to assure deadlock and livelock freedom.

Define $n-1$ adaptive planes, A_0 to A_{n-2}, as the combination of several sets of virtual channels.

$$A_i = d_{i,2} + d_{i+1,0} + d_{i+1,1}$$

Each adaptive plane involves only two dimensions[4]. Three virtual channels in each dimension are needed to support the $n-1$ adaptive planes. More precisely, the first and last need only one and two respectively, but the maximum number of virtual channels for any dimension is three.

Planar-Adaptive Routing Algorithm:

High-level (between adaptive planes)

1. For $i = 0$, $i < (n-1)$ do
   Route adaptively in A_i, see low-level routing.
   end

[4] The order of dimensions is arbitrary.

2. After exiting the loop, it can only be necessary to correct the address in d_{n-1}. If necessary, route in $d_{n-1,2}$ to the destination.

Low-level (within adaptive plane A_i)

Adaptive plane A_i contains virtual channels $d_{i,2}$, $d_{i+1,0}$, and $d_{i+1,1}$. Within the plane, route adaptively with respect to dimensions d_i and d_{i+1} by choosing any channel that leads closer to the destination. In order to prevent deadlock, the traffic is divided into two classes: *increasing* packets need to increase their d_i address and *decreasing* packets need to decrease their d_i address. Denote the channels which increase an address in a dimension as $d_{i,2}+$, those that decrease a $d_{i,2}-$. Divide the virtual channels in A_i into two separate virtual networks. Note that there is no coupling between the increasing and decreasing networks.

Increasing Network: $d_{i,2}+, d_{i+1,0}$

Decreasing Network: $d_{i,2}-, d_{i+1,1}$

Increasing traffic is routed in the increasing network. Decreasing traffic is routed in the decreasing network. Within each, traffic is routed adaptively towards its destination in any of the productive channels.

When the d_i address is correct, routing is completed in plane A_i, so proceed to the next high-level step.

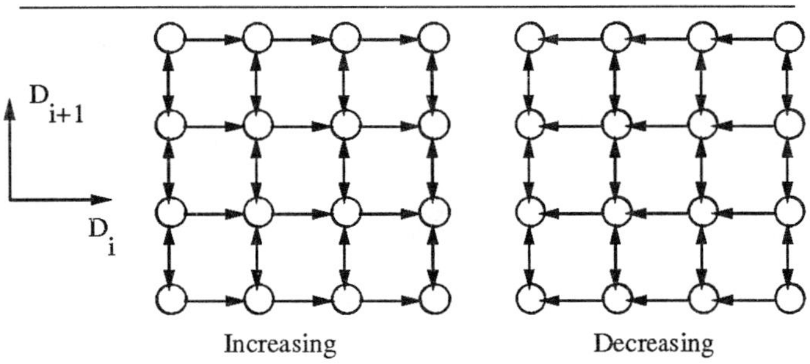

Figure 6: The channels for an adaptive plane A_i. The increasing and decreasing networks are logically decoupled as they contain disjoint sets of virtual channels.

In the high-level routing, the basic idea is to route successively in the adaptive planes. Routing in adaptive plane A_i reduces the distance in d_i to zero. The separate increasing and decreasing networks in each adaptive plane are shown in Figure 6. Packets do not pass between them. After routing in all of the adaptive planes, the packet has reached its destination. For d_{n-1}, there cannot be any adaptivity left for a minimal router, so the packet is routed directly to its destination.

In the low-level routing, the scheme is adaptive, as multiple paths can be chosen within each adaptive plane. In each adaptive plane, the packet completes its routing in at least one dimension. If in plane A_i, the d_{i+1} distance is reduced to zero first, routing continues in d_i exclusively, until the d_i distance is reduced to zero. The adaptive routing system is low cost, requiring only three virtual channels for an n-dimensional network.

5.3 Deadlock Freedom

Planar-adaptive routing is deadlock-free. Our proof decomposes the network into the adaptive planes, shows that routing in each plane is deadlock-free, and then shows that cycles cannot form between planes. Consequently, the planar-adaptive routing algorithm is free from deadlocks.

Theorem 1: Planar-adaptive routing is deadlock free with only three virtual channels.

Lemma 1.1 Routing within each adaptive plane, A_i, is deadlock free.

Proof of Lemma 1.1:

Recall that each adaptive plane is divided into two networks which are completely separate.

Increasing Network: $d_{i,2}+, d_{i+1,0}$

Decreasing Network: $d_{i,2}-, d_{i+1,1}$

The packets in d_i+ can only depend only on d_i+ and $d_{i+1,0}$ channels. The packets d_i- can only depend only on d_i- and $d_{i+1,1}$. Without loss of generality we consider only the increasing network. Suppose a cycle forms within the increasing network. Because our grid is rectangular, the cycle must have a d_i- edge. Packets in the increasing network cannot use a d_i- edge, therefore no cycle can form. A symmetric argument applies for the decreasing network. □

Lemma 1.2

Routing between adaptive planes is deadlock free. No cycles which cross between adaptive planes are possible.

Proof of Lemma 1.2:

Each adaptive plane A_i routes traffic into A_{i+1}. Assume a cycle of size m occurs:

$$Cycle = A_{C1}, A_{C2} ... A_{Cm}$$

For each link in the cycle, the high-level algorithm assures that the adaptive planes are traversed in numerical order. This means that in our cycle, we must have $Ci < C(i+1)$. But the $<$ operator is transitive, this means by walking around the cycle, we can derive the constraint that $Ci < Ci$ which is a contradiction. Therefore, no cycles can form and routing between adaptive plains is deadlock-free. □

Proof of Theorem 1:

By Lemma 1.1, routing within each adaptive plane is deadlock-free. By Lemma 1.2, routing between adaptive planes is deadlock-free. There are no other dependences within the network, therefore planar-adaptive routing is deadlock-free. □

Planar-adaptive routing allows some flexibility in routing at very low hardware cost. A primary concern in adaptive networks is how much it costs to prevent deadlock. To assure deadlock-free routing, the planar scheme requires only three virtual channels for k-ary n-cubes without wraparound channels. This is a dramatic improvement over previously published schemes [17, 5]. As shown in Figure 3, the Linder-Harden scheme deadlock prevention scheme requires 2^{n-1} virtual channels, a significant hardware overhead. Equally important, deadlock and livelock are avoided without any complex reversal counting [5] or aging schemes [18]. This means that planar-adaptive routers will be very simple and can make routing decisions very rapidly. As a result, they may run faster than adaptive routers requiring complex techniques for deadlock and livelock prevention. While speed is important, planar-adaptive routers have other features which enhance their attractiveness. Planar-adaptive routers can be extended to support fault-tolerance and in-order message transmission.

5.4 Fault Tolerance

Planar-adaptive networks can be augmented with misrouting to support fault-tolerance. The resulting networks can tolerate large numbers of faults, yet still deliver all packets to their destinations. The networks remain provably deadlock-free, and we give a proof of deadlock-freedom below. Circumventing faulty regions with only local information requires packet misrouting. Introducing misrouting also introduces the possibility of livelock, so we show that the resulting networks are livelock-free by proving that all packets make progress toward their destinations.

Planar-adaptive networks tolerate faults by routing around them. The basic idea is to use the flexibility of the adaptive routing algorithm to circumvent any faulty channels. We assume that all channel and node faults are detected. Then, all faulty regions are augmented until they are convex by running the deactivation algorithm given below. If faulty regions are not naturally convex, good nodes and channels are marked as faulty until the regions become convex. After the deactivation algorithm has been run, the convexity of faulty regions is ensured and packet routing can begin. Subject to the convexity constraint, planar-adaptive will route packets to all parts of the machine which remain connected.

Fault-Tolerant, Planar-Adaptive Routing:

High-level First, define a new adaptive plane with the previously-unused channels below.

$$A_{n-1} = d_{n-1,2} + d_{0,0} + d_{0,1}$$

For adaptive planes A_0 to A_{n-1}, route between adaptive planes using the low-level routing algorithm given below.

Low-level For each adaptive plane, A_i, route the packet as follows (when $i+1 = n$, use 0, i.e. compute $i+1$ modulo n).

1. If not blocked by fault, route as in the fault-free case.
2. If blocked by a fault in dimension d_{i+1}, route in d_i.
3. If blocked by a fault in d_i, route in d_{i+1}.
4. If blocked by a fault in d_i and the d_{i+1} distance has already been reduced to zero, it is necessary to misroute. If we were routing in d_{i+1}, continue to route in the same direction. If we were routing in d_i, the pick an arbitrary d_{i+1} direction and begin misrouting. At the first opportunity, route in d_i toward the destination. Continue to route in d_i only until it is possible to correct d_{i+1}. At that point, route in d_{i+1} to distance zero in this dimension[5], then revert to step 1.
5. Note that we cannot be blocked in d_{i+1} and have reduced the d_i distance to zero. If this were the case, we would have proceeded to the next adaptive plane.

Steps 2 and 3 make use of the adaptivity in routing to circumvent faults. Step 4 deals with the case where misrouting is necessary. Packets are routed around convex faulty regions in adaptive plane A_i by moving along d_{i+1} until reaching the corner of the faulty region. After reaching the corner, the packet follows the profile of the faulty region around until it has corrected its d_{i+1} address. An example is shown in Figure 7.

Though step 4 may appear somewhat complicated, correct implementation is simple. We need only tag packets that are overshooting. When they have completed step 4, they are untagged and resume from step 1.

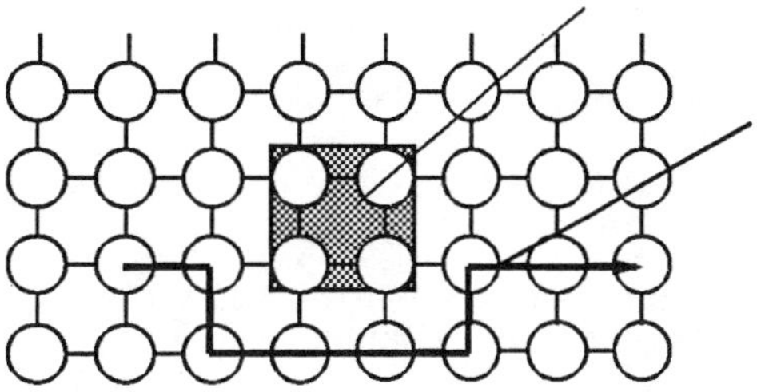

Figure 7: A packet can be routed around convex faulty regions. A packet might get trapped by concave faulty regions.

Deactivating nodes To assure that the faulty regions are convex, despite arbitrary channel failures, nodes deactivate themselves and all of their channels (by telling their neighbors) according to the following rule:

Faulty channel marking rule: For any two dimensions, d_i and d_j, $i \neq j$ if a node has channels marked as faulty in both d_i and d_j, mark all other channels as faulty. Channels which lead to the boundary are counted as faulty for the purposes of this algorithm. If a node has all of its channels marked faulty, it deactivates itself.

Some convex and non-convex faulty regions are shown in Figure 8. Our marking scheme will reduce the number of nodes available, however this may be a reasonable compromise for minimal increase in router complexity to support fault tolerance. Devising a routing scheme which maintains maximal connectivity and deadlock-freedom requires non-local information and perhaps programmable routing tables. The incorporation of such features is likely to significantly reduce router speed.

Misrouting and Deadlock Freedom

Theorem 2: Fault-tolerant, planar-adaptive routing is deadlock-free.

Lemma 2.1: Fault tolerant,planar-adaptive routing is deadlock-free within an adaptive plane.

Proof of Lemma 2.1:

Consider adaptive plane A_i. Misrouting only occurs when a message is forced to "overshoot" its destination in d_{i+1}. Overshoot in dimension d_i does not occur if the d_i distance ever reaches zero because then the packet would pass into plane A_{i+1}. Consider the two adaptive networks in the plane:

Increasing: $d_{i,2}+, d_{i+1,0}$

[5] This must be possible, as faulty regions are convex.

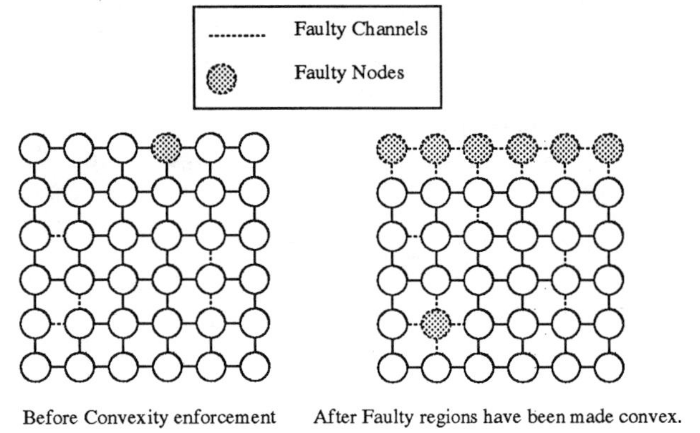

Figure 8: The deactivation removes any concave features and makes then convex. The picture illustrates the cases of a single faulty channel, a pair of faulty channels in the same dimension, a pair of faulty channels in different dimensions and a faulty node on the boundary.

Decreasing: $d_{i,2}-, d_{i+1,1}$

Without loss of generality, assume we are in the increasing network and we overshoot increasing d_{i+1}. Overshooting in d_{i+1} adds no additional dependences between virtual channels, as routing continues in the $d_{i,2}+$, $d_{i+1,0}+$. When we reach the end of the d_{i+1} edge of the faulty region, we resume routing in d_i+ towards the destination. Upon reaching the other side of the faulty region, we begin to correct our overshoot by routing in $d_{i+1,0}-$. All of this routing occurs in the increasing network (virtual channels $d_{i,2}+, d_{i+1,0}$). No new dependences have been added that did not exist in the network with no faults. Therefore, no deadlocks can have been introduced. By symmetry, this argument applies to both the increasing and decreasing networks. Thus fault-tolerant, planar-adaptive routing is deadlock free within an adaptive plane. □

Proof of Theorem 2:

By Lemma 2.1, fault-tolerant, planar-adaptive routing is deadlock-free within each adaptive plane. As in the fault-free case, packets only pass from lower-numbered adaptive planes to higher ones. Therefore, fault-tolerant, planar-adaptive routing is deadlock-free. □

Theorem 3: Fault-tolerant, planar-adaptive routing will route packets to all non-faulty nodes in the presence of convex faulty regions.

Lemma 3.1: In the presence of convex faulty regions, within each adaptive plane, A_i, planar-adaptive routing eventually reduces the distance to the destination in d_i to zero. This assures that packets eventually make progress to the next adaptive plane.

Proof of Lemma 3.1:

If there are no faults, the proof follows from the monotonic reduction in d_i or d_{i+1} distance with each routing step. Eventually, the d_i distance is reduced to zero.

If there are faults, misrouting may cause the d_{i+1} distance to increase temporarily. However the d_i distance is monotonic non-increasing. This can be seen from the routing algorithm within an adaptive plane. However,

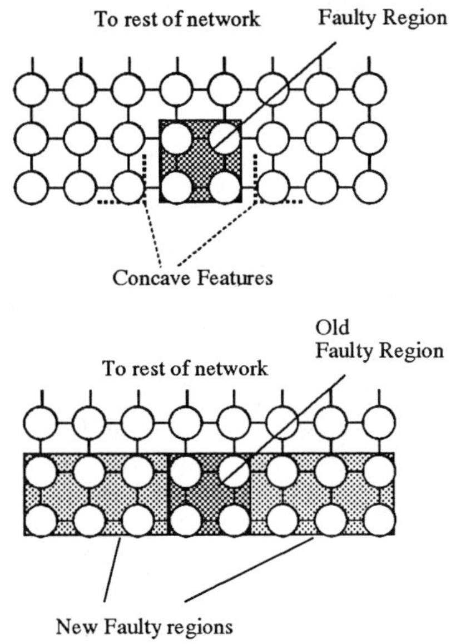

Figure 9: A faulty region which abuts the boundary of a k-ary n-cube with no wraparounds forms a concave feature. Additional nodes will be deactivated by our convexity-ensuring algorithm.

for each misrouting to circumvent a faulty region, the d_i distance decreases by at least one. Each misrouting requires at most $k-1$ steps (the maximum distance in one dimension). We cannot hit the boundary, as such would be a concave feature (see Figure 9). Faulty regions are convex, so they must have a corner. When the corner is reached, turning and routing in d_i reduces the d_i distance by at least one. Thus the d_i distance must be reduced by at least one for each k routing steps. A packet can only experience k misroutings in one plane, so the maximum number routing steps in one adaptive plane is k^2. The lemma is proved. □

Proof of Theorem 3:

Assume there exists a non-faulty node p that the fault-tolerant, planar-adaptive routing cannot reach. That means at some stage we are blocked from making progress towards the destination. By Lemma 3.1, routing in each adaptive plane A_i must complete successfully within k^2 routing steps. Successful completion implies that the distance in dimension d_i is reduced to zero, and it never again increases. The one exception to this rule is d_0, which we reuse in the final adaptive plane A_{n-1}. This case is considered below. Thus at the end of $(n-1)*k^2$ steps, are guaranteed to have routed successfully in all dimensions except d_{n-1}.

In the final adaptive plane (A_{n-1}), by Lemma 3.1 routing will successfully reduce the d_{n-1} distance to zero. However, if after doing so, we cannot reach p, it must be that we are blocked by faults in d_0. When we entered A_{n-1}, the d_0 distance was zero. Because our faulty regions are convex, we know that any errors introduced in d_0 are immediately correctable on the other side of the faulty region. Thus the only time that we route successfully in d_{n-1}, yet cannot correct d_0 is if the destination node lies within a faulty region. This means that node p must be faulty. This contradicts our assumption. Therefore, fault-tolerant planar adaptive routing will route packets to all non-faulty nodes in the presence of convex faulty regions. □

Livelock freedom Supporting fault tolerance requires the introduction of misrouting. If packets can move away from their destinations, there is a possibility of livelock.

Theorem 4: Planar-adaptive routing is livelock-free.

Proof of Theorem 4:

Each packet makes progress towards its destination. The maximum length of any misrouting is k, the extent of the network in any one dimension. For each k misrouting steps in d_{i+1}, the packet makes at least one step towards its destination in dimension in d_i. Since all packets are guaranteed to make progress towards their destination, there can be no livelock. □

As the scale and application domain of parallel machines continue to increase, fault-tolerance is of growing importance. Planar-adaptive routing supports the implementation of fault-tolerance with several desirable characteristics. First, there is virtually no overhead when systems are operating fault-free. Second, the routing scheme in the presence of faults remains simple, so good performance is possible. Finally, the reconfiguration algorithm for nodes and their channels is simple and use simple, local operations to ensure that all faulty regions in the network are convex.

6 Order-Preserving Packet Transmission

For some classes of traffic, preserving packet transmission order is important. Landin and Haridi showed that in-order packet delivery, or "race-free" networks can significantly reduce the number of packets required to implement serialization protocols for coherent shared memory [16]. Not only does the lesser packet requirement reduce network loading, it also may improve a critical performance feature, memory operation latency, by eliminating waits for acknowledgements in the protocol. In a number of other shared-memory protocols, preserving message-transmission order may also simplify the protocol and/or improve its performance [2, 10].

Our minimal, adaptive routing algorithms support both in-order packet delivery and adaptive, unordered packet delivery simultaneously. All traffic must be specified as ordered or unordered. Planar-adaptive routing guarantees in-order packet delivery for the ordered traffic both in the fault-free case, and in the presence of static faults[6]. For simplicity, we assume only one "virtual lane" [7] per virtual channel, so packets routed along a single path cannot pass each other. In a multi-lane virtual channel system, passing can be prevented by limiting the ordered traffic for each node to one lane.

In any network that uses multipath routing, preserving packet transmission order is difficult. Selecting paths dynamically, as in adaptive routing systems only worsens the situation. Data networks such as the Arpanet use packet sequence numbers and reordering (message reassembly). Such schemes are impractical in multiprocessor routing networks as maintaining sequence numbers for hundreds or thousands of nodes, both incoming and outgoing, is expensive. Further, the reassembly control and buffer space impose a significant hardware overhead.

[6]The set of faulty channels is assumed not to be changing during the packet routing.

Order Preserving, Planar-adaptive routing:

This algorithm applies for networks with no faulty channels. Route as in planar-adaptive routing algorithm, with the following change to the low-level algorithm:

1. In adaptive plane A_i, only route in d_i.

This change reduces the planar-adaptive scheme to dimension-order routing. It is more restrictive than the planar-adaptive algorithm, so our network is guaranteed to be deadlock free, even in the presence of unordered, adaptive traffic. Informally, since dimension-order routing uses only one path between each source and destination, packets traveling along the same path cannot pass each other, so transmission order is preserved.

Order Preserving, Fault-tolerant, Planar-adaptive routing:

This algorithm applies to networks with a static set of faulty channels, guaranteed to be in convex regions as described above.

High-level Route as in Fault-tolerant, planar-adaptive routing, with the following modified low-level routing algorithm. The only change is shown in italics. Note also that in step 4, return to step 1 now refers to our modified step 1.

Low-level For each adaptive plane, A_i, route the packet as follows.

Route as in the fault-tolerant, planar-adaptive algorithm with the following change to step 1, the other steps remain the same.

1. If not blocked by fault, *route in* d_i.

Since we have only modified the algorithm to bias our "adaptive" choices, the network is still deadlock-free and guaranteed to deliver all messages.

Theorem 5: The order-preserving, fault-tolerant, planar adaptive routing algorithm preserves message transmission order. (In the proof, we refer to it as simply the "routing algorithm").

Proof of Theorem 5:

The routing algorithm specifies a unique path through the network for each source-destination pair. At each step of the routing algorithm, there is no choice in which channel the packet will be routed in next. Since there is a single path, and packets on the same path may not pass each other, in-order packet delivery is assured. □

The planar-adaptive routing scheme can be generalized to support both in-order and out-of-order packet delivery traffic simultaneously. Under such conditions, deadlock and livelock freedom is still assured. The motivation for this is simple. In many cases, implicit synchronization may render the preservation of packet transmission order unnecessary. Such traffic should profit from the full advantage of adaptive routing. In other cases, as we have discussed, the preservation of transmission order makes an important difference in algorithm and communication efficiency. A particularly important case is implementing memory coherence protocols.

7 Implementation Issues

Planar-adaptive routing is of practical significance. Restricting the adaptivity reduces the hardware cost of adaptive routing by reducing the number of virtual channels required to prevent deadlock. Fewer virtual channels may allow the construction of faster routers (fewer buffer loads to drive), or the additional hardware available may be used to incorporate other performance enhancing features such as more "virtual lanes" [7].

Planar-adaptive routing is relatively low cost. Compared to Linder and Harden's scheme, planar-adaptive routing requires significantly fewer virtual channels. Planar adaptive routing requires only three buffers per physical channel, allowing the construction of very small, fast routers. In addition, the overall hardware resources consumed by the router will be smaller, broadening the applicability of the routers.

Planar-adaptive routers allow significantly lower switching complexity. The planar-adaptive algorithm allows an internal router organization without large crossbars. Even without considering the overhead for deadlock-prevention, a fully adaptive router must be able to connect each input to $n-1$ outputs. This is necessary to allow routing in arbitrary dimensions with equal speed. Supporting the symmetric adaptivity with high performance usually implies a number of nxn crossbars – one for each virtual network. See Figure 10. and the switch complexity. As shown in Figure 11, the switching hardware in a planar-adaptive routing can be partitioned into smaller crossbars of size 4x4. This significantly reduces the amount of hardware required and should reduce the time to setup and drive data across the switches. Low connectivity requirements also make it possible to use organizations which allow the router performance to be further optimized for high-speed, low latency performance [9, 8].

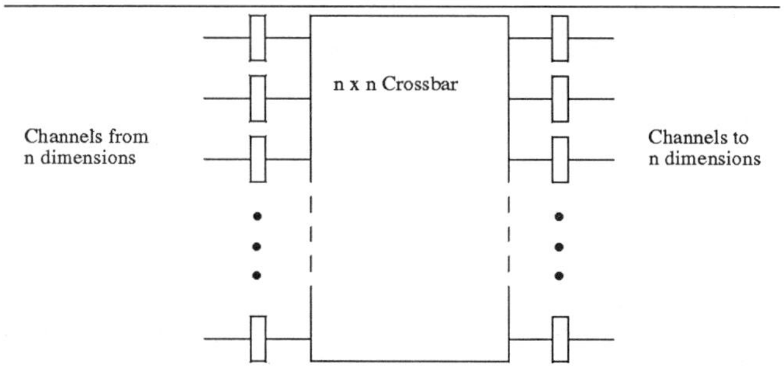

Figure 10: The minimal connectivity requirements for a fully adaptive router in a k-ary n-cube requires at least nxn connectivity. This is shown here as a crossbar.

The extensions to planar-adaptive routing for fault tolerance and packet ordering add only slightly to the router complexity. A single bit in message headers can be used to tag packets that are currently undergoing misrouting. The routing logic examines the tag when

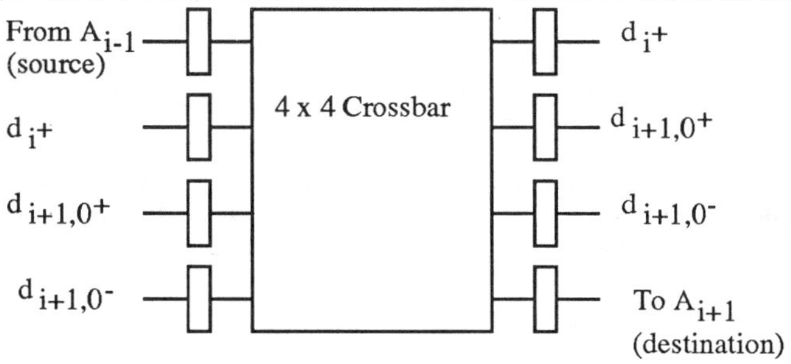

Figure 11: The planar adaptive router module for A_i. It only requires a fixed connectivity of $4x4$, permitting a smaller crossbar. A planar adaptive router can be built by composing such modules.

selecting paths and uses that and a simple routing function to make routing decisions. As in the fault-tolerant case, the messages which require in-order transmission are tagged as such and the tag serves as an input to the routing logic. The tag simply biases all adaptive choices to a preferred dimension, reducing the routing to something close to dimension-order routing.

One pragmatic concern in adaptive routing techniques concerns the encoding of destination information into packet headers. For packet routers to have single-cycle node latency, they must receive all routing inputs as soon as the message begins to arrive. In addition, they must make routing decisions in a single cycle. In fully-adaptive routers, the routing inputs may include the entire destination address, not just a few dimensions. Fitting the entire address into a single cycle channel transfer (many networks have one or two byte-wide channels) is difficult. Planar-adaptive routing limits the routing inputs to only two dimensions at a time. Fitting two dimensions of information into a single cycle channel transfer is much easier. As a packet is routed in successive adaptive planes, different information comes to the front of the message header as routing information becomes unnecessary and is stripped off.

8 Discussion and Conclusions

We have presented a simple class of adaptive routers for k-ary n-cubes, called *planar-adaptive* routers. These routers are provably deadlock-free and simple enough for high-performance implementation. Specifically, their virtual channel requirements are fixed and do not grow as the dimension of the network is increased. Planar-adaptive routing can be used to build adaptive networks for meshes of arbitrary dimension with only three virtual channels. This is less than the exponential number of virtual channels required by the Linder-Harden scheme even at $n = 3$, a three-dimensional network. If higher-dimensional networks are considered, planar adaptive routers are *much* simpler. In addition, restricting the adaptivity in routing also allows the router switches to be partitioned. Not only does this reduce their cost, but it makes it possible to tune them for low-latency and high speed.

We have also described several simple extensions to the basic planar adaptive router. These extensions support fault-tolerantand order-preserving packet transmission. Both extensions require minimal hardware support, no additional virtual channels, and are provably deadlock and livelock-free.

Many parametric questions remain for planar-adaptive routers. How should dimensions be ordered, particularly, relative to allocation practices. How does the limited adaptivity interact with various communication patterns? Can extra resources be used to further improve network performance by adding virtual-channel flow control ideas? Is such necessary, given planar adaptivity? Can these networks support large and small packet traffic simultaneously?

Deeper evaluation of planar-adaptive must involve simulation and implementation of the routing algorithms due to their complex dynamics. We are currently pursuing register-level simulation as well as prototype hardware construction. Both random traffic, synthetic loads, and actual packet traffic loads will be used to evaluate network performance. In addition, the development of careful characterization of the cost of various extensions will be pursued with great interest.

Beyond the basic evaluation of planar-adaptive routing lies a deeper question. How much adaptivity do routing networks need? We have described only a single instance of a family of adaptive routing algorithms. The family can be extended naturally to higher degrees of adaptivity (allowing routing in the f-flat of a n-dimensional space for f degress of adaptivity). The planar-adaptive case allows routing in a 2-flat of an n-dimensional network.

Another unanswered question is how to best make use of the flexibility and control offered by planar-adaptive routing. A problem in current day, mesh-based multicomputers is the sharing of communication resources amongst multiprogrammed jobs. Sharing such resources can lead to unpredictable performance. The ideas in planar-adaptive routing provides a way of allowing flexible use of network resources, yet restricting their use.

References

[1] Anant Agarwal. Limits on interconnection network performance. *IEEE Transactions on Parallel and Distributed Systems*, 2(4):398–412, 1991.

[2] David Chaiken, Craig Fields, Kiyoshi Kurihara, and Anant Agarwal. Directory-based cache coherence in large-scale multiprocessors. *IEEE Computer*, June 1990.

[3] W. Dally and C. Seitz. Deadlock-free message routing in multiprocessor interconnection networks. *IEEE Transactions on Computers*, C-36(5), 1987.

[4] W. J. Dally. Performance analysis of *k*-ary *n*-cube interconnection networks. *IEEE Transactions on Computers*, 39(6), June 1990.

[5] W. J. Dally and H. Aoki. Deadlock-free adaptive routing in multicomputer networks using virtual channels. *IEEE Transactions on Parallel and Distributed Systems*, To appear.

[6] William J. Dally. *A VLSI Architecture for Concurrent Data Structures*. Kluwer Academic Publishers, Boston, Mass., 1987.

[7] William J. Dally. Virtual channel flow control. In *Proceedings of the 17th International Symposium on Computer Architecture*. IEEE Computer Society, 1990.

[8] William J. Dally, Andrew Chien, Stuart Fiske, Waldemar Horwat, John Keen, Michael Larivee, Rich Lethin, Peter Nuth, Scott Wills, Paul Carrick, and Greg Fyler. The j-machine: A fine-grain concurrent computer. In *Information Processing 89, Proceedings of the IFIP Congress*, pages 1147–1153, August 1989.

[9] William J. Dally and Paul Song. Design of a self-timed vlsi multicomputer communication controller. In *Proceedings of the International Conference on Computer Design*, pages 230–4. IEEE Computer Society, 1987.

[10] Michel et. al. Dubois. Synchronization, coherence and event ordering in multiprocessors. *IEEE Computer*, (9-21), February 1988.

[11] D. Gelernter. A dag-based algorithm for prevention of store-and-forward deadlock in packet networks. *IEEE Transactions on Computers*, C-30(10):709–15, October 1981.

[12] K. D. Gunther. Prevention of deadlocks in packet-switched data transport systems. *IEEE Transactions on Communications*, COM-29(4), 1981.

[13] P. Kermani and L. Kleinrock. Virtual cut-through: a new computer communications switching technique. *Computer Networks*, 3(4):267–86, 1979.

[14] S. Konstantinidou. Adaptive, minimal routing in hypercubes. In W. J. Dally, editor, *Proceedings of the 6th MIT Conference on Advanced Research in VLSI*, pages 139–53. MIT Press, 1990.

[15] S. Konstantinidou and L. Snyder. Chaos router: architecture and performance. In *Proceedings of the International Symposium on Computer Architecture*, pages 212–21, 1991.

[16] A. Landin, E. Hagersten, and S. Haridi. Race-free interconnection networks and multiprocessor consistency. In *Proceedings of the International Symposium on Computer Architecture*, pages 106–115, 1991.

[17] D. Linder and J. Harden. An adaptive and fault tolerant wormhole routing strategy for k-ary n-cubes. *IEEE Transactions on Computers*, C-40(1):2–12, January 1991.

[18] J. Ngai. *A Framework for Adaptive Routing in Multicomputer Networks*. PhD thesis, California Institute of Technology, Computer Science Department, 1989. Caltech-CS-TR-89-09.

[19] J. Ngai and C. Seitz. A framework for adaptive routing in multicomputer networks. In *Proceedings of the 1989 ACM Symposium on Parallel Algorithms and Architectures*, 1989.

[20] S. Lillevik, Intel Corporation. Touchstone program overview. In *Proceedings of the Fifth Distributed Memory Computers Conference*, 1990.

[21] Charles L. Seitz. The cosmic cube. *Communications of the ACM*, 28(1):22–33, January 1985.

[22] Charles L. Seitz, William C. Athas, Charles M. Flaig, Alain J. Martin, Jakov Seizovic, Craig S. Steele, and Wen-King Su. The architecture and programming of the ametek series 2010 multicomputer. In *Proceedings of the Third Conference on Hypercube Computers*, pages 33–6. Association for Computing Machinery, ACM Press, January 1988.

The Turn Model for Adaptive Routing *

Christopher J. Glass and *Lionel M. Ni*

Advanced Computer Systems Laboratory
Department of Computer Science
Michigan State University
East Lansing, MI 48824-1027
{glass,ni}@cps.msu.edu

Abstract

We present a model for designing wormhole routing algorithms that are deadlock free, livelock free, minimal or nonminimal, and maximally adaptive. A unique feature of this model is that it is not based on adding physical or virtual channels to network topologies (though it can be applied to networks with extra channels). Instead, the model is based on analyzing the directions in which packets can turn in a network and the cycles that the turns can form. Prohibiting just enough turns to break all of the cycles produces routing algorithms that are deadlock free, livelock free, minimal or nonminimal, and maximally adaptive for the network. In this paper, we focus on the two most common network topologies for wormhole routing, n-dimensional meshes and k-ary n-cubes, without extra channels. In an n-dimensional mesh, just a quarter of the turns must be prohibited to prevent deadlock. The remaining three quarters of the turns permit partial adaptiveness in routing. Partially adaptive routing algorithms are described for 2D meshes, n-dimensional meshes, k-ary n-cubes, and hypercubes. Simulations of partially adaptive and nonadaptive routing algorithms for 2D meshes and hypercubes show that which algorithm has the lowest latencies and highest sustainable throughput depends on the pattern of message traffic. For nonuniform traffic, partially adaptive routing algorithms perform better than nonadaptive ones.

1 Introduction

Direct networks have become a popular interconnection architecture for constructing large-scale multiprocessors, such as multicomputers and scalable shared-memory multiprocessors. Direct networks offer massive parallelism [1, 2, 3, 4, 5] and are far more scalable than other approaches to multiprocessor interconnection. Systems based on direct networks are organized as ensembles of nodes, where each node has its own processor, local memory, and other supportive devices. The nodes communicate by sending messages. The network connects each node directly to only a few other nodes, its *neighbors*. Which nodes are neighbors is defined by the *topology* of the network. A node communicates with a node that is not its neighbor by sending a message through one of its neighbors. To handle the complexities of routing messages in the direct network, each node often has a *router*. The router controls local input and output channels, which connect it to local devices, and network input and output channels, which connect it to neighboring routers.

*This work was supported in part by the NSF grant ECS-88-14027.

Wormhole routing [6] is becoming a popular switching technique in direct networks. Wormhole routing switches a message along a network by first dividing the message into packets and the packets into *flow control digits* or *flits*. It then routes the flits in each packet through the network in a pipeline fashion. *Header flits* contain all of the routing information for a packet and lead each packet through the network. When the header flits reach a router that has no suitable output channel available, all of the flits in the packet wait where they are for a suitable channel to become available. One of the attractions of wormhole routing is that each router requires just enough buffer space to store a few flits for each channel. The *store-and-forward* and *virtual cut-through* switching techniques [7] require enough buffer space to store an entire packet for each channel. Another attraction of wormhole routing is that its communication latencies are low. In the absence of contention, the latencies for store-and-forward are proportional to the *product* of packet length and distance to travel [8]. The latencies for wormhole routing, virtual cut-through, and *circuit switching*, on the other hand, are proportional to the *sum* of packet length and distance to travel. Wormhole routing also has some advantages over circuit switching. Channel reservation and release are an integral part of wormhole routing, but are separate phases in circuit switching. Wormhole routing also permits routers to replicate flits and output them over multiple channels, making multicast and broadcast communications possible [9, 1].

The majority of network topologies for wormhole routing are *n-dimensional meshes* and *k-ary n-cubes*, particularly low-dimensional meshes and *hypercubes*. A 2D mesh is used in the Intel Touchstone DELTA [2], the Intel Paragon, and the Symult 2010 [10]; a 3D mesh is used in the MIT J-machine [11], and the Caltech MOSAIC; and a hypercube is used in the nCUBE-2 [1]. Formally, an n-dimensional mesh has $k_0 \times k_1 \times \cdots \times k_{n-2} \times k_{n-1}$ nodes, k_i nodes along each dimension i, where $k_i \geq 2$. Each node $\mathbf{X}$ is identified by n coordinates, $(x_0, x_1, \ldots, x_{n-2}, x_{n-1})$, where $0 \leq x_i \leq k_i - 1$ for $0 \leq i \leq n-1$. Two nodes $\mathbf{X}$ and $\mathbf{Y}$ are neighbors if and only if $x_i = y_i$ for all i, $0 \leq i \leq n-1$, except one, j, where $y_j = x_j \pm 1$. Thus, nodes have from n to $2n$ neighbors, depending on their location in the mesh. In a k-ary n-cube [8], all nodes have the same number of neighbors. The definition of a k-ary n-cube differs from that of an n-dimensional mesh in that all of the k_i's are equal to k and two nodes $\mathbf{X}$ and $\mathbf{Y}$ are neighbors if and only if $x_i = y_i$ for all i, $0 \leq i \leq n-1$, except one, j, where $y_j = (x_j \pm 1) \bmod k$. The change to modular arithmetic in the definition adds wraparound channels to the k-ary n-cube, giving it symmetry. Every node has n neighbors if $k = 2$ and $2n$ neighbors if $k > 2$. Another topology with symmetry is the hypercube, which is a special case of both n-dimensional meshes and k-ary n-cubes. A hypercube is an n-dimensional mesh in which $k_i = 2$ for $0 \leq i \leq n-1$ or a 2-ary n-cube.

Meshes and k-ary n-cubes are popular in part because their regular topologies simplify routing. In general, low-dimensional meshes are preferred over high-dimensional meshes and k-ary n-cubes. Low-dimensional meshes have low, fixed node degrees, which makes them more scalable than high-dimensional meshes and k-ary n-cubes. They also have fewer channels and higher channel bandwidth per bisection density and have lower contention and blocking latencies, which result in lower communication latencies and higher hot-spot throughputs [8]. On the other hand, high-dimensional meshes and k-ary n-cubes have some advantages that partially offset those of low-dimensional meshes. They tend to have lower diameters, which shortens path lengths. They also have more paths between pairs of nodes, which permits more fault tolerance. Finally, the symmetry of k-ary n-cubes can make it easier to spread packet traffic more evenly.

Algorithms for routing message packets through a network topology should have three characteristics: low communication latency, high network throughput, and ease of implementation in VLSI. Features contributing to ease of implementation are little hardware for channels, buffers, and control logic. Features contributing to low latency and high throughput are freedom from deadlock, freedom from indefinite postponement, freedom from livelock, fault tolerance, routing packets along short paths, spreading packet traffic evenly, and routing packets adaptively. Many of these terms require some definition (partly because they have been used in different ways by different authors). *Deadlock* occurs when a packet waits for an event that cannot happen. For example, a packet may wait for a network resource to be released by a packet that is, in turn, waiting for the first packet to release some resource. In wormhole routing, such a *circular wait* condition will cause deadlock, because a packet holds resources while waiting and excludes other packets from acquiring the held resources. *Indefinite postponement* is similar to deadlock, but occurs when a packet waits for an event that can happen but never does. For example, a packet may wait forever to acquire a network resource for which other packets are always competing successfully. The issue here is *fairness*. Both deadlock and indefinite postponement can stop a packet from being injected into a network or from moving once it is in the network. In contrast, livelock does not stop a packet's movement, but rather its progress toward the destination. *Livelock* occurs when the routing of a packet never leads it to its destination. Livelock is possible only when routing is *adaptive* (not along a predetermined path) and *nonminimal* (possibly away from or equidistant to the destination at times). *Minimal* routing, in contrast, restricts packets to shortest paths. Although minimal routing may initially sound more promising, nonminimal routing provides better fault tolerance.

Of these features, the most important is freedom from deadlock. Deadlock can keep many or all packets from reaching their destinations and occurs readily unless a routing algorithm includes preventive measures. Indefinite postponement and livelock are less likely to occur and are generally easier to prevent. Adaptiveness is also an important feature, because it contributes to several of the other features [12]. It provides alternative paths for packets that encounter continuously blocked channels, faulty hardware, or hot spots in traffic patterns.

The drawback to previous routing algorithms for meshes and k-ary n-cubes is that they either sacrifice adaptiveness for deadlock freedom or achieve adaptiveness and deadlock freedom at the expense of adding physical or virtual channels. The popular *xy routing algorithm* for 2D meshes [10, 2] routes a packet first along the x dimension (dimension 0) and then along the y dimension (dimension 1). The *e-cube routing algorithm* for hypercubes [13] routes a packet first along the lowest dimension and then along higher and higher dimensions. Ordering the dimensions in this way ensures that the xy and e-cube algorithms avoid deadlock, but it also ensures nonadaptiveness. Another popular way to avoid deadlock, and possibly to provide adaptiveness, is to add *virtual channels* to networks. Dally and Seitz [14] introduced the idea for nonadaptive routing, and several researchers [15, 12, 16] have extended it to adaptive routing. Adding a virtual channel to a physical channel is less expensive than adding a new physical channel, but it is not free. It involves adding buffer space and control logic to the two routers at the ends of the physical channel so that the virtual channels can share the physical channel and routers. It also reduces the bandwidths of the virtual channels already sharing the physical channel. An advantage of adding virtual or physical channels, however, is that they can support routing algorithms with a high degree of adaptiveness. A minimal, *fully adaptive* algorithm can route packets along any of the shortest paths in the topology. Dally [17] and Linder and Harden [16] describe such an algorithm for 2D meshes. A *partially adaptive* algorithm cannot route packets along every shortest path.

This paper presents a model for designing wormhole routing algorithms that are deadlock free, livelock free, minimal or nonminimal, and maximally adaptive for networks. A unique feature of this model is that it is not based on adding physical or virtual channels to network topologies (though it can be applied to networks with extra channels). Instead, the model is based on analyzing the directions in which packets can turn in a network and the cycles that the turns can form. Section 2 presents the model in general terms and applies it to n-dimensional meshes without extra channels. Sections 3, 4, and 5 describe many of the partially adaptive routing algorithms derived for 2D meshes, n-dimensional meshes and k-ary n-cubes, and hypercubes respectively. Simulations studying the performance of partially adaptive and nonadaptive algorithms in 2D meshes and hypercubes for different patterns of message traffic are described in Section 6. Section 7 concludes the paper.

2 Turn Model

Deadlock in wormhole routing is caused by packets waiting on each other in a cycle. Figure 1 shows one way that deadlock can occur in a 2D mesh. Four packets travelling in different directions try to turn left and wind up in a circular wait. If only one of the packets had not turned, this deadlock would have been avoided. This suggests that, by prohibiting certain turns in a network, a routing algorithm might prevent deadlock altogether. The routing algorithm would have to prohibit at least one turn in each of the many possible cycles. At the same time, the algorithm would have to leave a path between every pair of nodes. In addition, it should not prohibit more turns than necessary; otherwise, the adaptiveness of the algorithm would be reduced.

To solve this problem of designing wormhole routing algorithms that are deadlock free and maximally adaptive for a network, we propose the *turn model*. The model involves analyzing the directions in which packets can turn in the network and the cycles that the turns can form. It prohibits just enough turns to break all of the cycles. Routing algorithms that employ the remaining turns are deadlock free, livelock free, minimal or nonminimal, and maximally adaptive for the network. The model produces partially adaptive routing algorithms for such basic topologies as mesh-connected, k-ary n-cube, hexagonal, octagonal, and cube-connected cycle networks. Adding extra physical or virtual channels to the topologies allows the model to produce fully adaptive routing algorithms, the topic of a forthcoming paper [18]. The current paper focuses on improving performance without the expense of extra channels, as might be done by changing the routing algorithms in existing routers.

The steps of the turn model are given in more detail below. Unless specified otherwise, the term "channel" will be used to indicate either a virtual or physical channel.

1. Partition the channels in the network into sets according to the directions in which they route packets. If each node has v channels in a physical direction, treat these channels as being in v distinct *virtual directions* and divide them into v distinct sets accordingly. Put any wraparound channels (for tori) in a separate set to be incorporated during Step 5.

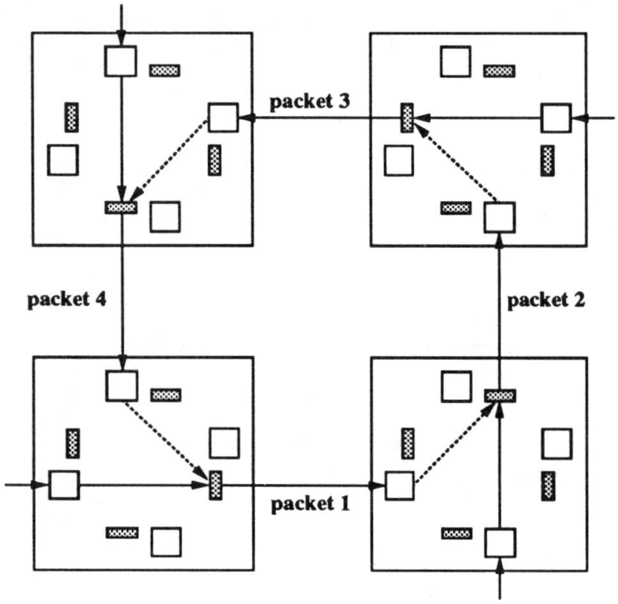

Figure 1. A wormhole deadlock involving four routers and four packets in a 2D mesh.

2. Identify the possible turns from one virtual direction to another, ignoring 180-degree and 0-degree turns. A 0-degree turn is only possible when there are multiple channels in one direction. It represents a transition from one set of channels to another when the two sets route packets in the same physical direction, but different virtual directions.

3. Identify the cycles that these abstract turns can form. Generally, identifying the simplest cycles in each plane of the topology is adequate.

4. Prohibit one turn in each abstract cycle so as to prevent deadlock. The turns must be chosen carefully in order to break every possible cycle, including complex cycles not identified in Step 3. A useful approach is first to break the cycles in each plane and then to check whether this allows more complex cycles.

5. Incorporate as many turns as possible from the set of wraparound channels, without reintroducing cycles. At least one turn for each wraparound channel can always be incorporated.

6. Incorporate as many 180-degree and 0-degree turns as possible, without reintroducing cycles.

Routing algorithms that route packets along the sets of channels identified in Step 1 and use only the turns from one set to another allowed by Steps 4, 5, and 6 are deadlock free, livelock free, minimal or nonminimal, and maximally adaptive for the network. They are deadlock free because breaking all of the cycles prevents circular waits. (We demonstrate deadlock freedom for individual routing algorithms later.) Preventing circular waits in this way means that it is possible to number the channels in the network so that each algorithm routes every packet along channels in strictly decreasing (or increasing) order [14]. This, together with the fact that a network contains a finite number of channels, means that a packet will reach its destination after a limited number of hops. Thus, routing is livelock free. Routing is maximally adaptive for the network because the model prohibits the minimum number of turns from one direction to another. The algorithms the model produces will also be nonminimal, but can easily be made minimal by modifying them to use channels only when they lead toward the destination. Nonminimal routing is more adaptive and fault tolerant, though.

To make the steps of the turn model clearer, the remainder of this section applies them to n-dimensional meshes, starting with 2D meshes. For 2D meshes, we first simplify the terminology used in the definition of n-dimensional meshes. Dimensions 0 and 1 become x and y. The lengths of the dimensions, k_0 and k_1, become m and n. The directions $-x$, $+x$, $-y$, and $+y$ become west, east, south, and north. From these four directions, eight 90-degree turns can be formed: left and right turns when travelling west, east, south, and north. The eight turns form two abstract cycles as shown in Figure 2. The xy routing algorithm prevents deadlock by prohibiting four of the turns (Figure 3). The remaining four turns cannot form a cycle; they also do not allow any adaptiveness. Deadlock can be prevented by prohibiting fewer than four turns, however. In fact, only two turns need to be prohibited, one from each abstract cycle, allowing for some adaptiveness in routing. Prohibiting any two turns will not prevent deadlock, however, as Figure 4 illustrates. The three left turns allowed in Figure 4a are equivalent to the prohibited right turn in Figure 4b, and the three right turns allowed in Figure 4b are equivalent to the prohibited left turn in Figure 4a. Thus, both cycles still exist and deadlock is possible (Figure 4c). Section 3 describes which pairs of turns can be prohibited to prevent deadlock and describes the partially adaptive routing algorithms based on these turns.

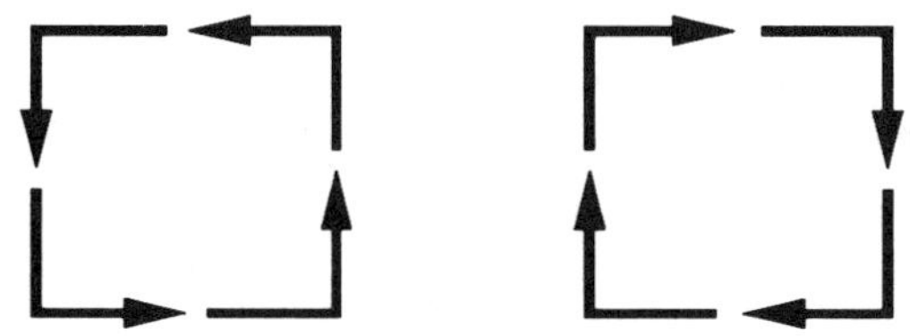

Figure 2. The possible abstract cycles and turns in a 2D mesh.

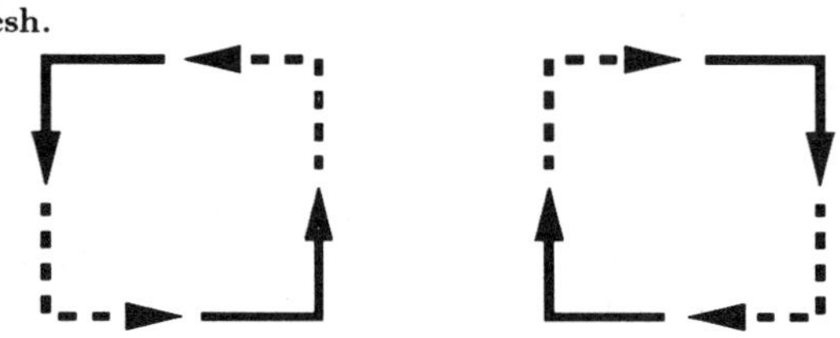

Figure 3. Only four turns (solid lines) are allowed in the xy routing algorithm.

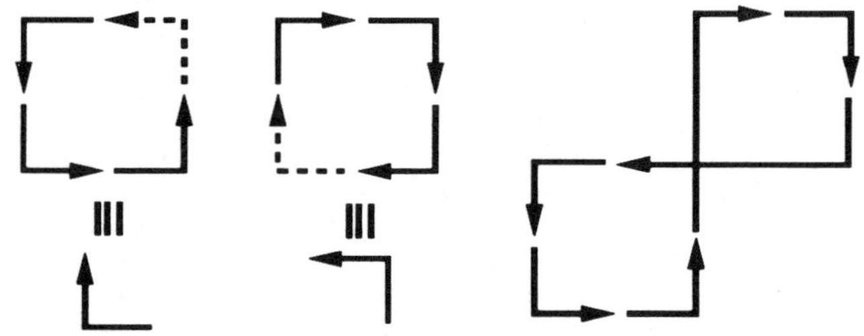

Figure 4. Six turns that complete the abstract cycles and allow deadlock.

In an n-dimensional mesh, each node has up to $2n$ input channels and $2n$ output channels. For each of these $2n$ directions, there are $2n-2$ possible 90-degree turns to a different direction, making $4n(n-1)$ total turns. These turns form two abstract cycles in each of the $n(n-1)/2$ planes, making $n(n-1)$ total cycles of four turns.

Theorem 1 *The minimum number of turns that must be prohibited to prevent deadlock in an n-dimensional mesh is $n(n-1)$, or a quarter of the possible turns.*

Proof: The $4n(n-1)$ turns in an n-dimensional mesh can be partitioned into $n(n-1)$ abstract cycles of four turns each. Each of the $n(n-1)/2$ planes contains two of these cycles. At least one of the four turns in each cycle must be prohibited in order to prevent these cycles. Therefore, prohibiting a quarter of the turns is necessary to prevent deadlock. □

In the following sections, we introduce specific partially adaptive routing algorithms based on the turn model for 2D mesh, n-dimensional mesh, k-ary n-cube, and hypercube topologies. A detailed study for the 3D mesh can be found in [19].

3 Partially Adaptive Routing in 2D Meshes

In a 2D mesh, there are four directions, eight 90-degree turns, and two abstract cycles of four turns. One turn from each cycle must be prohibited to prevent deadlock. Of the 16 different ways to prohibit these two turns, 12 prevent deadlock (see Figure 4 for a deadlock case) and three are unique if symmetry is taken into account.

3.1 West-First Routing Algorithm

Figure 5a shows one way to prohibit two turns in a 2D mesh. The prohibited turns are the two to the west. Therefore, to travel west, a packet must start out in that direction. This suggests the *west-first routing algorithm*: route a packet first west, if necessary, and then adaptively south, east, and north. Example paths for the west-first algorithm are shown in Figure 5b. In this figure, black squares represent nodes, and gray bars indicate blocked channels requiring that packets wait (dashed lines) or take alternative paths. Note that both minimal and nonminimal paths are shown.

Proof that the west-first partially adaptive algorithm is deadlock free is based on the work of Dally and Seitz [14], who show that a routing algorithm is deadlock free if the channels in the interconnection network can be numbered so that the algorithm routes every packet along channels with strictly decreasing (or increasing) numbers. Because the west-first algorithm routes packets first west and then in the other directions, we assign lower numbers to westward channels the farther west they are, and assign still lower numbers to eastward, northward, and southward channels the farther east they are.

Theorem 2 *The west-first routing algorithm is deadlock free.*

Proof: Assign each channel in the $m \times n$ mesh a two-digit number a, b in base r, where r is the greater of $3m-2$ and $n-1$. Figure 6 shows the particular numbers to assign to the channels leaving node (x, y). Figure 7 illustrates the numbering of a 4×4 mesh. To show that west-first routes every packet along channels with strictly decreasing numbers, it is sufficient to show that, for each channel into an arbitrary node, the algorithm can only route the packet out along a channel with a lower number. Figure 8 shows the four possible cases. Examination shows that, in each case, the channels used to route a packet out of a node have lower numbers than the input channel. Note that in part (c) a packet can make a 180-degree turn. This turn is only useful for nonminimal routing. □

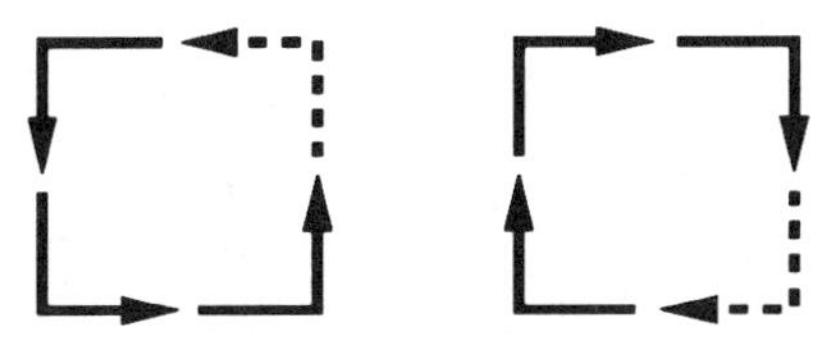

(a) The six turns allowed (solid lines) by the west-first algorithm.

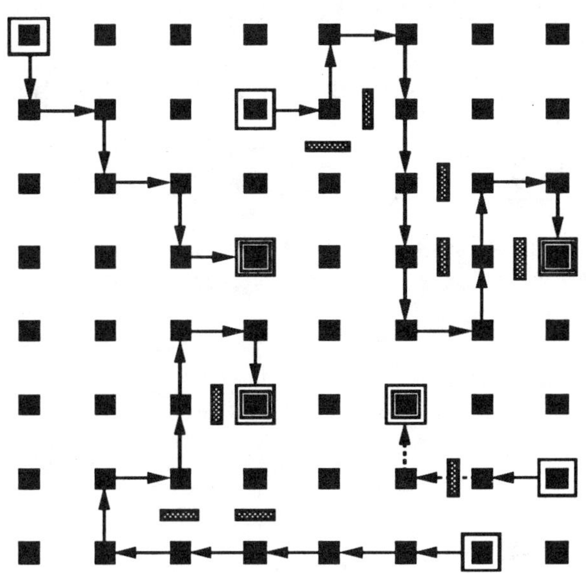

(b) Examples of the west-first algorithm in an 8×8 mesh.

Figure 5. The west-first routing algorithm for 2D meshes.

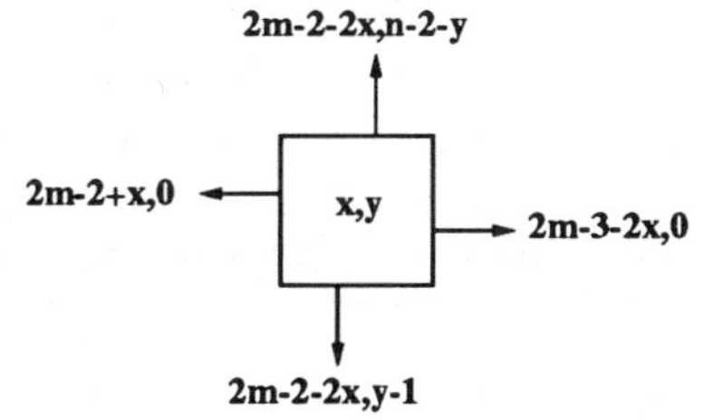

Figure 6. Numbering of the channels leaving each node (x, y) for the west-first routing algorithm.

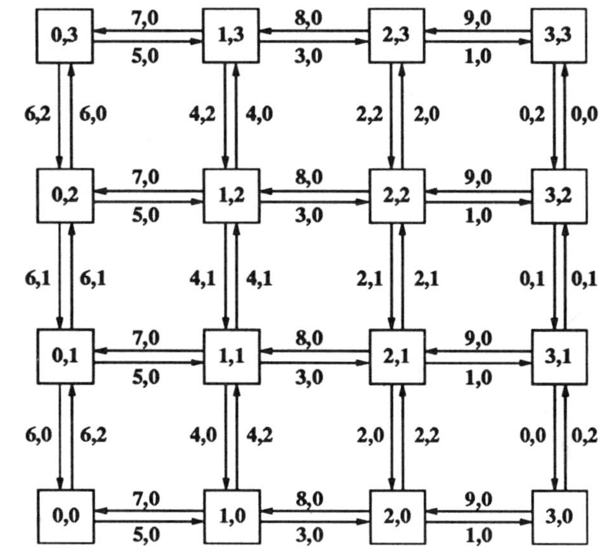

Figure 7. Numbering of a 4 × 4 mesh for the west-first routing algorithm.

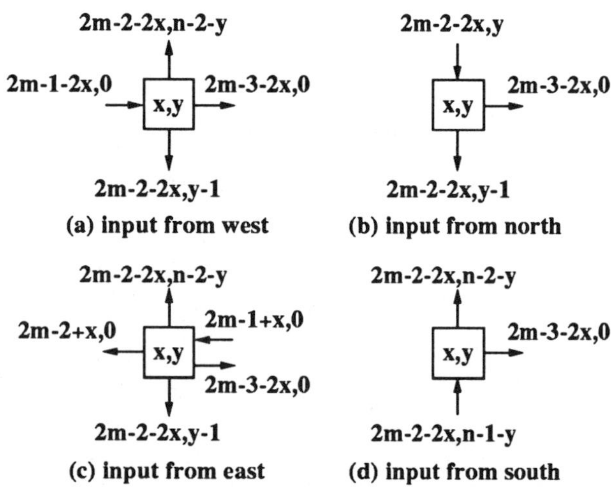

Figure 8. For each input channel, the output channels allowed by the west-first routing algorithm have lower numbers.

3.2 North-Last Routing Algorithm

Figure 9a shows another way to prohibit two turns in a 2D mesh. The prohibited turns are the two when travelling north. Therefore, a packet should only travel north when that is the last direction it needs to travel. This suggests the *north-last routing algorithm*: route a packet first adaptively west, south, and east, and then north. Example paths for the north-last algorithm are shown in Figure 9b.

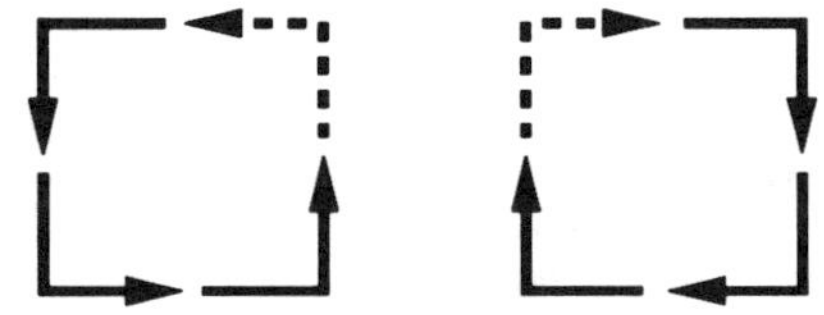

(a) The six turns allowed (solid lines) by the north-last algorithm.

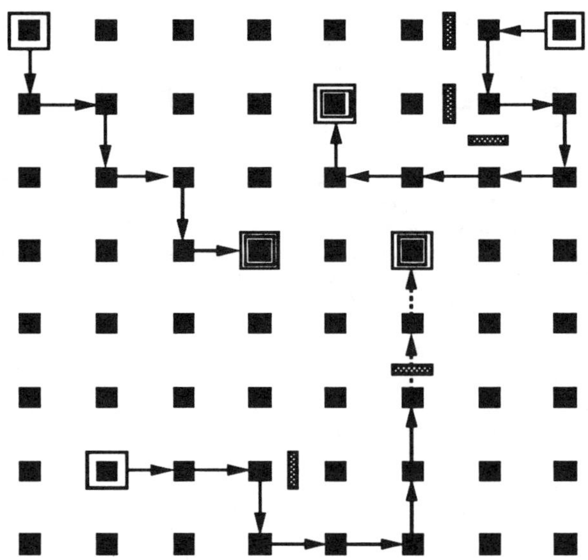

(b) Examples of the north-last algorithm in an 8 × 8 mesh.

Figure 9. The north-last routing algorithm for 2D meshes.

Theorem 3 *The north-last routing algorithm is deadlock free.*

Proof: The proof is similar to that for Theorem 2. Rotate Figures 6 and 7 counterclockwise 90 degrees, and reverse the directions of the channels. The figures now show that north-last routes every packet along channels with strictly increasing numbers. □

3.3 Negative-First Routing Algorithm

Figure 10a shows a third way to prohibit two turns in a 2D mesh. The prohibited turns are the two from a positive direction to a negative direction. Therefore, to travel in a negative direction, a packet must start out in a negative direction. This suggests the *negative-first routing algorithm*: route a packet first adaptively west and south, and then adaptively east and north. Yantchev and Jesshope propose a similar algorithm [15], but only for minimal routing. The negative-first algorithm can be either minimal or nonminimal, the nonminimal version being more adaptive and fault tolerant. Example paths for the negative-first algorithm are shown in Figure 10b.

Theorem 4 *The negative-first routing algorithm is deadlock free.*

The proof is a special case of the one given for n-dimensional meshes in Section 4.

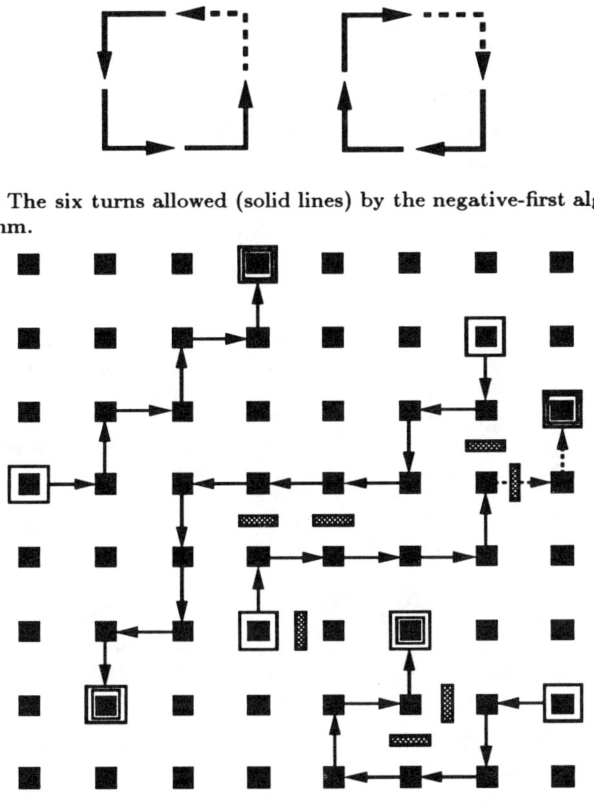

(a) The six turns allowed (solid lines) by the negative-first algorithm.

(b) Examples of the negative-first algorithm in an 8 × 8 mesh.

Figure 10. The negative-first routing algorithm for 2D meshes.

3.4 Degree of Adaptiveness

How adaptive are these partially adaptive routing algorithms? Let $S_{algorithm}$ be the number of shortest paths the algorithm allows from source node (s_x, s_y) to destination node (d_x, d_y). Also, let f be a fully adaptive algorithm, p be one of the three partially adaptive algorithms, $\Delta x = |d_x - s_x|$, and $\Delta y = |d_y - s_y|$. Then,

$$S_f = \frac{(\Delta x + \Delta y)!}{\Delta x! \Delta y!}$$

$$S_{west-first} = \begin{cases} \frac{(\Delta x+\Delta y)!}{\Delta x!\Delta y!} & \text{if } d_x \geq s_x \\ 1 & \text{otherwise} \end{cases}$$

$$S_{north-last} = \begin{cases} \frac{(\Delta x+\Delta y)!}{\Delta x!\Delta y!} & \text{if } d_y \leq s_y \\ 1 & \text{otherwise} \end{cases}$$

$$S_{negative-first} = \begin{cases} \frac{(\Delta x+\Delta y)!}{\Delta x!\Delta y!} & \text{if } (d_x \leq s_x \text{ and } d_y \leq s_y) \\ & \text{or } (d_x \geq s_x \text{ and } d_y \geq s_y) \\ 1 & \text{otherwise} \end{cases}$$

For minimal routing algorithms, the larger $S_{algorithm}$ is, the more adaptive the algorithm is. For the three partially adaptive routing algorithms, however, $S_p = 1$ for at least half of the source-destination pairs. Another measure of the degree to which a minimal routing algorithm is adaptive is the ratio $S_{algorithm}/S_f$. S_p/S_f ranges from 0 to 1, but averaged across all source-destination pairs, $S_p/S_f > 1/2$, which indicates a significant degree of adaptiveness. Note that $S_p = 1$ for a source-destination pair does not imply that algorithm p is nonadaptive for that pair. The partially adaptive algorithms all permit nonminimal routing. In the case of the negative-first algorithm, this means that routing can be adaptive even when $d_x \leq s_x$ and $d_y \geq s_y$ or when $d_x \geq s_x$ and $d_y \leq s_y$. For an illustration of this, see the bottom path in Figure 10b.

4 Partially Adaptive Routing in n-Dimensional Networks

This section describes the adaptive routing algorithms resulting from the application of the turn model to n-dimensional meshes and k-ary n-cubes. In general, these topologies are not practical unless n is small or the k's equal 2.

4.1 n-Dimensional Meshes

Of the many routing algorithms formed by prohibiting one turn per cycle, three are noteworthy for their simplicity. They are analogs of the west-first, north-last, and negative-first routing algorithms for 2D meshes. The analog of the west-first routing algorithm is the *all-but-one-negative-first routing algorithm*: route a packet first adaptively in the negative directions of all but one dimension $(n - 1)$ and then adaptively in the other directions. The analog of the north-last routing algorithm is the *all-but-one-positive-last routing algorithm*: route a packet first adaptively in the negative directions and the positive direction of one dimension (0) and then adaptively in the other directions. The analog of the negative-first routing algorithm is also called the *negative-first routing algorithm*: route a packet first adaptively in the negative directions and then adaptively in the positive directions. All of these algorithms are deadlock free, but the only proof we present is for the negative-first algorithm.

Theorem 5 *The negative-first routing algorithm for n-dimensional meshes is deadlock free.*

Proof: Let K be the sum of the k_i for an n-dimensional mesh, and let X be the sum of the x_i for any node $(x_0, x_1, \ldots, x_{n-2}, x_{n-1})$. Number each channel leaving a node in a positive direction $K - n + X$ and each channel leaving a node in a negative direction $K - n - X$. Then, if a packet enters a node when travelling in a negative direction, it enters along a channel numbered $K - n - X - 1$, which is less than $K - n - X$ and $K - n + X$, the numbers of the channels leaving the node in the negative and positive directions. If a packet enters a node when travelling in a positive direction, it enters along a channel numbered $K - n + X - 1$, which is less than $K - n + X$, the number of the channels leaving the node in the positive directions. Therefore, the negative-first algorithm routes every packet along channels with strictly increasing numbers and is deadlock free. □

The negative-first algorithm is deadlock free as a result of prohibiting just one turn per abstract cycle, the turn from a positive direction to a negative direction. Therefore, prohibiting some quarter of the turns is sufficient to prevent deadlock in an n-dimensional mesh. Combining this with Theorem 1, we have the following theorem, which supports our claim that the turn model produces maximally adaptive routing algorithms.

Theorem 6 *Prohibiting some quarter of the turns (that is, $n(n-1)$) in an n-dimensional mesh is necessary and sufficient to prevent deadlock.*

As the number of dimensions increases, the minimal partially adaptive algorithms are more likely to be able to route messages adaptively. $S_p = 1$ less often, especially when the k_i are large. But averaged across all source-destination pairs, $S_p/S_f > 1/2^{n-1}$, indicating that the degree of adaptiveness relative to fully adaptive algorithms decreases as n increases. Again, adaptiveness can be increased by nonminimal routing.

4.2 k-ary n-cubes

The partially adaptive routing algorithms for meshes can be extended to use the wraparound channels of k-ary n-cubes. One way is to allow a packet to be routed along a wraparound channel only on its first hop. To prove that the routing is still deadlock free, number the mesh channels as before and assign the wraparound channels a number that is either greater than or less than those of the mesh channels, depending on whether packets are routed along channels in strictly decreasing or increasing order in the proof. The negative-first algorithm can be extended to k-ary n-cubes in another way: classify each wraparound channel according to the direction in which it routes packets and then apply the negative-first algorithm. Thus, a node at the east edge of the mesh channels will have two channels to the west: a mesh channel to the node immediately to its west and a wraparound channel to a node at the west edge of the mesh channels. Again, the proof of deadlock freedom is a simple modification of the proof for meshes.

Note that all of these routing algorithms are strictly nonminimal. For k-ary n-cubes with $k > 4$, it is impossible to construct deadlock-free routing algorithms that are minimal without adding extra channels. This is a result of the many cycles that do not involve turns in the topology. By adding channels to a k-ary n-cube, Linder and Harden [16] construct a routing algorithm that is deadlock free, minimal, and fully adaptive. They add, however, enough channels to partition the k-ary n-cube into 2^{n-1} subnetworks with $n+1$ levels per subnetwork and k^n channels per level.

5 p-cube Routing in Hypercubes

Hypercubes are a special case of both n-dimensional meshes and k-ary n-cubes. Consequently, the partially adaptive routing algorithms for hypercubes are special cases of the algorithms for n-dimensional meshes and k-ary n-cubes. Proofs that the routing algorithms are deadlock free are corollaries of the proofs for the more general cases.

The special case of the negative-first algorithm has a particularly compact expression, the *p-cube routing algorithm*. Let **S** be the binary address of the source node for a packet, **C** be the binary address of the node the header flits currently occupy, and **D** be the binary address of the destination node. The p-cube routing algorithm has two phases. In the case of minimal routing, the first phase routes the packet along a dimension i for which $c_i = 1$ and $d_i = 0$. When there is no such dimension, the second phase routes the packet along a dimension i for which $c_i = 0$ and $d_i = 1$. These steps are easily computed using bitwise logic operations as shown in Figure 11. If nonminimal routing is desired, because of its increased adaptiveness and fault tolerance, the first phase can also route the packet along any dimension i for which $c_i = 1$ and $d_i = 1$. Then, the steps can be computed as shown in Figure 12. In both of these algorithms, the only input transmitted in the header flits is **D**. **C** is a unique constant for each router, and p depends on which input buffer the header flits occupy in the router. Konstantinidou proposes an algorithm similar to p-cube [20], but only for minimal routing.

The number of shortest paths from **S** to **D**, S_{p-cube}, is $h_1!h_0!$, where $|\mathbf{X}|$ represents the number of 1's in the binary number **X**, $h_1 = |(\mathbf{S} \wedge \bar{\mathbf{D}})|$, and $h_0 = |(\bar{\mathbf{S}} \wedge \mathbf{D})|$. For a fully adaptive routing algorithm, f, $S_f = h!$, where $h = h_1 + h_0 = |(\mathbf{S} \oplus \mathbf{D})|$ is the Hamming distance between **S** and **D**. The other measure of the degree of adaptiveness for the p-cube routing is $S_{p-cube}/S_f = 1/\binom{h}{h_1}$.

Algorithm: Minimal p-cube routing for hypercubes.
Input: Current address, **C**, and destination address, **D**.
Procedure:

1. If $\mathbf{C} = \mathbf{D}$, route the packet to the local processor and exit.
2. $\mathbf{R} = \mathbf{C} \wedge \bar{\mathbf{D}}$.
3. If $\mathbf{R} = 0$, then $\mathbf{R} = \bar{\mathbf{C}} \wedge \mathbf{D}$.
4. Route the packet along any available channel in a dimension i for which $r_i = 1$.

Figure 11. The minimal p-cube routing algorithm for hypercubes.

Overall, the p-cube routing algorithm offers a choice of many shortest paths, especially when compared to the nonadaptive e-cube routing algorithm. The following table illustrates this for a binary 10-cube where the source node (1011010100) sends a message to the destination node (0010111001). For this example, $h = 6$, $h_0 = 3$, and $h_1 = 3$. One of the 36 possible shortest paths is shown. For each node transmitting the message, the number of choices based on the p-cube routing is also shown. The number of choices in parentheses indicates the additional choices available with nonminimal routing.

Algorithm: Nonminimal p-cube routing for hypercubes.
Input: Current address, **C**; destination address, **D**; and whether the last hop was in a positive direction, p.
Procedure:

1. If $\mathbf{C} = \mathbf{D}$, route the packet to the local processor and exit.
2. If $p = 1$, then $\mathbf{R} = \bar{\mathbf{C}} \wedge \mathbf{D}$.
3. Else if $\mathbf{C} \wedge \bar{\mathbf{D}} = 0$, then $\mathbf{R} = \mathbf{C} \vee (\bar{\mathbf{C}} \wedge \mathbf{D})$.
4. Else $\mathbf{R} = \mathbf{C}$.
5. Route the packet along any available channel in a dimension i for which $r_i = 1$.

Figure 12. The minimal p-cube routing algorithm for hypercubes.

address	choices	dimension taken	comment
1011010100	3(+2)	2	source
1011010000	2(+2)	9	phase 1
0011010000	1(+2)	6	phase 1
0010010000	3	5	phase 2
0010110000	2	0	phase 2
0010110001	1	3	phase 2
0010111001			destination

6 Simulation Experiments

To compare the partially adaptive routing algorithms all-but-one-negative-first (ABONF), all-but-one-positive-last (ABOPL), and negative-first (NF) with the nonadaptive routing algorithms xy and e-cube, we simulate a 16×16 mesh and a binary 8-cube for three different traffic patterns. Each of these topologies contains 256 nodes. A pair of unidirectional channels connects each pair of neighboring routers and each router to its local processor. All of the channels have the same bandwidth, 20 flits/μsec. Each input channel into a router has a buffer the size of a single flit. The routers operate asynchronously and synchronize to simultaneously transmit the flits in a packet.

The processors generate messages at time intervals chosen from a negative exponential distribution. Each message has an equal probability of being one packet of 10 or 200 flits. Messages that are blocked from immediately entering the network are queued at the source processor. Messages that arrive at a destination processor are immediately consumed. When multiple input channels contain header flits waiting for the same available output channel, an *input selection policy* must arbitrate. The policy used is called *local first-come-first-served* and decides in favor of the header flits that arrived in the router first. This policy is fair and therefore prevents indefinite postponement. When a header flit in an input channel has multiple output channels available to it, an *output selection policy* must arbitrate. The policy used is called xy and decides in favor of the output channel along the lowest dimension. All routing is minimal.

For each simulation, two characteristics of network performance are measured: average communication latency (in μsec) and average sustainable network throughput (in flits delivered per μsec). The throughput is sustainable when the number of packets queued at their source processors is small and bounded.

Obviously, the network performance is largely determined by the message traffic pattern, which is application dependent. Three network workloads are considered: *uniform*, *matrix-transpose*, and *reverse-flip*. The uniform pattern sends each message to any of the other processors with equal probability. In the mesh, the matrix-transpose pattern sends each message from the processor at row i and column j to the one at row j and column i. In the hypercube, a matrix-transpose pattern is derived by mapping a 16 × 16 mesh to the hypercube so that neighbors in the mesh are neighbors in the hypercube. Messages are then sent to the nodes dictated by the matrix transpose in the mesh. The resulting pattern in the hypercube sends each message from the processor at $(x_0, x_1, x_2, x_3, x_4, x_5, x_6, x_7)$ to the one at $(\bar{x_4}, x_5, x_6, x_7, \bar{x_0}, x_1, x_2, x_3)$. The reverse-flip pattern sends each message from the processor at $(x_0, x_1, x_2, x_3, x_4, x_5, x_6, x_7)$ to the one at $(\bar{x_7}, \bar{x_6}, \bar{x_5}, \bar{x_4}, \bar{x_3}, \bar{x_2}, \bar{x_1}, \bar{x_0})$.

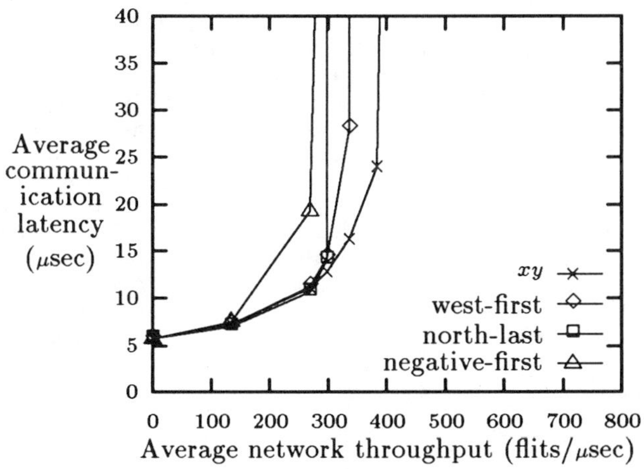

Figure 13. Comparison of routing algorithms for uniform traffic in a 16 × 16 mesh.

The simulations indicate that, for uniform traffic in the mesh and hypercube, the nonadaptive routing algorithms have lower latencies at high throughputs than the partially adaptive algorithms (Figure 13). At low throughputs, the algorithms perform about the same. For the nonuniform traffic patterns, the partially adaptive routing algorithms have the lower latencies, especially at high throughputs (Figures 14, 15, and 16). For matrix-transpose traffic in both the mesh and hypercube, the maximum sustainable throughput of the partially adaptive algorithms is twice that of the nonadaptive algorithms. For reverse-flip traffic, the maximum sustainable throughput of the partially adaptive algorithms is four times that of the nonadaptive e-cube algorithm.

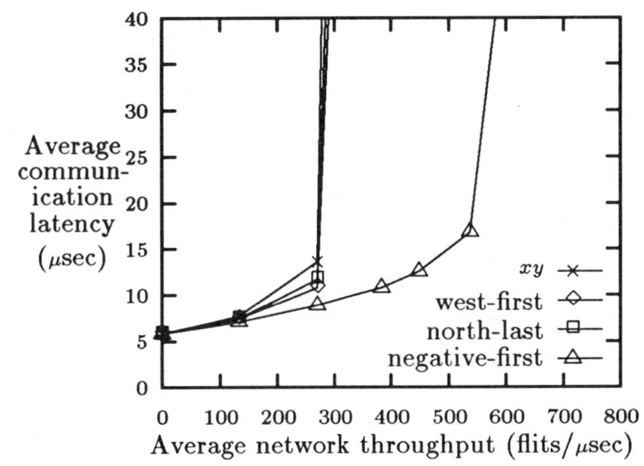

Figure 14. Comparison of routing algorithms for matrix-transpose traffic in a 16 × 16 mesh.

Overall in the hypercube, the highest sustainable throughputs are for the partially adaptive algorithms and reverse-flip traffic. These throughputs are 50% higher than the next highest sustainable throughput in the hypercube, which occurs for the e-cube algorithm and uniform traffic. This improvement in throughput is not due to shorter path lengths for reverse-flip traffic. The average path length for reverse-flip traffic is 4.27 hops, versus 4.01 hops for uniform traffic. Overall in the mesh, the highest sustainable throughput is for the negative-first algorithm and matrix-transpose traffic. This throughput is 30% higher than the second highest sustainable throughput in the mesh, which occurs for the xy algorithm and uniform traffic. Again, average path length is longer for matrix-transpose traffic (11.34 hops) than for uniform traffic (10.61 hops).

The reason the nonadaptive routing algorithms perform better than the partially adaptive routing algorithms for uniform traffic is that they happen to embody global, long-term information about this traffic pattern. From a global, long-term point of view, the uniform traffic pattern starts with message traffic spread evenly across the mesh or hypercube, and the xy and e-cube algorithms maintain that evenness. The adaptive algorithms, on the other hand, select channels based on local, short-term information. These selections tend to benefit just the routed packet and only for the immediate future and tend to interfere with other packets. The result is that the evenness of uniform traffic is not maintained as well as when global information is used.

Despite the superior performance of the nonadaptive routing algorithms for uniform traffic, the partially adaptive algorithms probably provide better performance in real systems. Uniform traffic has been used in many previous simulation studies, but we know of no real applications that generate uniform traffic. A traffic pattern is determined by the application and how its processes are mapped to the nodes of the network. For most applications, each node will communicate with some nodes much more than others. Nonuniform traffic presents a problem for the xy and e-cube algorithms because they are nonadaptive. Just as they maintain the evenness of uniform traffic, they blindly maintain the unevenness of nonuniform traffic. The result, as the figures illustrate, is often poor performance.

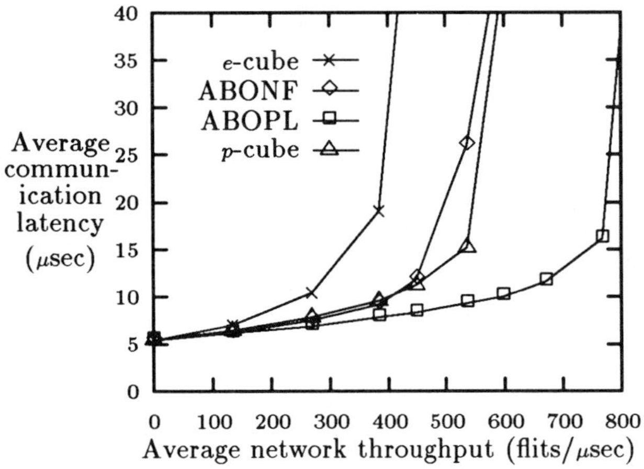

Figure 15. Comparison of routing algorithms for matrix-transpose traffic in an 8-cube.

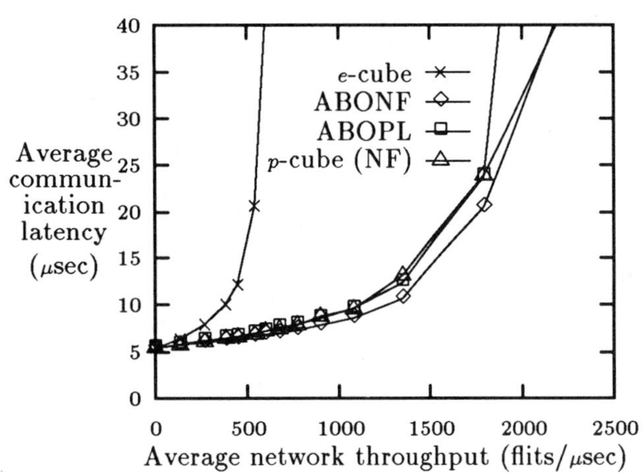

Figure 16. Comparison of routing algorithms for reverse-flip traffic in an 8-cube.

7 Conclusions and Future Work

Our goal has been to make the best use of the channels in wormhole-routed interconnection networks. Analyzing the directions in which packets can turn in a network and prohibiting the minimum number of turns that break all of the cycles produces routing algorithms that are deadlock free, livelock free, minimal or nonminimal, and maximally adaptive. Deadlock freedom and livelock freedom are essential for routing algorithms. Adaptiveness increases the chances that packets can avoid hot spots and faulty hardware and decreases the chances of indefinite postponement and livelock. Nonminimal routing allows even greater hot-spot avoidance and fault tolerance. The turn model, unlike other approaches to designing adaptive routing algorithms, is applicable to networks with only the channels required by the network topologies (as well as to networks with extra physical or virtual channels). Applied to n-dimensional meshes and k-ary n-cubes without extra channels, the turn model produces several new, partially adaptive routing algorithms. Simulations of these partially adaptive routing algorithms indicate that they can perform better than nonadaptive algorithms for nonuniform patterns of message traffic.

While the turn model has many advantages, it also has some disadvantages. Adaptive routing can require more complex control logic for route selection than does nonadaptive routing, and this may increase node delay. Part of the complexity is due to the need for a router to decide between multiple output channels, all of which lead to the destination. Another part of the complexity is due to the need for a router to base the route selection on more header information. For dimension-order routing, a router typically bases a selection on the distance remaining in one of the dimensions. For adaptive routing, a router must base a selection on the distance remaining in more than one, or all, dimensions. Every extra bit of header information that is required for the router to select an output channel increases router storage requirements and makes communication latencies more like those of store and forward.

There are many directions for future work. In [19], we investigate the effects of different input and output selection policies on network performance. In [18], we illustrate the application of the turn model to networks that include extra virtual or physical channels. Other models for designing adaptive routing algorithms are based on adding extra channels to networks, but do not produce routing algorithms that are maximally adaptive for the enhanced networks. Another obvious extension of our work is to apply the turn model to other topologies, such as hexagonal, octagonal, and cube-connected cycle networks, all of which permit adaptive routing without the addition of channels. In such topologies, the turns are not necessarily 90-degrees and the abstract cycles are not necessarily formed by four turns. A final important task is the identification of realistic workload distributions, so that the results of future simulations can be more meaningful.

Acknowledgments

The authors wish to thank Dr. Philip K. McKinley for helping us develop the simulator.

References

1. NCUBE Company, *NCUBE 6400 Processor Manual*, 1990.

2. Intel Corporation, *A Touchstone DELTA System Description*, 1991.

3. S. B. Borkar, R. Cohn, G. Cox, S. Gleason, T. Gross, H. T. Kung, M. Lam, B. Moore, C. Peterson, J. Pieper, L. Rankin, P. S. Tseng, J. Sutton, J. Urbanski, and J. Webb, "iWarp: An integrated solution to high-speed parallel computing," in *Proceedings of Supercomputing'88*, pp. 330–339, Nov. 1988.

4. D. Lenoski, J. Laudon, K. Gharachorloo, A. Gupta, and J. Hennessy, "The directory-based cache coherence protocol for the DASH multiprocessor," in *Proc. of the 17th International Symposium on Computer Architecture*, pp. 148–159, May 1990.

5. A. Agarwal, B.-H. Lim, D. Kranz, and J. Kubiatowicz, "APRIL: A processor architecture for multiprocessing multiprocessor," in *Proc. of the 17th International Symposium on Computer Architecture*, pp. 104–114, May 1990.

6. W. J. Dally and C. L. Seitz, "The torus routing chip," *Journal of Distributed Computing*, vol. 1, no. 3, pp. 187–196, 1986.

7. P. Kermani and L. Kleinrock, "Virtual cut-through: A new computer communication switching technique," *Computer Networks*, vol. 3, no. 4, pp. 267–286, 1979.

8. W. J. Dally, "Performance analysis of k-ary n-cube interconnection networks," *IEEE Transactions on Computers*, vol. C-39, pp. 775–785, June 1990.

9. X. Lin and L. M. Ni, "Deadlock-free multicast wormhole routing in in multicomputer networks," in *Proceedings of the 18th Annual International Symposium on Computer Architecture*, pp. 116–125, May 1991.

10. C. L. Seitz, W. C. Athas, C. M. Flaig, A. J. Martin, J. Seizovic, C. S. Steele, and W.-K. Su, "The architecture and programming of the Ametek Series 2010 multicomputer," in *Proceedings of the Third Conference on Hypercube Concurrent Computers and Applications, Volume I*, (Pasadena, CA), pp. 33–36, Association for Computing Machinery, Jan. 1988.

11. W. J. Dally, "The J-machine: System support for Actors," in *Actors: Knowledge-Based Concurrent Computing* (Hewitt and Agha, eds.), MIT Press, 1989.

12. W. J. Dally and H. Aoki, "Adaptive routing using virtual channels," tech. rep., Massachusetts Institute of Technology, Laboratory for Computer Science, Sept. 1990.

13. H. Sullivan and T. R. Bashkow, "A large scale, homogeneous, fully distributed parallel machine," in *Proceedings of the 4th Annu. Symp. Comput. Architecture*, vol. 5, pp. 105–124, Mar. 1977.

14. W. J. Dally and C. L. Seitz, "Deadlock-free message routing in multiprocessor interconnection networks," *IEEE Transactions on Computers*, vol. C-36, pp. 547–553, May 1987.

15. J. T. Yantchev and C. R. Jesshope, "Adaptive, low latency, deadlock-free packet routing for networks of processors," in *IEE Proceedings, Pt. E*, vol. 136(3), pp. 178–186, May 1988.

16. D. H. Linder and J. C. Harden, "An adaptive and fault tolerant wormhole routing strategy for k-ary n-cubes," *IEEE Transactions on Computers*, vol. 40, pp. 2–12, Jan. 1991.

17. W. J. Dally, "Fine-grain message passing concurrent computers," in *Proc. of the Third Conference on Hypercube Concurrent Computers*, vol. 1, (Pasadena, CA.), pp. 2–12, Jan. 1988.

18. C. J. Glass and L. M. Ni, "Maximally fully adaptive routing in 2d meshes," Tech. Rep. MSU-CPS-ACS-51, Dept. of Computer Science, Michigan State University, East Lansing, Michigan, Jan. 1992.

19. C. J. Glass and L. M. Ni, "Adaptive routing in mesh-connected networks," in *Proceedings of the 12th International Conference on Distributed Computing Systems*, June 1992.

20. S. Konstantinidou, "Adaptive, minimal routing in hypercubes," in *Proc. of the 6th MIT Conference: Advanced Research in VLSI*, pp. 139–153, 1990.

Low-Latency Message Communication Support for the AP1000

Toshiyuki Shimizu, Takeshi Horie, and Hiroaki Ishihata

Fujitsu Laboratories Limited
1015 Kamikodanaka, Nakahara-ku,
Kawasaki 211, Japan
toshi@flab.fujitsu.co.jp

ABSTRACT

Low-latency communication is the key to achieving a high-performance parallel computer. In using state-of-the-art processors, we must take cache memory into account. This paper presents an architecture for low-latency message communication and implementation, and performance evaluation.

We developed a message controller (MSC) to support low-latency message passing communication for the AP1000, to minimize message handling overhead. MSC sends messages directly from cache memory and automatically receives messages in the circular buffer. We designed communication functions between cells and evaluated communication performance by running benchmark programs such as the Pingpong benchmark, the LINPACK benchmark, the SLALOM benchmark, and a solver using the scaled conjugate gradient method.

Keywords: message handling, message-passing, cache memory, low-latency, parallel computer.

1 Introduction

Key issues in implementing a high-performance parallel computer include the utilization of high-speed processing elements, incorporation of a low-latency, high-throughput interprocessor communication facility, and minimization of message handling time.

In this paper, we present the communications scheme designed for the AP1000, a 2-D toroidal mesh MIMD computer. Our technique involves sending messages directly from the sender's cache memory to the receiver's buffer. This communication method can easily be incorporated into ordinary message passing models, and minimizes message handling overhead.

After a review of previous work and problems encountered, we introduce our scheme in detail, describe our hardware and software implementations, then conclude by presenting performance results.

Review of present communications techniques

Many distributed memory parallel processors (DMPP) have been proposed. The Cosmic Cube[1], MarkIIIfp[2], and J-Machine[3] have been developed for research purposes, and the iPSC[4], nCUBE, and Transputer have been developed as commercial products. In a larger parallel computer, the DMPP is easily expandable and is cost-effective. However, it is not easy to obtain good results for many applications. Some algorithms require much communication to execute in parallel when there are many processing elements.

To run a program efficiently, communication time should be minimized. Minimizing communication latency and widening communication throughput are critical issues in developing a DMPP. A large system that has hundreds or thousands of processor elements attempting to communicate with each other has a large message handling overhead for small messages. Much research has been done to widen communication throughput[5], and to minimize communication latency[6, 7] and message handling overhead[3, 8, 9, 10, 11].

Kermani and Kleinrock avoided the interaction of intermediate processors between sender and receiver by incorporating virtual cut-through[6]. Dally proposed wormhole routing to avoid buffering messages at processors between the sender and receiver[7]. Dally also proposed virtual channels to increase communication throughput and prevent deadlock[5].

As network latency decreases and throughput increases, the time consumed by the sending and receiving processors becomes dominant. The iWarp supports systolic communication, which is very efficient at sending and receiving when messages are well scheduled[11].

© 1992 ACM 0-89791-509-7/92/0005/0288 $1.50

However, it is usually difficult to write tightly scheduled programs because predicting and scheduling messages is difficult.

Nikhil and Papadopoulos introduced the *T processor for fast execution of data flow computation[9]. A synchronization processor is attached to support remote data (token) access and process scheduling. The functions for handling tokens can apply to efficient message passing functions. Since the token length is limited, messages would be partitioned in many tokens and processed. The amount of the data actually transferred would be large, which may cause network congestion. The total throughput of data movement is limited.

Hsu and Banerjee developed a message passing coprocessor (MPC) to accelerate message communication by supporting process scheduling, message buffer management, and buffer copying[10]. To use the MPC, an application program has to request buffers for messages to be sent and to release buffers that hold unneeded received messages. These restrictions can eliminate copying.

A message-driven processor has well-designed mechanisms for receiving messages[3, 8]. Although these mechanisms were designed to handle messages produced by object-oriented programs, such techniques may also be applied to achieve efficient message passing.

However, all the above designs fail to take advantage of possible speedups offered by communicating directly to-and-from cache memory. All state-of-the-art RISC processors include cache memory, and we must realize that data which is to be sent from a processor is often already cached.

Communications on the AP1000

We introduce a new technique, which we call "line-sending," by which messages may be sent from a processor directly from its cache memory, bypassing DMA and main memory access. This technique eliminates time needed to copy data from user memory to system memory, flush the cache, process interrupts, and initialize the DMA controller. In the AP1000, the line-sending function is implemented in a single VLSI chip, the message controller (MSC).

Our message controller also manages the reception of messages from the network directly into a circular buffer, which we call "buffer-receiving." This is performed as soon as the data arrives, and does not require a processor interruption. Also, because the MSC has direct access to main memory, the usual DMA controller is not used in receiving messages. Incoming messages are immediately stored by the MSC in a circular buffer allocated in the user space. This buffer may be accessed by the user directly.

In the next section, we present an analysis of the performance of our communications techniques.

2 Analysis of message communication

This section summarizes the message passing mechanism, and discusses the overhead for sending and receiving messages.

2.1 Conventional message passing mechanism

Message communication in conventional machines is shown in Figure 1.

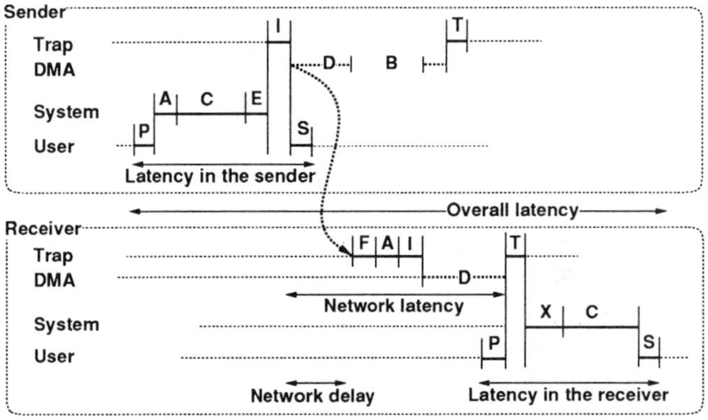

Figure 1: Steps for sending and receiving a message

The steps indicated in the figure are as follows:

A: Allocates the buffer for saving messages

B: Blocked by the network congestion

C: Copies a message to or from the system message buffer

D: Transfers data to or from devices by DMA

E: Enqueues the messages in a trap routine that will invoke the DMA transfer

F: Finds the origin of the interrupt

I: Initiates DMA

P: Checks parameters and calls system service routines

S: Checks the status and reports it

T: Checks the transfer status

X: Extracts a specified message from the receive buffer

We will describe the timing diagrams. A user program on a sender calls the library to send a message. Parameter checking is done by the library routine (P), buffer[1] for the sent message to be stored in is allocated (A), the message is copied to the allocated buffer (C), message to be transferred is enqueued (E), the DMA controller is initialized and is started (I), and control is returned to the user program (S).

[1] Send buffer is usually an uncached area to eliminate flushing after copy.

After DMA is started, the message arrives at the receiver and a trap occurs (F), the receiver allocates buffer space[2] for the message (A) and starts the DMA controller (I). While (F), (A), and (I) are processed by the receiver, the network is stopped, then sending DMA is blocked (B). When DMA transfer is done, status checking and initialization for another transfer is processed (T).

A user program on a receiver calls the library to receive a message. After parameter checking is done by the library routine (P) and DMA transfer is finished (T), the CPU finds the message in the buffer (X), and copies it to the user buffer (C), and checks status and returns control to the user program (S).

Even if we use machines with a high-performance network, messages are blocked by F, A, and I. *Network latency*, the time from the sender starts transferring to the receiver receives all the data, is $D + F + A + I + network\ delay$.

If the receiving DMA is started before message arrival, F, A, and I can be preprocessed. In this case, sending is not blocked and latency is reduced. However, without examining the message size, a large message buffer should be used for DMA.

Latency in the sender, in which the user program on the sender is blocked, is $P+A+C+E+I+S$. *Latency in the receiver*, in which the user program on the receiver is blocked, is $P + T + X + C + S$. These are the best cases. If a message has not arrived, the user program is suspended.

Overall latency is the most important, it is the time from when the sender calls to the time the receiver can access the message. Latency in the sender and receiver is important because it shows how long the user program is blocked by message passing.

All symbols in Figure 1 show the message handling overhead, except D. They should be reduced or eliminated for faster execution of parallel programs. Data copying, C, can be eliminated if a pointer to the message buffer is returned and the user can access the buffer area. The iPSC[4] provides isend() and irecv() to avoid copying.

The MPC[10] processes the message buffer management, interrupt handling, and buffer copying to reduce the overall latency. The MPC succeeds in releasing the CPU from processing message handling and accelerates copying and interrupt handling. Stage F is eliminated, and stage A and I are preprocessed. Latency in the sender and receiver is thus reduced. However, although a similar sequence of message copying and interrupt handling is executed by the MPC, the overall latency is still long.

[2]This buffer is usually an uncached area to eliminate invalidation before use.

The MDP[8] allows access to the incoming message. This mechanism reduces overall latency and allows pipelining execution. Since the MDP uses a send instruction to send messages, the timing of sending is different from Figure 1. Data can be sent immediately. Message handling routines should be carefully designed since interruption is disabled while messages are sent. The MDP does not apparently to utilize cache memory.

2.2 Line sending and buffer receiving

To perform message passing on a processor with cache memory, some problems should be considered.

- Message buffer for receiving should not be cached or should be invalidated before receiving. That is because the received message is not accessed if the data had been in cache memory. Old data might be read from cache memory.
- To use a copyback cache, flushing or copying the data to uncached area should be done before invoking DMA for sending. This is because the newest data is not always in main memory where DMA access can take place.

Accessing uncached data is very slow, and invalidating cache memory is expensive. Flushing the cache or copying to an uncachable area causes a problem with overhead.

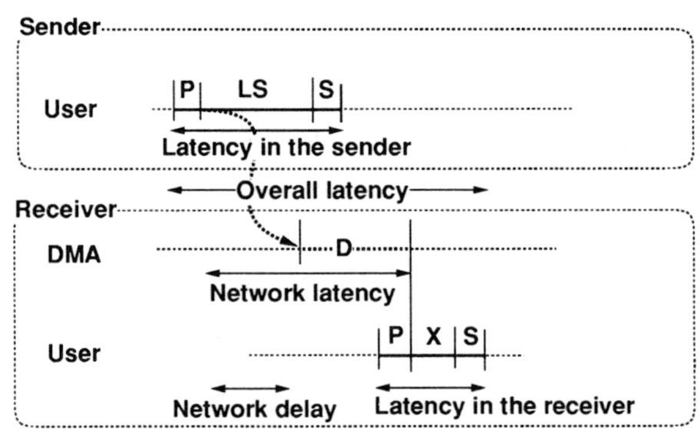

Figure 2: Message passing performed by the MSC

We propose a message transfer scheme using line sending and buffer receiving. This method utilizes cache memory and eliminates unneeded operations. Figure 2 illustrates message passing. LS is the line sending and the other symbols are the same as in Figure 1. LS is faster than memory copying because it can move data in a block with one operation, but the copy function needs a load and store operation using a register.

Line sending and buffer receiving have the following advantages:

- Line sending sends data directly from cache memory in a similar manner to cache flushing. This scheme eliminate copying, DMA initialization, and interrupt processing. A, E, and I for sending are eliminated, And C is replaced by LS.

- Line sending is not buffered, and data is transferred immediately.

- Receiving DMA is always enabled, so a message is transferred on arrival. Received messages are stored in the large circular buffer. An interrupt is not needed to control DMA. The sender is not blocked because newly arrived data is immediately processed. F, A, and I for receiving are eliminated.

- Since all operations are done in user mode, no operating system service calls are needed. Traps only occur when the network is busy.

Line sending and buffer receiving promise good performance which can utilize cache memory and eliminate overhead, A, C, E, I, F, X, and T, completely. However, there are the following problems:

- Line sending is controlled by the CPU, and other calculation can not be done while messages are being sent.

- Line sending may produce a trap when the network is busy, this depends on network utilization of the application program.

- Message passing is done by cache line size and is aligned. Handling a misaligned message is difficult.

- Receiving by the ring buffer is complicated compared with ordinary approaches. To look for the desired message and treat wraparound message seems to be difficult and expensive.

We will show that the above problems can be made negligible in Section 6.

3 MSC

This section discusses the hardware design which implements line sending and buffer receiving. To implement line sending and buffer receiving, the message handling hardware (MSC) incorporates a cache controller and a DMA controller. Figure 3 shows the MSC configuration.

Memory, other devices, and the MSC are connected by a local bus called LBUS. The CPU and cache memory are connected to the MSC. During normal operation, the MSC works as a direct-mapped cache memory controller with a copyback policy. The line size is four words. Wbuf is a write buffer that is used to write data to memory or devices.

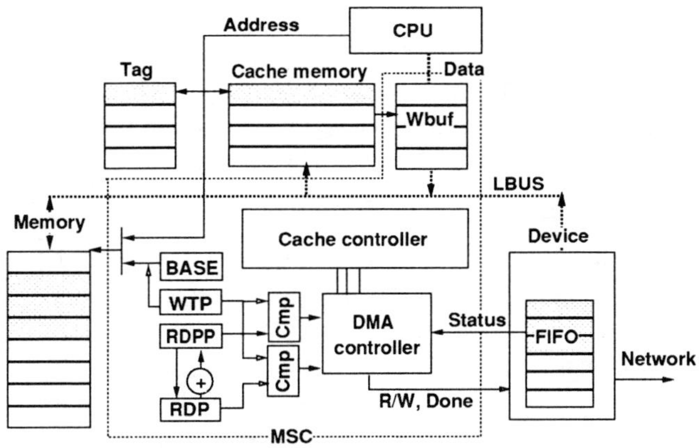

Figure 3: MSC configuration

3.1 Line sending

A line sending function sends a cache line message like that of a cache flush. DMA is activated automatically even when there is no specified data in the cache. The arrows in Figure 4 indicate when there is data movement: HIT when there is data in the cache, and MISS when the cache is invalid. The figure also shows a normal cache flush (FLUSH) for comparison.

Initiating line sending similar to cache memory control commands is implemented by a simple store instruction. The 6 MSBs of the address are decoded as commands. The function for line send and line send with end bit are assigned to 0x3b and 0x3c. This operation is different from the sending by program mode, which reads data from memory to the register and writes data to the device. Line sending doesn't load and store data but specifies the address of data. Cache line data is sent by a store instruction.

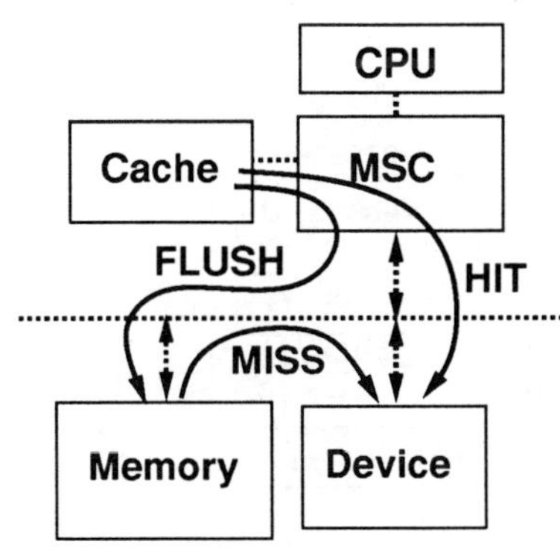

Figure 4: Data movement during line sending

When an CPU initiates a line sending command, the MSC checks the tag memory to see if the data is in the cache or in main memory. It simultaneously checks the output network device status to see if the device can accept the data, and checks that the local bus is ready, and that no other DMA is activated to write the same network device. If all devices are ready and data is in the cache, data is read from the cache and written to the Wbuf (HIT). If data is not in the cache, DMA to one cache line is invoked, and the data is read from main memory and written to the device (MISS). When line send with end bit is specified, the data ends the message.

The CPU is blocked until the status has been checked and data has been moved from the cache to Wbuf or DMA is initiated. The CPU does not wait for all the data to be written to the device. To implement this mechanism, the devices must have a FIFO deeper than the cache line size. Because it is not known when a whole line is sent to the network, MSC checks the FIFO status to see whether there is room for the message.

If devices are busy, a data access exception is reported to the CPU, and a trap occurs. This trap enables the CPU to retry line sending and avoid deadlock.

Line sending will not invalidate the cache entry or write back to main memory. Because this data may be accessed again, invalidation might lose the newest data, and flushing is expensive. Programs often modify a part of the messages and send again.

3.2 Buffer receiving

Buffer receiving (Figure 5) corresponds to any asynchronous data transfer request. Hardware monitors the ring buffer for overflow, notifies the CPU of such an error by an interrupt, or stops transferring until data reading produces a receive area in the buffer. The accessed area is released and returned to the MSC as a receive buffer by modifying the register.

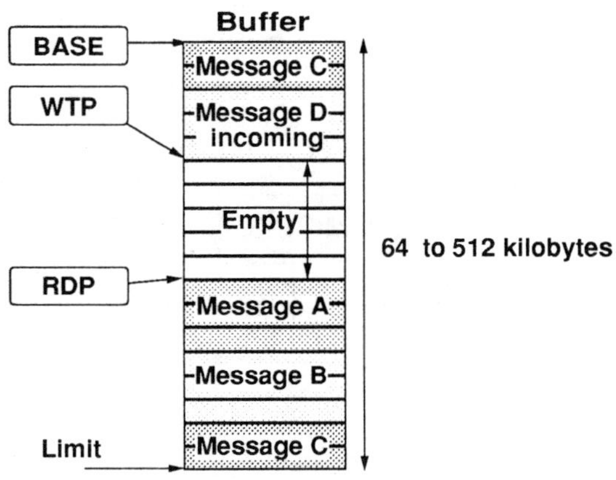

Figure 5: Buffer receiving

Data movement is done in 4-word aligned blocks. This is the same as the cache line size so that the LBUS can move quickly.

The BASE, write pointer (WTP), and read pointer (RDP) are registers (Figure 3). The BASE holds the buffer address. A pair of pointers to the circular buffer, WTP and RDP, points to the data that has been received from other processors but which has not yet been read by the CPU. The WTP points to the address where the next received data is to be stored. It is updated by the hardware after each data is stored. The RDP points to the address that the CPU is currently accessing. The CPU writes any value to the RDP to dispose of data which is no longer needed.

When data arrives from a network device, the MSC checks that the WTP value does not exceed the RDP. If the WTP and RDP hold the same value, no more data can be received, and the MSC suspends transfer or notifies the CPU by generating an interrupt signal.

The WTP is initialized to the top of the buffer address (base address), and RDP is initialized to the bottom address (Limit: base address + buffer size - 1)[3]. The buffer size can be between 64 to 512 kilobytes.

A received message is not written to the cache memory directly. That is because it may cause the replacement of the cached data which is used before the message.

4 Software implementation

As described in Section 3, the MSC only supports simple mechanisms. A software library provides a more general interface for message passing. We developed basic send and receive functions, send() and recvs(). We show how alignment problems are handled.

We also describe global operation functions such as global sum, minimum, and maximum. Global operations require a lot of small message communication (4 bytes or 8 bytes). To get good performance, specially formatted messages are used.

It is important that the operating system we use schedules processes only when the process calls the receive message function in order to reduce process switches. Since any other process will run concurrently in send and receive functions, we don't have to disable interrupts.

This section explains how these routines are implemented.

4.1 Message format for send and receive

Table 1 lists the message format for ordinary message transfer.

[3] The address is always aligned on a cache line, and the base address must be aligned according to the buffer size.

Table 1: Message format

Offset	Field	Size
0	Routing header	4 Bytes
4	Message length	4 Bytes
8	Alignment of message start	4 Bytes
12	Cell IDx of sender	4 Bytes
16	Cell IDy of sender	4 Bytes
24	Message ID for trace	4 Bytes
28	Message type	4 Bytes
32	Message body	Any

The *routing header* contains a hardware header to specify the destination cell. We assume that only the header word is used by the hardware. The other words are used by software.

Cell IDx and *Cell IDy* identify the source processor with the relative distance. *Alignment of message* specifies the message start alignment from offset 32. *Message length*, which holds the message size, and *alignment of message*, enable the handling of byte alignment messages. Since cache line size is 16 bytes, alignment varies from 0 to 15. There is no restriction on the message length.

4.2 Send message function

`send()` sends a message specified by the address (p) and size to a cell specified by cid. The message type can be specified. The code is as follows:

```
send(cid, type, p, size)
{
  Set message info. to the header in buffer q;
  LSEND(q);
  LSEND(q+16);
  do size/cache_line_size-1 times {
    LSEND(p);
    Increment p;
  }
  LSENDE(p);
}
```

LSEND(p) and LSENDE(p) invoke line send functions with and without an end bit. These are written as follows:

```
st %r0,[%r1+%r2] ;LSEND(p), %r1=p,%r2=0xec000000
st %r0,[%r1+%r2] ;LSENDE(p),%r1=p,%r2=0xf0000000
```

4.3 Receive message function

`recvs()` waits until a message is received from a specified cell. It avoids unneeded copies and can return control if there is no appropriate message. The code is as follows:

```
recvs(cid, type)
{
  Return NULL if no message has been received;
  Pick up a header from top of the ring buf.(RDP);
  forever {
    if header is marked 'USED' {
      Invalidate this message area;
      Increment RDP to skip this message;
    } else if message is found {
      Mark a header 'USED';
      Wait until the whole message is received;
      Copy data only if wraparound occurred;
      Return the message address;
    }
    if no more messages {
      Return NULL;
    }
    Pick up the next message header;
  }
}
```

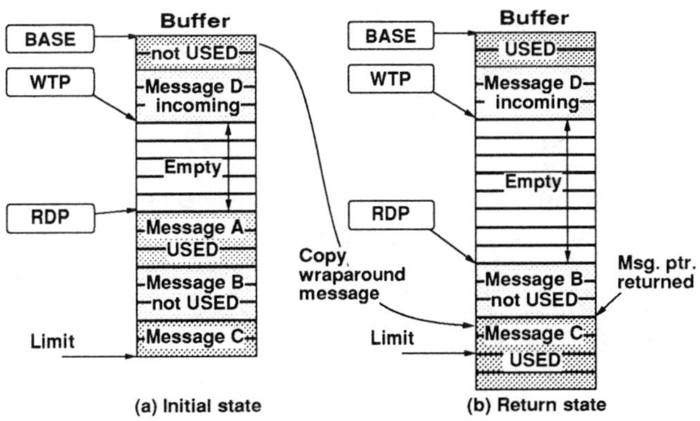

Figure 6: Ring buffer operation

Figure 6 shows how a ring buffer is used and wraparound data is managed. When recvs() is called to find message C, the buffer is in the initial state (a). Message A is accessed first, but, since message A is marked 'USED', message area A is invalidated[4] and the RDP is incremented to the beginning of message B. Message B is not 'USED' but does not match, so message C is picked up. This is a match, but has wraparound, so the remainder of the message is appended to the end of the buffer (limit). Message C is marked 'USED' and is returned with the message address (msg. ptr.). When

[4] to confirm a newly arrived message, which is stored in main memory is accessed

function recvs() exits, the buffer status is as shown in (b).

4.4 Global operations

A parallel computer often uses global operations such as sum, maximum, and minimum. The functions are briefly explained below:

dmax() gets the cell ID and maximum value in double-precision data for all the cells.

dsum() sums the double-precision data for all cells.

A call to global function *func*(), such as dmax() and dsum(), in a cell must be complemented by a call to *func*() in all other cells. All functions perform binary tree communication to get information from all cells.

Line sending and buffer receiving are used to implement the above, using the special formatted messages listed in Table 2.

Index of DATA identifies the origin of the data.

Table 2: Message format for global operations

Offset	Field	Size
0	Routing header (with func.)	4 Bytes
4	Index of DATA (cid)	4 Bytes
8	DATA (float, int, double)	8 Bytes

By using this format, messages can be packed within one cache line to get good performance. The lower nine bits of the *routing header* indicate which global operation should be done.

5 AP1000 architecture

This section overviews the hardware architecture of the AP1000[12]. Figure 7 shows the AP1000 system configuration. Each processing element, or cell, is connected by three independent networks, the T-net, B-net, and S-net. The total number of cells varies from 16 to 1024.

To obtain high-throughput and low-latency communication, we choose a two-dimensional torus topology for the interprocessor communication, T-net. We developed a routing controller (RTC), for the T-net which is designed to run a routing scheme that incorporates the structured buffer pool algorithm into wormhole routing[13]. This scheme provides low-latency, high-throughput communication, and avoids deadlock. The RTC handles the flow control and routing in communication between cells. The RTC connects four neighbors with a 16-bit data bus and uses a transfer rate of 25 megabytes per second per channel. The RTC also provides broadcast facilities on the T-net.

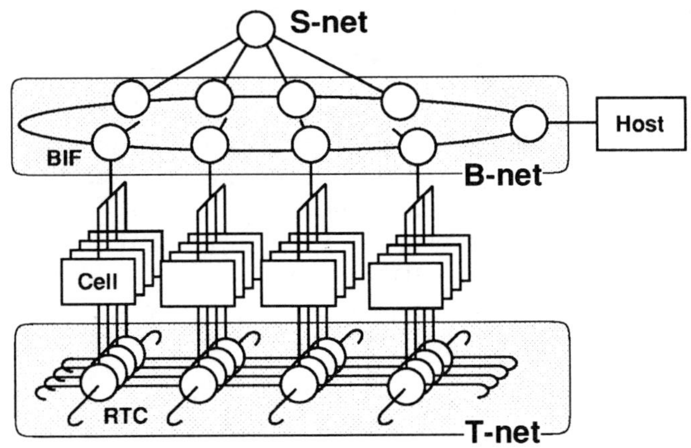

Figure 7: AP1000 system configuration

In the cell processor, network devices and the MSC are connected by a local bus, the LBUS. The network devices have a FIFO 8 words deep. The device decodes the FIFO status for the MSC.

We use a SPARC IU and FPU for the cell processor, which operates at 25 MHz. The IU and FPU are connected to a simple direct-mapped cache. The cache has a capacity of 128 kilobytes with a line size of 16 bytes. The cache controller in the MSC controls general-purpose SRAM by copyback.

The local memory for the processing elements is managed by the DRAM controller called DRAMC. The DRAMC controls 16 megabytes of memory. It takes 160 ns for word write access and 400 ns for block write access. Because wait cycles are inserted for read accesses, it takes 400 ns for word read access and 640 ns for block read access.

6 Performance results

To evaluate the line sending and buffer receiving, we ran several benchmark programs. The Pingpong benchmark[14] evaluates the overall latency of message communication. From the results of global functions we can evaluate the effect of the special format messages. We can see how much effect communication speedup has on larger applications.

6.1 Pingpong benchmark

To determine the effects of message handling, the time taken to send various lengths of messages from a master cell to a slave cell and back was measured. In the experiment, cell (0,0) sends a message to cell (4, 1), then cell(4, 1) returns the message to cell (0, 0). Since wormwhole routing is used, distance does not affect the result. Half of this time is used for sending the message.

It is the overall latency discussed in Section 2. The other cells are idle and have no effect on the communication cells.

Figure 8 shows the time required to handle a message versus the message size in bytes. Normal refers to the timing of the ordinary DMA transfer functions. All functions used here return the address of the received message. There is no copy overhead on receiving. BR refers to timing with buffer receiving, recvs(). LS refers to line sending, send(), while LS+BR refers to both BR and LS.

Table 3 summarizes the overhead of transferring modes. The symbols have the same meaning in Section 2, and $S_s = A + E + C + I$, $N_d = Network\ delay$, and $S_r = F + A + I + T$. Table 3 also shows the Pingpong time when data size is small (10 bytes) and large (10 kilobytes)[5].

For small data sizes, copying time is negligible. The difference between BR and LS+BR is the setup time for send, and is about $28\mu s$ (61.3 − 32.8). The result of Normal and LS for sending of small data sizes is limited by the setup time for receiving. The setup time for receiving is about $78\mu s$ (111 − 32.8).

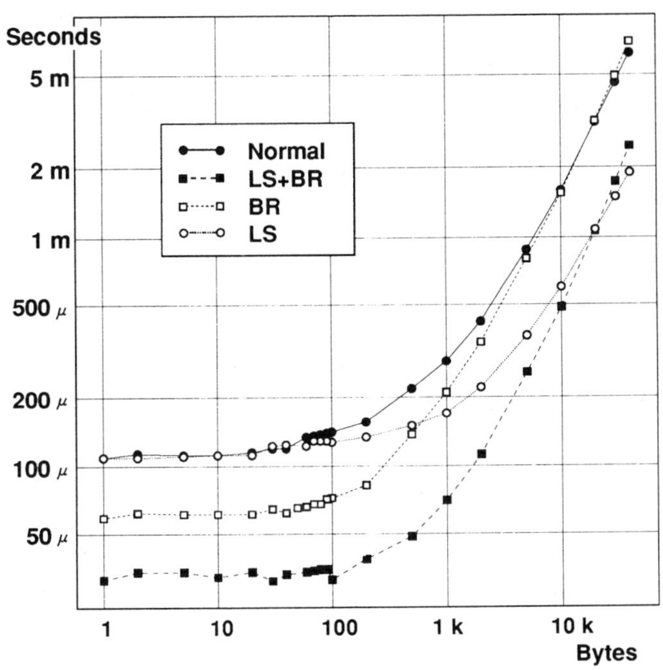

Figure 8: Pingpong performance

In LS mode, receiving interrupts degrade the performance for smaller-sized messages. BR avoids interrupt overhead when receiving messages, and performance is good for smaller-sized messages. When sending is performed by DMA, setup time degrades the performance for smaller-sized messages.

For large data transfer, copying time for sending is the dominating factor. In the LS+BR mode, memory copying is eliminated, so performance is good even when messages are large.

Table 3: Summary of overhead (microseconds)

Mode	Over all latency	10 B	10 KB
Normal	$P, S_s, N_d, S_r, D, X, S$	112	1591
LS	$P, N_d, S_r, max(LS, D), X, S$	111	597
BR	P, S_s, N_d, D, X, S	61.3	1554
LS+BR	$P, N_d, max(LS, D), X, S$	32.8	491

6.2 Global operation performance

Table 4 lists the timing of global operations[6]. Cache refers to using line sending and buffer receiving with the format described in Table 2.

Table 4: Performance of global functions (microseconds)

Func.	Cells	Normal	LS	BR	LS+BR	Cache
dmax	64	1,970	1,840	975	597	136
	256	2,630	2,460	1,320	809	198
	512	2,970	2,770	1,480	913	224
dsum	64	1,990	1,850	983	586	119
	256	2,660	2,470	1,320	792	163
	512	3,000	2,800	1,500	911	190

The results of Normal, LS, BR, and LS+BR is similar to the results for the Pingpong benchmark. The best results were obtained by using a cache format message. Because the message size is one third that of ordinary messages, data transfer timing is reduced. The result of dsum() is faster than dmax() because dmax() needs more calculation, such as setting the index.

6.3 Results of larger applications

Table 5 lists the results of benchmarks with and without message handling functions. Figure 9 shows performance results normalized by normal mode.

The benchmarks are briefly explained as follows:

[5]In this measurement, the BR, LS, and LS+BR modes were called using the same user interface as used by the normal mode. Thus, the results are slower than native functions of AP1000. The time using the native functions, xy_send and xy_recv, is $19.4\mu s$ for 10 bytes data.

[6]Better performance may be achieved by using the native library calls, which utilize the RTC broadcast functions, as given here:

Cells	64	256	512
dmax	92.1	121	139
dsum	74.8	98.4	114

Table 5: Performance results

Application name	Cells (conf)	Problem size	Timing (seconds) Normal	LS	BR	LS+BR	Speedup ratio (Normal/LS+BR)
LINPACK	64	1000	8.73	7.95	6.65	4.83	1.81
	(8x8)	2000	35.8	33.0	31.4	26.2	1.37
		4000	197	187	186	170	1.16
	256	1000	7.44	6.51	5.12	3.05	2.44
	(16x16)	2000	21.0	18.5	15.8	10.8	1.94
		4000	80.4	71.7	69.2	54.9	1.46
SCG	256	100	1.65	1.70	0.93	0.61	2.70
	(16x16)	200	4.22	4.21	2.69	1.98	2.13
		400	14.3	13.7	11.58	9.97	1.43
	512	100	1.71	1.76	0.93	0.58	2.95
	(16x32)	200	3.89	3.98	2.29	1.63	2.39
		400	12.2	12.4	9.34	7.51	1.62
SLALOM	16	1067	64.9	65.4	61.9	59.8	1.09
	64	1666	66.9	67.7	63.2	60.1	1.11
	256	2205	68.3	70.2	64.7	60.2	1.13

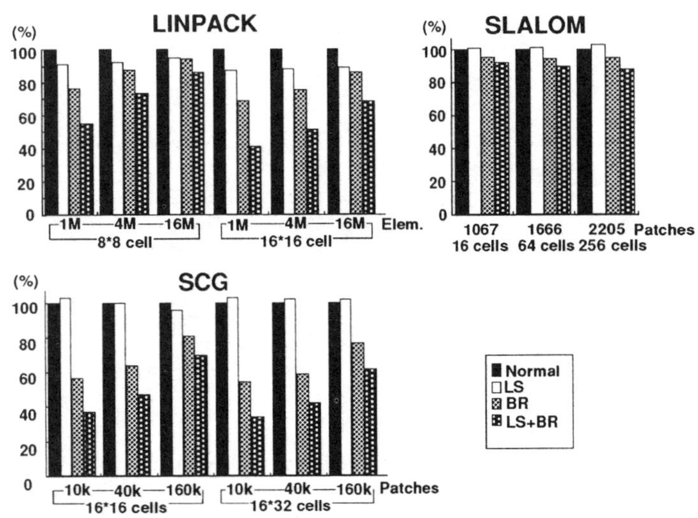

Figure 9: Normalized performance results

LU decomposition: LINPACK

This program was originally written by Prof. Brent to perform the LINPACK benchmark[15] The results reflect the problem area of solving dense systems of equations using block LU decomposition. Problem size n refers to a matrix of $n \times n$ elements. Note that in this measurement, broadcast functions of RTC are not used. Thus, the results reported here are slower than those in [16].

Scaled conjugate gradient method: SCG

SCG solves the two-dimensional finite difference method using the scaled conjugate gradient method in which coefficient matrix is scaled by diagonal elements. Problem size n refers to a $n \times n$ mesh size to be partitioned. The matrix to be solved is $n^2 \times n^2$ in size.

Slalom benchmark: SLALOM

SLALOM[17] is a computer benchmark which solves an optical radiosity in the interior of a box. The problem size is set to the number of patches that LS+BR mode can calculate in one minute.

These results reflect the results of the communication performance. LS+BR shows better performance overall the items. Receiving overhead, such as interrupts, is also dominant for large applications. When receiving overhead is reduced, reducing the sending overhead is effective. The problems we pointed out in Section 2.2, including line sending using the CPU, effects of the trap, and complicated ring buffer operation, become negligible.

7 Conclusion

We have introduced a scheme to perform interprocessor communication in a distributed memory parallel computer by using line sending and buffer receiving. We evaluated it by running several benchmarks, and proved that these mechanisms to support low-latency communication can speed up applications, even if these functions consume CPU time.

Reducing the overhead of sending messages speeds up the communication performance of a parallel machine which already has efficient receiving mechanisms. It is important to utilize cache memory for message passing functions. Line sending can initiate message transfer directly and immediately, and can be started in same way whether data is cached or not.

For buffer receiving, considerable overhead may be introduced in message searching, because in the current implementation, messages are searched from the oldest to the newest. If message arrival is scheduled well, messages that arrive first are read out first, and overhead is kept very small. However, if messages are not read out soon and remain in the ring buffer, the search time increases.

If many messages arrive at the same time, the ring buffer overflows. To prevent this, we should consider message scheduling. However, buffer receiving tolerates some misordered messages.

When a message is wrapped around in the ring buffer, a remainder of the message is appended to the bottom of the ring buffer. This is not a good approach because it wastes memory and requires copying. Invalidation of areas in the ring buffer that have been read are processed by software. These do not affect the present results.

Current implementations of line sending are blocked by network congestion, which is reported by the occurrence of traps. This does not cause performance problems, as the cost of a trap is negligible.

Our results show that line sending and buffer receiving can speed up many kinds of applications.

Acknowledgments

We thank Dr. Ishii, Mr. Shiraishi, and Mr. Uchida for their helpful suggestions, Prof. Richard Brent at Australian National University for use of the LU decomposition program, and Mr. Kenichi Hayashi for use of the SCG method program. We also thank the referees for their helpful comments and suggestions.

REFERENCES

[1] Charles L. Seitz, "The Cosmic Cube," in *Communications of the ACM*, 28(1): pp. 22–33, Jan. 1985.

[2] J. Tuazon, J. Peterson and M. Pniel, "Mark IIIfp Hypercube Concurrent Processor Architecture," in *Proc. 3rd Conf. on Hypercube Concurrent Computers and Applications*, Pasadena, CA, pp. 71–80, Jan. 1988.

[3] W. J. Dally et al., "The J-Machine: A Fine-Grain Concurrent Computer," in *Information Processing 89*, Elsevier North Holland, 1989.

[4] Ramune Arlauskas, "iPSC/2 System: A Second Generation Hypercube," in *Third Conf. on Hypercube Concurrent Computers and Applications*, pp. 33–36, ACM, 1988.

[5] W. J. Dally, "Virtual-Channel Flow Control," in *Proc. of the 17th Int'l Symp. on Computer Architecture*, pp. 60–68, May 1990.

[6] P. Kermani and L. Kleinrock, "Virtual Cut Through: A New Computer Communication Switching Technique," *Computer Networks*, pp. 267–286, 1979.

[7] W. J. Dally and C. L. Seitz. "The Torus Routing Chip," *Distributed Computing*, pp. 187–196, 1986.

[8] W. J. Dally et al., "Message-Driven Processor Architecture Version 11," in *MIT Concurrent VLSI Architecture Memo 14*, A.I. Memo No. 1069, Aug. 1988.

[9] R. S. Nikhil and G. M. Papadopoulos. "*T: a Killer Micro for a Brave New World," *Technical Memorandum of MIT*, Computation Structures Group Memo 325.

[10] J. M. Hsu and P. Banerjee, "A Message Passing Coprocessor for Distributed Memory Multicomputers," in *Proc. of Super Computing 90*, pp. 720–729, 1990.

[11] S. Borkar et al., "Supporting Systolic and Memory Communication in iWarp," in *Proc. of the 17th Int'l Symp. on Computer Architecture*, pp. 70–81, May 1990.

[12] H. Ishihata, T. Horie, S. Inano, T. Shimizu, and S. Kato, "An Architecture of Highly Parallel Computer AP1000," *IEEE Pacific Rim Conf. on Communications, Computers, and Signal Processing*, May 1991, pp.13–16.

[13] T. Horie, H. Ishihata, T. Shimizu, and M. Ikesaka, "AP1000 Architecture and Performance of LU Decomposition," in *Proc. of 1991 Int'l Conf. on Parallel Processing*, August 1991, pp.634–635.

[14] R. Hockney, "Performance parameters and benchmarking of supercomputers," *Parallel computing*, Vol 17, 10&11, Dec. 1991, pp.1111–1130.

[15] J. J. Dongarra, "Performance of Various Computers Using Standard Linear Equations Software," *Technical Report*, University of Tennessee, May 8, 1991.

[16] R. P. Brent, "The LINPACK Benchmark on the AP1000: Preliminary Report," *Proc. of the Second Fujitsu-ANU CAP Workshop*, Australian National University, Nov. 28-29, 1991.

[17] J. Gustafson et al., "SLALOM UPDATE," *Supercomputing Review*, March 1991, pp.56–61.

Session 10: I/O Systems

Futurebus+ as an I/O Bus: Profile B

Barbara P. Aichinger
Digital Equipment Corporation

Abstract

The IEEE Futurebus+ is a very fast (3GB/sec.), industry standard backplane bus specification for computer systems. Futurebus+ was designed independent of any CPU architecture so it is truly open. With this open architecture Futurebus+ can be applied to many different computing applications. Profile B is a subset of the IEEE 896 Futurebus+ standard and targets high performance, general purpose computer I/O applications. This paper describes how and why the functional, electrical, mechanical and environmental characteristics were chosen.

What is Futurebus+?

Futurebus+ is a revised and expanded version of the original 1987 Futurebus standard (IEEE 896.1-1987). The wide acceptance of Futurebus+ started in 1988. Early that year the US Navy's Next Generation Computer Resources Program (NGCR) chartered a Backplane Working Group to develop a set of requirements for computers used in Mission Critical applications. A principal requirement was that the chosen standard would likely become a major commercial success, so that the Navy could capitalize upon the systems expertise and funding provided by commercial and industrial computer vendors. At the conclusion of this research, the Pentagon announced that all future US Navy Mission Critical Computer Resources will be based on the Futurebus+ standard. After this announcement, Futurebus+ received another boost from the VME International Trade Association. VITA members saw a need to develop a strategy which would lead to the definition of a new bus architecture to follow the widely successful IEEE 1014: VMEbus standard. In late 1988, VITA announced that it would join forces with the IEEE Futurebus+ Working Group to generate a new open computer bus standard. Shortly thereafter, the Multibus Manufacturers Group also agreed to join this effort.

Futurebus+ represents a major paradigm shift for the computer industry. It is the first completely comprehensive bus architecture designed to be an OPEN standard, that is, an interface specification for which there are no restrictions for who may use it. The Futurebus+ architecture was also designed to be scalable and will support multiple generations of computer technology.

Futurebus+ is a family of standards, but the three major documents that have dominated the Futurebus+ development are:

- IEEE 896.1 Futurebus+ Logical Layer Specification
- IEEE 896.2 Futurebus+ Physical Layer Specification
- IEEE P896.3 Futurebus+ Recommended Practices

Background on Profiles

The Futurebus+ family of specifications provides a rich set of "tools" with which to build optimal implementations for a wide spectrum of applications. When called up within profiles, these specifications and options are tightly constrained. This is to provide the implementor with clear, cost effective guidelines, which if followed, will maximize interoperability with any other implementation that follows the same guidelines.

In January of 1990, members of the IEEE 896 Working Group decided that a Futurebus+ profile to serve the needs of the I/O community should be formed. The Working Group recognized that this would allow computer manufacturers who adopted Futurebus+ as their I/O bus to maintain a consistent I/O interface over many years. This is a significant advantage to users who wish to exploit advancements in computer technology while maintaining application interfaces over time. With this mandate, the Profile B Working Group set out to subset the Futurebus+ architecture for use as a general-purpose, high performance computer I/O bus. The task of picking the right options from the broad spectrum of Futurebus+ features was completed in September of 1991 when Profile B became an IEEE standard.

Profile B Architecture

The architecture of Profile B is that of an I/O bus which is bridged by a Profile B system bridge to a system bus where the CPU and main memory reside. Profile B buses can also contain bridges to other buses, such as Sbus, Multibus II, Turbo Channel or VME. Profile B modules can also reside on Profile A (cache coherent, multiprocessor memory interconnect) and Profile F (performance optimized Profile A) buses when they act as the actual system bus. Profile B clearly specifies the functions, such as use of the status lines, timing, and transactions, that an I/O module should and should not perform. The objective is to maximize interoperability between the system and the I/O modules.

Figure 1 Profile B System Architecture

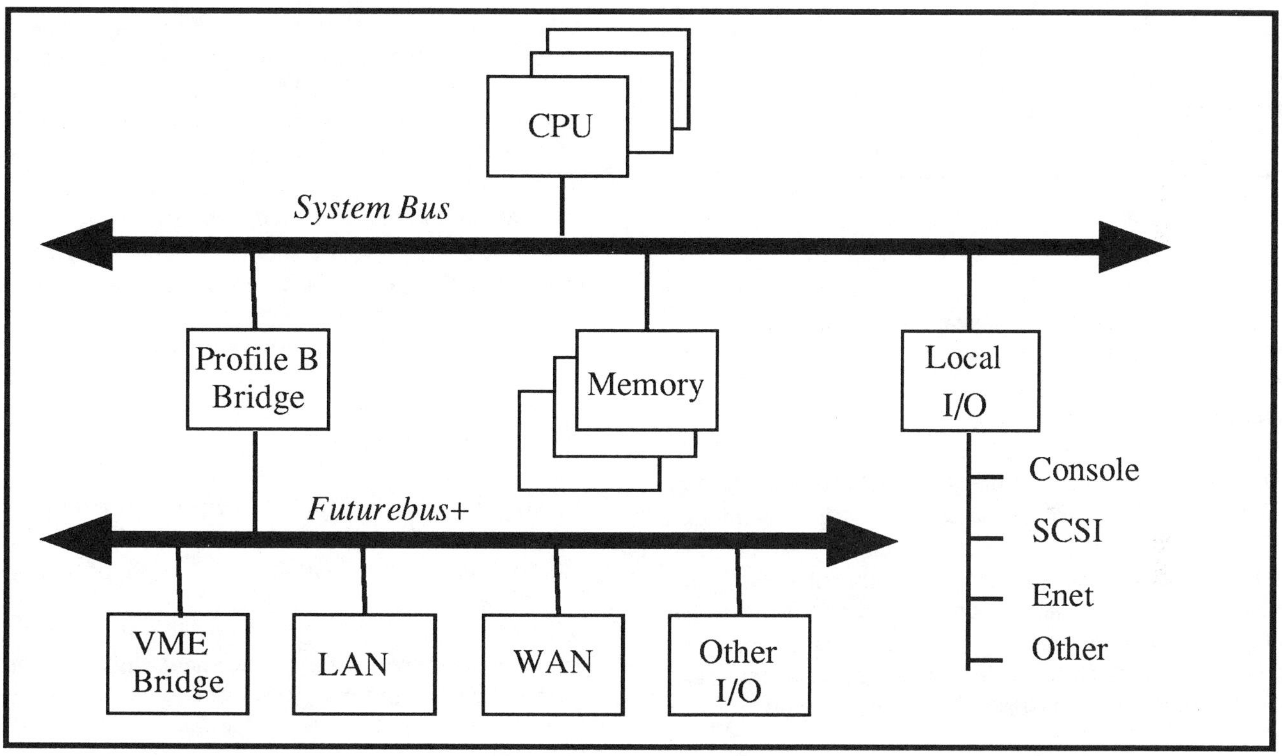

Register Set and DMA

To implement the Profile B architecture, the necessary register set and its characteristics needed to be defined. The minimum register set chosen consists of ROM registers, Futurebus+ Specific Registers, and Core Registers. Per the 896.2 standard these registers are mapped with a big endian data format. These registers serve three basic purposes:

- The first is to describe the modules capabilities.
- The second is to allow the system configuration process to enable or disable the modules capabilities.
- The third is to provide status on the modules operation.

With these registers, the system can configure the modules operation so that they match the systems and can read the modules status in the case of an error. The register set chosen proved to be cost effective and key to providing interoperability.

The Working Group recognized the need for a standardized software interface. The IEEE P1212 standard was chosen and Profile B recommends the circular queue DMA architecture.

The Working Group struggled with the data format for the DMA data and DMA control structures. Since Futurebus+ was designed to be independent of any particular CPU architecture, the Working Group compromised and specified that either big endian or little endian data formats may be supported on Profile B modules.

Arbitration

Profile B defaults to a central arbitration scheme at power-up. Central arbitration was chosen overwhelmingly by the Working Group because of its simplicity and high performance. In this scheme, every slot has two request lines and they come from each slot and go to the central arbiter, one grant line then comes from the central arbiter back to each slot. To help prevent deadlock situations and provide for real time applications, Profile B assigned priorities to the two request lines. The higher request (rq1*) was assigned to Read Response transactions. The lower request (rq0*) is for all other transactions.

Figure 2 Central Arbitration Block Diagram

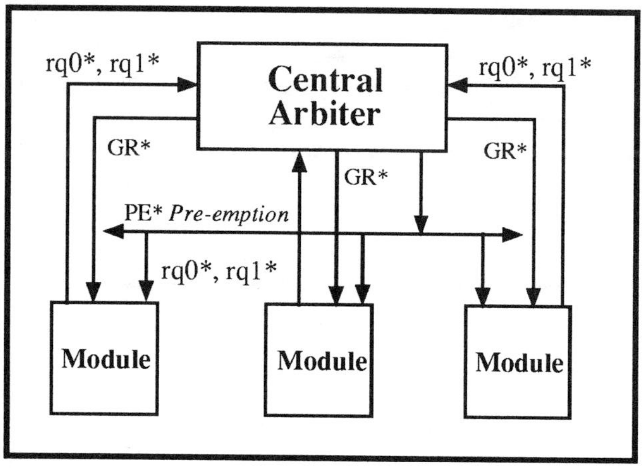

Read Response transactions are the result of a Read Request transaction that was split or pended. The 896.1 protocol allows a slave to transfer the requested read data back to the requester at a later time. Because the requester is *waiting* for the read data to be returned, Read Response transactions are given a high priority for bus tenure.

Futurebus+ central arbitration also includes a method of pre-emption. In most Profile B systems the pre-emption signal will be bused; that is, each slot will see the same signal as it is "daisy chained" along the backplane. The pre-emption line signals to the module that it must give up bus tenure after finishing its current transaction. This is particularly useful in Real-Time applications that need to obtain the bus in a fast and deterministic manner.

The arbitration scheme is mandated only to be fair in its allocation of bus tenure. The Working Group suspects that most Profile B systems will choose some type of round-robin arbitration scheme, since this method is both cost effective and uses a simple bus tenure algorithm.

The Arbitration Bus

Futurebus+ has an Arbitration Bus that uses a distributed parallel contention protocol. This bus can be used for three purposes:

- To send messages for the purpose of changing arbitration priority in a central arbitration based machine.
- For gaining bus tenure in a distributed arbitration based machine.
- For sending system wide notification information such as power fail.

The Profile B Working Group determined that this bus was not necessary for most I/O applications so its use is listed as optional. One use of the bus that was specified was for the transmission of the Power Fail message. I/O modules that do not need to receive Power Fail notification do not need to connect at all to the Arbitration Bus. All Profile B systems are required to send the Power Fail message just prior to power going down.

Live Insertion

Live Insertion is included in the Futurebus+ standard to answer the needs of computer vendors who sell into the high availability market. Due to growing importance, live insertion is supported in Profile B as an optional feature. The computer industry should expect to see more on this topic in the future, as high availability is becoming increasingly important to system vendors. The four levels of live insertion specified in the Futurebus+ IEEE 896.2 document, differ in reliability and system operation.

- On Level 0, live insertion is not implemented.
- Level 1 suspends transactions on Futurebus+ while modules are replaced.
- Level 2 provides for replacement while bus activity continues, but there may be transient faults or restrictions may be placed on the types of transactions allowed.
- Level 3 provides for replacement while bus activity continues without any restrictions.

Protocol

The Futurebus+ standard has built into the protocol and architecture various methods of allowing performance to improve over time. The data path is defined from 32 to 256 bits wide, which allows for throughput improvements simply by extending the width of the data path. Futurebus+ has a default method of transferring data called Compelled mode based on a handshake between the master and the slave, without which the master cannot proceed. This allows older, slower modules based on slower technologies to interoperate with new, higher performance modules based on faster technologies. A fast master slows down when speaking to a slow slave, and a fast slave acknowledges a slow master quickly, although the master does not proceed to the next phase of the transaction until it is ready.

Through technological advancements and the introduction

of packet mode, the performance of Futurebus+ will continue to improve as needed. Packet mode is a source-synchronized method that is optimized for block mode transfers. The transfer rate is configurable and was designed for high performance applications. When Profile B was made an IEEE standard in September of 1991, the packet mode protocol was not well understood and was still evolving. It was for this reason that the Profile B Working Group made this method of data transfer optional. That is, Profile B modules are not required to support packet mode.

Transactions

IEEE 896.1 specifies the logical layer for Futurebus+. The profiles provide a subset of this layer to better fit the particular application. Profile B allows the following transaction types:

- Read Unlocked
- Write Unlocked
- Address Only Unlocked
- Read Partial
- Write Partial
- Read Response

Because I/O data and control structures are rarely cached, the Working Group chose not to include any cached operations in Profile B. Split read transactions are supported under Profile B and are essential for bus bridges to slower buses or buses that experience a long read latency. Profile B supports only split read transactions, and only if the split is initiated by the module receiving the request. The Working Group strove for simplification and voted not to support broadcast, broadcall, wait, or transaction flag. Busy, however, is supported, and guidance is given around the use of busy to prevent starvation and deadlock conditions.

Signal Set Summary

The Profile B Working Group chose to use the entire 896.1 signal set with some restrictions. Below is a summary of the signal set .

INFORMATION LINES

AD[63..0]*	Address/Data
D[255..64]*	Data
BP[31..0]*	Bus Parity
TG[7..0]*	TaG
TP*	Tag Parity
CM[7..0]*	CoMmand
CP*	CommandParity
ST[7..0]*	STatus
CA[2..0]	CApability

SYNCHRONIZATION LINES

AS*,AK*,AI*	Address handshake
DS*,DK*,DI*	Data handshake
ET*	End of Tenure

ARBITRATED MESSAGE LINES

AB[7..0]*	Arbitration Bus
ABP*	Arbitration Bus Parity
AC[1..0]	Arbitration bus Condition
AP*,AQ*,AR*	Arbitration bus sync

RESET/BUS INITIALIZATION LINE

RE*	REset

CENTRAL ARBITRATION

RQ[1..0]*	ReQuest
GR*	GRant
PE*	Pre Emption

SLOT IDENTIFICATION

GA[4..0]*	Geographical Address

Diagnosability and Maintainability

Error checking and reporting plays a big role in the design of Profile B modules. Guidelines were put in place to avoid overburdening the error reporting tasks of the hardware while still allowing for system reliability and diagnosability. For example, only the slave module can drive the status lines during transactions. If the master detects an error, it is recorded in the master's error registers but not signaled on the bus. It is then up to the I/O module design whether to retry the errored transaction or report it to an upper layer of software. Also, it is the master's responsibility to know if the module to which it is targeting the transaction is a Profile B module. Profile B modules acting as slaves will ignore the assertion of non-Profile B supported status lines.

Maintaining the systems integrity is often an overlooked aspect when designing an architecture. The Profile B Working Group was fortunate enough to have some of the leading fault management and diagnostic engineers as members. It was these members that brought to light the importance of power up self test. In response to compelling arguments in favor of maintainability, Profile B mandates Built In power up Self Test (BIST) for all Profile B modules. It is recommended that all modules have test coverage of at least 90 percent of all testable logic.

Serial Bus and TAG Bus

Futurebus+ has an auxiliary bus to the main parallel bus called the TAG Bus. This bus follows the parallel bus in terms of protocol. However, its use is largely undefined. For interoperability reasons that could result from the incompatible use of the TAG bus, Profile B lists this bus as optional and most system vendors list it as not supported. Serial bus support is also optional in Profile B. Most Working Group members envisioned that serial bus could be used as an alternative access bus for test and maintenance.

Timing Requirements

To guarantee a minimum level of performance, Profile B includes timing requirements. Figure 3 shows a summary of these timing requirements. The entire set of timing requirements can be found in 896.2 Profile B.

Figure 3 Profile B Timing Diagram

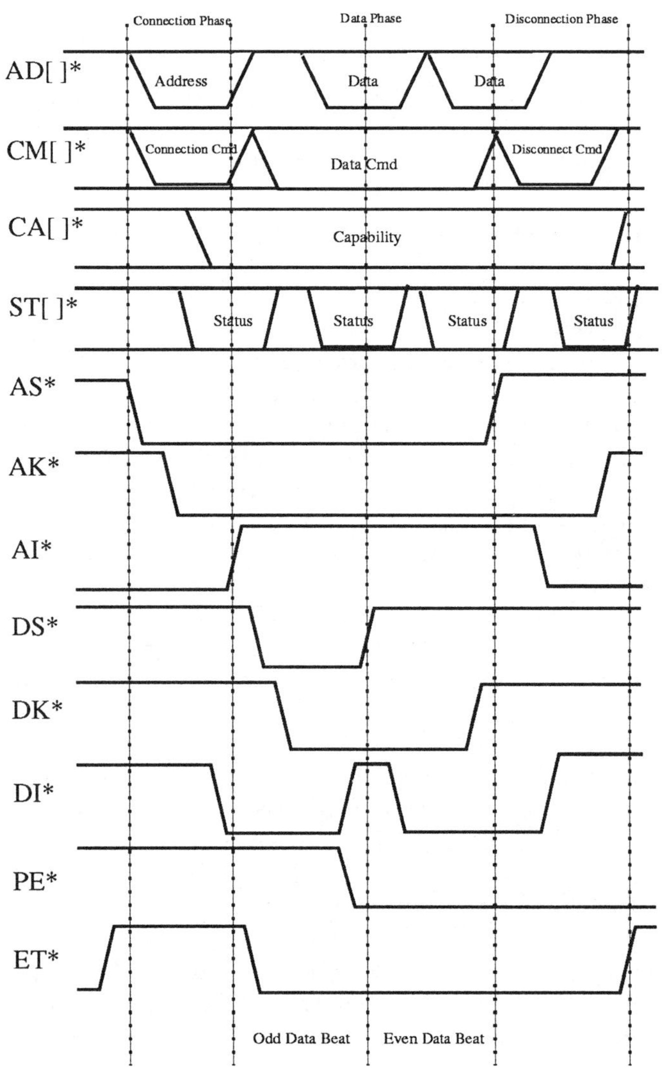

Table 1 Profile B Timing Parameters

Description	Max Value	Comment
AS* to ~ai*	100ns	
~AIf to ds*	50ns	If data phase
~AIf to ~as*	50ns	If address only
DS* to ~di*	2us	Compelled CSR read
~DS* to ~dk*	2us	Compelled CSR read
DS* to ~di*	50ns	Compelled write
~DS* to ~dk*	50ns	Compelled write
~DI to ~dk*	50ns	Compelled read/write
~DK to ds*	50ns	Compelled read/write
~AS* to ~ak*	100ns	Disconnect phase
last ~DK* to ~as*	25ns	Even beat to disconnect
last ~DI* to ~as*	25ns	Odd beat to disconnect
~AS* to ~dk*	50ns	Odd beat end
~AS* to ~di	50ns	Even beat end
~AKf to ~et*	40ns	Master turn off time

Electrical Specifications

The Futurebus+ protocol and architecture is based on a wired-or'd electrical environment. The 896 Working Group chose to base this electrical signaling environment on the IEEE 1194 specification. To create the full electrical specification that Futurebus+ needed, the Working Group formed a task force called the Futurebus+ Expert Electrical Task Force. Today, the work of this task force is summarized in Profile B and all other profiles in 896.2 reference these electrical specifications.

The electrical parameters, which ensure positive noise margins on all signals, include the characteristics of the backplane, the modules, and the backplane transceiver logic (BTL) transceivers.

The most important and controversial parameter specified is the module stub length, which is the length of the signal path on the module connecting the BTL transceiver to the Futurebus+ connector. Initially, a variety of stub lengths were used, based on the results of different analysis techniques of varying accuracy. The Expert Electrical Task Force performed extensive testing to prove that the correct stub length is 25mm, and that figure has been accepted by the IEEE 896 Working Group.

Profile B mandates the use of BTL transceivers for driving the backplane. The rise and fall times of these transceivers is carefully specified at 0.5V/ns, measured between 1.3V and 1.8V. These rise and fall times are measured with transceiver loading equivalent to 16.5 ohms tied to 2.1V DC. To guarantee incident wave switching, the stub length and the rise and fall times must be strictly adhered to.

Signal skew requirements are also an important parameter to consider when designing a Futurebus+ module. Module address and data signals must have propagation delays less than or equal to the strobe lines. The module design must take into account not only the logic but the effects of the connector, the stub length, the input capacitance of the transceiver, and the variations in the module stub impedance.

As mentioned, the Futurebus+ backplane is a bused wired-or'd circuit. The module must filter out the effects of the wired-or'd glitch. Glitch filters are required in Profile B on those signals (AI*, AK*, and RE*) that can be driven by several modules simultaneously. If a module supports the Arbitration Bus, additional filters are required. Since broadcast and broadcall are not supported, no glitch filters on DI* and DK* are required. Again, this was viewed as a cost savings and a simplification to the architecture.

Careful consideration was given to the power specifications currently listed in Profile B. Power guidelines and recommendations are listed for both module and system designs. With these specifications, a module designer can design a module knowing what to expect from the system. In turn, a systems designer can be assured that modules from different vendors will have compatible power requirements once plugged into that vendors system. Modules must produce published specifications for their current demand at each supply voltage level. It will then be the job of the system integrator to ensure that the system configuration can support the power demands of the installed option modules. The specified voltages are:

- 48 +/- V
- +5.0 V
- +3.3 V
- VBP (voltage Battery Powered)
- 0 V DC

The power-up sequencing is specified at:

- 48 +/- V
- +3.3V
- +5.0V
- +2.1V (present on the backplane only)

If battery back-up is not provided, then the voltage battery powered backup (VBP) power pins will be tied to +5V. The power down sequencing is:

- +5V
- +3.3V

The 48 +V/-V and the 2.1 voltages may go down either before or after the +3.3V or the +5.0V. Only the +5.0V in relationship to the +3.3V is specified in the profile. There are no mandated voltage levels to be provided by the system. However, the signal pins assigned to the above listed voltages are reserved, and no other voltage level can be substituted.

Mechanical Requirements

Profile B's mechanical requirements guarantee mechanical compatibility between subracks, backplanes, modules, and connectors. The profile only controls those dimensions which are required to ensure that subracks and modules will fit together. For the bulk of the mechanical work, the Profile A and B Working Groups joined their resources, and now compatible mechanical specification for Profiles A, B, and F appears in IEEE 896.2.

The highlights of the mechanical specifications are:

- Modules are 12 SU by 12 SU standard as defined by IEEE P1301 and 1301.1. An SU is 25mm.
- The subrack is 12 SU high by 300mm deep with a 30 mm separation plane.
- The front panel of the module is 30mm wide.

All I/O for a Profile B module must be through the module front panel. Provisions are made for optional I/O through the backplane, but only on the lower 80 pins of the E connector, and it must be duplicated through the front panel. All profiles in IEEE 896.2 have the same connector pinout.

The connector chosen for Futurebus+ was originally driven by the Navy's need for a connector that would allow a 0.6 inch spacing between modules. The decision was made to go with a 2mm metric connector that is high density, modular, and developed initially for cable interconnect but adapted for backplane use.

Environmental

Profile B systems are intended for use in open office or computer room applications, the environment of which is best described by the Class 4 Category of IEEE P1156. The profile specifies the minimum and maximum environmental conditions that a module must tolerate and the system must provide. Among these specifications are:

- Low temperature of 10 degrees C.
- High temperature of 45 degrees C.
- Airflow of at least 1.5 linear meters per second.

If modules require additional airflow they shall state so in their documentation.

Performance

Performance predictions for a Futurebus+ system will vary with the speed of the device operating on the bus at any given time. As mentioned previously, it is the slowest module involved in the transaction that determines the bus bandwidth. Today, the performance is dictated by the BTL transceiver propagation delay and transceiver-to-transceiver skew. In discrete designs, the designer has to contend with PAL and gate delays of the logic that sits behind the transceivers. In the very near future, silicon vendors will offer a protocol and data chip set solution that combines the logic that sits behind the transceivers into a single ASIC or a group of ASICs. This will increase the performance. Beyond that, we should expect to see the ASICs integrate the BTL transceivers into the protocol and data chips. This will offer the highest performance given the current backplane technology.

First generation Futurebus+ systems using only compelled mode have publicly demonstrated performance of 162 Mbytes/sec. As the propagation delay of the transceivers decrease, performance in the 200 Mbytes/sec range is expected within 1 year. Packet Mode will increase the performance into the 300 MB/sec range within the next 2 years or less. Figure 4 shows the performance predictions for Futurebus+.

Figure 4 Futurebus+ Performance Projections

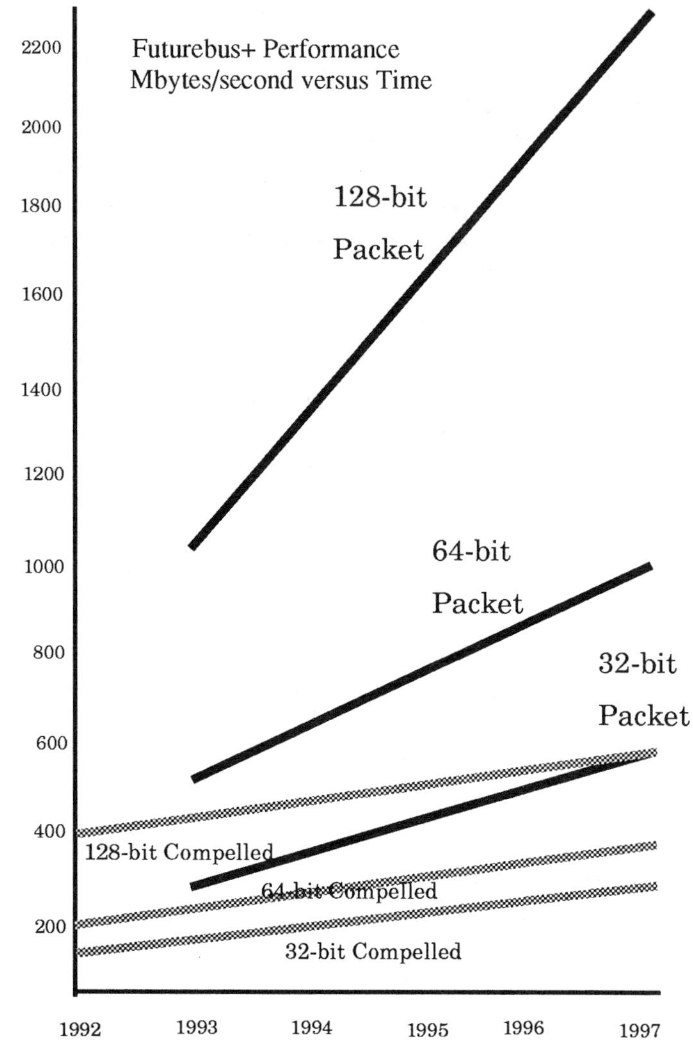

Summary

Open standards are becoming increasingly important in the computer industry and will continue to do so over the next decade. Architecting scalable standard buses as I/O buses allows the industry to continually improve CPU and memory interconnects while allowing for a consistent I/O interface to protect investments in user specific applications.

Commercially, Futurebus+ appears to be a success and enjoys the support of many computer vendors including Texas Instruments, Digital Equipment Corporation, AT&T, Unisys, Nanotek, Tektronix, Raytheon, Amdahl, Force Computers, Signetics, National Semiconductor, Sun Microsystems, Ironics, Hewlett-Packard, Future+ Systems and IBM. In addition, members of the U.S. Navy's Next-Generation Computer Research (NGCR) program plan to use Profile B modules in Futurebus+ NGCR systems.

About the Author

Barbara P. Aichinger is a Principal Engineer working in the Futurebus+ Technical Office at Digital Equipment Corporation. Barbara joined Digital in 1983 and has worked as the Project Leader for many of Digitals high performance CPU and I/O devices. She has been involved with the IEEE 896 Futurebus+ Working Group since early 1990 and served as editor and task group leader for IEEE 896.2 Profile B. Barbara has a BSEE from the University of Akron, Ohio and an MSEE from the University of Massachusetts, Lowell.

References

IEEE 896.1 Futurebus+ Logical Layer Specification

IEEE 896.2 Futurebus+ Physical Layer Specification

IEEE P1156.1 Environmental Core Specification

IEEE P1194.1 Electrical Characteristics of Backplane Transceiver Logic Interface Circuits

IEEE P1212 Control and Status Register Architecture

IEEE P1301 Standard for Metric Equipment Practice for Microcomputers Coordination Document

IEEE 1301.1 Detail Standard for a Metric Equipment Practice Using a 2mm Connector and Convection Cooling

Proceedings of OPEN BUS '91 Futurebus+ Profile B by Barbara P. Aichinger

Proceedings of BUSCON-WEST '92 The I/O Bus: Futurebus+ by Barbara P. Aichinger

A Study of I/O System Organizations

A. L. Narasimha Reddy
IBM Almaden Research Center
650 Harry Road, K56/802
San Jose, CA 95120
reddy@almaden.ibm.com.

Abstract

With the increasing processing speeds, it has become important to design powerful and efficient I/O systems. In this paper, we look at several design options in designing an I/O system and study their impact on the performance. Specifically, we use trace driven simulations to study a disk system with a nonvolatile cache. Some of the considered design parameters include the cache block size, the fetch size, the cache size and the disk access policy. We show that decoupling the fetch size and the cache block size results in significant performance improvements. A new write-back policy is presented that is shown to offer significant performance benefits. We show that optimal block size in a two-level memory hierarchy is dependent only on the latency, data rate product of the second level as previously conjectured. We also present results showing the effect of a split access operation of a disk read/write head.

1 Introduction

Processor speeds have been improving at a rapid pace over the last few years. It has been realized that if corresponding improvements in the I/O performance are not achieved, the system's performance may not improve at the same rate as of the processor speed improvements. Amdahl's rule of thumb for a balanced computer requires that a system should have 1 Mbyte of main memory capacity and 1 Mbit/sec of I/O bandwidth per 1 MIPS of CPU performance [1]. Recent measurements [2] show that the I/O requirements are nearly an order of magnitude higher, 1 Mbyte/sec of I/O bandwidth per 1 MIPS, for the current machines.

Several proposals have been made recently for employing multiple disk organizations [3, 4, 5, 6, 7]. Most of these studies have been aimed at improving the data throughput of the system. They also study the disk system independent of the other components of the system such as a disk cache or an I/O cache.

Disk cache or I/O cache is normally used to improve the performance of the disk system [8, 9]. We will use the term I/O cache or cache in this paper to denote a cache used within the I/O system, which may be physically located within the main memory (file cache) or within the disk subsystem (disk cache).

Studies so far have looked at the disk system or the I/O cache independently. In this paper, we study the interaction between the I/O cache and the disk system with the aim of understanding how the various policy decisions and system parameters affect the performance of the whole I/O system. There are several parameters and policies that influence the performance of the system. We study the impact of various parameters such as the cache size, block size and fetch size. The policies adopted at the disk system may impact the decisions at the cache. We consider the interaction of various disk policies and the cache design parameters to understand the total effect seen by the system.

The rest of the paper is organized as follows. Section 2 looks at the system model, defines various parameters used in the study and the various disk/cache management policies considered in the study. Section 3 describes our evaluation methodology. Section 4 describes the results of various experiments conducted. Section 5 concludes the paper by outlining the major results presented in the paper.

2 System Model

An I/O system in our model consists of a number of disks together with a cache as shown in Fig.1. Whenever data is written to the I/O system, it is written to the cache. The data is eventually written to the disk at a later time. A write is considered completed

© 1992 ACM 0-89791-509-7/92/0005/0308 $1.50

when the data is written to the cache. When a read request arrives at the I/O system, it is first checked to see if the requested block is in the cache. If it is, the requested block is returned to the system. If the requested block is not in the cache, the data is read from the disk. Whenever data is read from the disk, it is copied into the cache and returned to the system. A read request is considered complete when the requested block is returned to the system.

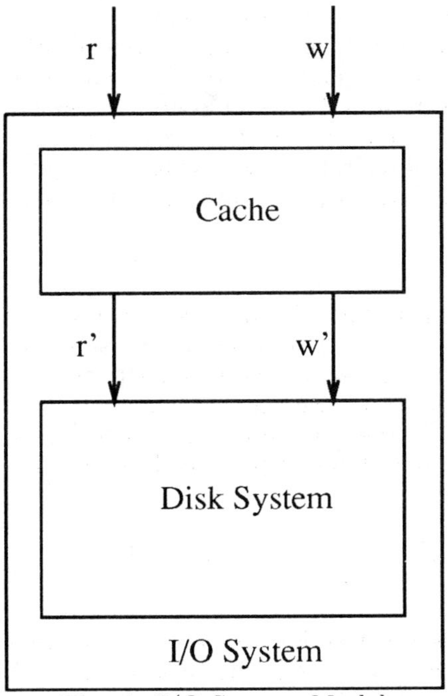

Fig. 1. I/O System Model.

There are four parameters in our model: cache size, cache block size, fetch size, and destage size. Cache size is the amount of cache space in the I/O system. Cache block size is the unit of space allocation in the cache. Fetch size is the amount of data fetched from the disk to the cache on a read miss in the cache. In our model, whenever data is written to disk, all blocks belonging to a *destage unit* are written together. We varied the destage size from fetch size to a track size of 32 kbytes. It was found that destage size of a track always resulted in better performance (lower writes at disk, better read response time and better disk utilization). Hence, we only consider destage sizes of a track in this paper, unless specifically mentioned otherwise. Request size is the number of sectors requested from the I/O system, sector being the smallest unit of data uniquely addressable on the disks. Request sizes are determined from the traces. We considered cache sizes of 1Mbytes to 16Mbytes for our simulations. Cache block sizes from 512 bytes to 32 Kbytes were considered. Fetch size was varied from 512 bytes to 32 Kbytes. The relation between the block size and the fetch size is as follows. The data is always transferred in units determined by the cache block size. For example, if a request asks for 7 sectors starting at sector numbered 3, when block size is 4 and the fetch size is 16, block numbers 1 (sectors 1,2,3,4), 2, 3, and 4, i.e., sectors 1,2,...16, will be brought into the cache. For the same request, if the block size is 2 and the fetch size is 16, block numbers 2 (sectors 3,4), 3, 4,5,6,7,8 and 9, i.e., sectors 3,4,...18, will be brought into the cache resulting in transfers of different sectors.

The following procedure is employed in determining how many sectors of data are to be brought into the cache on a request. If the request size is larger than the fetch size, the number of sectors brought in from the disk equals the request size, otherwise, it equals the fetch size. In other words, fetch size is the minimum number of sectors brought from the disk to the cache on a read miss.

On a miss, cache blocks may have to be written back to the disk. The LRU chain is scanned to see which blocks are at the head of the LRU chain. Since every miss results in fetching max(request size, fetch size) number of blocks, as many blocks have to be evicted from the cache on every miss. If these blocks at the head of the LRU chain were not dirty (i.e., don't have to be written back to the disk), servicing the miss would only involve reading the blocks from the disk to the cache. To facilitate this, the blocks at the head of the LRU chain can be continually written to the disk in the background. If this cleaning activity is carried out when the disk is idle, the cost of cleaning can be hidden from the response time. This is modeled in the following way in our simulations: the number of dirty blocks at the head of LRU chain to be cleaned for servicing the read miss is counted. The read request is issued to the disk system. After the read request is satisfied by a transfer of the requested blocks from the disk to the cache, we simulate the write back of the dirty blocks by issuing a write request to the disk system for an appropriate number of blocks. Even though, this modeling is not exact, it suffices for our evaluation purposes by simulating the write-back activity.

When the block size doesn't equal the fetch size, which blocks should be written back to the disk on a read miss? Should we strictly write the blocks at the head of the LRU chain? Should we write back the blocks that were brought together into the cache (based on the fetch size)? If we follow the first method, a write-back operation may actually involve writing a number of blocks that belong to different tracks and thus incurring a large cost. If we follow the second method, we have not decoupled the cache block size and the fetch size and we might as well have organized the cache on bigger blocks of fetch size. To alleviate these two problems, we adopt a method based on the above two ideas. Blocks at the head of LRU chain are scanned to iden-

Table 1. Disk parameters.

Avg. latency	8.3 ms
Avg. seek	14.2 ms
sectors/track	64
sector size	512 bytes
tracks/cylinder	19
cylinders/disk	746
seek cost function	nonlinear
latency cost function	uniform

tify the blocks that need to be written back. Once these blocks are identified, all the blocks that belong to the same track (destage unit) on the disk that are currently present in the cache are also written back to the disk. The blocks at the head of the LRU chain are considered evicted from the cache and the other blocks that may be written to the disk as a result of such an operation are left in the cache in a clean (i.e., not dirty) state. By adopting such a strategy, it is hoped that dirty blocks belonging to the same track are written to the disk in one single operation while still following an LRU replacement policy. It is possible, using such a write-back policy, a block at the tail of the LRU chain may repeatedly get written back to the disk as a result of evicting other dirty blocks at the head of the LRU chain that belong to the same track. The effectiveness of such a policy needs to be verified through simulations.

Disk service involves several components. A *seek* is performed to seek to the track on which the requested block of data resides. Rotational *latency* is paid to reach the first block of the request on the track. *Read time* or *transfer time* is the time spent in actually reading the data from the disk surface. The disk parameters used for simulations can be found in Table 1.

Disks are assumed to employ a SCAN algorithm for satisfying the disk requests. In this service policy, the disk arm moves outward from the center of the disk servicing requests in its path till it reaches the outermost track. Once it reaches the outermost track, it jumps to the innermost track with an outstanding request and starts the outward journey again. Reads and writes are treated in the same fashion once queued at the disk i.e., reads are not given higher priority over writes at the disk. However, writes to the disk are queued only during the periods when the disk is idle. If a read request is issued after a write request is queued, the read request may have to wait for the write request to complete. The employed SCAN policy also did rotational optimization: if two requests belonging to the same track are waiting to be serviced, they are served in the order that they may be read off from the disk surface, rather than in their arrival order. To further reduce rotational latency, we considered *split access* operations. If a request asks for n number of blocks, in normal operation, on an average half a rotation penalty is paid to get to the first block in the request and then the requested blocks are read from the disk. This operation may result in paying more than one revolution for reading/writing a single track. In split access operation, the disk starts servicing the request as soon as any of the requested blocks comes under the read-write head. For example, if a request asks for reading blocks numbered 1,2,3,4 from a track of eight blocks 1,2,...8, and the read-write head happens to get to block number 3 first, then blocks 3 and 4 are read, blocks 5,6,7,8 are skipped over and then blocks 1 and 2 are read. In such operation, a disk read/write of a single track will not take more than one single revolution.

In normal operation of serving the request from the first block, latency plus read time , on an average, equal

$$l_{max}/2 + n * R \quad (1)$$

for reading n blocks from a single track, where l_{max} is the time for one revolution and R is the data rate in secs/block. The seek time is not affected in employing the split access operation and hence we only look at the difference in the read time plus latency. In split access operation, the latency plus read time is given by the following:

$$f * l_{max} + (1-f) * ((1-f)\frac{l_{max}}{2} + n * R), \quad (2)$$

where f is the fraction of blocks on a track that are being read = n/N, N is the total number of blocks on a single track. The first term in the above expression counts the probability of finding the read/write head in the middle of the requested sequence (and hence paying a full revolution to serve the request) and the second term counts the probability of finding the read/write head positioned in the rest of the track. The above simplifies to

$$l_{max}/2 + l_{max} * f(1 - f/2). \quad (3)$$

This function grows less rapidly than the earlier function. For example, when f = 0.25, the above cost = $0.719 l_{max}$, when f = 0.5, it is $0.875 l_{max}$, and when f = 1, it is l_{max}. Hence, the split access operation of serving disk requests flattens the latency+read time cost function. This indicates that, split access operation may favor larger fetch sizes than normal mode operation. The effective average latency of a disk operation in split access operation = $l_{max}/2 + l_{max} * f(1 - f/2) - n * R$ = $\frac{l_{max}}{2}(1 - f^2)$, which again indicates that the transfers are more efficient as f approaches 1. The benefits of larger accesses in split access operation have to be weighed against the problem of cache pollution. This balance needs to be studied through simulations.

Table 2. Characteristics of the traces.

Trace	Reads		Writes		Trace length	System Capacity	Read ratio
	# of req.	kbytes	# of req.	kbytes	seconds	Mbytes (# of disks)	
1	37037	114462	30079	67752.5	3751.45	1672 (4)	0.55
2	46215	120931.5	23532	21474	6053.96	2926 (7)	0.66
3	49545	140215.5	54735	38211	2003.89	6688 (16)	0.48
4	54171	94569.5	48558	82833	5422.18	3344 (8)	0.53

3 Evaluation Methodology

Physical I/O traces were obtained from IBM AS/400 systems running real applications. Four traces were employed in this study. The characteristics of these traces can be found in Table 2. All the traces used in this study are from commercial environment with predominantly transaction oriented workloads. The first trace, Trace 1, has both interactive and batch requests. Trace 2 contains mostly batch requests. Trace 3 contains only interactive requests. Trace 4 is obtained from a server application, where the machine is used as a server for a number of terminals. Each trace entry contained the following information: the time the request was initiated, the disk address, the starting sector address on the disk, the number of sectors requested and whether the request is a read or a write operation. The AS/400 architecture is segment-based and distributes blocks of a file across the disks in the system. The file is initially allocated on a single disk, but further allocations of blocks to the same file can get distributed across all the disks. In this study, we do not consider the effects of file/block allocation on disks since the trace information we have is only from physical I/Os.

When a nonvolatile cache is used, the writes can be declared completed once the data is written to the cache. If sufficient clean (or empty) space is left in the cache for writes to take place without waiting for some dirty pages to be evicted to the cache, the write performance seen by the user is limited by how fast the data can be written to the cache. The dirty blocks in the cache can be written to the disk by a background process. This process may keep a certain number of clean blocks in the cache to ensure that the writes can be completed by writing to the cache. However, when a read request is issued to the I/O system, the read request is completed only when the requested block is returned to the user. Hence, the perceived performance of the I/O system is determined by how fast the read requests can be serviced (assuming that the load on the system is not so high as to be unable to keep writing the dirty blocks of data from the cache to the disk). Hence, in this paper, read response time is used as a measure of performance of the system. This is in contrast to the approach taken in [10, 11] where write bandwidth of the system is the primary concern.

Since disk accesses take considerably longer time compared to accesses from the cache, we consider the performance to be mainly dictated by the misses in the cache. Since write misses can be satisfied by writing the data blocks to the cache, read misses are considered to be the main determinants of performance. In the model we employ here, the read/write hits and write misses to cache are assumed to be satisfied in zero time. The response time for servicing a read miss is considered as the time for satisfying that request.

At each cache size, different block sizes and fetch sizes were considered for the I/O system organization. For each organization, the effective access time was computed. Effective access time of each organization is the sum of response times of all read misses divided by the total number of requests in the trace. In our model, read response time is the measure of performance. If we used only the read miss ratio as the measure, we would not account for the different costs associated with fetching different number of blocks from the disk. For each trace, the effective access time of each organization is computed. The access times of all the organizations are scaled with respect to the acess time of an organization with a block size of 4 kbytes and a fetch size of 4 kbytes to obtain their *relative access times*. Hence, by definition, for all traces, the relative access time of a system with a block size of 4 kbytes and a fetch size of 4 kbytes is 1.0. The relative access times of each organization are computed for all the four traces. Then, a geometric mean of these relative access times is computed for each organization. We call this the *normalized access time*. Normalized access time is used as the final measure of performance in our study. System organizations are compared on the basis of normalized access time. Lower the normalized access time, better the performance. This approach of evaluation is similar to the approach adopted by the SPEC benchmark group [12].

4 Results

In this section, we present the results obtained from the simulations.

4.1 Fetch size and Block size

Fig. 2. shows the performance of different organizations for a cache size of 1 Mbytes. The different organizations are compared on the basis of normalized access time, as explained earlier. It is observed that an organization with a fetch size of 4 kbytes and a block size of 512 bytes achieves the best performance. However, there are several other organizations with almost equal performance. It is also noted that at the optimal fetch size of 4 kbytes, the differences in performance due to varying the block size are about 10%. Among these organizations, a choice could be made based on some other criterion. For example, in this study, we did not include the cost of managing larger LRU chains with smaller block sizes. If these costs are a concern, among the organizations with almost equal performance in Fig.2., an organization with a slightly larger block size may be preferred. The relatively flat region around the optimal block size indicates that choosing a slightly different fetch size would not hurt performance drastically. It is noted that decoupling block size from fetch size produced considerable performance improvements (roughly 25% improvement from a block size = fetch size = 16k to 16k fetch size and 2 kbyte block size). Even when the cost of handling larger LRU chains is included, this benefit is likely to be significant since the cost of a disk access is much more expensive.

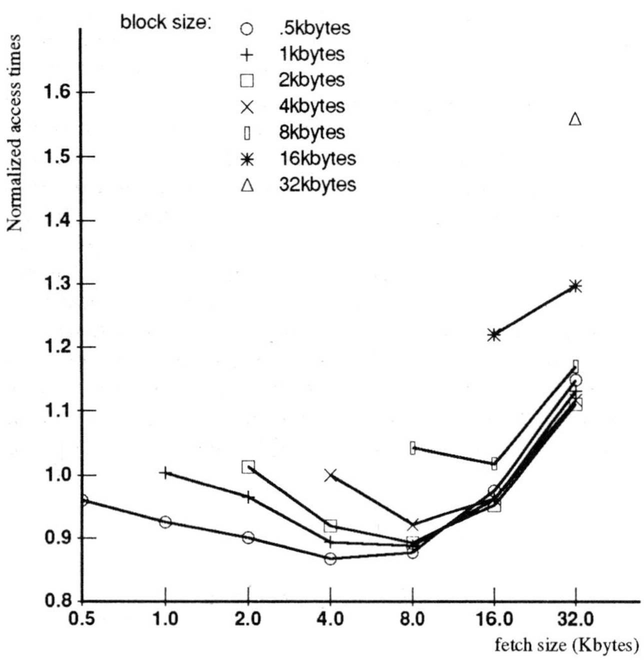

Fig. 2. Performance of various organizations at cache size = 1M.

4.2 Cache size

Fig. 3. shows the effect of cache size on the performance of various organizations when block size equals fetch size. To show the impact of cache size on the average access times, actual values are plotted in Fig. 3. rather than the normalized access times.

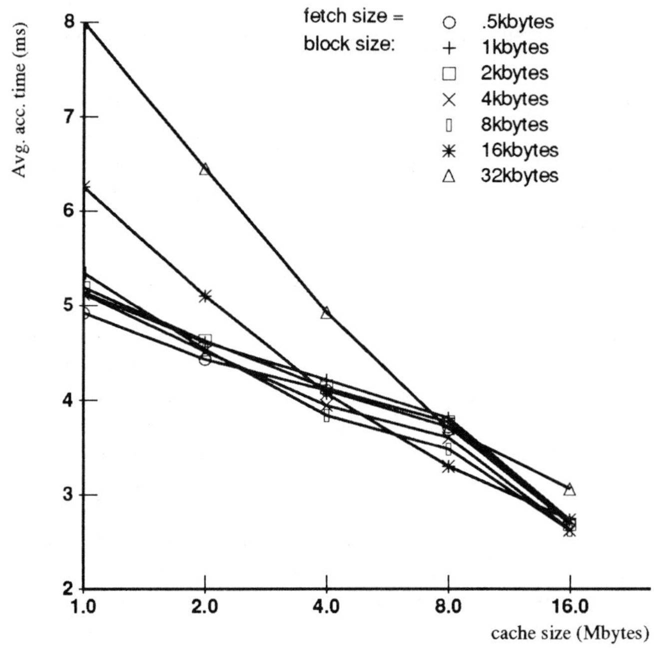

Fig. 3. Performance of various organizations at different cache sizes.

It is observed that the difference in performance between different organizations is more significant at smaller cache sizes than at larger cache sizes. It is also noted that organizations with fetch sizes larger than 8 kbytes have nearly equal performance at higher cache sizes even though they differ considerably at smaller cache sizes. Larger fetch size tries to exploit spatial locality. However, as a result of fetching more blocks into the cache, the cache may get polluted. At smaller cache sizes, this pollution is a bigger problem. But at larger cache sizes, this is less of a problem and hence the observed trend. This tends to indicate that if sufficiently large caches are employed, the implications of choice of other parameters are less significant. This fact is also observable in Fig. 4, which shows the performance of different organizations at a cache size of 16 Mbytes. It is observed that the normalized access times now range from 0.9 to 1.2 compared to a range of variation of 0.9 to 1.6 at a cache size of 1 Mbytes. It is also noted that the optimal fetch size has increased with an increase in cache size.

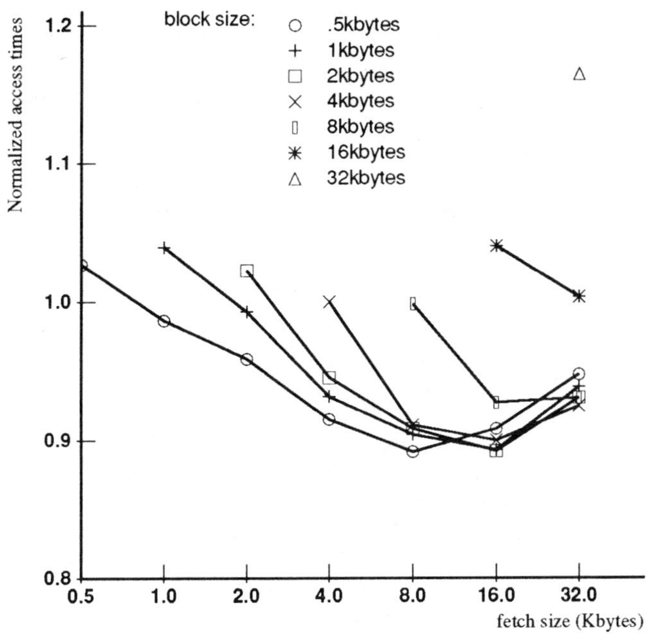

Fig. 4. Performance of various organizations at different cache sizes.

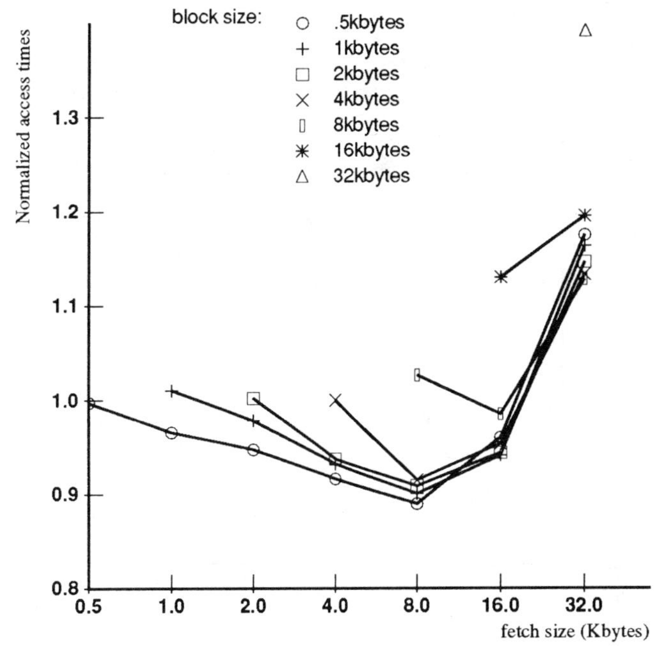

Fig. 5. Normal-mode performance at cache size = 16M.

4.3 Normal-mode Disk Operation

Fig. 5. shows the performance of various organizations at a cache size of 16 Mbytes, employing a normal-mode disk operation. The best fetch size for normal-mode operation is observed to be 8 Kbytes. In normal-mode operation, the latency cost of each disk access is higher than that in a split access operation. To offset this higher cost of latency, we fetch more data in each disk access in normal-mode operation. We observe that the performance in normal mode degrades quickly at larger fetch sizes compared to a more gradual degradation of performance in split access operation. This is as expected from the analysis earlier owing to a relatively flat read time plus latency cost of split access operations. At the optimal fetch size, the split access operation resulted in 5-10% (depending on cache size) performance improvement over normal mode operation of disks. In a more highly loaded environment, these performance gains are likely to be higher. To assess these possible improvements, we conducted two other experiments where the time between two requests was reduced by a factor of 2 and 4. Split access operation in these two cases resulted in 20% and 45% improvement in performance at the best fetch sizes.

4.4 Disk Reads and Writes

Fig.6. shows the fraction of total disk operations that are read operations as a function of block size and fetch size for Trace 1 at a cache size of 16 Mbytes. For this experiment, the destage size was made equal to the fetch size. As the fetch size is increased, reads constitute larger fraction of the total disk operations. At larger fetch sizes, smaller block sizes result in larger read ratios. With larger block sizes, there is a higher probability of a block being dirty and hence a miss results more often in an eviction of a dirty block and hence the resulting higher write ratios. The reason that the write ratio decreases with increasing fetch size is that the writes have more spatial locality than reads, at least for the traces under study. This can also be observed by the miss ratio curves shown in Fig. 7, where it is seen that writes have smaller miss ratios than reads. The read/write ratios in the I/O workload have significant impact on the performance in systems where the reads and writes have different costs such as disk arrays with parity protection. The larger the readratio, the better the performance of disk arrays since the writes are more expensive [?].

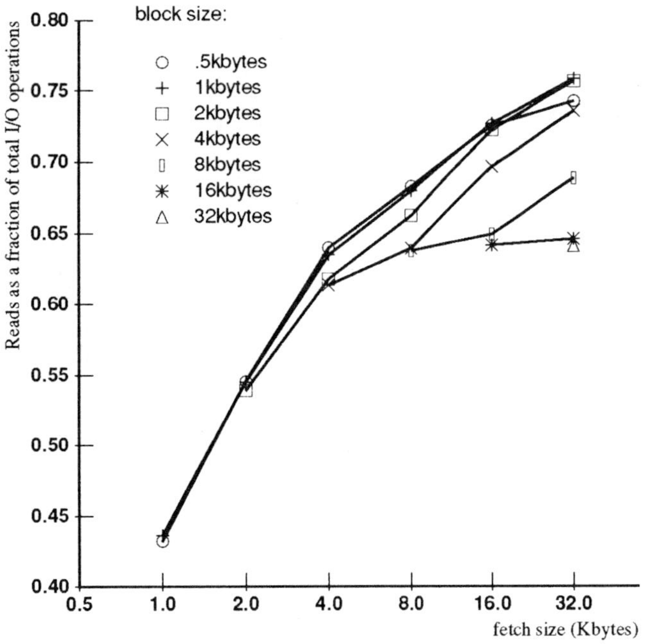

Fig. 6. Read ratio as a function of block size and fetch size -Trace 1.

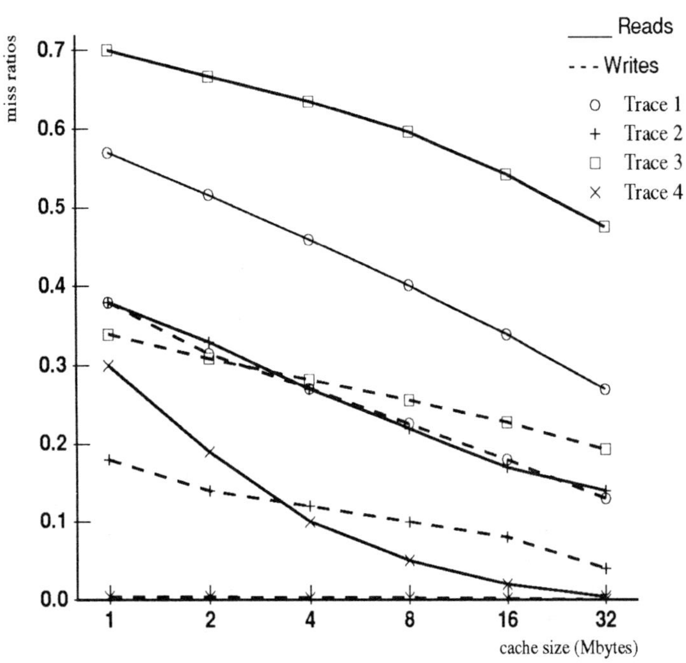

Fig. 7. Miss ratio as a function of block size.

From Fig. 6, it is seen that by choosing the block size and fetch size independent of each other, we can obtain desired workload characteristics. Besides the observed performance benefits in non-arrayed systems as reported in this paper, the ability to change the workload characteristics seen by the disk system is an important benefit of decoupling block size and fetch size. It is also observed from Fig. 6 and Table 2 that for some fetch sizes, the workload seen by the disk system after the cache has fewer fraction of write requests than that of the workload before the cache. All this discussion points to the fact that the write penalty of the array systems can be managed by using nonvolatile caches and appropriate cache management techniques.

4.5 Optimal Block Size

Previously, it was conjectured that the optimal block size for minimizing the access time in a two-level cache depended only on the product of the latency and the data rate of the second level cache and not on the individual parameters separately [14]. Similarly, optimal striping unit in a disk array system is shown to be directly related to the product of data rate and the positioning time of a disk [15]. We show that this is indeed the case in any two-level memory system under some assumptions. In fact, from the dimensions of the parameters alone, it could be argued that this has to be the case. Here, we present another simple argument to show why this is true. For the analysis here, we assume that the block size and the fetch size are equal. The cost of serving a miss is given by $c_b = c_0 + b * c_1$, where c_0 is the latency of the data access from the second level memory and c_1 is the time to access a unit of data. The optimal block size is one that minimizes the total cost of serving the misses, given by,

$$T_b = m_b * c_b, \tag{4}$$

where m_b is the total number of misses at block size b or alternately the miss ratio at that block size if we consider T_b to be normalized cost of serving misses. When the block size is increased, the miss ratio decreases till a point beyond which the miss ratio starts to increase again. There is no reason to choose the cache block size larger than this minimum point since both the miss ratio and the cost of serving a miss increase beyond this point. Assume that the cache block size at which this minimum in miss rate occurs to be b_{min}. The miss ratio in the range of $(1, b_{min})$ can be approximated by:

$$ln(m_b) = ln(m_{min}) + k * ln(b_{min}/b). \tag{5}$$

The above states that log of miss ratio is a linear function of log of the block size. This behavior is observed in several studies, for example [14, 16]. If we substitute the values of m_b and c_b from above and differentiate with respect to b to obtain the optimal block size, we find that the optimal block size is given by

$$b_{opt} = \frac{kc_0}{(1-k)c_1}. \tag{6}$$

This shows that the previous conjecture about optimal block size is indeed true. Typically, the miss ratio drops 20%-30% for every doubling of cache size in the range of (1, b_{min}) [14]. If this is the case, we can choose k to be approximately 0.33 in the above calculations to obtain $b_{opt} = c_0 / 2c_1$. Using the above equations, it can also be shown that the differences in performance around the optimal block size would be small.

In I/O systems, cache and the disks function as a two-level memory hierarchy. If the assumptions in the above analysis are valid in such a hierarchy, we could apply the analytical results to such a system as well. Even though disk access can fit the above cost model of accessing a block of size b, the latency parameter (or positioning time = rotational latency + seek time for disks) is not a constant, but is a random variable. We could approximate this by choosing average positioning time for this parameter. Another factor that is ignored in the above analysis is the queuing delays that may be incurred in the disk systems. If queuing delays are large, this model can not be applied to the disk systems. The constant factor relating the optimal block size to the latency and data rate parameters may depend on the workload characteristics. How the workload characteristics may impact these constants remains to be established.

Fig. 8. compares the performance of various organizations at a cache size of 16 Mbytes, using normal mode disk operation, at different data rates. For this set of experiments, the block size = fetch size = destage size. It is observed that the optimal block size doubled when the data rate of the disks is improved by a factor of two. This conforms to the above analysis. It is also noted that the variations in performance around the optimal configuration point are not very significant.

4.6 Write-back policy

Fig. 9. shows the effect of the write-back policy on the number of write operations for Trace 1 at the fetch size of 32 kbytes. The figure shows the number of write operations of the proposed write-back policy as a fraction of the number of write operations in a strict LRU policy. In a strict LRU policy, only the blocks at the head of the LRU chain are written to the disk. If n number of blocks are to be written to disk from the head of the LRU chain, these n number of blocks are grouped into as few write operations as possible based on their track location. It is seen that the proposed write-back policy considerably reduces the number of write operations seen at the disk. The write operations are reduced by more than half at a block size of 512 bytes. The reduction of the number of write operations is significant because of the earlier discussed write penalty in disk arrays. The policy is seen to be more effective at smaller block sizes. At smaller block sizes, it is more likely that blocks belonging to the same track are not bunched together in the LRU chain and hence a higher likelihood of the proposed write-back policy being effective at reducing the number of write operations.

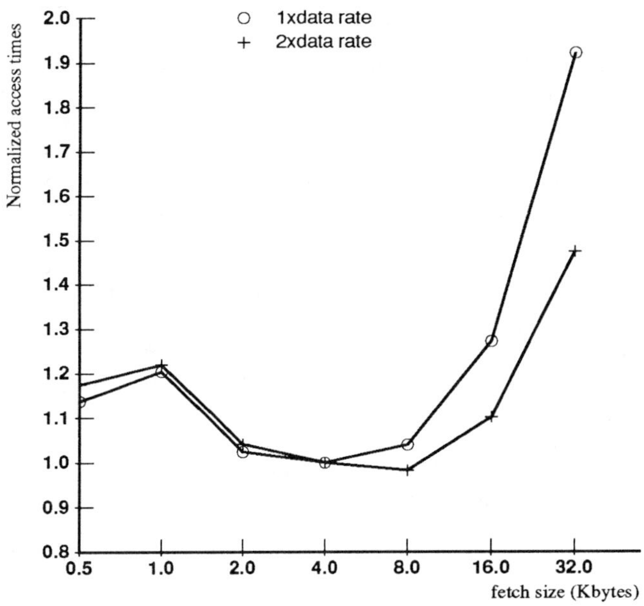

Fig. 8. Performance of various organizations at different data rates.

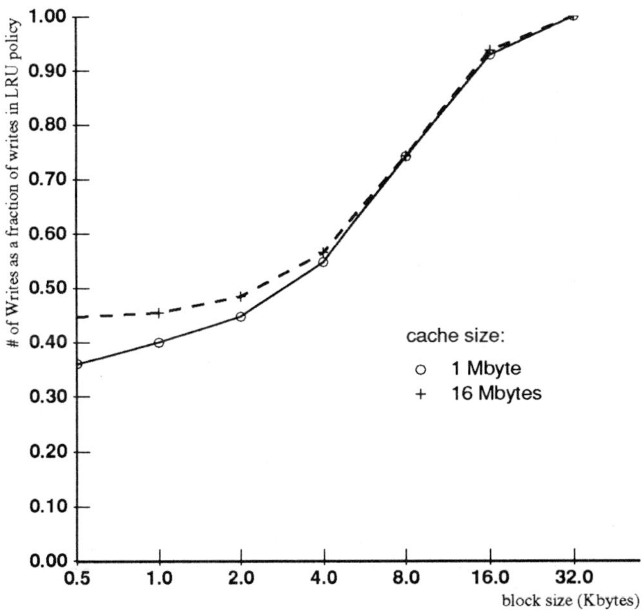

Fig. 9. Performance of write-back policy.

4.7 Impact of two levels of caching

In most systems, part of the main memory is used as an I/O cache (file cache). Besides this cache, the I/O system may have a cache on its own (disk cache). If I/O cache is used in two places, in the memory and the I/O system, the second level cache in the I/O system may be of little benefit depending on the size of the cache employed in the main memory. This is illustrated in Fig. 10. The figure shows the effective access times observed at the second level cache in the I/O system when the system has a first level I/O cache of 4 Mbytes, in both caches the block size and the fetch size being 4 kbytes. It is observed that up to a size of 4 Mbytes, there is very little improvement in access times. It is also observed that even at higher cache sizes, the second level in a two-level cache has effective access times that are higher than a single level cache of the same size. The reason for this is that the first level cache takes away much of locality and hence the second level cache observes higher miss ratios and hence higher effective access times than a single level cache of same size. This indicates that benefits of cache are more significant if the cache space is located in one level. This also raises the question that if there should be a cache close to the disk system since a main memory I/O cache reduces its benefit significantly.

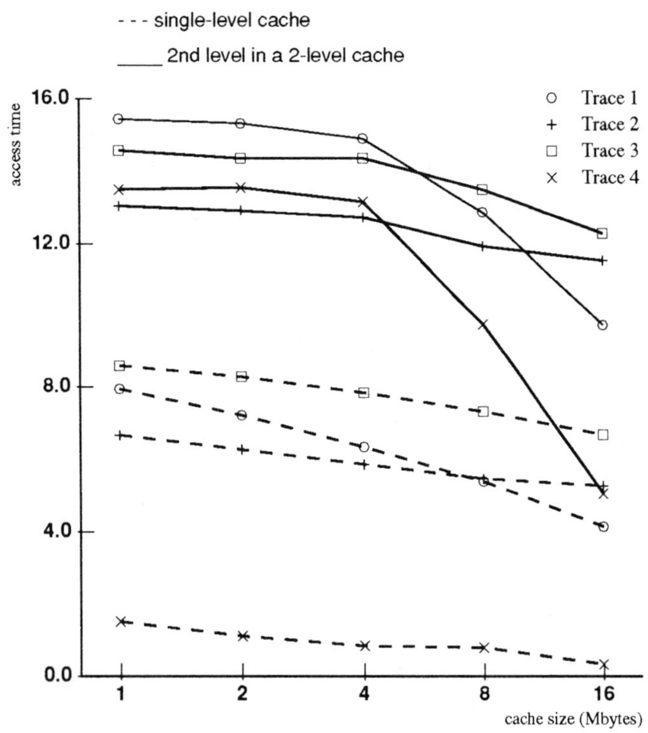

Fig. 10. Access times of a two-level cache.

Keeping the cache closer to the processor (in main memory) reduces page fault ratio and other processing overheads as well. Keeping it closer to the disks enables sharing the cache between different processors connected to the same I/O system. This question is also addressed in [17]. The optimal configuration for I/O caching (between main memory and the disk system) remains an open question and further study is required.

5 Conclusions and Future work

In this paper, we have presented a study of I/O system organizations. Several design choices and policies were evaluated through trace-driven simulations. It was shown that decoupling the cache block size and the fetch size yielded significant performance benefits. It was also shown that by suitably choosing these parameters, the read/write characteristics of the workload seen by the disk system can be considerably altered. This is particularly useful in I/O systems such as disk arrays where the costs of reads and writes are different. A new write-back policy presented in this paper is shown to reduce the number of disk write operations considerably. It was also shown that a previous conjecture about block size being determined by the product of latency and data rate is indeed true. It was shown that split access operation of disk could result in considerable performance benefits. Some results were presented to show the effects of two levels of caching in the I/O system.

The impact of various parameters and policies in a cached disk array system remains to be studied. The effect of two levels of caching is only briefly explored here. Given a performance goal, what is the best way to organize a cached I/O system at a fixed cost? We intend to pursue these questions in our future work.

6 Acknowledgements

Discussions with John Fu, of University of Illinois, Jai Menon, Dick Mattson, Robert Morris, Rich Freitas, John Palmer and Jim Brady, of IBM corporation, have been helpful.

References

[1] G. M. Amdahl. Validity of the single processor approach to achieving large scale computing capabilities. *Proc. AFIPS Spring Joint Comput. Conf.*, 30:483–485, April 1967.

[2] J. Akella and D. P. Siewiorek. Modeling and measurement of the impact of input/output on system performance. *Proc. of 18th Ann. Symp. on Computer Arch.*, May 1991.

[3] D. A. Patterson, G. Gibson, and R. H. Katz. A case for redundant arrays of inexpensive disks (RAID). *ACM SIGMOD Conference*, June 1988.

[4] A. L. Narasimha Reddy and P. Banerjee. An evaluation of multiple-disk I/O systems. *IEEE Trans. Comput.*, C-38, no. 12:1680–1690, Dec. 1989.

[5] K. Salem and H. Garcia-Molina. Disk striping. *Int. Conf. on Data Engineering*, pages 336–342, 1986.

[6] M. Livny, S. Khoshafian, and H. Boral. Multi-disk management algorithms. *Proc. ACM SIGMETRICS Conf.*, pages 69–77, May 1987.

[7] M. Y. Kim. Synchronized disk interleaving. *IEEE Trans. Comput.*, C-35, no. 11:978–988, Nov. 1986.

[8] A. J. Smith. Disk cache-miss ratio analysis and design considerations. *ACM Trans. on Comput. Systems*, 3, no. 3:161–203, Aug. 1985.

[9] J. K. Ousterhout, H. DaCosta, D. Harrison, J. Kunze, M. Kupfer, and J. Thompson. A trace-driven analysis of the unix 4.2 bsd file system. *Proc. 10th Symp. on Operating System Principles*, pages 15–24, Dec. 1985.

[10] J. Ousterhout and F. Douglis. Beating the I/O bottleneck: A case for log-structured file systems. *Tech. Rep., Dept. of EECS, Univ. of California, Berkeley*, Aug. 1988.

[11] M. Rosenblum and J. K. Ousterhout. The LFS storage manager. *Proc. of ACM Symp. on Oper. Syst. Principles*, 1991.

[12] The SPEC benchmark suite. SPEC, Fremont, CA, Dec. 1990.

[13] A. L. Narasimha Reddy. Reads and writes: when I/Os aren't quite the same. *IBM Tech. Report: RJ 8033*, March 1991.

[14] A. J. Smith. Line (block) size choice for cpu cache memories. *IEEE Trans. on Computers*, Sept. 1987.

[15] P. M. Chen and D. Patterson. Maximizing performance in a striped disk array. *Proc. 17th Ann. Int. Symp. on Computer Architecture*, June 1990.

[16] S. Przybylski. The performance impact of block sizes and fetch strategies. *Proc. of 17th Ann. Symp. on Computer Archicture*, May 1990.

[17] K. Li and K. Petersen. Evaluation of memory system extensions. *Proc. of 18th Ann. Symp. on Computer Arch.*, May 1991.

Comparison of Sparing Alternatives for Disk Arrays

Jai Menon and Dick Mattson

IBM Almaden Research Center
San Jose, California 95120-6099
Telephone: (408) 927-2070 *E-Mail: menonjm@ibm.com*

Abstract— This paper explores how choice of sparing methods impacts the performance of RAID level 5 (or parity striped) disk arrays. The three sparing methods examined are dedicated sparing, distributed sparing, and parity sparing. For database type workloads with random single block reads and writes, array performance is compared in four different modes - normal mode (no disks have failed), degraded mode (a disk has failed and its data has not been reconstructed), rebuild mode (a disk has failed and its data is being reconstructed), and copyback mode (which is needed for distributed sparing and parity sparing when failed disks are replaced with new disks). Attention is concentrated on small disk subsystems (fewer than 32 disks) where choice of sparing method has significant impact on array performance, rather than large disk subsystems (64 or more disks). It is concluded that, for disk subsystems with a small number of disks, distributed sparing offers major advantages over dedicated sparing in normal, degraded and rebuild modes of operation, even if one has to pay a copyback penalty. Furthermore, it is better than parity sparing in rebuild mode and similar to it in other operating modes, making it the sparing method of choice.

1. Introduction

A ***disk array*** is a set of disk drives (and controller) which can automatically recover data when one (or more) drives in the set fails. Such recovery is done using redundant data (parity) that is stored on the disks and is maintained by the controller. [11] gives a nice description of five types of disk arrays called RAID levels 1 through 5, and [3] describes a sixth type of disk array. The array parity technique is illustrated below on a 4+P disk array. In this diagram, Pi is a parity block that protects the four data blocks labelled Di.


```
        +------------------- P grp 1
        |     .   .   .          ...
        |                   +-P grp 8
        | Track 1    Track 2 |
Disk 1  D1 D2 D3 D4 D5 D6 D7 D8
Disk 2  D1 D2 D3 D4 D5 D6 D7 D8
Disk 3  D1 D2 D3 D4 D5 D6 D7 D8
Disk 4  D1 D2 D3 D4 P5 P6 P7 P8
Disk 5  P1 P2 P3 P4 D5 D6 D7 D8
```

Only two tracks (each with four blocks) are shown on each disk. A column consisting of 4 data blocks and a parity block is called a ***parity group***. There are eight parity groups in the diagram shown. The ***parity width*** of the array is the number of data blocks per parity group, 4 in the example. An array with small parity width (8 or smaller) is called a ***small array***; and an array with large parity width (say 16 or larger) a ***large array***. In the figure, P1 contains the parity or XOR of the 4 data blocks labeled D1 and these 5 blocks form a parity group. Similarly, P2 is the XOR of the blocks labeled D2, P3 the XOR of D3s, and so on. Such a disk array is robust against single disk crashes; if a disk were to fail, data on it can be recreated by reading data from the remaining four disks and performing the appropriate XOR operations.

Whenever the controller receives a request to write a data block, it must also update the corresponding parity block for consistency. If one of the D1 blocks is altered, the new value of P1 is calculated as:

```
new P1 = old D1 XOR new D1 XOR old P1
```

Since the parity must be altered each time the data is modified, these arrays require four disk accesses to write a data block: 1) Read the old data; 2) Read the old parity; 3) Write the new data; and 4) Write the new parity, where the reads must be completed before their corresponding writes can begin.

In the diagram, the parity blocks are ***rotated*** with the parity block for the 1st parity group on disk-5, the parity block for the 5th parity group on disk-4, etc. This organization is used for either a track striped RAID Level 5 or a parity striped array, and for small read/write requests there is little performance difference between them. The track striped RAID Level 5 disk array is the type considered in this paper.

To minimize the probability of losing data, arrays often use on-line spare disk drives (called ***dedicated sparing***) so that data on a failed disk drive can be immediately rebuilt to a spare drive. Two alternative forms of sparing have been proposed by [6] and [12]: ***distributed sparing*** (in which the spare space is distributed among the drives in an array); and ***parity sparing*** (in which the system starts with no spares, but when a disk fails, parity groups in different arrays are combined to form larger parity groups and arrays).

When all the drives in an array are operational, it is said to be in ***normal mode***. The array is said to be in ***degraded mode*** when a drive in the array has failed and no attempt has been made to rebuild the data that used to be on that drive and place it on another drive; and the array is said to be in ***rebuild mode*** during the time that data on the failed drive is being rebuilt and placed on another drive. If a second disk drive fails before the failed drive is replaced and data on it rebuilt, the array will lose data.

This paper shows that the choice of sparing method significantly impacts the performance of disk arrays. It gives an overview of the three sparing approaches, describes the models used to evaluate the performance of arrays, lists the cases that are analyzed (widths of arrays, drive and controller parameters, workload parameters, etc.), presents the results of the performance analysis and, finally, concludes that, all things considered, distributed sparing is the best method.

2. The Three Sparing Approaches

The traditional approach to sparing in arrays is called ***dedicated sparing*** [1] and is exemplified by the two N+P arrays (Disks 1-5 in array-1, disks 8-12 in array-2, and two spare disks, shared between the two arrays) shown in Figure 1. Each array has 4+1=5 disks holding N=4 disks worth of data. Each disk has K=6 regions, which in this paper represent disk tracks (which may contain several blocks), but regions could represent blocks, tracks, cylinders, etc. Each region is labelled; the region labelled "da1" is decoded as meaning "d" for data, "a" for data named "a", and "1" meaning it is in parity group 1. Similarly, the region labelled "p-1" stands for the parity information for parity group 1, "S-A" stands for a spare region called "A", and "Xa1" or "Ya1" stands for a non-accessable region (because the disk containing it is broken) that used to contain data named "a" and belonged to parity group "1". The spare disks are shared between the two arrays and are unused in normal operation. In each array, the N+1=5 disks operate as a 4+P array with rotated parity, each disk having K=6 regions. Corresponding regions from the N+1 disks form a ***parity group*** containing N+1 regions; so there are K parity groups in each array. The only disadvantage to dedicated sparing is that it does not utilize the spare disks in normal operation.

When a disk (e.g. Disk-3) fails, K regions from K different parity groups are lost. Each lost region can be rebuilt using the corresponding regions from the surviving disks. The rebuilt data can then be written to a region on the spare disk and read back to verify correctness. As can be seen from Figure 1, a disk failure requires 6 regions to be read from each of four disks, and 6 regions to be written and verified on a spare disk (Disk-6) which now replaces the broken disk. If a region is a track, at least 36 disk revolutions are needed to complete the rebuild of disk-3. If a second disk (Disk-5) should fail, the regions from it can be rebuilt and written and verified on the second spare disk (Disk-7) with an additional 36 revolutions.

```
            |       K=6 Regions               |        K=6 Regions
      Disk-1 |    da1 de2 di3 dm4 p-5 du6      |     da1 de2 di3 dm4 p-5 du6
Array Disk-2 |    db1 df2 dj3 p-4 dq5 dv6      |     db1 df2 dj3 p-4 dq5 dv6
  1   Disk-3 |  X dc1 dg2 p-3 dn4 dr5 dw6      |   X Xc1 Xg2 X-3 Xn4 Xr5 Xw6
      Disk-4 |    dd1 p-2 dk3 do4 ds5 dx6      |     dd1 p-2 dk3 do4 ds5 dx6
      Disk-5 |  Y p-1 dh2 dl3 dp4 dt5 p-6      |   Y Y-1 Yh2 Yl3 Yp4 Yt5 Y-6
------------    -------------------------        -------------------------
Spare Disk-6 |    S-A S-B S-C S-D S-E S-F      |     dc1 dg2 p-3 dn4 dr5 dw6
Spare Disk-7 |    S-G S-H S-I S-J S-K S-L      |     p-1 dh2 dl3 dp4 dt5 p-6
------------    -------------------------        -------------------------
      Disk-8 |    dy7 dC8 dG9 dKa p-b dSc      |     dy7 dC8 dG9 dKa p-b dSc
Array Disk-9 |    dz7 dD8 dH9 p-a dOb dTc      |     dz7 dD8 dH9 p-a dOb dTc
  2   Disk-10|    dA7 dE8 p-9 dLa dPb dUc      |     dA7 dE8 p-9 dLa dPb dUc
      Disk-11|    dB7 p-8 dI9 dMa dQb dVc      |     dB7 p-8 dI9 dMa dQb dVc
      Disk-12|    p-7 dF8 dJ9 dNa dRb p-c      |     p-7 dF8 dJ9 dNa dRb p-c

            |    (a) Before Any Failure       |    (b) After 2 Failures
```

Figure 1: Dedicated Sparing Approach

The ***distributed sparing*** approach ([6])is exemplified by the two N+P+S arrays (Disks 1-6 in array-1, disks 7-12 in array-2) shown in Figure 2 with each array using 4+1+1=6 disks holding N=4 disks worth of data. The data and parity regions are also called ***information regions*** to distinguish them from ***spare regions***. As can be seen from Figure 2, no two regions from a parity group are on the same disk, so if a disk (say Disk-3) fails, at most one information region from any parity group is lost and this lost region can be rebuilt from the remaining information regions of the parity group on the other disks and copied to a spare space region on still another disk. To rebuild the information regions on disk-3, four regions have to be read from each of 5 disks and one region has to be written and verified on each of 5 disks, for a total of 30 disk revolutions to complete the recovery process, but this is better than the 36 disk revolutions that were needed to complete a rebuild in the dedicated sparing approach.

As shown in Figure 2, if a second disk (Disk-6) fails, the regions from it can be rebuilt by reading 6 regions from 4 disks in Array-1, and writing and verifying 1 region on each of 6 disks in Array-2, for a total of 36 disk revolutions.

One would expect distributed sparing to be better than dedicated sparing because: in normal mode N+P+S disks are used instead of N+P; in degraded mode N+S disks are available instead of N and only (N+1)/(N+2) regions on a disk are lost as opposed to all regions for dedicated sparing; in rebuild mode fewer I/Os are needed to rebuild lost information and since the spare regions are distributed over many disks, the writing to spare regions can be done in parallel instead of being serialized onto one disk as in dedicated sparing. On the other hand, distributed sparing would have more disk failures that impact performance because all disk failures cause the array to operate in degraded mode, whereas, for dedicated sparing, failure of the spare disk has no performance effect.

Finally, to return to distributed spare space after a broken disk is replaced requires that information regions be copied-back to the new disk into their original locations. Since there is no urgency to do copyback (similar to the urgency to do rebuild), this ***copyback mode*** can be scheduled to happen when the system is not very busy, such as in the middle of the night, during lunch time, etc..

In later analysis, a system with two 4+P+S arrays using distributed sparing is examined. Figure 5 shows some of the relevant states of such a two array system, with starred states being the ones reported in this paper.

The ***parity sparing*** approach ([12]) is exemplified by the four 2+P arrays (Disks 1-3, 4-6, 7-9, and A-C in arrays 1,2,3, and 4) shown in Figure 3, with each array using 2+1=3 disks holding N=2 disks worth of data. Together, the two arrays (Disks 1,2,3 and Disks 4,5,6) hold four disks worth of data as in the previous examples, but there are no spare regions. When a disk (say Disk-3) fails, the broken 2+P array is combined with the other good 2+P array to form a larger good array of size 4+P. Forming the new and larger parity groups is somewhat complex, but can be deduced from Figure 3 where it is easy to see that to perform this combining operation, every data region on every surviving disk in array 1 must be read (8 reads), and every parity region on every surviving disk in array 1 must be read, written, and verified (4 reads + 4 writes + 4 verifies). Also, every parity region on every disk in array 2 must be read, written, and verified (6 reads + 6 writes + 6 verifies) for a total of 38 revolutions.

```
                  |     K=6 Regions             |      K=6 Regions
           Disk-1 |   da1 de2 di3 dm4 p-5 S-F   |   da1 de2 di3 dm4 p-5 dv6
           Disk-2 |   db1 df2 dj3 p-4 S-E du6   |   db1 df2 dj3 p-4 dq5 du6
     Array Disk-3 | X dc1 dg2 p-3 S-D dq5 dv6   | X Xc1 Xg2 X-3 X-D Xq5 Xv6
       1   Disk-4 |   dd1 p-2 S-C dn4 dr5 dw6   |   dd1 p-2 p-3 dn4 dr5 dw6
           Disk-5 |   p-1 S-B dk3 do4 ds5 dx6   |   p-1 dg2 dk3 do4 ds5 dx6
           Disk-6 | Y S-A dh2 dl3 dp4 dt5 p-6   | Y Yc1 Yh2 Yl3 Yp4 Yt5 Y-6
     ------------   -------------------------     -------------------------
           Disk-7 |   dy7 dC8 dG9 dKA p-B S-L   |   dy7 dC8 dG9 dKA p-B p-6
           Disk-8 |   dz7 dD8 dH9 p-A S-K dSC   |   dz7 dD8 dH9 p-A dt5 dSC
     Array Disk-9 |   dA7 dE8 p-9 S-J dOB dTC   |   dA7 dE8 p-9 dp4 dOB dTC
       2   Disk-10|   dB7 p-8 S-I dLA dPB dUC   |   dB7 p-8 dl3 dLA dPB dUC
           Disk-11|   p-7 S-H dI9 dMA dQB dVC   |   p-7 dh2 dI9 dMA dQB dVC
           Disk-12|   S-G dF8 dJ9 dNA dRB p-C   |   dc1 dF8 dJ9 dNA dRB p-C

                  |   (a) Before Any Failure    |   (b) After 2 Failures
```

Figure 2: Distributed Sparing Approach

```
           |        K=6 Regions             |        K=6 Regions
Array Disk-1  |   da1 de3 p-5 dm7 dq9 p-B    |   da1 de3 dj5 dm7 dq9 p-B
  1   Disk-2  |   db1 p-3 di5 dn7 p-9 duB    |   db1 df3 di5 dn7 p-9 duB
      Disk-3  | X p-1 df3 dj5 p-7 dr9 dvB    | X X-1 Xf3 Xj5 X-7 Xr9 XvB
              |   -----------------------    |   -----------------------
Array Disk-4  |   dc2 dg4 p-6 do8 dsA p-C    |   dc1 dg3 p-5 do7 ds9 dvB
  2   Disk-5  |   dd2 p-4 dk6 dp8 p-A dwC    |   dd1 p-3 dk5 dp7 dr9 dwB
      Disk-6  |   p-2 dh4 dl6 p-8 dtA dxC    |   p-1 dh3 dl5 p-7 dt9 dxB
              |   -----------------------    |   -----------------------
Array Disk-7  |   dyD dCF p-H dKJ dOL p-N    |   dyD dCF p-H dKJ dOL p-N
  3   Disk-8  |   dzD p-F dGH dLJ p-L dSN    |   dzD p-F dGH dLJ p-L dSN
      Disk-9  |   p-D dDF dHH p-J dPL dTN    |   p-D dDF dHH p-J dPL dTN
              |   -----------------------    |   -----------------------
Array Disk-10 |   dAE dEG p-I dMK dQM p-O    |   dAE dEG p-I dMK dQM p-O
  4   Disk-11 |   dBE p-G dII dNK p-M dUO    |   dBE p-G dII dNK p-M dUO
      Disk-12 |   p-E dFG dJI p-K dRM dVO    |   p-E dFG dJI p-K dRM dVO
              |                              |
              |   (a) Before Any Failure     |   (b) After Fail+Rebuild
```

Figure 3: Parity Sparing, before and after 1st Failure + Rebuild

```
              |        K=6 Regions           |        K=6 Regions
      Disk-1  |   da1 de3 dj5 dm7 dq9 p-B    |   da1 de3 dj5 dm7 dq9 p-B
      Disk-2  |   db1 df3 di5 dn7 p-9 duB    |   db1 df3 di5 dn7 p-9 duB
Array Disk-3  | X X-1 Xf3 Xj5 X-7 Xr9 XvB    | X X-1 Xf3 Xj5 X-7 Xr9 XvB
 12   Disk-4  |   dc1 dg3 p-5 do7 ds9 dvB    |   dc1 dg3 p-5 do7 ds9 dvB
      Disk-5  |   dd1 p-3 dk5 dp7 dr9 dwB    |   dd1 p-3 dk5 dp7 dr9 dwB
      Disk-6  | Y p-1 dh3 dl5 p-7 dt9 dxB    | Y Y-1 Yh3 Yl5 Y-7 Yt9 YxB
              |   -----------------------    |   -----------------------
Array Disk-7  |   dyD dCF p-H dKJ dOL S-F    |   dyD dCF p-H dKJ dOL dxb
  3   Disk-8  |   dzD p-F dGH dLJ S-E dSN    |   dzD p-F dGH dLJ dt9 dSN
      Disk-9  |   p-D dDF dHH S-D dPL dTN    |   p-D dDF dHH p-7 dPL dTN
              |                              |
Array Disk-10 |   dAD dEF S-C dMJ dQL p-N    |   dAD dEF dl5 dMJ dQL p-N
  4   Disk-11 |   dBD S-B dIH dNJ p-L dUN    |   dBD dh3 dIH dNJ p-L dUN
      Disk-12 |   S-A dFF dJH p-J dRL dVN    |   p-1 dFF dJH p-J dRL dVN
              |                              |
              |   (a) Just After 2nd Fail    |   (b) After 2nd Rebuild
```

Figure 4: Parity Sparing, before and after 2nd Failure + Rebuild

As shown in Figure 4, if a second disk (Disk-6) fails, the regions from it can be rebuilt by first reading all the old parity regions in arrays 3 and 4 (12 revolutions), forming a new parities by XORing pairs of parities together, then writing and verifying these 6 new parities (12 revolutions) into the locations shown in Figure 4, which has the effect of combining the two 2+P Arrays 3 and 4 to form a single 4+P+S array in 24 revolutions. Then the rebuilt information regions in array-12 can be placed in the spare regions of array-34, with 36 disk revolutions.

To perform the copyback operation, when the broken drive is replaced, the larger array is separated into two smaller arrays. This copying back of information can be scheduled to happen when the system is not very busy (lunch time, middle of the night, etc.).

In a later analysis, a system with four 2+P arrays will be examined. Figure 6 shows some of the relevant states of such a two array system, with starred states being the ones reported in this paper.

3. Brief Description of the Analysis

The results from [7] indicate that arrays without a non-volatile disk cache have poor performance; so all the analysis in this paper assumes a non-volatile disk cache. An analysis is presented for each sparing method when operating in normal mode, degraded mode, rebuild mode, and copyback mode (if it is necessary). Many simplifying assumptions are made to keep the analysis tractable, but, the analysis is accurate enough for performance comparisons between disk array subsystems using different sparing methods.

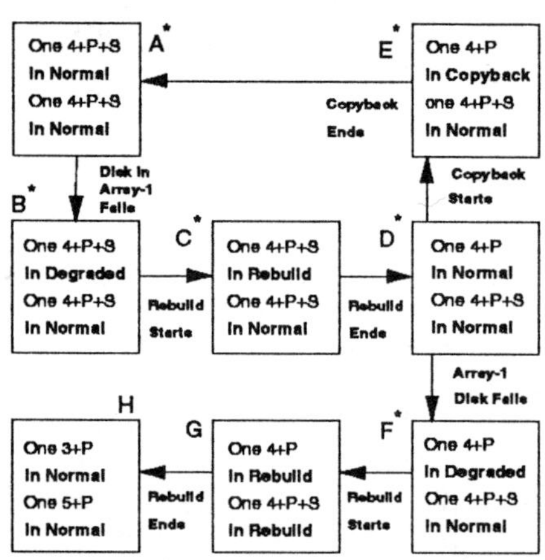

Figure 5: Distributed Sparing States

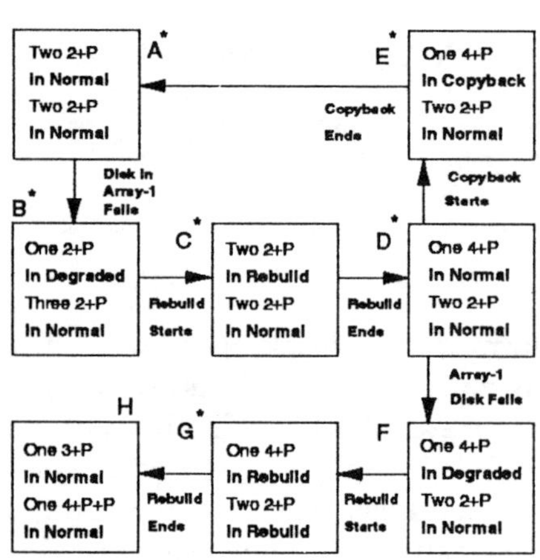

Figure 6: Parity Sparing States

The systems are modelled as a disk controller with a large non-volatile cache attached to arrays of disks. The controller consists of 4 processors [5] whose job is to examine a shared, non-volatile cache for hits and misses on read and write requests. If the block requested by a read is in cache, it is considered a ***read hit***; else it is a ***read miss***. Read hits are satisfied directly out of the cache, read misses require access of the disks. If the block written by a write request is in cache, it is a ***write hit*** else it is a ***write miss***. On a write hit or miss, the data block is accepted from the system and placed in the non-volatile cache after which the write is considered "done". This block is destaged to disk at some later time, along with other blocks that also need to be destaged and that are on the same track or cylinder. From the viewpoint of the disks, it sees only read misses and destages.

Traces from transaction-processing applications ([4]) indicate that, for large caches, it is very reasonable to set the write hit ratio to 1, since most database writes are preceded by reads which bring the blocks into the disk controller cache. This means that when a block is destaged, only 3 disk accesses are needed - read old parity, write new parity, write new data. Read old data is not needed, since it is always already in cache.

Write hits may be divided into hits on ***dirty regions*** (regions that have been previously written by the host system and are sitting in the cache waiting to be destaged) and hits on clean regions. If the system request rate is S and the fraction of requests that are write hits to clean regions is C, then the destage rate is SC regions/sec because, in steady state, the rate at which new dirty regions are created in cache must be equal to the rate at which dirty regions are destaged from cache. If X regions are destaged per destage, the destage rate can be expressed as SC/X destages/sec.

For normal mode performance, the system was modelled as an M/M/4 system (to represent the four storage directors managing the cache) which generates read misses and destages at some rate to be handled by N+1 or N+2 disks each of which is again represented as an M/M/1 queue.

There are three types of requests from the system - read hits, read misses and write hits. Read hits and write hits are satisfied directly by the cache; hence their response time is modelled as the response time of an M/M/4 system. Read misses first pass through the M/M/4 system with some response time, then enter the queue of one of the N+1 or N+2 devices with equal probability. The utilization of the devices is calculated easily, since the read miss rate and the destage rate are known, and the service time for a read miss and the service time for a destage are also known. All the quantities needed to calculate the read miss response time at the devices is thus known. The total read miss response time is calculated as the sum of the response time through the cache (M/M/4 queue) and the response time at the device (M/M/1 queue). The average request response time may now be calculated as a function of read hit response time, write hit response time and read miss response time.

Degraded Mode for Distributed Sparing was analyzed as follows. In normal mode an N + 2 array gets R read misses/sec and D destages/sec (3D destage operations) so that each device gets R/(N + 2) reads/sec and 3D/(N + 2) destages/sec. After the failure of one of the disks, the R/(N + 2) reads/sec to the failed device increases the traffic to each of the surviving disks by (R/(N + 2))*((N/(N + 1)) reads/sec (assuming the parity tracks are rotated across the devices at a rate that is relatively prime to the rate at which spare tracks are rotated across the devices).

The D/(N + 2) writes of data per second and the D/(N + 2) reads of parity and writes of parity that used to go to the failed device do not affect the traffic to the surviving disks in any way. So, in summary, each of the surviving disks get

$$\frac{(2N + 1) * R}{(N + 2) \times (N + 1)} \text{ reads/sec and}$$

$$\frac{3D}{N + 2} \text{ destages/sec}$$

The degraded mode analysis for dedicated and parity sparing followed a similar line of reasoning.

This paper introduces a new procedure for the ***Rebuild Mode Analysis***. Whereas [9] presented an excellent analysis of rebuild time for disk arrays, by considering three different rebuild strategies - ***baseline rebuild***, ***rebuild with redirection of reads***, and ***piggy-backing rebuild***, this paper considers only baseline rebuild (since most actual array implementations use this procedure), and it adds to the work of [9] by calculating the performance of the array to user requests during the rebuild process. In making this analysis, it is assumed that any updates to be made to the spare disk are held off (buffered in the controller) until rebuild completes. In addition, this paper makes two realistic assumptions not made in [9]; it is assumed that after a track of blocks is rebuilt and written to the spare device, it must be read back and ***verified*** for correctness; and it is assumed that user requests get priority over background rebuild activity.

Each device in the array will process user requests. Only when there are no user requests in its queue will a device attempt to rebuild the next sequential track. At the end of rebuilding this track, if a new user request has arrived, the device returns to handle the new user request. Otherwise, it continues to rebuild the next sequential track, always examining the queue for user requests at the end of each track rebuild.

Rebuild mode performance depends mostly on two key factors - the number of disks involved in rebuild and the performance of these drives before rebuild begins (typically the drives are in degraded mode before rebuild begins, though sometimes they are in normal mode when rebuild begins - e.g. for parity sparing). Interestingly, the total number of I/Os needed to complete the rebuild has only a secondary effect on rebuild performance, given the policy of giving user requests higher priority than rebuild work.

Next, consider the factors affecting rebuild time. The drive which takes the longest time to complete its portion of rebuild work determines rebuild time. Which drive takes the longest time to rebuild and the length of time this drive takes to complete rebuild is a function of the busyness of the drives before rebuild begins, the number of I/Os needed to complete rebuild on each of the drives, and whether these I/Os must wait for other rebuild I/Os on other drives to complete (e.g., a write I/O to the spare device cannot be started until read I/Os on corresponding tracks on surviving disks have been completed and the data to be written to the spare drive reconstructed). Once again, there need not be a strong correlation between the total number of I/Os needed to complete rebuild and rebuild time.

To conserve space, the more complicated analysis for ***Rebuild Mode Analysis for Parity Sparing*** is all that is presented in this paper. The analysis for dedicated and distributed sparing follows a similar pattern.

There are two cases to be considered - rebuild following the first failure when a broken N + 1 array and a good N + 1 array are combined into a 2N + 1 array; and rebuild following a second failure in a 2N + 1 array which causes two good N + 1 arrays to be combined to create spare space, and then the data on the broken disk in the 2N + 1 array is rebuilt to this spare space.

During ***Rebuild after first failure***, a broken N + 1 array and a good N + 1 array are combined to form a good 2N + 1 array. If there are T tracks per device, a surviving disk in the broken array must read TN/(N + 1) tracks and must read, write and verify T/(N + 1) tracks for a total of (TN + 3T)/(N + 1) I/Os. Also, a disk in the good array must read, write and verify T/(N + 1) tracks for a total of 3T/(N + 1) I/Os. These are the minimum number of I/Os needed - more I/Os may be needed in some cases to achieve proper parity distribution in the 2N + 1 array. Figure 7 shows a simplified Markov model of the states of a disk in the broken array and Figure 8 shows the states of a disk in the good array that was combined with the broken array. On a disk in the broken array, every data track (N/N + 1 of the tracks) is read, and every parity track (1/N + 1 of the tracks) is read, written and verified.

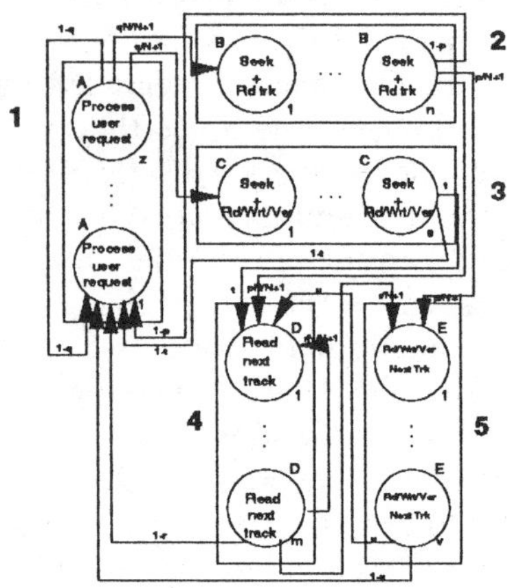

Figure 7: States of a Disk in Broken Array During Parity Sparing Rebuild

From Figure 7, there are five states for such a device - a first state in which it is processing user requests, a second state in which it is seeking and then reading a data track to be used for rebuild, a third state in which it is seeking, then reading/writing/verifying a parity track, a fourth state like the second one but without a seek and a fifth state like the third one but without a seek. Each of the states has substates - the first state has z substates, where z is the average time to handle a user request; the second state has n substates, where n is how long it takes to seek and then read a track; the third state has s substates, where s is how long it takes to seek to a track, then read it, write it back, and read it back again to verify it; the fourth state has m substates, where m is the time to read the next sequential track, and the fifth state has v substates, where v is the time to read, write, then read again the next sequential track.

From the last substate of the first state, a transition to the first substate of the second state is N times more likely than a transition to the first substate of the third state, since there are N times as many data tracks as parity tracks. Once it has completed reading/writing/verifying a parity track (last substate of state 3), it returns to process a user request with probability 1-t (t is the probability that no new user request arrived in time s) or it proceeds to read the next sequential data track with probability t. When it reaches the last substate of State 2 (handling a data track), it returns to process a user request with probability 1-p, or it proceeds to the next sequential data or parity track with probability p. Since data tracks are N times more likely than parity tracks, it transitions to a data track with probability $p/(N+1)$. The other transition probabilities are easy to figure out and the probability of being in any of the substates A, B, C, etc. can easily be computed and will not be included here.

It is easy to see that tracks are being rebuilt at a rate of $\mu = B + C + D + E$ tracks/time unit. If a disk has T tracks, all will have been processed in $T/(B + C + D + E)$ time units.

The performance of the array to user requests can be calculated by assuming that the device utilization as seen by user requests is $\rho_1 + \rho_2$, where ρ_1 is the utilization in degraded mode, and ρ_2 is the extra utilization as seen by user requests during the rebuild process (since rebuild activity can only be preempted on track boundaries). It is calculated as the arrival rate of user requests to a device in the array times the average delay seen by a user request because of rebuild. The average delay is

$$nB \times \frac{n}{2} + sC \times \frac{s}{2} + mD \times \frac{m}{2} + vE \times \frac{v}{2}$$

Next, consider the states of a disk in the good array being combined with the broken array. This is shown in Figure 8. This disk was operating in normal mode before rebuild began, unlike a disk in the

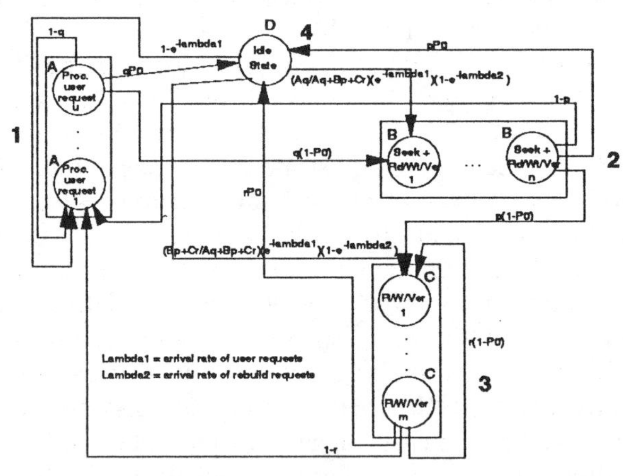

Figure 8: States of a Disk in Array Being Combined with for Parity Sparing

broken array which was operating in degraded mode when rebuild began. Also, this disk needs to only access its parity tracks (read/write/verify each parity track) whereas a disk in the broken array must access all its tracks. As a result, it is possible that a disk in the array being combined with could be in the idle state during rebuild - no user request to process and no rebuild work to do since it is being held up by the disks in the broken array which are yet to generate any rebuild work for it to do. Such a disk has four states - State 1 with u substates in which it is processing user requests, State 2 with n substates in which it seeks then reads/writes/verifies a parity track, State 3 with m substates in which it reads/writes/verifies a parity track, and State 4 in which it is idle. Values u, m and n are the time to process a user request, to read/write/verify a track, and seek time plus time to read/write/verify a track.

From the last substate of State 1, the disk returns to process a user request with probability 1-q, and leaves State 1 with probability q. If P0 is the probability of there being no rebuild request in the queue, then the disk transitions to State 4 with probability q*P0. Else, it transitions to the first substate of State 2. The transition probabilities out of the idle state require some explanation. If λ_1 is the arrival rate of user requests to the disk, and arrivals are Poisson, $e^{-\lambda_1}$ is the probability of no user request arrival in one time unit. So, $1-e^{-\lambda_1}$ is the probability that at least one user request arrives in unit time and is, therefore, the probability of a transition to the first substate of State 1 from the idle state. If λ_2 is the arrival rate of rebuild requests (this should be $(B+C+D+E)/(N+1)$, where B, C, D and E are as defined in Figure 7 and N is the parity width of the good array), then $(e^{-\lambda_1}) \times (1-(e^{-\lambda_2}))$ is the probability (K) that there was no user request but there was a rebuild request in unit time, so it is the probability that the disk must go to one of the two rebuild states 2 or 3. It will transition to State 2 (where a seek is required) if the idle state was entered last from State 1 after processing a user request; it will transition to State 3 (where a seek is not required, since the disk arm is already at the proper location) if the idle state was entered from one of the two rebuild states last. Hence, K is weighted by the probability that the last transition into the idle state was from State 1, to get the probability of a transition from State 4 to the first substate of State 2. Similarly, K is weighted by the probability that the last transition into the idle state was from one of the two rebuild states to get the probability of a transition from the idle state to the first substate of State 3. If the probability of being in any of the first substates is A, of being in any of the second substates is B, of being in any of the third substates is C and of being in any of the fourth substates is D, then, one skilled in the art can easily solve for A, B, C and D.

To consider ***Rebuild after Second Failure*** three arrays are affected - a $2N+1$ array (Array 1 say) which has just lost a disk and is operating in degraded mode; and two good $N+1$ arrays (Arrays 2 and 3, say) which are operating in normal mode. The two $N+1$ arrays are combined to form a $2N+1$ array and spare space distributed on $2N+2$ disks. Then, the data from the broken disk is rebuilt from the broken $2N+1$ array to the newly created spare space. The procedure operates as follows. Parity track 1 of the disk containing parity of all data track 1s from array 2, and parity track 1 of the disk containing parity of all data track 1s from array 3 are read and XORed together. The result is written back (and verified) to one of the two parity tracks just read from. The other parity track read from is freed up and can contain the rebuilt track 1 from the broken device. Track 1 from the broken device is rebuilt (by reading from 2N disks of Array 1 and XORing together) and it is then written into the freed up track (either on Array 2 or Array 3) and then read again for verification. The above procedure is now repeated for Track 2, and so on, until all tracks are rebuilt. It should be clear that on Arrays 2 and 3, a disk will read/write/verify every parity track ($1/N+1$ of the tracks), but it does not need to access the data tracks. On the other hand, on Array 1, a disk reads every track. The disks of Array 1 perform rebuild as fast as possible - they are not slowed down by any activity on Arrays 2 and 3. On the other hand, the disks of Arrays 2 and 3 are slowed down by how fast the Array 1 disks are rebuilding data to be written to spare space in Arrays 2 and 3. Hence, they may need to go to idle state (no user request, no rebuild work), since they may have to wait for a track to be rebuilt by Array 1. The model for the states of a disk in Array-2 or Array-3 is the same as in Figure 8. The model for the states of a disk in Array-1 is simple and is not shown although the performance results are shown later.

For ***Copyback Mode Analysis in Distributed Sparing*** an $N+1$ array and a spare device are combined to form an $N+2$ distributed spare array. On the spare device, $N+1/N+2$ of the tracks are written and verified. The copyback procedure has only two states, idle, and write + verify. Any writes to the spare device are buffered in the controller and not written to it until copyback mode completes. For a disk in the $N+1$ array, only $1/N+2$ of the tracks need to be read. Its procedure involves only three states, process user requests, seek + read_track, and read_track, which have u, n, and m substates respectively. The analysis of such a simple model is not included here, but the results are reported later, as are the results for copyback of parity sparing.

4. Assumptions and Cases

Other work indicates that, on very large systems with 64 or more drives, the extra performance provided by distributed or parity sparing is likely to be small. Hence, only small systems involving 12 disks, holding 8 disks worth of data are analyzed in this paper. These systems are those shown in Figure 1, Figure 2, and Figure 3, for dedicated, distributed, and parity sparing respectively. Each of these array organizations are analyzed with a non-volatile disk cache.

The performance of the subsystems for database and transaction processing applications are particularly interesting and ***Workload Parameters*** of single block read and write requests, no skew among the different devices in the array or between the different arrays in the subsystem, and random seeks were selected to represent such workloads. The read fraction r was set at 75%, the write hit ratio was set to 100%, the average block size read or written was set to 6250 bytes and the read hit ratio was set at 70% [4].

The ***Disk, Controller and Channel Parameters*** used in this study were: a disk average seek time of 10 msecs, latency of 5.6 msecs, and a data rate of 4.2 MB/sec.; a controller overhead of 1 msecs; and a channel data rate capability of 18 MB/sec. Finally, for the rebuild calculations, 30,000 tracks per device (15 tracks per cylinder and 2000 cylinders) was assumed.

5. Performance Results

The performance of the disk subsystems are presented as a curve of response time (including queuing delays) versus I/O rate, where the lower the response time curve over the range of I/O rates considered typical, the better the performance of the disk subsystem. [2] predicts that (on IBM systems) the I/O rate as a function of GB of data will vary between a low of 1 acc/sec/GB for user data to a high of 11 acc/sec/GB for system data (in the 1995 time period). Three GB disk drives are assumed in this study and the arrays with 8 drives worth of data would store approximately 25 GB. Therefore, I/O rates between 25 I/Os/sec for user data and 300 I/Os/sec for system data are the ones of interest. However, a common rule of thumb is to design disk subsystems to operate at twice the highest expected I/O rate, so all the curves show response times for I/O rates as high as 600 I/Os/sec.

Normal Mode Results are presented in Figure 9. The graphs indicate that the subsystem using distributed sparing has the same performance as the subsystem using parity sparing and both have better performance than the subsystem using dedicated sparing. Between 25 and 300 I/Os/sec parity sparing and distributed sparing have a maximum of 10% lower response times than the system using dedicated sparing. This is considered to be a significant performance difference, indicating that system designers should seriously consider one of these alternative sparing strategies when building small systems.

Also shown in Figure 9, is the performance of the three systems following the first failure and the subsequent rebuild. The dedicated sparing system has the same performance after rebuild as before. The distributed and parity sparing systems have the same performance, but it is different and worse than their original normal mode performance.

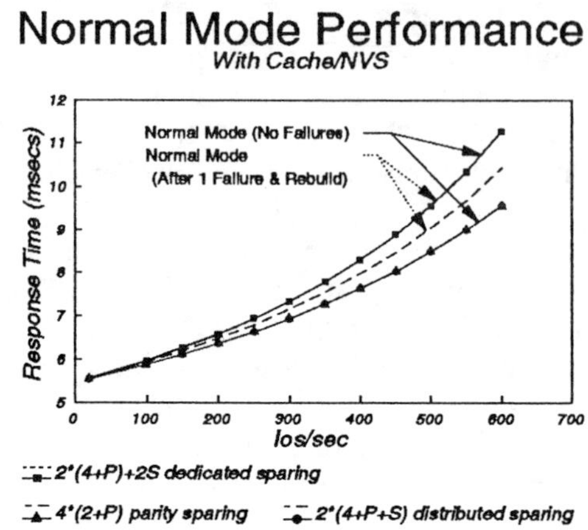

Figure 9: Normal Mode Performance

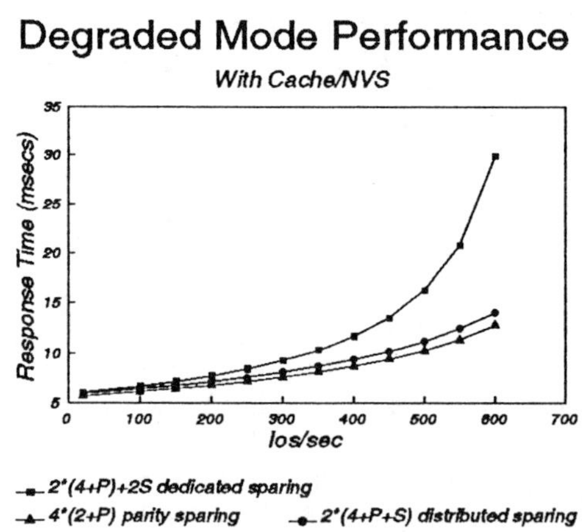

Figure 10: Average Degraded Mode Performance

At 300 I/Os/sec, the systems not using dedicated sparing have 5.7% lower response time than the system using dedicated sparing.

Degraded Mode Results are presented in Figure 10. At 300 I/Os/sec, the distributed sparing system has 13% lower response time and the parity sparing system has 18% lower response time than the system using dedicated sparing making it have the best performance in degraded mode. However, the degraded mode performance results are not as important as the rebuild mode performance results, since on a disk failure, the array controller will immediately switch into rebuild mode, spending as little time as possible in degraded mode.

Rebuild Mode Results are presented in Figure 11. Once again, dedicated sparing has the worst performance. At 300 I/Os/sec, distributed sparing has a 14% lower response time and parity sparing a 17.5% lower response time than dedicated sparing, making parity sparing the best performer in rebuild mode, but only 3.5% better than distributed sparing. Interestingly, however, as will be shown in Figure 13, the system using parity sparing takes longer to complete the rebuild than does the system using distributed sparing. For example, at 300 I/Os/sec, the distributed sparing system takes 10 minutes to complete the rebuild, whereas the parity sparing system (and the dedicated sparing system) take almost 17 minutes to complete the rebuild. To choose between parity sparing and distributed sparing, one must decide between a system that operates at a certain degraded performance level for only 10 minutes before returning to normal operation, versus a system that operates at a marginally better degraded performance level for a much longer 17 minutes before returning to normal operation.

Also shown in Figure 11 is the rebuild mode performance (after second failure). Note that the three systems are now almost identical in rebuild mode performance. To explain this, recall that rebuild mode performance depends on the number of disks executing user requests, the number of disks involved in rebuild and the mode of operation of these drives before rebuild begins. All the systems started with 12 disks; 10 of them were active for the dedicated sparing system and all 12 were active for the other two systems. During the rebuild following the first failure, the dedicated sparing system had 9 active disks handling user requests and data was being rebuilt to a tenth disk. During this same rebuild, the other two systems had 11 active disks handling user requests. The difference in performance between the systems was caused, in part, by the fact that the dedicated sparing system had 2 less active disks. During the rebuild following the second failure, the dedicated sparing system still has 9 active disks as before; however, the other two systems now have only 10 active disks handling user requests, so they have lost some of their advantage. Furthermore, only five disks are involved in dedicated sparing rebuild after the second failure; whereas all 10 surviving disks are involved during rebuild for the distributed and parity sparing systems. The combination of these factors makes rebuild performance as good for the dedicated sparing system as for the other systems.

Copyback Mode Results are presented in Figure 12.

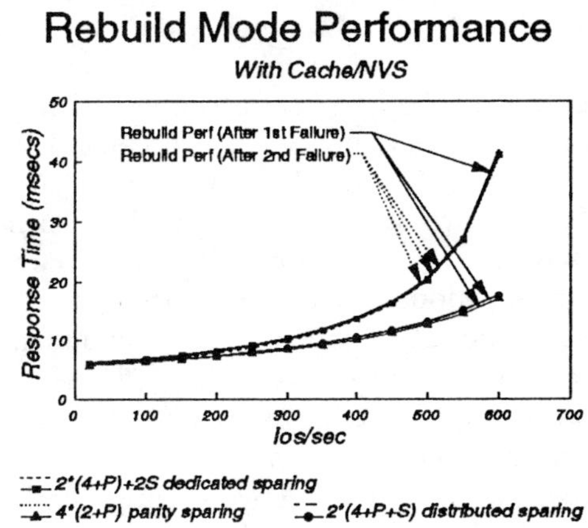

Figure 11: Average Rebuild Mode Performance

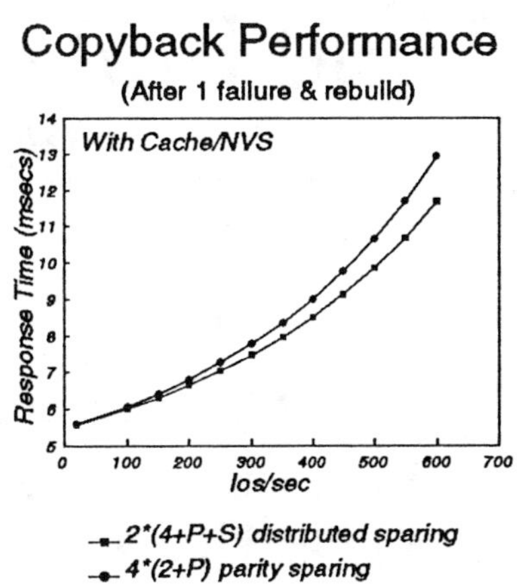

Figure 12: Average Copyback Mode Performance

The distributed sparing system has better copyback performance than the parity sparing system and it also takes less time to complete the copyback, though the differences are small; for example, at 300 I/Os/sec there is only a 4% difference in response times and the copyback times (see Figure 13) are 16 and 18 minutes, respectively. It is intriguing that the copyback time for the distributed sparing system is 16 minutes whereas the rebuild time (after first failure) was 10 minutes. This is because, during copyback, writing to a single device is the bottleneck, whereas, during rebuild, writing to all the devices in the array is possible, since spare space was distributed among all the devices.

The ***Results Summary*** is shown in Figure 13, where a plot of subsystem performance over time is shown for the three different systems. For performance, the response time at 300 I/Os/sec is shown. In the beginning, all subsystems are in normal mode and have the best performance. In this phase, the dedicated sparing system has the worst performance and the other two systems have the same performance. Then, the systems enter degraded mode briefly, before they enter rebuild mode. The amount of time spent in rebuild mode is shown to scale. In this mode, the dedicated sparing system has the worst performance and the parity sparing system has the best performance. However, the distributed sparing system recovers from rebuild mode the fastest. The distributed sparing system and the parity sparing system do not recover all the way back to the same performance they had in the original normal mode; they will not do so until copyback completes. The dedicated sparing system, on the other hand, recovers back to the same performance it had in the original normal mode following rebuild. Once rebuild completes, the distributed and parity sparing systems enter copyback mode. The distributed sparing system has better copyback mode performance and completes copyback faster than the parity sparing system. It is interesting to note that, during copyback, the distributed sparing system performance is only marginally worse than the dedicated sparing system performance in normal mode. Once copyback completes, all systems return to the original normal mode performance.

6. Conclusions

In this paper, disk subsystems built of arrays using traditional dedicated sparing are compared to disk subsystems built of arrays using newer techniques like distributed sparing and parity sparing. Since the newer techniques do not offer much performance gain for large subsystems with many drives, only small systems with 12 drives were considered - a 2*(4+P) system with two dedicated spares, a 2*(4+P+S) distributed spare system and a 4*(2+P) system with parity sparing. The performance of these systems were compared using

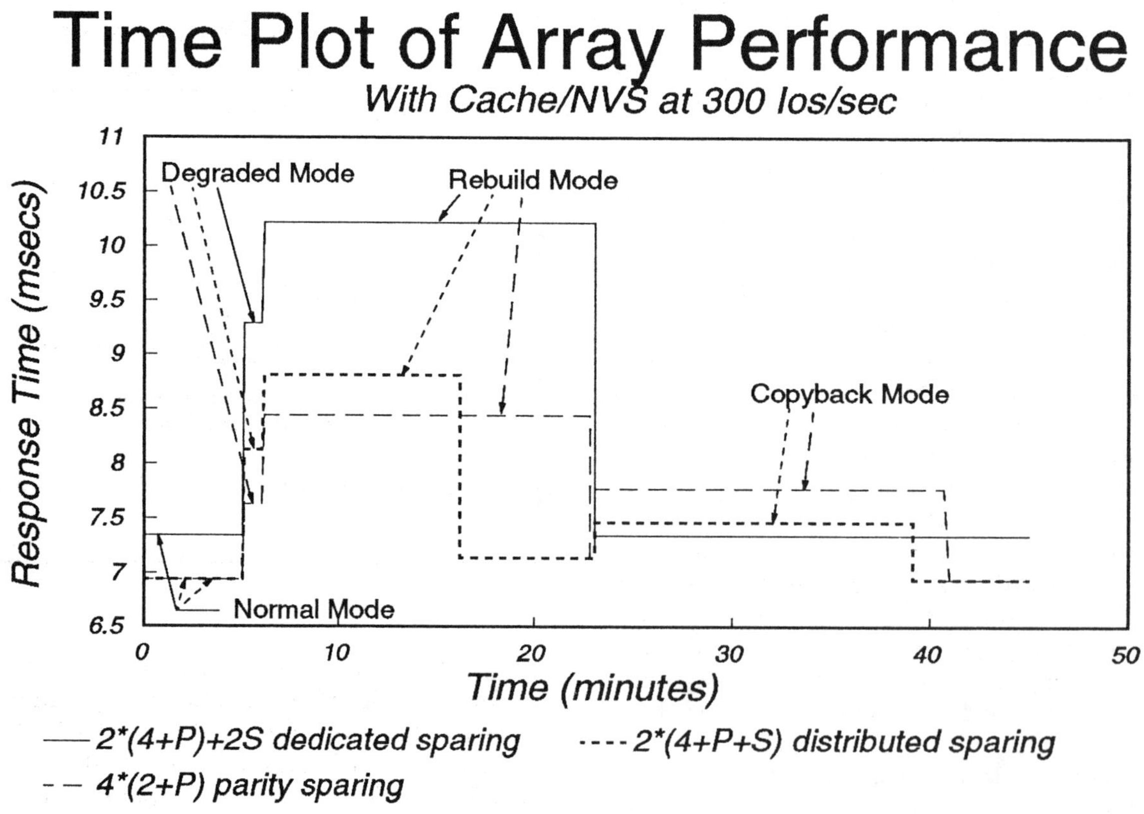

Figure 13: Time Plot at 300 I/Os/sec

analytical models in normal mode, degraded mode, rebuild mode and copyback mode; and rebuild and copyback times were also compared using another set of analytical models. Unlike previous work, the analysis of rebuild and copyback modes includes the realistic assumption that tracks that have been rebuilt or copied back will need to be verified. The models developed here extend considerably the work reported in [9] and [7].

The results showed that, for small subsystems, there is considerable performance leverage in using either distributed or parity sparing instead of dedicated sparing. Performance improvements ranging from 10% to 18% are possible by use of these alternative sparing techniques. The issue of whether distributed sparing or parity sparing was better was addressed next. The comparison was confined to one based on performance and ignored issues such as implementation complexity. There was no difference in performance between these two systems in normal mode, and only marginal performance differences in degraded, rebuild, and copyback modes. The distributed sparing system was marginally better in copyback time, and was considerably better in rebuild time. Since arrays with sparing should spend very little time, if any, in degraded mode, and since copyback can be scheduled to happen when the system is not very busy, the rebuild mode comparisons were the most significant. Unlike degraded mode, arrays will spend tens of minutes in rebuild mode, and the rebuild operation cannot be scheduled, since the system is operating with poor performance when a disk has failed and is exposed to data outage should a second disk fail before rebuild is done. In rebuild mode, parity sparing has marginally better performance, but, most significantly, distributed sparing takes much less time to complete the rebuild and return to normal mode. Thus, it is concluded that, distributed sparing is better than parity sparing which is better than dedicated sparing.

While the main result of this paper is that distributed sparing is the best sparing technique, the counter-intuitive result that there is no strong correlation between rebuild or copyback work and rebuild or copyback time is also significant. Copyback can take longer than rebuild, particularly for distributed sparing, even though less total work needs to be done during copyback. Also, for parity sparing, the best rebuild times are achieved by combining two good arrays to create spare space and then rebuilding the broken disk to spare space, rather than by merely combining the broken array with a good array.

7. References

1. Dunphy, R. H. et. al., Disk Drive Memory, *United States Patent* **4,914,656** (Apr. 1990).
2. Goldstein, S., Storage Performance - an Eight Year Outlook, *IBM Santa Teresa Technical Report* **TR 03.308** (Santa Teresa, July 1987).
3. Gray, J. N. et. al., Parity Striping of Disk Arrays: Low-Cost Reliable Storage With Acceptable Throughput, *16th International Conference on VLDB* (Australia, August 1990).
4. Hyde, J., Personal Communication, *IBM SSPD Performance Group* (1990).
5. Menon, J. M. and Hartung, M., The IBM 3990 Disk Cache, *Compcon 1988* (San Francisco, June 1988).
6. Menon, M. J., Mattson, R. L. and Spencer, N., Distributed Sparing for Improved Performance of Disk Arrays, *IBM Research Report* **RJ 7943** (Jan. 1991).
7. Menon, M. J. and Mattson, R. L., Performance of Arrays in Transaction Processing Environments, *IBM Research Report* **RJ 8230** (July 1991).
8. Menon, M. J. and Mattson, R. L., Comparison of Sparing Alternatives for Disk Arrays, *IBM Research Report* **RJ 8999** (Sept 1991).
9. Muntz, R. R. and Lui, C. S., Performance Analysis of Disk Arrays Under Failure, *16th VLDB Conference* (1990) pp. 162—173.
10. Nelson, R. and Tantawi, N., Approximate Analysis of Fork-Join Synchronization in Parallel Queues, *IEEE Transactions on Computers* **37,6** (June 1988) pp. 739—743.
11. Patterson, D. et. al., Reliable Arrays of Inexpensive Disks (RAID), *ACM SIGMOD Conference 1988* (Chicago, June 1988).
12. Reddy, A. L. and Banerjee, P., Gracefully Degradable Disk Arrays, *Proceedings of FTCS-21* (June 1991).

Session 11: Program Performance

Monitoring Program Behaviour on SUPRENUM

Markus Siegle, Richard Hofmann,
Institut für Informatik VII, Universität Erlangen-Nürnberg,
Martensstraße 3, 8520 Erlangen, Germany,
e-mail siegle@immd7.informatik.uni-erlangen.de

Abstract

It is often very difficult for programmers of parallel computers to understand how their parallel programs behave at execution time, because there is not enough insight into the interactions between concurrent activities in the parallel machine. Programmers do not only wish to obtain statistical information that can be supplied by profiling, for example. They need to have detailed knowledge about the functional behaviour of their programs. Considering performance aspects, they need timing information as well. Monitoring is a technique well suited to obtain information about both functional behaviour and timing. Global time information is essential for determining the chronological order of events on different nodes of a multiprocessor or of a distributed system, and for determining the duration of time intervals between events from different nodes. A major problem on multiprocessors is the absence of a global clock with high resolution. This problem can be overcome if a monitor system capable of supplying globally valid time stamps is used.

In this paper, the behaviour and performance of a parallel program on the SUPRENUM multiprocessor is studied. The method used for gaining insight into the runtime behaviour of a parallel program is hybrid monitoring, a technique that combines advantages of both software monitoring and hardware monitoring. A novel interface makes it possible to measure program activities on SUPRENUM. The SUPRENUM system and the ZM4 hardware monitor are briefly described. The example program under study is a parallel ray tracer. We show that hybrid monitoring is an excellent method to provide programmers with valuable information for debugging and tuning of parallel programs.

Keywords: debugging, event-driven monitoring, multiprocessor, parallel program, performance evaluation, ray tracing, SUPRENUM, tuning.

1 Introduction

It is often very difficult for programmers of parallel computers to understand how their parallel programs behave at execution time, because there is not enough insight into the interactions between concurrent activities in the parallel machine.

Programmers need to have detailed knowledge of the functional behaviour of their programs, and for the consideration of performance aspects they need timing information as well. Usually, methods such as profiling and accounting do not provide sufficient information, they only give summary statistical results. Therefore users often resort to rudimentary methods, such as writing log-files during program execution, in order to obtain debug information and performance information about their programs. But only a relatively small fraction of the needed information can be obtained that way. A major problem with multiprocessors is the absence of a global clock with high resolution. Global timing information is essential for determining the chronological order of events on different nodes of a multiprocessor or of a distributed system, and for determining the duration of time intervals between events from different nodes.

Facing this problem, our approach is to apply event-driven monitoring techniques [3] [8] [9] in order to find out how a parallel program behaves. In particular, we decided to use hybrid monitoring, which combines advantages of both hardware monitoring and software monitoring. Using software monitoring, it is relatively easy to relate the event traces obtained from the measurements to the measured program. But since monitoring is done within the object system (i.e. within the system under study), and therefore constitutes an extra workload, software monitoring changes the behaviour of the object system. Also, it is usually impossible to obtain global timing information because most parallel systems do not provide a global clock with high resolution. With hardware monitoring there is no intrusion and the timing problem can be solved by providing an external clock. But there is no easy way to relate the recorded signals to the source code of the measured program.

In hybrid monitoring, as in software monitoring, the program under study is instrumented by inserting additional instructions at points of interest. The execution of such a measurement instruction marks an event. It causes the output of measurement data, containing a token identifying the event and possibly some additional parameters, to an external interface. A hardware monitor is connected to the interface. It records the event stream coming from the interface, and stores the sequence of events together with the respective time stamps as an event trace. Since most of the work is done by the external hardware monitor, hybrid monitoring provides the capabilities of software monitoring at a much lower level of intrusion. The hardware monitor we use is a scalable distributed monitor system called ZM4. It is capable of simultaneously recording event streams coming from an arbitrary number of nodes. Since the ZM4 has a global clock with high resolution, events coming from different nodes can be chronologically ordered by their time stamps.

In this paper, we use hybrid monitoring techniques to study the behaviour of a parallel program on the German supercomputer SUPRENUM. The SUPRENUM project was launched in 1984 as a government-funded project, and implementation of a prototype started in 1986. The project resulted in a commercial product in 1990. SUPRENUM is a distributed-memory multiprocessor in which the processing nodes are interconnected by a hierarchical bus system. The SUPRENUM architecture and its software environment are discussed in more detail in Section 2.

In section 3 the essential features of the hardware monitor ZM4 are presented. Section 4 presents the application of our method to the implementation of a parallel ray tracing program on SUPRENUM. We show how measurements supported the implementation of a parallel program by providing programmers with valuable information about the behaviour of their program. Both debugging and tuning of the parallel program were supported considerably by the measurements.

2 The SUPRENUM Multiprocessor

2.1 Hardware Architecture

The SUPRENUM system [5] [11] [13] [2] is a MIMD-type multiprocessor consisting of up to 256 processors (nodes). It is a distributed-memory machine with a two-level interconnection network. All the elements comprising one processing node are accommodated on a single printed circuit board.

The main components of each node are a 32-Bit microprocessor (MC68020) operating at a clock rate of 20 MHz, 8 MByte of main memory protected by 2-Bit error-detection and 1-Bit error-correction logic, and four coprocessors:

- The paged memory management unit (PMMU) (MC68851) checks access rights and page violation when the node memory is being accessed by the CPU or at the beginning of DMA.
- The floating-point unit (FPU) (MC68882) executes scalar floating-point arithmetic.
- The vector floating-point unit (VFPU) consists of the Weitek chip set WTL2264/2265 and 64 KByte of fast static memory (vector cache). Peak performance is 10 MFlops for single-operation double-precision floating-point computations, and 20 MFlops in the case of chained operations. Peak performance is achieved even if one of the two operands is being read from main memory by DMA, provided a constant increment is used.
- The communication unit (CU) is a microprogrammable coprocessor which takes care of the data transfer between a node's main memory and other nodes in the system. The CPU initiates the communication. The communication unit then handles the entire data transfer including bus request, transfer with protocol checks, and bus release. The functions of the communication unit are realized mainly by gate arrays and hybrid modules.

Up to 16 processing nodes form a cluster. Nodes of the same cluster communicate via the cluster bus. In order to provide some degree of fault-tolerance, the cluster bus consists of two independent parallel buses, each having a transfer rate of 160 MByte/s. Thus the total bandwidth available for intra-cluster communication is 320 MByte/s.

Figure 1 (left) shows the components of one SUPRENUM cluster. In addition to the processing nodes, each cluster contains 3 or 4 special purpose nodes: there are up to 2 communication nodes which handle the communication between clusters. If a processing node in one cluster wants to communicate with another processing node in a different cluster, communication is done via a communication node. There is one disk controller node which can connect up to 4 disks to the cluster. Finally, there is one cluster diagnosis node which monitors the clusterbus and maintains statistical records. Only communication activities can be monitored by the diagnosis node.

The clusters are interconnected in a toroid structure by bit-serial buses, called SUPRENUM bus. Figure 1 (right) shows the 16 cluster SUPRENUM system and a front-end computer. A token ring protocol is employed for the SUPRENUM bus with a data transfer rate of 25 MByte/s. By duplicating the torus structure the bandwidth doubles and fault-tolerance is achieved because the clusters in a ring can always be reached via alternative routes.

2.2 The Programming Model

The SUPRENUM computer is a multi-user machine. Users can access the SUPRENUM kernel via a front-end computer. In order to execute a parallel program, a user must first request a certain number of clusters or nodes. If the requested number of resources is not available at the moment, the user has to wait. The code of the user program is then downloaded from the front-end computer to the partition assigned to the user. When the user's job terminates, all processors are released. There is a certain time limit which can be set by the operator, after which the resources assigned to a user are released, even if that user's job is not yet completed. This is done to prevent monopolization.

The following programming model is employed for SUPRENUM: user programs consist of one or more independent processes. A process can create other processes at any point of time. A user application starts with an initial process. Termination of the initial process causes termination of the whole application program. Otherwise a process can only be terminated by itself.

Processes communicate by sending and receiving messages. According to the specifications, both synchronous and asynchronous communication between processes are supported. Using synchronous communication, the sender of a message is blocked until the receiver of the message accepts the message. The sender cannot do any work while waiting for his communication partner to receive the message. In order to avoid this waiting time, asynchronous communication can be used. In this case the sender does not send the message directly to the receiver but to a mailbox associated with the receiver. The

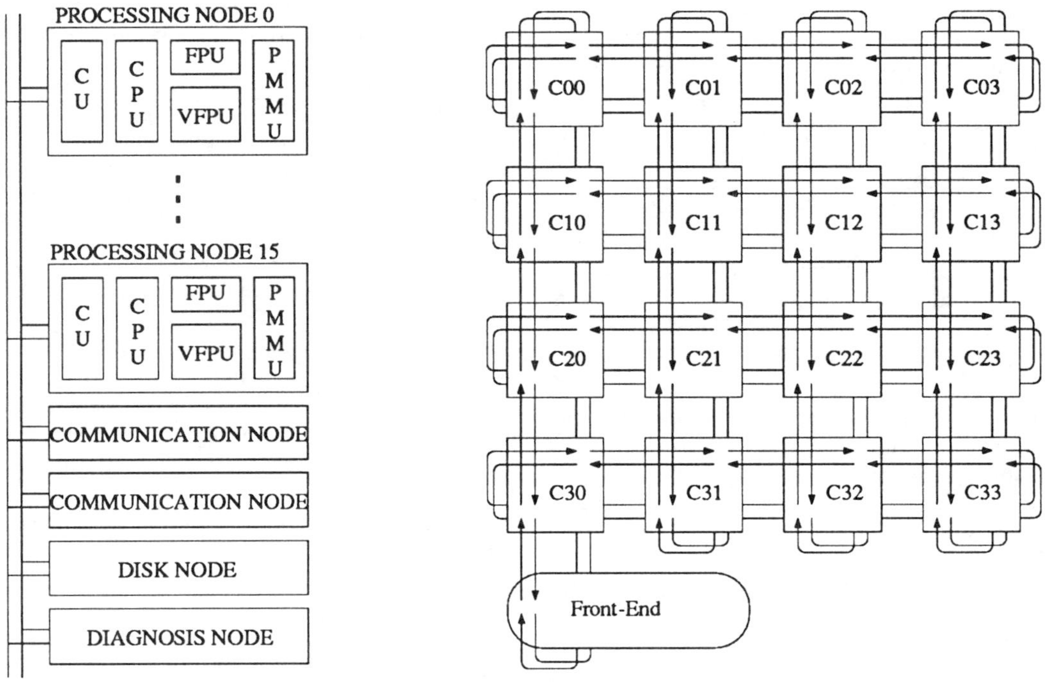

Figure 1: The SUPRENUM cluster (left) and the 16-cluster SUPRENUM system

sender can continue with his work once the message is placed in the receiver's mailbox. The message is actually read from the mailbox by the receiver at a later time. In Section 4 we will discuss the behaviour of SUPRENUM's synchronous and asynchronous communication in detail.

3 The Hardware Monitor ZM4

3.1 The ZM4 Architecture

The ZM4 is a hardware monitoring system which has been developed and built at the University of Erlangen-Nürnberg [4] (The name indicates that the ZM4 is the fourth generation of monitor systems built at our University). It is designed to measure arbitrary parallel and distributed systems. Consequently the ZM4 itself is a distributed system which is scalable and adaptable to any object system. This universality is an important feature of the ZM4, considering that most sophisticated monitoring systems are dedicated to one special object system [1] [3] [7] [14].

We now describe the components of the ZM4 in a bottom-up fashion. The central component of the ZM4 is the dedicated probe unit (DPU) which consists of probes interfacing to the object system, an event detector, and an event recorder. The event detector detects relevant measurement information coming from the object system interface. The probes and the event detector are the only parts of the ZM4 that depend on the object system.

The event recorder of the ZM4 is realized as a plug-in board for a monitor agent (MA). Standard PC/AT computers are used as monitor agents. One event recorder can record up to four independent event streams. Upon a request signal the event recorder inputs data coming from the event detector. It stores this data together with a time stamp and a flag field into a FIFO buffer of size $32K * 96$ bits. The contents of the FIFO buffer are written simultaneously onto the disk of the monitor agent. The FIFO is needed as a high-speed buffer to ensure that no events get lost during bursts of events.

The clock of the event recorder has a resolution of 100 ns. About 10000 events per second can be written from the FIFO buffer onto the disk of the monitor agent. This limit is due to the disk transfer rate of the monitor agent. However, a bandwidth of 120 MByte/s at the input of the FIFO allows for peak event rates of 10 millions of events per second during bursts of events.

In order to monitor larger object systems, two or more DPU's have to be employed. In this case the local clocks of the event recorders have to be synchronized to obtain globally valid time stamps. Another plug-in board, called measure tick generator (MTG), is used for that purpose. It constitutes the master part of the global clock of the ZM4. It is connected to the event recorders via the tick channel. The local clocks of the event recorders can be started simultaneously by a signal on the tick channel. A manchester-coded signal which is transmitted continuously via the tick channel prevents skewing of the local clocks. Thus the local clocks can provide globally valid timing information. For details about the global clock of the ZM4 see [4].

Up to four DPU's can be plugged into one monitor agent. If one wishes to use more than four DPU's, more than one monitor agent is needed. It is important to note that there is still only one measure tick generator connected to all event recorders by the tick channel. All monitor agents are connected to a control and evaluation computer (CEC) by the

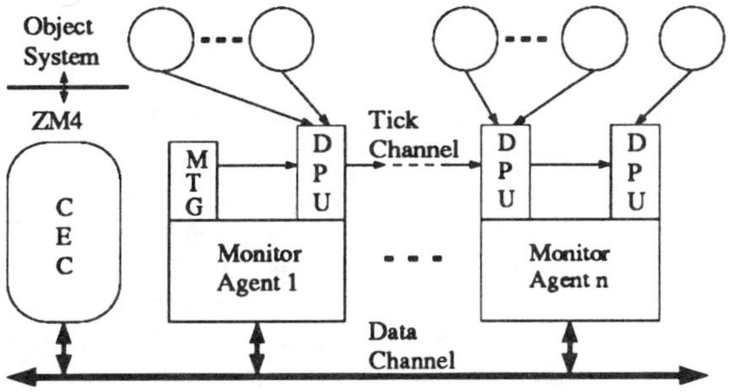

Figure 2: The ZM4 distributed, scalable hardware monitor

data channel (an Ethernet using TCP/IP). Figure 2 shows the general configuration of the ZM4.

When a measurement has been carried out, the event traces recorded by the event recorders and stored on the disks of the monitor agents are transmitted via the data channel to the control and evaluation computer. There the local traces can be merged to one global trace, since events can be sorted according to their globally valid time stamps. Evaluation of the global trace is done using the SIMPLE software package [10] [4] which provides tools for statistical analysis, visualization, and animation of measurement data.

3.2 Adaptation of ZM4 to SUPRENUM

As mentioned in the previous section, the interface between object system and event recorder depends on the object system. In the past, the ZM4 has been used for monitoring a great variety of object systems such as Transputers, high-speed networks, clusters of workstations, and robot systems. Each such object system may provide a different hardware interface to which measurement data is output.

In the case of SUPRENUM we considered two candidate interfaces for outputting measurement data. Each processing node has a serial terminal interface (V.24) and a seven segment display on its front cover. The terminal interface is intended to be used by service personnel. The seven segment display displays the internal state of communication firmware. Data transfer via the terminal interface is slow (less than 20 KBit/s). It would take more than 2.4 ms to output 48 bits of event data, not including time for context switching. Therefore we decided not to use the terminal interface.

The seven segment display is driven from a gate array on the processing node board. It can display only 16 different patterns. Under normal operating conditions, the seven segment display is not intended to be addressed by the user. We wished to output event data which is 48 bits wide via the seven segment display. To code the event, 16 bits of the event data are used, and a parameter field of 32 bits is provided for outputting additional information relevant at the point of the program where the event is initiated. In order to output 48 bits of data via a display which can only display 16 different patterns, we devised the following scheme: one pattern is used as a triggerword T which signals to the monitoring hardware that measurement data will follow. The 48 bits are output as a sequence of 16 pairs $T\ m_i$ like

$$T\ m_0\ T\ m_1\ \ldots\ T\ m_{15}$$

where each m_i is a pattern that encodes 3 bits of the original 48 bits. There are two essential conditions:

- The triggerword T must be reserved for this application, since it signals to the event detector that measurement data will follow.
- The output of a pair $T\ m_i$ must be an atomic action. No other information must be output to the seven segment display between T and m_i.

The routine that can be called from the user program in order to output data via the seven segment display was implemented in cooperation with the SUPRENUM company. It is called as

$$hybrid\_mon(p1, p2)$$

where $p1$ is a 16-Bit integer defining the event and $p2$ is a 32-Bit parameter which can be used to output additional relevant data. One call of the routine *hybrid_mon* takes less than one twentieth of the time that would be needed to output an event via the terminal interface. This results in a very low level of intrusion and ensures that the time needed to output an event is more than two orders of magnitude smaller than the duration of the measured activities.

An interface was built whose probes are plugged into the socket of the seven segment display on one side and which connects to the event recorder of the ZM4 on the other side as shown in Figure 3. Its event detector con-

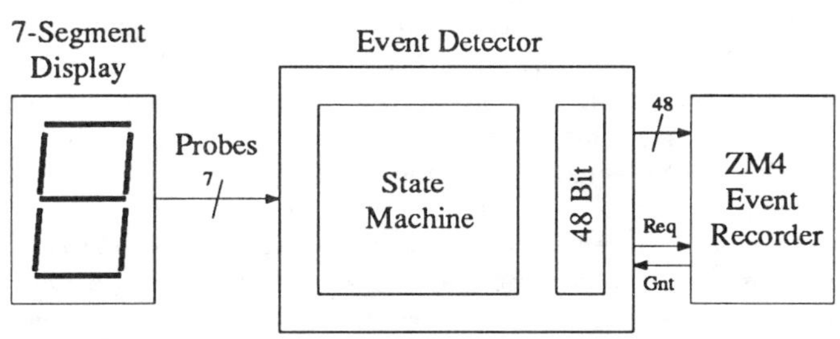

Figure 3: The interface between SUPRENUM and ZM4

tains recognition logic for the triggerword T and reconstructs the original 48 bits of the event data from the sequence $T\ m_0\ T\ m_1\ \ldots\ T\ m_{15}$. It is realized as a state machine in programmable logic. Once a 48-Bit event is assembled the interface issues a request signal and the event is recorded by the event recorder of the ZM4.

4 Performance Evaluation of a Parallel Ray Tracer

As mentioned in the introduction, the main difficulty when writing parallel programs is the lack of insight into the internal activities of the parallel program and into the mutual effect of the user program and the system software of the underlying parallel architecture. Programmers wish to know more about the functional behaviour as well as the performance of their parallel programs. These problems are also

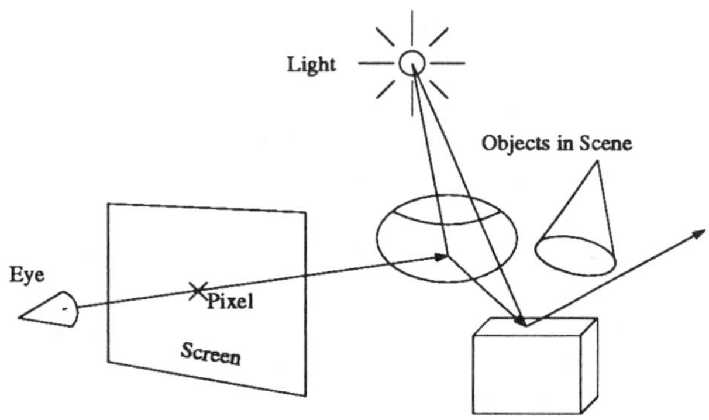

Figure 4: The basic concept of ray tracing

encountered by people writing programs for the SUPRENUM multiprocessor. In this paper, we investigate how hybrid monitoring techniques can support the implementation of parallel programs for a novel machine. Both debugging and tuning are addressed.

We have chosen ray tracing as an attractive example application, and we have implemented a parallel ray tracing program for SUPRENUM [12]. It is important to note that it was not the major aim of our work to build a highly sophisticated ray tracer, but to develop methods which make writing of correct and efficient parallel code easier.

4.1 Ray Tracing

An important field of research in computer graphics is the generation of realistic images from formal descriptions of a scene. Natural phenomena such as light and shadow, reflection and refraction, or depth of field have to be simulated in order to get such high-quality images. Ray tracing [15] [6] is one of the most sophisticated and most powerful methods for image generation.

The basic concept of ray tracing is illustrated in Figure 4. The idea is to follow the trajectory of a ray (the eye ray) originating at the eye of the observer and going through one particular pixel of the image plane into the scene. The colour value of the eye ray (i.e. of its associated pixel) has to be computed. To do this, the closest point of intersection between the ray and objects in the scene is determined. The colour value of the pixel depends on the surface properties of the object at the intersection point in various ways. First of all, the colour value depends on the colour of the object at the intersection point and how that point is being illuminated by light sources. If the object is "shiny", i.e. if light hitting the object is reflected, the colour value also depends on the colour of a reflected ray originating at the intersection point. Finally, if the object is not opaque, the colour value of the pixel also depends on the colour of a transmitted ray originating at the point of intersection. The colours of both the reflected ray and the transmitted ray are computed recursively. The colour of the eye ray is a combination of the colour of the object, the colour of the reflected ray, and the colour of the transmitted ray.

Ray tracing is a very time-consuming process. Note that 256K pixels have to be processed in order to compute a 512 by 512 image. Depending on the resolution of the image to be created, the complexity of the scene, and the shading model used, it can take between seconds and days to render a scene. This is a great challenge for computer architects and programmers. In the past many acceleration techniques for ray tracing have been suggested [6].

Parallelization is a very promising approach for improving the performance of a ray tracing program. By dividing the work to be done between a large number of processors, computation time can be reduced significantly. Many different ways to parallelize ray tracing have been proposed and tested. There are two basic schemes to distribute the computation between several processors:

- Using *object partitioning,* each processor takes care of a certain fraction of the objects in the scene to be rendered.
- With *ray partitioning,* different rays are processed by different processors.

The second scheme, *ray partitioning,* works as follows: each processor computes a part of the final image by computing the colour values of a subset of all rays which have to be processed. In doing this, each processor can work completely independently of all other processors involved. There is no communication between processors until the end, when the complete image is put together from the local results. For processing a ray, each processor needs information about the whole scene to be rendered. This means that the information contained in the scene description must be replicated on each processor, which requires redundant storage. This may be a disadvantage because scene descriptions are often very long and need a lot of memory.

With ray partitioning, it may either be predetermined which rays are processed by a particular processor (static ray partitioning), or the assignment of a ray to a processor may be made during the computation of an image (dynamic ray partitioning). The performance of static ray partitioning is often quite poor because the computation time for a single ray varies significantly, and therefore it is difficult to predict how long it will take to process a certain subset of rays. This results in a load balancing problem which can be at least partly solved by assigning discontinuous subsets of rays to the processors, instead of assigning continuous subsets such as rectangular patches to the processors.

4.2 Parallelizing Ray Tracing for SUPRENUM

For our parallelization of ray tracing we chose a dynamic ray partitioning approach in which the ray tracing algorithm is executed in a distributed manner by one master processor and several servant processors. As shown in Figure 5, the master communicates with all the servant processors, but there is no communication between any two servant processors. The master is responsible for control of the high-level flow of the algorithm, whereas the actual tracing of rays (the geometric intersection operations, mapping transformations, etc.) is executed by the servants.

Figure 6 shows the basic structure of the master and servant processes. The horizontal bars in the figure denote instrumentation points. At these points, measurement instructions were inserted into the program. The master adminis-

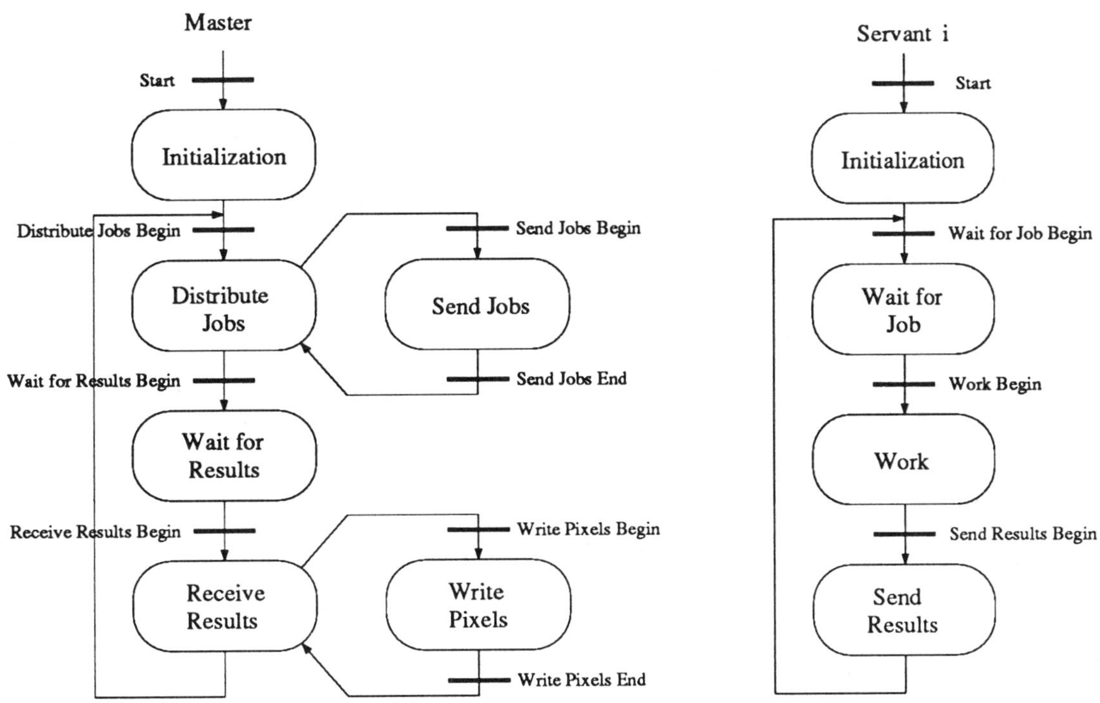

Figure 6: Basic structure of master and servant processes

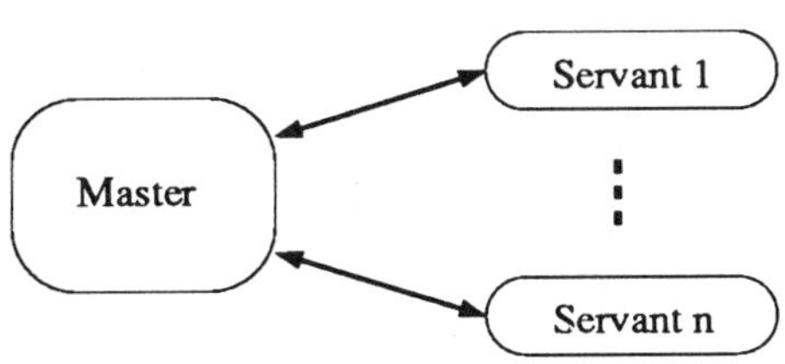

Figure 5: Process structure of the ray tracer

trates the work to be done. He always keeps a certain number of unfinished pixels in a queue. While there are more pixels to process, the master assigns jobs to the servants ("Distribute Jobs", "Send Jobs"), collects the results returned from the servants ("Receive Results"), and writes the output picture file ("Write Pixels"). The number of times the code for "Send Jobs" and "Write Pixels" is executed in each loop may vary. An oversampling scheme, in which more than one ray is computed per pixel in order to reduce aliasing problems, is also organized by the master. The jobs assigned to the servants consist of bundles of one or more rays whose colour values have to be computed.

The servants receive messages containing a job, trace the rays belonging to a job ("Work"), and return the results to the master ("Send Results"). They can work independently of each other because they all have the complete scene information available. Each servant has to communicate with the master to receive jobs and return results, but there is no communication between the servants.

The maximum number of outstanding jobs assigned by the master to one particular servant is limited by a window flow control scheme which works as follows: initially the master has a fixed number of credits from each servant. The master may send jobs to a servant as long as there are credits from that servant available. With each result the master gets one credit back from a servant. This load balancing scheme prevents flooding of the servants with jobs coming from the master, but it also ensures that the servants always have enough work to do to keep them busy.

The time to compute a ray varies considerably. For instance, a ray which does not intersect any object of the scene gets assigned the background colour of the picture without any further processing. A different ray may hit an object, generate secondary rays which in turn may generate more rays recursively, so that much more processing is required. The window flow control scheme described above guarantees that the activities of the servants are completely decoupled. Furthermore, the assignment of rays to processors is completely dynamic. Therefore processing of "long" rays on one servant does not cause other servants to wait.

It is easy to see that the master constitutes a hot-spot for communication because he must communicate with all the servants. We expected that this would not cause any problems, provided the following conditions hold:

- Communication is sufficiently fast.
- The time needed to process a ray is significantly longer than time needed to do administrative work associated with a ray.

4.3 Evolution of the Parallel Program

In this section we describe four versions of a parallel ray tracer. Evaluating measurements of each version motivated the changes introduced for the following version.

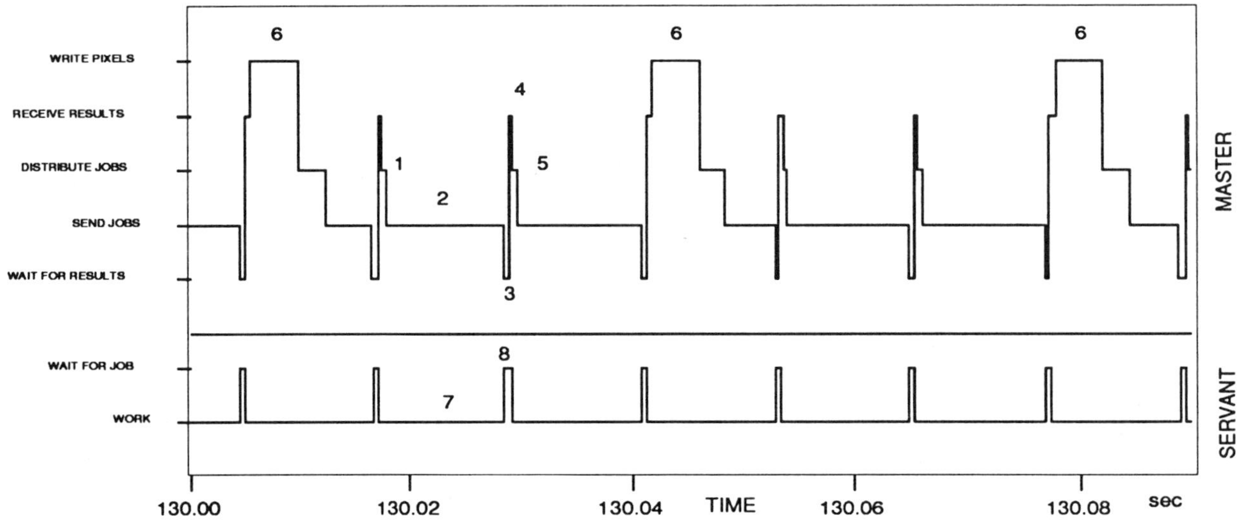

Figure 7: Behaviour of the mailbox communication (ray tracer on two processors)

Version 1: SUPRENUM's Mailbox Mechanism
We started by implementing a basic ray tracing program for SUPRENUM. The implementation of the first version was led by the following considerations:

It is important for the communication between the master and the servants that the sender of a message does not get blocked until the message is actually received by the receiver. Otherwise a lot of time would be spent idling while waiting for the communication partner. Therefore asynchronous communication has to be employed. In particular, we used the mailbox mechanism of the SUPRENUM system. A mailbox is a light-weight process owned by the receiving process. The sender of a message does not send the message directly to the receiver but to the receiver's mailbox. The receiver reads his mailbox whenever he wishes to do so. According to the specifications of SUPRENUM's mailbox mechanism the mailbox process is always in a receive state and therefore the sender of a message will never be blocked.

However, measurements of the mailbox communication between the master and one of the servants reveiled a different behaviour. Since the mailbox is a (light-weight) process, it must be actually running in order to receive a message. The mailbox process is running on the same processor as the receiving process (together with several other light-weight processes) in a time-sharing manner. The scheduling strategy used is plain round-robin. However, instead of using time-slicing, each process that is scheduled may either run until it gets blocked or until it decides to relinquish the processor deliberately. The sender of a message is blocked until the mailbox process on the receiver's processor is actually scheduled. This may not be the case until the receiver himself becomes blocked because he is waiting for a message or because he wants to send some message himself. Consequently, (asynchronous) mailbox communication behaves very much like synchronous communication. This can be observed in the Gantt-chart shown in Figure 7.

A Gantt-chart is a time-state diagram which depicts program activities during the measurement. For the diagram in Figure 7 we measured our ray tracing program running on two processors. The activities of the master processor and the servant processor are shown over a common time axis. Communication between the master and the servant is done using mailboxes. One can observe in the Gantt-chart that the master goes through the following stages (numbers refer to locations in the chart):

- During the activity "Distribute Jobs" (1) the master refills the pixel-queue and does some more administrative work.
- During "Send Jobs" (2) he sends a job (in this case consisting of a single ray) to the servant. After the send activity the activity "Wait for Results" (3) begins.
- In "Receive Results" (4) the master receives a message coming from the servant. The message contains results computed by the servant. However, these are not the results for the job just sent, but for a previous job (remember with the window flow control scheme the number of outstanding jobs per servant may be greater than one).
- "Receive Results" is followed by the next "Distribute Jobs" (5) activity.

Some of the master's cycles also contain a write activity (6) (in the window shown in Figure 7 this is the case in every third cycle). The duration of "Distribute Jobs" is significantly longer after such a write activity because new pixels must be inserted into the pixel-queue, after pixels whose computation is completed have been written onto disk.

The servant works on a job ("Work", 7), returns the results, and waits for the next job ("Wait for Job", 8). It can be seen that the servant spends most of the time in the "Work" state, so servant utilization in this measurement is very good. Since there is only one servant present, the master can easily keep him busy and the servant has always enough work to do.

It can be observed in the diagram in Figure 7 that the master becomes blocked during the "Send Jobs" activitiy. The transition from "Send Jobs" to "Wait for Results" ($2 \rightarrow 3$) on the master processor can only occur in a synchronized manner with the transition from "Work" to "Wait for Job" (7

→ 8) on the servant processor. This is a very disappointing result, because in using mailbox communication we expected that the master's "Send Jobs" and the servant's "Wait for Job" would be decoupled. The reason for the observed behaviour is as follows. The servant's mailbox process can only be scheduled after the servant relinquishes the processor because he is waiting for a message. Only then can the master place his message in the servant's mailbox. This results in a synchronous behaviour of SUPRENUM's mailbox communication.

We monitored another run of this version of our ray tracer. The behaviour of the program is illustrated in the Gantt-chart shown in Figure 8. These results were obtained from moni-

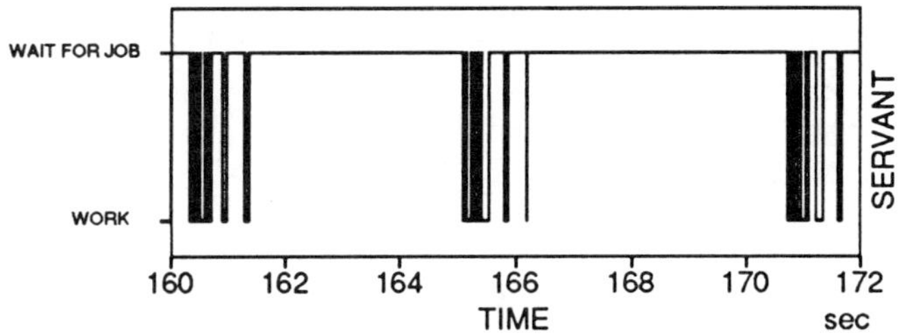

Figure 8: Servant utilization using mailbox communication(ray tracer on 16 processors)

toring the program when it was rendering a scene of moderate complexity (the scene contained 25 primitive objects). The program ran on 16 processors, i.e. there is one master and 15 servants. Only one servant is shown in the figure but the other servants behave similarly. It can be easily seen that the program's performance is very poor. The servants are only working about 15 % of the total time. Each servant spends the rest of the time waiting for the master to accept the results of the current job and to give the servant a new job. In this measurement the window size for the number of outstanding jobs per servant was 3, and a job consisted of one single ray.

Version 2: Communication Agents (one direction)
Having evaluated this and other measurements, we decided to implement our own asynchronous communication in order to avoid such long waiting times. For the communication from the master to the servants we introduced a pool of light-weight processes which we call communication agents. Their task is to forward a message from the master to one of the servants. The agents are running on the same processor as the master. Whenever the master wishes to send a message to a servant he indicates this fact to an agent, who is currently not engaged in some other communication, by setting a shared variable. This agent will forward the master's message to the servant. If no free agent is available a new agent is created and added to the pool. Measurements showed that the number of agents created remains quite small. After the indication the master relinquishes the processor and all agents will be scheduled. Context-switching between light-weight processes belonging to the same team of processes is cheap (less than 1 ms).

Ray tracing the same scene as above with the modified program, servant processor utilization improved to about 29 %, as can be seen in Figure 9 (during the measurement the servants spent about 29 % of the total time in the "Work" state). A pool of 5 communication agents was created for rendering this scene on 16 processors. For clarity of the figure only one communication agent is shown. Also, as before, only one servant's activities are shown in the figure.

Figure 9 (bottom) gives a more detailed view on the activities going on (numbers refer to locations in the chart): as in Figure 7, one can observe the cycles the master goes through. Again, writing the output file is not done in every cycle. In one of the cycles there are several pixels written to the output file at a time (1). This is because pixels have to be written in correct ordering. So, whenever a continuous stretch of pixels has been processed, the results are written onto disk. Waiting times of the master are not significant. Therefore one way to solve the still existing communication bottleneck at the master would be to reduce the number of messages sent, by sending jobs consisting of more than one ray, as described below.

For the Gantt-charts shown in Figure 7 and Figure 8 the beginning of the servants' "Send Results" activity had not been instrumented. In these charts there is a direct transition from "Work" to "Wait for Job". Since we wished to know the duration of the "Send Results" activity, we inserted an additional measurement instruction at the beginning of "Send Results" for the charts in Figure 9. In Figure 9 we can see that the servant goes through the stages "Work" (2), "Send Results" (3), and "Wait for Job" (4).

The behaviour of the communication agents can be observed in the Gantt-chart in Figure 9 (bottom): if an agent is scheduled ("Wake Up", 5) and finds that there is no message to be forwarded, he goes back to sleep immediately ("Sleep", 6). Otherwise he takes the message, forwards it to the receiver ("Forward", 7), is freed whenever the message is received by the receiver ("Freed", 8), and goes back to sleep ("Sleep", 9). It can be seen from the chart that the time an agent spends in the "Freed" state is extremely short (8).

Version 3: Communication Agents (both directions)
Using communication agents improved the servant processor utilization by almost 100 %, but a utilization of 29 % is still very poor. As introducing communication agents for sending messages from the master to the servants turned out to be helpful, we decided to use agents for the reverse communication (from a servant to the master) as well. Apart from this, we wanted to relieve the communication problem by reducing the total communication volume. Sending a message for every single ray is certainly not the best strategy. Therefore we reduced the number of messages to be sent by sending bundles of rays instead of single rays. More specifically, 50 rays are now sent to a servant at a time, and the servant returns 50 results in one message. Measurements showed that these changes resulted in a further improvement of the ray tracer's performance. Now the servant utilization was more than 46 %.

Version 4: Further Tuning
Measurement results from the previous version indicated that the communication hot-spot at the master is still the major problem. We wished to know whether it would be advantageous to further increase the bundle size and chose a bundle

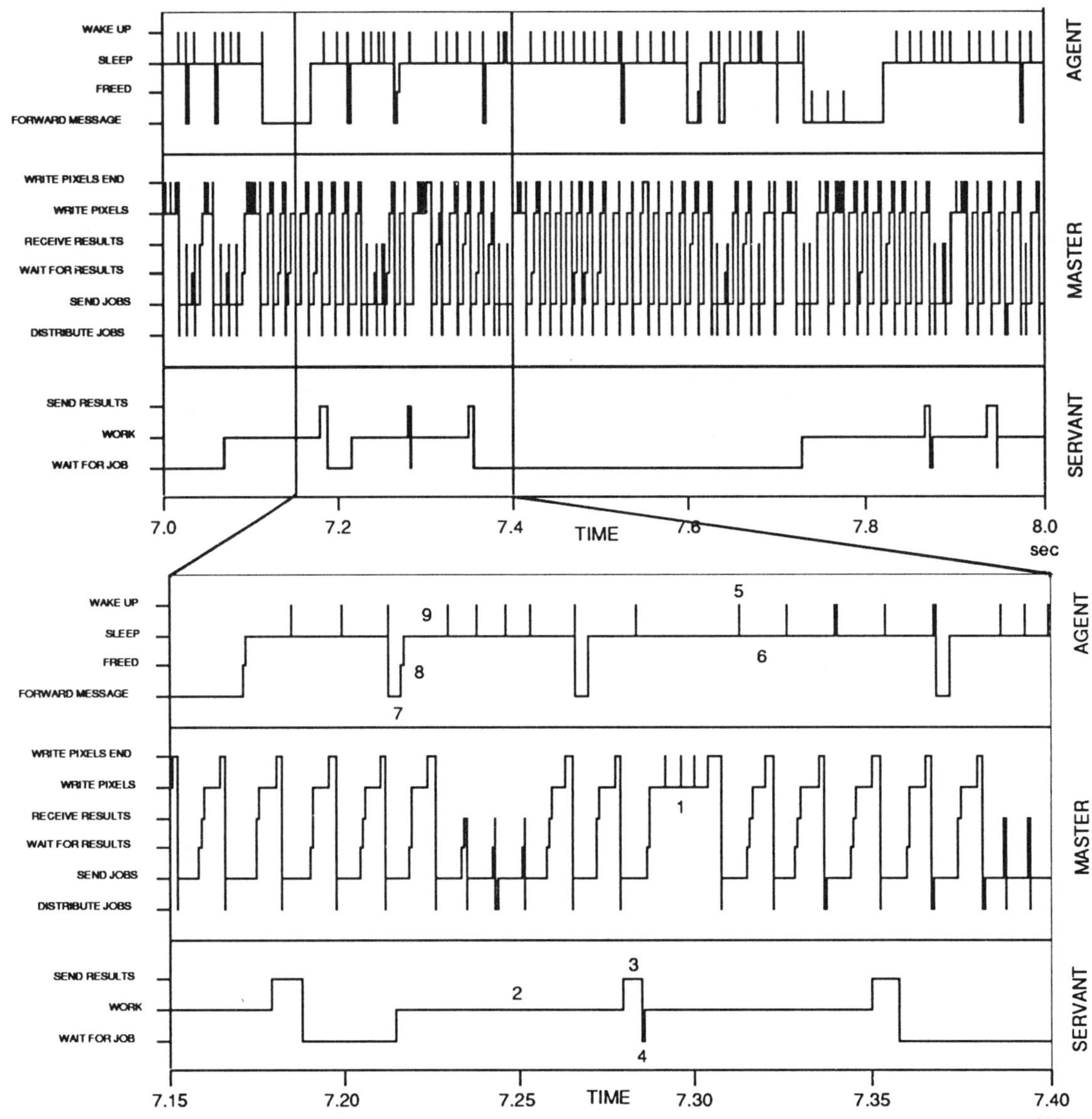

Figure 9: Using communication agents for master-servant communication, bottom shows more detailed view of measurement

size of 100 for the next measurement. A bundle size of 100 is still small compared to the total number of rays which have to be computed for a whole image (remember for a 512 by 512 image 256K rays have to be processed even if no oversampling is done). Therefore distributing jobs of size 100 to the servants does not cause any significant load balancing problems. Also, a minor programming error in the previous version of the program had been detected, namely the choice of an inadequate constant for the length of the master's queue of pixels to be computed. This lead to a situation in which there were not enough pixels in the pixel-queue to constitute a sufficient amount of work for the servants. With these changes our ray tracer finally achieved 60 % servant processor utilization when ray tracing the example scene. The improvement of servant utilization for the example scene using the four described versions of our program is shown in figure 10. For this scene, the initial servant utilization of about 15 % could be improved to 60 %.

Rendering Complex Scenes

The more complex a scene, the more time it takes to trace a single ray. More complex scenes result in a workload with relatively more computation and less communication, i.e. a good servant processor utilization can be achieved more easily when rendering complex scenes. As mentioned before, the example scene rendered during the measurements discussed above was only of moderate complexity. Therefore, this scene was a hard test candidate for our ray tracer. Rendering a more complex scene comprising more than 250 primitives (a fractal pyramid) we found that the servant processors reached a utilization of over 99 %. Due to the complexity of this scene the master did not become a bottleneck although he had to

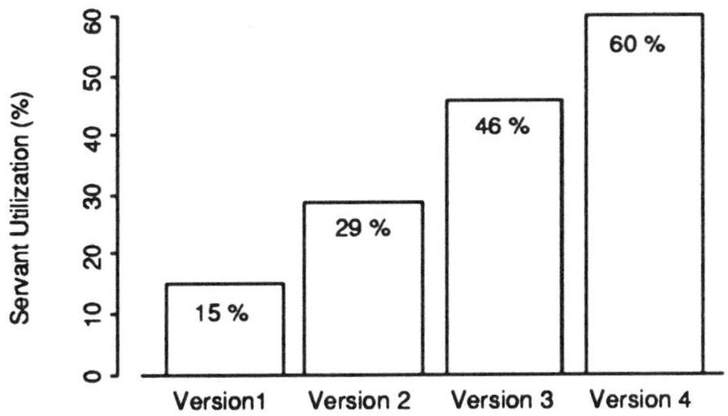

Figure 10: Improvement of servant utilization

keep 15 servants working. It should be mentioned that the utilization percentages given refer to the actual ray tracing phase of the program only, i.e. time for initializing the master process, creating the servant processes, and reading the scene description file is not taken into account. However, for ray tracing complex scenes, initialization is of orders of magnitude smaller than time needed for computation.

5 Conclusion

In this paper, we have described how hybrid monitoring techniques supported the development of a parallel program for the SUPRENUM multiprocessor. Hybrid monitoring proved to be an excellent method for debugging and tuning of parallel programs on a novel machine. The example application is a ray tracer parallelized according to a dynamic ray partitioning scheme. Measurements of the instrumented program were carried out using the hardware monitoring system ZM4.

Event-driven hybrid monitoring with global timing information provided insight into the runtime behaviour of the parallel program which could not have been gained using other methods. We have shown how a basic implementation of the ray tracer could be improved significantly with the help of measurements. Efficiency of the program could be increased dramatically.

It would certainly be very interesting to measure the operating system and not only the application program. Instrumenting SUPRENUM's operating system to find more detailed information about the behaviour of the node scheduling algorithm and internode communication is one of our goals.

In our future work we intend to make use of SUPRENUM's vector processing capabilities. More precisely, we plan to implement a hierarchical bounding volume scheme based on parallelopipeds. Plane intersection operations will be vectorized to further increase the performance of the servant processes.

References

[1] T. Bemmerl, R. Lindhof, and T. Treml. The Distributed Monitor System of TOPSYS. In H. Burkhart, editor, *CONPAR 90–VAPP IV, Joint International Conference on Vector and Parallel Processing. Proceedings*, pages 756–764, Zurich, Switzerland, September 1990. Springer, Berlin, LNCS 457.

[2] A. Böhm, J. Brehm, and H. Finnemann. Parallel Conjugate Gradient Algorithms for Solving the Neutron Diffusion Equation. In *International Conference on Supercomputing*, pages 163–172, Cologne, June 1991 1991. ACM Press.

[3] H. Burkhart and R. Millen. Performance Measurement Tools in a Multiprocessor Environment. *IEEE Transactions on Computers*, 38(5):725–737, May 1989.

[4] P. Dauphin, R. Hofmann, R. Klar, B. Mohr, A. Quick, M. Siegle, and F. Sötz. ZM4/SIMPLE: a General Approach to Performance–Measurement and –Evaluation of Distributed Systems. In T.L. Casavant and M. Singhal, editors, *Advances in Distributed Computing: Concepts and Design*. IEEE Computer Society Press, 1992.

[5] W.K. Giloi. SUPRENUM: A trendsetter in modern supercomputer development. *Parallel Computing, North–Holland*, 1988(7):283–296, 1988.

[6] A.S. Glassner. *An Introduction to Ray Tracing*. Academic Press Limited, London, San Diego, New York, Boston, Sydney, Tokyo, Toronto, 1989.

[7] A.D. Malony, D.A. Reed, and D.C. Rudolph. Integrating Performance Data Collection, Analysis, and Visualization. In M. Simmons and R. Koskela, editors, *Performance Instrumentation and Visualization*, chapter 6, pages 73–98. ACM Press, Frontier Series, Addison–Wesley Publishing Company, New York, 1990.

[8] B.P. Miller, M. Clark, J. Hollingsworth, S. Kierstead, S.-S. Lim, and T. Torzewski. IPS–2: The Second Generation of a Parallel Program Measurement System. *IEEE Transactions on Parallel and Distributed Systems*, 1(2):206–217, April 1990.

[9] A. Mink, R. Carpenter, G. Nacht, and J. Roberts. Multiprocessor Performance–Measurement Instrumentation. *Computer*, pages 63–75, September 1990.

[10] B. Mohr. SIMPLE: a Performance Evaluation Tool Environment for Parallel and Distributed Systems. In A. Bode, editor, *Distributed Memory Computing, 2nd European Conference, EDMCC2*, pages 80–89, Munich, Germany, April 1991. Springer, Berlin, LNCS 487.

[11] K. Peinze. The SUPRENUM preprototype: Status and experiences. *Parallel Computing, North–Holland*, 1988(7):297–313, 1988.

[12] J.-P. Richter. Parallelisierung des Ray Tracing Verfahrens. Internal study, Universität Erlangen–Nürnberg, IMMD VII, Januar 1992.

[13] K. Solchenbach and U. Trottenberg. SUPRENUM: System essentials and grid applications. *Parallel Computing, North–Holland*, 1988(7):265–281, 1988.

[14] J.J.P. Tsai, K. Fang, and H. Chen. A Noninvasive Architecture to Monitor Real–Time Distributed Systems. *Computer*, pages 11–23, March 1990.

[15] T. Whitted. An Improved Illumination Model for Shaded Display. *Communications of the ACM*, pages 343–349, June 1980.

Dynamic Dependency Analysis of Ordinary Programs [1]

Todd M. Austin and Gurindar S. Sohi

Computer Sciences Department
University of Wisconsin-Madison
1210 W. Dayton Street
Madison, WI 53706
{austin; sohi}@cs.wisc.edu

Abstract

A quantitative analysis of program execution is essential to the computer architecture design process. With the current trend in architecture of enhancing the performance of uniprocessors by exploiting fine-grain parallelism, first-order metrics of program execution, such as operation frequencies, are not sufficient; characterizing the exact nature of dependencies between operations is essential.

This paper presents a methodology for constructing the dynamic execution graph that characterizes the execution of an ordinary program (an application program written in an imperative language such as C or FORTRAN) from a serial execution trace of the program. It then uses the methodology to study parallelism in the SPEC benchmarks. We see that the parallelism can be bursty in nature (periods of lots of parallelism followed by periods of little parallelism), but the average parallelism is quite high, ranging from 13 to 23,302 operations per cycle. Exposing this parallelism requires renaming of both registers and memory, though renaming registers alone exposes much of this parallelism. We also see that fairly large windows of dynamic instructions would be required to expose this parallelism from a sequential instruction stream.

1 Introduction

Two things generally affect the advance of computer architectures: a better understanding of program execution, and new or better implementation technologies. It is therefore very important to understand the dynamics of program execution when considering the design of future-generation architectures.

To date, most processors have either executed instructions sequentially, or have overlapped the execution of a few instructions from a sequential instruction stream (via pipelining). For such processors, the relevant characteristics of dynamic program execution included operation frequencies, branch prediction accuracies, latencies of memory operations in cache-based memory systems, amongst others. The continuing trend in processor architecture is to boost the performance (of a single processor) by overlapping the execution of more and more operations, using fine-grain parallel processing models such as VLIW, superscalar, decoupled, systolic, or dataflow (in a complete or a restricted fashion). To aid the design of such processors, simple first-order metrics of the dynamic execution, such as operation frequencies and operation latencies, are not sufficient by themselves. What is needed is a thorough understanding of how the operations of a program interact, *i.e.*, what is the nature of dependencies between operations in the dynamic execution graph, how these are impacted by the processor model, and how they impact performance.

The dynamic execution of a program can be best described as a graph, where the nodes of the graph represent operations (or instructions), and the edges in the graph represent dependencies between operations. This paper focuses on a methodology for constructing and analyzing the graph representing the dynamic execution of a program, and considers its application to parallelism studies. In Section 2 we introduce and discuss the various dependencies that exist in program execution, show how they form a graph representing the order of computation in a program, and discuss some of the interesting metrics that can be obtained from this graph. In Section 3 we detail the extraction of these dynamic dependency graphs from the execution trace of a sequential program. Previous work is cited and the implementation of *Paragraph*, our tool for extracting and analyzing the graph, is discussed. Section 4 presents results of parallelism studies on the SPEC benchmarks, and Section 5 presents a summary and conclusions.

2 Program Dependencies and the Dynamic Dependency Graph

Program executions contain many dependencies. These dependencies force a specific order on the execution of the operations. Some dependencies are inherent to the execution of the program and cannot be removed, others can be removed, but usually not without costs in storage and possibly

[1] This work was supported by National Science Foundation Grant CCR-8919635.

execution speed.

2.1 Types of Dependencies

True Data Dependencies
Two operations share a true data dependency if one operation creates a value that is used by the other (also called a Read-After-Write or RAW dependency). The dependency forces an order upon operations such that source values are created before they are used in subsequent operations.

Storage Dependencies
Dependencies can also exist because of a limited amount of storage. Such storage dependencies require that a computation be delayed until the storage location for the result is no longer required by previous computation. Storage dependencies are often further classified and referred to as Write-After-Read (WAR) and Write-After-Write (WAW) dependencies. Since many different data values can reside in a single storage location over the lifetime of a program, synchronization is required to ensure a computation is accessing the correct value for that storage location. Violation of a storage dependency would result in the access of an uninitialized storage location, or another data value stored in the same storage location.

Control Dependencies
A control dependency is introduced when it is not known which instruction will be executed next until some (previous) instruction has completed. Such dependencies arise because of conditional branch instructions that choose between several paths of execution based upon the outcome of certain tests.

Resource Dependencies
Resource dependencies (sometimes called structural hazards) occur when operations must delay because some required physical resource has become exhausted. Examples of limiting resources in a processor include functional units, window slots, and physical registers (when renaming is supported.)

2.2 The Dynamic Dependency Graph

The *dynamic dependency graph (DDG)* is a partially ordered, directed, acyclic graph, where the nodes of the graph represent the computation that occurred during the execution of an instruction, and the edges represent the dependencies between the instructions in a dynamic execution of the program.

Figure 1 illustrates a simple program execution trace and the DDG extracted from the trace. The execution trace shows the instructions executed to evaluate the statement `S := A + B + C + D`. In the DDG, the operation at the tail of an edge depends on the execution of the operation at the head of the edge. The only dependencies that exists in this program trace are true data dependencies. This dependency requires that an operation not execute until its source values have been created. For example, the instruction `r4 <- r0 + r1` cannot execute until the value of `A` is loaded into `r0` by the instruction `load r0,A` and the value `B` is loaded into `r1` by the instruction `load r1,B`.

True data dependencies can only be removed by changing the algorithms used in the program and/or with compiler transformations that rewrite the code. Examples of algorithmic changes include the use of parallel (most likely logarithmic) algorithms instead of sequential algorithms (the algorithm used in Figure 1 is actually a parallel summation algorithm). Examples of compiler transformations include loop unrolling, invariant loop code motion, loop interchange, and strength reduction, amongst others.

Short of rewriting the program, the true data dependency is the only dependency in a program execution that cannot be removed. If all other dependencies are removed, the resulting graph is simply the *dynamic dataflow graph*.

Figure 2 shows the same computation as Figure 1 but augmented with storage dependencies. The storage dependencies are introduced by the reuse of register locations for different values. The storage dependency edges are annotated with a small, gray bubble. As shown in the figure, the order of execution is further constrained because the subexpression `C + D` cannot begin execution until the subexpression `A + B` has completed using the registers `r0` and `r1`.

Storage dependencies can always be removed by assigning a new storage location to each value created. This is commonly called *renaming*. When using unlimited renaming (assumed for the analysis in this paper), each datum created is a token, and each token is bound to a unique storage location. This results in the program execution having the property of *single-assignment*; that is, a location is assigned to at most once. Figure 1 uses a different storage location for each value created, thus no storage dependencies are created.

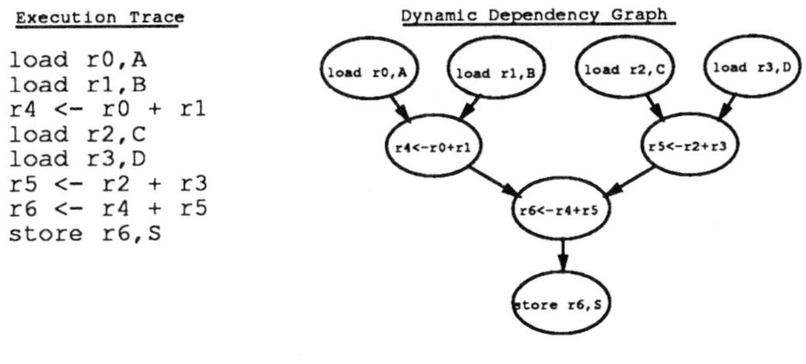

Figure 1: Dynamic Dependency Graph Example

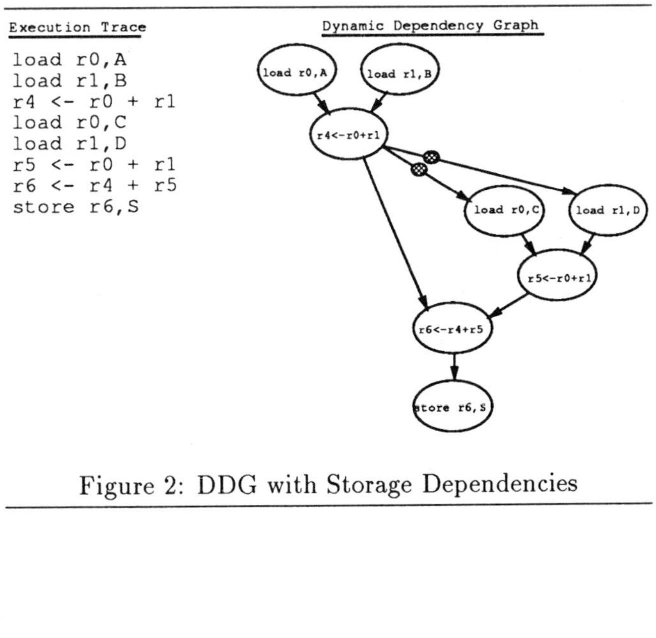

Figure 2: DDG with Storage Dependencies

Removing storage dependencies, via renaming, however, is not without cost. It is likely that during the life of a program, more values are created than could be stored in unique locations in a conventional, high-speed memory. Single-assignment storage allocation would not only be slow and expensive, it would also be wasteful, since a storage location could certainly be reused after the value contained within it was no longer required by another computation. Much research has been done attempting to efficiently implement single-assignment semantics on top of a conventional memory system. Most has been performed in the dataflow literature where the machines directly support single-assignment semantics [1, 6, 11]. The primary techniques used have been self-cleaning graphs, garbage collection, and explicit allocation/deallocation. Self-cleaning graphs can release token storage when the extent is limited to a single entry/single exit body of code; the technique is similar to stack allocation of local variables in imperative languages. Garbage collection is more appropriate when the extent of a variable is not known. The technique tends to be very expensive, and is generally avoided if possible. Often it is avoided by forcing the programmer or compiler to explicitly allocate and deallocate dynamic storage.

To understand how a control dependency could affect the placement of a computation in the DDG, consider Figure 3. The control dependency, shown as a dashed line, is introduced because it is not known which instructions will be executed after the compare and branch instructions until the execution of the `read r1` instruction. The `read r1` instruction reads a value from an input device into the register `r1`. Removing this dependency would require *a priori* knowledge of the input. If a reliable branch prediction method is not available, the `ble` instruction will cause the fetching of instructions to cease until the input has been read. This is illustrated in Figure 3 by the delay of the computation `C + D` until after the `read r1` instruction has completed. Since the compare and branch instructions only provide a mechanism to change the flow of control, and do not create any values, they are not included in the DDG. Operations that are not executed (*e.g.*, `r2 <- r0 + r1`) are also omitted from the DDG.

Figure 4 shows an example of resource dependencies. The processor executing the code fragment contains only two generic functional units (one is required for any instruction execution), thus at most two operations can coexist in any single level of the DDG.

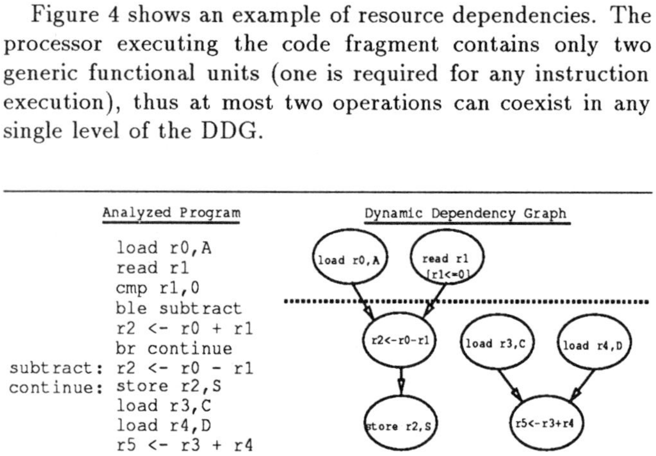

Figure 3: DDG with Control Dependencies

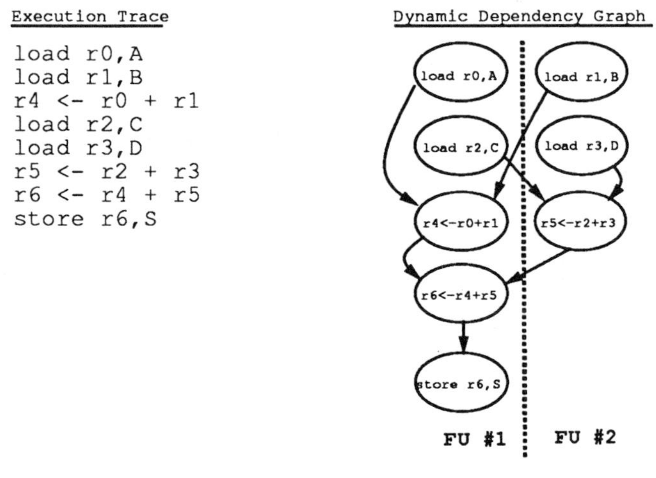

Figure 4: DDG with Resource Dependencies

2.3 DDG Analysis

Given the dependence relations between operations, we can construct the DDG, as illustrated in the previous section. Now let us consider what information can be obtained from the DDG.

The first, and perhaps most valuable, piece of information that we can obtain relates to the true nature of parallelism in program execution. If the DDG is topologically sorted, its height shows the minimum number of steps required to execute the program. This is a function of the dependencies in the graph and is termed the *critical path length* of the particular execution. For example, the DDG in Figure 1 has a critical path length of four, and the DDG of Figure 2 has a critical path length of six. Plotting the number of operations by level in the topologically sorted DDG yields the *parallelism profile* of the DDG. The average number of operations per level for the parallelism profile is the *available parallelism* in the application, and can be viewed as the speedup that could be attained by an abstract machine capable of extracting and executing the DDG from the program's execution trace. For example, the parallelism profile for Figure 1 has four operations in level one, two operations in level two, and one operation in levels three and four; the parallelism profile for Figure 2 has two, one, two, one, one and one operations in levels one, two, three, four, five and six, respectively.

We can also obtain the distribution of value lifetimes from the DDG. The value lifetimes are useful in determining the amount of temporary storage required to exploit the parallelism in the DDG. Likewise, we can also determine the resource requirements of an abstract machine that executes the DDG.

Next, we can obtain the distribution of the degree of sharing of each computed value (or token). Such a distribution is important not only for a possible dataflow realization of our abstract execution engine (by indicating how many operations can be "fired" when a token is created in an explicit token store machine, for example), but also for more conventional multiprocessor execution of the program. In a multiprocessor, different processors are responsible for execution of different parts of a (suitably constrained) DDG of a program. By measuring how much data flows from the nodes in one subgraph to another (albeit in a very constrained form of the DDG that matches the processor execution model), we can measure the degree of data sharing amongst the processors, for example.

By placing suitable constraints on the execution order, or the resources available, we can throttle the DDG to match a particular machine model. Thus, for example, we can obtain parallelism profiles for machines that cannot do storage renaming, or rename only registers, or for machines that have a limited number of ALUs, or for machines that have the ability to look at a fixed-size, contiguous window of instructions.

In Section 4 we shall see how the DDG analysis of the SPEC benchmarks can be carried out along these lines. There we shall consider parallelism studies, and how parallelism is impacted by various constraints placed on the execution of instructions, and consequently on the construction of the DDG.

3 DDG Extraction

Having introduced the concept of the dynamic dependency graph and illustrated the importance of DDG analysis, we now consider how we could construct the DDG of ordinary programs (*i.e.*, programs written in imperative languages), subject to various constraints, and how we could carry out its analysis. Before we describe our methodology, we briefly discuss the previous work in the area.

3.1 Previous Work

There has been a plethora of work in measuring the average parallelism in a (sequential) instruction stream [5, 9, 12, 13, 15]. These studies typically find the length of the critical path through the computation, and compute the average parallelism as the total number of instructions divided by the length of the critical path. (Some also measure the maximum width to determine the maximum number of resources required.) Because they are interested in only a single measure, namely the average or available parallelism, and not in other aspects of the DDG, they do not need to construct the entire DDG, or even parts of it. These studies typically evaluate how the average parallelism changes under various constraints such as register renaming, various branch prediction strategies, memory disambiguation strategies, changes in operation latencies, instruction window sizes, resource constraints, etc. Changes in a parameter result in changes to the critical path length (and the width of the DDG), and consequently to the average (and maximum) parallelism.

To the best of our knowledge, Kumar presented the first work that actually gathered the distribution of parallelism, *i.e.*, the parallelism profile, and the memory requirement profile of serial programs [8]. Kumar extracts parallelism profiles by rewriting FORTRAN programs such that the profile is generated during the execution of the program. Although the method would lend itself to any imperative language, it was only applied to FORTRAN. The operations in the DDG are FORTRAN statements that are assumed to execute in one unit of time. A notable, earlier work is that of Kuck et al. [7] in which program dependencies of FORTRAN programs were analyzed statically, and the resulting available parallelism was estimated from the analyzed code fragments.

A number of papers from the dataflow literature have included examples of DDG analysis [2, 3, 4, 10]. For example, Culler and Arvind [2] provide detailed parallelism profiles and waiting token (or storage usage) profiles for some dataflow programs. Their dataflow processor and language environment lends itself well to dataflow analysis. Instrumenting the dataflow processor's execution is sufficient to generate the parallelism profiles and critical path. Yet their environment lacks storage and most control dependencies, so their results will not include the effects they have on available parallelism. Therefore, it is not clear how their results would extend to programs written in imperative languages such as C or FORTRAN, and also how they could be applied to processors that have more restricted computation models.

Our method of extracting DDGs from serial traces is very similar in spirit to Kumar's method, though the actual implementation is completely different. While Kumar placed FORTRAN statements into the DDG, we instead place machine instructions into the DDG. This allows more precise control over the relative time taken for operations in the DDG, and finer-grain parallelism (such as that found *within* FORTRAN statements) will show up in our results. Moreover, since our technique builds the DDG from a serial execution trace, without modifications to the source program (like Kumar's method), it can be applied widely.

As we shall see in Section 4, our results agree with the conclusions of [3] and [8] that ordinary programs, not intended to execute in parallel environments, do indeed have a significant amount of fine-grain parallelism.

3.2 Paragraph: A Tool for DDG Analysis

All DDGs analyzed in this paper were extracted from serial program execution traces using *Paragraph*. This form of extraction was selected because it is the simplest to perform, and the results are very applicable to the development of processors that must extract parallelism from sequential instruction streams. Yet, extraction from serial traces has caveats that must be made apparent before interpreting the results in Section 4 or comparing them to similar studies that may be done. First, because the trace was generated by a serial program, it is impossible to create totally independent loop iterations (unless loop control instructions are specifically marked and the DDG analyzer can be instructed to treat them differently). Separate iterations of a loop will be connected by at least one recurrence from the loop counter. This results in reducing loop parallelism as the successive independent iterations unroll around the loop counter recurrence. The second caveat involves program transformations performed by compilers. The compiler can actually create a second order effect on the parallelism in the program. For instance, the MIPS compiler commonly performs loop unrolling which tends to decrease the recurrences created by loop counters, thus increasing the parallelism in the program.

Paragraph was developed to extract and analyze DDGs from serial traces produced on DECstation 3100/5000 workstations. The traces were captured with *Pixie*, a basic block execution profiler. *Paragraph* is fully parameterizable. The following parameters can be combined in any combination to see their effects on the parallelism profiles and critical paths.

- System Calls Stall: If this switch is set, an encountered system call is assumed to modify all live values in the program. This causes the placement of all computation after the system call to be in a lower level in the topologically sorted DDG than the system call. If the switch is not set, the system call instructions are assumed to modify nothing, and are ignored.
- Rename Registers: If this is switch is turned on, the storage dependencies on registers are not incorporated into the DDG.
- Rename Data: If this switch is turned on, the storage dependencies for the non-stack segments are not incorporated into the DDG.
- Rename Stack: If this switch is turned on, the storage dependencies for the stack segment are not incorporated into the DDG.
- Window Size: This indicates the number of contiguous instructions in the serial trace that can be considered at any one time when placing values into the DDG. The DDG is created by sliding the window across the entire trace. Once an instruction leaves the instruction window, due to displacement by instructions farther into the trace, it can no longer affect the placement of future instructions into the DDG.

Every trace analysis produces two metrics: the parallelism profile, and the critical path length. The parallelism profile is generated by recording in a hash table the DDG level of each live value. This hash table is called the *live well.* When an instruction is processed, its source values are located, by address or register number, in the hash table (because they are being referenced, they are alive and will be in the hash table). The value created by the newly encountered instruction will be available in the DDG level L_{dest} where:

$$L_{dest} = MAX(L_{src1}, L_{src2}) + t_{op}$$

L_{src1} and L_{src2} are the DDG levels in which the source values are first available for use by another computation, and t_{op} is the time in abstract machine steps (or DDG levels) to complete the operation. If the instruction has no dependencies, *e.g.*, a load immediate, it is placed in the topologically highest level in the DDG. The parallelism profile distribution is updated by incrementing a distribution entry indexed by L_{dest}. When the range of L_{dest} becomes too large to represent each possible value in a distribution, a range of L_{dest} values is mapped to each distribution entry, and in the final output, the average number of operations per level within the range is computed.

Paragraph's implementation is complicated by the need to continually release or reuse value storage in the live well. This is required because a typical program's DDG can contain billions of operations, and thus billions of values will be entered into the live well; many more than can be stored in conventional memories. When a value becomes *dead,* it can be removed from the live well. A value is dead when it will never again be referenced by an instruction in the trace. Two methods can be used to determine if a value is dead.

1. Process the trace in two passes, first in the reverse direction and then in the forward direction. If the instructions are processed in reverse, the first occurrence of a value is its last use, and value lifetime information can be easily inserted into the trace for use on a second, forward pass through the trace. The disadvantage of this approach is that the entire trace must be stored for reverse analysis.
2. Process the trace in a single pass in the forward direction. This method can only determine that a value has become dead after its storage location is reused. While this is not a problem for registers, many memory locations will be used during a program's execution necessitating the need to track many potentially dead values.

All the analyses of the SPEC benchmarks in Section 4 were performed in the forward direction, but a very large memory (32 MBytes) was required to hold the working set of *Paragraph.* A very space efficient hash table was used to minimize the per value memory overhead.

Two special cases must be handled when processing instructions. First, if an instruction uses a value that existed when the program began execution, *i.e.*, a pre-initialized register value, or a value from the DATA segment, the value is placed in the live well such that it was created in the level immediately preceding the topologically highest level in the DDG (the variable *highestLevel* records the topologically highest level in the DDG). This placement prevents a preexisting value from delaying any future computation placed in the DDG. Any values created using only the preexisting value will still be placed in the topologically highest level.

The second special case is the handling of system calls. *Paragraph* does not determine the exact side effects of a system call. Therefore, it must either assume that the system call modified all live values in the program, or that it modified nothing. The conservative assumption (all values modified) is implemented by placing a *firewall* in the DDG. A firewall prevents any later encountered instruction from executing (or firing) higher in the DDG than the firewall. The firewall must be placed immediately after the deepest computation in the DDG. This location is recorded by the variable *deepestLevelYetUsed*, and is possibly updated each time a computation is placed in the DDG. After placing a firewall in the DDG, the variable *highestLevel* is updated to the level immediately following the firewall. To ensure no computation is placed in the DDG prior to the last firewall, the placement function is redefined to be:

$$L_{dest} = MAX(L_{src1}, L_{src2}, highestLevel) + t_{op}$$

The firewall can also be used to represent the effect of a mispredicted conditional branch, resulting in all operations after the conditional branch being placed into the DDG with a control dependency to the firewall. Figure 5 shows the state of the live well after processing the trace in Figure 1. The edges between the records in the live well are not explicitly stored. They are only included to show the order in which values were placed into the live well. The value at the head of an edge was used as a source value to the operation that created the value at the tail of the edge. Each record contains

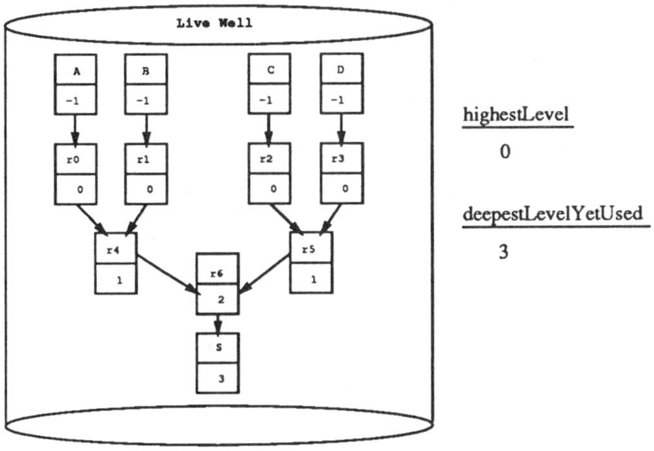

Figure 5: Live Well State After Processing Trace

the name of the location and the level in which the value was created. The variables A, B, C, and D are pre-initialized values from the DATA segment, and therefore are placed into the live well at level -1, the level immediately preceding the topologically highest level in the DDG.

The addition of storage dependencies can be implemented by further constraining the placement of computation in the DDG:

$$L_{dest} = MAX(L_{src1}, L_{src2}, highestLevel, D_{dest} + 1) + t_{op}$$

D_{dest} is the deepest level in the DDG of any computation that used a previous value stored in the same location as the destination value. Given this strategy of placement in the DDG, values stored in the same location will have non-intersecting lifetimes in the DDG.

Paragraph can optionally limit the number of viewable instructions when building the DDG. Figure 6 shows a conceptual view of the instruction window. The instruction window passes along the entire trace allowing at most W instructions to be viewed at any one time. As instructions enter the window, they are placed into a DDG being built in the window. Instructions ahead of the window are not considered for placement until they enter the instruction window. The first level available for placement is always the level at the bottom of the instruction window. As the instruction window moves along the trace, instructions displaced from the window can no longer affect the placement of other instructions. This is implemented by including a firewall with the operations displaced from the instruction window. The firewalls are shown as vertical dashed lines in Figure 6. The resulting DDG cannot contain more than W operations in any single level, *i.e.*, the case where all the instructions in the window are independent.

4 SPEC Benchmark Analysis

To demonstrate DDG analysis of ordinary programs, we present the results of some parallelism availability studies, using a DDG analysis of the SPEC benchmarks [14]. The affects on available parallelism due to system calls, renaming, and instruction window size are explored.

All traces were generated using *Pixie* on DECstation

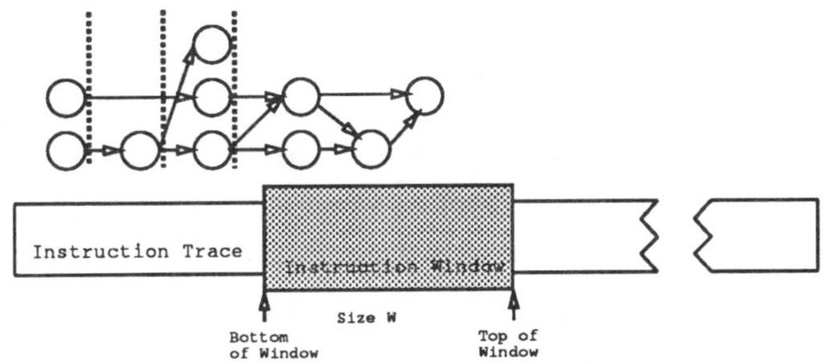

Figure 6: Paragraph Instruction Window

3100/5000 workstations. All the benchmarks were compiled with the MIPS 'C' and FORTRAN compilers, both version 2.1, at optimization level '-O3'. Table 1 shows the instruction latencies (in DDG levels) for each operation class in the MIPS processor. These values are used to determine how many levels an operation will span in the DDG before the value it creates is available for use by subsequent operations.

Table 1: Instruction Class Operation Times

Operation Class	Steps
Integer ALU	1
Integer Multiply	6
Integer Division	12
Floating Point Add/Sub	6
Floating Point Multiply	6
Floating Point Division	12
Load/Store	1
System Calls	1

Table 2 details the SPEC benchmarks, their arguments, and the inputs used. At most 100,000,000 instructions were traced due to time restrictions during the writing of this paper. Analyzed instructions are taken from the start of the program's instruction trace. The benchmarks *cc1* and *espresso* were completely analyzed.

To give an upper bound on the available parallelism, we first analyze DDGs containing only true data dependencies. Table 3 shows the critical path length, and available parallelism for the SPEC benchmarks. Figure 7 shows graphically the parallelism profiles for all benchmarks analyzed (note that the x and y scales differ for each benchmark.) The results in Table 3 are given for both conservative and optimistic system call assumptions; the results in Figure 7 are for conservative system call assumptions. System calls are relatively infrequent, the most frequent case being cc1 with a system call roughly every 14,861 instructions. Comparing the *Conservative* and *Optimistic* columns indicates the range in which the actual value of available parallelism lies. The conservative system call assumption does not hide much parallelism. For most of the benchmarks, the maximum absolute measurement error is very small, with *cc1* being the largest at 32%. For each analysis, all renaming is enabled, the window size is the same size as the trace (no control dependencies), and no functional unit resource restrictions are imposed.

The critical path lengths in Table 3 show the absolute

Table 2: SPEC Benchmarks Analyzed

Benchmark Name	Source Language	Benchmark Type	Arguments	Input	Total Instructions In Trace	Instructions Analyzed
cc1	C	Int	-O	explow.i	59,313,327	59,313,327
doduc	FORTRAN	FP	none	doducin	1,619,374,300	100,000,000
eqntott	C	Int	-s -.ioplte	int_pri_3.eqn	1,241,913,236	100,000,000
espresso	C	Int	-t	opa	119,134,865	119,134,865
fpppp	FORTRAN	FP	none	natoms4	2,396,679,406	100,000,000
matrix300	FORTRAN	FP	none	none	2,766,534,109	100,000,000
nasker	FORTRAN	FP	none	none	919,571,920	100,000,000
spice2g6	FORTRAN	Int and FP	none	greycode.in	28,696,843,509	100,000,000
tomcatv	FORTRAN	FP	none	none	1,872,460,468	100,000,000
xlisp	C	Int	none	li-input.lsp	1,234,252,567	100,000,000

Table 3: SPEC Benchmark Dataflow Results

Benchmark Name	Number of System Calls	Conservative		Optimistic		Maximum Measurement Error
		Critical Path Length	Available Parallelism	Critical Path Length	Available Parallelism	
cc1	3,991	1,321,698	36.21	903,622	52.95	0.32
doduc	428	877,872	103.59	848,052	107.22	0.03
eqntott	44	109,088	782.52	78,774	942.35	0.16
espresso	91	742,678	132.97	560,225	176.26	0.25
fpppp	30	49,24	1,999.86	48,484	2,032.78	0.02
matrix300	34	4,191	23,302.60	2,839	33,748.58	0.31
nasker	23	1,885,077	50.97	1,884,388	50.99	0.00
spice2g6	1,849	746,124	111.45	600,633	138.44	0.19
tomcatv	24	17,008	5,806.13	14,559	6,800.33	0.15
xlisp	3,470	5,650,548	13.28	5,640,833	13.30	0.00

minimum number of steps required to evaluate the computations in each benchmark. The available parallelism (and the parallelism profile) is computed only from instructions that create values (and thus are placed in the DDGs and parallelism profiles,) and does not include control instructions such as jumps and branches. (The average parallelism would be higher if these were included.) The results indicate that there is a significant amount of parallelism available in the applications. In fact, significantly more parallelism than was shown in [15] (compare the results with the "Perfect" results in [15]). However, as we will see, exploiting the available parallelism will require memory renaming and very large instruction windows for many of the benchmarks. Of course, perfect control flow and memory disambiguation is assumed in the dataflow analysis of Table 3 and Figure 7, whereas [15] places some limitations on their analysis that are representative of the current state-of-the-art.

Xlisp stands out as the benchmark with the least amount of parallelism. Further investigation revealed that the benchmark executes a Lisp program (li-input.lsp) that spends nearly all of its time in a *prog* structure. This construct provides an imperative programming framework in Lisp. The Lisp interpreter implements an abstract serial machine for the prog structure, thus re-introducing the control dependencies that are normally removed by *Paragraph.* The control dependencies show up as recurrences in the updating of the prog structure program counter. The resulting program's DDG is riddled with data dependencies, and thus provides little parallelism.

Time constraints prohibited us from running all the benchmarks to completion. Had we done so, we believe that the benchmarks with large amounts of parallelism (*i.e.*, few inter-instruction dependencies) would have continued to show an increase in the available parallelism, as independent instructions would be placed into the same DDG levels as earlier placed instructions. Benchmarks with smaller amounts of parallelism (*i.e.*, many inter-instruction dependencies) would probably reveal approximately the same amount of available parallelism, as dependent instructions would be placed into new levels of the DDG. Of course, later phases of a program could be very much unlike earlier phases, possibly exhibiting much more, or much less parallelism. This issue remains to be investigated.

Obtaining the parallelism shown in Table 3 will not be possible if storage and control dependencies cannot be removed. First consider the necessity to remove storage dependencies in order to expose parallelism. Table 4 shows the available parallelism when all storage dependencies (register and memory) are left in the DDG, when only memory storage dependencies are left in the DDG (registers renamed), when only non-stack memory storage dependencies are left in the DDG (registers and stack renamed), and when no storage dependencies are in the DDG. For all experiments, system calls force the insertion of a firewall, the instruction window size is the same size as the trace, and there are no functional unit resource restrictions.

The results illustrate that renaming must occur, otherwise the available parallelism in the trace will be substantially reduced. Without register renaming, very little parallelism is detected. This is to be expected since the use of a limited number of storage elements, namely 32 registers, for buffering the results of computations is a severe impediment to

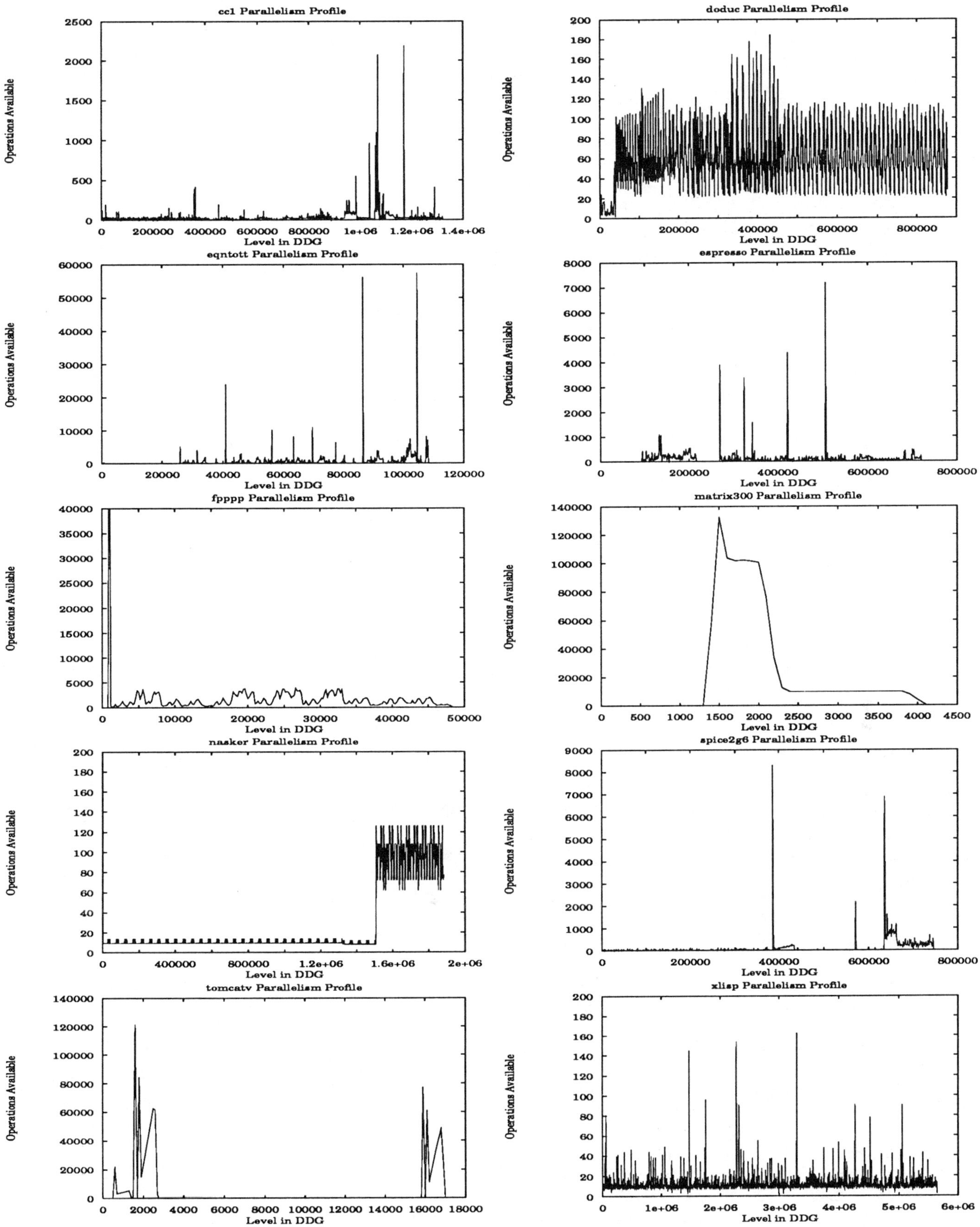

Figure 7: Parallelism Profiles for the SPEC Benchmarks

Table 4: SPEC Benchmarks under Different Renaming Conditions

Benchmark Name	Available Parallelism			
	No Renaming	Regs Renamed	Regs/Stack Renamed	Reg/Mem Renamed
cc1	3.65	33.70	36.19	36.21
doduc	1.62	29.97	103.59	103.59
eqntott	3.67	532.69	538.87	782.52
espresso	2.53	42.46	42.49	132.97
fpppp	1.69	18.34	81.32	1,999.86
matrix300	2.05	1,235.74	23,302.59	23,302.60
nasker	2.58	50.84	50.85	50.97
spice2g6	1.85	39.67	57.36	111.45
tomcatv	1.52	66.63	5,772.38	5,806.13
xlisp	3.32	13.27	13.28	13.28

parallelism. In most cases, renaming registers is enough to expose a sizable fraction the parallelism in the trace. The exception being *matrix300* and *tomcatv* where many of the values (vectors) used are not allocated to registers. The register renaming analysis assumed an infinite number of physical registers were available to rename logical registers.

As mentioned earlier, it is generally easier to rename variables resident on the stack, since their extent is known to be the same as the procedure using the values. If the stack and register values are renamed, only slightly more parallelism is exposed except for *tomcatv* and *matrix300*. Both *tomcatv* and *matrix300* manipulate arrays allocated on the stack. Since all values stored on the stack are renamed, including array accesses, the results are optimistic because it is unlikely that a stack based renaming technique could effectively rename array accesses.

The parallelism values presented in Table 3 and Figure 7 also assume that the entire trace (100,000,000 instructions in most cases) can be searched to find independent operations. For our next study, we vary the window size. This will demonstrate how many instructions in the dynamic instruction stream will have to be exposed before significant parallelism is realized. Figure 8 shows the percent of total available parallelism exposed as a function of instruction window size (note both axes are logarithmic scales.) Each point in the graph represents a full DDG extraction and analysis of up to 100,000,000 instructions (and requires approximately 10 hours on a DECstation 3100.) For each result, system calls force the insertion of a firewall, all renaming is enabled, and there are no functional unit resource restrictions. The instruction window size, described in Section 3, determines how much of the instruction trace is viewable when building the DDG.

Figure 8 indicates that very extensive look ahead, on the order of 100,000 instructions, will be required to garner all the available parallelism in *cc1*, *doduc*, *espresso*, *nasker*, and *spice*. For the applications with a large amount of available parallelism, *i.e.*, *eqntott*, *fpppp*, *matrix300*, and *tomcatv*, the number of instructions needed in the window greatly increases. For *matrix300*, only 3.8% of the total available parallelism (an average of 875 operations per level or cycle in the DDG) is exposed with a window size of 1,000,000 instructions. However, modest levels of parallelism (about 7-52 operations per cycle), certainly enough to fuel the next several generations of superscalar processors, can be obtained for all benchmarks with window sizes as small as 100 instructions.

It is unlikely that conventional superscaler designs could ever remove all control dependencies and completely exploit the parallelism in large instruction windows. This is because 1) the branch predictors currently available are not accurate enough to expose even hundreds of instructions, and 2) resolving dependencies between more than even a hundred instructions would require a prohibitive amount of associative logic. It is apparent that other methods of exposing independent instructions and resolving dependencies will be required.

5 Summary

In this paper, we presented a methodology for building and analyzing the dynamic dependency graph (DDG) of a program from a sequential execution trace of the program. The DDG of a program is a partially ordered, directed, acyclic graph where the nodes of the graph represent computation that occurred during the execution of the program, and the edges represent dependencies that force a specific order on the execution of the instructions. We also illustrated how the analysis of a (suitably constrained) DDG can yield valuable insight into the dynamics of program execution.

We then applied our DDG analysis methodology to study the parallelism in the SPEC benchmarks (for executions of 100 million instructions in most cases). We constructed parallelism profiles, measured the length of the critical path of computation through the programs, and measured the average (or available) parallelism. These studies indicated that there is a useful amount of parallelism in the benchmarks, ranging from 13 to 23,302 operations per cycle, but to fully expose this parallelism requires large instruction windows as well as the ability to rename both registers and memory. Renaming only registers exposed much of the parallelism in most of the cases. The parallelism profiles indicate that parallelism is bursty, with periods of lots of parallelism followed by periods of much less parallelism.

We also saw how the exposed parallelism was influenced by the size of the window of dynamic instructions. If we are interested in only small amounts of fine-grain parallelism (say less than 10 or 20 operations per cycle), then window sizes of a few hundred instructions are sufficient, but for larger levels of parallelism, much larger window sizes (on the order of thousands or tens of thousands of instructions) are required.

We feel that for a quantitative analysis of future-generation fine-grain parallel architectures, DDG analysis is

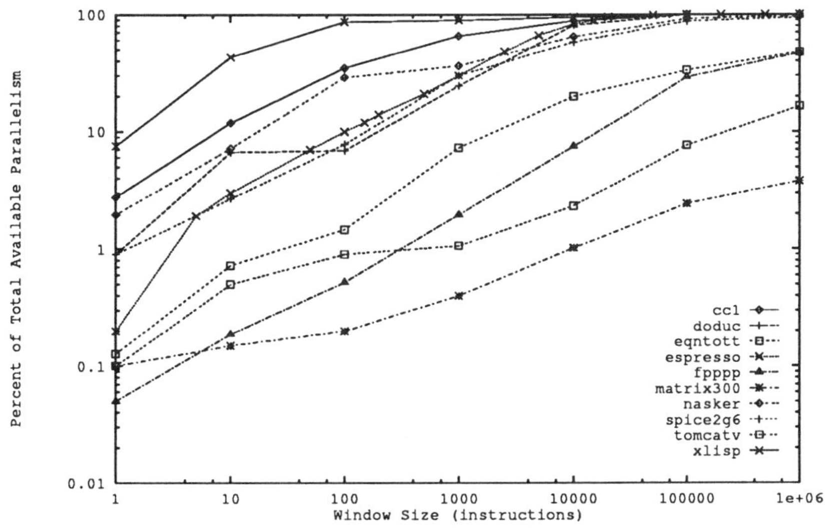

Figure 8: Window Size vs. Parallelism

going to be essential in understanding the dynamics of program execution on such machines, and strongly advocate the use of such analysis methods, despite their costs in execution time and resource requirements.

References

[1] Arvind, S. Brobst, "The Evolution of Dataflow Architectures from Static Dataflow to P-RISC," MIT Computation Structures Group Memo 316, August 1990.

[2] Arvind, D. E. Culler, "Resource Requirements of Dataflow Program," In *Proceedings of the 15th Annual International Symposium on Computer Architecture*, pp. 141-150, May 1988.

[3] Arvind, D. E. Culler, G. K. Maa, "Assessing the Benefits of Fine-grained Parallelism in Dataflow Programs," In *Proceedings of Supercomputing 88*, pp. 60-69, November 1988.

[4] Arvind, R. S. Nikhil, "A Dataflow Approach to General-purpose Parallel Computing," MIT Computation Structures Group Memo 302, July 1989.

[5] M. Butler, T. Yeh, Y. Patt, M. Alsup, H. Scales, M. Shebanow, "Single Instruction Stream Parallelism Is Greater than Two," In *Proceedings of the Eighteenth Annual Symposium on Computer Architecture*, pp. 276-286, May 1991.

[6] D. E. Culler, G. M. Papadopoulos, "The Explicit Token Store," In *Proceedings of the 17th Annual International Symposium on Computer Architecture*, pp. 82-91, May 1990.

[7] D. J. Kuck, et al., "Measurements of Parallelism in Ordinary FORTRAN Programs," Computer, vol 27, pp. 37-46, January 1974.

[8] M. Kumar, "Measuring Parallelism in Computation-Intensive Scientific/Engineering Application," IEEE Transactions on Computers, C-37, 9, pp. 1088-1098, September 1988.

[9] A. Nicolau, J. Fisher, "Measuring the Parallelism Available for Very Long Instruction Word Architectures," IEEE Transactions on Computers, C-33, 11, pp. 968-976, November 1984.

[10] R. S. Nikhil, "The Parallel Programming Language Id and its Compilation for Parallel Machines," MIT Computation Structures Group Memo 313, July 1990.

[11] G. M. Papadopoulos, "Implementation of a General Purpose Dataflow Multiprocessor," MIT Laboratory for Computer Science TR-432, December 1988.

[12] M. D. Smith, M. Johnson, M. A. Horowitz, "Limits on Multiple Instruction Issue," In *Third International Symposium on Architectural Support for Programming Languages and Operating Systems*, pp. 290-302, May 1991.

[13] G. S. Tjaden and M. J. Flynn. "Detection and Parallel Execution of Parallel Instructions," *IEEE Transactions on Computers*, C-19 (10), pp. 889-895, October 1970.

[14] J. Uniejewski, "SPEC Benchmark Suite: Designed for Today's Advanced Systems," *SPEC Newsletter*, Fall 1989.

[15] D. W. Wall, "Limits of Instructional-Level Parallelism," In *Proceedings of the Fourth International Conference on Architectural Support for Programming Languages and Operating Systems*, pp. 176-188, April 1991.

An Analysis of Loop Latency in Dataflow Execution

Walid A. Najjar W. Marcus Miller A. P. Wim Böhm

Department of Computer Science
Colorado State University
Fort Collins, CO 80523, USA

ABSTRACT

Recent evidence indicates that the exploitation of locality in dataflow programs could have a dramatic impact on performance. The current trend in the design of dataflow processors suggest a synthesis of traditional non-strict fine grain instruction execution and a strict coarse grain execution in order to exploit locality. While an increase in instruction granularity will favor the exploitation of locality within a single execution thread, the resulting grain size may increase latency among execution threads. In this paper, the resulting latency incurred through the partitioning of fine grain instructions into coarser grain threads is evaluated. We define the concept of a cluster *of fine grain instructions to quantify coarse grain input and output latencies using a set of numeric benchmarks. The results offer compelling evidence that the inner loops of a significant number of numeric codes would benefit from coarse grain execution. Based on cluster execution times, more than 60% of the measured benchmarks favor a coarse grain execution. In 63% of the cases the input latency to the cluster is the same in coarse or fine grain execution modes. These results suggest that the effects of increased instruction granularity on latency is minimal for a high percentage of the measured codes, and in large part is offset by available intra-thread locality. Furthermore, simulation results indicate that strict or non-strict data structure access does not change the basic cluster characteristics.*

*This work is in part supported by NSF Grants CCR-9010240 and MIP-9113268

1 INTRODUCTION

One major issue in the design of scalable high performance parallel architectures is the ability to tolerate and mask unpredictable fine-grain latency due to memory access or interprocessor communication [Smi90]. The fine-grain dataflow model of execution has been shown to provide both latency masking and an efficient hardware synchronization mechanism [AI87]. Dataflow machines employ large name spaces coupled with inexpensive synchronization at the instruction level which allows dataflow processors to mask latency at minimum cost. However, the general purpose matching mechanism employed in fine grain dataflow processors has precluded the exploitation of program and data locality. In fine grain dataflow execution, inherently sequential threads of code, fine grain execution give rise to pipeline stalls due to matching latency. With no capability to exploit locality within these threads, performance falls dramatically. Reducing matching store bandwidth through simplified operand matching schemes, coupled with the prospect of exploiting a high degree of locality has been the catalyst behind the design of new, second generation hybrid architectures [Ian88, SYH+89, GH90, PC90]. By increasing task granularity, hybrid machines execute portions of dataflow graphs as sequential threads, allowing them to exploit thread locality, while reducing matching store bandwidth.

Measuring temporal and spatial locality for a single thread of von Neumann code involves tracking the time between successive memory references. The asynchronous nature of fine grain dataflow execution tends to obscure the presence of program and data locality, making such measurements difficult. None the less, research in this area has revealed the presence of several forms of locality [MNB91].These results suggest there could be a significant performance improvement in the execution of coarse-grain dataflow graphs over fine-grain ones. Partitioning a dataflow graph in such a manner, would enable the processing elements to exploit *intra-thread* locality, while reducing matching store bandwidth. The problem addressed in this paper is that while a coarser granularity would favor the exploitation of locality *within a thread*, it might result in an increased latency *among threads* and thereby degrading performance. This paper reports on the quantitative evaluation of the increase in latency that a coarse-grain execution model would introduce.

The paper is organized as follows: section 2 defines the execution models used to quantify and evaluate inter-thread latency. The results obtained through simulation of a variety of benchmark programs are reported and discussed in section 3. The impact of strict and non-strict structure store access on cluster latency is presented and discussed in section 4. In section 5 these results are used in an analytic evaluation of a fine grain and coarse grain execution model. Section 6 offers concluding remarks.

2 DEFINITIONS AND MODELS

The objective of this paper is to quantitatively evaluate the added latency cost that is incurred in a coarse-grain dataflow execution model. In this section we define the execution models as well as the graph and timing parameters that will be used in the evaluation.

Definition 1 *A* **cluster** *of instructions is a connected directed acyclic graph with only* one output arc. *In a cluster each node is a fine grain instruction and the output is always generated by the last executing node.*

An example of a cluster is depicted in Figure 1. While a cluster could be any collection of fine grain instructions, in this paper we will focus on the body of loops as a specific type of cluster. Figure 3 shows the body of loop number 7 in the Livermore loops benchmark suite. Two parameters are associated with the graph of a cluster:

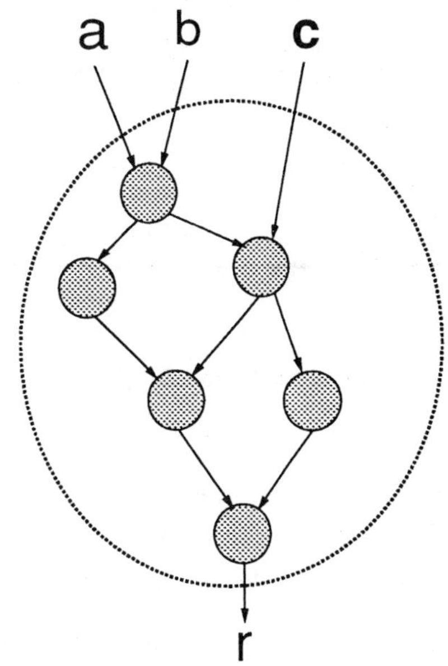

Figure 1: Typical cluster of fine grain instructions

- S_1 is the total number of instructions in the cluster, it is also a measure of its execution time on a sequential machine.

- S_∞ is the cluster critical path length, it is also a measure of its execution time on a machine with infinite hardware parallelism.

$\Pi = S_1/S_\infty$ is the average fine grain parallelism in the cluster. In the example of Figure 1 $S_1 = 6$, $S_\infty = 4$ and $\Pi = 1.5$.

Two execution models of a cluster are defined:

- *Fine grain* cluster execution model: any instruction in the cluster will execute as soon as its inputs are available, instructions execute in parallel assuming infinite hardware parallelism.

- *Coarse grain* cluster execution model: no instruction will execute until all the input tokens to the cluster have arrived. Instructions in the cluster are executed in a sequential non-pipelined mode.

For the sake of simplicity, we will assume, in both models, that all instructions execute in one time step and that communication overhead is negligible. The *ideal execution* model of a cluster is therefore a fine grain execution with infinite matching bandwidth. A *token generation* is the execution time of a single instruction under ideal execution, it will be used as the basic time unit in the remainder of this paper.

Figure 2: Relationship between input latency and output delay

Next we define a number of timing parameters that characterize the execution of a cluster under either fine or coarse grain models.

- t_0: the arrival time of the first input to the cluster,
- t_n: the arrival time of the last token in the cluster,
- t_r: the time at which the result is generated,

The relationships between these values, shown in Figure 2, are defined by:

- l: the delay between t_0 and t_n, $(l = t_n - t_0)$,
- d: the delay between the arrival of the last input token (t_n) and the first result token (t_r), $(d = t_r - t_n)$,
- l': the delay until the first fine grain instruction in the cluster can fire,

Notice that l and l' are not parameters of the cluster itself but rather depend on the execution of the program graph containing it.

For a cluster executed on a machine with infinite resources, $l \geq 0$, $l' \leq l$, and $1 \leq d \leq S_\infty$. For fine grain execution, $d < S_\infty$ implies some instructions may fire before all of the cluster's inputs have arrived, hence there will be some degree of pipelining and latency masking occurring within the cluster. The net effect is one of pipelining, in which one or more instructions begin execution before all cluster inputs have arrived thereby keeping the pipeline busy. Pipeline starvation could occur due to insufficient program parallelism in a dataflow machine [BG90]. Dataflow architectures such as the Monsoon circumvent the pipeline starvation problem by allowing the concurrent execution of multiple clusters (threads) per processor [TPB+91].

In general, for a cluster to be efficiently executed under a fine grain model, $\Pi \gg 1, S_\infty \gg d$, and $l \gg l'$. These conditions guarantee that the dataflow circular pipeline stays full, hence the cost of token matching and structure store latency can be hidden by fast context switching. A cluster may favor a coarse grain execution strategy for $l \approx l'$ or $d \approx S_\infty$, provided the average cluster parallelism, Π is reasonably small and the available intra-thread locality is high.

Based on these parameters, we can derive the following properties for an ideal execution model (i.e with zero matching costs):

1. $l = 0 \Rightarrow d = S_\infty$. By the definition of d, if no instruction in the cluster incurs any input latency, the cluster output delay will be equal to its critical path length.
2. $l' = l \Rightarrow d = S_\infty$. If $l = l'$, no instruction in the cluster can fire until all inputs have arrived, hence the number of generations between the nodes with input time t_n and the output time t_r is S_∞, and therefore $d = S_\infty$.
3. $l' + S_\infty \leq l + S_1$. This follows directly from the definitions of l' and l. $l' \leq l$ and $S_\infty \leq S_1$, hence for a dataflow machine with infinite resources, $l' + S_\infty \leq l + S_1$. Evidently, $l' + S_\infty$ is the lower bound on the execution time in the fine grain model and $l + S_1$ the upper bound on the execution time in the coarse grain model. This relationship will be investigated further in section 5.

3 LATENCY MEASUREMENTS

To quantify the cluster parameters, l, l', and d, a dataflow machine simulator based on the Manchester Data Flow Machine (MDFM) instruction set [BGK87] was used to trace the execution of clusters in a suite of benchmarks consisting of:

- Lawrence Livermore Loops (1-10, 13-15) [McM86, Feo87]
- Purdue Benchmarks (1-4, 7-14) [Ric85, Ric90]

The clusters were simply chosen as the inner loop in each benchmark. The cluster boundary was chosen such that the top level instruction in each cluster is an arithmetic instructions. In other words all the inputs to the cluster are inputs to an arithmetic instruction within that cluster.

Benchmarks were compiled from the single assignment language SISAL [MSA+85] into MDFM machine code. To study the effects of both strict and non-strict structure store access on cluster latency, all benchmarks were compiled using both strict and non-strict/no garbage collection options (see section 4). As an example, the Sisal code for Livermore Loop 7 as well as the cluster of instructions of its inner loop are shown in Figure 3. The opcodes MLR and ADR are multiply reals, and add reals respectively. With each input is also specified its arrival time, in generation numbers, obtained from the simulator after compiling the source code using strict structure store access and garbage collection enabled. For this loop $l' = 13, l = 14, d = 8, S_\infty = 8$, and $S_1 = 16$, yielding an average cluster parallelism of $\Pi = 1.8$.

Simulation results obtained for code generated using strict structures with garbage collection active are summarized in Table 1. The values in column SP will be discussed in section 5. The following observation can be made:

- l and l' are the same for 63% of the simulation runs, implying the token arrival to token result delay, d, is very nearly equal to S_∞ for these clusters. In these cases a coarse grain execution would not incur any additional latency over a fine grain one. Under these conditions there can be little pipelining of instruction execution, and therefore the overall execution time of the cluster is not affected by its execution mode.

- The average value of Π is small $\approx$ 1.3 for the Livermore Loops, and $\approx$ 1.1 for the Purdue benchmarks. This indicates that there is very little parallelism to exploit within these clusters (this result has been reported in [JW89]). Because Π is small, token matching and structure store latency cannot be masked in the fine grain execution of a single cluster per processor. One alternatives is to exploit inter-thread concurrency by executing multiple threads per processor as in the Monsoon architecture [TPB+91]. Another alternative is a coarse grain execution strategy which offers great potentials for exploiting intra-thread locality and also reducing matching store costs.

LL Loop	l'	l	d	S_∞	S_1	Π	SP
1	13	13	4	4	5	1.25	0.90
2	9	9	3	3	4	1.33	0.93
3	13	13	2	2	2	1	0.94
4	5	5	8	8	8	1	0.67
5	6	6	2	2	2	1	0.90
6	19	19	2	2	2	1	0.96
7	13	14	8	8	16	1.78	1.03
8	43	43	6	6	14	2.33	1.05
9	29	29	10	10	17	1.70	0.96
10	1	1	9	9	9	1	0.58
15	0	12	6	11	13	1.18	1.08
Purdue	l'	l	d	S_∞	S_1	Π	SP
1	0	0	4	4	4	1	0.62
2	0	12	2	6	6	1	1.19
3	1	1	41	41	41	1	0.52
4	0	1	2	3	3	1	1.00
7	0	7	4	5	6	1.2	0.93
8*	0	9	1	2	2	1	1.09
9	0	0	6	6	6	1	0.58
10*	0	0	2	2	2	1	0.75
11*	2	2	6	6	6	1	0.64
13	0	1	4	5	6	1.2	0.89
14*	1	17	8	15	17	1.13	1.06

Table 1: Timing and cluster parameters per benchmark – Strict structures (*: significant loop only).

4 STRICT AND NON-STRICT STRUCTURES

The MDFM code generation system can be configured to generate code for both strict and non-strict access to the structure store. The structure store accesses data without the use of tags, implementing the I-structure paradigm through a deferred read mechanism [GB88]. The structure store consist of an allocation unit, structure memory, a deferred access queue and a clearance unit. The allocation unit manages storage allotment, while the clearance unit performs garbage collection. Structure store access can be made asynchronously via a deferred access queue. When a read request is

```
type double = double_real;
type OneD  = array[double];
function Loop7(n:integer;R,T:double; U,Y,Z:OneD; returns OneD)
   for k in 1,n returns
      array of U[k]+R * (Z[k]+R * Y[k])
                  +T * (U[k+3]+R * (U[k+2]+R * U[k+1])
                  +T* (U[k+6] +R * (U[k+5]+R * U[k+4])))
   end for
end function
```

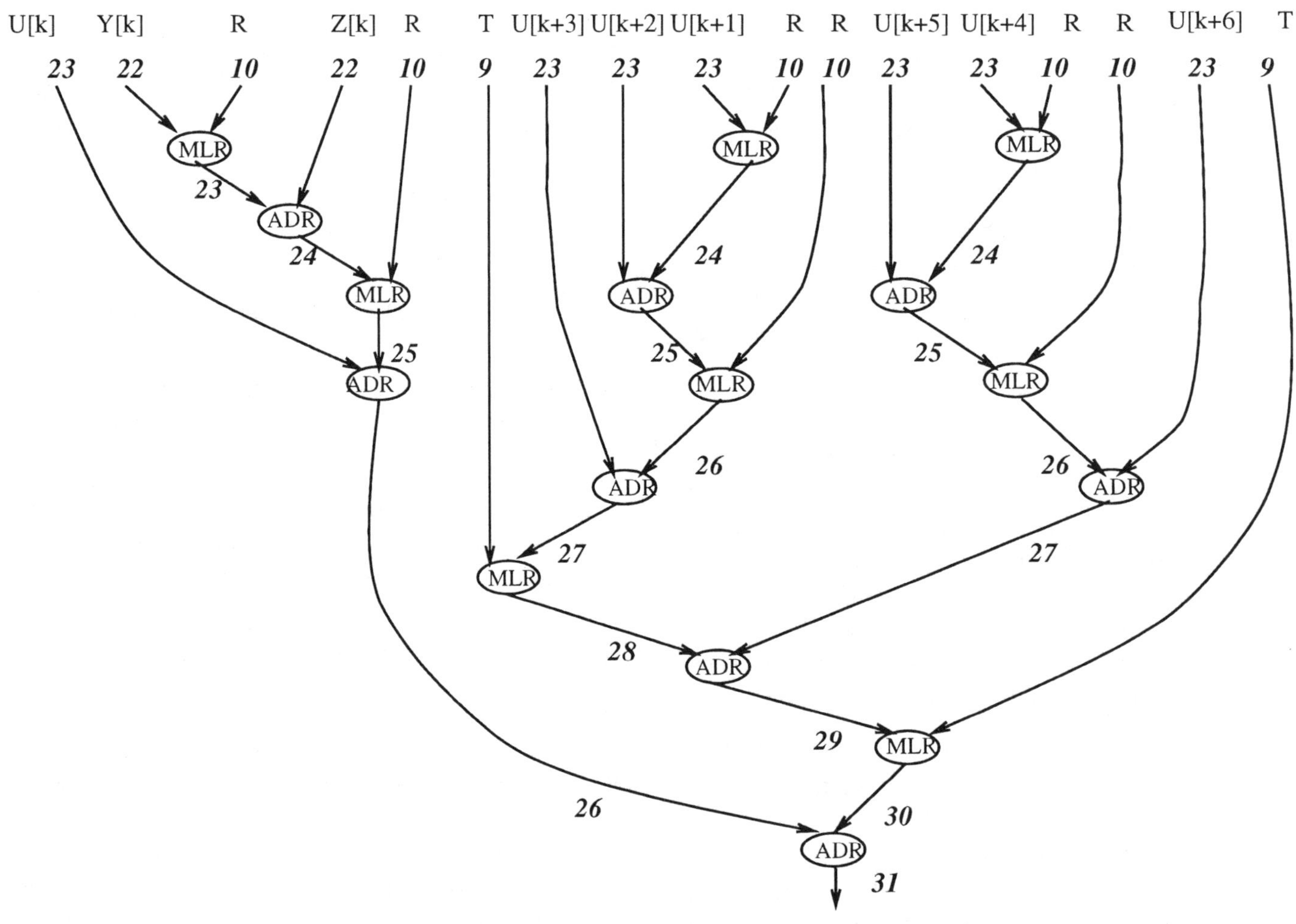

Figure 3: Cluster of instructions for Livermore loop 7

LL Loop	l'	l	d
1	7	7	4
2	0	1	3
3	7	7	2
4	6	8	8
5	2	2	2
6	6	6	2
7	7	8	8
8	13	13	6
9	10	12	10
10	1	1	9
15	0	17	6

Table 2: Timing and cluster parameters, Livermore loops – Non-Strict structures.

made for data not yet written, the request is held in the deferred access queue until the required data arrives. To compare the effects of strict and non-strict structure store access on cluster parameters, each benchmark was compiled to generate code for both paradigms.

For strict structure store access, the compiler generates code to ensure strictness, i.e. no instruction can access an array element until the entire data structure is built. The effect of strictness on cluster inputs is to delay the arrival of tokens transporting data structure elements. Simulation results indicate that the basic cluster characteristics do not change. Table 2 shows the timing parameters for a non-strict execution of some Livermore loops. Comparing these with the values in Table 1, the main conclusions that can be drawn are:

- The token arrival latencies l' and l, are in general longer for code compiled with strict structure store accesses than non-strict. This result is to be expected since no array element is available prior to completion of the whole array.
- In most of the cases in the strict execution we have $l = l'$ whereas it is not the case in the non-strict execution. Again this is to be expected since strict array creation makes all array elements available at the same time.

From these initial results we can conclude that a coarse grain execution is not hampered by strict array implementation whereas a non-strict array implementation would enhance fine grain execution. These initial results however, must be confirmed by larger benchmark programs.

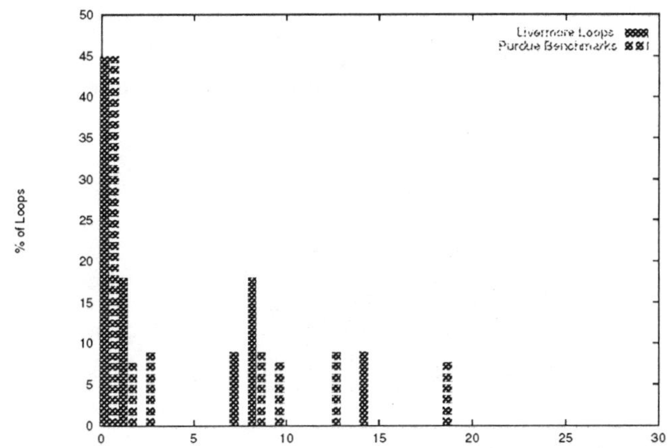

Figure 4: The distribution of Δ across benchmarks

5 ANALYSIS OF RESULTS

The results in the previous section describe the latency of input token arrival at cluster boundaries. In this section we analyze the effects of the input latency on the execution time of a cluster under the fine and coarse grain models of execution. Let T, T_{min}, T_{max} and Δ be defined as

$$T = t_r - t_0$$

$$T_{min} = l' + S_\infty$$

$$T_{max} = l + S_1$$

$$\Delta = l - l' + S_1 - S_\infty$$

T is the total delay in the cluster execution from the arrival of the first input to the availability of its output. T_{min} is the lower bound on T under the fine grain execution model and T_{max} is the upper bound on T under sequential coarse grain execution. The difference Δ can be viewed as a measure of the potential loss in performance between the coarse and fine grain models. Surprisingly, for the combined benchmarks, $T_{min} = T_{max}$ in 45% of the cases. Figure 4 plots the distribution of Δ for the Livermore loops and the Purdue benchmarks. Both sets of data exhibit similar behavior, a high percentage of benchmarks have values of T_{min} and T_{max} that are nearly equal. For the Livermore loops, $\Delta \leq 10$

for 85% of the measured code. For the Purdue benchmarks, $\Delta \leq 10$ in 75% of the cases. None of the measured values exceeded 20 token generations for either test suite.

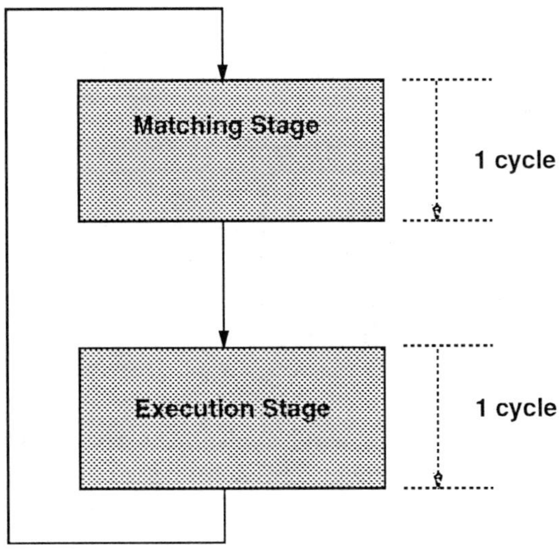

Figure 5: A two stage hybrid machine

The above analysis is based on a number of simplifications such as negligible matching costs and the pipelined nature of dataflow execution. The following analysis is based on a hypothetical dataflow machine depicted in Figure 5 where the matching stage and the execution stage both have a unit time delay. The machine can operate in both coarse and fine grain modes as defined in Section 2. In both modes an instruction will execute in one time step.

Let T_f and T_c represent the execution time in the fine and coarse grain modes respectively. They can be derived as

$$T_f = l + 2d$$

$$T_c = l + 1 + S_1$$

For a cluster of instructions executed in fine grain mode, a latency l' is incurred until the first instruction packet can fire. At time $t_0 + l$ there will be d instructions that will have to go through the two stages of the machine. In coarse grain mode the execution unit incurs a startup latency of l, until the matching unit collects all cluster inputs. The first instruction is ready to execute at time $l + 1$, all others instructions requiring an additional S_1 cycles to produce the final result.

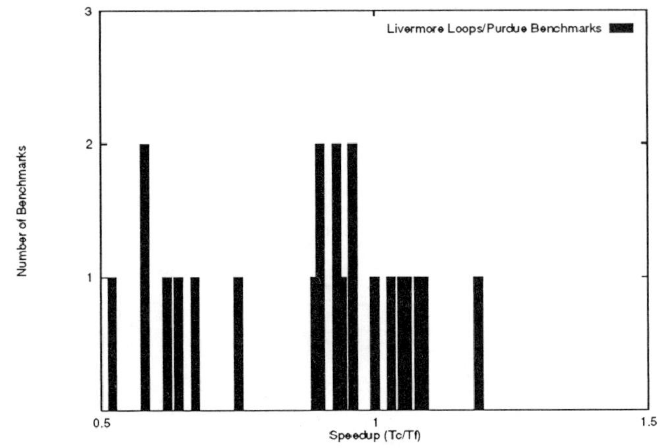

Figure 6: Distribution of speed-up

Let the speed-up achievable in the fine grain mode over the coarse grain one be defined by

$$SP = \frac{T_c}{T_f} = \frac{l + 1 + S_1}{l + 2d}$$

The fine grain mode outperforms the coarse grain mode when

$$T_c > T_f \Longleftrightarrow l + S_1 + 1 > l + 2d \Longleftrightarrow S_1 > 2d - 1$$

The values of SP are shown in Table 1, indicating that 60% of the benchmarks would benefit from a coarse grain execution. The distribution of the speed-up SP across the benchmarks is shown in Figure 6. It can be noted that all values of SP lie between 0.5 and 1.2 implying that a coarse grain execution would outperform a fine grain one by at most a factor of 2, while the fine grain execution will perform at most 20% better and that in only one case. While a factor of 2 is very significant in real architectures, it does not carry much weight in hypothetical architectures based on highly simplified approximations. These results are even more compelling considering that communication costs or resource conflicts have not been accounted for in the fine grain execution model.

A fine grain model of execution will perform well for small input latency l, and sufficiently large cluster parallelism. In this case a fine grain execution model can mask memory latency through fast and inexpensive synchronization. However, if cluster parallelism is small and input latency high, the fine grain model performs poorly because there is insufficient useful work to mask input latency. The full cost of token matching is incurred because there are no instructions in the execution unit's ready queue. By exploiting intra-thread locality, a coarse grain model can efficiently execute clusters consisting of sequential code with few synchronization points.

6 CONCLUSION

The architectural tradeoffs required to reduce synchronization cost, exploit locality and mask memory latency are among the most complex issues to be faced in the design of the next generation of high performance parallel processing systems. Although traditional dataflow processors provide efficient context switching and synchronization mechanisms they fail to exploit program or data locality. Hybrid style (dataflow/von Neumann) machines offer great potential to bridge the gap between costly synchronization and latency inherent in sequential execution and the ability to exploit locality in fine grain execution.

However, by relying on a coarser granularity of execution, hybrid machines could suffer from an increase in latency among execution threads. This paper reports on an experimental evaluation of inter-thread latency in dataflow program execution of a benchmark suite comprising numeric and non-numeric code.

The concept of a *cluster* of fine grain instructions is used to quantify input and output latencies under both coarse and fine grain execution models. The results show that in a large percentage of the cases (63%) there was no increase in latency between fine and a coarse grain execution models. An analysis of the execution of these clusters on an idealized hypothetical dataflow machine shows that a coarse grain execution will outperform a fine grain one in over 60% of the cases. In those cases where the fine grain model has a smaller execution time, the speed-up is less than 1.2 for the large majority of cases.

This work offers compelling evidence that the inner loops of a substantial number of numeric and non-numeric programs would benefit from a coarse grain hybrid execution strategy without any detrimental increase in latency.

REFERENCES

[AI87] Arvind and R.A. Iannucci. Two fundamentals issues in multiprocessors: the data-flow solutions. Technical Report LCS CSG 226-6, Laboratory for Computer Science, MIT, Cambrige Massachussett, May 1987.

[BG90] A. P. W. Böhm and J. R. Gurd. Iterative instructions in the Manchester dataflow computer. *IEEE Trans. on Parallel and Distributed Systems*, 1(2):129–139, 1990.

[BGK87] A.P.W. Böhm, J.R. Gurd, and C.C. Kirkham. The Manchester dataflow computing system. In J. Dongarra, editor, *Experimental Parallel Computing Architectures*, pages 177–219. North Holland, 1987.

[Feo87] J. T. Feo. The Livermore Loops in Sisal. Technical Report UCID-21159, Computing Research Group, Lawrence Livermore National Laboratory, Livermore, CA 94550, August 1987.

[GB88] J. R. Gurd and A. P. W. Böhm. Implicit parallel processing: SISAL on the Manchester dataflow computer. In G. Paul and G.S. Almasi, editors, *Parallel Systems and Computation*, pages 179–204. North Holland Publishing Company, 1988.

[GH90] V. G. Grafe and J. E. Hoch. The EPSILON-2 multiprocessor system. *Journal of Parallel and Distributed Computing*, 10(4), 1990.

[Ian88] R. A. Iannucci. A dataflow/von Neumann hybrid architecture. Technical Report MIT/LCS/TR-418, MIT Laboratory for Computer Science, May 1988.

[JW89] N. P. Jouppi and D. W. Wall. Available instruction-level parallelism for superscalar and superpipelined machines. Technical Report WRL Research Report 89/7, Western Research Laboratory, Palo Alta, CA, July 1989.

[McM86] F. H. McMahon. Livermore fortran kernels: A computer test of numerical performance range. Technical Report UCRL-53745, Lawrence Livermore National Laboratory, Livermore, CA, December 1986.

[MNB91] W. M. Miller, W. A. Najjar, and A. P. W. Böhm. A quantitative analysis of locality in dataflow programs. In 24th *International Symp. on Microarchitecture (MICRO-24), Albuquerque, NM*, pages 46–53, Nov 1991.

[MSA+85] J. McGraw, S. Skedzielewski, S. Allan, R. Oldehoeft, J. Glauert, C. Kirkham, B. Noyce, and R. Thomas. SISAL: Streams and Iteration in a Single Assignment Language: reference manual version 1.2. Manual M-146, Rev. 1, Lawrence Livermore National Laboratory, Livermore, CA, March 1985.

[PC90] G. M. Papadopolus and D. E. Culler. Monsoon: an explicit token-store architecture. In *Proceedings of the* 17th *Annual International Symposium on Computer Architecture*, June 1990.

[Ric85] J. R. Rice. Problems to test parallel and vector languages. Technical Report CSD-TR 516, Purdue University, 1985.

[Ric90] J. R. Rice. Problems to test parallel and vector languages - 2. Technical Report CSD-TR 1016, Purdue University, 1990.

[Smi90] B. Smith. The end of architecture (keynote address). In *Proceedings of the* 17th *Int. Symp. on Computer Architecture*, May 1990.

[SYH+89] S. Sakai, Y. Yamaguchi, K. Hiraki, Y. Kodama, and T. Yuba. An architecture of a data-flow single chip processor. In *Int. Symp. on Computer Architecture*, pages 46–53, May 1989.

[TPB+91] K. R. Traub, G. M. Papadopoulos, M. J. Beckerle, J. E. Hicks, and J. Young. Overview of the Monsoon Project. In *Int. Conf. on Computer Design*, pages 150–155. IEEE, October 1991.

Session 12: Vectors and Streams

A Novel Cache Design for Vector Processing

Qing Yang *
Dept. of Electrical Engineering
The University of Rhode Island
Kingston, RI 02881

Liping Wu Yang
Assoc. Data Inc.
200 Dyer Street
Providence, RI 02903

ABSTRACT

This paper introduces an innovative cache design for vector computers, called prime-mapped cache. By utilizing the special properties of a Mersenne prime, the new design does not increase the critical path length of a processor, nor does it increase the cache access time as compared to a direct-mapped cache. The prime-mapped cache minimizes cache miss ratio caused by line interferences that have been shown to be critical for numerical applications by previous investigators. We show that significant performance gains are possible by adding the proposed cache memory into an existing vector computer provided that application programs can be blocked. The performance gain will increase with the increase of the speed gap between processors and memories. We develop an analytical performance model based on a generic vector computation model to study the performance of the design. Our preliminary performance analysis on various vector access patterns shows that the prime-mapped cache can provide as much as a factor of 2 to 3 performance improvement over the conventional direct-mapped cache in the vector processing environment. Moreover, the additional hardware cost introduced by the new mapping scheme is negligible.

1 Introduction

While cache memories have been successfully used in general purpose computers to boost system performance [1], their effectiveness for vector processing has not been established. Most of existing supercomputer vector processors typically do not have cache memories because of perceived poor performance for vectorized numerical algorithms. This common believe results primarily from three considerations: First, numerical programs generally have data sets that are too large for the current cache sizes. Sweep accesses of a large vector may result in complete reloading of the cache before the processor reuses them. Secondly, address sequentiality which has been an important assumption in conventional caches may not be as good in vectorized numerical algorithms that usually access data with certain stride (unit or non-unit). And third, register files and highly interleaved memories have been commonly used to achieve high memory bandwidth required by vector processing. It is not clear whether cache memories can significantly improve the performance of such systems. However, with the rapid advances in device technology and increased speed gap between processor and memory [2], it has become increasingly important to study the performance of cache memories for vector processors [3]

The first concern about possible poor performance of vector cache memories (we will call a cache holding vector data a *vector cache*) has been studied by a number of researchers [4, 5, 6]. It is well known that the memory hierarchy can be better utilized if numerical algorithms are *blocked*. Instead of operating on an entire vector of large size, we can block the vector into several segments and perform computations on these segments. Blocking is a general program optimization technique that promotes data reuse in high speed memories. Lam et al. have recently studied the cache performance of a blocked matrix multiplication algorithm [4]. It is shown in their study that blocking factor (the size of inner loop) has significant impact on cache performance. In [5], So and Zecca presented an interesting performance study for vector caches by means of trace driven simulations [5]. They have shown that although the program locality of vector executions is significantly different from that of scalar executions the cache hit ratio is high enough to take advantage of a cache. Their study is based on traces of a set of fixed size programs that are either cache-optimized subroutines from the machine library or highly vectorized for vector machines. It is not clear how the cache behaves for generally blocked programs with different problem sizes.

Sequentiality of vector addresses depends on vector access stride that varies widely in numerical algorithms. Since the basic storage unit in a cache is a cache line that consists of a group of consecutive memory words, cache pollution may result if the access stride is not one. Fu and Patel [7] have recently presented a comprehensive study on the effects of cache line sizes on the performance of vector caches. They proposed two prefetching schemes, sequential-prefetching and stride-prefetching, to reduce the influence of long stride vector accesses. As shown in [7], certain performance improvements as result of the two prefetching schemes are obtained. However, the cache miss ratios for some applications considered in [7] are still as high as over 40% in some cases. This is because that not only does the poor sequentiality of vector data result in cache pollutions but also a large amount of *interference misses* [4].

In spite of the fact that most supercomputer vector machines use interleaved memory and large register files to speed up memory accesses, the increased speed gap between processor and memory may still favor a cache memory to bridge this gap. This is because not only is a register file relatively small that can hardly hold the working set of a program but also it requires extra efforts in software to manage it. Cache memory, on the other hands, is transpar-

*This research is supported in part by NSF under Grant No. CCR-8909672.

ent to programmers. Highly interleaved memory may provide enough bandwidth to single stream vector accesses, but the memory speed has to be extremely fast and the number of interleaved memory modules has to be excessively large in order to provide enough bandwidth for multiple stream vector accesses. Baily has shown in his study [8] that hundreds and even thousands of interleaved memory modules are needed to achieve a reasonable memory performance for multiple stream vector accesses. Furthermore, vector processing has become a mainstream form of computing ranging from superminis to workstations. Vector processors have also been incorporated into mainframes as built-in accelerators for computationally intensive applications. For these types of machines, a cache memory can be a cost-effective enhancement towards a smooth memory hierarchy [5, 7]. Several recent vector computers feature a cache-based memory hierarchy such as IBM 3090 [5], Alliant FX/8 and Vax/600.

It is clear from the above discussions that cache memories have a good performance potential for future vector processors. However, the question as to whether or not a cache memory can provide similar benefits for vector processors as it does for general purpose computers remains to be answered. A single miss in the vector cache results in a number of processor stall cycles equal to the entire memory access time, while the memory accesses of a vector processor without cache are fully pipelined. In order to benefit from a vector cache, the miss ratio must be kept extremely small. In general, cache misses can be classified into three categories [2]: compulsory, capacity, and conflicts. The compulsory misses are the misses in the initial loading of data, which can be properly pipelined in a vector computer. The capacity misses are due to the size limitation of a cache to hold data between references. If application algorithms are properly blocked as mentioned previously, the capacity misses can be attributed to the compulsory misses for the initial loading of each block of data provided that the block size is less than cache size. The last category, conflict misses, plays a key role in the vector processing environment. Conflicts can occur when two or more elements of the same vector are mapped to the same cache line or elements from two different vectors compete for the same cache line. The former is called *self-interference* whereas the latter is called *cross-interference* [4]. The recent study on blocked matrix multiplication algorithm [4] shows that the self-interference misses increase drastically and dominate cache misses after the fraction of a 16K-word cache being used exceeds 3%. It is also shown in [4] that an algorithm with one problem size can run at twice the speed of the same algorithm with a different size.

Since conflict misses that significantly degrade vector cache performance have a lot to do with vector access stride, one may wish to adjust the size of an application problem to make a good access stride for a given machine. However, not only does this approach give a programmer a burden of knowing architecture details of a machine but also infeasible for many applications. It is known that conflicts are minimum if the access stride is relative prime to the number of cache lines which is a power of 2 for direct or set-associative cache. Note that the stride required to access the major diagonal of a matrix is one greater than the stride required to access a row of the matrix stored in a column-major. Therefore, it is not possible to make both row access and major diagonal access efficient because one stride or the other is not relative prime to the cache size of any direct or set-associative cache.

In this paper, we propose a new cache design, called *prime – mapped* cache, in an attempt to minimize cache miss ratio. The main idea of the design is that memory data are mapped into cache lines according to a Mersenne prime. The cache access logic of the new mapping scheme keeps virtually the same as direct-mapped cache, resulting in no additional delay for cache accesses. At the meantime, the address generation takes no longer than the normal address calculation time due to the special properties of the Mersenne number. Moreover, generating addresses for cache access is done in parallel with normal address calculations resulting in no performance penalty. Thus, it has the advantages of both direct-mapped cache and fully associative cache if replacement is not considered. We also present an analytical model for two simple vector processor models: memory-register vector processor model and cache-based vector processor model. The advantage of an analytical modeling is that it provides us with a quick and insightful performance estimate of a given design without the limitation of application problem sizes [9]. Based on the analytical model, one can easily pinpoint where the potential performance bottleneck is. Furthermore, most numerical algorithms are highly structured, which makes analysis possible and fairly accurate. Our performance analysis on typical vector access patterns shows that the new cache design improves vector processing performance by a factor of 2-3 over conventional cache designs with negligibly additional hardware cost.

The paper is organized as follows. Section 2 presents the cache design and discussions on hardware issues. In Section 3, we present an analytical performance model for two vector processors with and without a cache. We will carry out performance analyses and comparisons for various approaches in Section 4. We consider three types of typical vector access patterns: random multi-stride access, subblock access, and FFT access in our performance analysis. Section 5 concludes the paper.

2 Minimizing Cache Misses

In this section, we consider several alternatives to reduce vector cache misses. By vector cache, we mean, in this paper, the cache that holds vector data accessed by vector load or store instructions. We assume that scalar data have a separate cache.

2.1 Can Associativity Help?

Since cache misses in a vector cache result mainly from line conflicts as discussed in the introduction, one would naturally think of set-associative-mapped cache with higher associativity or fully associative cache. It is well known that higher associativity has the advantages of less line conflicts and the flexibility of implementing a replacement algorithm such as LRU. Lam et al [4] have shown that the average miss rates of a set-associative cache are relatively lower than that of direct-mapped cache. However, the fraction of cache used in case of set-associative cache still remains very small (in the range of 20% to 60%) though it is larger than that of the direct-mapped cache. Moreover, the standard deviation of miss rate increases steadily with the blocking factor implying that the execution time for some problem sizes can be significantly worse than others. For the same cache size, increasing associativity results in decreased number of sets that data can be mapped to although several cache lines can be mapped to the same set. As a result, we will not see significant reduction in terms of interference misses. Furthermore, increasing the associativity also increases the cache hit time [10] which has negative effects on system performance. As to the replacement algorithm, due to the nature of numerical algorithms, we may not be able to take this advantage as we do for most other applications since serial access to vectors dictates against LRU replacement [3]. Whether there exists a better replacement algorithm needs further study.

2.2 Effects of Line Size

Cache line size is one of the most important parameters in a cache design. Larger cache line sizes reduce compulsory misses if an application has a high spatial locality. At the meantime, larger cache lines also reduces the number of lines in the cache, giving rise to more conflicts. In addition, non-unit access strides may also result in cache pollutions since the loaded excess data may never be used before being replaced. Cache pollution degrades cache performance significantly because not only do the unused data use cache space but also memory bandwidth [7]. Fu and Patel [7] observed that cache line sizes have unpredictable impacts on vector cache performance. The best cache line size of one program may be the worst for another program in a given cache design. For some applications, increasing cache line sizes even results in increased miss ratio, which is contradictory to common believe. Their observations suggest that an optimal cache line size for vector processing be difficult to determine unless all application programs have the same stride characteristics. There are also other considerations in deciding cache line size such as bus width, degree of memory interleaving etc.. Cache line size selection for the vector cache is more complicated than general purpose computers. In this paper, we will concentrate on fixed line size of 8 bytes or one double precision word.

2.3 Prime-Mapped Cache

We propose a cache design with a novel mapping scheme called **prime-mapping** that attempts to minimize interference misses. The idea behind the new design is simple. Instead of having 2^c cache lines in the cache, we allow only a prime number of cache lines to reside in the cache. Using a prime number in a memory system to avoid memory access conflicts was attempted before. In the early 70's, Budnik and Kuck suggested the use of prime number of memory modules in the context of a parallel computer [11]. The idea was latter developed by Burroughs in the design of the BSP computer [12]. However, addressing for such prime-number memory systems is much more complex than for memory systems in which the number of memory modules is a power of 2. This complicated addressing is more critical in cache design since we can not afford to allow any additional delay for cache accesses. Any increase in cache hit time will affect not only the average access time but also the clock rate of the CPU. Therefore, it is of essential importance that any attempt in designing a new cache must ensure no increase in the length of the critical path of a processor.

Our approach here is to utilize the special properties of a class of prime numbers: the Mersenne primes. A Mersenne number is of the form $2^c - 1$ for some c that makes $2^c - 1$ a prime. Examples of such c are 2, 3, 5, 7, 13, 17, and 19 etc.. A cache line with address A_l is mapped into line number $A_l \ mod \ (2^c - 1)$ in the cache. Since Mersenne number is a prime, a vector access to the cache with this mapping scheme can be made conflict-free. Meanwhile, the address space is also well utilized since the number of lines in the prime-mapped cache is just one less than a 2's power.

A detailed description of the *Prime-mapped* scheme is as follows: Each memory address, same as conventional cache-based computer system[10], is partitioned into three fields: $W = log_2(line\ size)$ bits of word address in a line (offset); $c = log_2(number\ of\ lines + 1)$ bits of index; and the remaining tag bits of tag. The access logic of the prime-mapped cache consists of three components: data memory, tag memory, and matching logic. Same as a direct-mapped cache, the data memory contains an address decoder and cached data; the tag memory stores tags corresponding to the cached lines; and the matching logic checks if the tag in an issued address matches the tag in the cache. The cache lookup process is exactly the same as the direct-mapped cache and hence takes the same amount of time as the direct-mapped cache. However, the index field used to access the data memory is not just a subfield of the original address word issued by the processor since the modulus for cache mapping is not a 2's power any more. It is the residue of the line address modulo a Mersenne number. How efficient this modular operation can be done is essential to the cache performance. In the following, we show how the index conversion can be done without adding additional delay in the address mapping process.

Figure 1 shows the block diagram of the address computation logic. It consists of two parallel parts: one normal address calculation unit that generates addresses for accessing the main memory and the other address generator that calculates addresses for accessing the vector cache. The normal address calculation unit is a part of address control logic or functional unit that any existing vector computers should have. The memory address of a vector element is calculated based on a vector stride and the address of the previous element of the vector. For generating a cache address, the tag field and the word (offset) field are the same as that for memory address. It is only the index field (c bits) that needs to be calculated in a Mersenne number form through the additional address generator. Since a Mersenne number is defined as an integer modulo $2^c - 1$, arithmetic operations are greatly simplified by noting that $2^c = 1$. Consider any two integers represented in c-bit binary form. If we add the two numbers we obtain a $(c+1)$-bit sum with the most significant bit being carry bit. But $2^c \equiv 1 \ mod \ (2^c - 1)$. Thus, addition modulo a Mersenne number is performed very simply by using a conventional full binary adder of c bits and by folding the most significant carry bit output back into the least significant carry bit input. Therefore, a c-bit full adder is sufficient to perform the address generation. The index field of the cache address of a vector element is obtained by adding the stride to the index field of the cache address of the previous element of the vector. Note that both the stride and the previous index value should be in the Mersenne number form as explained shortly. Because the addition is performed on a c-bit field which is a portion of a memory word, this process should take no longer than the normal address calculation process. Two addresses are therefore generated concurrently: one for cache access and the other for memory access in case of a cache miss.

It remains to consider how to generate the cache address of the first element of a vector and the vector stride in a Mersenne number form efficiently. Let the starting line address of a vector be A_{start} that consists of two fields: tag_A and $index_A$ with the lengths of each field being tag and c, respectively. We ignore the offset field of an address since a line is the basic unit for cache mapping. Suppose the least significant c bits of tag_A are represented by tag_{A1} and the second c bits are represented by tag_{A2} and so forth. In order to map the starting line of the vector into the prime-mapped cache, we need to perform a modular operation $A_{start} \ mod \ (2^c - 1)$. Since

$$A_{start} = index_A + 2^c tag_{A1} + 2^{2c} tag_{A2} + \cdots,$$

and $2^c \ mod \ (2^c - 1) = 1$, we can write

$$A_{start} \ mod \ (2^c - 1) = index_A + tag_{A1} + tag_{A2} + \cdots.$$

Therefore, to derive the index field of the starting line address of a vector, what we need to do is to perform a sequence of c bit additions. If the length of tag_A (tag) in bits is less than or comparable to the length of $index_A$ (c), then we just need one c-bit addition. In practice, this is often the case. For example, the cache size of the Alliant FX/8 is 128K bytes (16K double words) giving rise to an index length of 14 bits if the line size is 8 bytes. If the address length is 32 bits, the remaining tag field consists of maximum of 15 bits. We then need to perform a 14-bit addition and add back the most significant bit of the starting address into the least significant bit of the sum. Similarly, the VAX6000 Model 400 vector processor has a cache of 1 Mbytes that can easily make the tag field comparable to the index field. If it is desired in a design that the tag field be longer than the index field, we would need at most one more level of addition of c bits in calculating the index field of the starting address of a vector.

The address conversion logic for the starting element of a vector is also shown in Figure 1 assuming $tag \leq c$. Two multiplexors are used to select addends for the c−bit adder. The multiplexors will select two fields (tag and index) of the memory address word to do addition for the starting element. For all other elements of the vector, the multiplexors will select index value of the cache address of the previous element and the stride to do addition. The generation of the vector starting address for cache access can be done in parallel with the memory access of the vector element if the vector is accessed first time. It is saye to assume that a couple of stages of c bit additions can finish before the loaded memory data arrives in the vector cache. Thus, the loaded data can be written into the vector cache using the newly calculated index value. In this case, there is no performance penalty resulting from the address conversion. The converted cache address of the starting element can be stored in a special register for future reuses if the vector is going to be accessed again. Subsequent accesses to the elements in the same vector can be done using two possible addresses: cache addresses as discussed above or memory addresses if a miss occurs. The calculation of these addresses does not incur any additional delay compared to existing machines as evidenced previously.

Converting an integer stride into a Mersenne number can be done in the same way as for the starting address. That is, just additions are needed. This process can be done at the time when the vector stride is loaded into the vector stride register. However, a special register of c bits is needed to keep the converted stride as shown in Figure 1.

The additional hardware cost as result of this new mapping scheme includes 2 multiplexors, a full adder and a few registers as shown in Figure 1. Even a small percentage of performance improvement can justify such insignificant hardware cost. As will be evidenced latter in this paper, we expect to double and even triple the performance of direct-mapped cache and the performance of the machines without cache. However, there is still a trade-off between performance and hardware cost. The registers storing the starting addresses of vectors, for example, add more cost to the machine. If several vectors are accessed concurrently, we not only need more registers but also the control logic to control the access of these registers. If we can afford to spend 1 or 2 more cycles at each vector start-up time, we may eliminate these registers. Each time a vector is accessed again, we recalculate its starting address even though the vector is already in the cache. This recalculation requires just an addition of subwords which takes small and limited amount of time, and it may also be pipelined. On the other hand, if performance is absolutely important one can pay for the registers.

3 An Analytical Model

In this section, we present an analytical performance model based on the simple vector performance model given in [2]. It should be noted that the analysis and the numerical results presented here are not meant to be predictors of performance of any realistic computer system. Rather, they are meant to give a quick insight into the simplified vector processor models and to show some potential problems that might exist in a vector cache memory.

3.1 A Vector Computation Model

Two simplified vector processor models considered here are shown in Figures 2 and 3 which will be referred to as MM-model and CC-model, respectively. Both models have a vector processing unit, a set of vector registers with maximum vector length of V_L words, and a set of low order-bit interleaved memory modules (or banks) that are connected to the vector processor through three pipelined buses. Two of the three buses are read buses and the other is write bus. Each of these buses contains separate data bus and address bus. There are totally $M = 2^m$ interleaved memory banks each of which has the access time of t_m cycles. The second processor model (CC-model) shown in Figure 3 differs from the first one (MM-model) only in that it has a cache memory of size C lines between the processor and memories. We assume that this cache memory is used purely for vector data similar to the split vector cache of VAX/6000. It is assumed that a line of data can be transferred on one of the buses within one cycle.

Cache miss ratio has been used by many researchers as a performance measure to evaluate cache performance. However, it is not a very good performance measure in this context because we intend to compare the performance differences between the MM-model and the CC-model. The performance measures that we use in this paper are *total execution time* of an application program and *clock cycles per result* which is defined as the average number of clock cycles needed to produce one vector element result [2].

Our simplified computational model assumes that application programs are blocked into several segments. One of the vector data that an application program operates on is partitioned into several sub-blocks of size B each. We call this B a *blocking factor*. A sub-block of data may be used several times by one program segment. We define a reuse factor, R, as the number of times a block of data is reused. During each vector operation, the processor may load two vectors from the memory simultaneously or load just one vector with the other operand available in a register. It is assumed that the probability that the processor accesses two vector streams simultaneously from the memory during one vector operation is P_{ds} (double stream). The probability that the processor accesses just a single vector stream with the other operand available in a register is P_{ss} ($= 1 - P_{ds}$). The system performs operations similar to the SAXPY operations. The processor first loads one or two vectors into its registers and then performs arithmetic operations on the two vectors or on one vector and a scalar in a scalar register.

In order to simplify our analysis, we further assume that all single-stream vector accesses are evenly intercepted by one-double-stream accesses if $P_{ds} \neq 0$. In other words, every sequence of $\frac{BP_{ss}}{BP_{ds}} = \frac{P_{ss}}{P_{ds}}$ consecutive single-stream vector accesses is followed by one double stream vector access which is again followed by a statistically identical sequence of single stream accesses, and so forth. Thus, one can imagine one of the vectors of length B as a two dimensional matrix with $P_{ss}/P_{ds}+1$ columns and BP_{ds} rows. The vector length of each column is BP_{ds}. After every P_{ss}/P_{ds} column accesses of the imagined matrix, the processor loads two vectors to perform vector operations on the first and the second vector. Therefore, the length of the second vector can be considered as BP_{ds}.

Although the assumed computation model is simplified, it is very close to many realistic applications. For example, the blocked matrix multiplication algorithm in [4] has the blocking factor of b^2 since the matrices are blocked into submatrices of size $b \times b$. The reuse factor of each block is b and each sequence of $b-1$ single stream vector accesses is followed by a double stream access. Therefore, the fraction of time when the processor accesses a single vector stream is $(b-1)/b$ while the fraction of double stream accesses is $1/b$. The length of the first vector is then b^2 and the length of the second vector is b. Similarly, the blocked LU decomposition algorithm with a blocking factor of b^2 has an average reuse factor of $3b/2$ and the blocked FFT algorithm with a blocking factor of b has a reuse factor of $Log_2 b$.

The access strides of loading the two vectors are denoted by s_1 and s_2, respectively. Access strides vary widely depending on application programs. In general, unit stride occurs more frequently than other strides in most numerical algorithms [7]. We therefore use P_{std1} to denote the probability that an access stride is 1. If a stride is not 1, we assume that it takes any other integer values equally likely. A stride can take an integer value in the range of $(1, 2, \cdots, M)$ for the MM-model and in the range of $(1, 2, \cdots, C)$ for the CC-model due to modular operations. We also assume that writing results into memory or cache will not delay the normal vector operations. This assumption is not a severe restriction because it can be realized in real machines by having write buffers, separate data bus for writing and separate write port for memories [2].

In summary, our simple vector computational model consists of the following seven-tuple:

$$VCM = [B, R, P_{ds}, s_1, s_2, P_{std1}(s_1), P_{std1}(s_2)].$$

By properly selecting these model parameters, the model can fit into a variety of numerical algorithms and various vector access patterns. For example, if we set $VCM = [b, r, 1, 1, P, 1, 1/C]$, we have double stream vector accesses to columns and rows of a $b \times b$ submatrix of a $P \times Q$ matrix stored in column-major. Each pair of column and row are used for r times. If $VCM = [b, r, 0, P+1, -, 1/C, -]$ (The symbol "-" means undefined), then we have a single vector access stream to a major diagonal of a $b \times b$ submatrix of the same $P \times Q$ matrix.

3.2 Execution Time of the MM-Model

Let us consider the MM-model of Figure 2 first. The vector performance can be characterized by the execution time for a sequence of operations on a vector of length B, T_B, which is given by [2]

$$T_B = T_o + \lceil \frac{B}{V_L} \rceil \cdot T_{start} + B \cdot T^M_{elemt}, \quad (1)$$

where T_{start} is the start-up time for each inner most loop, T_o is the outer loop overhead which is assumed to be constant in our analysis, and T^M_{elemt} [1] is the time for processing one element of the vector ignoring the start-up time. The start-up time depends on the memory access time and the type of arithmetic operations to be performed. It should not be difficult to determine its value for a given set of system parameters. In our discussions, we assume T_{start} to be constant for a given memory access time. If the system is fully pipelined with one functional unit, T^M_{elemt} should be one in an ideal case. In reality, T^M_{elemt} is often greater than one because of stalls resulting from memory accesses, data dependencies and control dependencies. Since our primary interest here is memory system performance, we will concentrate on memory stalls only. The major source of memory stalls for vector processors is memory conflicts [13, 14, 8]. A number of storage schemes to minimize memory conflicts stands out in the literature. Some examples are [15, 13, 12, 11] to list a few. In our analysis, we consider only the low-order bit interleaving scheme although some conflict-free dynamic storage schemes can provide about 18% better performance than the simple interleaving [13]. In the following, we derive T^M_{elemt} by taking into account memory stalls.

Memory stalls can result from two types of bank conflicts: One is the conflicts between elements in the same vector (*self-interference*) denoted by I^M_s, and the other occurs between elements from two different vectors (*cross-interference*) denoted by I^M_c. Let us first consider the number of possible stall cycles of accessing one vector stream with stride s_1. When a vector access stream traverses across all memory banks (one sweep), the number of memory banks visited by the access stream is $M/gcd(M, s_1)$ [14, 15], where $gcd(M, s_1)$ is the greatest common divisor of M and s_1. If both t_m and V_L are greater than $M/gcd(M, s_1)$, memory conflicts occur. As a result, the first conflicting element is delayed by $t_m - M/gcd(M, s_1)$ cycles. There are $V_L/(M/gcd(M, s_1))$ such conflicts as seen by the contended memory bank. For a special case where $gcd(M, s_1) = 2^m = M$, each of $V_L - 1$ elements will be delayed by $t_m - 1$ cycles. Since M is a 2's power, $gcd(M, s_1)$ is in the form of 2^i for some $i = 1, \cdots m-1$. The number of possible values of s_1 within M such that $gcd(M, s_1) = 2^i$ $(i \in (1, \cdots m-1))$ is equal to the divisor function of $M/2^i$ which is given by $\phi(\frac{M}{2^i}) = \frac{M}{2^{i+1}} = 2^{m-i-1}$ [16]. For each such s_1, $\frac{V_L}{M/2^i} - 1$ sweeps are delayed by $(t_m - M/2^i)$ cycles. Recall that the probability of $s_1 = 1$ is P_{std1} and the probability of s_1 taking any other value $(2 \cdots M)$ is $\frac{1-P_{std1}}{M-1}$. Therefore the total number of stall cycles resulting from accessing a vector of length V_L, I^M_s, is given by

$$I^M_s = \frac{1-P_{std1}}{M-1}[\sum_{i=\lceil log_2 \frac{M}{t_m} \rceil}^{m-1} (t_m - \frac{M}{2^i})2^{m-i-1}(\frac{V_L}{M/2^i} - 1) + +(V_L - 1)(t_m - 1)].$$

The lower limit of the summation in the above equation is determined based on the condition $t_m \geq M/2^i$. Notice that the above equation assumes that $t_m < M$ so that unit stride

[1] For notational convenience, we use superscript M and C on a parameter to distinguish MM-model (Figure 2) and CC-model (Figure 3) vector processors, respectively.

does not incur any stalls. Simple algebraic manipulation leads to

$$I_s^M = V_L \frac{1-P_{std1}}{(M-1)} \cdot [t_m + \frac{t_m}{2} \lfloor log_2 t_m \rfloor - 2^{\lfloor log_2 t_m \rfloor}].$$

Next, let us consider memory stalls as result of cross-interferences between two vector access streams. Let s_2 be the stride of accessing the second vector stream and D be the memory bank difference between the starting addresses of the two vectors. We assume that D is uniformly distributed between 1 and M. If the memory bank address of the ith element of the first vector is is_1, the memory bank address of the jth element of the second vector is $js_2 + D$. Thus whenever the congruence, $s_1 i \equiv s_2 j + D (mod\ M)$, has solutions for $i \in (0, 1, \cdots, V_L - 1)$ and $j \in (0, 1, \cdots, V_L - 1)$ such that $\mid i - j \mid < t_m$, conflicts between the two access streams (cross interferences) occur. The number of stall cycles due to such a conflict is $t_m - \mid i - j \mid$. Therefore, the cross-interferences can be calculated by solving the above congruence equation with two variables [16]. We have written a program solving the congruence equation. The total number of stall cycles due to the cross-interference for a given set of s_1, s_2 and D is the accumulation of quantities $t_m - \mid i - j \mid$ for each pair of solution (i, j), where $i, j \in (0, 1, \cdots, V_L - 1)$. The final cross-interference, I_c^M, is averaged over all possible values of s_1, s_2 and D based on the given distributions discussed in the beginning of this section. T_{elemt}^M can now be expressed as

$$\begin{aligned} T_{elemt}^M &= 1 + average\ stall\ cycles\ per\ element \\ &= 1 + P_{ss} \frac{I_s^M}{V_L} + P_{ds} \frac{(2I_s^M + I_c^M)}{V_L}. \end{aligned} \quad (2)$$

Substituting Equation (2) into Equation (1) we get the execution time of one block. Assume that the total data size of a program is N which is blocked into several segments of length B. Taking into account the reuse factor, R, the total execution time T_N^M can be expressed as:

$$T_N^M = T_B \cdot R \cdot \lceil \frac{N}{B} \rceil. \quad (3)$$

3.3 Execution Time of Direct-Mapped CC-Model

Now let us consider the CC-model of Figure 3 that has a direct-mapped cache of size $C = 2^c$ lines. The processor initially loads one or two vectors into the cache while performing the designated vector operations. The process of the initial loading will take the amount of time given by Equation (1). After the vectors are loaded into the cache, the remaining operations on the same set of data are expected to be performed in the cache without accessing memories in an ideal situation. The total execution time of the CC-model (Figure 3) is given by

$$T_N^C = \{T_B + (R-1)[T_o + \lceil \frac{B}{V_L} \rceil (T_{start} - t_m) + BT_{elemt}^C]\} \lceil \frac{N}{B} \rceil, \quad (4)$$

where T_B covers the effects of compulsory and capacity misses as discussed above. Notice that the start up time after the initial vector loading is decreased by t_m since the reused vector is in the cache provided that it has not been replaced due to a conflict. Similar to the analysis of the MM-model, we use T_{elemt}^C to include memory stalls due to cache misses.

Suppose that the processor tries to load a vector of length B into the vector cache with a random stride s_1. The number of cache lines occupied by the vector is given by $C/gcd(C, s_1)$. Thus, there will be $B - C/gcd(C, s_1)$ self-interferences if B is greater than $C/gcd(C, s_1)$. Again the number of s_1's such that $gcd(C, s_1) = 2^{(c-i)}$ is 2^{i-1} (divisor function) [16]. If $gcd(C, s_1) = C$, then there would be $B - 1$ conflicts. Therefore, the average number of stalls due to self-interference misses in the B-element vector is given by

$$I_s^C(B) = \frac{1-P_{std1}}{C-1} [\sum_{i=1}^{c - \lceil log_2 \frac{C}{B} \rceil} (B - \frac{C}{2^{c-i}}) 2^{i-1} + B - 1] \cdot t_m, \quad (5)$$

where the upper limit of the summation is determined based on $B \geq C/2^i$. Notice that there is no self-interference if the access stride is one and the block size B is less than cache size. For every self-interference miss the processor stalls for t_m cycles. Simple algebraic manipulation leads to

$$I_s^C(B) = \frac{1-P_{std1}}{C-1} \frac{1}{3} (3B2^{\lfloor log_2 B \rfloor} - 2 \cdot 2^{2\lfloor log_2 B \rfloor} - 1) \cdot t_m. \quad (6)$$

For B being a power of 2, we have

$$I_s^C(B) = \frac{1-P_{std1}}{3(C-1)} (B^2 - 1) \cdot t_m.$$

The cross interference misses, I_c^C, can be calculated in a similar way as for the I_c^M or using the footprint model described in [3, 4] assuming that the two vectors are independent. The probability that any one element of the second vector falls into the footprint of the first vector is $\frac{B}{C}$. There are totally BP_{ds} elements in the second vector. Therefore, the total stalls due to cross-interferences are given by $I_c^C = \frac{B^2 P_{ds}}{C} t_m$. Thus, the time for processing one vector element, T_{elemt}^C, is

$$T_{elemt}^C = 1 + P_{ss} \frac{I_s^C(B)}{B} + P_{ds} \frac{(I_s^C(B) + I_s^C(BP_{ds}) + I_c^C)}{B}. \quad (7)$$

Substituting Equation (7) into Equation (4) we obtain the total execution time of the direct-mapped CC-model.

3.4 Analysis and Comparison of the Two Models

We now carry out a preliminary performance analysis for the two vector computers based on the simple analytical model presented above. We use the *average clock cycles per result* as a performance measure in our following discussions. It is obtained by dividing the total execution time by the product of N and R. In the following figures, we fix the values of V_L, T_o, and T_{start} at 64, 10, and $30 + t_m$ [2], respectively. The probability of unit stride access, P_{std1}, is also fixed at 0.25 which is the average value of the experimental data reported in [7].

Figure 4 shows the *average clock cycles per result* as a function of memory access time in terms of processor cycles. If memory access time is small, it can be seen from the figure that adding a direct-mapped cache memory does not help. The performance of the MM-model performs even better than the CC-model that has a cache memory. This is primarily due to the fact that any one of irregularly distributed cache misses results in a memory access that takes t_m cycles. The interleaved memory with pipelining may well satisfy the bandwidth requirement of the processor. However, as the speed gap between processor and memory increases, the performance of the CC-model takes over. With the blocking factor of 4K, the CC-model outperforms the MM-model after the memory access time exceeds 20 cycles. If the blocking factor is 2K, the CC-model shows better performance when the memory access time is over 7 cycles.

It is well known that cache performance depends on how often data are reused after they have been loaded into the cache. In Figure 4, the reuse factor is fixed at B. In order to observe how the reuse factor affect the performance of vector caches we plotted *clock cycles per result* as a function of reuse factor R while fixing the blocking factor at $1K$ as shown in Figure 5. Two curves are plotted for CC-model corresponding to memory access times of 8 and 16 cycles, and two other similar curves are plotted for the MM-model. As expected, the two processor models have the same performance when the reuse factor is 1. With the system parameters indicated in the figure, whenever the reuse factor is more than one, the CC-model performs better than the MM-model. Moreover, it can be seen in this figure that after the reuse factor exceeds certain value, the performance change is not significant.

We noticed earlier in Figure 4 that different blocking factors show different performances. To observe this effects more closely, we plotted the performance vs. blocking factors with other parameters being fixed at the values shown in Figure 6. For memory access time of 16 cycles, the blocking factor can not be more than 4K after which the vector cache performs poorly. The cross point is at the blocking factor being about 5K if memory access time is 32 cycles. However, our cache size for the CC-model is 8K words implying that only a small portion of the cache is utilized.

From the above three figures, the following observations are in order. First of all, as the memory access time increases with respect to the clock time of processors, vector cache memory can provide better performance than the machine without cache even with a small reuse factor; Secondly, the performance improvement of the direct-mapped cache for vector processor is limited as shown by these figures. Finally, the utilization of the vector cache is very poor in order to sustain a reasonable performance.

4 Performance of Prime-Mapped Cache

From the performance analysis presented in the last section, we observed that the performance gain resulting from adding a direct-mapped cache into a vector computer is not very impressive. In this section, we will show that the newly proposed cache mapping scheme can provide significant performance improvement over the conventional cache designs. Moreover, the cache utilization can be close to one without significant performance degradations. We consider three typical vector access patterns that are commonly encountered in vector processing: random multistride access, subblock access and FFT access. Unless otherwise specified, all the numerical results reported in this section are computed by fixing V_L, T_o, and T_{start} at 64, 10, and $30+t_m$ [2], respectively.

Random Stride Accesses

Since the modulus in the prime-mapped cache is a prime number, the self-interference misses occur only when the stride is an integral multiple of the cache size. Therefore, I_s^C is simply given by

$$I_s^C(B) = \frac{(1 - P_{std1})(B - 1)}{C - 1} t_m, \qquad (8)$$

assuming that the stride is uniformly distributed between 2 and C if it is not 1. For cross-interferences, the footprint model similar to the direct-mapped cache can be used to estimate I_c^C. Substituting Equation (8) into Equation (7) we obtain the time for processing one vector element for prime-mapped cache. The total execution time is calculated using Equation (4).

In Figure 7, we plotted the clock cycles per result as a function of memory access time. Compared to the previous figures, we increased the number of memory banks from 32 to 64. Although the performance of the direct-mapped cache catches up with the MM-model after the memory access time exceeds 24 cycles, average cycles per result of the CC-model keeps increasing. The prime-mapped cache, on the other hand, shows little change in performance as memory access time increases. It outperforms both the MM-model and the direct-mapped CC-model over entire range of memory times considered. When the memory access time matches the number of memory modules (64), the prime-mapped CC-model runs three times faster than the direct-mapped CC-model and almost five times faster than the MM-model.

As we observed in the last section, the blocking factor affect to a large extent the performance of direct-mapped vector cache. In order to observe this effect on prime-mapped cache, Figure 8 shows the performance as a function of blocking factor for the three machine models with the memory cycle time being half of the number of banks. As shown in the figure, average cycles per result for the direct-mapped cache quickly cross over that of the MM-model after the blocking factor is about 3K, while the average cycles per result for the prime-mapped cache remains flat. Thus, the prime-mapped cache is not very sensitive to the blocking factor for the random stride access.

In the above two figures, we have fixed the probability of accessing a vector with stride 1, P_{std1}, at 0.25. To examine the effect of this parameter on system performance, we plotted clock cycles per result by varying P_{std1} as shown in Figure 9. High probability of unit stride will reduce both memory conflicts and cache line conflicts. As shown in the figure, as this probability increases, the performance difference between the two mapping schemes comes close. When the probability of unit stride is 1, the performance of the two mapping schemes is the same. Whenever this probability is nonunit, the prime-mapped cache performs better than the direct-mapped cache.

Figure 10 shows the effect of proportion of double access streams on the performance of the three models. When the proportion of double access streams is large, cross-interferences between the two vectors in the cache becomes large. It is shown in the figure that the cycle time increases with the increase of the proportion of double stream accesses. Notice that the cross-interference in the prime-mapped cache is severer than that in direct-mapped cache because the footprint of the former is larger than the footprint of the latter. Nevertheless, the prime-mapped cache still performs better than the direct-mapped cache over all possible fractions of double stream accesses. The performance difference ranges from 40% to a factor of 2.

If we fix the stride of one vector at 1 and assume the other stride to be random, then we have accesses to rows and columns of a random sized matrix. Figure 11 shows the performance of such access patterns. If columns of the matrix were accessed more often than rows, we would expect small number of interferences in the direct-mapped cache because the stride is one for a column access. If rows were accessed more often, on the other hands, we would expect more interferences in the direct-mapped cache as shown in Figure 11. In both cases, however, the prime-mapped cache shows the same performance which is better than that of direct-mapped cache.

Sub-block Accesses

Sub-block accesses have proven to be important in many vector processing applications. Blocked matrix multiplication is an example that needs to access a submatrix of a large matrix. Let the original large matrix be dimensioned $P \times Q$, and the sub-block be dimensioned $b_1 \times b_2$. A sub-block access can be characterized as b_2 stride-1 accesses to column vectors of length b_1. The distance between the starting addresses of two successive column vectors is P.

Sub-block accesses can be easily made conflict free for any arbitrary two dimensional matrix by properly selecting blocking factors. Notice that this is either impossible or prohibitively costly for the MM-model since the modulus is a power of 2 [13]. Consider the above matrix with dimensions $P \times Q$ that is stored in a column-major. To make accesses to a sub-block of dimension $b_1 \times b_2$ conflict free in the prime-mapped cache, what we need to do is to select b_1 and b_2 in such a way that the following conditions are satisfied.

$$b_1 \leq min(P\ mode\ C,\ C - P\ mod\ C),\ and$$
$$b_2 \leq \lfloor \tfrac{C}{b_1} \rfloor.$$

A row-major storage can also be realized similarly by interchanging the corresponding dimensions. It can be easily shown that a sub-block with b_1 and b_2 satisfying the above conditions can be stored in the prime-mapped cache without self-interference. This is because that b_1 elements of any column vector are stored in consecutive memory locations and hence no conflict can occur among them. Moreover, since $(P\ mode\ C) \geq b_1$ the first elements of any two consecutive column vectors are mapped into two cache locations that are at least b_1 lines apart as long as $b_2 \leq \lfloor \frac{C}{b_1} \rfloor$. The fraction of the cache being used is $b_1 b_2 / C$. If we let $b_1 = min(P\ mode\ C,\ C - P\ mod\ C)$, and $b_2 = \lfloor \frac{C}{b_1} \rfloor$. then the cache utilization is close to 1. In other words, conflict free access is possible to the submatrix even with the cache utilization approaching 1.

FFT Accesses

The FFT accesses result from the Cooley and Tukey's Fast Fourier Transform (FFT) algorithm. One way to implement the FFT algorithm in a memory hierarchical system is to map the input data into a two dimensional array[17]. Suppose an N-point data array to be transformed can be represented as $N = B_2 \times B_1$. Then the input data can be considered to be a matrix of B_1 columns and B_2 rows. The matrix is stored in a column-major. The algorithm proceeds by first doing B_1-point row FFTs for B_2 times each of which is expected to be done within the local cache. After all B_2 row FFTs are done, we multiply twiddle factors and perform column FFTs for B_1 times. Again it is expected that each of the column FFTs is done inside the cache. If B_2 is less than the cache size, each of the column FFTs can be done in the cache without misses except for the compulsory misses since the array is stored in a column-major. However, the row FFTs of the first step may not be guaranteed to be done inside the cache without misses. Depending on the value of B_2, conflict misses may occur. The number of interference misses is obviously given by $B_1 - C/gcd(B_2, C)$ for $B_1 > C/gcd(B_2, C)$ assuming a lockup free cache.

The total execution time of this algorithm on the direct-mapped cache can be computed by using Equation (4) twice. First, we substitute B and R in (4) by B_1 and $log_2 B_1$, respectively. T^C_{elemt} should include the above self interferences for a given B_2. Notice that $P_{ds} = 0$ if we assume that twiddle factors are available in the registers. Second, Equation (4) is used again with B and R being replaced by B_2 and $log_2 B_2$, respectively. T^C_{elemt} can be considered to be 1 assuming that $B_2 < C$. The final total execution time is the sum of the above two times. The execution time of prime-mapped cache can be done similarly by noting that there are no self-interference misses unless $B_2 = C$. Compulsory misses (T_B) should also be adjusted based on the FFT stride characteristics.

Figure 12 shows the performance comparison of the FFT access on the two different cache organizations. The curves are the average clock cycles per point which is the total execution time divided by N. In the figure, we fix one dimension while varying the other. It is observed from these curves that the prime-mapped cache outperforms the direct-mapped cache by a factor of more than 2. The improvement is valid over all possible values of the blocking factor B_2. With the prime-mapped cache, an FFT algorithm can be implemented very easily. Optimization is guaranteed as long as the block size is less than the cache size.

5 Conclusions

In this paper, we have proposed an innovative cache mapping scheme for vector computers, called prime-mapped cache. The cache lookup time of the new mapping scheme keeps the same as direct-mapped cache. Generation of cache addresses for accessing the prime-mapped cache can be done in parallel with normal address calculations. This address generation takes shorter time than the normal address calculation due to the special properties of the Mersenne prime. Therefore, the new mapping scheme does not result in any performance penalty as far as the cache access time is concerned. The hardware cost introduced by the prime mapping scheme includes 2 multiplexors, a full adder and a few registers.

We have also developed an analytical performance model for a generic vector computational model that covers a wide spectrum of numerical algorithms. The analytical model is simple and precise for a given set of vector access patterns. Three typical vector access patterns have been considered in our performance analysis: random multistride, submatrix and FFT accesses. It is shown that the prime-mapped cache outperforms both the vector computer without cache and the vector computer with a direct-mapped cache for all vector access patterns considered. The performance improvement ranges from 40% to a factor of 3 depending on the memory cycle time, blocking factor and access patterns.

Our conclusion is that cache memory can improve the performance of vector processing provided that application programs can be blocked. With the new mapping scheme, the cache memory can provide significant performance improvement which will become larger as the speed gap between processor and memory increases. Further studies are needed to collect experimental data for the new design.

References

[1] A. J. Smith, "Cache memories," *Computing Surveys*, vol. 14, pp. 472–530, Sept. 1982.

[2] J. L. Hennessy and D. A. Patterson, *Computer Architecture, A Quantitative Approach.* Morgan Kaufmann, 1990.

[3] H. S. Stone, *High Performance Computer Architecture.* Addison-Wesley, 1990.

[4] M. S. Lam, E. E. Rothberg, and M. E. Wolf, "The cache performance and optimizations of blocked algorithms," in *Proc. of Arch. Supp. for Prog. Lang. and Opr. Sys.*, pp. 63–74, April 1991.

[5] K. So and V. Zecca, "Cache performance of vector processors," in *Proc. 15th. Int'l Symp. on Comp. Arch.*, pp. 261–268, 1988.

[6] D. Gannon, W. Jalby, and K. Gallivan, "Strategies for cache and local memory management by global program transformation," in *Int'l Conf. on Supercomputing*, 1987.

[7] J. W. C. Fu and J. H. Patel, "Data prefetching in multiprocessor vector cache memories," in *Proc. 18th. Int'l Symp. on Comp. Arch.*, pp. 54–63, 1991.

[8] D. H. Bailey, "Vector computer memory bank contention," *IEEE Trans. on Computers*, vol. C-36, pp. 293–298, MARCH 1987.

[9] Q. Yang, L. Bhuyan, and B.-C. Liu, "Analysis and comparison of cache coherence protocols for a packet-switched multiprocessor," *IEEE Trans. on Comput.*, vol. 38, pp. 1143–1153, August 1989. Special Issue on Distributed Computer Systems.

[10] M. D. Hill, "A case for direct-mapped caches," *IEEE Computer*, pp. 25–40, Dec. 1988.

[11] P. Budnik and D. J. Kuck, "Organization and use of parallel memories," *IEEE Trans. on Computers*, pp. 1566–1569, Dec. 1971.

[12] D. H. Lawrie and C. R. Vora, "The prime memory system for array access," *IEEE Trans. on Computers*, vol. C-31, pp. 435–441, May 1982.

[13] D. T. HarperIII, "Block, multistride vector, and FFT accesses in parallel memory systems," *IEEE Trans. on Parallel and Distributed Systems*, Jan. 1991.

[14] W. Oed and O. Lange, "On the effective bandwidth of interleaved memories in vector processor systems," *IEEE Trans. on Computers*, vol. C-34, pp. 949–957, Oct. 1985.

[15] R. Raghavan and J. P. Hayes, "On randomly interleaved memories," in *Proceedings of Supercomputing-90*, pp. 49–58, Nov. 1990.

[16] A. J. Pettofrezzo and D. R. Byrkit, *Elements of Number Theory.* Prentice-Hall, 1970.

[17] J. W. Cooley, *The Structure of FFT and Convolution Algorithms.* IBM T. J. Watson Research Center, 1990. Research Report.

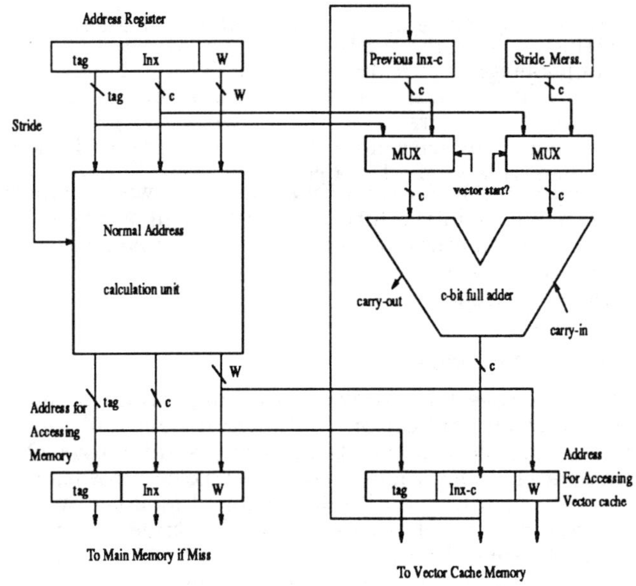

Figure 1. Address generation logic for the prime-mapped vector cache.

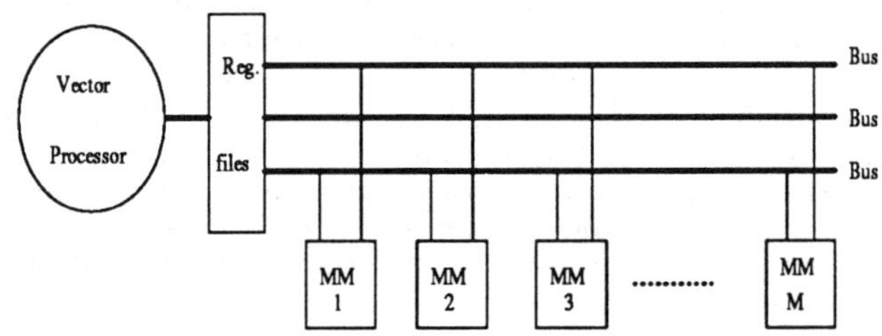

Figure 2. A vector computer model without cache (MM-model).

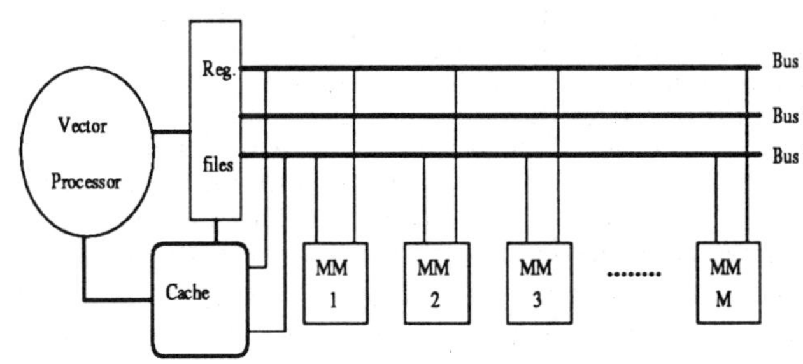

Figure 3. A vector computer with a cache memory (CC-model).

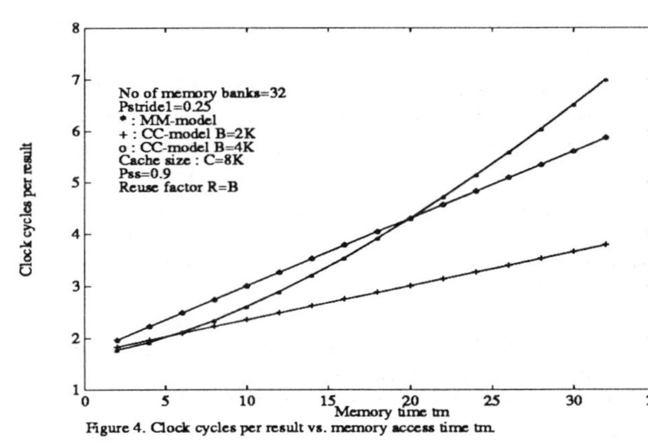

Figure 4. Clock cycles per result vs. memory access time tm.

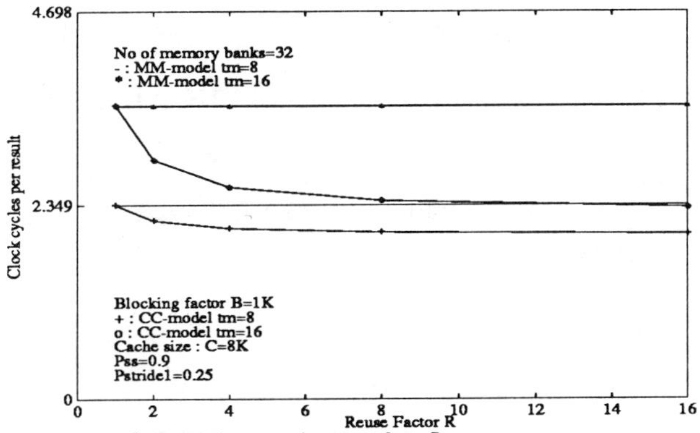

Figure 5. Clock cycles per result vs. reuse factor R.

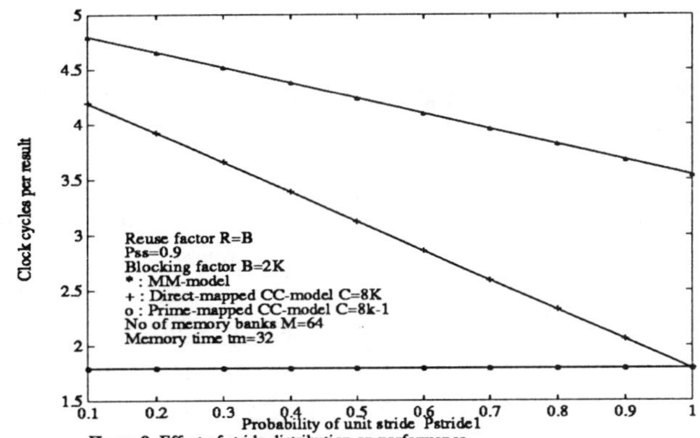

Figure 9. Effect of stride distribution on performance.

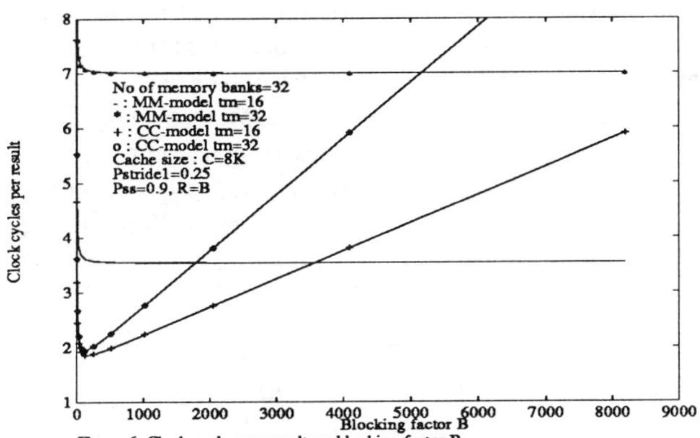

Figure 6. Clock cycles per result vs. blocking factor B.

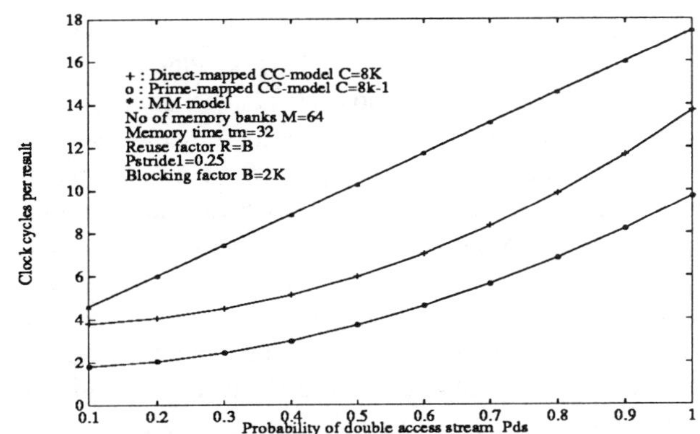

Figure 10. Clock cycles per result vs proportion of double stream accesses.

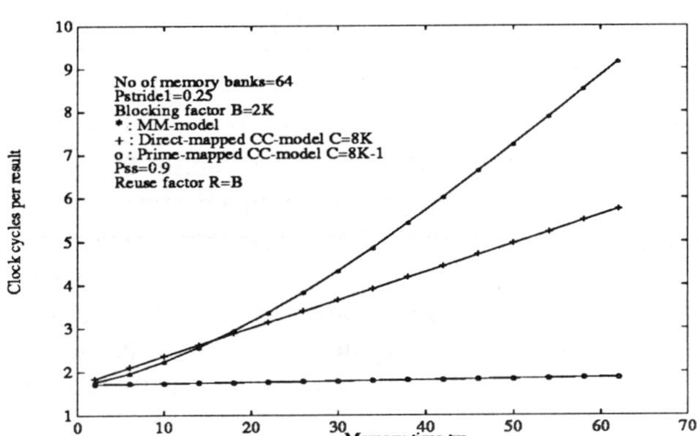

Figure 7. Comparison between direct-mapped cache and prime-mapped cache.

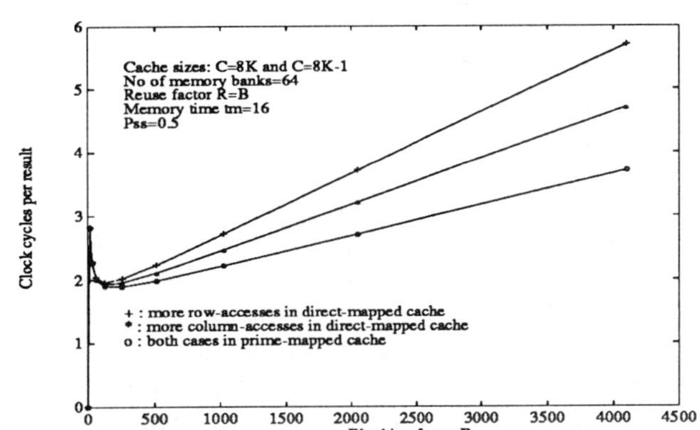

Figure 11. Performance of row and column accesses to a random sized matrix stored in column-major.

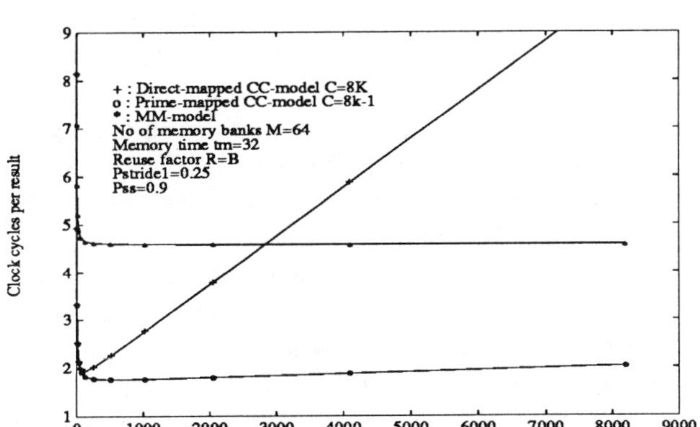

Figure 8. Comparison between direct-mapped cache and prime-mapped cache.

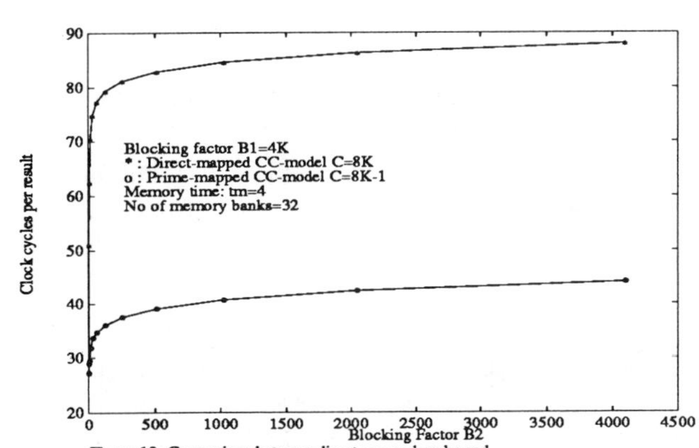

Figure 12. Comparison between direct-mapped cache and prime-mapped cache for FFT access.

INCREASING THE NUMBER OF STRIDES FOR CONFLICT-FREE VECTOR ACCESS

Mateo Valero, Tomás Lang, José M. Llabería, Montse Peiron, Eduard Ayguadé and Juan J. Navarro
Departament d'Arquitectura de Computadors, Universitat Politècnica de Catalunya
c/ Gran Capità s/n, Mòdul D-4, 08034 - Barcelona, SPAIN.
Phone: + 34 - 3 - 401 69 79, E_mail: mateo@ac.upc.es

ABSTRACT

Address transformation schemes, such as skewing and linear transformations, have been proposed to achieve conflict-free vector access for some strides in vector processors with multi-module memories. In this paper, we extend these schemes to achieve this conflict-free access for a larger number of strides. The basic idea is to perform an out-of-order access to vectors of fixed length, equal to that of the vector registers of the processor. Both matched and unmatched memories are considered; we show that the number of strides is even larger for the latter case. The hardware for address calculations and access control is described and shown to be of similar complexity as that required for access in order.

KEYWORDS

Vector processors, Multi-module memories, Vectors with constant stride, Conflict-free access.

1. Introduction

To have a sufficient memory bandwidth, the memory of fast processors is organized as several modules that can be accessed simultaneously. To achieve a memory throughput of one access per processor cycle, the number of memory modules should be at least equal to the ratio between the memory cycle and the processor cycle (matched memory system). However, to obtain this throughput, the request sequence has to be such that there are no conflicts in the accesses. This is achieved, for example, with conventional memory interleaving and for vectors with odd strides, but not for other strides or more unstructured patterns. This has motivated the proposal of other addressing schemes, the use of buffers, as well as the increase of the number of memory modules (unmatched memory system).

In this paper we consider ways of obtaining minimum latency for address streams which correspond to a single vector of constant stride, fixed length and any initial address. This addressing pattern is typical of vector processors (and scalar processors accessing vectors), but does appear also in general scalar processing when the processor has decoupled memory access and execute. In both cases, to overlap memory access and execution, the processor is decomposed into two independent modules, as shown in Figure 1. The memory-access module performs loads and stores to/from a "register file" and the execute unit obtains the operands from that file.

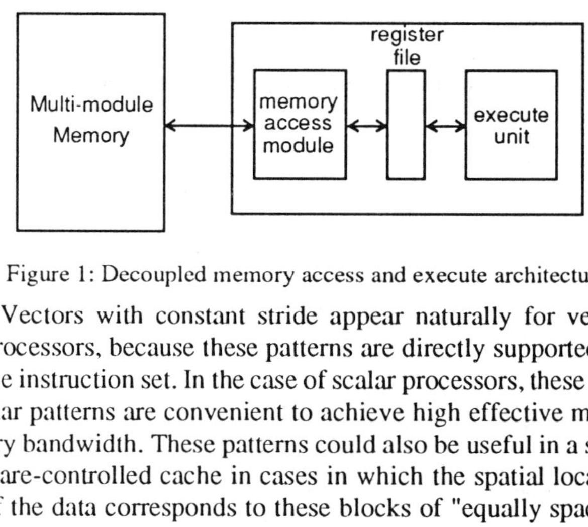

Figure 1: Decoupled memory access and execute architecture

Vectors with constant stride appear naturally for vector processors, because these patterns are directly supported by the instruction set. In the case of scalar processors, these regular patterns are convenient to achieve high effective memory bandwidth. These patterns could also be useful in a software-controlled cache in cases in which the spatial locality of the data corresponds to these blocks of "equally spaced" items.

We consider the case in which the processor accesses vectors of length equal to the number of elements of one of its vector registers, because this is the way the LOAD and STORE instructions operate. Since the size of the vectors is usually much larger than the size of vector registers, the above mentioned mode of operation requires strip-mining by the compiler so that a very high fraction of the accesses are of vectors of length equal to that of the registers. In Section 5, we discuss the access of shorter vectors.

Moreover, we propose that the elements of the vector be requested out of order and that the whole vector be stored in the vector register before its use by the processor. This prevents the chaining of LOAD/STOREs with other operations; however, this is reasonable because the complex timing of memory accesses make this chaining difficult anyhow. Even though this decoupled operation would be the default, we discuss in Section 5 that the proposed out-of-order access can support chained access/execute in cases where ordered access would make this mode of operation impractical.

The two main address transformation schemes proposed in the literature to achieve conflict-free access to vectors with strides that produce conflicts with conventional interleaving are skewing and linear transformations. These schemes were initially proposed for array processors [1, 2, 3, 4] and later for vector processors [5, 6, 7, 8], multiprocessors [9], and VLIW processors [10]. For vectors and a matched-memory system, they can provide conflict-free access to one family of strides, where the family defined by x is the set of strides $\sigma \cdot 2^x$ with σ odd [11]. Moreover, for the case in which different vectors are accessed with different strides, dynamic schemes based on skewing [11] and on linear transformations [6] were proposed. Linear transformations have the advantage over skewing that usually the module number is simpler to compute.

A larger number of families of conflict-free strides can be achieved by increasing the number of memory modules (unmatched memory system). If $M=2^m$ is the number of memory modules and $T=2^t$ is the ratio between the memory cycle and the processor cycle, then at most (m-t+1) families are conflict free, assuming that the elements are requested in order [6].

Although out of the scope of this paper, it is worthwhile to mention that techniques have also been proposed to improve efficiency for the cases in which conflict-free access is not achieved. For the skewing and linear schemes mentioned above, peak memory throughput can be obtained for x' < x for long vectors by the use of buffers [5]. Moreover, schemes based on linear transformations have been proposed to distribute randomly the modules corresponding to consecutive addresses, so that the various strides do not produce clustering to memory modules [8, 10, 12]. Recently a proposal has been made [13] for an analytical model that can be used to make comparisons among these linear transformations. For both schemes, most of the evaluations performed consider long vectors, so that the initial transient is not significant and the throughput is determined for the steady state. This throughput is evaluated as a function of several parameters, such as structure of the transformation, number of buffers, and number of memory modules. Although in [8, 10, 11] some measurements are given for short vectors, the effect of length is not discussed nor is the transformation determined with a vector length in mind.

To introduce the out-of-order accessing we use a matched memory system and a linear transformation of the addresses, although the same results can be obtained with interleaving (using an internal field of the address as module number) or with skewing. We show that this mode of accessing vectors of fixed size results in conflict-free accesses for a larger number of families of strides than ordered access. The case of unmatched memory system is also studied. The hardware required for address calculations is presented and the efficiency of the scheme is evaluated.

The results in this paper should be extended to the cases in which several vectors are accessed simultaneously by a single processor or by several processors in a multiprocessor system.

2. Model and Condition for Conflict-Free Access

We now describe the model of the memory subsystem, present some definitions and give the condition for conflict-free access.

Figure 2 shows the general structure of the system which has been used by previous authors. The memory is composed of $M=2^m$ modules and the module latency is of $T=2^t$ processor cycles. Each memory module has q input and q' output buffers. The processor requests one element per (processor) cycle unless it has to wait because the associated input memory buffer is full. The latency of the vector access is defined as the number of processor cycles from the time the processor sends the first address until the last element is received. We assume that the interconnection network is a single bus with a delay of one cycle. Therefore, the latency of a conflict-free access to a vector of length L is (T+L+1) cycles.

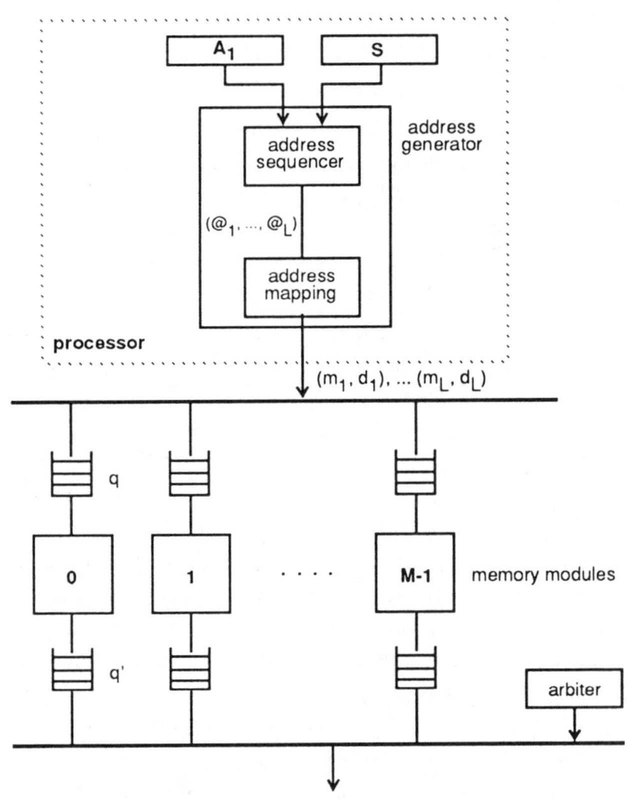

Figure 2: General structure of the system. $(@_1, ..., @_L)$ refers to any request ordering.

We consider the vector length L equal to 2^λ, with $\lambda \geq m$. The first element of the vector has address A_1 and consecutive elements are separated by a constant value S (the stride) so that the i-th element has address $A_1+S\cdot(i-1)$. Note that the vector can have any initial address. As done in [11], we classify the strides into families defined by x so that all strides $\sigma\cdot 2^x$ with σ odd belong to the same family.

Since the memory is organized in several modules, an address mapping is required which transforms the address A (one-dimensional) with binary representation $a_{n-1}, a_{n-2}, ..., a_1, a_0$ (in short also denoted $a_{n-1..0}$) into the two-dimensional space (module, displacement). Since conflicts depend only on the module number part, we only consider that component of the mapping. That is, the module number b with binary representation $b_{m-1..0}$ is given by b = F(A) where F is the memory-module component of the address mapping.

We now define the spatial and temporal distributions of the elements of a vector, since these determine the latency of the access.

Definition: The SPATIAL DISTRIBUTION of a vector in the multi-module memory is the M-tuple SD, where SD(i) is the number of vector elements in module i.

The spatial distribution is LATENCY-MATCHED (T-MATCHED) if $SD(i) \leq L/T$ for all i (this implies that at least T modules have $SD(i) > 0$). If the spatial distribution of a vector is T-matched we say that the VECTOR IS T-MATCHED.

Definition: The TEMPORAL DISTRIBUTION of a vector is the sequence of memory-module numbers $(m_1, ..., m_L)$ where m_i is the module corresponding to the i-th processor request. Note that the elements can be requested in any order.

Other authors use similar terms related with the spatial distribution, such as short-term and long-term equidistributed sequences [12], and with the temporal distribution, such as return numbers [14] and variability [13].

Definition: A temporal distribution is CONFLICT FREE when every element can be accessed as soon as it is requested (the corresponding memory module is not busy with a previous request). This is equivalent to stating that a temporal distribution is conflict free if any subset of T consecutively requested elements are located in T different memory modules. This is the condition we will require.

Moreover, from the last definition it follows directly that a necessary condition for a conflict-free temporal distribution is that the vector be T-matched. Because of this, to determine the conditions for a conflict-free temporal distribution, we first determine conditions for a T-matched vector and then consider access orders so that any T consecutive accesses are to different memory modules.

Since the spatial distribution is independent from the temporal distribution, to determine conditions for a T-matched vector we use the canonical temporal distribution, defined below, even though it might not be conflict free.

Definition: The CANONICAL TEMPORAL DISTRIBUTION of a vector is the temporal distribution when the elements are requested in order.

For linear mappings (and for skewing) the canonical temporal distribution is periodic. Consequently, we can define the canonical temporal distribution in one period and state Lemma 1, below.

Definition: The period P_x of an address mapping for a vector with stride $\sigma\cdot 2^x$ is the period of its canonical temporal distribution.

Definition: We call CTP_x the canonical temporal distribution in one period for a vector with stride $\sigma\cdot 2^x$.

Definition: CTP_x is T-matched if the spatial distribution in the period is T-matched.

Lemma 1: If CTP_x is T-matched and $L = k\cdot P_x$ with $k > 0$ then the vector is T-matched.

Proof: This is evident since if each period is T-matched and the vector length is a multiple of the period, the vector has to be T-matched. ❑

In summary, we consider vectors with $L = k\cdot P_x$, determine the conditions for having a T-matched CTP_x and then find a temporal distribution that has the property that any T consecutive requests go to different modules.

3. Matched Memory

We now discuss the matched-memory case (M=T) and generalize to the unmatched case in the next section.

For the matched-memory case, we choose F as the linear transformation

$$b_i = a_i \oplus a_{s+i} \qquad s \geq t,\ 0 \leq i \leq t-1 \qquad (1)$$

For the rest of this section we assume this mapping. It has the property that when the elements of the vector are requested in order the access is conflict free for vectors with strides of the family with x = s, of any length and with any initial address [6].

Figure 3 illustrates a portion of the mapping for m = t = 3 and s = 3.

The period for a stride $\sigma\cdot 2^x$ is $P_x = \lceil 2^{s+t-x} \rceil$ [6].

Lemma 2: Let $x \leq s$ and P_x be the corresponding period. Consider the grouping of these P_x elements into 2^{s-x} subsequences consisting of 2^t elements each. The i-th subsequence $(1 \leq i \leq 2^{s-x})$ contains the elements $(i + k_1\cdot 2^{s-x})$ with $0 \leq k_1 \leq 2^t-1$. For any of these subsequences, all its elements are located in different memory modules.

Proof: Let A_i, with binary representation $a_{n-1..0}$, be the address of the i-th element. For the mapping defined in (1), this element is located in module m_i such that

$$m_i = (a_{s+t-1} \oplus a_{t-1}, ..., a_{s+1} \oplus a_1, a_s \oplus a_0) = a_{s+t-1..s} \oplus a_{t-1..0}$$

Moreover, the element $i + k_1\cdot 2^{s-x}$ has address

$$A_i + k_1\cdot 2^{s-x}\cdot\sigma\cdot 2^x = A_i + k_1\cdot\sigma\cdot 2^s$$

and is located in module

$$((a_{s+t-1..s} + (k_1\cdot\sigma) \bmod 2^t) \bmod 2^t) \oplus a_{t-1..0}$$

Since σ is odd, the values $(k_1 \cdot \sigma) \bmod 2^t$ for $0 \le k_1 \le 2^t-1$ are all different. As the bits $a_{t-1..0}$ are independent of k_1, the 2^t elements are stored in different modules. ❑

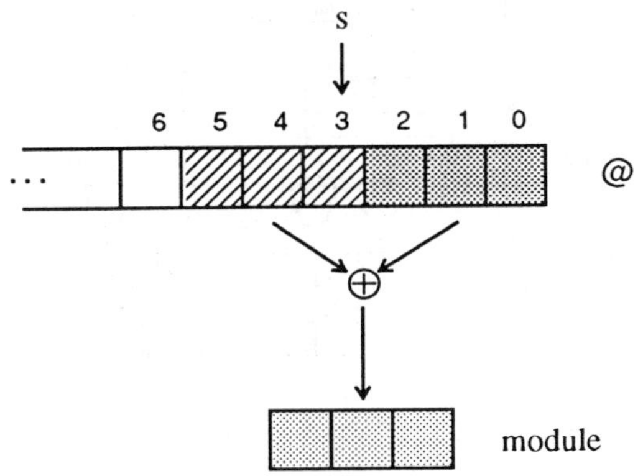

module	0	1	2	3	4	5	6	7
	0	1	2	3	4	5	6	7
	9	8	11	10	13	12	15	14
	18	19	16	17	22	23	20	21
	27	26	25	24	31	30	29	28
	36	37	38	39	32	33	34	35
	45	44	47	46	41	40	43	42
	54	55	52	53	50	51	48	49
	63	62	61	60	59	58	57	56
	64	65	66	67	68	69	70	71
				⋮				

Figure 3: XOR-based linear transformation and mapping of the address space when m=t=3 and s=3.

Lemma 3: The families of strides that produce T-matched CTP_x are those defined by $x = 0, 1, ..., s-1, s$.

Proof: If $x \le s$, because of Lemma 2 the elements $(i + k_1 \cdot 2^{s-x}) \bmod P_x$ for $0 \le k_1 \le 2^t-1$ are in different modules. Taking as values for $i = 1, 2, ..., 2^{s-x}$ we obtain 2^{s-x} subsequences of 2^t elements mapped into different modules, so each module contain 2^{s-x} elements; therefore CTP_x is T-matched. On the other hand, if $x > s$ the elements are mapped into just $\lceil 2^{s+t-x} \rceil$ modules, so not all modules are visited ($s+t-x < t = m$). Therefore, CTP_x is not T-matched. ❑

Theorem 1: The families of strides defined by $s-N \le x \le s$ where $N = \min(\lambda-t, s)$ produce T-matched vectors of length $L = 2^\lambda$.

Proof: For a vector to be T-matched it is sufficient that CTP_x be T-matched and that $L = k \cdot P_x$ (Lemma 1). Because of Lemma 3, CTP_x is T-matched for all $x \le s$. If $x \ge s-N$ then $x \ge s - (\lambda-t)$ for the definition of N; this can be rewritten as $\lambda \ge s + t - x$, or $L = k \cdot P_x$ for some $k > 0$. Therefore the vector is T-mached. ❑

Note that for $x < s-N$ when $\lambda-t < s$ it is possible for a vector with length $L = 2^\lambda$ to be T-matched, but this depends on its initial address. Since we consider vectors with any initial address, these cases are not of interest.

Corollary: For fixed λ and t, the value of s defines a window of families of strides that produce T-matched vectors.

Up to now we have shown the conditions for a vector to be T-matched. However, the access in order can lead to a high latency because of an unsuitable canonical temporal distribution. In the example of Figure 1, the vectors of length 64 are T-matched for $0 \le x \le 3$. Consider the access of a vector with stride 12 and whose first element is in position 16. Since $x = 2$ the period is $P_x = 16$ and the CTP_x is

$$2, 7, 5, 2, 0, 5, 3, 0, 6, 3, 1, 6, 4, 1, 7, 4$$

and this sequence is repeated for each of the four periods of the vector. The access is not conflict free. In fact only the family with $x = 3$ produces a conflict-free canonical temporal distribution.

3.1. Reordering

We now show how to reorder the access of the vector elements so as to achieve a better temporal distribution.

Theorem 2: The elements of a T-matched vector with length $L = k \cdot P_x$ for some $k > 0$ can be grouped in subsequences such that the temporal distribution of each subsequence is conflict free.

Proof: Since $L = k \cdot P_x$, the vector can be divided in k subvectors of length P_x. In each of these subvectors we use the 2^{s-x} subsequences defined in Lemma 2. Since the elements of each subsequence are mapped in different modules the temporal distribution of each subsequence is conflict free.❑

For the calculation of the addresses of the consecutive elements in a subsequence it is necessary to increment by $\sigma \cdot 2^s$, instead of $\sigma \cdot 2^x$ for the canonical order. The order of the subsequences is not important. One possibility is to request all subsequences in one period and then go to the following period, and so on. In such a case, the first elements of consecutive subsequences in one period are separated by $\sigma \cdot 2^x$, which is also the separation between the last element of one period and the first of the next. The control to perform the requests in this order is shown in Figure 4.

The hardware required to generate the addresses is shown in Figure 5. To simplify the implementation it is convenient that the compiler issues instructions to load the values $\sigma \cdot 2^x$, $\sigma \cdot 2^s$ and 2^{s-x}. If this is done, the complexity is practically the same as that for the case in which requests are in order.

For the previous example, for the first period we obtain two subsequences that contain the vector elements (0, 2, 4, 6, 8, 10, 12, 14) and (1, 3, 5, 7, 9, 11, 13, 15), respectively. These are located in modules (2, 5, 0, 3, 6, 1, 4, 7) and (7, 2, 5, 0, 3, 6, 1, 4). Note that even if each subsequence is conflict free, the access to the whole vector is not, because the temporal distributions of the different subsequences are not the same. Consequently, in the next section we give an additional reordering that provides this conflict-free access.

However, it is worth noticing that with two buffers at the input of each module and one buffer at the output, the above mentioned ordering produces a latency which is not greater than 2T+L cycles, that is, the increase in latency due to the non conflict-free access is at most of T-1 cycles [15].

```
SUB = A1      ;SUB is the initial address of the present
              ;subsequence
A = A1        ;A is the request address
for K=1 to 2^(λ-(s+t-x))     ;k is the period number
    for J=1 to 2^(s-x)       ;j is the subsequence number
        for I=2 to 2^t       ;the first address of each sub-
                             ;sequence is obtained outside
                             ;the loop
            A= A + σ·2^s
        end for
        if J<2^(s-x) then
            (SUB = SUB + σ·2^x || A = SUB + σ·2^x)
                             ;in parallel
    end for
    SUB = A + σ·2^x || A = A + σ·2^x
end for
```

Figure 4: Control to perform the memory requests.

3.2. Conflict-free Ordering

Even though the additional latency associated with the ordering described in the previous section is low in practice (since L>>T), we now propose a scheme that eliminates this additional latency and permits the access of the whole vector in a conflict-free manner.

To achieve this, it is necessary to incorporate a second reordering so that the temporal distribution of all subsequences is the same. However, this poses a problem with the calculation of the addresses inside the subsequences, since to have a simple incremental calculation (adding $\sigma \cdot 2^s$) it is necessary to do this in the order described in the previous section. The solution is to decouple the calculation of the addresses from the actual requests. This is achieved by calculating the addresses of subsequence i+1 while accessing subsequence i. Consequently, during the first 2^t cycles, it is necessary to calculate the addresses of the first subsequence (which are used immediately for memory access) and of the second subsequence (which are stored in a set of latches for access as the next subsequence). After that, for each subsequence, the addresses for access are obtained from the latches and a new address is calculated to store. Consequently, as shown in Figure 6, two address generators are needed, although one of them is only used in the first 2^t cycles. Moreover, it is necessary to store the temporal distribution of the first subsequence, which is used to control the order of the requests of the following subsequences. In addition to the latches in the processor, no buffers are needed in the memory modules.

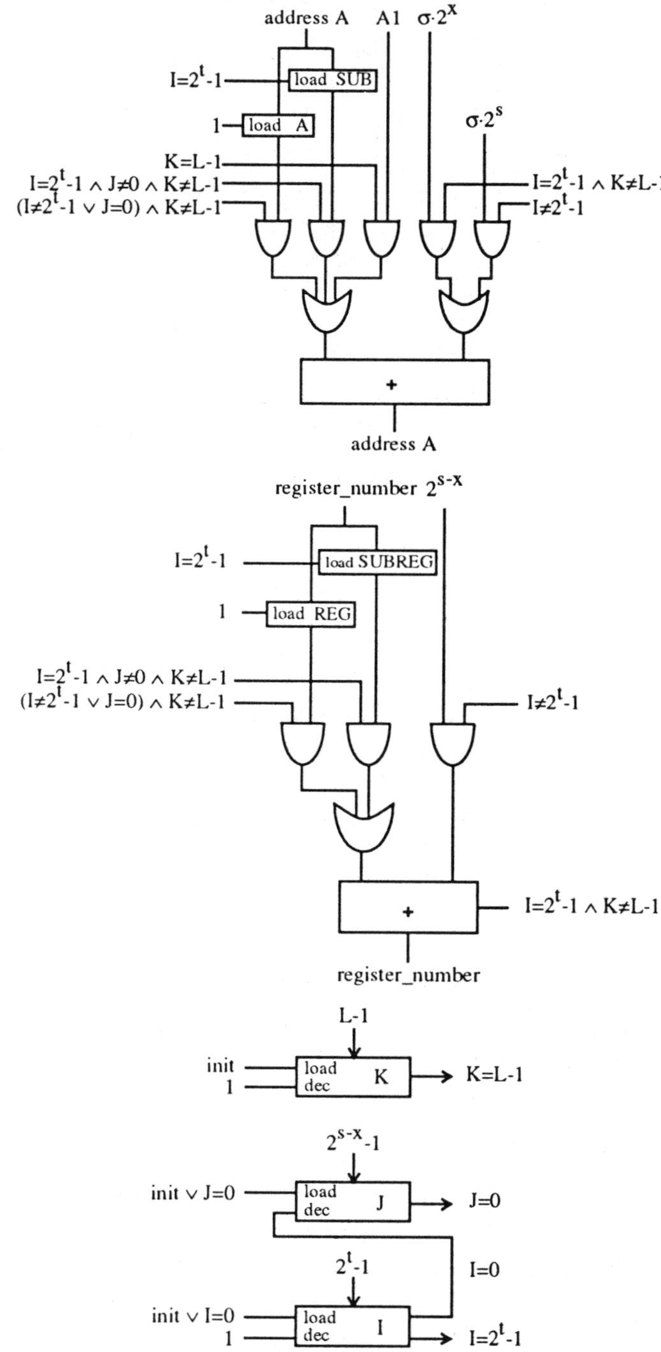

Figure 5: Hardware for address calculation and register addressing.

3.3. Choice of s

As shown previously, the proposed scheme achieves conflict-free access to the families of strides $\sigma \cdot 2^x$ such that $s\text{-}N \le x \le s$, and the choice of s determines the window of conflict-free strides. Since the family for x = 0 includes all the odd strides (and in particular stride one), it is certainly convenient to include this family by making $s \le \lambda\text{-}t$; the largest window occurs when $s = \lambda\text{-}t$. In such a case, the conflict-free strides belong to the families with $0 \le x \le \lambda\text{-}t$.

For example, for L = 128 and m = t = 3 we choose s = 4 and obtain conflict-free access for the families defined by x = 0, 1, 2, 3, 4.

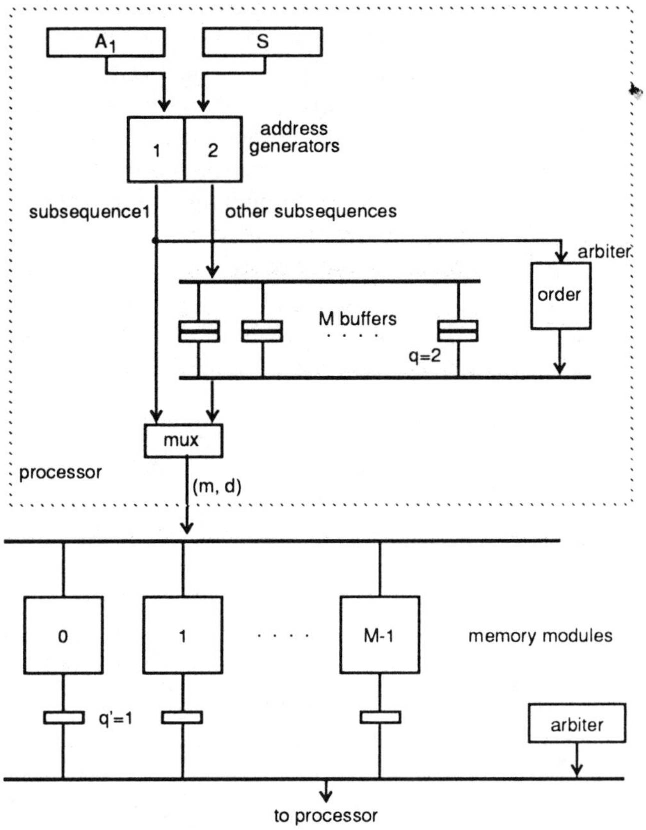

Figure 6: Architecture model for out-of-order memory accesses

4. Unmatched Memory

One way to increase the number of families of strides that produce conflict-free access, is to increase the number of modules (m > t).

A possible mapping for this case is to use the same one as defined in (1) replacing t by m. In such a case, the period P_x is $\lceil 2^{s+m-x} \rceil$, and for ordered access, any vector length and any initial address, conflict-free access is obtained for the families defined by x = s, s+1,..., s+m-t [6].

This can be combined with the technique presented in Section 3 for vectors of length L, so that conflict-free access is obtained for the families defined by

$$x = s\text{-}N, s\text{-}N+1, \ldots, s, s+1, \ldots, s+m-t$$

In this case, the vectors with strides belonging to the families x = s, s+1, ..., s+m-t are accessed in order and the rest are accessed out-of-order using the results of Section 3. In particular, if s = λ-t, the conflict-free families have $0 \le x \le \lambda+m-2t$.

4.1. A Better Mapping

We now consider a way of increasing the number of conflict-free strides for vectors of length L and out-of-order access. To simplify our discussion we consider the special case where m=2t. For this case we use F as the following mapping:

$$b_i = \begin{cases} a_i \oplus a_{s+i} & 0 \le i \le t-1, s \ge t \\ a_{y+i-t} & t \le i \le 2t-1, y \ge s+t \end{cases} \qquad (2)$$

For the rest of this section we assume this mapping. An example for t = 2, m = 4, s = 3 and y = 7 is given in Figure 7.

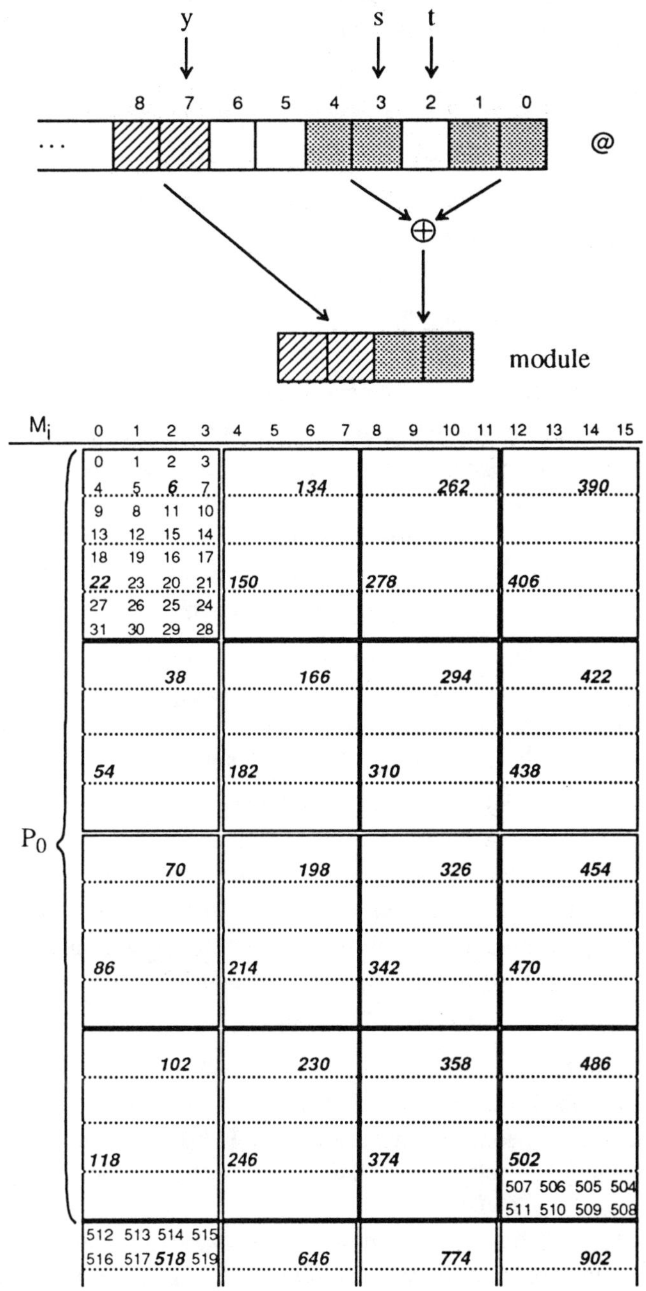

Figure 7: XOR-based transformation and mapping of the address space when m=4, t=2, s=3 and y=7. In italic the elements of a vector with λ=5 with initial address A_1=6 and stride S=16 are shown.

This mapping corresponds to a division of the modules into T sections of T modules and of the address space into blocks of 2^y locations; each block is mapped into one section, using the mapping defined by the lower t bits of b.

The period for a stride of the family $\sigma \cdot 2^x$ is $P_x = \lceil 2^{y+t-x} \rceil$.

Lemma 4: Let $x \leq y$ and P_x be the corresponding period. Consider the grouping of these P_x elements into 2^{y-x} subsequences consisting of 2^t elements each. The i-th subsequence ($1 \leq i \leq 2^{y-x}$) contains the elements ($i + k_1 \cdot 2^{y-x}$) with $0 \leq k_1 \leq 2^t-1$. For any of these subsequences, all its elements are located in different memory sections.

Proof: The addresses of the elements in the i-th subsequence are given by

$$A_i + k_1 \cdot 2^{y-x} \cdot \sigma \cdot 2^x = A_i + k_1 \cdot \sigma \cdot 2^y$$

with $0 \leq k_1 \leq 2^t-1$. Since σ is odd, all these addresses have different combinations in the bits $a_{y+t-1..y}$, so all 2^t sections are visited. ❑

Lemma 5: The families of strides that produce T-matched CTP_x are those defined by $x = 0, ..., y$.

Proof: Because of Lemma 4, there are 2^{y-x} elements of CTP_x mapped in each section. If $x \geq s+t$ all 2^{y-x} elements are located in the same module inside the section, so each one of the T modules that appear in CTP_x contain P_x/T elements. Therefore CTP_x is T-matched. If $x < s+t$, more modules are visited in each section, so each one contains less than P_x/T elements. CTP_x is, therefore, also T-matched.

On the other hand, if $x > y$ just $\lceil 2^{y+t-x} \rceil$ modules are visited, so CTP_x is not T-matched. ❑

Theorem 3: The families of strides defined by $x = s-N, ..., s$ and $x = y-R, ..., y$ where $N = \min(\lambda-t, s)$ and $R = \min(\lambda-t, y)$ produce T-matched vectors of length $L = 2^\lambda$.

Proof: Let $x = s-N, ..., s$, so $\lambda \geq s+t-x$. The elements ($i + k_1 \cdot 2^{s-x}$) with $0 \leq k_1 \leq 2^t-1$ have different combinations in the bits $a_{s+t-1..s}$ (see Lemma 2), and therefore are located in at least T modules, exactly T if the bits $a_{y+t-1..y}$ are not modified. Let's assume for the moment that those bits are not modified. Taking as values for $i = k_2 \cdot 2^{s+t-x} + k_3$ with $0 \leq k_2 \leq (L/2^{s+t-x})-1$ and $1 \leq k_3 \leq 2^{s-x}$ we obtain that each of the T modules contain L/T elements. If the bits $a_{y+t-1..y}$ are modified then the elements are distributed in more modules, containing each one less than L/T elements. Therefore, the vector is T-matched.

Let $x = y-R, ..., y$. Then, $\lambda \geq y+t-x$, so $L = k \cdot P_x$ for some $k > 0$. Moreover, because of Lemma 5, CTP_x is T-matched. Therefore the vector is T-matched. ❑

To correctly partition the set of families of strides, we will assume from now on that $y-R \geq s+1$; this implies $R = \lambda-t$ and $y \geq \lambda-t$. Therefore there are two groups of families of strides, those with x in [s-N, s] and those in [y-R, y]. As a consequence of the previous lemmas and theorem, depending on the value of x, one of the following subsequences is used:

i) for $s-N \leq x \leq s$, we define subsequences as stated in Lemma 2. We know that its elements are mapped into different modules because they have different combinations in the bits s+t-1..s; therefore the temporal distribution is conflict free. For some values of σ and A_1, also the bits y+t-1..y of the elements in one subsequence may vary; in this case many sections are visited in one subsequence, which also leads to a conflict-free temporal distribution of the subsequence.

ii) for $y-R \leq x \leq y$, we define subsequences as stated in Lemma 4. Its elements are mapped into different sections, so its temporal distribution is conflict free.

For example, consider the mapping shown in Figure 7 and let $x=4$, $\sigma=1$, $A_1=6$ and $L=32$. The elements of the period P_x are marked in italic in Figure 7. There are eight subsequences in one period, corresponding to the elements of the vector (0, 8, 16, 24), (1, 9, 17, 25), (2, 10, 18, 26), ..., (7, 15, 23, 31). These elements are located in the modules (2, 6, 10, 14), (0, 4, 8, 12), (2, 6, 10, 14), ..., (0, 4, 8, 12).

For the calculation of the addresses we could use the same algorithm as in section 3.1, where the increment of address in the inner loop is either $\sigma \cdot 2^s$ or $\sigma \cdot 2^y$.

As in section 3, we have obtained subsequences whose temporal distribution is conflict free; however this might not be the case for the whole vector. For example, consider $x=6$, $\sigma=3$ and $A_1=0$. In this case, $P_x=8$, so there are two subsequences in one CTP_x, corresponding to the vector elements (0, 2, 4, 6) and (1, 3, 5, 7). These elements are located in the modules (0, 12, 8, 4) and (4, 0, 12, 8) respectively. Again, next we give an additional reordering that provides conflict-free access to the whole vector.

4.2. Conflict-free reordering for unmatched memory

In the case of matched memory, all subsequences contain all modules, so it is sufficient to remember the order in which the first one is requested and use it to access the remaining subsequences. This is not the case for unmatched memory, since different subsequences may contain different modules.

To achieve the conflict-free access to the whole vector we will apply the same strategy as in section 3.2 with some modifications depending on the value of x, as explained below. The following definition is useful:

Definition: A section is composed of 2^t modules labeled 0 to 2^t-1. The SUPERMODULE i consists of the i-th module of each section. That is, the supermodule number of an address is determined by the bits $a_{s+t-1..s}$.

Two cases have to be considered, as follows:

i) $s-N \leq x \leq s$: for this case, as stated before, the subsequences used are those defined in Lemma 2. Since the 2^t elements in these subsequences have different combinations in the bits $a_{s+t-1..s}$, all supermodules appear in each subsequence. Therefore we can apply the same strategy as in section 3.2 but at the supermodule level, i.e.: the supermodule numbers of the first subsequence must be remembered and the elements of the remaining subsequences should be requested in the same "supermodule order" as the first one. Note that this implies that two latches are needed per supermodule, not per module. This results in $2 \cdot 2^t$ latches (not $2 \cdot 2^m$).

ii) $y-R \le x \le y$: now the subsequences are defined by Lemma 4. Since its elements are in different sections, it is sufficient to request each subsequence in the section order of the first subsequence.

In summary,

i) for $x \le s$ the supermodule order of the first subsequence is stored (bits $b_{t-1..0}$) and the latches are labeled by supermodule.

ii) for $x > s$, the section order of the first subsequence is stored (bits $b_{2t-1..t}$) and the latches are labeled by section.

4.3. Choice of s and y

For the reordering proposed, we know how to obtain a conflict-free access to the families with $x = s-N, \ldots, s$ and $x = y-R, \ldots, y$; making $y-R = s+1$ a single window of N+R+2 families is obtained. As discussed in Section 3, a convenient choice is $s=\lambda-t$; for this case, to achieve the largest possible single window, we choose

$$y = \lambda-t+1+\lambda-t= 2(\lambda-t)+1$$

Consequently, the conflict-free families correspond to

$$0 \le x \le 2(\lambda-t)+1$$

Compared to the mapping used at the beginning of Section 4, this provides $\lambda-t+1$ additional families.

For example, for L = 128, T = 8 and M = 64 we choose s = 4 and y = 9 and obtain conflict-free access for the families defined by x = 0, 1, ..., 9.

5. Evaluation

In this Section we present a discussion of the effectiveness of the proposed scheme, in terms of its efficiency, the cost of implementation, and its completeness to handle any stride and any vector length. Moreover, we comment on the possibility of using chaining of LOAD/STORE and EXECUTE in important particular cases.

A) Fraction of strides that are conflict free.

We now determine the fraction f of conflict-free strides for the choices of s and y presented in sections 3 and 4.

Since the fraction of strides belonging to family $\sigma \cdot 2^x$ is $1/2^{x+1}$, the fraction of conflict-free strides produced by a window from x=0 to x=w is

$$\sum_{i=0}^{w} \frac{1}{2^{i+1}} = 1 - \frac{1}{2^{w+1}}$$

Consequently, for the matched memory system case ($w=\lambda-t$) we get

$$f = 1 - \frac{1}{2^{\lambda-t+1}}$$

and for the unmatched case ($w = 2(\lambda-t)+1$)

$$f = 1 - \frac{1}{2^{2(\lambda-t+1)}}$$

For example, for L = 128 and M = T = 8, we choose s = 4 and get 31/32th conflict-free strides. Moreover, this set of strides probably includes the most-frequently used ones.

If we increase the number of memory modules to M = 64 and keep T = 8, for s = 4 and y = 9 we get 1023/1024th conflict-free strides.

B) Access of non conflict-free strides and efficiency assuming uniform distribution of strides.

The families of strides included in A) are conflict free so one element can be obtained from memory per cycle after the startup of T+1. The rest of families are not conflict free because the elements of vectors of the family with x=w+i (i > 0) are located in $\lceil 2^{t-i} \rceil$ modules and one element is accessed every $2^t / \lceil 2^{t-i} \rceil$ cycles in average. Consequently, the efficiency η can be approximated by

$$\eta = \frac{1}{1 + \frac{t}{2^{w+1}}}$$

where w is the boundary of the conflict-free window.

For the matched example given before the efficiency is $\eta=0.914$ whereas for the unmatched memory case it is $\eta=0.997$. In comparison, for ordered access the highest efficiency is obtained for s=0 (to have conflict-free access for odd strides). This results in $\eta=0.4$ for the matched memory case and $\eta=0.84$ for the unmatched one.

C) Vectors with length different than L.

As indicated in the introduction, the scheme is designed for vectors of length L equal to the number of elements of the vector registers. Also, we have indicated that a large fraction of the vectors will have this length since strip-mining is used for longer vectors. This leaves a small fraction of shorter vectors.

Moreover, in some vector processors there are vector registers of several lengths; normally these lengths are a multiple of the length of the shortest vector register. In such a case, L would correspond to the length of the smallest vector register and the others would have lengths which are a multiple of L. This situation can also appear in memory-access units for scalar processors, as discussed in the introduction.

Consequently, the following cases can occur:

i) the length of the vector is smaller than L. In this case two alternatives exist:
   - access the vector in order. This would produce the inefficiency of the resulting temporal distribution.
   - use the scheme presented in Sections 3 and 4 if the length V is related to the family of strides x so that

$$V = k \cdot 2^{w+t-x}$$

where w is either s or y. This is because this

length satisfies the requirements for the proposed reordering.

In general, divide the vector into two parts, one of length equal to V above and the other of the rest. Access the first part using the scheme of Sections 3 and 4 and the second part in order. This separation can be done by the compiler.

ii) the length of the vector is a multiple of L. This occurs for the case of multiple-size registers. In such a case the same scheme described in Sections 3 and 4 is used for each portion of length L. The overall efficiency is the same as for vectors of length L.

D) Complexity of the hardware: address calculation, buffers, arbitration, and register addressing.

As shown in Figure 6, the address calculation for conflict-free access in out-of-order mode requires two address generators instead of one for the standard ordered scheme. Moreover, it requires a buffer of size 2T, a queue to store the temporal distribution of the first subsequence and an arbiter to issue the remaining subsequences in the same order. Finally, a controller is required for the address calculations in the required order. We estimate that the hardware cost of these components is a minor part of the cost of the memory subsystem.

To achieve the required throughput, it might be necessary to pipeline the adder (this would also be needed in the standard ordered access and the latency of the adder would also have to be added to the latency of the vector access, unless several vector accesses are chained together). Moreover, the usual techniques have to be used to eliminate the dependencies in the calculation of successive addresses.

In addition to the buffers mentioned before, no additional ones are needed. This is in contrast with other proposals that include a significant number of buffers to eliminate the effect of an unsuitable temporal distribution.

To support the out-of-order access, elements of the vector register have to be addressed out of order. Consequently, this register has to be of the random access type, whereas for ordered access and return a FIFO organization is adequate.

E) Efficiency of more memory modules.

As has been seen in Section 4, the addition of modules to make the memory unmatched increases the number of families of strides that are conflict free. However, this is obtained at a large expense because to double the number of conflict-free families it is necessary to square the number of modules. This is aggravated by the fact that the added families contain fewer strides and that these strides are probably less frequently used.

Of course, the addition of memory modules can be justified by other reasons, such as simultaneous access to several vectors and non vector access.

F) Possibility of chaining of LOAD and EXECUTE.

As mentioned in the introduction, the complicated timing produced when access in order is coupled with buffers, makes it impractical to chain two instructions if one of the operands of the second is being obtained with a LOAD. In contrast, the scheme proposed produces one vector element each cycle in a deterministic order (for conflict-free strides). Consequently, it is possible to perform the chaining if the first instruction is executed using the same order of elements as the LOAD. Note that the sequence of addresses to the register elements is produced anyhow as part of the LOAD.

G) Maximum number of conflict-free families for the unmatched case.

The number of conflict-free families obtained in section 4 is not the maximum achievable with out-of-order access. In fact, it is possible to have t-1 more families [15]. However, the structure of the subsequences for these t-1 additional families is different that presented. Because of this, the inclusion of these families would complicate the hardware for address generation and access control.

H) Conflict-free families and vector length.

For unmatched memory, the access in order produces at most t+1 conflict-free families for any vector length (for $m = 2t$). In contrast, the scheme we propose produces only two conflict-free families for any vector length, but increases to $2(\lambda-t+1)$ the number of conflict-free families for vectors of length $L = 2^{\lambda}$.

6. Conclusions

In this paper we have considered the access of vectors of fixed length, equal to the length of a vector register. The access patterns correspond to constant strides and the vector can begin in any address. The basic idea we propose is an out-of-order access of the elements of the vector to achieve conflict-free access for all strides that produce T-matched vectors. We first consider the matched memory case, where M=T. In this case, we obtain a window of λ-t+1 families of strides that are conflict free, whereas previous schemes that perform the access in order result in a single conflict-free family (for vectors of any length). To achieve this, we divide the vector in subvectors which are accessed in a conflict-free manner. This by itself does not produce conflict-free access to the whole vector, although the added latency is low. To achieve the conflict-free access to the whole vector we propose that an additional set of T addresses be calculated and latched, so that the temporal distribution of all subsequences is the same. The analysis of the required hardware for address calculations shows that, with compiler support, the complexity is similar to that of the address generator for access in order.

We present then an extension of this scheme for the unmatched memory case. For a number of modules $M=T^2$, the size of the conflict-free window is doubled; this compares favorably to the t+1 conflict-free families obtained with ordered access. Note however, as we discuss in Section 5, that the resulting increase in efficiency from the matched to the unmatched case is obtained at the cost of squaring the number of memory modules.

We discuss also the access of vectors that are shorter than the size of the vector registers. In this case, depending on the stride family, we propose a combination of out-of-order and ordered access. If the length of the vector is known at compile time, the division of the vector in this two subvectors can be done by the compiler.

The ideas have been presented using an address mapping based on linear transformations. However, the same results can be achieved with interleaving or with skewing. For this, it is necessary to select in a suitable manner the bits that determine the module number in the interleaved case, and the number of rows to rotate for skewing. The difference between these schemes is the behavior for vectors of length smaller than L.

We plan to extend this work to the case in which several vectors are accessed simultaneously, either in a single processor with several memory ports or in a multiprocessor with vector processors. We also will explore further the use of these techniques for scalar processors with decoupled memory access and execute units.

7. Acknowledgments

This work has been supported by the Ministry of Education of Spain under contract TIC-299/89 and by the CEPBA (European Center for Parallelism of Barcelona).

8. References

1. P. Budnik and D. J. Kuck, "The Organization and Use of Parallel Memories", IEEE Trans. on Computers, vol. C-20, no. 12, pp. 1566-1569, 1971.
2. D.H. Lawrie, "Access and Alignment of Data in an Array Processor", IEEE Trans. on Computers, vol. C-24, no. 12, pp. 1145-1155, Dec. 1975.
3. J. Frailong, W. Jalby and J. Lenfant, "XOR-schemes: A Flexible Data Organization in Parallel Memories", Int'l Conference on Parallel Processing, pp. 276-283, 1985.
4. H.A.G. Wijshoff and J. van Leeuwen, "The Structure of Periodic Storage Schemes for Parallel Memories", IEEE Trans. on Computers, vol. C-34, pp. 501-505, June 1985.
5. D.T. Harper III and J.R. Jump, "Performance Evaluation of Vector Accesses in Parallel Memories Using a Skewed Storage Scheme", Int'l Symposium on Computer Architecture, pp. 324-328, 1986.
6. D.T. Harper III, "Block, Multistride Vector and FFT Accesses in Parallel Memory Systems", IEEE Trans. on Parallel and Distributed Systems, vol. 2, no. 1, pp. 43-51, 1991.
7. C-L. Chen and C-K Liao, "Analysis of Vector Access Performance on Skewed Interleaved Memory", Int'l Symposium on Computer Architecture, pp. 387-394, 1989.
8. S. Weiss, "An Aperiodic Storage Scheme to Reduce Memory Conflicts in Vector Processors", Int'l Symposium on Computer Architecture, pp. 380-386, 1989.
9. A. Norton and E. Melton, "A Class of Boolean Linear Transformations for Conflict-Free Power-of-Two Stride Access", Int'l Conference on Parallel Processing, pp. 247-254, 1987.
10. B. R. Rau, M. S. Schlansker and D. W. L. Yen, "The Cydra™ 5 Stride-Insensitive Memory System", Int'l Conference on Parallel Processing, pp. 242-246, 1989.
11. D.T. Harper III and D. A. Linebarger, "Conflict-Free Vector Access Using a Dynamic Storage Scheme", IEEE Trans. on Computers, vol. 40, no. 3, pp. 276-283, 1991.
12. B.R. Rau, "Pseudo-Randomly Interleaved Memory", Int'l Symposium on Computer Architecture, pp. 74-83, 1991.
13. D.T. Harper III and Y. Costa, "Analytical Estimation of Vector Access Performance in Parallel Memory Architectures", Internal Report, Dept. of Electrical Engineering. The University of Texas at Dallas, 1991.
14. W. Oed and O. Lange, "On the Effective Bandwidth of Interleaved Memories in Vector Processing Systems, IEEE Trans. on Computers, vol. C-34, no. 10, pp. 949-957, October 1985.
15. M. Valero et al., "Conflict-Free Access to Vectors", Research Report, Departament d'Arquitectura de Computadors, Universitat Politècnica de Catalunya, UPC/DAC RR91-22, October 1991.

Evaluation of the WM Architecture

Wm. A. Wulf
Computer Science Department
University of Virginia

Abstract

This report describes the results of studies of the WM architecture— its performance, the values of some of its key architectural parameters, the difficulty of compiling for it, and hardware implementation complexity. The studies confirm that, with comparable chip area and without heroic compiler technology, WM is capable of outperforming traditional scalar architectures by factors of 2-9. They also underscore the need to devise higher bandwidth memory systems.

Description of the WM Architecture

A more complete description of WM may be found in [Wul88, Wul90, Wul90b]; here we provide only enough to understand its evaluation.

The quest for greater instruction-level concurrency can be divided into two broad categories: those in which the the concurrency is starkly explicit in the programmer's model, and those in which it is not. VLIW machines are an example from the first category [Fis84], the second category includes the superscalar, superpiplined, and some decoupled access-execute architectures [cf, Jou89]. While potentially capable of less concurrency, the second category requires simpler compiler technology and thus it is interesting to investigate the degree of concurrency they can achieve.

WM falls more into this second category; the semantics of its instruction set are strictly sequential, but have been designed to allow concurrency in their implementation. Specifically, in WM eliminates a number of data and control dependencies common in conventional architectures — dependencies that appear purely as artifacts of the architecture. Elimination of these dependencies materially enhances the achievable concurrency.

The resulting design resembles a collection of cooperating software processes synchronized by first-in-first-out queues. Each of some 12 components operates independently and asynchronously — thus it faintly resembles data flow machines [Nik89] in that operations are performed as data becomes available. Figure 1 illustrates this model of the architecture.

The "instr fetch" unit is responsible for fetching instructions and enqueueing them for execution by the integer, floating-point, or control execution units; it proceeds as rapidly as possible, and blocks only when the various instruction queues are full or an unresolved conditional branch is encountered.

The integer and floating-point execution units (IEU, FEU) execute instructions in order from their respective instruction FIFOs. They proceed independently and block only when there is no instruction to execute or they need data that is not yet in their data FIFOs.

The "data fetch" and "data store" units, called "stream control units", asynchronously enqueue/dequeue a "stream" of data — a sequence of data values where the number and "stride" of the items are known in advance. They block only when an input FIFO is full, an output FIFO is empty, or no memory request is outstanding.

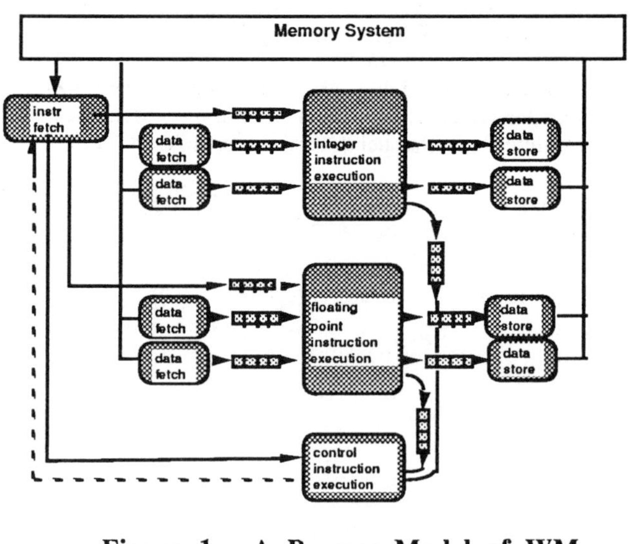

Figure 1: A Process Model of WM

© 1992 ACM 0-89791-509-7/92/0005/0382 $1.50

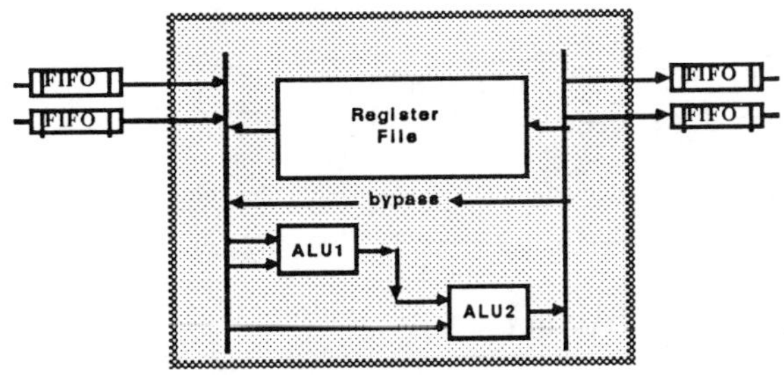

Figure 2: The Arithmetic Unit Model

The integer and floating-point execution units execute RISC-like, register-to-register operations of the form

$$r_d := (r_1 \ \underline{op}_1 \ r_2) \ \underline{op}_2 \ r_3$$

That is, three source operands and two operators are specified in each instruction. This leads to an explicitly pipelined[1] model of these execution units as shown in Figure 2, in which the inner operation ($\underline{op}_1$) of one instruction is performed concurrently with the outer operation ($\underline{op}_2$) of its predecessor. Thus, in principle, four arithmetic operations can be executing concurrently — two in the integer unit and two in the floating-point unit.

Load and store instructions are executed by the integer unit; they specify an address, a data size, and an execution unit. A Load causes the data at the specified address to be enqueued on the "input FIFO' of the specified execution unit. A Store causes data to be dequeued from the output FIFO of the specified execution unit and stored at the specified address. Both Load and Store specify the address as a two operator, three operand expression syntactically and semantically identical to an integer instruction.

The operands of an integer or floating instruction may be the contents of a register, a value from one of the FIFO's, or, in the case of the integer unit, a 5-bit literal. The register names 0 and 1 are reserved to name the FIFOs; thus an instruction names (and dequeues) a value from memory simply by naming, say, r0 in a source context. Similarly, an instruction enqueues a value to be stored by naming r0 in a destination context.

Relationals are explicit operators in both arithmetic units; they produce *two results* — a condition code and their left operand. Thus, for example,

```
r5 := (r5 < 10) + 1
```

[1] Note that an *implementation* may use more (or less) pipelining; what we describe here is the degree of pipelining evident to the programmer in the architectural definition.

has the effect of both testing and incrementing r5. Valid programs must dynamically pair relationals and conditional jumps. Condition code values produced by relationals are enqueued in a FIFO by the arithmetic units and dequeued by the control execution unit. A conditional branch may be executed as soon as its condition code is available, even if there are as yet unexecuted instructions between the one that produced the condition and the conditional jump. Since unconditional jumps can always be executed (they simply affect the location from which the instruction FIFOs are filled), the control execution unit only blocks when it encounters a conditional jump and there is no condition code in its FIFOs.

The semantics of the instruction set are such that, with two minor exceptions, the meaning of a program is as if its instructions were executed sequentially. The exceptions are that the result of an instruction is not available as the inner operand of its successor, and that no guarantees exist about memory hazards between the integer and floating units. Explicit synchronization is possible, however.

One version of the inner loop code for the dot product of two vectors is shown in Figure 3. In this code "r0-r31" denote registers in the integer unit and "f0-f31" denote registers in the floating-point unit; the assembler uses the register names to distinguish between integer and floating-point instructions.

Walking through this loop,

- the first two instructions are "load 32-bit floating-point value"; they request that a[i] and b[i] be enqueued in the floating-point input FIFO (r4 holds i, r6 and r7 are the base addresses of a and b respectively; "<<" is a left shift used to scale i),

- the third instruction increments and tests i (the condition code is enqueued for the control unit),

- the fourth instruction forms the partial sum (note the references to f0 access and dequeue the values of a[i] and b[i]), and finally

- the last instruction tests whether the condition code generated above is true, and if so loops back.

This sequential explanation is correct; but the execution of the code involves a good deal of concurency. For example, the first three instructions will be enqueued for execution by the IEU, the fourth for the FEU and the last for the CEU. Since the data will likely not be available the first time that the floating-point operation is enqued, that instruction will block but the IEU and CEU will continue. A second or third floating operation may be enqueued before the data value arrives in the FEU data FIFO. [Smi84] and [Soh84] have called this phenomenon *slip*. In this case slip may allow the integer unit to get several loop iterations ahead of the floating-point unit.

```
Loop: L32f     (r4<<2)+r6   -- enqueue 32-bit floating value of a[i]
      L32f     (r4<<2)+r7   -- enqueue 32-bit floating value of b[i]
      r4 :=    (r4+1)<r5    -- increment and test i
      f4 :=    (f0*f0)+f4   -- form sum += a[i]*b[i]
      JIT  Loop             -- test
```

Figure 3: WM Code for Dot Product

A better coding of the dot product example would use WM's streaming capability. A single instruction, *stream-in*, informs a stream control unit that a sequence of operands is to be read from memory — starting at a specified location, with a specified stride and count. The count of the number of operands not yet committed to be processed is maintained, and can be tested by a special conditional jump, JNI (Jump of stream count Not zero in the Integer unit). Thus, dot product becomes:

```
      Sin32F   f0,r6,r5,4
      Sin32F   f1,r7,r5,4
Loop: f4 := (f0*f1)+f4
      JNI    f0, Loop
```

The JNI can be overlapped with the execution of the computation, so this version of the loop issues two floating-point operation per floating-point multiply time. Equivalently, each iteration completes in one floating multiply time.

Relation of WM to Other Architectures

In either of the above examples, the exact degree of concurrency, and hence performance, will depend on several factors — including the relative performance of the floating and integer units, the nature of the memory and cache, etc. This is quantified later. However, the fact that the semantics are those of a sequential machine is *very* important. It is this essential property that avoids the need for heroic compilation techniques; specifically the detection of streaming is a relatively simple extension of familiar scalar optimizations [Dav90]. This too is discussed later.

In summary, the performance of WM arises from

- the ability to issue 2 arithmetic operations per instruction,
- the asynchronous and concurrent issue and execution of integer and floating-point instructions,
- masking of memory latency by the data FIFOs,
- the asynchronous and overlapped handling of control (jumps), and
- the asynchronous generation of load/store operations by the streaming units.

Architecture is, we believe, about the *composition* of components — deciding what to include, what to exclude, how to integrate the chosen components, what interactions can and cannot be exploited by compilers and applications, etc. We hope to have stood on the shoulders of our predecessors in selecting and integrating components. We specifically note

- the notion of a "decoupled access/execute architecture" (DAE), separating hardware that generates memory requests from that which operates on the requested values, was discovered independently by several researchers in the early 80's [Ple83, Smi84, Goo85, Smi87]. The technique is used in the ZS-1 [Smi87], and in restricted form in the Intel i860 [Int89].

- [Smi84] introduces the use of FIFOs to interface the processor to memory and to synchronize condition codes between the decoupled units. A very restricted form of the idea was used in the Stretch in the early 60's [Buc62].

- the issue of multiple scalar operations in a single instruction is an old trick in digital signal processors, is the essence of "chaining" in vector processors, is behind VLIW machines[Fis84], and in a restricted form is in the "multiply-accumulate" instructions of recent scalar machines [IBM90, Int89]. Architectures that use this approach have been called "superscalar"[Jou89].

The contribution of WM, we believe, comes from the synergistic interplay of these features, tempered by a healthy dose of our experience with optimizing compilers. The way in which the decoupling was done, the role played by FIFOs, and the form of the multiple operations per instruction all strongly affected each other. The result is descended from, but not really *like* any of the other machines mentioned above. For example,

- the decoupled architectures of both Smith and Davidson [Smi84, Ple83] contain two processors — one to manage data access and the other to manage execution of data manipulation. The two processors are controlled by distinct programs. WM has two data manipulation processors, one of which happens to be able to issue memory access commands. It has eight additional simple processors, the stream control units, that manage data access of a special form (vectors). Our model actually corresponds most closely to a theoretical model proposed by Pratt [Pra78] that separates the result-forming "kernel" of a computation from its control skeleton.

- Smith discusses, but discards, the notion of merging the two programs of a DAE [Smi84]. We not only merge them, but enforce sequential semantics on the merged program. This was a crucial decision with respect to compilability. Whereas Smith asserts that techniques such as trace-scheduling are necessary for the general case of a 2-program DAE, a minor extension of traditional scalar optimization techniques are adequate for WM [Dav90].

- To our knowledge, WM is the first design intended for general-purpose computation to use the 3-operand, 2-operator instruction format, although it is an obvious instance of the general notion of superscalar instructions. We suspect that the reason is that most designers' initial intuition is that the format will not be used very often; that certainly was our initial reaction. As reported later, that intuition is wrong.

As is indicated by the preliminary performance data described in Section 3, it appears as though WM's synergy has had a significant impact on performance. Whereas studies such as [Smi84] and [Jou89] predict concurrency of a factor of two or a bit better, we regularly see factors of four or more. On some highly structured tight loops, such as SAXPY, dot product or string copy, we see factors of six to nine.

Some Preliminary Results

It is difficult to compare an unimplemented architecture to existing implementations of extant architectures; it is even more difficult to compare it to other unimplemented ones. Thus, although we have attempted some implementation-independent comparisons [Gri90, Wul90], our main focus was on

- how well the unusual features of the WM architecture are utilized by real programs,
- the value of various architectural parameters, such as FIFO size, needed to achieve good performance,
- testing the hypothesis that the single, semantically sequential program does not lose performance compared to the separate programs of Smith-style DAEs,
- consideration of various memory system designs to support the memory bandwidth required,
- exploration of the hardware design space to ascertain whether there are any "gottchas",
- exploration of the compilation issues posed by WM, and verification of the hypothesis that scalar optimization techniques are adequate,

Some of these are discussed in more detail below.

An Implementation-Independent Comparison

[Gri90] undertook an implementation-independent study and compared five architectures on three small benchmarks. The method involved uncovering the inherent data and control dependencies in the benchmarks and using these with two real arithmetic unit times, to derive a set of equations for the *virtual clock cycles* for each benchmark. In effect, the methodology assumed that each implementation "threw hardware at the problem", and so was constrained only by the inherent dependencies in the program. While unrealistic from a cost/performance perspective, the methodology does fairly represent "the best that can be done" by each of the architectures.

The study was hampered by the tedious nature of the manual process, hence the small number of architectures and benchmarks. The architectures were the MILSTD 1750, a hypothetical pipelined version of the MILSTD 1750, the MIPS R-3000, the Sun SPARC, the Intel i860, and WM. The three benchmarks were dot product, UNIX string compare, and an infinite-impulse response filter. The component times used were proportional to commercially available Weitek and BIT floating-point parts.

At least for this small set of machines and benchmarks, the architectures seemed to fall into three classes — (1) the non-pipelined 1750, (2) the pipelined 1750, MIPS, SPARC, and i860, and (3) WM. There was surprisingly little difference between the machines in the middle, tending to confirm the observations in [Col85] that many reported differences have more to do with implementation than architecture. Between the classes, however, there were significant differences — with WM generally 2-8 times faster than the middle bunch and those an additional factor of two faster than the non-pipelined 1750.

Observed Concurrency

An alternative to direct comparisons is to determine the degree of concurrency possible from the WM mechanisms. Representative of such results was a study to investigate the effect of operation times on concurrency[Wul89a]. A set of 9 benchmarks was studied:

FFT	Fast Fourier Transform (from the Stanford Benchmarks)
IIR	an Infinite Impulse Response Filter. This loop is interesting because it contains a recurrence, and hence cannot be vectorized.
DOT	dot product (from the Stanford Benchmarks)
LLL5	the 5th Livermore Loop. This loop is interesting because it also contains a recurrence.
Whet-p3	the P3 subroutine from the Whetstone benchmark. This subroutine is interesting

	because it has strong data dependencies that generally interfere with the use of a pipelined arithmetic unit. It is the one case in which explicit nop's had to be installed to accommodate WM's data dependency rule (the fact that the result of an instruction is not available as the inner operand of the immediate succeeding instruction).
STRCPY	the UNIX string copy utility
STRCMP	the UNIX string compare utility
SAXPY	the SAXPY subroutine from LINPACK
LINKLIST	a linked list search routine that searches for the largest element in some field of the list; this routine is pessimal for WM since it cannot be streamed, it uses only the integer execution unit, and, as it turns out, it uses only one operation/instruction.

Two sets of operation times were considered: times proportional to a commercial BIT and Weitek components, respectively. The BIT times were used because they represent a very fast, non-pipelined part. The Weitek times were chosen because the represent something like a worst-case; the part is heavily pipelined, but we used it as though it were not. The relative times were:

BIT	all operations require unit time except integer and floating divide (2 each)
Weitek	the Weitek part is pipelined; the times used were those to complete a full operation; all operations require unit time except floating divide (12), integer divide (10), floating multiply (4), other floating operations (2), and integer multiply (2).

	Ops/Cycle	
Benchmark	BIT Times	Weitek Times
FFT	2.40	1.69
IIR	1.97	1.37
DOT	6.80	2.72
LLL5	4.55	2.20
Whet-p3	1.33	1.13
STRCPY	5.94	5.94
STRCMP	3.94	3.94
SAXPY	8.82	3.23
LINKLIST	1.54	1.54

Figure 4: WM Concurrency in Various Benchmarks

The results are shown in Figure 4. As is obvious, one shouldn't use a pipelined ALU in non-pipelined mode — we observed more than a factor of two reduction in concurrency using times proportional to the Weitek part.

On a more serious level, it is interesting that each of the examples achieves some degree of concurrency, and that it often arises from different sources. In the examples with vector or string data, streaming is a large contributor, but they all also benefit from multiple operations per instruction — especially SAXPY. IIR, which uses only integer operations, does not benefit from the decoupling of execution units, but does benefit from streaming and some multiple operation instructions; it is hurt by Weitek's slow integer-multiply time. LINKLIST, which we had anticipated would get no concurrency at all, is able to fully overlap the execution of its conditional jumps.

Instruction FIFO Sizes

The instruction FIFOs are what permit sequential program semantics while simultaneously allowing *slip*, as in decoupled access architectures. Thus, one suspects that the depth of these FIFOs may significantly affect performance. This was studied by Kester [Kes90].

The FIFOs need to be deep enough so that neither of the execution units is starved (idle) simply because the instruction FIFO of the other unit is full, and hence the next instruction for this unit is hidden. The compiler can assist by interleaving instructions for the two units (program semantics are invariant so long as the order of instructions for each unit is maintained separately).This optimization is trivial, at least within a basic block. Thus, if N_i and N_f are the number of integer and floating-point instructions in a basic block respectively, the longest string of integer and floating-point instructions in a basic block need be no more than $\lceil N_i / N_f \rceil$ and $\lceil N_f / N_i \rceil$ respectively. These are also the maximum number of FIFO entries needed to prevent starvation.

The WM simulator was instrumented to collect these data dynamically, so that the most frequently executed basic blocks are weighted most heavily. As might be expected, the results are not very interesting for programs that heavily exploit streaming, such as many scientific computations. For these the critical concurrency is between the stream units and one of the execution units, and slip between the execution units is irrelevant. For programs such as the Whetstone benchmark that do not stream heavily, however, we get results like those shown below. Thus, for example, 6.5% of the basic blocks require an instruction depth of 2 for the IEU and 1 for the FEU in order to prevent a loss of performance from instruction starvation. It is encouraging that quite modest depths — three or four — are enough to prevent performance degradation due to starvation in all cases.

Integer Instruction FIFO Depth Needed	Floating-point Instruction FIFO Depth Needed				
	0	1	2	3	4
0	18.1	5.7	0.4	0.0	0.0
1	18.3	10.4	2.7	5.5	0.0
2	9.2	6.5	0.0	0.0	0.0
3	10.5	4.3	0.0	0.0	0.0
4	1.6	5.0	0.0	0.0	0.0

Figure 5: Percentage of Basic Blocks Requiring Various Instruction FIFO Depths

FORTRAN	WM
`do 10, i=1,N`	`L:   f0:=(f4*f1)+f0`
`10 y(i) = y(i)+a*x(i)`	`     JNI    f0, L`

Figure 6: Fortran and WM encoding of Dot Product

```
do {
  w[i+k].rp = z[i].rp+z[m+i].rp ;
  w[i+k].ip = z[i].ip+z[m+i].ip ;
  w[i+j].rp =
    e[k+1].rp*(z[i].rp-z[i+m].rp)-
    e[k+1].ip*(z[i].ip-z[i+m].ip);
  w[i+j].ip =
    e[k+1].rp*(z[i].ip-z[i+m].ip)+
    e[k+1].ip*(z[i].rp-z[i+m].rp) ;
  i = i+1 ;
  } while ( i <= j );
```

Figure 7: Inner Loop of the Stanford FFT Benchmark

Data FIFO Size

The data FIFOs allow a program to issue memory requests early, and hence at least partially mask the effects of memory latency. Thus, an obvious question is how large these FIFOs should be — or, alternatively, how is performance affected by their sizes? This was studied by both Kester[Kes90] and Wad [Wul91].

The answer to this question is, in part, dependent on the compiler's ability to move load operations to earlier in the instruction stream. However, we can get an upper bound on the size required by considering only streaming code. A stream control unit will request the next read as soon as there is room in the FIFO; thus, it behaves like a program with explicit loads

The more interesting cases with respect to FIFO depth are those in which the average bandwidth required by the processor is less than that provided by the memory system — but the peak bandwidth is greater. To illustrate we'll consider the inner loop of the Stanford FFT benchmark and assume all floating operations require a single cycle. The loop requires 12 cycles and exhibits the following pattern of memory requests:

Remembering that this "wraps around", it's easy to see that the peak bandwidth required is 7 references in 7 cycles (4 reads and 3 writes), but the *average* bandwidth required is the 8 references in 12 cycles. The need for the maximum number of FIFO entries happens when the average bandwidth required by the cpu and provided by the memory system are the same — which gives rise to an actual memory reference pattern such as

This particular example requires two entries in both the input and output FIFOs to smooth the bursty cpu requests. Detailed analyses by Wad[Wul91] have confirmed that four entries are adequate in all but artificially contrived cases; the real problem will be providing enough sustained bandwidth to routines such as SAXPY.

Hardware Feasibility Explorations

Our hardware implementation efforts focused on two primary topics: (1) the implementation of the Stream Control Unit (SCU), and (2) the modeling of the WM architecture using the VHSIC Hardware Description Language (VHDL). An independent study, albeit for somewhat different purposes was done by Seitz [Sei90].

Implementation of the Stream Control Unit : The goals of designing the SCU were: (1) to develop a set of reusable elements that could be employed to implement other features of the WM computer, (2) to obtain realistic estimates of speed, power, area, and pin counts for the SCU and other modules, and (3) to evaluate multiple SCU designs and determine an optimal implementation.

Based on the IC designs which were developed, a complete 32-bit SCU is estimated to require approximately 50,000 transistors. Tradeoffs between speed and size can substantially reduce the transistor count, if necessary. A prototype SCU with an 8-bit datapath and four address generation units was implemented [Pam90]. The prototype was thoroughly tested and functions correctly.

VHDL Model of the WM Architecture: A functional model of the WM architecture has been developed using the VHSIC Hardware Description Language (VHDL)[Sal89]. The model is implementation independent in that the WM's architecture is described without including features which would imply or preclude any legal WM implementations. The model serves as a workbench in which the performance effects of varying system buffer sizes, memory delays, operator delays, and so forth, can be observed. In addition, the modular nature of the model will facilitate the gradual transition from implementation-independent to implementation-dependent descriptions as behavioral model elements are replaced with structural descriptions in the model.

Seitz Study: As an educational experiment, Professor Chuck Seitz, at CalTech, created a project for his VLSI class during the Spring of 1990 based on the WM specifications. The class was broken into teams with each team assuming the responsibility of the architecture, modeling, and simulation of a portion of the WM machine. A complete switch-level model was developed with supporting simulation (COSMOS) for a machine that included an IFU, an IEU, and FIFOs (no FEU was included in the design but hooks for later addition of an FEU were). Hardware to support streaming was included but not address translation hardware. A 16K byte instruction cache was also included in the design. It was estimated that the full design would consume approximately 100 mm^2 of silicon.

Compiler Explorations

To verify that WM requires only minor extensions of traditional scalar optimizations Davidson produced a high quailty compiler for it [Dav90].

The compiler translates Kernighan and Ritchie C source into WM assembly language. The compiler is implemented using a machine independent front-end that generates code for an abstract, stack-based machine. The back-end of the compiler consists of a retargetable optimizer driven by a machine description. The stack-based intermediate language is powerful enough to support additional Algol-like languages such as Pascal and Ada with minor extensions.

The following optimizations are implemented [Ben88]: unreachable code elimination, branch chaining, branch minimumization, peephole optimization, common subexpression elimination, constant folding, copy propagation, global register allocation via graph coloring, dead variable elimination, code motion, strength reduction, induction variable elimination, recurrence elimination via software pipelining and instruction scheduling. The only WM-specific optimizations were to detect streaming opportunities and issuing load and conditional instructions as soon as possible; both of these are extensions of conventional scalar techniques [Dav90].

The quality of the code produced is illustrated by the following coding of the 5th Livermore Loop. This example is interesting because it contains a recurrence (x[i] is a function of x[i-1]); such situations, also called "loop carried dependencies", must be detected by vectorizing and parallelizing compilers to prevent incorrect vectorization and/or concurrent execution of the loop body.

```
for (i = 2; i < n; i++)
    x[i] = z[i] * (y[i] - x[i-1]);
```

The compiler produced the code shown in Figure 8; the code has been slightly hand-edited to insert comments and to change nmeumonics to conform to the most recent machine definition (the compiler is slightly behind the definition). We assume that the integer registers r20, r22, and r23 contain the addresses of x, z, and y respectively; r21 contains n. Register 31 in both the IEU and FEU is "always zero"; stores into it (as in the first 2 lines) do not affect its value.

The key point, of course, is that the actual loop is the three instructions beginning at L20. The JNI, like other jumps, can be overlapped with the floating-point operations, thus this code produces a new x[i] every other floating-point cycle.

Utilization of Two Operations/Instruction

The WM C compiler was instrumented to collect data on the nature of the code generated, including the number of times that two operations per instruction are used. As shown in Figure 9, over a fairly large benchmark sample, about 30% of all instructions use both operations — or, equivalently, almost half of all operations are contained in such instructions.

Instructions that do not fit the 2-op format (e.g., branches) were not counted. Of those that use the 2-op format, we counted those that used zero, one or two operations (zero operations occur in an instruction is used for a simple register-to-register transfer). The rightmost column shows the percentage of operations appearing in the 2-op format.

```
        r31 := (r21-1)<=0     -- check if loop should be executed
   l64f r31 := (8) + r20      -- generate memory request for x[1]
        r24 := (r21) - 1      -- compute number of items to stream
        f22 := f0             -- dequeue x[1]
 jumpIT L1                    -- jump if loop not to be executed
        r19 := (16) + r22     -- compute address of z[2]
  Si64f f1,r19,r24,8          -- stream in z[2], z[3],...,z[n]
        r19 := (16) + r23     -- compute address of y[2]
 Sin64f f0,r19,r24,8          -- stream in y[2], y[3],...,y[n]
        r19 := (16) + r20     -- compute address of x[2]
Sout64f f0,r19,r24,8          -- stream out x[2], x[3],..,x[n]
L2:     f22 := (f0-f22)*f1    -- compute x[i] (nb, dequeues z[i] & y[i])
        f0 := (f31)+f22       -- store x[i] (nb, f22 == next x[i-1])
 Jni f1 L2                    -- jump if stream count not zero
L1:
```

Figure 8: Compiled Code for the 5th Livermore Loop

Program name	0 ops	1 ops	2 ops	% 2 ops
ackerman	7	10	8	44%
banner	65	45	14	24%
bubblesort	30	29	22	43%
compact	533	417	137	25%
dhrystone	134	110	58	35%
grep	287	186	78	30%
linpack	377	252	201	44%
od	440	362	136	27%
othello	576	366	229	39%
puzzle	150	223	73	25%
queens	29	23	12	34%
quicksort	87	66	69	51%
sieve	8	18	6	25%
shellsort	26	28	27	49%
whetstone	417	173	77	31%
TOTALS:	3166	2308	1147	33%

Figure 9: Utilization of Two Operations per Instruction Stanford Benchmarks

These are static measures, of course. Our intuition is that the number would be larger if measured dynamically because (1) of increment-and-test combinations, and (2) the WM-equivalents of common "addressing modes" use two operations (e.g., "scaled indexing"). While the intuition certainly holds for the type of programs we have executed, we cannot confirm it in general because of the limited and artificial nature of those programs that can be executed on a simulator.

Summary

At this point quite a bit about the potential performance of the WM architecture. We know that modest levels of concurency in the range of 2-9 are possible over a reasonably broad range of applications. We know that each of the kinds of concurrency contributes to the total performance in some applications. We know that a surprising number of operations fit the 2-operator/instruction format. We know that modest values for the architectural parameters such as FIFO size are adequate to achieve this level of performance. We know that non-heroic compilation techniques are adequate to achieve this performance. Finally, we have indications that implementation will consume chip area comparable to that of a conventional RISC design.

We also know the probable Achilles heel of the architecture, namely the need to build a memory system capable of supplying the bandwidth that the processor can absorb. It is -- fortunately or unfortunately -- a problem that has to be faced by all of the newer architectures. Even traditional RISC designs are oustripping the bandwidth capabilities of commercial memory components.

Acknowledgements

Many people have contributed to the results reported here. My special thanks go to: Jim Aylor, Barry Johnson, Anita Jones, Jack Davidson, Andrew Grimshaw, Charlie Hitchcock, Chuck Seitz and his students, Ricky Benitez, Peter Kester, Sally McKee, Ramesh Peri, Max Salinas, and Rohit Wad.

Bibliography

[Ben88] Benitez, M. E. and J. W. Davidson, "A Portable Global Optimizer and Linker", in

Proceedings of the SIGPLAN '88 Symposium on Programming Language Design and Implementation, June 1988, pp. 329-338.

[Buc62] Bucholz, W. (ed), "Planning a Computer System", McGraw Hill, 1962.

[Col85] Colwell, R., et. al., "Computers, Complexity, and Controversy", IEEE Computer, September 1985

[Dav90] Davidson, Jack W., and Benitez, Manuel E. "Code Generation for Streaming: An Access/Execute Mechanism", Fourth International Conference on Architectural Support for Programming Languages and Operating Systems, April 1991.

[Dav90a] Davidson, Jack W., and Benitez, Manuel E., Private Communication.

[Fis84] Fisher, J. A., "The VLIW Machine: A Multiprocessor for Compiling Scientific Code", in *IEEE Computer*, vol. 17, no. 7, July 1984, pp 45-53.

[Gri90] Grimshaw, A. S., Chisholm, D., Segal, B., Benitez, R., Salinas, M., Kester, P., and S. T. McCalla, "Implementation Independent Architectural Comparison", Computer Science TR-90-12, University of Virginia, June, 1990.

[Goo85] Goodman, J. R., et. al., "PIPE: A VLSI Decoupled Architecture", Twelfth Annual International Symposium on Computer Architecture, June 1985.

[IBM90] Special Issue on the RISC System/6000, IBM Journal of Research and Development, v34, n1, Janurary 1990.

[Int89] Intel Corporation, *i860™ 64-Bit Microprocessor Programmer's Reference Manual*, 1989.

[Jou89] Jouppi, N. P., D. W. Wall, "Available Instruction-Level Parallelism for Superscalar and Superpiplined Machines", *Third International Conference on Architectural Support for Programming Languages and Operating Systems,* April 1989.

[Kes90] Kester, Peter, "Performance of the WM Architecture". University of Virginia Computer Science Technical Report & Masters Thesis, 1990.

[Nik89] Nikhil, R. S., and Arvind, "Can Dataflow Subsume von Neuman Computing?", Sixteenth Annual International Symposium on Computer Architecture, June 1989.

[Pam90] Pamidi, Sunil. "A VLSI Implementation of the Stream Control Unit for the WM Machine", University of Virginia, Department of Electrical Engineering Master of Science Thesis, May 1990.

[Ple83] Pleszkun, A. R., and Davidson, E. S., "A Structured Memory Access Architecture", 1983 International Conference on Parallel Processing, August 1983.

[Pra78] Pratt, T., "Program Analysis and Optimization through Kernel-Control Decomposition", Acta Informatica v9, 1978.

[Sal89] Salinas, Jr., M. H., "An Implementation Independent Model of the WM Computer Architecture", Masters Thesis, Department of Electrical Engineering, University of Virginia, December, 1989.

[Sei90] Seitz, C., Private Communication.

[Smi84] Smith, J. E., "Decoupled Access/Execute Computer Architectures", ACM Transactions of Computer Systems", vol 2, no 4, November 1984.

[Smi87] Smith, J. E., et. al., "The ZS-1 Central Processor", in *Second International Conference on Architectural Support for Programming Languages and Operating Systems,* October 1987.

[Soh84] Sohi, G. S., and Davidson, E. S., "Performance of the Structured Memory Access (SMA) Architecture", 1984 International Conference on Parallel Processing, August 1984.

[Wul88] Wulf, Wm. A., "The WM Computer Architecture", in *Computer Architecture News*, v16, n1, March 1988.

[Wul89a] Wulf, Wm. A., A. K. Jones, P. J. Kester, "WM Machine Architecture Measurement; An Initial Analysis", University of Virginia internal report, May 17, 1989.

[Wul89b] Wulf, Wm. A.,"The WM Computer Architecture; Definition and Rationale", version 2, University of Virginia Technical Report TR-88-22, February 1989.

[Wul90] Wulf, Wm. A., and Charles Hitchcock, "The WM Family of Computer Architectures", University of Virginia Technical Report TR-90-05, March 1990.

[Wul90b] Wulf, Wm. A., "The WM Computer Architecture; Principles of Operation", University of Virginia Technical Report TR-90-02, January 1990.

[Wul91] Wulf, Wm. A. and Wad, R. "WM FIFO: SIze Analysis", University of Virgina Technical Report TR-91-16, July 1991

Session 13: System Performance

The Impact of Communication Locality on Large-Scale Multiprocessor Performance

Kirk L. Johnson
Laboratory for Computer Science
Massachusetts Institute of Technology
Cambridge, Massachusetts 02139

Abstract

As multiprocessor sizes scale and computer architects turn to interconnection networks with non-uniform communication latencies, the lure of exploiting communication locality to increase performance becomes inevitable. Models that accurately quantify locality effects provide invaluable insight into the importance of exploiting locality as machine sizes and features change. This paper presents a framework for modeling the impact of communication locality on system performance. The framework provides a means for combining simple models of application, processor, and network behavior to obtain a combined model that accurately reflects feedback effects between processors and networks. We introduce a model that characterizes application behavior with three parameters that capture computation grain, sensitivity to communication latency, and amount of locality present at execution time. The combined model is validated with measurements taken from a detailed simulator for a complete multiprocessor system. Using the combined model, we show that exploiting communication locality provides gains which are at most linear in the factor by which average communication distance is reduced when the number of outstanding communication transactions per processor is bounded. The combined model is also used to obtain rough upper bounds on the performance improvement from exploiting locality to minimize communication distance.

1 Introduction

At the heart of any multiprocessor lies the interconnection network through which processing nodes communicate with one another. The simplest types of interconnection networks allow all distinct pairs of processors to communicate with the same latency, ignoring contention effects. The simplicity of the cost model provided by such *uniform communication latency* (UCL) interconnection networks affords simplicity in software systems (e.g. compilers, schedulers, operating systems) built upon architectures that use such networks. Unfortunately, mechanisms used to implement UCL networks are not *scalable*. Single-level shared-bus architectures are limited by bus bandwidth and are unable to support reasonable communication loads from more than a few dozen processors. Full crossbars might provide nearly uniform communication latencies, but excessive hardware requirements prevent them from being scalable. Indirect, multistage networks that circumvent the bandwidth problems of buses and quadratic hardware requirements of full crossbars provide bandwidth which scales with machine size. But this increased bandwidth comes at a price: *all* communication latency increases with the number of processors in the system.[1]

Because the construction of scalable UCL networks appears to be intractable, future large-scale multiprocessors will probably use some type of *non-uniform communication latency* (NUCL) interconnection network (e.g. meshes, trees). In such networks, all processors are able to communicate with one another, but latencies may vary greatly. In terms of average communication latency between all pairs of processors, such networks may do no better than the most efficient UCL networks. However, as machine sizes scale, NUCL networks have an advantage: some processors can remain "close" to one another, regardless of machine size; other processors gradually become "further" away. The smaller the distance between a pair of communicating processors, the lower the communication latency. Moreover, the network bandwidth required for communication typically decreases with communication distance.

This difference gives NUCL architectures an advantage over UCL architectures. As machine sizes scale, applications running on UCL architectures face increasing latencies for all communication. On the other hand, with NUCL architectures, some applications can be organized such that communication patterns tend to favor nearby processors. Such applications should experience performance gains commensurate with the degree that communication latencies can be reduced.

We prefer UCL and NUCL over the more conventional UMA (*uniform memory access*) and NUMA (*non-uniform memory access*) nomenclature, because the conventional terms imply shared-memory semantics. UCL and NUCL capture the same fundamental difference for a more general class of architectures.

1.1 What is Locality?

Applications often take advantage of *communication locality* to realize performance gains. Communication locality is a property of both applications and architectures. *Application locality* (or *algorithmic locality*) is that which is present in the organization of an application, independent of architectural details. *Architectural locality* represents the ability of an architecture to exploit

[1] Conventional wisdom dictates that this increase is logarithmic in the number of processors in the system; proponents of "three-space realizability" arguments claim a somewhat higher rate [9].

© 1992 ACM 0-89791-509-7/92/0005/0392 $1.50

application locality.

Two components contribute to application locality. The first, *temporal locality*, represents the effect of decreasing the communication frequency between application threads. Applications that minimize inter-thread communication by maximizing data reuse tend to exhibit good temporal locality. The second component, *physical locality*, represents the effect of affinity in the communication patterns amongst an application's threads. Applications tend to have good physical locality to the extent that their inter-thread communication graphs have relatively low bisection width and high diameter. An application in which all distinct pairs of threads communicate equally has no physical locality.

With this understanding, the fundamental difference between UCL and NUCL architectures becomes clear. Both classes of architectures allow exploitation of temporal locality, but UCL architectures are only able to exploit physical locality to the extent that threads can be collocated when there are more threads than processors. In addition to being able to collocate threads, NUCL architectures can exploit physical locality by placing communicating threads on processors such that average communication distance is minimized.

1.2 Managing Communication Latency

As machine sizes scale, communication latencies will also increase. Architects have proposed many approaches for managing that latency; these approaches can be divided into three broad categories.

- Those that attempt to *avoid* long latency operations. These approaches exploit temporal locality in the application and focus on enhancing data reuse (e.g. caches, compilation for data locality).
- Those that attempt to *reduce* communication latency. These approaches exploit physical locality in the application and focus on minimizing communication distance.
- Those that attempt to *tolerate* long latency operations. These approaches typically focus on software paradigms and processor architectures which allow useful work to overlap long latency operations (e.g. multithreading, relaxed memory consistency models, data prefetching).

This paper focuses on the impact of the latter two approaches on multiprocessor performance. Numerous researchers have demonstrated the importance of the first approach (exploiting temporal locality); compilation techniques for increasing temporal locality continue to be an active area of research [10, 12].

1.3 Contributions of this Paper

This paper describes a framework for analyzing the impact of communication costs on end application performance for a broad class of multiprocessors. This framework is then used to quantify the impact of physical locality in large-scale multiprocessors using interconnection networks organized as k-ary n-dimensional meshes.

The modeling framework provides a mechanism for combining separate models of applications, communication mechanisms (e.g. coherence protocols), and interconnection networks. Each of the component models can be changed independently of the others; this provides a means of gauging the importance of particular application or architectural features in controlled experiments. Component models are combined such that applications receive feedback from interconnection networks and only proceed at rates appropriate to observed communication latencies. The application model introduced in this paper characterizes application behavior with three parameters: the application's computational grain size, its ability to tolerate communication latency, and the amount of physical locality present at execution time. Model predictions agree closely with measurements taken from detailed simulations of a complete multiprocessor system.

We demonstrate that under a reasonable set of assumptions about processor and application behavior, the impact of contention in k-ary n-dimensional mesh networks is bounded. In particular, we use the combined model to show that when the number of outstanding communication transactions per processor is bounded, average per-hop communication latency in large machines approaches a constant value; this effect is observable in machines with a few thousand processors. Because average per-hop latency approaches a constant value under this condition, average communication latencies are linear in communication distance.

This fact has profound impact on the performance improvements available by exploiting physical locality. Any gain due to exploiting physical locality is bounded by the degree to which communication latencies are reduced. Since communication latencies are linear in communication distance, exploiting physical locality to reduce communication distances provides gains which are at most linear in the factor by which communication distances are reduced.

We also use the combined model to obtain rough upper bounds on the performance improvement possible by exploiting physical locality in two-dimensional mesh networks. In the architecture used in the simulation experiments, network switches are clocked twice as fast as processors. Under these conditions, our analysis indicates that these upper bounds are around two for machines with 1,000 processors and roughly 50 for machines with a million processors. By using the model to investigate the impact of changing the relative balance between computation and communication speeds, we demonstrate that these bounds are significantly larger for architectures with less bandwidth-rich interconnection networks—decreasing the relative speed of the network by a factor of eight increases the upper bounds by approximately a factor of three.

1.4 Overview

The rest of this paper is organized as follows: Section 2 describes the modeling framework and its components. Section 3 describes the set of experiments used to verify the model. The section concludes by presenting results from these experiments and noting that they agree closely with the values predicted by the model. Section 4 uses the model to predict performance across a wide range of machine configurations. Section 5 provides a brief overview of related work. Section 6 closes with a summary of our major results. Finally, Appendix A summarizes the nomenclature used in the rest of the paper.

2 A Framework for Modeling

This section presents a framework for modeling the impact of communication costs on application performance. The framework consists of three components: an application model describes processor behavior in terms of abstract communication transactions, a transaction model describes the resources required to satisfy communication transactions, and a network model characterizes the behavior of the underlying interconnection network. The application and transaction models are combined to obtain a node model which describes the behavior of individual multiprocessor nodes as seen by the interconnection network. The final combined model is obtained by joining the node and network models. These models are joined such that applications effectively receive feedback from the network and only inject messages at rates appropriate to the message latencies they actually observe.

In order to compare application performance for different machine configurations and applications with different amounts of physical locality, a metric of performance is needed. This framework uses average transaction rate as a basis for such comparisons, as discussed in Section 2.6. Simulation results demonstrating the accuracy of the model are presented in Section 3.

2.1 Application Model

The application model describes the behavior of individual processors running their portion of an application by indicating how per-processor communication transaction issue rate depends on transaction latency. The model captures both application- and processor-specific details. It characterizes not only the basic computational grain size of an application but also how behavior changes when transaction latencies increase. Computational grain size is an informal notion; another common term for the same notion is computation-to-communication ratio. In this paper, this notion is captured by T_r, the average amount of useful work done by a thread between successive communication transactions. The dependence of processor behavior on observed transaction latency is captured by the *latency sensitivity*, s, as described below. We show that s is intimately related to the degree to which an architecture and application utilize multiple outstanding communication transactions.

For architectures with UCL interconnection networks, these two parameters (T_r and s) are sufficient to characterize application behavior. For architectures with NUCL interconnection networks, additional information about communication patterns that exist during application execution (e.g. which processing nodes communicate with one another) is also necessary. These patterns depend on the amount of physical locality present in an application, the topology of the interconnection network, and the degree to which the mapping used to assign application threads to processors exploits these features to minimize communication distances. Because good metrics for these factors are still an area of active research, this paper uses an operational definition of physical locality. All information about communication patterns is captured by a single number: average communication distance d, measured in network hops. This parameter captures the amount of physical locality present at execution time. For interconnection networks with topologies more complex than that of the k-ary n-dimensional meshes used in this paper, more detailed representations might be necessary.

For the applications and architecture described in this paper, communication transactions are cache coherency transactions. The development of the framework does not depend on this fact; given an appropriate transaction model, the framework could be used to model applications and architectures that utilize other styles of interprocessor communication.

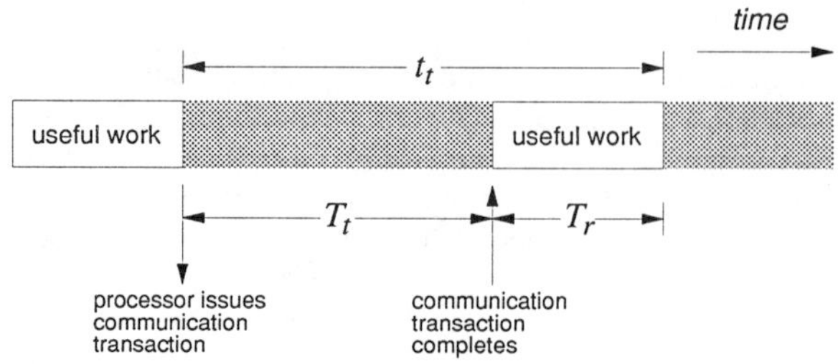

Figure 1: A simple processor in action. Shaded regions between periods of useful work represent time spent waiting for communication transactions to complete.

In order to derive a simple application model from first principles, consider an application for which the average run length between successive communication transactions by a thread is T_r cycles. Assume each transaction takes an average of T_t cycles to complete. When processors can only support a single outstanding communication transaction, as depicted in Figure 1, the average *inter-transaction issue time* t_t is given by

$$t_t = T_r + T_t \tag{1}$$

or

$$T_t = t_t - T_r \tag{2}$$

That is, inter-transaction issue time and average transaction latency T_t are linearly related with a slope of 1 and intercept determined by the computational grain of the application. In what follows, such relationships between t_t and T_t will be referred to as *application transaction curves*.

Extending this model to accommodate processor architectures capable of supporting multiple outstanding transactions is straightforward. Consider, for example, the case of block multithreaded processors with p hardware contexts and a context switch time of T_s cycles (see Figure 2). Each thread runs until it issues a communication transaction, at which time the processor switches contexts and restarts execution of the next thread. Such processors have two basic modes of operation. In the first mode, transaction latencies are small enough to ensure that transactions always complete before the invoking thread is ready to run again. The following inequality expresses this condition:

$$T_t < pT_s + (p-1)T_r \tag{3}$$

When operating in the first mode, processors are completely able to mask communication latency. A new transaction is invoked every $T_s + T_r$ cycles, thus the average inter-transaction issue time is simply

$$t_t = T_r + T_s \tag{4}$$

This equation represents the minimum inter-transaction issue time for a given application when using multithreaded processors.

When the inequality in Equation (3) does not hold, processors operate in a second mode where they are no longer able to completely mask communication latencies. When operating in the

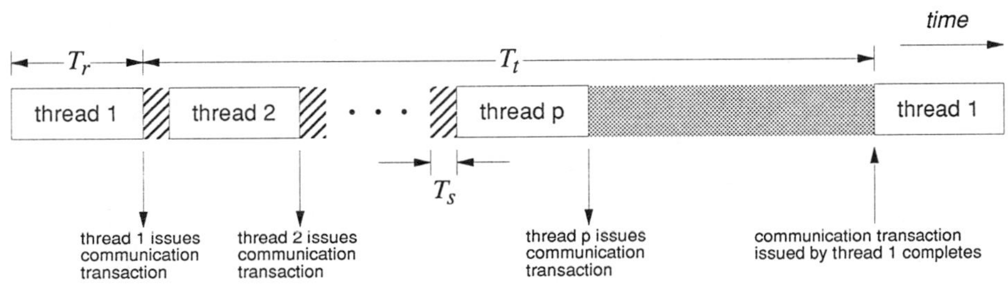

Figure 2: A block multithreaded processor in action. Hashed regions between thread runs represent context switching time; the shaded region at the right represents time spent waiting for communication transactions to complete.

second mode, processors invoke p transactions every $T_r + T_t$ cycles (see Figure 2), thus the average inter-transaction issue time is given by

$$t_t = \frac{T_r + T_t}{p} \tag{5}$$

or

$$T_t = pt_t - T_r \tag{6}$$

As with non-multithreaded processors, application behavior is characterized by a linear relationship between t_t and T_t. In fact, the only difference due to p-multithreaded processors is an extra factor of p in the slope of the $t_t - T_t$ relationship (compare Equations (2) and (6)) and the lower bound on average inter-transaction issue time given by Equation (4).

None of the experiments described in this paper yielded inter-transaction issue times approaching the lower bound given in Equation (4). Thus the rest of this paper drops explicit references to this bound.

Increases in the slope of an application transaction curve indicate decreased sensitivity of application performance to increases in transaction latency. For example, consider two applications, $\mathcal{A}$ and $\mathcal{B}$, such that the slope of $\mathcal{B}$'s application transaction curve is twice that of $\mathcal{A}$. If an increase in transaction latency of x cycles causes $\mathcal{A}$'s average inter-transaction issue time to increase by y cycles, then a similar increase in the transaction latency observed by $\mathcal{B}$ will only increase $\mathcal{B}$'s average inter-transaction issue time by $y/2$ cycles.

Extending the application model to accommodate other mechanisms for supporting multiple outstanding transactions (e.g. weak ordering, data prefetching) is equally straightforward. The impact of all such mechanisms is essentially the same: applications for which processors keep an average of k transactions outstanding have application transaction curves with slopes k times greater than those for the same application running on processors which can only support a single outstanding transaction. Since increases in slope indicate decreased sensitivity to communication latency, this corresponds nicely with the intuition that architectures embodying such mechanisms should be less sensitive to increasing communication latencies.

Note that the constant offset in the application model (Equation (6)) depends on an application's computational grain, as captured by T_r. When the same application model is used to characterize application behavior for a range of machine configurations, there is an implicit assumption that problem size is being scaled such that T_r remains constant. For many applications this may require using problem sizes proportional to the total number of hardware contexts available.

2.2 Transaction Model

The transaction model describes the resources required to satisfy a communication transaction. It encompasses two pieces of information: the average number of network messages which must be sent to satisfy a transaction and the average latency of a transaction.

Intuitively, transaction latency T_t consists of some fixed delay plus a component dependent on average message latency T_m. The fixed delay arises from factors such as message sending and receiving overhead, processing necessary to maintain coherence in cache-coherent systems, and the like. Thus average transaction latency is modeled as

$$T_t = cT_m + T_f \tag{7}$$

where c indicates the extent to which transaction latency depends on message latency, and T_f represents any fixed delay inherent in the transaction mechanism. In essence, c is the number of messages in the "critical path" of a transaction. For simple transaction mechanisms which require only single message exchanges between peers, $c = 2$.

The average number of messages required to satisfy a communication transaction is assumed to be some constant g. Observe that the average inter-message injection time t_m for an individual node and the average inter-transaction issue time t_t are related by a factor of g:

$$t_t = gt_m \tag{8}$$

2.3 Node Model

The node model describes the behavior of a multiprocessor node from the perspective of the interconnection network. The node model indicates how fast nodes will inject messages into the interconnection network as a function of average message latency. In essence, the node model provides the same information for messages that the application model provides for transactions.

The node model is derived from the application and transaction models by substituting Equations (7) and (8) into Equation (6) and simplifying.

$$T_m = \frac{pg}{c}t_m - \frac{T_r + T_f}{c} \tag{9}$$

Not surprisingly, Equation (9) indicates that average inter-message injection time t_m and average message latency T_m are linearly related. The slope of the relationship depends on the constants from the transaction model and the slope of the application transaction curve; the intercept on the computational grain and constants from the transaction model. Such relationships between t_m and T_m will be referred to as *application message curves*.

The intuition about the slope of application transaction curves applies to application message curves as well: the greater the slope of an application message curve, the less sensitive t_m is to increases in T_m. Accordingly, we will refer to the slope of an application message curve as the *latency sensitivity* s. Larger values of s correspond to decreased sensitivity of application performance to changes in average message latency. Note that s is proportional to p, the average number of outstanding transactions, where the constant of proportionality is determined by the parameters of the transaction model.

2.4 Network Model

The network model describes the behavior of the interconnection network by providing average message latency as a function of average message size, message injection rate, and average communication distance. In this paper, we use a model for packet-switched, buffered mesh networks, but the framework can easily accommodate models for other types of packet-switched networks such as that for indirect networks given in [8]. We believe that modifications to allow for circuit-switched networks would be straightforward.

The network model used in this paper is that for packet-switched k-ary n-dimensional torus networks with separate unidirectional channels in both mesh directions presented by Agarwal in [1]. The model assumes that messages are wormhole routed according to an e-cube routing scheme [6]. In this model, channel utilization ρ and average message latency T_m are given by

$$\rho = \frac{r_m B k_d}{2} \quad (10)$$

$$T_m = n k_d T_h + B \quad (11)$$

where

r_m is the average message injection rate for each node. r_m is related to the average inter-message injection time according to

$$r_m = \frac{1}{t_m} \quad (12)$$

B is the average message size, in flits

k_d is the average distance per dimension each message must travel, which is given by the average communication distance d divided by the number of dimensions n:

$$k_d = \frac{d}{n} \quad (13)$$

T_h is the average per-hop latency for the head of a message, which is given by

$$T_h = 1 + \left(\frac{\rho B}{1-\rho}\right)\left(\frac{k_d - 1}{k_d^2}\right)\left(\frac{n+1}{n}\right) \quad (14)$$

Average communication distance d (and thus k_d) depends on the amount of physical locality in an application and the extent to which good thread-to-processor mappings are used. In addition to reducing average communication distance, good mappings can also lead to lower values of T_h, the average per-hop latency. This happens because reductions in k_d provide corresponding reductions in channel utilization ρ (see Equations (10) and (14)). Thus the benefits of exploiting physical locality are twofold: both communication distance and network contention are reduced.

This paper extends Agarwal's basic network model slightly. First, as given, Equation (14) is only valid for $k_d \geq 1$. Good mappings of applications that exhibit a considerable degree of physical locality can easily violate this condition. Under these circumstances, messages will tend to encounter very little contention delay. Thus, for $k_d < 1$, T_h is taken to be 1.

A second extension reflects the effect of contention for the channels which connect processing nodes to the network. An accurate network model must account for this factor, for it can become significant in the presence of long messages or high message rates. For the experiments described in Section 3, contention for these channels added two to five network cycles to the average message latency. Extending the model to account for this contention introduces additional complexity to the solution of the combined model without providing further insight into the issues at hand. Accordingly, this paper does not treat such an extension. The modeled values shown in Sections 3 and 4, however, reflect the inclusion of this factor as discussed in [7].

2.5 Combined Model

We obtain the combined model by using the node and network models to provide feedback to one another so that individual nodes "back off" as message latencies increase, injecting messages into the network at rates appropriate to the message latencies they actually observe. Equating the right hand sides of Equations (9) and (11) provides us with a quadratic polynomial in r_m, the average message injection rate. Given values for the various application and network model parameters, the quadratic is easily solved; the resulting value of r_m represents the predicted per-node message injection for the application and network described by the given parameter values. Other values of interest (e.g. channel utilization, average inter-transaction issue time) are obtained by substituting the predicted value of r_m into the appropriate model equations.

2.6 Performance Metrics

In order to compare performance of different machine configurations, a performance metric is needed. Such a metric should relate directly to end performance—the rate at which useful work gets done.

Within the framework presented in this paper, the average amount of useful work each thread performs between issuing communication transactions is assumed to be some constant T_r. Since the average inter-transaction issue time is t_t, the rate at which useful work gets done can be computed directly as T_r/t_t. Note that this value is proportional to the average transaction issue rate r_t, where r_t is given by

$$r_t = \frac{1}{t_t} \quad (15)$$

When T_r is held constant, r_t serves as a good metric of per-processor performance—increases in r_t are indicative of proportional increases in actual per-processor performance. A good metric of aggregate performance for an N-processor machine is thus

Nr_t. For a particular application model, the performance obtained with two different machine configurations can be compared by computing the ratio of the aggregate performance obtained in each case. Similar computations can be used to compare the performance of different application models for a particular machine configuration.

3 Experimentation

This section describes the simulation experiments used to validate the combined model. It begins with a description of the multiprocessor architecture for which the simulations were run, followed by a description of the application code used. The section concludes with a presentation of simulation results validating the models developed in Section 2.

3.1 The Architecture

The architecture simulated in these experiments is that of the MIT Alewife machine [2]. The basic Alewife architecture consists of processor/memory nodes communicating over a packet-switched interconnection network organized as a low-dimensional mesh.

Each processor/memory node consists of a Sparcle processor [3], a floating-point coprocessor, several megabytes of DRAM, a 64-kilobyte unified instruction/data cache (direct mapped, 16-byte lines), and a controller that serves as both memory and network interface. In order to support block multithreading, Sparcle provides four hardware contexts. Switches between hardware contexts can be effected in 11 cycles. In addition to providing the processor direct access to message sending and receiving facilities, the memory/network interface implements the LimitLESS protocol [4] to provide coherent caches and shared memory. Components on a processor/memory node are clocked at 33 to 40 MHz.

The mesh-organized interconnection network provides two eight-bit unidirectional channels between each neighboring pair of nodes; one for each direction. The bandwidth of each channel is around 60 to 80 Mbytes/sec; network switches are clocked twice as fast as processors. The base delay through a network switch is a single network cycle. Each network switch is connected to its corresponding processing node through a pair of eight-bit channels; one channel is used to deliver messages from the node to the network, the other to deliver messages from the network to the processing node. A moderate amount of buffering is provided on each switch. Messages are wormhole routed according to an e-cube routing scheme [6].

All simulations were run assuming a 64-node machine organized as a two-dimensional, radix-eight torus. The simulator used provides instruction level simulation of Sparcle and cycle-by-cycle simulation of the cache, controller, and network components.

3.2 The Application

The model of the previous section described application behavior in terms of computation grain T_r, latency sensitivity s, and average communication distance d. In order to validate the model, we devised a synthetic application with several interesting properties. First, it has a particularly small computation grain size. As the goal of these experiments was to measure the impact of varying communication costs on end performance, this is useful—intuition dictates that these effects should be more pronounced in applications with small computation grain. Second, the application has particularly good physical locality: its 64 threads communicate with one another according to a radix-eight two-dimensional torus organization. This allowed us to drastically vary average communication distance by using different thread-to-processor mappings. Third, by using the block multithreading features of Sparcle to vary the number of transactions the application kept outstanding, we could vary the latency sensitivity of the application.

Each of the simulation experiments used the same application code. In that code, each thread maintains a single word of state in local memory and repeatedly iterates through a simple inner-loop. During the course of one pass through the inner-loop, a thread reads the value from each of its neighbors' state words, performs some trivial computation, and writes a new value to its own state word. Threads make no effort to synchronize with one another.

Note that inter-thread communication takes place through shared memory. Each time a thread reads a neighbor's state or updates its own state, inter-thread communication is effected, if necessary, through appropriate cache-coherency transactions. Because Alewife provides coherent caches and all threads run the same inner-loop, the great majority of attempts to read a neighbor's state word cause cache-coherency traffic—it is likely one thread will update its state word before another can read it twice. Similarly, when a thread updates its local state word, cache-coherency traffic will usually be needed to invalidate read copies of the word from neighboring threads' caches.

Two parameters were varied across the suite of simulations. First, by using different thread-to-processor mappings, the average number of hops required to communicate between neighboring threads in the application's communication graph could be changed drastically. Average communication distances for the nine mappings used in these experiments ranged from one to just over six network hops.[2]

The second parameter that was changed between experiments was the degree of multithreading, p. In each case, the simulation run consisted of as many independent instances of the basic application as there were hardware contexts, with exactly one thread from each application instance resident on every processor. No data was shared between application instances, thus threads on the same node do not communicate with one another. Experiments were run with one, two, and four hardware contexts.

A priori knowledge of the cache line size and details of the coherency protocol provides the expected average message size and average number of messages per transaction; these values are 96 bits ($B = 12$ flits, assuming 8-bit network channels) and $g = 3.2$ messages per transaction, respectively.

3.3 Verification of the Model

The rest of this section presents experimental results which demonstrate the accuracy of the combined model.

Figure 3 shows application message curves as measured for the simulation experiments described earlier in this section. As predicted by Equation (9), t_m and T_m are linearly related. Note that increasing the number of contexts causes the application message curve slope to increase in the expected manner. That is, the

[2] Randomly chosen thread-to-processor mappings on a machine of this size lead to expected average communication distances of just over four network hops (see Equation (17)).

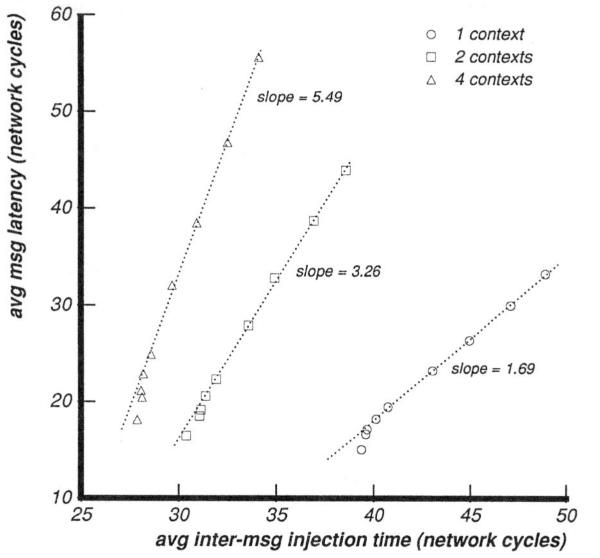

Figure 3: Average inter-message injection time t_m vs. average message latency T_m. Symbols denote simulation results; dotted lines represent linear regressions of measured values.

slope for two contexts is roughly twice the slope for one context, and so on.

Several phenomena cause the increases in slope to be slightly less than expected. Most of the difference can be attributed to an unfavorable interaction between the asynchronous nature of the application code used in the experiments and the cache coherence protocol.[3] Because of this interaction, the constant c in Equation (7) increases with the number of contexts; in the experiments with four contexts, c is measured to be 15 percent larger than in experiments with one context. Since c occurs in the denominator of the slope of the node model (Equation (9)), increases in c manifest themselves as decreases in application message curve slope.

Figures 4 and 5 plot average communication distance against average message rate and average message latency. Symbols indicate results from individual simulation runs; dotted curves show the values predicted by the model. Note that predicted values for message rate are consistently within a few percent of measured values and predicted values for message latency track measured values to within a few network cycles.

4 Results and Discussion

A number of interesting questions can be addressed given a model that accurately describes the effects of changing communication costs on application behavior. This section provides analysis and discussion of two such issues. First, we show that when the number of outstanding communication transactions per processor is bounded, communication latencies in large machines are linear in communication distance. Because of this fact, the exploitation of physical locality provides gains which are at most linear in the factor by which average communication distance is reduced.

Second, we use the combined model to obtain rough upper bounds on the performance improvement possible from exploit-

[3] No real applications have exhibited this behavior.

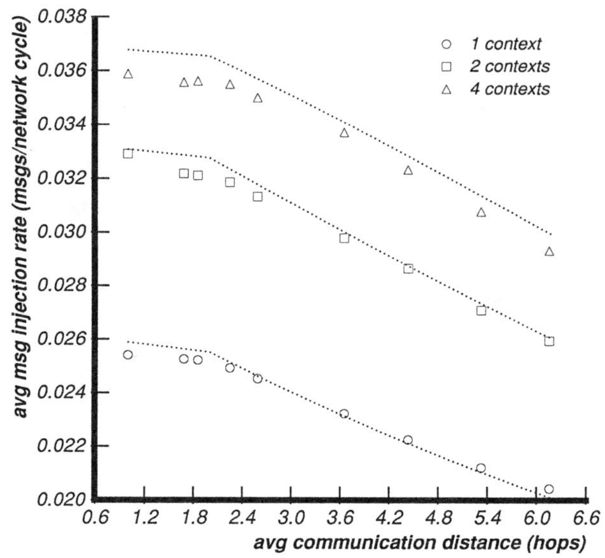

Figure 4: Average communication distance d vs. average message injection rate r_m. Symbols denote simulation results; dotted lines show values predicted by combined model.

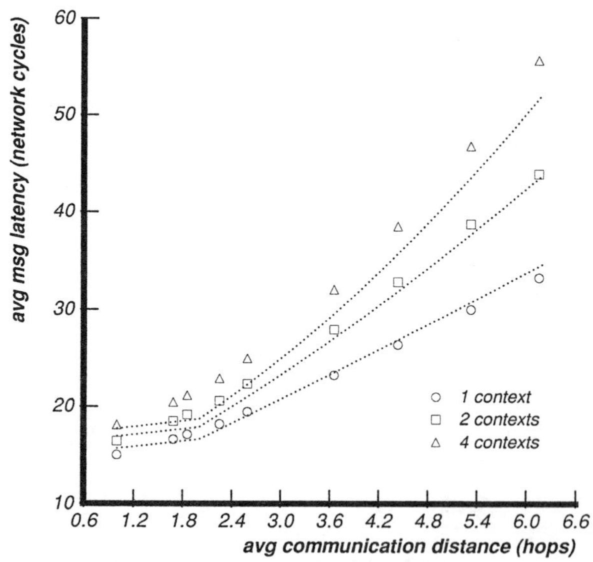

Figure 5: Average communication distance d vs. average message latency T_m. Symbols denote simulation results; dotted lines show values predicted by combined model.

ing physical locality in two-dimensional mesh networks. For the architecture described in Section 3, we show that these bounds are somewhat less than one might expect. We establish that this is due to the relatively high bandwidth provided by the network used in that architecture and show that the bounds increase when less bandwidth-rich interconnection networks are used—decreasing the relative speed of the network by a factor of eight leads to upper bounds that are roughly three times larger.

4.1 Bandwidth vs. Latency

As machine sizes scale, applications with little physical locality place increasing bandwidth demands on interconnection networks. Increases in application bandwidth requirements in turn cause contention effects to become more pronounced. Using the framework presented in this paper, we demonstrate that under a reasonable set of assumptions about application and processor behavior, the impact of contention effects is bounded, even for very large machines and communication-intensive applications that induce heavy network loads. Consequently, we show that the performance benefit from exploiting physical locality to reduce communication distances is at most linear in the factor that average communication distance is reduced.

By combining Equations (10), (11), and (14), one can show that as average communication distances increase, the average time it takes a message to travel a single network hop approaches a limiting value given by

$$T_h = \frac{Bs}{2n} \qquad (16)$$

See [7] for details. Note that this limiting value depends only on average message size B, latency sensitivity s, and network dimension n. For a given application and architecture, B and n are constants, while s is linearly related to p, the average number of outstanding communication transactions.[4]

Intuitively, T_h approaches this limiting value because of the linkage between application and network behavior. If each node can only have some finite number of transactions outstanding (i.e. s is finite), increasing transaction latencies cause transaction issue rates to fall. This negative feedback keeps processors from loading interconnection networks to a point where communication latencies become unbounded.

Thus, as machine sizes scale and communication distances increase, T_h approaches the value given by Equation (16). In turn, this implies that average communication latency is linear in communication distance. Note that processor architectures able to support multiple outstanding transactions afford higher values of s, which lead to proportional increases in the limiting value of T_h.

These conclusions have a profound impact on the potential benefit of physical locality. Any gain due to exploiting physical locality is bounded by the degree by which communication latencies are reduced. Since communication latencies are linear in communication distance, reducing average communication distance by some factor x can only provide performance gains which are linear in x.

The smaller the computational grain of an application, the faster the limiting value of T_h will be approached. For applications with small computational grain, the limiting case can be

[4] For realistic applications and architectures, s is finite.

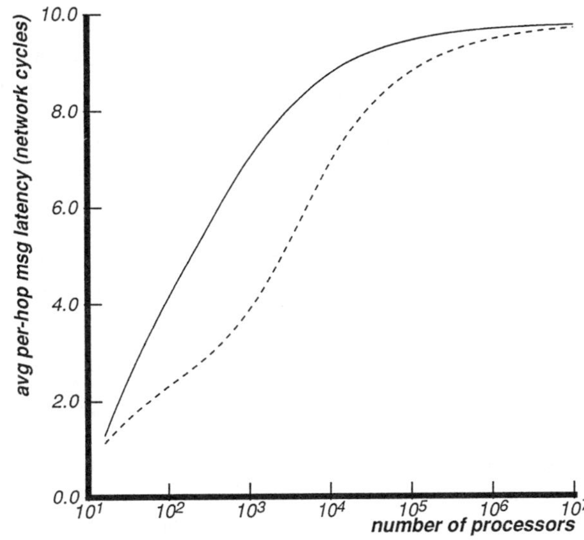

Figure 6: Average per-hop message latency T_h vs. number of processors N. The solid line represents the application of Section 3 running with two hardware contexts, assuming random communication patterns. The dashed line shows the impact of increasing the computation grain of that application by a factor of ten.

approached for relatively small machines. For example, consider Figure 6. T_h is plotted against machine size for two applications; a two-dimensional interconnection network is assumed. The solid curve represents the application of Section 3 running on a multithreaded processor with two hardware contexts. The dashed curve shows the effect of artificially increasing the computational grain size by a factor of ten. In this case ($s = 3.26$, $B = 12$, $n = 2$), the limiting value of T_h is approximately 9.8 network cycles. For the application with smaller computational grain size, T_h reaches over eighty percent of its limiting value with a few thousand processors. When the grain size is increased, T_h still approaches the same limiting value, albeit quite a bit more slowly, as expected. Curves for one and four hardware contexts behave similarly.

4.2 Physical Locality

Intuition dictates that application performance should benefit from thread-to-processor mappings that reduce overall communication distance. The more physical locality present in an application, the greater the gains possible through reducing communication distances. This section demonstrates that while such gains are certainly possible, they are somewhat less than one might initially expect for the architecture described in Section 3—no more than a factor of two or so for a 1,000 processor machine. An examination of the factors leading to this less-than-expected impact indicates that it is primarily due to the relatively high ratio of communication bandwidth to computation speed in that architecture. Recomputing the gains for architectures with progressively slower networks confirms this fact showing that larger gains are possible when processors are faster relative to the speed of the interconnection network.

Any application with finite latency sensitivity s will be communication-bound for large enough message latency T_m. Once T_m exceeds some threshold, increases in communication latencies will cause proportional decreases in application performance.

Equation (9) indicates that the smaller an application's computational grain size, the lower this threshold will be. Further, the lower this threshold, the greater the impact exploiting physical locality can have on end performance—reductions in communication latency are more beneficial when applications are already communication-bound. Thus, for an application with substantial physical locality and a very small computational grain size, comparing the performance obtained with best-case mappings and mappings which ignore physical locality provides a rough upper bound on the potential benefit of exploiting physical locality for *any* application. Since the application described in Section 3 has the desired properties, it is well suited for use in this comparison.

Random mappings represent the expected case when applications possess no physical locality or physical locality is ignored when mapping threads to processors. Under these circumstances, essentially random communication patterns result. For torus-connected k-ary n-dimensional interconnection networks, assuming random communication patterns and nodes that never send messages to themselves, the average distance traversed by a message, d, is given by[5]

$$d = \frac{nk^{n+1}}{4(k^n - 1)} \quad (17)$$

See [1] or [11] for details.

For this application and network, because the communication patterns of the application are the same as the network topology, an ideal mapping in which every communication requires but a single network hop is trivially obtained. Such a mapping represents the expected best case.

As discussed in Section 2.6, average transaction issue rate is a good metric of per-processor performance. Thus, in order to compare performance obtained with different mappings of a particular application on a given machine configuration, it is sufficient to compute the ratio of the transaction issue rates obtained in each case. When this ratio compares the performance of ideal and random mappings for a given machine size N, it is termed the *expected gain* due to exploitation of physical locality.

Figure 7 shows a log-log plot of expected gain against machine sizes from ten to a million processors for the application of Section 3 running with one, two, and four hardware contexts. The curves are strikingly similar—each starts at unity gain for ten processors, reaches a gain of two at around 1,000 processors, then quickly enters a region where the randomly-mapped application is communication-bound. Expected gains for one million processors range from 40 to 55. Recall that because the application being measured has very small computation grain, these are rough upper bounds on the gains available to any application.

Initially, an expected gain of only a factor of two for a 1,000 processor machine seems somewhat surprising. On a machine of that size, average communication distance for random mappings is nearly a factor of 16 larger than the single-hop distances afforded by an ideal mapping. Further, there's good reason to expect that for random mappings, T_h will be substantially larger, by a factor of four or more, than for an ideal mapping (see Figure 6). It is reasonable to expect, then, that the nk_dT_h term of Equation (11) will be a factor of 50 or 100 larger for a random mapping than for an ideal mapping.

[5] Equation (17) is only exact for even values of k. For odd values of k, the correct value is smaller by $\frac{nk^{n-1}}{4(k^n-1)}$. Since this term is $O(\frac{1}{k})$, it rapidly becomes insignificant as k increases.

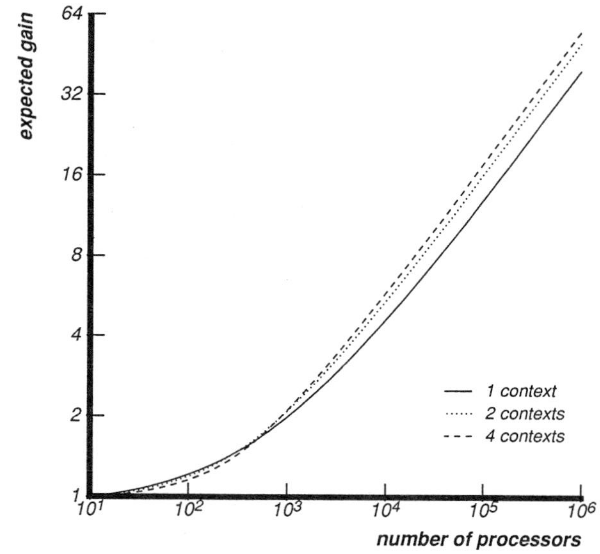

Figure 7: Expected gain due to exploitation of physical locality vs. number of processors (two-dimensional mesh). Each curve compares performance of ideal mapping vs. random mapping for a given degree of processor multithreading.

These results indicate that a large disparity exists between the magnitudes of the difference in communication costs and the difference in end performance when comparing ideal and random mappings. By using the application and network models from Section 2, the degree to which various factors contribute to end performance can be quantified. Such a breakdown allows identification of the phenomena that lead to the apparent disparity.

Substituting Equations (7) and (11) into Equation (6) and solving for the average inter-transaction issue time t_t gives:

$$t_t = \frac{c}{p}nk_dT_h + \frac{c}{p}B + \frac{T_f}{p} + \frac{T_r}{p} \quad (18)$$

Each of the four terms in Equation (18) represents the contribution to t_t from a distinct component:

$\frac{c}{p}nk_dT_h$ represents the contribution from *variable message overhead*—those components of message latency that increase with increased communication distance.

$\frac{c}{p}B$ represents the contribution from *fixed message overhead*—those components of message latency that are fixed with respect to changes in communication distance.

$\frac{T_f}{p}$ represents the contribution from *fixed transaction overhead*—those components of transaction latency that are constant with respect to message latency.

$\frac{T_r}{p}$ represents the contribution from *actual CPU cycles*.

Of these four components, only variable message overhead increases with communication distance. Thus the exploitation of physical locality can only affect the contribution of variable message overhead.

Figure 8 plots the contribution of each of these components for ideal and random mappings of the application of Section 3 on a 1,000 processor machine for one, two, and four hardware

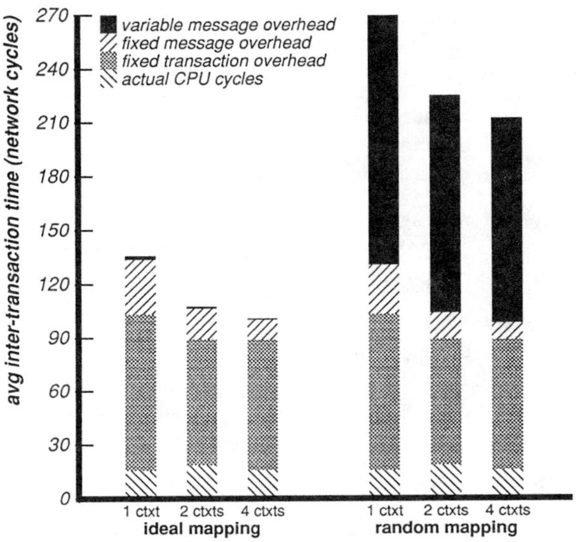

Figure 8: Breakdown of factors contributing to average inter-transaction issue time t_t for ideal and random mappings (1000 processors, $k = 10$, $n = 2$).

contexts. In moving from ideal to random mappings, the absolute contribution of fixed components declines slightly (no more than a few cycles)[6], while the contribution of variable message overhead increases drastically, as expected. Because these drastic increases only serve to bring the contribution due to variable message overhead on par with that from the fixed components, their net impact on inter-transaction issue time is limited to a factor of two or so.

In each of the six cases shown in Figure 8, fixed transaction overhead constitutes around two-thirds of the total fixed component. While this might seem inordinately large, in absolute terms, it corresponds to around 1 or 1.5 μs, assuming the timings discussed in Section 3. Further, recall that for this application an average transaction requires three or four network messages. This fixed overhead of 1 or 1.5 μs includes not only the sending and receiving overhead for those messages, but also any memory accesses and cache coherency processing necessary to complete a transaction.

When the relative balance of computation speed and communication bandwidth isn't as skewed in favor of communication as for the architecture described in Section 3, the fraction of inter-transaction time due to fixed transaction overhead and actual CPU cycles is reduced. Such a reduction increases the relative magnitude of increases in communication costs, thus allowing greater gains when physical locality is exploited.

Table 1 shows the impact of reducing network speed relative to processor speed by factors of two, four, and eight for the one context application for thousand- and million-processor machines. Similar results are obtained with two and four hardware contexts. As expected, the greater the relative cost of communication, the greater the benefit of exploiting physical locality.

Increasing the network dimension n affords both shorter average communication distances for random mappings on machines of a given size (see Equation (17)) and lower values of T_h for large machines (see Equation (16)). Because both of these effects

[6] This decline is due to decreased contention for processor-network channels, as discussed in Section 2.4.

Network Speed	Expected gain for 10^3 processors	Expected gain for 10^6 processors
2x faster	2.1	41.2
same	3.1	68.3
2x slower	4.5	101.6
4x slower	5.9	134.3

Table 1: Impact of reducing relative network speed on expected gains. Network speed is measured relative to processor speed; "2x faster" represents the architecture described in Section 3.

reduce communication latencies when random mappings are used without changing the situation when ideal mappings are used, the impact of exploiting physical locality on end performance is lower when higher dimensional networks ($n > 2$) are used.

5 Related Work

In [5], Chittor and Enbody present data obtained from running experiments similar to those described in Section 3 on the Ametek 2010, a distributed-memory, mesh-connected multiprocessor somewhat similar to that used in this paper. For the sizes of machines measured (up to 144 nodes), they note that the effect of contention for network resources, while observable, does not significantly impact end performance. From their measurements, they extrapolate that the impact of network contention will be far more substantial as machine sizes scale. Both conclusions are well borne out by the model presented in this paper.

On a different tack, Scherson and Corbett [11] introduce a framework for bounding the maximum expected speedup of different types of applications running on mesh-connected multiprocessors. Because they assume that communication latency is proportional to communication distance, the results presented in this paper lend credence to their model.

Finally, Agarwal [1] presents the network model described in Section 2. He uses the model to demonstrate that exploitation of physical locality enables networks to provide lower message latencies for a given message injection rate. However, because fixed message rates are assumed, independent of observed message latencies, the absolute conclusions drawn about the impact of exploiting physical locality are only appropriate for applications that are completely insensitive to changes in communication latency.

6 Summary

For multiprocessors with NUCL interconnection networks, physical locality will become an important element of the performance equation as machine sizes continue to increase. This paper develops a framework that allows accurate modeling of these effects. Using this framework, we obtain rough upper bounds on the performance impact of exploiting physical locality in architectures utilizing two-dimensional mesh interconnects.

We introduce a novel application model that characterizes application and processor behavior with three parameters relating to computation grain, latency sensitivity, and physical locality. We present a framework for combining this model with models for communication mechanisms and interconnection networks. Behavior predicted by the combined model agrees closely with that observed in detailed simulations of a complete multiprocessor system.

Previous studies of interconnection network behavior (e.g. [1]) fail to account for the feedback between networks and applications. We show that when the number of communication transactions each multiprocessor node can have outstanding is bounded, this feedback prevents processors from loading k-ary n-dimensional mesh interconnection networks to a point where communication latencies become unbounded. In fact, we show that when this condition is met, average per-hop communication latency approaches a constant value, the value of which is determined by average message size B, an application's latency sensitivity s (which is proportional to the average number of transactions a node keeps outstanding), and the network dimension n. Further, we demonstrate that this limiting value can be approached on machines with a few thousand processors. Finally, because average per-hop latencies are limited in this manner, we conclude that exploiting physical locality to reduce average communication distance can only provide performance improvements that are linear in the factor by which communication distance is reduced.

Using the modeling framework, we show that for two-dimensional mesh interconnects and the architecture used in the simulation experiments (in which processors are clocked half as fast as network switches), upper bounds on the performance improvement from exploiting physical locality are around two for machines with 1,000 processors and roughly 50 for machines with a million processors. Decreasing the relative network speed leads to larger upper bounds—slowing the network by a factor of eight increased these bounds by roughly a factor of three.

Finally, Figure 8 demonstrates the conventional maxim that fixed communication overheads must be small to support efficient execution of applications with small computation grain. The figure also raises an interesting corollary to this bit of common wisdom: The smaller the computation grain that can be efficiently supported, the larger the potential benefit of exploiting physical locality.

We believe that these basic results, suitably modified, will continue to hold for architectures using interconnection network topologies other than the k-ary n-dimensional meshes used in this paper.

7 Acknowledgments

The research reported in this paper is funded in part by NSF grant # MIP-9012773, in part by DARPA contract # N00014-87-K-0825, and in part by a NSF Presidential Young Investigator Award.

A Nomenclature

n mesh network dimension
k mesh network radix (side length)
N total number of processors

T_r average thread run length between successive communication transactions
s latency sensitivity
d average communication distance

p degree of hardware multithreading
T_s context switch time
c number of messages in "critical path" of a transaction
g average number of messages per transaction
T_f fixed component of transaction model

T_t average transaction latency
t_t average per-processor inter-transaction issue time
r_t average per-processor transaction issue rate

T_m average message latency
t_m average per-processor inter-message injection time
r_m average per-processor message injection rate

B average message size (in flits)
k_d average distance a message travels in each dimension
ρ network channel utilization
T_h average per-hop message latency

References

[1] Anant Agarwal. Limits on Interconnection Network Performance. *IEEE Transations on Parallel and Distributed Systems*, pages 398–412, October 1991.

[2] Anant Agarwal, David Chaiken, Kirk Johnson, David Kranz, John Kubiatowicz, Kiyoshi Kurihara, Beng-Hong Lim, Gino Maa, and Dan Nussbaum. The MIT Alewife Machine: A Large-Scale Distributed-Memory Multiprocessor. Technical Report MIT/LCS/TM-454, MIT Laboratory for Computer Science, June 1991.

[3] Anant Agarwal, Beng-Hong Lim, David Kranz, and John Kubiatowicz. APRIL: A Processor Architecture for Multiprocessing. In *Proceedings of the 17th Annual International Symposium on Computer Architecture*, pages 104–114, June 1990.

[4] David Chaiken, John Kubiatowicz, and Anant Agarwal. LimitLESS Directories: A Scalable Cache Coherence Scheme. In *Proceedings of the Fourth International Conference on Architectural Support for Programming Languages and Operating Systems (ASPLOS IV)*, pages 224–234, April 1991.

[5] Suresh Chittor and Richard Enbody. Performance Evaluation of Mesh-Connected Wormhole-Routed Networks for Interprocessor Communication in Multicomputers. In *Proceedings of Supercomputing '90*, pages 647–656, November 1990.

[6] William J. Dally. Performance Analysis of *k*-ary *n*-cube Interconnection Networks. *IEEE Transations on Computers*, pages 775–785, June 1990.

[7] Kirk Johnson and Anant Agarwal. The Impact of Communication Locality on Large-Scale Multiprocessor Performance. Technical Report MIT/LCS/TM-463, MIT Laboratory for Computer Science, February 1992.

[8] Clyde P. Kruskal and Marc Snir. The Performance of Multistage Interconnection Networks for Multiprocessors. *IEEE Transactions on Computers*, pages 1091–1098, December 1983.

[9] Dan Nussbaum and Anant Agarwal. Scalability of Parallel Machines. *Communications of the ACM*, pages 56–61, March 1991.

[10] G. N. S. Prasanna. Structure Driven Multiprocessor Compilation of Numeric Problems. Technical Report MIT/LCS/TR-502, MIT Laboratory for Computer Science, April 1991.

[11] Isaac D. Scherson and Peter F. Corbett. Communications Overhead and the Expected Speedup of Multidimensional Mesh-Connected Parallel Processors. *Journal of Parallel and Distributed Computing*, pages 86–96, January 1991.

[12] Michael E. Wolf and Monica S. Lam. A Data Locality Optimizing Algorithm. In *Proceedings of the ACM SIGPLAN '91 Conference on Programming Language Design and Implementation*, pages 30–44, June 1991.

Performance of the SCI Ring

Steven L. Scott, James R. Goodman and Mary K. Vernon

Department of Computer Sciences
University of Wisconsin - Madison

Abstract

The Scalable Coherent Interface (SCI) is an emerging IEEE standard that provides computer-bus-like services to a set of nodes via fast, unidirectional links. This paper presents the first detailed performance study of the SCI ring, using both analytical models and simulation. Performance is analyzed for uniform and non-uniform traffic, and the effect of the ring's flow control protocol is studied.

The queueing model is based on an M/G/1 queue, augmented to include the effect of packet trains on the mean and variance of the source transmission time. The model is validated against simulation results, and shown to be quantitatively accurate for uniform workloads, and at least qualitatively accurate for non-uniform workloads. The flow control mechanism is shown to effectively prevent node starvation and reduce the ability of nodes to unfairly consume ring bandwidth, but at the cost of decreased overall ring utilization. The SCI ring is also compared to a standard bus, modeled with a simple M/G/1 queue, and shown to provide substantially higher throughputs and lower latency than a bus with realistic clock speeds.

1. INTRODUCTION

The Scalable Coherent Interface (SCI) is a proposed IEEE standard that provides very-high-performance, bus-like functionality to a large number of processor nodes [IEEE91, Gust92]. Using a packet-based communication protocol based on unidirectional links connected in a ring, it provides a shared-memory interface, including cache coherence, to the nodes. The protocol has been developed over a period of approximately four years, has included participation by representatives of dozens of companies and many universities and has assembled appropriate expertise in many different disciplines to solve the plethora of problems associated with a novel design.

The SCI includes protocols at three different levels: the physical level, the logical level, and the cache-coherence level. The logical level provides the protocol for reliably transmitting packets between nodes. The node interface consists of two unidirectional links, an input and an output, which are used to connect nodes together in the basic topology of a ring. The ring can in theory be arbitrarily large, but performance considerations lead to the expectation that a ring will be limited to a modest number of processors, numbering at most a few dozen and perhaps as few as two. Larger systems can be built by connecting together multiple rings by means of switches, that is, nodes containing more than a single interface.

The ring is unusual in that each node provides a bypass buffer capable of storing temporarily a packet arriving from its upstream neighbor while it is transmitting a packet. This buffer allows nodes to transmit concurrently rather than having to wait for a token, but results in long latency if all nodes happen to initiate transmission simultaneously on an idle ring. Because of the novel construction of the ring and the attendant clock rates achievable in the design, very high performance is expected, and a peak bandwidth of one gigabyte per second is easy to demonstrate. The nature of the protocol, however, makes both the achievable bandwidth and the observed latency much harder to predict. Reported here is the most detailed study to date attempting to analyze the performance of a single ring. It includes analyzing the performance under a variety of conditions, including the number of nodes in the ring, the service rate of queues, the size of packets, and the distribution of sources and destinations for the packets. In addition, a mechanism to assure fairness in the ring is investigated to assess its impact on the performance. The SCI protocol does provide priority scheduling, but this aspect of the protocol is not investigated in this study. The ring is studied both by the use of an analytical model and through simulation.

The remainder of the paper is organized as follows. Section 2 of the paper describes the protocol of the SCI logical layer. Section 3 describes the analytical model. Section 4 presents and analyzes the results of the study, and Section 5 summarizes the conclusions.

2. THE SCI LOGICAL-LEVEL PROTOCOL

The key idea behind the SCI logical level protocol is the use of unidirectional, point-to-point links that can be clocked at a rate independent of the signal latency between nodes. The basic building block of an SCI system is a *ring* (sometimes called a *ringlet*) of two or more nodes connected by these links. The protocol is designed such that short of an actual hardware failure packets are guaranteed to be accepted by each node that they pass through as they traverse the ring. Therefore, a node can output a *symbol* of information on every clock cycle, and there is *no* direct feedback from a node to its upstream neighbor. A packet might not be accepted by its *destination*, however, due to queue congestion. The protocol uses packet-level acknowledgements to deal with this issue.

2.1. Basic Protocol

This section presents a summary of the basic protocol. Details such as ring initialization and error detection/recovery are not covered, nor is all the functionality of the standard presented. Buffer management is somewhat simplified; we assume a single transmit and receive queue per node, whereas the actual system requires dual queues in order to support a higher level protocol. The cache coherence level of the SCI standard is not considered at all. Much more detail can be found in the standard [IEEE91].

A packet traversing an SCI ring is sent from a *source* node to a *target* node in the form of a *send packet*. The target node then *strips* the send packet, and returns an *echo packet* around the remainder of the ring. This echo packet tells the source node whether or not the send packet was accepted by the target. If the packet was not accepted, then the source must retransmit it.

A send packet consists of a 16 byte header and an optional data component of up to 256 bytes. The header contains command and control information, a 16-bit CRC (Cyclic Redundancy Check) and a 64-bit memory address (16-bit node id and 48-bit intra-node address). We assume a data component size of 64 bytes, which corresponds to the SCI cache line size. Echo packets are 8 bytes long. We assume a 16 bit link width (the standard defines both a 16 bit copper implementation and a serial, fiber optic implementation)

Figure 1 shows a block diagram of an SCI node and ring interface. A node transmits a symbol onto its output link on every SCI cycle. When a node has no packet to transmit, it sends an *idle symbol*. When a source desires to send a packet over the ring, it places the packet in its transmit queue. If the ring buffer is empty and the node is not currently transmitting a packet from the stripper, the send packet is immediately output onto the ring. When a source packet is transmitted, a copy must either must be saved at the head of the queue (thus blocking further transmissions) or placed into an optional *active buffer*. The copy is either discarded or used for retransmission when the echo packet is received.

Upon arrival at the downstream node, a send packet is parsed and either stripped or *passed* along the ring. In the absence of contention, a passing packet may be routed directly from the *stripper* to the output link. If the ring buffer is not empty or the transmit queue at the node is currently transmitting a packet, the passing packet is routed into the ring buffer. If a passing packet and a source packet are ready to transmit on the same cycle, the transmit queue is given priority and the passing packet is routed to the ring buffer.

When the transmit queue is done transmitting a packet, if the ring buffer has accumulated any symbols, output resumes from the ring buffer (which may still be receiving symbols from the stripper). This is known as the *recovery stage*, and lasts until the ring buffer is completely emptied. The node is not allowed to transmit another source packet during the recovery stage. To empty the ring buffer, the node either must see gaps in the stream of incoming packets, or create gaps in the packet stream by stripping packets for which it is the target. During these gaps, the buffer can be drained while not being simultaneously filled. If the ring buffer is empty after a source transmission completes, then there is no recovery stage.

When a send packet reaches its target, it is stripped and either placed into the receive queue (space permitting) or discarded. The node uses the bandwidth created by stripping the packet to insert idle symbols, transmit symbols from the transmit queue or drain the ring buffer. The last four symbols of the send packet are replaced with an echo packet that continues its way

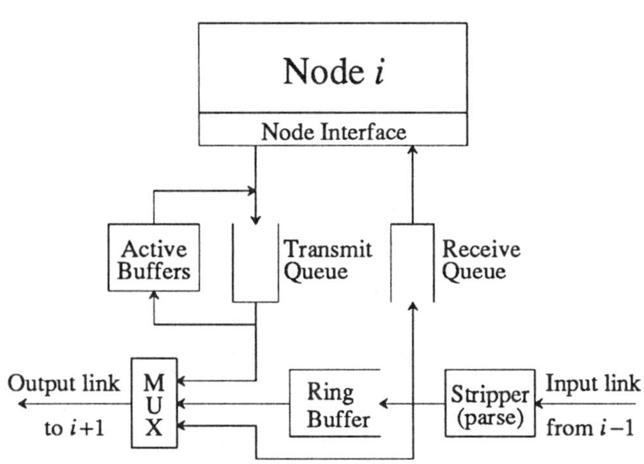

Figure 1: An SCI Node

around the ring to the packet's source. At the source, the echo packet is matched with a saved send packet in an active buffer or at the head of the transmit queue, and the appropriate action is taken (discarding or retransmitting the send packet).

One last feature of the protocol that needs mentioning is that packets are always separated by at least one idle symbol. This allows the stripper to periodically delete an idle symbol, if necessary to adjust for a slowly varying clock period between neighbors (this is known as *elasticity*). It also assures timely distribution of priority and other information carried in the idle symbols. We do not consider elasticity or priorities here, but *do* require the intervening idle symbols. For the purposes of the basic model, this is equivalent to increasing the length of all packets by one symbol.

2.2. Flow Control

The basic protocol described above works fine for uniform traffic rates and routing distributions. However, it allows for nodes to be unfairly starved in the presence of certain non-uniform traffic patterns. Consider a node that partially fills its ring buffer during a transmit queue transmission. If the node then receives a continuous stream of passing packets, then its recovery stage can take arbitrarily long, denying it the chance to transmit another packet. For this reason, the SCI protocol includes a flow control mechanism that uses *go bits* in the idle symbols to enforce an approximate round robin ordering under heavy loads. The flow control mechanism is complicated by a priority mechanism that partitions the ring's bandwidth between high and low priority nodes. While the priority mechanism has certain special uses, such as in real-time systems, it is not likely to be used for general purpose multiprocessors. We assume that all nodes have equal priority, and present the simpler flow control mechanism that results.

Each idle symbol contains a go bit which is either set (making it a *go-idle*) or cleared (making it a *stop-idle*). The stripper passes all idles and passing packets (as well as echos for packets that it strips) to the transmitter stage of the node interface. When it strips a packet, it fills the empty slots with idle symbols. When a node is not transmitting a packet from its transmit queue and is not in the recovery stage, it simply passes all symbols -- send, echo and idle -- from the stripper to its output link. Whenever the transmitter emits a go-idle, it continues to emit go-idles until the next packet boundary, possibly converting passing stop-idles into go-idles (this is called go-bit *extension*).

A node may *only* transmit a source packet immediately following a go-idle. During transmission of a packet, a node maintains the inclusive-OR of all go bits it receives from the stripper. If the ring buffer does not fill up at all during transmission, then the node postpends an idle symbol to its packet using the saved go bit it maintained during the transmission, and then continues to either transmit another source packet or output symbols from the stripper.

If the ring buffer *does* fill up at all during transmit queue transmission, then the node enters the recovery stage. All idles sent during the recovery stage, including the idle postpended to the original source transmission, are stop-idles. The node continues, however, to maintain the inclusive-OR of go bits it receives throughout the recovery stage. When the recovery stage ends (the last symbol is drained from the ring buffer), the saved go bit is released in the postpending idle just as it was for the postpending idle of a source transmission when the recovery state was not entered.

The stop idles that are transmitted during a recovery stage inhibit the downstream neighbors from sending new packets and eventually provide enough slack for the node to drain its ring buffer and send a packet. In the absence of contention, all idles on the ring will be go-idles, and a newly arriving send packet can always be sent immediately.

3. ANALYTICAL MODEL

This section presents an analytical performance model of the SCI ring. The model is useful for a variety of reasons: it allows the quick exploration of a large state space, it's precisely defined and can be implemented by other researchers and engineers, and it helps us gain insight into the processes being modeled. Results from the model, as well as from detailed simulations, will be presented in section 4.

The model is based upon an approximate, iterative solution of the M/G/1 queue [Klei75] (see Figure 2). It does not consider flow control, limited active buffers or target queue overflow. The effect of these factors can be determined from simulation results. The model does consider, and effectively deals with, ring buffer fill-up during transmit queue transmissions, the transmission recovery process, the formation and effect of packet trains[1], non-homogeneous packet arrival rates and non-uniform packet destination probabilities, delays due to queueing in ring buffers and variance of transmit queue service times. We present only a summary of the model here, highlighting the important aspects of the approach.

3.1. Model Inputs

Inputs to the model are the ring size (N), packet arrival rates (λ_i), routing probabilities (z_{ij}), packet lengths (l_{addr}, l_{data}, l_{echo}), packet type ratio (f_{data}, f_{addr}), transmission delay (T_{wire}) and parsing delay (T_{parse}). Note that each node has a distinct arrival rate and a distinct, possibly non-uniform packet destination probability distribution.

3.2. Discussion of Model Equations

The model equations are given in Appendix A. Equations (1) through (14) are straightforward. In the first twelve equations quantities such as mean and variance of packets lengths, link utilizations, and various throughputs and ratios are derived directly from the inputs. Note that packet lengths include the idle symbols. The model then ignores these idles and considers only the remaining "free" idles.

Two key assumptions in the model are that the number of idle symbols between packet trains is geometrically distributed and that packet trains contain a geometrically distributed number of packets[2]. Thus the probability than an idle symbol is directly followed by a packet, $P_{pkt,i}$, is the inverse of the mean time between packet trains (Equation (15)), and the expected remaining length of a passing packet train that is interrupted by the arrival of a packet from the transmit queue is equal to the mean length of a packet train (first occurrence of $l_{train,i}$ in Equation (16)).

The transmit queue service time includes the recovery period, which lasts until the ring buffer is empty. Thus total service time is equal to the time that would elapse if we were to simply discard the send packet and wait until a number of idle symbols equal to the length of the packet passed through the node. The first half of Equation (16) accounts for the possible residual life of a passing packet train when a send packet arrives to an idle transmit queue. The second half accounts for the remaining time taken to observe the required number of idle symbols. After each of the idle symbols, another packet train passes through with probability $P_{pkt,i}$.

Equations (18) - (22) compute new estimates of coupling probabilities. The second term of Equation (18) considers new couplings that are formed when a source packet is injected at node i. Equation (19) calculates the mean number of coupled packets that enter the stripper at node i for each packet stripped, where stripped packets include echo packets that are consumed and send packets that are converted into echo packets. Equation (21) considers couplings from the upstream neighbor that are destroyed by the stripper at node i. Equation (22) computes the net effect of stripping packets and removing couplings. Note that we assume in these equations that coupling probabilities are not correlated with packet length. The relation between service time and coupling probabilities is cyclic. The equations are solved iteratively until the coupling probabilities converge.

After the above convergence, several metrics can be computed. The variance of the packet train length (Equation (24)) is computed using the geometric distribution of the number of packets in a packet train. The variance of the transmit queue service time (Equation (26)) is computed using the binomial distribution of the number of packet trains arriving during the transmission/recovery period. The variance calculation in Equation (26) also assumes that the total recovery time is a constant (Equation (25)) times the last term of Equation (16). That is, we assume a strong correlation between the delay due to packet trains arriving during the recovery period (the last term of Equation (16)) and the residual life of a passing packet train (the first half of Equation (16)). Finally, the mean backlog seen by a passing packet at node i (Equation (32)) is computed by dividing the total backlog created by an injected packet, by the mean number of passing packets per injected packet.

Experience implementing this model has shown that convergence is faster for smaller ring sizes. We required average change in coupling probabilities to be less than 10^{-5} for convergence. Approximately 10 iterations were needed for N=4, 30 for N=16 and 110 for N=64. Total time to solve the model for N=64 on a DECstation 3100 is about 1 second. Comparable simulation time (simulating 9.3 million cycles, as was done for this paper) is over 4 hours.

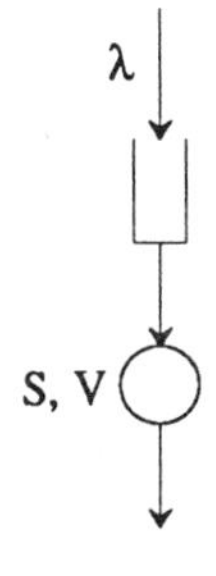

$$c = \frac{\sqrt{V}}{S} \qquad \rho = \lambda S$$

$$Q = \rho + \frac{\rho^2(1+c^2)}{2(1-\rho)}$$

$$L = \frac{Var(S)+S^2}{2S}$$

$$W = (Q-\rho)S + \rho L$$

Figure 2: The M/G/1 queue

λ - arrival rate; S - mean service time; V - variance of service time; c - coefficient of variation; ρ - utilization; Q - mean queue length; L - mean residual life; W - mean wait time

[1]Note that these packet trains arise from collisions between passing packets and source packets as well as from the insertion of trains at source nodes.

[2] We comment on the accuracy of these and other model assumptions in section 4.9.

4. RESULTS

This section presents results derived from both the analytical model and a detailed, parameter-driven simulator of the SCI ring. The inputs to the model and to the simulator are identical. The ring is modeled as an open system (Poisson arrivals), with the arrival rates, packet lengths, mix of packet types, routing probabilities, ring size, wire transmission delay and packet parsing delay specified as inputs. The simulator has the additional ability to consider flow control and limited buffer space (active buffers and receive queues). Since the ring is modeled as an open system, latency becomes infinite as saturation is reached. An actual system, of course, would have a limit to the number of queued or outstanding requests, and nodes would be stalled at some point rather than continuing to add requests. Section 4.6 illustrates the component of total delay due to queueing.

The unit of length in the model and simulator is one link width, and the unit of time is one clock cycle. We assume (as per the standard) a 16-bit link with a 2 ns cycle time. Using these assumptions, we present output latencies in *ns* and throughputs in *bytes per ns*. Throughputs are calculated using the entire packet, including address, command and control information. Section 4.7 considers sustained data throughput using a read request/read response model.

Many other parameters have been fixed or limited in order to make the problem space tractable. Since the number of nodes in a ring is expected to be small, we analyzed ring sizes of 4 and 16 nodes. Except where noted, we assumed that 60% of send packets were address/command only (16 bytes), and 40% included data blocks (80 bytes) (we refer to these as address packets and data packets for the remainder of the paper). This corresponds to a workload in which most of the traffic consists of paired address and data packets. We assume a fixed minimum delay of 4 cycles per node traversed by a packet: one cycle to gate a symbol onto an output link, one cycle for the symbol to reach its downstream neighbor and two cycles to parse a symbol before routing it to the local node or to the next output link. Message latencies also include one cycle to originally queue the packet, and a delay equal to the packet length to consume the packet as it arrives at the target node. We assume unlimited active buffers at each node, but only one or two active buffers are actually needed to approximate this [Scot91].

The simulator implements the protocol described in section 2 on a cycle by cycle basis, explicitly tracking each symbol on the ring. Simulations were run for 9.3 million cycles each, and 90% confidence intervals were computed using the method of batched means. Confidence intervals were generally under or about 1%, except near saturation, where they sometimes increased to a few percent.

4.1. Uniform traffic

Figure 3 shows the performance of 4- and 16-node SCI rings with uniform arrival rates and routing probabilities and no flow control. Each graph includes three sets of data, one with all address packets, one with all data packets and one with 40% data packets. Both simulation and model results are shown. The model is very accurate for the 4-node ring. For the 16-node ring, the model is accurate for the all-address-packet workload, but underestimates latency under moderate to heavy loading for the other workloads. Even for the worst case, however, the model provides a good estimate for the behavior of the ring. The reason for the error is identified and discussed in section 4.9.

Throughput is higher for the workload with larger packet sizes. There are two reasons for this. First, a smaller proportion of the ring bandwidth is used for the idle symbols that must separate each packet (we include only bytes within packets in the throughput measure). Second, the bandwidth consumed by echo packets becomes smaller relative to the bandwidth used by send packets. Throughput could also be increased by use of packet locality. Unlike a shared bus, a ring requires less bandwidth if the packets are sent a shorter distance (message latency is similarly reduced). For the purposes of this paper, we assume equally distributed destinations.

Figure 4 illustrates the effect of flow control on uniform traffic for ring sizes of 4 and 16. Each graph includes two sets of data, one with all address packets, and one with all data packets. Results for the mixed address/data workload fall in between these. We can see that even with uniform traffic loading, flow control significantly reduces the maximum throughput. The reason for this is that there are times when a node cannot transmit a source packet, even though there are available slots in which to do so, because another node has stopped sending go bits in order to clear its ring buffer. The degradation is greater for the 16-node ring than for the 4-node ring. Simulations indicate that the throughput degradation from flow control is greatest for ring sizes in the 10 to 20 range, and actually lessens slightly for larger rings [Scot91].

4.2. Node Starvation

This section examines the situation in which a node is inhibited from transmitting by reducing the number of breaks it sees in its pass-though traffic. Figure 5 presents the performance for 4- and 16-node rings where all nodes are routing uniformly, except that no packets are routed to node 0 (the starved node). Mean message latencies are plotted for individual source nodes (labeled P0, P1, *etc.*). In Figure 5(a), we see that P0 saturates before the other nodes. As the throughput per node reaches about 3.2 bytes/node/ns, P0's arrivals can no longer be satisfied and its message latency goes to infinity (recall that this is simulated as an open system). As P1, P2 and P3 increase their throughput beyond this point, the realized throughput of P0 is actually driven back down to 0. This causes the unusual shape in the curves for P1 and P2. P1, P2 and P3 all reach the same saturation bandwidth.

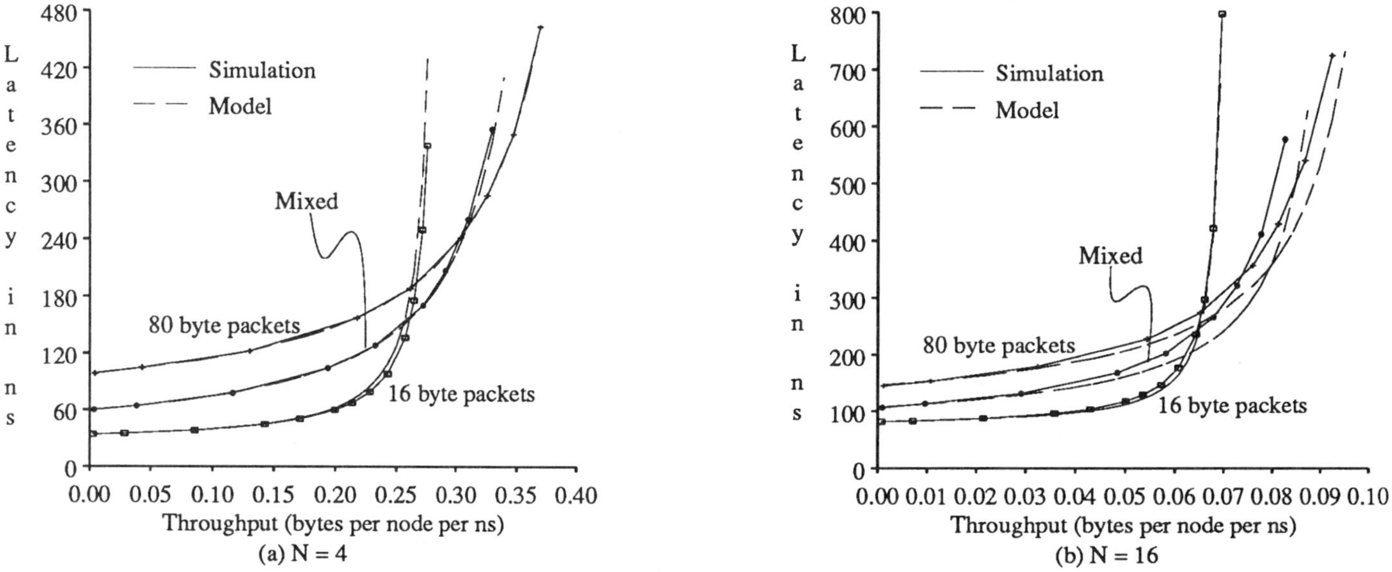

Figure 3: Uniform traffic without flow control

The equations in the model assume that the system is not in saturation, so in order to model the behavior after P0 has saturated, the model detects saturated queues, and automatically throttles back the corresponding arrival rates to keep the transmit queue utilization at exactly one. The model qualitatively predicts correct behavior, including the throttling of P0's throughput and the corresponding inflection points in the P1 curve. However, the model underestimates the impact of the non-uniform traffic, and quantitative error is fairly large when the starved node is in saturation.

For a ring size of 16 (Figure 5(b)), the disparity between nodes is not as pronounced. The starved node reaches almost as high a bandwidth as the other nodes before it saturates. This is because the non-uniform routing causes smaller differences in link utilizations for the larger ring. The model correctly predicts the spread in performance between the starved node (P0) and the least affected node (P15). The absolute error, however, is fairly significant under heavy loads.

Figure 6 demonstrates the effect of flow control on node starvation. Parts (a) and (b) show the message latency for each node as the traffic is varied. In parts (c) and (d), the ring is in saturation (all nodes are trying to send as often as possible), and the realized throughput for each node is shown.

In Figure 6(a), we see that the addition of flow control reduces the disparity between the performance of the four nodes, but at an overall reduction in throughput. The throughput of P0 is not driven back down by the other nodes, as it is without flow control. Note, however, that the performance is not fully equalized; P0 achieves a smaller maximum throughput than P1, P1 achieves a smaller maximum throughput than P2, *etc*.

Figure 6(c) shows the saturation bandwidths for the 4-node ring with P0 still being starved. Without flow control, P1, P2 and P3 all achieve the same throughput, but P0 is *completely* starved.

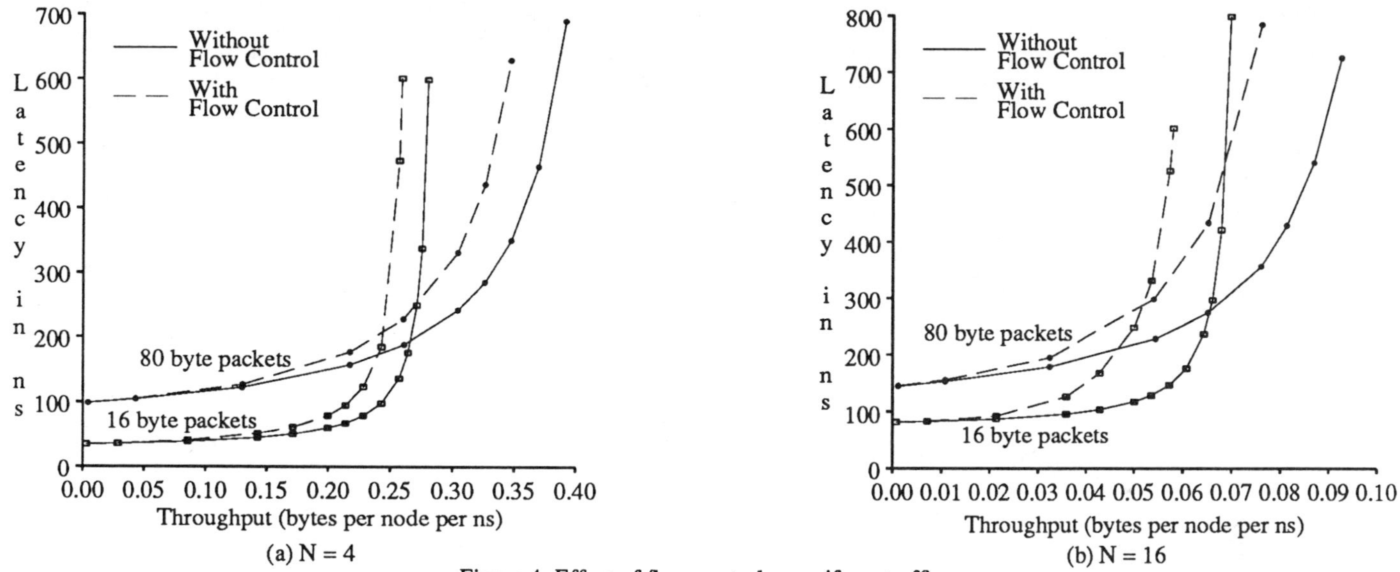

Figure 4: Effect of flow control on uniform traffic

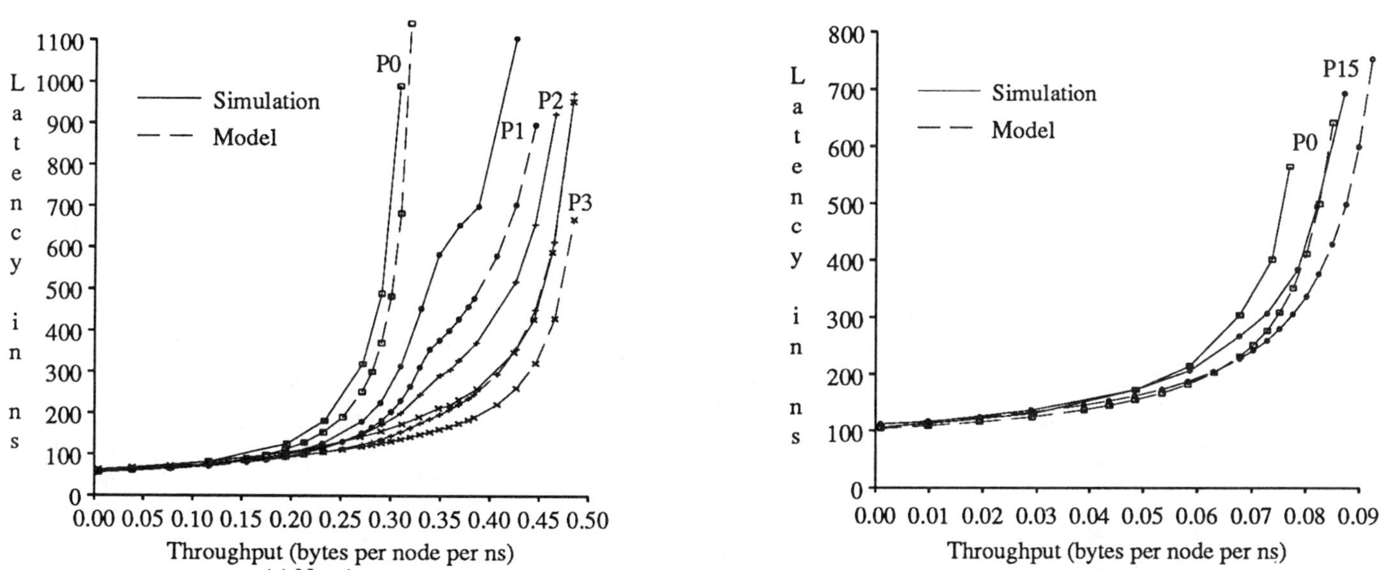

Figure 5: Node starvation without flow control

Because the ring is fully utilized and it is not receiving any packets, it has no opportunities in which to transmit a packet (*i.e*: it enters an infinite recovery stage). The flow control mechanism successfully deals with this problem. With flow control, the total ring throughput is reduced slightly, and the throughput of the non-starved nodes is reduced significantly, but the starved node is no longer kept from transmitting. The flow control mechanism does not achieve full equal partitioning of bandwidth, however. The throughput of a node is limited by how quickly it can empty its ring buffer after a transmission, and the flow control protocol guarantees that even a starved node will make forward progress in the recovery stage by throttling downstream transmissions and thus creating gaps in its incoming packet stream. However, a node whose pass-through traffic is lower overall (due to non-uniform traffic) will still be able to recovery more quickly on average.

Figure 6(b) shows the effect of flow control for a ring size of 16 with P0 being starved. The addition of flow control almost completely equalizes the performance of the various nodes (again at an overall reduction in ring capacity). Figure 6(d) shows the saturation bandwidths for the 16-node ring. Although the impact on P0 was small under light to medium traffic, P0 is completely starved when the ring is fully loaded. Flow control reduces the realized throughput of the non-starved nodes and allows the starved node to transmit. The bandwidth is much more equally divided than it was for the 4-node ring. This is because the differences in link utilizations caused by the non-uniform traffic are smaller for the larger ring.

4.3. Hot Sender

In this section, we examine the ring's behavior in the presence of a "hot sender" (a node that attempts to use as much ring bandwidth as possible). Figure 7 presents the performance for 4- and 16-node rings where packet destinations are uniformly distributed, but node 0 always wants to transmit a packet. P1, the first downstream node from the hot sender, is severely affected by the extra traffic. The hot node degrades the performance of all other nodes on the ring, affecting the closest nodes more heavily.

The model is very accurate for a ring size of four (Figure 7(a)). For a ring size of 16 (Figure 7(b)), the model is qualitatively accurate, but slightly underestimates latency for most of the nodes, and significantly overestimates the latency for the immediate downstream neighbor of the hot node (the reason that the model overestimates P1's latency is actually that it underestimates P0's latency (the hot node), allowing P0 to send more than it would in reality).

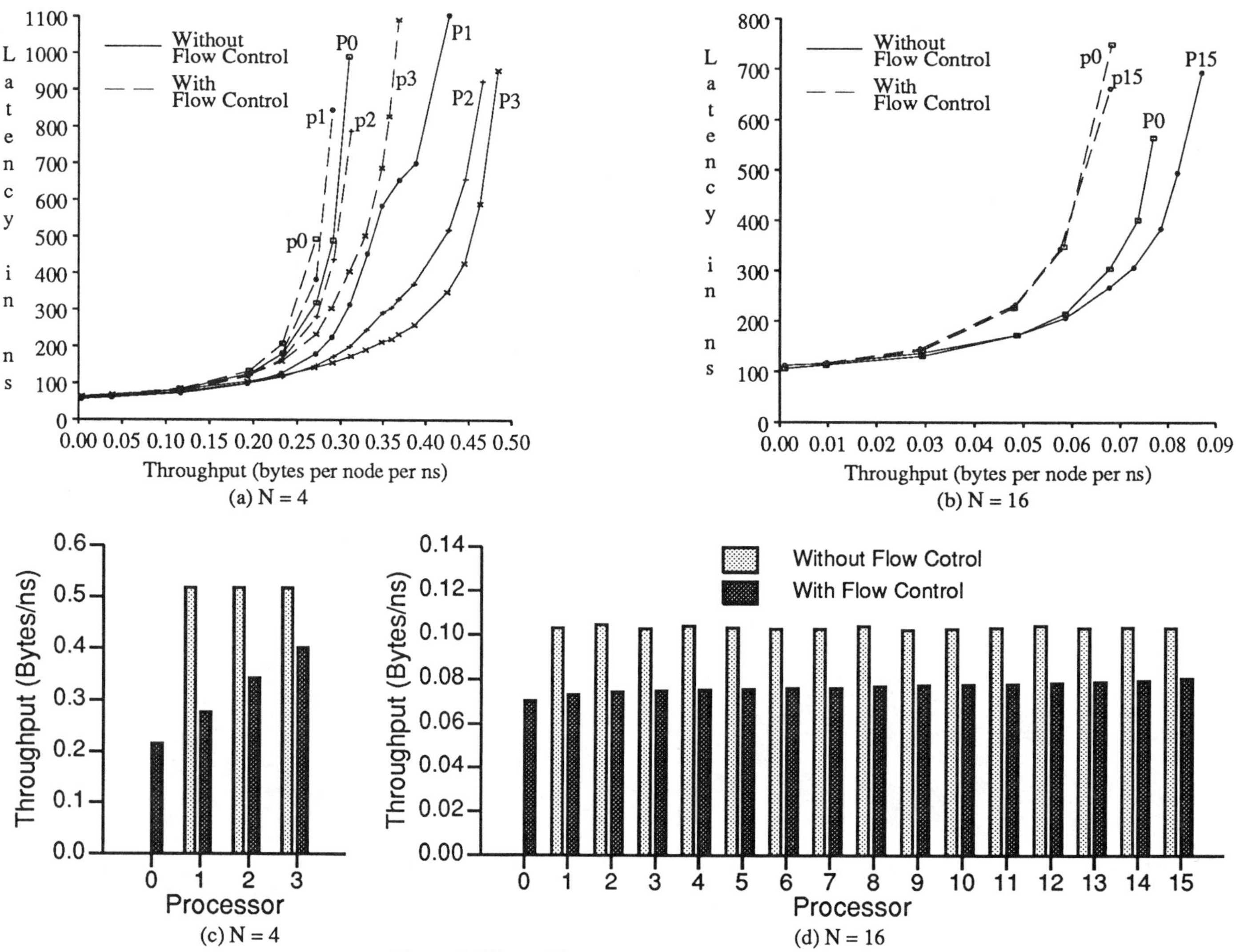

Figure 6: Effect of flow control on node starvation

Figure 8 demonstrates the effect of flow control on a hot sender. Parts (a) and (b) show the message latencies for each node as a function of throughput. The addition of flow control equalizes the effect of the hot node on the message latency for the other nodes on the ring. Performance is improved for some nodes and degraded for others, but the hot node's downstream neighbor is no longer severely penalized.

This phenomenon can be clearly seen in parts (c) and (d), which show vertical slices of the throughput-latency curves under moderate throughput from the "cold" nodes (0.194 bytes/ns in Figure 8(c), 0.048 bytes/ns in Figure 8(d)). Without flow control, the mean message latencies experienced by the cold nodes vary significantly, with the closest downstream nodes being affected the most. With flow control, the hot node affects all other nodes approximately equally. The nearest downstream node, in particular, is no longer subjected to extremely large latencies. The improved ring fairness is achieved at the expense of the hot sender's throughput. Without flow control, it realizes a rate of 0.670 bytes/ns on the 4-node ring. With flow control, it realizes only 0.550 bytes/ns. For the 16-node ring, the hot sender's throughput is reduced from 0.526 bytes/ns to 0.293 bytes/ns. For certain applications, most notably real-time systems, it may be desirable to allow one node or a set of nodes to consume more than their share of ring bandwidth. SCI provides a priority mechanism to satisfy this requirement.

In addition to hot senders and node starvation, we have examined producer-consumer and other non-uniform workloads. Though not presented here, the results are similar. The flow control mechanism reduces the effects of greedy nodes on the rest of the ring, and provides all nodes with a reasonable approximation to their share of the bandwidth, regardless of the non-uniformities present in the communication pattern.

4.4. Comparison to a Conventional Bus

This section compares the SCI ring to a conventional, synchronous bus. The prime advantage of SCI, at the logical-layer level, is its use of fast, point-to-point links. The unidirectional nature of the communication allows the cycle time to be limited only by the speed of the technology. Standard ECL circuitry available in 1992 allows a 2 ns clock. To compare this against a conventional bus, we developed a simple M/G/1 bus model. The model assumes no overhead for arbitration, and single-cycle synchronous transmission in 32-bit chunks. The pin-out for an SCI interface is also 32 bits (16-bit input link plus 16-bit output link).

Figure 9 compares the throughput-latency characteristics of an SCI ring to a bus as the bus cycle time is varied. Data for the SCI ring are from the simulator with flow control in effect. We assume a workload of 60% address packets (16 bytes) and 40% data packets (80 bytes). Ring/bus sizes of 4 and 16 nodes are used. If a synchronous bus had the same cycle time as the SCI ring, it would clearly provide better performance. This is due not only to the bus' greater width, but to the single cycle broadcast latency. With a bus cycle time of 4ns, latency is still lower when lightly loaded, but the maximum throughput is also lower. This is due to the bus' lack of concurrency.

As the bus cycle time is increased, the latency goes up significantly, and the maximum throughput drops off significantly. Realistic bus cycle times range from 20 to 100 ns. A typical high performance shared bus has a 30 ns cycle time. The Stardent Titan graphics supercomputer uses a 31.25 ns bus [Siew91], for example, and the Silicon Graphics Power Series computers use a 30 ns bus [Grap89]. The ELXSI System 6400 used expensive twisted-pair ECL with differential signaling for their shared backplane, achieving a cycle time of 25 ns [Olso83]. The SCI ring provides far greater bandwidth and lower latency than a bus of comparable width running at 20 ns or slower.

As the number of nodes on a ring increases, the average message latency will increase. As the number of nodes on a bus increases, the average message latency will also increase, due to greater contention for the bus and because the cycle time of the bus will have to be increased to accommodate the greater capacitive loading and longer physical distances. Because of the increased cycle time, the total bandwidth of the bus will decrease as well. The cycle time of an SCI ring is independent of ring size.

4.5. Sustained Data Throughput using a Request/Response Model

This section considers total sustained data transfer rates on a ring. We assume that the ring traffic consists solely of read request packets and their associated read response packets. Latencies represent an address packet transmission from a processor to a memory, followed by a data packet transmission from the memory to the processor including receipt of the entire data block (memory

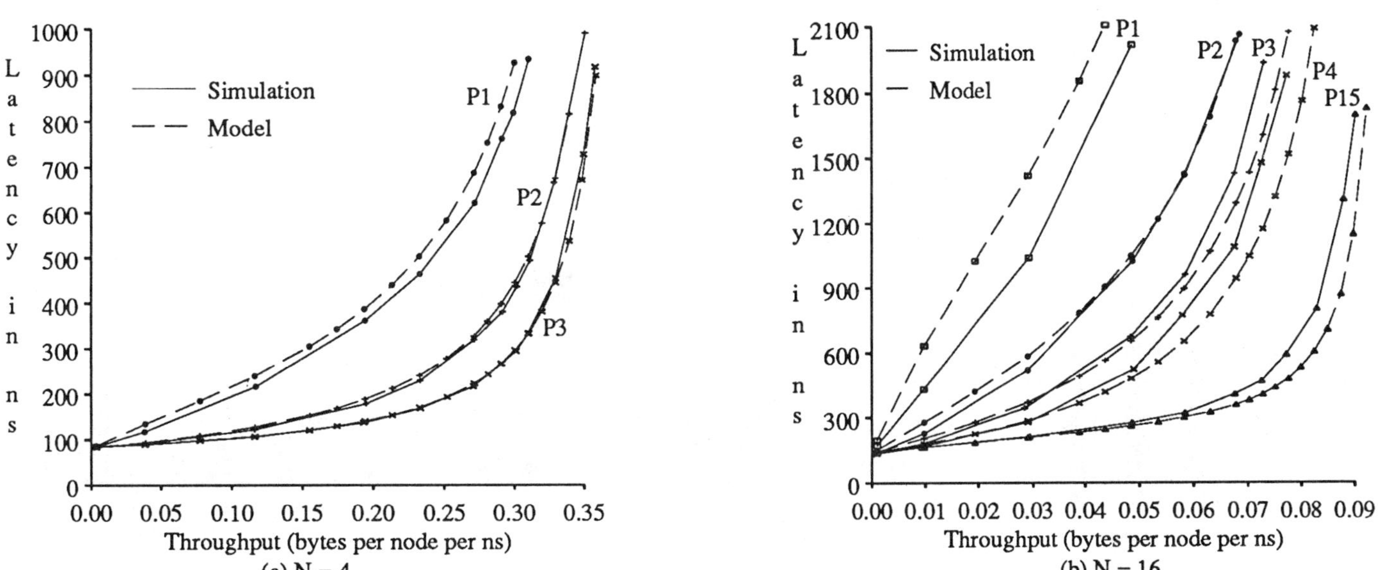

(a) N = 4

(b) N = 16

Figure 7: Hot sender without flow control

lookup time is not included). We use a data block size of 64 bytes, and the throughput includes only the data bytes.

The results are shown in Figure 10. Since an address packet is 16 bytes and a data packet includes a 16 byte header along with the 64 bytes of data, exactly two thirds of the send packet symbols contain data. The actual data throughput is thus two thirds of the total throughput. The throughput shown in Figure 10 is the *total* ring throughput, measured in gigabytes per second.

4.6. Breakdown of Message Latency

In this section, we break the mean message latency into several components. Figure 11 plots results from the analytical model for ring sizes of 4 and 16. The packet traffic is uniform, with 40% of the packets containing 64-byte data blocks. The latency is broken into 4 components. The *Fixed* curve represents latency due to wire transmission delay and fixed switching overheads. The *Transit* curve represents the time from when a transmit queue begins transmitting until the packet is consumed at the destination. The difference between these two curves is due to delays passing through the ring buffers. The *Idle Source* curve represents the latency seen by a packet arriving at an idle transmit queue (there are no packets in front of it and the node is not in the recovery stage). The difference between the *Transit* curve and this curve represents the time a source packet may have to wait while a packet finishes passing through the node. The *Total* curve represents total, end-to-end latency. The gap between the *Transit* curve and this curve represents the total time a packet is queued at a transmit queue before receiving permission to transmit.

Most of the latency under heavy loads is due to waiting in the transmit queues. In a closed system (where there is a limit on the number of queued packets), the delay due to transmit queueing would level off at some point. Delay due to buffer backlog becomes more significant relative to transmit queueing delay as the ring size is increased from 4 to 16. For very large rings, transmission delay becomes dominant except when the ring is very close to saturation.

4.7. Discussion of Model

Below we identify several possible sources of error in our analytical model, and discuss the likely significance of each.

First, we assume geometrically distributed inter-packet-train spacing, whereas simulations show that certain lengths of spaces are much more common. For example, the space created

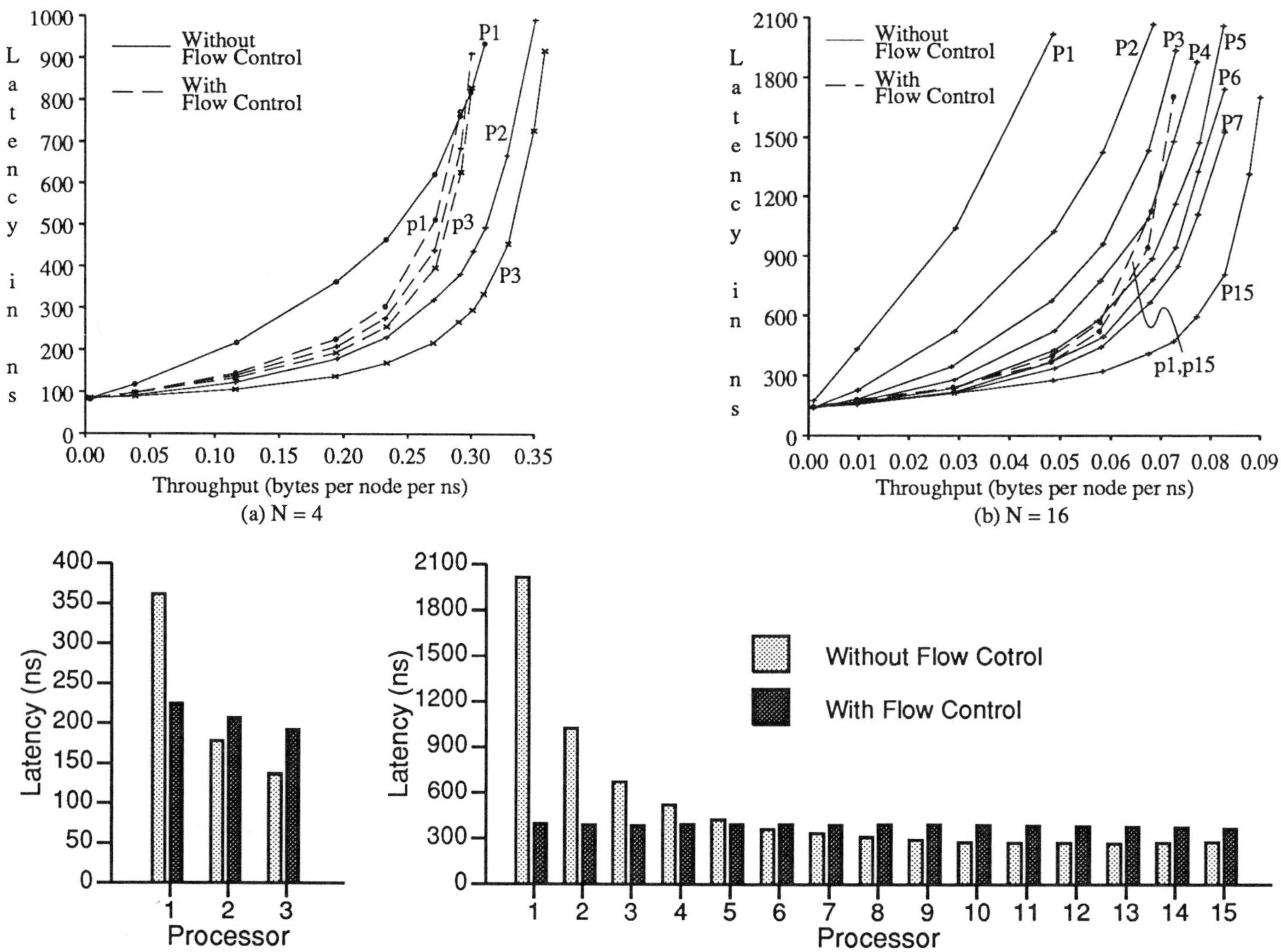

Figure 8: Effect of flow control on hot sender

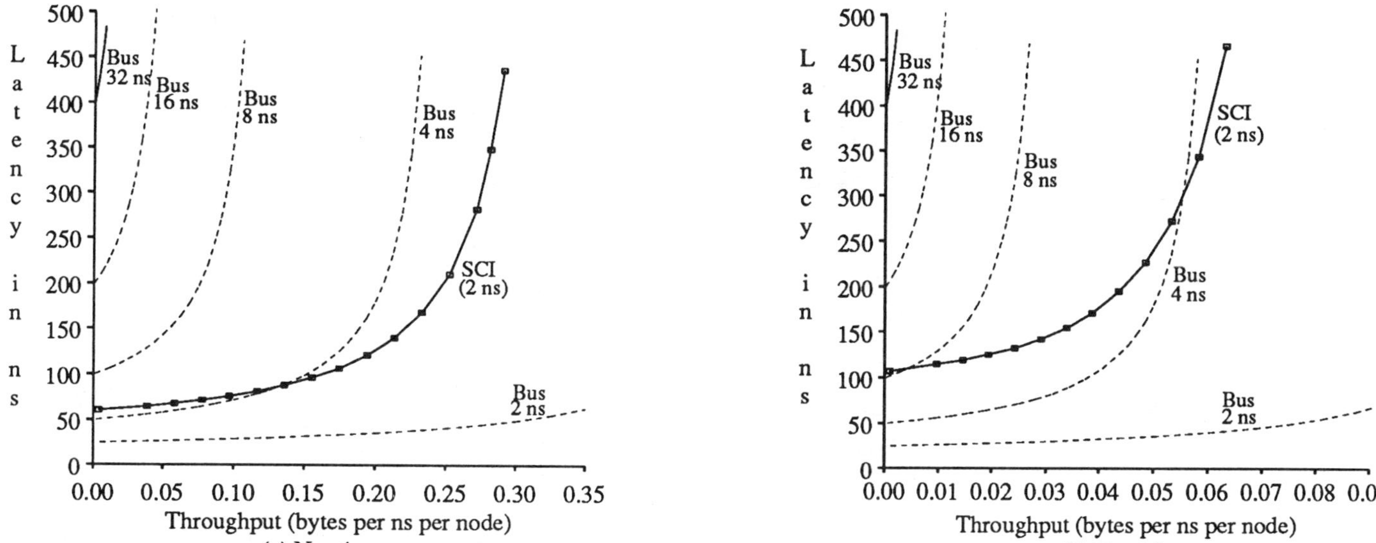

(a) N = 4 (b) N = 16

Figure 9: SCI ring vs conventional bus

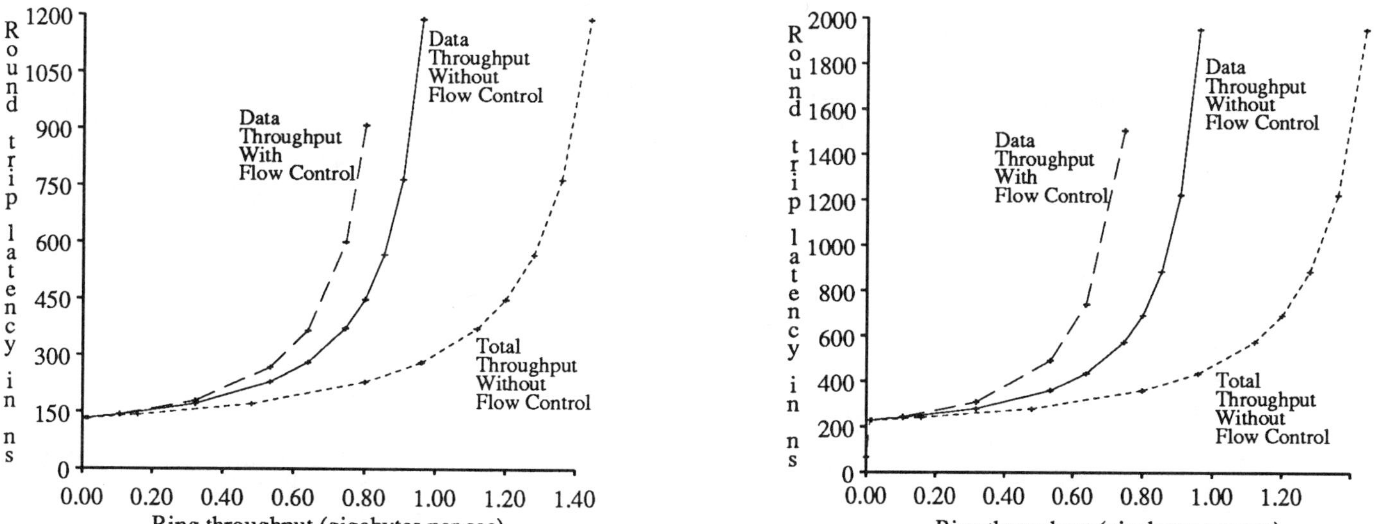

(a) N = 4 (b) N = 16

Figure 10: Sustained data throughput

by replacing an address packet with an echo packet occurs with high frequency. However, simulation estimates of the coefficient of variation of the inter-packet-train spacing, are very close to 1. Thus, we do not anticipate that this assumption causes significant error.

Second, in computing the variance of the recovery period, we do not know the correlation between the residual life of a passing packet train and the remaining portion. We assume a correlation of one, and treat the portion due to residual life of a passing packet train as a constant multiplier to the remaining recovery time (Equation (25)). This slightly overestimates the service time variance, but we do not believe this causes significant error.

Finally, we assume that the transmit queue utilization and the pass-through ring utilization are independent. That is, the model assumes we see the same rate of passing packets regardless of whether the transmit queue is in use. *This is the primary source of error in the model*. We have found using the simulator that the pass-through traffic tends to be lower than average when the transmit queue is idle, and higher than average when the transmit queue is active (during the transmission/recovery stage). This causes the model to underestimate the length of the recovery stage, thus underestimating the overall message latency. The error increases as the mean length of the recovery period increases, which causes the error to grow for larger rings and packet sizes.

Two worthwhile directions for future research are to reduce the error in the current model and to extend the model to account for flow control.

5. CONCLUSIONS

This paper presented a performance study of the SCI ring, including a description of the logical-level protocol, an efficient, analytical performance model, and extensive simulation results. The performance of the SCI ring was analyzed under uniform and non-uniform workloads and with and without the flow control mechanism. The SCI ring was also compared to a conventional shared bus.

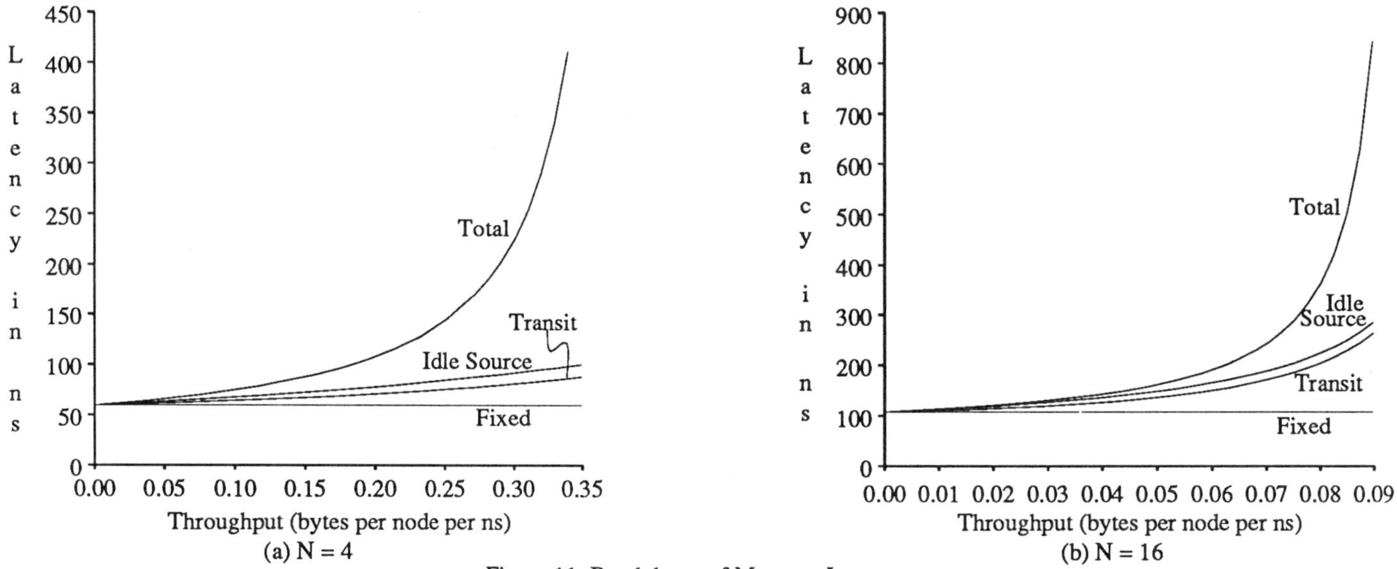

Figure 11: Breakdown of Message Latency

The analytical model developed for the SCI ring did not consider the flow control mechanism, but was found to be accurate for both uniform and non-uniform communication patterns. Where quantitative error was greater, qualitative behavior was still predicted correctly. The primary source of error in the model was identified, and will be the topic of further research, along with extensions to model flow control mechanisms.

The SCI flow control mechanism effectively prevents node starvation, providing all nodes with their approximate fair share of the ring bandwidth. Non-uniform routing still affects the realized node throughputs to some extent, however, with the effect being greater for smaller ring sizes. The flow control mechanism also equalizes the negative impact that a hot node has on the rest of the ring. Without flow control, the downstream neighbors of a hot node see substantially increased message latencies.

The fairness provided by the flow control mechanism comes at the cost of overall ring throughput. Maximum throughput is reduced by up to 30%. The impact is greatest for ring sizes of 8 to 32, and is negligible for a ring size of 2. We are investigating possible modifications to the flow control mechanism that would gracefully increase ring throughput in return for reduced fairness.

In comparing the SCI ring to a conventional bus, the clock speed was considered along with the number of cycles needed to convey a message. Although the number of cycles is larger for the ring, the faster clock speed gives a significant advantage. A 32-bit bus would have to have a 4 ns clock to be competitive with a 16-bit wide SCI ring with a 2 ns clock (and even then it would have a lower saturation bandwidth). While a 2 ns clock for SCI is realizable in 1992 with standard ECL circuitry, typical high performance multiprocessor buses have cycle times of about 30 ns.

With a 16-bit width and 2 ns cycle time, the SCI ring provides a total peak throughput of over 1 gigabyte per second. Communication locality and larger packet sizes increase this number, while flow control overhead decreases it. Given a read request/read response model and 64-byte data blocks, a total data transfer rate of approximately 600-800 megabytes per second can be sustained over a single ring. The flow control mechanism partitions this bandwidth fairly among all participating nodes. The SCI standard leaves room for future improvements by both increasing the link width and decreasing the cycle time.

Acknowledgements

The authors gratefully acknowledge the assistance of Dave James, Ross Johnson and Alain Kagi in clarifying several important concepts in the SCI standard. Thanks also to Rich Maclin and Ross Johnson for providing valuable mathematical assistance. In addition we have received much help from other SCI colleagues too numerous to mention, but especially from Dave Gustavson, Stein Gjessing, Ernst Kristiansen, and Hans Wiggers.

Steven Scott was supported by a fellowship from the Fannie and John Hertz Foundation. This work was also supported by National Science Foundation grants #CCR-892766 and #CCR-9024144.

References

[Grap89] Silicon Graphics Inc., Power Series, Silicon Graphics Technical Report, 1989.

[Gust92] Gustavson, D. B., The Scalable Coherent Interface and Related Standards Projects, *IEEE Micro* **12**(1), February 1992, 10-22.

[IEEE91] IEEE, SCI-Scalable Coherent Interface, P1596/D2.00 18Nov91, Draft for Recirculation to the Balloting Body, prepared by the P1596 Ballot Review Committee of the IEEE Microprocessor Standards Committee, 1991.

[Klei75] Kleinrock, L., *Queueing Systems, Volume I,* John Wiley and Sons, New York, 1975.

[Olso83] Olson, R. A., B. Kumar, and L. E. Shar, Messages and Multiprocessing in the ELXSI System 6400, *COMPCON83*, February 1983, 21-24.

[Scot91] Scott, S. L., J. R. Goodman, and M. K. Vernon, Analysis of the SCI Ring, Computer Sciences Technical Report #1055, University of Wisconsin-Madison, Madison, WI 53706, November 1991.

[Siew91] Siewiorek, D. P. and P. J. Koopman, Jr., *The Architecture of Supercomputers: Titan, A Case Study,* Academic Press, San Diego, CA, 1991.

Appendix A — Performance Model Equations

Model inputs:

N	Number of nodes per ring
$z_{i,j}$	Fraction of node i's packets routed to node j
λ_i	Transmit queue packet arrival rate at node i
f_{data}	Fraction of send packets that are data packets
f_{addr}	Fraction of send packets that are addr packets
l_{data}	Length (in symbols) of a data packet (including postpended idle)
l_{addr}	Length of an address packet
l_{echo}	Length of an echo packet
T_{wire}	Number of cycles to traverse a wire
T_{parse}	Number of cycles to parse a packet

Preliminary calculations:

l_{send} Mean length of a send packet

$$l_{send} = f_{data}\, l_{data} + f_{addr}\, l_{addr} \tag{1}$$

X_i Mean throughput at node i

$$X_i = \lambda_i\,(l_{send} - 1) \tag{2}$$

λ_{ring} Total packet arrival rate

$$\lambda_{ring} = \sum_{i=0}^{N-1} \lambda_i \tag{3}$$

$r_{echo,i}$ Rate of echo packets passing through node i

$$r_{echo,i} = \sum_{j \neq i} \lambda_j \sum_{\substack{k=j+1 \\ (mod\, N)}}^{i} z_{jk} \tag{4}$$

$r_{data,i}$ Rate of data packets passing through node i

$$r_{data,i} = f_{data} \sum_{j \neq i} \lambda_j \sum_{\substack{k=i+1 \\ (mod\, N)}}^{j-1} z_{jk} \tag{5}$$

$r_{addr,i}$ Rate of address packets passing through node i

$$r_{addr,i} = f_{addr} \sum_{j \neq i} \lambda_j \sum_{\substack{k=i+1 \\ (mod\, N)}}^{j-1} z_{jk} \tag{6}$$

$r_{pass,i}$ Total rate of packets passing through node i

$$r_{pass,i} = r_{echo,i} + r_{data,i} + r_{addr,i} = \sum_{j \neq i} \lambda_j \tag{7}$$

$r_{rcv,i}$ Rate of packets routed to node i

$$r_{rcv,i} = \sum_{j \neq i} \lambda_j z_{ji} \tag{8}$$

$n_{pass,i}$ Mean number of passed packets per injected packet at node i

$$n_{pass,i} = \frac{r_{pass,i}}{\lambda_i} \tag{9}$$

$U_{pass,i}$ Utilization of node i's output link by passing packets

$$U_{pass,i} = r_{data,i} l_{data} + r_{addr,i} l_{addr} + r_{echo,i} l_{echo} \tag{10}$$

$l_{pkt,i}$ Mean length of a passing packet at node i

$$l_{pkt,i} = \frac{U_{pass,i}}{r_{pass,i}} \tag{11}$$

$L_{pkt,i}$ Residual life of passing packet at node i

$$L_{pkt,i} = \left[\frac{r_{data,i} l_{data}^2 + r_{addr,i} l_{addr}^2 + r_{echo,i} l_{echo}^2}{2U_{pass,i}}\right] - \frac{1}{2} \tag{12}$$

Calculations inside iteration:

$n_{train,i}$ Mean number of packets in a passing packet train at node i

$$n_{train,i} = \frac{1}{1 - C_{pass,i}} \tag{13}$$

$l_{train,i}$ Mean length of passing packet train at node i

$$l_{train,i} = l_{pkt,i} n_{train,i} \tag{14}$$

$P_{pkt,i}$ Probability that an idle symbol passing through node i is directly followed by a packet

$$P_{pkt,i} = \frac{U_{pass,i}}{(1 - U_{pass,i}) l_{train,i}} \tag{15}$$

S_i Mean transmit queue service time at node i

$$S_i = (1-\rho_i) U_{pass,i} [L_{pkt,i} + (C_{pass,i} - P_{pkt,i}) l_{train,i}] + l_{send}\,(1 + P_{pkt,i} l_{train,i}) \tag{16}$$

ρ_i Utilization of transmit queue at node i

$$\rho_i = \lambda_i S_i \tag{17}$$

Calculating new coupling probabilities:

$C_{link,i}$ Probability that packet on node i's output link immediately follows its predecessor

$$C_{link,i} = \frac{1}{(n_{pass} + 1)} \left[n_{pass,i} C_{pass,i} + [\rho_i + (1-\rho_i) U_{pass,i}] + P_{pkt,i} l_{send} \right] \tag{18}$$

$F_{in,i}$ Mean number of "following" packets entering stripper i per stripped packet

$$F_{in,i} = C_{link,i-1} \left[\frac{\lambda_{ring}}{\lambda_i + r_{rcv,i}} \right] \tag{19}$$

$P_{uncouple}$ Probability a stripped packet at node i causes the following packet to become uncoupled, given there is a following packet

$$P_{uncouple,i} = \left[\frac{\lambda_i}{\lambda_i + r_{rcv,i}} \right] \left[\frac{\lambda_{ring} - \lambda_i - r_{rcv,i}}{\lambda_{ring}} \right] \tag{20}$$

F_{out} Mean number of "following" packets leaving stripper i per stripped packet

$$F_{out,i} = (1 - C_{link,i-1})^2 F_{in,i} + C_{link,i-1}(1 - C_{link,i-1})(F_{in,i} - 1) + C_{link,i-1}^2 (F_{in,i} - 1 - P_{uncouple,i}) + (1 - C_{link,i-1}) C_{link,i-1} (F_{in,i} - P_{uncouple,i}) \tag{21}$$

$C_{pass,i}$ Probability that passing packet at node i immediately follows its predecessor

$$C_{pass,i} = \frac{F_{out,i}(\lambda_i + r_{rcv,i})}{\lambda_{ring} - \lambda_i} \tag{22}$$

Calculating final model outputs:

$V_{pkt,i}$ Variance of passing packet length at node i

$$V_{pkt,i} = \frac{1}{r_{pass,i}} \Big[r_{data,i}(l_{data} - l_{pkt,i})^2 + r_{addr,i}(l_{addr} - l_{pkt,i})^2 + r_{echo,i}(l_{echo} - l_{pkt,i})^2 \Big] \quad (23)$$

$V_{train,i}$ Variance of passing packet train length at node i

$$V_{train,i} = \frac{V_{pkt,i}}{(1 - C_{pass,i})} + \frac{l_{pkt,i}{}^2 C_{pass,i}}{(1 - C_{pass,i})^2} \quad (24)$$

$\psi_{type,i}$ Constant multiplier for approximate variance calculation

$$\psi_{type,i} = \frac{(1-\rho_i)U_{pass,i}[L_{pkt,i} + (C_{pass,i} - P_{pkt,i})l_{train,i}] + l_{type}P_{pkt,i}l_{train,i}}{l_{type}P_{pkt,i}l_{train,i}} \quad (25)$$

where $type \in \{addr, data\}$

$V_{addr,i}$ Variance of service time for an address packet injected at node i

$V_{data,i}$ Variance of service time for a data packet injected at node i

$$V_{type,i} = \left[\sum_{j=1}^{l_{type}} \binom{l_{type}}{j} P_{pkt,i}{}^j (1 - P_{pkt,i})^{l_{type}-j} (jV_{train,i} + [jl_{train,i}]^2) - (l_{train,i}P_{pkt,i}l_{type})^2 \right] \psi^2_{type,i} \quad (26)$$

V_i Overall variance of service time for an packet injected at node i

$$V_i = f_{data}(V_{data,i} + S_{data,i}{}^2) + f_{addr}(V_{addr,i} + S_{addr,i}{}^2) - S_i{}^2 \quad (27)$$

c_i Coefficient of variation of S_i

$$c_i = \frac{\sqrt{V_i}}{S_i} \quad (28)$$

Q_i Mean transmit queue length at node i

$$Q_i = \rho_i + \frac{\rho_i{}^2 (1 + c_i{}^2)}{2(1 - \rho_i)} \quad (29)$$

L_i Mean residual life of transmit queue service time at node i

$$L_i = \frac{V_i + S_i{}^2}{2S_i} \quad (30)$$

W_i Mean wait time in transmit queue at node i

$$W_i = (Q_i - \rho_i)S_i + \rho_i L_i \quad (31)$$

B_i Mean backlog at node i seen by a passing packet

$$B_i = \left[(1-\rho_i)U_{pass,i}(C_{pass,i} - P_{pkt\,i})l_{send}n_{train,i} + f_{data}P_{pkt,i}l_{data}\left[\frac{l_{data}+1}{2}\right]n_{train,i} + f_{addr}P_{pkt,i}l_{addr}\left[\frac{l_{addr}+1}{2}\right]n_{train,i} \right] \frac{1}{n_{pass,i}} \quad (32)$$

T_i Mean transit time for node i (once transmission begins)

$$T_i = 1 + T_{wire} + t_{parse} + l_{send} + \sum_{j \neq i} z_{ij} \sum_{\substack{k=i+1 \\ (mod\ N)}}^{j-1} (1 + T_{wire} + t_{parse} + B_k) \quad (33)$$

R_i Mean response time of a packet transmission from node i

$$R_i = W_i + (1-\rho_i)U_{pass,i}L_{pkt,i} + T_i \quad (34)$$

Tradeoffs in Supporting Two Page Sizes*

Madhusudhan Talluri,[†] *Shing Kong,*[‡] *Mark D. Hill,*[†] *David A. Patterson*[††]

[†]Computer Sciences Dept.
University of Wisconsin
Madison, Wisconsin 53706
talluri@cs.wisc.edu

[‡]Sun Microsystems Laboratories, Inc.
Mail Stop: 29-225
2550 Garcia Ave.
Mountain View, CA 94043-1100

[††]CS Division, UC Berkeley
571 Evans Hall
Berkeley, CA 94720

ABSTRACT

As computer system main memories get larger and processor cycles-per-instruction (CPIs) get smaller, the time spent in handling translation lookaside buffer (TLB) misses could become a performance bottleneck. We explore relieving this bottleneck by (a) increasing the page size and (b) supporting two page sizes.

We discuss how to build a TLB to support two page sizes and examine both alternatives experimentally with a dozen uniprogrammed, user-mode traces for the SPARC architecture. Our results show that increasing the page size to 32KB causes both a significant increase in average working set size (e.g., 60%) and a significant reduction in the TLB's contribution to CPI, CPI_{TLB}, (namely a factor of eight) compared to using 4KB pages. Results for using two page sizes, 4KB and 32KB pages, on the other hand, show a small increase in working set size (about 10%) and variable decrease in CPI_{TLB}, (from negligible to as good as found with the 32KB page size). CPI_{TLB} when using two page sizes is consistently better for fully associative TLBs than for set-associative ones.

Our results are preliminary, however, since (a) our traces do not include multiprogramming or operating system behavior, and (b) our page-size assignment policy may not reflect a real operating system's policy.

Keywords: Address translation, page size, translation lookaside buffer, virtual memory, working set size

* Talluri is supported in part by a summer internship at Sun Microsystems Laboratories, Inc. and by National Science Foundation Award (MIPS-8957278); Kong is supported by Sun Microsystems Laboratories, Inc.; Hill is supported in part by a National Science Foundation Presidential Young Investigator Award (MIPS-8957278) with matching funds from A.T.& T. Bell Laboratories, Cray Research Foundation and Digital Equipment Corporation; Patterson is supported in part by DARPA/NASA Ames Research Center, Grant Number: NAG2-591.

1. Introduction

A *translation lookaside buffer (TLB)* is a fast buffer containing recently used virtual-to-physical address translations [ClE85, HeP90, SaB81, Smi82]. Most computers that support paged virtual memory [Den70] use TLBs to reduce average address translation time.

Ten years ago, TLB miss handling was responsible for only a small fraction of a machine's cycles-per-instruction (CPI). A TLB could map a substantial fraction of main memory (e.g., 0.5MB), machines had large CPIs (e.g., 10 cycles), and programs had small working sets. For example, Clark and Emer [ClE85] report that the VAX-11/780 loses only 5% of its performance to TLB misses. Wood *et al.* [WEG86] report TLB miss rates to be around 0.03 - 3% for some machines built in the early 1980s.

However, technological and architectural trends have led to increasing main memory sizes, decreasing CPIs, and programs with larger working sets. Today's workstations can have memories larger than 32MB and an average CPI of two cycles or less. In a few years, we expect main memories of 256MB and CPIs of 0.5 cycles to be common. The larger memories are needed to support programs with larger working sets or to keep resident the working sets of multiple programs. Thus, TLB miss handling may become a performance bottleneck unless TLBs miss less often despite having to map larger working sets.

One way of improving TLB performance is to make the TLB hold more entries. The extent to which the TLB size can be increased depends on whether the level-one cache uses physical tags. If it uses physical tags, then TLB access must complete before the cache access does (even if the cache uses virtual index as in the MIPS R4000). Furthermore, for superscalar machines that may do multiple memory references per cycle, the TLB may need to be multi-ported. Therefore, if the TLB gets too large, it will adversely affect the latency of every memory reference.

If the level-one cache uses virtual tags, it is much more straightforward to build a large TLB, since it is accessed only on level-one cache misses. To date, few computer designers have used virtually-tagged caches due to concerns about the complexity of handling synonyms (i.e., multiple virtual addresses that map to the same physical address), cache flushes on context switches and mul-

© 1992 ACM 0-89791-509-7/92/0005/0415 $1.50

tiprocessor issues.

A second method for improving TLB performance is to make the page size larger. The advantages are that the TLB maps more memory "for free", the size of operating system data structures decreases, and disk paging is more efficient (since the delay of disk head movement is amortized over more data transferred). There are, however, several reasons why typical page sizes have not increased. First, page sizes are much harder to change than cache block sizes. Page size is an architectural parameter, not just an implementation issue, as it affects memory management by the operating system. Thus, established architectures like the IBM 370 and DEC VAX-11 still use their original page size. Second, as we will show, larger pages result in larger working sets due to internal fragmentation [Den70], i.e., memory wasted due to the page size being larger than what the program needs. Third, the protection granularity becomes coarser. Appel and Li [ApL91] describe some applications that would benefit from smaller pages.

A third method for improving TLB performance is to use two page sizes and to require page sizes to be powers of two and pages to be aligned (i.e., a page of size B must be placed in virtual and physical memory at an address that is a multiple of B). If the large page size can be judiciously used, this method can make the TLB map more memory without a significant impact on working set size and no effect on minimum protection granularity.

However, supporting multiple page sizes has several disadvantages. First, like a larger page size, this change impacts a computer's architecture. Second, new TLB implementations must be built to handle multiple page sizes, which is not straightforward (Section 2). Third, software must select a proper page-size assignment policy to take advantage of the larger pages. Fourth, memory management and page replacement policies must accommodate multiple page sizes. Fifth, external fragmentation is now possible, which does not exist with a single page size. External fragmentation is waste due to the page size being larger than a contiguous region of available memory.

Nevertheless, supporting two page sizes is much simpler than supporting Multics-style segments [Org72] or many page sizes. Supporting segments that can be of arbitrary length starting at arbitrary addresses, requires TLBs to form physical addresses by addition than by concatenation, and software for mitigating external fragmentation is harder. Supporting multiple page sizes that are aligned and all powers of two, allows physical addresses to be formed by concatenation, but still requires software to handle external fragmentation and makes the use of set-associative TLBs difficult.

We are aware of two supercomputers and four recent microprocessor architectures that support multiple page sizes. However, there has been little software support for general use of the larger pages. The CDC CYBER 200 [CDC81] supported two page sizes (64KB and a selectable smaller page size) using a fully associative page table. The ETA10 [ETA86] supercomputer supports two page sizes — a large page size of 64KW or 256KW and a small page size of 1KW, 2KW or 8KW (word is 64 bits). The R4000 [Sla91] supports thirteen page sizes (4KB to 16MB) and has a 48-entry fully associative TLB. SuperSPARC [BIK92] supports four pages sizes (4KB, 256KB, 16MB and 4GB) using a 64-entry fully-associative TLB. Hewlett Packard's PA-RISC 1.1 Architecture [HP90] has a 4-entry fully associative Block TLB for large pages (256KB to 16MB), and a separate fully-associative TLB for 4KB pages. The Intel i860 XP microprocessor [INT91] supports one very large page size with a 16-entry TLB for 4MB pages and a separate 64-entry TLB for 4KB pages (both TLBs are four-way set-associative). All require pages to be aligned.

In this study we compare use of two page sizes versus a single page size. We explore the utility of a medium-sized page (e.g. 32KB) instead of megabyte-sized pages that will be used in specific applications only. We consider examining multiple page sizes beyond our scope for two reasons. First, we think it prudent to initially examine the simpler extension. Second, we do not know of a good operating system policy for selecting among many page sizes.

In this paper we show that increasing page size dramatically improves TLB performance at the cost of a large increase in working set size. By using a combination of small and large pages, i.e., 4KB and 32KB, preliminary studies show that it is possible to improve TLB performance with little increase in working set size. For some programs, we show that using two page sizes can result in a better performance than using a single page size of 8KB. We also explore ways to build set-associative TLBs to support two page sizes.

This paper leaves open research issues related to efficient TLB miss handling, page-size assignment policies, memory management and page replacement policies for multiple page size systems.

The remainder of this paper consists of five sections. Section 2 explores some ways to build set-associative TLBs to support two page sizes. Section 3 describes our experimental methodology, metrics and page-size assignment policy. Section 4 discusses the variation of working set size with page size. Section 5 presents results of TLB performance for different page sizes. Finally, we conclude mentioning some open problems that need to be solved before multiple page sizes can be used.

2. Implementing TLBs that Support Two Page Sizes

2.1. Fully Associative TLBs

The most straightforward way to support more than one page size is to use a fully associative TLB. The tag in each TLB entry contains the page size, in addition to enough bits to store the virtual page number for the smallest page size. Hit/miss detection logic uses the page size to select the actual page number for virtual address tag comparison. The page size is also used when forming the physical address.

However, while the fully associative TLB solution is conceptually simple, it can be very expensive to implement. Each TLB entry must (logically) have its own comparator for the virtual address tag comparison logic. Although this may be the only feasible solution if one wants to support more than two page sizes, it may be overkill if one wants to support only two page sizes.

2.2. Set-Associative TLBs

If we restrict ourselves to two page sizes, which are powers of two and aligned, it is possible to build a set-associative TLB. Given that we have two page sizes, which bits do we use to index the set-associative TLB? We could use (a) the page number of the small page, (b) the page number of the large page or (c) the exact page number.

We discuss the three options next, where we assume the small page size to be 4KB and the large page size to be 32KB. For purposes of illustration, we use a 16-bit virtual address, byte addressing and assume bit<0> is the least significant bit of the address.

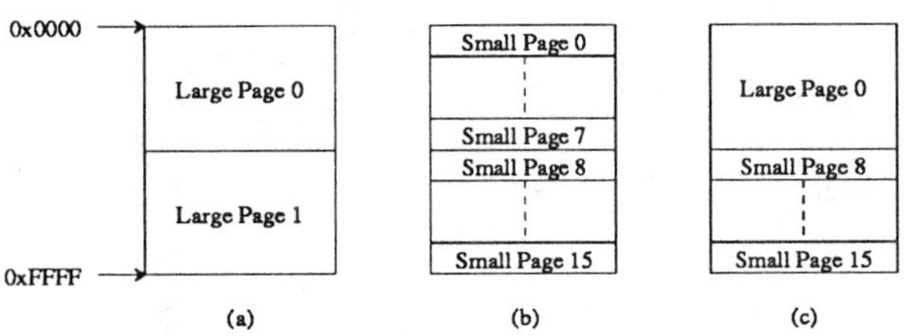

Figure 2.1. Virtual Address Space.

The 32KB page must be aligned on a 32KB boundary. The 16-bit address space can consist of: (a) two 32KB pages, or (b) 16 4KB pages, or (c) a combination of one 32KB and eight 4KB pages.

Indexing the TLB by the Page Number of the Small Page. Consider a direct-mapped TLB with two entries. The TLB is indexed with the least significant bit of the small page number, bit<12>, of the virtual address. This works fine in the case shown in Figure 2.1(b), where the entire address space consists of small pages. On the other hand, if the address space has large pages as in Figures 2.1(a) or 2.1(c), each large page can be mapped to *both* entry 0 and entry 1, depending on the value of bit<12>, which is part of its page offset. This negates the very reason to support both large and small pages. We conclude that using the least significant bits of the small page number to index a set-associative TLB supporting two page sizes does not work.

Indexing the TLB by the Page Number of the Large Page. Again, consider a direct-mapped TLB with two entries. The TLB is indexed with the large page number, bit<15> of the virtual address. This works fine when the entire address space consists of large pages only, as in Figure 2.1(a). On the other hand, if small pages are used, as in Figures 2.1(b) or 2.1(c), eight consecutive small pages compete for the same TLB entry. For example in Figure 2.1(b), Small pages 0-7 all compete for TLB entry 0. This causes many conflict misses due to collisions within a TLB set. We expect this collision cost is not as large as it sounds, because:

a) If the consecutive small pages are indeed being used together, the operating system should allocate them together as a large page, as shown in Figure 2.1(c).

b) If all the small pages are accessed sequentially (but not in a loop), then only entry 0 is used instead of overwriting the rest of the TLB. Hence, it is a good idea to index the TLB with the large page number if one is using small pages for a sequential scan.

c) We can reduce the collision cost by increasing the degree of associativity. In this example, if we increase the degree of associativity to eight, then each of small pages can have their own TLB entry, though they all map to set 0.

If only 32KB pages are used, this scheme degenerates to using a TLB supporting 32KB pages only. If only 4KB pages are used (i.e., no large pages are used, though the hardware supports them), then the collision cost of a set-associative TLB becomes significant and this TLB performs worse than TLBs supporting only 4KB pages (Section 5.2.1).

Indexing the TLB by the Exact Page Number. Again, consider a direct-mapped TLB with two entries. The TLB is indexed by the large page number (bit<15>) when we have a large page and by the least significant bit of the small page number (bit<12>) when we have a small page. However, we do not know the page size, when we access the TLB. We can follow any of three strategies to index the TLB :

(a) Parallel access: Build a dual-ported or replicated TLB that can be indexed by both the small and large page numbers simultaneously.

(b) Sequential access: First assume the incoming address belongs to a small page and index the TLB with the small page number. If we have a miss, reprobe [KJL89] the TLB with the large page number.

(c) Split TLBs: Have a separate TLB for each page size. This is similar to supporting split instruction and data TLBs. Access both TLBs in parallel using different page numbers (small and large).

Option (a) can be expensive and it is not clear whether it is much easier to build than a fully associative TLB. Option (b) results in the TLB hit cost of one page being higher than the other. It is not clear this gives any performance advantage for using the larger page size. Option (c) will result in unused hardware if pages are not appropriately distributed between the two page sizes.

2.3. How to Handle Misses in a TLB that Supports Two Page Sizes

The time taken to handle a miss, the *miss penalty*, is an important parameter in determining TLB performance [HeP90]. Supporting two page sizes makes miss handling more difficult as we do not know the page size for the memory reference that caused the miss. We can expect the miss penalty for a TLB supporting two page sizes to be larger than for a TLB supporting a single page size.

The precise impact of two page sizes on the miss penalty can be determined only by knowing the data structures used by the operating system. We assume that a TLB miss causes a software exception, which invokes a TLB miss-handling routine to scan the software data structures and supply the required translation entry. We estimate that miss-handling routines that support two page sizes take about 25% longer to execute than similar routines for a single page size. This estimate is based on routines written in assembly code for the SPARC architecture [SPA91].

Typical miss handlers use the least significant bits of the page number to index into a data structure, and this is more complicated with two page sizes. A multi-level table or split tables accessed by trying all page sizes in some order may be candidates for page-table data structures. Use of a software cache of translation entries indexed using techniques similar to those discussed above might be advantageous. Precise miss-handling techniques and software data structures that can be used in page tables for two page sizes are beyond the scope of this paper.

3. Methodology

We conducted extensive trace-driven simulations to study the working set sizes and TLB performance when using a single page size and two page sizes. This section details the workloads, metrics, simulation techniques and policy for page-size assignment used in the experiments.

3.1. Workloads

Table 3.1 lists the details of the workloads used to generate the traces for the simulations. All the workloads are uniprogrammed, user-only traces for the SPARC architecture. The programs represent different application categories, reference a large amount of memory and are relatively long. Trace lengths are number of memory references made by the programs. "WS Size" is the average working set size for the program when using 4KB pages, with the working set parameter T equal to ten million references. We simulated the SPEC benchmarks [SPE89] by executing the programs and dynamically generating traces of their memory references, using the tracing tools **shade** [Cme91] and **shadow** [Hsu89].

We would prefer traces with multiprogrammed and operating-system behavior to exercise large TLBs. Since our tracing tools did not allow us to generate such traces, we could not consider them in this study. The only public-domain traces with operating system behavior that we are aware of are the ATUM traces [ASH86]. We do not use these traces as they are too short to exercise the TLBs and the page-size assignment policy.

3.2. Metrics

In choosing a new page size scheme — a single larger page size or a two page size scheme — we tradeoff increased memory demands against better TLB performance. We quantify increased memory demands with the metric *normalized working set size*, $WS_{Normalized}$, which represents the increase in average working set size with

Program	Application	Trace Length (million)	Average WS Size (KB)	Average refs. per instruction
li	int SPEC	6512	146	1.313
espresso	int SPEC	632	168	1.280
fpppp	FP SPEC	2166	221	1.497
doduc	SPEC	1698	246	1.291
x11perf	graphics	83	433	1.207
eqntott	int SPEC	1662	753	1.151
worm	graphics	104	1115	1.207
nasa7	FP SPEC	9247	1124	1.395
xnews	X server	644	1259	1.187
matrix300	FP SPEC	2347	1484	1.385
tomcatv	FP SPEC	2297	2948	1.413
verilog	logic sim.	729	15059	1.264

Table 3.1. Workloads.

respect to using 4KB pages. We measure TLB performance using contribution to CPI due to TLB miss handling, CPI_{TLB}.

We derive $WS_{Normalized}$ as follows. $W(t, T, ps)$ is the set of distinct pages referenced in the interval $[t-T+1, t]$, where T is a parameter of the working set algorithm [Den68] and ps specifies either a single page size or multiple page sizes and how to select between them. The *working set size*, $w(t, T, ps)$, is the sum of the sizes of pages in $W(t, T, ps)$. The *average working set size* is $s(T, ps) = \frac{1}{k}\sum_{t=0}^{k} w(t, T, ps)$, where k is the number of memory references in the program. Finally, *normalized working set size*, $WS_{Normalized}(ps)$, is:

$$WS_{Normalized}(ps) = \frac{s(T, ps)}{s(T, 4KB)}.$$

$WS_{Normalized}$ represents the increase in average working set size when using a new page size combination, ps, with respect to the average working set size for 4KB pages. For example, a $WS_{Normalized}(32KB)$ of 1.5 means that the average working set size increased by 50% by changing the page size from 4KB to 32KB. It is difficult to relate $WS_{Normalized}$ directly to a change in program execution time without considering many system-specific parameters such as physical memory size, page replacement policy, multiprogrammed workload, etc. However, unless memory is underutilized, increased working set size would either require more physical memory to run the same program or would increase the page fault rate.

We measure TLB performance as the contribution to CPI due to TLB miss handling, CPI_{TLB}. This metric can be directly related to program execution time [HeP90]. CPI_{TLB} is calculated as follows :

$$CPI_{TLB} = (TLB\ misses\ per\ instruction) \times (TLB\ miss\ penalty).$$

From trace-driven simulations, we calculate the *TLB misses per instruction (MPI)* factor. The TLB miss penalty depends on both hardware and software and is more difficult to estimate (see Section 2.3). In this paper we assume the miss penalty to be twenty cycles, which is a reasonable estimate for TLB misses handled in software. Other metrics used to measure TLB performance can easily be calculated from CPI_{TLB} and RPI (References per instruction from table 3.1),

$$\textit{TLB misses per instruction } (MPI) = \frac{CPI_{TLB}}{20},$$

$$\textit{TLB miss ratio} = \frac{MPI}{RPI}.$$

Our studies assume a 25% increase in miss penalty for a TLB supporting two page sizes.(Section 2.3). The increase also will account for the costs of *page promotion* (Section 3.4). Further, the results do not change significantly with moderate changes in the miss penalty.

Another metric that is of interest is the increase in miss penalty that can be tolerated when using two page sizes to give the same CPI_{TLB} as using a single page size of 4KB, called the *critical miss penalty increase*, $\Delta\hat{mp}(ps)$ =

$$\left(\frac{MPI(4KB)}{MPI(ps)} - 1\right) \times 100\% = \left(1.25 \times \frac{CPI_{TLB}(4KB)}{CPI_{TLB}(ps)} - 1\right) \times 100\%$$

For the two page sizes, we use 4KB and 32KB pages. We also have similar data for combinations of 4KB/16KB and 4KB/64KB, but space constraints prevent us from presenting them here.

3.3. Simulation Technique

Due to the large number of different TLB configurations that needed to be simulated and the long running time of the trace-driven simulations, it was not feasible to perform simulations one at a time.

We performed TLB simulations with the cache simulator **tycho. Tycho** implements all-associativity simulation [HiS89], a variation of stack simulation [MGS70]. We modified **tycho** to handle using index bits other than the least significant bits of the page number and to support two page sizes. Using **tycho** it was possible to simulate many TLB configurations (84 in our case) in one simulation in about double the simulation time for a comparable single TLB simulation.

We also used stack simulation techniques to calculate average working set sizes. Slutz and Traiger[1] [SlT74] show that working set size calculation for different page sizes and different values of T can be done using stack simulation. We modified the algorithm, which requires T counters, to use very few counters, making it feasible to run simulations for large values of T (namely 100 million).

For each trace, we simulated more than one thousand TLB configurations and calculated average working set sizes for sixty-three page size/T combinations. We consumed 5.5 months of CPU time to collect the data, a subset of which we present in this paper.

1. We do not use Slutz's algorithm for multiple page sizes [Slu75] because it does not allow page sizes to change dynamically, which we assume in our page-size assignment policy (Section 3.4).

3.4. Policy for Page-Size Assignment

To test the performance of TLBs supporting two page sizes, we need a policy to assign page sizes to regions of the address space. We need a complete implementation of the operating system to do an accurate page-size assignment. In the absence of any real operating system policy, we use the following method to arrive at a page-size assignment. We do the assignment dynamically during the simulation, looking at the last T references.

We treat the virtual address space as chunks of 32KB each. Each chunk consists of eight blocks of 4KB. During the simulation we maintain a list of all the blocks accessed in the last T references. We map each chunk as either one large page of 32KB or eight small pages of 4KB each. The decision on whether or not to promote a chunk to a large page depends on the number of blocks accessed within the window of the last T references. If all the blocks in a chunk have been accessed, then the chunk should certainly be mapped as a large page. If only one block has been accessed then the chunk should remain mapped as small pages. The threshold we use to promote is whether half or more of the blocks in a chunk have been accessed. In this way, at worst we only double the working set size (in reality the increase is much less).

This policy uses the inherent spatial locality in the programs without the compiler or operating system taking care to align data structures on page boundaries. With software support for proper packing of data and code, more large pages would be used, which would lead to better TLB performance and smaller working set size increases.

There are some costs associated with promoting a chunk from small pages to a large page : (a) cost of updating the mapping data structures and invalidating TLB entries for the small pages, (b) copying the small pages already in memory to one large page and (c) paging in/zeroing the small pages not resident in memory. This will increase the CPI_{TLB} for the two-page-size schemes. We expect these costs to be low as page promotions are not frequent. Further, these costs can be folded into the extra miss penalty we assume for the two-page-size schemes.

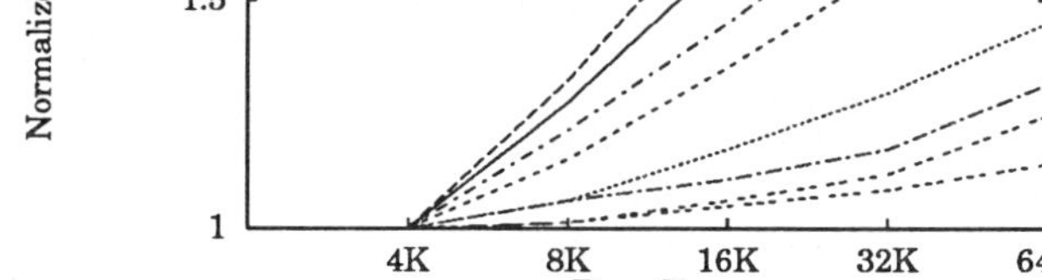

Figure 4.1.

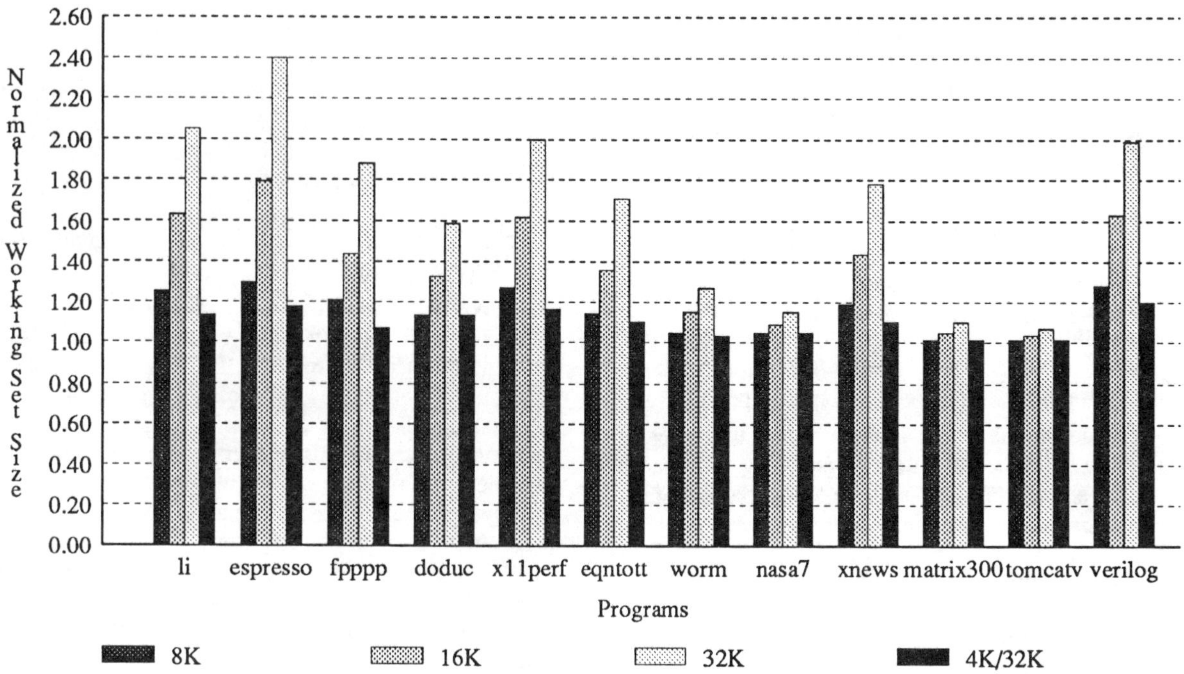

Figure 4.2. Normalized Working Set Sizes (T = 10M).

4. Results of Working Set Size Calculations

In this section we study the variation of working set sizes when using page sizes larger than 4KB. The working set size of a program is a measure of the memory cost of using larger pages. Though current operating systems do not use the working set policy for page replacement, we consider the working set size a good estimate of programs' memory demands.

Figure 4.1 shows the variation of $WS_{Normalized}$ with page size for T = 10 million references. The X-axis shows the page size and the Y-axis shows $WS_{Normalized}$ (both axes are logarithmic). The graph shows that the working set size increases quite significantly by using larger page sizes.

Doubling the page size increases working set size by only 1% to 30%. Doubling the page size does not double the working set size because programs exhibit spatial locality [Den70]. Programs like *matrix300* and *tomcatv*, that traverse all their address space in a linear looping fashion, already have most of their address space in the working set and increasing page size does not affect their working set sizes much. Programs that have a sparse address space (e.g., *li*) or have good temporal locality in a small region of the address space (e.g., *espresso*) show large increases in working set sizes.

$WS_{Normalized}$ is approximately proportional to the page size. Though the exact values may change, the qualitative trend is not sensitive to varying T through 10, 25 and 50 million references. Averaging across all the traces, $WS_{Normalized}(32KB)$ is 1.67 and $WS_{Normalized}(64KB)$ is 2.03, for T = 10 million references.

Figure 4.2 shows $WS_{Normalized}$ for the various programs for single page sizes from 8KB to 32KB and the two-page-size scheme using a combination of 4KB and 32KB pages. Recall that $WS_{Normalized}$ is 1.0 for 4KB pages.

The working set size increase resulting from two page sizes is less than for any single page size larger than 4KB. Across all the programs, $WS_{Normalized}(4KB/32KB)$ is only 1.01 to 1.22 (average 1.1). Further, this increase is insensitive to the value of T, varying by only a few percent.

Our results show that there is a significant increase in working set size by using a larger single page size. We conclude that the memory cost of using two page sizes is small and might be a better option than using a single larger page size, even if that single page size is 8KB.

5. Results of TLB Simulations

The main motivation for using large pages is to improve the effectiveness of TLBs. In this section we present results of preliminary studies comparing single-page-size TLBs with those that can support two page sizes. Space constraints allow us to present data for only three sample TLB organizations, one fully associative and two set-associative.

We divide the traced programs into two categories based on their working set sizes. The small programs have a working set size of less than 1MB and the large programs have working sets larger than 1MB (Table 3.1). The traces are displayed in ascending order of working set size, so that effects due to working set size, if any, may be observed.

We do not use large TLBs ($\geq$ 64 entries) in our study. Large TLBs in combination with large pages have negligible miss rates for our workloads, making it impossible to make comparisons. Nevertheless, our current results are our best estimate of the relative behavior of future TLBs,

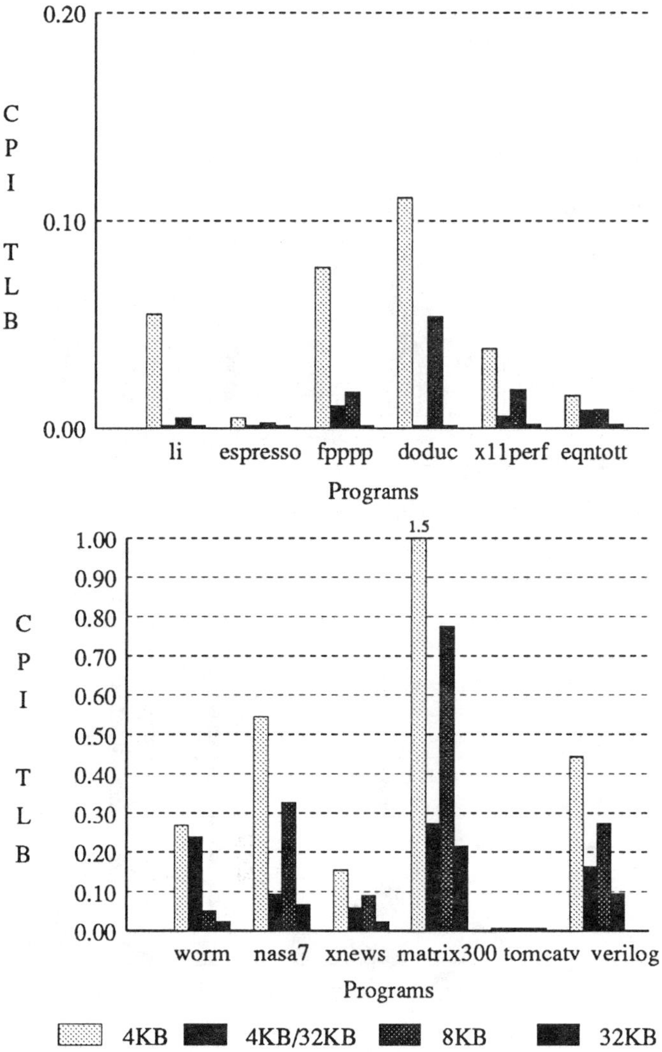

Figure 5.1. CPI contribution for 16-entry fully associative TLB.

which will be larger, but exercised by user programs with larger working set sizes in multiprogrammed workloads that include operating system behavior.

5.1. Fully Associative TLBs

Figure 5.1 shows CPI_{TLB} for a 16-entry fully associative TLB. Using a single large page size (32KB) gives the best CPI_{TLB}. The TLB now maps eight times more memory than when using a single page size of 4KB and the CPI_{TLB} reduces by approximately a factor of eight. Using a single page size of 8KB doubles the mapped area and nearly halves the CPI_{TLB}.

CPI_{TLB} when using two page sizes are only slightly worse than that obtained when using a single large page size of 32KB. The difference in CPI_{TLB} is mostly due to the increase in miss penalty when using two page sizes. The results show that there is a significant benefit in using a combination of large and small pages. Further the improvement does not require a large increase in working set size (Section 4).

For many programs the two-page-sizes scheme has lower CPI_{TLB} than using a single page size of 8KB. The use of large pages (32KB) in the two-page-sizes scheme has the potential to map a much larger area than a single page size of 8KB. Further, using two page sizes has a penalty comparable in working set size to using a single page size of 8KB. It should be noted, however, that the choice of page sizes is an architectural issue and the decision should not be based on any particular implementation.

5.2. Two-Way Set-Associative TLBs

Figure 5.2 shows the CPI_{TLB} for 16-entry and 32-entry, two-way set-associative TLBs. The histograms compare CPI_{TLB} when using the exact index for the two-page-sizes scheme with CPI_{TLB} for a single page size TLB. We use exact indexing for the two-page-sizes TLBs as we expect this to do the best. Section 5.2.1 compares the different indexing schemes. The results for two-way set-associative TLBs are, however, not as regular as in the fully associative case.

Using large pages lowers the CPI_{TLB} quite significantly because the same TLB now maps a larger region of memory. *Matrix300* is an extreme example: CPI_{TLB} reduces from 1.56 for 4KB pages to 0.11 for 32KB pages (for a 32-entry TLB). Using a single page size of 32KB has the lowest CPI_{TLB}. A single page size of 8KB, also produces a significant improvement in CPI_{TLB}.

For eight of the twelve programs, using two page sizes delivers lower CPI_{TLB} than using a single page size of 4KB, even with the increased miss penalty for the two-page-sizes scheme. The improvement in CPI_{TLB} varies from very large (e.g., *matrix300, nasa7*) to moderate (e.g., *verilog, xnews*). This shows that it is possible to support two page sizes using set-associative TLBs while improving TLB effectiveness. However, for a couple of programs (e.g., *espresso, worm*) there is a degradation in CPI_{TLB} by using two page sizes. This is due to insufficient use of large pages during page-size assignment and the larger miss penalty for the two-page-sizes scheme.

$WS_{Normalized}$ for the two-page-sizes scheme and for a single page size of 8KB are comparable. Comparing CPI_{TLB} in the two cases, however, there are no clear trends. For a 16-entry TLB, the small programs seem to benefit more from using two page sizes. On the other hand, for a 32-entry TLB, the small programs seem to benefit more from a single 8KB page size. For large matrix-manipulation programs (e.g., *nasa7* and *matrix300*) using two page sizes is a better option as they use mostly large pages and get CPI_{TLB} comparable to using 32KB pages. The results might suggest that increasing the page size to 8KB is better than using two page sizes. However, as programs continue to get larger, there may be more benefit in moving to a combination of small and large pages than to a single page size of 8KB.

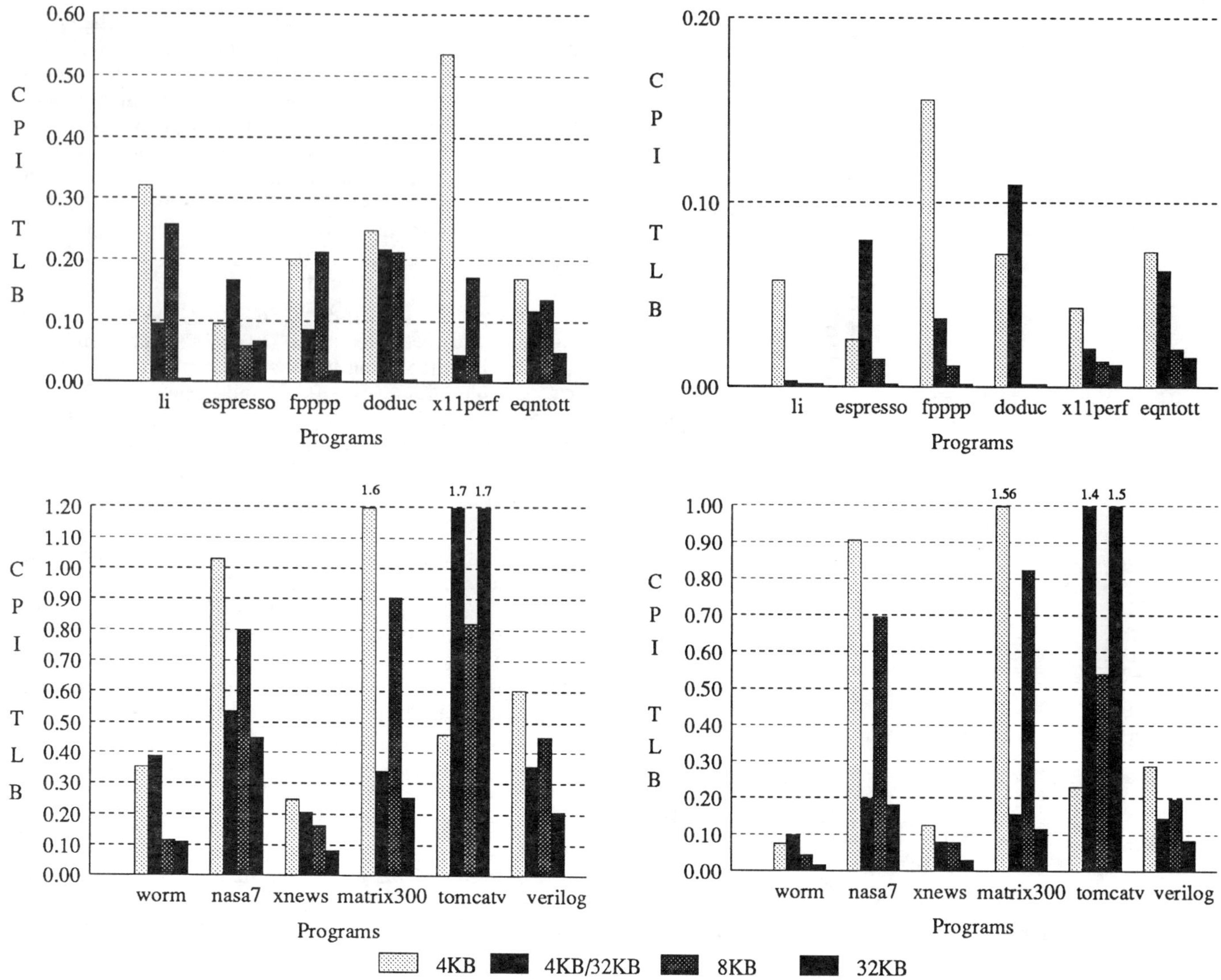

Figure 5.2. CPI contribution for set-associative TLB.

(16 entry, two-way) (32 entry, two-way)

To consider the effect of increase in miss penalty for TLBs supporting two page sizes, we look at the critical miss penalty increase. $\Delta\hat{mp}(4KB/32KB)$ varies from 30% to 1200% for programs that show an improvement in CPI_{TLB} when using two page sizes. This shows that even with a 30% increase in miss penalty for two page sizes, the same trends/results will hold. We conclude that a moderate increase in miss penalty when using two page sizes can be tolerated to give better performance than when using a single page size of 4KB.

Though there is a general trend of decreasing CPI_{TLB} when using larger pages, there are some exceptions. For example, *Tomcatv* has a quickly degrading CPI_{TLB} for increasing page sizes for two-way set-associative TLBs. The program's access pattern causes the TLB to thrash even with larger pages. Alexander *et al.* [AKB85] report similar behavior for different traces. We do not see any such anomalies for higher associativities, which indicates that they are due to interaction between the access pattern and the bits used to index the TLB.

The results show that there is potential for improving CPI_{TLB} by using a combination of small and large page sizes. We have also shown that a moderate increase in miss penalties for the more complicated TLBs does not affect the trends. Since the policy for allocation of pages (Section 3.4) is not realistic however, these results are only preliminary. Furthermore, with a real operating system using two page sizes, we expect the allocation pattern to change and result in different TLB behavior — set conflicts are sensitive to allocation of data structures in the virtual address space. Exact performance gains for using two page sizes can only be estimated with realistic policies for page-size assignment, more accurate estimates for miss penalty, estimates of the impact of increased working set size on the system page fault rate, and studies of larger and multiprogrammed workloads.

Program	4KB	4KB large index	4KB/32KB large index	4KB/32KB exact index
16-entry, two-way				
li	0.320	0.452	0.026	0.095
espresso	0.095	0.310	0.170	0.166
fpppp	0.201	0.174	0.082	0.086
doduc	0.248	0.488	0.058	0.216
x11perf	0.536	0.360	0.039	0.045
eqntott	0.170	0.207	0.178	0.118
worm	0.352	0.468	0.489	0.389
nasa7	1.029	1.149	0.635	0.537
xnews	0.247	0.297	0.178	0.205
matrix300	1.624	1.604	0.322	0.339
tomcatv	0.461	2.608	2.246	1.752
verilog	0.604	0.821	0.357	0.357
32-entry, two-way				
li	0.058	0.273	0.013	0.003
espresso	0.026	0.113	0.032	0.080
fpppp	0.156	0.141	0.041	0.037
doduc	0.072	0.294	0.016	0.109
x11perf	0.043	0.352	0.033	0.021
eqntott	0.074	0.094	0.052	0.063
worm	0.077	0.376	0.353	0.100
nasa7	0.907	0.815	0.296	0.199
xnews	0.126	0.211	0.086	0.080
matrix300	1.568	1.557	0.152	0.156
tomcatv	0.232	2.464	2.020	1.437
verilog	0.288	0.619	0.180	0.145

Table 5.1. Comparison of indexing schemes.

5.2.1. Comparison of Indexing Schemes for Set-Associative TLBs

Table 5.1 compares CPI_{TLB} using different indexing schemes for 16- and 32-entry two-way set-associative TLBs supporting two page sizes.

Exact indexing is intuitively the better indexing scheme. Although there are more cases where the exact index does better than the large page index, in more than 50% of the programs the CPI_{TLB} are roughly comparable. The two indexing schemes differ only in how they handle small pages. This comparable behavior might be due to the following (a) There may be few small pages (e.g., for *matrix300*). Hence, the CPI_{TLB} is similar to using all large pages and the indexing scheme for the small pages has little effect. (b) In our page-size assignment, small pages are used only if 1, 2 or 3 of the blocks in a large-page region are accessed. Associativity covers the cases of one or two blocks. So the large page index does worse only if three blocks in a large page region are accessed. We expect this to be infrequent.

Use of large page index is based on assumptions of allocation of enough large pages (Section 2.2). Suppose that a system supports two page sizes and uses the large page index, but the software does not allocate any large pages. The simulations show that this results in a severe degradation in CPI_{TLB} (compare the first two columns in Table 5.1). The degradation occurs because the bits used as the large page index are a poor choice if one is using only small pages. Thus, the effectiveness of hardware to support two page sizes depends on the operating system to do a good page-size assignment. Without software support, hardware supporting two page sizes may do worse than when supporting a single page size of 4KB. This is an important issue if the new hardware has to work with older versions of the operating system.

6. Summary and Conclusions

As main memories get larger and processor cycles-per-instruction (CPI) get smaller, the time spent in handling TLB misses is becoming more significant. It may not be possible to increase the number of TLB entries to map the gigantic memories of the future when using a physically tagged level-one cache without adversely affecting the latency of all memory references. Two alternatives for making a TLB more effective are (a) increasing the page size and (b) supporting two page sizes.

We experimentally examined both alternatives with a dozen uniprogrammed, user-mode traces for the SPARC architecture. Our results show that increasing the page size to 32KB reduces the TLB's contribution to CPI, CPI_{TLB}, by factors of about three to eight (sometimes more) compared to using 4KB pages. However, this CPI decrease is accompanied by a significant increase in average working set size (e.g., 60%). Without making many additional assumptions it is not possible to translate the increased working set size to a CPI penalty. Nevertheless, unless main memory is underutilized, larger working sets either demand a larger main memory, cause a higher page fault rate, or both.

Our results show that the use of two page sizes — 4KB and 32KB — keeps the increase in average working set size modest (about 10%), and makes CPI_{TLB} reductions that depend on whether the TLB is fully associative or set-associative. Results for a 16-entry fully associative TLB show that performance of two page sizes is mostly comparable to using the large page size. With two-way set-associative TLBs, due to the complexity of indexing with two page sizes, the results range from no improvement to CPI_{TLB} comparable to using 32KB pages. In a few cases, there is even a degradation in CPI_{TLB} resulting from using two page sizes. Furthermore, CPI_{TLB} is adversely affected by using the large page index if the operating system does not allocate any large pages.

We also compared using two page sizes with increasing the single page size to 8KB. Results show that (a) both cause a similar, modest increase in average working set size, (b) using two page sizes leads to a lower CPI_{TLB} with a fully associative TLB, but (c) results are mixed for set-associative TLBs due to indexing issues.

Even if all our assumptions are accurate, our results neither conclusively reject nor conclusively support the use of two page sizes. Furthermore, there are three important reasons not to infer too much from our results. First, the two-page-size results critically depend on the operating system's policy and mechanism for selecting between the two page sizes. Instead of modifying the operating system, we used traces generated with current software and dynamically remapped page sizes in response to usage patterns. A real page-mapping policy may perform much better (e.g., by reorganizing code and data for the new page sizes) or much worse (e.g., mapping policies might use less dynamic information). Second, despite consuming nearly 5.5 months of CPU simulation time, our traces are inadequate to exercise large TLBs, in part, because they do not include the effect of multiprogramming and operating systems behavior. Third, the selection of page size or sizes is determined by more factors than we have examined, including disk performance, paging performance and protection granularity. Furthermore, the selection of page size is typically an architectural, not an implementation, decision. Thus, one should not be satisfied that a page size is good for a particular machine, but ask whether it is likely to be good for most implementation technologies and workloads the architecture is likely to encounter in the future. One should not, for example, select page sizes that require the use of a fully associative TLB unless one expects that most future technologies will support fully associative TLBs well.

We hope that this paper motivates more research, particularly operating system research, to solve the problems associated with supporting multiple page sizes and to see whether they should be the preferred alternative.

7. Acknowledgements

We would like to thank R. Cmelik, D. Ditzel, Ed Kelly, Y. Khalidi, S. Kleiman, S. Richardson, G. Taylor, D. Williams and M. Wing among others at Sun Microsystems, Inc. and Sun Microsystems Laboratories, Inc. for their help with this research; D. Chenevert, M. Choudhary, S. Jain, R. Lee, V. Matena, G. Maturana, R. Subrahmaniam and R. Yung for helping with the traces; S. Adve, S. Chessin, S. Muchnick, A. Pai, S. Vajapeyam and D. Wood for their comments and help in writing this paper.

References

[ASH86] A. AGARWAL, R. L. SITES and M. HOROWITZ, ATUM: A New Technique for Capturing Address Traces Using Microcode, *Proc. Thirteenth Intl. Symp. on Computer Architecture* , June 1986, 119-129.

[AKB85] C. A. ALEXANDER, W. M. KESHLEAR and F. BRIGGS, Translation Buffer Performance in a UNIX Environment, *Computer Architecture News*, December 1985, 2-14.

[ApL91] A. W. APPEL and K. LI, Virtual Memory Primitives for User Programs, *Proc. 4th Intl. Conf. on Architectural Support for Programming Languages and Operating Systems*, April 1991, 96-107.

[BlK92] G. BLANCK and S. KRUEGER, The SuperSPARC Microprocessor, *COMPCON*, San Fransisco, February, 1992, 136-141.

[ClE85] D. W. CLARK and J. S. EMER, Performance of the VAX-11/780 Translation Buffer: Simulation and Measurement, *ACM Transactions on Computer Systems 3*, 1 (February 1985), 31-62.

[Cme91] R. F. CMELIK, Introduction to SpixTools, Sun Microsystems Technical Memorandum, June 1991.

[CDC81] *CDC CYBER 200 Model 205 Computer System, Hardware Reference Manual*, Control Data Corporation, 1981.

[Den68] P. J. DENNING, The Working Set Model for Program Behavior, *Communications of the ACM 11*, 5 (May 1968), 323-333.

[Den70] P. J. DENNING, Virtual Memory, *Computing Surveys 2*, 3 (September 1970), 153-189.

[ETA86] *Mainframe Subsystem Instruction Specification for the ETA10, Rev: B*, ETA Systems, Inc., March 1986.

[HeP90] J. L. HENNESSY and D. A. PATTERSON, *Computer Architecture A Quantitative Approach*, Morgan Kaufmann Publishers Inc., 1990.

[HP90] *PA RISC 1.1 Architecture and Instruction Set Reference Manual*, Hewlett Packard, November 1990.

[HiS89] M. D. HILL and A. J. SMITH, Evaluating Associativity in CPU Caches, *IEEE Trans. on Computers C-38*, 12 (December 1989), 1612-1630.

[Hsu89] P. Y. HSU, Introduction to SHADOW, Sun Microsystems Technical Memorandum, July 1989.

[INT91] *Overview of the i860 XP Supercomputing Microprocessor*, Intel Corporation, 1991.

[KJL89] R. E. KESSLER, R. JOOSS, A. LEBECK and M. D. HILL, Inexpensive Implementations of Set-Associativity, *Proc. 16th Symp. on Computer Architecture* , June 1989, 131-139.

[MGS70] R. L. MATTSON, J. GECSEI, D. R. SLUTZ and I. L. TRAIGER, Evaluation Techniques for Storage Hierarchies, *IBM Systems Journal 9*, 2 (1970), 78-117.

[Org72] E. J. ORGANICK, *The Multics System: An Examination of Its Structure*, MIT Press, Cambridge, MA, 1972.

[SPA91] *The SPARC Architecture Manual, Version 8*, SPARC International Inc., Menlo Park, CA., 1991.

[SPE89] SPEC, Newsletter, Vol. 1, 1989.

[SaB81] M. SATYANARAYANAN and D. BHANDARKAR, Design Trade-offs in VAX-11 Translation Buffer Organization, *IEEE Computer 14*, 12 (December 1981), 103-111.

[Sla91] M. SLATER, MIPS Previews 64-Bit R4000 Architecture, *Microprocessor Report 5*, 2 (February 6, 1991), 1,6-9,18.

[SIT74] D. R. SLUTZ and I. L. TRAIGER, A Note on the Calculation of the Average Working Set Size, *Communications of the ACM 17*, 10 (October 1974), 563-565.

[Slu75] D. R. SLUTZ, A Relation Between Working Set and Optimal Algorithms for Segment Reference Strings, IBM Research Report RJ 1623, July 1975.

[Smi82] A. J. SMITH, Cache Memories, *Computing Surveys 14*, 3 (September, 1982), 473 - 530.

[WEG86] D. A. WOOD, S. J. EGGERS, G. GIBSON, M. D. HILL, J. PENDLETON, S. A. RITCHIE, R. H. KATZ and D. A. PATTERSON, An In-Cache Address Translation Mechanism, *Proc. 13th Intl. Symp. on Computer Architecture*, Tokyo, Japan, June 1986.

Poster Abstracts

OPAC: A Floating-Point Coprocessor Dedicated To Compute-Bound Kernels [a]

André Seznec Karl Courtel[b]

IRISA, Campus de Beaulieu
35042 Rennes Cedex
FRANCE
Email: seznec@irisa.irisa.fr

ABSTRACT

In many applications, the main part of the computations may be encapsulated in compute-bounds kernels. Achieving high performance on compute-bound primitives at a low hardware cost has became an important challenge. OPAC was designed as the basic cell of a floating-point coprocessor dedicated to the execution of compute-bound kernels. Due to efficient hardware mechanisms for controlling and sequencing a pipeline performance close to a floating-point multiply-add per cycle per cell is reached on applications such as solving linear systems, FFTs or correlations in a microprocessor environment.

[a]This work was partially supported by the French Ministry of Defense under Grant DRET-INRIA No 88.34.191.00.470.75.01 and the CNRS (PRC-ANMand GCIS)

[b]at present, BULL S.A., Les Clayes-sous-Bois

Parallel Electro-Optical Rule-Based System for Fast Execution of Expert Systems

Ahmed Louri Jongwhoa Na

Department of Electrical and Computer Engineering
University of Arizona
Tucson, AZ 85721
Email: louri@paris.ece.arizona.edu
(602) 621 - 2318

ABSTRACT

A hybrid electro-optical rule-based system (EORBS) is proposed for the fast and parallel implementation of rule-based systems (RBS's). The EORBS is a hybrid system in which electronics is used for the user interface and optics for the inference engine. The EORBS utilizes two-dimensional optical planes as basic computational entities, and is therefore able to provide concurrent inferencing. Unlike conventional RBS's, EORBS provides parallel matching, selection and rule-firing. The thereotical performance of EORBS is estimated and is shown superior to pure electornic RBS's.

A New Compiler-Directed Cache Coherence Scheme for Shared Memory Multiprocessors with Fast and Parallel Explicit Invalidation

Ahmed Louri Hongki Sung

Department of Electrical and Computer Engineering
University of Arizona
Tucson, AZ 85721
Email: louri@paris.ece.arizona.edu
(602) 621 - 2318

ABSTRACT

We propose a novel compiler-directed cache management scheme which allows parallel invalidation of a subset of array elements. The scheme limits non-stale data invalidations using a novel memory allocation technique. Its correctness is proved using a flow graph model. It is also shown that the scheme provides more cacheability than the previous compiler-directed ones and has lower overhead in determining read hit at runtime. A new performance parameter called unwanted invalidation ratio, for compiler-directed coherence schemes is also proposed.

The Time-Constrained Barrier Synchronizer and its Applications in Parallel Systems

Der-Chung Cheng Kanad Ghose

Department of Computer Science
State University of New York
Binghamton, NY 13902-6000
Email: ghose@bingvaxu.cc.binghamton.edu
(607)-777-4608/(607)-777-4802

ABSTRACT

A barrier synchronizer, allowing processors to participate dynamically by letting them register their intent to participate within a timeout period, is presented. The synchronizer allows some applications - like software combining and highly concurrent queue operations - to be implemented in a rather unconventional but highly efficient manner. The barrier synchronizer generates successive time windows, allowing requests within the same window to be combined, thus ensuring a more-or-less fixed latency for the Fetch-and-Op primitive.

Architecture of a Graphics Processor

Gautam B. Singh

Department of Electrical and Computer Engineering
Wayne State University
Detroit, Michigan 48202
Email: gsingh@ece.wayne.edu

ABSTRACT

The design principles that were applied in the design of the integer-RISC machine, are applied to the design of the Reduced Instruction Set Graphics Processor. The processor instruction is defined after critical evaluation of the common graphics operations. Single cycle operations (in a *pure RISC* style) are performed through instructions for primitive graphics *as well as* general purpose computations. This processor is envisioned to become the CPU of choice for the ergonomic applications that rely heavily on graphics capabilities for user interface bandwidth improvement. The motivation for integrating graphics with general-purpose computations stems from the performance enhancement acheived due to increased integration levels, and the program portability offered by a single processor based systems.

Performance Evaluation of Disk Subsystems

Ruben Yomtov

Unisys Corporation
San Jose, California

ABSTRACT

Mainframe Central Processor Unit (CPU) speed/performance has increased by more than two orders of magnitude since the 1970's. However, the I/O subsystem performance has only quadrupled in the same period of time. There is a need for a computer architecture with an effective storage hierarchy to complement improvements made in the CPU performance.

This paper presents a technique to cal;culate the I/O performance of disk subsystems withe and without disk cache buffers. Through a series of calculation it is shown that the best way to improve I/O performance is to increase the number of data paths and use disk memory caching.

Prefetch Unit for Vector Operations on Scalar Computers

Ivan Sklenar

The Institute of Physics CSAV
Cukrovarnicka 10
CS-162 00 Praha 6
Czechoslovakia
Tel: (0042-2-)312 07 41
FAX: (0042-2-)312 31 84
Email: SKLENAR@CSPGFU11.BITNET

ABSTRACT

Current caches are not adequate for vector operations. A new kind of support for vector operations, called prefetch unit, is designed to improve the performance of the scalar (SISD) processors. The prefetch unit can be used for any SISD architecture and also for many kinds of MIMD architectures. It may run in parallel and asynchronously with other parts of processor. It keeps trace of the history of memory references, and initializes rarely any superfluous prefetches.

Enhancing Boosting with Semantic Register in a Superscalar Processor

Feipei Lai Meng-chou Chang

Dept. of Electrical Engineering
Dept. of Computer Science and Information Engineering
National Taiwan University
Taipei, Taiwan, ROC

ABSTRACT

IAS-S Supports boosting with "semantic register" and boosting boundary register to remove the dependences caused by conditional branches. In IAS-S, there is no dedicated shadow register file, and multiple levels of boosting is supported without multiple copies of register files. Any general-purpose register in IAS-S can be regarded as a sequential register or a shadow register flexibly. Furthermore, multi-way jump mechanism is combined with boosting to reduce the penalty due to frequent control transfers.

Data Path Issues in a Highly Concurrent Machine

Augustus K. Uht Darin B. Johnson

Dept. of Computer Science and Engineering
University of California, San Diego
La Jolla, California, USA 92093-0114

ABSTRACT

It is desirable to achieve high read bandwidths for the processing elements of highly concurrent SISD computers, both while keeping the register and memory write bandwidths low, and while keeping the interconnection networks simple. Solutions to these problems are proposed, simulated, verified, and measured. New techniques called write elimination and write liberation are presented that also greatly reduce the complexity of the data cache. The elimination of addressable hardware registers is also achieved.

Memory Management Support for Tiled Array Organization

Gary Newman

Kodak Electronic Printing Systems
Billerica, Massachusetts
Email: gnewman@keps.kodak.com

ABSTRACT

A novel method is described which adds support for sub-array ordered (tiled) arrays to a conventional MMU. The resulting pages contain two dimensional tiles of data rather than one dimensional strips, making tiled virtual memory transparently available to general purpose application programs. The method is further extended to support sub-arrays with three or more dimensions. The image MMU of the Kodak Prophecy Color Publishing System is shown as a product implementation for color picture arrays.

Performance of Multiple-Bus Multiprocessor Under Non-Uniform Memory Reference Model

M.A. Sayeed   M. Atiquzzaman

Department of Electrical Engineering
King Fahd University of Petroleum and Minerals
Dhahran 31261, Saudi Arabia
Department of Computer Science and Engineering
La Trobe University
Bundoora, Victoria 3083, Australia
Email: atiq@latcs1.lat.oz.au

ABSTRACT

Performance evaluation of multiple-bus multiprocessor systems is usually carried out under the assumption of uniform memory reference model. Hot spots arising in multiprocessor systems due to the use of shared variables, synchronization primitives etc., give rise to non-uniform memory reference patterns. The objective of this paper is to study the performance of multiple bus multiprocessor system in the presence of hot spots. Analytic expressions for the average memory bandwidth and probability of acceptance of prioritized processors have been derived. The results are validated by simulation results.
Keywords: Multiple bus interconnection, performance evaluation, memory bandwidth, blocking probability, multiprocessors.

Seamless - A Latency-Tolerant RISC-Based Multiprocessor Architecture

Samuel A. Fineberg   Thomas L. Casavant   Brent H. Pease

Parallel Processing Laboratory
Department of Electrical and Computer Engineering
University of Iowa
Iowa City, IA 52242, USA
(319) 335-5953
Email: tomc@eng.uiowa.edu

ABSTRACT

The Seamless parallel system being developed at the University of Iowa ECE Department provides a method for providing latency tolerance in physically-distributed memory systems utilizing "off-the-shelf" RISC CPUs without incurring the overhead of multithreading. Seamless encompasses an *evolutionary* new programming model emphasizing data locality that views communication as data movement rather than message passing I/O. A hardware Locality Manager is added to each processing element to perform this data movement concurrently with computation.

A Class of Prefetch Schemes for On-Chip Data Caches

Anujan Varma   Gunjan Sinha

Computer Engineering Department
University of California
Santa Cruz, CA 95064
Olivetti Advanced Technology Center
20399 Stevens Creek Blvd.
Cupertino, CA 95014

ABSTRACT

We introduce and evaluate a class of prefetch schemes for on-chip data caches in high-performance RISC processors. These schemes are conservative, initiating a prefetch only when a sequential pattern of references have been observed. Performance results based on traces of five programs in the SPEC suite on an IBM RS/6000 show that these schemes result in a significant reduction in miss ratio without the large increase in memory traffic associated with earlier schemes.

Performance Improvement for Vector Pipeline Multiprocessor Systems Using a Disordered Execution Model

M. Tahar Kechadi   J-L. Dekeyser   Ph. Marquet   Ph. Preux

Univercité des Sciences et Technologies de Lille
Laboratoire d'Informatique Fondamentale de Lille
Lille, FRANCE

ABSTRACT

Memory contention may cause dramatic loss of performance in vector pipeline multiprocessor systems. To enhance memory performance, the disordered execution model aims at scheduling vector element accesses in order to avoid memory confli cts. This scheduling relies on memory bank activities at access issue time. A disorde red pipeline execution is associated with disordered memory access in order to maint ain the chaining of all processor functional units. An analytical model and simulations demonstrate the interest of this model.

Pipelining and Bypassing in a VLIW Processor

Arthur Abnous Nader Bagherzadeh

University of California, Irvine

ABSTRACT

This paper describes issues involved in the bypassing mechanism for a VLIW processor and its relation to the pipeline structure of the processor. We will first describe the pipeline structure of our processor and analyze its performance and compare it to typical RISC-style pipeline structures given the context of a processor with multiple functional units. Next, we shall study the performance effects of various bypassing schemes in terms of their effectiveness in resolving pipeline data hazards and their effect on the processor cycle time.

Synthesis of Application-Specific Heterogeneous Multiprocessor Systems

Shiv Prakash Alice C. Parker

Electrical Engineering - Systems
University of Southern California
Los Angeles, CA 90089-2562

ABSTRACT

Heterogeneous systems can achieve enhanced performance and/or cost-effectiveness over homogeneous systems. SOS, a formal method to synthesize optimal heterogeneous systems for given applications, involves creation and solution of a mixed integer-linear programming model. A primary component of the model is the set of relations to be satisfied to ensure proper ordering of various events in the task execution, and completeness and correctness of the system. Experiments indicate SOS can be useful in designing heterogeneous systems.

A Partitioned Translation Lookaside Buffer Approach to Reducing Address Bandwidth

Matthew Farrens   Arvin Park   Rob Fanfelle   Pius Ng   Gary Tyson

Department of Computer Science
University of California
Davis, CA 95616
tel: (916) 752-9678 fax: (916) 752-4767
Email: farrens@cs.ucdavis.edu, park@cs.ucdavis.edu

ABSTRACT

Simulations indicate a simple modification of existing virtual memory hardware can significantly reduce the number of pins required to transmit address information from processor to off-chip memory. This modification consists of partitioning a TLB so that virtual page numbers are stored in a cache on the processor and corresponding real page numbers are stored in registers at the memory, making it possible to transmit a small register index instead of the entire real page number.

Architectural and Implementation Tradeoffs in the Design of Multiple-Context Processors

James Laudon   Anoop Gupta   Mark Horowitz

Computer Systems Laboratory
Stanford University, CA 94305
Email: laudon@pepper.stanford.edu

ABSTRACT

We examine two multiple-context schemes in the context of scalable shared-memory multiprocessors. The blocked scheme switches between contexts at cache misses. The proposed interleaved scheme switches between available contexts on a cycle-by-cycle basis, while providing full pipeline interlocks for good single-context performance. We show the interleaved scheme to have a performance advantage over the blocked scheme due to its ability to hide pipeline dependencies and reduce the context switch cost. We also show that, while the implementation of the interleaved scheme is more complex, this complexity is not overwhelming.

Implications of Hierarchical N-body Methods for Multiprocessor Architecture

Jaswinder Pal Singh

Computer Systems Laboratory
Stanford University
Stanford, CA 94305

ABSTRACT

We first examine the key architectural implications of realistically scaling a representative member of this important class of applications. Using scaling methods that reflect the concerns of an application scientist leads to different conclusions than does naive scaling in terms of data set size. In particular, we show that under the most realistic scaling model, both the communication to computation ratio and the amount of cache memory per processor required for effective performance increase with scaling. We then examine the effect of a shared address space versus message passing as the communication abstraction. We show that the lack of a shared address space substantially increases the programming complexity and performance overheads of a message-passing implementation.

Expanded Delta Networks for Very Large Parallel Computers

Brian D. Alleyne Isaac D. Scherson

Department of Electrical Engineering
Princeton University
Princeton, New Jersey 08544
(714) 856-7713
Email: alleyne@ics.uci.edu
Dept. of Information and Computer Science
University of California, Irvine
Irvine, California 92717
(714) 856-8144
Email: isaac@ics.uci.edu

ABSTRACT

We analyze a generalization of the traditional delta network, dubbed *Expanded Delta Network* (EDN), which provides multiple paths that can be exploited to reduce contention. In massively parallel SIMD computers, the trend is to put a large number of processors on a chip, but due to I/O constraints only a subset of the processors may have access to the network at any time. This leads to the Restricted Access Expanded Delta Network of which the MasPar MP-1 router network is an example.
Keywords: interconnection networks, delta networks, crossbar, hyperbar, clustering, capacity, SIMD.

This research was supported in part by the Air Force Office of Scientific Research under grant number AFOSR-90-0144 and NSF under grant number MIP9106949.

Directory-Based Cache Coherency Protocol for a Ring-Connected Multiprocessor-Array

Wisam Michael

University of Southern California
Los Angeles, CA 90089

ABSTRACT

The main goal of this paper is to demonstrate that a multiprocessor with very fast poit-to-point interconnection can be 10 times faster than a bus-based one. In this work, we presented a two-dimensional ring-connected system where the processing-nodes are arranged in rows and columns and interconnected through horizontal and vertical unidirectional 64-bit links (similar to the Illiac 4). After presenting the architecture for the processing-nodes, the pipelined feature of the network and the cache-coherency protocol, we discussed some implementation issues for the system. Using trace-driven simulation, some performance results for the new system and for a bus-based two-dimensional system (similar to the Wisconsin multicube) were presented to show the superiority of using point-to-point interconnections instead of busses.

Revisit The Case For Direct-Mapped Caches: A Case For Two-Way Set-Associative Level-Two Caches

Konrad Lai　　Wen-Hann Wang　　Jim Quinlan

Architecture Development Lab
Intel Corporation
Hillsboro, OR 97124

ABSTRACT

In this paper we argue that a two-way second-level cache is a better design choice than a direct-mapped organization. We show two-way caches are as simple to implement as direct-mapped caches. If the cache controller contains tags, the data array can be organized as a single bank of standard SRAM. Otherwise, both tag and data can be organized as a single SRAM bank. Our simulation results show these novel two-way organizations outperform the direct-mapped approach.

Analysis of Multithreaded Microprocessors under Multiprogramming

David E. Culler Michial Gunter James C. Lee

Computer Science Division — EECS
University of California, Berkeley

ABSTRACT

We examine multithreading to improve uniprocessor cost/performance on multiple processes. Processor utilization and cache behavior are studied analytically and under simulation by interleaving reference traces to model timesharing and multithreading. Multithreading a small number of threads is superior with large on-chip caches and significant memory latency. The switch need not be extremely fast. Surprisingly, miss ratios under multithreading may be lower than under timesharing, because switch-on-miss multithreading favors processes with better cache behavior.

Cache Write Generate For High Performance Parallel Processing

C.M. Wittenbrink A.K. Somani C.H. Chen

Department of Electrical Engineering and
Department of Computer Science and Engineering
University of Washington, FT-10
Seattle, WA 98195
(206) 685-1602
Email: somani@ee.washington.edu

ABSTRACT

We present, Generate, a new cache write handling scheme that avoids unnecessary reads from main memory, reduces bus contention, and increases the available bandwidth of the memory. Cache Write Generate increases the amount of CPU execution and memory load/store overlap, and decreases the memory cycle time. We compare the performance of cache write generate with write around and write allocate in single processor and shared bus multiprocessors and demonstrate a speedup of 1.2 to 1.5 over allocate and write around.

Integrated Computer Architecture Development System

Walter H. Burkhardt Stefan Rust

Institut fuer Informatik
Universitaet Stuttgart
Breitwiesenstr. 20-22
D-7000 Stuttgart-80
Email: burkhardt@ifi.informatik.uni-stuttgart.dbp.de
Fax: 1-49-711-780-1044

ABSTRACT

Development in systems architecture of separate soft- and hardware components introduces high inefficiencies, due to redundancies and seldom used functions on the levels of implementation. A better approach offers a methodology for an integrated software, firmware, and hardware design. Required are, however, immense computer re- sources with graphical capabilities. But it gives help in the development under constraints. We present such a system and show its capabilities in the development of a defect-free sorter module.

Keywords: Application-Specific-Architecture, Integrated design and development systems, CAD, Performance.

Author Index